Merriam-Webster's
Pocket
Dictionary

Merriam-Webster's
Pocket
Dictionary

Merriam-Webster, Incorporated
Springfield, Massachusetts

A GENUINE MERRIAM-WEBSTER

The name *Webster* alone is no guarantee of excellence.
It is used by a number of publishers and may serve
mainly to mislead an unwary buyer.

Merriam-Webster™ is the name you should look for
when you consider the purchase of dictionaries or other
fine reference books. It carries the reputation of a
company that has been publishing since 1831 and is your
assurance of quality and authority.

Copyright © 1995 by Merriam-Webster, Incorporated
Philippines Copyright 1995 by Merriam-Webster, Incorporated

Library of Congress Cataloging in Publication Data

Main entry under title:

Merriam-Webster's pocket dictionary.
    p.   cm.
  ISBN 0-87779-500-2
  1. English language—Dictionaries.
PE1628.M38   1995
423—dc20   95-4773
                         CIP

Made in the United State of America
2122NFWP01

Preface

Merriam-Webster's Pocket Dictionary is an extremely concise reference to those words which form the very core of the English vocabulary. It is based on the earlier *Webster's Vest Pocket Dictionary,* but it has been expanded and updated to cover new vocabulary that has entered the language since the publication of that dictionary. This dictionary is the smallest of the family of dictionaries published by Merriam-Webster. It is intended to serve as a quick reference, especially for questions of spelling, pronunciation, and hyphenation of the most common words in everyday use.

This dictionary shares many details of presentation with the more comprehensive members of the Merriam-Webster family, such as *Merriam-Webster's Collegiate Dictionary, Tenth Edition.* However, conciseness of presentation necessarily requires special treatment of entries, and this book has a number of special features uniquely its own. Users need to be familiar with the following major features of this dictionary.

Main entries follow one another in alphabetical order. Centered periods within the entries show points at which a hyphen may be put when the word is broken at the end of a line.

Homographs (words spelled the same but having different meanings) are run in to a single main entry when they are closely related. Second and succeeding homographs are represented by a swung dash: ~ Homographs of distinctly different origin (as ¹**date** and ²**date**) are given separate entries with preceding raised numerals.

Variant spellings that are quite common appear at the main entry following a comma (as **judg•ment, judge•ment**) and following other boldface entry words, such as inflected forms and run-on entries.

Inflected forms of nouns, verbs, adjectives, and adverbs are shown when they are irregular—as when requiring the dropping of a final *e* or changing a final *y* to *i* before the suffix: (as **waged; wag•ing** at **wage**) or when the form of the base word itself changes: (as **rode** . . .; **rid•den** at **ride**)—or when there might be doubt about their spelling: (as *pl* **egos** at **ego**). They are given either in full (as **bet•ter** . . .; **best** at **good**) or cut back to a convenient point of division (as **-ut•ed; -ut•ing** at **dis•trib•ute**). Common variants of inflected forms are shown even if they are regular (as **burst** *or* **burst•ed** at burst). When the inflected forms of a verb involve no irregularity except the doubling of a final consonant, the double consonant is shown instead of full or cutback inflected forms (as *vb* **-gg-** at **lug**). A variant or inflected form whose alphabetical place is distant from the main entry is entered at its own place with a cross-reference in small capital letters to the main entry (as **hung** *past of* HANG).

Several other kinds of entries are also found in this dictionary. A **run-in entry** is a term related to a main entry that appears within a definition (as **small intestine** at **in•tes•tine**). It is set off by parentheses. Derivative words, made up usually of the main entry and a common word element, such as a suffix, are shown as **undefined run-on entries** following all definitions of a main entry. These are set off by a dash (as — **gar•den•er** at **gar•den**). The meaning of an undefined run-on entry can be inferred from the meaning of the main entry where it appears and that of the added word element, shown elsewhere in the book. A **run-on phrase** is a group of two or more words having the main entry as a major element and having a special meaning of its own (as **in force** at **force** or **look after** at **look**). Run-on phrases are always defined.

Lists of undefined words formed by the addition of a common English prefix to a word entered in the dictionary and having meanings that can be inferred from the meaning of the root word and that of the prefix will be found at entries for the following prefixes: *anti-, bi-, co-, counter-, extra-, hyper-, in-, inter-, mini-, multi-, non-, over-, post-, pre-, re-, self-, sub-, super-, un-,* and *vice-.*

Pronunciation information is either given explicitly or implied for every entry in the dictionary. Pronunciation respellings are placed within reversed slanted lines (as \jē'ämətrē\ at **ge•om•e•try**). Where the pronunciation is not indicated at a particular entry, or is indicated in a cutback form, the full pronunciation is to be inferred from an earlier indicated pronunciation. A full list of the pronunciation symbols used is shown on the page following this Preface.

The grammatical function of entry words is indicated by an italic **functional label** (as *vb, n,* or *prefix*).

Hyphens that are a fixed part of hyphenated compounds (such as *self-conscious*) are converted to a special "double hyphen" when the compound appears in lightface type and that hyphen comes at the end of a line in this dictionary. This indicates to you that the hyphen is to be retained when the word is not at the end of a line. Fixed hyphens in boldface entry words are shown as short boldface dashes, which are a bit larger than ordinary hyphens. These short dashes or long hyphens in bold-face words are retained at the end of a line in this dictionary.

Guide words are used at the top of pages to indicate the range of entries on those pages. In choosing guide words for a page, we select the alphabetically first and last spelled-out bold-face words or phrases on that page. This means that any boldface entry—main entry, variant spelling, inflected form, run-in or run-on entry—can be used as a guide word. Please keep this in mind if the word used as a guide word does not happen to be the first or last main entry on the page. The guide words them-selves are in alphabetical order throughout the book, so occa-sionally it has been necessary to modify this rule. When the alphabetically last entry on one page would come later than the alphabetically first entry on the following page, a different word is chosen as guide word. On pages that contain a substantial number of undefined words following a prefix entry, that prefix may be used as the first or last guide word.

All **abbreviations** used in this book are listed, along with a number of other common abbreviations, in a special section immediately following the dictionary proper. This Abbreviations section is followed in turn by a brief **Handbook of Style** dis-cussing and illustrating the chief points of English punctuation, italicization, capitalization, and the formation of plurals.

Pronunciation Symbols

ə	banana, collide, abut; raised \ᵊ\ in \ᵊl\, \ᵊn\ as in battle, cotton, in \lᵊ\, mᵊ\, rᵊ\ as in French table, prisme, titre	œ	French bœuf, German Hölle
ˈə, ˌə	humbug, abut	œ̄	French feu, German Höhle
ər	operation, further	ȯi	toy, sawing
a	map, patch	p	pepper, lip
ā	day, fate	r	rarity
ä	bother, cot, father	s	source, less
ȧ	father as pronounced by those who do not rhyme it with *bother*	sh	shy, mission
aú	now, out	t	tie, attack
b	baby, rib	th	thin, ether
ch	chin, catch	th	then, either
d	did, adder	ü	boot, few \ˈfyü\
e	set, red	u̇	put, pure \ˈpyu̇r\
ē	beat, nosebleed, easy	ue	German füllen
f	fifty, cuff	ue̅	French rue, German fühlen
g	go, big	v	vivid, give
h	hat, ahead	w	we, away
hw	whale	y	yard, cue \ˈkyü\; raised \ʸ\ indicates that a preceding \l\, \n\, or \w\ is modified by the placing of the tongue tip against the lower front teeth, as in French *digne* \dēnʸ\
i	tip, banish		
ī	site, buy	z	zone, raise
j	job, edge	zh	vision, pleasure
k	kin, cook	\	slant line used in pairs to mark the beginning and end of a transcription
k̲	German ich, Buch		
l	lily, cool	ˈ	mark at the beginning of a syllable that has primary (strongest) stress: \ˈpenmən.ship\
m	murmur, dim		
n	nine, own; raised \ⁿ\ indicates that a preceding vowel or diphthong is pronounced through both nose and mouth, as in French *bon* \bōⁿ\	ˌ	mark at the beginning of a syllable that has secondary (next-strongest) stress: \ˈpenmənˌship\
ŋ	sing, singer, finger, ink		
ō	bone, hollow		
ȯ	saw, cork		

A

¹a \'ā\ *n, pl* **a's** *or* **as** \'āz\ : 1st letter of the alphabet

²a \ə, 'ā\ *indefinite article* : one or some—used to indicate an unspecified or unidentified individual

aard·vark \'ärd,värk\ *n* : ant-eating African mammal

aback \ə'bak\ *adv* : by surprise

aba·cus \'abəkəs\ *n, pl* **aba·ci** \'abə,sī, -,kē\ *or* **aba·cus·es** : calculating instrument using rows of beads

abaft \ə'baft\ *adv* : toward or at the stern

ab·a·lo·ne \,abə'lōnē\ *n* : large edible shellfish

¹aban·don \ə'bandən\ *vb* : give up without intent to reclaim —**aban·don·ment** *n*

²abandon *n* : thorough yielding to impulses

aban·doned \ə'bandənd\ *adj* : morally unrestrained

abase \ə'bās\ *vb* **abased; abas·ing** : lower in dignity —**abase·ment** *n*

abash \ə'bash\ *vb* : embarrass —**abash·ment** *n*

abate \ə'bāt\ *vb* **abat·ed; abat·ing** : decrease or lessen

abate·ment \ə'bātmənt\ *n* : tax reduction

ab·at·toir \'abə,twär\ *n* : slaughterhouse

ab·bess \'abəs\ *n* : head of a convent

ab·bey \'abē\ *n, pl* **-beys** : monastery or convent

ab·bot \'abət\ *n* : head of a monastery

ab·bre·vi·ate \ə'brēvē,āt\ *vb* **-at·ed; -at·ing** : shorten —**ab·bre·vi·a·tion** \ə,brēvē'āshən\ *n*

ab·di·cate \'abdi,kāt\ *vb* **-cat·ed; -cat·ing** : renounce —**ab·di·ca·tion** \,abdi-'kāshən\ *n*

ab·do·men \'abdəmən, ab'dōmən\ *n* **1** : body area between chest and pelvis **2** : hindmost part of an insect —**ab·dom·i·nal** \ab'dämənᵊl\ *adj* —**ab·dom·i·nal·ly** *adv*

ab·duct \ab'dəkt\ *vb* : kidnap —**ab·duc·tion** \-'dəkshən\ *n* —**ab·duc·tor** \-tər\ *n*

abed \ə'bed\ *adv or adj* : in bed

ab·er·ra·tion \,abə'rāshən\ *n* : deviation or distortion —**ab·er·rant** \a'berənt\ *adj*

abet \ə'bet\ *vb* **-tt-** : incite or encourage —**abet·tor, abet·ter** \-ər\ *n*

abey·ance \ə'bāəns\ *n* : state of inactivity

ab·hor \ab'hór, ab-\ *vb* **-rr-** : hate —**ab·hor·rence** \-əns\ *n* —**ab·hor·rent** \-ənt\ *adj*

abide \ə'bīd\ *vb* **abode** \-'bōd\ *or* **abid·ed; abid·ing 1** : endure **2** : remain, last, or reside

ab·ject \'ab,jekt, ab'-\ *adj* : low in spirit or hope —**ab·jec·tion** \ab'jekshən\ *n* —**ab·ject·ly** *adv* —**ab·ject·ness** *n*

ab·jure \ab'júr\ *vb* **1** : renounce **2** : abstain from —**ab·ju·ra·tion** \,abjə'rāshən\ *n*

ablaze \ə'blāz\ *adj or adv* : on fire

able \'ābəl\ *adj* **abler** \-blər\; **ablest** \-bləst\ **1** : having sufficient power, skill, or resources **2** : skilled or efficient —**abil·i·ty** \ə'bilətē\ *n* —**ably** \'āblē\ *adv*

-able, -ible \əbəl\ *adj suffix* **1** : capable of, fit for, or worthy of **2** : tending, given, or liable to

ab·lu·tion \ə'blüshən, a'blü-\ *n* : washing of one's body

ab·ne·gate \'abni,gāt\ *vb* **-gat·ed; -gat·ing 1** : relinquish **2** : renounce —**ab·ne·ga·tion** \,abni'gāshən\ *n*

ab·nor·mal \ab'nórməl\ *adj* : deviating from the normal or average —**ab·nor·mal·i·ty** \,abnər'malətē, -nór-\ *n* —**ab·nor·mal·ly** *adv*

aboard \ə'bōrd\ *adv* : on, onto, or within a car, ship, or aircraft ~ *prep* : on or within

abode \ə'bōd\ *n* : residence

abol·ish \ə'bälish\ *vb* : do away with —**ab·o·li·tion** \,abə'lishən\ *n*

abom·i·na·ble \ə'bämənəbəl\ *adj* : thoroughly unpleasant or revolting

abom·i·nate \ə'bämə,nāt\ *vb* **-nat·ed**

-nat·ing : hate —abom·i·na·tion \ə,bämə'nāshən\ n

ab·orig·i·nal \,abə'rijənəl\ adj 1 : original 2 : primitive

ab·orig·i·ne \-'rijənē\ n : original inhabitant

abort \ə'bȯrt\ vb : terminate prematurely —abor·tive \-'bȯrtiv\ adj

abor·tion \ə'bȯrshən\ n : spontaneous or induced termination of pregnancy

abound \ə'baund\ vb : be plentiful

about \ə'baut\ adv : around ~ prep 1 : on every side of 2 : on the verge of 3 : having as a subject

above \ə'bəv\ adv : in or to a higher place ~ prep 1 : in or to a higher place than 2 : more than

above·board adv or adj : without deception

abrade \ə'brād\ vb abrad·ed; abrad·ing : wear away by rubbing —abra·sion \-'brāzhən\ n

abra·sive \ə'brāsiv\ n : substance for grinding, smoothing, or polishing ~ adj 1 : tending to abrade 2 : causing irritation —abra·sive·ly adv —abra·sive·ness n

abreast \ə'brest\ adv or adj 1 : side by side 2 : up to a standard or level

abridge \ə'brij\ vb abridged; abridg·ing : shorten or condense —abridg·ment, abridge·ment n

abroad \ə'brȯd\ adv or adj 1 : over a wide area 2 : outside one's country

ab·ro·gate \'abrəgāt\ vb -gat·ed; -gat·ing : annul or revoke —ab·ro·ga·tion \,abrə'gāshən\ n

abrupt \ə'brəpt\ adj 1 : sudden 2 : so quick as to seem rude —abrupt·ly adv

ab·scess \'ab,ses\ n : collection of pus surrounded by inflamed tissue —ab·scessed \-,sest\ adj

ab·scond \ab'skänd\ vb : run away and hide

ab·sent \'absənt\ adj : not present ~ ab·sent \ab'sent\ vb : keep oneself away —ab·sence \'absəns\ n —ab·sen·tee \,absən'tē\ n

ab·sent·mind·ed \,absənt'mindəd\ adj : unaware of one's surroundings or action —ab·sent·mind·ed·ly adv —ab·sent·mind·ed·ness n

ab·so·lute \'absə,lüt, ,absə'-\ adj 1 : pure 2 : free from restriction 3 : definite —ab·so·lute·ly adv

ab·so·lu·tion \,absə'lüshən\ n : remission of sins

ab·solve \əb'zälv, -'sälv\ vb -solved; -solv·ing : set free of the consequences of guilt

ab·sorb \əb'sȯrb, -'zȯrb\ vb 1 : suck up or take in as a sponge does 2 : engage (one's attention) —ab·sor·ben·cy \-'sȯrbənsē, -'zȯr-\ n —ab·sor·bent \-bənt\ adj or n —ab·sorb·ing adj —ab·sorb·ing·ly adv

ab·sorp·tion \əb'sȯrpshən, -'zȯrp-\ n : process of absorbing —ab·sorp·tive \-tiv\ adj

ab·stain \əb'stān\ vb : refrain from doing something —ab·stain·er n —ab·sten·tion \-'stenchən\ n —ab·sti·nence \'abstənəns\ n

ab·ste·mi·ous \əb'stēmēəs\ adj : sparing in use of food or drink —ab·ste·mi·ous·ly adv —ab·ste·mi·ous·ness n

ab·stract \ab'strakt, 'ab,-\ adj 1 : expressing a quality apart from an object 2 : not representing something specific ~ \'ab,-\ n : summary ~ \ab'-, 'ab,-\ vb 1 : remove or separate 2 : make an abstract of —ab·stract·ly adv —ab·stract·ness n

ab·strac·tion \ab'strakshən\ n 1 : act of abstracting 2 : abstract idea or work of art

ab·struse \əb'strüs, ab-\ adj : hard to understand —ab·struse·ly adv —ab·struse·ness n

ab·surd \əb'sərd, -'zərd\ adj : ridiculous or unreasonable —ab·sur·di·ty \-ətē\ n —ab·surd·ly adv

abun·dant \ə'bəndənt\ adj : more than enough —abun·dance \-dəns\ n —abun·dant·ly adv

abuse \ə'byüz\ vb abused; abus·ing 1 : misuse 2 : mistreat 3 : attack with words ~ \-'byüs\ n 1 : corrupt practice 2 : improper use 3 : mistreatment 4 : coarse and insulting speech —abus·er n —abu·sive \-'byüsiv\ adj —abu·sive·ly adv —abu·sive·ness n

abut \ə'bət\ vb -tt- : touch along a border —abut·ter n

abut·ment \ə'bətmənt\ n : part of a bridge that supports weight

abys·mal \ə'bizməl\ adj 1 : immeasurably deep 2 : wretched —abys·mal·ly adv

abyss \ə'bis\ n : immeasurably deep gulf

-ac \,ak\ n suffix : one affected with

aca·cia \ə'kāshə\ n : leguminous tree or shrub

ac·a·dem·ic \,akə'demik\ adj 1 : relating

to schools or colleges **2** : theoretical —**ac·a·dem·i·cal·ly** \-ik/lē\ adv

acad·e·my \ə'kadəmē\ n, pl **-mies 1** : private high school **2** : society of scholars or artists

acan·thus \ə'kanthəs\ n, pl **acanthus 1** : prickly Mediterranean herb **2** : ornament representing acanthus leaves

ac·cede \ak'sēd\ vb **-ced·ed; -ced·ing 1** : become a party to an agreement **2** : express approval **3** : enter upon an office

ac·cel·er·ate \ik'selə₁rāt, ak-\ vb **-at·ed; -at·ing 1** : bring about earlier **2** : speed up —**ac·cel·er·a·tion** \-₁selə'rāshən\ n

ac·cel·er·a·tor \ik'selə₁rātər, ak-\ n : pedal for controlling the speed of a motor vehicle

ac·cent \'ak₁sent\ n **1** : distinctive manner of pronunciation **2** : prominence given to one syllable of a word **3** : mark (as ´, `, ^) over a vowel in writing or printing to indicate pronunciation ~ \'ak,-, ak'-\ vb : emphasize —**ac·cen·tu·al** \ak'senchəwəl\ adj

ac·cen·tu·ate \ak'sencha₁wāt\ vb **-at·ed; -at·ing** : stress or show off by a contrast —**ac·cen·tu·a·tion** \-₁sencha'wāshən\ n

ac·cept \ik'sept, ak-\ vb **1** : receive willingly **2** : agree to —**ac·cept·abil·i·ty** \ik₁septə'bilətē, ak-\ n —**ac·cept·able** \-'septəbəl\ adj —**ac·cep·tance** \-'septəns\ n

ac·cess \'ak₁ses\ n : capability or way of approaching —**ac·ces·si·bil·i·ty** \ik₁sesə'bilətē, ak-\ n —**ac·ces·si·ble** \-'sesəbəl\ adj

ac·ces·sion \ik'seshən, ak-\ n **1** : something added **2** : act of taking office

ac·ces·so·ry \ik'sesərē, ak-\ n, pl **-ries 1** : nonessential addition **2** : one guilty of aiding a criminal —**accessory** adj

ac·ci·dent \'aksədənt\ n **1** : event occurring by chance or unintentionally **2** : chance —**ac·ci·den·tal** \₁aksə'dent³l\ adj —**ac·ci·den·tal·ly** adv

ac·claim \ə'klām\ vb or n : praise

ac·cla·ma·tion \₁aklə'māshən\ n **1** : eager applause **2** : unanimous vote

ac·cli·mate \'aklə₁māt, ə'klīmət\ vb **-mat·ed; -mat·ing** : acclimatize —**ac·cli·ma·tion** \₁aklə'māshən, -₁klī-\ n

ac·cli·ma·tize \ə'klīmə₁tīz\ vb **-tized; -tiz·ing** : accustom to a new climate or situation —**ac·cli·ma·ti·za·tion** \-₁klīmətə'zāshən\ n

ac·co·lade \'akə₁lād\ n : expression of praise

ac·com·mo·date \ə'kämə₁dāt\ vb **-dated; -dat·ing 1** : adapt **2** : provide with something needed **3** : hold without crowding

ac·com·mo·da·tion \ə₁kämə'dāshən\ n **1** : quarters —usu. pl. **2** : act of accommodating

ac·com·pa·ny \ə'kəmpənē\ vb **-nied; -ny·ing 1** : go or occur with **2** : play supporting music —**ac·com·pa·ni·ment** \-nəmənt\ n —**ac·com·pa·nist** \-nist\ n

ac·com·plice \ə'kämpləs, -'kəm-\ n : associate in crime

ac·com·plish \ə'kämplish, -'kəm-\ vb : do, fulfill, or bring about —**ac·com·plished** adj —**ac·com·plish·er** n —**ac·com·plish·ment** n

ac·cord \ə'kórd\ vb **1** : grant **2** : agree ~ n **1** : agreement **2** : willingness to act —**ac·cor·dance** \-'kórd³ns\ n —**ac·cor·dant** \-³nt\ adj

ac·cord·ing·ly \ə'kórdiŋlē\ adv : consequently

according to prep **1** : in conformity with **2** : as stated by

ac·cor·di·on \ə'kórdēən\ n : keyboard instrument with a bellows and reeds ~ adj : folding like an accordion bellows —**ac·cor·di·on·ist** \-nist\ n

ac·cost \ə'kóst\ vb : approach and speak to esp. aggressively

ac·count \ə'kaúnt\ n **1** : statement of business transactions **2** : credit arrangement with a vendor **3** : report **4** : worth **5** : sum deposited in a bank ~ vb : give an explanation

ac·count·able \ə'kaúntəbəl\ adj : responsible —**ac·count·abil·i·ty** \-₁kaúntə'bilətē\ n

ac·coun·tant \ə'kaúnt³nt\ n : one skilled in accounting —**ac·coun·tan·cy** \-³nsē\ n

ac·count·ing \ə'kaúntiŋ\ n : financial record keeping

ac·cou·tre, ac·cou·ter \ə'kütər\ vb **-tred** or **-tered; -tring** or **-ter·ing** \-'kütəriŋ, -'kütriŋ\ : equip

ac·cou·tre·ment, ac·cou·ter·ment \ə'kütərmənt, -'kütər-\ n **1** : accessory item —usu. pl. **2** : identifying characteristic

ac·cred·it \ə'kredət\ vb 1 : approve officially 2 : attribute —**ac·cred·i·ta·tion** \-,kredə'tāshən\ n

ac·crue \ə'krü\ vb -crued; -cru·ing : be added by periodic growth —**ac·cru·al** \-əl\ n

ac·cu·mu·late \ə'kyümyə,lāt\ vb -lat·ed; -lat·ing : collect or pile up —**ac·cu·mu·la·tion** \-,kyümyə'lāshən\ n —**ac·cu·mu·la·tor** \-'kyümyə,lātər\ n

ac·cu·rate \'akyərət\ adj : free from error —**ac·cu·ra·cy** \-rəsē\ n —**ac·cu·rate·ly** adv —**ac·cu·rate·ness** n

ac·cursed \ə'kərst, -'kərsəd\, **ac·curst** \ə'kərst\ adj 1 : being under a curse 2 : damnable

ac·cuse \ə'kyüz\ vb -cused; -cus·ing : charge with an offense —**ac·cu·sa·tion** \,akyə'zāshən\ n —**ac·cus·er** n

ac·cused \ə'kyüzd\ n, pl -cused : defendant in a criminal case

ac·cus·tom \ə'kəstəm\ vb : make familiar through use or experience

ace \'ās\ n : one that excels

acer·bic \ə'sərbik, a-\ adj : sour or biting in temper, mood, or tone

acet·amin·o·phen \ə,sētə'minəfən\ n : pain reliever

ac·e·tate \'asə,tāt\ n : fabric or plastic derived from acetic acid

ace·tic acid \ə'sētik-\ n : acid found in vinegar

acet·y·lene \ə'set³lən, -³l,ēn\ n : colorless gas used as a fuel in welding

ache \'āk\ vb ached; ach·ing 1 : suffer a dull persistent pain 2 : yearn —**ache** n

achieve \ə'chēv\ vb achieved; achiev·ing : gain by work or effort —**achieve·ment** n —**achiev·er** n

ac·id \'asəd\ adj 1 : sour or biting to the taste 2 : sharp in manner 3 : of or relating to an acid ~ n : sour water-soluble chemical compound that reacts with a base to form a salt —**acid·ic** \ə'sidik\ adj —**acid·i·fy** \ə'sidə,fī\ vb —**acid·i·ty** \-ətē\ n —**acid·ly** adv

ac·knowl·edge \ik'nälij, ak-\ vb -edged; -edg·ing 1 : admit as true 2 : admit the authority of 3 : express thanks for —**ac·knowl·edg·ment** n

ac·me \'akmē\ n : highest point

ac·ne \'aknē\ n : skin disorder marked esp. by pimples

ac·o·lyte \'akə,līt\ n : assistant to a member of clergy in a religious service

acorn \'ā,kȯrn, -kərn\ n : nut of the oak

acous·tic \ə'küstik\ adj : relating to hearing or sound —**acous·ti·cal** \-stikəl\ adj —**acous·ti·cal·ly** \-klē\ adv

acous·tics \ə'küstiks\ n sing or pl 1 : science of sound 2 : qualities in a room that affect how sound is heard

ac·quaint \ə'kwānt\ vb 1 : inform 2 : make familiar

ac·quain·tance \ə'kwānt³ns\ n 1 : personal knowledge 2 : person with whom one is acquainted —**ac·quain·tance·ship** n

ac·qui·esce \,akwē'es\ vb -esced; -esc·ing : consent or submit —**ac·qui·es·cence** \-'es³ns\ n —**ac·qui·es·cent** \-³nt\ adj —**ac·qui·es·cent·ly** adv

ac·quire \ə'kwīr\ vb -quired; -quir·ing : gain

ac·qui·si·tion \,akwə'zishən\ n : a gaining or something gained —**acqui·si·tive** \ə'kwizətiv\ adj

ac·quit \ə'kwit\ vb -tt- 1 : pronounce not guilty 2 : conduct (oneself) usu. well —**ac·quit·tal** \-³l\ n

acre \'ākər\ n 1 pl : lands 2 : 4840 square yards

acre·age \'ākərij\ n : area in acres

ac·rid \'akrəd\ adj : sharp and biting —**acrid·i·ty** \a'kridətē, ə-\ n —**ac·rid·ly** adv —**ac·rid·ness** n

ac·ri·mo·ny \'akrə,mōnē\ n, pl -nies : harshness of language or feeling —**ac·ri·mo·ni·ous** \,akrə'mōnēəs\ adj —**ac·ri·mo·ni·ous·ly** adv

ac·ro·bat \'akrə,bat\ n : performer of tumbling feats —**ac·ro·bat·ic** \,akrə'batik\ adj

across \ə'krȯs\ adv 1 : to or on the opposite side ~ prep 1 : to or on the opposite side of 2 : on so as to cross

acryl·ic \ə'krilik\ n 1 : plastic used for molded parts or in paints 2 : synthetic textile fiber

act \'akt\ n 1 : thing done 2 : law 3 : main division of a play ~ vb 1 : perform in a play 2 : conduct oneself 3 : operate 4 : produce an effect

action \'akshən\ n 1 : legal proceeding 2 : manner or method of performing 3 : activity 4 : thing done over a period of time or in stages 5 : combat 6 : events of a literary plot 7 : operating mechanism

ac·ti·vate \'aktə,vāt\ *vb* **-vat·ed; -vat·ing** : make active or reactive —**ac·ti·va·tion** \,aktə'vāshən\ *n*

ac·tive \'aktiv\ *adj* **1** : causing action or change **2** : lively, vigorous, or energetic **3** : erupting or likely to erupt **4** : now in operation —**active** *n* —**ac·tive·ly** *adv*

ac·tiv·i·ty \ak'tivətē\ *n, pl* **-ties 1** : quality or state of being active **2** : what one is actively doing

ac·tor \'aktər\ *n* : one that acts

ac·tress \'aktrəs\ *n* : woman who acts in plays

ac·tu·al \'akchəwəl\ *adj* : really existing —**ac·tu·al·i·ty** \,akchə'walətē\ *n* —**ac·tu·al·iza·tion** \,akchəwələ'zāshən\ *n* —**ac·tu·al·ize** \'akchəwə,līz\ *vb* —**ac·tu·al·ly** *adv*

ac·tu·ary \'akchə,werē\ *n, pl* **-ar·ies** : one who calculates insurance risks and premiums —**ac·tu·ar·i·al** \,akchə'werēəl\ *adj*

ac·tu·ate \'akchə,wāt\ *vb* **-at·ed; -at·ing** : put into action —**ac·tu·a·tor** \-,wātər\ *n*

acu·men \ə'kyümən\ *n* : mental keenness

acu·punc·ture \'akyù,pəŋkchər\ *n* : treatment by puncturing the body with needles —**acu·punc·tur·ist** \,akyù'pəŋkchərist\ *n*

acute \ə'kyüt\ *adj* **acut·er; acut·est 1** : sharp **2** : containing less than 90 degrees **3** : mentally alert **4** : severe —**acute·ly** *adv* —**acute·ness** *n*

ad \'ad\ *n* : advertisement

ad·age \'adij\ *n* : old familiar saying

ad·a·mant \'adəmənt, -,mant\ *adj* : insistent —**ad·a·mant·ly** *adv*

adapt \ə'dapt\ *vb* : adjust to be suitable for a new use or condition —**adapt·abil·i·ty** \ə,daptə'bilətē\ *n* —**adapt·able** *adj* —**ad·ap·ta·tion** \,ad-,ap'tāshən, -əp-\ *n* —**adapter** *n* —**adap·tive** \ə'daptiv\ *adj*

add \'ad\ *vb* **1** : join to something else so as to increase in amount **2** : say further **3** : find a sum —**ad·di·tion** \ə'dishən\ *n*

ad·der \'adər\ *n* **1** : poisonous European snake **2** : No. American snake

ad·dict \'adikt\ *n* : one who is psychologically or physiologically dependent (as on a drug) ~ \ə'dikt\ *vb* : cause to become an addict —**ad·dic·tion** \ə'dikshən\ *n* —**ad·dic·tive** \-'diktiv\ *adj*

ad·di·tion·al \ə'dishənəl\ *adj* : existing as a result of adding —**ad·di·tion·al·ly** *adv*

ad·di·tive \'adətiv\ *n* : substance added to another

ad·dle \'ad⁹l\ *vb* **-dled; -dling** : confuse

ad·dress \ə'dres\ *vb* **1** : direct one's remarks to **2** : mark an address on ~ \ə'dres, 'ad,res\ *n* **1** : formal speech **2** : place where a person may be reached or mail may be delivered

ad·duce \ə'düs, -'dyüs\ *vb* **-duced; -duc·ing** : offer as proof

ad·e·noid \'ad,nòid, -°nòid\ *n* : enlarged tissue near the opening of the nose into the throat —usu. pl. —**adenoid, ad·e·noi·dal** \-òl\ *adj*

adept \ə'dept\ *adj* : highly skilled —**adept·ly** *adv* —**adept·ness** *n*

ad·e·quate \'adikwət\ *adj* : good or plentiful enough —**ad·e·qua·cy** \-kwəsē\ *n* —**ad·e·quate·ly** *adv*

ad·here \ad'hir, əd-\ *vb* **-hered; -her·ing 1** : remain loyal **2** : stick fast —**ad·her·ence** \-'hirəns\ *n* —**ad·her·ent** \-ənt\ *adj or n*

ad·he·sion \ad'hēzhən, əd-\ *n* : act or state of adhering

ad·he·sive \-'hēsiv, -ziv\ *adj* : tending to adhere ~ *n* : adhesive substance

adieu \ə'dü, -'dyü\ *n, pl* **adieus** *or* **adieux** \-'düz,-'dyüz\ : farewell

ad·ja·cent \ə'jāsənt\ *adj* : situated near or next

ad·jec·tive \'ajiktiv\ *n* : word that serves as a modifier of a noun —**ad·jec·ti·val** \,ajik'tīvəl\ *adj* —**ad·jec·ti·val·ly** *adv*

ad·join \ə'jóin\ *vb* : be next to

ad·journ \ə'jərn\ *vb* : end a meeting —**ad·journ·ment** *n*

ad·judge \ə'jəj\ *vb* **-judged; -judg·ing 1** : think or pronounce to be **2** : award by judicial decision

ad·ju·di·cate \ə'jüdi,kāt\ *vb* **-cat·ed; -cat·ing** : settle judicially —**ad·ju·di·ca·tion** \ə,jüdi'kāshən\ *n*

ad·junct \'aj,əŋkt\ *n* : something joined or added but not essential

ad·just \ə'jəst\ *vb* : fix, adapt, or set right —**ad·just·able** *adj* —**ad·just·er, ad·jus·tor** \ə'jəstər\ *n* —**ad·just·ment** \-mənt\ *n*

ad·ju·tant \'ajətənt\ *n* : aide esp. to commanding officer

ad-lib \'ad'lib\ *vb* **-bb-** : speak without preparation **—ad-lib** *n or adj*

ad-min-is-ter \əd'minəstər\ *vb* **1** : manage **2** : give out esp. in doses **—ad-min-is-tra-ble** \-strəbəl\ *adj* **—ad-min-is-trant** \-strənt\ *n*

ad-min-is-tra-tion \əd,minə'strāshən, ad-\ *n* **1** : process of managing **2** : persons responsible for managing **—ad-min-is-tra-tive** \əd'minə,strātiv\ *adj* **—ad-min-is-tra-tive-ly** *adv*

ad-min-is-tra-tor \əd'minə,strātər\ *n* : one that manages

ad-mi-ra-ble \'admərəbəl\ *adj* : worthy of admiration **—ad-mi-ra-bly** \-blē\ *adv*

ad-mi-ral \'admərəl\ *n* : commissioned officer in the navy ranking next below a fleet admiral

ad-mire \əd'mīr\ *vb* **-mired; -mir-ing** : have high regard for **—ad-mi-ra-tion** \,admə'rāshən\ *n* **—ad-mir-er** *n* **—ad-mir-ing-ly** *adv*

ad-mis-si-ble \əd'misəbəl\ *adj* : that can be permitted **—ad-mis-si-bil-i-ty** \-,misə'bilətē\ *n*

ad-mis-sion \əd'mishən\ *n* **1** : act of admitting **2** : admittance or a fee paid for this **3** : acknowledgment of a fact

ad-mit \əd'mit\ *vb* **-tt-** **1** : allow to enter **2** : permit **3** : recognize as genuine **—ad-mit-ted-ly** *adv*

ad-mit-tance \əd'mit°ns\ *n* : permission to enter

ad-mix-ture \ad'mikschər\ *n* **1** : thing added in mixing **2** : mixture

ad-mon-ish \əd'mänish\ *vb* : rebuke **—ad-mon-ish-ment** \-mənt\ *n* **—ad-mo-ni-tion** \,admə'nishən\ *n* **—ad-mon-i-to-ry** \əd'mänə,tōrē\ *adj*

ado \ə'dü\ *n* **1** : fuss **2** : trouble

ado-be \ə'dōbē\ *n* : sun-dried building brick

ad-o-les-cence \,ad°l'es°ns\ *n* : period of growth between childhood and maturity **—ad-o-les-cent** \-°nt\ *adj or n*

adopt \ə'däpt\ *vb* **1** : take (a child of other parents) as one's own child **2** : take up and practice as one's own **—adop-tion** \-'däpshən\ *n*

adore \ə'dōr\ *vb* **adored; ador-ing 1** : worship **2** : be extremely fond of **—ador-able** *adj* **—ador-ably** *adv* **—ad-o-ra-tion** \,adə'rāshən\ *n*

adorn \ə'dörn\ *vb* : decorate with ornaments **—adorn-ment** *n*

adrift \ə'drift\ *adv or adj* **1** : afloat without motive power or moorings **2** : without guidance or purpose

adroit \ə'dröit\ *adj* : dexterous or shrewd **—adroit-ly** *adv* **—adroit-ness** *n*

adult \ə'dəlt, 'ad,əlt\ *adj* : fully developed and mature ~ *n* : grown-up person **—adult-hood** *n*

adul-ter-ate \ə'dəltə,rāt\ *vb* **-at-ed; -at-ing** : make impure by mixture **—adul-ter-a-tion** \-,dəltə'rāshən\ *n*

adul-tery \ə'dəltərē\ *n, pl* **-ter-ies** : sexual unfaithfulness of a married person **—adul-ter-er** \-tərər\ *n* **—adul-ter-ess** \-tərəs\ *n* **—adul-ter-ous** \-tərəs\ *adj*

ad-vance \əd'vans\ *vb* **-vanced; -vanc-ing 1** : bring or move forward **2** : promote **3** : lend ~ *n* **1** : forward movement **2** : improvement **3** : offer ~ *adj* : being ahead of time **—ad-vance-ment** *n*

ad-van-tage \əd'vantij\ *n* **1** : superiority of position **2** : benefit or gain **—ad-van-ta-geous** \,ad,van'tājəs, -vən-\ *adj* **—ad-van-ta-geous-ly** *adv*

ad-vent \'ad,vent\ *n* **1** *cap* : period before Christmas **2** : a coming into being or use

ad-ven-ti-tious \,advən'tishəs\ *adj* : accidental **—ad-ven-ti-tious-ly** *adv*

ad-ven-ture \əd'venchər\ *n* **1** : risky undertaking **2** : exciting experience **—ad-ven-tur-er** \-chərər\ *n* **—ad-ven-ture-some** \-chərsəm\ *adj* **—ad-ven-tur-ous** \-chərəs\ *adj*

ad-verb \'ad,vərb\ *n* : word that modifies a verb, an adjective, or another adverb **—ad-ver-bi-al** \ad'vərbēəl\ *adj* **—ad-ver-bi-al-ly** *adv*

ad-ver-sary \'advər,serē\ *n, pl* **-sar-ies** : enemy or rival **—adversary** *adj*

ad-verse \ad'vərs, 'ad-,\ *adj* : opposing or unfavorable **—ad-verse-ly** *adv*

ad-ver-si-ty \əd'vərsətē\ *n, pl* **-ties** : hard times

ad-vert \ad'vərt\ *vb* : refer

ad-ver-tise \'advər,tīz\ *vb* **-tised; -tis-ing** : call public attention to **—ad-ver-tise-ment** \,advər'tīzmənt, əd-'vərtəzmənt\ *n* **—ad-ver-tis-er** *n*

ad-ver-tis-ing \'advər,tīziŋ\ *n* : business of preparing advertisements

ad-vice \əd'vīs\ *n* : recommendation with regard to a course of action

ad-vis-able \əd'vīzəbəl\ *adj* : wise or prudent **—ad-vis-abil-i-ty** \-,vīzə-'bilətē\ *n*

ad·vise \əd'vīz\ *vb* -vised; -vis·ing : give advice to —**ad·vis·er, ad·vis·or** \-'vīzər\ *n*

ad·vise·ment \əd'vīzmənt\ *n* : careful consideration

ad·vi·so·ry \əd'vīzərē\ *adj* : having power to advise

ad·vo·cate \'advəkət, -,kāt\ *n* : one who argues or pleads for a cause or proposal ~ \-,kāt\ *vb* -cat·ed; -cat·ing : recommend —**ad·vo·ca·cy** \-vəkə-sē\ *n*

adze \'adz\ *n* : tool for shaping wood

ae·gis \'ējəs\ *n* : protection or sponsorship

ae·on \'ēən, 'ē,än\ *n* : indefinitely long time

aer·ate \'ar,āt\ *vb* -at·ed; -at·ing : supply or impregnate with air —**aer·a·tion** \,ar'āshən\ *n* —**aer·a·tor** \'ar,ātər\ *n*

ae·ri·al \'arēəl\ *adj* : inhabiting, occurring in, or done in the air ~ *n* : antenna

ae·rie \'arē, 'irē\ *n* : eagle's nest

aer·o·bic \,ar'ōbik\ *adj* : using or needing oxygen

aer·o·bics \-biks\ *n sing or pl* : exercises that produce a marked increase in respiration and heart rate

aero·dy·nam·ics \,arōdī'namiks\ *n* : science of bodies in motion in a gas —**aero·dy·nam·ic** \-ik\ *adj* —**aero·dy·nam·i·cal·ly** \-iklē\ *adv*

aero·nau·tics \,arə'nótiks\ *n* : science dealing with aircraft —**aero·nau·ti·cal** \-ikəl\ *adj*

aero·sol \'arə,säl, -,sól\ *n* **1** : liquid or solid particles suspended in a gas **2** : substance sprayed as an aerosol

aero·space \'arō,spās\ *n* : earth's atmosphere and the space beyond —**aero·space** *adj*

aes·thet·ic \es'thetik\ *adj* : relating to beauty —**aes·thet·i·cal·ly** \-iklē\ *adv*

aes·thet·ics \-'thetiks\ *n* : branch of philosophy dealing with beauty

afar \ə'fär\ *adv* : from, at, or to a great distance —**afar** *n*

af·fa·ble \'afəbəl\ *adj* : easy to talk to —**af·fa·bil·i·ty** \,afə'bilətē\ *n* —**af·fa·bly** \'afəblē\ *adv*

af·fair \ə'far\ *n* : something that relates to or involves one

¹af·fect \ə'fekt, a-\ *vb* : assume or feign for effect —**af·fec·ta·tion** \,af,ek'tāshən\ *n*

²affect *vb* : produce an effect on

af·fect·ed \ə'fektəd, a-\ *adj* **1** : pre-

tending to some trait **2** : artificially assumed to impress —**af·fect·ed·ly** *adv*

af·fect·ing \ə'fektiŋ, a-\ *adj* : arousing pity or sorrow —**af·fect·ing·ly** *adv*

af·fec·tion \ə'fekshən\ *n* : kind or loving feeling —**af·fec·tion·ate** \-shənət\ *adj* —**af·fec·tion·ate·ly** *adv*

af·fi·da·vit \,afə'dāvət\ *n* : sworn statement

af·fil·i·ate \ə'filē,āt\ *vb* -at·ed; -at·ing : become a member or branch —**af·fil·i·ate** \-ēət\ *n* —**af·fil·i·a·tion** \-,filē-'āshən\ *n*

af·fin·i·ty \ə'finətē\ *n, pl* -ties : close attraction or relationship

af·firm \ə'fərm\ *vb* : assert positively —**af·fir·ma·tion** \,afər'māshən\ *n*

af·fir·ma·tive \ə'fərmətiv\ *adj* : asserting the truth or existence of something ~ *n* : statement of affirmation or agreement

af·fix \ə'fiks\ *vb* : attach

af·flict \ə'flikt\ *vb* : cause pain and distress to —**af·flic·tion** \-'flikshən\ *n*

af·flu·ence \'af,lüəns; a'flü-, ə-\ *n* : wealth —**af·flu·ent** \-ənt\ *adj*

af·ford \ə'ford\ *vb* **1** : manage to bear the cost of **2** : provide

af·fray \ə'frā\ *n* : fight

af·front \ə'frənt\ *vb or n* : insult

af·ghan \'af,gan, -gən\ *n* : crocheted or knitted blanket

afire \ə'fīr\ *adj or adv* : being on fire

aflame \ə'flām\ *adj or adv* : flaming

afloat \ə'flōt\ *adj or adv* : floating

afoot \ə'füt\ *adv or adj* **1** : on foot **2** : in progress

afore·said \ə'for,sed\ *adj* : said or named before

afraid \ə'frād, *South also* ə'fred\ *adj* : filled with fear

afresh \ə'fresh\ *adv* : anew

aft \'aft\ *adv* : to or toward the stern or tail

af·ter \'aftər\ *adv* : at a later time ~ *prep* **1** : behind in place or time **2** : in pursuit of ~ *conj* : following the time when ~ *adj* **1** : later **2** : located toward the back

af·ter·life \'aftər,līf\ *n* : existence after death

af·ter·math \-,math\ *n* : results

af·ter·noon \,aftər'nün\ *n* : time between noon and evening

af·ter·thought *n* : later thought

af·ter·ward \'aftərwərd\, **af·ter·wards** \-wərdz\ *adv* : at a later time

again \ə'gen, -'gin\ adv 1 : once more 2 : on the other hand 3 : in addition

against \ə'genst\ prep 1 : directly opposite to 2 : in opposition to 3 : so as to touch or strike

agape \ə'gāp, -'gap\ adj or adv : having the mouth open in astonishment

ag·ate \'agət\ n : quartz with bands or masses of various colors

age \'āj\ n 1 : length of time of life or existence 2 : particular time in life (as majority or the latter part) 3 : quality of being old 4 : long time 5 : period in history ~ vb : become old or mature

-age \ij\ n suffix 1 : aggregate 2 : action or process 3 : result of 4 : rate of 5 : place of 6 : state or rank 7 : fee

aged adj 1 : \'ājəd\ : old 2 : \'ājd\ : allowed to mature

age·less \'ājləs\ adj : eternal

agen·cy \'ājənsē\ n, pl -cies 1 : one through which something is accomplished 2 : office or function of an agent 3 : government administrative division

agen·da \ə'jendə\ n : list of things to be done

agent \'ājənt\ n 1 : means 2 : person acting or doing business for another

ag·gran·dize \ə'gran,dīz, 'agrən-\ vb -dized; -diz·ing : make great or greater —**ag·gran·dize·ment** \ə'grandəzmənt, -,dīz-; ,agrən'dīz-\ n

ag·gra·vate \'agrə,vāt\ vb -vat·ed; -vat·ing 1 : make more severe 2 : irritate —**ag·gra·va·tion** \,agrə'vāshən\ n

ag·gre·gate \'agrigət\ adj : formed into a mass ~ \-,gāt\ vb -gat·ed; -gat·ing : collect into a mass ~ \-gət\ n 1 : mass 2 : whole amount

ag·gres·sion \ə'greshən\ n 1 : unprovoked attack 2 : hostile behavior —**ag·gres·sor** \-'gresər\ n

ag·gres·sive \ə'gresiv\ adj 1 : easily provoked to fight 2 : hard working and enterprising —**ag·gres·sive·ly** adv —**ag·gres·sive·ness** n

ag·grieve \ə'grēv\ vb -grieved; -griev·ing 1 : cause grief to 2 : inflict injury on

aghast \ə'gast\ adj : struck with amazement or horror

agile \'ajəl\ adj : able to move quickly and easily —**agil·i·ty** \ə'jilətē\ n

ag·i·tate \'ajə,tāt\ vb -tat·ed; -tat·ing 1 : shake or stir back and forth 2 : excite or trouble the mind of 3 : try to arouse public feeling —**ag·i·ta·tion** \,ajə-'tāshən\ n —**ag·i·ta·tor** \'ajə-,tātər\ n

ag·nos·tic \ag'nästik, əg-\ n : one who doubts the existence of God

ago \ə'gō\ adj or adv : earlier than the present

agog \ə'gäg\ adj : full of excitement

ag·o·nize \'agə,nīz\ vb -nized; -niz·ing : suffer mental agony —**ag·o·niz·ing·ly** adv

ag·o·ny \'agənē\ n, pl -nies : extreme pain or mental distress

agrar·i·an \ə'grerēən\ adj : relating to land ownership or farming interests —**agrarian** n —**agrar·i·an·ism** n

agree \ə'grē\ vb agreed; agree·ing 1 : be of the same opinion 2 : express willingness 3 : get along together 4 : be similar 5 : be appropriate, suitable, or healthful

agree·able \-əbəl\ adj 1 : pleasing 2 : willing to give approval —**agree·able·ness** n —**agree·ably** adv

agree·ment \-mənt\ n 1 : harmony of opinion or purpose 2 : mutual understanding or arrangement

ag·ri·cul·ture \'agri,kəlchər\ n : farming —**ag·ri·cul·tur·al** \,agri'kəl-chərəl\ adj —**ag·ri·cul·tur·ist** \-rist\, **ag·ri·cul·tur·al·ist** \-rəlist\ n

aground \ə'graünd\ adv or adj : on or onto the bottom or shore

ague \'āgyü\ n 1 : fever with recurrent chills and sweating 2 : malaria

ahead \ə'hed\ adv or adj 1 : in or toward the front 2 : into or for the future 3 : in a more advantageous position

ahead of prep 1 : in front of or advance of 2 : in excess of

ahoy \ə'hói\ interj —used in hailing

aid \'ād\ vb : provide help or support ~ n : help

aide \'ād\ n : helper

AIDS \'ādz\ n : serious disease of the human immune system

ail \'āl\ vb 1 : trouble 2 : be ill

ai·le·ron \'ālə,rän\ n : movable part of an airplane wing

ail·ment \'ālmənt\ n : bodily disorder

aim \'ām\ vb 1 : point or direct (as a weapon) 2 : direct one's efforts ~ n 1 : an aiming or the direction of aiming 2 : object or purpose —**aim·less** adj —**aim·less·ly** adv —**aim·less·ness** n

air \'ar\ n 1 : mixture of gases surrounding the earth 2 : melody 3 : outward appearance **4** : artificial manner **5** : compressed air **6** : travel by or use of aircraft **7** : medium of transmission of radio waves ~ *vb* **1** : expose to the air **2** : broadcast —**air·borne** \-,bōrn\ *adj*

air–condition *vb* : equip with an apparatus (**air conditioner**) for filtering and cooling the air

air·craft *n, pl* **aircraft** : craft that flies

Aire·dale terrier \'ar,dāl-\ *n* : large terrier with a hard wiry coat

air·field *n* : airport or its landing field

air force *n* : military organization for conducting warfare by air

air·lift *n* : a transporting of esp. emergency supplies by aircraft —**airlift** *vb*

air·line *n* : air transportation system —**air·lin·er** *n*

air·mail *n* : system of transporting mail by airplane —**airmail** *vb*

air·man \-mən\ *n* **1** : aviator **2** : enlisted man in the air force in one of the 3 ranks below sergeant **3** : enlisted man in the air force ranking just below airman first class

airman basic *n* : enlisted man of the lowest rank in the air force

airman first class *n* : enlisted man in the air force ranking just below sergeant

air·plane *n* : fixed-wing aircraft heavier than air

air·port *n* : place for landing aircraft and usu. for receiving passengers

air·ship *n* : powered lighter-than-air craft

air·strip *n* : airfield runway

air·tight *adj* : tightly sealed to prevent flow of air

air·waves \'ar,wāvz\ *n pl* : medium of transmission of radio waves

airy \'arē\ *adj* **air·i·er; -est** **1** : delicate **2** : breezy

aisle \'īl\ *n* : passage between sections of seats

ajar \ə'jär\ *adj or adv* : partly open

akim·bo \ə'kimbō\ *adj or adv* : having the hand on the hip and the elbow turned outward

akin \ə'kin\ *adj* **1** : related by blood **2** : similar in kind

-al \əl\ *adj suffix* : of, relating to, or characterized by

al·a·bas·ter \'alə,bastər\ *n* : white or translucent mineral

alac·ri·ty \ə'lakrətē\ *n* : cheerful readiness

alarm \ə'lärm\ *n* **1** : warning signal or device **2** : fear at sudden danger ~ *vb* **1** : warn **2** : frighten

alas \ə'las\ *interj* —used to express unhappiness, pity, or concern

al·ba·tross \'albə,trós, -,träs\ *n, pl* **-tross** *or* **-trosses** : large seabird

al·be·it \ól'bēət, al-\ *conj* : even though

al·bi·no \al'bīnō\ *n, pl* **-nos** : person or animal with abnormally white skin —**al·bi·nism** \'albə,nizəm\ *n*

al·bum \'albəm\ *n* **1** : book for displaying a collection (as of photographs) **2** : collection of recordings

al·bu·men \al'byümən\ *n* **1** : white of an egg **2** : albumin

al·bu·min \-mən\ *n* : protein found in blood, milk, egg white, and tissues

al·che·my \'alkəmē\ *n* : medieval chemistry —**al·che·mist** \'alkəmist\ *n*

al·co·hol \'alkə,hól\ *n* **1** : intoxicating agent in liquor **2** : liquor —**alcoholic** *adj*

al·co·hol·ic \,alkə'hólik, -'häl-\ *n* : person affected with alcoholism

al·co·hol·ism \'alkə,hól,izəm\ *n* : addiction to alcoholic beverages

al·cove \'al,kōv\ *n* : recess in a room or wall

al·der·man \'óldərmən\ *n* : city official

ale \'āl\ *n* : beerlike beverage —**ale·house** *n*

alert \ə'lərt\ *adj* **1** : watchful **2** : quick to perceive and act ~ *n* : alarm ~ *vb* : warn —**alert·ly** *adv* —**alert·ness** *n*

ale·wife *n* : fish of the herring family

al·fal·fa \al'falfə\ *n* : cloverlike forage plant

al·ga \'algə\ *n, pl* **-gae** \'al,jē\ : any of a group of lower plants that includes seaweed —**al·gal** \-gəl\ *adj*

al·ge·bra \'aljəbrə\ *n* : branch of mathematics using symbols —**al·ge·bra·ic** \,aljə'brāik\ *adj* —**al·ge·bra·i·cal·ly** \-'brāəklē\ *adv*

alias \'ālēəs, 'ālyəs\ *adv* : otherwise called ~ *n* : assumed name

al·i·bi \'alə,bī\ *n* **1** : defense of having been elsewhere when a crime was committed **2** : justification ~ *vb* **-bied; -bi·ing** : offer an excuse

alien \'ālēən, 'ālyən\ *adj* : foreign ~ *n* **1** : foreign-born resident **2** : extraterrestrial

alien·ate \'ālēə,nāt, 'ālyə-\ *vb* **-at·ed; -at·ing** : cause to be no longer friendly —**alien·ation** \,ālēə'nāshən, ,ālyə-\ *n*

alight \ə'līt\ vb : dismount

align \ə'līn\ vb : bring into line —**align-er** n —**align-ment** n

alike \ə'līk\ adj : identical or very similar ~ adv : equally

al-i-men-ta-ry \ˌalə'mentərē\ adj : relating to or functioning in nutrition

al-i-mo-ny \'alə,mōnē\ n, pl -nies : money paid to a separated or divorced spouse

alive \ə'līv\ adj 1 : having life 2 : lively or animated

al-ka-li \'alkə,lī\ n, pl -lies or -lis : strong chemical base —**al-ka-line** \-kələn, -,līn\ adj —**al-ka-lin-i-ty** \ˌalkə'linətē\ n

all \'ȯl\ adj 1 : the whole of 2 : greatest possible 3 : every one of ~ adv 1 : wholly 2 : so much 3 : for each side ~ pron 1 : whole number or amount 2 : everything or everyone

Al-lah \'älə, 'al-\ n : God of Islam

all-around adj : versatile

al-lay \ə'lā\ vb 1 : alleviate 2 : calm

al-lege \ə'lej\ vb -leged; -leg-ing : assert without proof —**al-le-ga-tion** \ˌali-gāshən\ n —**al-leg-ed-ly** \ə'lejədlē\ adv

al-le-giance \ə'lējəns\ n : loyalty

al-le-go-ry \'alə,gȯrē\ n, pl -ries : story in which figures and actions are symbols of general truths —**al-le-gor-i-cal** \ˌalə'gȯrikəl\ adj

al-le-lu-ia \ˌalə'lüyə\ interj : hallelujah

al-ler-gen \'alərjən\ n : something that causes allergy —**al-ler-gen-ic** \ˌalər-'jenik\ adj

al-ler-gy \'alərjē\ n, pl -gies : abnormal reaction to a substance —**al-ler-gic** \ə'lərjik\ adj —**al-ler-gist** \'alərjist\ n

al-le-vi-ate \ə'lēvē,āt\ vb -at-ed; -at-ing : relieve or lessen —**al-le-vi-a-tion** \ə,lēvē'āshən\ n

al-ley \'alē\ n, pl -leys 1 : place for bowling 2 : narrow passage between buildings

al-li-ance \ə'līəns\ n : association

al-li-ga-tor \'alə,gātər\ n : large aquatic reptile related to the crocodiles

al-lit-er-a-tion \ə,litə'rāshən\ n : repetition of initial sounds of words —**al-lit-er-a-tive** \-'litə,rātiv\ adj

al-lo-cate \'alə,kāt\ vb -cat-ed; -cat-ing : assign —**al-lo-ca-tion** \ˌalə'kāshən\ n

al-lot \ə'lät\ vb -tt- : distribute as a share —**al-lot-ment** n

al-low \ə'laù\ vb 1 : admit or concede 2 : permit —**al-low-able** adj

al-low-ance \-əns\ n 1 : allotted share 2 : money given regularly for expenses

al-loy \'al,ȯi\ n : metals melted together —**al-loy** \ə'lȯi\ vb

all right adv or adj 1 : satisfactorily 2 : yes 3 : certainly

all-spice \'ȯl,spīs\ n : berry of a West Indian tree made into a spice

al-lude \ə'lüd\ vb -lud-ed; -lud-ing : refer indirectly —**al-lu-sion** \-'lüzhən\ n —**al-lu-sive** \-'lüsiv\ adj —**al-lu-sive-ly** adv —**al-lu-sive-ness** n

al-lure \ə'lùr\ vb -lured; -lur-ing : entice ~ n : attractive power

al-ly \ə'lī, 'al,ī\ vb -lied; -ly-ing : enter into an alliance —**al-ly** \'al,ī, ə'lī\ n

-al-ly \əlē\ adv suffix : -ly

al-ma-nac \'ȯlmə,nak, 'al-\ n : annual information book

al-mighty \ȯl'mītē\ adj : having absolute power

al-mond \'ämənd , 'am-, 'alm-, 'älm-\ n : tree with nutlike fruit kernels

al-most \'ȯl,mōst, ȯl-'\ adv : very nearly

alms \'ämz, 'älmz, 'almz\ n, pl **alms** : charitable gift

aloft \ə'lȯft\ adv : high in the air

alo-ha \ä'lōhä\ interj —used to greet or bid farewell

alone \ə'lōn\ adj 1 : separated from others 2 : not including anyone or anything else —**alone** adv

along \ə'lȯŋ\ prep 1 : in line with the direction of 2 : at a point on or during ~ adv 1 : forward 2 : as a companion 3 : all the time

along-side adv or prep : along or by the side

alongside of prep : alongside

aloof \ə'lüf\ adj : indifferent and reserved —**aloof-ness** n

aloud \ə'laùd\ adv : so as to be heard

al-paca \al'pakə\ n 1 : So. American mammal related to the llama 2 : alpaca wool or cloth made of this

al-pha-bet \'alfə,bet, -bət\ n : ordered set of letters of a language —**al-pha-bet-i-cal** \ˌalfə'betikəl\, **al-pha-bet-ic** \-'betik\ adj —**al-pha-bet-i-cal-ly** \-klē\ adv

al-pha-bet-ize \'alfəbə,tīz\ vb -ized; -iz-ing : arrange in alphabetical order —**al-pha-bet-iz-er** n

al-ready \ȯl'redē\ adv : by a given time

al-so \'ȯlsō\ adv : in addition

al·tar \'ȯltər\ n : structure for rituals

al·ter \'ȯltər\ vb : make different —**al·ter·a·tion** \,ȯltə'rāshən\ n

al·ter·ca·tion \,ȯltər'kāshən\ n : dispute

al·ter·nate \'ȯltərnət, 'al-\ adj 1 : arranged or succeeding by turns 2 : every other ~ \-,nāt\ vb -**nat·ed;** -**nat·ing** : occur or cause to occur by turns ~ \-nət\ n : substitute —**al·ter·nate·ly** adv —**al·ter·na·tion** \,ȯltər'nāshən, ,al-\ n

alternating current n : electric current that regularly reverses direction

al·ter·na·tive \ȯl'tərnətiv, al-\ adj : offering a choice —**alternative** n

al·ter·na·tor \'ȯltər,nātər, 'al-\ n : alternating-current generator

al·though \ȯl'thō\ conj : even though

al·tim·e·ter \al'timətər, 'altə,mētər\ n : instrument for measuring altitude

al·ti·tude \'altə,tüd, -,tyüd\ n 1 : distance up from the ground 2 : angular distance above the horizon

al·to \'altō\ n, pl -**tos** : lower female choral voice

al·to·geth·er \,ȯltə'gethər\ adv 1 : wholly 2 : on the whole

al·tru·ism \'altrü,izəm\ n : concern for others —**al·tru·ist** \-ist\ n —**al·tru·is·tic** \,altrü'istik\ adj —**al·tru·is·ti·cal·ly** \-tiklē\ adv

al·um \'aləm\ n : crystalline compound containing aluminum

alu·mi·num \ə'lümənəm\ n : silver-white malleable ductile light metallic element

alum·na \ə'ləmnə\ n, pl -**nae** \-,nē\ : woman graduate

alum·nus \ə'ləmnəs\ n, pl -**ni** \-,nī\ : graduate

al·ways \'ȯlwēz, -wāz\ adv 1 : at all times 2 : forever

am pres 1st sing of BE

amal·gam \ə'malgəm\ n 1 : mercury alloy 2 : mixture

amal·gam·ate \ə'malgə,māt\ vb -**at·ed;** -**at·ing** : unite —**amal·ga·ma·tion** \-,malgə'māshən\ n

am·a·ryl·lis \,amə'riləs\ n : bulbous herb with clusters of large colored flowers like lilies

amass \ə'mas\ vb : gather

am·a·teur \'amə,tər, -,tùr, -,tyùr, -,chùr, -chər\ n 1 : person who does something for pleasure rather than for pay 2 : person who is not expert —

am·a·teur·ish \,amə'tərish, -'tùr-, -'tyùr-\ adj —**am·a·teur·ism** \'amə,tər,izəm, -,tùr-, -,tyùr-, -,chùr-, -chər-\ n

am·a·to·ry \'amə,tōrē\ adj : of or expressing sexual love

amaze \ə'māz\ vb **amazed; amaz·ing** : fill with wonder —**amaze·ment** n —**amaz·ing·ly** adv

am·a·zon \'amə,zän, -zən\ n : tall strong woman —**am·a·zo·ni·an** \,amə'zō-nēən\ adj

am·bas·sa·dor \am'basədər\ n : representative esp. of a government —**am·bas·sa·do·ri·al** \-,basə'dōrēəl\ adj —**am·bas·sa·dor·ship** n

am·ber \'ambər\ n : yellowish fossil resin or its color

am·ber·gris \'ambər,gris, -,grēs\ n : waxy substance from certain whales used in making perfumes

am·bi·dex·trous \,ambi'dekstrəs\ adj : equally skilled with both hands —**am·bi·dex·trous·ly** adv

am·bi·ence, am·bi·ance \'ambēəns, 'ämbē,äns\ n : pervading atmosphere

am·big·u·ous \am'bigyəwəs\ adj : having more than one interpretation —**am·bi·gu·i·ty** \,ambə'gyüətē\ n

am·bi·tion \am'bishən\ n : eager desire for success or power —**am·bi·tious** \shəs\ adj —**am·bi·tious·ly** adv

am·biv·a·lence \am'bivələns\ n : simultaneous attraction and repulsion —**am·biv·a·lent** \-lənt\ adj

am·ble \'ambəl\ vb -**bled; -bling** : go at a leisurely gait —**amble** n

am·bu·lance \'ambyələns\ n : vehicle for carrying injured or sick persons

am·bu·la·to·ry \'ambyələ,tōrē\ adj 1 : relating to or adapted to walking 2 : able to walk about

am·bush \'am,bùsh\ n : trap by which a surprise attack is made from a place of hiding —**ambush** vb

ame·lio·rate \ə'mēlyə,rāt\ vb -**rat·ed;** -**rat·ing** : make or grow better —**ame·lio·ra·tion** \-,mēlyə'rāshən\ n

amen \'ā'men, 'ä-\ interj —used for affirmation esp. at the end of prayers

ame·na·ble \ə'mēnəbəl, -'men-\ adj : ready to yield or be influenced

amend \ə'mend\ vb 1 : improve 2 : alter in writing

amend·ment \-mənt\ n : change made in a formal document (as a law)

amends \ə'mendz\ *n sing or pl* : compensation for injury or loss

ame·ni·ty \ə'menətē, -'mē-\ *n, pl* **-ties 1** : agreeableness **2** *pl* : social conventions **3** : something serving to comfort or accommodate

am·e·thyst \'aməthəst\ *n* : purple gemstone

ami·a·ble \'āmēəbəl\ *adj* : easy to get along with —**ami·a·bil·i·ty** \,āmē-ə-'bilətē\ *n* —**ami·a·bly** \'āmēəblē\ *adv*

ami·ca·ble \'amikəbəl\ *adj* : friendly —**am·i·ca·bly** \-blē\ *adv*

amid \ə'mid\, **amidst** \-'midst\ *prep* : in or into the middle of

amino acid \ə'mēnō-\ *n* : nitrogen-containing acid

amiss \ə'mis\ *adv* : in the wrong way ~ *adj* : wrong

am·me·ter \'am,ētər\ *n* : instrument for measuring electric current

am·mo·nia \ə'mōnyə\ *n* **1** : colorless gaseous compound of nitrogen and hydrogen **2** : solution of ammonia in water

am·mu·ni·tion \,amyə'nishən\ *n* **1** : projectiles fired from guns **2** : explosive items used in war

am·ne·sia \am'nēzhə\ *n* : sudden loss of memory —**am·ne·si·ac** \-zē,ak, -zhē-\, **am·ne·sic** \-zik, -sik\ *adj or n*

am·nes·ty \'amnəstē\ *n, pl* **-ties** : a pardon for a group —**amnesty** *vb*

amoe·ba \ə'mēbə\ *n, pl* **-bas** *or* **-bae** \-,bē\ : tiny one-celled animal that occurs esp. in water —**amoe·bic** \-'bik\ *adj*

amok \ə'mək, -'mäk\ *adv* : in a violent or uncontrolled way

am·o·rous \'amərəs\ *adj* **1** : inclined to love **2** : being in love **3** : indicative of love —**am·o·rous·ly** *adv* —**am·o·rous·ness** *n*

amor·phous \ə'mórfəs\ *adj* : shapeless

am·or·tize \'amər,tīz, ə'mór-\ *vb* **-tized; -tiz·ing** : get rid of (as a debt) gradually with periodic payments —**amor·ti·za·tion** \,amərtə'zāshən, ə,mórt-\ *n*

amount \ə'maúnt\ *vb* **1** : be equivalent **2** : reach a total ~ *n* : total number or quantity

amour \ə'múr, ä-, a-\ *n* **1** : love affair **2** : lover

am·pere \'am,pir\ *n* : unit of electric current

am·per·sand \'ampər,sand\ *n* : character & used for the word *and*

am·phib·i·ous \am'fibēəs\ *adj* **1** : able to live both on land and in water **2** : adapted for both land and water —**am·phib·i·an** \-ən\ *n*

am·phi·the·ater \'amfə,thēətər\ *n* : oval or circular structure with rising tiers of seats around an arena

am·ple \'ampəl\ *adj* **-pler** \-plər\; **-plest** \-pləst\ **1** : large **2** : sufficient —**am·ply** \-plē\ *adv*

am·pli·fy \'amplə,fī\ *vb* **-fied; -fy·ing** : make louder, stronger, or more thorough —**am·pli·fi·ca·tion** \,ampləfə'kāshən\ *n* —**am·pli·fi·er** \'amplə,fīər\ *n*

am·pli·tude \-,tüd, -,tyüd\ *n* **1** : fullness **2** : extent of a vibratory movement

am·pu·tate \'ampyə,tāt\ *vb* **-tat·ed; -tat·ing** : cut off (a body part) —**am·pu·ta·tion** \,ampyə'tāshən\ *n* —**am·pu·tee** \,ampyə'tē\ *n*

amuck \ə'mək\ *var of* AMOK

am·u·let \'amyələt\ *n* : ornament worn as a charm against evil

amuse \ə'myüz\ *vb* **amused; amus·ing 1** : engage the attention of in an interesting and pleasant way **2** : make laugh —**amuse·ment** *n*

an \ən, 'an\ *indefinite article* : a —used before words beginning with a vowel sound

-an \ən\, **-ian** \ēən\, **-ean** \ēən\ *n suffix* **1** : one that belongs to **2** : one skilled in ~ *adj suffix* **1** : of or belonging to **2** : characteristic of or resembling

anach·ro·nism \ə'nakrə,nizəm\ *n* : one that is chronologically out of place —**anach·ro·nis·tic** \ə,nakrə'nistik\ *adj*

an·a·con·da \,anə'kändə\ *n* : large So. American snake

ana·gram \'anə,gram\ *n* : word or phrase made by transposing the letters of another word or phrase

anal \'ān°l\ *adj* : relating to the anus

an·al·ge·sic \,an°l'jēzik, -sik\ *n* : pain reliever

anal·o·gy \ə'naləjē\ *n, pl* **-gies 1** : similarity between unlike things **2** : example of something similar —**a·log·i·cal** \,an°l'äjikəl\ *adj* —**ana·log·i·cal·ly** \-iklē\ *adv* —**anal·o·gous** \ə'naləgəs\ *adj*

anal·y·sis \ə'naləsəs\ *n, pl* **-y·ses** \-,sēz\ **1** : examination of a thing to deter-

mine its parts **2** : psychoanalysis —
an·a·lyst \'an⁴l̄ist\ *n* —**an·a·lyt·ic**
\,an⁴l'itik\, **an·a·lyt·i·cal** \-ikəl\ *adj*
—**an·a·lyt·i·cal·ly** \-iklē\ *adv*
an·a·lyze \'an⁴l,īz\ *vb* -**lyzed**; -**lyz·ing**
: make an analysis of
an·ar·chism \'anər,kizəm, -,när-\ *n*
: theory that all government is undesirable —**an·ar·chist** \-kist\ *n or adj*
—**an·ar·chis·tic** \,anər'kistik\ *adj*
an·ar·chy \'anərkē, -,när-\ *n* : lack of
government or order —**an·ar·chic** \a-
'närkik\ *adj* —**an·ar·chi·cal·ly** \-iklē\
adv
anath·e·ma \ə'nathəmə\ *n* **1** : solemn
curse **2** : person or thing accursed or
intensely disliked
anat·o·my \ə'natəmē\ *n, pl* -**mies**
: science dealing with the structure
of organisms —**an·a·tom·ic** \,anə-
'tämik\, **an·a·tom·i·cal** \-ikəl\ *adj*
—**an·a·tom·i·cal·ly** *adv* —**anat·
o·mist** \ə'natəmist\ *n*
-**ance** \əns\ *n suffix* **1** : action or process
2 : quality or state **3** : amount or degree
an·ces·tor \'an,sestər\ *n* : one from
whom an individual is descended
an·ces·tress \-trəs\ *n* : female ancestor
an·ces·try \-trē\ *n* **1** : line of descent **2**
: ancestors —**an·ces·tral** \an'sestrəl\
adj
an·chor \'aŋkər\ *n* : heavy device that
catches in the sea bottom to hold a
ship in place ~ *vb* : hold or become
held in place by or as if by an anchor
—**an·chor·age** \-korij\ *n*
an·chor·man \'aŋkər,man\ *n* : news
broadcast coordinator
an·cho·vy \'an,chōvē, an'chō-\ *n, pl*
-**vies** *or* -**vy** : small herringlike fish
an·cient \'ānshənt\ *adj* **1** : having existed for many years **2** : belonging to
times long past —**ancient** *n*
-**ancy** \ənsē\ *n suffix* : quality or state
and \ənd, 'and\ *conj* —used to indicate
connection or addition
and·iron \'an,dīərn\ *n* : one of 2 metal
supports for wood in a fireplace
an·drog·y·nous \an'dräjənəs\ *adj* **1**
: having characteristics of both male
and female **2** : suitable for either sex
an·ec·dote \'anik,dōt\ *n* : brief story —
an·ec·dot·al \,anik'dōt⁴l\ *adj*
ane·mia \ə'nēmēə\ *n* : blood deficiency
—**ane·mic** \ə'nēmik\ *adj*
anem·o·ne \ə'nemənē\ *n* : small herb
with showy usu. white flowers

an·es·the·sia \,anəs'thēzhə\ *n* : loss of
bodily sensation
an·es·thet·ic \,anəs'thetik\ *n* : agent that
produces anesthesia —**anesthetic** *adj*
—**anes·the·tist** \ə'nesthətist\ *n* —
anes·the·tize \-thə,tīz\ *vb*
anew \ə'nü, -'nyü\ *adv* : over again
an·gel \'ānjəl\ *n* : spiritual being superior to humans —**an·gel·ic** \an'jelik\,
an·gel·i·cal \-ikəl\ *adj* —**an·gel·i·
cal·ly** *adv*
an·ger \'aŋgər\ *n* : strong feeling of displeasure ~ *vb* : make angry
an·gi·na \an'jīnə\ *n* : painful disorder of
heart muscles —**an·gi·nal** \an'jīn⁴l\
adj
¹an·gle \'aŋgəl\ *n* **1** : figure formed by
the meeting of 2 lines in a point **2**
: sharp corner **3** : point of view ~ *vb*
-**gled**; -**gling** : turn or direct at an angle
²angle *vb* -**gled**; -**gling** : fish with
a hook and line —**an·gler** \-glər\ *n* —
an·gle·worm *n* —**an·gling** *n*
an·go·ra \aŋ'gōrə, an-\ *n* : yarn or cloth
made from the hair of an Angora goat
or rabbit
an·gry \'aŋgrē\ *adj* -**gri·er**; -est : feeling
or showing anger —**an·gri·ly** \-grəlē\
adv
an·guish \'aŋgwish\ *n* : extreme pain or
distress of mind —**an·guished**
\-gwisht\ *adj*
an·gu·lar \'aŋgyələr\ *adj* **1** : having
many or sharp angles **2** : thin and
bony —**an·gu·lar·i·ty** \,aŋgyə'larətē\
n
an·i·mal \'anəməl\ *n* **1** : living being capable of feeling and voluntary motion
2 : lower animal as distinguished
from humans
an·i·mate \'anəmət\ *adj* : having life ~
\-,māt\ *vb* -**mat·ed**; -**mat·ing** **1** : give
life or vigor to **2** : make appear to
move —**an·i·mat·ed** *adj*
an·i·ma·tion \,anə'māshən\ *n* **1** : liveliness **2** : animated cartoon
an·i·mos·i·ty \,anə'mäsətē\ *n, pl* -**ties**
: resentment
an·i·mus \'anəməs\ *n* : deep-seated hostility
an·ise \'anəs\ *n* : herb related to the carrot with aromatic seeds (**ani·seed**
\-,sēd\) used in flavoring
an·kle \'aŋkəl\ *n* : joint or region between the foot and the leg —**an·kle·
bone** *n*

an·nals \'an^əlz\ *n pl* : chronological record of history —**an·nal·ist** \-^əlist\ *n*

an·neal \ə'nēl\ *vb* 1 : make less brittle by heating and then cooling 2 : strengthen or toughen

an·nex \ə'neks, 'an,eks\ *vb* : assume political control over (a territory) ~ \'an,eks, -iks\ *n* : added building —**an·nex·a·tion** \,an,ek'sāshən\ *n*

an·ni·hi·late \ə'nīə,lāt\ *vb* -**lat·ed; -lat·ing** : destroy —**an·ni·hi·la·tion** \-,nīə'lāshən\ *n*

an·ni·ver·sa·ry \,anə'vərsərē\ *n, pl* -**ries** : annual return of the date of a notable event or its celebration

an·no·tate \'anə,tāt\ *vb* -**tat·ed; -tat·ing** : furnish with notes —**an·no·ta·tion** \,anə'tāshən\ *n* —**an·no·ta·tor** \'anə,tātər\ *n*

an·nounce \ə'naúns\ *vb* -**nounced; -nounc·ing** : make known publicly —**an·nounce·ment** *n* —**an·nounc·er** *n*

an·noy \ə'nói\ *vb* : disturb or irritate —**an·noy·ance** \-əns\ *n* —**an·noy·ing·ly** \-'nóiiŋlē\ *adv*

an·nu·al \'anyəwəl\ *adj* 1 : occurring once a year 2 : living only one year —**annual** *n* —**an·nu·al·ly** *adv*

an·nu·ity \ə'nüətē, -'nyü-\ *n, pl* -**ties** : amount payable annually or the right to such a payment

an·nul \ə'nəl\ *vb* -**ll-** : make legally void —**an·nul·ment** *n*

an·ode \'an,ōd\ *n* 1 : positive electrode 2 : negative battery terminal —**an·od·ic** \a'nädik\

anoint \ə'nóint\ *vb* : apply oil to as a rite —**anoint·ment** *n*

anom·a·ly \ə'näməlē\ *n, pl* -**lies** : something abnormal or unusual —**anom·a·lous** \-ləs\ *adj*

anon·y·mous \ə'nänəməs\ *adj* : of unknown origin —**an·o·nym·i·ty** \,anə'nimətē\ *n* —**anon·y·mous·ly** *adv*

an·oth·er \ə'nəthər\ *adj* 1 : any or some other 2 : one more ~ *pron* 1 : one more 2 : one different

an·swer \'ansər\ *n* 1 : something spoken or written in reply to a question 2 : solution to a problem ~ *vb* 1 : reply to 2 : be responsible 3 : be adequate —**an·swer·er** *n*

an·swer·able \-rəbəl\ *adj* : responsible

ant \'ant\ *n* : small social insect —**ant·hill** *n*

-ant \ənt\ *n suffix* 1 : one that performs or causes an action 2 : thing that is

acted upon ~ *adj suffix* 1 : performing an action or being in a condition 2 : causing an action or process

an·tag·o·nism \an'tagə,nizəm\ *n* : active opposition or hostility —**an·tag·o·nist** \-ənist\ *n* —**an·tag·o·nis·tic** \-,tagə'nistik\ *adj*

an·tag·o·nize \an'tagə,nīz\ *vb* -**nized; -niz·ing** : cause to be hostile

ant·arc·tic \ant'ärktik, -'ärtik\ *adj* : relating to the region near the south pole

antarctic circle *n* : circle parallel to the equator approximately 23°27′ from the south pole

an·te·bel·lum \,anti'beləm\ *adj* : existing before the U.S. Civil War

an·te·ce·dent \,antə'sēd^ənt\ *n* : one that comes before —**antecedent** *adj*

an·te·lope \'ant^əl,ōp\ *n, pl* -**lope** *or* -**lopes** : deerlike mammal related to the ox

an·ten·na \an'tenə\ *n, pl* -**nae** \-,nē\ *or* -**nas** 1 : one of the long slender paired sensory organs on the head of an arthropod 2 *pl* -**nas** : metallic device for sending or receiving radio waves

an·te·ri·or \an'tirēər\ *adj* : located before in place or time

an·them \'anthəm\ *n* : song or hymn of praise or gladness

an·ther \'anthər\ *n* : part of a seed plant that contains pollen

an·thol·o·gy \an'thäləjē\ *n, pl* -**gies** : literary collection

an·thra·cite \'anthrə,sīt\ *n* : hard coal

an·thro·poid \'anthrə,póid\ *n* : large ape —**anthropoid** *adj*

an·thro·pol·o·gy \,anthrə'päləjē\ *n* : science dealing with humans —**an·thro·po·log·i·cal** \-pə'läjikəl\ *adj* —**an·thro·pol·o·gist** \-'päləjist\ *n*

anti- \,antē, -,tī, **ant-, anth-** *prefix* 1 : opposite in kind, position, or action 2 : opposing or hostile toward 3 : defending against 4 : curing or treating

antiabortion	antiart
antiacademic	antiauthoritar-
antiadministra-	ian
tion	antiauthority
antiaggression	antibacterial
antiaircraft	antibias
antialien	antiblack
antiapartheid	antibourgeois
antiaristocratic	antiboycott

antibureau-
   cratic
antiburglar
antiburglary
antibusiness
anticancer
anticapitalism
anticapitalist
anti-Catholic
anticensorship
anti-Christian
anti-Chris-
   tianity
antichurch
anticigarette
anticlerical
anticollision
anticolonial
anticommunism
anticommunist
anticonserva-
   tion
anticonserva-
   tionist
anticonsumer
anticonven-
   tional
anticorrosion
anticorrosive
anticorruption
anticrime
anticruelty
anticult
anticultural
antidandruff
antidemocratic
antidiscrimina-
   tion
antidrug
antidumping
antiestablish-
   ment
antievolution
antievolutionary
antifamily
antifascism
antifascist
antifatigue
antifemale
antifeminine
antifeminism
antifeminist
antifertility
antiforeign
antiforeigner
antifraud
antigambling
antiglare

antigovernment
antiguerrilla
antigun
antihijack
antihomosexual
antihuman
antihumanism
antihumanistic
antihunting
anti-imperial-
   ism
anti-imperialist
anti-inflation
anti-inflationary
anti-institu-
   tional
anti-integration
anti-intellectual
anti-intellectual-
   ism
antijamming
anti-Jewish
antilabor
antiliberal
antiliberalism
antilitter
antilittering
antilynching
antimale
antimanage-
   ment
antimaterialism
antimaterialist
antimicrobial
antimilitarism
antimilitarist
antimilitary
antimiscegena-
   tion
antimonopolist
antimonopoly
antimosquito
antinoise
antiobesity
antiobscenity
antipapal
antipersonnel
antipolice
antipollution
antiporno-
   graphic
antipornogra-
   phy
antipoverty
antiprofiteering
antiprogressive
antiprostitution
antirabies

antiracketeering
antiradical
antirape
antirealism
antirecession
antireform
antireligious
antirevolution-
   ary
antiriot
antiromantic
antirust
antisegregation
antisex
antisexist
antisexual
antishoplifting
antislavery
antismoking
antismuggling
antismut
antispending
antistrike
antistudent
antisubmarine
antisubversion
antisubversive
antisuicide
antitank

antitax
antitechnologi-
   cal
antitechnology
antiterrorism
antiterrorist
antitheft
antitobacco
antitotalitarian
antitoxin
antitraditional
antitrust
antituberculosis
antitumor
antityphoid
antiulcer
antiunemploy-
   ment
antiunion
antiuniversity
antiurban
antiviolence
antiviral
antivivisection
antiwar
anti-West
anti-Western
antiwhite
antiwoman

an·ti·bi·ot·ic \,antēbī'ätik, -bē-\ *n* : substance that inhibits harmful microorganisms —**antibiotic** *adj*

an·ti·body \'anti,bädē\ *n* : bodily substance that counteracts the effects of a foreign substance or organism

an·tic \'antik\ *n* : playful act ~ *adj* : playful

an·tic·i·pate \an'tisə,pāt\ *vb* -**pat·ed; -pat·ing 1** : be prepared for **2** : look forward to —**an·tic·i·pa·tion** \-,tisə-'pāshən\ *n* —**an·tic·i·pa·to·ry** \-'tisəpə,tōrē\ *adj*

an·ti·cli·max \,antē'klī,maks\ *n* : something strikingly less important than what has preceded it —**an·ti·cli·mac·tic** \-klī'maktik\ *adj*

an·ti·dote \'anti,dōt\ *n* : remedy for poison

an·ti·freeze \'anti,frēz\ *n* : substance to prevent a liquid from freezing

an·ti·mo·ny \'antə,mōnē\ *n* : brittle white metallic chemical element

an·tip·a·thy \an'tipəthē\ *n, pl* -**thies** : strong dislike

an·ti·quar·i·an \,antə'kwerēən\ *adj* : relating to antiquities or old books

—an·ti·quar·i·an n —an·ti·quari·an·ism n

an·ti·qua·ry \'antə,kwerē\ n, pl -quar·ies : one who collects or studies antiquities

an·ti·quat·ed \'antə,kwātəd\ adj : out-of-date

an·tique \an'tēk\ adj : very old or out-of-date —antique n

an·tiq·ui·ty \an'tikwətē\ n, pl -ties 1 : ancient times 2 pl : relics of ancient times

an·ti·sep·tic \,antə'septik\ adj : killing or checking the growth of germs —antiseptic n —an·ti·sep·ti·cal·ly \-ti-klē\ adv

an·tith·e·sis \an'tithəsəs\ n, pl -eses \-,sēz\ : direct opposite

ant·ler \'antlər\ n : solid branched horn of a deer —ant·lered \-lərd\ adj

ant·onym \'antə,nim\ n : word of opposite meaning

anus \'ānəs\ n : the rear opening of the alimentary canal

an·vil \'anvəl\ n : heavy iron block on which metal is shaped

anx·i·ety \aŋ'zīətē\ n, pl -eties : uneasiness usu. over an expected misfortune

anx·ious \'aŋkshəs\ adj 1 : uneasy 2 : earnestly wishing —anx·ious·ly adv

any \'enē\ adj 1 : one chosen at random 2 : of whatever number or quantity ~ pron 1 : any one or ones 2 : any amount ~ adv : to any extent or degree

any·body \-,bədē, -,bäd-\ pron : anyone

any·how \-,haù\ adv 1 : in any way 2 : nevertheless

any·more \,enē'mōr\ adv : at the present time

any·one \-'enē,wən\ pron : any person

any·place adv : anywhere

any·thing pron : any thing whatever

any·time adv : at any time whatever

any·way adv : anyhow

any·where adv : in or to any place

aor·ta \ā'ortə\ n, pl -tas or -tae \-,ē\ : main artery from the heart —aor·tic \ā'ortik\ adj

apart \ə'pärt\ adv 1 : separately in place or time 2 : aside 3 : to pieces

apart·heid \ə'pär,tāt, -,tīt\ n : racial segregation

apart·ment \ə'pärtmənt\ n : set of usu. rented rooms

ap·a·thy \'apəthē\ n : lack of emotion or interest —ap·a·thet·ic \,apə'thetik\

adj —ap·a·thet·i·cal·ly \-iklē\ adv

ape \'āp\ n : large tailless primate ~ vb aped; ap·ing : imitate

ap·er·ture \'apər,chúr, -chər\ n : opening

apex \'ā,peks\ n, pl apex·es or api·ces \'āpə,sēz, 'apə-\ : highest point

aphid \'āfid, 'a-\ n : small insect that sucks plant juices

aph·o·rism \'afə,rizəm\ n : short saying stating a general truth —aph·o·ris·tic \,afə'ristik\ adj

aph·ro·dis·i·ac \,afrə'dēzē,ak, -'diz-\ n : substance that excites sexual desire

api·a·rist \'āpēərist\ n : beekeeper —api·ary \-,pē,erē\ n

apiece \ə'pēs\ adv : for each one

aplen·ty \ə'plentē\ adj : plentiful or abundant

aplomb \ə'pläm, -'pləm\ n : complete calmness or self-assurance

apoc·a·lypse \ə'päkə,lips\ n : writing prophesying a cataclysm in which evil forces are destroyed —apoc·alyp·tic \-,päkə'liptik\ adj

apoc·ry·pha \ə'päkrəfə\ n : writings of dubious authenticity —apoc·ry·phal \-fəl\ adj

apol·o·get·ic \ə,pälə'jetik\ adj : expressing apology —apol·o·get·i·cal·ly \-iklē\ adv

apol·o·gize \ə'pälə,jīz\ vb -gized; -giz·ing : make an apology —apol·o·gist \-jist\ n

apol·o·gy \ə'päləjē\ n, pl -gies 1 : formal justification 2 : expression of regret for a wrong

ap·o·plexy \'apə,pleksē\ n : sudden loss of consciousness caused by rupture or obstruction of an artery of the brain —ap·o·plec·tic \,apə'plektik\ adj

apos·ta·sy \ə'pästəsē\ n, pl -sies : abandonment of a former loyalty —apos·tate \ə'päs,tāt\ adj or n

apos·tle \ə'päsəl\ n : disciple or advocate —apos·tle·ship n —ap·os·tol·ic \,apə'stälik\ adj

apos·tro·phe \ə'pästrə,fē\ n : punctuation mark ' to indicate the possessive case or the omission of a letter or figure

apoth·e·cary \ə'päthə,kerē\ n, pl -car·ies : druggist

ap·pall \ə'pól\ vb : fill with horror or dismay

ap·pa·ra·tus \,apə'ratəs, -'rāt-\ n, pl -tus·es or -tus 1 : equipment 2 : complex machine or device

ap·par·el \ə'parəl\ n : clothing

ap·par·ent \ə'parənt\ adj 1 : visible 2 : obvious 3 : seeming —**ap·par·ent·ly** adv

ap·pa·ri·tion \apə'rishən\ n : ghost

ap·peal \ə'pēl\ vb 1 : try to have a court case reheard 2 : ask earnestly 3 : have an attraction —**appeal** n

ap·pear \ə'pir\ vb 1 : become visible or evident 2 : come into the presence of someone 3 : seem

ap·pear·ance \ə'pirəns\ n 1 : act of appearing 2 : outward aspect

ap·pease \ə'pēz\ vb -**peased**; -**peas·ing** : pacify with concessions —**ap·pease·ment** n

ap·pel·late \ə'pelət\ adj : having power to review decisions

ap·pend \ə'pend\ vb : attach

ap·pend·age \ə'pendij\ n : something attached

ap·pen·dec·to·my \apən'dektəmē\ n, pl -**mies** : surgical removal of the appendix

ap·pen·di·ci·tis \ə,pendə'sītəs\ n : inflammation of the appendix

ap·pen·dix \ə'pendiks\ n, pl -**dix·es** or -**di·ces** \-də,sēz\ 1 : supplementary matter 2 : narrow closed tube extending from lower right intestine

ap·pe·tite \'apə,tīt\ n 1 : natural desire esp. for food 2 : preference

ap·pe·tiz·er \-,tīzər\ n : food or drink to stimulate the appetite

ap·pe·tiz·ing \-ziŋ\ adj : tempting to the appetite —**ap·pe·tiz·ing·ly** adv

ap·plaud \ə'plȯd\ vb : show approval esp. by clapping

ap·plause \ə'plȯz\ n : a clapping in approval

ap·ple \'apəl\ n : rounded fruit with firm white flesh

ap·ple·jack \-,jak\ n : brandy made from cider

ap·pli·ance \ə'plīəns\ n : household machine or device

ap·pli·ca·ble \'aplikəbəl, ə'plikə-\ adj : capable of being applied —**ap·pli·ca·bil·i·ty** \,aplikə'bilətē, ə,plikə-\ n

ap·pli·cant \'aplikənt\ n : one who applies

ap·pli·ca·tion \aplə'kāshən\ n 1 : act of applying or thing applied 2 : constant attention 3 : request

ap·pli·ca·tor \'aplə,kātər\ n : device for applying a substance

ap·pli·qué \,aplə'kā\ n : cut-out fabric decoration —**appliqué** vb

ap·ply \ə'plī\ vb -**plied**; -**ply·ing** 1 : place in contact 2 : put to practical use 3 : devote (one's) attention or efforts to something 4 : submit a request 5 : have reference or a connection

ap·point \ə'pȯint\ vb 1 : set or assign officially 2 : equip or furnish —**ap·poin·tee** \ə,pȯin'tē, ,a-\ n

ap·point·ment \ə'pȯintmənt\ n 1 : act of appointing 2 : nonelective political job 3 : arrangement for a meeting

ap·por·tion \ə'pȯrshən\ vb : distribute proportionately —**ap·por·tion·ment** n

ap·po·site \'apəzət\ adj : suitable —**ap·po·site·ly** adv —**ap·po·site·ness** n

ap·praise \ə'prāz\ vb -**praised**; -**prais·ing** : set value on —**ap·prais·al** \-'prāzəl\ n —**ap·prais·er** n

ap·pre·cia·ble \ə'prēshəbəl\ adj : considerable —**ap·pre·cia·bly** \-blē\ adv

ap·pre·ci·ate \ə'prēshē,āt\ vb -**ated**; -**at·ing** 1 : value justly 2 : be grateful for 3 : increase in value —**ap·pre·ci·a·tion** \-,prēshē'āshən\ n

ap·pre·cia·tive \ə'prēshətiv, -shē,āt-\ adj : showing appreciation

ap·pre·hend \,apri'hend\ vb 1 : arrest 2 : look forward to in dread 3 : understand —**ap·pre·hen·sion** \-'henchən\ n

ap·pre·hen·sive \-'hensiv\ adj : fearful —**ap·pre·hen·sive·ly** adv —**ap·pre·hen·sive·ness** n

ap·pren·tice \ə'prentəs\ n : person learning a craft ~ vb -**ticed**; -**tic·ing** : employ or work as an apprentice —**ap·pren·tice·ship** n

ap·prise \ə'prīz\ vb -**prised**; -**pris·ing** : inform

ap·proach \ə'prōch\ vb 1 : move nearer or be close to 2 : make initial advances or efforts toward —**approach** n —**ap·proach·able** adj

ap·pro·ba·tion \,aprə'bāshən\ n : approval

ap·pro·pri·ate \ə'prōprē,āt\ vb -**at·ed**; -**at·ing** 1 : take possession of 2 : set apart for a particular use ~ \-'prēət\ adj : suitable —**ap·pro·pri·ate·ly** adv —**ap·pro·pri·ate·ness** n —**ap·pro·pri·a·tion** \ə,prōprē'āshən\ n

ap·prov·al \ə'prüvəl\ n : act of approving

ap·prove \ə'prüv\ *vb* **-proved; -prov-ing** : accept as satisfactory

ap·prox·i·mate \ə'präksəmət\ *adj* : nearly correct or exact ~ \-,māt\ *vb* **-mat·ed; -mat·ing** : come near —**ap·prox·i·mate·ly** *adv* —**ap·prox-i·ma·tion** \-,präksə'māshən\ *n*

ap·pur·te·nance \ə'pərt³nəns\ *n* : accessory —**ap·pur·te·nant** \'pərt-³nənt\ *adj*

apri·cot \'aprə,kät, 'ā-\ *n* : peachlike fruit

April \'āprəl\ *n* : 4th month of the year having 30 days

apron \'āprən\ *n* : protective garment

ap·ro·pos \,aprə'pō, 'aprə,pō\ *adv* : suitably ~ *adj* : being to the point

apropos of *prep* : with regard to

apt \'apt\ *adj* **1:** suitable **2** : likely **3** : quick to learn —**apt·ly** *adv* —**apt·ness** *n*

ap·ti·tude \'aptə,tüd, -tyüd\ *n* **1** : capacity for learning **2** : natural abil-ity

aqua \'akwə, 'äk-\ *n* : light greenish blue color

aquar·i·um \ə'kwareēəm\ *n, pl* **-i·ums** *or* **-ia** \-ēə\ : glass container for aquatic animals and plants

aquat·ic \ə'kwätik, -'kwat-\ *adj* : of or relating to water —**aquatic** *n*

aq·ue·duct \'akwə,dəkt\ *n* : conduit for carrying running water

aqui·line \'akwə,līn, -lən\ *adj* : curved like an eagle's beak

-ar \ər\ *adj suffix* **1** : of, relating to, or being **2** : resembling

ara·besque \,arə'besk\ *n* : intricate de-sign

ara·ble \'arəbəl\ *adj* : fit for crops

ar·bi·ter \'ärbətər\ *n* : final authority

ar·bi·trary \'ärbə,treñ\ *adj* **1** : selected at random **2** : autocratic —**ar·bi-trari·ly** \,ärbə'trerəlē\ *adv* —**ar·bi-trari·ness** \'ärbə,trerēnəs\ *n*

ar·bi·trate \'ärbə,trāt\ *vb* **-trat·ed; -trat·ing** : settle a dispute as arbitrator —**ar·bi·tra·tion** \,ärbə'trāshən\ *n*

ar·bi·tra·tor \'ärbə,trātər\ *n* : one cho-sen to settle a dispute

ar·bor \'ärbər\ *n* : shelter under branches or vines

ar·bo·re·al \är'bōrēəl\ *adj* : living in trees

arc \'ärk\ *n* **1** : part of a circle **2** : bright sustained electrical discharge ~ *vb* **arced** \'ärkt\; **arc·ing** \'ärkiŋ\ : form an arc

ar·cade \är'kād\ *n* : arched passageway between shops

ar·cane \är'kān\ *adj* : mysterious or se-cret

¹arch \'ärch\ *n* : curved structure span-ning an opening ~ *vb* : cover with or form into an arch

²arch *adj* **1** : chief —usu. in combina-tion **2** : mischievous —**arch·ly** *adv* —**arch·ness** *n*

ar·chae·ol·o·gy, ar·che·ol·o·gy \,ärkē-'äləjē\ *n* : study of past human life —**ar·chae·o·log·i·cal** \-kēə'läjikəl\ *adj* —**ar·chae·ol·o·gist** \-kē'äləjist\ *n*

ar·cha·ic \är'kāik\ *adj* : belonging to an earlier time —**ar·cha·i·cal·ly** \-iklē\ *adv*

arch·an·gel \'ärk,ānjəl\ *n* : angel of high rank

arch·bish·op \'ärch'bishəp\ *n* : chief bishop —**arch·bish·op·ric** \-ə,prik\ *n*

arch·di·o·cese \'är'dīəsəs, -,sēz, -,sēs\ *n* : diocese of an archbishop

arch·ery \'ärchərē\ *n* : shooting with bow and arrows —**ar·cher** \-chər\ *n*

ar·che·type \'ärki,tīp\ *n* : original pat-tern or model

ar·chi·pel·a·go \,ärkə'pelə,gō, ,ärchə-\ *n, pl* **-goes** *or* **-gos** : group of islands

ar·chi·tect \'ärkə,tekt\ *n* : building de-signer

ar·chi·tec·ture \'ärkə,tekchər\ *n* **1** : building design **2** : style of building **3** : manner of organizing elements —**ar·chi·tec·tur·al** \,ärkə'tekchərəl, -'tekshrəl\ *adj* —**ar·chi·tec·tur·al·ly** *adv*

ar·chives \'är,kīvz\ *n pl* : public records or their storage place —**archi·vist** \'ärkəvist, -,kī-\ *n*

arch·way \-,wā\ *n* : passageway under an arch

arc·tic \'ärktik, 'ärt-\ *adj* **1** : relating to the region near the north pole **2** : frigid

arctic circle *n* : circle parallel to the equator approximately 23°27′ from the north pole

ar·dent \'ärd³nt\ *adj* : characterized by warmth of feeling —**ar·dent·ly** *adv*

ar·dor \'ärdər\ *n* : warmth of feeling

ar·du·ous \'ärjəwəs\ *adj* : difficult —**ar·du·ous·ly** *adv* —**ar·du·ous·ness** *n*

are *pres 2d sing or pres pl of* BE

area \'arēə\ *n* **1** : space for something **2** : amount of surface included **3** : region **4** : range covered by a thing or concept

ar·e·a code *n* : 3-digit area-identifying telephone number

are·na \ə'rēnə\ *n* 1 : enclosed exhibition area 2 : sphere of activity

ar·gon \'är,gän\ *n* : colorless odorless gaseous chemical element

ar·got \'ärgət, -,gō\ *n* : special language (as of the underworld)

ar·gu·able \'ärgyəwəbəl\ *adj* : open to dispute

ar·gue \'ärgyü\ *vb* **-gued; -gu·ing** 1 : give reasons for or against something 2 : disagree in words

ar·gu·ment \'ärgyəmənt\ *n* 1 : reasons given to persuade 2 : dispute with words

ar·gu·men·ta·tive \,ärgyə'mentətiv\ *adj* : inclined to argue

ar·gyle \'är,gīl\ *n* : colorful diamond pattern in knitting

ar·ia \'ärēə\ *n* : opera solo

ar·id \'arəd\ *adj* : very dry —**arid·i·ty** \ə'ridətē\ *n*

arise \ə'rīz\ *vb* **arose** \-'rōz\ **aris·en** \-'riz³n\ **aris·ing** \-'rīziŋ\ 1 : get up 2 : originate

ar·is·to·cra·cy \,arə'stäkrəsē\ *n, pl* **-cies** : upper class —**aris·to·crat** \ə'ristə,krat\ *n* —**aris·to·crat·ic** \ə,ristə'kratik\ *adj*

arith·me·tic \ə'rithmə,tik\ *n* : mathematics that deals with numbers —**ar·ith·met·ic** \,arith'metik\ **ar·ith·met·i·cal** \-ikəl\ *adj*

ark \'ärk\ *n* : big boat

¹arm \'ärm\ *n* 1 : upper limb 2 : branch —**armed** \'ärmd\ *adj* —**arm·less** *adj*

²arm *vb* : furnish with weapons ~ *n* 1 : weapon 2 : branch of the military forces 3 *pl* : family's heraldic designs

ar·ma·da \är'mädə, -'mäd-\ *n* : naval fleet

ar·ma·dil·lo \,ärmə'dilō\ *n, pl* **-los** : burrowing mammal covered with bony plates

ar·ma·ment \'ärməmənt\ *n* : military arms and equipment

ar·ma·ture \'ärmə,chùr, -chər\ *n* : rotating part of an electric generator or motor

armed forces *n pl* : military

ar·mi·stice \'ärməstəs\ *n* : truce

ar·mor \'ärmər\ *n* : protective covering —**armored** \-mərd\ *adj*

ar·mory \'ärmərē\ *n, pl* **-mories** : factory or storehouse for arms

arm·pit *n* : hollow under the junction of the arm and shoulder

ar·my \'ärmē\ *n, pl* **-mies** 1 : body of men organized for war esp. on land 2 : great number

aro·ma \ə'rōmə\ *n* : usu. pleasing odor —**ar·o·mat·ic** \,arə'matik\ *adj*

around \ə'raùnd\ *adv* 1 : in or along a circuit 2 : on all sides 3 : near 4 : in an opposite direction ~ *prep* 1 : surrounding 2 : along the circuit of 3 : to or on the other side of 4 : near

arouse \ə'raùz\ *vb* **aroused; arous·ing** 1 : awaken from sleep 2 : stir up —**arous·al** \-'raùzəl\ *n*

ar·raign \ə'rān\ *vb* 1 : call before a court to answer to an indictment 2 : accuse —**ar·raign·ment** *n*

ar·range \ə'rānj\ *vb* **-ranged; -rang·ing** 1 : put in order 2 : settle or agree on 3 : adapt (a musical composition) for voices or instruments —**ar·range·ment** *n* —**ar·rang·er** *n*

ar·ray \ə'rā\ *vb* 1 : arrange in order 2 : dress esp. splendidly ~ *n* 1 : arrangement 2 : rich clothing 3 : imposing group

ar·rears \ə'rirz\ *n pl* : state of being behind in paying debts

ar·rest \ə'rest\ *vb* 1 : stop 2 : take into legal custody —**arrest** *n*

ar·rive \ə'rīv\ *vb* **-rived; -riv·ing** 1 : reach a destination, point, or stage 2 : come near in time —**ar·riv·al** \-əl\ *n*

ar·ro·gant \'arəgənt\ *adj* : showing an offensive sense of superiority —**ar·ro·gance** \-gəns\ *n* —**ar·ro·gant·ly** *adv*

ar·ro·gate \-,gāt\ *vb* **-gat·ed; -gat·ing** : to claim without justification

ar·row \'arō\ *n* : slender missile shot from a bow —**ar·row·head** *n*

ar·royo \ə'róiō, -ə\ *n, pl* **-royos** 1 : watercourse 2 : gully

ar·se·nal \'ärs³nəl\ *n* 1 : place where arms are made or stored 2 : store

ar·se·nic \'ärs³nik\ *n* : solid grayish poisonous chemical element

ar·son \'ärs³n\ *n* : willful or malicious burning of property —**arson·ist** \-ist\ *n*

art \'ärt\ *n* 1 : skill 2 : branch of learning 3 : creation of things of beauty or works so produced 4 : ingenuity

ar·te·rio·scle·ro·sis \ar,tirēöskIə'rōsəs\ *n* : hardening of the arteries —**ar·te·rio·scle·rot·ic** \-'rätik\ *adj or n*

ar·tery \'ärtərē\ *n, pl* **-ter·ies** 1 : tubular vessel carrying blood from the heart

2 : thoroughfare —**ar·te·ri·al** \är'tireəl\ adj

art·ful \-fəl\ adj 1 : ingenious 2 : crafty —**art·ful·ly** adv —**art·ful·ness** n

ar·thri·tis \är'thrītəs\ n, pl **-ti·des** \-'thritə,dēz\ : inflammation of the joints —**ar·thrit·ic** \-,'thritik\ adj or n

ar·thro·pod \'ärthrə,päd\ n : invertebrate animal (as an insect or crab) with segmented body and jointed limbs —**arthropod** adj

ar·ti·choke \'ärtə,chōk\ n : tall thistlelike herb or its edible flower head

ar·ti·cle \'ärtikəl\ n 1 : distinct part of a written document 2 : nonfactional published piece of writing 3 : word (as an, the) used to limit a noun 4 : item or piece

ar·tic·u·late \är'tikyələt\ adj : able to speak effectively ~ \-,lāt\ vb **-lat·ed; -lat·ing** 1 : utter distinctly 2 : unite by joints —**ar·tic·u·late·ly** adv —**ar·tic·u·late·ness** n —**ar·tic·u·la·tion** \-,tikyə'lāshən\ n

ar·ti·fact \'ärtə,fakt\ n : object of esp. prehistoric human workmanship

ar·ti·fice \'ärtəfəs\ n 1 : trick or trickery 2 : ingenious device or ingenuity

ar·ti·fi·cial \,ärtə'fishəl\ adj 1 : manmade 2 : not genuine —**ar·ti·fi·ci·al·i·ty** \-,fishē'alətē\ n —**ar·ti·fi·cial·ly** adv —**ar·ti·fi·cial·ness** n

ar·til·lery \är'tilərē\ n, pl **-ler·ies** : large caliber firearms

ar·ti·san \'ärtəzən, -sən\ n : skilled craftsman

art·ist \'ärtist\ n : one who creates art —**ar·tis·tic** \är'tistik\ adj —**ar·tis·ti·cal·ly** \-iklē\ adv —**ar·tis·try** \'ärtəstrē\ n

art·less \'ärtləs\ adj : sincere or natural —**art·less·ly** adv —**art·less·ness** n

arty \'ärtē\ adj **art·i·er; -est** : pretentiously artistic —**art·i·ly** \'ärtəlē\ adv —**art·i·ness** n

-ary \,erē\ adj suffix : of, relating to, or connected with

as \əz, ,az\ adv 1 : to the same degree 2 : for example ~ conj 1 : in the same way or degree as 2 : while 3 : because 4 : though ~ pron —used after same or such ~ prep : in the capacity of

as·bes·tos \as'bestəs, az-\ n : fibrous incombustible mineral

as·cend \ə'send\ vb : move upward —**as·cen·sion** \-'senchən\ n

as·cen·dan·cy \ə'sendənsē\ n : domination

as·cen·dant \ə'sendənt\ n : dominant position ~ adj 1 : moving upward 2 : dominant

as·cent \ə'sent\ n 1 : act of moving upward 2 : degree of upward slope

as·cer·tain \,asər'tān\ vb : determine —**as·cer·tain·able** adj

as·cet·ic \ə'setik\ adj : self-denying —**ascetic** n —**as·cet·i·cism** \-'setə,sizəm\ n

as·cribe \ə'skrīb\ vb **-cribed; -crib·ing** : attribute —**as·crib·able** adj —**as·crip·tion** \-'skripshən\ n

asep·tic \ā'septik\ adj : free of disease germs

1ash \'ash\ n : tree related to the olives

2ash n : matter left when something is burned —**ash·tray** n

ashamed \ə'shāmd\ adj : feeling shame —**asham·ed·ly** \-'shāmədlē\ adv

ash·en \'ashən\ adj : deadly pale

ashore \ə'shōr\ adv : on or to the shore

aside \ə'sīd\ adv 1 : toward the side 2 : out of the way

aside from prep 1 : besides 2 : except for

as·i·nine \'asˀn,īn\ adj : foolish —**asi·nin·i·ty** \,asˀn'inətē\ n

ask \'ask\ vb 1 : call on for an answer or help 2 : utter (a question or request) 3 : invite

askance \ə'skans\ adv 1 : with a side glance 2 : with mistrust

askew \ə'skyü\ adv or adj : out of line

asleep \ə'slēp\ adv or adj 1 : sleeping 2 : numbed 3 : inactive

as long as conj 1 : on condition that 2 : because

as of prep : from the time of

as·par·a·gus \ə'sparəgəs\ n : tall herb related to the lilies or its edible stalks

as·pect \'as,pekt\ n 1 : way something looks to the eye or mind 2 : phase

as·pen \'aspən\ n : poplar

as·per·i·ty \a'sperətē, ə-\ n, pl **-ties** 1 : roughness 2 : harshness

as·per·sion \ə'spərzhən\ n : remark that hurts someone's reputation

as·phalt \'as,folt\ n : dark tarlike substance used in paving

as·phyx·ia \as'fiksēə\ n : lack of oxygen causing unconsciousness

as·phyx·i·ate \-sē,āt\ vb **-at·ed; -at·ing** : suffocate —**as·phyx·i·a·tion** \-,fiksē'āshən\ n

as·pi·ra·tion \ˌaspəˈrāshən\ *n* : strong desire to achieve a goal

as·pire \əˈspīr\ *vb* **-pired; -pir·ing** : have an ambition —**as·pi·rant** \ˈaspərənt, əˈspīrənt\ *n*

as·pi·rin \ˈasprən\ *n, pl* **aspirin** *or* **as·pi·rins** : pain reliever

ass \ˈas\ *n* **1** : long-eared animal related to the horse **2** : stupid person

as·sail \əˈsāl\ *vb* : attack violently —**as·sail·able** *adj* —**as·sail·ant** *n*

as·sas·si·nate \əˈsasᵊnˌāt\ *vb* **-nated; -nat·ing** : murder esp. for political reasons —**as·sas·sin** \-ˈsasᵊn\ *n* —**as·sas·si·na·tion** \-ˌsasᵊnˈāshən\ *n*

as·sault \əˈsȯlt\ *n or vb* : attack

as·say \ˈasˌā, aˈsā\ *n* : analysis (as of an ore) to determine quality or properties —**as·say** \aˈsā, ˈasˌā\ *vb*

as·sem·ble \əˈsembəl\ *vb* **-bled; -bling** **1** : collect into one place **2** : fit together the parts of

as·sem·bly \-blē\ *n, pl* **-blies 1** : meeting **2** *cap* : legislative body **3** : a fitting together of parts

as·sem·bly·man \-mən\ *n* : member of a legislative assembly

as·sem·bly·wom·an \-ˌwu̇-mən\ *n* : woman who is a member of a legislative assembly

as·sent \əˈsent\ *vb or n* : consent

as·sert \əˈsərt\ *vb* **1** : declare **2** : defend —**as·ser·tion** \-ˈsərshən\ *n* —**as·sert·ive** \-ˈsərtiv\ *adj* —**as·sert·ive·ness** *n*

as·sess \əˈses\ *vb* **1** : impose (as a tax) **2** : evaluate for taxation —**as·sess·ment** *n* —**as·ses·sor** \-ər\ *n*

as·set \ˈasˌet\ *n* **1** *pl* : individually owned property **2** : advantage or resource

as·sid·u·ous \əˈsijəwəs\ *adj* : diligent —**as·si·du·i·ty** \ˌasəˈdüətē, -ˈdyü-\ *n* —**as·sid·u·ous·ly** *adv* —**as·sid·u·ous·ness** *n*

as·sign \əˈsīn\ *vb* **1** : transfer to another **2** : appoint to a duty **3** : designate as a task **4** : attribute —**as·sign·able** *adj* —**as·sign·ment** *n*

as·sim·i·late \əˈsiməˌlāt\ *vb* **-lated; -lat·ing** **1** : absorb as nourishment **2** : understand —**as·sim·i·la·tion** \-ˌsiməˈlāshən\ *n*

as·sist \əˈsist\ *vb* : help —**assist** *n* —**as·sis·tance** \-ˈsistəns\ *n* —**as·sis·tant** \-tənt\ *n*

as·so·ci·ate \əˈsōshēˌāt, -sē-\ *vb* **-at·ed; -at·ing 1** : join in companionship or partnership **2** : connect in thought —**as·so·ci·ate** \-shēət, -sēət\ *n* —**as·so·ci·a·tion** \-ˌsōshēˈāshən, -sē-\ *n*

as soon as *conj* : when

as·sort·ed \əˈsȯrtəd\ *adj* : consisting of various kinds

as·sort·ment \-mənt\ *n* : assorted collection

as·suage \əˈswāj\ *vb* **-suaged; -suag·ing** : ease or satisfy

as·sume \əˈsüm\ *vb* **-sumed; -sum·ing 1** : take upon oneself **2** : pretend to have or be **3** : take as true

as·sump·tion \əˈsəmpshən\ *n* : something assumed

as·sure \əˈshu̇r\ *vb* **-sured; -sur·ing 1** : give confidence or conviction to **2** : guarantee —**as·sur·ance** \-əns\ *n*

as·ter \ˈastər\ *n* : herb with daisylike flowers

as·ter·isk \ˈastəˌrisk\ *n* : a character * used as a reference mark or as an indication of omission of words

astern \əˈstərn\ *adv or adj* **1** : behind **2** : at or toward the stern

as·ter·oid \ˈastəˌrȯid\ *n* : small planet between Mars and Jupiter

asth·ma \ˈazmə\ *n* : disorder marked by difficulty in breathing —**asth·mat·ic** \azˈmatik\ *adj or n*

astig·ma·tism \əˈstigməˌtizəm\ *n* : visual defect —**as·tig·mat·ic** \ˌastigˈmatik\ *adj*

as to *prep* **1** : concerning **2** : according to

as·ton·ish \əˈstänish\ *vb* : amaze —**as·ton·ish·ing·ly** *adv* —**as·ton·ish·ment** *n*

as·tound \əˈsta͏u̇nd\ *vb* : fill with confused wonder —**as·tound·ing·ly** *adv*

astrad·dle \əˈstradᵊl\ *adv or prep* : so as to straddle

as·tral \ˈastrəl\ *adj* : relating to or coming from the stars

astray \əˈstrā\ *adv or adj* : off the right path

astride \əˈstrīd\ *adv* : with legs apart or one on each side ~ *prep* : with one leg on each side of

as·trin·gent \əˈstrinjənt\ *adj* : causing shrinking or puckering of tissues —**as·trin·gen·cy** \-jənsē\ *n* —**astrin·gent** *n*

as·trol·o·gy \əˈsträləjē\ *n* : prediction of events by the stars —**as·trol·o·ger** \-əjər\ *n* —**as·tro·log·i·cal** \ˌastrə-ˈläjikəl\ *adj*

as•tro•naut \'astrə,nȯt\ *n* : space traveler

as•tro•nau•tics \,astrə'nȯtiks\ *n* : construction and operation of spacecraft —**as•tro•nau•tic** \-ik\, **as•tro•nau•ti•cal** \-ikəl\ *adj*

as•tro•nom•i•cal \,astrə'nämikəl\ *adj* 1 : relating to astronomy 2 : extremely large

as•tron•o•my \ə'stränəmē\ *n, pl* **-mies** : study of the celestial bodies —**as•tron•o•mer** \-əmər\ *n*

as•tute \ə'stüt, -'styüt\ *adj* : shrewd —**as•tute•ly** *adv* —**as•tute•ness** *n*

asun•der \ə'səndər\ *adv or adj* 1 : into separate pieces 2 : separated

asy•lum \ə'sīləm\ *n* 1 : refuge 2 : institution for care esp. of the insane

asym•met•ri•cal \,āsə'metrikəl\, **asym•met•ric** \-trik\ *adj* : not symmetrical —**asym•me•try** \,ā'simətrē\ *n*

at \ət, 'at\ *prep* 1 —used to indicate a point in time or space 2 —used to indicate a goal 3 —used to indicate condition, means, cause, or manner

at all *adv* : without restriction or under any circumstances

ate *past of* EAT

-ate \ət, ,āt\ *n suffix* 1 : office or rank 2 : group of persons holding an office or rank ~ *adj suffix* 1 : brought into or being in a state 2 : marked by having

athe•ist \'āthēist\ *n* : one who denies the existence of God —**athe•ism** \-,izəm\ *n* —**athe•is•tic** \,āthē'istik\ *adj*

ath•ero•scle•ro•sis \,athərōsklə'rōsəs\ *n* : arteriosclerosis with deposition of fatty substances in the arteries —**ath•ero•scle•rot•ic** \-'rätik\ *adj*

ath•lete \'ath,lēt\ *n* : one trained to compete in athletics

ath•let•ics \ath'letiks\ *n sing or pl* : exercises and games requiring physical skill —**ath•let•ic** \-ik\ *adj*

-ation \'āshən\ *n suffix* : action or process

-ative \,ātiv, ətiv\ *adj suffix* 1 : of, relating to, or connected with 2 : tending to

at•las \'atləs\ *n* : book of maps

at•mo•sphere \'atmə,sfir\ *n* 1 : mass of air surrounding the earth 2 : surrounding influence —**at•mo•spher•ic** \,atmə'sfirik, -'sfer-\ *adj* —**at•mo•spher•i•cal•ly** \-iklē\ *adv*

atoll \'a,tȯl, 'ā-, -,täl\ *n* : ring-shaped coral island

at•om \'atəm\ *n* 1 : tiny bit 2 : smallest particle of a chemical element that can exist alone or in combination

atom•ic \ə'tämik\ *adj* 1 : relating to atoms 2 : nuclear

atomic bomb *n* : bomb utilizing the energy released by splitting the atom

at•om•iz•er \'atə,mīzər\ *n* : device for dispersing a liquid as a very fine spray

atone \ə'tōn\ *vb* **atoned; aton•ing** : make amends —**atone•ment** *n*

atop \ə'täp\ *prep* : on top of ~ *adv or adj* : on, to, or at the top

atri•um \'ātrēəm\ *n, pl* **atria** \-trēə\ *or* **atriums** 1 : open central room or court 2 : heart chamber that receives blood from the veins

atro•cious \ə'trōshəs\ *adj* : appalling or abominable —**atro•cious•ly** *adv* —**atro•cious•ness** *n*

atroc•i•ty \ə'träsətē\ *n, pl* **-ties** : savage act

at•ro•phy \'atrəfē\ *n, pl* **-phies** : wasting away of a bodily part or tissue —**at•ro•phy** *vb*

at•ro•pine \'atrə,pēn\ *n* : drug used esp. to relieve spasms

at•tach \ə'tach\ *vb* 1 : seize legally 2 : bind by personalities 3 : join —**at•tach•ment** *n*

at•ta•ché \,atə'shā, ,a,ta-, ə,ta-\ *n* : technical expert on a diplomatic staff

at•tack \ə'tak\ *vb* 1 : try to hurt or destroy with violence or words 2 : set to work on ~ *n* 1 : act of attacking 2 : fit of sickness

at•tain \ə'tān\ *vb* 1 : achieve or accomplish 2 : reach —**at•tain•abil•i•ty** \ə,tānə'bilətē\ *n* —**at•tain•able** *adj* —**at•tain•ment** *n*

at•tempt \ə'tempt\ *vb* : make an effort toward —**attempt** *n*

at•tend \ə'tend\ *vb* 1 : handle or provide for the care of something 2 : accompany 3 : be present at 4 : pay attention —**at•ten•dance** \-'tendəns\ *n* —**at•ten•dant** \-dənt\ *adj or n*

at•ten•tion \ə'tenchən\ *n* 1 : concentration of the mind on something 2 : notice or awareness —**at•ten•tive** \-'tentiv\ *adj* —**at•ten•tive•ly** *adv* —**at•ten•tive•ness** *n*

at•ten•u•ate \ə'tenyə,wāt\ *vb* **-at•ed; -at•ing** 1 : make or become thin 2 : weaken —**at•ten•u•a•tion** \-,tenyə-'wāshən\ *n*

at·test \ə'test\ *vb* : certify or bear witness —**at·tes·ta·tion** \ˌa,tes'tāshən\ *n*

at·tic \'atik\ *n* : space just below the roof

at·tire \ə'tīr\ *vb* **-tired; -tir·ing** : dress —**attire** *n*

at·ti·tude \'atə,tüd, -,tyüd\ *n* **1** : posture or relative position **2** : feeling, opinion, or mood

at·tor·ney \ə'tərnē\ *n, pl* **-neys** : legal agent

at·tract \ə'trakt\ *vb* **1** : draw to oneself **2** : have emotional or aesthetic appeal for —**at·trac·tion** \-'trakshən\ *n* —**at·trac·tive** \-'traktiv\ *adj* —**at·trac·tive·ly** *adv* —**at·trac·tive·ness** *n*

at·tri·bute \'atrə,byüt\ *n* : inherent characteristic ~ \ə'tribyət\ *vb* **-trib·ut·ed; -trib·ut·ing 1** : regard as having a specific cause or origin **2** : regard as a characteristic —**at·trib·ut·able** *adj* —**at·tri·bu·tion** \ˌatrə'byüshən\ *n*

at·tune \ə'tün, -'tyün\ *vb* : bring into harmony

au·burn \'ȯbərn\ *adj* : reddish brown

auc·tion \'ȯkshən\ *n* : public sale of property to the highest bidder —**auction** *vb* —**auc·tion·eer** \ˌȯkshə'nir\ *n*

au·di·ble \'ȯdəbəl\ *adj* : capable of being heard —**au·di·bly** \-blē\ *adv*

au·di·ence \'ȯdēəns\ *n* **1** : formal interview **2** : group of listeners or spectators

au·dio \'ȯdē,ō\ *adj* : relating to sound or its reproduction ~ *n* : television sound

au·dio·vi·su·al \ˌȯdēō'vizhəwəl\ *adj* : relating to both hearing and sight

au·dit \'ȯdət\ *vb* : examine financial accounts —**audit** *n* —**au·di·tor** \'ȯdətər\ *n*

au·di·tion \ȯ'dishən\ *n* : tryout performance —**audition** *vb*

au·di·to·ri·um \ˌȯdə'tōrēəm\ *n, pl* **-ri·ums** *or* **-ria** \-'rēə\ : room or building used for public performances

au·di·to·ry \'ȯdə,tōrē\ *adj* : relating to hearing

au·ger \'ȯgər\ *n* : tool for boring

aug·ment \ȯg'ment\ *vb* : enlarge or increase —**aug·men·ta·tion** \ˌȯgmən'tāshən\ *n*

au·gur \'ȯgər\ *n* : prophet ~ *vb* : predict —**au·gu·ry** \'ȯgyərē, -gər-\ *n*

au·gust \ȯ'gəst\ *adj* : majestic

Au·gust \'ȯgəst\ *n* : 8th month of the year having 31 days

auk \'ȯk\ *n* : stocky diving seabird

aunt \'ant, 'ȧnt\ *n* **1** : sister of one's father or mother **2** : wife of one's uncle

au·ra \'ȯrə\ *n* **1** : distinctive atmosphere **2** : luminous radiation

au·ral \'ȯrəl\ *adj* : relating to the ear or to hearing

au·ri·cle \'ȯrikəl\ *n* : atrium or ear-shaped pouch in the atrium of the heart

au·ro·ra bo·re·al·is \ə'rȯrə,bȯrē'aləs\ *n* : display of light in the night sky of northern latitudes

aus·pic·es \'ȯspəsəz, -,sēz\ *n pl* : patronage and protection

aus·pi·cious \ȯ'spishəs\ *adj* : favorable

aus·tere \ȯ'stir\ *adj* : severe —**aus·tere·ly** *adv* —**aus·ter·i·ty** \ȯ'sterətē\ *n*

au·then·tic \ə'thentik, ȯ-\ *adj* : genuine —**au·then·ti·cal·ly** \-iklē\ *adv* —**au·then·tic·i·ty** \ˌȯ,then'tisətē\ *n*

au·then·ti·cate \ə'thenti,kāt, ȯ-\ *vb* **-cat·ed; -cat·ing** : prove genuine —**au·then·ti·ca·tion** \-ˌthenti'kāshən\ *n*

au·thor \'ȯthər\ *n* **1** : writer **2** : creator —**au·thor·ship** *n*

au·thor·i·tar·i·an \ə,thärə'terēən, ə-, -,thȯr-\ *adj* : marked by blind obedience to authority

au·thor·i·ta·tive \ə'thärə,tātiv, ȯ-, -'thȯr-\ *adj* : being an authority —**au·thor·i·ta·tive·ly** *adv* —**au·thor·i·ta·tive·ness** *n*

au·thor·i·ty \ə'thärətē, ȯ-, -'thȯr-\ *n, pl* **-ties 1** : expert **2** : right, responsibility, or power to influence **3** *pl* : persons in official positions

au·tho·rize \'ȯthə,rīz\ *vb* **-rized; -riz·ing** : permit or give official approval for —**au·tho·ri·za·tion** \ˌȯthərə'zāshən\ *n*

au·to \'ȯtō\ *n, pl* **autos** : automobile

au·to·bi·og·ra·phy \ˌȯtəbī'ägrəfē, -bē-\ *n* : writer's own life story —**au·to·bi·og·ra·pher** \-fər\ *n* —**au·to·bio·graph·i·cal** \-ˌbīə'grafikəl\ *adj*

au·toc·ra·cy \ȯ'täkrəsē\ *n, pl* **-cies** : government by one person having unlimited power —**au·to·crat** \'ȯtə,krat\ *n* —**au·to·crat·ic** \ˌȯtə'kratik\ *adj* —**au·to·crat·i·cal·ly** \-iklē\ *adv*

au·to·graph \'ȯtə,graf\ *n* : signature ~ *vb* : write one's name on

au·to·mate \'ȯtə,māt\ *vb* **-mat·ed; -mat·ing** : make automatic —**au·to·ma·tion** \ˌȯtə'māshən\ *n*

au·to·mat·ic \,ȯtə'matik\ *adj* 1 : involuntary 2 : designed to function without human intervention ~ *n* : automatic device (as a firearm) —**au·to·mat·i·cal·ly** \-iklē\ *adv*

au·tom·a·ton \ȯ'tämətən, -,tän\ *n, pl* **-a·tons** *or* **-a·ta** \-tə, -,tä\ : robot

au·to·mo·bile \,ȯtəmō'bēl, -'mō,bēl\ *n* : 4-wheeled passenger vehicle with its own power source

au·to·mo·tive \,ȯtə'mōtiv\ *adj* : relating to automobiles

au·ton·o·mous \ȯ'tänəməs\ *adj* : self-governing —**au·ton·o·mous·ly** *adv* —**au·ton·o·my** \-mē\ *n*

au·top·sy \'ȯ,täpsē, 'ȯtəp-\ *n, pl* **-sies** : medical examination of a corpse

au·tumn \'ȯtəm\ *n* : season between summer and winter —**au·tum·nal** \ȯ-'təmnəl\ *adj*

aux·il·ia·ry \ȯg'zilyərē, -lərē\ *adj* 1 : being a supplement or reserve 2 : accompanying a main verb form to express person, number, mood, or tense —**auxiliary** *n*

avail \ə'vāl\ *vb* : be of use or make use ~ *n* : use

avail·able \ə'vāləbəl\ *adj* 1 : usable 2 : accessible —**avail·abil·i·ty** \-,vālə-'bilətē\ *n*

av·a·lanche \'avə,lanch\ *n* : mass of sliding or falling snow or rock

av·a·rice \'avərəs\ *n* : greed —**av·a·ri·cious** \,avə'rishəs\ *adj*

avenge \ə'venj\ *vb* **avenged; aveng·ing** : take vengeance for —**aveng·er** *n*

av·e·nue \'avə,nü, -,nyü\ *n* 1 : way of approach 2 : broad street

av·er·age \'avrij\ *adj* 1 : being about midway between extremes 2 : ordinary ~ *vb* 1 : be usually 2 : find the mean of ~ *n* : mean

averse \ə'vərs\ *adj* : feeling dislike or reluctance —**aver·sion** \-'vərzhən\ *n*

avert \ə'vərt\ *vb* : turn away

avi·ary \'āvē,erē\ *n, pl* **-ar·ies** : place where birds are kept

avi·a·tion \,āvē'āshən, av-\ *n* : operation or manufacture of airplanes —**avi·a·tor** \'āvē,ātər, 'av-\ *n*

avid \'avəd\ *adj* 1 : greedy 2 : enthusiastic —**avid·i·ty** \ə'vidətē, a-\ *n* —**avid·ly** *adv*

av·o·ca·do \,avə'kädō, ,äv-\ *n, pl* **-dos** : tropical fruit with green pulp

av·o·ca·tion \,avə'kāshən\ *n* : hobby

avoid \ə'vȯid\ *vb* 1 : keep away from 2 : prevent the occurrence of 3 : refrain from —**avoid·able** *adj* —**avoidance** \-ᵊns\ *n*

avoir·du·pois \,avərdə'pȯiz\ *n* : system of weight based on the pound of 16 ounces

avow \ə'vau̇\ *vb* : declare openly —**avow·al** \-'vau̇əl\ *n*

await \ə'wāt\ *vb* : wait for

awake \ə'wāk\ *vb* **awoke** \-'wōk\; **awok·en** \-'wōkən\ *or* **awaked; awak·ing** : wake up —**awake** *adj*

awak·en \ə'wākən\ *vb* **-ened; -en·ing** : wake up

award \ə'wȯrd\ *vb* : give (something won or deserved) ~ *n* 1 : judgment 2 : prize

aware \ə'war\ *adj* : having realization or consciousness —**aware·ness** *n*

awash \ə'wȯsh, -'wäsh\ *adv or adj* : flooded

away \ə'wā\ *adv* 1 : from this or that place or time 2 : out of the way 3 : in another direction 4 : from one's possession ~ *adj* 1 : absent 2 : distant

awe \'ȯ\ *n* : respectful fear or wonder ~ *vb* **awed; aw·ing** : fill with awe —**awe·some** \-səm\ *adj* —**awe·struck** *adj*

aw·ful \'ȯfəl\ *adj* 1 : inspiring awe 2 : extremely disagreeable 3 : very great —**aw·ful·ly** *adv*

awhile \ə'hwīl\ *adv* : for a while

awk·ward \'ȯkwərd\ *adj* 1 : clumsy 2 : embarrassing —**awk·ward·ly** *adv* —**awk·ward·ness** *n*

awl \'ȯl\ *n* : hole-making tool

aw·ning \'ȯniŋ\ *n* : window cover

awry \ə'rī\ *adv or adj* : wrong

ax, axe \'aks\ *n* : chopping tool

ax·i·om \'aksēəm\ *n* : generally accepted truth —**ax·i·om·at·ic** \,aksēə-'matik\ *adj*

ax·is \'aksəs\ *n, pl* **ax·es** \-,sēz\ : center of rotation —**ax·i·al** \-sēəl\ *adj* —**ax·i·al·ly** *adv*

ax·le \'aksəl\ *n* : shaft on which a wheel revolves

aye \'ī\ *adv* : yes ~ *n* : a vote of yes

aza·lea \ə'zālyə\ *n* : rhododendron with funnel-shaped blossoms

az·i·muth \'azəməth\ *n* : horizontal direction expressed as an angle

azure \'azhər\ *n* : blue of the sky —**azure** *adj*

B

b \'bē\ *n, pl* **b's** *or* **bs** \'bēz\ : 2d letter of the alphabet

bab•ble \'babəl\ *vb* **-bled; -bling** 1 : utter meaningless sounds 2 : talk foolishly or too much —**babble** *n* —**bab•bler** *n*

babe \'bāb\ *n* : baby

ba•bel \'bābəl, 'bab-\ *n* : noisy confusion

ba•boon \ba'bün\ *n* : large Asian or African ape with a doglike muzzle

ba•by \'bābē\ *n, pl* **-bies** : very young child ~ *vb* **-bied; -by•ing** : pamper —**baby** *adj* —**ba•by•hood** *n* —**ba•by•ish** *adj*

ba•by-sit *vb* **-sat; -sit•ting** : care for children while parents are away —**baby-sit•ter** *n*

bac•ca•lau•re•ate \,bakə'lórēət\ *n* : bachelor's degree

bac•cha•na•lia \,bakə'nālyə\ *n, pl* **-lia** : drunken orgy —**bac•cha•na•lian** \-yən\ *adj or n*

bach•e•lor \'bachələr\ *n* 1 : holder of lowest 4-year college degree 2 : unmarried man —**bach•e•lor•hood** *n*

ba•cil•lus \bə'siləs\ *n, pl* **-li** \-,ī\ : rod-shaped bacterium —**bac•il•lary** \'basə,lerē\ *adj*

back \'bak\ *n* 1 : part of a human or animal body nearest the spine 2 : part opposite the front 3 : player farthest from the opponent's goal ~ *adv* 1 : to or at the back 2 : ago 3 : to or in a former place or state 4 : in reply ~ *adj* 1 : located at the back 2 : not paid on time 3 : moving or working backward 4 : not current ~ *vb* 1 : support 2 : go or cause to go back 3 : form the back of —**back•ache** *n* —**back•er** *n* —**back•ing** *n* —**back•less** *adj* —**back•rest** *n*

back•bite *vb* **-bit; -bit•ten; -bit•ing** : say spiteful things about someone absent —**back•bit•er** *n*

back•bone *n* 1 : bony column in the back that encloses the spinal cord 2 : firm character

back•drop *n* : painted cloth hung across the rear of a stage

back•fire *n* : loud noise from the wrongly timed explosion of fuel in an engine ~ *vb* 1 : make or undergo a backfire 2 : have a result opposite of that intended

back•gam•mon \'bak,gamən\ *n* : board game

back•ground *n* 1 : scenery behind something 2 : sum of a person's experience or training

back•hand *n* : stroke (as in tennis) made with the back of the hand turned forward —**backhand** *adj or vb* —**back•hand•ed** *adj*

back•lash *n* : adverse reaction

back•log *n* : accumulation of things to be done —**backlog** *vb*

back•pack *n* : camping pack carried on the back ~ *vb* : hike with a backpack —**back•pack•er** *n*

back•slide *vb* **-slid; -slid** *or* **-slid•den** \-,slidᵊn\; **-slid•ing** : lapse in morals or religious practice —**back•slid•er** *n*

back•stage *adv or adj* : in or to an area behind a stage

back-up *n* : substitute

back•ward \'bakwərd\, **back•wards** *adv* 1 : toward the back 2 : with the back foremost 3 : in a reverse direction 4 : toward an earlier or worse state ~ *adj* 1 : directed, turned, or done backward 2 : retarded in development —**back•ward•ness** *n*

back•woods *n pl* : remote or isolated place

ba•con \'bākən\ *n* : salted and smoked meat from a pig

bac•te•ri•um \bak'tirēəm\ *n, pl* **-ria** \-ēə\ : microscopic plant —**bac•te•ri•al** \-ēəl\ *adj* —**bac•te•ri•o•log•ic** \-,tir-ēə'läjik\, **bac•te•ri•o•log•i•cal** \-əl\ *adj* —**bac•te•ri•ol•o•gist** \-ē'älə-jist\ *n* —**bac•te•ri•ol•o•gy** \-jē\ *n*

bad \'bad\ *adj* **worse** \'wərs\; **worst** \'wərst\ 1 : not good 2 : naughty 3 : faulty 4 : spoiled —**bad** *n or adv* —**bad•ly** *adv* —**bad•ness** *n*

bade *past of* BID

badge \'baj\ *n* : symbol of status

bad·ger \'bajər\ *n* : burrowing mammal ~ *vb* : harass

bad·min·ton \'bad‚mint³n\ *n* : tennis-like game played with a shuttlecock

baf·fle \'bafəl\ *vb* **-fled; -fling** : perplex ~ *n* : device to alter flow (as of liquid or sound) —**baf·fle·ment** *n*

bag \'bag\ *n* : flexible usu. closable container ~ *vb* **-gg-** 1 : bulge out 2 : put in a bag 3 : catch in hunting

bag·a·telle \‚bagə'tel\ *n* : trifle

ba·gel \'bāgəl\ *n* : hard doughnut-shaped roll

bag·gage \'bagij\ *n* : traveler's bags and belongings

bag·gy \'bagē\ *adj* **-gi·er; -est** : puffed out like a bag —**bag·gi·ly** *adv* —**bag·gi·ness** *n*

bag·pipe *n* : musical instrument with a bag, a tube with valves, and sounding pipes —often pl.

¹**bail** \'bāl\ *n* : container for scooping water out of a boat —**bail** *vb* —**bail·er** *n*

²**bail** *n* 1 : security given to guarantee a prisoner's appearance in court 2 : release secured by bail ~ *vb* : bring about the release of by giving bail

bai·liff \'bāləf\ *n* 1 : British sheriff's aide 2 : minor officer of a U.S. court

bai·li·wick \'bāli‚wik\ *n* : one's special field or domain

bail·out \'bā‚laut\ *n* : rescue from financial distress

bait \'bāt\ *vb* 1 : harass with dogs usu. for sport 2 : furnish (a hook or trap) with bait ~ *n* : lure esp. for catching animals

bake \'bāk\ *vb* **baked; bak·ing** : cook in dry heat esp. in an oven ~ *n* : party featuring baked food —**bak·er** *n* —**bak·ery** \'bākərē\ *n* —**bake·shop** *n*

bal·ance \'baləns\ *n* 1 : weighing device 2 : counteracting weight, force, or influence 3 : equilibrium 4 : that which remains ~ *vb* **-anced; -anc·ing** 1 : compute the balance 2 : equalize 3 : bring into harmony or proportion —**bal·anced** *adj*

bal·co·ny \'balkōnē\ *n, pl* **-nies** : platform projecting from a wall

bald \'bold\ *adj* 1 : lacking a natural or usual covering (as of hair) 2 : plain —**bald·ing** *adj* —**bald·ly** *adv* —**bald·ness** *n*

bal·der·dash \'boldər‚dash\ *n* : nonsense

bale \'bāl\ *n* : large bundle ~ *vb* **baled; bal·ing** : pack in a bale —**bal·er** *n*

bale·ful \'bālfəl\ *adj* 1 : deadly 2 : ominous

balk \'bok\ *n* : hindrance ~ *vb* 1 : thwart 2 : stop short and refuse to go on —**balky** *adj*

¹**ball** \'bol\ *n* 1 : rounded mass 2 : game played with a ball ~ *vb* : form into a ball

²**ball** *n* : large formal dance —**ballroom** *n*

bal·lad \'baləd\ *n* 1 : narrative poem 2 : slow romantic song —**bal·lad·eer** \‚balə'dir\ *n*

bal·last \'baləst\ *n* : heavy material to steady a ship or balloon ~ *vb* : provide with ballast

bal·le·ri·na \‚balə'rēnə\ *n* : female ballet dancer

bal·let \'ba‚lā, ba'lā\ *n* : theatrical dancing

bal·lis·tics \bə'listiks\ *n sing or pl* : science of projectile motion —**ballistic** *adj*

bal·loon \bə'lün\ *n* : inflated bag ~ *vb* 1 : travel in a balloon 2 : swell out —**bal·loon·ist** *n*

bal·lot \'balət\ *n* 1 : paper used to cast a vote 2 : system of voting ~ *vb* : vote

bal·ly·hoo \'balē‚hü\ *n* : publicity —**bal·ly·hoo** *vb*

balm \'bäm, 'bälm\ *n* 1 : fragrant healing or soothing preparation 2 : spicy fragrant herb

balmy \'bämē, 'bälmē\ *adj* **balm·i·er; -est** : gently soothing —**balm·i·ness** *n*

ba·lo·ney \bə'lōnē\ *n* : nonsense

bal·sa \'bolsə\ *n* : very light wood of a tropical tree

bal·sam \-səm\ *n* 1 : aromatic resinous plant substance 2 : balsam-yielding plant —**bal·sam·ic** \bol'samik\ *adj*

bal·us·ter \'baləstər\ *n* : upright support for a rail

bal·us·trade \-‚strād\ *n* : row of balusters topped by a rail

bam·boo \bam'bü\ *n* : tall tropical grass with strong hollow stems

bam·boo·zle \bam'büzəl\ *vb* **-zled; -zling** : deceive

ban \'ban\ *vb* **-nn-** : prohibit ~ *n* : legal prohibition

ba·nal \bə'näl, -'nal; 'bān³l\ *adj*

: ordinary and uninteresting —**ba·nal·i·ty** \bə'nalətē\ n

ba·nana \bə'nanə\ n : elongated fruit of a treelike tropical plant

1band \'band\ n 1 : something that ties or binds 2 : strip or stripe different (as in color) from nearby matter 3 : range of radio wavelengths ~ vb 1 : enclose with a band 2 : unite for a common end —**band·ed** adj —**band·er** n

2band n 1 : group 2 : musicians playing together

ban·dage \'bandij\ n : material used esp. in dressing wounds ~ vb : dress or cover with a bandage

ban·dan·na, ban·dana \ban'danə\ n : large colored figured handkerchief

ban·dit \'bandət\ n : outlaw or robber —**ban·dit·ry** \-dətrē\ n

band·stand n : stage for band concerts

band·wag·on n : candidate, side, or movement gaining support

1ban·dy \'bandē\ vb -died; -dy·ing : exchange in rapid succession

2bandy adj : curved outward

bane \'bān\ n 1 : poison 2 : cause of woe —**bane·ful** adj

1bang \'baŋ\ vb : strike, thrust, or move usu. with a loud noise ~ n 1 : blow 2 : sudden loud noise ~ adv : directly

2bang n : fringe of short hair over the forehead —usu. pl. ~ vb : cut in bangs

ban·gle \'baŋgəl\ n : bracelet

ban·ish \'banish\ vb 1 : force by authority to leave a country 2 : expel —**ban·ish·ment** n

ban·is·ter \-əstər\ n 1 : baluster 2 : handrail

ban·jo \'ban,jō\ n, pl -jos : stringed instrument with a drumlike body —**ban·jo·ist** n

1bank \'baŋk\ n 1 : piled-up mass 2 : rising ground along a body of water 3 : sideways slope along a curve ~ vb 1 : form a bank 2 : cover (as a fire) to keep inactive 3 : incline (an airplane) laterally

2bank n : tier of objects

3bank n 1 : money institution 2 : reserve supply ~ vb : conduct business in a bank —**bank·book** n —**bank·er** n —**bank·ing** n

bank·rupt \'baŋ,krəpt\ n : one required by law to forfeit assets to pay off debts ~ adj 1 : legally a bankrupt 2 : lacking something essential —

bankrupt vb —**bank·rupt·cy** \-,krəp-sē\ n

ban·ner \'banər\ n : flag ~ adj : excellent

banns \'banz\ n pl : announcement in church of a proposed marriage

ban·quet \'baŋkwət\ n : ceremonial dinner —**banquet** vb

ban·shee \'banshē\ n : wailing female spirit that foretells death

ban·tam \'bantəm\ n : miniature domestic fowl

ban·ter \'bantər\ n : good-natured joking —**banter** vb

ban·yan \'banyən\ n : large tree that grows new trunks from the limbs

bap·tism \'bap,tizəm\ n : Christian rite signifying spiritual cleansing —**bap·tis·mal** \bap'tizməl\ adj

bap·tize \bap'tīz, 'bap,tīz\ vb -tized; -tiz·ing : administer baptism to

bar \'bär\ n 1 : long narrow object used esp. as a lever, fastening, or support 2 : barrier 3 : body of practicing lawyers 4 : wide stripe 5 : food counter 6 : place where liquor is served 7 : vertical line across the musical staff ~ vb -rr- 1 : obstruct with a bar 2 : shut out 3 : prohibit ~ prep : excluding —**barred** adj —**bar·room** n —**bar·tend·er** n

barb \'bärb\ n : sharp projection pointing backward —**barbed** adj

bar·bar·ian \bär'barēən\ adj 1 : relating to people considered backward 2 : not refined —**barbarian** n

bar·bar·ic \'bärik\ adj : barbarian

bar·ba·rous \'bärbərəs\ adj 1 : lacking refinement 2 : mercilessly cruel —**bar·ba·rism** \-bə,rizəm\ n —**bar·bar·i·ty** \bär'barətē\ n —**bar·ba·rous·ly** adv

bar·be·cue \'bärbi,kyü\ n : gathering at which barbecued food is served ~ vb -cued; -cu·ing : cook over hot coals or on a spit often with a highly seasoned sauce

bar·ber \'bärbər\ n : one who cuts hair

bar·bi·tu·rate \bär'bichərət\ n : sedative or hypnotic drug

bard \'bärd\ n : poet

bare \'bar\ adj **bar·er**; **bar·est** : naked 2 : not concealed 3 : empty 4 : leaving nothing to spare 5 : plain ~ vb **bared**; **bar·ing** : make or lay bare —**bare·foot, bare·foot·ed** adv or adj —**bare·hand·ed** adv or adj —

bare·head·ed *adv or adj* — **bare·ly** *adv* — **bare·ness** *n*

bare·back, **bare·backed** *adv or adj* : without a saddle

bare·faced *adj* : open and esp. brazen

bar·gain \'bärgən\ *n* 1 : agreement 2 : something bought for less than its value ~ *vb* 1 : negotiate 2 : barter

barge \'bärj\ *n* : broad flat-bottomed boat ~ *vb* **barged; barg·ing** : move rudely or clumsily —**barge·man** *n*

bar·i·tone \'barə,tōn\ *n* : male voice between bass and tenor

bar·i·um \'barēəm\ *n* : silver-white metallic chemical element

¹bark \'bärk\ *vb* 1 : make the sound of a dog 2 : speak in a loud curt tone ~ *n* : sound of a barking dog

²bark *n* : tough corky outer covering of a woody stem or root ~ *vb* : remove bark or skin from

³bark *n* : sailing ship with a fore-and-aft rear sail

bark·er \'bärkər\ *n* : one who calls out to attract people to a show

bar·ley \'bärlē\ *n* : cereal grass or its seeds

barn \'bärn\ *n* : building for keeping hay or livestock —**barn·yard** *n*

bar·na·cle \'bärnikəl\ *n* : marine crustacean

barn·storm *vb* : tour through rural districts giving performances

ba·rom·e·ter \bə'rämətər\ *n* : instrument for measuring atmospheric pressure —**baro·met·ric** \,barə'metrik\ *adj*

bar·on \'barən\ *n* : British peer —**bar·on·age** \-ij\ *n* —**ba·ro·ni·al** \bə-'rōnēəl\ *adj* —**bar·ony** \'barənē\ *n*

bar·on·ess \-ənəs\ *n* 1 : baron's wife 2 : woman holding a baronial title

bar·on·et \-ənət\ *n* : man holding a rank between a baron and a knight —**bar·on·et·cy** \-sē\ *n*

ba·roque \bə'rōk, -'räk\ *adj* : elaborately ornamented

bar·racks \'baräks\ *n sing or pl* : soldiers' housing

bar·ra·cu·da \,barə'küdə\ *n, pl* **-da** *or* **-das** : large predatory sea fish

bar·rage \bə'räzh, -'räj\ *n* : heavy artillery fire

bar·rel \'barəl\ *n* 1 : closed cylindrical container 2 : amount held by a barrel 3 : cylindrical part ~ *vb* **-reled** *or* **-relled; -rel·ing** *or* **-rel·ling** 1 : pack

in a barrel 2 : move at high speed —**bar·reled** *n*

bar·ren \'barən\ *adj* 1 : unproductive of life 2 : uninteresting —**bar·ren·ness** *n*

bar·rette \bä'ret, bə-\ *n* : clasp for a woman's hair

bar·ri·cade \'barə,kād, ,barə'-\ *n* : barrier —**barricade** *vb*

bar·ri·er \'barēər\ *n* : something that separates or obstructs

bar·ring \'bäriŋ\ *prep* : omitting

bar·ris·ter \'barəstər\ *n* : British trial lawyer

bar·row \'barō\ *n* : wheelbarrow

bar·ter \'bärtər\ *vb* : trade by exchange of goods —**barter** *n*

ba·salt \bə'sȯlt, 'bā,-\ *n* : dark fine-grained igneous rock —**ba·sal·tic** \bə'sȯltik\ *adj*

¹base \'bās\ *n, pl* **bas·es** 1 : bottom 2 : fundamental part 3 : beginning point 4 : supply source of a force 5 : compound that reacts with an acid to form a salt ~ *vb* **based; bas·ing** : establish —**base·less** *adj*

²base *adj* **bas·er; bas·est** 1 : inferior 2 : contemptible —**base·ly** *adv* —**base·ness** *n*

base·ball *n* : game played with a bat and ball by 2 teams

base·ment \-mənt\ *n* : part of a building below ground level

bash \'bash\ *vb* : strike violently ~ *n* : heavy blow

bash·ful \-fəl\ *adj* : self-conscious —**bash·ful·ness** *n*

ba·sic \'bāsik\ *adj* 1 : relating to or forming the base or essence 2 : relating to a chemical base —**ba·si·cal·ly** *adv* —**ba·sic·i·ty** \bā'sisətē\ *n*

ba·sil \'bazəl, 'bās-, 'bāz-\ *n* : aromatic mint

ba·sil·i·ca \bə'silikə\ *n* : important church or cathedral

ba·sin \'bās⁰n\ *n* 1 : large bowl or pan 2 : region drained by a river

ba·sis \'bāsəs\ *n, pl* **ba·ses** \-,sēz\ 1 : something that supports 2 : fundamental principle

bask \'bask\ *vb* : enjoy pleasant warmth

bas·ket \'baskət\ *n* : woven container —**bas·ket·ful** *n*

bas·ket·ball *n* : game played with a ball on a court by 2 teams

bas-re·lief \,bäri'lēf\ *n* : flat sculpture with slightly raised design

¹bass \'bas\ *n, pl* **bass** *or* **bass·es** : spiny-finned sport and food fish

²bass \'bās\ n **1** : deep tone **2** : lowest choral voice

bas·set hound \'basət-\ n : short-legged dog with long ears

bas·si·net \‚basə'net\ n : baby's bed

bas·soon \bə'sün, ba-\ n : low-pitched wind instrument

bas·tard \'bastərd\ n **1** : illegitimate child **2** : offensive person ~ adj **1** : illegitimate **2** : inferior —**bas·tard·ize** vb —**bas·tardy** n

¹baste \'bāst\ vb **bast·ed; bast·ing** : sew temporarily with long stitches

²baste vb **bast·ed; bast·ing** : moisten at intervals while cooking

bas·tion \'baschən\ n : fortified position

¹bat \'bat\ n **1** : stick or club **2** : sharp blow ~ vb **-tt-** : hit with a bat

²bat n : small flying mammal

³bat vb **-tt-** : wink or blink

batch \'bach\ n : quantity used or produced at one time

bate \'bāt\ vb **bat·ed; bat·ing** : moderate or reduce

bath \'bath, 'bàth\ n, pl **baths** \'bathz, 'bàths, 'baths, 'bàths\ **1** : a washing of the body **2** : water for washing the body **3** : liquid in which something is immersed **4** : bathroom **5** : large financial loss —**bath·tub** n

bathe \'bàth\ vb **bathed; bath·ing 1** : wash in liquid **2** : flow against so as to wet **3** : shine light over **4** : take a bath or a swim —**bath·er** n

bath·robe n : robe worn around the house

bath·room n : room with a bathtub or shower and usu. a sink and toilet

ba·tiste \bə'tēst\ n : fine sheer fabric

ba·ton \bə'tän\ n : musical conductor's stick

bat·tal·ion \bə'talyən\ n : military unit composed of a headquarters and two or more companies

bat·ten \'batᵊn\ n : strip of wood used to seal or reinforce ~ vb : furnish or fasten with battens

¹bat·ter \'batər\ vb : beat or damage with repeated blows

²batter n : mixture of flour and liquid

³batter n : player who bats

bat·tery \'batərē\ n, pl **-ter·ies 1** : illegal beating of a person **2** : group of artillery guns **3** : group of electric cells

bat·ting \'batin\ n : layers of cotton or wool for stuffing

bat·tle \'batᵊl\ n : military fighting ~ vb **-tled; -tling** : engage in battle —**bat·tle·field** n

bat·tle–ax n : long-handled ax formerly used as a weapon

bat·tle·ment \-mənt\ n : parapet on top of a wall

bat·tle·ship n : heavily armed warship

bat·ty \'batē\ adj **-ti·er; -est** : crazy

bau·ble \'bòbəl\ n : trinket

bawdy \'bòdē\ adj **bawd·i·er; -est** : obscene or lewd —**bawd·i·ly** adv —**bawd·i·ness** n

bawl \'bòl\ vb : cry loudly ~ n : long loud cry

¹bay \'bā\ adj : reddish brown ~ n : bay-colored animal

²bay n : European laurel

³bay n **1** : compartment **2** : area projecting out from a building and containing a window (**bay window**)

⁴bay vb : bark with deep long tones ~ n **1** : position of one unable to escape danger **2** : baying of dogs

⁵bay n : body of water smaller than a gulf and nearly surrounded by land

bay·ber·ry \-‚berē\ n : shrub bearing small waxy berries

bay·o·net \'bāənət, ‚bāə'net\ n : dagger that fits on the end of a rifle ~ vb **-net·ed; -net·ing** : stab with a bayonet

bay·ou \'bīü, -ō\ n : creek flowing through marshy land

ba·zaar \bə'zär\ n **1** : market **2** : fair for charity

ba·zoo·ka \-'zükə\ n : weapon that shoots armor-piercing rockets

BB n : small shot pellet

be \'bē\ vb **was** \'wəz, 'wäz\, **were** \'wər\; **been** \'bin\; **be·ing** \'bēin\; **am** \əm, 'am\, **is** \'iz, əz\, **are** \ər, 'är\ **1** : equal **2** : exist **3** : occupy a certain place **4** : occur ~ verbal auxiliary — used to show continuous action or to form the passive voice

beach \'bēch\ n : sandy shore of a sea, lake, or river ~ vb : drive ashore

beach·comb·er \-‚kōmər\ n : one who searches the shore for useful objects

beach·head n : shore area held by an attacking force in an invasion

bea·con \'bēkən\ n : guiding or warning light or signal

bead \'bēd\ n : small round body esp. strung on a thread ~ vb : form into a bead —**bead·ing** n —**beady** adj

bea·gle \'bēgəl\ n : small short-legged hound

beak \'bēk\ *n* : bill of a bird —**beaked** *adj*

bea·ker \'bēkər\ *n* **1** : large drinking cup **2** : laboratory vessel

beam \'bēm\ *n* **1** : large long piece of timber or metal **2** : ray of light **3** : directed radio signals for the guidance of pilots ~ *vb* **1** : send out light **2** : smile **3** : aim a radio broadcast

bean \'bēn\ *n* : edible plant seed borne in pods

¹bear \'bar\ *n, pl* **bears** *or pl* **bear** : large heavy mammal with shaggy hair **2** : gruff or sullen person —**bear·ish** *adj*

²bear *vb* **bore** \'bōr\; **borne** \'bōrn\ **bear·ing 1** : carry **2** : give birth to or produce **3** : endure **4** : press **5** : go in an indicated direction —**bear·able** *adj* —**bear·er** *n*

beard \'bird\ *n* **1** : facial hair on a man **2** : tuft like a beard ~ *vb* : confront boldly —**beard·ed** *adj* —**beard·less** *adj*

bear·ing *n* **1** : way of carrying oneself **2** : supporting object or purpose **3** : significance **4** : machine part in which another part turns **5** : direction with respect esp. to compass points

beast \'bēst\ *n* **1** : animal **2** : brutal person —**beast·li·ness** *n* —**beast·ly** *adj*

beat \'bēt\ *vb* **beat; beat·en** \'bēt³n\ *or* **beat; beat·ing 1** : strike repeatedly **2** : defeat **3** : act or arrive before **4** : throb ~ *n* **1** : single stroke or pulsation **2** : rhythmic stress in poetry or music ~ *adj* : exhausted —**beat·er** *n*

be·a·tif·ic \,bēə'tifik\ *adj* : blissful

be·at·i·fy \bē'atə,fī\ *vb* **-fied; -fy·ing** : make happy or blessed —**be·at·i·fi·ca·tion** \-,atəfə'kāshən\ *n*

be·at·i·tude \-'atə,tüd, -,tyüd\ *n* : saying in the Sermon on the Mount (Matthew 5:3-12) beginning "Blessed are"

beau \'bō\ *n, pl* **beaux** \'bōz\ *or* **beaus** : suitor

beau·ty \'byütē\ *n, pl* **-ties** : qualities that please the senses or mind —**beau·te·ous** \-ēəs\ *adj* —**beau·te·ous·ly** *adv* —**beau·ti·fi·ca·tion** \,byütəfə'kāshən\ *n* —**beau·ti·fi·er** \'byütə,fīər\ *n* —**beau·ti·ful** \-ifəl\ *adj* —**beau·ti·ful·ly** *adv* —**beau·ti·fy** \-ə,fī\ *vb*

bea·ver \'bēvər\ *n* : large fur-bearing rodent

be·cause \bi'kòz, -'kəz\ *conj* : for the reason that

because of *prep* : by reason of

beck \'bek\ *n* : summons

beck·on \'bekən\ *vb* : summon esp. by a nod or gesture

be·come \bi'kəm\ *vb* **-came** \-'kām\; **-come; -com·ing 1** : come to be **2** : be suitable —**be·com·ing** *adj* —**be·com·ing·ly** *adv*

bed \'bed\ *n* **1** : piece of furniture to sleep on **2** : flat or level surface ~ *vb* **-dd-** : put or go to bed —**bed·spread** *n*

bed·bug *n* : wingless bloodsucking insect

bed·clothes *n pl* : bedding

bed·ding *n* **1** : sheets and blankets for a bed **2** : soft material (as hay) for an animal's bed

be·deck \bi'dek\ *vb* : adorn

be·dev·il \-'devəl\ *vb* : harass

bed·lam \'bedləm\ *n* : uproar and confusion

be·drag·gled \bi'dragəld\ *adj* : dirty and disordered

bed·rid·den \'bed,rid³n\ *adj* : kept in bed by illness

bed·rock *n* : solid subsurface rock —**bedrock** *adj*

¹bee \'bē\ *n* : 4-winged honey-producing insect —**bee·hive** *n* —**bee·keep·er** *n* —**bees·wax** *n*

²bee *n* : neighborly work session

beech \'bēch\ *n, pl* **beech·es** *or* **beech** : tree with smooth gray bark and edible nuts (**beech·nuts**) —**beech·en** \-ən\ *adj*

beef \'bēf\ *n, pl* **beefs** \'bēfs\ *or* **beeves** \'bēvz\ : flesh of a steer, cow, or bull ~ *vb* : strengthen —used with *up* —**beef·steak** *n*

bee·line *n* : straight course

been *past part of* BE

beep \'bēp\ *n* : short usu. high-pitched warning sound —**beep** *vb* —**beep·er** *n*

beer \'bir\ *n* : alcoholic drink brewed from malt and hops —**beery** *adj*

beet \'bēt\ *n* : garden root vegetable

bee·tle \'bēt³l\ *n* : 4-winged insect

be·fall \bi'fòl\ *vb* **-fell; -fall·en** : happen to

be·fit \bi'fit\ *vb* : be suitable to

be·fore \bi'fōr\ *adv* **1** : in front **2** : earlier ~ *prep* **1** : in front of **2** : earlier than ~ *conj* : earlier than

be·fore·hand *adv or adj* : in advance

be·friend \bi'frend\ *vb* : act as friend to

be·fud·dle \-'fəd⁹l\ *vb* : confuse

beg \'beg\ *vb* -**gg**- : ask earnestly

be·get \bi'get\ *vb* -**got**; -**got·ten** *or* -**got**; -**get·ting** : become the father of

beg·gar \'begər\ *n* : one that begs ~ *vb* : make poor —**beg·gar·ly** *adj* — **beg·gary** *n*

be·gin \bi'gin\ *vb* -**gan** \-'gan\; -**gun** \-'gən\; -**gin·ning 1** : start **2** : come into being —**be·gin·ner** *n*

be·gone \bi'gȯn\ *vb* : go away

be·go·nia \-'gōnyə\ *n* : tropical herb with waxy flowers

be·grudge \-'grəj\ *vb* **1** : concede reluctantly **2** : look upon disapprovingly

be·guile \-'gīl\ *vb* -**guiled**; -**guil·ing 1** : deceive **2** : amuse

be·half \-'haf, -'häf\ *n* : benefit

be·have \-'hāv\ *vb* -**haved**; -**hav·ing** : act in a certain way

be·hav·ior \-'hāvyər\ *n* : way of behaving —**be·hav·ior·al** \-əl\ *adj*

be·head \-'hed\ *vb* : cut off the head of

be·hest \-'hest\ *n* : command

be·hind \bi'hīnd\ *adv* : at the back ~ *prep* **1** : in back of **2** : less than **3** : supporting

be·hold \-'hōld\ *vb* -**held**; -**hold·ing** : see —**be·hold·er** *n*

be·hold·en \-'hōldən\ *adj* : indebted

be·hoove \-'hüv\ *vb* -**hooved**; -**hoov·ing** : be necessary for

beige \'bāzh\ *n* : yellowish brown — **beige** *adj*

be·ing \'bēiŋ\ *n* **1** : existence **2** : living thing

be·la·bor \bi'lābər\ *vb* : carry on to absurd lengths

be·lat·ed \-'lātəd\ *adj* : delayed

belch \'belch\ *vb* **1** : expel stomach gas orally **2** : emit forcefully —**belch** *n*

be·lea·guer \bi'lēgər\ *vb* **1** : besiege **2** : harass

bel·fry \'belfrē\ *n, pl* -**fries** : bell tower

be·lie \bi'lī\ *vb* -**lied**; -**ly·ing 1** : misrepresent **2** : prove false

be·lief \bə'lēf\ *n* **1** : trust **2** : something believed

be·lieve \-'lēv\ *vb* -**lieved**; -**liev·ing 1** : trust in **2** : accept as true **3** : hold as an opinion —**be·liev·able** *adj* —**be·liev·ably** *adv* —**be·liev·er** *n*

be·lit·tle \bi'lit⁹l\ *vb* -**lit·tled**; -**lit·tling 1** : disparage **2** : make seem less

bell \'bel\ *n* : hollow metallic device that rings when struck ~ *vb* : provide with a bell

bel·la·don·na \belə'dänə\ *n* : poisonous herb yielding a drug

belle \'bel\ *n* : beautiful woman

bel·li·cose \'beli,kōs\ *adj* : pugnacious —**bel·li·cos·i·ty** \,beli'käsətē\ *n*

bel·lig·er·ent \bə'lijərənt\ *adj* **1** : waging war **2** : truculent —**bel·lig·er·ence** \-rəns\ *n* —**bel·lig·er·en·cy** \-rənsē\ *n* —**belligerent** *n*

bel·low \'belō\ *vb* : make a loud deep roar or shout —**bellow** *n*

bel·lows \-ōz, -əz\ *n sing or pl* : device with sides that can be compressed to expel air

bell·weth·er \'bel'wethər, -,weth-\ *n* : leader

bel·ly \'belē\ *n, pl* -**lies** : abdomen ~ *vb* -**lied**; -**ly·ing** : bulge

be·long \bi'lȯŋ\ *vb* **1** : be suitable **2** : be owned **3** : be a part of

be·long·ings \-iŋz\ *n pl* : possessions

be·loved \bi'ləvəd, -'ləvd\ *adj* : dearly loved —**beloved** *n*

be·low \-'lō\ *adv* : in or to a lower place ~ *prep* : lower than

belt \'belt\ *n* **1** : strip (as of leather) worn about the waist **2** : endless band to impart motion **3** : distinct region ~ *vb* **1** : put a belt around **2** : thrash

be·moan \bi'mōn\ *vb* : lament

be·muse \-'myüz\ *vb* : confuse

bench \'bench\ *n* **1** : long seat **2** : judge's seat **3** : court

bend \'bend\ *vb* **bent** \'bent\; **bending 1** : curve or cause a change of shape in **2** : turn in a certain direction ~ *n* **1** : act of bending **2** : curve

be·neath \bi'nēth\ *adv or prep* : below

bene·dic·tion \,benə'dikshən\ *n* : closing blessing

bene·fac·tor \'benə,faktər\ *n* : one who gives esp. charitable aid

be·nef·i·cence \bə'nefəsəns\ *n* : quality of doing good —**be·nef·i·cent** \-sənt\ *adj*

ben·e·fi·cial \,benə'fishəl\ *adj* : being of benefit —**ben·e·fi·cial·ly** *adv*

ben·e·fi·cia·ry \-'fishē,erē, -'fishərē\ *n, pl* -**ries** : one who receives benefits

ben·e·fit \'benə,fit\ *n* **1** : something that does good **2** : help **3** : fund-raising event —**benefit** *vb*

be·nev·o·lence \bə'nevələns\ *n* **1** : charitable nature **2** : act of kindness —**be·nev·o·lent** \-lənt\ *adj* —**be·nev·o·lent·ly** *adv*

be·night·ed \bi'nītəd\ *adj* : ignorant

be·nign \bi'nīn\ *adj* 1 : gentle or kindly 2 : not malignant —**be·nig·ni·ty** \-'nignətē\ *n*

be·nig·nant \-'nignənt\ *adj* : benign

bent \'bent\ *n* : aptitude or interest

be·numb \bi'nəm\ *vb* : make numb esp. by cold

ben·zene \'ben,zēn\ *n* : colorless flammable liquid

be·queath \bi'kwēth, -'kwēth\ *vb* 1 : give by will 2 : hand down

be·quest \bi'kwest\ *n* : something bequeathed

be·rate \-'rāt\ *vb* : scold harshly

be·reaved \-'rēvd\ *adj* : suffering the death of a loved one ~ *n, pl* **bereaved** : one who is bereaved —**be·reave·ment** *n*

be·reft \-'reft\ *adj* : deprived of or lacking something

be·ret \bə'rā\ *n* : round soft visorless cap

beri·beri \,berē'berē\ *n* : thiamine-deficiency disease

berm \'bərm\ *n* : bank of earth

ber·ry \'berē\ *n, pl* **-ries** : small pulpy fruit

ber·serk \bər'sərk, -'zərk\ *adj* : crazed —**berserk** *adv*

berth \'bərth\ *n* 1 : place where a ship is anchored 2 : place to sit or sleep esp. on a ship 3 : job ~ *vb* : to bring or come into a berth

ber·yl \'berəl\ *n* : light-colored silicate mineral

be·seech \bi'sēch\ *vb* **-sought** \-'sȯt\ *or* **-seeched; -seech·ing** : entreat

be·set \-'set\ *vb* 1 : harass 2 : hem in

be·side \-'sīd\ *prep* 1 : by the side of 2 : besides

be·sides \-'sīdz\ *adv* 1 : in addition 2 : moreover ~ *prep* 1 : other than 2 : in addition to

be·siege \-'sēj\ *vb* : lay siege to —**be·sieg·er** *n*

be·smirch \bi'smərch\ *vb* : soil

be·sot \-'sät\ *vb* **-tt-** : become drunk

be·speak \bi'spēk\ *vb* **-spoke; -spo·ken; -speak·ing** 1 : address 2 : indicate

best \'best\ *adj, superlative of* GOOD 1 : excelling all others 2 : most productive 3 : largest ~ *adv, superlative of* WELL 1 : in the best way 2 : most ~ *n* : one that is best ~ *vb* : outdo

bes·tial \'beschəl, 'bēs-\ *adj* 1 : relating to beasts 2 : brutish —**bes·ti·al·i·ty** \,beschē'alətē, ,bēs-\ *n*

be·stir \bi'stər\ *vb* : rouse to action

best man *n* : chief male attendant at a wedding

be·stow \bi'stō\ *vb* : give —**be·stow·al** \-əl\ *n*

bet \'bet\ *n* 1 : something risked or pledged on the outcome of a contest 2 : the making of a bet ~ *vb* **bet; bet·ting** 1 : risk (as money) on an outcome 2 : make a bet with

be·tide \bi'tīd\ *vb* : happen to

be·to·ken \bi'tōkən\ *vb* : give an indication of

be·tray \bi'trā\ *vb* 1 : seduce 2 : report or reveal to an enemy by treachery 3 : abandon 4 : prove unfaithful to 5 : reveal unintentionally —**be·tray·al** *n* —**be·tray·er** *n*

be·troth \-'trȯth, -'trȯth, -'trȯth, *or with* th\ *vb* : promise to marry —**be·troth·al** *n* —**be·trothed** *n*

bet·ter \'betər\ *adj, comparative of* GOOD 1 : more than half 2 : improved in health 3 : of higher quality ~ *adv, comparative of* WELL 1 : in a superior manner 2 : more ~ *n* 1 : one that is better 2 : advantage ~ *vb* 1 : improve 2 : surpass —**bet·ter·ment** \-mənt\ *n*

bet·tor, bet·ter \'betər\ *n* : one who bets

be·tween \bi'twēn\ *prep* 1 —used to show two things considered together 2 : in the space separating 3 —used to indicate a comparison or choice ~ *adv* : in an intervening space or interval

bev·el \'bevəl\ *n* : slant on an edge ~ *vb* **-eled** *or* **-elled; -el·ing** *or* **-el·ling** 1 : cut or shape to a bevel 2 : incline

bev·er·age \'bevrij\ *n* : drink

bevy \'bevē\ *n, pl* **bev·ies** : large group

be·wail \bi'wāl\ *vb* : lament

be·ware \-'war\ *vb* : be cautious

be·wil·der \-'wildər\ *vb* : confuse —**be·wil·der·ment** *n*

be·witch \-'wich\ *vb* 1 : affect by witchcraft 2 : charm —**be·witch·ment** *n*

be·yond \bē'yänd\ *adv* 1 : farther 2 : besides ~ *prep* 1 : on or to the farther side of 2 : out of the reach of 3 : besides

bi- \'bī, ,bī\ *prefix* 1 : two 2 : coming or occurring every two 3 : twice, doubly, or on both sides

bicolored	bicultural
biconcave	bidirectional
biconcavity	bifunctional
biconvex	bimetal
biconvexity	bimetallic

binational　　bipolar
biparental　　biracial

bi·an·nu·al \ˌbīˈanyəwəl\ adj : occurring twice a year —**bi·an·nu·al·ly** adv

bi·as \ˈbīəs\ n 1 : line diagonal to the grain of a fabric 2 : prejudice ~ vb -**ased** or -**assed**; -**as·ing** or -**as·sing** : prejudice

bib \ˈbib\ n : shield tied under the chin to protect the clothes while eating

Bi·ble \ˈbībəl\ n 1 : sacred scriptures of Christians 2 : sacred scriptures of Judaism or of some other religion —**bib·li·cal** \ˈbiblikəl\ adj

bib·li·og·ra·phy \ˌbibleˈägrəfē\ n, pl -**phies** : list of writings on a subject or of an author —**bib·li·og·ra·pher** \-fər\ n —**bib·li·o·graph·ic** \-lēəˈgrafik\ adj

bi·cam·er·al \ˈbīˈkamərəl\ adj : having 2 legislative chambers

bi·car·bon·ate \-ˈkärbəˌnāt, -nət\ n : acid carbonate

bi·cen·ten·ni·al \ˌbīsenˈtenēəl\ n : 200th anniversary —**bicentennial** adj

bi·ceps \ˈbīˌseps\ n : large muscle of the upper arm

bick·er \ˈbikər\ vb or n : squabble

bi·cus·pid \bīˈkəspəd\ n : double-pointed tooth

bi·cy·cle \ˈbīˌsikəl\ n : 2-wheeled vehicle moved by pedaling ~ vb -**cled**; -**cling** : ride a bicycle —**bi·cy·cler** \-klər\ n **bi·cy·clist** \-list\ n

bid \ˈbid\ vb **bade** \ˈbad, ˈbād\ or **bid**; **bid·den** \ˈbidᵊn\ or **bid**; **bid·ding** 1 : order 2 : invite 3 : express 4 : make a bid ~ n 1 : act of bidding 2 : buyer's proposed price —**bid·da·ble** \-əbəl\ adj —**bid·der** n

bide \ˈbīd\ vb **bode** \ˈbōd\ or **bid·ed**; **bided**; **bid·ing** 1 : wait 2 : dwell

bi·en·ni·al \bīˈenēəl\ adj 1 : occurring once in 2 years 2 : lasting 2 years —**biennial** n —**bi·en·ni·al·ly** adv

bier \ˈbir\ n : stand for a coffin

bi·fo·cals \ˈbīˌfōkəlz\ n pl : eyeglasses that correct for near and distant vision

big \ˈbig\ adj -**gg**- : large in size, amount, or scope —**big·ness** n

big·a·my \ˈbigəmē\ n : marrying one person while still married to another —**big·a·mist** \-mist\ n —**big·a·mous** \-məs\ adj

big·horn n, pl -**horn** or -**horns** : wild mountain sheep

bight \ˈbīt\ n 1 : loop of a rope 2 : bay

big·ot \ˈbigət\ n : one who is intolerant of others —**big·ot·ed** \-ətəd\ adj —**big·ot·ry** \-ətrē\ n

big shot n : important person

big·wig n : big shot

bike \ˈbīk\ n : bicycle or motorcycle

bi·ki·ni \bəˈkēnē\ n : woman's brief 2-piece bathing suit

bi·lat·er·al \bīˈlatərəl\ adj : involving 2 sides —**bi·lat·er·al·ly** adv

bile \ˈbīl\ n 1 : greenish liver secretion that aids digestion 2 : bad temper

bi·lin·gual \bīˈliŋgwəl\ adj : using 2 languages

bil·ious \ˈbilyəs\ adj : irritable —**bil·ious·ness** n

bilk \ˈbilk\ vb : cheat

¹bill \ˈbil\ n : jaws of a bird together with their horny covering ~ vb : caress fondly —**billed** adj

²bill n 1 : draft of a law 2 : list of things to be paid for 3 : printed advertisement 4 : piece of paper money ~ vb : submit a bill or account to

bill·board n : surface for displaying advertising bills

bil·let \ˈbilət\ n : soldiers' quarters ~ vb : lodge in a billet

bill·fold n : wallet

bil·liards \ˈbilyərdz\ n : game of driving balls into one another or into pockets on a table

bil·lion \ˈbilyən\ n, pl **billions** or **billion** : 1000 millions —**billion** adj —**bil·lionth** \-yənth\ adj or n

bil·low \ˈbilō\ n 1 : great wave 2 : rolling mass ~ vb : swell out —**bil·lowy** \ˈbiləwē\ adj

billy goat n : male goat

bin \ˈbin\ n : storage box

bi·na·ry \ˈbinərē\ adj : consisting of 2 things —**binary** n

bind \ˈbīnd\ vb **bound** \ˈbau̇nd\; **bind·ing** 1 : tie 2 : obligate 3 : unite into a mass 4 : bandage —**bind·er** n —**binding** n

binge \ˈbinj\ n : spree

bin·go \ˈbiŋgō\ n, pl -**gos** : game of covering numbers on a card

bin·oc·u·lar \bīˈnäkyələr, bə-\ adj : of or relating to both eyes ~ n : binocular optical instrument —usu. pl.

bio·chem·is·try \ˌbīōˈkeməstrē\ n : chemistry dealing with organisms —**bio·chem·i·cal** adj or n —**bio·chem·ist** n

bio·de·grad·able \ˌbīōdiˈgrādəbəl\ adj : able to be reduced to harmless products by organisms —**bio·de·grad·abil·i·ty** n —**bio·deg·ra·da·tion** n —**bio·de·grade** vb

bi·og·ra·phy \bīˈägrəfē, bē-\ n, pl **-phies** : written history of a person's life —**bi·og·ra·pher** \-fər\ n —**bi·o·graph·i·cal** \ˌbīōˈgrafikəl\ adj

bi·ol·o·gy \bīˈäləjē\ n : science of living beings and life processes —**bi·o·log·ic** \ˌbīəˈläjik\, **bi·o·log·i·cal** \-əl\ adj —**bi·ol·o·gist** \bīˈäləjist\ n

bio·phys·ics \ˌbīōˈfiziks\ n : application of physics to biological problems —**bio·phys·i·cal** adj —**bio·phys·i·cist** n

bi·op·sy \ˈbīˌäpsē\ n, pl **-sies** : removal of live bodily tissue for examination

bio·tech·nol·o·gy \ˌbīōtekˈnäləjē\ n : manufacture of products using techniques involving the manipulation of DNA

bi·par·ti·san \bīˈpärtəzən, -sən\ adj : involving members of 2 parties

bi·ped \ˈbīˌped\ n : 2-footed animal

birch \ˈbərch\ n : deciduous tree with close-grained wood —**birch, birch·en** \-ən\ adj

bird \ˈbərd\ n : warm-blooded egg-laying vertebrate with wings and feathers —**bird·bath** n —**bird·house** n —**bird·seed** n

bird's-eye \ˈbərdzˌī\ adj 1 : seen from above 2 : cursory

birth \ˈbərth\ n 1 : act or fact of being born or of producing young 2 : origin —**birth·day** n —**birth·place** n —**birth·rate** n

birth·mark n : unusual blemish on the skin at birth

birth·right n : something one is entitled to by birth

bis·cuit \ˈbiskət\ n : small bread made with leavening other than yeast

bi·sect \ˈbīˌsekt\ vb : divide into 2 parts —**bi·sec·tion** \ˈbīˌsekshən\ n —**bi·sec·tor** \-tər\ n

bish·op \ˈbishəp\ n : clergy member higher than a priest

bish·op·ric \-shəˌprik\ n 1 : diocese 2 : office of bishop

bis·muth \ˈbizməth\ n : heavy brittle metallic chemical element

bi·son \ˈbīsᵊn, ˈbīz-\ n, pl **-son** : large shaggy wild ox of central U.S.

bis·tro \ˈbēstrō, ˈbis-\ n, pl **-tros** : small restaurant or bar

¹**bit** \ˈbit\ n 1 : part of a bridle that goes in a horse's mouth 2 : drilling tool

²**bit** n 1 : small piece or quantity 2 : small degree

bitch \ˈbich\ n : female dog ~ vb : complain

bite \ˈbīt\ vb **bit** \ˈbit\; **bit·ten** \ˈbitᵊn\; **bit·ing** \ˈbītiŋ\ 1 : to grip or cut with teeth or jaws 2 : dig in or grab and hold 3 : sting 4 : take bait ~ n 1 : act of biting 2 : bit of food 3 : wound made by biting —**bit·ing** adj

bit·ter \ˈbitər\ adj 1 : having an acrid lingering taste 2 : intense or severe 3 : extremely harsh or resentful —**bit·ter·ly** adv —**bit·ter·ness** n

bit·tern \ˈbitərn\ n : small heron

bi·tu·mi·nous coal \bəˈtümənəs-, -ˈtyü-\ n : coal that yields volatile waste matter when heated

bi·valve \ˈbīˌvalv\ n : animal (as a clam) with a shell of 2 parts —**bivalve** adj

biv·ouac \ˈbivəˌwak\ n : temporary camp ~ vb **-ouacked; -ouack·ing** : camp

bi·zarre \bəˈzär\ adj : very strange —**bi·zarre·ly** adv

blab \ˈblab\ vb **-bb-** : talk too much

black \ˈblak\ adj 1 : of the color black 2 : Negro 3 : soiled 4 : lacking light 5 : wicked or evil 6 : gloomy ~ n 1 : black pigment or dye 2 : something black 3 : color of least lightness 4 : person of a dark-skinned race ~ vb : blacken —**black·ing** n —**black·ish** adj —**black·ly** adv —**black·ness** n

black-and-blue adj : darkly discolored from bruising

black·ball \ˈblakˌbȯl\ vb 1 : ostracize 2 : boycott —**blackball** n

black·ber·ry \ˈblakˌberē\ n : black or purple fruit of a bramble

black·bird n : bird of which the male is largely or wholly black

black·board n : dark surface for writing on with chalk

black·en \ˈblakən\ vb 1 : make or become black 2 : defame

black·guard \ˈblagərd, -ˌärd\ n : scoundrel

black·head n : small dark oily mass plugging the outlet of a skin gland

black hole n : invisible extremely massive celestial object

black·jack n 1 : flexible leather-covered club 2 : card game ~ vb : hit with a blackjack

black·list *n* : list of persons to be punished or boycotted —**blacklist** *vb*

black·mail *n* **1** : extortion by threat of exposure **2** : something extorted by blackmail —**blackmail** *vb* —**black·mail·er** *n*

black·out *n* **1** : darkness due to electrical failure **2** : brief fainting spell —**black out** *vb*

black·smith *n* : one who forges iron

black·top *n* : dark tarry material for surfacing roads —**blacktop** *vb*

blad·der \'bladər\ *n* : sac into which urine passes from the kidneys

blade \'blād\ *n* **1** : leaf esp. of grass **2** : something resembling the flat part of a leaf **3** : cutting part of an instrument or tool —**blad·ed** \'blādəd\ *adj*

blame \'blām\ *vb* **blamed; blam·ing 1** : find fault with **2** : hold responsible or responsible for —**blam·able** *adj* —**blame** *n* —**blame·less** *adj* —**blame·less·ly** *adv* —**blame·wor·thi·ness** *n* —**blame·worthy** *adj*

blanch \'blanch\ *vb* : make or become white or pale

bland \'bland\ *adj* **1** : smooth in manner **2** : soothing **3** : tasteless —**bland·ly** *adv* —**bland·ness** *n*

blan·dish·ment \'blandishmənt\ *n* : flattering or coaxing speech or act

blank \'blaŋk\ *adj* **1** : showing or causing a dazed look **2** : lacking expression **3** : empty **4** : free from writing **5** : downright ~ *n* **1** : an empty space **2** : form with spaces to write in **3** : unfinished form (as of a key) **4** : cartridge with no bullet ~ *vb* : cover or close up —**blank·ly** *adv* —**blank·ness** *n*

blan·ket \'blaŋkət\ *n* **1** : heavy covering for a bed **2** : covering layer ~ *vb* : cover ~ *adj* : applying to a group

blare \'blar\ *vb* **blared; blar·ing** : make a loud harsh sound —**blare** *n*

blar·ney \'blärnē\ *n* : skillful flattery

bla·sé \blä'zā\ *adj* : indifferent to pleasure or excitement

blas·pheme \blas'fēm\ *vb* **-phemed; -phem·ing** : speak blasphemy —**blas·phem·er** *n*

blas·phe·my \'blasfəmē\ *n, pl* **-mies** : irreverence toward God or anything sacred —**blas·phe·mous** *adj*

blast \'blast\ *n* **1** : violent gust of wind **2** : explosion ~ *vb* : shatter by or as if by explosive —**blast off** *vb* : take off esp. in a rocket

bla·tant \'blāt°nt\ *adj* : offensively showy —**bla·tan·cy** \-°nsē\ *n* —**bla·tant·ly** *adv*

¹blaze \'blāz\ *n* **1** : fire **2** : intense direct light **3** : strong display ~ *vb* **blazed; blaz·ing** : burn or shine brightly

²blaze *n* **1** : white stripe on an animal's face **2** : trail marker esp. on a tree ~ *vb* **blazed; blaz·ing** : mark with blazes

blaz·er \-ər\ *n* : sports jacket

bleach \'blēch\ *vb* : whiten —**bleach** *n*

bleach·ers \-ərz\ *n sing or pl* : uncovered stand for spectators

bleak \'blēk\ *adj* **1** : desolately barren **2** : lacking cheering qualities —**bleak·ish** *adj* —**bleak·ly** *adv* —**bleak·ness** *n*

blear \'blir\ *adj* : dim with water or tears

bleary \'blirē\ *adj* : dull or dimmed esp. from fatigue

bleat \'blēt\ *n* : cry of a sheep or goat or a sound like it —**bleat** *vb*

bleed \'blēd\ *vb* **bled** \'bled\; **bleed·ing 1** : lose or shed blood **2** : feel distress **3** : flow from a wound **4** : draw fluid from **5** : extort money from —**bleed·er** *n*

blem·ish \'blemish\ *vb* : spoil by a flaw ~ *n* : noticeable flaw

¹blench \'blench\ *vb* : flinch

²blench *vb* : grow or make pale

blend \'blend\ *vb* **1** : mix thoroughly **2** : combine into an integrated whole —**blend** *n* —**blend·er** *n*

bless \'bles\ *vb* **blessed** \'blest\; **bless·ing 1** : consecrate by religious rite **2** : invoke divine care for **3** : make happy —**bless·ed** \'blesəd\, **blest** \'blest\ *adj* —**bless·ed·ly** \'blesədlē\ *adv* —**bless·ed·ness** \'blesədnəs\ *n* —**bless·ing** *n*

blew *past of* BLOW

blight \'blīt\ *n* **1** : plant disorder marked by withering or an organism causing it **2** : harmful influence **3** : deteriorated condition ~ *vb* : affect with or suffer from blight

blimp \'blimp\ *n* : airship holding form by pressure of contained gas

blind \'blīnd\ *adj* **1** : lacking or quite deficient in ability to see **2** : not intelligently controlled **3** : having no way out ~ *vb* **1** : to make blind **2** : dazzle ~ *n* **1** : something to conceal or darken **2** : place of concealment —**blind·ly** *adv* —**blind·ness** *n*

blind·fold vb : cover the eyes of — **blindfold** n

blink \'bliŋk\ vb 1 : wink 2 : shine intermittently ~ n : wink

blink·er n : a blinking light

bliss \'blis\ n 1 : complete happiness 2 : heaven or paradise —**bliss·ful** adj —**bliss·ful·ly** adv

blis·ter \'blistər\ n 1 : raised area of skin containing watery fluid 2 : raised or swollen spot ~ vb : develop or cause blisters

blithe \'blīth, 'blīth\ adj **blith·er; blith·est** :- cheerful —**blithe·ly** adv — **blithe·some** \-səm\ adj

blitz \'blits\ n 1 : series of air raids 2 : fast intensive campaign —**blitz** vb

bliz·zard \'blizərd\ n : severe snowstorm

bloat \'blōt\ vb : swell

blob \'bläb\ n : small lump or drop

bloc \'bläk\ n : group working together

block \'bläk\ n 1 : solid piece 2 : frame enclosing a pulley 3 : quantity considered together 4 : large building divided into separate units 5 : a city square or the distance along one of its sides 6 : obstruction 7 : interruption of a bodily or mental function ~ vb : obstruct or hinder

block·ade \blä'kād\ n : isolation of a place usu. by troops or ships —**block·ade** vb —**block·ad·er** n

block·head n : stupid person

blond, blonde \'bländ\ adj 1 : fair in complexion 2 : of a light color — **blond, blonde** n

blood \'bləd\ n 1 : red liquid that circulates in the heart, arteries, and veins of animals 2 : lifeblood 3 : lineage — **blood·ed** adj —**blood·less** adj — **blood·stain** n —**blood·stained** adj — **blood·suck·er** n —**blood·suck·ing** n —**bloody** adj

blood·cur·dling adj : terrifying

blood·hound n : large hound with a keen sense of smell

blood·mo·bile \-mō,bēl\ n : truck for collecting blood from donors

blood·shed n : slaughter

blood·shot adj : inflamed to redness

blood·stream n : blood in a circulatory system

blood·thirsty adj : eager to shed blood —**blood·thirst·i·ly** adv —**blood·thirst·i·ness** n

bloom \'blüm\ n 1 : flower 2 : period of

flowering 3 : fresh or healthy look ~ vb 1 : yield flowers 2 : mature — **bloomy** adj

bloo·mers \'blümərz\ n pl : woman's underwear of short loose trousers

bloop·er \'blüpər\ n : public blunder

blos·som \'bläsəm\ n or vb : flower

blot \'blät\ n 1 : stain 2 : blemish ~ vb **-tt-** 1 : spot 2 : dry with absorbent paper —**blot·ter** n

blotch \'bläch\ n : large spot —**blotch** vb —**blotchy** adj

blouse \'blaus, 'blauz\ n : loose garment reaching from the neck to the waist

¹**blow** \'blō\ vb **blew** \'blü\; **blown** \'blōn\; **blow·ing** 1 : move forcibly 2 : send forth a current of air 3 : sound 4 : shape by blowing 5 : explode 6 : bungle — n 1 : gale 2 : act of blowing —**blow·er** n —**blowy** adj

²**blow** n 1 : forcible stroke 2 pl : fighting 3 : calamity

blow·out n : bursting of a tire

blow·torch n : small torch that uses a blast of air

¹**blub·ber** \'bləbər\ n : fat of whales

²**blubber** vb : cry noisily

blud·geon \'bləjən\ n : short club ~ vb : hit with a bludgeon

blue \'blü\ adj **blu·er; blu·est** 1 : of the color blue 2 : melancholy ~ n : color of the clear sky —**blu·ish** \-ish\ adj

blue·bell n : plant with blue bell-shaped flowers

blue·ber·ry \-,berē\ n : edible blue or blackish berry

blue·bird n : small bluish songbird

blue·fish n : bluish marine food fish

blue jay n : American crested jay

blue·print n 1 : photographic print in white on blue of a mechanical drawing 2 : plan of action —**blueprint** vb

blues \'blüz\ n pl 1 : depression 2 : music in a melancholy style

¹**bluff** \'bləf\ adj 1 : rising steeply with a broad flat front 2 : frank ~ n : cliff

²**bluff** vb : deceive by pretense ~ n : act of bluffing —**bluff·er** \-ər\ n

blu·ing, blue·ing \'blüiŋ\ n : laundry preparation to keep fabrics white

blun·der \'bləndər\ vb 1 : move clumsily 2 : make a stupid mistake ~ n : bad mistake

blun·der·buss \-,bəs\ n : obsolete short-barreled firearm

blunt \'blənt\ adj 1 : not sharp 2

: tactless ~ *vb* : make dull —**blunt-ly** *adv* —**blunt-ness** *n*

blur \'blər\ *n* **1** : smear 2 : something perceived indistinctly ~ *vb* **-rr-** : cloud or obscure —**blur-ry** \-ē\ *adj*

blurb \'blərb\ *n* : short publicity notice

blurt \'blərt\ *vb* : utter suddenly

blush \'bləsh\ *n* : reddening of the face —**blush** *vb* —**blush-ful** *adj*

blus-ter \'bləstər\ *vb* **1** : blow violently 2 : talk or act with boasts or threats —**bluster** *n* —**blus-tery** *adj*

boa \'bōə\ *n* **1** : a large snake (as the **boa con-stric-tor** \-kən'striktər\) that crushes its prey 2 : fluffy scarf

boar \'bōr\ *n* : male swine

board \'bōrd\ *n* **1** : long thin piece of sawed lumber 2 : flat thin sheet esp. for games 3 : daily meals furnished for pay 4 : official body ~ *vb* **1** : go aboard 2 : cover with boards 3 : supply meals to —**board-er** *n*

board-walk *n* : wooden walk along a beach

boast \'bōst\ *vb* : praise oneself or one's possessions —**boast** *n* —**boast-er** *n*—**boast-ful** *adj* —**boast-ful-ly** *adv*

boat \'bōt\ *n* : small vessel for traveling on water —**boat** *vb* —**boat-man** \-mən\ *n*

boat-swain \'bōsᵊn\ *n* : ship's officer in charge of the hull

¹**bob** \'bäb\ *vb* **-bb- 1** : move up and down 2 : appear suddenly

²**bob** *n* **1** : float 2 : woman's short hair-cut ~ *vb* : cut hair in a bob

bob-bin \'bäbən\ *n* : spindle for holding thread

bob-ble \'bäbəl\ *vb* **-bled; -bling** : fumble —**bobble** *n*

bob-cat *n* : small American lynx

bob-o-link \'bäbə,liŋk\ *n* : American songbird

bob-sled \'bäb,sled\ *n* : racing sled —**bobsled** *vb*

bob-white \'bäb'hwīt\ *n* : quail

¹**bock** \'bäk\ *n* : dark beer

¹**bode** \'bōd\ *vb* **bod-ed; bod-ing** : indicate by signs

²**bode** *past of* BIDE

bod-ice \'bädəs\ *n* : close-fitting top of dress

bod-i-ly \'bädᵊlē\ *adj* : relating to the body ~ *adv* **1** : in the flesh 2 : as a whole

body \'bädē\ *n, pl* **bod-ies 1** : the physical whole of an organism 2 : human being 3 : main part 4 : mass of matter

5 : group —**bod-ied** *adj* —**bod-i-less** \-iləs, -'iləs\ *adj* —**body-guard** *n*

bog \'bäg, 'bog\ *n* : swamp ~ *vb* **-gg-** : sink in or as if in a bog —**bog-gy** *adj*

bo-gey \'bùgē, 'bō-\ *n, pl* **-geys** : someone or something frightening

bog-gle \'bägəl\ *vb* **-gled; -gling** : overwhelm with amazement

bo-gus \'bōgəs\ *adj* : fake

bo-he-mi-an \bō'hēmēən\ *n* : one living unconventionally —**bohemian** *adj*

¹**boil** \'bòil\ *n* : inflamed swelling

²**boil** *vb* **1** : heat to a temperature (**boil-ing point**) at which vapor forms 2 : cook in boiling liquid 3 : be agitated —**boil** *n*

boil-er \'bòilər\ *n* : tank holding hot water or steam

bois-ter-ous \'bòistərəs\ *adj* : noisily turbulent —**bois-ter-ous-ly** *adv*

bold \'bōld\ *adj* **1** : courageous 2 : insolent 3 : daring —**bold-ly** *adv* —**bold-ness** *n*

bo-le-ro \bə'lerō\ *n, pl* **-ros 1** : Spanish dance 2 : short open jacket

boll \'bōl\ *n* : seed pod

boll weevil *n* : small grayish weevil that infests the cotton plant

bo-lo-gna \bə'lōnē\ *n* : large smoked sausage

bol-ster \'bōlstər\ *n* : long pillow ~ *vb* **-stered; -ster-ing** : support

bolt \'bōlt\ *n* **1** : flash of lightning 2 : sliding bar used to fasten a door 3 : roll of cloth 4 : threaded pin used with a nut ~ *vb* **1** : move suddenly 2 : fasten with a bolt 3 : swallow hastily

bomb \'bäm\ *n* : explosive device ~ *vb* : attack with bombs —**bomb-proof** *adj*

bom-bard \bäm'bärd, bəm-\ *vb* : attack with or as if with artillery —**bom-bard-ment** *n*

bom-bar-dier \,bämbə'dir\ *n* : one who releases the bombs from a bomber

bom-bast \'bäm,bast\ *n* : pretentious language —**bom-bas-tic** \bäm'bastik\ *adj*

bomb-er *n* **1** : one that bombs 2 : airplane for dropping bombs

bomb-shell *n* **1** : bomb 2 : great surprise

bona fide \'bōnə,fīd, 'bän-; ,bōnə'fīdē\ *adj* **1** : made in good faith 2 : genuine

bo-nan-za \bə'nanzə\ *n* : something yielding a rich return

bon-bon \'bän,bän\ *n* : piece of candy

bond \'bänd\ *n* **1** : fetters 2 : uniting

force **3** : obligation made binding by money **4** : interest-bearing certificate ~ *vb* **1** : insure **2** : cause to adhere —**bond·hold·er** *n*

bond·age \'bändij\ *n* : slavery —**bond·man** \-mən\ *n* —**bond·wom·an** *n*

^1**bonds·man** \'bändzmən\ *n* : slave

^2**bondsman** *n* : surety

bone \'bōn\ *n* : skeletal material ~ *vb* **boned; bon·ing** : to free from bones —**bone·less** *adj* —**bony** \'bōnē\ *adj*

bon·er \'bōnər\ *n* : blunder

bon·fire \'bän,fīr\ *n* : outdoor fire

bo·ni·to \bə'nētō\ *n, pl* **-tos** *or* **-to** : medium-sized tuna

bon·net \'bänət\ *n* : hat for a woman or infant

bo·nus \'bōnəs\ *n* : extra payment

boo \'bü\ *n, pl* **boos** : shout of disapproval —**boo** *vb*

boo·by \'bübē\ *n, pl* **-bies** : dunce

book \'buk\ *n* **1** : paper sheets bound into a volume **2** : long literary work or a subdivision of one ~ *vb* : reserve —**book·case** *n* —**book·let** \-lət\ *n* —**book·mark** *n* —**book·sell·er** *n* —**book·shelf** *n*

book·end *n* : support to hold up a row of books

book·ie \-ē\ *n* : bookmaker

book·ish \-ish\ *adj* : fond of books and reading

book·keep·er *n* : one who keeps business accounts —**book·keep·ing** *n*

book·mak·er *n* : one who takes bets —**book·mak·ing** *n*

book·worm *n* : one devoted to reading

^1**boom** \'büm\ *n* **1** : long spar to extend the bottom of a sail **2** : beam projecting from the pole of a derrick

^2**boom** *vb* **1** : make a deep hollow sound **2** : grow rapidly esp. in value ~ *n* **1** : booming sound **2** : rapid growth

boo·mer·ang \'bümə,raŋ\ *n* : angular club that returns to the thrower

^1**boon** \'bün\ *n* : benefit

^2**boon** *adj* : congenial

boon·docks \'bün,däks\ *n pl* : rural area

boor \'bur\ *n* : rude person —**boor·ish** *adj*

boost \'büst\ *vb* **1** : raise **2** : promote —**boost** *n* —**boost·er** *n*

boot \'büt\ *n* **1** : covering for the foot and leg **2** : kick ~ *vb* : kick

boo·tee, boo·tie \'bütē\ *n* : infant's knitted sock

booth \'büth\ *n, pl* **booths** \'büthz,

'büths\ : small enclosed stall or seating area

boot·leg \'büt,leg\ *vb* : make or sell liquor illegally —**bootleg** *adj or n* —**boot·leg·ger** *n*

boo·ty \'bütē\ *n, pl* **-ties** : plunder

booze \'büz\ *vb* **boozed; booz·ing** : drink liquor to excess ~ *n* : liquor —**booz·er** *n* —**boozy** *adj*

bo·rax \'bōr,aks\ *n* : crystalline compound of boron

bor·der \'bordər\ *n* **1** : edge **2** : boundary ~ *vb* **1** : put a border on **2** : be close

^1**bore** \'bōr\ *vb* **bored; bor·ing 1** : pierce **2** : make by piercing ~ *n* : cylindrical hole or its diameter —**bor·er** *n*

^2**bore** *past of* BEAR

^3**bore** *n* : one that is dull ~ *vb* **bored; bor·ing** : tire with dullness —**bore·dom** \'bōrdəm\ *n*

born \'born\ *adj* **1** : brought into life **2** : being such by birth

borne *past part of* BEAR

bo·ron \'bōr,än\ *n* : dark-colored chemical element

bor·ough \'bərō\ *n* : incorporated town or village

bor·row \'bärō\ *vb* **1** : take as a loan **2** : take into use

bo·som \'büzəm, 'bü-\ *n* : breast ~ *adj* : intimate —**bo·somed** *adj*

boss \'bos\ *n* : employer or supervisor ~ *vb* : supervise —**bossy** *adj*

bot·a·ny \'bätᵊnē\ *n* : plant biology —**bo·tan·i·cal** \bə'tanikəl\ *adj* —**bot·a·nist** \'bätᵊnist\ *n* —**bot·a·nize** \-ᵊn,īz\ *vb*

botch \'bäch\ *vb* : do clumsily —**botch** *n*

both \'bōth\ *adj or pron* : the one and the other ~ *conj* —used to show each of two is included

both·er \'bäthər\ *vb* **1** : annoy or worry **2** : take the trouble —**bother** *n* —**both·er·some** \-səm\ *adj*

bot·tle \'bätᵊl\ *n* : container with a narrow neck and no handles ~ *vb* **bot·tled; bot·tling** : put into a bottle

bot·tle·neck *n* : place or cause of congestion

bot·tom \'bätəm\ *n* **1** : supporting surface **2** : lowest part or place —**bottom** *adj* —**bot·tomed** *adj* —**bot·tom·less** *adj*

bot·u·lism \'bächə,lizəm\ *n* : acute food poisoning

bou·doir \'bü,dwär, 'bü-, ,bü'-, ,bù'-\ *n* : woman's private room

bough \'baù\ *n* : large tree branch

bought *past of* BUY

bouil·lon \'bü,yän; 'bùl,yän, -yən\ *n* : clear soup

boul·der \'bōldər\ *n* : large rounded rock —**boul·dered** *adj*

bou·le·vard \'bùlə,värd, 'bü-\ *n* : broad thoroughfare

bounce \'baùns\ *vb* **bounced; bounc·ing** 1 : spring back 2 : make bounce —**bounce** *n* —**bouncy** \'baùnsē\ *adj*

1bound \'baùnd\ *adj* : intending to go

2bound *n* : limit or boundary ~ *vb* : be a boundary of —**bound·less** *adj* —**bound·less·ness** *n*

3bound *adj* 1 : obliged 2 : having a binding 3 : determined 4 : incapable of failing

4bound *n* : leap ~ *vb* : move by springing

bound·ary \'baùndrē\ *n, pl* **-aries** : line marking extent or separation

boun·ty \'baùntē\ *n, pl* **-ties** 1 : generosity 2 : reward —**boun·te·ous** \-ēəs\ *adj* —**boun·te·ous·ly** *adv* —**boun·ti·ful** \-ifəl\ *adj* —**boun·ti·ful·ly** *adv*

bou·quet \bō'kā, bü-\ *n* 1 : bunch of flowers 2 : fragrance

bour·bon \'bərbən\ *n* : corn whiskey

bour·geoi·sie \,bùrzh,wä'zē\ *n* : middle class of society —**bour·geois** \'bùrzh,wä, bùrzh'wä\ *n or adj*

bout \'baùt\ *n* 1 : contest 2 : outbreak

bou·tique \bü'tēk\ *n* : specialty shop

bo·vine \'bō,vīn, -,vēn\ *adj* : relating to cattle —**bovine** *n*

1bow \'baù\ *vb* 1 : submit 2 : bend the head or body ~ *n* : act of bowing

2bow \'bō\ *n* 1 : bend or arch 2 : weapon for shooting arrows 3 : knot with loops 4 : rod with stretched horsehairs for playing a stringed instrument ~ *vb* : curve or bend —**bow·man** \-mən\ *n* —**bow·string** *n*

3bow \'baù\ *n* : forward part of a ship —**bow** *adj*

bow·els \'baùəls\ *n pl* 1 : intestines 2 : inmost parts

bow·er \'baùər\ *n* : arbor

1bowl \'bōl\ *n* : concave vessel or part —**bowl·ful** \-,fùl\ *n*

2bowl *n* : round ball for bowling ~ *vb* : roll a ball in bowling —**bowl·er** *n*

bowl·ing *n* : game in which balls are rolled to knock down pins

1box \'bäks\ *n, pl* **box** *or* **box·es** : evergreen shrub —**box·wood** \-,wùd\ *n*

2box *n* 1 : container usu. with 4 sides and a cover 2 : small compartment ~ *vb* : put in a box

3box *n* : slap ~ *vb* 1 : slap 2 : fight with the fists —**box·er** *n* —**box·ing** *n*

box·car *n* : roofed freight car

box office *n* : theater ticket office

boy \'bói\ *n* : male child —**boy·hood** *n* —**boy·ish** *adj* —**boy·ish·ly** *adv* —**boy·ish·ness** *n*

boy·cott \-,kät\ *vb* : refrain from dealing with —**boycott** *n*

boy·friend \'bói,frend\ *n* 1 : male friend 2 : woman's regular male companion

brace \'brās\ *n* 1 : crank for turning a bit 2 : something that resists weight or supports 3 : punctuation mark {or} ~ *vb* **braced; brac·ing** 1 : make taut or steady 2 : invigorate 3 : strengthen

brace·let \'brāslət\ *n* : ornamental band for the wrist or arm

brack·et \'brakət\ *n* 1 : projecting support 2 : punctuation mark [or] 3 : class ~ *vb* 1 : furnish or fasten with brackets 2 : place within brackets 3 : group

brack·ish \-ish\ *adj* : salty

brad \'brad\ *n* : nail with a small head

brag \'brag\ *vb* -**gg**- : boast —**brag** *n*

brag·gart \'bragərt\ *n* : boaster

braid \'brād\ *vb* : interweave ~ *n* : something braided

braille \'brāl\ *n* : system of writing for the blind using raised dots

brain \'brān\ *n* 1 : organ of thought and nervous coordination enclosed in the skull 2 : intelligence ~ *vb* : smash the skull of —**brained** *adj* —**brain·less** *adj* —**brainy** *adj*

braise \'brāz\ *vb* **braised; brais·ing** : cook (meat) slowly in a covered dish

brake \'brāk\ *n* : device for slowing or stopping ~ *vb* **braked; brak·ing** : slow or stop by a brake

bram·ble \'brambəl\ *n* : prickly shrub

bran \'bran\ *n* : edible cracked grain husks

branch \'branch\ *n* 1 : division of a plant stem 2 : part ~ *vb* 1 : develop branches 2 : diverge —**branched** *adj*

brand \'brand\ *n* 1 : identifying mark made by burning 2 : stigma 3 : distinctive kind (as of goods from one firm) ~ *vb* : mark with a brand

bran·dish \'brandish\ *vb* : wave

brand–new adj : unused

bran·dy \'brandē\ n, pl **-dies** : liquor distilled from wine

brash \'brash\ adj 1 : impulsive 2 : aggressively self-assertive

brass \'bras\ n 1 : alloy of copper and zinc 2 : brazen self-assurance 3 : high-ranking military officers — **brassy** adj

bras·siere \brə'zir\ n : woman's undergarment to support the breasts

brat \'brat\ n : ill-behaved child — **brat·ti·ness** n —**brat·ty** adj

bra·va·do \brə'vädō\ n, pl **-does** or **-dos** : false bravery

1brave \'brāv\ adj **brav·er; brav·est** : showing courage ~ vb **braved; brav·ing** : face with courage — **brave·ly** adv —**brav·ery** \-ərē\ n

2brave n : American Indian warrior

bra·vo \'brävō\ n, pl **-vos** : shout of approval

brawl \'brȯl\ n : noisy quarrel or violent fight —**brawl** vb —**brawl·er** n

brawn \'brȯn\ n : muscular strength — **brawny** \-ē\ adj —**brawn·i·ness** n

bray \'brā\ n : harsh cry of a donkey — **bray** vb

bra·zen \'brāz³n\ adj 1 : made of brass 2 : bold —**bra·zen·ly** adv —**bra·zen·ness** n

bra·zier \'brāzhər\ n : charcoal grill

breach \'brēch\ n 1 : breaking of a law, obligation, or standard 2 : gap ~ vb : make a breach in

bread \'bred\ n : baked food made of flour ~ vb : cover with bread crumbs

breadth \'bredth\ n : width

bread·win·ner n : wage earner

break \'brāk\ vb **broke** \'brōk\; **bro·ken** \'brōkən\; **break·ing** 1 : knock into pieces 2 : transgress 3 : force a way into or out of 4 : exceed 5 : interrupt 6 : fail ~ n 1 : act or result of breaking 2 : stroke of good luck —**break·able** adj or n —**break·age** \'brākij\ n — **break·er** n —**break in** vb 1 : enter by force 2 : interrupt 3 : train — **break out** vb 1 : erupt with force 2 : develop a rash

break·down n : physical or mental failure —**break down** vb

break·fast \'brekfəst\ n : first meal of the day —**breakfast** vb

breast \'brest\ n 1 : milk-producing gland esp. of a woman 2 : front part of the chest

breast·bone n : sternum

breath \'breth\ n 1 : slight breeze 2 : air breathed in or out —**breath·less** adj —**breath·less·ly** adv —**breath·less·ness** n —**breathy** \'brethē\ adj

breathe \'brēth\ vb **breathed; breath·ing** 1 : draw air into the lungs and expel it 2 : live 3 : utter

breath·tak·ing adj : exciting

breech·es \'brichəz\ n pl : trousers ending near the knee

breed \'brēd\ vb **bred** \'bred\; **breed·ing** 1 : give birth to 2 : propagate 3 : raise ~ n 1 : kind of plant or animal usu. developed by humans 2 : class — **breed·er** n

breeze \'brēz\ n : light wind ~ vb **breezed; breez·ing** : move fast — **breezy** adj

breth·ren \'brethrən, -ərn\ pl of BROTHER

bre·via·ry \'brēvərē, 'brē-, -vyərē, -vē,erē\ n, pl **-ries** : prayer book used by Roman Catholic priests

brev·i·ty \'brevətē\ n, pl **-ties** : shortness or conciseness

brew \'brü\ vb : make by fermenting or steeping —**brew** n —**brew·er** n — **brew·ery** \'brüərē, 'brürē\ n

bri·ar var of BRIER

bribe \'brīb\ vb **bribed; brib·ing** : corrupt or influence by gifts ~ n : something offered or given in bribing —**brib·able** adj —**brib·ery** \-ərē\ n

bric–a–brac \'brikə,brak\ n pl : small ornamental articles

brick \'brik\ n : building block of baked clay —**brick** vb —**brick·lay·er** n — **brick·lay·ing** n

bride \'brīd\ n : woman just married or about to be married —**brid·al** \-³l\ adj

bride·groom n : man just married or about to be married

brides·maid n : woman who attends a bride at her wedding

1bridge \'brij\ n 1 : structure built for passage over a depression or obstacle 2 : upper part of the nose 3 : compartment from which a ship is navigated 4 : artificial replacement for missing teeth ~ vb : build a bridge over —**bridge·able** adj

2bridge n : card game for 4 players

bri·dle \'brīd³l\ n : headgear to control a horse ~ vb **-dled; -dling** 1 : put a bridle on **2** : restrain **3** : show hostility or scorn

brief \'brēf\ *adj* **1** : short or concise ~ *n* : concise summary (as of a legal case) ~ *vb* : give final instructions or essential information to —**brief·ly** *adv* —**brief·ness** *n*

brief·case *n* : case for papers

¹bri·er \'brīər\ *n* : thorny plant

²brier *n* : heath of southern Europe

¹brig \'brig\ *n* : 2-masted ship

²brig *n* : jail on a naval ship

bri·gade \brig'ād\ *n* **1** : large military unit **2** : group organized for a special activity

brig·a·dier general \ˌbrigə'dir-\ *n* : officer ranking next below a major general

brig·and \'brigənd\ *n* : bandit —**brig·and·age** \-ij\ *n*

bright \'brīt\ *adj* **1** : radiating or reflecting light **2** : cheerful **3** : intelligent —**bright·en** \-ᵊn\ *vb* —**bright·en·er** \'brītᵊnər\ *n* —**bright·ly** *adv* —**bright·ness** *n*

bril·liant \'brilyənt\ *adj* **1** : very bright **2** : splendid **3** : very intelligent —**bril·liance** \-yəns\ *n* —**bril·lian·cy** \-yənsē\ *n* —**bril·liant·ly** *adv*

brim \'brim\ *n* : edge or rim ~ *vb* : be or become full —**brim·less** *adj* —**brimmed** *adj*

brim·ful \-'fül\ *adj* : full to the brim

brim·stone *n* : sulfur

brin·dled \'brindᵊld\ *adj* : gray or tawny with dark streaks or flecks

brine \'brīn\ *n* **1** : salt water **2** : ocean —**brin·i·ness** *n* —**briny** *adj*

bring \'briŋ\ *vb* **brought** \'brot\; **bring·ing 1** : cause to come with one **2** : persuade **3** : produce **4** : sell for —**bring·er** *n* —**bring about** *vb* : make happen —**bring up** *vb* **1** : care for and educate **2** : cause to be noticed

brink \'briŋk\ *n* : edge

bri·quette, bri·quet \bri'ket\ *n* : pressed mass (as of charcoal)

brisk \'brisk\ *adj* **1** : lively **2** : invigorating —**brisk·ly** *adv* —**brisk·ness** *n*

bris·ket \'briskət\ *n* : breast or lower chest of a quadruped

bris·tle \'brisəl\ *n* : short stiff hair ~ *vb* **-tled; -tling 1** : stand erect **2** : show angry defiance **3** : appear as if covered with bristles —**bris·tly** *adj*

brit·tle \'britᵊl\ *adj* **-tler; -tlest** : easily broken —**brit·tle·ness** *n*

broach \'brōch\ *n* : pointed tool (as for opening casks) ~ *vb* **1** : pierce (as a cask) to open **2** : introduce for discussion

broad \'brod\ *adj* **1** : wide **2** : spacious **3** : clear or open **4** : obvious **5** : tolerant in outlook **6** : widely applicable **7** : dealing with essential points —**broad·en** \-ᵊn\ *vb* —**broad·ly** *adv* —**broad·ness** *n*

broad·cast *n* **1** : transmission by radio waves **2** : radio or television program ~ *vb* **-cast; -cast·ing 1** : scatter or sow in all directions **2** : make widely known **3** : send out on a broadcast —**broad·cast·er** *n*

broad·cloth *n* : fine cloth

broad·loom *adj* : woven on a wide loom esp. in solid color

broad-mind·ed *adj* : tolerant of varied opinions —**broad-mind·ed·ly** *adv* —**broad-mind·ed·ness** *n*

broad·side *n* **1** : simultaneous firing of all guns on one side of a ship **2** : verbal attack

bro·cade \brō'kād\ *n* : usu. silk fabric with a raised design

broc·co·li \'bräkəlē\ *n* : green vegetable akin to cauliflower

bro·chure \brō'shùr\ *n* : pamphlet

brogue \'brōg\ *n* : Irish accent

broil \'broil\ *vb* : cook by radiant heat —**broil** *n*

broil·er *n* **1** : utensil for broiling **2** : chicken fit for broiling

¹broke \'brōk\ *past of* BREAK

²broke *adj* : out of money

bro·ken \'brōkən\ *adj* : imperfectly spoken —**bro·ken·ly** *adv*

bro·ken·heart·ed \-'härtəd\ *adj* : overcome by grief or despair

bro·ker \'brōkər\ *n* : agent who buys and sells for a fee —**broker** *vb* —**bro·ker·age** \-kərij\ *n*

bro·mine \'brō,mēn\ *n* : deep red liquid corrosive chemical element

bron·chi·tis \brän'kītəs, bräŋ-\ *n* : inflammation of the bronchi

bron·chus \'bräŋkəs\ *n, pl* **-chi** \-,kī, -,kē\ : division of the windpipe leading to a lung —**bron·chi·al** \-kēəl\ *adj*

bronze \'bränz\ *vb* **bronzed; bronz·ing** : make bronze in color ~ *n* **1** : alloy of copper and tin **2** : yellowish brown —**bronzy** \-ē\ *adj*

brooch \'brōch, 'brüch\ *n* : ornamental clasp or pin

brood \'brüd\ *n* : family of young ~ *vb*

1 : sit on eggs to hatch them 2 : ponder ~ adj : kept for breeding — **brood·er** n —**brood·ing·ly** adv

¹brook \'brůk\ vb : tolerate

²brook n : small stream

broom \'brům, 'brům\ n 1 : flowering shrub 2 : implement for sweeping — **broom·stick** n

broth \'broth\ n, pl **broths** \'broths, 'brothz\ : liquid in which meat has been cooked

broth·el \'bräthəl, 'broth-\ n : house of prostitutes

broth·er \'brəthər\ n, pl **brothers** also **breth·ren** \'brethrən, -ərn\ 1 : male sharing one or both parents with another person 2 : kinsman — **broth·er·hood** n —**broth·er·li·ness** n —**broth·er·ly** adj

broth·er–in–law n, pl **brothers–in–law** : brother of one's spouse or husband of one's sister or husband of one's spouse's sister

brought past of BRING

brow \'braů\ n 1 : eyebrow 2 : forehead 3 : edge of a steep place

brow·beat vb -beat; -beat·en or -beat; -beat·ing : intimidate

brown \'braůn\ adj 1 : of the color brown 2 : of dark or tanned complexion ~ n : a color like that of coffee ~ vb : make or become brown — **brown·ish** adj

browse \'braůz\ vb **browsed; brows·ing** 1 : graze 2 : look over casually — **brows·er** n

bru·in \'brüən\ n : bear

bruise \'brüz\ vb **bruised; bruis·ing** 1 : make a bruise on 2 : become bruised ~ n : surface injury to flesh

brunch \'brənch\ n : late breakfast, early lunch, or combination of both

bru·net, bru·nette \brü'net\ adj : having dark hair and usu. dark skin —**brunet, brunette** n

brunt \'brənt\ n : main impact

¹brush \'brəsh\ n 1 : small cut branches 2 : coarse shrubby vegetation

²brush n : bristles set in a handle used esp. for cleaning or painting 2 : light touch ~ vb 1 : apply a brush to 2 : remove with or as if with a brush 3 : dismiss in an offhand way 4 : touch lightly —**brush up** vb : renew one's skill

³brush n : skirmish

brush–off n : curt dismissal

brusque \'brəsk\ adj : curt or blunt in manner —**brusque·ly** adv

bru·tal \'brüt°l\ adj : like a brute and esp. cruel —**bru·tal·i·ty** \brü'talətē\ n —**bru·tal·ize** \'brüt°l,īz\ vb —**bru·tal·ly** \-°lē\ adv

brute \'brüt\ adj 1 : relating to beasts 2 : unreasoning 3 : purely physical ~ n 1 : beast 2 : brutal person —**brut·ish** \-ish\ adj

bub·ble \'bəbəl\ vb -bled; -bling : form, rise in, or give off bubbles ~ n : globule of gas in or covered with a liquid —**bub·bly** \-əlē\ adj

bu·bo \'bübō, 'byü-\ n, pl **buboes** : inflammatory swelling of a lymph gland —**bu·bon·ic** \bü'bänik, 'byü-\ adj

buc·ca·neer \,bəkə'nir\ n : pirate

buck \'bək\ n, pl **buck** or **bucks** 1 : male animal (as a deer) 2 : dollar ~ vb 1 : jerk forward 2 : oppose

buck·et \'bəkət\ n : pail —**buck·et·ful** n

buck·le \'bəkəl\ n 1 : clasp (as on a belt) for two loose ends 2 : bend or fold ~ vb -led; -ling 1 : fasten with a buckle 2 : apply oneself 3 : bend or crumple

buck·ler \'bəklər\ n : shield

buck·shot n : coarse lead shot

buck·skin n : soft leather (as from the skin of a buck) —**buckskin** adj

buck·tooth n : large projecting front tooth —**buck–toothed** adj

buck·wheat n : herb whose seeds are used as a cereal grain or the seeds themselves

bu·col·ic \byü'kälik\ adj : pastoral

bud \'bəd\ n 1 : undeveloped plant shoot 2 : partly opened flower ~ vb -dd- 1 : form or put forth buds 2 : be or develop like a bud

Bud·dhism \'bü,dizəm, 'bů-\ n : religion of eastern and central Asia —**Bud·dhist** \'büdist, 'bůd-\ n or adj

bud·dy \'bədē\ n, pl -dies : friend

budge \'bəj\ vb **budged; budg·ing** : move from a place

bud·get \'bəjət\ n 1 : estimate of income and expenses 2 : plan for coordinating income and expenses 3 : money available for a particular use —**budget** vb or adj —**bud·get·ary** \-ə,terē\ adj

buff \'bəf\ n 1 : yellow to orange yellow color 2 : enthusiast ~ adj : of the color buff ~ vb : polish

buf·fa·lo \'bəfə,lō\ n, pl -lo or -loes : wild ox (as a bison)

¹buf·fer \'bəfər\ n : shield or protector

²buffer n : one that buffs

1buf·fet \'bəfət\ *n* : blow or slap ~ *vb* : hit esp. repeatedly

2buf·fet \bə'fā, bü-\ *n* **1** : sideboard **2** : meal at which people serve themselves

buf·foon \ˌbə'fün\ *n* : clown —**buf·foon·ery** \-ərē\ *n*

bug \'bəg\ *n* **1** : small usu. obnoxious crawling creature usu. **2** : 4-winged sucking insect **3** : unexpected imperfection **4** : disease-producing germ **5** : hidden microphone ~ *vb* **-gg- 1** : pester **2** : conceal a microphone in

bug·a·boo \'bəgəˌbü\ *n, pl* **-boos** : bogey

bug·bear *n* : source of dread

bug·gy \'bəgē\ *n, pl* **-gies** : light carriage

bu·gle \'byügəl\ *n* : trumpetlike brass instrument —**bu·gler** \-glər\ *n*

build \'bild\ *vb* **built** \'bilt\; **build·ing 1** : put together **2** : establish **3** : increase ~ *n* : physique —**build·er** *n*

build·ing \'bildiŋ\ *n* **1** : roofed and walled structure **2** : art or business of constructing buildings

bulb \'bəlb\ *n* **1** : large underground plant bud **2** : rounded or pear-shaped object —**bul·bous** \-əs\ *adj*

bulge \'bəlj\ *n* : swelling projecting part ~ *vb* **bulged; bulg·ing** : swell out

bulk \'bəlk\ *n* **1** : magnitude **2** : indigestible food material **3** : large mass **4** : major portion ~ *vb* : cause to swell or bulge —**bulky** \-ē\ *adj*

bulk·head *n* : ship's partition

1bull \'bül\ *n* **1** : large adult male animal (as of cattle) ~ *adj* : male

2bull *n* **1** : papal letter **2** : decree

bull·dog *n* : compact short-haired dog

bull·doze \-ˌdōz\ *vb* **1** : move or level with a tractor (**bull·doz·er**) having a broad blade **2** : force

bul·let \'bülət\ *n* : missile to be shot from a gun —**bul·let·proof** *adj*

bul·le·tin \'bülətən\ *n* **1** : brief public report **2** : periodical

bull·fight *n* : sport of taunting and killing bulls —**bull·fight·er** *n*

bull·frog *n* : large deep-voiced frog

bull·head·ed *adj* : stupidly stubborn

bul·lion \'bülyən\ *n* : gold or silver esp. in bars

bull·ock \'bülək\ *n* **1** : young bull **2** : steer

bull's-eye *n, pl* **bull's-eyes** : center of a target

bul·ly \'bülē\ *n, pl* **-lies** : one who hurts or intimidates others ~ *vb* **-lied; -ly·ing** : act like a bully toward

bul·rush \'bül,rəsh\ *n* : tall coarse rush or sedge

bul·wark \'bül,wərk, -,wórk; 'bəl,wərk\ *n* **1** : wall-like defense **2** : strong support or protection

bum \'bəm\ *vb* **-mm- 1** : wander as a tramp **2** : get by begging ~ *n* : idle worthless person ~ *adj* : bad

bum·ble·bee \'bəmbəl,bē\ *n* : large hairy bee

bump \'bəmp\ *vb* : strike or knock forcibly ~ *n* **1** : sudden blow **2** : small rounded swelling —**bumpy** *adj*

1bum·per \'bəmpər\ *adj* : unusually large

2bump·er \'bəmpər\ *n* : shock-absorbing bar at either end of a car

bump·kin \'bəmpkən\ *n* : awkward country person

bun \'bən\ *n* : sweet biscuit or roll

bunch \'bənch\ *n* : group ~ *vb* : form into a group —**bunchy** *adj*

bun·dle \'bənd⁼l\ *n* **1** : several items bunched together **2** : something wrapped for carrying **3** : large amount ~ *vb* **-dled; -dling** : gather into a bundle

bun·ga·low \'bəngə,lō\ *n* : one-story house

bun·gle \'bəngəl\ *vb* **-gled; -gling** : do badly —**bungle** *n* —**bun·gler** *n*

bun·ion \'bənyən\ *n* : inflamed swelling of the first joint of the big toe

1bunk \'bəŋk\ *n* : built-in bed that is often one of a tier ~ *vb* : sleep

2bunk *n* : nonsense

bun·ker \-ər\ *n* **1** : storage compartment **2** : protective embankment

bun·kum, bun·combe \'bəŋkəm\ *n* : nonsense

bun·ny \'bənē\ *n, pl* **-nies** : rabbit

1bun·ting \'bəntiŋ\ *n* : small finch

2bunting *n* : flag material

buoy \'büē, 'bói\ *n* : floating marker anchored in water ~ *vb* **1** : keep afloat **2** : raise the spirits of —**buoy·an·cy** \'bóiənsē, 'büyən-\ *n* —**buoy·ant** \-yənt\ *adj*

bur, burr \'bər\ *n* : rough or prickly covering of a fruit —**bur·ry** *adj*

bur·den \'bərd⁼n\ *n* **1** : something carried **2** : something oppressive **3** : cargo ~ *vb* : load or oppress —**bur·den·some** \-səm\ *adj*

bur·dock \'bər,däk\ *n* : tall coarse herb with prickly flower heads

bu·reau \'byùrō\ n **1** : chest of drawers **2** : administrative unit **3** : business office

bu·reau·cra·cy \byù'räkrəsē\ n, pl **-cies 1** : body of government officials **2** : unwieldy administrative system — **bu·reau·crat** \'byùrə,krat\ n — **bu·reau·crat·ic** \,byùrə'kratik\ adj

bur·geon \'bərjən\ vb : grow

bur·glary \'bərglərē\ n, pl **-glar·ies** : forcible entry into a building to steal — **bur·glar** \-glər\ n — **bur·glar·ize** \'bərglə,rīz\ vb

bur·gle \'bərgəl\ vb **-gled; -gling** : commit burglary on or in

Bur·gun·dy \'bərgəndē\ n, pl **-dies** : kind of table wine

bur·i·al \'berēəl\ n : act of burying

bur·lap \'bər,lap\ n : coarse fabric usu. of jute or hemp

bur·lesque \bər'lesk\ n **1** : witty or derisive imitation **2** : broadly humorous variety show ~ vb **-lesqued; -lesqu·ing** : mock

bur·ly \'bərlē\ adj **-li·er; -est** : strongly and heavily built

burn \'bərn\ vb **burned** \'bərnd, 'bərnt\ or **burnt** \'bərnt\; **burn·ing 1** : be on fire **2** : feel or look as if on fire **3** : alter or become altered by or as if by fire or heat **4** : cause or make by fire ~ n : injury or effect produced by burning — **burn·er** n

bur·nish \'bərnish\ vb : polish

burp \'bərp\ n or vb : belch

bur·ro \'bərō, 'bùr-\ n, pl **-os** : small donkey

bur·row \'bərō\ n : hole in the ground made by an animal ~ vb : make a burrow — **bur·row·er** n

bur·sar \'bərsər\ n : treasurer esp. of a college

bur·si·tis \bər'sītəs\ n : inflammation of a sac (**bur·sa** \'bərsə\) in a joint

burst \'bərst\ vb **burst** or **burst·ed; burst·ing 1** : fly apart or into pieces **2** : enter or emerge suddenly ~ n : sudden outbreak or effort

bury \'berē\ vb **bur·ied; bury·ing 1** : deposit in the earth **2** : hide

bus \'bəs\ n, pl **bus·es** or **bus·ses** : large motor-driven passenger vehicle ~ vb **bused** or **bussed; bus·ing** or **bus·sing** : travel or transport by bus

bus·boy n : waiter's helper

bush \'bùsh\ n **1** : shrub **2** : rough un-

cleared country **3** : a thick tuft or mat — **bushy** adj

bush·el \'bùshəl\ n : 4 pecks

bush·ing \'bùshiŋ\ n : metal lining used as a guide or bearing

busi·ness \'biznəs, -nəz\ n **1** : vocation **2** : commercial or industrial enterprise **3** : personal concerns — **busi·ness·man** \-,man\ n — **busi·ness·wom·an** \-,wùmən\ n

¹bust \'bəst\ n **1** : sculpture of the head and upper torso **2** : breasts of a woman

²bust vb **1** : burst or break **2** : tame ~ n **1** : punch **2** : failure

¹bus·tle \'bəsəl\ vb **-tled; -tling** : move or work briskly ~ n : energetic activity

²bustle n : pad or frame formerly worn under a woman's skirt

busy \'bizē\ adj **busi·er; -est 1** : engaged in action **2** : being in use **3** : full of activity ~ vb **bus·ied; busy·ing** : make or keep busy — **busi·ly** adv

busy·body n : meddler

but \'bət\ conj **1** : if not for the fact **2** : that **3** : without the certainty that **4** : rather **5** : yet ~ prep : other than

butch·er \'bùchər\ n **1** : one who slaughters animals or dresses their flesh **2** : brutal killer **3** : bungler — **butcher** vb — **butch·ery** \-ərē\ n

but·ler \'bətlər\ n : chief male household servant

¹butt \'bət\ vb : strike with a butt ~ n : blow with the head or horns

²butt n **1** : target **2** : victim

³butt vb : join edge to edge

⁴butt n : large end or bottom

⁵butt n : large cask

butte \'byüt\ n : isolated steep hill

but·ter \'bətər\ n : solid edible fat churned from cream ~ vb : spread with butter — **but·tery** adj

but·ter·cup n : yellow-flowered herb

but·ter·fat n : natural fat of milk and of butter

but·ter·fly n : insect with 4 broad wings

but·ter·milk n : liquid remaining after butter is churned

but·ter·nut n : edible nut of a tree related to the walnut or this tree

but·ter·scotch \-,skäch\ n : candy made from sugar, corn syrup, and water

but·tocks \'bətəks\ n pl : rear part of the hips

but·ton \'bət⁹n\ *n* **1** : small knob for fastening clothing **2** : buttonlike object ~ *vb* : fasten with buttons

but·ton·hole *n* : hole or slit for a button ~ *vb* : hold in talk

but·tress \'bətrəs\ *n* **1** : projecting structure to support a wall **2** : support — **buttress** *vb*

bux·om \'bəksəm\ *adj* : full-bosomed

buy \'bī\ *vb* **bought** \'bȯt\; **buy·ing** : purchase ~ *n* : bargain —**buy·er** *n*

buzz \'bəz\ *vb* : make a low humming sound ~ *n* : act or sound of buzzing

buz·zard \'bəzərd\ *n* : large bird of prey

buzz·er *n* : signaling device that buzzes

buzz·word \'bəz,wərd\ *n* : word or phrase in vogue

by \'bī\ *prep* **1** : near **2** : through **3** : beyond **4** : throughout **5** : no later than — *adv* **1** : near **2** : farther

by·gone \'bī,gȯn\ *adj* : past —**bygone** *n*

by·law, bye·law *n* : organization's rule

by·line *n* : writer's name on an article

by·pass *n* : alternate route ~ *vb* : go around

by-prod·uct *n* : product in addition to the main product

by·stand·er *n* : spectator

by·way \'bī,wā\ *n* : side road

by·word *n* : proverb

C

c \'sē\ *n, pl* **c's** *or* **cs** \'sēz\ : 3d letter of the alphabet

cab \'kab\ *n* **1** : light closed horse-drawn carriage **2** : taxicab **3** : compartment for a driver —**cab·bie, cabby** *n* —**cab·stand** *n*

ca·bal \kə'bal\ *n* : group of conspirators

ca·bana \kə'banə, -nyə\ *n* : shelter at a beach or pool

cab·a·ret \,kabə'rā\ *n* : nightclub

cab·bage \'kabij\ *n* : vegetable with a dense head of leaves

cab·in \-ən\ *n* **1** : private room on a ship **2** : small house **3** : airplane compartment

cab·i·net \'kabnət\ *n* **1** : display case or cupboard **2** : advisory council of a head of state —**cab·i·net·mak·er** *n* —**cab·i·net·mak·ing** *n* —**cab·i·net·work** *n*

ca·ble \'kābəl\ *n* **1** : strong rope, wire, or chain **2** : cablegram **3** : bundle of electrical wires ~ *vb* **-bled; -bling** : send a cablegram to

ca·ble·gram \-,gram\ *n* : message sent by a submarine telegraph cable

ca·boose \kə'büs\ *n* : crew car on a train

ca·cao \kə'kaù, -'kāȯ\ *n, pl* **cacaos** : So. American tree whose seeds (**cacao beans**) yield cocoa and chocolate

cache \'kash\ *n* **1** : hiding place **2** : something hidden —**cache** *vb*

ca·chet \ka'shā\ *n* : prestige or a feature conferring this

cack·le \'kakəl\ *vb* **-led; -ling** : make a cry or laugh like the sound of a hen —**cackle** *n* —**cack·ler** *n*

ca·coph·o·ny \ka'käfənē\ *n, pl* **-nies** : harsh noise —**ca·coph·o·nous** \-nəs\ *adj*

cac·tus \'kaktəs\ *n, pl* **cac·ti** \-,tī\ *or* **-tus·es** : drought-resistant flowering plant with scales or prickles

cad \'kad\ *n* : ungentlemanly person — **cad·dish** \-ish\ *adj* —**cad·dish·ly** *adv* —**cad·dish·ness** *n*

ca·dav·er \kə'davər\ *n* : dead body — **ca·dav·er·ous** \-ərəs\ *adj*

cad·die, cad·dy \'kadē\ *n, pl* **-dies** : golfer's helper —**caddie, caddy** *vb*

cad·dy \'kadē\ *n, pl* **-dies** : small tea chest

ca·dence \'kād⁹ns\ *n* : measure of a rhythmical flow —**ca·denced** \-⁹nst\ *adj*

ca·det \kə'det\ *n* : student in a military academy

cadge \'kaj\ *vb* **cadged; cadg·ing** : beg —**cadg·er** *n*

cad·mi·um \'kadmēəm\ *n* : grayish metallic chemical element

cad·re \'ka-,rē\ *n* : nucleus of highly trained people

ca·fé \ka'fā, kə-\ *n* : restaurant

caf·e·te·ria \,kafə'tirēə\ *n* : self-service restaurant

caf·feine \ka'fēn, 'ka,fēn\ *n* : stimulating alkaloid in coffee and tea

cage \'kāj\ *n* : box of wire or bars for confining an animal ~ *vb* **caged; caging** : put or keep in a cage

ca·gey \-ē\ *adj* **-gi·er; -est** : shrewd — **ca·gi·ly** *adv* — **ca·gi·ness** *n*

cais·son \'kā,sän, -sən\ *n* 1 : ammunition carriage 2 : watertight chamber for underwater construction

ca·jole \kə'jōl\ *vb* **-joled; -joling** : persuade or coax — **ca·jol·ery** \-ərē\ *n*

cake \'kāk\ *n* 1 : food of baked or fried usu. sweet batter 2 : compacted mass ~ *vb* **caked; cak·ing** 1 : form into a cake 2 : encrust

cal·a·bash \'kalə,bash\ *n* : gourd

cal·a·mine \'kalə,mīn\ *n* : lotion of oxides of zinc and iron

ca·lam·i·ty \kə'lamətē\ *n, pl* **-ties** : disaster — **ca·lam·i·tous** \-əs\ *adj* — **ca·lam·i·tous·ly** *adv* — **ca·lam·i·tous·ness** *n*

cal·ci·fy \'kalsə,fī\ *vb* **-fied; -fy·ing** : harden — **cal·ci·fi·ca·tion** \,ka lsəfə'kāshən\ *n*

cal·ci·um \'kalsēəm\ *n* : silver-white soft metallic chemical element

cal·cu·late \'kalkyə,lāt\ *vb* **-lat·ed; -lat·ing** 1 : determine by mathematical processes 2 : judge — **cal·cu·la·ble** \-ləbəl\ *adj* — **cal·cu·la·tion** \,kalkyə·'lāshən\ *n* — **cal·cu·la·tor** \'kal kyə,lātər\ *n*

cal·cu·lat·ing *adj* : shrewd

cal·cu·lus \'kalkyələs\ *n, pl* **-li** \-,lī\ : higher mathematics dealing with rates of change

cal·dron *var of* CAULDRON

cal·en·dar \'kaləndər\ *n* : list of days, weeks, and months

¹calf \'kaf, 'kåf\ *n, pl* **calves** \'kavz, 'kåvz\ : young cow or related mammal — **calf·skin** *n*

²calf *n, pl* **calves** : back part of the leg below the knee

cal·i·ber, cal·i·bre \'kaləbər\ *n* 1 : diameter of a bullet or shell or of a gun bore 2 : degree of mental or moral excellence

cal·i·brate \'kalə,brāt\ *vb* **-brat·ed; -brat·ing** : adjust precisely — **cal·i·bra·tion** \,kalə'brāshən\ *n*

cal·i·co \'kali,kō\ *n, pl* **-coes** *or* **-cos** 1 : printed cotton fabric 2 : animal with fur having patches of different colors

cal·i·pers \'kaləpərz\ *n* : measuring instrument with two adjustable legs

ca·liph \'kāləf, 'kal-\ *n* : title of head of Islam — **ca·liph·ate** \-,āt, -ət\ *n*

cal·is·then·ics \,kaləs'theniks\ *n sing or pl* : stretching and jumping exercises — **cal·is·then·ic** *adj*

calk \'kók\ *var of* CAULK

call \'ról\ *vb* 1 : shout 2 : summon 3 : demand 4 : telephone 5 : make a visit 6 : name — **call** *n* — **call·er** *n* — **call down** *vb* : reprimand — **call off** *vb* : cancel

call·ing *n* : vocation

cal·li·ope \kə'līə,pē, 'kalē,ōp\ *n* : musical instrument of steam whistles

cal·lous \'kaləs\ *adj* 1 : thickened and hardened 2 : unfeeling ~ *vb* : make callous — **cal·los·i·ty** \ka'läsətē\ *n* — **cal·lous·ly** *adv* — **cal·lous·ness** *n*

cal·low \'kalō\ *adj* : inexperienced or innocent — **cal·low·ness** *n*

cal·lus \'kaləs\ *n* : callous area on skin or bark ~ *vb* : form a callus

calm \'käm, 'kälm\ *n* 1 : period or condition of peacefulness or stillness ~ *adj* : still or tranquil ~ *vb* : make calm — **calm·ly** *adv* — **calm·ness** *n*

ca·lor·ic \kə'lórik\ *adj* : relating to heat or calories

cal·o·rie \'kalərē\ *n* : unit for measuring heat and energy value of food

ca·lum·ni·ate \kə'ləmnē,āt\ *vb* **-at·ed; -at·ing** : slander — **ca·lum·ni·a·tion** \-,ləmnē'āshən\ *n*

ca·lum·ny \'kaləmnē\ *n, pl* **-nies** : false and malicious charge — **ca·lum·ni·ous** \kə'ləmnēəs\ *adj*

calve \'kav, 'kåv\ *vb* **calved; calv·ing** : give birth to a calf

calves *pl of* CALF

ca·lyp·so \kə'lipsō\ *n, pl* **-sos** : West Indian style of music

ca·lyx \'kāliks, 'kal-\ *n, pl* **-lyx·es** *or* **-ly·ces** \-lə,sēz\ : sepals of a flower

cam \'kam\ *n* : machine part that slides or rotates irregularly to transmit linear motion

ca·ma·ra·de·rie \,käm'rädərē, ,käm-, -mə'-, -'rad-\ *n* : fellowship

cam·bric \'kāmbrik\ *n* : fine thin linen or cotton fabric

came *past of* COME

cam·el \'kaməl\ *n* : large hoofed mammal of desert areas

ca·mel·lia \kə'mēlyə\ *n* : shrub or tree grown for its showy roselike flowers or the flower itself

cam·eo \'kamē,ō\ n, pl **-eos** : gem carved in relief

cam·era \'kamrə\ n : box with a lens for taking pictures —**cam·era·man** \-,man, -mən\ n

cam·ou·flage \'kamə,fläzh, -,fläj\ vb : hide by disguising —**camouflage** n

camp \'kamp\ n 1 : place to stay temporarily esp. in a tent 2 : group living in a camp ~ vb : make or live in a camp —**camp·er** n —**camp·ground** n —**camp·site** n

cam·paign \kam'pān\ n : series of military operations or of activities meant to gain a result —**campaign** vb

cam·pa·ni·le \,kampə'nēlē, -'nēl\ n, pl **-ni·les** or **-ni·li** \-'nēlē\ : bell tower

cam·phor \'kamfər\ n : gummy volatile aromatic compound from an evergreen tree (**cam·phor tree**)

cam·pus \'kampəs\ n : grounds and buildings of a college or school

1can \kən, 'kan\ vb, past **could** \kəd, 'kúd\; pres sing & pl **can** 1 : be able to 2 : be permitted to by conscience or feeling 3 : have permission or liberty to

2can \'kan\ n : metal container ~ vb **-nn-** : preserve by sealing in airtight cans or jars —**can·ner** n —**can·nery** \-ərē\ n

ca·nal \kə'nal\ n 1 : tubular passage in the body 2 : channel filled with water

can·a·pé \'kanəpē, -,pā\ n : appetizer

ca·nard \kə'närd\ n : false report

ca·nary \-'nerē\ n, pl **-nar·ies** : yellow or greenish finch often kept as a pet

can·cel \'kansəl\ vb **-celed** or **-celled**; **-cel·ing** or **-cel·ling** 1 : cross out 2 : destroy, neutralize, or match the force or effect of —**cancel** n —**can·cel·la·tion** \,kansə'lāshən\ n —**can·cel·er, can·cel·ler** n

can·cer \'kansər\ n 1 : malignant tumor that tends to spread 2 : slowly destructive evil —**can·cer·ous** \-ərəs\ adj —**can·cer·ous·ly** adv

can·de·la·bra \,kandə'läbrə, -'lab-\ n : candelabrum

can·de·la·brum \-rəm\ n, pl **-bra** \-rə\ : ornamental branched candlestick

can·did \'kandəd\ adj 1 : frank 2 : unposed —**can·did·ly** adv —**can·did·ness** n

can·di·date \'kandə,dāt, -dət\ n : one who seeks an office or membership —**can·di·da·cy** \-dəsē\ n

can·dle \'kand²l\ n : tallow or wax molded around a wick and burned to give light —**can·dle·light** n —**can·dle·stick** n

can·dor \'kandər\ n : frankness

can·dy \'kandē\ n, pl **-dies** : food made from sugar ~ vb **-died; -dy·ing** : encrust in sugar

cane \'kān\ n 1 : slender plant stem 2 : a tall woody grass or reed 3 : stick for walking or beating ~ vb : caned; **can·ing** 1 : beat with a cane 2 : weave or make with cane —**can·er** n

ca·nine \'kā,nīn\ adj : relating to dogs ~ n 1 : pointed tooth next to the incisors 2 : dog

can·is·ter \'kanəstər\ n : cylindrical container

can·ker \'kaŋkər\ n : mouth ulcer —**can·ker·ous** \-kərəs\ adj

can·na·bis \'kanəbəs\ n : preparation derived from hemp

can·ni·bal \'kanəbəl\ n : human or animal that eats its own kind —**can·ni·bal·ism** \-bə,lizəm\ n —**can·ni·bal·is·tic** \,kanəbə'listik\ adj

can·ni·bal·ize \'kanəbə,līz\ vb **-ized; -iz·ing** 1 : take usable parts from 2 : practice cannibalism

can·non \'kanən\ n, pl **-nons** or **-non** : large heavy gun —**can·non·ball** n —**can·non·eer** \,kanə'nir\ n

can·non·ade \,kanə'nād\ n : heavy artillery fire ~ vb **-ad·ed; -ad·ing** : bombard

can·not \'kan,ät; kə'nät\ : can not —**cannot but** : be bound to

can·ny \'kanē\ adj **-ni·er; -est** : shrewd —**can·ni·ly** adv —**can·ni·ness** n

ca·noe \kə'nü\ n : narrow sharp-ended boat propelled by paddles —**canoe** vb —**ca·noe·ist** n

1can·on \'kanən\ n 1 : regulation governing a church 2 : authoritative list 3 : an accepted principle

2canon n : clergy member in a cathedral

ca·non·i·cal \kə'nänikəl\ adj 1 : relating to or conforming to a canon 2 : orthodox —**ca·non·i·cal·ly** adv

can·on·ize \'kanə,nīz\ vb **-ized** \-,nīzd\, **-iz·ing** : recognize as a saint —**can·on·iza·tion** \,kanənə'zāshən\ n

can·o·py \'kanəpē\ n, pl **-pies** : overhanging cover —**canopy** vb

1cant \'kant\ n 1 : slanting surface 2 : slant ~ vb 1 : tip up 2 : lean to one side

2cant vb : talk hypocritically ~ n 1 : jargon 2 : insincere talk

can't \'kant, 'kȧnt\ : can not

can·ta·loupe \'kant³l,ōp\ n : muskmelon with orange flesh

can·tan·ker·ous \kan'taŋkərəs\ adj : hard to deal with —**can·tan·ker·ous·ly** adv —**can·tan·ker·ous·ness** n

can·ta·ta \kən'tätə\ n : choral work

can·teen \kan'tēn\ n 1 : place of recreation for service personnel 2 : water container

can·ter \'kantər\ n : slow gallop —**canter** vb

can·ti·cle \'kantikəl\ n : liturgical song

can·ti·le·ver \'kant³l,ēvər, -,ev-\ n : beam or structure supported only at one end

can·to \'kan,tō\ n, pl **-tos** : major division of a long poem

can·tor \'kantər\ n : synagogue official who sings liturgical music

can·vas \'kanvəs\ n 1 : strong cloth orig. used for making tents and sails 2 : set of sails 3 : oil painting

can·vass \-vəs\ vb : solicit votes, orders, or opinions from ~ n : act of canvassing —**can·vass·er** n

can·yon \'kanyən\ n : deep valley with steep sides

cap \'kap\ n 1 : covering for the head 2 : top or cover like a cap 3 : upper limit ~ vb **-pp-** 1 : provide or protect with a cap 2 : climax —**cap·ful** \-,ful\ n

ca·pa·ble \'kāpəbəl\ adj : able to do something —**ca·pa·bil·i·ty** \,kāpə'bilə-tē\ n —**ca·pa·bly** \'kāpəblē\ adv

ca·pa·cious \kə'pāshəs\ adj : able to contain much

ca·pac·i·tance \kə'pasətəns\ n : ability to store electrical energy

ca·pac·i·tor \-ətər\ n : device for storing electrical energy

ca·pac·i·ty \-ətē\ n, pl **-ties** 1 : ability to contain 2 : volume 3 : ability 4 : role or job ~ adj : equaling maximum capacity

¹**cape** \'kāp\ n : point of land jutting out into water

²**cape** n : garment that drapes over the shoulders

¹**ca·per** \'kāpər\ n : flower bud of a shrub pickled for use as a relish

²**caper** n : leap or prance about ~ n 1 : frolicsome leap 2 : escapade

cap·il·lary \'kapə,lerē\ adj 1 : resembling a hair 2 : having a very small bore ~ n, pl **-lar·ies** : tiny thin-walled blood vessel

¹**cap·i·tal** \'kapət³l\ adj 1 : punishable by death 2 : being in the series A, B, C rather than a, b, c 3 : relating to capital 4 : excellent ~ n 1 : capital letter 2 : seat of government 3 : wealth 4 : total face value of a company's stock 5 : investors as a group

²**capital** n : top part of a column

cap·i·tal·ism \-,izəm\ n : economic system of private ownership of capital

cap·i·tal·ist \-ist\ n 1 : person with capital invested in business 2 : believer in capitalism ~ adj 1 : owning capital 2 : practicing, advocating, or marked by capitalism —**cap·i·tal·is·tic** \,kapət³l'istik\ adj —**cap·i·tal·is·ti·cal·ly** \-klē\ adv

cap·i·tal·ize \-,īz\ vb **-ized; -iz·ing** 1 : write or print with a capital letter 2 : use as capital 3 : supply capital for 4 : turn something to advantage —**cap·i·tal·iza·tion** \,kapət³lə-'zāshən\ n

cap·i·tol \'kapət³l\ n : building in which a legislature sits

ca·pit·u·late \kə'pichə,lāt\ vb **-lat·ed; -lat·ing** : surrender —**ca·pit·u·la·tion** \-,pichə'lāshən\ n

ca·pon \'kā,pän, -pən\ n : castrated male chicken

ca·price \kə'prēs\ n : whim —**ca·pri·cious** \-'prishəs\ adj —**ca·pri·cious·ly** adv —**ca·pri·cious·ness** n

cap·size \'kap,sīz, kap'sīz\ vb **-sized; -siz·ing** : overturn

cap·stan \'kapstən, -,stan\ n : upright winch

cap·sule \'kapsəl, -,sül\ n 1 : enveloping cover (as for medicine) 2 : small pressurized compartment for astronauts ~ adj : very brief or compact —**cap·su·lar** \-sələr\ adj —**cap·su·lat·ed** \-sə,lātəd\ adj

cap·tain \'kaptən\ n 1 : commander of a body of troops 2 : officer in charge of a ship 3 : commissioned officer in the navy ranking next below a rear admiral or a commodore 4 : commissioned officer (as in the army) ranking next below a major 5 : leader ~ vb : be captain of —**cap·tain·cy** n

cap·tion \'kapshən\ n 1 : title 2 : explanation with an illustration —**caption** vb

cap·tious \'kapshəs\ adj : tending to find fault —**cap·tious·ly** adv

cap·ti·vate \'kaptə,vāt\ vb -**vat·ed;** -**vat·ing** : attract and charm —**cap·ti·va·tion** \,kaptə'vāshən\ n —**cap·ti·va·tor** \'kaptə,vātər\ n

cap·tive \-tiv\ adj **1** : made prisoner **2** : confined or under control —**captive** n —**cap·tiv·i·ty** \kap'tivətē\ n

cap·tor \'kaptər\ n : one that captures

cap·ture \-chər\ n : seizure by force or trickery ~ vb -**tured;** -**tur·ing** : take captive

car \'kär\ n **1** : vehicle moved on wheels **2** : cage of an elevator

ca·rafe \kə'raf, -'räf\ n : decanter

car·a·mel \'karəməl, 'kärməl\ n **1** : burnt sugar used for flavoring and coloring **2** : firm chewy candy

1carat var of KARAT

2car·at \'karət\ n : unit of weight for precious stones

car·a·van \'karə,van\ n : travelers journeying together (as in a line)

car·a·way \'karə,wā\ n : aromatic herb with seeds used in seasoning

car·bine \'kär,bēn, -,bīn\ n : short-barreled rifle

car·bo·hy·drate \,kärbō'hī,drāt, -drət\ n : compound of carbon, hydrogen, and oxygen

car·bon \'kärbən\ n **1** : chemical element occurring in nature esp. as diamond and graphite **2** : piece of carbon paper or a copy made with it

1car·bon·ate \'kärbə,nāt, -nət\ n : salt or ester of a carbon-containing acid

2car·bon·ate \-,nāt\ vb -**at·ed;** -**at·ing** : impregnate with carbon dioxide —**car·bon·ation** \,kärbə'nāshən\ n

carbon paper n : thin paper coated with a pigment for making copies

car·bun·cle \'kär,bəŋkəl\ n : painful inflammation of the skin and underlying tissue

car·bu·re·tor \'kärbə,rātər, -byə-\ n : device for mixing fuel and air

car·cass \'kärkəs\ n : dead body

car·cin·o·gen \kär'sinəjən\ n : agent causing cancer —**car·ci·no·gen·ic** \,kärs'nō'jenik\ adj

car·ci·no·ma \,kärs'n'ōmə\ n, pl -**mas** or -**ma·ta** \-mətə\ : malignant tumor —**car·ci·no·ma·tous** \-mətəs\ adj

1card \'kärd\ vb : comb (fibers) before spinning ~ n : device for carding fibers —**card·er** n

2card n **1** : playing card **2** pl : game played with playing cards **3** : small flat piece of paper

card·board n : stiff material like paper

car·di·ac \'kärdē,ak\ adj : relating to the heart

car·di·gan \'kärdigən\ n : sweater with an opening in the front

1car·di·nal \'kärd³nəl\ n **1** : official of the Roman Catholic Church **2** : bright red songbird

2cardinal adj : of basic importance

cardinal number n : number (as 1, 82, 357) used in counting

car·di·ol·o·gy \,kärdē'äləjē\ n : study of the heart —**car·di·ol·o·gist** \-jist\ n

car·dio·vas·cu·lar \-ō'vaskyələr\ adj : relating to the heart and blood vessels

care \'ker\ n **1** : anxiety **2** : watchful attention **3** : supervision ~ vb **cared;** **car·ing 1** : feel anxiety or concern **2** : like **3** : provide care —**care·free** adj —**care·ful** \-fəl\ adj —**care·ful·ly** adv —**care·ful·ness** n —**care·giv·er** \-,givər\ n —**care·less** adj —**care·less·ly** adv —**care·less·ness** n

ca·reen \kə'rēn\ vb **1** : sway from side to side **2** : career

ca·reer \kə'rir\ n : vocation ~ vb : go at top speed

ca·ress \kə'res\ n : tender touch ~ vb : touch lovingly or tenderly

car·et \'karət\ n : mark ‿ showing where something is to be inserted

care·tak·er n : one in charge for another or temporarily

car·go \'kärgō\ n, pl -**goes** or -**gos** : transported goods

car·i·bou \'karə,bü\ n, pl -**bou** or -**bous** : large No. American deer

car·i·ca·ture \'karikə,chúr\ n : distorted representation for humor or ridicule —**caricature** vb —**car·i·ca·tur·ist** \-ist\ n

car·ies \'karēz\ n, pl **caries** : tooth decay

car·il·lon \'karə,län\ n : set of tuned bells

car·mine \'kärmən, -,mīn\ n : vivid red

car·nage \'kärnij\ n : slaughter

car·nal \'kärn³l\ adj : sensual —**car·nal·i·ty** \kär'nalətē\ n —**car·nal·ly** adv

car·na·tion \kär'nāshən\ n : showy flower

car·ni·val \'kärnəvəl\ n **1** : festival **2** : traveling enterprise offering amusements

car·ni·vore \-,vōr\ n : flesh-eating ani-

-mal —**car·niv·o·rous** \kär'nivərəs\ adj —**car·niv·o·rous·ly** adv —**car·niv·o·rous·ness** n

car·ol \'karəl\ n : song of joy —**carol** vb —**car·ol·er, car·ol·ler** \-ələr\ n

car·om \-əm\ n or vb : rebound

ca·rouse \kə'rauz\ vb -**roused; -rous·ing** : drink and be boisterous —**ca·rouse** n —**ca·rous·er** n

car·ou·sel, car·rou·sel \,karə'sel, 'karə,-\ n : merry-go-round

¹carp \'kärp\ vb : find fault

²carp n, pl **carp** or **carps** : freshwater fish

car·pel \'kärpəl\ n : modified leaf forming part of the ovary of a flower

car·pen·ter \'kärpəntər\ n : one who builds with wood —**carpenter** vb —**car·pen·try** \-trē\ n

car·pet \'kärpət\ n : fabric floor covering ~ vb : cover with a carpet —**car·pet·ing** \-iŋ\ n

car·port n : open-sided automobile shelter

car·riage \'karij\ n 1 : conveyance 2 : manner of holding oneself 3 : wheeled vehicle

car·ri·on \'karēən\ n : dead and decaying flesh

car·rot \'karət\ n : orange root vegetable

car·ry \'karē\ vb -**ried; -ry·ing** 1 : move while supporting 2 : hold (oneself) in a specified way 3 : support 4 : keep in stock 5 : reach to a distance 6 : win —**car·ri·er** \-ēər\ n —**carry on** vb 1 : conduct 2 : behave excitedly —**carry out** vb : put into effect

cart \'kärt\ n : wheeled vehicle ~ vb : carry in a cart —**cart·age** \-ij\ n —**cart·er** n

car·tel \kär'tel\ n : business combination designed to limit competition

car·ti·lage \'kärt⁰lij\ n : elastic skeletal tissue —**car·ti·lag·i·nous** \kärt⁰l'ajənəs\ adj

car·tog·ra·phy \kär'tägrəfē\ n : making of maps —**car·tog·ra·pher** \-fər\ n

car·ton \'kärt⁰n\ n : cardboard box

car·toon \kär'tün\ n 1 : humorous drawing 2 : comic strip —**cartoon** vb —**car·toon·ist** n

car·tridge \'kärtrij\ n 1 : tube containing powder and a bullet or shot for a firearm 2 : container of material for insertion into an apparatus

carve \'kärv\ vb **carved; carv·ing** 1 : cut with care 2 : cut into pieces or slices —**carv·er** n

cas·cade \kas'kād\ n : small steep waterfall ~ vb -**cad·ed; -cad·ing** : fall in a cascade

¹case \'kās\ n 1 : particular instance 2 : convincing argument 3 : inflectional form esp. of a noun or pronoun 4 : fact 5 : lawsuit 6 : instance of disease —**in case** : as a precaution —**in case of** : in the event of

²case n 1 : box 2 : outer covering ~ vb : encase 1 : enclose 2 : inspect

case·ment \-mənt\ n : window that opens like a door

cash \'kash\ n 1 : ready money 2 : money paid at the time of purchase ~ vb : give or get cash for

ca·shew \'kashü, kə'shü\ n : tropical American tree or its nut

¹cash·ier \ka'shir\ vb : dismiss in disgrace

²cash·ier n : person who receives and records payments

cash·mere \'kazh,mir, 'kash-\ n : fine goat's wool or a fabric of this

ca·si·no \kə'sēnō\ n, pl -**nos** : place for gambling

cask \'kask\ n : barrel-shaped container for liquids

cas·ket \'kaskət\ n : coffin

cas·se·role \'kasə,rōl\ n : baking dish or the food cooked in this

cas·sette \kə'set, ka-\ n : case containing magnetic tape

cas·sock \'kasək\ n : long clerical garment

cast \'kast\ vb **cast; cast·ing** 1 : throw 2 : deposit (a ballot) 3 : assign parts in a play 4 : mold ~ n 1 : throw 2 : appearance 3 : rigid surgical dressing 4 : actors in a play

cas·ta·nets \,kastə'nets\ n pl : shells clicked together in the hand

cast·away \'kastə,wā\ n : survivor of a shipwreck —**castaway** adj

caste \'kast\ n : social class or rank

cast·er \'kastər\ n : small wheel on furniture

cas·ti·gate \'kastə,gāt\ vb -**gat·ed; -gat·ing** : chastise severely —**cas·ti·ga·tion** \,kastə'gāshən\ n —**cas·ti·ga·tor** \'kastə,gātər\ n

cast iron n : hard brittle alloy of iron

cas·tle \'kasəl\ n : fortified building

cast-off adj : thrown away —**cast·off** n

cas·trate \'kas,trāt\ vb -**trat·ed; -trat·ing** : remove the testes of —**cas·tra·tion** \ka'strāshən\ n

ca·su·al \'kazhəwəl\ adj 1 : happening

by chance **2** : showing little concern **3** : informal —**ca·su·al·ly** \-ē-lē\ *adv* — **ca·su·al·ness** *n*

ca·su·al·ty \-tē\ *n*, *pl* **-ties 1** : serious or fatal accident **2** : one injured, lost, or destroyed

ca·su·ist·ry \'kazhəwəstrē\ *n*, *pl* **-ries** : rationalization —**ca·su·ist** \-wist\ *n*

cat \'kat\ *n* **1** : small domestic mammal **2** : related animal (as a lion) — **cat·like** *adj*

cat·a·clysm \'katə,klizəm\ *n* : violent change —**cat·a·clys·mal** \,katə'klizməl\, **cat·a·clys·mic** \-'klizmik\ *adj*

cat·a·comb \'katə,kōm\ *n* : underground burial place

cat·a·log, cat·a·logue \'kat^əl,óg\ *n* **1** : list **2** : book containing a description of items ~ *vb* **-loged** *or* **-logued**; **-log·ing** *or* **-logu·ing 1** : make a catalog of **2** : enter in a catalog —**cat·a·log·er, cat·a·logu·er** *n*

ca·tal·pa \kə'talpə\ *n* : tree with broad leaves and long pods

ca·tal·y·sis \kə'taləsəs\ *n*, *pl* **-y·ses** \-,sēz\ : increase in the rate of chemical reaction caused by a substance (**cat·a·lyst** \'kat^əlist\) that is itself unchanged —**cat·a·lyt·ic** \,kat^əl'itik\ *adj*

cat·a·ma·ran \katəmə'ran\ *n* : boat with twin hulls

cat·a·mount \'katə,maúnt\ *n* : cougar

cat·a·pult \'katə,pəlt, -,púlt\ *n* : device for hurling or launching —**catapult** *vb*

cat·a·ract \'katə,rakt\ *n* **1** : large waterfall **2** : cloudiness of the lens of the eye

ca·tarrh \kə'tär\ *n* : inflammation of the nose and throat

ca·tas·tro·phe \kə'tastrə,fē\ *n* **1** : great disaster or misfortune **2** : utter failure —**cat·a·stroph·ic** \,katə'sträfik\ *adj* —**cat·a·stroph·i·cal·ly** \-iklē\ *adv*

cat·bird *n* : American songbird

cat·call *n* : noise of disapproval

catch \'kach, 'kech\ *vb* **caught** \'kót\; **catch·ing 1** : capture esp. after pursuit **2** : trap **3** : detect esp. by surprise **4** : grasp **5** : get entangled **6** : become affected with or by **7** : seize and hold firmly ~ *n* **1** : act of catching **2** : something caught **3** : something that fastens **4** : hidden difficulty — **catch·er** *n*

catch·ing \-iŋ\ *adj* : infectious

catch·up \'kechəp, 'kach-; 'katsəp\ *var of* KETCHUP

catch·word *n* : slogan

catchy \-ē\ *adj* **catch·i·er; -est** : likely to catch interest

cat·e·chism \'katə,kizəm\ *n* : set of questions and answers esp. to teach religious doctrine

cat·e·gor·i·cal \,katə'górikəl\ *adj* : absolute —**cat·e·gor·i·cal·ly** \-klē\ *adv*

cat·e·go·ry \'katə,gōrē\ *n*, *pl* **-ries** : group or class —**cat·e·go·ri·za·tion** \,katigərə'zāshən\ *n* —**cat·e·go·rize** \'katigə,rīz\ *vb*

ca·ter \'kātər\ *vb* **1** : provide food for **2** : supply what is wanted —**ca·ter·er** *n*

cat·er·cor·ner \,katē'kórnər, ,katə-, ,kitē-\, **cat·er·cor·nered** *adv or adj* : in a diagonal position

cat·er·pil·lar \'katər,pilər\ *n* : butterfly or moth larva

cat·er·waul \'katər,wól\ *vb* : make the harsh cry of a cat —**caterwaul** *n*

cat·fish *n* : big-headed fish with feelers about the mouth

cat·gut *n* : tough cord made usu. from sheep intestines

ca·thar·sis \kə'thärsəs\ *n*, *pl* **ca·thar·ses** \-,sēz\ : a purging —**ca·thar·tic** \kə-'thärtik\ *adj or n*

ca·the·dral \-'thēdrəl\ *n* : principal church of a diocese

cath·e·ter \'kathətər\ *n* : tube for insertion into a body cavity

cath·ode \'kath,ōd\ *n* **1** : negative electrode **2** : positive battery terminal — **ca·thod·ic** \ka'thädik\ *adj*

cath·o·lic \'kathəlik\ *adj* **1** : universal **2** *cap* : relating to Roman Catholics

Cath·o·lic *n* : member of the Roman Catholic Church —**Ca·thol·i·cism** \kə'thälə,sizəm\ *n*

cat·kin \'katkən\ *n* : long dense flower cluster

cat·nap *n* : short light nap —**catnap** *vb*

cat·nip \-,nip\ *n* : aromatic mint relished by cats

cat's-paw *n*, *pl* **cat's-paws** : person used as if a tool

cat·sup \'kechəp, 'kach-; 'katsəp\ *var of* KETCHUP

cat·tail *n* : marsh herb with furry brown spikes

cat·tle \'kat^əl\ *n pl* : domestic bovines —**cat·tle·man** \-mən, -,man\ *n*

cat·ty \'katē\ *adj* **-ti·er; -est** : mean or spiteful —**cat·ti·ly** *adv* —**cat·ti·ness** *n*

cat·walk \'kat-,wôk\ n : high narrow walk

Cau·ca·sian \kô'kāzhən\ adj : relating to the white race —**Caucasian** n

cau·cus \'kôkəs\ n : political meeting —**caucus** vb

caught past of CATCH

cauldron \'kóldrən\ n : large kettle

cau·li·flow·er \'kóli,flaůər, 'käl-\ n : vegetable having a compact head of usu. white undeveloped flowers

caulk \'kók\ vb : make seams watertight —**caulk** n —**caulk·er** n

caus·al \'kózəl\ adj : relating to or being a cause —**cau·sal·i·ty** \kó'zalətē\ n —**caus·al·ly** \'kózəlē\ adv

cause \'kóz\ n 1 : something that brings about a result 2 : reason 3 : lawsuit 4 : principle or movement to support ~ vb caused; caus·ing : be the cause of —**cau·sa·tion** \kó'zāshən\ n —**caus·ative** \'kózətiv\ adj —**cause·less** adj —**caus·er** n

cause·way n : raised road esp. over water

caus·tic \'kóstik\ adj 1 : corrosive 2 : sharp or biting —**caustic** n

cau·ter·ize \'kótə,rīz\ vb -ized; -iz·ing : burn to prevent infection or bleeding —**cau·ter·i·za·tion** \,kótərə'zāshən\ n

cau·tion \'kóshən\ n 1 : warning 2 : care or prudence ~ vb : warn —**cau·tion·ary** \-shə,nerē\ adj

cau·tious \'kóshəs\ adj : taking caution —**cau·tious·ly** adv —**cau·tious·ness** n

cav·al·cade \,kavəl'kād, 'kavəl,-\ n 1 : procession on horseback 2 : series

cav·a·lier \,kavə'lir\ n : mounted soldier ~ adj : disdainful or arrogant —**cav·a·lier·ly** adv

cav·al·ry \'kavəlrē\ n, pl -ries : troops on horseback or in vehicles —**cav·al·ry·man** \-mən, -,man\ n

cave \'kāv\ n : natural underground chamber —**cave in** vb : collapse

cav·ern \'kavərn\ n : large cave —**cav·ern·ous** adj —**cav·ern·ous·ly** adv

cav·i·ar, cav·i·are \'kavē,är, 'käv-\ n : salted fish roe

cav·il \'kavəl\ vb -iled or -illed; -il·ing or -il·ling : raise trivial objections —**cavil** n —**cav·il·er, cav·il·ler** n

cav·i·ty \'kavətē\ n, pl -ties 1 : unfilled place within a mass 2 : decay in a tooth

ca·vort \kə'vórt\ vb : prance or caper

caw \'kó\ vb : utter the harsh call of the crow —**caw** n

cay·enne pepper \,kī'en-, ,kā-\ n : ground dried fruits of a hot pepper

CD \,sē'dē\ n : compact disc

cease \'sēs\ vb ceased; ceas·ing : stop

cease·less \-ləs\ adj : continuous

ce·dar \'sēdər\ n : cone-bearing tree with fragrant durable wood

cede \'sēd\ vb ced·ed; ced·ing : surrender —**ced·er** n

ceil·ing \'sēliŋ\ n 1 : overhead surface of a room 2 : upper limit

cel·e·brate \'selə,brāt\ vb -brat·ed; -brat·ing 1 : perform with appropriate rites 2 : honor with ceremonies 3 : extol —**cel·e·brant** \-brənt\ n —**cel·e·bra·tion** \,selə'brāshən\ n —**cel·e·bra·tor** \'selə,brātər\ n

cel·e·brat·ed \-əd\ adj : renowned

ce·leb·ri·ty \sə'lebrətē\ n, pl -ties 1 : renown 2 : well-known person

ce·ler·i·ty \sə'lerətē\ n : speed

cel·ery \'selərē\ n, pl -er·ies : herb grown for crisp edible stalks

ce·les·ta \sə'lestə\, **ce·leste** \sə'lest\ n : keyboard musical instrument

ce·les·tial \sə'leschəl\ adj 1 : relating to the sky 2 : heavenly

cel·i·ba·cy \'seləbəsē\ n 1 : state of being unmarried 2 : abstention from sexual intercourse —**cel·i·bate** \'sɛ:-labət\ n or adj

cell \'sel\ n 1 : small room 2 : tiny mass of protoplasm that forms the fundamental unit of living matter 3 : container holding an electrolyte for generating electricity —**celled** adj

cel·lar \'selər\ n : room or area below ground

cel·lo \'chelō\ n, pl -los : bass member of the violin family —**cel·list** \-ist\ n

cel·lo·phane \'selə,fān\ n : thin transparent cellulose wrapping

cel·lu·lar \'selyələr\ adj : relating to or consisting of cells

cel·lu·lose \'selyə,lōs\ n : complex plant carbohydrate

Cel·sius \'selsēəs\ adj : relating to a thermometer scale on which the freezing point of water is 0° and the boiling point is 100°

ce·ment \si'ment\ n 1 : powdery mixture of clay and limestone that hardens when wetted 2 : binding agent ~ vb : unite or cover with cement —**ce·ment·er** n

cem·e·tery \'semə,terē\ n, pl **-ter·ies** : burial ground

cen·ser \'sensər\ n : vessel for burning incense

cen·sor \'sensər\ n : one with power to suppress anything objectionable (as in printed matter) ~ vb : be a censor of —**cen·so·ri·al** \sen'sōrēəl\ adj —**cen·sor·ship** \-,ship\ n

cen·so·ri·ous \sen'sōrēəs\ adj : critical —**cen·so·ri·ous·ly** adv —**cen·so·ri·ous·ness** n

cen·sure \'senchər\ n : official reprimand ~ vb **-sured; -sur·ing** : find blameworthy —**cen·sur·able** adj

cen·sus \'sensəs\ n : periodic population count —**census** vb

cent \'sent\ n : monetary unit equal to 1/100 of a basic unit of value

cen·taur \'sen,tȯr\ n : mythological creature that is half man and half horse

cen·ten·ni·al \sen'tenēəl\ n : 100th anniversary —**centennial** adj

cen·ter \'sentər\ n 1 : middle point 2 : point of origin or greatest concentration 3 : region of concentrated population 4 : player near the middle of the team ~ vb 1 : place, fix, or concentrate at or around a center 2 : have a center —**cen·ter·piece** n

cen·ti·grade \'sentə,grād, 'sänt-\ adj : Celsius

cen·ti·me·ter \'sentə,mētər, 'sänt-\ n : 1/100 meter

cen·ti·pede \'sentə,pēd\ n : long flat many-legged arthropod

cen·tral \'sentrəl\ adj 1 : constituting or being near a center 2 : essential or principal —**cen·tral·ly** adv

cen·tral·ize \-trə,līz\ vb **-ized; -iz·ing** : bring to a central point or under central control —**cen·tral·i·za·tion** \,sentrələ'zāshən\ n —**cen·tral·iz·er** n

cen·tre \'sentər\ chiefly Brit var of CENTER

cen·trif·u·gal \sen'trifyəgəl, -'trifigəl\ adj : acting in a direction away from a center or axis

cen·tri·fuge \'sentrə,fyüj\ n : machine that separates substances by spinning

cen·trip·e·tal \sen'tripət'l\ adj : acting in a direction toward a center or axis

cen·tu·ri·on \sen'chúrēən, -'túr-\ n : Roman military officer

cen·tu·ry \'senchərē\ n, pl **-ries** : 100 years

ce·ram·ic \sə'ramik\ n 1 pl : art or process of shaping and hardening articles from clay 2 : product of ceramics —**ceramic** adj

ce·re·al \'sirēəl\ adj : made of or relating to grain or to the plants that produce it ~ n 1 : grass yielding edible grain 2 : food prepared from a cereal grain

cer·e·bel·lum \,serə'beləm\ n, pl **-bel·lums** or **-bel·la** \-'belə\ : part of the brain controlling muscular coordination —**cer·e·bel·lar** \-ər\ adj

ce·re·bral \sə'rēbrəl, 'serə-\ adj 1 : relating to the brain, intellect, or cerebrum 2 : appealing to the intellect

cerebral palsy n : disorder caused by brain damage and marked esp. by defective muscle control

cer·e·brate \'serə,brāt\ vb **-brat·ed; -brat·ing** : think —**cer·e·bra·tion** \,serə'brāshən\ n

ce·re·brum \sə'rēbrəm, 'serə-\ n, pl **-brums** or **-bra** \-brə\ : part of the brain that contains the higher nervous centers

cer·e·mo·ny \'serə,mōnē\ n, pl **-nies** 1 : formal act prescribed by law, ritual, or convention 2 : prescribed procedures —**cer·e·mo·ni·al** \,serə'mōnēəl\ adj or n —**cer·e·mo·ni·ous** \-nēəs\ adj

ce·rise \sə'rēs\ n : moderate red

cer·tain \'sərt'n\ adj 1 : settled 2 : true 3 : specific but not named 4 : bound 5 : assured ~ pron : certain ones —**cer·tain·ly** adv —**cer·tain·ty** \-tē\ n

cer·tif·i·cate \sər'tifikət\ n : document establishing truth or fulfillment

cer·ti·fy \'sərtə,fī\ vb **-fied; -fy·ing** 1 : verify 2 : endorse —**cer·ti·fi·able** \-,fīəbəl\ adj —**cer·ti·fi·ably** \-blē\ adv —**cer·ti·fi·ca·tion** \,sərtəfə'kāshən\ n —**cer·ti·fi·er** n

cer·ti·tude \'sərtə,tüd, -,tyüd\ n : state of being certain

cer·vix \'sərviks\ n, pl **-vi·ces** \-və-,sēz\ or **-vix·es** 1 : neck 2 : narrow end of the uterus —**cer·vi·cal** \-vikəl\ adj

ce·sar·e·an \si'zarēən\ n : surgical operation to deliver a baby —**cesarean** adj

ce·si·um \'sēzēəm\ n : silver-white soft ductile chemical element

ces·sa·tion \se'sāshən\ n : a halting

ces·sion \'seshən\ n : a yielding

cess·pool \'ses,pül\ n : underground sewage pit

Cha·blis \'shab,lē; sha'blē\ n, pl **Cha·blis** \-,lēz, -'blēz\ : dry white wine

chafe \\'chāf\\ *vb* **chafed; chaf•ing 1** : fret **2** : make sore by rubbing

chaff \\'chaf\\ *n* **1** : debris separated from grain **2** : something worthless

chafing dish \\'chāfiŋ-\\ *n* : utensil for cooking at the table

cha•grin \shə'grin\ *n* : embarrassment or humiliation ~ *vb* : cause to feel chagrin

chain \\'chān\\ *n* **1** : flexible series of connected links **2** *pl* : fetters **3** : linked series ~ *vb* : bind or connect with a chain

chair \\'cher\\ *n* **1** : seat with a back **2** : position of authority or dignity **3** : chairman ~ *vb* : act as chairman of

chair•man \-mən\ *n* : presiding officer **—chair•man•ship** *n*

chair•wom•an \-,wümən\ *n* : woman who acts as a presiding officer

chaise longue \\'shāz'lôŋ\\ *n, pl* **chaise longues** \-lôŋ, -'lôŋz\ : long chair for reclining

cha•let \sha'lā\ *n* : Swiss mountain cottage with overhanging roof

chal•ice \\'chaləs\\ *n* : eucharistic cup

chalk \\'chôk\\ *n* **1** : soft limestone **2** : chalky material used as a crayon ~ *vb* : mark with chalk **—chalky** *adj* — **chalk up** *vb* **1** : credit **2** : achieve

chalk•board *n* : blackboard

chal•lenge \\'chalənj\\ *vb* **-lenged; -leng•ing 1** : dispute **2** : invite or dare to act or compete **—challenge** *n* **—chal•leng•er** *n*

cham•ber \\'chāmbər\\ *n* **1** : room **2** : enclosed space **3** : legislative meeting place or body **4** *pl* : judge's consultation room **—cham•bered** *adj*

cham•ber•maid *n* : bedroom maid

chamber music *n* : music by a small group for a small audience

cha•me•leon \kə'mēlyən\ *n* : small lizard whose skin changes color

cham•ois \\'shamē\\ *n, pl* **cham•ois** \-ē, -ēz\ **1** : goatlike antelope **2** : soft leather

¹champ \\'champ, 'chämp\\ *vb* : chew noisily

²champ \\'champ\\ *n* : champion

cham•pagne \sham'pān\ *n* : sparkling white wine

cham•pi•on \\'champēən\\ *n* **1** : advocate or defender **2** : winning contestant ~ *vb* : protect or fight for

cham•pi•on•ship \-,ship\ *n* **1** : title of a champion **2** : contest to pick a champion

chance \\'chans\\ *n* **1** : unpredictable element of existence **2** : opportunity **3** : probability **4** : risk **5** : raffle ticket ~ *vb* **chanced; chanc•ing 1** : happen **2** : encounter unexpectedly **3** : risk **—chance** *adj*

chan•cel \\'chansəl\\ *n* : part of a church around the altar

chan•cel•lery, chan•cel•lory \\'chansələrē\\ *n, pl* **-leries** *or* **-lories 1** : position of a chancellor **2** : chancellor's office

chan•cel•lor \-sələr\ *n* **1** : chief or high state official **2** : head of a university **—chan•cel•lor•ship** *n*

chan•cre \\'shaŋkər\\ *n* : skin ulcer esp. from syphilis

chancy \\'chansē\\ *adj* **chanc•i•er; -est** : risky

chan•de•lier \,shandə'lir\ *n* : hanging lighting fixture

chan•dler \\'chandlər\\ *n* : provisions dealer **—chan•dlery** *n*

change \\'chānj\\ *vb* **changed; chang•ing 1** : make or become different **2** : exchange **3** : give or receive change for ~ *n* **1** : a changing **2** : excess from a payment **3** : money in smaller denominations **4** : coins **—change•able** *adj* **—change•less** *adj* **—chang•er** *n*

chan•nel \\'chan³l\\ *n* **1** : deeper part of a waterway **2** : means of passage or communication **3** : strait **4** : broadcast frequency ~ *vb* **-neled** *or* **-nelled; -nel•ing** *or* **-nel•ling** : make or direct through a channel

chant \\'chant\\ *vb* : sing or speak in one tone **—chant** *n* **—chant•er** *n*

chan•tey, chan•ty \\'shantē, 'chant-\\ *n, pl* **-teys** *or* **-ties** : sailors' work song

Cha•nu•kah \\'känəkə, 'hän-\\ *var of* HANUKKAH

cha•os \\'kā,äs\\ *n* : complete disorder **—cha•ot•ic** \kā'ätik\ *adj* **—cha•ot•i•cal•ly** \-iklē\ *adv*

¹chap \\'chap\\ *n* : fellow

²chap *vb* **-pp-** : dry and crack open usu. from wind and cold

cha•pel \\'chapəl\\ *n* : private or small place of worship

chap•er•on, chap•er•one \\'shapə,rōn\\ *n* : older person who accompanies young people at a social gathering ~ *vb* **-oned; -on•ing** : act as chaperon at or for **—chap•er•on•age** \-ij\ *n*

chap•lain \\'chaplən\\ *n* : clergy member in a military unit or a prison **—chap•lain•cy** \-sē\ *n*

chap·ter \\'chaptər\ *n* **1** : main book division **2** : branch of a society

char \\'chär\ *vb* **-rr- 1** : burn to charcoal **2** : scorch

char·ac·ter \\'kariktər\ *n* **1** : letter or graphic mark **2** : trait or distinctive combination of traits **3** : peculiar person **4** : fictional person **—char·ac·ter·i·za·tion** \,kariktərə'zāshən\ *n* **—char·ac·ter·ize** \\'kariktə,rīz\ *vb*

char·ac·ter·is·tic \,kariktə'ristik\ *adj* : typical ~ *n* : distinguishing quality **—char·ac·ter·is·ti·cal·ly** \-tiklē\ *adv*

cha·rades \shə'rādz\ *n sing or pl* : pantomime guessing game

char·coal \\'chär,kōl\ *n* : porous carbon prepared by partial combustion

chard \\'chärd\ *n* : leafy vegetable

charge \\'chärj\ *vb* **charged; charg·ing 1** : give an electric charge to **2** : impose a task or responsibility on **3** : command **4** : accuse **5** : rush forward in assault **6** : assume a debt for **7** : fix as a price ~ *n* **1** : excess or deficiency of electrons in a body **2** : tax **3** : responsibility **4** : accusation **5** : cost **6** : attack **—charge·able** *adj*

charg·er \-ər\ *n* : horse ridden in battle

char·i·ot \\'chareət\ *n* : ancient 2-wheeled vehicle **—char·i·o·teer** \,chareə'tir\ *n*

cha·ris·ma \kə'rizmə\ *n* : special ability to lead **—char·is·mat·ic** \,karəz'matik\ *adj*

char·i·ty \\'charətē\ *n, pl* **-ties 1** : love for mankind **2** : generosity or leniency **3** : alms **4** : institution for relief of the needy **—char·i·ta·ble** \-əbəl\ *adj* **—char·i·ta·ble·ness** *n* **—char·i·ta·bly** \-blē\ *adv*

char·la·tan \\'shärlətən\ *n* : impostor

charm \\'chärm\ *n* **1** : something with magic power **2** : appealing trait **3** : small ornament ~ *vb* : fascinate **—charm·er** *n* **—charm·ing** *adj* **—charm·ing·ly** *adv*

char·nel house \\'chärnˀl-\ *n* : place for dead bodies

chart \\'chärt\ *n* **1** : map **2** : diagram ~ *vb* **1** : make a chart of **2** : plan

char·ter \-ər\ *n* **1** : document granting rights **2** : constitution ~ *vb* **1** : establish by charter **2** : rent **—char·ter·er** *n*

char·treuse \shär'trüz, -'trüs\ *n* : brilliant yellow green

char·wom·an \\'chär,wúmən\ *n* : cleaning woman

chary \\'charē\ *adj* **chari·er; -est** : cautious **—chari·ly** \\'charəlē\ *adv*

¹chase \\'chās\ *vb* **chased; chas·ing 1** : follow trying to catch **2** : drive away **—chase** *n* **—chas·er** *n*

²chase *vb* **chased; chas·ing** : decorate (metal) by embossing or engraving

chasm \\'kazəm\ *n* : gorge

chas·sis \\'chasē, 'shasē\ *n, pl* **chas·sis** \-ēz\ : supporting structural frame

chaste \\'chāst\ *adj* **chast·er; chast·est 1** : abstaining from all or unlawful sexual relations **2** : modest or decent **3** : severely simple **—chaste·ly** *adv* **—chaste·ness** *n* **—chas·ti·ty** \\'chastətē\ *n*

chas·ten \\'chāsˀn\ *vb* : discipline

chas·tise \chas'tīz\ *vb* **-tised; -tis·ing 1** : punish **2** : censure **—chas·tise·ment** \-mənt, 'chastəz-\ *n*

chat \\'chat\ *n* : informal talk **—chat** *vb* **—chat·ty** \-ē\ *adj*

châ·teau \sha'tō\ *n, pl* **-teaus** \-'tōz\ *or* **-teaux** \-'tō, -'tōz\ **1** : large country house **2** : French vineyard estate

chat·tel \\'chatˀl\ *n* : item of tangible property other than real estate

chat·ter \\'chatər\ *vb* **1** : utter rapidly succeeding sounds **2** : talk fast or too much **—chatter** *n* **—chat·ter·er** *n*

chat·ter·box *n* : incessant talker

chauf·feur \\'shōfər, shō'fər\ *n* : hired car driver ~ *vb* : work as a chauffeur

chau·vin·ism \\'shōvə,nizəm\ *n* **1** : excessive patriotism **—chau·vin·ist** \-vənist\ *n* **—chau·vin·is·tic** \,shō-və'nistik\ *adj*

cheap \\'chēp\ *adj* **1** : inexpensive **2** : shoddy **—cheap** *adv* **—cheap·en** \\'chēpən\ *vb* **—cheap·ly** *adv* **—cheap·ness** *n*

cheap·skate *n* : stingy person

cheat \\'chēt\ *n* **1** : act of deceiving **2** : one that cheats ~ *vb* **1** : deprive through fraud or deceit **2** : violate rules dishonestly **—cheat·er** *n*

check \\'chek\ *n* **1** : sudden stoppage **2** : restraint **3** : test or standard for testing **4** : written order to a bank to pay money **5** : ticket showing ownership **6** : slip showing an amount due **7** : pattern in squares or fabric in such a pattern **8** : mark placed beside an item noted ~ *vb* **1** : slow down or stop **2** : restrain **3** : compare or correspond with a source or original **4** : inspect or test for condition **5** : mark with a check **6** : leave or accept for safe-keeping or shipment **7** : checker — **check-in** vb : report one's arrival — **check out** vb : settle one's account and leave

1check-er \-ər\ n : piece in checkers ~ vb : mark with different colors or into squares

2checker n : one that checks

check-er-board \-,bȯrd\ n : board of 64 squares of alternate colors

check-ers \'chekərz\ n : game for 2 played on a checkerboard

check-mate vb : thwart completely — **checkmate** n

check-point n : place where traffic is checked

check-up n : physical examination

ched-dar \'chedər\ n : hard smooth cheese

cheek \'chēk\ n **1** : fleshy side part of the face **2** : impudence — **cheeked** \'chēkt\ adj — **cheeky** adj

cheep \'chēp\ vb : utter faint shrill sounds — **cheep** n

cheer \'chir\ n **1** : good spirits **2** : food and drink for a feast **3** : shout of approval or encouragement ~ vb **1** : give hope or courage to **2** : make or become glad **3** : urge on or applaud with shouts — **cheer-er** n — **cheer-ful** \-fəl\ adj — **cheer-ful-ly** adv — **cheer-ful-ness** n — **cheer-lead-er** n — **cheer-less** adj — **cheer-less-ly** adv — **cheer-less-ness** n

cheery \'chirē\ adj **cheer-i-er; -est** : cheerful — **cheer-i-ly** adv — **cheer-i-ness** n

cheese \'chēz\ n : curd of milk usu. pressed and cured — **cheesy** adj

cheese-cloth n : lightweight coarse cotton gauze

chee-tah \'chētə\ n : spotted swift-moving African cat

chef \'shef\ n : chief cook

chem-i-cal \'kemikəl\ adj **1** : relating to chemistry **2** : working or produced by chemicals ~ n : substance obtained by chemistry — **chem-i-cal-ly** \-klē\ adv

che-mise \shə'mēz\ n **1** : woman's one-piece undergarment **2** : loose dress

chem-ist \'kemist\ n **1** : one trained in chemistry **2** Brit : pharmacist

chem-is-try \-istrē\ n, pl **-tries** : science that deals with the composition and properties of substances

che-mo-ther-a-py \,kēmō'therəpē, ,kemō-\ n : use of chemicals in the treatment of disease — **che-mo-ther-a-peu-tic** adj

che-nille \shə'nēl\ n : yarn with protruding pile or fabric of such yarn

cheque \'chek\ chiefly Brit var of CHECK 4

cher-ish \'cherish\ vb : hold dear

cher-ry \'cherē\ n, pl **-ries** : small fleshy fruit of a tree related to the roses or the tree or its wood

cher-ub \'cherəb\ n **1** pl **-u-bim** \-ə,bim, -yə-\ : angel **2** pl **-ubs** : chubby child — **che-ru-bic** \chə'rübik\ adj

chess \'ches\ n : game for 2 played on a checkerboard — **chess-board** n — **chess-man** n

chest \'chest\ n **1** : boxlike container **2** : part of the body enclosed by the ribs and breastbone — **chest-ed** adj

chest-nut \'ches,nət\ n : nut of a tree related to the beech or the tree

chev-i-ot \'shevēət, -vē-\ n **1** : heavy rough wool fabric **2** : soft-finished cotton fabric

chev-ron \'shevrən\ n : V-shaped insignia

chew \'chü\ vb : crush or grind with the teeth ~ n : something to chew — **chew-able** adj — **chew-er** n — **chewy** adj

chic \'shēk\ n : smart elegance of dress or manner ~ adj **1** : stylish **2** : currently fashionable

chi-ca-nery \shik'ānərē\ n, pl **-ner-ies** : trickery

chick \'chik\ n : young chicken or bird

chick-a-dee \-ə,dē\ n : small grayish American bird

chick-en \'chikən\ n **1** : common domestic fowl or its flesh used as food **2** : coward

chicken pox n : acute contagious virus disease esp. of children

chi-cle \'chikəl\ n : gum from a tropical evergreen tree

chic-o-ry \'chikərē\ n, pl **-ries** : herb used in salad or its dried ground root used to adulterate coffee

chide \'chīd\ vb **chid** \'chid\ or **chid-ed** \'chīdəd\; **chid** or **chid-den** \'chid°n\ or **chid-ed**; **chid-ing** \'chīdiŋ\ : scold

chief \'chēf\ n : leader ~ adj **1** : highest in rank **2** : most important — **chief-dom** n — **chief-ly** adv

chief-tain \'chēftən\ n : chief

chif-fon \shif'än, 'shif,-\ n : sheer fabric

chig·ger \'chigər\ n : bloodsucking mite

chi·gnon \'shēn,yän\ n : knot of hair

chil·blain \'chil,blān\ n : sore or inflamed swelling caused by cold

child \'chīld\ n, pl **chil·dren** \'children\ **1** : unborn or recently born person **2** : son or daughter —**child·bear·ing** n or adj —**child·birth** n —**child·hood** n —**child·ish** adj —**child·ish·ly** adv —**child·ish·ness** n —**child·less** adj —**child·less·ness** n —**child·like** adj —**child·proof** \-,prüf\ adj

chili, chile, chil·li \'chilē\ n, pl **chil·ies** or **chil·es** or **chil·lies** **1** : hot pepper **2** : spicy stew of ground beef, chilies, and beans

chill \'chil\ vb : make or become cold or chilly ~ adj : moderately cold ~ n **1** : feeling of coldness with shivering **2** : moderate coldness

chilly \-ē\ adj **chil·li·er; -est** : noticeably cold —**chill·i·ness** n

chime \'chīm\ n : set of tuned bells or their sound ~ vb : make bell-like sounds —**chime in** vb : break into or join in a conversation

chi·me·ra, chi·mae·ra \kī'mirə, kə-\ n : imaginary monster **2** : illusion —**chi·me·ri·cal** \-'merikəl\ adj

chim·ney \'chimnē\ n, pl **-neys 1** : passage for smoke **2** : glass tube around a lamp flame

chimp \'chimp, 'shimp\ n : chimpanzee

chim·pan·zee \,chim,pan'zē, ,shim-; chim'panzē, shim-\ n : small ape

chin \'chin\ n : part of the face below the mouth —**chin·less** adj

chi·na \'chīnə\ n **1** : porcelain ware **2** : domestic pottery

chin·chil·la \chin'chilə\ n : small So. American rodent with soft pearl-gray fur or this fur

chink \'chink\ n : small crack ~ vb : fill chinks of

chintz \'chints\ n : printed cotton cloth

chip \'chip\ n **1** : small thin flat piece cut or broken off **2** : thin crisp morsel of food **3** : counter used in games **4** : flaw where a chip came off **5** : small slice of semiconductor containing electronic circuits ~ vb **-pp-** : cut or break chips from —**chip in** vb : contribute

chip·munk \-,məŋk\ n : small striped ground-dwelling rodent

chip·per \-ər\ adj : lively and cheerful

chi·rop·o·dy \kə'räpədē, shə-\ n : podiatry —**chi·rop·o·dist** \-ədist\ n

chi·ro·prac·tic \'kīrə,praktik\ n : system of healing based esp. on manipulation of body structures —**chi·ro·prac·tor** \-tər\ n

chirp \'chərp\ n : short sharp sound like that of a bird or cricket —**chirp** vb

chis·el \'chizəl\ n : sharp-edged metal tool ~ vb **-eled** or **-elled; -el·ing** or **-el·ling 1** : work with a chisel **2** : cheat —**chis·el·er** \-ələr\ n

chit \'chit\ n : signed voucher for a small debt

chit·chat \-,chat\ n : casual conversation —**chitchat** vb

chiv·al·rous \'shivəlrəs\ adj **1** : relating to chivalry **2** : honest, courteous, or generous —**chiv·al·rous·ly** adv —**chiv·al·rous·ness** n

chiv·al·ry \-rē\ n, pl **-ries 1** : system or practices of knighthood **2** : spirit or character of the ideal knight —**chi·val·ric** \shə'valrik\ adj

chive \'chīv\ n : herb related to the onion

chlo·ride \'klōr,īd\ n : compound of chlorine

chlo·ri·nate \-ə,nāt\ vb **-nat·ed; -nat·ing** : treat or combine with chlorine —**chlo·ri·na·tion** \,klōrə'nāshən\ n

chlo·rine \'klōr,ēn\ n : chemical element that is a heavy strong-smelling greenish yellow irritating gas

chlo·ro·form \'klōrə,form\ n : etherlike colorless heavy fluid ~ vb : anesthetize or kill with chloroform

chlo·ro·phyll \'klōrə,fil\ n : green coloring matter of plants

chock \'chäk\ n : wedge for blocking the movement of a wheel —**chock** vb

chock-full \'chək'ful, 'chäk-\ adj : full to the limit

choc·o·late \'chäkələt, 'chok-\ n **1** : ground roasted cacao beans or a beverage made from them **2** : candy made of or with chocolate **3** : dark brown

choice \'chois\ n **1** : act or power of choosing **2** : one selected **3** : variety offered for selection ~ adj **choic·er; choic·est 1** : worthy of being chosen **2** : selected with care **3** : of high quality

choir \'kwīr\ n : group of singers esp. in church —**choir·boy** n —**choir·mas·ter** n

choke \'chōk\ vb **choked; chok·ing 1** : hinder breathing **2** : clog or obstruct ~ n **1** : a choking or sound of choking **2** : valve for controlling air intake in a gasoline engine

chok·er \-ər\ n : tight necklace

cho·ler \'kälər, 'kō-\ n : bad temper — **cho·ler·ic** \'kälərik, kə'ler-\ adj

chol·era \'kälərə\ n : disease marked by severe vomiting and dysentery

cho·les·ter·ol \kə'lestə,rōl, -,rȯl\ n : waxy substance in animal tissues

choose \'chüz\ vb **chose** \'chōz\; **cho·sen** \'chōz°n\; **choos·ing 1** : select after consideration **2** : decide **3** : prefer — **choos·er** n

choosy, choos·ey \'chüzē\ adj **choos·i·er; -est** : fussy in making choices

chop \'chäp\ vb **-pp- 1** : cut by repeated blows **2** : cut into small pieces ~ n **1** : sharp downward blow **2** : small cut of meat often with part of a rib

chop·per \-ər\ n **1** : one that chops **2** : helicopter

chop·py \-ē\ adj **-pi·er; -est 1** : rough with small waves **2** : jerky or disconnected —**chop·pi·ly** adv —**chop·pi·ness** n

chops \'chäps\ n pl : fleshy covering of the jaws

chop·sticks n pl : pair of sticks used in eating in oriental countries

cho·ral \'kōrəl\ adj : relating to or sung by a choir or chorus or in chorus — **cho·ral·ly** adv

cho·rale \kə'ral, -'räl\ n **1** : hymn tune or harmonization of a traditional melody **2** : chorus or choir

1chord \'kȯrd\ n : harmonious tones sounded together

2chord n **1** : cordlike anatomical structure **2** : straight line joining 2 points on a curve

chore \'chōr\ n **1** pl : daily household or farm work **2** : routine or disagreeable task

cho·re·og·ra·phy \,kōrē'ägrəfē\ n, pl **-phies** : art of composing and arranging dances —**cho·reo·graph** \'kōrēə,graf\ vb —**cho·re·og·ra·pher** \,kō-rē'ägrəfər\ n —**cho·reo·graph·ic** \-ēə'grafik\ adj

cho·ris·ter \'kōrəstər\ n : choir singer

chor·tle \'chȯrt°l\ vb **-tled; -tling** : laugh or chuckle —**chortle** n

cho·rus \'kōrəs\ n **1** : group of singers or dancers **2** : part of a song repeated at intervals **3** : composition for a chorus ~ vb : sing or utter together

chose past of CHOOSE

cho·sen \'chōz°n\ adj : favored

1chow \'chaù\ n : food

2chow n : thick-coated muscular dog

chow·der \'chaùdər\ n : thick soup usu. of seafood and milk

chow mein \'chaù'mān\ n : thick stew of shredded vegetables and meat

chris·ten \'kris°n\ vb **1** : baptize **2** : name —**chris·ten·ing** n

Chris·ten·dom \-dəm\ n : areas where Christianity prevails

Chris·tian \'krischən\ n : adherent of Christianity ~ adj : relating to or professing a belief in Christianity or Jesus Christ —**Chris·tian·ize** \'krischə-,nīz\ vb

Chris·ti·an·i·ty \,krischē'anətē\ n : religion derived from the teachings of Jesus Christ

Christian name n : first name

Christ·mas \'krisməs\ n : December 25 celebrated as the birthday of Christ

chro·mat·ic \krō'matik\ adj **1** : relating to color **2** : proceeding by half steps of the musical scale

chrome \'krōm\ n : chromium or something plated with it

chro·mi·um \-ēəm\ n : a bluish white metallic element used esp. in alloys

chro·mo·some \'krōmə,sōm, -,zōm\ n : part of a cell nucleus that contains the genes —**chro·mo·som·al** \,krō-mə'sōməl, -'zō-\ adj

chron·ic \'kränik\ adj : frequent or persistent —**chron·i·cal·ly** \-iklē\ adv

chron·i·cle \'kränikəl\ n : history ~ vb **-cled; -cling** : record —**chron·i·cler** \-iklər\ n

chro·nol·o·gy \krə'näləjē\ n, pl **-gies** : list of events in order of their occurrence —**chron·o·log·i·cal** \,krä-n°l'äjikəl\ adj —**chron·o·log·i·cal·ly** \-iklē\ adv

chro·nom·e·ter \krə'nämətər\ n : very accurate timepiece

chrys·a·lis \'krisələs\ n, pl **chrys·al·i·des** \kris'alə,dēz\ or **chrys·a·lis·es** : insect pupa enclosed in a shell

chry·san·the·mum \kris'anthəməm\ n : plant with showy flowers

chub·by \'chəbē\ adj **-bi·er; -est** : fat — **chub·bi·ness** n

1chuck \'chək\ vb **1** : tap **2** : toss ~ n **1** : light pat under the chin **2** : toss

2chuck n **1** : cut of beef **2** : machine part that holds work or another part

chuck·le \'chəkəl\ vb **-led; -ling** : laugh quietly —**chuckle** n

chug \'chəg\ n : sound of a laboring engine ~ *vb* **-gg-** : work or move with chugs

chum \'chəm\ *n* : close friend ~ *vb* **-mm-** : be chums —**chum·my** \-ē\ *adj*

chump \'chəmp\ *n* : fool

chunk \'chəŋk\ *n* 1 : short thick piece 2 : sizable amount

chunky \-ē\ *adj* **chunk·i·er; -est** 1 : stocky 2 : containing chunks

church \'chərch\ *n* 1 : building esp. for Christian public worship 2 : whole body of Christians 3 : denomination 4 : congregation —**church·go·er** *n* — **church·go·ing** *adj or n*

church·yard *n* : cemetery beside a church

churl \'chərl\ *n* : rude ill-bred person — **churl·ish** *adj*

churn \'chərn\ *n* : container in which butter is made ~ *vb* 1 : agitate in a churn 2 : shake violently

chute \'shüt\ *n* : trough or passage

chut·ney \'chətnē\ *n, pl* **-neys** : sweet and sour relish

chutz·pah \'hütspə, 'kùt-, -spä\ *n* : nerve or insolence

ci·ca·da \sə'kādə\ *n* : stout-bodied insect with transparent wings

ci·der \'sīdər\ *n* : apple juice

ci·gar \sig'är\ *n* : roll of leaf tobacco for smoking

cig·a·rette \sigə'ret, 'sigə,ret\ *n* : cut tobacco rolled in paper for smoking

cinch \'sinch\ *n* 1 : strap holding a saddle or pack in place 2 : sure thing — **cinch** *vb*

cin·cho·na \siŋ'kōnə\ *n* : So. American tree that yields quinine

cinc·ture \'siŋkchər\ *n* : belt or sash

cin·der \'sindər\ *n* 1 *pl* : ashes 2 : piece of partly burned wood or coal

cin·e·ma \'sinəmə\ *n* : movies or a movie theater —**cin·e·mat·ic** \,sinə'matik\ *adj*

cin·na·mon \'sinəmən\ *n* : spice from an aromatic tree bark

ci·pher \'sīfər\ *n* 1 : zero 2 : code

cir·ca \'sərkə\ *prep* : about

cir·cle \'sərkəl\ *n* 1 : closed symmetrical curve 2 : cycle 3 : group with a common tie ~ *vb* **-cled; -cling** 1 : enclose in a circle 2 : move or revolve around

cir·cuit \'sərkət\ *n* 1 : boundary 2 : regular tour of a territory 3 : complete path of an electric current 4 : group of electronic components

cir·cu·itous \,sər'kyüətəs\ *adj* : circular or winding

cir·cuit·ry \'sərkətrē\ *n, pl* **-ries** : arrangement of an electric circuit

cir·cu·lar \'sərkyələr\ *adj* 1 : round 2 : moving in a circle ~ *n* : advertising leaflet —**cir·cu·lar·i·ty** \,sərkyə-'larətē\ *n*

cir·cu·late \'sərkyə,lāt\ *vb* **-lat·ed; -lat·ing** : move or cause to move in a circle or from place to place or person to person —**cir·cu·la·tion** \,sərkyə'lā-shən\ *n* —**cir·cu·la·to·ry** \'sərkyələ-,tōrē\ *adj*

cir·cum·cise \'sərkəm,sīz\ *vb* **-cised; -cis·ing** : cut off the foreskin of —**cir·cum·ci·sion** \,sərkəm'sizhən\ *n*

cir·cum·fer·ence \sər'kəmfrəns\ *n* : perimeter of a circle

cir·cum·flex \'sərkəm,fleks\ *n* : phonetic mark (as ´)

cir·cum·lo·cu·tion \,sərkəmlō'kyüshən\ *n* : excessive use of words

cir·cum·nav·i·gate \,sərkəm'navə,gāt\ *vb* : sail completely around —**cir·cum·nav·i·ga·tion** *n*

cir·cum·scribe \'sərkəm,skrīb\ *vb* 1 : draw a line around 2 : limit

cir·cum·spect \'sərkəm,spekt\ *adj* : careful —**cir·cum·spec·tion** \,sər-kəm'spekshən\ *n*

cir·cum·stance \'sərkəm,stans\ *n* 1 : fact or event 2 *pl* : surrounding conditions 3 *pl* : financial situation —**cir·cum·stan·tial** \,sərkəm-'stanchəl\ *adj*

cir·cum·vent \,sərkəm'vent\ *vb* : get around esp. by trickery —**cir·cum·ven·tion** \-'venchən\ *n*

cir·cus \'sərkəs\ *n* : show with feats of skill, animal acts, and clowns

cir·rho·sis \sə'rōsəs\ *n, pl* **-rho·ses** \-,sēz\ : fibrosis of the liver —**cir·rhot·ic** \-'rätik\ *adj or n*

cir·rus \'sirəs\ *n, pl* **-ri** \-,rī\ : wispy white cloud

cis·tern \'sistərn\ *n* : underground water tank

cit·a·del \'sitəd'l, -ə,del\ *n* : fortress

cite \'sīt\ *vb* **cit·ed; cit·ing** 1 : summon before a court 2 : quote 3 : refer to esp. in commendation —**ci·ta·tion** \sī'tāshən\ *n*

cit·i·zen \'sitəzən\ *n* : member of a country —**cit·i·zen·ry** \-rē\ *n* —**cit·i·zen·ship** *n*

cit·ron \'sitrən\ *n* : lemonlike fruit

cit·rus \'sitrəs\ *n, pl* **-rus** *or* **-rus·es** : evergreen tree or shrub grown for its fruit (as the orange or lemon)

city \'sitē\ *n, pl* **cit·ies** : place larger or more important than a town

civ·ic \'sivik\ *adj* : relating to citizenship or civil affairs

civ·ics \-iks\ *n* : study of citizenship

civ·il \'sivəl\ *adj* **1** : relating to citizens **2** : polite **3** : relating to or being a lawsuit —**civ·il·ly** *adv*

ci·vil·ian \sə'vilyən\ *n* : person not in a military, police, or fire-fighting force

ci·vil·i·ty \sə'vilətē\ *n, pl* **-ties** : courtesy

civ·i·li·za·tion \,sivələ'zāshən\ *n* **1** : high level of cultural development **2** : culture of a time or place

civ·i·lize \'sivə,līz\ *vb* **-lized; -liz·ing** : raise from a primitive stage of cultural development —**civ·i·lized** *adj*

civil liberty *n* : freedom from arbitrary governmental interference —usu. pl.

civil rights *n pl* : nonpolitical rights of a citizen

civil service *n* : government service

civil war *n* : war among citizens of one country

clack \'klak\ *vb* : make or cause a clatter —**clack** *n*

clad \'klad\ *adj* : covered

claim \'klām\ *vb* **1** : demand or take as the rightful owner **2** : maintain ~ *n* **1** : demand of right or ownership **2** : declaration **3** : something claimed —**claim·ant** \-ənt\ *n*

clair·voy·ant \klar'vöiənt\ *adj* : able to perceive things beyond the senses —**clair·voy·ance** \-əns\ *n* —**clairvoy·ant** *n*

clam \'klam\ *n* : bivalve mollusk

clam·ber \'klambər\ *vb* : climb awkwardly

clam·my \'klamē\ *adj* **-mi·er; -est** : being damp, soft, and usu. cool —**clam·mi·ness** *n*

clam·or \-ər\ *n* **1** : uproar **2** : protest —**clamor** *vb* —**clam·or·ous** *adj*

clamp \'klamp\ *n* : device for holding things together —**clamp** *vb*

clan \'klan\ *n* : group of related families —**clan·nish** *adj* —**clan·nish·ness** *n*

clan·des·tine \klan'destən\ *adj* : secret

clang \'klaŋ\ *n* : loud metallic ringing —**clang** *vb*

clan·gor \-ər, -gər\ *n* : jumble of clangs

clank \'klaŋk\ *n* : brief sound of struck metal —**clank** *vb*

clap \'klap\ *vb* **-pp- 1** : strike noisily **2** : applaud ~ *n* **1** : loud crash **2** : noise made by clapping the hands

clap·board \'klabərd, 'klap-, -,bōrd\ *n* : narrow tapered board used for siding

clap·per \'klapər\ *n* : tongue of a bell

claque \'klak\ *n* **1** : group hired to applaud at a performance **2** : group of sycophants

claret \'klarət\ *n* : dry red wine

clar·i·fy \'klarə,fī\ *vb* **-fied; -fy·ing** : make or become clear —**clar·i·fi·ca·tion** \,klarəfə'kāshən\ *n*

clar·i·net \,klarə'net\ *n* : woodwind instrument shaped like a tube —**clar·i·net·ist, clar·i·net·tist** \-ist\ *n*

clar·i·on \'klarēən\ *adj* : loud and clear

clar·i·ty \'klarətē\ *n* : clearness

clash \'klash\ *vb* **1** : make or cause a clash **2** : be in opposition or disharmony ~ *n* **1** : crashing sound **2** : hostile encounter

clasp \'klasp\ *n* **1** : device for holding things together **2** : embrace or grasp ~ *vb* **1** : fasten **2** : embrace or grasp

class \'klas\ *n* **1** : group of the same status or nature **2** : social rank **3** : course of instruction **4** : group of students ~ *vb* : classify —**class·less** *adj* —**class·mate** *n* —**class·room** *n*

clas·sic \'klasik\ *adj* **1** : serving as a standard of excellence **2** : classical ~ *n* : work of enduring excellence and esp. of ancient Greece or Rome —**clas·si·cal** \-ikəl\ *adj* —**clas·si·cal·ly** \-klē\ *adv* —**clas·si·cism** \'klasə,sizəm\ *n* —**clas·si·cist** \-sist\ *n*

clas·si·fied \'klasə,fīd\ *adj* : restricted for security reasons

clas·si·fy \-,fī\ *vb* **-fied; -fy·ing** : arrange in or assign to classes —**clas·si·fi·ca·tion** \,klasəfə'kāshən\ *n* —**clas·si·fi·er** \'klasə,fiər\ *n*

clat·ter \'klatər\ *n* : rattling sound —**clatter** *vb*

clause \'klóz\ *n* **1** : separate part of a document **2** : part of a sentence with a subject and predicate

claus·tro·pho·bia \,klóstrə'fōbēə\ *n* : fear of closed or narrow spaces —**claus·tro·pho·bic** \-bik\ *adj*

clav·i·chord \'klavə,kórd\ *n* : early keyboard instrument

clav·i·cle \'klavikəl\ *n* : collarbone

claw \'kló\ *n* : sharp curved nail or process (as on the toe of an animal) ~ *vb* : scratch or dig —**clawed** *adj*

clay \'klā\ *n* : plastic earthy material —**clay·ey** \-ē, -ā\ *adj*

clean \'klēn\ *adj* **1** : free from dirt or disease **2** : pure or honorable **3**

: thorough ~ *vb* : make or become clean —**clean** *adv* —**clean·er** *n*

clean·ly \-lē\ *adv* —**clean·ness** *n*

clean·ly \'klenlē\ *adj* -**li·er**; -**est** : clean —**clean·li·ness** *n*

cleanse \'klenz\ *vb* **cleansed**; **cleans·ing** : make clean —**cleans·er** *n*

clear \'klir\ *adj* **1** : bright 2 : free from clouds 3 : transparent 4 : easily heard, seen or understood 5 : free from doubt 6 : free from restriction or obstruction ~ *vb* **1** : make or become clear 2 : go away 3 : free from accusation or blame 4 : explain or settle 5 : net 6 : jump or pass without touching ~ *n* : clear space or part —**clear** *adv* —**clear·ance** \'klirəns\ *n*

clear·ing \'klirin\ *n* : land cleared of wood

clear·ly *adv* **1** : in a clear manner 2 : it is obvious that

cleat \'klēt\ *n* : projection that strengthens or prevents slipping

cleav·age \'klēvij\ *n* **1** : a splitting apart 2 : depression between a woman's breasts

¹cleave \'klēv\ *vb* **cleaved** \'klēvd\ *or* **clove** \'klōv\; **cleav·ing** : adhere

²cleave *vb* **cleaved** \'klēvd\; **cleav·ing** : split apart

cleav·er \'klēvər\ *n* : heavy chopping knife

clef \'klef\ *n* : sign on the staff in music to show pitch

cleft \'kleft\ *n* : crack

clem·ent \'klemənt\ *adj* **1** : merciful 2 : temperate or mild —**clem·en·cy** \-ənsē\ *n*

clench \'klench\ *vb* **1** : hold fast 2 : close tightly

cler·gy \'klərjē\ *n* : body of religious officials —**cler·gy·man** \-jimən\ *n*

cler·ic \'klerik\ *n* : member of the clergy

cler·i·cal \-ikəl\ *adj* **1** : relating to the clergy 2 : relating to a clerk or office worker

clerk \'klərk, *Brit* 'klärk\ *n* **1** : official responsible for record-keeping 2 : person doing general office work 3 : salesperson in a store —**clerk** *vb* —**clerk·ship** *n*

clev·er \'klevər\ *adj* **1** : resourceful 2 : marked by wit or ingenuity —**clev·er·ly** *adv* —**clev·er·ness** *n*

clew *var of* CLUE

cli·ché \kli'shā\ *n* : trite phrase —**cli·chéd** \-'shād\ *adj*

click \'klik\ *n* : slight sharp noise ~ *vb* : make or cause to make a click

cli·ent \'klīənt\ *n* **1** : person who engages professional services 2 : customer

cli·en·tele \,klīən'tel, ,klē-\ *n* : body of customers

cliff \'klif\ *n* : high steep face of rock

cli·mate \'klīmət\ *n* : average weather conditions over a period of years —**cli·mat·ic** \klī'matik\ *adj*

cli·max \'klī,maks\ *n* : the highest point ~ *vb* : come to a climax —**cli·mac·tic** \klī'maktik\ *adj*

climb \'klīm\ *vb* **1** : go up or down by use of hands and feet 2 : rise ~ *n* : a climbing —**climb·er** *n*

clinch \'klinch\ *vb* **1** : fasten securely 2 : settle 3 : hold fast or firmly —**clinch** *n* —**clinch·er** *n*

cling \'klin\ *vb* **clung** \'klən\; **cling·ing** **1** : adhere firmly 2 : hold on tightly

clin·ic \'klinik\ *n* : facility for diagnosis and treatment of outpatients —**clin·i·cal** \-əl\ *adj* —**clin·i·cal·ly** \-klē\ *adv*

clink \'klink\ *vb* : make a slight metallic sound —**clink** *n*

clin·ker \'klinkər\ *n* : fused stony matter esp. in a furnace

¹clip \'klip\ *vb* -**pp-** : fasten with a clip ~ *n* : device to hold things together

²clip *vb* -**pp-** **1** : cut or cut off 2 : hit ~ *n* **1** : clippers 2 : sharp blow 3 : rapid pace

clip·per \'klipər\ *n* **1** *pl* : implement for clipping 2 : fast sailing ship

clique \'klēk, 'klik\ *n* : small exclusive group of people

cli·to·ris \'klitərəs, kli'tōrəs\ *n*, *pl* **cli·to·ri·des** \-'tōrə,dēz\ : small organ at the front of the vulva

cloak \'klōk\ *n* **1** : loose outer garment 2 : something that conceals ~ *vb* : cover or hide with a cloak

clob·ber \'kläbər\ *vb* : hit hard

clock \'kläk\ *n* : timepiece not carried on the person ~ *vb* : record the time of

clock·wise \-,wīz\ *adv or adj* : in the same direction as a clock's hands move

clod \'kläd\ *n* **1** : lump esp. of earth 2 : dull insensitive person

clog \'kläg\ *n* **1** : restraining weight 2 : thick-soled shoe ~ *vb* -**gg-** **1** : impede with a clog 2 : obstruct passage through 3 : become plugged up

clois·ter \'klóistər\ *n* **1** : monastic establishment **2** : covered passage ~ *vb* : shut away from the world

clone \'klōn\ *n* **1** : offspring produced from a single organism **2** : copy

¹close \'klōz\ *vb* **closed; clos•ing 1** : shut **2** : cease operation **3** : terminate **4** : bring or come together ~ *n* : conclusion or end

²close \'klōs\ *adj* **clos•er; clos•est 1** : confining **2** : secretive **3** : strict **4** : stuffy **5** : having little space between items **6** : fitting tightly **7** : near **8** : intimate **9** : accurate **10** : nearly even **—close** *adv* **—close•ly** *adv* **—close•ness** *n*

clos•et \'kläzət, 'klóz-\ *n* : small compartment for household utensils or clothing ~ *vb* : take into a private room for a talk

clo•sure \'klōzhər\ *n* **1** : act of closing **2** : something that closes

clot \'klät\ *n* : dried mass of a liquid **—clot** *vb*

cloth \'klóth\ *n, pl* **cloths** \'klóthz, 'klóths\ **1** : fabric **2** : tablecloth

clothe \'klōth\ *vb* **clothed** *or* **clad** \'klad\; **cloth•ing** : dress

clothes \'klōthz, 'klōz\ *n pl* **1** : clothing **2** : bedclothes

cloth•ier \'klōthyər, -thēər\ *n* : maker or seller of clothing

cloth•ing \'klōthiŋ\ *n* : covering for the human body

cloud \'klaúd\ *n* **1** : visible mass of particles in the air **2** : something that darkens, hides, or threatens ~ *vb* : darken or hide **—cloud•i•ness** *n* **—cloud•less** *adj* **—cloudy** *adj*

cloud•burst *n* : sudden heavy rain

clout \'klaút\ *n* **1** : blow **2** : influence ~ *vb* : hit forcefully

¹clove \'klōv\ *n* : section of a bulb

²clove *past of* CLEAVE

³clove *n* : dried flower bud of an East Indian tree used as a spice

clo•ver \'klōvər\ *n* : leguminous herb with usu. 3-part leaves

clo•ver•leaf *n, pl* **-leafs** *or* **-leaves** : highway interchange

clown \'klaún\ *n* : funny costumed entertainer esp. in a circus ~ *vb* : act like a clown **—clown•ish** *adj* **—clown•ish•ly** *adv* **—clown•ish•ness** *n*

cloy \'klói\ *vb* : disgust with excess **cloy•ing•ly** \-iŋlē\ *adv*

club \'kləb\ *n* **1** : heavy wooden stick **2** : playing card of a suit marked with a black figure like a clover leaf **3**

: group associated for a common purpose ~ *vb* **-bb-** : hit with a club

club•foot *n* : misshapen foot twisted out of position from birth **—club•foot•ed** \-,fútəd\ *adj*

cluck \'klək\ *n* : sound made by a hen **—cluck** *vb*

clue \'klü\ *n* : piece of evidence that helps solve a problem ~ *vb* **clued; clue•ing** *or* **clu•ing** : provide with a clue

clump \'kləmp\ *n* **1** : cluster **2** : heavy tramping sound ~ *vb* : tread heavily

clum•sy \'kləmzē\ *adj* **-si•er; -est 1** : lacking dexterity, nimbleness, or grace **2** : tactless **—clum•si•ly** *adv* **—clum•si•ness** *n*

clung *past of* CLING

clunk•er \'kləŋkər\ *n* : old automobile

clus•ter \'kləstər\ *n* : group ~ *vb* : grow or gather in a cluster

clutch \'kləch\ *vb* : grasp ~ *n* **1** : grasping hand or claws **2** : control or power **3** : coupling for connecting two working parts in machinery

clut•ter \'klətər\ *vb* : fill with things that get in the way **—clutter** *n*

co- *prefix* : with, together, joint, or jointly

coact	cofounder
coactor	coheir
coauthor	coheiress
coauthorship	cohost
cocaptain	cohostess
cochairman	coinvent
cochampion	coinventor
cocomposer	coinvestigator
coconspirator	coleader
cocreator	comanagement
codefendant	comanager
codesign	co-organizer
codevelop	co-own
codeveloper	co-owner
codirect	copartner
codirector	copartnership
codiscoverer	copresident
codrive	coprincipal
codriver	coprisoner
coedit	coproduce
coeditor	coproducer
coexecutor	coproduction
coexist	copromoter
coexistence	coproprietor
coexistent	copublish
cofeature	copublisher
cofinance	corecipient
cofound	coresident

cosignatory cowinner
cosigner coworker
cosponsor cowrite
costar

coach \'kōch\ n 1 : closed 2-door 4-wheeled carriage 2 : railroad passenger car 3 : bus 4 : 2d-class air travel 5 : one who instructs or trains performers ~ vb : instruct or direct as a coach

co·ag·u·late \kō'agyə,lāt\ vb **-lat·ed; -lat·ing** : clot —**co·ag·u·lant** \-lənt\ n —**co·ag·u·la·tion** \-,agyə'lāshən\ n

coal \'kōl\ n 1 : ember 2 : black solid mineral used as fuel —**coal·field** n

co·alesce \,kōə'les\ vb **alesced; -alesc·ing** : grow together —**co·ales·cence** \-'les³ns\ n

co·ali·tion \-'lishən\ n : temporary alliance

coarse \'kōrs\ adj **coars·er; coars·est** 1 : composed of large particles 2 : rough or crude —**coarse·ly** adv —**coars·en** \-³n\ vb —**coarse·ness** n

coast \'kōst\ n : seashore ~ vb : move without effort —**coast·al** \-³l\ adj

coast·er \-ər\ n 1 : one that coasts 2 : plate or mat to protect a surface

coast guard n : military force that guards or patrols a coast —**coast-guards·man** \'kōst,gärdzmən\ n

coast·line n : shape of a coast

coat \'kōt\ n 1 : outer garment for the upper body 2 : external growth of fur or feathers 3 : covering layer ~ vb : cover with a coat —**coat·ed** adj —**coat·ing** n

coax \'kōks\ vb : move to action or achieve by gentle urging or flattery

cob \'käb\ n : corncob

co·balt \'kō,bolt\ n : shiny silver-white magnetic metallic chemical element

cob·ble \'käbəl\ vb **cob·bled; cob·bling** : make or put together hastily

cob·bler \'käblər\ n 1 : shoemaker 2 : deep-dish fruit pie

cob·ble·stone n : small round paving stone

co·bra \'kōbrə\ n : venomous snake

cob·web \'käb,web\ n : network spun by a spider or a similar filament

co·caine \kō'kān, 'kō,kān\ n : drug obtained from the leaves of a So. American shrub (**co·ca** \'kōkə\)

coch·lea \'kōklēə, 'käk-\ n, pl **-chle·ae** or **-chle·ae** \-lē,ē, -,ī\ : the usu. spiral

part of the inner ear —**coch·le·ar** \-lēər\ adj

cock \'käk\ n 1 : male fowl 2 : valve or faucet ~ vb 1 : draw back the hammer of a firearm 2 : tilt to one side —**cock·fight** n

cock·ade \kä'kād\ n : badge on a hat

cock·a·too \'käkə,tü\ n, pl **-toos** : large Australian crested parrot

cock·eyed \'käk'īd\ adj 1 : tilted to one side 2 : slightly crazy

cock·le \'käkəl\ n : edible shellfish

cock·pit \'käk,pit\ n : place for a pilot, driver, or helmsman

cock·roach n : nocturnal insect often infesting houses

cock·tail \'käk,tāl\ n 1 : iced drink of liquor and flavorings 2 : appetizer

cocky \'käkē\ adj **cock·ier; -est** : overconfident —**cock·i·ly** \-əlē\ adv —**cock·i·ness** n

co·coa \'kōkō\ n 1 : cacao 2 : powdered chocolate or a drink made from this

co·co·nut \'kōkə,nət\ n : large nutlike fruit of a tropical palm (**coconut palm**)

co·coon \kə'kün\ n : case protecting an insect pupa

cod \'käd\ n, pl **cod** : food fish of the No. Atlantic

cod·dle \'käd³l\ vb **-dled; -dling** : pamper

code \'kōd\ n 1 : system of laws or rules 2 : system of signals

co·deine \'kō,dēn\ n : narcotic drug used in cough remedies

cod·ger \'käjər\ n : odd fellow

cod·i·cil \'kädəsəl, -,sil\ n : postscript to a will

cod·i·fy \'kädə,fī, 'kōd-\ vb **-fied; -fy·ing** : arrange systematically —**cod·i·fi·ca·tion** \,kädəfə'kāshən, ,kōd-\ n

co·ed \'kō,ed\ n : female student in a coeducational institution —**coed** adj

co·ed·u·ca·tion \,kō-\ n : education of the sexes together —**co·ed·u·ca·tion·al** adj

co·ef·fi·cient \,kōə'fishənt\ n 1 : number that is a multiplier of another 2 : number that serves as a measure of some property

co·erce \kō'ərs\ vb **-erced; -erc·ing** : force —**co·er·cion** \-'ərzhən, -shən\ n —**co·er·cive** \-'ərsiv\ adj

cof·fee \'kofē\ n : drink made from the roasted and ground seeds (**coffee**

beans) of a tropical shrub —**cof·fee·house** n —**cof·fee·pot** n

cof·fer \'kȯfər\ n : box for valuables

cof·fin \-fən\ n : box for burial

cog \'käg\ n : tooth on the rim of a gear —**cogged** \'kägd\ adj —**cog·wheel** n

co·gent \'kōjənt\ adj : compelling or convincing —**co·gen·cy** \-jənsē\ n

cog·i·tate \'käjə,tāt\ vb -**tat·ed; -tat·ing** : think over —**cog·i·ta·tion** \,käjə'tā-shən\ n —**cog·i·ta·tive** \'käjə,tātiv\ adj

co·gnac \'kōn,yak\ n : French brandy

cog·nate \'käg,nāt\ adj : related —**cog·nate** n

cog·ni·tion \käg'nishən\ n : act or process of knowing —**cog·ni·tive** \'kägnətiv\ adj

cog·ni·zance \'kägnəzəns\ n : notice or awareness —**cog·ni·zant** \'kägnəzənt\ adj

co·hab·it \kō'habət\ vb : live together as husband and wife —**co·hab·i·ta·tion** \-,habə'tāshən\ n

co·here \kō'hir\ vb -**hered; -her·ing** : stick together

co·her·ent \-'hirənt\ adj 1 : able to stick together 2 : logically consistent —**co·her·ence** \-əns\ n —**co·her·ent·ly** adv

co·he·sion \-'hēzhən\ n : a sticking together —**co·he·sive** \-siv\ adj —**co·he·sive·ly** adv —**co·he·sive·ness** n

co·hort \'kō,hȯrt\ n 1 : group of soldiers 2 : companion

coif·fure \kwä'fyūr\ n : hair style

coil \'kȯil\ vb : wind in a spiral ~ n : series of loops (as of rope)

coin \'kȯin\ n : piece of metal used as money ~ vb 1 : make (a coin) by stamping 2 : create —**coin·age** \-ij\ n —**coin·er** n

co·in·cide \,kōən'sīd, 'kōən,sīd\ vb -**cid·ed; -cid·ing** 1 : be in the same place 2 : happen at the same time 3 : be alike —**co·in·ci·dence** \kō-'insədəns\ n —**co·in·ci·dent** \-ənt\ adj —**co·in·ci·den·tal** \-,insə'dentᵊl\ adj

co·itus \'kōətəs\ n : sexual intercourse —**co·ital** \-ətᵊl\ adj

coke \'kōk\ n : fuel made by heating soft coal

co·la \'kōlə\ n : carbonated soft drink

col·an·der \'kələndər, 'käl-\ n : perforated utensil for draining food

cold \'kōld\ adj 1 : having a low or below normal temperature 2 : lacking

warmth of feeling 3 : suffering from lack of warmth ~ n 1 : low temperature 2 : minor respiratory illness —**cold·ly** adv —**cold·ness** n —**in cold blood** : with premeditation

cold-blood·ed adj 1 : cruel or merciless 2 : having a body temperature that varies with the temperature of the environment

cole·slaw \'kōl,slȯ\ n : cabbage salad

col·ic \'kälik\ n : sharp abdominal pain —**col·icky** adj

col·i·se·um \,kälə'sēəm\ n : arena

col·lab·o·rate \kə'labə,rāt\ vb -**rat·ed; -rat·ing** 1 : work jointly with others 2 : help the enemy —**col·lab·o·ra·tion** \-,labə'rāshən\ n —**col·lab·o·ra·tor** \-'labə,rātər\ n

col·lapse \kə'laps\ vb -**lapsed; -laps·ing** 1 : fall in 2 : break down physically or mentally 3 : fold down ~ n : breakdown —**col·laps·ible** adj

col·lar \'kälər\ n : part of a garment around the neck ~ vb 1 : seize by the collar 2 : grab —**col·lar·less** adj

col·lar·bone n : bone joining the breastbone and the shoulder blade

col·lards \'kälərdz\ n pl : kale

col·late \kə'lāt; 'käl,āt, 'kōl-\ vb -**lat·ed; -lat·ing** 1 : compare carefully 2 : assemble in order

col·lat·er·al \kə'latərəl\ adj 1 : secondary 2 : descended from the same ancestors but not in the same line 3 : similar ~ n : property used as security for a loan

col·league \'käl,ēg\ n : associate

col·lect \kə'lekt\ vb 1 : bring, come, or gather together 2 : receive payment of ~ adv or adj : to be paid for by the receiver —**col·lect·ible, col·lect·able** adj —**col·lec·tion** \-'lekshən\ n —**col·lec·tor** \-'lektər\ n

col·lec·tive \-tiv\ adj : denoting or shared by a group ~ n : a cooperative unit —**col·lec·tive·ly** adv

col·lege \'kälij\ n : institution of higher learning granting a bachelor's degree —**col·le·gian** \kə'lējən\ n —**col·le·giate** \kə'lējət\ adj

col·lide \kə'līd\ vb -**lid·ed; -lid·ing** : strike together —**col·li·sion** \-'li-zhən\ n

col·lie \'kälē\ n : large long-haired dog

col·loid \'käl,ȯid\ n : tiny particles in suspension in a fluid —**col·loi·dal** \kə'lȯidᵊl\ adj

col·lo·qui·al \kə'lōkwēəl\ adj : used in

informal conversation —**col·lo·qui·al·ism** \-ə,lizəm\ *n*

col·lo·quy \'käləkwē\ *n, pl* **-quies** : formal conversation or conference

col·lu·sion \kə'lüzhən\ *n* : secret cooperation for deceit —**col·lu·sive** \-'lüsiv\ *adj*

co·logne \kə'lōn\ *n* : perfumed liquid

¹**co·lon** \'kōlən\ *n, pl* **colons** *or* **co·la** \-lə\ : lower part of the large intestine —**co·lon·ic** \kō'länik\ *adj*

²**colon** *n, pl* **colons** : punctuation mark : used esp. to direct attention to following matter

col·o·nel \'kərnᵊl\ *n* : commissioned officer (as in the army) ranking next below a brigadier general

col·o·nize \'kälə,nīz\ *vb* **-nized; -niz·ing** 1 : establish a colony in 2 : settle —**col·o·ni·za·tion** \kälənə'zāshən\ *n* —**col·o·niz·er** *n*

col·on·nade \,kälə'nād\ *n* : row of supporting columns

col·o·ny \'kälənē\ *n, pl* **-nies** 1 : people who inhabit a new territory or the territory itself 2 : animals of one kind (as bees) living together —**co·lo·nial** \kə'lōnēəl\ *adj or n* —**col·o·nist** \'kälənist\ *n*

col·or \'kələr\ *n* 1 : quality of visible things distinct from shape that results from light reflection 2 *pl* : flag 3 : liveliness ~ *vb* 1 : give color to 2 : blush —**col·or·fast** *adj* —**col·or·ful** *adj* —**col·or·less** *adj*

col·or-blind *adj* : unable to distinguish colors —**color blindness** *n*

col·ored \'kələrd\ *adj* 1 : having color 2 : of a race other than the white ~ *n, pl* **colored** *or* **coloreds** : colored person

co·los·sal \kə'läsəl\ *adj* : very large or great

co·los·sus \-əs\ *n, pl* **-si** \-'läs,ī\ : something of great size or scope

colt \'kōlt\ *n* : young male horse —**colt·ish** *adj*

col·umn \'käləm\ *n* 1 : vertical section of a printed page 2 : regular feature article (as in a newspaper) 3 : pillar 4 : row (as of soldiers) —**co·lum·nar** \kə'ləmnər\ *adj* —**col·um·nist** \'käləmnist\ *n*

co·ma \'kōmə\ *n* : deep prolonged unconsciousness —**co·ma·tose** \-,tōs, 'kämə-\ *adj*

comb \'kōm\ *n* 1 : toothed instrument for arranging the hair 2 : crest on a

fowl's head —**comb** *vb* —**combed** \'kōmd\ *adj*

com·bat \kəm'bat, 'käm,bat\ *vb* **-bat·ed** *or* **-bat·ted; -bat·ing** *or* **-bat·ting** : fight —**com·bat** \'käm,bat\ *n* —**com·bat·ant** \kəm'batᵊnt *n* —**com·bat·ive** \kəm'bativ\ *adj*

com·bi·na·tion \,kämbə'nāshən\ *n* 1 : process or result of combining 2 : code for opening a lock

com·bine \kəm'bīn\ *vb* **-bined; -bin·ing** : join together ~ \'käm,bīn\ *n* 1 : association for business or political advantage 2 : harvesting machine

com·bus·ti·ble \kəm'bəstəbəl\ *adj* : apt to catch fire —**com·bus·ti·bil·i·ty** \-,bəstə'bilətē\ *n* —**combustible** *n*

com·bus·tion \-'bəschən\ *n* : process of burning

come \'kəm\ *vb* **came** \'kām\; **come; com·ing** 1 : move toward or arrive at something 2 : reach a state 3 : originate or exist 4 : amount —**come clean** *vb* : confess —**come into** *vb* : acquire, achieve —**come off** *vb* : succeed —**come to** *vb* : regain consciousness —**come to pass** : happen —**come to terms** : reach an agreement

come·back *n* 1 : retort 2 : return to a former position —**come back** *vb*

co·me·di·an \kə'mēdēən\ *n* 1 : comic actor 2 : funny person 3 : entertainer specializing in comedy

co·me·di·enne \-,mēdē'en\ *n* : a woman who is a comedian

com·e·dy \'kämədē\ *n, pl* **-dies** 1 : an amusing play 2 : humorous entertainment

come·ly \'kəmlē\ *adj* **-li·er; -est** : attractive —**come·li·ness** *n*

com·et \'kämət\ *n* : small bright celestial body having a tail

com·fort \'kəmfərt\ *n* 1 : consolation 2 : well-being or something that gives it ~ *vb* 1 : give hope to 2 : console —**com·fort·able** \'kəmftəbəl, 'kəmfərt-\ *adj* —**com·fort·ably** \-blē\ *adv* —**com·fort·less** *adj*

com·fort·er \'kəmfərtər\ *n* 1 : one that comforts 2 : quilt

com·ic \'kämik\ *adj* 1 : relating to comedy 2 : funny ~ *n* 1 : comedian 2 : sequence of cartoons —**com·i·cal** *adj*

com·ing \'kəmin\ *adj* : next

com·ma \'kämə\ *n* : punctuation mark , used esp. to separate sentence parts

com·mand \kə'mand\ *vb* **1** : order **2** : control ~ *n* **1** : act of commanding **2** : an order given **3** : mastery **4** : troops under a commander —**com·man·dant** \'kämən,dant, -,dänt\ *n*

com·man·deer \,kär ən'dir\ *vb* : seize by force

com·mand·er \kə'mandər\ *n* **1** : officer commanding an army or subdivision of an army **2** : commissioned officer in the navy ranking next below a captain

com·mand·ment \-'mandmənt\ *n* : order

command sergeant major *n* : noncommissioned officer in the army ranking above a first sergeant

com·mem·o·rate \kə'memə,rāt\ *vb* **-rat·ed; -rat·ing** : celebrate or honor —**com·mem·o·ra·tion** \-,memə'rāshən\ *n* —**com·mem·o·ra·tive** \-'memrətiv, -'memə,rāt-\ *adj*

com·mence \kə'mens\ *vb* **-menced; -menc·ing** : start

com·mence·ment \-mənt\ *n* **1** : beginning **2** : graduation ceremony

com·mend \kə'mend\ *vb* **1** : entrust **2** : recommend **3** : praise —**commend·able** \-əbəl\ *adj* —**com·men·da·tion** \,kämən'dāshən, -,en-\ *n*

com·men·su·rate \kə'mensərət, -'mench-\ *adj* : equal in measure or extent

com·ment \'käm,ent\ *n* : statement of opinion or remark —**comment** *vb*

com·men·tary \-ən,terē\ *n, pl* **-tar·ies** : series of comments

com·men·ta·tor \-ən,tātər\ *n* : one who discusses news

com·merce \'kämərs\ *n* : business

com·mer·cial \kə'mərshəl\ *adj* : designed for profit or for mass appeal ~ *n* : broadcast advertisement —**commer·cial·ize** \-,īz\ *vb* —**com·mer·cial·ly** \-ē\ *adv*

com·min·gle \kə'miŋgəl\ *vb* : mix

com·mis·er·ate \kə'mizə,rāt\ *vb* **-at·ed; at·ing** : sympathize —**com·mis·era·tion** \-,mizə'rāshən\ *n*

com·mis·sary \'kämə,serē\ *n, pl* **-sar·ies** : store esp. for military personnel

com·mis·sion \kə'mishən\ *n* **1** : order granting power or rank **2** : panel to judge, approve, or act **3** : the doing of an act **4** : agent's fee ~ *vb* **1** : confer rank or authority to or for **2** : request something be done

com·mis·sion·er \-shənər\ *n* **1** : member of a commission **2** : head of a government department

com·mit \kə'mit\ *vb* **-tt-** **1** : turn over to someone for safekeeping or confinement **2** : perform or do **3** : pledge —**com·mit·ment** *n*

com·mit·tee \kə'mitē\ *n* : panel that examines or acts on something

com·mo·di·ous \kə'mōdēəs\ *adj* : spacious

com·mod·i·ty \kə'mädətē\ *n, pl* **-ties** : article for sale

com·mo·dore \'kämə,dōr\ *n* **1** : former commissioned officer in the navy ranking next below a rear admiral **2** : officer commanding a group of merchant ships

com·mon \'kämən\ *adj* **1** : public or shared by several **3** : widely known, found, or observed **4** : ordinary ~ *n* : community land —**com·mon·ly** *adv* —**in common** : shared together

com·mon·place \'kämən,plās\ *n* : cliché ~ *adj* : ordinary

common sense *n* : good judgment

com·mon·weal \-,wēl\ *n* : general welfare

com·mon·wealth \-,welth\ *n* : state

com·mo·tion \kə'mōshən\ *n* : disturbance

¹com·mune \kə'myün\ *vb* **-muned; -mun·ing** : communicate intimately

²com·mune \'käm,yün; kə'myün\ *n* : community that shares all ownership and duties —**com·mu·nal** \-ᵊl\ *adj*

com·mu·ni·cate \kə'myünə,kāt\ *vb* **-cat·ed; -cat·ing** **1** : make known **2** : transmit **3** : exchange information or opinions —**com·mu·ni·ca·ble** \-'myünikəbəl\ *adj* —**com·mu·ni·ca·tion** \-,myünə'kāshən\ *n* —**com·mu·ni·ca·tive** \-'myüni,kātiv, -kət-\ *adj*

Com·mu·nion \kə'myünyən\ *n* : Christian sacrament of partaking of bread and wine

com·mu·ni·qué \kə'myünə,kā, -,myünə'kā\ *n* : official bulletin

com·mu·nism \'kämyə,nizəm\ *n* **1** : social organization in which goods are held in common **2** *cap* : political doctrine based on revolutionary Marxist socialism —**com·mu·nist** \-nist\ *n or adj, often cap* —**com·mu·nis·tic** \,kämyə'nistik\ *adj, often cap*

com·mu·ni·ty \kə'myünətē\ *n, pl* **-ties**

: body of people living in the same place under the same laws

com·mute \kə'myüt\ vb **-mut·ed; -mut·ing 1** : reduce (a punishment) **2** : travel back and forth regularly ~ n : trip made in commuting —**com·mu·ta·tion** \ˌkämyə'tāshən\ n —**com·mut·er** n

¹**com·pact** \kəm'pakt, 'käm,pakt\ adj **1** : hard **2** : small or brief ~ vb : pack together ~ \'käm,pakt\ n **1** : cosmetics case **2** : small car —**com·pact·ly** adv —**com·pact·ness** n

²**com·pact** \'käm,pakt\ n : agreement

compact disc n : plastic-coated disc with laser-readable recorded music

com·pan·ion \kəm'panyən\ n **1** : close friend **2** : one of a pair —**com·pan·ion·able** adj —**com·pan·ion·ship** n

com·pa·ny \'kəmpənē\ n, pl **-nies 1** : business organization **2** : group of performers **3** : guests **4** : infantry unit

com·par·a·tive \kəm'parətiv\ adj **1** : relating to or being an adjective or adverb form that denotes increase **2** : relative —**comparative** n —**com·par·a·tive·ly** adv

com·pare \kəm'par\ vb **-pared; -par·ing 1** : represent as similar **2** : check for likenesses or differences ~ n : comparison —**com·pa·ra·ble** \'kämprəbəl\ adj

com·par·i·son \kəm'parəsən\ n **1** : act of comparing **2** : change in the form and meaning of an adjective or adverb to show different levels of quality, quantity, or relation

com·part·ment \kəm'pärtmənt\ n : section or room

com·pass \'kəmpəs, 'käm-\ n **1** : scope **2** : device for drawing circles **3** : device for determining direction

com·pas·sion \kəm'pashən\ n : pity —**com·pas·sion·ate** \-ənət\ adj

com·pat·i·ble \-'patəbəl\ adj : harmonious —**com·pat·i·bil·i·ty** \-ˌpatə'bilətē\ n

com·pa·tri·ot \kəm'pātrēət, -trē,ät\ n : fellow countryman

com·pel \kəm'pel\ vb **-ll- :** cause through necessity

com·pen·di·ous \kam'pendēəs\ adj **1** : concise and comprehensive **2** : comprehensive

com·pen·di·um \-'pendēəm\ n, pl **-di·ums** or **-dia** \-dēə\ : summary

com·pen·sate \'kämpən,sāt\ vb **-sat·ed;**

-sat·ing 1 : offset or balance **2** : repay —**com·pen·sa·tion** \ˌkämpən'sāshən\ n —**com·pen·sa·to·ry** \kəm'pensə-ˌtōrē\ adj

com·pete \kəm'pēt\ vb **-pet·ed; -pet·ing** : strive to win —**com·pe·ti·tion** \ˌkämpə'tishən\ n —**com·pet·i·tive** \kəm'petətiv\ adj —**com·pet·i·tive·ness** n —**com·pet·i·tor** \kəm'petətər\ n

com·pe·tent \'kämpətənt\ adj : capable —**com·pe·tence** \-əns\ n —**com·pe·ten·cy** \-ənsē\ n

com·pile \kəm'pīl\ vb **-piled; -pil·ing** : collect or compose from several sources —**com·pi·la·tion** \ˌkämpə-'lāshən\ n —**com·pil·er** \kəm'pīlər\ n

com·pla·cen·cy \kəm'plāsənsē\ n : self-satisfaction —**com·pla·cent** \-ᵊnt\ adj

com·plain \kəm'plān\ vb **1** : express grief, pain, or discontent **2** : make an accusation —**com·plain·ant** n —**com·plain·er** n

com·plaint \-'plānt\ n **1** : expression of grief or discontent **2** : ailment **3** : formal accusation

com·ple·ment \'kämpləmənt\ n **1** : something that completes **2** : full number or amount ~ \-ˌment\ vb : complete —**com·ple·men·ta·ry** \ˌkämplə'mentərē\ adj

com·plete \kəm'plēt\ adj **-plet·er; -est 1** : having all parts **2** : finished **3** : total ~ vb **-plet·ed; -plet·ing 1** : make whole **2** : finish —**com·plete·ly** adv —**com·plete·ness** n —**com·ple·tion** \-'plēshən\ n

com·plex \käm'pleks, kəm-; 'käm-ˌpleks\ adj **1** : having many parts **2** : intricate ~ \'käm,pleks\ n : psychological problem —**com·plex·i·ty** \käm'pleksətē, kəm-\ n

com·plex·ion \kəm'plekshən\ n : hue or appearance of the skin esp. of the face —**com·plex·ioned** adj

com·pli·cate \'kämplə,kāt\ vb **-cat·ed; -cat·ing** : make complex or hard to understand —**com·pli·cat·ed** \-əd\ adj —**com·pli·ca·tion** \ˌkämplə-'kāshən\ n

com·plic·i·ty \kəm'plisətē\ n. pl **-ties** : participation in guilt

com·pli·ment \'kämpləmənt\ n **1** : flattering remark **2** pl : greeting ~ \-ˌment\ vb : pay a compliment to

com·pli·men·ta·ry \,kämplə'mentərē\ adj **1** : praising **2** : free

com·ply \kəm'plī\ vb **-plied; -ply·ing** : conform or yield **—com·pli·ance** \-əns\ n **—com·pli·ant** \-ənt\ n

com·po·nent \kəm'pōnənt, 'käm,pō-\ n : part of something larger ~ adj : serving as a component

com·port \kəm'pōrt\ vb **1** : agree **2** : behave **—com·port·ment** \-mənt\ n

com·pose \kəm'pōz\ vb **-posed; -pos·ing 1** : create (as by writing) or put together **2** : set type **—com·pos·er** n **—com·po·si·tion** \,kämpə'zishən\ n

com·pos·ite \käm'päzət, kəm-\ adj : made up of diverse parts **—com·posite** n

com·post \'käm,pōst\ n : decayed organic fertilizing material

com·po·sure \kəm'pōzhər\ n : calmness

com·pote \'käm,pōt\ n : fruits cooked in syrup

[1]com·pound \'käm,paund, käm'paund\ vb **1** : combine or add **2** : pay (interest) on principal and accrued interest ~ \'käm,paund\ adj : made up of 2 or more parts ~ \'käm,paund\ n : something that is compound

[2]com·pound \'käm,paund\ n : enclosure

com·pre·hend \,kämpri'hend\ vb **1** : understand **2** : include **—com·pre·hen·si·ble** \-'hensəbəl\ adj **—com·pre·hen·sion** \-'henchən\ n **—com·pre·hen·sive** \-siv\ adj

com·press \kəm'pres\ vb : squeeze together ~ \'käm,pres\ n : pad for pressing on a wound **—com·pres·sion** \-'preshən\ n **—com·pres·sor** \-'presər\ n

compressed air n : air under pressure greater than that of the atmosphere

com·prise \kəm'prīz\ vb **-prised; -pris·ing 1** : contain or cover **2** : be made up of

com·pro·mise \'kämprə,mīz\ vb **-mised; -mis·ing** : settle differences by mutual concessions **—compromise** n

comp·trol·ler \kən'trōlər, 'kämp,trō-\ n : financial officer

com·pul·sion \kəm'pəlshən\ n **1** : coercion **2** : irresistible impulse **—com·pul·sive** \-siv\ adj **—com·pul·sory** \-'pəlsərē\ adj

com·punc·tion \-'pənkshən\ n : remorse

com·pute \-'pyüt\ vb **-put·ed; -put·ing**

: calculate **—com·pu·ta·tion** \,kämpyü'tāshən\ n

com·put·er \kəm'pyütər\ n : electronic data processing machine **—com·put·er·iza·tion** \-,pyütərə'zāshən\ n **—com·put·er·ize** \-'pyütə,rīz\ vb

com·rade \'käm,rad, -rəd\ n : companion **—com·rade·ship** n

[1]con \'kän\ adv : against ~ n : opposing side or person

[2]con \"\ vb **-nn-** : swindle

con·cave \kän'kāv, 'kän,kāv\ adj : curved like the inside of a sphere **—con·cav·i·ty** \kän'kavətē\ n

con·ceal \kən'sēl\ vb : hide **—con·ceal·ment** n

con·cede \-'sēd\ vb **-ced·ed; -ced·ing** : grant

con·ceit \-'sēt\ n : excessively high opinion of oneself **—con·ceit·ed** \-əd\ adj

con·ceive \-'sēv\ vb **-ceived; -ceiv·ing 1** : become pregnant **2** : think of **—con·ceiv·able** \-'sēvəbəl\ adj **—con·ceiv·ably** \-blē\ adv

con·cen·trate \'känsən,trāt\ vb **-trat·ed; -trat·ing 1** : gather together **2** : make stronger **3** : fix one's attention ~ n : something concentrated **—con·cen·tra·tion** \,känsən'trāshən\ n

con·cen·tric \kən'sentrik\ adj : having a common center

con·cept \'kän,sept\ n : thought or idea

con·cep·tion \kən'sepshən\ n **1** : act of conceiving **2** : idea

con·cern \kən'sərn\ vb **1** : relate to **2** : involve ~ n **1** : affair **2** : worry **3** : business **—con·cerned** \-'sərnd\ adj **—con·cern·ing** \-'sərnin\ prep

con·cert \'kän,sərt\ n **1** : agreement or joint action **2** : public performance of music **—con·cert·ed** \kən'sərtəd\ adj

con·cer·ti·na \,känsər'tēnə\ n : accordionlike instrument

con·cer·to \kən'chertō\ n, pl **-ti** \-tē\ or **-tos** : orchestral work with solo instruments

con·ces·sion \-'seshən\ n **1** : act of conceding **2** : something conceded **3** : right to do business on a property

conch \'känk, 'känch\ n, pl **conchs** \'känks\ or **conch·es** \'känchəz\ : large spiral-shelled marine mollusk

con·cil·ia·to·ry \kən'silēə,tōrē\ adj : mollifying

con·cise \kən'sīs\ adj : said in few words **—con·cise·ly** adv **—con·cise·ness** n **—con·ci·sion** \kən'sizhən\ n

con·clave \'kän,klāv\ n : private meeting

con·clude \kən'klüd\ vb **-clud·ed;**
-clud·ing 1 : end **2** : decide **—con·**
clu·sion \-'klüzhən\ n **—con·clu·sive**
\-siv\ adj **—con·clu·sive·ly** adv

con·coct \kən'käkt, kän-\ vb : prepare or
devise **—con·coc·tion** \-'käkshən\
n

con·com·i·tant \-'kämətənt\ adj : accompanying **—concomitant** n

con·cord \'kän,kȯrd, 'käŋ-\ n : agreement

con·cor·dance \kən'kȯrdəns\ n **1**
: agreement **2** : index of words **—**
con·cor·dant \-ᵊnt\ adj

con·course \'kän,kȯrs\ n : open space
where crowds gather

con·crete \kän'krēt, 'kän,krēt\ adj **1**
: naming something real **2** : actual or
substantial **3** : made of concrete **—**
\'kän,krēt, kän'krēt\ n : hard building
material made of cement, sand,
gravel, and water

con·cre·tion \kän'krēshən\ n : hard
mass

con·cu·bine \'käŋkyu̇,bīn\ n : mistress

con·cur \kən'kər\ vb **-rr-** : agree **—con·**
cur·rence \-'kərəns\ n

con·cur·rent \-ənt\ adj : happening at
the same time

con·cus·sion \kən'kəshən\ n **1** : shock **2**
: brain injury from a blow

con·demn \-'dem\ vb **1** : declare to be
wrong, guilty, or unfit for use **2**
: sentence **—con·dem·na·tion** \,kän-
,dem'nāshən\ n

con·dense \kən'dens\ vb **-densed;**
-dens·ing 1 : make or become more
compact **2** : change from vapor to liquid **—con·den·sa·tion** \,kän,den-
'sāshən, -dən-\ n **—con·dens·er** n

con·de·scend \,kändi'send\ vb **1** : lower
oneself **2** : act haughtily **—con·de·**
scen·sion \-'senchən\ n

con·di·ment \'kändəmənt\ n : pungent
seasoning

con·di·tion \kən'dishən\ n **1** : necessary
situation or stipulation **2** pl : state of
affairs **3** : state of being ~ vb : put
into proper condition **—con·di·tion·**
al \kən'dishənəl\ adj **—con·di·tion·**
al·ly \-ē\ adv

con·do·lence \kən'dōləns\ n : expression of sympathy—usu. pl.

con·do·min·i·um \,kändə'minēəm\ n,
pl **-ums** : individually owned apartments

con·done \kən'dōn\ vb **-doned; -don·**
ing : overlook or forgive

con·dor \'kändər, -,dȯr\ n : large western American vulture

con·du·cive \kən'düsiv, -'dyü-\ adj
: tending to help or promote

con·duct \'kän,dəkt, kän-\ n **1** : management
2 : behavior ~ \kən'dəkt\ vb **1** : guide
2 : manage or direct **3** : be a channel
for **4** : behave **—con·duc·tion**
\-'dəkshən\ n **—con·duc·tive** \-'dək-
tiv\ adj **—con·duc·tiv·i·ty** \,kän,dək-
'tivətē\ n **—con·duc·tor** \-'dəktər\
n

con·duit \'kän,düət, -,dyü-\ n : channel
(as for conveying fluid)

cone \'kōn\ n **1** : scaly fruit of pine
and related trees **2** : solid figure
having a circular base and tapering
sides

con·fec·tion \kən'fekshən\ n : sweet
dish or candy **—con·fec·tion·er**
\-shənər\ n

con·fed·er·a·cy \kən'fedərəsē\ n, pl
-cies 1 : league **2** cap : 11 southern
states that seceded from the U.S. in
1860 and 1861

con·fed·er·ate \-rət\ adj **1** : united in a
league **2** cap : relating to the Confederacy ~ n **1** : ally **2** cap : adherent of
the Confederacy ~ \-'fedə,rāt\ vb **-at·**
ed; -at·ing : unite **—con·fed·er·a·**
tion \-,fedə'rāshən\ n

con·fer \kən'fər\ vb **-rr- 1** : give **2**
: meet to exchange views **—con·fer·**
ee \,känfə'rē\ n **—con·fer·ence**
\'känfərəns\ n

con·fess \kən'fes\ vb **1** : acknowledge or
disclose one's misdeed, fault, or sin **2**
: declare faith in **—con·fes·sion**
\-'feshən\ n **—con·fes·sion·al** \-'fesh-
ənəl\ n or adj

con·fes·sor \kən'fesər, 2 also 'kän,fes-\
n **1** : one who confesses **2** : priest who
hears confessions

con·fet·ti \kən'fetē\ n : bits of paper or
ribbon thrown in celebration

con·fi·dant \'känfə,dant, -,dänt\ n : one
to whom secrets are confided

con·fide \kən'fīd\ vb **-fid·ed; -fid·ing 1**
: share private thoughts **2** : reveal in
confidence

con·fi·dence \'känfədəns\ n **1** : trust **2**
: self-assurance **3** : something confided **—con·fi·dent** \-ənt\ adj **—con·**
fi·den·tial \,känfə'denchəl\ adj **—**
con·fi·den·tial·ly \-ē\ adv **—con·fi·**
dent·ly adv

con·fig·u·ra·tion \kən,figyə'rāshən\ n
: arrangement

con·fine \kən'fīn\ *vb* **-fined; -fin·ing 1** : restrain or restrict to a limited area **2** : imprison **—con·fine·ment** *n* **—con·fin·er** *n*

confines \'kän,fīnz\ *n pl* : bounds

con·firm \kən'fərm\ *vb* **1** : ratify **2** : verify **3** : admit as a full member of a church or synagogue **—con·fir·ma·tion** \,känfər'māshən\ *n*

con·fis·cate \'känfə,skāt\ *vb* **-cat·ed; -cat·ing** : take by authority **—con·fis·ca·tion** \,känfə'skāshən\ *n* **—con·fis·ca·to·ry** \kən'fiskə,tōrē\ *adj*

con·fla·gra·tion \,känflə'grāshən\ *n* : great fire

con·flict \'kän,flikt\ *n* **1** : war **2** : clash of ideas ~ \kən'flikt\ *vb* : clash

con·form \kən'form\ *vb* **1** : make or be like **2** : obey **—con·for·mi·ty** \kən'formətē\ *n*

con·found \kən'faúnd, kän-\ *vb* : confuse

con·front \kən'frənt\ *vb* : oppose or face **—con·fron·ta·tion** \,känfrən-'tā-shən\ *n*

con·fuse \kən'fyüz\ *vb* **-fused; -fus·ing 1** : make mentally uncertain **2** : jumble **—con·fu·sion** \-'fyüzhən\ *n*

con·fute \-'fyüt\ *vb* **-fut·ed; -fut·ing** : overwhelm by argument

con·geal \kən'jēl\ *vb* **1** : freeze **2** : become thick and solid

con·ge·nial \kən'jēnēəl\ *adj* : kindred or agreeable **—con·ge·ni·al·i·ty** *n*

con·gen·i·tal \kən'jenət*ə*l\ *adj* : existing from birth

con·gest \kən'jest\ *vb* : overcrowd or overfill **—con·ges·tion** \-'jeschən\ *n* **—con·ges·tive** \-'jestiv\ *adj*

con·glom·er·ate \kən'glämərət\ *adj* : made up of diverse parts ~ \-ə,rāt\ *vb* **-at·ed; -at·ing** : form into a mass ~ \-ərət\ *n* : diversified corporation **—con·glom·er·a·tion** \-,glämə'rā-shən\ *n*

con·grat·u·late \kən'grachə,lāt, -'graj-\ *vb* **-lat·ed; -lat·ing** : express pleasure to for good fortune **—con·grat·u·la·tion** \-,grachə'lāshən, -,graj-\ *n* **—con·grat·u·la·to·ry** \-'grachələ,tōrē-'graj-\ *adj*

con·gre·gate \'kängri,gāt\ *vb* **-gat·ed; -gat·ing** : assemble

con·gre·ga·tion \,kängri'gāshən\ *n* **1** : assembly of people at worship **2** : religious group **—con·gre·ga·tion·al** \-shənəl\ *adj*

con·gress \'käŋgrəs\ *n* : assembly of delegates or of senators and representatives **—con·gres·sio·nal** \kən-'greshənəl, kän-\ *adj* **—con·gress·man** \'käŋgrəsmən\ *n* **—con·gress·wom·an** *n*

con·gru·ence \kən'grüəns, 'käŋgrə-wəns\ *n* : likeness **—con·gru·ent** \-ənt\ *adj*

con·gru·ity \kən'grüətē, kän-\ *n* : correspondence between things **—con·gru·ous** \'käŋgrəwəs\ *adj*

con·ic \'känik\ *adj* : relating to or like a cone **—con·i·cal** \-ikəl\ *adj*

co·ni·fer \'känəfər, 'kōn-\ *n* : cone-bearing tree **—co·nif·er·ous** \kō'nifərəs\ *adj*

con·jec·ture \kən'jekchər\ *n* or *vb* : guess **—con·jec·tur·al** \-əl\ *adj*

con·join \kən'join\ *vb* : join together **—con·joint** \-'joint\ *adj*

con·ju·gal \'känjigəl, kən'jü-\ *adj* : relating to marriage

con·ju·gate \'känjə,gāt\ *vb* **-gat·ed; -gat·ing** : give the inflected forms of (a verb) **—con·ju·ga·tion** \,känjə-'gāshən\ *n*

con·junc·tion \kən'jəŋkshən\ *n* **1** : combination **2** : occurrence at the same time **3** : a word that joins other words together **—con·junc·tive** \-tiv\ *adj*

con·jure \'känjər, 'kən-\ *vb* **-jured; -jur·ing 1** : summon by sorcery **2** : practice sleight of hand **3** : entreat **—con·jur·er, con·ju·ror** \'känjərər, 'kən-\ *n*

con·nect \kə'nekt\ *vb* : join or associate **—con·nect·able** *adj* **—con·nec·tion** \-'nekshən\ *n* **—con·nec·tive** \-tiv\ *n or adj* **—con·nec·tor** *n*

con·nive \kə'nīv\ *vb* **-nived; -niv·ing 1** : pretend ignorance of wrongdoing **2** : cooperate secretly **—con·niv·ance** *n*

con·nois·seur \,känə'sər, -'sür\ *n* : expert judge esp. of art

con·note \kə'nōt\ *vb* **-not·ed; -not·ing** : suggest additional meaning **—con·no·ta·tion** \,känə'tāshən\ *n*

con·nu·bi·al \kə'nübēəl, -'nyü-\ *adj* : relating to marriage

con·quer \'käŋkər\ *vb* : defeat or overcome **—con·quer·or** \-kərər\ *n*

con·quest \'kän,kwest, 'käŋ-\ *n* **1** : act of conquering **2** : something conquered

con·science \'känchəns\ *n* : awareness of right and wrong

con·sci·en·tious \,känchē'enchəs\ *adj*

: honest and hard-working —**con·sci·en·tious·ly** adv

con·scious \'känchəs\ adj 1 : aware 2 : mentally awake or alert 3 : intentional —**con·scious·ly** adv —**con·scious·ness** n

con·script \kən'skript\ vb : draft for military service —**con·script** \'kän‚skript\ n —**con·scrip·tion** \kən'skripshən\ n

con·se·crate \'känsə‚krāt\ vb **-crat·ed; -crat·ing** 1 : declare sacred 2 : devote to a solemn purpose —**con·se·cra·tion** \‚känsə'krāshən\ n

con·sec·u·tive \kən'sekyətiv\ adj : following in order —**con·sec·u·tive·ly** adv

con·sen·sus \-'sensəs\ n 1 : agreement in opinion 2 : collective opinion

con·sent \-'sent\ vb : give permission or approval —**consent** n

con·se·quence \'känsə‚kwens\ n 1 : result or effect 2 : importance —**con·se·quent** \-kwənt, -‚kwent\ adj —**con·se·quent·ly** adv

con·se·quen·tial \‚känsə'kwenchəl\ adj : important

con·ser·va·tion \‚känsər'vāshən\ n : planned management of natural resources —**con·ser·va·tion·ist** \-shənist\ n

con·ser·va·tive \kən'sərvətiv\ adj 1 : disposed to maintain the status quo 2 : cautious —**con·ser·va·tism** \-və‚tizəm\ n —**conservative** n —**con·ser·va·tive·ly** adv

con·ser·va·to·ry \kən'sərvə‚tōrē\ n, pl **-ries** : school for art or music

con·serve \-'sərv\ vb **-served; -serv·ing** : keep from wasting ~ \'kän‚sərv\ n : candied fruit or fruit preserves

con·sid·er \kən'sidər\ vb 1 : think about 2 : give thoughtful attention to 3 : think that —**con·sid·er·ate** \-'sidərət\ adj —**con·sid·er·a·tion** \-‚sidə'rāshən\ n

con·sid·er·able \-'sidərəbəl\ adj 1 : significant 2 : noticeably large —**con·sid·er·a·bly** \-blē\ adv

con·sid·er·ing prep : taking notice of

con·sign \kən'sīn\ vb 1 : transfer 2 : send to an agent for sale —**con·sign·ee** \‚känsə'nē, -‚sī-; kən‚sī-\ n —**con·sign·ment** \kən'sīnmənt\ n —**con·sign·or** \‚känsə'nȯr, -‚sī-; kən‚sī-\ n

con·sist \kən'sist\ vb 1 : be inherent —

used with in 2 : be made up —used with of

con·sis·ten·cy \-'sistənsē\ n, pl **-cies** 1 : degree of thickness or firmness 2 : quality of being consistent

con·sis·tent \-tənt\ adj : being steady and regular —**con·sis·tent·ly** adv

¹**con·sole** \kən'sōl\ vb **-soled; -sol·ing** : soothe the grief of —**con·so·la·tion** \‚känsə'lāshən\ n

²**con·sole** \'kän‚sōl\ n : cabinet or part with controls

con·sol·i·date \kən'sälə‚dāt\ vb **-dat·ed; -dat·ing** : unite or compact —**con·sol·i·da·tion** \-‚sälə'dāshən\ n

con·som·mé \‚känsə'mā\ n : clear soup

con·so·nance \'känsənəns\ n : agreement or harmony —**con·so·nant** \-nənt\ adj —**con·so·nant·ly** adv

con·so·nant \-nənt\ n 1 : speech sound marked by constriction or closure in the breath channel 2 : letter other than a, e, i, o, and u —**con·so·nan·tal** \‚känsə'nant³l\ adj

con·sort \'kän‚sȯrt\ n : spouse ~ \kən'sȯrt\ vb : keep company

con·spic·u·ous \kən'spikyəwəs\ adj : very noticeable —**con·spic·u·ous·ly** adv

con·spire \kən'spīr\ vb **-spired; -spir·ing** : secretly plan an unlawful act —**con·spir·a·cy** \-'spirəsē\ n —**con·spir·a·tor** \-'spirətər\ n —**con·spir·a·to·ri·al** \-‚spirə'tōrēəl\ adj

con·sta·ble \'känstəbəl, 'kən-\ n : police officer

con·stab·u·lary \kən'stabyə‚lerē\ n, pl **-lar·ies** : police force

con·stant \'känstənt\ adj 1 : steadfast or faithful 2 : not varying 3 : continually recurring ~ n : something unchanging —**con·stan·cy** \-stənsē\ n —**con·stant·ly** adv

con·stel·la·tion \‚känstə'lāshən\ n : group of stars

con·ster·na·tion \-stər'nāshən\ n : amazed dismay

con·sti·pa·tion \‚känstə'pāshən\ n : difficulty of defecation —**con·sti·pate** \'känstə‚pāt\ vb

con·stit·u·ent \kən'stichəwənt\ adj 1 : component 2 : having power to elect ~ n 1 : component part 2 : one who may vote for a representative —**con·stit·u·en·cy** \-wənsē\ n

con·sti·tute \'känstə‚tüt, -‚tyüt\ vb

-tut·ed; -tut·ing 1 : establish 2 : be all or a basic part of

con·sti·tu·tion \,känstə'tüshən, -'tyü-\ n 1 : physical composition or structure 2 : the basic law of an organized body or the document containing it —con·sti·tu·tion·al \-əl\ adj —con·sti·tu·tion·al·i·ty \-,tüshə'nalətē, -,tyü-\ n

con·strain \kən'strān\ vb 1 : compel 2 : confine 3 : restrain —con·straint \-'strānt\ n

con·strict \-'strikt\ vb : draw or squeeze together —con·stric·tion \-'strik-shən\ n —con·stric·tive \-'striktiv\ adj

con·struct \kən'strəkt\ vb : build or make —con·struc·tion \-'strəkshən\ n —con·struc·tive \-tiv\ adj

con·strue \kən'strü\ vb -strued; -stru·ing : explain or interpret

con·sul \känsəl\ n 1 : Roman magistrate 2 : government commercial official in a foreign country —con·sul·ar \-sələr\ adj —con·sul·ate \-lət\ n

con·sult \kən'səlt\ vb 1 : ask the advice or opinion of 2 : confer —con·sul·tant \-ənt\ n —con·sul·ta·tion \,känsəl'tāshən\ n

con·sume \kən'süm\ vb -sumed; -sum·ing : eat or use up —con·sum·able adj —con·sum·er n

con·sum·mate \kən'səmət\ adj : complete or perfect ~ \'känsə,māt\ vb -mat·ed; -mat·ing : make complete —con·sum·ma·tion \,känsə'māshən\ n

con·sump·tion \kən'səmpshən\ n 1 : act of consuming 2 : use of goods 3 : tuberculosis —con·sump·tive \-tiv\ adj or n

con·tact \'kän,takt\ n 1 : a touching 2 : association or relationship 3 : connection or communication ~ vb 1 : come or bring into contact 2 : communicate with

con·ta·gion \kən'tājən\ n 1 : spread of disease by contact 2 : disease spread by contact —con·ta·gious \-jəs\ adj

con·tain \-'tān\ vb 1 : enclose or include 2 : have or hold within 3 : restrain —con·tain·er n —con·tain·ment n

con·tam·i·nate \kən'tamə,nāt\ vb -nat·ed; -nat·ing : soil or infect by contact or association —con·tam·i·na·tion \-,tamə'nāshən\ n

con·tem·plate \'käntəm,plāt\ vb -plat·ed; -plat·ing : view or consider thoughtfully —con·tem·pla·tion \,käntəm'plāshən\ n —con·tem·pla·tive \kən'templətiv; 'käntəm,plāt-\ adj

con·tem·po·ra·ne·ous \kən,tempə-'rānēəs\ adj : contemporary

con·tem·po·rary \kən'tempə,rerē\ adj 1 : occurring at or existing at the same time 2 : of the same age —contemporary n

con·tempt \kən'tempt\ n 1 : feeling of scorn 2 : state of being despised 3 : disobedience to a court or legislature —con·tempt·ible \-'temptəbəl\ adj

con·temp·tu·ous \-'tempchəwəs\ adj : feeling or expressing contempt —con·temp·tu·ous·ly adv

con·tend \-'tend\ vb 1 : strive against rivals or difficulties 2 : argue 3 : maintain or claim —con·tend·er n

¹con·tent \kən'tent\ adj : satisfied ~ vb : satisfy ~ n : ease of mind —con·tent·ed adj —con·tent·ed·ly adv —con·tent·ed·ness n —con·tent·ment n

²con·tent \'kän,tent\ n 1 pl : something contained 2 pl : subject matter (as of a book) 3 : essential meaning 4 : proportion contained

con·ten·tion \kən'tenchən\ n : state of contending —con·ten·tious \-chəs\ adj —con·ten·tious·ly adv

con·test \kən'test\ vb : dispute or challenge ~ \'kän,test\ n 1 : struggle 2 : game —con·test·able \kən'testəbəl\ adj —con·tes·tant \-'testənt\ n

con·text \'kän,tekst\ n : words surrounding a word or phrase

con·tig·u·ous \kən'tigyəwəs\ adj : connected to or adjoining —con·ti·gu·i·ty \,käntə'gyüətē\ n

con·ti·nence \'känt³nəns\ n : self-restraint —con·ti·nent \-ənt\ adj

con·ti·nent \'känt³nənt\ n : great division of land on the globe —con·ti·nen·tal \,känt³n'ent³l\ adj

con·tin·gen·cy \kən'tinjənsē\ n, pl -cies : possible event

con·tin·gent \-jənt\ adj : dependent on something else ~ n : a quota from an area or group

con·tin·u·al \kən'tinyəwəl\ adj 1 : continuous 2 : steadily recurring —con·tin·u·al·ly \-ē\ adv

con·tin·ue \kən'tinyü\ vb -tin·ued; -tin·u·ing 1 : remain in a place or condition 2 : endure 3 : resume after an intermission 4 : extend —

con·tin·u·ance \-yǝwǝns\ n —con·tin·u·a·tion \-,tinyǝ'wāshǝn\ n

con·tin·u·ous \-'tinyǝwǝs\ adj : continuing without interruption —con·ti·nu·ity \,känt'n'üǝtē, -'yü-\ n —con·tin·u·ous·ly adv

con·tort \kǝn'tȯrt\ vb : twist out of shape —con·tor·tion \-'tȯrshǝn\ n

con·tour \'kän,tu̇r\ n 1 : outline 2 pl : shape

con·tra·band \'käntrǝ,band\ n : illegal goods

con·tra·cep·tion \,käntrǝ'sepshǝn\ n : prevention of conception —con·tra·cep·tive \-'septiv\ adj or n

con·tract \'kän,trakt\ n : binding agreement ~ \kǝn'trakt, 1 usu 'kän,trakt\ vb 1 : establish or undertake by contract 2 : become ill with 3 : make shorter —con·trac·tion \kǝn'trak·shǝn\ n —con·trac·tor \'kän,traktǝr, kǝn'trak-\ n —con·trac·tu·al \kǝn-'trakchǝwǝl\ adj —con·trac·tu·al·ly adv

con·tra·dict \,käntrǝ'dikt\ vb : state the contrary of —con·tra·dic·tion \-'dik-shǝn\ n —con·tra·dic·to·ry \-'dik-tǝrē\ adj

con·tral·to \kǝn'traltō\ n, pl -tos : lowest female singing voice

con·trap·tion \kǝn'trapshǝn\ n : device or contrivance

con·trary \'kän,trerē; 4 often kǝn'trerē\ adj 1 : opposite in character, nature, or position 2 : mutually opposed 3 : unfavorable 4 : uncooperative or stubborn —con·trar·i·ly \-,trerǝlē, -'trer-\ adv —con·trari·wise \-,wīz\ adv —con·trary \'kän,trerē\ n

con·trast \'kän,trast\ n 1 : unlikeness shown by comparing 2 : unlike color or tone of adjacent parts ~ \kǝn'trast\ vb 1 : show differences 2 : compare so as to show differences

con·tra·vene \,käntrǝ'vēn\ vb -vened; -ven·ing : go or act contrary to

con·trib·ute \kǝn'tribyǝt\ vb -ut·ed; -ut·ing : give or help along with others —con·tri·bu·tion \,käntrǝ'byüshǝn\ n —con·trib·u·tor \kǝn'tribyǝtǝr\ n —con·trib·u·to·ry \-yǝ,tōrē\ adj

con·trite \'kän,trīt, kǝn'trīt\ adj : repentant —con·tri·tion \kǝn-'trishǝn\ n

con·trive \kǝn'trīv\ vb -trived; -triv·ing 1 : devise or make with ingenuity 2

: bring about —con·triv·ance \-'trīvǝns\ n —con·triv·er n

con·trol \-'trōl\ vb -ll- 1 : exercise power over 2 : dominate or rule ~ n 1 : power to direct or regulate 2 : restraint 3 : regulating device —con·trol·la·ble adj —con·trol·ler \-'trōlǝr, 'kän,-\ n

con·tro·ver·sy \'käntrǝ,vǝrsē\ n, pl -sies : clash of opposing views —con·tro·ver·sial \,käntrǝ'vǝrshǝl, -sēǝl\ adj

con·tro·vert \'käntrǝ,vǝrt, ,käntrǝ'-\ vb : contradict —con·tro·vert·ible adj

con·tu·ma·cious \,käntǝ'māshǝs, -tyǝ-\ adj : rebellious

con·tu·me·ly \kǝn'tümǝlē, 'käntu̇,mēlē, -tyü-\ n : rudeness

con·tu·sion \kǝn'tüzhǝn, -tyü-\ n : bruise —con·tuse \-'tüz, -'tyüz\ vb

co·nun·drum \kǝ'nǝndrǝm\ n : riddle

con·va·lesce \,känvǝ'les\ vb -lesced; -lesc·ing : gradually recover health —con·va·les·cence \-'ns\ n —con·va·les·cent \-'nt\ adj or n

con·vec·tion \kǝn'vekshǝn\ n : circulation in fluids due to warmer portions rising and colder ones sinking —con·vec·tion·al \-'vekshǝnǝl\ adj —con·vec·tive \-'vektiv\ adj

con·vene \kǝn'vēn\ vb -vened; -ven·ing : assemble or meet

con·ve·nience \-'vēnyǝns\ n 1 : personal comfort or ease 2 : device that saves work

con·ve·nient \-nyǝnt\ adj 1 : suited to one's convenience 2 : near at hand —con·ve·nient·ly adv

con·vent \'känvǝnt, -,vent\ n : community of nuns

con·ven·tion \kǝn'venchǝn\ n 1 : agreement esp. between nations 2 : large meeting 3 : body of delegates 4 : accepted usage or way of behaving —con·ven·tion·al \-'venchǝnǝl\ adj —con·ven·tion·al·ly adv

con·verge \kǝn'vǝrj\ vb -verged; -verg·ing : approach a single point —con·ver·gence \-'vǝrjǝns\ n —con·ver·gent \-jǝnt\ adj

con·ver·sant \-'vǝrs'nt\ adj : having knowledge and experience

con·ver·sa·tion \,känvǝr'sāshǝn\ n : an informal talking together —con·ver·sa·tion·al \-shǝnǝl\ adj

¹con·verse \kǝn'vǝrs\ vb -versed; -vers·ing : engage in conversation —con·verse \'kän,vǝrs\ n

²con·verse \kən'vərs, 'kän,vers\ adj
: opposite —con·verse \'kän,vərs\ n
—con·verse·ly adv

con·ver·sion \kən'vərzhən\ n 1 : change
2 : adoption of religion

con·vert \kən'vərt\ vb 1 : turn from one
belief or party to another 2 : change
~ \'kän,vərt\ n : one who has under-
gone religious conversion —con·
vert·er, con·ver·tor \kən'vərtər\ n—
con·vert·ible adj

con·vert·ible \kən'vərtəbəl\ n : automobile with a removable top

con·vex \kän'veks, 'kän,-, kən'-\ adj
: curved or rounded like the outside
of a sphere —con·vex·i·ty \kən-
'veksətē, kän-\ n

con·vey \kən'vā\ vb -veyed; -vey·ing
: transport or transmit —con·vey·
ance \-'vāəns\ n —con·vey·or \-ər\
n

con·vict \kən'vikt\ vb : find guilty ~
\'kän,vikt\ n : person in prison

con·vic·tion \kən'vikshən\ n 1 : act of
convicting 2 : strong belief

con·vince \-'vins\ vb -vinced; -vinc·ing
: cause to believe —con·vinc·ing·ly
adv

con·viv·ial \-'vivyəl, -'vivēəl\ adj
: cheerful or festive —con·viv·i·al·i-
ty \-,vivē'alətē\ n

con·voke \kən'vōk\ vb -voked; -vok·ing
: call together to a meeting —con·vo-
ca·tion \,känvə'kāshən\ n

con·vo·lut·ed \'känvə,lütəd\ adj 1
: intricately folded 2 : intricate

con·vo·lu·tion \,känvə'lüshən\ n : con-
voluted structure

con·voy \'kän,voi, kən'voi\ vb
: accompany for protection ~ \'kän,-
,voi\ n : group of vehicles or ships
moving together

con·vul·sion \kən'vəlshən\ n : violent
involuntary muscle contraction —
con·vulse \-'vəls\ vb —con·vul·sive
\-'vəlsiv\ adj

coo \'kü\ n : sound of a pigeon —coo
vb

cook \'kük\ n : one who prepares food
~ vb : prepare food —cook·book n
—cook·er n —cook·ery n —cookware n

cook·ie, cooky \'kükē\ n, pl -ies : small
sweet flat cake

cool \'kül\ adj 1 : moderately cold 2
: not excited 3 : unfriendly ~ vb
: make or become cool ~ n 1 : cool
time or place 2 : composure —cool-

ant \-ənt\ n —cool·er n —
cool·ly adv —cool·ness n

coo·lie \'külē\ n : unskilled Oriental laborer

coop \'küp, 'küp\ n : enclosure usu. for
poultry ~ vb : confine in or as if in a
coop

co-op \'kō,äp\ n : cooperative

coo·per \'küpər, 'küp-\ n : barrel maker
—cooper vb

co·op·er·ate \kō'äpə,rāt\ vb : act jointly
—co·op·er·a·tion \-,äpə'rāshən\ n

co·op·er·a·tive \kō'äpərətiv, -'äpə,rāt-\
adj : willing to work with others ~ n
: enterprise owned and run by those
using its services

co-opt \kō'äpt\ vb 1 : elect as a col-
league 2 : take over

co·or·di·nate \-'ȯrd⁾nət\ adj : equal esp.
in rank ~ n : any of a set of numbers
used in specifying the location of a
point on a surface or in space ~ \-⁾n-
,āt\ vb -nat·ed; -nat·ing 1 : make or
become coordinate 2 : work or act together harmoniously —co·or·
di·nate·ly adv —co·or·di·na·tion
\-,ȯrd⁾n'āshən\ n —co·or·di·na·tor
\-⁾n,ātər\ n

coot \'küt\ n 1 : dark-colored duckling
bird 2 : harmless simple person

cop \'käp\ n : police officer

¹cope \'kōp\ n : cloaklike ecclesiastical
vestment

²cope vb coped; cop·ing : deal with difficulties

co·pi·lot \'kō,pīlət\ n : assistant airplane
pilot

cop·ing \'kōpiŋ\ n : top layer of a wall

co·pi·ous \'kōpēəs\ adj : very abundant
—co·pi·ous·ly adv —co·pi·ous·ness
n

cop·per \'käpər\ n 1 : malleable reddish
metallic chemical element 2 : penny
—cop·pery adj

cop·per·head n : largely coppery brown
venomous snake

co·pra \'kōprə\ n : dried coconut meat

copse \'käps\ n : thicket

cop·u·la \'käpyələ\ n : verb linking subject and predicate —cop·u·la·tive
\-,lātiv\ adj

cop·u·late \'käpyə,lāt\ vb -lat·ed; -lat·
ing : engage in sexual intercourse —
cop·u·la·tion \,käpyə'lāshən\ n

copy \'käpē\ n, pl cop·ies 1 : imitation
or reproduction of an original 2
: writing to be set for printing ~ vb
cop·ied; copy·ing 1 : make a copy of

2 : imitate —**cop·i·er** \-ər\ n —**copyist** n

copy·right n : sole right to a literary or artistic work ~ vb : get a copyright on

co·quette \kō'ket\ n : flirt

cor·al \'kórəl\ n **1** : skeletal material of colonies of tiny sea polyps **2** : deep pink —**coral** adj

cord \'kórd\ n **1** : usu. heavy string **2** : long slender anatomical structure **3** : measure of firewood equal to 128 cu. ft. **4** : small electrical cable ~ vb **1** : tie or furnish with a cord **2** : pile (wood) in cords

cor·dial \'kórjəl\ adj : warmly welcoming ~ n : liqueur —**cor·di·al·i·ty** \,kórjē'alətē, kórd'yal-\ n —**cordial·ly** \'kórjəlē\ adv

cor·don \'kórd'n\ n : encircling line of troops or police —**cordon** vb

cor·do·van \'kórdəvən\ n : soft fine-grained leather

cor·du·roy \'kórdə,ròi\ n **1** : heavy ribbed fabric **2** pl : trousers of corduroy

core \'kōr\ n **1** : central part of some fruits **2** : inmost part ~ vb **cored; coring** : take out the core of —**cor·er** n

cork \'kórk\ n **1** : tough elastic bark of a European oak (**cork oak**) **2** : stopper of cork ~ vb : stop up with a cork —**corky** adj

cork·screw \'kórk,skrü\ n : device for drawing corks from bottles

cor·mo·rant \'kórmərənt, -,rant\ n : dark seabird

¹corn \'kórn\ n : cereal grass or its seeds ~ vb : cure or preserve in brine —**corn·meal** n —**corn·stalk** n —**corn·starch** n

²corn n : local hardening and thickening of skin

corn·cob n : axis on which the kernels of Indian corn are arranged

cor·nea \'kórnēə\ n : transparent part of the coat of the eyeball —**cor·ne·al** adj

cor·ner \'kórnər\ n **1** : point or angle formed by the meeting of lines or sides **2** : place where two streets meet **3** : inescapable position **4** : control of the supply of something ~ vb **1** : drive into a corner **2** : get a corner on **3** : turn a corner

cor·ner·stone n **1** : stone at a corner of a wall **2** : something basic

cor·net \kór'net\ n : trumpetlike instrument

cor·nice \'kórnəs\ n : horizontal wall projection

cor·nu·co·pia \,kórnə'kōpēə, -nyə-\ n : goat's horn filled with fruits and grain emblematic of abundance

co·rol·la \kə'rälə\ n : petals of a flower

cor·ol·lary \'kórə,lerē\ n, pl **-lar·ies 1** : logical deduction **2** : consequence or result

co·ro·na \kə'rōnə\ n : shining ring around the sun seen during eclipses

cor·o·nary \'kórə,nerē\ adj : relating to the heart or its blood vessels ~ n **1** : thrombosis of an artery supplying the heart **2** : heart attack

cor·o·na·tion \,kórə'nāshən\ n : crowning of a monarch

cor·o·ner \'kórənər\ n : public official who investigates causes of suspicious deaths

¹cor·po·ral \'kórpərəl\ adj : bodily

²corporal n : noncommissioned officer ranking next below a sergeant

cor·po·ra·tion \,kórpə'rāshən\ n : legal creation with the rights and liabilities of a person —**cor·po·rate** \'kórpərət\ adj

cor·po·re·al \kór'pōrēəl\ adj : physical or material —**cor·po·re·al·ly** adv

corps \'kōr\ n, pl **corps** \'kōrz\ **1** : subdivision of a military force **2** : working group

corpse \'kórps\ n : dead body

cor·pu·lence \'kórpyələns\ n : obesity —**cor·pu·lent** \-lənt\ adj

cor·pus \'kórpəs\ n, pl **-po·ra** \-pərə\ **1** : corpse **2** : body of writings

cor·pus·cle \'kór,pəsəl\ n : blood cell

cor·ral \kə'ral\ n : enclosure for animals —**corral** vb

cor·rect \kə'rekt\ vb **1** : make right **2** : chastise ~ adj **1** : true or factual **2** : conforming to a standard —**cor·rec·tion** \-'rekshən\ n —**cor·rec·tive** \-'rektiv\ adj —**cor·rect·ly** adv —**cor·rect·ness** n

cor·re·late \'kórə,lāt\ vb **-lat·ed; -lat·ing** : show a connection between —**cor·re·late** \-lət, -,lāt\ n —**cor·re·la·tion** \,kórə'lāshən\ n

cor·rel·a·tive \kə'relətiv\ adj : regularly used together —**correlative** n

cor·re·spond \,kórə'spänd\ vb **1** : match **2** : communicate by letter —**cor·re·spon·dence** \-'spändəns\ n —**cor·re·spond·ing·ly** \-'spändiŋlē\ adv

cor·re·spon·dent \-'spändənt\ *n* **1**
: person one writes to **2** : reporter

cor·ri·dor \'kórədər, -,dór\ *n* : passageway connecting rooms

cor·rob·o·rate \kə'räbə,rāt\ *vb* **-rat·ed;
-rat·ing** : support with evidence —
cor·rob·o·ra·tion \-,räbə'rāshən\ *n*

cor·rode \kə'rōd\ *vb* **-rod·ed; -rod·ing**
: wear away by chemical action —
cor·ro·sion \-'rōzhən\ *n* —**cor·ro·
sive** \-'rōsiv\ *adj or n*

cor·ru·gate \'kórə,gāt\ *vb* **-gat·ed; -gat·
ing** : form into ridges and grooves —
cor·ru·gat·ed *adj* —**cor·ru·ga·tion**
\,kórə'gāshən\ *n*

cor·rupt \kə'rəpt\ *vb* **1** : change from
good to bad **2** : bribe ~ *adj* : morally
debased —**cor·rupt·ible** *adj* —**cor·
rup·tion** \-'rəpshən\ *n*

cor·sage \kór'säzh, -'säj\ *n* : bouquet
worn by a woman

cor·set \'kórsət\ *n* : woman's stiffened
undergarment

cor·tege \kór'tezh, 'kór,-\ *n* : funeral
procession

cor·tex \'kór,teks\ *n, pl* **-ti·ces**
\'kórtə,sēz\ *or* **-tex·es** : outer or covering layer of an organism or part (as
the brain) —**cor·ti·cal** \'kórtikəl\ *adj*

cor·ti·sone \'kórtə,sōn, -,zōn\ *n* : adrenal
hormone

cos·met·ic \käz'metik\ *n* : beautifying
preparation ~ *adj* : relating to beautifying

cos·mic \'käzmik\ *adj* **1** : relating to the
universe **2** : vast or grand

cos·mo·naut \'käzmə,nót\ *n* : Soviet or
Russian astronaut

cos·mo·pol·i·tan \,käzmə'pälət∂n\ *adj*
: belonging to all the world —**cos·
mopolitan** *n*

cos·mos \'käzməs, -,mōs, -,mäs\ *n*
: universe

cos·sack \'käs,ak, -ək\ *n* : Russian czar-
ist cavalryman

cost \'kóst\ *n* **1** : amount paid for something **2** : loss or penalty ~ *vb* **cost;
cost·ing 1** : require so much in payment **2** : cause to pay, suffer, or lose
—**cost·li·ness** \-lēnəs\ *n* —**cost·ly**
\-lē\ *adj*

cos·tume \'käs,tüm, -,tyüm\ *n* : clothing

co·sy \'kōzē\ *var of* COZY

cot \'kät\ *n* : small bed

cote \'kōt, 'kät\ *n* : small shed or coop

co·te·rie \'kōtə,rē, ,kōtə'-\ *n* : exclusive
group of persons

co·til·lion \kō'tilyən\ *n* : formal ball

cot·tage \'kätij\ *n* : small house

cot·ton \'kät∂n\ *n* : soft fibrous plant
substance or thread or cloth made of
it —**cot·ton·seed** *n* —**cot·tony** *adj*

cot·ton·mouth *n* : poisonous snake

couch \'kauch\ *vb* **1** : lie or place on a
couch **2** : phrase ~ *n* : bed or sofa

cou·gar \'kügər, -,gär\ *n* : large tawny
wild American cat

cough \'kóf\ *vb* : force air from the lungs
with short sharp noises —**cough** *n*

could \'kud\ *past of* CAN

coun·cil \'kaunsəl\ *n* **1** : assembly or
meeting **2** : body of lawmakers —
coun·cil·lor, coun·cil·or \-sələr\ *n* —
coun·cil·man \-mən\ *n* —**coun·cil·
wom·an** *n*

coun·sel \'kaunsəl\ *n* **1** : advice **2**
: deliberation together **3** *pl* **-sel**
: lawyer ~ *vb* **-seled** *or* **-selled; -sel-
ing** *or* **-sel·ling 1** : advise **2** : consult
together —**coun·sel·or, coun·sel·lor**
\-sələr\ *n*

¹count \'kaunt\ *vb* **1** : name or indicate
one by one to find the total number **2**
: recite numbers in order **3** : rely **4**
: be of value or account ~ *n* **1** : act
of counting or the total obtained by
counting **2** : charge in an indictment
—**count·able** *adj*

²count *n* : European nobleman

coun·te·nance \'kaunt∂nəns\ *n* : face or
facial expression ~ *vb* **-nanced;
-nanc·ing** : allow or encourage

¹coun·ter \'kauntər\ *n* **1** : piece for reckoning or games **2** : surface over which
business is transacted

²counter *n* : one that counts

³coun·ter *vb* : oppose ~ *adv* : in an
opposite direction ~ *n* : offsetting
force or move ~ *adj* : contrary

counter- *prefix* **1** : contrary or opposite
2 : opposing **3** : retaliatory

counteraccusa-tion	countercharge
counteraggres-sion	counterclaim
counterargue	countercom-plaint
counterassault	countercoup
counterattack	countercriticism
counterbid	counterdemand
counterblock-ade	counterdemon-stration
counterblow	counterdemon-strator
countercam-paign	countereffort
	counterevidence

counterguerrilla
counterinfla-
tionary
counterinflu-
ence
countermeasure
countermove
countermove-
ment
counteroffer
counterpetition
counterploy
counterpower
counterpressure
counterpropa-
ganda
counterproposal
counterprotest
counterquestion
counterraid
counterrally
counterreform

counterresponse
counterretalia-
tion
counterrevolu-
tion
counterrevolu-
tionary
counterstrategy
counterstyle
countersue
countersugges-
tion
countersuit
counterten-
dency
counterterror
counterterror-
ism
counterterrorist
counterthreat
counterthrust
countertrend

coun·ter·act vb : lessen the force of — **coun·ter·ac·tive** adj

coun·ter·bal·ance n : balancing influence or weight ~ vb : oppose or balance

coun·ter·clock·wise adv or adj : opposite to the way a clock's hands move

coun·ter·feit \'kaúntər,fit\ vb 1 : copy in order to deceive 2 : pretend ~ adj : spurious ~ n : fraudulent copy — **coun·ter·feit·er** n

coun·ter·mand \-,mand\ vb : supersede with a contrary order

coun·ter·pane \-,pān\ n : bedspread

coun·ter·part n : one that is similar or corresponds

coun·ter·point n : music with interwoven melodies

coun·ter·sign n : secret signal ~ vb : add a confirming signature to

count·ess \'kaúntəs\ n : wife or widow of a count or an earl or a woman holding that rank in her own right

count·less \-ləs\ adj : too many to be numbered

coun·try \'kəntrē\ n, pl -**tries 1** : nation **2** : rural area — adj : rural — **coun·try·man** \-mən\ n

coun·try·side n : rural area or its people

coun·ty \'kaúntē\ n, pl -**ties** : local government division esp. of a state

coup \'kü\ n, pl **coups** \'küz\ **1** : brilliant sudden action or plan **2** : sudden overthrow of a government

coupe \'küp\ n : 2-door automobile with an enclosed body

cou·ple \'kəpəl\ vb -**pled; -pling** : link together ~ n **1** : pair **2** : two persons closely associated or married

cou·pling \'kəpliŋ\ n : connecting device

cou·pon \'kü,pän, 'kyü-\ n : certificate redeemable for goods or a cash discount

cour·age \'kərij\ n : ability to conquer fear or despair — **cou·ra·geous** \kə'rājəs\ adj

cou·ri·er \'kúrēər, 'kər-\ n : messenger

course \'kōrs\ n **1** : progress **2** : ground over which something moves **3** : part of a meal served at one time **4** : method of procedure **5** : subject taught in a series of classes ~ vb **coursed; cours·ing 1** : hunt with dogs **2** : run speedily — **of course** : as might be expected

court \'kōrt\ n **1** : residence of a sovereign **2** : sovereign and his or her officials and advisers **3** : area enclosed by a building **4** : space marked for playing a game **5** : place where justice is administered ~ vb : woo — **court·house** n — **court·room** n — **court·ship** \-,ship\ n

cour·te·ous \'kərtēəs\ adj : showing politeness and respect for others — **cour·te·ous·ly** adv

cour·te·san \'kōrtəzən, 'kərt-\ n : prostitute

cour·te·sy \'kərtəsē\ n, pl -**sies** : courteous behavior

court·ier \'kōrtēər, 'kōrtyər\ n : person in attendance at a royal court

court·ly \'kōrtlē\ adj -**li·er; -est** : polite or elegant — **court·li·ness** n

court–mar·tial n, pl **courts–martial** : military trial court — **court–martial** vb

court·yard n : enclosure open to the sky that is attached to a house

cous·in \'kəzᵊn\ n : child of one's uncle or aunt

cove \'kōv\ n : sheltered inlet or bay

co·ven \'kəvən\ n : group of witches

cov·e·nant \'kəvənənt\ n : binding agreement — **cov·e·nant** \-nənt, -,nant\ vb

cov·er \'kəvər\ vb **1** : place something over or upon **2** : protect or hide **3** : include or deal with ~ n : something that covers — **cov·er·age** \-ərij\ n

cov·er·let \-lət\ n : bedspread

co·vert \'kō,vərt, 'kəvərt\ adj : secret ~ \'kəvərt, 'kō-\ n : thicket that shelters animals

cov·et \'kəvət\ vb : desire enviously — **cov·et·ous** adj

cov·ey \'kəvē\ n, pl **-eys 1** : bird with her young **2** : small flock (as of quail)

¹cow \'kau̇\ n : large adult female animal (as of cattle) —**cow·hide** n

²cow vb : intimidate

cow·ard \'kau̇ərd\ n : one who lacks courage —**cow·ard·ice** \-əs\ n — **cow·ard·ly** adv or adj

cow·boy n : a mounted ranch hand who tends cattle

cow·er \'kau̇ər\ vb : shrink from fear or cold

cow·girl n : woman ranch hand who tends cattle

cowl \'kau̇l\ n : monk's hood

cow·lick \'kau̇,lik\ n : turned-up tuft of hair that resists control

cow·slip \-,slip\ n : yellow flower

cox·swain \'käksən, -,swän\ n : person who steers a boat

coy \'kȯi\ adj : shy or pretending shyness

coy·ote \'kī,ōt, kī'ōtē\ n, pl **coy·otes** or **coyote** : small No. American wolf

coz·en \'kəzⁿn\ vb : cheat

co·zy \'kōzē\ adj **-zi·er; -est** : snug

crab \'krab\ n : short broad shellfish with pincers

crab·by \'krabē\ adj **-bi·er; -est** : cross

¹crack \'krak\ vb **1** : break with a sharp sound **2** : fail in tone **3** : break without completely separating ~ n **1** : sudden sharp noise **2** : witty remark **3** : narrow break **4** : sharp blow **5** : try

²crack adj : extremely proficient

crack·down n : disciplinary action — **crack down** vb

crack·er \-ər\ n : thin crisp bakery product

crack·le \'krakəl\ vb **-led; -ling 1** : make snapping noises **2** : develop fine cracks in a surface —**crackle** n

crack·pot \'krak,pät\ n : eccentric

crack–up n : crash

cra·dle \'krādⁿl\ n : baby's bed ~ vb **-dled; -dling 1** : place in a cradle **2** : hold securely

craft \'kraft\ n **1** : occupation requiring special skill **2** : craftiness **3** pl usu **craft** : structure designed to provide transportation **4** pl usu **craft** : small boat —**crafts·man** \'kraftsmən\ n — **crafts·man·ship** \-,ship\ n

crafty \'kraftē\ adj **craft·i·er; -est** : sly —**craft·i·ness** n

crag \'krag\ n : steep cliff —**crag·gy** \-ē\ adj

cram \'kram\ vb **-mm- 1** : eat greedily **2** : pack in tight **3** : study intensely for a test

cramp \'kramp\ n **1** : sudden painful contraction of muscle **2** pl : sharp abdominal pains ~ vb **1** : affect with cramp **2** : restrain

cran·ber·ry \'kran,berē\ n : red acid berry of a trailing plant

crane \'krān\ n **1** : tall wading bird **2** : machine for lifting heavy objects ~ vb **craned; cran·ing** : stretch one's neck to see

cra·ni·um \'krānēəm\ n, pl **-ni·ums** or **-nia** \-nēə\ : skull —**cra·ni·al** \-əl\ adj

crank \'kraŋk\ n **1** : bent lever turned to operate a machine **2** : eccentric ~ vb : start or operate by turning a crank

cranky \'kraŋkē\ adj **crank·i·er; -est** : irritable

cran·ny \'kranē\ n, pl **-nies** : crevice

craps \'kraps\ n : dice game

crash \'krash\ vb **1** : break noisily **2** : fall and hit something with noise and damage ~ n **1** : loud sound **2** : action of crashing **3** : failure

crass \'kras\ adj : crude or unfeeling

crate \'krāt\ n : wooden shipping container —**crate** vb

cra·ter \'krātər\ n : volcanic depression

cra·vat \krə'vat\ n : necktie

crave \'krāv\ vb **craved; crav·ing** : long for —**crav·ing** n

cra·ven \'krāvən\ adj : cowardly —**craven** n

craw·fish \'krȯ,fish\ n : crayfish

crawl \'krȯl\ vb **1** : move slowly (as by drawing the body along the ground) **2** : swarm with creeping things ~ n : very slow pace

cray·fish \'krā,fish\ n : lobsterlike freshwater crustacean

cray·on \'krā,än, -ən\ n : stick of chalk or wax used for drawing or coloring —**crayon** vb

craze \'krāz\ vb **crazed; craz·ing** : make or become insane ~ n : fad

cra·zy \'krāzē\ adj **cra·zi·er; -est 1** : mentally disordered **2** : wildly impractical —**cra·zi·ly** adv —**cra·zi·ness** n

creak \'krēk\ vb or n : squeak —**creaky** adj

cream \'krēm\ n **1** : yellowish fat-rich part of milk **2** : thick smooth sauce.

confection, or cosmetic **3** : choicest part ~ *vb* : beat into creamy consistency —**creamy** *adj*

cream·ery \-ərē\ *n, pl* -**er·ies** : place where butter and cheese are made

crease \'krēs\ *n* : line made by folding —**crease** *vb*

cre·ate \krē'āt\ *vb* -**at·ed; -at·ing** : bring into being —**cre·ation** \krē'āshən\ *n* —**cre·ative** \-'ātiv\ *adj* —**cre·ativi·ty** \,krēā'tivətē\ *n* —**cre·ator** \krē'ātər\ *n*

crea·ture \'krēchər\ *n* : lower animal or human being

cre·dence \'krēd³ns\ *n* : belief

cre·den·tials \kri'denchəlz\ *n* : evidence of qualifications or authority

cred·i·ble \'kredəbəl\ *adj* : believable —**cred·i·bil·i·ty** \,kredə'bilətē\ *n*

cred·it \'kredət\ *n* **1** : balance in a person's favor **2** : time given to pay for goods **3** : belief **4** : esteem **5** : source of honor ~ *vb* **1** : believe **2** : give credit to

cred·it·able \-əbəl\ *adj* : worthy of esteem or praise —**cred·it·ably** \-əblē\ *adv*

cred·i·tor \-ər\ *n* : person to whom money is owed

cred·u·lous \'krejələs\ *adj* : easily convinced —**cre·du·li·ty** \kri'dülətē, -'dyü-\ *n*

creed \'krēd\ *n* : statement of essential beliefs

creek \'krēk, 'krik\ *n* : small stream

creel \'krēl\ *n* : basket for carrying fish

creep \'krēp\ *vb* **crept** \'krept\; **creep·ing 1** : crawl **2** : grow over a surface like ivy —**creep** *n* —**creep·er** *n*

cre·mate \'krē,māt\ *vb* -**mat·ed; -mat·ing** : burn up (a corpse) —**cre·ma·tion** \kri'māshən\ *n* —**cre·ma·to·ry** \'krēmə,tōrē, 'krem-\ *n*

cre·o·sote \'krēə,sōt\ *n* : oily wood preservative

crepe, crêpe \'krāp\ *n* : light crinkled fabric

cre·scen·do \krə'shendō\ *adv or adj* : growing louder —**crescendo** *n*

cres·cent \'kres³nt\ *n* : shape of the moon between new moon and first quarter

crest \'krest\ *n* **1** : tuft on a bird's head **2** : top of a hill or wave **3** : part of a coat of arms ~ *vb* : rise to a crest —**crest·ed** \-əd\ *adj*

crest·fall·en *adj* : sad

cre·tin \'krēt³n\ *n* : stupid person

cre·vasse \kri'vas\ *n* : deep fissure esp. in a glacier

crev·ice \'krevəs\ *n* : narrow fissure

crew \'krü\ *n* : body of workers (as on a ship) —**crew·man** \-mən\ *n*

crib \'krib\ *n* **1** : manger **2** : grain storage bin **3** : baby's bed ~ *vb* -**bb-** : put in a crib

crib·bage \'kribij\ *n* : card game scored by moving pegs on a board (**cribbage board**)

crick \'krik\ *n* : muscle spasm

¹**crick·et** \'krikət\ *n* : insect noted for the chirping of the male

²**cricket** *n* : bat and ball game played on a field with wickets

cri·er \'krīər\ *n* : one who calls out announcements

crime \'krīm\ *n* : serious violation of law

crim·i·nal \'krimən³l\ *adj* : relating to or being a crime or its punishment ~ *n* : one who commits a crime

crimp \'krimp\ *vb* : cause to become crinkled, wavy, or bent —**crimp** *n*

crim·son \'krimzən\ *n* : deep red —**crimson** *adj*

cringe \'krinj\ *vb* **cringed; cring·ing** : shrink in fear

crin·kle \'kriŋkəl\ *vb* -**kled; -kling** : wrinkle —**crinkle** *n* —**crin·kly** \-klē\ *adj*

crin·o·line \'krin³lən\ *n* **1** : stiff cloth **2** : full stiff skirt or petticoat

crip·ple \'kripəl\ *n* : disabled person ~ *vb* -**pled; -pling** : disable

cri·sis \'krīsəs\ *n, pl* **cri·ses** \-,sēz\ : decisive or critical moment

crisp \'krisp\ *adj* **1** : easily crumbled **2** : firm and fresh **3** : lively **4** : invigorating —**crisp** *vb* —**crisp·ly** *adv* —**crisp·ness** *n* —**crispy** *adj*

criss·cross \'kris,krós\ *n* : pattern of crossed lines ~ *vb* : mark with or follow a crisscross

cri·te·ri·on \krī'tirēən\ *n, pl* -**ria** \-ēə\ : standard

crit·ic \'kritik\ *n* : judge of literary or artistic works

crit·i·cal \-ikəl\ *adj* **1** : inclined to criticize **2** : being a crisis **3** : relating to criticism or critics —**crit·i·cal·ly** \-iklē\ *adv*

crit·i·cize \'kritə,sīz\ *vb* -**cized; -cizing 1** : judge as a critic **2** : find fault —**crit·i·cism** \-ə,sizəm\ *n*

cri·tique \krə'tēk\ *n* : critical estimate

croak \'krōk\ *n* : hoarse harsh cry (as of a frog) —**croak** *vb*

cro·chet \krō'shā\ n : needlework done with a hooked needle —**crochet** vb

crock \'kräk\ n : thick earthenware pot or jar —**crock·ery** \-ərē\ n

croc·o·dile \'kräkə,dīl\ n : large reptile of tropical waters

cro·cus \'krōkəs\ n, pl -cus·es : herb with spring flowers

crone \'krōn\ n : ugly old woman

cro·ny \'krōnē\ n, pl -nies : chum

crook \'krük\ n 1 : bent or curved tool or part 2 : thief ~ vb : curve sharply

crook·ed \'krükəd\ adj 1 : bent 2 : dishonest —**crook·ed·ness** n

croon \'krün\ vb : sing softly —**croon·er** n

crop \'kräp\ n 1 : pouch in the throat of a bird or insect 2 : short riding whip 3 : something that can be harvested ~ vb -pp- 1 : trim 2 : appear unexpectedly —used with up

cro·quet \krō'kā\ n : lawn game of driving balls through wickets

cro·quette \-'ket\ n : mass of minced food deep-fried

cro·sier \'krōzhər\ n : bishop's staff

cross \'kròs\ n 1 : figure or structure consisting of an upright and a cross piece 2 : interbreeding of unlike strains ~ vb 1 : intersect 2 : cancel 3 : go or extend across 4 : interbreed ~ adj 1 : going across 2 : contrary 3 : marked by bad temper —**cross·ing** n —**cross·ly** adv

cross·bow \-,bō\ n : short bow mounted on a rifle stock

cross·breed vb -bred; -breed·ing : hybridize

cross–ex·am·ine vb : question about earlier testimony —**cross–ex·am·i·na·tion** n

cross–eyed adj : having the eye turned toward the nose

cross–re·fer vb : refer to another place (as in a book) —**cross–ref·er·ence** n

cross·roads n : place where 2 roads cross

cross section n : representative portion

cross·walk n : path for pedestrians crossing a street

cross·ways adv : crosswise

cross·wise \-,wīz\ adv : so as to cross something —**crosswise** adj

crotch \'kräch\ n : angle formed by the parting of 2 legs or branches

crotch·ety \'krächətē\ adj : cranky, ill-natured

crouch \'kraüch\ vb : stoop over —**crouch** n

croup \'krüp\ n : laryngitis of infants

crou·ton \'krü,tän\ n : bit of toast

¹crow \'krō\ n : large glossy black bird

²crow vb 1 : make the loud sound of the cock 2 : gloat ~ n : cry of the cock

crow·bar n : metal bar used as a pry or lever

crowd \'kraüd\ vb : collect or cram together ~ n : large number of people

crown \'kraün\ n 1 : wreath of honor or victory 2 : royal headdress 3 : top or highest part ~ vb 1 : place a crown on 2 : honor —**crowned** \'kraünd\ adj

cru·cial \'krüshəl\ adj : vitally important

cru·ci·ble \'krüsəbəl\ n : heat-resisting container

cru·ci·fix \'krüsə,fiks\ n : representation of Christ on the cross

cru·ci·fix·ion \,krüsə'fikshən\ n : act of crucifying

cru·ci·fy \'krüsə,fī\ vb -fied; -fy·ing 1 : put to death on a cross 2 : persecute

crude \'krüd\ adj crud·er; -est 1 : not refined 2 : lacking grace or elegance ~ n : unrefined petroleum —**crude·ly** adv —**cru·di·ty** \-ətē\ n

cru·el \'krüəl\ adj -el·er or -el·ler; -el·est or -el·lest : causing suffering to others —**cru·el·ly** \-ē\ adv —**cru·el·ty** \tē\ n

cru·et \'krüət\ n : bottle for salad dressings

cruise \'krüz\ vb cruised; cruis·ing 1 : sail to several ports 2 : travel at the most efficient speed —**cruise** n

cruis·er \'krüzər\ n 1 : warship 2 : police car

crumb \'krəm\ n : small fragment

crum·ble \'krəmbəl\ vb -bled; -bling : break into small pieces —**crum·bly** \-blē\ adj

crum·ple \'krəmpəl\ vb -pled; -pling 1 : crush together 2 : collapse

crunch \'krənch\ vb : chew or press with a crushing noise ~ n : crunching sound —**crunchy** adj

cru·sade \krü'sād\ n 1 cap : medieval Christian expedition to the Holy Land 2 : reform movement —**crusade** vb —**cru·sad·er** n

crush \'krəsh\ vb 1 : squeeze out of shape 2 : grind or pound to bits 3 : suppress ~ n 1 : severe crowding 2 : infatuation

crust \\'krəst\ *n* **1** : hard outer part of bread or a pie **2** : hard surface layer —**crust•al** *adj* —**crusty** *adj*

crus•ta•cean \\,krəs'tāshən\ *n* : aquatic arthropod having a firm shell

crutch \\'krəch\ *n* : support for use by the disabled in walking

crux \\'krəks, 'krùks\ *n, pl* **crux•es 1** : hard problem **2** : crucial point

cry \\'krī\ *vb* **cried; cry•ing 1** : call out **2** : weep ~ *n, pl* **cries 1** : shout **2** : fit of weeping **3** : characteristic sound of an animal

crypt \\'kript\ *n* : underground chamber

cryp•tic \\'kriptik\ *adj* : enigmatic

cryp•tog•ra•phy \\krip'tägrəfē\ *n* : coding and decoding of messages —**cryp•tog•ra•pher** \\-fər\ *n*

crys•tal \\'kristᵊl\ *n* **1** : transparent quartz **2** : something (as glass) like crystal **3** : body formed by solidification that has a regular repeating atomic arrangement —**crys•tal•line** \\-tələn\ *adj*

crys•tal•lize \\-tə,līz\ *vb* **-lized; -liz•ing** : form crystals or a definite shape —**crys•tal•li•za•tion** \\,kristələ'zāshən\ *n*

cub \\'kəb\ *n* : young animal

cub•by•hole \\'kəbē,hōl\ *n* : small confined space

cube \\'kyüb\ *n* **1** : solid having 6 equal square sides **2** : product obtained by taking a number **3** times as a factor ~ *vb* **cubed; cub•ing 1** : raise to the 3d power **2** : form into a cube : cut into cubes —**cu•bic** \\'kyübik\ *adj*

cu•bi•cle \\-bikəl\ *n* : small room

cu•bit \\'kyübət\ *n* : ancient unit of length equal to about 18 inches

cuck•old \\'kəkəld, 'kük-\ *n* : man whose wife is unfaithful —**cuckold** *vb*

cuck•oo \\'kükü, 'kük-\ *n, pl* **-oos** : brown European bird ~ *adj* : silly

cu•cum•ber \\'kyü,kəmbər\ *n* : fleshy fruit related to the gourds

cud \\'kəd\ *n* : food chewed again by ruminating animals

cud•dle \\'kədᵊl\ *vb* **-dled; -dling** : lie close

cudg•el \\'kəjəl\ *n or vb* : club

¹cue \\'kyü\ *n* : signal —**cue** *vb*

²cue *n* : stick used in pool

¹cuff \\'kəf\ *n* **1** : part of a sleeve encircling the wrist **2** : folded trouser hem

²cuff *vb or n* : slap

cui•sine \\kwi'zēn\ *n* : manner of cooking

cu•li•nary \\'kələ,nerē, 'kyülə-\ *adj* : of or relating to cookery

cull \\'kəl\ *vb* : select

cul•mi•nate \\'kəlmə,nāt\ *vb* **-nat•ed; -nat•ing** : rise to the highest point —**cul•mi•na•tion** \\,kəlmə'nāshən\ *n*

cul•pa•ble \\'kəlpəbəl\ *adj* : deserving blame

cul•prit \\'kəlprət\ *n* : guilty person

cult \\'kəlt\ *n* **1** : religious system **2** : faddish devotion —**cult•ist** *n*

cul•ti•vate \\'kəltə,vāt\ *vb* **-vat•ed; -vat•ing 1** : prepare for crops **2** : foster the growth of **3** : refine —**cul•ti•va•tion** \\,kəltə'vāshən\ *n*

cul•ture \\'kəlchər\ *n* **1** : cultivation **2** : refinement of intellectual and artistic taste **3** : particular form or stage of civilization —**cul•tur•al** \\'kəlchərəl\ *adj* —**cul•tured** \\'kəlchərd\ *adj*

cul•vert \\'kəlvərt\ *n* : drain crossing under a road or railroad

cum•ber•some \\'kəmbərsəm\ *adj* : awkward to handle due to bulk

cu•mu•la•tive \\'kyümyələtiv, -,lāt-\ *adj* : increasing by additions

cu•mu•lus \\'kyümyələs\ *n, pl* **-li** \\-,lī, -,lē\ : massive rounded cloud

cun•ning \\'kəniŋ\ *adj* **1** : crafty **2** : clever **3** : appealing ~ *n* **1** : skill **2** : craftiness

cup \\'kəp\ *n* **1** : small drinking vessel **2** : contents of a cup **3** : a half pint ~ *vb* **-pp-** : shape like a cup —**cup•ful** *n*

cup•board \\'kəbərd\ *n* : small storage closet

cup•cake *n* : small cake

cu•pid•i•ty \\kyu'pidətē\ *n, pl* **-ties** : excessive desire for money

cu•po•la \\'kyüpələ, -,lō\ *n* : small rooftop structure

cur \\'kər\ *n* : mongrel dog

cu•rate \\'kyürət\ *n* : member of the clergy —**cu•ra•cy** \\-əsē\ *n*

cu•ra•tor \\kyu'rātər\ *n* : one in charge of a museum or zoo

curb \\'kərb\ *n* **1** : restraint **2** : raised edging along a street ~ *vb* : hold back

curd \\'kərd\ *n* : coagulated milk

cur•dle \\'kərdᵊl\ *vb* **-dled; -dling 1** : form curds **2** : sour

cure \\'kyür\ *n* **1** : recovery from disease **2** : remedy ~ *vb* **cured; cur•ing 1** : restore to health **2** : process for storage or use —**cur•able** *adj*

cur•few \\'kər,fyü\ *n* : requirement to be off the streets at a set hour

cu•rio \\'kyürē,ō\ *n, pl* **-ri•os** : rare or unusual article

cu·ri·ous \'kyurēəs\ *adj* **1** : eager to learn **2** : strange —**cu·ri·os·i·ty** \,kyurē'äsətē\ *n* —**cu·ri·ous·ness** *n*

curl \'kərl\ *vb* **1** : form into ringlets **2** : curve ~ *n* **1** : ringlet of hair **2** : something with a spiral form —**curl·er** *n* —**curly** *adj*

cur·lew \'kərlü, -lyü\ *n, pl* **-lews** *or* **-lew** : long-legged brownish bird

curli·cue \'kərli,kyü\ *n* : fanciful curve

cur·rant \'kərənt\ *n* **1** : small seedless raisin **2** : berry of a shrub

cur·ren·cy \'kərənsē\ *n, pl* **-cies** **1** : general use or acceptance **2** : money

cur·rent \'kərənt\ *adj* : occurring in or belonging to the present ~ *n* **1** : swiftest part of a stream **2** : flow of electricity

cur·ric·u·lum \kə'rikyələm\ *n, pl* **-la** \-lə\ : course of study

¹cur·ry \'kərē\ *vb* **-ried; -ry·ing** : brush (a horse) with a wire brush (**curry·comb** \-,kōm\) —**curry fa·vor** : seek favor by flattery

²curry *n, pl* **-ries** : blend of pungent spices or a food seasoned with this

curse \'kərs\ *n* **1** : a calling down of evil or harm upon one **2** : affliction ~ *vb* **cursed; curs·ing** **1** : call down injury upon **2** : swear at **3** : afflict

cur·sor \'kərsər\ *n* : indicator on a computer screen

cur·so·ry \'kərsərē\ *adj* : hastily done

curt \'kərt\ *adj* : rudely abrupt —**curt·ly** *adv* —**curt·ness** *n*

cur·tail \kər'tāl\ *vb* : shorten —**cur·tail·ment** *n*

cur·tain \'kərtᵊn\ *n* : hanging screen that can be drawn back or raised —**curtain** *vb*

curt·sy, curt·sey \'kərtsē\ *n, pl* **-sies** *or* **-seys** : courteous bow made by bending the knees —**curtsy, curtsey** *vb*

cur·va·ture \'kərvə,chūr\ *n* : amount or state of curving

curve \'kərv\ *vb* **curved; curv·ing** : bend from a straight line or course ~ *n* **1** : a bending without angles **2** : something curved

cush·ion \'kushən\ *n* **1** : soft pillow **2** : something that eases or protects ~ *vb* **1** : provide with a cushion **2** : soften the force of

cusp \'kəsp\ *n* : pointed end

cus·pid \'kəspəd\ *n* : a canine tooth

cus·pi·dor \'kəspə,dȯr\ *n* : spittoon

cus·tard \'kəstərd\ *n* : sweetened cooked mixture of milk and eggs

cus·to·dy \'kəstədē\ *n, pl* **-dies** : immediate care or charge —**cus·to·di·al** \,kəs'tōdēəl\ *adj* —**cus·to·di·an** \-ēən\ *n*

cus·tom \'kəstəm\ *n* **1** : habitual course of action **2** *pl* : import taxes ~ *adj* : made to personal order —**cus·tom·ari·ly** \,kəstə'merəlē\ *adv* —**custom·ary** \'kəstə,merē\ *adj* —**custom-built** *adj* —**cus·tom-made** *adj*

cus·tom·er \'kəstəmər\ *n* : buyer

cut \'kət\ *vb* **cut; cut·ting** **1** : penetrate or divide with a sharp edge **2** : experience the growth of (a tooth) through the gum **3** : shorten **4** : remove by severing **5** : intersect ~ *n* **1** : something separated by cutting **2** : reduction —**cut in** *vb* : thrust oneself between others

cu·ta·ne·ous \kyu'tānēəs\ *adj* : relating to the skin

cute \'kyüt\ *adj* **cut·er; -est** : pretty

cu·ti·cle \'kyütikəl\ *n* : outer layer (as of skin)

cut·lass \'kətləs\ *n* : short heavy curved sword

cut·lery \'kətlərē\ *n* : cutting utensils

cut·let \-lət\ *n* : slice of meat

cut·ter \'kətər\ *n* **1** : tool or machine for cutting **2** : small armed motorboat **3** : light sleigh

cut·throat *n* : murderer ~ *adj* : ruthless

-cy \sē\ *n suffix* **1** : action or practice **2** : rank or office **3** : body **4** : state or quality

cy·a·nide \'sīə,nīd, -nəd\ *n* : poisonous chemical salt

cy·cle \'sīkəl, 4 also 'sikəl\ *n* **1** : period of time for a series of repeated events **2** : recurring round of events **3** : long period of time **4** : bicycle or motorcycle ~ *vb* **-cled; -cling** : ride a cycle —**cy·clic** \'sīklik, 'sik-\, **cy·cli·cal** \-əl\ *adj* —**cy·clist** \'sīklist, 'sik-\ *n*

cy·clone \'sī,klōn\ *n* : tornado —**cy·clon·ic** \sī'klänik\ *adj*

cy·clo·pe·dia, cy·clo·pae·dia \,sīklə'pēdēə\ *n* : encyclopedia

cyl·in·der \'siləndər\ *n* **1** : long round body or figure **2** : rotating chamber in a revolver **3** : piston chamber in an engine —**cy·lin·dri·cal** \sə'lindrikəl\ *adj*

cym·bal \'simbəl\ *n* : one of 2 concave brass plates clashed together

cyn·ic \'sinik\ *n* : one who attributes all actions to selfish motives —**cyn·i·cal** \-ikəl\ *adj* —**cyn·i·cism** \-ə,sizəm\ *n*

cy·no·sure \'sīnə,shúr. 'sin-\ n : center of attraction

cy·press \'sīprəs\ n : evergreen tree related to the pines

cyst \'sist\ n : abnormal bodil[...]
cys·tic \'sistik\ adj

czar \'zär\ n : ruler of Russia unt[...] **—czar·ist** n or adj

D

d \'dē\ n, pl **d's** or **ds** \'dēz\ : 4th letter of the alphabet

¹dab \'dab\ n : gentle touch or stroke ~ vb **-bb-** : touch or apply lightly

²dab n : small amount

dab·ble \'dabəl\ vb **-bled; -bling 1** : splash **2** : work without serious effort **—dab·bler** \-blər\ n

dachs·hund \'däks,hunt\ n : small dog with a long body and short legs

dad \'dad\ n : father

dad·dy \'dadē\ n, pl **-dies** : father

daf·fo·dil \'dafə,dil\ n : narcissus with trumpetlike flowers

daft \'daft\ adj : foolish **—daft·ness** n

dag·ger \'dagər\ n : knife for stabbing

dahl·ia \'dalyə. 'dàl-\ n : tuberous herb with showy flowers

dai·ly \'dālē\ adj **1** : occurring. done. or used every day or every weekday **2** : computed in terms of one day ~ n. pl **-lies** : daily newspaper **—daily** adv

dain·ty \'dāntē\ n, pl **-ties** : something delicious ~ adj **-ti·er; -est** : delicately pretty **—dain·ti·ly** adv **—dain·ti·ness** n

dairy \'darē\ n. pl **-ies** : farm that produces or company that processes milk **—dairy·maid** n **—dairy·man** \-mən. -,man\ n

da·is \'dāəs\ n : raised platform (as for a speaker)

dai·sy \'dāzē\ n, pl **-sies** : tall leafy-stemmed plant bearing showy flowers

dale \'dāl\ n : valley

dal·ly \'dalē\ vb **-lied; -ly·ing 1** : flirt **2** : dawdle **—dal·li·ance** \-əns\ n

dal·ma·tian \dal'māshən\ n : large dog having a spotted white coat

¹dam \'dam\ n : female parent of a domestic animal

²dam n : barrier to hold back water **—dam** vb

dam·age \'damij\ n **1** : loss or harm due to injury **2** pl : compensation for loss

or injury ~ vb **-aged; -ag·ing** : do damage to

dam·ask \'daməsk\ n : firm lustrous figured fabric

dame \'dām\ n : woman of rank or authority

damn \'dam\ vb **1** : condemn to hell **2** : curse **—dam·na·ble** \-nəbəl\ adj **—dam·na·tion** \dam'nāshən\ n **—damned** adj

damp \'damp\ n : moisture ~ vb **1** : reduce the draft in **2** : restrain **3** : moisten ~ adj : moist **—damp·ness** n

damp·en \'dampən\ vb **1** : diminish in activity or vigor **2** : make or become damp

damp·er \'dampər\ n : movable plate to regulate a flue draft

dam·sel \'damzəl\ n : young woman

dance \'dans\ vb **danced; danc·ing** : move rhythmically to music ~ n : act of dancing or a gathering for dancing **—danc·er** n

dan·de·li·on \'dand³l,īən\ n : common yellow-flowered herb

dan·der \'dandər\ n : temper

dan·druff \'dandrəf\ n : whitish thin dry scales of skin on the scalp

dan·dy \'dandē\ n, pl **-dies 1** : man too concerned with clothes **2** : something excellent ~ adj **-di·er; -est** : very good

dan·ger \'dānjər\ n **1** : exposure to injury or evil **2** : something that may cause injury **—dan·ger·ous** \'dānjərəs\ adj

dan·gle \'dangəl\ vb **-gled; -gling 1** : hang and swing freely **2** : be left without support or connection **3** : allow or cause to hang **4** : offer as an inducement

dank \'dank\ adj : unpleasantly damp

dap·per \'dapər\ adj : neat and stylishly dressed

ap·ple \'dapəl\ *vb* **-pled; -pling :** mark with colored spots

are \'dar\ *vb* **dared; dar·ing 1 :** have sufficient courage **2 :** urge or provoke to contend **—dare** *n* **—dar·ing** \'darin\ *n or adj*

dare·dev·il *n* : recklessly bold person

dark \'därk\ *adj* **1 :** having little or no light **2 :** not light in color **3 :** gloomy **~** *n* : absence of light **—dark·en** \-ən\ *vb* **—dark·ly** *adv* **—dark·ness** *n*

dar·ling \'därlin\ *n* **1 :** beloved **2 :** favorite **~** *adj* **1 :** dearly loved **2 :** very pleasing

darn \'därn\ *vb* : mend with interlacing stitches **—darn·er** *n*

dart \'därt\ *n* **1 :** small pointed missile **2** *pl* : game of throwing darts at a target **3 :** tapering fold in a garment **4 :** quick movement **~** *vb* : move suddenly or rapidly

dash \'dash\ *vb* **1 :** smash or knock or hurl violently **3 :** ruin **4 :** perform or finish hastily **5 :** move quickly **~** *n* **1 :** sudden burst, splash, or stroke **2 :** punctuation mark **—3 :** tiny amount **4 :** showiness or liveliness **5 :** sudden rush **6 :** short race **7 :** dashboard

dash·board *n* : instrument panel

dash·ing \'dashin\ *adj* : dapper and charming

das·tard \'dastərd\ *n* : one who sneakingly commits malicious acts

das·tard·ly \-lē\ *adj* : base or malicious

da·ta \'dātə, 'dat-, 'dät-\ *n sing or pl* : factual information

da·ta·base \-,bās\ *n* : data organized for computer search

¹date \'dāt\ *n* : edible fruit of a palm

²date *n* **1 :** day, month, or year when something is done or made **2 :** historical time period **3 :** social engagement or the person one goes out with **~** *vb* **dat·ed; dat·ing 1 :** determine or record the date of **2 :** have a date with **3 :** originate **—to date :** up to now

dat·ed \-əd\ *adj* : old-fashioned

da·tum \'dātəm, 'dat-, 'dät-\ *n, pl* **-ta** \-ə\, *or* **-tums** : piece of data

daub \'dob\ *vb* : smear **~** *n* : something daubed on **—daub·er** *n*

daugh·ter \'dotər\ *n* : human female offspring

daugh·ter-in-law *n, pl* **daughters-in-law** : wife of one's son

daunt \'dont\ *vb* : lessen the courage of

daunt·less \-ləs\ *adj* : fearless

dav·en·port \'davən,port\ *n* : sofa

daw·dle \'dod⁰l\ *vb* **-dled; -dling 1 :** waste time **2 :** loiter

dawn \'don\ *vb* **1 :** grow light as the sun rises **2 :** begin to appear, develop, or be understood **~** *n* : first appearance (as of daylight)

day \'dā\ *n* **1 :** period of light between one night and the next **2 :** 24 hours **3 :** specified date **4 :** particular time or age **5 :** period of work for a day **—day·light** *n* **—day·time** *n*

day·break *n* : dawn

day·dream *n* : fantasy of wish fulfillment **—daydream** *vb*

daylight saving time *n* : time one hour ahead of standard time

daze \'dāz\ *vb* **dazed; daz·ing 1 :** stun by a blow **2 :** dazzle **—daze** *n*

daz·zle \'dazəl\ *vb* **-zled; -zling 1 :** overpower with light **2 :** impress greatly **—dazzle** *n*

DDT \,dē,dē'tē\ *n* : long-lasting insecticide

dea·con \'dēkən\ *n* : subordinate church officer

dea·con·ess \'dēkənəs\ *n* : woman who assists in church ministry

dead \'ded\ *adj* **1 :** lifeless **2 :** unresponsive or inactive **3 :** exhausted **4 :** obsolete **5 :** precise **~** *n, pl* **dead 1 :** one that is dead **—usu. with** *the* **2 :** most lifeless time **~** *adv* **1 :** completely **2 :** directly **—dead·en** \'ded⁰n\ *vb*

dead·beat *n* : one who will not pay debts

dead end *n* : end of a street with no exit **—dead-end** *adj*

dead heat *n* : tie in a contest

dead·line *n* : time by which something must be finished

dead·lock *n* : struggle that neither side can win **—deadlock** *vb*

dead·ly \'dedlē\ *adj* **-li·er; -est 1 :** capable of causing death **2 :** very accurate **3 :** fatal to spiritual progress **4 :** suggestive of death **5 :** very great **~** *adv* : extremely **—dead·li·ness** *n*

dead·pan *adj* : expressionless **—dead·pan** *n or vb or adv*

dead·wood *n* : something useless

deaf \'def\ *adj* : unable or unwilling to hear **—deaf·en** \-ən\ *vb* **—deaf·ness** *n*

deaf-mute *n* : deaf person unable to speak

deal \'dēl\ n 1 : indefinite quantity 2 : distribution of playing cards 3 : negotiation or agreement 4 : treatment received 5 : bargain ~ vb dealt \'delt\; deal·ing \'dēliŋ\ 1 : distribute playing cards 2 : be concerned with 3 : administer or deliver 4 : take action 5 : sell 6 : reach a state of acceptance —deal·er n —deal·ing n

dean \'dēn\ n 1 : head of a group of clergy members 2 : university or school administrator 3 : senior member

dear \'dir\ adj 1 : highly valued or loved 2 : expensive ~ n : loved one —dear·ly adv —dear·ness n

dearth \'dərth\ n : scarcity

death \'deth\ n 1 : end of life 2 : cause of loss of life 3 : state of being dead 4 : destruction or extinction —death·less adj —death·ly adj or adv

de·ba·cle \di'bäkəl, -'bakəl\ n : disaster or fiasco

de·bar \di'bär\ vb : bar from something

de·bark \-'bärk\ vb : disembark —de·bar·ka·tion \,dē,bär'kāshən\ n

de·base \di'bās\ vb : disparage —de·base·ment n

de·bate \-'bāt\ vb -bat·ed; -bat·ing : discuss a question by argument —de·bat·able adj —debate n —de·bat·er n

de·bauch \-'bóch\ vb : seduce or corrupt —de·bauch·ery \-ərē\ n

de·bil·i·tate \-'bilə,tāt\ vb -tat·ed; -tat·ing : make ill or weak

de·bil·i·ty \-'bilətē\ n, pl -ties : physical weakness

debit \'debət\ n : account entry of a payment or debt ~ vb : record as a debit

deb·o·nair \,debə'nar\ adj : suave

de·bris \də'brē, dā-; 'dā,brē\ n, pl -bris \-'brēz, -,brēz\ : remains of something destroyed

debt \'det\ n 1 : sin 2 : something owed 3 : state of owing —debt·or \-ər\ n

de·bunk \dē'bəŋk\ vb : expose as false

de·but \'dā,byü,dā'byü\ n 1 : first public appearance 2 : formal entrance into society —debut vb —deb·u·tante \'debyü,tänt\ n

de·cade \'dek,ād, -əd; de'kād\ n : 10 years

dec·a·dence \'dekədəns, di'kād°ns\ n : deterioration —dec·a·dent \-ənt, -°nt\ adj or n

de·cal \'dē,kal, di'kal, 'dekəl\ n : picture or design for transfer from prepared paper

de·camp \di'kamp\ vb : depart suddenly

de·cant \di'kant\ vb : pour gently

de·cant·er \-ər\ n : ornamental bottle

de·cap·i·tate \di'kapə,tāt\ vb -tat·ed; -tat·ing : behead —de·cap·i·ta·tion \-,kapə'tāshən\ n

de·cay \di'kā\ vb 1 : decline in condition 2 : decompose —decay n

de·cease \-'sēs\ n : death —decease vb

de·ceit \-'sēt\ n 1 : deception 2 : dishonesty —de·ceit·ful \-fəl\ adj —de·ceit·ful·ly adv —de·ceit·ful·ness n

de·ceive \-'sēv\ vb -ceived; -ceiv·ing : trick or mislead —de·ceiv·er n

de·cel·er·ate \dē'selə,rāt\ vb -at·ed; -at·ing : slow down

De·cem·ber \di'sembər\ n : 12th month of the year having 31 days

de·cent \'dēs°nt\ adj 1 : good, right, or just 2 : clothed 3 : not obscene 4 : fairly good —de·cen·cy \-°nsē\ n —de·cent·ly adv

de·cep·tion \di'sepshən\ n 1 : act or fact of deceiving 2 : fraud —de·cep·tive \-'septiv\ adj —de·cep·tive·ly adv —de·cep·tive·ness n

de·cide \di'sīd\ vb -cid·ed; -cid·ing 1 : make a choice or judgment 2 : bring to a conclusion 3 : cause to decide

de·cid·ed adj 1 : unquestionable 2 : resolute —de·cid·ed·ly adv

de·cid·u·ous \di'sijəwəs\ adj : having leaves that fall annually

dec·i·mal \'desəməl\ n : fraction in which the denominator is a power of 10 expressed by a point (**decimal point**) placed at the left of the numerator —decimal adj

de·ci·pher \di'sīfər\ vb : make out the meaning of —de·ci·pher·able adj

de·ci·sion \-'sizhən\ n 1 : act or result of deciding 2 : determination

de·ci·sive \-'sīsiv\ adj 1 : having the power to decide 2 : conclusive 3 : showing determination —de·ci·sive·ly adv —de·ci·sive·ness n

deck \'dek\ n 1 : floor of a ship 2 : pack of playing cards ~ vb 1 : array or dress up 2 : knock down

de·claim \di'klām\ vb : speak loudly or impressively —dec·la·ma·tion \,deklə'māshən\ n

de·clare \di'klar\ vb -clared; -clar·ing 1 : make known formally 2 : state emphatically —dec·la·ra·tion \,deklə-

'rāshən\ *n* —**de·clar·a·tive** \di'klarə-
tiv\ *adj* —**de·clar·a·to·ry** \di'klarə,tōrē\ *adj* —**de·clar·er** *n*

de·clen·sion \di'klenchən\ *n* : inflectional forms of a noun, pronoun,
or adjective

de·cline \di'klīn\ *vb* -**clined**; -**clin·ing** 1
: turn or slope downward 2 : wane 3
: refuse to accept 4 : inflect ~ *n* 1
: gradual wasting away 2 : change to
a lower state or level 3 : a descending
slope —**de·clin·a·tion** \,deklə-'nā-
shən\ *n*

de·code \dē'kōd\ *vb* : decipher (a coded
message) —**de·cod·er** *n*

de·com·mis·sion \,dēkə'mishən\ *vb*
: remove from service

de·com·pose \,dēkəm'pōz\ *vb* 1
: separate into parts 2 : decay —
de·com·po·si·tion \dē,kämpə'zishən\
n

de·con·ges·tant \,dēkən'jestənt\ *n*
: agent that relieves congestion

de·cor, dé·cor \dā'kór, 'dā,kór\ *n* : room
design or decoration

dec·o·rate \'dekə,rāt\ *vb* -**rat·ed**; -**rat·
ing** 1 : add something attractive to 2
: honor with a medal —**dec·o·ra·tion**
\,dekə'rāshən\ *n* —**dec·o·ra·tive**
\'dekərətiv\ *adj* —**dec·o·ra·tor**
\'dekə,rātər\ *n*

de·co·rum \di'kōrəm\ *n* : proper behavior —**de·co·rous** \'dekərəs, di'kōrəs\
adj

de·coy \'dē,kói, di'-\ *n* : something that
tempts or draws attention from another ~ *vb* : tempt

de·crease \di'krēs\ *vb* -**creased**; -**creas·
ing** : grow or cause to grow less —
decrease \'dē,krēs\ *n*

de·cree \di'krē\ *n* : official order —**de·
cree** *vb*

de·crep·it \di'krepət\ *adj* : impaired by
age

de·cre·scen·do \,dākrə'shendō\ *adv* or
adj : with a decrease in volume

de·cry \di'krī\ *vb* : express strong disapproval of

ded·i·cate \'dedi,kāt\ *vb* -**cat·ed**; -**cat·
ing** 1 : set apart for a purpose (as
honor or worship) 2 : address to
someone as a compliment —**ded·i·
ca·tion** \,dedi'kāshən\ *n* —**ded·i·ca·
to·ry** \'dedikə,tōrē\ *adj*

de·duce \di'düs, -'dyüs\ *vb* -**duced**;
-**duc·ing** : derive by reasoning —
de·duc·ible *adj*

de·duct \-'dəkt\ *vb* : subtract —**deduct·
ible** *adj*

de·duc·tion \-'dəkshən\ *n* 1
: subtraction 2 : reasoned conclusion
—**de·duc·tive** \-'dəktiv\ *adj*

deed \'dēd\ *n* 1 : exploit 2 : document
showing ownership ~ *vb* : convey by
deed

deem \'dēm\ *vb* : think

deep \'dēp\ *adj* 1 : extending far or a
specified distance down, back,
within, or outward 2 : occupied 3
: dark and rich in color 4 : low in tone
~ *adv* 1 : deeply 2 : far along in time
~ *n* : deep place —**deep·en** \'dēpən\
vb —**deep·ly** *adv*

deep-seat·ed \-'sētəd\ *adj* : firmly established

deer \'dir\ *n, pl* **deer** : ruminant mammal
with antlers in the male —**deer·skin**
n

de·face \di'fās\ *vb* : mar the surface of
—**de·face·ment** *n* —**de·fac·er** *n*

de·fame \di'fām\ *vb* -**famed**; -**fam·ing**
: injure the reputation of —**def·a·ma·
tion** \,defə'māshən\ *n* —**de·fam·a·to·
ry** \di'famə,tōrē\ *adj*

de·fault \di'fólt\ *n* : failure in a duty —
default *vb* —**de·fault·er** *n*

de·feat \di'fēt\ *vb* 1 : frustrate 2 : win
victory over ~ *n* : loss of a battle or
contest

def·e·cate \'defi,kāt\ *vb* -**cat·ed**; -**cat·ing**
: discharge feces from the bowels —
def·e·ca·tion \,defi'kāshən\ *n*

de·fect \'dē,fekt, di'fekt\ *n* : imperfection ~ \di'-\ *vb* : desert —**de·
fection** \-'fekshən\ *n* —**de·fec·tor**
\-'fektər\ *n*

de·fec·tive \di'fektiv\ *adj* : faulty or deficient —**defective** *n*

de·fend \-'fend\ *vb* 1 : protect from danger or harm 2 : take the side of —
de·fend·er *n*

de·fen·dant \-'fendənt\ *n* : person
charged or sued in a court

de·fense \-'fens\ *n* 1 : act of defending
2 : something that defends 3 : party,
group, or team that opposes another
—**de·fense·less** *adj* —**de·fen·si·ble**
adj —**de·fen·sive** *adj or n*

[1]**de·fer** \di'fər\ *vb* -**rr**- : postpone —**de·
fer·ment** \di'fərmənt\ *n* —**de·fer·ra·
ble** \-əbəl\ *adj*

[2]**defer** *vb* -**rr**- : yield to the opinion or
wishes of another —**def·er·ence**
\'defrəns\ *n* —**def·er·en·tial** \,defə-
'renchəl\ *adj*

de·fi·ance \di'fīəns\ *n* : disposition to resist —**de·fi·ant** \-ənt\ *adj*

de·fi·cient \di'fishənt\ *adj* 1 : lacking something necessary 2 : not up to standard —**de·fi·cien·cy** \-'fishənsē\ *n*

def·i·cit \'defəsət\ *n* : shortage esp. in money

de·file \di'fīl\ *vb* **-filed; -fil·ing** 1 : make filthy or corrupt 2 : profane or dishonor —**de·file·ment** *n*

de·fine \di'fīn\ *vb* **-fined; -fin·ing** 1 : fix or mark the limits of 2 : clarify in outline 3 : set forth the meaning of —**de·fin·able** *adj* —**de·fin·ably** *adv* —**de·fin·er** *n* —**def·i·ni·tion** \,defə-'nishən\ *n*

def·i·nite \'defənət\ *adj* 1 : having distinct limits 2 : clear in meaning, intent, or identity 3 : typically designating an identified or immediately identifiable person or thing —**def·i·nite·ly** *adv*

de·fin·i·tive \di'finətiv\ *adj* 1 : conclusive 2 : authoritative

de·flate \di'flāt\ *vb* **-flat·ed; -flat·ing** 1 : release air or gas from 2 : reduce —**de·fla·tion** \-'flāshən\ *n*

de·flect \'flekt\ *vb* : turn aside —**de·flec·tion** \-'flekshən\ *n*

de·fog \-'fòg, -'fäg\ *vb* : remove condensed moisture from —**de·fog·ger** *n*

de·fo·li·ate \dē'fōlē,āt\ *vb* **-at·ed; -at·ing** : deprive of leaves esp. prematurely —**de·fo·li·ant** \-lēənt\ *n* —**de·fo·li·a·tion** \-,fōlē'āshən\ *n*

de·form \di'fòrm\ *vb* 1 : distort 2 : disfigure —**de·for·ma·tion** \,dē,fòr-'māshən, ,defər-\ *n* —**de·for·mi·ty** \di'fòrmətē\ *n*

de·fraud \di'fròd\ *vb* : cheat

de·fray \-'frā\ *vb* : pay

de·frost \-'fròst\ *vb* 1 : thaw out 2 : free from ice —**de·frost·er** *n*

deft \'deft\ *adj* : quick and skillful —**deft·ly** *adv* —**deft·ness** *n*

de·funct \di'fəŋkt\ *adj* : dead

de·fy \-'fī\ *vb* **-fied; -fy·ing** 1 : challenge 2 : boldly refuse to obey

de·gen·er·ate \di'jenərət\ *adj* : degraded or corrupt ~ *n* : degenerate person ~ \-ə,rāt\ *vb* : become degenerate —**de·gen·er·a·cy** \-rəsē\ *n* —**de·gen·er·a·tion** \-,jenə'rāshən\ *n* —**de·gen·er·a·tive** \-'jenə,rātiv\ *adj*

de·grade \di'grād\ *vb* 1 : reduce from a higher to a lower rank or degree 2 : debase 3 : decompose

de·grad·able \-əbəl\ *adj* —**deg·ra·da·tion** \,degrə'dāshən\ *n*

de·gree \di'grē\ *n* 1 : step in a series 2 : extent, intensity, or scope 3 : title given to a college graduate 4 : a 360th part of the circumference of a circle 5 : unit for measuring temperature

de·hy·drate \dē'hī,drāt\ *vb* 1 : remove water from 2 : lose liquid —**de·hy·dra·tion** \,dēhī'drāshən\ *n*

de·i·fy \'dēə,fī, 'dā-\ *vb* **-fied; -fy·ing** 1 : make a god of —**de·i·fi·ca·tion** \,dēəfə'kāshən, ,dā-\ *n*

deign \'dān\ *vb* : condescend

de·i·ty \'dēətē, 'dā-\ *n, pl* **-ties** 1 *cap* : God 2 : a god or goddess

de·ject·ed \di'jektəd\ *adj* : sad —**de·jec·tion** \-shən\ *n*

de·lay \di'lā\ *n* : a putting off of something ~ *vb* 1 : postpone 2 : stop or hinder for a time

de·lec·ta·ble \di'lektəbəl\ *adj* : delicious

del·e·gate \'deligət, -,gāt\ *n* : representative ~ \-,gāt\ *vb* **-gat·ed; -gat·ing** 1 : entrust to another 2 : appoint as one's delegate —**del·e·ga·tion** \,deli'gāshən\ *n*

de·lete \di'lēt\ *vb* **-let·ed; -let·ing** : eliminate something written —**de·le·tion** \-'lēshən\ *n*

del·e·te·ri·ous \,delə'tirēəs\ *adj* : harmful

de·lib·er·ate \di'libərət\ *adj* 1 : determined after careful thought 2 : intentional 3 : not hurried ~ \-ə,rāt\ *vb* **-at·ed; -at·ing** : consider carefully —**de·lib·er·ate·ly** *adv* —**de·lib·er·ate·ness** *n* —**de·lib·er·a·tion** \-,libə'rāshən\ *n* —**de·lib·er·a·tive** \-'libə,rātiv, -rət-\ *adj*

del·i·ca·cy \'delikəsē\ *n, pl* **-cies** 1 : something special and pleasing to eat 2 : fineness 3 : frailty

del·i·cate \'delikət\ *adj* 1 : subtly pleasing to the senses 2 : dainty and charming 3 : sensitive or fragile 4 : requiring fine skill or tact —**del·i·cate·ly** *adv*

del·i·ca·tes·sen \,delikə'tes⁰n\ *n* : store that sells ready-to-eat food

de·li·cious \di'lishəs\ *adj* : very pleasing esp. in taste or aroma —**de·li·cious·ly** *adv* —**de·li·cious·ness** *n*

de·light \di'līt\ *n* 1 : great pleasure 2 : source of great pleasure ~ *vb* 1 : take great pleasure 2 : satisfy greatly —**de·light·ful** \-fəl\ *adj* —**de·light·ful·ly** *adv*

de·lin·eate \di'linē,āt\ *vb* **-eat·ed; -eat·ing** : sketch or portray —**de·lin·ea·tion** \-,linē'āshən\ *n*

de·lin·quent \-'liŋkwənt\ *n* : delinquent person — *adj* **1** : violating duty or law **2** : overdue in payment —**de·lin·quen·cy** \-kwənsē\ *n*

de·lir·i·um \di'lirēəm\ *n* : mental disturbance —**de·lir·i·ous** \-ēəs\ *adj*

de·liv·er \di'livər\ *vb* **1** : set free **2** : hand over **3** : assist in birth **4** : say or speak **5** : send to an intended destination —**de·liv·er·ance** \-ərəns\ *n* —**de·liv·er·er** *n* —**de·liv·ery** \-ərē\ *n*

dell \'del\ *n* : small secluded valley

del·ta \'deltə\ *n* : triangle of land at the mouth of a river

de·lude \di'lüd\ *vb* **-lud·ed; -lud·ing** : mislead or deceive

del·uge \'delyüj\ *n* **1** : flood **2** : drenching rain ~ *vb* **-uged; -ug·ing** **1** : flood **2** : overwhelm

de·lu·sion \di'lüzhən\ *n* : false belief

de·luxe \di'lùks, -'ləks, -'lüks\ *adj* : very luxurious or elegant

delve \'delv\ *vb* **delved; delv·ing 1** : dig **2** : seek information in records

dem·a·gogue, dem·a·gog \'demə,gäg\ *n* : politician who appeals to emotion and prejudice —**dem·a·gogu·ery** \-,gägərē\ *n* —**dem·a·gogy** \-,gägē, -,gäjē\ *n*

de·mand \di'mand\ *n* **1** : act of demanding **2** : something claimed as due **3** : ability and desire to buy **4** : urgent need ~ *vb* **1** : ask for with authority **2** : require

de·mar·cate \di'mär,kāt, 'dē,mär-\ *vb* **-cat·ed; -cat·ing** : mark the limits of —**de·mar·ca·tion** \,dē,mär'kāshən\ *n*

de·mean \di'mēn\ *vb* : degrade

de·mean·or \-'mēnər\ *n* : behavior

de·ment·ed \-'mentəd\ *adj* : crazy

de·mer·it \-'merət\ *n* : mark given an offender

demi·god \'demi,gäd\ *n* : mythological being less powerful than a god

de·mise \di'mīz\ *n* **1** : death **2** : loss of status

demi·tasse \'demi,tas\ *n* : small cup of coffee

de·mo·bi·lize \di'mōbə,līz, dē-\ *vb* : disband from military service —**de·mo·bi·li·za·tion** \-,mōbələ'zāshən\ *n*

de·moc·ra·cy \di'mäkrəsē\ *n, pl* **-cies 1** : government in which the supreme power is held by the people **2**

: political unit with democratic government

dem·o·crat \'demə,krat\ *n* : adherent of democracy

dem·o·crat·ic \,demə'kratik\ *adj* : relating to or favoring democracy —**dem·o·crat·i·cal·ly** \-tiklē\ *adv* —**de·moc·ra·tize** \di'mäkrə,tīz\ *vb*

de·mol·ish \di'mälish\ *vb* **1** : tear down or smash **2** : put an end to —**de·mo·li·tion** \,demə'lishən, ,dē-\ *n*

de·mon \'dēmən\ *n* : evil spirit —**de·mon·ic** \di'mänik\ *adj*

dem·on·strate \'demən,strāt\ *vb* **-strat·ed; -strat·ing 1** : show clearly or publicly **2** : prove **3** : explain —**de·mon·stra·ble** \di'mänstrəbəl\ *adj* —**de·mon·stra·bly** \-blē\ *adv* —**dem·on·stra·tion** \,demən'strāshən\ *n* —**de·mon·stra·tive** \di'mänstrətiv\ *adj or n* —**dem·on·stra·tor** \'demən,strātər\ *n*

de·mor·al·ize \di'mórə,līz\ *vb* : destroy the enthusiasm of

de·mote \di'mōt\ *vb* **-mot·ed; -mot·ing** : reduce to a lower rank —**de·mo·tion** \-'mōshən\ *n*

de·mur \di'mər\ *vb* **-rr-** : object —**de·mur** *n*

de·mure \di'myùr\ *adj* : modest —**de·mure·ly** *adv*

den \'den\ *n* **1** : animal's shelter **2** : hiding place **3** : cozy private little room

de·na·ture \dē'nāchər\ *vb* **-tured; -tur·ing** : make (alcohol) unfit for drinking

de·ni·al \di'nīəl\ *n* : rejection of a request or of the validity of a statement

den·i·grate \'deni,grāt\ *vb* **-grat·ed; -grat·ing** : speak ill of

den·im \'denəm\ *n* **1** : durable twilled cotton fabric **2** *pl* : pants of denim

den·i·zen \'denəzən\ *n* : inhabitant

de·nom·i·na·tion \di,nämə'nāshən\ *n* **1** : religious body **2** : value or size in a series —**de·nom·i·na·tion·al** \-shə-nəl\ *adj*

de·nom·i·na·tor \-'nämə,nātər\ *n* : part of a fraction below the line

de·note \di'nōt\ *vb* **1** : mark out plainly **2** : mean —**de·no·ta·tion** \,dēnō'tāshən\ *n* —**de·no·ta·tive** \'dēnō-,tātiv, di'nōtətiv\ *adj*

de·noue·ment \,dā,nü'mäⁿ\ *n* : final outcome (as of a drama)

de·nounce \di'naùns\ *vb* **-nounced; -nounc·ing 1** : pronounce blameworthy or evil **2** : inform against

dense \\'dens\ *adj* **dens•er; -est 1** : thick, compact, or crowded **2** : stupid — **dense•ly** *adv* — **dense•ness** *n* — **den•si•ty** \\'densətē\ *n*

dent \\'dent\ *n* : small depression — **dent** *vb*

den•tal \\'dentᵊl\ *adj* : relating to teeth or dentistry

den•ti•frice \\'dentəfrəs\ *n* : preparation for cleaning teeth

den•tin \\'dentᵊn\, **den•tine** \\'den,tēn, 'den-\ *n* : bonelike component of teeth

den•tist \\'dentist\ *n* : one who cares for and replaces teeth — **den•tist•ry** *n*

den•ture \\'denchər\ *n* : artificial teeth

de•nude \\di'nüd, -'nyüd\ *vb* **-nud•ed; -nud•ing** : strip of covering

de•nun•ci•a•tion \\di,nənsē'āshən\ *n* : act of denouncing

de•ny \\-'nī\ *vb* **-nied; -ny•ing 1** : declare untrue **2** : disavow **3** : refuse to grant

de•odor•ant \\dē'ōdərənt\ *n* : preparation to prevent unpleasant odors — **de•odor•ize** \\-,rīz\ *vb*

de•part \\di'pärt\ *vb* **1** : go away or away from **2** : die — **de•par•ture** \\-'pärchər\ *n*

de•part•ment \\di'pärtmənt\ *n* **1** : area of responsibility or interest **2** : functional division — **de•part•men•tal** \\di,pärt'mentᵊl, ,dē-\ *adj*

de•pend \\di'pend\ *vb* **1** : rely for support **2** : be determined by or based on something else — **de•pend•abil•i•ty** \\-,pendə'bilətē\ *n* — **de•pend•able** *adj* — **de•pen•dence** \\di'pendəns\ *n* — **de•pen•den•cy** \\-dənsē\ *n* — **de•pen•dent** \\-ənt\ *adj or n*

de•pict \\di'pikt\ *vb* : show by or as if by a picture — **de•pic•tion** \\-'pikshən\ *n*

de•plete \\di'plēt\ *vb* **-plet•ed; -plet•ing** : use up resources of — **de•ple•tion** \\-'plēshən\ *n*

de•plore \\-'plōr\ *vb* **-plored; -plor•ing** : regret strongly — **de•plor•able** \\-əbəl\ *adj*

de•ploy \\-'plói\ *vb* : spread out for battle — **de•ploy•ment** \\-mənt\ *n*

de•port \\di'pōrt\ *vb* **1** : behave **2** : send out of the country — **de•por•ta•tion** \\,dē,pōr'tāshən\ *n* — **de•port•ment** \\di'pōrtmənt\ *n*

de•pose \\-'pōz\ *vb* **-posed; -pos•ing 1** : remove (a ruler) from office **2** : testify — **de•po•si•tion** \\,depə-'zishən, ,dē-\ *n*

de•pos•it \\di'päzət\ *vb* **-it•ed; -it•ing**

: place esp. for safekeeping ~ *n* **1** : state of being deposited **2** : something deposited **3** : act of depositing **4** : natural accumulation — **de•pos•i•tor** \\-'päzətər\ *n*

de•pos•i•to•ry \\di'päzə,tōrē\ *n, pl* **-ries** : place for deposit

de•pot \\/ *usu* 'depō, 2 *usu* 'dēp-\ *n* **1** : place for storage **2** : bus or railroad station

de•prave \\di'prāv\ *vb* **-praved; -prav•ing** : corrupt morally — **de•praved** *adj* — **de•prav•i•ty** \\-'pravətē\ *n*

dep•re•cate \\'depri,kāt\ *vb* **-cat•ed; -cat•ing 1** : express disapproval of **2** : belittle — **dep•re•ca•tion** \\,depri-'kāshən\ *n* — **dep•re•ca•to•ry** \\'depri-kə,tōrē\ *adj*

de•pre•ci•ate \\di'prēshē,āt\ *vb* **-at•ed; -at•ing 1** : lessen in value **2** : belittle — **de•pre•ci•a•tion** \\-,prēshē'āshən\ *n*

dep•re•da•tion \\,deprə'dāshən\ *n* : a laying waste or plundering — **dep•re•date** \\'deprə,dāt\ *vb*

de•press \\di'pres\ *vb* **1** : press down **2** : lessen the activity or force of **3** : discourage **4** : decrease the market value of — **de•pres•sant** \\-ᵊnt\ *n or adj* — **de•pressed** *adj* — **de•pres•sive** \\-iv\ *adj or n* — **de•pres•sor** \\-ər\ *n*

de•pres•sion \\di'preshən\ *n* **1** : act of depressing or state of being depressed **2** : depressed place **3** : period of low economic activity

de•prive \\-'prīv\ *vb* **-prived; -priv•ing** : take or keep something away from — **de•pri•va•tion** \\,deprə'vāshən\ *n*

depth \\'depth\ *n, pl* **depths 1** : something that is deep **2** : distance down from a surface **3** : distance from front to back **4** : quality of being deep

dep•u•ta•tion \\,depyə'tāshən\ *n* : delegation

dep•u•ty \\'depyətē\ *n, pl* **-ties** : person appointed to act for another — **dep•u•tize** \\-yə,tīz\ *vb*

de•rail \\di'rāl\ *vb* : leave the rails — **de•rail•ment** *n*

de•range \\-'rānj\ *vb* **-ranged; -rang•ing 1** : disarrange or upset **2** : make insane — **de•range•ment** *n*

der•by \\'dərbē, *Brit* 'där-\ *n, pl* **-bies 1** : horse race **2** : stiff felt hat with dome-shaped crown

de•reg•u•late \\dē'regyù,lāt\ *vb* : remove restrictions on — **de•reg•u•la•tion** \\-,regyù'lāshən\ *n*

der•e•lict \\'derə,likt\ *adj* **1** : abandoned

2 : negligent ~ *n* **1** : something abandoned **2** : bum —**der·e·lic·tion** \ˌderəˈlikshən\ *n*

de·ride \diˈrīd\ *vb* **-rid·ed; -rid·ing** : make fun of —**de·ri·sion** \-ˈrizhən\ *n* —**de·ri·sive** \-ˈrīsiv\ *adj* —**de·ri·sive·ly** *adv* —**de·ri·sive·ness** *n*

de·rive \diˈrīv\ *vb* **-rived; -riv·ing 1** : obtain from a source or parent **2** : come from a source **3** : infer or deduce —**der·i·va·tion** \ˌderəˈvāshən\ *n* —**de·riv·a·tive** \diˈrivətiv\ *adj or n*

der·ma·tol·o·gy \ˌdərməˈtäləjē\ *n* : study of the skin and its disorders —**der·ma·tol·o·gist** \-jist\ *n*

de·rog·a·tive \diˈrägətiv\ *adj* : derogatory

de·rog·a·to·ry \diˈrägəˌtōrē\ *adj* : intended to lower the reputation

der·rick \ˈderik\ *n* **1** : hoisting apparatus **2** : framework over an oil well

de·scend \diˈsend\ *vb* **1** : move or climb down **2** : derive **3** : extend downward **4** : appear suddenly (as in an attack) —**de·scen·dant, de·scen·dent** \-ənt\ *adj or n* —**de·scent** \diˈsent\ *n*

de·scribe \-ˈskrīb\ *vb* **-scribed; -scrib·ing** : represent in words —**de·scrib·able** *adj* —**de·scrip·tion** \-ˈskripshən\ *n* —**de·scrip·tive** \-ˈskriptiv\ *adj*

de·scry \diˈskrī\ *vb* **-scried; -scry·ing** : catch sight of

des·e·crate \ˈdesiˌkrāt\ *vb* **-crat·ed; -crat·ing** : treat (something sacred) with disrespect —**des·e·cra·tion** \ˌdesiˈkrāshən\ *n*

de·seg·re·gate \dēˈsegrəˌgāt\ *vb* : eliminate esp. racial segregation in —**de·seg·re·ga·tion** *n*

¹**des·ert** \ˈdezərt\ *n* : dry barren region —**desert** *adj*

²**de·sert** \diˈzərt\ *n* : what one deserves

³**de·sert** \diˈzərt\ *vb* : abandon —**de·sert·er** *n* —**de·ser·tion** \-ˈzərshən\ *n*

de·serve \-ˈzərv\ *vb* **-served; -serv·ing** : be worthy of

des·ic·cate \ˈdesiˌkāt\ *vb* **-cat·ed; -cat·ing** : dehydrate —**des·ic·ca·tion** \ˌdesiˈkāshən\ *n*

de·sign \diˈzīn\ *vb* **1** : create and work out the details of **2** : make a pattern or sketch of ~ *n* **1** : mental project or plan **2** : purpose **3** : preliminary sketch **4** : underlying arrangement of elements **5** : decorative pattern —**de·sign·er** *n*

des·ig·nate \ˈdezigˌnāt\ *vb* **-nat·ed; -nat·ing 1** : indicate, specify, or name **2** : appoint —**des·ig·na·tion** \ˌdezigˈnāshən\ *n*

de·sire \diˈzīr\ *vb* **-sired; -sir·ing 1** : feel desire for **2** : request ~ *n* **1** : strong conscious impulse to have, be, or do something **2** : something desired —**de·sir·abil·i·ty** \-ˌzīrəˈbilətē\ *n* —**de·sir·able** \-ˈzīrəbəl\ *adj* —**de·sir·able·ness** *n* —**de·sir·ous** \-ˈzīrəs\ *adj*

de·sist \diˈzist, -ˈsist\ *vb* : stop

desk \ˈdesk\ *n* : table esp. for writing and reading

des·o·late \ˈdesələt, ˈdez-\ *adj* **1** : lifeless **2** : disconsolate ~ \-ˌlāt\ *vb* **-lat·ed; -lat·ing** : lay waste —**des·o·la·tion** \ˌdesəˈlāshən, ˌdez-\ *n*

de·spair \diˈspar\ *vb* : lose all hope ~ *n* : loss of hope

des·per·a·do \ˌdespəˈrädō, -ˈrād-\ *n, pl* **-does** *or* **-dos** : desperate criminal

des·per·ate \ˈdesprət\ *adj* **1** : hopeless **2** : rash **3** : extremely intense —**des·per·ate·ly** *adv* —**des·per·a·tion** \ˌdespəˈrāshən\ *n*

de·spi·ca·ble \diˈspikəbəl, ˈdespik-\ *adj* : deserving scorn

de·spise \diˈspīz\ *vb* **-spised; -spis·ing** : feel contempt for

de·spite \-ˈspīt\ *prep* : in spite of

de·spoil \diˈspȯil\ *vb* : strip of possessions or value

de·spon·den·cy \-ˈspändənsē\ *n* : dejection —**de·spon·dent** \-dənt\ *adj*

des·pot \ˈdespət, -ˌpät\ *n* : tyrant —**des·pot·ic** \desˈpätik\ *adj* —**des·po·tism** \ˈdespəˌtizəm\ *n*

des·sert \diˈzərt\ *n* : sweet food, fruit, or cheese ending a meal

des·ti·na·tion \ˌdestəˈnāshən\ *n* : place where something or someone is going

des·tine \ˈdestən\ *vb* **-tined; -tin·ing 1** : designate, assign, or determine in advance **2** : direct

des·ti·ny \ˈdestənē\ *n, pl* **-nies** : that which is to happen in the future

des·ti·tute \ˈdestəˌtüt, -ˌtyüt\ *adj* **1** : lacking something **2** : very poor —**des·ti·tu·tion** \ˌdestəˈtüshən, -ˈtyü-\ *n*

de·stroy \diˈstrȯi\ *vb* : kill or put an end to

de·stroy·er \-ˈstrȯiər\ *n* **1** : one that destroys **2** : small speedy warship

de·struc·tion \-ˈstrəkshən\ *n* **1** : action of destroying **2** : ruin —

de·struc·ti·bil·i·ty \-,strəktə'bilətē\ n
—**de·struc·ti·ble** \-'strəktəbəl\ adj
de·struc·tive \-'strəktiv\ adj

de·sul·to·ry \'desəl,tōrē\ adj : aimless

de·tach \di'tach\ vb : separate

de·tached \-'tacht\ adj 1 : separate 2
: aloof or impartial

de·tach·ment \-'tachmənt\ n 1
: separation 2 : troops or ships on special service 3 : aloofness 4
: impartiality

de·tail \di'tāl, 'dē,tāl\ n : small item or
part ~ vb : give details of

de·tain \di'tān\ vb 1 : hold in custody 2
: delay

de·tect \di'tekt\ vb : discover —**detect-
able** adj —**de·tec·tion** \-'tekshən\ n
—**de·tec·tor** \-tər\ n

de·tec·tive \-'tektiv\ n : one who investigates crime

dé·tente \dā'tänt\ n : relaxation of ten-
sions between nations

de·ten·tion \di'tenchən\ n : confinement

de·ter \-'tər\ vb -**rr**- : discourage or prevent —**de·ter·rence** \-əns\ n —
de·ter·rent \-ənt\ adj or n

de·ter·gent \di'tərjənt\ n : cleansing
agent

de·te·ri·o·rate \-'tirēə,rāt\ vb -**rat·ed;
-rat·ing** : make or become worse —
de·te·ri·o·ra·tion \-,tirēə'rāshən\ n

de·ter·mi·na·tion \di,tərmə'nāshən\ n 1
: act of deciding or fixing 2 : firm
purpose

de·ter·mine \-'tərmən\ vb -**mined;
-min·ing** 1 : decide on, establish, or
settle 2 : find out 3 : bring about as a
result

de·test \-'test\ vb : hate —**de·test·able**
adj —**de·tes·ta·tion** \,dē,tes'tāshən\ n

det·o·nate \'detⁿ,āt\ vb -**nat·ed; -nat·
ing** : explode —**det·o·na·tion**
\,detⁿ'āshən\ n —**det·o·na·tor**
\'detⁿ,ātər\ n

de·tour \'dē,tur\ n : temporary indirect
route —**detour** vb

de·tract \di'trakt\ vb : take away —**de-
trac·tion** \-'trakshən\ n —**de·trac·tor**
\-'traktər\ n

det·ri·ment \'detrəmənt\ n : damage —
det·ri·men·tal \,detrə'mentⁿl\ adj —
det·ri·men·tal·ly adv

deuce \'düs, 'dyüs\ n 1 : 2 in cards or
dice 2 : tie in tennis 3 : devil —used
as an oath

deut·sche mark \'dóichə-\ n : monetary
unit of Germany

de·val·ue \dē'val,yü\ vb : reduce the
value of —**de·val·u·a·tion** n

dev·as·tate \'devə,stāt\ vb -**tat·ed; -tat·
ing** : ruin —**dev·as·ta·tion** \,devə-
'stāshən\ n

de·vel·op \di'veləp\ vb 1 : grow, increase, or evolve gradually 2 : cause
to grow, increase, or reach full potential —**de·vel·op·er** n —**de·vel·op·
ment** n —**de·vel·op·men·tal** \-,veləp-
'mentⁿl\ adj

de·vi·ate \'dēvē,āt\ vb -**at·ed; -at·ing**
: change esp. from a course or standard —**de·vi·ant** \-vēənt\ adj or n —
de·vi·ate \-vēət, -vē,āt\ n —**de·vi·a·
tion** \,dēvē'āshən\ n

de·vice \di'vīs\ n 1 : specialized piece of
equipment or tool 2 : design

dev·il \'devəl\ n 1 : personified supreme
spirit of evil 2 : demon 3 : wicked
person ~ vb -**iled** or -**illed; -il·ing** or
-**il·ling** 1 : season highly 2 : pester —
dev·il·ish \'devəlish\ adj —**dev·il·ry**
\'devəlrē\, **dev·il·try** \-trē\ n

de·vi·ous \'dēvēəs\ adj : tricky

de·vise \di'vīz\ vb -**vised; -vis·ing**
1 : invent 2 : plot 3 : give by will

de·void \-'void\ adj : entirely lacking

de·vote \di'vōt\ vb -**vot·ed; -vot·ing** : set
apart for a special purpose

de·vot·ed adj : faithful

dev·o·tee \,devə'tē, -'tā\ n : ardent follower

de·vo·tion \di'vōshən\ n 1 : prayer —
usu. pl. 2 : loyalty and dedication —
de·vo·tion·al \-shənəl\ adj

de·vour \di'vaùər\ vb : consume raven-
ously —**de·vour·er** n

de·vout \-'vaút\ adj 1 : devoted to religion 2 : serious —**de·vout·ly** adv —
de·vout·ness n

dew \'dü, 'dyü\ n : moisture condensed
at night —**dew·drop** n —**dewy** adj

dex·ter·ous \'dekstrəs\ adj : skillful with
the hands —**dex·ter·i·ty** \dek'sterətē\
n —**dex·ter·ous·ly** adv

dex·trose \'dek,strōs\ n : plant or blood
sugar

di·a·be·tes \,dīə'bētēz, -'bētəs\ n
: disorder in which the body has too
little insulin and too much sugar —
di·a·bet·ic \-'betik\ adj or n

di·a·bol·ic \-'bälik\, **di·a·bol·i·cal** \-ikəl\
adj : fiendish

di·a·crit·ic \-'kritik\ n : mark accompanying a letter and indicating a specific
sound value —**di·a·crit·i·cal** \-'kri-
tikəl\ adj

di·a·dem \'dīə,dem\ *n* : crown

di·ag·no·sis \,dīig'nōsəs, -əg-\ *n, pl* **-no·ses** \-,sēz\ : identifying of a disease from its symptoms —**di·ag·nose** \'dīig,nōs, -əg-\ *vb* —**di·ag·nos·tic** \,dīig'nästik, -əg-\ *adj*

di·ag·o·nal \dī'agənəl\ *adj* : extending from one corner to the opposite corner ~ *n* : diagonal line, direction, or arrangement —**di·ag·o·nal·ly** *adv*

di·a·gram \'dīə,gram\ *n* : explanatory drawing or plan ~ *vb* **-gramed** *or* **-grammed**; **-gram·ing** *or* **gram·ming** : represent by a diagram —**di·a·gram·mat·ic** \,dīəgrə'matik\ *adj*

di·al \'dīəl\ *n* **1** : face of a clock, meter, or gauge **2** : control knob or wheel ~ *vb* **-aled** *or* **-alled**; **-al·ing** *or* **-al·ling** : turn a dial to call, operate, or select

di·a·lect \'dīə,lekt\ *n* : variety of language confined to a region or group

di·a·logue \-,log\ *n* : conversation

di·am·e·ter \dī'amətər\ *n* **1** : straight line through the center of a circle **2** : thickness

di·a·met·ric \,dīə'metrik\, **di·a·met·ri·cal** \-'trikəl\ *adj* : completely opposite —**di·a·met·ri·cal·ly** \-klē\ *adv*

di·a·mond \'dīmənd, 'dīə-\ *n* **1** : hard brilliant mineral that consists of crystalline carbon **2** : flat figure having 4 equal sides, 2 acute angles, and 2 obtuse angles **3** : playing card of a suit marked with a red diamond **4** : baseball field

di·a·per \'dīpər\ *n* : baby's garment for receiving bodily wastes ~ *vb* : put a diaper on

di·a·phragm \'dīə,fram\ *n* **1** : sheet of muscle between the chest and abdominal cavity **2** : contraceptive device

di·ar·rhea \,dīə'rēə\ *n* : abnormally watery discharge from bowels

di·a·ry \'dīərē\ *n, pl* **-ries** : daily record of personal experiences —**di·a·rist** \'dīərist\ *n*

di·a·tribe \'dīə,trīb\ *n* : biting or abusive denunciation

dice \'dīs\ *n, pl* **dice** : die or a game played with dice ~ *vb* **diced**; **dic·ing** : cut into small cubes

dick·er \'dikər\ *vb* : bargain

dic·tate \'dik,tāt\ *vb* **-tat·ed**; **-tat·ing 1** : speak for a person or a machine to record **2** : command ~ *n* : order —**dic·ta·tion** \dik'tāshən\ *n*

dic·ta·tor \'dik,tātər\ *n* : person ruling absolutely and often brutally —**dic·ta·to·ri·al** \,diktətōrēəl\ *adj* —**dic·ta·tor·ship** \dik'tātər,ship, 'dik,-\ *n*

dic·tion \'dikshən\ *n* **1** : choice of the best word **2** : precise pronunciation

dic·tio·nary \-shə,nerē\ *n, pl* **-nar·ies** : reference book of words with information about their meanings

dic·tum \'diktəm\ *n, pl* **-ta** \-tə\ : authoritative or formal statement

did *past of* DO

di·dac·tic \dī'daktik\ *adj* : intended to teach a moral lesson

¹die \'dī\ *vb* **died; dy·ing** \'dīiŋ\ **1** : stop living **2** : pass out of existence **3** : stop or subside **4** : long

²die \'dī\ *n* **1** *pl* **dice** \'dīs\ : small marked cube used in gambling **2** *pl* **dies** \'dīz\ : form for stamping or cutting

die·sel \'dēzəl, -səl\ *n* : engine in which high compression causes ignition of the fuel

di·et \'dīət\ *n* : food and drink regularly consumed (as by a person) ~ *vb* : eat less or according to certain rules —**di·etary** \'dīə,terē\ *adj or n* —**di·et·er** *n*

di·etet·ics \,dīə'tetiks\ *n sing or pl* : science of nutrition —**di·etet·ic** *adj* —**di·eti·tian, di·eti·cian** \-'tishən\ *n*

dif·fer \'difər\ *vb* **1** : be unlike **2** : vary **3** : disagree —**dif·fer·ence** \'difrəns\ *n*

dif·fer·ent \-rənt\ *adj* : not the same —**dif·fer·ent·ly** *adv*

dif·fer·en·ti·ate \,difə'renchē,āt\ *vb* **-at·ed**; **-at·ing 1** : make or become different **2** : distinguish —**dif·fer·en·ti·a·tion** \-,renchē'āshən\ *n*

dif·fi·cult \'difikəlt\ *adj* : hard to do, understand, or deal with

dif·fi·cul·ty \-kəltē\ *n, pl* **-ties 1** : difficult nature **2** : great effort **3** : something hard to do, understand, or deal with

dif·fi·dent \'difədənt\ *adj* : reserved —**dif·fi·dence** \-əns\ *n*

dif·fuse \dif'yüs\ *adj* **1** : wordy **2** : not concentrated ~ \-'yüz\ *vb* **-fused**; **-fus·ing** : pour out or spread widely —**dif·fu·sion** \-'yüzhən\ *n*

dig \'dig\ *vb* **dug** \'dəg\; **dig·ging 1** : turn up soil **2** : hollow out or form by removing earth **3** : uncover by turning up earth ~ *n* **1** : thrust **2**

: cutting remark **—dig in** vb **1**
: establish a defensive position **2**
: begin working or eating **—dig up**
vb : discover

¹di·gest \'dī‚jest\ n : body of information in shortened form

²di·gest \dī'jest, də-\ vb **1** : think over **2**
: convert (food) into a form that can
be absorbed **3** : summarize **—di·gest·ible** adj **—di·ges·tion** \-'jeschən\ n **—di·ges·tive** \-'jestiv\ adj

dig·it \'dijət\ n **1** : any of the figures 1
to 9 inclusive and usu. the symbol 0
2 : finger or toe

dig·i·tal \-³l\ adj : providing information in numerical digits **—dig·i·tal·ly**
adv

dig·ni·fy \'dignə‚fī\ vb **-fied; -fy·ing**
: give dignity or attention to

dig·ni·tary \-‚terē\ n, pl **-taries** : person
of high position

dig·ni·ty \'dignətē\ n, pl **-ties 1** : quality
or state of being worthy or honored **2**
: formal reserve (as of manner)

di·gress \dī'gres, də-\ vb : wander from
the main subject **—di·gres·sion**
\-'greshən\ n

dike \'dīk\ n : earth bank or dam

di·lap·i·dat·ed \də'lapə‚dātəd\ adj
: fallen into partial ruin **—di·lap·i·da·tion** \-‚lapə'dāshən\ n

di·late \dī'lāt, 'dī‚lāt\ vb **-lat·ed; -lat·ing**
: swell or expand **—di·la·ta·tion**
\‚dilə'tāshən\ n **—di·la·tion** \dī-
'lāshən\ n

dil·a·to·ry \'dilə‚tōrē\ adj **1** : delaying **2**
: tardy or slow

di·lem·ma \də'lemə\ n **1** : undesirable
choice **2** : predicament

dil·et·tante \'dilə‚tänt, -‚tant; ‚dilə'tänt,
-'tant\ n, pl **-tantes** or **-tan·ti** \-'tänte,
-'tantē\ : one who dabbles in a field
of interest

dil·i·gent \'dilajant\ adj : attentive and
busy **—dil·i·gence** \-jəns\ n **—dil·i·gent·ly** adv

dill \'dil\ n : herb with aromatic leaves
and seeds

dil·ly·dal·ly \'dilē‚dalē\ vb : waste time
by delay

di·lute \dī'lüt, də-\ vb **-lut·ed; -lut·ing**
: lessen the consistency or strength
of by mixing with something else
~ adj : weak **—di·lu·tion** \-'lüshən\
n

dim \'dim\ adj **-mm- 1** : not bright or
distinct **2** : having no luster **3** : not
seeing or understanding clearly **—**

dim vb **—dim·ly** adv **—dim·mer** n
—dim·ness n

dime \'dīm\ n : U.S. coin worth 1/10
dollar

di·men·sion \də'menchən, dī-\ n **1**
: measurement of extension (as in
length, height, or breadth) **2** : extent
—di·men·sion·al \-'menchənəl\ adj

di·min·ish \də'minish\ vb **1** : make less
or cause to appear less **2** : dwindle

di·min·u·tive \də'minyətiv\ adj : extremely small

dim·ple \'dimpəl\ n : small depression
esp. in the cheek or chin

din \'din\ n : loud noise

dine \'dīn\ vb **dined; din·ing** : eat dinner

din·er \'dīnər\ n **1** : person eating dinner
2 : railroad dining car or restaurant
resembling one

din·ghy \'dinē, -gē, -kē\ n, pl **-ghies**
: small boat

din·gy \'dinjē\ adj **-gi·er; -est 1** : dirty **2**
: shabby **—din·gi·ness** n

din·ner \'dinər\ n : main daily meal

di·no·saur \'dīnə‚sȯr\ n : extinct often
huge reptile

dint \'dint\ n : force—in the phrase by
dint of

di·o·cese \'dīəsəs, -‚sēz, -‚sēs\ n, pl
-ce·ses \-əz, 'dīə‚sēz\ : territorial jurisdiction of a bishop **—di·oc·e·san**
\dī'äsəsən, ‚dīə'sēz³n\ adj or n

dip \'dip\ vb **-pp- 1** : plunge into a liquid
2 : take out with a ladle **3** : lower and
quickly raise again **4** : sink or slope
downward suddenly ~ n **1** : plunge
into water for sport **2** : sudden downward movement or incline **—dip·per**
n

diph·the·ria \dif'thirēə\ n : acute contagious disease

diph·thong \'dif‚thȯn\ n : two vowel
sounds joined to form one speech
sound (as ou in out)

di·plo·ma \də'plōmə\ n, pl **-mas**
: record of graduation from a school

di·plo·ma·cy \-məsē\ n **1** : business of
conducting negotiations between
nations **2** : tact **—di·plo·mat** \'dip-
lə‚mat\ n **—dip·lo·mat·ic** \‚dip-
lə'matik\ adj

dire \'dīr\ adj **dir·er; -est 1** : very horrible **2** : extreme

di·rect \də'rekt, dī-\ vb **1** : address **2**
: cause to move or to follow a certain
course **3** : show (someone) the way **4**
: regulate the activities or course of **5**
: request with authority ~ adj **1**

: leading to or coming from a point without deviation or interruption **2** : frank —**direct** *adj* —**di·rect·ly** *adv* —**di·rect·ness** *n* —**di·rec·tor** \-tər\ *n*

direct current *n* : electric current flowing in one direction only

di·rec·tion \də'rekshən, dī-\ *n* **1** : supervision **2** : order **3** : course along which something moves —**di·rec·tion·al** \-shənəl\ *adj*

di·rec·tive \-tiv\ *n* : order

di·rec·to·ry \-tərē\ *n, pl* **-ries** : alphabetical list of names and addresses

dirge \'dərj\ *n* : funeral hymn

di·ri·gi·ble \'dirəjəbəl, də'rijə-\ *n* : airship

dirt \'dərt\ *n* **1** : mud, dust, or grime that makes something unclean **2** : soil

dirty \-ē\ *adj* **dirt·i·er; -est 1** : not clean **2** : unfair **3** : indecent ~ *vb* **dirt·ied; dirty·ing** : make or become dirty —**dirt·i·ness** *n*

dis·able \dis'ābəl\ *vb* **-abled; -abling** : make unable to function —**dis·abil·i·ty** \,disə'bilətē\ *n*

dis·abuse \,disə'byüz\ *vb* : free from error or misconception

dis·ad·van·tage \,disəd'vantij\ *n* : something that hinders success —**dis·ad·van·ta·geous** *adj*

dis·af·fect \disə'fekt\ *vb* : cause discontent in —**dis·af·fec·tion** *n*

dis·agree \,disə'grē\ *vb* **1** : fail to agree **2** : differ in opinion —**dis·agree·ment** *n*

dis·agree·able \-əbəl\ *adj* : unpleasant

dis·al·low \,disə'laü\ *vb* : refuse to admit or recognize

dis·ap·pear \,disə'pir\ *vb* **1** : pass out of sight **2** : cease to be —**dis·ap·pear·ance** *n*

dis·ap·point \,disə'pȯint\ *vb* : fail to fulfill the expectation or hope of —**dis·ap·point·ment** *n*

dis·ap·prove \-ə'prüv\ *vb* **1** : condemn or reject **2** : feel or express dislike or rejection —**dis·ap·prov·al** *n* —**dis·ap·prov·ing·ly** *adv*

dis·arm \dis'ärm\ *vb* **1** : take weapons from **2** : reduce armed forces **3** : make harmless or friendly —**dis·ar·ma·ment** \-'ärməmənt\ *n*

dis·ar·range \,disə'rānj\ *vb* : throw into disorder —**dis·ar·range·ment** *n*

dis·ar·ray \,disə'rā\ *n* : disorder

di·sas·ter \diz'astər, dis-\ *n* : sudden great misfortune —**di·sas·trous** \-'astrəs\ *adj*

dis·avow \,disə'vaü\ *vb* : deny responsibility for —**dis·avow·al** \-'vaüəl\ *n*

dis·band \dis'band\ *vb* : break up the organization of

dis·bar \dis'bär\ *vb* : expel from the legal profession —**dis·bar·ment** *n*

dis·be·lieve \disbi'lēv\ *vb* : hold not worthy of belief —**dis·be·lief** *n*

dis·burse \dis'bərs\ *vb* **-bursed; -burs·ing** : pay out —**dis·burse·ment** *n*

disc *var of* DISK

dis·card \dis'kärd, 'dis,kärd\ *vb* : get rid of as unwanted —**dis·card** \'dis,kärd\ *n*

dis·cern \dis'ərn, diz-\ *vb* : discover with the eyes or the mind —**dis·cern·ible** *adj* —**dis·cern·ment** *n*

dis·charge \dis'chärj, 'dis,chärj\ *vb* **1** : unload **2** : shoot **3** : set free **4** : dismiss from service **5** : let go or let off **6** : give forth fluid ~ \'dis,-, dis'-\ *n* **1** : act of discharging **2** : a flowing out (as of blood) **3** : dismissal

dis·ci·ple \di'sīpəl\ *n* : one who helps spread another's teachings

dis·ci·pli·nar·i·an \,disəplə'nerēən\ *n* : one who enforces order

dis·ci·pline \'disəplən\ *n* **1** : field of study **2** : training that corrects, molds, or perfects **3** : punishment **4** : control gained by obedience or training ~ *vb* **-plined; -plin·ing 1** : punish **2** : train in self-control —**dis·ci·plin·ary** \'disəplə,nerē\ *adj*

dis·claim \dis'klām\ *vb* : disavow

dis·close \-'klōz\ *vb* : reveal —**dis·clo·sure** \-'klōzhər\ *n*

dis·col·or \dis'kələr\ *vb* : change the color of esp. for the worse —**dis·col·or·ation** \dis,kələ'rāshən\ *n*

dis·com·fit \dis'kəmfət\ *vb* : upset —**dis·com·fi·ture** \dis'kəmfə,chür\ *n*

dis·com·fort \dis'kəmfərt\ *n* : uneasiness

dis·con·cert \,diskən'sərt\ *vb* : upset

dis·con·nect \,diskə'nekt\ *vb* : undo the connection of

dis·con·so·late \dis'känsələt\ *adj* : hopelessly sad

dis·con·tent \diskən'tent\ *n* : uneasiness of mind —**dis·con·tent·ed** *adj*

dis·con·tin·ue \,diskən'tinyü\ *vb* : end —**dis·con·tin·u·ance** *n* —**dis·con·ti·nu·i·ty** \dis,käntə'nüətē, -'nyü-\ *n*

—**dis·con·tin·u·ous** \ˌdiskən'tin-yəwəs\ adj

dis·cord \'dis,kȯrd\ n : lack of harmony —**dis·cor·dant** \dis'kȯrd°nt\ adj — **dis·cor·dant·ly** adv

dis·count \'dis,kaůnt\ n : reduction from a regular price ~ \'dis,-, dis'-\ vb 1 : reduce the amount of 2 : disregard —**discount** adj —**dis·count·er** n

dis·cour·age \dis'kərij\ vb -**aged**; -ag· **ing** 1 : deprive of courage, confidence, or enthusiasm 2 : dissuade — **dis·cour·age·ment** n

dis·course \'dis,kȯrs\ n 1 : conversation 2 : formal treatment of a subject ~ \dis'-\ vb -**coursed**; -**cours·ing** : talk at length

dis·cour·te·ous \dis'kərtēəs\ adj : lacking courtesy —**dis·cour·te·ous· ly** adv —**dis·cour·te·sy** n

dis·cov·er \dis'kəvər\ vb 1 : make known 2 : obtain the first sight or knowledge of 3 : find out —**dis·cov· er·er** n —**dis·cov·ery** \-ōrē\ n

dis·cred·it \dis'kredət\ vb 1 : disbelieve 2 : destroy confidence in ~ n 1 : loss of reputation 2 : disbelief —**dis·cred· it·able** adj

dis·creet \dis'krēt\ adj : capable of keep· ing a secret —**dis·creet·ly** adv

dis·crep·an·cy \dis'krepənsē\ n, pl -**cies** : difference or disagreement

dis·crete \dis'krēt, 'dis,-\ adj : in· dividually distinct

dis·cre·tion \dis'kreshən\ n 1 : discreet quality 2 : power of decision or choice —**dis·cre·tion·ary** adj

dis·crim·i·nate \dis'krimə,nāt\ vb -**nat·ed**; -**nat·ing** 1 : distinguish 2 : show favor or disfavor unjustly — **dis·crim·i·na·tion** \-,krimə'nāshən\ n —**dis·crim·i·na·to·ry** \-'krimənə- ,tōrē\ adj

dis·cur·sive \dis'kərsiv\ adj : passing from one topic to another —**dis· cur·sive·ly** adv —**dis·cur·sive·ness** n

dis·cus \'diskəs\ n, pl -**cus·es** : disk hurled for distance in a contest

dis·cuss \dis'kəs\ vb : talk about or pre· sent —**dis·cus·sion** \-'kəshən\ n

dis·dain \dis'dān\ n : feeling of con· tempt ~ vb : look upon or reject with disdain —**dis·dain·ful** \-fəl\ adj — **dis·dain·ful·ly** adv

dis·ease \di'zēz\ n : condition of a body that impairs its functioning — **dis·eased** \-'zēzd\ adj

dis·em·bark \ˌdisəm'bärk\ vb : get off a ship —**dis·em·bar·ka·tion** \dis- ,em,bär'kashən\ n

dis·em·bod·ied \ˌdisəm'bädēd\ adj : having no substance or reality

dis·en·chant \ˌdisən'chant\ vb : to free from illusion —**dis·en·chant·ment** n

dis·en·chant·ed \-'chantəd\ adj : disappointed

dis·en·gage \ˌdis-ən'gāj\ vb : release —**dis· en·gage·ment** n

dis·en·tan·gle \ˌdisən'tangəl\ vb : free from entanglement

dis·fa·vor \dis'fāvər\ n : disapproval

dis·fig·ure \dis'figyər\ vb : spoil the ap· pearance of —**dis·fig·ure·ment** n

dis·fran·chise \dis'fran,chīz\ vb : deprive of the right to vote — **dis·fran·chise·ment** n

dis·gorge \dis'gȯrj\ vb : spew forth

dis·grace \dis'grās\ vb : bring disgrace to ~ n 1 : shame 2 : cause of shame —**dis·grace·ful** \-fəl\ adj —**dis· grace·ful·ly** adv

dis·grun·tle \dis'grənt°l\ vb -**tled**; -**tling** : put in bad humor

dis·guise \dis'gīz\ vb -**guised**; -**guis·ing** : hide the true identity or nature of ~ n : something that conceals

dis·gust \dis'gəst\ n : strong aversion ~ vb : provoke disgust in —**dis·gust· ed·ly** adv —**dis·gust·ing·ly** adv

dish \'dish\ n 1 : vessel for serving food or the food it holds 2 : food prepared in a particular way ~ vb : put in a dish —**dish·cloth** n —**dish·rag** n — **dish·wash·er** n —**dish·wa·ter** n

dis·har·mo·ny \dis'härmənē\ n : lack of harmony —**dis·har·mo·ni·ous** \dishär'mōnēəs\ adj

dis·heart·en \dis'härt°n\ vb : discourage

dis·shev·el \di'shevəl\ vb -**eled** or -**elled**; -**el·ing** or -**el·ling** : throw into disor· der —**dis·shev·eled**, **dis·shev·elled** adj

dis·hon·est \dis'änəst\ adj : not honest —**dis·hon·est·ly** adv —**dis·hon·es·ty** n

dis·hon·or \dis'änər\ n or vb : disgrace —**dis·hon·or·able** adj —**dis·hon· or·ably** adv

dis·il·lu·sion \ˌdisə'lüzhən\ vb : to free from illusion —**dis·il·lu·sion·ment** n

dis·in·cli·na·tion \ˌdis,inklə'nāshən\ n : slight aversion —**dis·in·cline** \dis'in'klīn\ vb

dis·in·fect \ˌdisən'fekt\ vb : destroy dis· ease germs in or on —**dis·in·fec·tant**

\-'fektənt\ *adj or n* —**dis·in·fec·tion**
\-'fekshən\ *n*

dis·in·gen·u·ous \,dis·ᵊn'jenyəwəs\ *adj*
: lacking in candor

dis·in·her·it \-ᵊn'herət\ *vb* : prevent
from inheriting property

dis·in·te·grate \'dis'intə,grāt\ *vb* : break
into parts or small bits —**dis·in·te·gra·tion** \dis,intə'grāshən\ *n*

dis·in·ter·est·ed \'dis'intərəstəd, -,res-\
adj 1 : not interested 2 : not prejudiced —**dis·in·ter·est·ed·ness** *n*

dis·joint·ed \'dis'jóintəd\ *adj* 1
: separated at the joint 2 : incoherent

disk \'disk\ *n* : something round and flat

dis·like \'dis'līk\ *vb* : regard with dislike
~ *n* : feeling that something is unpleasant and to be avoided

dis·lo·cate \'dislō,kāt, dis'-\ *vb* : move
out of the usual or proper place —
dis·lo·ca·tion \,dislō'kāshən\ *n*

dis·lodge \'dis'läj\ *vb* : force out of a
place

dis·loy·al \'dis'lóiəl\ *adj* : not loyal —
dis·loy·al·ty *n*

dis·mal \'dizməl\ *adj* : showing or causing gloom —**dis·mal·ly** *adv*

dis·man·tle \dis'mantᵊl\ *vb* -**tled; -tling**
: take apart

dis·may \dis'mā\ *vb* -**mayed; -may·ing**
: discourage —**dismay** *n*

dis·mem·ber \dis'member\ *vb* : cut into
pieces —**dis·mem·ber·ment** *n*

dis·miss \dis'mis\ *vb* 1 : send away 2
: remove from service 3 : put aside or
out of mind —**dis·miss·al** *n*

dis·mount \dis'maúnt\ *vb* 1 : get down
from something 2 : take apart

dis·obey \,disə'bā\ *vb* : refuse to obey
—**dis·obe·di·ence** \-'bēdēəns\ *n* —
dis·obe·di·ent \-ənt\ *adj*

dis·or·der \dis'órdər\ *n* 1 : lack of order
2 : breach of public order 3
: abnormal state of body or mind —
disorder *vb* —**dis·or·der·li·ness** *n* —
dis·or·der·ly *adj*

dis·or·ga·nize \dis'órgə,nīz\ *vb* : throw
into disorder —**dis·or·ga·ni·za·tion** *n*

dis·own \dis'ōn\ *vb* : repudiate

dis·par·age \-'parij\ *vb* -**aged; -ag·ing**
: say bad things about —**dis·par·age·ment** *n*

dis·pa·rate \dis'parət, 'dispərət\ *adj*
: different in quality or character —
dis·par·i·ty \dis'parətē\ *n*

dis·pas·sion·ate \dis'pashənət\ *adj* : not
influenced by strong feeling —
dis·pas·sion·ate·ly *adv*

dis·patch \dis'pach\ *vb* 1 : send 2 : kill
3 : attend to rapidly 4 : defeat ~ *n* 1
: message 2 : news item from a correspondent 3 : promptness and efficiency —**dis·patch·er** *n*

dis·pel \dis'pel\ *vb* -**ll-** : clear away

dis·pen·sa·ry \-'pensərē\ *n, pl* -**ries**
: place where medical or dental aid is
provided

dis·pen·sa·tion \,dispən'sāshən\ *n* 1
: system of principles or rules 2
: exemption from a rule 3 : act of dispensing

dis·pense \dis'pens\ *vb* -**pensed; -pens·ing** 1 : portion out 2 : make up and
give out (remedies) —**dis·pens·er** *n* —
dispense with : do without

dis·perse \-'pərs\ *vb* -**persed; -pers·ing**
: scatter —**dis·per·sal** \-'pərsəl\ *n* —
dis·per·sion \-'pərzhən\ *n*

dis·place \-'plās\ *vb* 1 : expel or force to
flee from home or native land 2 : take
the place of —**dis·place·ment** \-mənt\
n

dis·play \-'plā\ *vb* : present to view —
display *n*

dis·please \-'plēz\ *vb* : arouse the dislike
of —**dis·plea·sure** \-'plezhər\ *n*

dis·port \dis'pōrt\ *vb* 1 : amuse 2 : frolic

dis·pose \dis'pōz\ *vb* -**posed; -pos·ing** 1
: give a tendency to 2 : settle —**dis·pos·able** \-'pōzəbəl\ *adj* —**dis·pos·al**
\-'pōzəl\ *n* —**dis·pos·er** *n* —**dispose**
of 1 : determine the fate, condition, or
use of 2 : get rid of

dis·po·si·tion \,dispə'zishən\ *n* 1 : act or
power of disposing of 2 : arrangement
3 : natural attitude

dis·pos·sess \,dispə'zes\ *vb* : deprive of
possession or occupancy —**dis·pos·ses·sion** \-'zeshən\ *n*

dis·pro·por·tion \,disprə'pōrshən\ *n*
: lack of proportion —**dis·pro·por·tion·ate** \-shənət\ *adj*

dis·prove \dis'prüv\ *vb* : prove false —
dis·proof *n*

dis·pute \dis'pyüt\ *vb* -**put·ed; -put·ing**
1 : argue 2 : deny the truth or rightness of 3 : struggle against or over ~
n : debate or quarrel —**dis·put·able**
\-əbəl, 'dispyət-\ *adj* —**dis·pu·ta·tion**
\,dispyə'tāshən\ *n*

dis·qual·i·fy \dis'kwälə,fī\ *vb* : make ineligible —**dis·qual·i·fi·ca·tion** *n*

dis·qui·et \dis'kwīət\ *vb* : make uneasy
or restless ~ *n* : anxiety

dis·re·gard \,disri'gärd\ *vb* : pay no attention to ~ *n* : neglect

dis·re·pair \disri'par\ n : need of repair

dis·rep·u·ta·ble \dis'repyətəbəl\ adj : having a bad reputation

dis·re·pute \disri'pyüt\ n : low regard

dis·re·spect \disri'spekt\ n : lack of respect —**dis·re·spect·ful** adj

dis·robe \dis'rōb\ vb : undress

dis·rupt \dis'rəpt\ vb : throw into disorder —**dis·rup·tion** \-'rəpshən\ n —**dis·rup·tive** \-'rəptiv\ adj

dis·sat·is·fac·tion \dis,satəs'fakshən\ n : lack of satisfaction

dis·sat·is·fy \dis'satəs,fī\ vb : fail to satisfy

dis·sect \dis'sekt\ vb : cut into parts esp. to examine —**dis·sec·tion** \-'sekshən\ n

dis·sem·ble \di'sembəl\ vb -**bled; -bling** : disguise feelings or intention —**dis·sem·bler** n

dis·sem·i·nate \di'semə,nāt\ vb -**nat·ed; -nat·ing** : spread around —**dis·sem·i·na·tion** \-,semə'nāshən\ n

dis·sen·sion \di'senchən\ n : discord

dis·sent \di'sent\ vb : object or disagree ~ n : difference of opinion —**dis·sent·er** n —**dis·sen·tient** \-'senchənt\ adj or n

dis·ser·ta·tion \,disər'tāshən\ n : long written study of a subject

dis·ser·vice \dis'sərvəs\ n : injury

dis·si·dent \'disədənt\ n : one who differs openly with an establishment —**dis·si·dence** \-əns\ n —**dissident** adj

dis·sim·i·lar \di'simələr\ adj : different —**dis·sim·i·lar·i·ty** \di,simə'larətē\ n

dis·si·pate \'disə,pāt\ vb -**pat·ed; -pat·ing** 1 : break up and drive off 2 : squander —**dis·si·pa·tion** \,disə'pāshən\ n

dis·so·ci·ate \dis'ōsē,āt, -shē-\ vb -**at·ed; -at·ing** : separate from association —**dis·so·ci·a·tion** \dis,ōsē'āshən, -shē-\ n

dis·so·lute \'disə,lüt\ adj : loose in morals or conduct

dis·so·lu·tion \,disə'lüshən\ n : act or process of dissolving

dis·solve \di'zälv\ vb 1 : break up or bring to an end 2 : pass or cause to pass into solution

dis·so·nance \'disənəns\ n : discord —**dis·so·nant** \-nənt\ adj

dis·suade \di'swād\ vb -**suad·ed; -suad·ing** : persuade not to do something —**dis·sua·sion** \-'swāzhən\ n

dis·tance \'distəns\ n 1 : measure of separation in space or time 2 : reserve

dis·tant \-tənt\ adj 1 : separate in space 2 : remote in time, space, or relationship 3 : reserved —**dis·tant·ly** adv

dis·taste \dis'tāst\ n : dislike —**dis·taste·ful** adj

dis·tem·per \dis'tempər\ n : serious virus disease of dogs

dis·tend \dis'tend\ vb : swell out —**dis·ten·sion, dis·ten·tion** \-'tenchən\ n

dis·till \dis'til\ vb : obtain by distillation —**dis·til·late** \'distə,lāt, -lət\ n —**dis·till·er** n —**dis·till·ery** \di'stilərē\ n

dis·til·la·tion \,distə'lāshən\ n : purification of liquid by evaporating then condensing

dis·tinct \dis'tiŋkt\ adj 1 : distinguishable from others 2 : readily discerned —**dis·tinc·tive** \-tiv\ adj —**dis·tinc·tive·ly** adv —**dis·tinc·tive·ness** n —**dis·tinct·ly** adv —**dis·tinct·ness** n

dis·tinc·tion \-'tiŋkshən\ n 1 : act of distinguishing 2 : difference 3 : special recognition

dis·tin·guish \-'tiŋgwish\ vb 1 : perceive as different 2 : set apart 3 : discern 4 : make outstanding —**dis·tin·guish·able** adj —**dis·tin·guished** \-gwisht\ adj

dis·tort \dis'tort\ vb : twist out of shape, condition, or true meaning —**dis·tor·tion** \-'torshən\ n

dis·tract \dis'trakt\ vb : divert the mind or attention of —**dis·trac·tion** \-'strakshən\ n

dis·traught \dis'trot\ adj : agitated with mental conflict

dis·tress \-'tres\ n 1 : suffering 2 : misfortune 3 : state of danger or great need ~ vb : subject to strain or distress —**dis·tress·ful** adj

dis·trib·ute \-'tribyət\ vb -**ut·ed; -ut·ing** 1 : divide among many 2 : spread or hand out —**dis·tri·bu·tion** \,distrə-'byüshən\ n —**dis·trib·u·tive** \dis-'tribyətiv\ adj —**dis·trib·u·tor** \-ər\ n

dis·trict \dis,trikt\ n : territorial division

dis·trust \dis'trəst\ vb or n : mistrust —**dis·trust·ful** \-fəl\ adj

dis·turb \dis'tərb\ vb 1 : interfere with 2 : destroy the peace, composure, or order of —**dis·tur·bance** \-'tərbəns\ n —**dis·turb·er** n

dis·use \dis'yüs\ n : lack of use

ditch \'dich\ n : trench ~ vb 1 : dig a ditch in 2 : get rid of

dith•er \'dithər\ n : highly nervous or excited state

dit•to \'ditō\ n, pl **-tos** : more of the same

dit•ty \'ditē\ n, pl **-ties** : short simple song

di•uret•ic \,dīyu'retik\ adj : tending to increase urine flow —**diuretic** n

di•ur•nal \dī'ərnªl\ adj 1 : daily 2 : of or occurring in the daytime

di•van \'dī,van, di'-\ n : couch

dive \'dīv\ vb **dived** \'dīvd\ or **dove** \'dōv\; **dived**; **div•ing** 1 : plunge into water headfirst 2 : submerge 3 : descend quickly ~ n 1 : act of diving 2 : sharp decline —**div•er** n

di•verge \də'vərj, dī-\ vb **-verged**; **-verg•ing** 1 : move in different directions 2 : differ —**di•ver•gence** \-'vərjəns\ n —**di•ver•gent** \-jənt\ adj

di•vers \'dīvərz\ adj : various

di•verse \dī'vərs, də-, 'dī,vərs\ adj : involving different forms —**di•ver•si•fi•ca•tion** \də,vərsəfə'kāshən, dī-\ n —**di•ver•si•fy** \-'vərsə,fī\ vb —**di•ver•si•ty** \-sətē\ n

di•vert \də'vərt, dī-\ vb 1 : turn from a course or purpose 2 : distract 3 : amuse —**di•ver•sion** \-'vərzhən\ n

di•vest \dī'vest, də-\ vb : strip of clothing, possessions, or rights

di•vide \də'vīd\ vb **-vid•ed**; **-vid•ing** 1 : separate 2 : distribute 3 : share 4 : subject to mathematical division ~ n : watershed —**di•vid•er** n

div•i•dend \'divə,dend\ n 1 : individual share 2 : bonus 3 : number to be divided

div•i•na•tion \,divə'nāshən\ n : practice of trying to foretell future events

di•vine \də'vīn\ adj **-vin•er**; **-est** 1 : relating to or being God or a god 2 : supremely good ~ n : clergy member ~ vb **-vined**; **-vin•ing** 1 : infer 2 : prophesy —**di•vine•ly** adv —**di•vin•er** n —**di•vin•i•ty** \də'vinətē\ n

di•vis•i•ble \-'vizəbəl\ adj : capable of being divided —**di•vis•i•bil•i•ty** \-,vizə'bilətē\ n

di•vi•sion \-'vizhən\ n 1 : distribution 2 : part of a whole 3 : disagreement 4 : process of finding out how many times one number is contained in another

di•vi•sive \də'vīsiv, -'vi-, -ziv\ adj : creating dissension

di•vi•sor \-'vīzər\ n : number by which a dividend is divided

di•vorce \də'vōrs\ n : legal breaking up of a marriage —**divorce** vb

di•vor•cée \-,vōr'sā, -'sē\ n : divorced woman

di•vulge \də'vəlj, dī-\ vb **-vulged**; **-vulg•ing** : reveal

diz•zy \'dizē\ adj **-zi•er**; **-est** 1 : having a sensation of whirling 2 : causing or caused by giddiness —**diz•zi•ly** adv —**diz•zi•ness** n

DNA \,dē,en'ā\ n : compound in cell nuclei that is the basis of heredity

do \'dü\ vb **did** \'did\; **done** \'dən\; **do•ing** \'düiŋ\; **does** \'dəz\ 1 : work to accomplish (an action or task) 2 : behave 3 : prepare or fix up 4 : fare 5 : finish 6 : serve the needs or purpose of 7 —used as an auxiliary verb —**do away with** 1 : get rid of 2 : destroy —**do by** : deal with —**do•er** \'düər, 'dü-\ n —**do in** vb 1 : ruin 2 : kill

doc•ile \'däsəl\ adj : easily managed —**do•cil•i•ty** \dä'silətē\ n

¹dock \'däk\ vb 1 : shorten 2 : reduce

²dock n 1 : berth between 2 piers to receive ships 2 : loading wharf or platform ~ vb : bring or come into dock —**dock•work•er** n

³dock n : place in a court for a prisoner

dock•et \'däkət\ n 1 : record of the proceedings in a legal action 2 : list of legal causes to be tried —**docket** vb

doc•tor \'däktər\ n 1 : person holding one of the highest academic degrees 2 : one (as a surgeon) skilled in healing arts ~ vb 1 : give medical treatment to 2 : repair or alter —**doc•tor•al** \-tərəl\ adj

doc•trine \'däktrən\ n : something taught —**doc•tri•nal** \-trənªl\ adj

doc•u•ment \'däkyəmənt\ n : paper that furnishes information or legal proof —**doc•u•ment** \-,ment\ vb —**doc•u•men•ta•tion** \,däkyəmən-'tāshən\ n —**doc•u•ment•er** n

doc•u•men•ta•ry \,däkyə'mentərē\ adj 1 : of or relating to documents 2 : giving a factual presentation —**documentary** n

dod•der \'dädər\ vb : become feeble usu. from age

dodge \'däj\ vb **dodged**; **dodg•ing** 1 : move quickly aside or out of the way of 2 : evade —**dodge** n

do•do \'dōdō\ n, pl **-does** or **-dos** 1 : heavy flightless extinct bird 2 : stupid person

doe \'dō\ n, pl **does** or **doe** : adult female deer —**doe·skin** \-,skin\ n

does pres 3d sing of DO

doff \'däf\ vb : remove

dog \'dog\ n : flesh-eating domestic mammal ~ vb 1 : hunt down or track like a hound 2 : harass —**dog·catch·er** n —**dog·gy** \-ē\ n or adj —**dog·house** n

dog-ear \'dog,ir\ n : turned-down corner of a page —**dog-ear** vb —**dog-eared** \-,ird\ adj

dog·ged \'dógəd\ adj : stubbornly determined

dog·ma \'dógmə\ n : tenet or code of tenets

dog·ma·tism \-,tizəm\ n : unwarranted stubbornness of opinion —**dog·ma·tic** \dog'matik\ adj

dog·wood n : flowering tree

doi·ly \'dóilē\ n, pl -lies : small decorative mat

do·ings \'düiŋz\ n pl : events

dol·drums \'dōldrəmz,'däl-\ n pl : spell of listlessness, despondency, or stagnation

dole \'dōl\ n : distribution esp. of money to the needy or unemployed —**dole out** vb : give out esp. in small portions

dole·ful \'dōlfəl\ adj : sad —**dole·ful·ly** adv

doll \'däl, 'dol\ n : small figure of a person used esp. as a child's toy

dol·lar \'dälər\ n : any of various basic monetary units (as in the U.S. and Canada)

dol·ly \'dälē\ n, pl -lies : small cart or wheeled platform

dol·phin \'dälfən\ n 1 : sea mammal related to the whales 2 : saltwater food fish

dolt \'dōlt\ n : stupid person —**dolt·ish** adj

-dom \dəm\ n suffix 1 : office or realm 2 : state or fact of being 3 : those belonging to a group

do·main \dō'mān, də-\ n 1 : territory over which someone reigns 2 : sphere of activity or knowledge

dome \'dōm\ n 1 : large hemispherical roof 2 : roofed stadium

do·mes·tic \də'mestik\ adj 1 : relating to the household or family 2 : relating and limited to one's own country 3 : tame ~ n : household servant —**do·mes·ti·cal·ly** \-tiklē\ adv

do·mes·ti·cate \-ti,kāt\ vb -cat·ed;

-cat·ing : tame —**do·mes·ti·ca·tion** \-,mesti'kāshən\ n

do·mi·cile \'dämə,sīl, 'dō-; 'däməsəl\ n : home —**domicile** vb

dom·i·nance \'dämənəns\ n : control —**dom·i·nant** \-nənt\ adj

dom·i·nate \-,nāt\ vb -nat·ed; -nat·ing 1 : have control over 2 : rise high above —**dom·i·na·tion** \,dämə'nāshən\ n

dom·i·neer \,dämə'nir\ vb : exercise arbitrary control

do·min·ion \də'minyən\ n 1 : supreme authority 2 : governed territory

dom·i·no \'dämə,nō\ n, pl -noes or -nos : flat rectangular block used as a piece in a game (**dominoes**)

don \'dän\ vb -nn- : put on (clothes)

do·nate \'dō,nāt\ vb -nat·ed; -nat·ing : make a gift of —**do·na·tion** \dō-'nāshən\ n

¹done \'dən\ past part of DO

²done adj 1 : finished or ended 2 : cooked sufficiently

don·key \'däŋkē, 'dəŋ-\ n, pl -keys : sturdy domestic ass

do·nor \'dōnər\ n : one that gives

doo·dle \'düd⁰l\ vb -dled; -dling : draw or scribble aimlessly —**doodle** n

doom \'düm\ n 1 : judgment 2 : fate 3 : ruin —**doom** vb

door \'dōr\ n : passage for entrance or a movable barrier that can open or close such a passage —**door·jamb** n —**door·knob** n —**door·mat** n —**door·step** n —**door·way** n

dope \'dōp\ n 1 : narcotic preparation 2 : stupid person 3 : information ~ vb **doped; dop·ing** : drug

dor·mant \'dormənt\ adj : not actively growing or functioning —**dor·man·cy** \-mənsē\ n

dor·mer \'dormər\ n : window built upright in a sloping roof

dor·mi·to·ry \'dormə,tōrē\ n, pl -ries : residence hall (as at a college)

dor·mouse \'dor,maùs\ n : squirrellike rodent

dor·sal \'dorsəl\ adj : relating to or on the back —**dor·sal·ly** adv

do·ry \'dōrē\ n, pl -ries : flat-bottomed boat

dose \'dōs\ n : quantity (as of medicine) taken at one time ~ vb **dosed; dos·ing** : give medicine to —**dos·age** \'dōsij\ n

dot \'dät\ n 1 : small spot 2 : small round

mark made with or as if with a pen ~ *vb* **-tt-** : mark with dots

dot·age \'dōtij\ *n* : senility

dote \'dōt\ *vb* **dot·ed; dot·ing 1** : act feeblemindedly **2** : be foolishly fond

dou·ble \'dəbəl\ *adj* **1** : consisting of 2 members or parts **2** : being twice as great or as many **3** : folded in two — *n* **1** : something twice another **2** : one that resembles another ~ *adv* : doubly ~ *vb* **-bled; -bling 1** : make or become twice as great **2** : fold or bend **3** : clench

dou·ble-cross *vb* : deceive by trickery —**dou·ble-cross·er** *n*

dou·bly \'dəblē\ *adv* : to twice the degree

doubt \'daut\ *vb* **1** : be uncertain about **2** : mistrust **3** : consider unlikely ~ *n* **1** : uncertainty **2** : mistrust **3** : inclination not to believe —**doubt·ful** \-fəl\ *adj* —**doubt·ful·ly** *adv* —**doubt·less** \-ləs\ *adv*

douche \'düsh\ *n* : jet of fluid for cleaning a body part

dough \'dō\ *n* : stiff mixture of flour and liquid —**doughy** \'dō·ē\ *adj*

dough·nut \-,nət\ *n* : small fried ring-shaped cake

dough·ty \'dautē\ *adj* **-ti·er; -est** : able, strong, or valiant

dour \'dauər, 'dur\ *adj* **1** : severe **2** : gloomy or sullen —**dour·ly** *adv*

douse \'daus, 'dauz\ *vb* **doused; dousing 1** : plunge into or drench with water **2** : extinguish

¹**dove** \'dəv\ *n* : small wild pigeon

²**dove** \'dōv\ *past of* DIVE

dove·tail \'dəv,tāl\ *vb* : fit together neatly

dow·a·ger \'dauijər\ *n* **1** : widow with wealth or a title **2** : dignified elderly woman

dowdy \'daudē\ *adj* **dowd·i·er; -est** : lacking neatness and charm

dow·el \'dauəl\ *n* **1** : peg used for fastening two pieces **2** : wooden rod

dow·er \'dauər\ *n* : property given a widow for life ~ *vb* : supply with a dower

¹**down** \'daun\ *adv* **1** : toward or in a lower position or state **2** : to a lying or sitting position **3** : as a cash deposit **4** : on paper ~ *adj* **1** : lying on the ground **2** : directed or going downward **3** : being at a low level ~ *prep* : toward the bottom of ~ *vb* **1** : cause to go down **2** : defeat

²**down** *n* : fluffy feathers

down·cast *adj* **1** : sad **2** : directed down

down·fall *n* : ruin or cause of ruin

down·grade *n* : downward slope ~ *vb* : lower in grade or position

down·heart·ed *adj* : sad

down·pour *n* : heavy rain

down·right *adv* **1** : thoroughly ~ *adj* : absolute or thorough

downs \'daunz\ *n pl* : rolling treeless uplands

down·size \'daun,sīz\ *vb* : reduce in size

down·stairs *adv* : on or to a lower floor and esp. the main floor —**downstairs** *adj or n*

down-to-earth *adj* : practical

down·town *adv* : to, toward, or in the business center of a town —**down·town** *n or adj*

down·trod·den \'daun,träd²n\ *adj* : suffering oppression

down·ward \'daunwərd\, **down·wards** \-wərdz\ *adv* : to a lower place or condition —**downward** *adj*

down·wind *adv or adj* : in the direction the wind is blowing

downy \'daunē\ *adj* **-i·er; -est** : resembling or covered with down

dow·ry \'daurē\ *n, pl* **-ries** : property a woman gives her husband in marriage

dox·ol·o·gy \däk'säləjē\ *n, pl* **-gies** : hymn of praise to God

doze \'dōz\ *vb* **dozed; doz·ing** : sleep lightly —**doze** *n*

doz·en \'dəz²n\ *n, pl* **-ens** *or* **-en** : group of 12 —**doz·enth** \-²nth\ *adj*

drab \'drab\ *adj* **-bb-** : dull —**drab·ly** *adv* —**drab·ness** *n*

dra·co·ni·an \drā'kōnēən, dra-\ *adj, often cap* : harsh, cruel

draft \'draft, 'draft\ *n* **1** : act of drawing or hauling **2** : act of drinking **3** : amount drunk at once **4** : preliminary outline or rough sketch **5** : selection from a pool or the selection process **6** : order for the payment of money **7** : air current ~ *vb* **1** : select usu. on a compulsory basis **2** : make a preliminary sketch, version, or plan of ~ *adj* : drawn from a container —**draft·ee** \draf'tē, draf-\ *n* —**drafty** \'draftē\ *adj*

drafts·man \'draftsmən, 'draft-\ *n* : person who draws plans

drag \'drag\ *n* **1** : something dragged over a surface or through water **2** : something that hinders progress or is boring **3** : act or an instance of dragging ~ vb -gg- 1 : haul 2 : move or work with difficulty 3 : pass slowly 4 : search or fish with a drag — **drag·ger** n

drag·net \-ˌnet\ n 1 : trawl 2 : planned actions for finding a criminal

drag·on \ˈdragən\ n : fabled winged serpent

drag·on·fly n : large 4-winged insect

drain \ˈdrān\ vb 1 : draw off or flow off gradually or completely 2 : exhaust ~ n : means or act of draining — **drain·age** \-ij\ n —**drain·er** n —**drain·pipe** n

drake \ˈdrāk\ n : male duck

dra·ma \ˈdrämə, ˈdram-\ n 1 : composition for theatrical presentation esp. on a serious subject 2 : series of events involving conflicting forces — **dra·mat·ic** \drəˈmatik\ adj —**dra·mat·i·cal·ly** \-iklē\ adv —**dram·a·tist** \ˈdramətist, ˈdräm-\ n —**dram·a·ti·za·tion** \ˌdramətəˈzāshən, ˌdräm-\ n —**dra·ma·tize** \ˈdramə,tīz, ˈdräm-\ vb

drank past of DRINK

drape \ˈdrāp\ vb **draped; drap·ing** 1 : cover or adorn with folds of cloth 2 : cause to hang in flowing lines or folds ~ n : curtain

drap·ery \ˈdrāpərē\ n, pl **-er·ies** : decorative fabric hung esp. as a heavy curtain

dras·tic \ˈdrastik\ adj : extreme or harsh —**dras·ti·cal·ly** \-tiklē\ adj

draught \ˈdraft\, **draughty** \ˈdraftē\ chiefly Brit var of DRAFT, DRAFTY

draw \ˈdró\ vb **drew** \ˈdrü\; **drawn** \ˈdrón\; **draw·ing** 1 : move or cause to move (as by pulling) 2 : attract or provoke 3 : extract 4 : take or receive (as money) 5 : bend a bow in preparation for shooting 6 : leave a contest undecided 7 : sketch 8 : write out 9 : deduce ~ n 1 : act, process, or result of drawing 2 : tie —**draw out** : cause to speak candidly —**draw up** 1 : write out 2 : pull oneself erect 3 : bring or come to a stop

draw·back n : disadvantage

draw·bridge n : bridge that can be raised

draw·er \ˈdrór, ˈdróər\ n 1 : one that draws 2 : sliding boxlike compartment 3 pl : underpants

draw·ing \ˈdróiŋ\ n 1 : occasion of choosing by lot 2 : act or art of mak-

ing a figure, plan, or sketch with lines 3 : something drawn

drawl \ˈdról\ vb : speak slowly —**drawl** n

dread \ˈdred\ vb : feel extreme fear or reluctance ~ n : great fear ~ adj : causing dread —**dread·ful** \-fəl\ adj —**dread·ful·ly** adv

dream \ˈdrēm\ n 1 : series of thoughts or visions during sleep 2 : dreamlike vision 3 : something notable 4 : ideal ~ vb **dreamed** \ˈdremt, ˈdrēmd\ or **dreamt** \ˈdremt\ **dream·ing** 1 : have a dream 2 : imagine —**dream·er** n —**dream·like** adj —**dreamy** adj

drea·ry \ˈdrirē\ adj **-ri·er; -est** : dismal —**drea·ri·ly** \ˈdrirəlē\ adv

¹dredge \ˈdrej\ n : machine for removing earth esp. from under water ~ vb **dredged; dredg·ing** : dig up or search with a dredge —**dredg·er** n

²dredge vb **dredged; dredg·ing** : coat (food) with flour

dregs \ˈdregz\ n pl 1 : sediment 2 : most worthless part

drench \ˈdrench\ vb : wet thoroughly

dress \ˈdres\ vb 1 : put clothes on 2 : decorate 3 : prepare (as a carcass) for use 4 : apply dressings, remedies, or fertilizer to ~ n 1 : apparel 2 : single garment of bodice and skirt ~ adj : suitable for a formal event —**dress·mak·er** n —**dress·mak·ing** n

dress·er \ˈdresər\ n : bureau with a mirror

dress·ing n 1 : act or process of dressing 2 : sauce or a seasoned mixture 3 : material to cover an injury

dressy \ˈdresē\ adj **dress·i·er; -est** 1 : showy in dress 2 : stylish

drew past of DRAW

drib·ble \ˈdribəl\ vb **-bled; -bling** 1 : fall or flow in drops 2 : drool —**dribble** n

drier comparative of DRY

driest superlative of DRY

drift \ˈdrift\ n 1 : motion or course of something drifting 2 : mass piled up by wind 3 : general intention or meaning ~ vb 1 : float or be driven along (as by a current) 2 : wander without purpose 3 : pile up under force —**drift·er** n —**drift·wood** n

¹drill \ˈdril\ vb 1 : bore with a drill 2 : instruct by repetition ~ n 1 : tool for boring holes 2 : regularly practiced exercise —**drill·er** n

²drill n : seed-planting implement

³drill n : twill-weave cotton fabric

drily var of DRYLY

drink \'driŋk\ vb **drank** \'draŋk\; **drunk** \'drəŋk\ or **drank**; **drink·ing** 1 : swallow liquid 2 : absorb 3 : drink alcoholic beverages esp. to excess ~ n 1 : beverage 2 : alcoholic liquor —**drink·able** adj —**drink·er** n

drip \'drip\ vb **-pp-** : fall or let fall in drops ~ n 1 : a dripping 2 : sound of falling drops

drive \'drīv\ vb **drove** \'drōv\; **driv·en** \'drivən\; **driv·ing** 1 : urge or force onward 2 : direct the movement or course of 3 : compel 4 : cause to become 5 : propel forcefully ~ n 1 : trip in a vehicle 2 : intensive campaign 3 : aggressive or dynamic quality 4 : basic need —**driv·er** n

drive–in adj : accommodating patrons in cars —**drive–in** n

driv·el \'drivəl\ vb **-eled** or **-elled**; **-el·ing** or **-el·ling** 1 : drool 2 : talk stupidly ~ n : nonsense

drive·way n : usu. short private road from the street to a house

driz·zle \'drizəl\ n : fine misty rain —**drizzle** vb

droll \'drōl\ adj : humorous or whimsical —**droll·ery** \-ərē\ n —**drol·ly** adv

drom·e·dary \'drämə,derē\ n, pl **-dar·ies** : speedy one-humped camel

drone \'drōn\ n 1 : male honeybee 2 : deep hum or buzz ~ vb **droned; dron·ing** : make a dull monotonous sound

drool \'drül\ vb : let liquid run from the mouth

droop \'drüp\ vb 1 : hang or incline downward 2 : lose strength or spirit —**droop** n —**droopy** \-ē\ adj

drop \'dräp\ n 1 : quantity of fluid in one spherical mass 2 pl : medicine used by drops 3 : decline or fall 4 : distance something drops ~ vb **-pp-** 1 : fall in drops 2 : let fall 3 : convey 4 : go lower or become less strong or less active —**drop·let** \-lət\ n —**drop back** : move toward the rear —**drop behind** : fail to keep up —**drop in** : pay an unexpected visit

drop·per n : device that dispenses liquid by drops

drop·sy \'dräpsē\ n : edema

dross \'dräs\ n : waste matter

drought \'draut\ n : long dry spell

¹drove \'drōv\ n : crowd of moving people or animals

²drove past of DRIVE

drown \'draun\ vb 1 : suffocate in water 2 : overpower or become overpowered

drowse \'drauz\ vb **drowsed; drows·ing** : doze —**drowse** n

drowsy \'drauzē\ adj **drows·i·er; -est** : sleepy —**drows·i·ly** adv —**drows·i·ness** n

drub \'drəb\ vb **-bb-** : beat severely

drudge \'drəj\ vb **drudged; drudg·ing** : do hard or boring work —**drudge** n —**drudg·ery** \-ərē\ n

drug \'drəg\ n 1 : substance used as or in medicine 2 : narcotic ~ vb **-gg-** : affect with drugs —**drug·gist** \-ist\ n —**drug·store** n

dru·id \'drüəd\ n : ancient Celtic priest

drum \'drəm\ n 1 : musical instrument that is a skin-covered cylinder beaten usu. with sticks 2 : drum-shaped object (as a container) ~ vb **-mm-** 1 : beat a drum 2 : drive, force, or bring about by steady effort —**drum·beat** n —**drum·mer** n

drum·stick n 1 : stick for beating a drum 2 : lower part of a fowl's leg

drunk \'drəŋk\ adj : having the faculties impaired by alcohol ~ n : one who is drunk —**drunk·ard** \'drəŋkərd\ n —**drunk·en** \-kən\ adj —**drunk·en·ly** adv —**drunk·en·ness** n

dry \'drī\ adj **dri·er** \'drīər\; **dri·est** \'drīəst\ 1 : lacking water or moisture 2 : thirsty 3 : marked by the absence of alcoholic beverages 4 : uninteresting 5 : not sweet ~ vb **dried; dry·ing** : make or become dry —**dry·ly** adv —**dry·ness** n

dry–clean vb : clean (fabrics) chiefly with solvents other than water —**dry cleaning** n

dry·er \'drīər\ n : device for drying

dry goods n pl : textiles, clothing, and notions

dry ice n : solid carbon dioxide

du·al \'düəl, 'dyü-\ adj : twofold —**du·al·ism** \-ə,lizəm\ n —**du·al·i·ty** \dü'alətē, dyü-\ n

dub \'dəb\ vb **-bb-** : name

du·bi·ous \'dübēəs, 'dyü-\ adj 1 : uncertain 2 : questionable —**du·bi·ous·ly** adv —**du·bi·ous·ness** n

du·cal \'dükəl, 'dyü-\ adj : relating to a duke or dukedom

duch·ess \'dəchəs\ n 1 : wife of a duke 2 : woman holding a ducal title

duchy \'dē-\ *n, pl* **-ies** : territory of a duke or duchess

¹duck \'dək\ *n, pl* : swimming bird related to the goose and swan — *vb* **1** : thrust or plunge under water **2** : lower the head or body suddenly **3** : evade —**duck·ling** \-liŋ\ *n*

²duck *n* : cotton fabric

duct \'dəkt\ *n* : canal for conveying a fluid —**duct·less** \-ləs\ *adj*

duc·tile \'dəkt⁹l\ *adj* : able to be drawn out or shaped —**duc·til·i·ty** \,dək-'tilətē\ *n*

dude \'düd, 'dyüd\ *n* **1** : dandy **2** : guy

dud·geon \'dəjən\ *n* : ill humor

due \'dü, 'dyü\ *adj* **1** : owed **2** : appropriate **3** : attributable **4** : scheduled ~ *n* **1** : something due **2** *pl* : fee ~ *adv* : directly

du·el \'düəl, 'dyü-\ *n* : combat between 2 persons —**duel** *vb* —**du·el·ist** *n*

du·et \dü'et, dyü-\ *n* : musical composition for 2 performers

due to *prep* : because of

dug *past of* DIG

dug·out \'dəg,aút\ *n* **1** : boat made by hollowing out a log **2** : shelter made by digging

duke \'dük, 'dyük\ *n* : nobleman of the highest rank —**duke·dom** *n*

dull \'dəl\ *adj* **1** : mentally slow **2** : blunt **3** : not brilliant or interesting —**dull** *vb* —**dul·lard** \'dələrd\ *n* —**dull·ness** *n* —**dul·ly** *adv*

du·ly \'dülē, 'dyü-\ *adv* : in a due manner or time

dumb \'dəm\ *adj* **1** : mute **2** : stupid —**dumb·ly** *adv*

dumb·bell \'dəm,bel\ *n* **1** : short bar with weights on the ends used for exercise **2** : stupid person

dumb·found, dum·found \,dəm'faúnd\ *vb* : amaze

dum·my \'dəmē\ *n, pl* **-mies 1** : stupid person **2** : imitative substitute

dump \'dəmp\ *vb* : let fall in a pile ~ *n* : place for dumping something (as refuse) —**in the dumps** : sad

dump·ling \'dəmpliŋ\ *n* : small mass of boiled or steamed dough

dumpy \'dəmpē\ *adj* **dump·i·er; -est** : short and thick in build

¹dun \'dən\ *adj* : brownish gray

²dun *vb* **-nn-** : hound for payment of a debt

dunce \'dəns\ *n* : stupid person

dune \'dün, 'dyün\ *n* : hill of sand

dung \'dəŋ\ *n* : manure

dun·ga·ree \,dəŋgə'rē\ *n* **1** : blue denim **2** *pl* : work clothes made of dungaree

dun·geon \'dənjən\ *n* : underground prison

dunk \'dəŋk\ *vb* : dip or submerge temporarily in liquid

duo \'düö, 'dyüö\ *n, pl* **du·os** : pair

du·o·de·num \,düə'dēnəm, dyü-; dú-'äd⁹nəm, dyü-\ *n, pl* **-na** \-'dēnə, -⁹nə\ *or* **-nums** : part of the small intestine nearest the stomach — **du·o·de·nal** \-'dēn⁹l, -⁹nəl\ *adj*

dupe \'düp, dyüp\ *n* : one easily deceived or cheated —**dupe** *vb*

du·plex \'dü,pleks, 'dyü-\ *adj* : double ~ *n* : 2-family house

du·pli·cate \'düplikət, 'dyü-\ *adj* **1** : consisting of 2 identical items **2** : being just like another ~ *n* : exact copy ~ \-,kāt\ *vb* **-cat·ed; -cat·ing 1** : make an exact copy of **2** : repeat or equal —**du·pli·ca·tion** \,düpli-'kāshən, ,dyü-\ *n* —**du·pli·ca·tor** \'düpli,kātər, dyü-\ *n*

du·plic·i·ty \dú'plisətē, ,dyü-\ *n, pl* **-ties** : deception

du·ra·ble \'dúrəbəl, 'dyúr-\ *adj* : lasting a long time —**du·ra·bil·i·ty** \,dúrə'bilətē, ,dyúr-\ *n*

du·ra·tion \dú'rāshən, dyú-\ *n* : length of time something lasts

du·ress \dú'res, dyú-\ *n* : coercion

dur·ing \'düriŋ, 'dyúr-\ *prep* **1** : throughout **2** : at some point in

dusk \'dəsk\ *n* : twilight —**dusky** *adj*

dust \'dəst\ *n* : powdered matter ~ *vb* **1** : remove dust from **2** : sprinkle with fine particles —**dust·er** *n* —**dust·pan** *n* —**dusty** *adj*

du·ty \'dütē, 'dyü-\ *n, pl* **-ties 1** : action required by one's occupation or position **2** : moral or legal obligation **3** : tax —**du·te·ous** \-əs\ *adj* —**du·ti·able** \-əbəl\ *adj* —**du·ti·ful** \dütifəl, 'dyü-\ *adj*

dwarf \'dwórf\ *n, pl* **dwarfs** \'dwórfs\ *or* **dwarves** \'dwórvz\ : one that is much below normal size ~ *vb* **1** : stunt **2** : cause to seem smaller —**dwarf·ish** *adj*

dwell \'dwel\ *vb* **dwelt** \'dwelt\ *or* **dwelled** \'dweld, 'dwelt\; **dwell·ing 1** : reside **2** : keep the attention directed —**dwell·er** *n* —**dwell·ing** *n*

dwin·dle \'dwind⁹l\ *vb* **-dled; -dling** : become steadily less

dye \'dī\ *n* : coloring material ~ *vb* **dyed; dye·ing** : give a new color to

dying *pres part of* DIE

dyke *var of* DIKE

dy·nam·ic \dī'namik\ *adj* **1** : relating to physical force producing motion **2** : energetic or forceful

dy·na·mite \'dīnə,mīt\ *n* : explosive made of nitroglycerin —**dynamite** *vb*

dy·na·mo \-,mō\ *n, pl* **-mos** : electrical generator

dy·nas·ty \'dīnəstē, -,nas-\ *n, pl* **-ties** : succession of rulers of the same family —**dy·nas·tic** \dī'nastik\ *adj*

dys·en·tery \'dis³n,terē\ *n, pl* **-ter·ies** : disease marked by diarrhea

dys·lex·ia \dis'leksēə\ *n* : disturbance of the ability to read —**dys·lex·ic** \-sik\ *adj*

dys·pep·sia \-'pepshə, -sēə\ *n* : indigestion —**dys·pep·tic** \-'peptik\ *adj or n*

dys·tro·phy \'distrəfē\ *n, pl* **-phies** : disorder involving nervous and muscular tissue

E

e \'ē\ *n, pl* **e's** *or* **es** \'ēz\ : 5th letter of the alphabet

each \'ēch\ *adj* : being one of the class named ~ *pron* : every individual one ~ *adv* : apiece

ea·ger \'ēgər\ *adj* : enthusiastic or anxious —**ea·ger·ly** *adv* —**ea·ger·ness** *n*

ea·gle \'ēgəl\ *n* : large bird of prey

-ean —see -AN

¹ear \'ir\ *n* : organ of hearing or the outer part of this —**ear·ache** *n* —**eared** *adj* —**ear·lobe** \-,lōb\ *n*

²ear *n* : fruiting head of a cereal

ear·drum *n* : thin membrane that receives and transmits sound waves in the ear

earl \'ərl\ *n* : British nobleman —**earl·dom** \-dəm\ *n*

ear·ly \'ərlē\ *adj* **-li·er; -est** **1** : relating to or occurring near the beginning or before the usual time **2** : ancient —**early** *adv*

ear·mark *vb* : designate for a specific purpose

earn \'ərn\ *vb* **1** : receive as a return for service **2** : deserve

ear·nest \'ərnəst\ *n* : serious state of mind —**earnest** *adj* —**ear·nest·ly** *adv* —**ear·nest·ness** *n*

earn·ings \'ərninz\ *n pl* : something earned

ear·phone *n* : device that reproduces sound and is worn over or in the ear

ear·ring *n* : earlobe ornament

ear·shot *n* : range of hearing

earth \'ərth\ *n* **1** : soil or land **2** : planet inhabited by man —**earth·li·ness** *n*

—**earth·ly** *adj* —**earth·ward** \-wərd\ *adv*

earth·en \'ərthən\ *adj* : made of earth or baked clay —**earth·en·ware** \-,war\ *n*

earth·quake *n* : shaking or trembling of the earth

earth·worm *n* : long segmented worm

earthy \'ərthē\ *adj* **earth·i·er; -est** **1** : relating to or consisting of earth **2** : practical **3** : coarse —**earth·i·ness** *n*

ease \'ēz\ *n* **1** : comfort **2** : naturalness of manner **3** : freedom from difficulty ~ *vb* **eased; eas·ing 1** : relieve from distress **2** : lessen the tension of **3** : make easier

ea·sel \'ēzəl\ *n* : frame to hold a painter's canvas

east \'ēst\ *adv* : to or toward the east ~ *adj* : situated toward or at or coming from the east ~ *n* **1** : direction of sunrise **2** *cap* : regions to the east —**east·er·ly** \'ēstərlē\ *adv or adj* —**east·ward** *adv or adj* —**east·wards** *adv*

Eas·ter \'ēstər\ *n* : church feast celebrating Christ's resurrection

east·ern \'ēstərn\ *adj* **1** *cap* : relating to a region designated East **2** : lying toward or coming from the east —**East·ern·er** *n*

easy \'ēzē\ *adj* **eas·i·er; -est** **1** : marked by ease **2** : lenient —**eas·i·ly** \'ēzəlē\ *adv* —**eas·i·ness** \-ēnəs\ *n*

easy·go·ing *adj* : relaxed and casual

eat \'ēt\ *vb* **ate** \'āt\; **eat·en** \'ēt³n\; **eat·ing 1** : take in as food **2** : use up or corrode —**eat·able** *adj or n* —**eat·er** *n*

eaves \ˈēvz\ n pl : overhanging edge of a roof

eaves·drop vb : listen secretly —**eaves·drop·per** n

ebb \ˈeb\ n 1 : outward flow of the tide 2 : decline ~ vb 1 : recede from the flood state 2 : wane

eb·o·ny \ˈebənē\ n, pl **-nies** : hard heavy wood of tropical trees ~ adj 1 : made of ebony 2 : black

ebul·lient \i'bulyənt, -'bəl-\ adj : exuberant —**ebul·lience** \-yəns\ n

ec·cen·tric \ik'sentrik\ adj 1 : odd in behavior 2 : being off center —**eccentric** n —**ec·cen·tri·cal·ly** \-triklē\ adv —**ec·cen·tric·i·ty** \,ek,sen'trisətē\ n

ec·cle·si·as·tic \ik,lēzē'astik\ n : clergyman

ec·cle·si·as·ti·cal \-tikəl\, **ecclesiastic** adj : relating to a church —**ec·cle·si·as·ti·cal·ly** \-tiklē\ adv

ech·e·lon \ˈeshə,län\ n 1 : steplike arrangement 2 : level of authority

echo \ˈekō\ n, pl **ech·oes** : repetition of a sound caused by a reflection of the sound waves —**echo** vb

éclair \ā'klar\ n : custard-filled pastry

eclec·tic \e'klektik, i-\ adj : drawing or drawn from varied sources

eclipse \i'klips\ n : total or partial obscuring of one celestial body by another —**eclipse** vb

ecol·o·gy \i'käləjē, e-\ n, pl **-gies** : science concerned with the interaction of organisms and their environment —**eco·log·i·cal** \,ēkə'läjikəl, ,ek-\ adj —**eco·log·i·cal·ly** adv —**ecol·o·gist** \i'kälə,jist, e-\ n

eco·nom·ic \,ekə'nämik, ,ēkə-\ adj : relating to the producing and the buying and selling of goods and services

eco·nom·ics \-'nämiks\ n : branch of knowledge dealing with goods and services —**econ·o·mist** \i'känəmist\ n

econ·o·mize \i'känə,mīz\ vb **-mized; -miz·ing** : be thrifty —**econ·o·miz·er** n

econ·o·my \-əmē\ n, pl **-mies** 1 : thrifty use of resources 2 : economic system —**eco·nom·i·cal** \,ekə'nämikəl, ,ēkə-\ adj —**eco·nom·i·cal·ly** adv —**economy** adj

ecru \ˈekrü, ˈākrü\ n : beige

ec·sta·sy \ˈekstəsē\ n, pl **-sies** : extreme emotional excitement —**ec·stat·ic** \ek'statik, ik-\ adj —**ec·stat·i·cal·ly** \-iklē\ adv

ec·u·men·i·cal \,ekyə'menikəl\ adj : promoting worldwide Christian unity

ec·ze·ma \ig'zēmə, 'egzəmə, 'eksə-\ n : itching skin inflammation

1-ed \d after a vowel or b, g, j, l, m, n, ŋ, r, th, v, z, zh; əd, id after d, t; t after other sounds\ vb suffix or adj suffix 1 —used to form the past participle of regular verbs 2 : having or having the characteristics of

2-ed vb suffix —used to form the past tense of regular verbs

ed·dy \ˈedē\ n, pl **-dies** : whirlpool —**eddy** vb

ede·ma \i'dēmə\ n : abnormal accumulation of fluid in the body tissues —**edem·a·tous** \-'demətəs\ adj

Eden \ˈēdⁿ\ n : paradise

1edge \ˈej\ n 1 : cutting side of a blade 2 : line where something begins or ends ~ vb **edged; edg·ing** 1 : give or form an edge 2 : move gradually 3 : narrowly defeat —**edg·er** n

edge·wise \-,wīz\ adv : sideways

edgy \ˈejē\ adj **edg·i·er; -est** : nervous —**edg·i·ness** n

ed·i·ble \ˈedəbəl\ adj : fit or safe to be eaten —**ed·i·bil·i·ty** \,edə'bilətē\ n —**edible** n

edict \ˈē,dikt\ n : order or decree

ed·i·fi·ca·tion \,edəfə'kāshən\ n : instruction or information —**ed·i·fy** \ˈedə,fī\ vb

ed·i·fice \ˈedəfəs\ n : large building

ed·it \ˈedət\ vb 1 : revise and prepare for publication 2 : delete —**ed·i·tor** \-ər\ n —**ed·i·tor·ship** n

edi·tion \i'dishən\ n 1 : form in which a text is published 2 : total number published at one time

ed·i·to·ri·al \,edə'tōrēəl\ adj 1 : relating to an editor or editing 2 : expressing opinion ~ n : article (as in a newspaper) expressing the views of an editor —**ed·i·to·ri·al·ize** \-ē∂,līz\ vb —**ed·i·to·ri·al·ly** adv

ed·u·cate \ˈejə,kāt\ vb **-cat·ed; -cat·ing** 1 : give instruction to 2 : develop mentally and morally 3 : provide with information —**ed·u·ca·ble** \ˈejəkəbəl\ adj —**ed·u·ca·tion** \,ejə'kāshən\ n —**ed·u·ca·tion·al** \-shənəl\ adj —**ed·u·ca·tor** \-ər\ n

eel \ˈēl\ n : snakelike fish

ee·rie \ˈirē\ adj **-ri·er; -est** : weird —**ee·ri·ly** \ˈirəlē\ adv

ef·face \i'fās, e-\ vb **-faced; -fac·ing**

: obliterate by rubbing out —**ef-face-ment** n

ef-fect \i'fekt\ n **1** : result **2** : meaning **3** : influence **4** pl : goods or possessions ~ vb : cause to happen —**in effect** : in substance

ef-fec-tive \i'fektiv\ adj **1** : producing a strong or desired effect **2** : being in operation —**ef-fec-tive-ly** adv —**ef-fec-tive-ness** n

ef-fec-tu-al \i'fekchəwəl\ adj : producing an intended effect —**ef-fec-tu-al-ly** adv —**ef-fec-tu-al-ness** n

ef-fem-i-nate \ə'femənət\ adj : unsuitably womanish —**ef-fem-i-na-cy** \-nəsē\ n

ef-fer-vesce \,efər'ves\ vb -**vesced;** -**vesc-ing 1** : bubble and hiss as gas escapes **2** : show exhilaration —**ef-fer-ves-cence** \-'ves^ə ns\ n —**ef-fer-ves-cent** \-°nt\ adj —**ef-fer-ves-cent-ly** adv

ef-fete \e'fēt\ adj **1** : worn out **2** : weak or decadent **3** : effeminate

ef-fi-ca-cious \,efə'kāshəs\ adj : effective —**ef-fi-ca-cy** \'efəkəsē\ n

ef-fi-cient \i'fishənt\ adj : working well with little waste —**ef-fi-cien-cy** \-ənsē\ n —**ef-fi-cient-ly** adv

ef-fi-gy \'efəjē\ n, pl -**gies** : usu. crude image of a person

ef-flu-ent \'e,flüənt, e'flü-\ n : something that flows out —**effluent** adj

ef-fort \'efərt\ n **1** : a putting forth of strength **2** : use of resources toward a goal **3** : product of effort —**ef-fort-less** adj —**ef-fort-less-ly** adv

ef-fron-tery \i'frəntərē\ n, pl -**ter-ies** : insolence

ef-fu-sion \i'fyüzhən, e-\ n : a gushing forth —**ef-fu-sive** \-'fyüsiv\ adj —**ef-fu-sive-ly** adv

¹egg \'eg, 'āg\ vb : urge to action

²egg n **1** : rounded usu. hard-shelled reproductive body esp. of birds and reptiles from which the young hatches **2** : ovum —**egg-shell** n

egg-nog \-,näg\ n : rich drink of eggs and cream

egg-plant n : edible purplish fruit of a plant related to the potato

ego \'ēgō\ n, pl **egos** : self-esteem

ego-cen-tric \,ēgō'sentrik\ adj : self-centered

ego-tism \'ēgə,tizəm\ n : exaggerated sense of self-importance —**ego-tist**

\-tist\ n —**ego-tis-tic** \,ēgə'tistik\, **ego-tis-ti-cal** \-tikəl\ adj —**ego-tis-ti-cal-ly** adv

egre-gious \i'grējəs\ adj : notably bad —**egre-gious-ly** adv

egress \'ē,gres\ n : a way out

egret \'ēgrət, i'gret, 'egrət\ n : long-plumed heron

ei-der-down \'īdər,daún\ n : soft down obtained from a northern sea duck (**ei-der**)

eight \'āt\ n **1** : one more than 7 **2** : 8th in a set or series **3** : something having 8 units —**eight** adj or $pron$ —**eighth** \'āt th\ adj or adv or n

eigh-teen \āt'tēn\ n : one more than 17 —**eigh-teen** adj or $pron$ —**eigh-teenth** \-'tēnth\ adj or n

eighty \'ātē\ n, pl **eight-ies** : 8 times 10 —**eight-i-eth** \'ātēəth\ adj or n —**eighty** adj or $pron$

ei-ther \'ēthər, 'ī-\ adj **1** : both **2** : being the one or the other of two ~ $pron$: one of two or more ~ $conj$: one or the other

ejac-u-late \i'jakyə,lāt\ vb -**lat-ed;** -**lat-ing 1** : say suddenly **2** : eject a fluid (as semen) —**ejac-u-la-tion** \-,jak-yə'lāshən\ n

eject \i'jekt\ vb : drive or throw out —**ejec-tion** \-'jekshən\ n

eke \'ēk\ vb **eked; ek-ing** : barely gain with effort —usu. with out

elab-o-rate \i'labərət\ adj **1** : planned in detail **2** : complex and ornate ~ \-ə,rāt\ vb -**rat-ed;** -**rat-ing** : work out in detail —**elab-o-rate-ly** adv —**elab-o-rate-ness** n —**elab-o-ra-tion** \-,labə'rāshən\ n

elapse \i'laps\ vb **elapsed; elaps-ing** : slip by

elas-tic \i'lastik\ adj **1** : springy **2** : flexible ~ n **1** : elastic material **2** : rubber band —**elas-tic-i-ty** \-,las-'tisətē, ,ē,las-\ n

elate \i'lāt\ vb **elat-ed; elat-ing** : fill with joy —**ela-tion** \-'lāshən\ n

el-bow \'el,bō\ n **1** : joint of the arm **2** : elbow-shaped bend or joint ~ vb : push aside with the elbow

el-der \'eldər\ adj : older ~ n **1** : one who is older **2** : church officer

el-der-ber-ry \'eldər,berē\ n : edible black or red fruit or a tree or shrub bearing these

el-der-ly \'eldərlē\ adj : past middle age

el-dest \'eldəst\ adj : oldest

elect \i'lekt\ adj : elected but not yet in

office ~ *n* **elect** *pl* : exclusive group ~ *vb* : choose esp. by vote —**election** \i'lekshən\ *n* —**elective** \i'lektiv\ *n or adj* —**elector** \i'lektər\ *n* —**electoral** \-tərəl\ *adj*

elec·tor·ate \i'lektərət\ *n* : body of persons entitled to vote

electric \i'lektrik\ *adj* 1 : *or* **electrical** \-trikəl\ : relating to or run by electricity 2 : thrilling —**electrical·ly** *adv*

electrician \i,lek'trishən\ *n* : person who installs or repairs electrical equipment

electric·ity \-'trisətē\ *n, pl* **-ties** 1 : fundamental form of energy occurring naturally (as in lightning) or produced artificially 2 : electric current

electrify \i'lektrə,fī\ *vb* **-fied; -fy·ing** 1 : charge with electricity 2 : equip for use of electric power 3 : thrill —**electrifi·ca·tion** \-,lektrəfə'kāshən\ *n*

electrocar·dio·gram \i,lektrō'kärdē-ə,gram\ *n* : tracing made by an electrocardiograph

electrocar·dio·graph \-,graf\ *n* : instrument for monitoring heart function

electro·cute \i'lektrə,kyüt\ *vb* **-cut·ed; -cut·ing** : kill by an electric shock —**electro·cu·tion** \-,lektrə'kyüshən\ *n*

electrode \i'lek,trōd\ *n* : conductor at a nonmetallic part of a circuit

electrol·y·sis \i,lek'träləsəs\ *n* 1 : production of chemical changes through passage of an electric current through a substance 2 : destruction of hair roots with an electric current —**electro·lytic** \-trə'litik\ *adj*

electro·lyte \i'lektrə,līt\ *n* : nonmetallic electric conductor

electro·mag·net \i,lektrō'magnət\ *n* : magnet made using electric current

electro·mag·ne·tism \-nə,tizəm\ *n* : natural force responsible for interactions between charged particles —**electro·mag·net·ic** \-'mag'netik\ *adj* —**electro·mag·net·i·cal·ly** \-iklē\ *adv*

electron \i'lek,trän\ *n* : negatively charged particle within the atom

electron·ic \i,lek'tränik\ *adj* : relating to electrons or electronics —**electron·i·cal·ly** \-iklē\ *adv*

electron·ics \-iks\ *n* : physics of electrons and their use esp. in devices

electro·plate \i'lektrə,plāt\ *vb* : coat (as with metal) by electrolysis

ele·gance \'eligəns\ *n* : refined gracefulness —**ele·gant** \-gənt\ *adj* —**ele·gant·ly** *adv*

ele·gy \'eləjē\ *n, pl* **-gies** : poem expressing grief for one who is dead—**ele·gi·ac** \,elə'jīak, -,ak\ *adj*

ele·ment \'eləmənt\ *n* 1 *pl* : weather conditions 2 : natural environment 3 : constituent part 4 *pl* : simplest principles 5 : substance that has atoms of only one kind —**ele·men·tal** \,elə'mentᵊl\ *adj*

ele·men·ta·ry \,elə'mentrē\ *adj* 1 : simple 2 : relating to the basic subjects of education

ele·phant \'eləfənt\ *n* : huge mammal with a trunk and 2 ivory tusks

ele·vate \'elə,vāt\ *vb* **-vat·ed; -vat·ing** 1 : lift up 2 : exalt

ele·va·tion \,elə'vāshən\ *n* : height or a high place

ele·va·tor \'elə,vātər\ *n* 1 : cage or platform for raising or lowering something 2 : grain storehouse

elev·en \i'levən\ *n* 1 : one more than 10 2 : 11th in a set or series 3 : something having 11 units —**eleven** *adj or pron* —**elev·enth** \-ənth\ *adj or n*

elf \'elf\ *n, pl* **elves** \'elvz\ : mischievous fairy —**elf·in** \'elfən\ *adj* —**elf·ish** \'elfish\ *adj*

elic·it \i'lisət\ *vb* : draw forth

el·i·gi·ble \'eləjəbəl\ *adj* : qualified to participate or to be chosen —**el·i·gi·bil·i·ty** \,eləjə'bilətē\ *n* —**eligible** *n*

elim·i·nate \i'limə,nāt\ *vb* **-nat·ed; -nat·ing** : get rid of —**elim·i·na·tion** \i,limə'nāshən\ *n*

elite \ā'lēt\ *n* : choice or select group

elix·ir \i'liksər\ *n* : medicinal solution

elk \'elk\ *n* : large deer

el·lipse \i'lips, e-\ *n* : oval

el·lip·sis \-lipsəs\ *n, pl* **-lip·ses** \-,sēz\ 1 : omission of a word 2 : marks (as . . .) to show omission

el·lip·ti·cal \-tikəl\, **el·lip·tic** \-tik\ *adj* 1 : relating to or shaped like an ellipse 2 : relating to or marked by ellipsis

elm \'elm\ *n* : tall shade tree

el·o·cu·tion \,elə'kyüshən\ *n* : art of public speaking

elon·gate \i'lȯŋ,gāt\ *vb* **-gat·ed; -gat·ing** : make or grow longer —**elon·ga·tion** \,ē,lȯŋ'gāshən\ *n*

elope \i'lōp\ *vb* eloped; elop·ing : run

away esp. to be married —**elope‧ment** *n* —**elop‧er** *n*

el‧o‧quent \'elǝkwǝnt\ *adj* : forceful and persuasive in speech —**el‧o‧quence** \-kwǝns\ *n* —**el‧o‧quent‧ly** *adv*

else \'els\ *adv* **1** : in a different way, time, or place **2** : otherwise ~ *adj* **1** : other **2** : more

else‧where *adv* : in or to another place

elu‧ci‧date \i'lüsǝ,dāt\ *vb* -**dat‧ed**; -**dat‧ing** : explain —**elu‧ci‧da‧tion** \i,lüsǝ'dāshǝn\ *n*

elude \ē'lüd\ *vb* **elud‧ed**; **elud‧ing** : evade —**elu‧sive** \ē'lüsiv\ *adj* —**elu‧sive‧ly** *adv* —**elu‧sive‧ness** *n*

elves *pl of* ELF

ema‧ci‧ate \i'māshē,āt\ *vb* -**at‧ed**; -**at‧ing** : become or make very thin —**ema‧ci‧a‧tion** \i,māsē'āshǝn, -shē-\ *n*

em‧a‧nate \'emǝ,nāt\ *vb* -**nat‧ed**; -**nat‧ing** : come forth —**em‧a‧na‧tion** \,emǝ'nāshǝn\ *n*

eman‧ci‧pate \i'mansǝ,pāt\ *vb* -**pat‧ed**; -**pat‧ing** : set free —**eman‧ci‧pa‧tion** \i,mansǝ'pāshǝn\ *n* —**eman‧ci‧pa‧tor** \i'mansǝ,pātǝr\ *n*

emas‧cu‧late \i'maskyǝ,lāt\ *vb* -**lat‧ed**; -**lat‧ing** **1** : castrate **2** : weaken —**emas‧cu‧la‧tion** \i,maskyǝ'lāshǝn\ *n*

em‧balm \im'bäm, -'bälm\ *vb* : preserve (a corpse) —**em‧balm‧er** *n*

em‧bank‧ment \im'baŋkmǝnt\ *n* : protective barrier of earth

em‧bar‧go \im'bärgō\ *n*, *pl* -**goes** : ban on trade —**embargo** *vb*

em‧bark \-'bärk\ *vb* **1** : go on board a ship or airplane **2** : make a start —**em‧bar‧ka‧tion** \,em,bär'kāshǝn\ *n*

em‧bar‧rass \im'barǝs\ *vb* : cause distress and self-consciousness —**em‧bar‧rass‧ment** *n*

em‧bas‧sy \'embǝsē\ *n*, *pl* -**sies** : residence and offices of an ambassador

em‧bed \im'bed\ *vb* -**dd**- : fix firmly

em‧bel‧lish \-'belish\ *vb* : decorate —**em‧bel‧lish‧ment** *n*

em‧ber \'embǝr\ *n* : smoldering fragment from a fire

em‧bez‧zle \im'bezǝl\ *vb* -**zled**; -**zling** : steal (money) by falsifying records —**em‧bez‧zle‧ment** *n* —**em‧bez‧zler** \-ǝlǝr\ *n*

em‧bit‧ter \im'bitǝr\ *vb* : make bitter

em‧bla‧zon \-'blāzᵊn\ *vb* : display conspicuously

em‧blem \'emblǝm\ *n* : symbol —**em‧blem‧at‧ic** \,emblǝ'matik\ *adj*

em‧body \im'bädē\ *vb* -**bod‧ied**; -**body‧ing** : give definite form or expression to —**em‧bodi‧ment** \-'bädimǝnt\ *n*

em‧boss \-'bäs, -'bós\ *vb* : ornament with raised work

em‧brace \-'brās\ *vb* -**braced**; -**brac‧ing** **1** : clasp in the arms **2** : welcome **3** : include —**embrace** *n*

em‧broi‧der \-'bróidǝr\ *vb* : ornament with or do needlework —**em‧broi‧dery** \-ǝrē\ *n*

em‧broil \im'bróil\ *vb* : involve in conflict or difficulties

em‧bryo \'embrē,ō\ *n* : living being in its earliest stages of development —**em‧bry‧on‧ic** \,embrē'änik\ *adj*

emend \ē'mend\ *vb* : correct —**emen‧da‧tion** \,ē,men'dāshǝn\ *n*

em‧er‧ald \'emrǝld, 'emǝ-\ *n* : green gem ~ *adj* : bright green

emerge \i'mǝrj\ *vb* **emerged**; **emerg‧ing** : rise, come forth, or appear —**emer‧gence** \-'mǝrjǝns\ *n* —**emer‧gent** \-jǝnt\ *adj*

emer‧gen‧cy \i'mǝrjǝnsē\ *n*, *pl* -**cies** : condition requiring prompt action

em‧ery \'emǝrē\ *n*, *pl* -**er‧ies** : dark granular mineral used for grinding

emet‧ic \i'metik\ *n* : agent that induces vomiting —**emetic** *adj*

em‧i‧grate \'emǝ,grāt\ *vb* -**grat‧ed**; -**grat‧ing** : leave a country to settle elsewhere —**em‧i‧grant** \-igrǝnt\ *n* —**em‧i‧gra‧tion** \,emǝ'grāshǝn\ *n*

em‧i‧nence \'emǝnǝns\ *n* **1** : prominence or superiority **2** : person of high rank

em‧i‧nent \-nǝnt\ *adj* : prominent —**em‧i‧nent‧ly** *adv*

em‧is‧sary \'emǝ,serē\ *n*, *pl* -**sar‧ies** : agent

emis‧sion \ē'mishǝn\ *n* : substance discharged into the air

emit \ē'mit\ *vb* -**tt**- : give off or out

emol‧u‧ment \i'mälyǝmǝnt\ *n* : salary or fee

emote \i'mōt\ *vb* **emot‧ed**; **emot‧ing** : express emotion

emo‧tion \i'mōshǝn\ *n* : intense feeling —**emo‧tion‧al** \-shǝnǝl\ *adj* —**emo‧tion‧al‧ly** *adv*

em‧per‧or \'empǝrǝr\ *n* : ruler of an empire

em‧pha‧sis \'emfǝsǝs\ *n*, *pl* -**pha‧ses** \-,sēz\ : stress

em‧pha‧size \-,sīz\ *vb* -**sized**; -**siz‧ing** : stress

em‧phat‧ic \im'fatik, em-\ *adj* : uttered

with emphasis **—em·phat·i·cal·ly** \-iklē\ *adv*

em·pire \'em,pīr\ *n* : large state or a group of states

em·pir·i·cal \im'pirikəl\ *adj* : based on observation **—em·pir·i·cal·ly** \-iklē\ *adv*

em·ploy \im'ploi\ *vb* 1 : use 2 : occupy ~ *n* : paid occupation **—em·ploy·ee, em·ploye** \im,ploi'ē, -'ploi,ē\ *n* **—em·ploy·er** *n* **—em·ploy·ment** \-mənt\ *n*

em·pow·er \im'pauər\ *vb* : give power to **—em·pow·er·ment** *n*

em·press \'emprəs\ *n* 1 : wife of an emperor 2 : woman emperor

emp·ty \'emptē\ *adj* 1 : containing nothing 2 : not occupied 3 : lacking value, sense, or purpose ~ *vb* **-tied; -ty·ing** : make or become empty **—emp·ti·ness** \-tēnəs\ *n*

emu \'ēmyü\ *n* : Australian bird related to the ostrich

em·u·late \'emyə,lāt\ *vb* **-lat·ed; -lat·ing** : try to equal or excel **—em·u·la·tion** \,emyə'lāshən\ *n*

emul·si·fy \i'məlsə,fī\ *vb* **-fied; -fy·ing** : convert into an emulsion **—emul·si·fi·ca·tion** \i,məlsəfə'kāshən\ *n* **—emul·si·fi·er** \-'məlsə,fīər\ *n*

emul·sion \i'məlshən\ *n* 1 : mixture of mutually insoluble liquids 2 : light-sensitive coating on photographic film

-en \ən, ³n\ *vb suffix* 1 : become or cause to be 2 : cause or come to have

en·able \in'ābəl\ *vb* **-abled; -abling** : give power, capacity, or ability to

en·act \in'akt\ *vb* 1 : make into law 2 : act out **—en·act·ment** *n*

enam·el \in'aməl\ *n* 1 : glasslike substance used to coat metal or pottery 2 : hard outer layer of a tooth 3 : glossy paint **—enamel** *vb*

en·am·or \in'amər\ *vb* : excite with love

en·camp \in'kamp\ *vb* : make camp **—en·camp·ment** *n*

en·case \in'kās\ *vb* : enclose in or as if in a case

-ence \əns, ³ns\ *n suffix* 1 : action or process 2 : quality or state

en·ceph·a·li·tis \in,sefə'lītəs\ *n, pl* **-lit·i·des** \-'litə,dēz\ : inflammation of the brain

en·chant \in'chant\ *vb* 1 : bewitch 2 : fascinate **—en·chant·er** *n* **—en·chant·ment** *n* **—en·chant·ress** \-'chantrəs\ *n*

en·cir·cle \in'sərkəl\ *vb* : surround

en·close \in'klōz\ *vb* 1 : shut up or surround 2 : include **—en·clo·sure** \in-'klōzhər\ *n*

en·co·mi·um \en'kōmēəm\ *n, pl* **-mi·ums** *or* **-mia** \-mēə\ : high praise

en·com·pass \in'kəmpəs, -'käm-\ *vb* : surround or include

en·core \'än,kōr\ *n* : further performance

en·coun·ter \in'kauntər\ *vb* 1 : fight 2 : meet unexpectedly **—encounter** *n*

en·cour·age \in'kərij\ *vb* **-aged; -ag·ing** 1 : inspire with courage and hope 2 : foster **—en·cour·age·ment** *n*

en·croach \in'krōch\ *vb* : enter upon another's property or rights **—en·croach·ment** *n*

en·crust \in'krəst\ *vb* : form a crust on

en·cum·ber \in'kəmbər\ *vb* : burden **—en·cum·brance** \-brəns\ *n*

-en·cy \ənsē, ³n-\ *n suffix* : -ence

en·cyc·li·cal \in'siklikəl, en-\ *n* : papal letter to bishops

en·cy·clo·pe·dia \in,sīklə'pēdēə\ *n* : reference work on many subjects **—en·cy·clo·pe·dic** \-'pēdik\ *adj*

end \'end\ *n* 1 : point at which something stops or no longer exists 2 : cessation 3 : purpose ~ *vb* 1 : stop or finish 2 : be at the end of **—end·ed** *adj* **—end·less** *adj* **—end·less·ly** *adv*

en·dan·ger \in'dānjər\ *vb* : bring into danger

en·dear \in'dir\ *vb* : make dear **—en·dear·ment** \-mənt\ *n*

en·deav·or \in'devər\ *vb or n* : attempt

end·ing \'endiŋ\ *n* : end

en·dive \'en,dīv\ *n* : salad plant

en·do·crine \'endəkrən, -,krīn, -,krēn\ *adj* : producing secretions distributed by the bloodstream

en·dorse \in'dórs\ *vb* **-dorsed; -dors·ing** 1 : sign one's name to 2 : approve **—en·dorse·ment** *n*

en·dow \in'daù\ *vb* 1 : furnish with funds 2 : furnish naturally **—en·dow·ment** *n*

en·dure \in'dúr, -'dyúr\ *vb* **-dured; -dur·ing** 1 : last 2 : suffer patiently 3 : tolerate **—en·dur·able** *adj* **—en·dur·ance** \-əns\ *n*

en·e·ma \'enəmə\ *n* : injection of liquid into the rectum

en·e·my \'enə-mē\ *n, pl* **-mies** : one that attacks or tries to harm another

en·er·get·ic \,enər'jetik\ *adj* : full of energy or activity **—en·er·get·i·cal·ly** \-iklē\ *adv*

en·er·gize \'enər.jīz\ *vb* **-gized; -giz·ing** : give energy to

en·er·gy \'enərjē\ *n, pl* **-gies 1** : capacity for action **2** : vigorous action **3** : capacity for doing work

en·er·vate \'enər.vāt\ *vb* **-vat·ed; -vat·ing** : make weak or listless **—en·er·va·tion** \.enər'vāshən\ *n*

en·fold \in'fōld\ *vb* : surround or embrace

en·force \-'fōrs\ *vb* **1** : compel **2** : carry out **—en·force·able** \-əbəl\ *adj* **—en·force·ment** *n*

en·fran·chise \-'fran.chīz\ *vb* **-chised; -chis·ing** : grant voting rights to **—en·fran·chise·ment** \-.chīzmənt, -chəz-\ *n*

en·gage \in'gāj\ *vb* **-gaged; -gag·ing 1** : participate or cause to participate **2** : bring or come into working contact **3** : bind by a pledge to marry **4** : hire **5** : bring or enter into conflict **—en·gage·ment** \-mənt\ *n*

en·gag·ing *adj* : attractive

en·gen·der \in'jendər\ *vb* **-dered; -der·ing** : create

en·gine \'enjən\ *n* **1** : machine that converts energy into mechanical motion **2** : locomotive

en·gi·neer \.enjə'nir\ *n* **1** : one trained in engineering **2** : engine operator ~ *vb* : lay out or manage as an engineer

en·gi·neer·ing \-iŋ\ *n* : practical application of science and mathematics

en·grave \in'grāv\ *vb* **-graved; -gra·ving** : cut into a surface **—en·grav·er** *n* **—en·grav·ing** *n*

en·gross \-'grōs\ *vb* : occupy fully

en·gulf \-'gəlf\ *vb* : swallow up

en·hance \-'hans\ *vb* **-hanced; -hanc·ing** : improve in value **—en·hance·ment** *n*

enig·ma \i'nigmə\ *n* : puzzle or mystery **—enig·mat·ic** \.enig'matik, .ē-\ *adj* **—enig·mat·i·cal·ly** *adv*

en·join \in'jóin\ *vb* **1** : command **2** : forbid

en·joy \-'jói\ *vb* : take pleasure in **—en·joy·able** *adj* **—en·joy·ment** *n*

en·large \-'lärj\ *vb* **-larged; -larg·ing** : make or grow larger **—en·large·ment** *n* **—en·larg·er** *n*

en·light·en \-'līt^ən\ *vb* : give knowledge or spiritual insight to **—en·light·en·ment** *n*

en·list \-'list\ *vb* **1** : join the armed forces **2** : get the aid of **—en·list·ee** \-.lis'tē\ *n* **—en·list·ment** \-'listmənt\ *n*

en·liv·en \in'līvən\ *vb* : give life or spirit to

en·mi·ty \'enmətē\ *n, pl* **-ties** : mutual hatred

en·no·ble \in'ōbəl\ *vb* **-bled; -bling** : make noble

en·nui \.än'wē\ *n* : boredom

enor·mi·ty \i'nórmətē\ *n, pl* **-ties 1** : great wickedness **2** : huge size

enor·mous \i'nórməs\ *adj* : great in size, number, or degree **—enor·mous·ly** *adv* **—enor·mous·ness** *n*

enough \i'nəf\ *adj* : adequate ~ *adv* **1** : in an adequate manner **2** : in a tolerable degree ~ *pron* : adequate number, quantity, or amount

en·quire \in.kwīr\, **en·qui·ry** \'in.kwīrē, in'-; 'inkwərē, 'iŋ-\ *var of* INQUIRE, INQUIRY

en·rage \in'rāj\ *vb* : fill with rage

en·rich \-'rich\ *vb* : make rich **—en·rich·ment** *n*

en·roll, en·rol \-'rōl\ *vb* **-rolled; -roll·ing 1** : enter on a list **2** : become enrolled **—en·roll·ment** *n*

en route \äⁿ'rüt, en-, in-\ *adv or adj* : on or along the way

en·sconce \in'skäns\ *vb* **-sconced; -sconc·ing** : settle snugly

en·sem·ble \än'sämbəl\ *n* **1** : small group **2** : complete costume

en·shrine \in'shrīn\ *vb* **1** : put in a shrine **2** : cherish

en·sign \'ensən, *1 also* 'en.sīn\ *n* **1** : flag **2** : lowest ranking commissioned officer in the navy

en·slave \in'slāv\ *vb* : make a slave of **—en·slave·ment** *n*

en·snare \-'snar\ *vb* : trap

en·sue \-'sü\ *vb* **-sued; -su·ing** : follow as a consequence

en·sure \-'shůr\ *vb* **-sured; -sur·ing** : guarantee

en·tail \-'tāl\ *vb* : involve as a necessary result

en·tan·gle \-'taŋgəl\ *vb* : tangle **—en·tan·gle·ment** *n*

en·ter \'entər\ *vb* **1** : go or come in or into **2** : start **3** : set down (as in a list)

en·ter·prise \'entər.prīz\ *n* **1** : an undertaking **2** : business organization **3** : initiative

en·ter·pris·ing \-.prīziŋ\ *adj* : showing initiative

en·ter·tain \.entər'tān\ *vb* **1** : treat or receive as a guest **2** : hold in mind **3** : amuse **—en·ter·tain·er** *n* **—en·ter·tain·ment** *n*

en•thrall, en•thral \in'thrȯl\ vb **-thralled; -thrall•ing** : hold spellbound

en•thu•si•asm \-'thüzē,azəm, -'thyü-\ n : strong excitement of feeling or its cause —**en•thu•si•ast** \-,ast, -əst\ n —**en•thu•si•as•tic** \-,thüzē'astik, -,thyü-\ adj —**en•thu•si•as•ti•cal•ly** \-tiklē\ adv

en•tice \-'tīs\ vb **-ticed; -tic•ing** : tempt —**en•tice•ment** n

en•tire \in'tīr\ adj : complete or whole —**en•tire•ly** adv —**en•tire•ty** \-'tīrətē, -'tīrtē\ n

en•ti•tle \-'tīt⁹l\ vb **-tled; -tling 1** : name **2** : give a right to

en•ti•ty \'entətē\ n, pl **-ties** : something with separate existence

en•to•mol•o•gy \,entə'mäləjē\ n : study of insects —**en•to•mo•log•i•cal** \-mə'läjikəl\ adj —**en•to•mol•o•gist** \-'mäləjist\ n

en•tou•rage \,äntü'räzh\ n : retinue

en•trails \'entrəlz, -,trālz\ n pl : intestines

¹**en•trance** \'entrəns\ n **1** : act of entering **2** : means or place of entering —**en•trant** \'entrənt\ n

²**en•trance** \in'trans\ vb **-tranced; -tranc•ing** : fascinate or delight

en•trap \in'trap\ vb : trap —**en•trap•ment** n

en•treat \-'trēt\ vb : ask urgently —**en•treaty** \-'trētē\ n

en•trée, en•tree \'än,trā\ n : principal dish of the meal

en•trench \in'trench\ vb : establish in a strong position —**en•trench•ment** n

en•tre•pre•neur \,äntrəprə'nər\ n : organizer or promoter of an enterprise

en•trust \in'trəst\ vb : commit to another with confidence

en•try \'entrē\ n, pl **-tries 1** : entrance **2** : an entering in a record or an item so entered

en•twine \in'twīn\ vb : twine together or around

enu•mer•ate \i'nümə,rāt, -'nyü-\ vb **-at•ed; -at•ing 1** : count **2** : list —**enu•mer•a•tion** \i,nümə'rāshən, -,nyü-\ n

enun•ci•ate \ē'nənsē,āt\ vb **-at•ed; -at•ing 1** : announce **2** : pronounce —**enun•ci•a•tion** \-,nənsē'āshən\ n

en•vel•op \in'veləp\ vb : surround —**en•vel•op•ment** n

en•ve•lope \'envə,lōp, 'än-\ n : paper container for a letter

en•vi•ron•ment \in'vīrənmənt\ n : surroundings —**en•vi•ron•men•tal** \-,vīrən'ment⁹l\ adj

en•vi•ron•men•tal•ist \-⁹list\ n : person concerned about the environment

en•vi•rons \in'vīrənz\ n pl : vicinity

en•vis•age \in'vizij\ vb **-aged; -ag•ing** : have a mental picture of

en•vi•sion \in'vizhən\ vb : picture to oneself

en•voy \'en,vȯi, 'än-\ n : diplomat

en•vy \'envē\ n **1** : resentful awareness of another's advantage **2** : object of envy ~ vb **-vied; -vy•ing** : feel envy toward or on account of —**en•vi•able** \-vēəbəl\ adj —**en•vi•ous** \-vēəs\ adj —**en•vi•ous•ly** adv

en•zyme \'en,zīm\ n : biological catalyst

eon \'ēən, ē,än\ var of AEON

ep•au•let \,epə'let\ n : shoulder ornament on a uniform

ephem•er•al \i'femərəl\ adj : short-lived

ep•ic \'epik\ n : long poem about a hero —**epic** adj

epi•cure \'epi,kyur\ n : person with fastidious taste esp. in food and wine —**epi•cu•re•an** \,epikyu'rēən, -'kyurē-\ n or adj

ep•i•dem•ic \,epə'demik\ adj : affecting many persons at one time —**epidemic** n

epi•der•mis \,epə'dərməs\ n : outer layer of skin

ep•i•gram \'epə,gram\ n : short witty poem or saying —**ep•i•gram•mat•ic** \,epəgrə'matik\ adj

ep•i•lep•sy \'epə,lepsē\ n, pl **-sies** : nervous disorder marked by convulsive attacks —**ep•i•lep•tic** \,epə'leptik\ adj or n

epis•co•pal \i'piskəpəl\ adj : governed by bishops

ep•i•sode \'epə,sōd, -,zōd\ n : occurrence —**ep•i•sod•ic** \,epə'sädik, -'zäd-\ adj

epis•tle \i'pisəl\ n : letter

ep•i•taph \'epə,taf\ n : inscription in memory of a dead person

ep•i•thet \'epə,thet, -thət\ n : characterizing often abusive word or phrase

epit•o•me \i'pitəmē\ n **1** : summary **2** : ideal example —**epit•o•mize** \-,mīz\ vb

ep•och \'epək, 'ep,äk\ n : extended period —**ep·och·al** \'epəkəl, 'ep͵äkəl\ *adj*

ep·oxy \'ep͵äksē, ep'äksē\ *n* : synthetic resin used esp. in adhesives ~ *vb* **-ox·ied** *or* **-oxyed; -oxy·ing** : glue with epoxy

equa·ble \'ekwəbəl, 'ēkwə-\ *adj* : free from unpleasant extremes —**equa·bil·i·ty** \͵ekwə'bilətē, ͵ē-\ *n* —**equa·bly** \-blē\ *adv*

equal \'ēkwəl\ *adj* : of the same quantity, value, quality, number, or status as another ~ *n* : one that is equal ~ *vb* **equaled** *or* **equalled; equal·ing** *or* **equal·ling** : be or become equal to —**equal·i·ty** \i'kwälətē\ *n* —**equal·ize** \'ēkwə͵līz\ *vb* —**equal·ly** \'ēkwəlē\ *adv*

equa·nim·i·ty \͵ēkwə'nimətē, ek-\ *n, pl* **-ties** : calmness

equate \i'kwāt\ *vb* **equat·ed; equat·ing** : treat or regard as equal

equa·tion \i'kwāzhən, -shən\ *n* : mathematical statement that two things are equal

equa·tor \i'kwātər\ *n* : imaginary circle that separates the northern and southern hemispheres —**equa·to·ri·al** \͵ēkwə'tōrēəl, ͵ek-\ *adj*

eques·tri·an \i'kwestrēən\ *adj* : relating to horseback riding ~ *n* : horseback rider

equi·lat·er·al \͵ēkwə'latərəl\ *adj* : having equal sides

equi·lib·ri·um \-'librēəm\ *n, pl* **-ri·ums** *or* **-ria** \-rēə\ : state of balance

equine \'ē͵kwīn, 'ek͵wīn\ *adj* : relating to the horse —**equine** *n*

equi·nox \'ēkwə͵näks, 'ek-\ *n* : time when day and night are everywhere of equal length

equip \i'kwip\ *vb* **-pp-** : furnish with needed resources —**equip·ment** \-mənt\ *n*

eq·ui·ta·ble \'ekwətəbəl\ *adj* : fair

eq·ui·ty \'ekwətē\ *n, pl* **-ties 1** : justice **2** : value of a property less debt

equiv·a·lent \i'kwivələnt\ *adj* : equal —**equiv·a·lence** \-ləns\ *n* —**equivalent** *n*

equiv·o·cal \i'kwivəkəl\ *adj* : ambiguous or uncertain

equiv·o·cate \i'kwivə͵kāt\ *vb* **-cat·ed; -cat·ing 1** : use misleading language **2** : avoid answering definitely —**equiv·o·ca·tion** \i͵kwivə'kāshən\ *n*

1-er \ər\ *adj suffix or adv suffix* —used to form the comparative degree of ad-

jectives and adverbs and esp. those of one or two syllables

2-er \ər\, **-ier** \ēər, yər\, **-yer** \yər\ *n suffix* **1** : one that is associated with **2** : one that performs or is the object of an action **3** : one that is

era \'irə, 'erə, 'ērə\ *n* : period of time associated with something

erad·i·cate \i'radə͵kāt\ *vb* **-cat·ed; -cat·ing** : do away with

erase \i'rās\ *vb* **erased; eras·ing** : rub or scratch out —**eras·er** *n* —**era·sure** \i'rāshər\ *n*

ere \'er\ *prep or conj* : before

erect \i'rekt\ *adj* : not leaning or lying down ~ *vb* **1** : build **2** : bring to an upright position —**erec·tion** \i'rekshən\ *n*

er·mine \'ərmən\ *n* : weasel with white winter fur or its fur

erode \i'rōd\ *vb* **erod·ed; erod·ing** : wear away gradually

ero·sion \i'rōzhən\ *n* : process of eroding

erot·ic \i'rätik\ *adj* : sexually arousing —**erot·i·cal·ly** \-iklē\ *adv* —**erot·i·cism** \i'rätə͵sizəm\ *n*

err \'er, 'ər\ *vb* : be or do wrong

er·rand \'erənd\ *n* : short trip taken to do something often for another

er·rant \-ənt\ *adj* **1** : traveling about **2** : going astray

er·rat·ic \ir'atik\ *adj* **1** : eccentric **2** : inconsistent —**er·rat·i·cal·ly** \-iklē\ *adv*

er·ro·ne·ous \ir'ōnēəs, e'rō-\ *adj* : wrong —**er·ro·ne·ous·ly** *adv*

er·ror \'erər\ *n* **1** : something that is not accurate **2** : state of being wrong

er·satz \'er͵säts\ *adj* : phony

erst·while \'ərst͵hwīl\ *adv* : in the past ~ *adj* : former

er·u·di·tion \͵erə'dishən, ͵eryə-\ *n* : great learning —**er·u·dite** \'erə͵dīt, 'eryə-\ *adj*

erupt \i'rəpt\ *vb* : burst forth esp. suddenly and violently —**erup·tion** \i'rəpshən\ *n* —**erup·tive** \-tiv\ *adj*

-ery \ərē\ *n suffix* **1** : character or condition **2** : practice **3** : place of action

1-es \əz, iz *after* s, z, sh, ch; z *after* v or a vowel\ *n pl suffix* —used to form the plural of some nouns

2-es *vb suffix* —used to form the 3d person singular present of some verbs

es·ca·late \'eskə͵lāt\ *vb* **-lat·ed; -lat·ing** : become quickly larger or greater —**es·ca·la·tion** \͵eskə'lāshən\ *n*

es·ca·la·tor \\'eskə,lātər\\ n : moving stairs

es·ca·pade \\'eskə,pād\\ n : mischievous adventure

es·cape \is'kāp\ vb **-caped; -cap·ing** : get away or get away from ~ n 1 : flight from or avoidance of something unpleasant 2 : leakage 3 : means of escape ~ adj : providing means of escape **—es·cap·ee** \is,kā'pē, ,es-\ n

es·ca·role \\'eskə,rōl\\ n : salad green

es·carp·ment \is'kärpmənt\ n : cliff

es·chew \is'chü\ vb : shun

es·cort \\'es,kórt\\ n : one accompanying another **—es·cort** \is'kórt, es-\ vb

es·crow \\'es,krō\\ n : deposit to be delivered upon fulfillment of a condition

esoph·a·gus \i'säfəgəs\ n, pl **-gi** \-,gī, -,jī\ : muscular tube connecting the mouth and stomach

es·o·ter·ic \,esə'terik\ adj : mysterious or secret

es·pe·cial·ly \is'peshəlē\ adv : particularly or notably

es·pi·o·nage \\'espē,näzh, -nij\\ n : practice of spying

es·pous·al \is'pauzəl\ n 1 : betrothal 2 : wedding 3 : a taking up as a supporter **—es·pouse** \-'pauz\ vb

es·pres·so \e'spresō\ n, pl **-sos** : strong steam-brewed coffee

es·py \is'pī\ vb **-pied; -py·ing** : catch sight of

es·quire \\'es,kwīr\\ n —used as a title of courtesy

-ess \əs, ,es\ n suffix : female

es·say \\'es,ā\\ n : literary composition ~ vb \e'sā, 'es,ā\ : attempt **—es·say·ist** \\'es,āist\\ n

es·sence \\'es^ⁿs\\ n 1 : fundamental nature or quality 2 : extract 3 : perfume

es·sen·tial \i'senchəl\ adj : basic or necessary **—essential** n **—es·sen·tial·ly** adv

-est \əst, ist\ adj suffix or adv suffix —used to form the superlative degree of adjectives and adverbs and esp. those of 1 or 2 syllables

es·tab·lish \is'tablish\ vb 1 : bring into existence 2 : put on a firm basis 3 : cause to be recognized

es·tab·lish·ment \-mənt\ n 1 : business or a place of business 2 : an establishing or being established 3 : controlling group

es·tate \is'tāt\ n 1 : one's possessions 2 : large piece of land with a house

es·teem \is'tēm\ n or vb : regard

es·ter \\'estər\\ n : organic chemical compound

esthetic var of AESTHETIC

es·ti·ma·ble \\'estəməbəl\\ adj : worthy of esteem

es·ti·mate \\'estə,māt\\ vb **-mat·ed; -mat·ing** : judge the approximate value, size, or cost ~ \-mət\ n 1 : rough or approximate calculation 2 : statement of the cost of a job **—es·ti·ma·tion** \,estə'māshən\ n **—es·ti·ma·tor** \\'estə,mātər\\ n

es·trange \is'trānj\ vb **-tranged; -trang·ing** : make hostile **—es·trange·ment** n

es·tro·gen \\'estrəjən\\ n : hormone that produces female characteristics

es·tu·ary \\'eschə,werē\\ n, pl **-ar·ies** : arm of the sea at a river's mouth

et cet·era \et'setərə, -'setrə\ : and others esp. of the same kind

etch \\'ech\\ vb : produce by corroding parts of a surface with acid **—etch·er** n **—etch·ing** n

eter·nal \i'tərn^əl\ adj : lasting forever **—eter·nal·ly** adv

eter·ni·ty \-nətē\ n, pl **-ties** : infinite duration

eth·ane \\'eth,ān\\ n : gaseous hydrocarbon

eth·a·nol \\'ethə,nól, -,nōl\\ n : alcohol

ether \\'ēthər\\ n : light flammable liquid used as an anesthetic

ethe·re·al \i'thirēəl\ adj 1 : celestial 2 : exceptionally delicate

eth·i·cal \\'ethikəl\\ adj 1 : relating to ethics 2 : honorable **—eth·i·cal·ly** adv

eth·ics \-iks\ n sing or pl 1 : study of good and evil and moral duty 2 : moral principles or practice

eth·nic \\'ethnik\\ adj : relating to races or groups of people with common customs ~ n : member of a minority ethnic group

eth·nol·o·gy \eth'näləjē\ n : study of the races of human beings **—eth·no·log·i·cal** \,ethnə'läjikəl\ adj **—eth·nol·o·gist** \eth'näləjist\ n

et·i·quette \\'etikət, -,ket\\ n : good manners

et·y·mol·o·gy \,etə'mäləjē\ n, pl **-gies** 1 : history of a word 2 : study of etymologies **—et·y·mo·log·i·cal** \-mə'läjikəl\ adj **—et·y·mol·o·gist** \-'mäləjist\ n

eu·ca·lyp·tus \,yükə'liptəs\ n, pl **-ti** \-,tī\ or **-tus·es** : Australian evergreen tree

Eu·cha·rist \'yükərəst\ n : Communion —**eu·cha·ris·tic** \,yükə'ristik\ adj

eu·lo·gy \'yüləjē\ n, pl **-gies** : speech in praise —**eu·lo·gis·tic** \,yülə'jistik\ adj —**eu·lo·gize** \'yülə,jīz\ vb

eu·nuch \'yünək\ n : castrated man

eu·phe·mism \'yüfə,mizəm\ n : substitution of a pleasant expression for an unpleasant or offensive one —**eu·phe·mis·tic** \,yüfə'mistik\ adj

eu·pho·ni·ous \yu'fōnēəs\ adj : pleasing to the ear —**eu·pho·ny** \'yüfənē\ n

eu·pho·ria \yu'fōrēə\ n : elation —**eu·phor·ic** \-'fōrik\ adj

eu·tha·na·sia \,yüthə'nāzhə, -zhēə\ n : mercy killing

evac·u·ate \i vakyə,wāt\ vb **-at·ed; -at·ing 1** : discharge wastes from the body **2** : remove or withdraw from —**evac·u·a·tion** \i,vakyə'wāshən\ n

evade \i'vād\ vb **evad·ed; evad·ing** : manage to avoid

eval·u·ate \i'valyə,wāt\ vb **-at·ed; -at·ing** : appraise —**eval·u·a·tion** \i,valyə'wāshən\ n

evan·gel·i·cal \,ē,van'jelikəl, ,evən-\ adj : relating to the Christian gospel

evan·ge·lism \i'vanjə,lizəm\ n : the winning or revival of personal commitments to Christ —**evan·ge·list** \i'vanjəlist\ n —**evan·ge·lis·tic** \i,vanjə'listik\ adj

evap·o·rate \i'vapə,rāt\ vb **-rat·ed; -rat·ing 1** : pass off in or convert into vapor **2** : disappear quickly —**evap·o·ra·tion** \i,vapə'rāshən\ n —**evap·o·ra·tor** \i'vapə,rātər\ n

eva·sion \i'vāzhən\ n : act or instance of evading —**eva·sive** \i'vāsiv\ adj —**eva·sive·ness** n

eve \'ēv\ n : evening

even \'ēvən\ adj **1** : smooth **2** : equal or fair **3** : fully revenged **4** : divisible by 2 ~ adv **1** : already **2** —used for emphasis ~ vb : make or become even —**even·ly** adv —**even·ness** n

eve·ning \'ēvniŋ\ n : early part of the night

event \i'vent\ n **1** : occurrence **2** : noteworthy happening **3** : eventuality —**event·ful** adj

even·tu·al \i'venchəwəl\ adj : later —**even·tu·al·ly** adv

even·tu·al·i·ty \i,venchə'walətē\ n, pl **-ties** : possible occurrence or outcome

ev·er \'evər\ adv **1** : always **2** : at any time **3** : in any case

ev·er·green adj : having foliage that remains green —**evergreen** n

ev·er·last·ing \,evər'lastiŋ\ adj : lasting forever

every \'evrē\ adj **1** : being each one of a group **2** : all possible

every·body \'evri,bädē, -bəd-\ pron : every person

every·day adj : ordinary

every·one \-,wən\ pron : every person

every·thing pron : all that exists

every·where adv : in every place or part

evict \i'vikt\ vb : force (a person) to move from a property —**evic·tion** \i-'vikshən\ n

ev·i·dence \'evədəns\ n **1** : outward sign **2** : proof or testimony

ev·i·dent \-dənt\ adj : clear or obvious —**ev·i·dent·ly** \-ədəntlē, -ə,dent-\ adv

evil \'ēvəl\ adj **evil·er** or **evil·ler; evil·est** or **evil·lest** : wicked ~ n **1** : sin **2** : source of sorrow or distress —**evil·do·er** \,ēvəl'düər\ n —**evil·ly** adv

evince \i'vins\ vb **evinced; evinc·ing** : show

evis·cer·ate \i'visə,rāt\ vb **-at·ed; -at·ing** : remove the viscera of —**evis·cer·a·tion** \i,visə'rāshən\ n

evoke \i'vōk\ vb **evoked; evok·ing** : call forth or up —**evo·ca·tion** \,ēvō-'kāshən, ,evə-\ n —**evoc·a·tive** \i-'väkətiv\ adj

evo·lu·tion \,evə'lüshən\ n : process of change by degrees —**evo·lu·tion·ary** \-shə,nerē\ adj

evolve \i'välv\ vb **evolved; evolv·ing** : develop or change by degrees

ewe \'yü\ n : female sheep

ewer \'yüər\ n : water pitcher

ex·act \ig'zakt\ vb : compel to furnish ~ adj : precisely correct —**ex·act·ing** adj —**ex·ac·tion** \-'zakshən\ n —**ex·ac·ti·tude** \-'zaktə,tüd, -,tyüd\ n —**ex·act·ly** adv —**ex·act·ness** n

ex·ag·ger·ate \ig'zajə,rāt\ vb **-at·ed; -at·ing** : say more than is true —**ex·ag·ger·at·ed·ly** adv —**ex·ag·ger·a·tion** \-,zajə'rāshən\ n —**ex·ag·ger·a·tor** \-'zajə,rātər\ n

ex·alt \ig'zolt\ vb : glorify —**ex·al·ta·tion** \,eg,zol'tāshən, ,ek,sol-\ n

ex·am \ig'zam\ n : examination

ex·am·ine \-ən\ vb **-ined; -in·ing 1** : inspect closely **2** : test by questioning —**ex·am·i·na·tion** \-,zamə'nā-shən\ n example 115 exerciser

ex·am·ple \ig'zampəl\ n 1 : representative sample 2 : model 3 : problem to be solved for teaching purposes

ex·as·per·ate \ig'zaspə,rāt\ vb -at·ed; -at·ing : thoroughly annoy —**ex·as·per·a·tion** \-,zaspə'rāshən\ n

ex·ca·vate \'ekskə,vāt\ vb -vat·ed; -vat·ing : dig or hollow out —**ex·ca·va·tion** \,ekskə'vāshən\ n —**ex·ca·va·tor** \'ekskə,vātər\ n

ex·ceed \ik'sēd\ vb 1 : go or be beyond the limit of 2 : do better than

ex·ceed·ing·ly adv : extremely

ex·cel \ik'sel\ vb -ll- : do extremely well or far better than

ex·cel·lence \'eksələns\ n : quality of being excellent

ex·cel·len·cy \lənsē\ n, pl -cies —used as a title of honor

ex·cel·lent \'eksələnt\ adj : very good —**ex·cel·lent·ly** adv

ex·cept \ik'sept\ vb : omit ~ prep : excluding ~ conj : but —**ex·cep·tion** \-'sepshən\ n

ex·cep·tion·al \-'sepshənəl\ adj : superior —**ex·cep·tion·al·ly** adv

ex·cerpt \'ek,sərpt, 'eg,zərpt\ n : brief passage ~ \ek'-, eg'-, 'ek,-, 'eg,-\ vb : select an excerpt

ex·cess \ik'ses, 'ek,ses\ n : amount left over —**excess** adj —**ex·ces·sive** \ik'sesiv\ adj —**ex·ces·sive·ly** adv

ex·change \iks'chānj, 'eks,chānj\ n 1 : the giving or taking of one thing in return for another 2 : marketplace esp. for securities ~ vb -changed; -chang·ing : transfer in return for some equivalent —**ex·change·able** \iks'chānjəbəl\ adj

¹ex·cise \'ek,sīz, -,sīs\ n : tax

²ex·cise \ik'sīz\ vb -cised; -cis·ing : cut out —**ex·ci·sion** \-'sizhən\ n

ex·cite \ik'sīt\ vb -cit·ed; -cit·ing 1 : stir up 2 : kindle the emotions of —**ex·cit·abil·i·ty** \-,sītə'bilətē\ n —**ex·cit·able** \-'sītəbəl\ adj —**ex·ci·ta·tion** \,ek,sī'tāshən, -sə-\ n —**ex·cit·ed·ly** adv —**ex·cite·ment** \ik'sītmənt\ n

ex·claim \iks'klām\ vb : cry out esp. in delight —**ex·cla·ma·tion** \,ekskla'māshən\ n —**ex·clam·a·to·ry** \iks'klamə,tōrē\ adj

exclamation point n : punctuation mark ! used esp. after an interjection or exclamation

ex·clude \iks'klüd\ vb -clud·ed; -clud-ing : leave out —**ex·clu·sion** \-'klüzhən\ n

ex·clu·sive \-'klüsiv\ adj 1 : reserved for particular persons 2 : stylish 3 : sole —**exclusive** n —**ex·clu·sive·ly** adv —**ex·clu·sive·ness** n

ex·com·mu·ni·cate \,ekskə'myünə,kāt\ vb : expel from a church —**ex·com·mu·ni·ca·tion** \-,myünə'kāshən\ n

ex·cre·ment \'ekskrəmənt\ n : bodily waste —**ex·cre·men·tal** \,ekskrə-'ment³l\ adj

ex·crete \ik'skrēt\ vb -cret·ed; -cret·ing : eliminate wastes from the body —**ex·cre·tion** \-'skrēshən\ n —**ex·cre·to·ry** \'ekskrə,tōrē\ adj

ex·cru·ci·at·ing \ik'skrüshē,ātiŋ\ adj : intensely painful —**ex·cru·ci·at·ing·ly** adv

ex·cul·pate \'ekskəl,pāt\ vb -pat·ed; -pat·ing : clear from alleged fault

ex·cur·sion \ik'skərzhən\ n : pleasure trip

ex·cuse \ik'skyüz\ vb -cused; -cus·ing 1 : pardon 2 : release from an obligation 3 : justify ~ \-'skyüs\ n 1 : justification 2 : apology

ex·e·cute \'eksi,kyüt\ vb -cut·ed; -cut·ing 1 : carry out fully 2 : enforce 3 : put to death —**ex·e·cu·tion** \,eksi-'kyüshən\ n —**ex·e·cu·tion·er** \-shənər\ n

ex·ec·u·tive \ig'zekyətiv\ adj : relating to the carrying out of decisions, plans, or laws ~ n 1 : branch of government with executive duties 2 : administrator

ex·ec·u·tor \-yətər\ n : person named in a will to execute it

ex·ec·u·trix \ig'zekyə,triks\ n, pl **ex·ec·u·tri·ces** \-,zekyə'trī-,sēz\ or **ex·ec·u·trix·es** : woman executor

ex·em·pla·ry \ig'zemplərē\ adj : so commendable as to serve as a model

ex·em·pli·fy \-plə,fī\ vb -fied; -fy·ing : serve as an example of —**ex·em·pli·fi·ca·tion** \-,zempləfə'kāshən\ n

ex·empt \ig'zempt\ adj : being free from some liability ~ vb : make exempt —**ex·emp·tion** \-'zempshən\ n

ex·er·cise \'eksər,sīz\ n 1 : a putting into action 2 : exertion to develop endurance or a skill 3 pl : public ceremony ~ vb -cised; -cis·ing 1 : exert 2 : engage in exercise —**ex·er·cis·er** n

ex·ert \ig'zərt\ vb : put into action —**ex·er·tion** \-'zərshən\ n

ex·hale \eks'hāl\ vb **-haled; -hal·ing** : breathe out —**ex·ha·la·tion** \eksho'lāshən\ n

ex·haust \ig'zòst\ vb **1** : draw out or develop completely **2** : use up **3** : tire or wear out ~ n : waste steam or gas from an engine or a system for removing it —**ex·haus·tion** \-'zòschən\ n —**ex·haus·tive** \-'zòstiv\ adj

ex·hib·it \ig'zibət\ vb : display esp. publicly ~ n **1** : act of exhibiting **2** : something exhibited —**ex·hi·bi·tion** \,eksə'bishən\ n —**ex·hib·i·tor** \ig-'zibətər\ n

ex·hil·a·rate \ig'zilə,rāt\ vb **-rat·ed; -rat·ing** : thrill —**ex·hil·a·ra·tion** \-,zilə'rāshən\ n

ex·hort \-'zòrt\ vb : urge earnestly —**ex·hor·ta·tion** \,eks,òr'tāshən, ,egz-, -ər-\ n

ex·hume \igz'üm, -'yüm; iks'yüm, -'hyüm\ vb **-humed; -hum·ing** : dig up (a buried corpse) —**ex·hu·ma·tion** \,eksyü'māshən, -hyü-; ,egzü-, -zyü-\ n

ex·i·gen·cies \'eksəjənsēz, ig'zijən-\ n pl : requirements (as of a situation)

ex·ile \'eg,zīl, 'ek,sīl\ n **1** : banishment **2** : person banished from his or her country —**exile** vb

ex·ist \ig'zist\ vb **1** : have real or actual being **2** : live —**ex·is·tence** \-əns\ n —**ex·is·tent** \-ənt\ adj

ex·it \'egzət, 'eksət\ n **1** : departure **2** : way out of an enclosed space **3** : way off an expressway —**exit** vb

ex·o·dus \'eksədəs\ n : mass departure

ex·on·er·ate \ig'zänə,rāt\ vb **-at·ed; -at·ing** : free from blame —**ex·on·er·a·tion** \-,zänə'rāshən\ n

ex·or·bi·tant \ig'zòrbətənt\ adj : exceeding what is usual or proper

ex·or·cise \'ek,sòr,sīz, -sər-\ vb **-cised; -cis·ing** : drive out (as an evil spirit) —**ex·or·cism** \-,sizəm\ n —**ex·or·cist** \-,sist\ n

ex·ot·ic \ig'zätik\ adj : foreign or strange —**exotic** n —**ex·ot·i·cal·ly** \-iklē\ adv

ex·pand \ik'spand\ vb : enlarge

ex·panse \-'spans\ n : very large area

ex·pan·sion \-'spanchən\ n **1** : act or process of expanding **2** : expanded part

ex·pan·sive \-'spansiv\ adj **1** : tending to expand **2** : warmly benevolent **3** : of large extent —**ex·pan·sive·ly** adv —**ex·pan·sive·ness** n

ex·pa·tri·ate \ek'spātrē,āt, -ət\ n : exile —**expatriate** \-,āt\ adj or vb

ex·pect \ik'spekt\ vb **1** : look forward to **2** : consider probable or one's due —**ex·pec·tan·cy** \-ənsē\ n —**ex·pec·tant** \-ənt\ adj —**ex·pec·tant·ly** adv —**ex·pec·ta·tion** \,ek,spek'tāshən\ n

ex·pe·di·ent \ik'spēdēənt\ adj : convenient or advantageous rather than right or just ~ n : convenient often makeshift means to an end

ex·pe·dite \'ekspə,dīt\ vb **-dit·ed; -dit·ing** : carry out or handle promptly —**ex·pe·dit·er** n

ex·pe·di·tion \,ekspə'dishən\ n : long journey for work or research or the people making this

ex·pe·di·tious \-əs\ adj : prompt and efficient

ex·pel \ik'spel\ vb **-ll-** : force out

ex·pend \-'spend\ vb **1** : pay out **2** : use up —**ex·pend·able** adj

ex·pen·di·ture \-'spendichər, -də,chùr\ n : act of using or spending

ex·pense \ik'spens\ n : cost —**ex·pen·sive** \-'spensiv\ adj —**ex·pen·sive·ly** adv

ex·pe·ri·ence \ik'spirēəns\ n **1** : a participating in or living through an event **2** : an event that affects one **3** : knowledge from doing ~ vb **-enced; -enc·ing** : undergo

ex·per·i·ment \ik'sperəmənt\ n : test to discover something ~ vb : make experiments —**ex·per·i·men·tal** \-,sperə'ment°l\ adj —**ex·per·i·men·ta·tion** \-mən'tāshən\ n —**ex·per·i·men·ter** \-'sperə,mentər\ n

ex·pert \'ek,spərt\ adj : thoroughly skilled ~ n : person with special skill —**ex·pert·ly** adv —**ex·pert·ness** n

ex·per·tise \,ekspər'tēz\ n : skill

ex·pi·ate \'ekspē,āt\ vb : make amends for —**ex·pi·a·tion** \,ekspē'āshən\ n

ex·pire \ik'spīr, ek-\ vb **-pired; -pir·ing 1** : breathe out **2** : die **3** : end —**ex·pi·ra·tion** \,ekspə'rāshən\ n

ex·plain \ik'splān\ vb **1** : make clear **2** : give the reason for —**ex·plain·able** \-əbəl\ adj —**ex·pla·na·tion** \,eksplə-'nāshən\ n —**ex·plan·a·to·ry** \ik-'splanə,tòrē\ adj

ex·ple·tive \'eksplətiv\ n : usu. profane exclamation

ex·pli·ca·ble \ek'splikəbəl, 'eksplik-\ adj : capable of being explained

ex·plic·it \ik'splisət\ *adj* : absolutely clear or precise —**ex·plic·it·ly** *adv* — **ex·plic·it·ness** *n*

ex·plode \ik'splōd\ *vb* -**plod·ed; -plod·ing** 1 : discredit 2 : burst or cause to burst violently 3 : increase rapidly

ex·ploit \'ek,sploit\ *n* : heroic act ~ \ik-'sploit\ *vb* 1 : utilize 2 : use unfairly —**ex·ploi·ta·tion** \,ek,sploi'tāshən\ *n*

ex·plore \ik'splōr\ *vb* -**plored; -plor·ing** : examine or range over thoroughly —**ex·plo·ra·tion** \,eksplə'rāshən\ *n* —**ex·plor·a·to·ry** \ik'splōrə,tōrē\ *adj* —**ex·plor·er** *n*

ex·plo·sion \ik'splōzhən\ *n* : process or instance of exploding

ex·plo·sive -siv\ *adj* 1 : able to cause explosion 2 : likely to explode —**ex·plosive** *n* —**ex·plo·sive·ly** *adv*

ex·po·nent \ik'spōnənt, 'ek,spō-\ *n* 1 : mathematical symbol showing how many times a number is to be repeated as a factor 2 : advocate —**ex·po·nen·tial** \,ekspə'nenchəl\ *adj* —**ex·po·nen·tial·ly** *adv*

ex·port \ek'spōrt, 'ek,spōrt\ *vb* : send to foreign countries —**export** \'ek,-\ *n* —**ex·por·ta·tion** \,ek,spōr'tāshən\ *n* —**ex·port·er** \ek'spōrtər, 'ek,spōrt-\ *n*

ex·pose \ik'spōz\ *vb* -**posed; -pos·ing** 1 : deprive of shelter or protection 2 : subject (film) to light 3 : make known —**ex·po·sure** \-'spōzhər\ *n*

ex·po·sé, ex·po·se \,ekspō'zā\ *n* : exposure of something discreditable

ex·po·si·tion \,ekspə'zishən\ *n* : public exhibition

ex·pound \ik'spaund\ *vb* : set forth or explain in detail

¹ex·press \-'spres\ *adj* 1 : clear 2 : specific 3 : traveling at high speed with few stops —**express** *adv or n* — **ex·press·ly** *adv*

²express *vb* 1 : make known in words or appearance 2 : press out (as juice)

ex·pres·sion \-'spreshən\ *n* 1 : utterance 2 : mathematical symbol 3 : significant word or phrase 4 : look on one's face —**ex·pres·sion·less** *adj* —**ex·pres·sive** \-'spresiv\ *adj* —**ex·pres·sive·ness** *n*

ex·press·way \ik'spres,wā\ *n* : high-speed divided highway with limited access

ex·pul·sion \ik'spəlshən\ *n* : an expelling or being expelled

ex·pur·gate \'ekspər,gāt\ *vb* -**gat·ed; -gat·ing** : censor —**ex·pur·ga·tion** \,ekspər'gāshən\ *n*

ex·qui·site \ek'skwizət, 'ekskwiz-\ *adj* 1 : flawlessly beautiful and delicate 2 : keenly discriminating

ex·tant \'ekstənt, ek'stant\ *adj* : existing

ex·tem·po·ra·ne·ous \ek,stempə'rā-nēəs\ *adj* : impromptu —**ex·tem·po·ra·ne·ous·ly** *adv*

ex·tend \ik'stend\ *vb* 1 : stretch forth or out 2 : prolong 3 : enlarge —**ex·tend·able, -'stendəbəl\ *adj*

ex·ten·sion \-'stenchən\ *n* 1 : an extending or being extended 2 : additional part 3 : extra telephone line

ex·ten·sive \-'stensiv\ *adj* : of considerable extent —**ex·ten·sive·ly** *adv*

ex·tent \-'stent\ *n* : range, space, or degree to which something extends

ex·ten·u·ate \ik'stenyə,wāt\ *vb* -**at·ed; -at·ing** : lessen the seriousness of —**ex·ten·u·a·tion** \-,stenyə'wāshən\ *n*

ex·te·ri·or \ek'stirēər\ *adj* : external ~ *n* : external part or surface

ex·ter·mi·nate \ik'stərmə,nāt\ *vb* -**nat·ed; -nat·ing** : destroy utterly —**ex·ter·mi·na·tion** \-,stərmə'nāshən\ *n* —**ex·ter·mi·na·tor** \-'stərmə,nātər\ *n*

ex·ter·nal \ek'stərn°l\ *adj* : relating to or on the outside —**ex·ter·nal·ly** *adv*

ex·tinct \ik'stiŋkt\ *adj* : no longer existing —**ex·tinc·tion** \-'stiŋkshən\ *n*

ex·tin·guish \-'stiŋgwish\ *vb* : cause to stop burning —**ex·tin·guish·able** *adj* —**ex·tin·guish·er** *n*

ex·tir·pate \'ekstər,pāt\ *vb* -**pat·ed; -pat·ing** : destroy

ex·tol \ik'stōl\ *vb* -**ll-** : praise highly

ex·tort \-'stort\ *vb* : obtain by force or improper pressure —**ex·tor·tion** \-'storshən\ *n* —**ex·tor·tion·er** *n* —**ex·tor·tion·ist** *n*

ex·tra \'ekstrə\ *adj* 1 : additional 2 : superior —**extra** *n or adv*

extra- *prefix* : outside or beyond

ex·tract \ik'strakt\ *vb* 1 : pull out forcibly 2 : withdraw (as a juice) ~ \'ek,-\ *n* 1 : excerpt 2 : product (as a juice) obtained by extracting —**ex·tract·able** *adj* —**ex·trac·tion** \ik-'strakshən\ *n* —**ex·trac·tor** \-tər\ *n*

ex·tra·cur·ric·u·lar \,ekstrəkə'rikyələr\ *adj* : lying outside the regular curriculum

ex·tra·dite \'ekstrə,dīt\ *vb* -**dit·ed; -dit·ing** : bring or deliver a suspect to a different jurisdiction for trial —**ex·tra·di·tion** \,ekstrə'dishən\ *n*

ex·tra·mar·i·tal \\,ekstrə'marət³l\\ *adj* : relating to sexual relations of a married person outside of the marriage

ex·tra·ne·ous \\ek'strānēəs\\ *adj* : not essential or relevant —**ex·tra·ne·ous·ly** *adv*

ex·traor·di·nary \\ik'strȯrd³n,erē, ,ekstrə'ȯrd-\\ *adj* : notably unusual or exceptional —**ex·traor·di·nar·i·ly** \\ik-,strȯrd³n'erəlē, ,ekstrə,ȯrd-\\ *adv*

ex·tra·sen·so·ry \\,ekstrə'sensərē\\ *adj* : outside the ordinary senses

ex·tra·ter·res·tri·al \\,ekstrətə'restrēəl\\ *n* : one existing or coming from outside the earth ~ *adj* : relating to an extraterrestrial

ex·trav·a·gant \\ik'stravigənt\\ *adj* : wildly excessive, lavish, or costly — **ex·trav·a·gance** \\-gəns\\ *n* —**ex·trav·a·gant·ly** *adv*

ex·trav·a·gan·za \\-,stravə'ganzə\\ *n* : spectacular event

ex·tra·ve·hic·u·lar \\,ekstrəvē'hikyələr\\ *adj* : occurring outside a spacecraft

ex·treme \\ik'strēm\\ *adj* **1** : very great or intense **2** : very severe **3** : not moderate **4** : most remote ~ *n* **1** : extreme state **2** : something located at one end or the other of a range —**ex·treme·ly** *adv*

ex·trem·i·ty \\-'stremətē\\ *n, pl* **-ties 1** : most remote part **2** : human hand or foot **3** : extreme degree or state (as of need)

ex·tri·cate \\'ekstrə,kāt\\ *vb* **-cat·ed; -cat·ing** : set or get free from an entanglement or difficulty —**ex·tri·ca·ble** \\ik-'strikəbəl, ek-; 'ekstrik-\\ *adj* **ex·tri·ca·tion** \\,ekstrə'kāshən\\ *n*

ex·tro·vert \\'ekstrə,vərt\\ *n* : gregarious person —**ex·tro·ver·sion** \\,ekstrə-'vərzhən\\ *n* —**ex·tro·vert·ed** \\'ekstrə-,vərtəd\\ *adj*

ex·trude \\ik'strüd\\ *vb* **-trud·ed; -trud·ing** : to force or push out

ex·u·ber·ant \\ig'zübərənt\\ *adj* : joyously unrestrained —**ex·u·ber·ance** \\-rəns\\ *n* —**ex·u·ber·ant·ly** *adv*

ex·ude \\ig'züd\\ *vb* **-ud·ed; -ud·ing 1** : discharge slowly through pores **2** : display conspicuously

ex·ult \\ig'zəlt\\ *vb* : rejoice —**ex·ul·tant** \\-'zəlt³nt\\ *adj* —**ex·ul·tant·ly** *adv* — **ex·ul·ta·tion** \\,eksəl'tāshən, ,egzəl-\\ *n* —**ey** —see -Y

eye \\'ī\\ *n* **1** : organ of sight consisting of a globular structure (**eye·ball**) in a socket of the skull with thin movable covers (**eye·lids**) bordered with hairs (**eye·lash·es**) **2** : vision **3** : judgment **4** : something suggesting an eye ~ *vb* **eyed; eye·ing** *or* **ey·ing** : look at — **eye·brow** \\-,braủ\\ *n* —**eyed** \\'īd\\ *adj* —**eye·strain** *n*

eye·drop·per *n* : dropper

eye·glass·es *n pl* : glasses

eye·let \\'ilət\\ *n* : hole (as in cloth) for a lacing or rope

eye·open·er *n* : something startling — **eye·open·ing** *adj*

eye·piece *n* : lens at the eye end of an optical instrument

eye·sight *n* : sight

eye·sore *n* : unpleasant sight

eye·tooth *n* : upper canine tooth

eye·wit·ness *n* : person who actually sees something happen

ey·rie \\'īrē, *or like* AERIE\\ *var of* AERIE

F

f \\'ef\\ *n, pl* **f's** *or* **fs** \\'efs\\ : 6th letter of the alphabet

fa·ble \\'fābəl\\ *n* **1** : legendary story **2** : story that teaches a lesson —**fa·bled** \\-bəld\\ *adj*

fab·ric \\'fabrik\\ *n* **1** : structure **2** : material made usu. by weaving or knitting fibers

fab·ri·cate \\'fabri,kāt\\ *vb* **-cat·ed; -cat·ing 1** : construct **2** : invent —**fab·ri·ca·tion** \\,fabri'kāshən\\ *n*

fab·u·lous \\'fabyələs\\ *adj* **1** : like, told in, or based on fable **2** : incredible or marvelous —**fab·u·lous·ly** *adv*

fa·cade \\fə'säd\\ *n* **1** : principal face of a building **2** : false or superficial appearance

face \\'fās\\ *n* **1** : front or principal surface (as of the head) **2** : presence **3** : facial expression **4** : grimace **5** : outward appearance ~ vb **faced; fac•ing 1** : challenge or resist firmly or brazenly **2** : cover with different material **3** : sit or stand with the face toward **4** : have the front oriented toward —**faced** \'fāst\ adj —**face•less** adj n —**fa•cial** \'fāshəl\ adj or n

face•down adv : with the face downward

face-lift \'fās,lift\ n **1** : cosmetic surgery on the face **2** : modernization

fac•et \'fasət\ n **1** : surface of a cut gem **2** : phase —**fac•et•ed** adj

fa•ce•tious \fə'sēshəs\ adj : jocular —**fa•ce•tious•ly** adv —**fa•ce•tious•ness** n

fac•ile \'fasəl\ adj **1** : easy **2** : fluent

fa•cil•i•tate \fə'silə,tāt\ vb -**tat•ed; -tat•ing** : make easier

fa•cil•i•ty \fə'silətē\ n, pl -**ties 1** : ease in doing or using **2** : something built or installed to serve a purpose or facilitate an activity

fac•ing \'fāsiŋ\ n : lining or covering or material for this

fac•sim•i•le \fak'siməlē\ n : exact copy

fact \'fakt\ n **1** : act or action **2** : something that exists or is real **3** : piece of information —**fac•tu•al** \'fakchəwəl\ adj —**fac•tu•al•ly** adv

fac•tion \'fakshən\ n : part of a larger group —**fac•tion•al•ism** \-shənə,lizəm\ n

fac•tious \'fakshəs\ adj : causing discord

fac•ti•tious \fak'tishəs\ adj : artificial

fac•tor \'faktər\ n **1** : something that has an effect **2** : gene **3** : number used in multiplying

fac•to•ry \'faktərē\ n, pl -**ries** : place for manufacturing

fac•to•tum \fak'tōtəm\ n : person (as a servant) with varied duties

fac•ul•ty \'fakəltē\ n, pl -**ties 1** : ability to act **2** : power of the mind or body **3** : body of teachers or department of instruction

fad \'fad\ n : briefly popular practice or interest —**fad•dish** adj —**fad•dist** n

fade \'fād\ vb **fad•ed; fad•ing 1** : wither **2** : lose or cause to lose freshness or brilliance **3** : grow dim **4** : vanish

fag \'fag\ vb -**gg- 1** : drudge **2** : tire or exhaust

fag•ot, fag•got \'fagət\ n : bundle of twigs

Fahr•en•heit \'farən,hīt\ adj : relating to a thermometer scale with the boiling

point at 212 degrees and the freezing point at 32 degrees

fail \'fāl\ vb **1** : decline in health **2** : die away **3** : stop functioning **4** : be unsuccessful **5** : become bankrupt **6** : disappoint **7** : neglect ~ n : act of failing

fail•ing n : slight defect in character or conduct ~ prep : in the absence of lack of

faille \'fīl\ n : closely woven ribbed fabric

fail•ure \'fālyər\ n **1** : absence of expected action or performance **2** : bankruptcy **3** : deficiency **4** : one that has failed

faint \'fānt\ adj **1** : cowardly or spiritless **2** : weak and dizzy **3** : lacking vigor **4** : indistinct ~ vb : lose consciousness ~ n : act or condition of fainting —**faint•heart•ed** adj —**faint•ly** adv —**faint•ness** n

¹fair \'far\ adj **1** : pleasing in appearance **2** : not stormy or cloudy **3** : just or honest **4** : conforming with the rules **5** : open to legitimate pursuit or attack **6** : light in color **7** : adequate —**fair•ness** n

²fair adv, chiefly Brit : FAIRLY

³fair n : exhibition for judging or selling

fair•ly \'farlē\ adv **1** : in a manner of speaking **2** : without bias **3** : somewhat

fairy \'farē\ n, pl **fair•ies** : usu. small imaginary being —**fairy tale** n

fairy•land \-,land\ n **1** : land of fairies **2** : beautiful or charming place

faith \'fāth\ n, pl **faiths** \'fāths, 'fāthz\ **1** : allegiance **2** : belief and trust in God **3** : confidence **4** : system of religious beliefs —**faith•ful** \-fəl\ adj —**faith•ful•ly** adv —**faith•ful•ness** n: —**faith•less** adj —**faith•less•ly** adv —**faith•less•ness** n

fake \'fāk\ vb **faked; fak•ing 1** : falsify **2** : counterfeit ~ n : copy, fraud, or impostor ~ adj : not genuine —**fak•er** n

fa•kir \fə'kir\ n : wandering beggar of India

fal•con \'falkən, 'fól-\ n : small longwinged hawk used esp. for hunting —**fal•con•ry** \-rē\ n

fall \'fól\ vb **fell** \'fel\ **fall•en** \fólən\; **fall•ing 1** : go down by gravity **2** : hang freely **3** : go lower **4** : be defeated or ruined **5** : commit a sin **6**

: happen at a certain time **7** : become gradually ~ *n* **1** : act of falling **2** : autumn **3** : downfall **4** *pl* : waterfall **5** : distance something falls

fal·la·cy \'faləsē\ *n, pl* **-cies 1** : false idea **2** : false reasoning —**fal·la·cious** \fə'lāshəs\ *adj*

fal·li·ble \'faləbəl\ *adj* : capable of making a mistake —**fal·li·bly** \-blē\ *adv*

fall·out *n* **1** : radioactive particles from a nuclear explosion **2** : secondary effects

fal·low \'falō\ *adj* **1** : plowed but not planted **2** : dormant —**fallow** *n or vb*

false \'fóls\ *adj* **fals·er; fals·est 1** : not genuine, true, faithful, or permanent **2** : misleading —**false·ly** *adv* —**false·ness** *n* —**fal·si·fi·ca·tion** \,fólsəfə-'kāshən\ *n* —**fal·si·fy** \'fólsə,fī\ *vb* —**fal·si·ty** \'fólsətē\ *n*

false·hood \'fóls,hùd\ *n* : lie

fal·set·to \fól'setō\ *n, pl* **-tos** : artificially high singing voice

fal·ter \'fóltər\ *vb* **-tered; -ter·ing 1** : move unsteadily **2** : hesitate —**fal·ter·ing·ly** *adv*

fame \'fām\ *n* : public reputation —**famed** \'fāmd\ *adj*

fa·mil·ial \fə'milyəl\ *adj* : relating to a family

¹fa·mil·iar \fə'milyər\ *n* **1** : companion **2** : guardian spirit

²familiar *adj* **1** : closely acquainted **2** : forward **3** : frequently seen or experienced —**fa·mil·iar·i·ty** \fə,mil-'yaratē, -,milē'yar-\ *n* —**fa·mil·iar·ize** \fə'milyə,rīz\ *vb* —**fa·mil·iar·ly** *adv*

fam·i·ly \'famlē\ *n, pl* **-lies 1** : persons of common ancestry **2** : group living together **3** : parents and children **4** : group of related individuals

fam·ine \'famən\ *n* : extreme scarcity of food

fam·ish \'famish\ *vb* : starve

fa·mous \'fāməs\ *adj* : widely known or celebrated

fa·mous·ly *adv* : very well

¹fan \'fan\ *n* : device for producing a current of air ~ *vb* **-nn- 1** : move air with a fan **2** : direct a current of air upon **3** : stir to activity

²fan *n* : enthusiastic follower or admirer

fa·nat·ic \fə'natik\, **fa·nat·i·cal** \-ikəl\ *adj* : excessively enthusiastic or devoted —**fanatic** *n* —**fa·nat·i·cism** \-'natə,sizəm\ *n*

fan·ci·er \'fansēər\ *n* : one devoted to raising a particular plant or animal

fan·cy \'fansē\ *n, pl* **-cies 1** : liking **2** : whim **3** : imagination ~ *vb* **-cied; -cy·ing 1** : like **2** : imagine —*adj* **-cier; -est 1** : not plain **2** : of superior quality —**fan·ci·ful** \-sifəl\ *adj* —**fan·ci·ful·ly** \-fəlē\ *adv* —**fan·ci·ly** *adv*

fan·dan·go \fan'dangō\ *n, pl* **-gos** : lively Spanish dance

fan·fare \'fan,far\ *n* **1** : a sounding of trumpets **2** : showy display

fang \'fang\ *n* : long sharp tooth

fan·light *n* : semicircular window

fan·ta·sia \fan'tāzhə, -zēə; ,fantə'zēə\ *n* : music written to fancy rather than to form

fan·tas·tic \fan'tastik\ *adj* **1** : imaginary or unrealistic **2** : exceedingly or unbelievably great —**fan·tas·ti·cal·ly** \-tiklē\ *adv*

fan·ta·sy \'fantəsē\ *n* **1** : imagination **2** : product (as a daydream) of the imagination **3** : fantasia —**fan·ta·size** \'fantə,sīz\ *vb*

far \'fär\ *adv* **farther** \-thər\ *or* **further** \'fər-\; **farthest** *or* **furthest** \-thəst\ **1** : at or to a distance **2** : much **3** : to a degree **4** : to an advanced point or extent —*adj* **farther** *or* **further**; **farthest** *or* **furthest 1** : remote **2** : long **3** : being more distant

far·away *adj* : distant

farce \'färs\ *n* **1** : satirical comedy with an improbable plot **2** : ridiculous display —**far·ci·cal** \-sikəl\ *adj*

¹fare \'far\ *vb* **fared; far·ing** : get along

²fare *n* **1** : price of transportation **2** : range of food

fare·well \far'wel\ *n* **1** : wish of welfare at parting **2** : departure —**farewell** *adj*

far·fetched \'fär'fecht\ *adj* : improbable

fa·ri·na \fə'rēnə\ *n* : fine meal made from cereal grains

farm \'färm\ *n* : place where something is raised for food ~ *vb* **1** : use (land) as a farm **2** : raise plants or animals for food —**farm·er** *n* —**farm·hand** \-,hand\ *n* —**farm·house** *n* —**farm·ing** *n* —**farm·land** \-,land\ *n* —**farm·yard** *n*

far-off *adj* : remote in time or space

far·ri·er \'farēər\ *n* : blacksmith who shoes horses

far·row \'farō\ *vb* : give birth to a litter of pigs —**farrow** *n*

far·sight·ed *adj* **1** : better able to see distant things near than **2** : judicious or shrewd —**far·sight·ed·ness** *n*

far·ther \\'färthər\ *adv* **1** : at or to a greater distance or more advanced point **2** : to a greater degree or extent ~ *adj* : more distant

far·ther·most *adj* : most distant

far·thest \\'färthəst\ *adj* : most distant ~ *adv* **1** : to or at the greatest distance **2** : to the most advanced point **3** : by the greatest extent

fas·ci·cle \\'fasikəl\ *n* **1** : small bundle **2** : division of a book published in parts —**fas·ci·cled** \-kəld\ *adj*

fas·ci·nate \\'fas⁰n,āt\ *vb* -**nat·ed; -nat·ing** : transfix and hold spellbound —**fas·ci·na·tion** \,fas⁰n'āshən\ *n*

fas·cism \\'fash,izəm\ *n* : dictatorship that exalts nation and race —**fas·cist** \-ist\ *n or adj* —**fas·cis·tic** \fa'shistik\ *adj*

fash·ion \\'fashən\ *n* **1** : manner **2** : prevailing custom or style ~ *vb* : form or construct —**fash·ion·able** \-ənəbəl\ *adj* —**fash·ion·ably** \-blē\ *adv*

¹fast \\'fast\ *adj* **1** : firmly fixed, bound, or shut **2** : faithful **3** : moving or acting quickly **4** : indicating ahead of the correct time **5** : deep and undisturbed **6** : permanently dyed **7** : wild or promiscuous ~ *adv* **1** : so as to be secure or bound **2** : soundly or deeply **3** : swiftly

²fast *vb* : abstain from food or eat sparingly ~ *n* : act or time of fasting

fas·ten \\'fas⁰n\ *vb* : attach esp. by pinning or tying —**fas·ten·er** *n* —**fas·ten·ing** *n*

fas·tid·i·ous \fas'tidēəs\ *adj* : hard to please —**fas·tid·i·ous·ly** *adv* —**fas·tid·i·ous·ness** *n*

fat \\'fat\ *adj* -**tt-** **1** : having much fat **2** : thick ~ *n* : animal tissue rich in greasy or oily matter —**fat·ness** *n* —**fat·ten** \\'fat⁰n\ *vb* —**fat·ty** *adj or n*

fa·tal \\'fāt⁰l\ *adj* : causing death or ruin —**fa·tal·i·ty** \fā'talətē, fə-\ *n* —**fa·tal·ly** *adv*

fa·tal·ism \\'fāt⁰l,izəm\ *n* : belief that fate determines events —**fa·tal·ist** \-ist\ *n* —**fa·tal·is·tic** \,fāt⁰l'istik\ *adj* —**fa·tal·is·ti·cal·ly** \-tiklē\ *adv*

fate \\'fāt\ *n* **1** : principle, cause, or will held to determine events **2** : end or outcome —**fat·ed** *adj* —**fate·ful** \-fəl\ *adj* —**fate·ful·ly** *adv*

fa·ther \\'fäthər, 'fath-\ *n* **1** : male parent **2** *cap* : God **3** : originator —**father** *vb* —**fa·ther·hood** \-,húd\ *n* —

fa·ther·land \-,land\ *n* —**fa·ther·less** *adj* —**fa·ther·ly** *adj*

father–in–law *n, pl* **fa·thers–in–law** : father of one's spouse

fath·om \\'fathəm\ *n* : nautical unit of length equal to 6 feet ~ *vb* : understand —**fath·om·able** *adj* —**fath·om·less** *adj*

fa·tigue \fə'tēg\ *n* **1** : weariness from labor or use **2** : tendency to break under repeated stress ~ *vb* -**tigued; -tigu·ing** : tire out

fat·u·ous \\'fachəwəs\ *adj* : foolish or stupid —**fat·u·ous·ly** *adv* —**fat·u·ous·ness** *n*

fau·cet \\'fosət, 'fäs-\ *n* : fixture for drawing off a liquid

fault \\'folt\ *n* **1** : weakness in character **2** : something wrong or imperfect **3** : responsibility for something wrong **4** : fracture in the earth's crust ~ *vb* : find fault in or with —**fault·find·er** *n* —**fault·find·ing** *n* —**fault·i·ly** \\'foltəlē\ *adv* —**fault·less** *adj* —**fault·less·ly** *adv* —**faulty** *adj*

fau·na \\'fonə\ *n* : animals or animal life esp. of a region —**fau·nal** \-⁰l\ *adj*

faux pas \\'fō'pä\ *n, pl* **faux pas** *same or* -'päz\ : social blunder

fa·vor \\'fāvər\ *n* **1** : approval **2** : partiality **3** : act of kindness ~ *vb* : regard or treat with favor —**fa·vor·able** \\'fāvərəbəl\ *adj* —**fa·vor·ably** \-blē\ *adv*

fa·vor·ite \\'fāvərət\ *n* : one favored —**favorite** *adj* —**fa·vor·it·ism** \-,izəm\ *n*

¹fawn \\'fon\ *vb* : seek favor by groveling

²fawn *n* : young deer

faze \\'fāz\ *vb* **fazed; faz·ing** : disturb the composure of

fear \\'fir\ *n* : unpleasant emotion caused by expectation or awareness of danger ~ *vb* : be afraid of —**fear·ful** \-fəl\ *adj* —**fear·ful·ly** *adv* —**fear·less** *adj* —**fear·less·ly** *adv* —**fear·less·ness** *n* —**fear·some** \-səm\ *adj*

fea·si·ble \\'fēzəbəl\ *adj* : capable of being done —**fea·si·bil·i·ty** \,fēzə'bilətē\ *n* —**fea·si·bly** \\'fēzəblē\ *adv*

feast \\'fēst\ *n* **1** : large or fancy meal **2** : religious festival ~ *vb* : eat plentifully

feat \\'fēt\ *n* : notable deed

feath·er \\'fethər\ *n* : one of the light horny outgrowths that form the external covering of a bird's body —

feath·er \'feṯẖər\ vb —**feath·ered** \-ərd\ adj — **feath·er·less** adj —**feath·ery** adj

fea·ture \'fēchər\ n 1 : shape or appearance of the face 2 : part of the face 3 : prominent characteristic 4 : special attraction ~ vb : give prominence to —**fea·ture·less** adj

Feb·ru·ary \'febyə,werē, 'febə-, 'febrə-\ n : 2d month of the year having 28 and in leap years 29 days

fe·ces \'fē,sēz\ n pl : intestinal body waste —**fe·cal** \-kəl\ adj

feck·less \'fekləs\ adj : irresponsible

fe·cund \'fekənd, 'fē-\ adj : prolific —**fe·cun·di·ty** \fi'kəndətē, fe-\ n

fed·er·al \'fedrəl, -dərəl\ adj : of or constituting a government with power distributed between a central authority and constituent units —**fed·er·al·ism** \-rə,lizəm\ n —**fed·er·al·ist** \-list\ n or adj —**fed·er·al·ly** adv

fed·er·ate \'fedə,rāt\ vb -**at·ed; -at·ing** : join in a federation

fed·er·a·tion \,fedə'rāshən\ n : union of organizations

fe·do·ra \fi'dōrə\ n : soft felt hat

fed up adj : out of patience

fee \'fē\ n : fixed charge

fee·ble \'fēbəl\ adj -**bler; -blest** : weak or ineffective —**fee·ble·mind·ed** \,fēbəl'mīndəd\ adj —**fee·ble·mind·ed·ness** n —**fee·ble·ness** n —**fee·bly** \-blē\ adv

feed \'fēd\ vb **fed** \'fed\; **feed·ing** 1 : give food to 2 : eat 3 : furnish ~ n : food for livestock —**feed·er** n

feel \'fēl\ vb **felt** \'felt\; **feel·ing** 1 : perceive or examine through physical contact 2 : think or believe 3 : be conscious of 4 : seem 5 : have sympathy ~ n 1 : sense of touch 2 : quality of a thing imparted through touch —**feel·er** n

feel·ing \'fēliŋ\ n 1 : sense of touch 2 : state of mind 3 pl : sensibilities 4 : opinion

feet pl of FOOT

feign \'fān\ vb : pretend

feint \'fānt\ n : mock attack intended to distract attention —**feint** vb

fe·lic·i·tate \fi'lisə,tāt\ vb -**tat·ed; -tat·ing** : congratulate —**fe·lic·i·ta·tion** \-,lisə'tāshən\ n

fe·lic·i·tous \fi'lisətəs\ adj : aptly expressed —**fe·lic·i·tous·ly** adv

fe·lic·i·ty \-'lisətē\ n, pl -**ties** 1 : great happiness 2 : pleasing faculty esp. in art or language

fe·line \'fē,līn\ adj : relating to cats —**feline** n

¹fell \'fel\ vb : cut or knock down

²fell past of FALL

fel·low \'felō\ n 1 : companion or associate 2 : man or boy —**fel·low·ship** \-,ship\ n

fel·low·man \,felō'man\ n : kindred human being

fel·on \'felən\ n : one who has committed a felony

fel·o·ny \'felənē\ n, pl -**nies** : serious crime —**fe·lo·ni·ous** \fə'lōnēəs\ adj

¹felt \'felt\ n : cloth made of pressed wool and fur

²felt past of FEEL

fe·male \'fē,māl\ adj : relating to or being the sex that bears young —**female** n

fem·i·nine \'femənən\ adj : relating to the female sex —**fem·i·nin·i·ty** \,femə'ninətē\ n

fem·i·nism \'femə,nizəm\ n : organized activity on behalf of women's rights —**fem·i·nist** \-nist\ n or adj

fe·mur \'fēmər\ n, pl **fe·murs** or **fem·o·ra** \'femərə\ : long bone of the thigh —**fem·o·ral** \'femərəl\ adj

fence \'fens\ n : enclosing barrier esp. of wood or wire ~ vb **fenced; fenc·ing** 1 : enclose with a fence 2 : practice fencing —**fenc·er** n

fenc·ing \'fensiŋ\ n 1 : combat with swords for sport 2 : material for building fences

fend \'fend\ vb : ward off

fend·er \'fendər\ n : guard over an automobile wheel

fen·nel \'fenᵊl\ n : herb related to the carrot

fer·ment \fər'ment\ vb : cause or undergo fermentation ~ \'fər,ment\ n : agitation

fer·men·ta·tion \,fərmən'tāshən, -,men-\ n : chemical decomposition of an organic substance in the absence of oxygen

fern \'fərn\ n : flowerless seedless green plant

fe·ro·cious \fə'rōshəs\ adj : fierce or savage —**fe·ro·cious·ly** adv —**fe·ro·cious·ness** n —**fe·roc·i·ty** \-'räsətē\ n

fer·ret \'ferət\ n : white European polecat ~ vb : find out by searching

fer·ric \'ferik\, **fer·rous** \'ferəs\ adj : relating to or containing iron

fer·rule \'ferəl\ n : metal band or ring

fer·ry \'ferē\ vb -ried; -ry·ing : carry by boat over water ~ n, pl -ries : boat used in ferrying —**fer·ry·boat** n

fer·tile \'fərt°l\ adj 1 : producing plentifully 2 : capable of developing or reproducing —**fer·til·i·ty** \fər'tilətē\ n

fer·til·ize \'fərt°l,īz\ vb -ized; -iz·ing : make fertile —**fer·til·iza·tion** \,fərt°lə'zāshən\ n —**fer·til·iz·er** n

fer·vid \'fərvəd\ adj : ardent or zealous —**fer·vid·ly** adv

fer·vor \'fərvər\ n : passion —**fer·ven·cy** \-vənsē\ n —**fer·vent** \-vənt\ adj —**fer·vent·ly** adv

fes·ter \'festər\ vb 1 : form pus 2 : become more bitter or malignant

fes·ti·val \'festəvəl\ n : time of celebration

fes·tive \-tiv\ adj : joyous or happy —**fes·tive·ly** adv —**fes·tiv·i·ty** \fes'tivətē\ n

fes·toon \fes'tün\ n : decorative chain or strip hanging in a curve —**festoon** vb

fe·tal \'fēt°l\ adj : of, relating to, or being a fetus

fetch \'fech\ vb 1 : go or come after and bring or take back 2 : sell for

fetch·ing \'fechiŋ\ adj : attractive —**fetch·ing·ly** adv

fête \'fāt, 'fet\ n : lavish party ~ vb fêt·ed; fêt·ing : honor or commemorate with a fête

fet·id \'fetəd\ adj : having an offensive smell

fe·tish \'fetish\ n 1 : object believed to have magical powers 2 : object of unreasoning devotion or concern

fet·lock \'fet,läk\ n : projection on the back of a horse's leg above the hoof

fet·ter \'fetər\ n : chain or shackle for the feet —**fetter** vb

fet·tle \'fet°l\ n : state of fitness

fe·tus \'fētəs\ n : vertebrate not yet born or hatched

feud \'fyüd\ n : prolonged quarrel —**feud** vb

feu·dal \'fyüd°l\ adj : of or relating to feudalism

feu·dal·ism \-,izəm\ n : medieval political order in which land is granted in return for service —**feu·dal·is·tic** \,fyüd°l'istik\ adj

fe·ver \'fēvər\ n 1 : abnormal rise in body temperature 2 : state of height-

ened emotion —**fe·ver·ish** adj —**fe·ver·ish·ly** adv

few \'fyü\ pron : not many ~ adj : some but not many —often with a ~ n : small number —often with a

few·er \-ər\ pron : smaller number of things

fez \'fez\ n, pl **fez·zes** : round flat-crowned hat

fi·an·cé \,fē,än'sā\ n : man one is engaged to

fi·an·cée \,fē,än'sā\ n : woman one is engaged to

fi·as·co \fē'asko\ n, pl **-coes** : ridiculous failure

fi·at \'fēat, -,at, -,ät; 'fīət, -,at\ n : decree

fib \'fib\ n : trivial lie —**fib** vb —**fib·ber** n

fi·ber, fi·bre \'fībər\ n 1 : threadlike substance or structure (as a muscle cell or fine root) 2 : indigestible material in food 3 : element that gives texture or substance —**fi·brous** \-brəs\ adj

fi·ber·board n : construction material made of compressed fibers

fi·ber·glass n : glass in fibrous form in various products (as insulation)

fi·bril·la·tion \,fibrə'lāshən, ,fīb-\ n : rapid irregular contractions of heart muscle —**fi·bril·late** \'fibrə,lāt, 'fīb-\ vb

fib·u·la \'fibyələ\ n, pl **-lae** \-lē, -lī\ or **-las** : outer of the two leg bones below the knee —**fib·u·lar** \-lər\ adj

fick·le \'fikəl\ adj : unpredictably changeable —**fick·le·ness** n

fic·tion \'fikshən\ n : a made-up story or literature consisting of made up —**fic·tion·al** \-shənəl\ adj

fic·ti·tious \fik'tishəs\ adj : made up or pretended

fid·dle \'fid°l\ n : violin ~ vb -dled; -dling 1 : play on the fiddle 2 : move the hands restlessly —**fid·dler** \'fidlər, -°lər\ n

fid·dle·sticks n : nonsense —used as an interjection

fi·del·i·ty \fə'delətē, fī-\ n, pl **-ties** 1 : quality or state of being faithful 2 : quality of reproduction

fid·get \'fijət\ n 1 pl : restlessness 2 : one that fidgets ~ vb : move restlessly —**fid·gety** adj

fi·du·cia·ry \fə'düshē,erē, -'dyü-, -shərē\ adj : held or holding in trust —**fiduciary** n

field \'fēld\ n 1 : open country 2

: cleared land **3** : land yielding some special product **4** : sphere of activity **5** : area for sports **6** : region or space in which a given effect (as magnetism) exists ~ *vb* : put into the field —**field** *adj* —**field•er** *n*

fiend \'fēnd\ *n* **1** : devil **2** : extremely wicked person —**fiend•ish** *adj* —**fiend•ish•ly** *adv*

fierce \'firs\ *adj* **fierc•er; -est 1** : violently hostile or aggressive **2** : intense **3** : menacing looking —**fierce•ly** *adv* —**fierce•ness** *n*

fi•ery \'fī(ə)rē\ *adj* **fi•er•i•er; -est 1** : burning **2** : hot or passionate —**fi•er•i•ness** \'fī(ə)rēnəs\ *n*

fi•es•ta \fē'estə\ *n* : festival

fife \'fīf\ *n* : small flute

fif•teen \fif'tēn\ *n* : one more than 14 — **fifteen** *adj or pron* —**fif•teenth** \-'tēnth\ *adj or n*

fifth \'fifth\ *n* **1** : one that is number 5 in a countable series **2** : one of 5 equal parts of something —**fifth** *adj or adv*

fif•ty \'fiftē\ *n, pl* **-ties** : 5 times 10 — **fif•ti•eth** \-tēəth\ *adj or n* —**fifty** *adj or pron*

fif•ty-fif•ty *adv or adj* : shared equally

fig \'fig\ *n* : pear-shaped edible fruit

fight \'fīt\ *vb* **fought** \'fot\; **fight•ing 1** : contend against another in battle **2** : box **3** : struggle ~ *n* **1** : hostile encounter **2** : boxing match **3** : verbal disagreement —**fight•er** *n*

fig•ment \'figmənt\ *n* : something imagined or made up

fig•u•ra•tive \'figyərətiv, -gə-\ *adj* : metaphorical —**fig•u•ra•tive•ly** *adv*

fig•ure \'figyər, -gər\ *n* **1** : symbol representing a number **2** *pl* : arithmetical calculations **3** : price **4** : shape or outline **5** : illustration **6** : pattern or design **7** : prominent person ~ *vb* **-ured; -ur•ing 1** : be important **2** : calculate —**fig•ured** *adj*

fig•u•rine \,figyə'rēn\ *n* : small statue

fil•a•ment \'filəmənt\ *n* : fine thread or threadlike part —**fil•a•men•tous** \,filə'mentəs\ *adj*

fil•bert \'filbərt\ *n* : edible nut of a European hazel

filch \'filch\ *vb* : steal furtively

¹file \'fīl\ *n* : tool for smoothing or sharpening ~ *vb* **filed; fil•ing** : rub or smooth with a file

²file *vb* **filed; fil•ing 1** : arrange in order **2** : enter or record officially ~ *n* : device for keeping papers in order

³file *n* : row of persons or things one behind the other ~ *vb* **filed; fil•ing** : march in file

fil•ial \'filēəl, 'filyəl\ *adj* : relating to a son or daughter

fil•i•bus•ter \'filə,bəstər\ *n* : long speeches to delay a legislative vote — **filibuster** *vb* —**fil•i•bus•ter•er** *n*

fil•i•gree \'filə,grē\ *n* : ornamental designs of fine wire —**fil•i•greed** \-,grēd\ *adj*

fill \'fil\ *vb* **1** : make or become full **2** : stop up **3** : feed **4** : satisfy **5** : occupy fully **6** : spread through ~ *n* **1** : full supply **2** : material for filling —**fill•er** *n* —**fill in** *vb* **1** : provide information to or for **2** : substitute

fil•let \'filət, fi'lā, 'fil,ā\ *n* : piece of boneless meat or fish ~ *vb* : cut into fillets

fill•ing *n* : material used to fill something

fil•ly \'filē\ *n, pl* **-lies** : young female horse

film \'film\ *n* **1** : thin skin or membrane **2** : thin coating or layer **3** : strip of material used in taking pictures **4** : movie ~ *vb* : make a movie of — **filmy** *adj*

film•strip *n* : strip of film with photographs for still projection

fil•ter \'filtər\ *n* **1** : device for separating matter from a fluid **2** : device (as on a camera lens) that absorbs light ~ *vb* **1** : pass through a filter **2** : remove by means of a filter —**fil•ter•able** *adj* —**fil•tra•tion** \fil'trāshən\ *n*

filth \'filth\ *n* : repulsive dirt or refuse —**filth•i•ness** *n* —**filthy** \'filthē\ *adj*

fin \'fin\ *n* **1** : thin external process controlling movement in an aquatic animal **2** : fin-shaped part (as on an airplane) **3** : flipper —**finned** \'find\ *adj*

fi•na•gle \fə'nāgəl\ *vb* **-gled; -gling** : get by clever or tricky means —**fi•na•gler** *n*

fi•nal \'fīn⁰l\ *adj* **1** : not to be changed **2** : ultimate **3** : coming at the end — **final** *n* —**fi•nal•ist** \'fīn⁰list\ *n* —**fi•nal•i•ty** \fī'nalətē, fə-\ *n* —**fi•nal•ize** \-,īz\ *vb* —**fi•nal•ly** *adv*

fi•na•le \fə'nalē, fi'näl-\ *n* : last or climactic part

fi•nance \fə'nans, 'fī,nans\ *n* **1** *pl* : money resources **2** : management of money affairs ~ *vb* **-nanced; -nanc•ing 1** : raise funds for **2** : give necessary funds to **3** : sell on credit

fi·nan·cial \fə'nanchəl, fī-\ *adj* : relating to finance — **fi·nan·cial·ly** *adv*

fi·nan·cier \,finən'sir, ,fī,nan-\ *n* : person who invests large sums of money

finch \'finch\ *n* : songbird (as a sparrow or linnet) with a strong bill

find \'fīnd\ *vb* **found** \'fau̇nd\; **find·ing** **1** : discover or encounter **2** : obtain by effort **3** : experience or feel **4** : gain or regain the use of **5** : decide on (a verdict) ~ *n* **1** : act or instance of finding **2** : something found — **find·er** *n* — **find·ing** *n* — **find out** *vb* : learn, discover, or verify something

fine \'fīn\ *n* : money paid as a penalty ~ *vb* **fined**; **fin·ing** : impose a fine on — *adj* **fin·er**; **-est 1** : free from impurity **2** : small or thin **3** : not coarse **4** : superior in quality or appearance — *adv* : finely — **fine·ly** *adv* — **fine·ness** *n*

fin·ery \'fīnərē\ *n*, *pl* **-er·ies** : showy clothing and jewels

fi·nesse \fə'nes\ *n* **1** : delicate skill **2** : craftiness — **finesse** *vb*

fin·ger \'fiŋgər\ *n* **1** : one of the 5 divisions at the end of the hand and esp. one other than the thumb **2** : something like a finger **3** : part of a glove for a finger ~ *vb* **1** : touch with the fingers **2** : identify as if by pointing — **fin·gered** *adj* — **fin·ger·nail** *n* — **fin·ger·tip** *n*

fin·ger·ling \-gərliŋ\ *n* : small fish

fin·ger·print *n* : impression of the pattern of marks on the tip of a finger — **fingerprint** *vb*

fin·icky \'finikē\ *adj* : excessively particular in taste or standards

fin·ish \'finish\ *vb* **1** : come or bring to an end **2** : use or dispose of entirely **3** : put a final coat or surface on ~ *n* **1** : end **2** : final treatment given a surface — **fin·ish·er** *n*

fi·nite \'fī,nīt\ *adj* : having definite limits

fink \'fiŋk\ *n* : contemptible person

fiord *var of* FJORD

fir \'fər\ *n* : erect evergreen tree or its wood

fire \'fīr\ *n* **1** : light or heat and esp. the flame of something burning **2** : destructive burning (as of a house) **3** : enthusiasm **4** : the shooting of weapons ~ *vb* **fired**; **fir·ing 1** : kindle **2** : stir up or enliven **3** : dismiss from employment **4** : shoot **5** : bake —

fire·bomb *n or vb* — **fire·fight·er** *n* — **fire·less** *adj* — **fire·proof** *adj or vb* — **fire·wood** *n*

fire·arm *n* : weapon (as a rifle) that works by an explosion of gunpowder

fire·ball *n* **1** : ball of fire **2** : brilliant meteor

fire·boat *n* : boat equipped for fighting fire

fire·box *n* **1** : chamber (as of a furnace) that contains a fire **2** : fire-alarm box

fire·break *n* : cleared land for checking a forest fire

fire·bug *n* : person who deliberately sets destructive fires

fire·crack·er *n* : small firework that makes noise

fire·fly *n* : night-flying beetle that produces a soft light

fire·man \'fīrmən\ *n* **1** : person trained to put out fires **2** : stoker

fire·place *n* : opening made in a chimney to hold an open fire

fire·plug *n* : hydrant

fire·side *n* **1** : place near the fire or hearth **2** : home — *adj* : having an informal quality

fire·trap *n* : place apt to catch on fire

fire·work *n* : device that explodes to produce noise or a display of light

¹firm \'fərm\ *adj* **1** : securely fixed in place **2** : strong or vigorous **3** : not subject to change **4** : resolute ~ *vb* : make or become firm — **firm·ly** *adv* — **firm·ness** *n*

²firm *n* : business enterprise

fir·ma·ment \'fərməmənt\ *n* : sky

first \'fərst\ *adj* **1** : being number one **2** : foremost ~ *adv* **1** : before any other **2** : for the first time ~ *n* **1** : number one **2** : one that is first — **first class** *n* — **first-class** *adj or adv* — **first·ly** *adv* — **first-rate** *adj or adv*

first aid *n* : emergency care

first lieutenant *n* : commissioned officer ranking next below a captain

first sergeant *n* **1** : noncommissioned officer serving as the chief assistant to the commander of a military unit **2** : rank in the army below a command sergeant major and in the marine corps below a sergeant major

firth \'fərth\ *n* : estuary

fis·cal \'fiskəl\ *adj* : relating to money — **fis·cal·ly** *adv*

fish \'fish\ *n*, *pl* **fish** *or* **fish·es** : water animal with fins, gills, and usu. scales

~ *vb* **1** : try to catch fish **2** : grope — **fish•er** *n* —**fish•hook** *n* —**fish•ing** *n*

fish•er•man \-mən\ *n* : one who fishes

fish•ery \'fishərē\ *n, pl* **-er•ies** : fishing business or a place for this

fishy \'fishē\ *adj* **fish•i•er; -est 1** : relating to or like fish **2** : questionable

fis•sion \'fishən, 'fizh-\ *n* : splitting of an atomic nucleus —**fis•sion•able** \-ənəbəl\ *adj*

fis•sure \'fishər\ *n* : crack

fist \'fist\ *n* : hand doubled up —**fist•ed** \'fistəd\ *adj* —**fist•ful** \-,fül\ *n*

fist•i•cuffs \'fisti,kəfs\ *n pl* : fist fight

¹**fit** \'fit\ *n* : sudden attack of illness or emotion

²**fit** *adj* **-tt- 1** : suitable **2** : qualified **3** : sound in body — *vb* **-tt- 1** : be suitable to **2** : insert or adjust correctly **3** : make room for **4** : supply or equip **5** : belong — ~ *n* : state of fitting or being fitted —**fit•ly** *adv* —**fit•ness** *n* —**fit•ter** *n*

fit•ful \'fitfəl\ *adj* : restless —**fit•ful•ly** *adv*

fit•ting *adj* : suitable — ~ *n* : a small part

five \'fīv\ *n* **1** : one more than 4 **2** : 5th in a set or series **3** : something having 5 units —**five** *adj or pron*

fix \'fiks\ *vb* **1** : attach **2** : establish **3** : make right **4** : prepare **5** : improperly influence — ~ *n* **1** : predicament **2** : determination of location —**fix•er** *n*

fix•a•tion \fik'sāshən\ *n* : obsessive attachment —**fix•ate** \'fik,sāt\ *vb*

fixed \'fikst\ *adj* **1** : stationary **2** : settled —**fixed•ly** \'fiksədlē\ *adv* —**fixed•ness** \-nəs\ *n*

fix•ture \'fikschər\ *n* : permanent part of something

fizz \'fiz\ *vb* : make a hissing sound — *n* : effervescence

fiz•zle \'fizəl\ *vb* **-zled; -zling 1** : fizz **2** : fail — ~ *n* : failure

fjord \fē'órd\ *n* : inlet of the sea between cliffs

flab \'flab\ *n* : flabby flesh

flab•ber•gast \'flabər,gast\ *vb* : astound

flab•by \'flabē\ *adj* **-bi•er; -est** : not firm —**flab•bi•ness** *n*

flac•cid \'flaksəd, 'flasəd\ *adj* : not firm

¹**flag** \'flag\ *n* : flat stone

²**flag** *n* **1** : fabric that is a symbol (as of a country) **2** : something used to signal — *vb* **-gg- 1** : signal with a flag — **flag•pole** *n* —**flag•staff** *n*

³**flag** *vb* **-gg- :** lose strength or spirit

flag•el•late \'flajə,lāt\ *vb* **-lat•ed; -lat•ing** : whip —**flag•el•la•tion** \,flajə-'lāshən\ *n*

flag•on \'flagən\ *n* : container for liquids

fla•grant \'flāgrənt\ *adj* : conspicuously bad —**fla•grant•ly** *adv*

flag•ship *n* : ship carrying a commander

flag•stone *n* : flag

flail \'flāl\ *n* : tool for threshing grain — *vb* : beat with or as if with a flail

flair \'flar\ *n* : natural aptitude

flak \'flak\ *n, pl* **flak 1** : antiaircraft fire **2** : criticism

flake \'flāk\ *n* : small flat piece — *vb* : **flaked; flak•ing** : separate or form into flakes

flam•boy•ant \flam'bóiənt\ *adj* : showy —**flam•boy•ance** \-əns\ *n* —**flam•boy•ant•ly** *adv*

flame \'flām\ *n* **1** : glowing part of a fire **2** : state of combustion **3** : burning passion —**flame** *vb* —**flam•ing** *adj*

fla•min•go \flə'mingō\ *n, pl* **-gos** : long-legged long-necked tropical water bird

flam•ma•ble \'flaməbəl\ *adj* : easily ignited

flange \'flanj\ *n* : rim

flank \'flaŋk\ *n* : side of something — *vb* **1** : attack or go around the side of **2** : be at the side of

flan•nel \'flan⁹l\ *n* : soft napped fabric

flap \'flap\ *n* **1** : slap **2** : something flat that hangs loose — *vb* **-pp- 1** : move (wings) up and down **2** : swing back and forth noisily

flap•jack \-,jak\ *n* : pancake

flare \'flar\ *vb* **flared; flar•ing** : become suddenly bright or excited — ~ *n* : blaze of light

flash \'flash\ *vb* **1** : give off a sudden flame or burst of light **2** : appear or pass suddenly — ~ *n* **1** : sudden burst of light or inspiration **2** : instant — *adj* : coming suddenly

flash•light *n* : small battery-operated light

flashy \'flashē\ *adj* **flash•i•er; -est** : showy —**flash•i•ly** *adv* —**flash•i•ness** *n*

flask \'flask\ *n* : flattened bottle

flat \'flat\ *adj* **-tt- 1** : smooth **2** : broad and thin **3** : definite **4** : uninteresting **5** : deflated **6** : below the true pitch — ~ *n* **1** : level surface of land **2** : flat note in music **3** : apartment **4** : deflated tire — *adv* **-tt- 1** : exactly **2** : below the true pitch — *vb* **-tt- :** make

flat —**flat·ly** adv —**flat·ness** n —
flat·ten \-ᵊn\ vb

flat·car n : railroad car without sides

flat·fish n : flattened fish with both eyes on the upper side

flat·foot n, pl **flat·feet** : foot condition in which the arch is flattened —**flat·foot·ed** adj

flat-out adj 1 : being maximum effort or speed 2 : downright

flat·ter \'flatər\ vb 1 : praise insincerely 2 : judge or represent too favorably —**flat·ter·er** n —**flat·tery** \'flatərē\ n

flat·u·lent \'flachələnt\ adj : full of gas —**flat·u·lence** \-ləns\ n

flat·ware n : eating utensils

flaunt \'flȯnt\ vb : display ostentatiously —**flaunt** n

fla·vor \'flāvər\ n 1 : quality that affects the sense of taste 2 : something that adds flavor ~ vb : give flavor to —**fla·vor·ful** adj —**fla·vor·ing** n —**fla·vor·less** adj

flaw \'flȯ\ n : fault —**flaw·less** adj —**flaw·less·ly** adv —**flaw·less·ness** n

flax \'flaks\ n : plant from which linen is made

flax·en \'flaksən\ adj : made of or like flax

flay \'flā\ vb 1 : strip off the skin of 2 : criticize harshly

flea \'flē\ n : leaping bloodsucking insect

fleck \'flek\ vb or n : streak or spot

fledg·ling \'flejliŋ\ n : young bird

flee \'flē\ vb **fled** \'fled\; **flee·ing** : run away

fleece \'flēs\ n : sheep's wool ~ vb **fleeced; fleec·ing** 1 : shear 2 : get money from dishonestly —**fleecy** adj

¹**fleet** \'flēt\ vb : pass rapidly ~ adj 1 : swift —**fleet·ing** adj —**fleet·ness** n

²**fleet** n : group of ships

fleet admiral n : commissioned officer of the highest rank in the navy

flesh \'flesh\ n 1 : soft parts of an animal's body 2 : soft plant tissue (as fruit pulp) —**fleshed** \'flesht\ adj —**flesh out** vb : make fuller —**fleshy** adj

flesh·ly \'fleshlē\ adj : sensual

flew past of FLY

flex \'fleks\ vb : bend

flex·i·ble \'fleksəbəl\ adj 1 : capable of being flexed 2 : adaptable —**flex·i·bil·i·ty** \,fleksə'bilətē\ n —**flex·i·bly** \-əblē\ adv

flick \'flik\ n : light jerky stroke ~ vb 1 : strike lightly 2 : flutter

flick·er \'flikər\ vb 1 : waver 2 : burn unsteadily ~ n 1 : sudden movement 2 : wavering light

fli·er \'flīər\ n 1 : aviator 2 : advertising circular

¹**flight** \'flīt\ n 1 : act or instance of flying 2 : ability to fly 3 : a passing through air or space 4 : series of stairs —**flight·less** adj

²**flight** n : act or instance of running away

flighty \-ē\ adj **flight·i·er; -est** : capricious or silly —**flight·i·ness** n

flim·flam \'flim,flam\ n : trickery

flim·sy \-zē\ adj **-si·er; -est** 1 : not strong or well made 2 : not believable —**flim·si·ly** adv —**flim·si·ness** n

flinch \'flinch\ vb : shrink from pain

fling \'fliŋ\ vb **flung** \'fləŋ\; **fling·ing** 1 : move brusquely 2 : throw ~ n 1 : act or instance of flinging 2 : attempt 3 : period of self-indulgence

flint \'flint\ n : hard quartz that gives off sparks when struck with steel —**flinty** adj

flip \'flip\ vb **-pp-** 1 : cause to turn over quickly or many times 2 : move with a quick push ~ adj : insolent —**flip** n

flip·pant \'flipənt\ adj : not serious enough —**flip·pan·cy** \-ənsē\ n

flip·per \'flipər\ n : paddlelike limb (as of a seal) for swimming

flirt \'flərt\ vb 1 : be playfully romantic 2 : show casual interest ~ n : one who flirts —**flir·ta·tion** \,flər'tāshən\ n —**flir·ta·tious** \-shəs\ adj

flit \'flit\ vb **-tt-** : dart

float \'flōt\ n 1 : something that floats 2 : vehicle carrying an exhibit ~ vb 1 : rest on or in a fluid without sinking 2 : wander 3 : finance by issuing stock or bonds —**float·er** n

flock \'fläk\ n : group of animals (as birds) or people ~ vb : gather or move as a group

floe \'flō\ n : mass of floating ice

flog \'fläg\ vb **-gg-** : beat with a rod or whip —**flog·ger** n

flood \'fləd\ n 1 : great flow of water over the land 2 : overwhelming volume ~ vb : cover or fill esp. with water —**flood·wa·ter** n

floor \'flōr\ n 1 : bottom of a room on which one stands 2 : story of a building 3 : lower limit ~ vb 1 : furnish with a floor **2** : knock down **3** : amaze —**floor·board** n —**floor·ing** \-iŋ\ n

floo·zy, floo·zie \'flüzē\ n, pl **-zies** : promiscuous young woman

flop \'fläp\ vb **-pp- 1** : flap **2** : slump heavily **3** : fail —**flop** n

flop·py \'fläpē\ adj **-pi·er; -est** : soft and flexible

flo·ra \'flōrə\ n : plants or plant life of a region

flo·ral \'flōrəl\ adj : relating to flowers

flor·id \'flórəd\ adj **1** : very flowery in style **2** : reddish

flo·rist \'flórist\ n : flower dealer

floss \'fläs\ n **1** : soft thread for embroidery **2** : thread used to clean between teeth —**floss** vb

flo·ta·tion \flō'tāshən\ n : process or instance of floating

flo·til·la \flō'tilə\ n : small fleet

flot·sam \'flätsəm\ n : floating wreckage

¹flounce \'flaúns\ vb **flounced; flounc·ing** : move with exaggerated jerky motions —**flounce** n

²flounce n : fabric border or wide ruffle

¹floun·der \'flaúndər\ n, pl **flounder** or **flounders** : flatfish

²flounder vb **1** : struggle for footing **2** : proceed clumsily

flour \'flaúər\ n : finely ground meal ~ vb : coat with flour —**floury** adj

flour·ish \'flərish\ vb **1** : thrive **2** : wave threateningly ~ n **1** : embellishment **2** : fanfare **3** : wave **4** : showiness of action

flout \'flaút\ vb : treat with disdain

flow \'flō\ vb **1** : move in a stream **2** : proceed smoothly and readily ~ n : uninterrupted stream

flow·er \'flaúər\ n **1** : showy plant shoot that bears seeds **2** : state of flourishing ~ vb **1** : produce flowers **2** : flourish —**flow·ered** adj —**flow·er·i·ness** n —**flow·er·less** adj —**flow·er·pot** n —**flow·ery** \-ē\ adj

flown past part of FLY

flu \'flü\ n **1** : influenza **2** : minor virus ailment

flub \'fləb\ vb **-bb-** : bungle —**flub** n

fluc·tu·ate \'fləkchə‚wāt\ vb **-at·ed; -at·ing** : change rapidly esp. up and down —**fluc·tu·a·tion** \‚fləkchə'wāshən\ n

flue \'flü\ n : smoke duct

flu·ent \'flüənt\ adj : speaking with ease —**flu·en·cy** \-ənsē\ n —**flu·ent·ly** adv

fluff \'fləf\ n **1** : something soft and light **2** : blunder ~ vb **1** : make fluffy **2** : make a mistake —**fluffy** \-ē\ adj

flu·id \'flüəd\ adj : flowing ~ n : substance that can flow —**flu·id·i·ty** \flü'idətē\ n —**flu·id·ly** adv

fluid ounce n : unit of liquid measure equal to ¹⁄₁₆ pint

fluke \'flük\ n : stroke of luck

flume \'flüm\ n : channel for water

flung past of FLING

flunk \'fləŋk\ vb : fail in school work

flun·ky, flun·key \'fləŋkē\ n, pl **-kies** or **keys** : lackey

flu·o·res·cence \‚flùr'es⁹ns, ‚flór-\ n : emission of light after initial absorption —**flu·o·resce** \-'es\ vb —**flu·o·res·cent** \-'es⁹nt\ adj

flu·o·ri·date \'flórə‚dāt, 'flúr-\ vb **-dat·ed; -dat·ing** : add fluoride to —**flu·o·ri·da·tion** \‚flórə'dāshən, ‚flúr-\ n

flu·o·ride \'flór‚īd, 'flúr-\ n : compound of fluorine

flu·o·rine \'flúr‚ēn, -ən\ n : toxic gaseous chemical element

flu·o·ro·car·bon \‚flórō'kärbən, ‚flúr-\ n : compound containing fluorine and carbon

flu·o·ro·scope \'flúrə‚skōp\ n : instrument for internal examination —**flu·o·ro·scop·ic** \‚flúrə'skäpik\ adj —**flu·o·ros·co·py** \‚flúr'äskəpē\ n

flur·ry \'flərē\ n, pl **-ries 1** : light snowfall **2** : bustle **3** : brief burst of activity —**flurry** vb

¹flush \'fləsh\ vb : cause (a bird) to fly from cover

²flush n **1** : sudden flow (as of water) **2** : surge of emotion **3** : blush ~ vb **1** : blush **2** : wash out with a rush of liquid ~ adj **1** : filled to overflowing **2** : of a reddish healthy color **3** : smooth or level **4** : abutting —**flush** adv

³flush n : cards of the same suit

flus·ter \'fləstər\ vb : upset —**fluster** n

flute \'flüt\ n **1** : pipelike musical instrument **2** : groove —**fluted** adj —**flut·ing** n —**flut·ist** \-ist\ n

flut·ter \'flətər\ vb **1** : flap the wings rapidly **2** : move with quick wavering or flapping motions **3** : behave in an agitated manner ~ n **1** : a fluttering **2** : state of confusion —**flut·tery** \-ərē\ adj

flux \'fləks\ n : state of continuous change

¹fly \'flī\ vb **flew** \'flü\; **flown** \'flōn\; **fly·ing 1** : move through the air with wings **2** : float or soar **3** : flee **4**

: move or pass swiftly **5** : operate an airplane

²fly n, pl **flies** : garment closure

³fly n, pl **flies** : winged insect

fly•er var of FLIER

fly•pa•per n : sticky paper for catching flies

fly•speck n **1** : speck of fly dung **2** : something tiny

fly•wheel n : rotating wheel that regulates the speed of machinery

foal \ˈfōl\ n : young horse —**foal** vb

foam \ˈfōm\ n **1** : mass of bubbles on top of a liquid **2** : material of cellular form ~ vb : form foam —**foamy** adj

fob \ˈfäb\ n : short chain for a pocket watch

fo'c'sle var of FORECASTLE

fo•cus \ˈfōkəs\ n, pl **-ci** \-ˌsī\ **1** : point at which reflected or refracted rays meet **2** : adjustment (as of eyeglasses) for clear vision **3** : central point ~ vb : bring to a focus —**fo•cal** \-kəl\ adj —**fo•cal•ly** adv

fod•der \ˈfädər\ n : food for livestock

foe \ˈfō\ n : enemy

fog \ˈfȯg, ˈfäg\ n **1** : fine particles of water suspended near the ground **2** : mental confusion ~ vb **-gg-** : obscure or be obscured with fog —**fog•gy** adj

fog•horn n : warning horn sounded in a fog

fo•gy \ˈfōgē\ n, pl **-gies** : person with old-fashioned ideas

foi•ble \ˈfȯibəl\ n : minor character fault

¹foil \ˈfȯil\ vb : defeat ~ n : light fencing sword

²foil n **1** : thin sheet of metal **2** : one that sets off another by contrast

foist \ˈfȯist\ vb : force another to accept

¹fold \ˈfōld\ n **1** : enclosure for sheep **2** : group with a common interest

²fold vb **1** : lay one part over another **2** : embrace ~ n : part folded

fold•er \ˈfōldər\ n **1** : one that folds **2** : circular **3** : folded cover or envelope for papers

fol•de•rol \ˈfäldəˌräl\ n : nonsense

fo•liage \ˈfōlēij, -lij\ n : plant leaves

fo•lio \ˈfōlēˌō\ n, pl **-li•os** : sheet of paper folded once

folk \ˈfōk\ n, pl **folk** or **folks 1** : people in general **2** **folks** pl : one's family ~ adj : relating to the common people

folk•lore n : customs and traditions of a people —**folk•lor•ist** n

folksy \ˈfōksē\ adj **folks•i•er; -est** : friendly and informal

fol•li•cle \ˈfälikəl\ n : small anatomical cavity or gland

fol•low \ˈfälō\ vb **1** : go or come after **2** : pursue **3** : obey **4** : proceed along **5** : keep one's attention fixed on **6** : result from —**fol•low•er** n

fol•low•ing \ˈfäləwiŋ\ adj : next ~ n : group of followers ~ prep : after

fol•ly \ˈfälē\ n, pl **-lies** : foolishness

fo•ment \fōˈment\ vb : incite

fond \ˈfänd\ adj **1** : strongly attracted **2** : affectionate **3** : dear —**fond•ly** adv —**fond•ness** n

fon•dle \ˈfänd°l\ vb **-dled; -dling** : touch lovingly

fon•due \fänˈdü, -ˈdyü\ n : preparation of melted cheese

font \ˈfänt\ n **1** : baptismal basin **2** : fountain

food \ˈfüd\ n : material eaten to sustain life

fool \ˈfül\ n **1** : stupid person **2** : jester ~ vb **1** : waste time **2** : meddle **3** : deceive —**fool•ery** \ˈfüləre\ n —**fool•ish•ness** n —**fool•proof** adj

fool•ish \ˈfülish\ adj —**fool•ish•ly** adv —**fool•ish•ness** n —**fool•proof** adj

fool•har•dy \ˈfülˌhärdē\ adj : rash —**fool•har•di•ness** n

foot \ˈfut\ n, pl **feet** \ˈfēt\ **1** : end part of a leg **2** : unit of length equal to ⅓ yard **3** : unit of verse meter **4** : bottom —**foot•age** \-ij\ n —**foot•ed** adj —**foot•path** n —**foot•print** n —**foot•race** n —**foot•rest** n —**foot•wear** n

foot•ball n : ball game played by 2 teams on a rectangular field

foot•bridge n : bridge for pedestrians

foot•hill n : hill at the foot of higher hills

foot•hold n : support for the feet

foot•ing n **1** : foothold **2** : basis

foot•lights n pl : stage lights along the floor

foot•lock•er n : small trunk

foot•loose adj : having no ties

foot•man \ˈfutmən\ n : male servant

foot•note n : note at the bottom of a page

foot•step n **1** : step **2** : distance covered by a step **3** : footprint

foot•stool n : stool to support the feet

foot•work n : skillful movement of the feet (as in boxing)

fop \ˈfäp\ n : dandy —**fop•pery** \-əre\ n —**fop•pish** adj

for \ˈfȯr\ prep **1** —used to show preparation or purpose **2** : because of **3** —

used to show a recipient **4** : in support of **5** : so as to support or help cure **6** : so as to be equal to **7** : concerning **8** : through the period of ~ *conj* : because

for·age \'fórij\ *n* : food for animals ~ *vb* **-aged; -ag·ing 1** : hunt food **2** : search for provisions

for·ay \'fór,ā\ *n or vb* : raid

1for·bear \fór'bar\ *vb* **-bore** \-'bōr\; **-borne** \-'bōrn\; **-bear·ing 1** : refrain from **2** : be patient —**for·bear·ance** \-'barəns\ *n*

2forbear *var of* FOREBEAR

for·bid \fər'bid\ *vb* **-bade** \-'bad, -'bād\ *or* **-bad** \-'bad\; **-bid·den** \-'bid³n\; **-bid·ding 1** : prohibit **2** : order not to do something

for·bid·ding *adj* : tending to discourage

force \'fórs\ *n* **1** : exceptional strength or energy **2** : military strength **3** : body (as of persons) available for a purpose **4** : violence **5** : influence (as a push or pull) that causes motion ~ *vb* **forced; forc·ing 1** : compel **2** : gain against resistance **3** : break open —**force·ful** \-fəl\ *adj* —**force·ful·ly** *adv* —**in force 1** : in great numbers **2** : valid

for·ceps \'fórsəps\ *n, pl* **forceps** : surgical instrument for grasping objects

forc·ible \'fórsəbəl\ *adj* **1** : done by force **2** : showing force —**forc·i·bly** \-blē\ *adv*

ford \'fórd\ *n* : place to wade across a stream ~ *vb* : wade across

fore \'fór\ *adv* : in or toward the front ~ *adj* : being or coming before in time, place, or order ~ *n* : front

fore-and-aft *adj* : lengthwise

fore·arm \'fór,ärm\ *n* : part of the arm between the elbow and the wrist

fore·bear \'fór,bar\ *n* : ancestor

fore·bod·ing \fór'bōdiŋ\ *n* : premonition of disaster —**fore·bod·ing** *adj*

fore·cast \'fór,kast\ *vb* **-cast; -cast·ing** : predict —**forecast** *n* —**fore·cast·er** *n*

fore·cas·tle \'fōksəl\ *n* : forward part of a ship

fore·close \fór'klōz\ *vb* : take legal measures to terminate a mortgage — **fore·clo·sure** \-'klōzhər\ *n*

fore·fa·ther \'fór,fäthər\ *n* : ancestor

fore·fin·ger \'fór,fiŋgər\ *n* : finger next to the thumb

fore·foot \'fór,fút\ *n* : front foot of a quadruped

fore·front \'fór,frant\ *n* : foremost position or place

1fore·go \fór'gō\ *vb* **-went; -gone; -go·ing** : precede

2forego *var of* FORGO

fore·go·ing *adj* : preceding

fore·gone *adj* : determined in advance

fore·ground \'fór,graúnd\ *n* : part of a scene nearest the viewer

fore·hand \-,hand\ *n* : stroke (as in tennis) made with the palm of the hand turned forward —**forehand** *adj*

fore·head \'fórəd, 'fór,hed\ *n* : part of the face above the eyes

for·eign \'fórən\ *adj* **1** : situated outside a place or country and esp. one's own country **2** : belonging to a different place or country **3** : not pertinent **4** : related to or dealing with other nations —**for·eign·er** \-ər\ *n*

fore·know \fór'nō\ *vb* **-knew; -known; -know·ing** : know beforehand —**fore·knowl·edge** *n*

fore·leg \'fór,leg\ *n* : front leg

fore·lock \fór,läk\ *n* : front lock of hair

fore·man \'fórmən\ *n* **1** : spokesman of a jury **2** : workman in charge

fore·most \'fór,mōst\ *adj* : first in time, place, or order —**foremost** *adv*

fore·noon \'fór,nün\ *n* : morning

fo·ren·sic \fə'rensik\ *adj* : relating to courts or public speaking or debate

fo·ren·sics \-siks\ *n pl* : art or study of speaking or debating

fore·or·dain \,fórór'dān\ *vb* : decree beforehand

fore·quar·ter \'fór,kwórtər\ *n* : front half on one side of the body of a quadruped

fore·run·ner \'fór,rənər\ *n* : one that goes before

fore·see \fór'sē\ *vb* **-saw; -seen; -see·ing** : see or realize beforehand —**fore·see·able** *adj*

fore·shad·ow \fór,shadō\ *vb* : hint or suggest beforehand

fore·sight \'fór,sīt\ *n* : care or provision for the future —**fore·sight·ed** *adj* —**fore·sight·ed·ness** *n*

for·est \'fórəst\ *n* : large thick growth of trees and underbrush —**for·est·ed** \'fórəstəd\ *adj* —**for·est·er** \-əstər\ *n* —**for·est·land** \-,land\ *n* —**for·est·ry** \-əstrē\ *n*

fore·stall \fór'stól, fór-\ *vb* : prevent by acting in advance

fore·swear *var of* FORSWEAR

fore·taste \'fōr,tāst\ *n* : advance indication or notion ~ *vb* : anticipate

fore·tell \fōr'tel\ *vb* **-told; -tell·ing** : predict

fore·thought \'fōr,thot\ *n* : foresight

for·ever \fōr'evər\ *adv* 1 : for a limitless time 2 : always

for·ev·er·more \-,evər'mōr\ *adv* : forever

fore·warn \fōr'wōrn\ *vb* : warn beforehand

fore·word \'fōrwərd\ *n* : preface

for·feit \'fōrfət\ *n* : something forfeited ~ *vb* : lose or lose the right to by an error or crime —**for·fei·ture** \-fə-,chür\ *n*

¹**forge** \'fōrj\ *n* : smithy ~ *vb* **forged; forg·ing** 1 : form (metal) by heating and hammering 2 : imitate falsely esp. to defraud —**forg·er** *n* —**forg·ery** \-ərē\ *n*

²**forge** *vb* **forged; forg·ing** : move ahead steadily

for·get \fər'get\ *vb* **-got** \-'gät\; **-got·ten** \-'gät²n\ *or* **-got; -get·ting** 1 : be unable to think of or recall 2 : fail to think of at the proper time —**for·get·ta·ble** *adj* —**for·get·ful** \-fəl\ *adj* — **for·get·ful·ly** *adv*

for·get-me-not *n* : small herb with blue or white flowers

for·give \fər'giv\ *vb* **-gave** \-'gāv\; **-giv·en** \-'givən\; **-giv·ing** : pardon — **for·giv·able** *adj* —**for·give·ness** *n*

for·giv·ing *adj* 1 : able to forgive 2 : allowing room for error or weakness

for·go, fore·go \fōr'gō\ *vb* **-went; -gone; -go·ing** : do without

fork \'fōrk\ *n* 1 : implement with prongs for lifting, holding, or digging 2 : forked part 3 : a dividing into branches or a place where something branches ~ *vb* 1 : divide into branches 2 : move with a fork — **forked** \'fōrkt, 'fōrkəd\ *adj*

fork·lift *n* : machine for lifting with steel fingers

for·lorn \fər'lōrn\ *adj* 1 : deserted 2 : wretched —**for·lorn·ly** *adv*

form \'fōrm\ *n* 1 : shape 2 : set way of doing or saying something 3 : document with blanks to be filled in 4 : manner of performing with respect to what is expected 5 : mold 6 : kind or variety 7 : one of the ways in which a word is changed to show difference in use ~ *vb* 1 : give form or shape to 2 : train 3 : develop 4 : constitute —

for·ma·tive \'fōrmətiv\ *adj* — **form·less** \-ləs\ *adj*

formal \'fōrməl\ *adj* : following established custom ~ *n* : formal social event —**formal·i·ty** \fōr'malətē\ *n* —**for·mal·ize** \'fōrmə,līz\ *vb* —**for·mal·ly** *adv*

form·al·de·hyde \fōr'maldə,hīd\ *n* : colorless pungent gas used as a preservative and disinfectant

format \'fōr,mat\ *n* : general style or arrangement of something —**format** *vb*

for·ma·tion \fōr'māshən\ *n* 1 : a giving form to something 2 : something formed 3 : arrangement

for·mer \'fōrmər\ *adj* : coming before in time —**for·mer·ly** *adv*

for·mi·da·ble \'fōrmədəbəl, fōr'mid-\ *adj* 1 : causing fear or dread 2 : very difficult —**for·mi·da·bly** \-blē\ *adv*

for·mu·la \'fōrmyələ\ *n, pl* **-las** *or* **-lae** \-,lē, -lī\ 1 : set form of words for ceremonial use 2 : recipe 3 : milk mixture for a baby 4 : group of symbols or figures briefly expressing information 5 : set form or method

for·mu·late \-,lāt\ *vb* **-lat·ed; -lat·ing** : design, devise —**for·mu·la·tion** \,fōrmyə'lāshən\ *n*

for·ni·ca·tion \,fōrnə'kāshən\ *n* : illicit sexual intercourse —**for·ni·cate** \'fōrnə,kāt\ *vb* —**for·ni·ca·tor** \-,kātər\ *n*

for·sake \fər'sāk\ *vb* **-sook** \-'sük\; **-sak·en** \-'sākən\; **-sak·ing** : renounce completely

for·swear \fōr'swar\ *vb* **-swore; -sworn; -swear·ing** 1 : renounce under oath 2 : perjure

for·syth·ia \fər'sithēə\ *n* : shrub grown for its yellow flowers

fort \'fōrt\ *n* 1 : fortified place 2 : permanent army post

forte \'fōrt, 'fōr,tā\ *n* : something at which a person excels

forth \'fōrth\ *adv* : forward

forth·com·ing *adj* 1 : coming or available soon 2 : open and direct

forth·right *adj* : direct —**forth·right·ly** *adv* —**forth·right·ness** *n*

forth·with *adv* : immediately

for·ti·fy \'fōrtə,fī\ *vb* **-fied; -fy·ing** : make strong —**for·ti·fi·ca·tion** \,fōrtəfə'kāshən\ *n*

for·ti·tude \'fōrtə,tüd, -,tyüd\ *n* : ability to endure

fort·night \'fōrt,nīt\ n : 2 weeks —**fort·night·ly** adj or adv

for·tress \'fōrtrəs\ n : strong fort

for·tu·itous \fòr'tüətəs, -'tyü-\ adj : accidental

for·tu·nate \'fòrchənət\ adj 1 : coming by good luck 2 : lucky —**for·tu·nate·ly** adv

for·tune \'fòrchən\ n 1 : prosperity attained partly through luck 2 : good or bad luck 3 : destiny 4 : wealth

for·tune-tel·ler \-,telər\ n : one who foretells a person's future —**for·tune-tell·ing** \-iŋ\ n or adj

for·ty \'fòrtē\ n, pl **forties** : 4 times 10 —**for·ti·eth** \-ēəth\ adj or n —**forty** adj or pron

fo·rum \'fōrəm\ n, pl **-rums** 1 : Roman marketplace 2 : medium for open discussion

for·ward \'fòrwərd\ adj 1 : being near or at or belonging to the front 2 : brash ~ adv : toward what is in front ~ n : player near the front of his team ~ vb 1 : help onward 2 : send on —**for·ward·er** \-wərdər\ n —**for·ward·ness** n

for·wards \'fòrwərdz\ adv : forward

fos·sil \'fäsəl\ n : preserved trace of an ancient plant or animal ~ adj : being or originating from a fossil —**fos·sil·ize** vb

fos·ter \'fòstər\ adj : being, having, or relating to substitute parents ~ vb : help to grow or develop

fought past of FIGHT

foul \'faůl\ adj 1 : offensive 2 : clogged with dirt 3 : abusive 4 : wet and stormy 5 : unfair ~ n 1 : a breaking of the rules in a game ~ adv : foully ~ vb 1 : make or become foul or filthy 2 : tangle —**foul·ly** adv —**foul-mouthed** \-'maůthd, -'maůtht\ adj —**foul·ness** n

fou·lard \fů'lärd\ n : lightweight silk

foul-up n : error or state of confusion —**foul up** vb : bungle

¹**found** \'faůnd\ past of FIND

²**found** vb : establish —**found·er** n

foun·da·tion \faůn'dāshən\ n 1 : act of founding 2 : basis for something 3 : endowed institution 4 : supporting structure —**foun·da·tion·al** \-shənəl\ adj

foun·der \'faůndər\ vb : sink

found·ling \'faůndliŋ\ n : abandoned infant that is found

found·ry \'faůndrē\ n, pl **-dries** : place where metal is cast

fount \'faůnt\ n : fountain

foun·tain \'faůntªn\ n 1 : spring of water 2 : source 3 : artificial jet of water

four \'fōr\ n 1 : one more than 3 2 : 4th in a set or series 3 : something having 4 units —**four** adj or pron

four·fold adj : quadruple —**four·fold** adv

four·score adj : 80

four·some \'fōrsəm\ n : group of 4

four·teen \fōr'tēn\ n : one more than 13 —**fourteen** adj or pron —**four·teenth** \-'tēnth\ adj or n

fourth \'fōrth\ n 1 : one that is 4th 2 : one of 4 equal parts of something —**fourth** adj or adv

fowl \'faůl\ n, pl **fowl** or **fowls** 1 : bird 2 : chicken

fox \'fäks\ n, pl **fox·es** 1 : small mammal related to wolves 2 : clever person ~ vb : trick —**foxy** \'fäksē\ adj

fox·glove n : flowering plant that provides digitalis

fox·hole \'fäks,hōl\ n : pit for protection against enemy fire

foy·er \'fòiər, 'fòi,yā\ n : entrance hallway

fra·cas \'frākəs, 'frak-\ n, pl **-cas·es** \-əsəz\ : brawl

frac·tion \'frakshən\ n 1 : number indicating one or more equal parts of a whole 2 : portion —**frac·tion·al** \-shənəl\ adj —**frac·tion·al·ly** adv

frac·tious \'frakshəs\ adj : hard to control

frac·ture \'frakchər\ n : a breaking of something —**fracture** vb

frag·ile \'frajəl, -,īl\ adj : easily broken —**fra·gil·i·ty** \frə'jiləte\ n

frag·ment \'fragmənt\ n : part broken off ~ \-,ment\ vb : break into parts —**frag·men·tary** \'fragmən,terē\ adj —**frag·men·ta·tion** \,fragmən'tāshən, -,men-\ n

fra·grant \'frāgrənt\ adj : sweet-smelling —**fra·grance** \-grəns\ n —**fra·grant·ly** adv

frail \'frāl\ adj : weak or delicate —**frail·ty** \-tē\ n

frame \'frām\ vb **framed; fram·ing** 1 : plan 2 : formulate 3 : construct or arrange 4 : enclose in a frame 5 : make appear guilty ~ n 1 : makeup of the body 2 : supporting or enclosing structure 3 : state or disposition (as of mind) —**frame·work** n

franc \'frank\ n : monetary unit (as of France)

fran·chise \'fran,chīz\ n 1 : special privilege 2 : the right to vote —**franchisee** \,fran,chī'zē, -chə-\ n

fran·gi·ble \'franjəbəl\ adj : breakable —**fran·gi·bil·i·ty** \,franjə'bilətē\ n

¹frank \'frank\ adj : direct and sincere —**frank·ly** adv —**frank·ness** n

²frank vb : mark (mail) with a sign showing it can be mailed free ~ n : sign on franked mail

frank·furt·er \'frankfərtər, -,fərt-\, **frank·furt** \-fərt\ n : cooked sausage

frank·in·cense \'frankən,sens\ n : incense resin

fran·tic \'frantik\ adj : wildly excited —**fran·ti·cal·ly** \-iklē\ adv

fra·ter·nal \frə'tərn³l\ adj 1 : brotherly 2 : of a fraternity —**fra·ter·nal·ly** adv

fra·ter·ni·ty \frə'tərnətē\ n, pl -ties : men's student social group

fra·ter·nize \'fratər,nīz\ vb -nized; -nizing 1 : mingle as friends 2 : associate with members of a hostile group —**fra·ter·ni·za·tion** \,fratərnə'zāshən\ n

frat·ri·cide \'fratrə,sīd\ n : killing of a sibling —**frat·ri·cid·al** \,fratrə'sīd³l\ adj

fraud \'frod\ n : trickery —**fraud·u·lent** \'frojələnt\ adj —**fraud·u·lent·ly** adv

fraught \'frot\ adj : full of or accompanied by something specified

¹fray \'frā\ n : fight

²fray vb 1 : wear by rubbing 2 : separate the threads of 3 : irritate

fraz·zle \'frazəl\ vb -zled; -zling : wear out ~ n : exhaustion

freak \'frēk\ n 1 : something abnormal or unusual 2 : enthusiast —**freak·ish** adj —**freak out** vb 1 : experience nightmarish hallucinations from drugs 2 : distress or become distressed

freck·le \'frekəl\ n : brown spot on the skin —**freckle** vb

free \'frē\ adj **freer**; **fre·est** 1 : having liberty or independence 2 : not taxed 3 : given without charge 4 : voluntary 5 : not in use 6 : not fastened ~ adv : without charge ~ vb **freed**; **freeing** : set free —**free** adv —**free·born** adj —**free·dom** \'frēdəm\ n —**free·ly** adv

free·boot·er \-,bütər\ n : pirate

free-for-all n : fight with no rules

free·load vb : live off another's generosity —**free·load·er** n

free·stand·ing adj : standing without support

free·way \'frē,wā\ n : expressway

free will n : independent power to choose —**free·will** adj

freeze \'frēz\ vb **froze** \'frōz\; **fro·zen** \'frōz³n\; **freezing** 1 : harden into ice 2 : become chilled 3 : damage by frost 4 : stick fast 5 : become motionless 6 : fix at one stage or level ~ n 1 : very cold weather 2 : state of being frozen —**freez·er** n

freeze-dry vb : preserve by freezing then drying —**freeze-dried** adj

freight \'frāt\ n 1 : carrying of goods or payment for this 2 : shipped goods ~ vb : load or ship goods —**freight·er** n

french fry vb : fry in deep fat —**french fry** n

fre·net·ic \fri'netik\ adj : frantic —**fre·net·i·cal·ly** \-iklē\ adv

fren·zy \'frenzē\ n, pl -zies : violent agitation —**fren·zied** \-zēd\ adj

fre·quen·cy \'frēkwənsē\ n, pl -cies 1 : frequent or regular occurrence 2 : number of cycles or sound waves per second

fre·quent \'frēkwənt\ adj : happening often ~ \frē'kwent, 'frēkwənt\ vb : go to habitually —**fre·quent·er** n —**fre·quent·ly** adv

fres·co \'freskō\ n, pl -coes : painting on fresh plaster

fresh \'fresh\ adj 1 : not salt 2 : pure 3 : not preserved 4 : not stale 5 : like new 6 : insolent —**fresh·en** \-ən\ vb —**fresh·ly** adv —**fresh·ness** n

fresh·et \-ət\ n : overflowing stream

fresh·man \-mən\ n : first-year student

fresh·wa·ter n : water that is not salty

fret \'fret\ vb -tt- 1 : worry or become irritated 2 : fray 3 : agitate ~ n 1 : worn spot 2 : irritation —**fret·ful** \-fəl\ adj —**fret·ful·ly** adv —**fret·ful·ness** n

fri·a·ble \'frīəbəl\ adj : easily pulverized

fri·ar \'frīər\ n : member of a religious order

fri·ary \-ē\ n, pl -ar·ies : monastery of friars

fric·as·see \'frikə,sē, ,frikə'-\ n : meat stewed in a gravy ~ vb -seed; -see·ing : stew in gravy

fric·tion \'frikshən\ n 1 : a rubbing between 2 surfaces 2 : clash of opinions —**fric·tion·al** adj

Fri·day \'frīdā\ n : 6th day of the week

friend \'frend\ n : person one likes —

friend·less \'frēz\ *adj* —**friend·li·ness** \-lēnəs\ *n* —**friend·ly** *adj* —**friend·ship** \-,ship\ *n*

frieze \'frēz\ *n* : ornamental band around a room

frig·ate \'frigət\ *n* : warship smaller than a destroyer

fright \'frīt\ *n* : sudden fear —**fright·en** \-ᵊn\ *vb* —**fright·ful** \-fəl\ *adj* —**fright·ful·ly** *adv* —**fright·ful·ness** *n*

frig·id \'frijəd\ *adj* : intensely cold —**fri·gid·i·ty** \frij'idətē\ *n*

frill \'fril\ *n* **1** : ruffle **2** : pleasing but nonessential addition —**frilly** *adj*

fringe \'frinj\ *n* **1** : ornamental border of short hanging threads or strips **2** : edge —**fringe** *vb*

frisk \'frisk\ *vb* **1** : leap about **2** : search (a person) esp. for weapons

frisky \'friskē\ *adj* **frisk·i·er; -est** : playful —**frisk·i·ly** *adv* —**frisk·i·ness** *n*

¹frit·ter \'fritər\ *n* : fried batter containing fruit or meat

²fritter *vb* : waste little by little

friv·o·lous \'frivələs\ *adj* : not important or serious —**fri·vol·i·ty** \friv'älətē\ *n* —**friv·o·lous·ly** *adv*

frizz \'friz\ *vb* : curl tightly —**frizz** *n* —**frizzy** *adj*

fro \'frō\ *adv* : away

frock \'fräk\ *n* **1** : loose outer garment **2** : dress

frog \'frog, 'fräg\ *n* **1** : leaping amphibian **2** : hoarseness **3** : ornamental braid fastener **4** : small holder for flowers

frog·man \-,man, -mən\ *n* : underwater swimmer

frol·ic \'frälik\ *vb* **-icked; -ick·ing** : romp ~ *n* : fun —**frol·ic·some** \-səm\ *adj*

from \'frəm, 'främ\ *prep* —used to show a starting point

frond \'fränd\ *n* : fern or palm leaf

front \'frənt\ *n* **1** : face **2** : behavior **3** : main side of a building **4** : forward part **5** : boundary between air masses ~ *vb* **1** : have the main side adjacent to something **2** : serve as a front —**fron·tal** \-ᵊl\ *adj*

front·age \'frəntij\ *n* : length of boundary line on a street

fron·tier \,frən'tir\ *n* : outer edge of settled territory —**fron·tiers·man** \-'tirzmən\ *n*

fron·tis·piece \'frəntə,spēs\ *n* : illustration facing a title page

frost \'frost\ *n* **1** : freezing temperature **2** : ice crystals on a surface ~ *vb* **1** : cover with frost **2** : put icing on (a cake) —**frosty** *adj*

frost·bite \-,bīt\ *n* : partial freezing of part of the body —**frost·bit·ten** \-,bitᵊn\ *adj*

frost·ing *n* : icing

froth \'froth\ *n, pl* **froths** \'froths, 'frothz\ : bubbles on a liquid —**frothy** *adj*

fro·ward \'frōwərd\ *adj* : willful

frown \'fraún\ *vb or n* : scowl

frow·sy, frow·zy \'fraúzē\ *adj* **-si·er or -zi·er; -est** : untidy

froze *past of* FREEZE

frozen *past of* FREEZE

fru·gal \'frügəl\ *adj* : thrifty —**fru·gal·i·ty** \frü'galətē\ *n* —**fru·gal·ly** *adv*

fruit \'früt\ *n* **1** : usu. edible and sweet part of a seed plant **2** : result ~ *vb* : bear fruit —**fruit·cake** *n* —**fruit·ed** \-əd\ *adj* —**fruit·ful** *adj* —**fruit·ful·ness** *n* —**fruit·less** *adj* —**fruit·less·ly** *adv* —**fruity** *adj*

fru·ition \frü'ishən\ *n* : completion

frum·py \'frəmpē\ *adj* **frump·i·er; -est** : dowdy

frus·trate \'frəs,trāt\ *vb* **-trat·ed; -trat·ing** **1** : block **2** : cause to fail —**frus·trat·ing·ly** *adv* —**frus·tra·tion** \,frəs-'trāshən\ *n*

¹fry \'frī\ *vb* **fried; fry·ing** **1** : cook esp. with fat or oil **2** : be cooked by frying ~ *n, pl* **fries** **1** : something fried **2** : social gathering with fried food

²fry *n, pl* **fry** : recently hatched fish

fud·dle \'fədᵊl\ *vb* **-dled; -dling** : muddle

fud·dy-dud·dy \'fədē,dədē\ *n, pl* **-dies** : one who is old-fashioned or unimaginative

fudge \'fəj\ *vb* **fudged; fudg·ing** : cheat or exaggerate ~ *n* : creamy candy

fu·el \'fyüəl\ *n* : material burned to produce heat or power ~ *vb* **-eled or -elled; -el·ing or -el·ling** : provide with or take in fuel

fu·gi·tive \'fyüjətiv\ *adj* **1** : running away or trying to escape **2** : not lasting —**fugitive** *n*

-ful \fəl\ *adj suffix* **1** : full of **2** : having the qualities of **3** : -able ~ *n suffix* : quantity that fills

ful·crum \'fülkrəm, 'fəl-\ *n, pl* **-crums or -cra** \-krə\ : support on which a lever turns

ful·fill, ful·fil \ful'fil\ vb -filled; -fill·ing 1 : perform 2 : satisfy —**ful·fill·ment** n

¹**full** \'ful\ adj 1 : filled 2 : complete 3 : rounded 4 : having an abundance of something ~ adv : entirely ~ n : utmost degree —**full·ness** n —**ful·ly** adv

²**full** vb : shrink and thicken woolen cloth —**full·er** n

full-fledged \'ful'flejd\ adj : fully developed

ful·some \'fulsəm\ adj : copious verging on excessive

fum·ble \'fəmbəl\ vb -bled; -bling : fail to hold something properly —**fumble** n

fume \'fyüm\ n : irritating gas ~ vb fumed; fum·ing 1 : give off fumes 2 : show annoyance

fu·mi·gate \'fyümə,gāt\ vb -gat·ed; -gat·ing : treat with pest-killing fumes —**fu·mi·gant** \'fyümigant\ n —**fu·mi·ga·tion** \,fyümə'gāshən\ n

fun \'fən\ n 1 : something providing amusement or enjoyment 2 : enjoyment ~ adj : full of fun

func·tion \'fəŋkshən\ n 1 : special purpose 2 : formal ceremony or social affair ~ vb : have or carry on a function —**func·tion·al** \-shənəl\ adj —**func·tion·al·ly** adv

func·tion·ary \-shə,nerē\ n, pl -ar·ies : official

fund \'fənd\ n 1 : store 2 : sum of money intended for a special purpose 3 pl : available money ~ vb : provide funds for

fun·da·men·tal \,fəndə'ment³l\ adj 1 : basic 2 : of central importance or necessity —**fundamental** n —**fun·da·men·tal·ly** adv

fu·ner·al \'fyünərəl\ n : ceremony for a dead person —**funeral** adj —**fu·ne·re·al** \fyü'nirēəl\ adj

fun·gi·cide \'fənjə,sīd, 'fəŋgə-\ n : agent that kills fungi —**fun·gi·cid·al** \,fənjə'sīd³l, ,fəŋgə-\ adj

fun·gus \'fəŋgəs\ n, pl **fun·gi** \'fən,jī, 'fəŋ,gī\ : lower plant that lacks chlorophyll —**fun·gal** \'fəŋgəl\ adj —**fun·gous** \-gəs\ adj

funk \'fəŋk\ n : state of depression

funky \'fəŋkē\ adj **funk·i·er; -est** : unconventional and unsophisticated

fun·nel \'fən³l\ n 1 : cone-shaped utensil with a tube for directing the flow of a liquid 2 : ship's smokestack ~ vb -neled; -nel·ing : move to a central point or into a central channel

fun·nies \'fənēz\ n pl : section of comic strips

fun·ny \'fənē\ adj -ni·er; -est 1 : amusing 2 : strange

fur \'fər\ n 1 : hairy coat of a mammal 2 : article of clothing made with fur —**fur** adj —**furred** \'fərd\ adj —**fur·ry** \-ē\ adj

fur·bish \'fərbish\ vb : make lustrous or new looking

fu·ri·ous \'fyúrēəs\ adj : fierce or angry —**fu·ri·ous·ly** adv

fur·long \'fər,lóŋ\ n : a unit of distance equal to 220 yards

fur·lough \'fərlō\ n : authorized absence from duty —**furlough** vb

fur·nace \'fərnəs\ n : enclosed structure in which heat is produced

fur·nish \'fərnish\ vb 1 : provide with what is needed 2 : make available for use

fur·nish·ings \-iŋs\ n pl 1 : articles or accessories of dress 2 : furniture

fur·ni·ture \'fərnichər\ n : movable articles for a room

fu·ror \'fyúr,ór\ n 1 : anger 2 : sensational craze

fur·ri·er \'fərēər\ n : dealer in furs

fur·row \'fərō\ n 1 : trench made by a plow 2 : wrinkle or groove —**furrow** vb

fur·ther \'fərthər\ adv 1 : at or to a more advanced point 2 : more ~ adj : additional ~ vb : promote —**fur·ther·ance** \-ərəns\ n

fur·ther·more \'fərthər,mōr\ adv : in addition

fur·ther·most \-,mōst\ adj : most distant

fur·thest \'fərthəst\ adv or adj : farthest

fur·tive \'fərtiv\ adj : slyly or secretly done —**fur·tive·ly** adv —**fur·tive·ness** n

fu·ry \'fyúrē\ n, pl -ries 1 : intense rage 2 : violence

¹**fuse** \'fyüz\ n 1 : cord lighted to transmit fire to an explosive 2 usu **fuze** : device for exploding a charge ~, **fuze** vb fused or fuzed; fus·ing or fuz·ing : equip with a fuse

²**fuse** vb fused; fus·ing 1 : melt and run together 2 : unite ~ n : electrical safety device —**fus·ible** adj

fu·se·lage \'fyüsə,läzh, -zə-\ n : main body of an aircraft

fu·sil·lade \'fyüsə,läd, -,läd, ,fyüsə'-, -zə-\ n : volley of fire

fu·sion \'fyüzhən\ *n* **1** : process of merging by melting **2** : union of atomic nuclei

fuss \'fəs\ *n* **1** : needless bustle or excitement **2** : show of attention **3** : objection or protest ~ *vb* : make a fuss

fuss·bud·get \-,bəjət\ *n* : one who fusses or is fussy about trifles

fussy \'fəsē\ *adj* **fuss·i·er; -est 1** : irritable **2** : paying very close attention to details —**fuss·i·ly** *adv* —**fuss·i·ness** *n*

fu·tile \'fyüt⁰l, 'fyü,tīl\ *adj* : useless or vain —**fu·til·i·ty** \fyü'tilətē\ *n*

fu·ture \'fyüchər\ *adj* : coming after the present ~ *n* **1** : time yet to come **2** : what will happen —**fu·tur·is·tic** \,fyüchə'ristik\ *adj*

fuze *var of* FUSE

fuzz \'fəz\ *n* : fine particles or fluff

fuzzy \-ē\ *adj* **fuzz·i·er; -est 1** : covered with or like fuzz **2** : indistinct —**fuzz·i·ness** *n*

-fy \,fī\ *vb suffix* : make —**-fi·er** \,fīər\ *n suffix*

G

g \'jē\ *n, pl* **g's** *or* **gs** \'jēz\ **1** : 7th letter of the alphabet **2** : unit of gravitational force

gab \'gab\ *vb* **-bb-** : chatter —**gab** *n* —**gab·by** \'gabē\ *adj*

gab·ar·dine \'gabər,dēn\ *n* : durable twilled fabric

ga·ble \'gābəl\ *n* : triangular part of the end of a building —**ga·bled** \-bəld\ *adj*

gad \'gad\ *vb* **-dd-** : roam about —**gad·der** *n*

gad·fly *n* : persistently critical person

gad·get \'gajət\ *n* : device —**gad·get·ry** \'gajətrē\ *n*

gaff \'gaf\ *n* : metal hook for lifting fish —**gaff** *vb*

gaffe \'gaf\ *n* : social blunder

gag \'gag\ *vb* **-gg-** **1** : prevent from speaking or crying out by stopping up the mouth **2** : retch or cause to retch ~ *n* **1** : something that stops up the mouth **2** : laugh-provoking remark or act

gage *var of* GAUGE

gag·gle \'gagəl\ *n* : flock of geese

gai·ety \'gāətē\ *n, pl* **-eties** : high spirits

gai·ly \'gālē\ *adv* : in a gay manner

gain \'gān\ *n* **1** : profit **2** : obtaining of profit or possessions **3** : increase ~ *vb* **1** : get possession of **2** : win **3** : arrive at **4** : increase or increase in **5** : profit —**gain·er** *n* —**gain·ful** *adj* —**gain·ful·ly** *adv*

gain·say \gān'sā\ *vb* **-said** \-'sād, -'sed\; **-say·ing; -says** \-'sāz, -'sez\ : deny or dispute —**gain·say·er** *n*

gait \'gāt\ *n* : manner of walking or running —**gait·ed** *adj*

gal \'gal\ *n* : girl

ga·la \'gālə, 'galə, 'gälə\ *n* : festive celebration —**gala** *adj*

gal·axy \'galəksē\ *n, pl* **-ax·ies** : very large group of stars —**ga·lac·tic** \gə'laktik\ *adj*

gale \'gāl\ *n* **1** : strong wind **2** : outburst

¹gall \'gól\ *n* **1** : bile **2** : insolence

²gall \'gól\ *n* **1** : skin sore caused by chafing **2** : swelling of plant tissue caused by parasites ~ *vb* **1** : chafe **2** : irritate or vex

gal·lant \gə'lant, -'länt; 'galənt\ *n* : man very attentive to women ~ \'galənt; gə'lant, -'länt\ *adj* **1** : splendid **2** : brave **3** : polite and attentive to women —**gal·lant·ly** *adv* —**gal·lant·ry** \'galəntrē\ *n*

gall·blad·der *n* : pouch attached to the liver in which bile is stored

gal·le·on \'galyən\ *n* : large sailing ship formerly used esp. by the Spanish

gal·lery \'galərē\ *n, pl* **-ler·ies 1** : outdoor balcony **2** : long narrow passage or hall **3** : room or building for exhibiting art **4** : spectators —**gal·ler·ied** \-rēd\ *adj*

gal·ley \'galē\ *n, pl* **-leys 1** : old ship propelled esp. by oars **2** : kitchen of a ship or airplane

gal·li·um \'galēəm\ *n* : bluish white metallic chemical element

gal·li·vant \'galə,vant\ *vb* : travel or roam about for pleasure

gal·lon \'galən\ *n* : unit of liquid measure equal to 4 quarts

gal·lop \'galəp\ *n* : fast 3-beat gait of a horse —**gallop** *vb* —**gal·lop·er** *n*

gal·lows \'galōz\ *n, pl* -**lows** *or* -**lows·es** : upright frame for hanging criminals

gall·stone *n* : abnormal concretion in the gallbladder or bile passages

ga·lore \gə'lōr\ *adj* : in abundance

ga·losh \gə'läsh\ *n* : overshoe —usu. pl.

gal·va·nize \'galvə‚nīz\ *vb* -**nized;** -**niz·ing** 1 : shock into action 2 : coat (iron or steel) with zinc —**gal·va·ni·za·tion** \‚galvənə'zāshən\ *n* —**gal·va·niz·er** *n*

gam·bit \'gambit\ *n* 1 : opening tactic in chess 2 : stratagem

gam·ble \'gambəl\ *vb* -**bled;** -**bling** 1 : play a game for stakes 2 : bet 3 : take a chance ~ *n* : risky undertaking —**gam·bler** \-blər\ *n*

gam·bol \'gambəl\ *vb* -**boled** *or* -**bolled;** -**bol·ing** *or* -**bol·ling** : skip about in play —**gambol** *n*

game \'gām\ *n* 1 : playing activity 2 : competition according to rules 3 : animals hunted for sport or food ~ *vb* gamed; gam·ing : gamble ~ *adj* 1 : plucky 2 : lame —**game·ly** *adv* —**game·ness** *n*

game·cock *n* : fighting cock

game·keep·er *n* : person in charge of game animals or birds

gam·ete \gə'mēt, 'gam‚ēt\ *n* : mature germ cell —**ga·met·ic** \gə'metik\ *adj*

ga·mine \ga'mēn\ *n* : charming tomboy

gam·ut \'gamət\ *n* : entire range or series

gamy *or* **gam·ey** \'gāmē\ *adj* gam·i·er; -est : having the flavor of game esp. when slightly tainted —**gam·i·ness** *n*

¹gan·der \'gandər\ *n* : male goose

²gander *n* : glance

gang \'gaŋ\ *n* 1 : group of persons working together 2 : group of criminals ~ *vb* : attack in a gang —**with** *up*

gan·gling \'gaŋgliŋ\ *adj* : lanky

gan·gli·on \'gaŋglēən\ *n, pl* -**glia** \-glēə\ : mass of nerve cells

gang·plank *n* : platform used in boarding or leaving a ship

gan·grene \'gaŋ‚grēn, gaŋ'-; 'gan‚-, gan-\ *n* : local death of body tissue —**gangrene** *vb* —**gan·gre·nous** \'gaŋgrənəs\ *adj*

gang·ster \'gaŋstər\ *n* : member of criminal gang

gang·way \-‚wā\ *n* : passage in or out

gan·net \'ganət\ *n* : large fish-eating marine bird

gan·try \'gantrē\ *n, pl* -**tries** : frame structure supported over or around something

gap \'gap\ *n* 1 : break in a barrier 2 : mountain pass 3 : empty space

gape \'gāp\ *vb* gaped; gap·ing 1 : open widely 2 : stare with mouth open —**gape** *n*

ga·rage \gə'räzh, -'räj\ *n* : shelter or repair shop for automobiles ~ *vb* -raged; -rag·ing : put or keep in a garage

garb \'gärb\ *n* : clothing ~ *vb* : dress

gar·bage \'gärbij\ *n* 1 : food waste 2 : trash —**gar·bage·man** *n*

gar·ble \'gärbəl\ *vb* -**bled;** -**bling** : distort the meaning of

gar·den \'gärdᵊn\ *n* 1 : plot for growing fruits, flowers, or vegetables 2 : public recreation area ~ *vb* : work in a garden —**gar·den·er** \'gärdᵊnər\ *n*

gar·de·nia \gär'dēnyə\ *n* : tree or shrub with fragrant white or yellow flowers or the flower

gar·gan·tuan \gär'ganchəwən\ *adj* : having tremendous size or volume

gar·gle \'gärgəl\ *vb* -**gled;** -**gling** : rinse the throat with liquid —**gargle** *n*

gar·goyle \'gär‚goil\ *n* : waterspout in the form of a grotesque human or animal

gar·ish \'garish\ *adj* : offensively bright or gaudy

gar·land \'gärlənd\ *n* : wreath ~ *vb* : form into or deck with a garland

gar·lic \'gärlik\ *n* : herb with pungent bulbs used in cooking —**gar·licky** \-likē\ *adj*

gar·ment \'gärmənt\ *n* : article of clothing

gar·ner \'gärnər\ *vb* : acquire by effort

gar·net \'gärnət\ *n* : deep red mineral

gar·nish \'gärnish\ *vb* : add decoration to (as food) —**garnish** *n*

gar·nish·ee \‚gärnə'shē\ *vb* -**eed;** -**ee·ing** : take (as a debtor's wages) by legal authority

gar·nish·ment \'gärnishmənt\ *n* : attachment of property to satisfy a creditor

gar·ret \'garət\ *n* : attic

gar·ri·son \'garəsən\ *n* : military post or the troops stationed there —**garrison** *vb*

gar·ru·lous \'garələs\ *adj* : talkative —

gar·ru·li·ty \gə'rülətē\ n —**gar·ru·lous·ly** adv —**gar·ru·lous·ness** n

gar·ter \'gärtər\ n : band to hold up a stocking or sock

gas \'gas\ n, pl **gas·es 1** : fluid (as hydrogen or air) that tends to expand indefinitely **2** : gasoline ~ vb **gassed; gas·sing 1** : treat with gas **2** : fill with gasoline —**gas·eous** \'gasēəs, 'gashəs\ adj

gash \'gash\ n : deep long cut —**gash** vb

gas·ket \'gaskət\ n : material or a part used to seal a joint

gas·light n : light of burning illuminating gas

gas·o·line \'gasə,lēn, ,gasə'-\ n : flammable liquid from petroleum

gasp \'gasp\ vb **1** : catch the breath audibly **2** : breathe laboriously —**gasp** n

gas·tric \'gastrik\ adj : relating to or located near the stomach

gas·tron·o·my \gas'tränəmē\ n : art of good eating —**gas·tro·nom·ic** \,gastrə'nämik\ adj

gate \'gāt\ n : an opening for passage in a wall or fence —**gate·keep·er** n —**gate·post** n

gate·way n : way in or out

gath·er \'gathər\ vb **1** : bring or come together **2** : harvest **3** : pick up little by little **4** : deduce —**gath·er·er** n —**gath·er·ing** n

gauche \'gōsh\ adj : crude or tactless

gaudy \'gȯdē\ adj **gaud·i·er; -est** : tastelessly showy —**gaud·i·ly** \'gȯdᵊlē\ adv —**gaud·i·ness** n

gauge \'gāj\ n : instrument for measuring ~ vb **gauged; gaug·ing** : measure

gaunt \'gȯnt\ adj : thin or emaciated —**gaunt·ness** n

¹gaunt·let \-lət\ n **1** : protective glove **2** : challenge to combat

²gauntlet n : ordeal

gauze \'gȯz\ n : thin often transparent fabric —**gauzy** adj

gave past of GIVE

gav·el \'gavəl\ n : mallet of a presiding officer, auctioneer, or judge

gawk \'gȯk\ vb : stare stupidly

gawky \-ē\ adj **gawk·i·er; -est** : clumsy

gay \'gā\ adj **1** : merry **2** : bright and lively **3** : homosexual —**gay** n

gaze \'gāz\ vb **gazed; gaz·ing** : fix the eyes in a steady intent look —**gaze** n —**gaz·er** n

ga·zelle \gə'zel\ n : small swift antelope

ga·zette \-'zet\ n : newspaper

gaz·et·teer \,gazə'tir\ n : geographical dictionary

gear \'gir\ n **1** : clothing **2** : equipment **3** : toothed wheel —**gear** vb

gear·shift n : mechanism by which automobile gears are shifted

geek \'gēk\ n : socially inept person

geese pl of GOOSE

gei·sha \'gāshə, 'gē-\ n, pl -**sha** or -**shas** : Japanese girl or woman trained to entertain men

gel·a·tin \'jelətᵊn\ n : sticky substance obtained from animal tissues by boiling —**ge·lat·i·nous** \jə'latᵊnəs\ adj

geld \'geld\ vb : castrate

geld·ing \-iŋ\ n : castrated horse

gem \'jem\ n : cut and polished valuable stone —**gem·stone** n

gen·der \'jendər\ n **1** : sex **2** : division of a class of words (as nouns) that determines agreement of other words

gene \'jēn\ n : segment of DNA that controls inheritance of a trait

ge·ne·al·o·gy \,jēnē'äləjē, ,jen-, -'al-\ n, pl -**gies** : study of family pedigrees —**ge·ne·a·log·i·cal** \-ēə'läjikəl\ adj —**ge·ne·a·log·i·cal·ly** adv —**ge·ne·al·o·gist** \-ē'äləjist, -'al-\ n

genera pl of GENUS

gen·er·al \'jenrəl, 'jenə-\ adj **1** : relating to the whole **2** : applicable to all of a group **3** : common or widespread ~ n **1** : something that involves or is applicable to the whole **2** : commissioned officer in the army, air force, or marine corps ranking above a lieutenant general —**gen·er·al·ly** adv —**in general** : for the most part

gen·er·al·i·ty \,jenə'ralətē\ n, pl -**ties** : general statement

gen·er·al·ize \'jenrə,līz, 'jenə-\ vb -**ized; -iz·ing** : reach a general conclusion esp. on the basis of particular instances —**gen·er·al·iza·tion** \,jenrələ'zāshən, ,jenə-\ n

general of the air force : commissioned officer of the highest rank in the air force

general of the army : commissioned officer of the highest rank in the army

gen·er·ate \'jenə,rāt\ vb -**at·ed; -at·ing** : create or produce

gen·er·a·tion \,jenə'rāshən\ n **1** : living beings constituting a single step in a

generative   139   gestation

line of descent **2** : production —**gen·er·a·tive** \'jenə,rātiv, -rət-\ adj

gen·er·a·tor \'jenə,rātər\ n **1** : one that generates **2** : machine that turns mechanical into electrical energy

ge·ner·ic \jə'nerik\ adj **1** : general **2** : not protected by a trademark **3** : relating to a genus —**generic** n

gen·er·ous \'jenərəs\ adj **1** : freely giving or sharing —**gen·er·os·i·ty** \,jenə-'räsətē\ n —**gen·er·ous·ly** adv —**gen·er·ous·ness** n

ge·net·ics \jə'netiks\ n : biology dealing with heredity and variation —**ge·net·ic** \-ik\ adj —**ge·net·i·cal·ly** adv —**ge·net·i·cist** \-'netəsist\ n

ge·nial \'jēnēəl\ adj : cheerful —**ge·ni·al·i·ty** \,jēnē'alətē\ n —**ge·nial·ly** adv

ge·nie \'jēnē\ n : supernatural spirit that often takes human form

gen·i·tal \'jenətəl\ adj : concerned with reproduction —**gen·i·tal·ly** \-təlē\ adv

gen·i·ta·lia \,jenə'tālyə\ n pl : external genital organs

gen·i·tals \'jenətəlz\ n pl : genitalia

ge·nius \'jēnyəs\ n **1** : single strongly marked capacity **2** : extraordinary intellectual power or a person having such power

geno·cide \'jenə,sīd\ n : systematic destruction of a racial or cultural group

genre \'zhänrə, 'zhāⁿrə\ n : category esp. of literary composition

gen·teel \jen'tēl\ adj : polite or refined

gen·tile \'jen,tīl\ n : person who is not Jewish —**gentile** adj

gen·til·i·ty \jen'tilətē\ n, pl -ties **1** : good birth and family **2** : good manners

gen·tle \'jentəl\ adj -tler; -tlest **1** : of a family of high social station **2** : not harsh, stern, or violent **3** : soft or delicate ~ vb -tled; -tling : make gentle —**gen·tle·ness** n —**gen·tly** adv

gen·tle·man \-mən\ n : man of good family or manners —**gen·tle·man·ly** adv

gen·tle·wom·an \-,wùmən\ n : woman of good family or breeding

gen·try \'jentrē\ n, pl -tries : people of good birth or breeding

gen·u·flect \'jenyə,flekt\ vb : bend the knee in worship —**gen·u·flec·tion** \,jenyə'flekshən\ n

gen·u·ine \'jenyəwən\ adj : being the same in fact as in appearance —**gen·u·ine·ly** adv —**gen·u·ine·ness** n

ge·nus \'jēnəs\ n, pl **gen·era** \'jenərə\ : category of biological classification

ge·ode \'jē,ōd\ n : stone having a mineral-lined cavity

geo·des·ic \,jēə'desik, -'dēs-\ adj : made of a framework of linked polygons

ge·og·ra·phy \jē'ägrəfē\ n **1** : study of the earth and its climate, products, and inhabitants **2** : natural features of a region —**ge·og·ra·pher** \-fər\ n —**geo·graph·ic** \,jēə'grafik\, **geo·graph·i·cal** \-ikəl\ adj —**geo·graph·i·cal·ly** adv

ge·ol·o·gy \jē'äləjē\ n : study of the history of the earth and its life esp. as recorded in rocks —**geo·log·ic** \,jēə'läjik\, **geo·log·i·cal** \-ikəl\ adj —**geo·log·i·cal·ly** adv —**ge·ol·o·gist** \jē'äləjist\ n

ge·om·e·try \jē'ämətrē\ n, pl -tries : mathematics of the relations, properties, and measurements of solids, surfaces, lines, and angles —**geo·met·ric** \,jēə-'metrik\, **geo·met·ri·cal** \-rikəl\ adj

geo·ther·mal \,jēō'thərməl\ adj : relating to or derived from the heat of the earth's interior

ge·ra·ni·um \jə'rānēəm\ n : garden plant with clusters of white, pink, or scarlet flowers

ger·bil \'jərbəl\ n : burrowing desert rodent

ge·ri·at·ric \,jerē'atrik\ adj **1** : relating to aging or the aged **2** : old

ge·ri·at·rics \-triks\ n : medicine dealing with the aged and aging

germ \'jərm\ n **1** : microorganism **2** : source or rudiment

ger·mane \jər'mān\ adj : relevant

ger·ma·ni·um \-'mānēəm\ n : grayish white hard chemical element

ger·mi·cide \'jərmə,sīd\ n : agent that destroys germs —**ger·mi·cid·al** \,jərmə'sīdəl\ adj

ger·mi·nate \'jərmə,nāt\ vb -nat·ed; -nat·ing : begin to develop —**ger·mi·na·tion** \,jərmə'nāshən\ n

ger·ry·man·der \'jerē'mandər, 'jerē,-, ,gerē'-, ,gerē,-\ vb : divide into election districts so as to give one political party an advantage —**gerrymander** n

ger·und \'jerənd\ n : word having the characteristics of both verb and noun

ge·sta·po \gə'stäpō\ n, pl -pos : secret police

ges·ta·tion \je'stāshən\ n : pregnancy or incubation —**ges·tate** \'jes,tāt\ vb

ges·ture \'jeschər\ *n* **1** : movement of the body or limbs that expresses something **2** : something said or done for its effect on the attitudes of others —**ges·tur·al** \-chərəl\ *adj* —**gesture** *vb*

ge·sund·heit \gə'zùnt,hīt\ *interj* —used to wish good health to one who has just sneezed

get \'get\ *vb* **got** \'gät\; **got** *or* **got·ten** \'gät⁰n\; **get·ting 1** : gain or be in possession of **2** : succeed in coming or going **3** : cause to come or go or to be in a certain condition or position **4** : become **5** : be subjected to **6** : understand **7** : be obliged —**get along** *vb* **1** : get by **2** : be on friendly terms —**get by** *vb* : meet one's needs

get·away \'getə,wā\ *n* **1** : escape **2** : a starting or getting under way

gey·ser \'gīzər\ *n* : spring that intermittently shoots up hot water and steam

ghast·ly \'gastlē\ *adj* **-li·er; -est** : horrible or shocking

gher·kin \'gərkən\ *n* : small pickle

ghet·to \'getō\ *n, pl* **-tos** *or* **-toes** : part of a city in which members of a minority group live

ghost \'gōst\ *n* : disembodied soul —**ghost·ly** *adv*

ghost·write *vb* **-wrote; -writ·ten** : write for and in the name of another —**ghost·writ·er** *n*

ghoul \'gül\ *n* : legendary evil being that feeds on corpses —**ghoul·ish** *adj*

GI \jē'ī\ *n, pl* **GI's** *or* **GIs** : member of the U.S. armed forces

gi·ant \'jīənt\ *n* **1** : huge legendary being **2** : something very large or very powerful —**giant** *adj*

gib·ber \'jibər\ *vb* **-bered; -ber·ing** : speak rapidly and foolishly

gib·ber·ish \'jibərish\ *n* : unintelligible speech or language

gib·bon \'gibən\ *n* : manlike ape

gibe \'jīb\ *vb* **gibed; gib·ing** : jeer at —**gibe** *n*

gib·lets \'jibləts\ *n pl* : edible fowl viscera

gid·dy \'gidē\ *adj* **-di·er; -est 1** : silly **2** : dizzy —**gid·di·ness** *n*

gift \'gift\ *n* **1** : something given **2** : talent —**gift·ed** *adj*

gi·gan·tic \jī'gantik\ *adj* : very big

gig·gle \'gigəl\ *vb* **-gled; -gling** : laugh in a silly manner —**giggle** *n* —**gig·gly** \-əlē\ *adj*

gig·o·lo \'jigə,lō\ *n, pl* **-los** : man living on the earnings of a woman

Gi·la monster \'hēlə-\ *n* : large venomous lizard

gild \'gild\ *vb* **gild·ed** \'gildəd\ *or* **gilt** \'gilt\; **gild·ing** : cover with or as if with gold

gill \'gil\ *n* : organ of a fish for obtaining oxygen from water

gilt \'gilt\ *adj* : gold-colored ~ *n* : gold or goldlike substance on the surface of an object

gim·bal \'gimbəl, 'jim-\ *n* : device that allows something to incline freely

gim·let \'gimlət\ *n* : small tool for boring holes

gim·mick \'gimik\ *n* : new and ingenious scheme, feature, or device —**gim·mick·ry** *n* —**gim·micky** \-ikē\ *adj*

gimpy \'gimpē\ *adj* : lame

¹**gin** \'jin\ *n* : machine to separate seeds from cotton —**gin** *vb*

²**gin** *n* : clear liquor flavored with juniper berries

gin·ger \'jinjər\ *n* : pungent aromatic spice from a tropical plant —**gin·ger·bread** *n*

gin·ger·ly *adj* : very cautious or careful —**gingerly** *adv*

ging·ham \'giŋəm\ *n* : cotton clothing fabric

gin·gi·vi·tis \,jinjə'vītəs\ *n* : inflammation of the gums

gink·go \'giŋkō\ *n, pl* **-goes** *or* **-gos** : tree of eastern China

gin·seng \'jin,siŋ, -,seŋ, -,saŋ\ *n* : aromatic root of a Chinese herb

gi·raffe \jə'raf\ *n* : African mammal with a very long neck

gird \'gərd\ *vb* **gird·ed** \'gərdəd\ *or* **girt** \'gərt\; **gird·ing 1** : encircle or fasten with or as if with a belt **2** : prepare

gird·er \'gərdər\ *n* : horizontal supporting beam

gir·dle \'gərd⁰l\ *n* : woman's supporting undergarment ~ *vb* : surround

girl \'gərl\ *n* **1** : female child **2** : young woman **3** : sweetheart —**girl·hood** \-,hùd\ *n* —**girl·ish** *adj*

girlfriend *n* : frequent or regular female companion of a boy or man

girth \'gərth\ *n* : measure around something

gist \'jist\ *n* : main point or part

give \'giv\ *vb* **gave** \'gāv\; **giv·en** \'givən\; **giv·ing 1** : put into the possession or keeping of another **2** : pay

3 : perform 4 : contribute or donate 5 : produce 6 : utter 7 : yield to force, strain, or pressure ~ n : capacity or tendency to yield to force or strain — **give in** vb : surrender — **give out** vb : become used up or exhausted — **give up** vb 1 : let out of one's control 2 : cease from trying, doing, or hoping

give·away \ˈgiv-ə-wā\ n 1 : unintentional betrayal 2 : something given freely

giv·en \ˈgivən\ adj 1 : prone or disposed 2 : having been specified

giz·zard \ˈgizərd\ n : muscular usu. horny-lined enlargement following the crop of a bird

gla·cial \ˈglāshəl\ adj 1 : relating to glaciers 2 : very slow — **gla·cial·ly** adv

gla·cier \ˈglāshər\ n : large body of ice moving slowly

glad \ˈglad\ adj **-dd-** 1 : experiencing or causing pleasure, joy, or delight 2 : very willing — **glad·den** \-ᵊn\ vb — **glad·ly** adv — **glad·ness** n

glade \ˈglād\ n : grassy open space in a forest

glad·i·a·tor \ˈglādē-ātər\ n : one who fought to the death for the entertainment of ancient Romans — **glad·i·a·to·ri·al** \ˌgladēəˈtōrēəl\ adj

glad·i·o·lus \ˌglādēˈōləs\ n, pl **-li** \-ˌlē, -ˌlī\ : plant related to the irises

glam·our, glam·or \ˈglamər\ n : romantic or exciting attractiveness — **glam·or·ize** \-ə,rīz\ vb — **glam·or·ous** \-ərəs\ adj

glance \ˈglans\ vb **glanced; glanc·ing** 1 : strike and fly off to one side 2 : give a quick look ~ n : quick look

gland \ˈgland\ n : group of cells that secretes a substance — **glan·du·lar** \ˈglanjələr\ adj

glans \ˈglanz\ n, pl **glan·des** \ˈglan,dēz\ : conical vascular body forming the end of the penis or clitoris

glare \ˈglar\ vb **glared; glar·ing** 1 : shine with a harsh dazzling light 2 : stare angrily ~ n 1 : harsh dazzling light 2 : angry stare

glar·ing \ˈglariŋ\ adj : painfully obvious — **glar·ing·ly** adv

glass \ˈglas\ n 1 : hard usu. transparent material made by melting sand and other materials 2 : something made of glass 3 pl : lenses used to correct defects of vision — **glass** adj — **glass·ful** \-ˌful\ n — **glass·ware** \-ˌwar\ n — **glassy** adj

glass·blow·ing n : art of shaping a mass of molten glass by blowing air into it — **glass·blow·er** n

glau·co·ma \glau'kōmə, glȯ-\ n : state of increased pressure within the eyeball

glaze \ˈglāz\ vb **glazed; glaz·ing** 1 : furnish with glass 2 : apply glaze to ~ n : glassy surface or coating

gla·zier \ˈglāzhər\ n : one who sets glass in window frames

gleam \ˈglēm\ n 1 : transient or partly obscured light 2 : faint trace ~ vb : send out gleams

glean \ˈglēn\ vb : collect little by little — **glean·able** adj — **glean·er** n

glee \ˈglē\ n : joy — **glee·ful** adj

glen \ˈglen\ n : narrow hidden valley

glib \ˈglib\ adj **-bb-** : speaking or spoken with ease — **glib·ly** adv

glide \ˈglīd\ vb **glid·ed; glid·ing** : move or descend smoothly and effortlessly — **glide** n

glid·er \ˈglīdər\ n 1 : winged aircraft having no engine 2 : swinging porch seat

glim·mer \ˈglimər\ vb : shine faintly or unsteadily ~ n 1 : faint light 2 : small amount

glimpse \ˈglimps\ vb **glimpsed; glimps·ing** : take a brief look at — **glimpse** n

glint \ˈglint\ vb : gleam or sparkle — **glint** n

glis·ten \ˈglisᵊn\ vb : shine or sparkle by reflection — **glisten** n

glit·ter \ˈglitər\ vb : shine with brilliant or metallic luster ~ n : small glittering ornaments — **glit·tery** adj

gloat \ˈglōt\ vb : think of something with triumphant delight

glob \ˈgläb\ n 1 : large rounded lump

glob·al \ˈglōbəl\ adj : worldwide — **glob·al·ly** adv

globe \ˈglōb\ n 1 : sphere 2 : the earth or a model of it

glob·u·lar \ˈgläbyələr\ adj 1 : round 2 : made up of globules

glob·ule \ˈgläbyül\ n : tiny ball

glock·en·spiel \ˈgläkən,shpēl\ n : portable musical instrument consisting of tuned metal bars

gloom \ˈglüm\ n 1 : darkness 2 : sadness — **gloom·i·ly** adv — **gloom·i·ness** n — **gloomy** adj

glop \ˈgläp\ n : messy mass or mixture

glo·ri·fy \ˈglōrə,fī\ vb **-fied; -fy·ing** 1 : make to seem glorious 2 : worship — **glo·ri·fi·ca·tion** \ˌglōrəfəˈkāshən\ n

glo·ry \'glōrē\ *n, pl* **-ries 1 :** praise or honor offered in worship **2 :** cause for praise or renown **3 :** magnificence **4 :** heavenly bliss ~ *vb* **-ried; -ry·ing :** rejoice proudly **—glo·ri·ous** \'glōrēəs\ *adj* **—glo·ri·ous·ly** *adv*

¹gloss \'gläs, 'glós\ *n* **:** luster **—gloss·i·ly** \-əlē\ *adv* **—gloss·i·ness** \-ēnəs\ *n* **— gloss over** *vb* **1 :** mask the true nature of **2 :** deal with only superficially **—glossy** \-ē\ *adj*

²gloss *n* **:** brief explanation or translation ~ *vb* **:** translate or explain

glos·sa·ry \'gläsərē, 'glós-\ *n, pl* **-ries :** dictionary **—glos·sar·i·al** \glä-'sarēəl, glós-\ *adj*

glove \'gləv\ *n* **:** hand covering with sections for each finger

glow \'glō\ *vb* **1 :** shine with or as if with intense heat **2 :** show exuberance ~ *n* **:** brightness or warmth of color or feeling

glow·er \'glaůər\ *vb* **:** stare angrily **— glower** *n*

glow·worm *n* **:** insect or insect larva that emits light

glu·cose \'glü,kōs\ *n* **:** sugar found esp. in blood, plant sap, and fruits

glue \'glü\ *n* **:** substance used for sticking things together **—glue** *vb* **— glu·ey** \'glüē\ *adj*

glum \'gləm\ *adj* **-mm- 1 :** sullen **2 :** dismal

glut \'glət\ *vb* **-tt- :** fill to excess **—glut** *n*

glu·ten \'glüt°n\ *n* **:** gluey protein substance in flour

glu·ti·nous \'glüt°nəs\ *adj* **:** sticky

glut·ton \'glət°n\ *n* **:** one who eats to excess **—glut·ton·ous** \'glət°nəs\ *adj* **—glut·tony** \'glət°nē\ *n*

gnarled \'närld\ *adj* **1 :** knotty **2 :** gloomy or sullen

gnash \'nash\ *vb* **:** grind (as teeth) together

gnat \'nat\ *n* **:** small biting fly

gnaw \'nó\ *vb* **:** bite or chew on **— gnaw·er** *n*

gnome \'nōm\ *n* **:** dwarf of folklore **— gnom·ish** *adj*

gnu \'nü, 'nyü\ *n, pl* **gnu** *or* **gnus :** large African antelope

go \'gō\ *vb* **went** \'went\, **gone** \'gón, 'gän\, **go·ing** \'góiŋ\, **goes** \'gōz\ **1 :** move, proceed, run, or pass **2 :** leave **3 :** extend or lead **4 :** sell or amount **—with** *for* **5 :** happen **6 —**used in present participle to show intent or

imminent action **7 :** become **8 :** fit or harmonize **9 :** belong ~ *n, pl* **goes 1 :** act or manner of going **2 :** vigor **3 :** attempt **—go back on :** betray **—go by the board :** be discarded **—go for :** favor **—go off :** explode **—go one better :** outdo **—go over 1 :** examine **2 :** study **—go to town :** be very successful **—on the go :** constantly active

goad \'gōd\ *n* **:** something that urges **— goad** *vb*

goal \'gōl\ *n* **1 :** mark to reach in a race **2 :** purpose **3 :** object in a game through which a ball is propelled

goal·ie \'gōlē\ *n* **:** player who defends the goal

goal·keep·er *n* **:** goalie

goat \'gōt\ *n* **:** horned ruminant mammal related to the sheep **—goat·skin** *n*

goa·tee \gō'tē\ *n* **:** small pointed beard

¹gob \'gäb\ *n* **:** lump

¹gob·ble \'gäbəl\ *vb* **-bled; -bling :** eat greedily

²gobble *vb* **-bled; -bling :** make the noise of a turkey **(gobbler)**

gob·ble·dy·gook \'gäbəldē,guk, -'gük\ *n* **:** nonsense

gob·let \'gäblət\ *n* **:** large stemmed drinking glass

gob·lin \'gäblən\ *n* **:** ugly mischievous sprite

god \'gäd, 'gód\ *n* **1** *cap* **:** supreme being **2 :** being with supernatural powers **— god·like** *adj* **—god·ly** *adj*

god·child *n* **:** person one sponsors at baptism **—god·daugh·ter** *n* **—god·son** *n*

god·dess \'gädəs, 'gód-\ *n* **:** female god

god·less \-ləs\ *adj* **:** not believing in God **—god·less·ness** *n*

god·par·ent *n* **:** sponsor at baptism **— god·fa·ther** *n* **—god·moth·er** *n*

god·send \-,send\ *n* **:** something needed that comes unexpectedly

goes *pres 3d sing of* GO

go-get·ter \'gō,getər\ *n* **:** enterprising person **—go-get·ting** \-iŋ\ *adj or n*

gog·gle \'gägəl\ *vb* **-gled; -gling :** stare wide-eyed

gog·gles \-əlz\ *n pl* **:** protective glasses

go·ings-on \,gōiŋz'ón, -'än\ *n pl* **:** events

goi·ter \'góitər\ *n* **:** abnormally enlarged thyroid gland

gold \'gōld\ *n* **:** malleable yellow metallic chemical element **—gold·smith** \-,smith\ *n*

gold·brick \-,brik\ n : person who shirks duty —**goldbrick** vb

gold·en \'gōldən\ adj 1 : made of, containing, or relating to gold 2 : having the color of gold 3 : precious or favorable

gold·en·rod \'gōldən,räd\ n : herb having tall stalks with tiny yellow flowers

gold·finch \'gōld,finch\ n : yellow American finch

gold·fish \-,fish\ n : small usu. orange or golden carp

golf \'gälf, 'golf\ n : game played by hitting a small ball (**golf ball**) with clubs (**golf clubs**) into holes placed in a field (**golf course**) —**golf** vb —**golf·er** n

go·nad \'gō,nad\ n : sex gland

gon·do·la \'gändələ (usual for 1), gän-'dō-\ n 1 : long narrow boat used on the canals of Venice 2 : car suspended from a cable

gon·do·lier \,gändə'lir\ n : person who propels a gondola

gone \'gon\ adj : past 2 : involved

gon·er \'gonər\ n : hopeless case

gong \'gäŋ, 'goŋ\ n : metallic disk that makes a deep sound when struck

gon·or·rhea \,gänə'rēə\ n : bacterial inflammatory venereal disease of the genital tract —**gon·or·rhe·al** \-'rēəl\ adj

goo \'gü\ n : thick or sticky substance —**goo·ey** \-ē\ adj

good \'gud\ adj **bet·ter** \'betər\; **best** \'best\ 1 : satisfactory 2 : salutary 3 : considerable 4 : desirable 5 : well-behaved, kind, or virtuous ~ n 1 : something good 2 : benefit 3 pl : personal property 4 pl : wares ~ adv : well —**good·heart·ed** \-'härtəd\ adj —**good-look·ing** adj —**good-na·tured** \-'nāchərd\ adj —**good·ness** n —**good-tem·pered** \-'tempərd\ adj —**for good** : forever

good–bye, good–by \gud'bī\ n : parting remark

good-for-noth·ing n : idle worthless person

Good Friday n : Friday before Easter observed as the anniversary of the crucifixion of Christ

good·ly adj **-li·er; -est** : considerable

good·will n 1 : good intention 2 : kindly feeling

goody \'gudē\ n, pl **good·ies** : something that is good esp. to eat

goody–goody adj : affectedly or annoy-ingly sweet or self-righteous —**goody–goody** n

goof \'güf\ vb 1 : blunder 2 : waste time —usu. with off or around —**goof** n —**goof–off** n

goofy \'güfē\ adj **goof·i·er; -est** : crazy —**goof·i·ness** n

goose \'güs\ n, pl **geese** \'gēs\ : large bird with webbed feet

goose·ber·ry \'güs,berē, 'güz-\ n : berry of a shrub related to the currant

goose bumps n pl : roughening of the skin caused by fear, excitement, or cold

goose·flesh n : goose bumps

goose pimples n pl : goose bumps

go·pher \'gōfər\ n : burrowing rodent

¹**gore** \'gōr\ n : blood

²**gore** vb **gored; gor·ing** : pierce or wound with a horn or tusk

¹**gorge** \'gorj\ n : narrow ravine

²**gorge** vb **gorged; gorg·ing** : eat greedily

gor·geous \'gorjəs\ adj : supremely beautiful

go·ril·la \gə'rilə\ n : African manlike ape

gory \'gōrē\ adj **gor·i·er; -est** : bloody

gos·hawk \'gäs,hok\ n : long-tailed hawk with short rounded wings

gos·ling \'gäzliŋ, 'goz-\ n : young goose

gos·pel \'gäspəl\ n 1 : teachings of Christ and the apostles 2 : something accepted as infallible truth —**gospel** adj

gos·sa·mer \'gäsəmər, gäz-\ n 1 : film of cobweb 2 : light filmy substance

gos·sip \'gäsəp\ n 1 : person who reveals personal information 2 : rumor or report of an intimate nature ~ vb : spread gossip —**gos·sipy** \-ē\ adj

got past of GET

Goth·ic \'gäthik\ adj : relating to a medieval style of architecture

gotten past part of GET

gouge \'gauj\ n 1 : rounded chisel 2 : cavity or groove scooped out ~ vb **gouged; goug·ing** 1 : cut or scratch a groove in 2 : overcharge

gou·lash \'gü,läsh, -,lash\ n : beef stew with vegetables and paprika

gourd \'gōrd, 'gurd\ n 1 : any of a group of vines including the cucumber, squash, and melon 2 : inedible hardshelled fruit of a gourd

gour·mand \'gur,mänd\ n : person who loves good food and drink

gour·met \'gu̇r,mā, gu̇r'mā\ *n* : connoisseur of food and drink

gout \'gau̇t\ *n* : disease marked by painful inflammation and swelling of the joints —**gouty** *adj*

gov·ern \'gəvərn\ *vb* 1 : control and direct policy in 2 : guide or influence strongly 3 : restrain —**gov·ern·ment** \-ərmənt\ *n* —**gov·ern·men·tal** \,gəvər'ment∂l\ *adj*

gov·ern·ess \'gəvərnəs\ *n* : female teacher in a private home

gov·er·nor \'gəvənər, 'gəvər-\ *n* 1 : head of a political unit 2 : automatic speed-control device —**gov·er·nor·ship** *n*

gown \'gau̇n\ *n* 1 : loose flowing outer garment 2 : woman's formal evening dress —**gown** *vb*

grab \'grab\ *vb* -**bb**- : take by sudden grasp —**grab** *n*

grace \'grās\ *n* 1 : unmerited divine assistance 2 : short prayer before or after a meal 3 : respite 4 : ease of movement or bearing ~ *vb* **graced; grac·ing** 1 : honor 2 : adorn —**grace·ful** \-fəl\ *adj* —**grace·ful·ly** *adv* —**grace·ful·ness** *n* —**grace·less** *adj*

gra·cious \'grāshəs\ *adj* : marked by kindness and courtesy or charm and taste —**gra·cious·ly** *adv* —**gra·cious·ness** *n*

grack·le \'grakəl\ *n* : American blackbird

gra·da·tion \grā'dāshən, grə-\ *n* : step, degree, or stage in a series

grade \'grād\ *n* 1 : stage in a series, order, or ranking 2 : division of school representing one year's work 3 : mark of accomplishment in school 4 : degree of slope ~ *vb* **grad·ed; grad·ing** 1 : arrange in grades 2 : make level or evenly sloping 3 : give a grade to —**grad·er** *n*

grade school *n* : school including the first 4 or 8 grades

gra·di·ent \'grādēənt\ *n* : slope

grad·u·al \'grajəwəl\ *adj* : going by steps or degrees —**grad·u·al·ly** *adv*

grad·u·ate \'grajəwət\ *n* : holder of a diploma ~ *adj* : of or relating to studies beyond the bachelor's degree ~ \-ə,wāt\ *vb* **-at·ed; -at·ing** 1 : grant or receive a diploma 2 : mark with degrees of measurement —**grad·u·a·tion** \,grajə'wāshən\ *n*

graf·fi·to \grə'fētō, grɑ-\ *n, pl* **-ti** \-ē\ : inscription on a wall

graft \'graft\ *vb* : join one thing to another so that they grow together ~ *n* 1 : grafted plant 2 : the getting of money dishonestly or the money so gained —**graft·er** *n*

grain \'grān\ *n* 1 : seeds or fruits of cereal grasses 2 : small hard particle 3 : arrangement of fibers in wood —**grained** \'grānd\ *adj* —**grainy** *adj*

gram \'gram\ *n* : metric unit of weight equal to 1/1000 kilogram

gram·mar \'gramər\ *n* : study of words and their functions and relations in the sentence —**gram·mar·i·an** \grə'mareən\ *n* —**gram·mat·i·cal** \-'matikəl\ *adj* —**gram·mat·i·cal·ly** *adv*

grammar school *n* : grade school

gra·na·ry \'grānərē, 'gran-\ *n, pl* **-ries** : storehouse for grain

grand \'grand\ *adj* 1 : large or striking in size or scope 2 : fine and imposing 3 : very good —**grand·ly** *adv* —**grand·ness** *n*

grand·child \-,chīld\ *n* : child of one's son or daughter —**grand·daugh·ter** *n* —**grand·son** *n*

gran·deur \'granjər\ *n* : quality or state of being grand

gran·dil·o·quence \gran'diləkwəns\ *n* : pompous speaking —**gran·dil·o·quent** \-kwənt\ *adj*

gran·di·ose \'grandē,ōs, ,grandē'-\ *adj* 1 : impressive 2 : affectedly splendid —**gran·di·ose·ly** *adv*

grand·par·ent \'grand,parənt\ *n* : parent of one's father or mother —**grand·fa·ther** \-,fäthər, -,fåth-\ *n* —**grand·mother** \-,məthər\ *n*

grand·stand \-,stand\ *n* : usu. roofed stand for spectators

grange \'grānj\ *n* : farmers association

gran·ite \'granət\ *n* : hard igneous rock

grant \'grant\ *vb* 1 : consent to 2 : give 3 : admit as true ~ *n* 1 : act of granting 2 : something granted —**grant·ee** \grant'ē\ *n* —**grant·er** \'grantər\ *n* —**grant·or** \-ər, -,ȯr\ *n*

gran·u·late \'granyə,lāt\ *vb* **-lat·ed; -lat·ing** : form into grains or crystals —**gran·u·la·tion** \,granyə'lāshən\ *n*

gran·ule \'granyül\ *n* : small particle —**gran·u·lar** \-yələr\ *adj* —**gran·u·lar·i·ty** \,granyə'larətē\ *n*

grape \'grāp\ *n* : smooth juicy edible berry of a woody vine (**grape·vine**)

grape·fruit *n* : large edible yellow-skinned citrus fruit graph 145 grid

graph \graf\ *n* : diagram that shows relationships between things —**graph** *vb*

graph·ic \grafik\ *adj* **1** : vividly described **2** : relating to the arts (**graphic arts**) of representation and printing on flat surfaces ~ *n* **1** : picture used for illustration **2** *pl* : computer screen display —**graph·i·cal·ly** \-iklē\ *adv*

graph·ite \graf₁fīt\ *n* : soft carbon used for lead pencils and lubricants

grap·nel \grapnəl\ *n* : small anchor with several claws

grap·ple \grapəl\ *vb* -**pled**; -**pling 1** : seize or hold with or as if with a hooked implement **2** : wrestle

grasp \grasp\ *vb* **1** : take or seize firmly **2** : understand ~ *n* **1** : one's hold or control **2** : one's reach **3** : comprehension

grass \gras\ *n* : plant with jointed stem and narrow leaves —**grassy** *adj*

grass·hop·per \-₁häpər\ *n* : leaping plant-eating insect

grass·land *n* : land covered with grasses

¹**grate** \grāt\ *n* **1** : grating **2** : frame of iron bars to hold burning fuel

²**grate** *vb* **grat·ed**; -**ing 1** : pulverize by rubbing against something rough **2** : irritate —**grat·er** *n* —**grat·ing·ly** *adv*

grate·ful \grātfəl\ *adj* : thankful or appreciative —**grate·ful·ly** *adv* —**grate·ful·ness** *n*

grat·i·fy \gratə₁fī\ *vb* -**fied**; -**fy·ing** : give pleasure to —**grat·i·fi·ca·tion** \₁gratəfə'kāshən\ *n*

grat·ing \grātiŋ\ *n* : framework with bars across it

gra·tis \gratəs, 'grāt-\ *adv or adj* : free

grat·i·tude \gratə₁tüd, -₁tyüd\ *n* : state of being grateful

gra·tu·itous \grə'tüətəs, -'tyü-\ *adj* **1** : free **2** : uncalled-for

gra·tu·ity \-ətē\ *n, pl* -**ities** : tip

¹**grave** \grāv\ *n* : place of burial —**grave·stone** *n* —**grave·yard** *n*

²**grave** *adj* **grav·er**; **grav·est 1** : threatening great harm or danger **2** : solemn —**grave·ly** *adv* —**grave·ness** *n*

grav·el \gravəl\ *n* : loose rounded fragments of rock —**grav·el·ly** *adj*

grav·i·tate \gravə₁tāt\ *vb* -**tat·ed**; -**tat·ing** : move toward something

grav·i·ta·tion \₁gravə'tāshən\ *n* : natural force of attraction that tends to draw bodies together —**grav·i·ta·tion·al** \-shənəl\ *adj* —**grav·i·ta·tion·al·ly** *adv*

grav·i·ty \gravətē\ *n, pl* -**ties 1** : serious importance **2** : gravitation

gra·vy \grāvē\ *n, pl* -**vies** : sauce made from thickened juices of cooked meat

gray \grā\ *adj* **1** : of the color gray **2** : having gray hair ~ *n* : neutral color between black and white ~ *vb* : make or become gray —**gray·ish** \-ish\ *adj* —**gray·ness** *n*

¹**graze** \grāz\ *vb* **grazed**; **graz·ing** : feed on herbage or pasture —**graz·er** *n*

²**graze** *vb* **grazed**; **graz·ing** : touch lightly in passing

grease \grēs\ *n* : thick oily material or fat ~ \grēs, 'grēz\ *vb* **greased**; **greas·ing** : smear or lubricate with grease —**greasy** \grēsē, -zē\ *adj*

great \grāt\ *adj* **1** : large in size or number **2** : larger than usual —**great·ly** *adv* —**great·ness** *n*

grebe \grēb\ *n* : diving bird related to the loon

greed \grēd\ *n* : selfish desire beyond reason —**greed·i·ly** \-ᵊlē\ *adv* —**greed·i·ness** \-ēnəs\ *n* —**greedy** \grēdē\ *adj*

green \grēn\ *adj* **1** : of the color green **2** : unripe **3** : inexperienced ~ *vb* : become green ~ *n* **1** : color between blue and yellow **2** *pl* : leafy parts of plants —**green·ish** *adj* —**green·ness** *n*

green·ery \grēnərē\ *n, pl* -**eries** : green foliage or plants

green·horn *n* : inexperienced person

green·house *n* : glass structure for the growing of plants

greet \grēt\ *vb* **1** : address with expressions of kind wishes **2** : react to —**greet·er** *n*

greet·ing *n* **1** : friendly address on meeting **2** *pl* : best wishes

gre·gar·i·ous \gri'garēəs\ *adj* : social or companionable —**gre·gar·i·ous·ly** *adv* —**gre·gar·i·ous·ness** *n*

grem·lin \gremlən\ *n* : small mischievous gnome

gre·nade \grə'nād\ *n* : small missile filled with explosive or chemicals

grew *past of* GROW

grey *var of* GRAY

grey·hound \grā₁haúnd\ *n* : tall slender dog noted for speed

grid \grid\ *n* **1** : grating **2** : evenly

spaced horizontal and vertical lines (as on a map)

grid·dle \'grid^əl\ n : flat metal surface for cooking

grid·iron \'grid,īərn\ n 1 : grate for broiling 2 : football field

grief \'grēf\ n 1 : emotional suffering caused by or as if by bereavement 2 : disaster

griev·ance \'grēvəns\ n : complaint

grieve \'grēv\ vb **grieved; griev·ing** : feel or cause to feel grief or sorrow

griev·ous \'grēvəs\ adj 1 : oppressive 2 : causing grief or sorrow —**griev·ous·ly** adv

grill \'gril\ vb 1 : cook on a grill 2 : question intensely ~ n 1 : griddle 2 : informal restaurant

grille, grill \'gril\ n : grating forming a barrier or screen —**grill·work** n

grim \'grim\ adj -**mm**- 1 : harsh and forbidding in appearance 2 : relentless —**grim·ly** adv —**grim·ness** n

gri·mace \'griməs, grim'ās\ n : facial expression of disgust —**grimace** vb

grime \'grīm\ n : embedded or accumulated dirt —**grimy** adj

grin \'grin\ vb -**nn**- : smile so as to show the teeth —**grin** n

grind \'grīnd\ vb **ground** \'graúnd\; **grind·ing** 1 : reduce to powder 2 : wear down or sharpen by friction 3 : operate or produce by turning a crank ~ n : monotonous labor or routine —**grind·er** n —**grind·stone** \'grīn,stōn\ n

grip \'grip\ vb -**pp**- : seize or hold firmly ~ n 1 : grasp 2 : control 3 : device for holding

gripe \'grīp\ vb **griped; grip·ing** 1 : cause pains in the bowels 2 : complain —**gripe** n

grippe \'grip\ n : influenza

gris·ly \'grizlē\ adj -**li·er; -est** : horrible or gruesome

grist \'grist\ n : grain to be ground or already ground —**grist·mill** n

gris·tle \'grisəl\ n : cartilage —**gris·tly** \-lē\ adj

grit \'grit\ n 1 : hard sharp granule 2 : material composed of granules 3 : unyielding courage ~ vb -**tt**- : press with a grating noise —**grit·ty** adj

grits \'grits\ n pl : coarsely ground hulled grain

griz·zled \'grizəld\ adj : streaked with gray

groan \'grōn\ vb 1 : moan 2 : creak under a strain —**groan** n

gro·cer \'grōsər\ n : food dealer —**gro·cery** \'grōsrē, 'grōsh-, -ərē\ n

grog \'gräg\ n : rum diluted with water

grog·gy \-ē\ adj -**gi·er; -est** : dazed and unsteady on the feet —**grog·gi·ly** adv —**grog·gi·ness** n

groin \'gròin\ n : juncture of the lower abdomen and inner thigh

grom·met \'grämət, 'gräm-\ n : eyelet

groom \'grüm, 'grùm\ n 1 : one who cares for horses 2 : bridegroom ~ vb 1 : clean and care for (as a horse) 2 : make neat or attractive 3 : prepare

groove \'grüv\ n 1 : long narrow channel 2 : fixed routine —**groove** vb

grope \'grōp\ vb **groped; grop·ing** : search for by feeling

gros·beak \'grōs,bēk\ n : finch with large conical bill

¹**gross** \'grōs\ adj 1 : glaringly noticeable 2 : bulky 3 : consisting of an overall total exclusive of deductions 4 : vulgar ~ n : the whole before any deductions ~ vb : earn as a total —**gross·ly** adv —**gross·ness** n

²**gross** n, pl **gross** : 12 dozen

gro·tesque \grō'tesk\ adj 1 : absurdly distorted or repulsive 2 : ridiculous —**gro·tesque·ly** adv

grot·to \'grätō\ n, pl -**toes** : cave

grouch \'graúch\ n : complaining person —**grouch** vb —**grouchy** adj

¹**ground** \'graúnd\ n 1 : bottom of a body of water 2 pl : sediment 3 : basis for something 4 : surface of the earth 5 : conductor that makes electrical connection with the earth or a framework ~ vb 1 : force or bring down to the ground 2 : give basic knowledge to 3 : connect with an electrical ground —**ground·less** adj

²**ground** past of GRIND

ground·hog n : woodchuck

ground·wa·ter n : underground water

ground·work n : foundation

group \'grüp\ n : number of associated individuals ~ vb : gather or collect into groups

grou·per \'grüpər\ n : large fish of warm seas

grouse \'graús\ n, pl **grouse** or **grouses** : ground-dwelling game bird

grout \'graút\ n : mortar for filling cracks —**grout** vb

grove \'grōv\ n : small group of trees

grov·el \'grävəl, 'gräv-\ vb -**eled** or

-elled; -el•ing or -el•ling : abase oneself

grow \ˈgrō\ vb **grew** \ˈgrü\; **grown** \ˈgrōn\; **grow•ing 1** : come into existence and develop to maturity **2** : be able to grow **3** : advance or increase **4** : become **5** : cultivate —**grow•er** n

growl \ˈgraůl\ vb : utter a deep threatening sound —**growl** n

grown–up \ˈgrōn,əp\ n : adult —**grown–up** adj

growth \ˈgrōth\ n **1** : stage in growing **2** : process of growing **3** : result of something growing

grub \ˈgrəb\ vb **-bb- 1** : root out by digging **2** : search about ~ n **1** : thick wormlike larva **2** : food

grub•by \ˈgrəbē\ adj **-bi•er; -est** : dirty —**grub•bi•ness** n

grub•stake n : supplies for a prospector

grudge \ˈgrəj\ vb **grudged; grudg•ing** : be reluctant to give ~ n : feeling of ill will

gru•el \ˈgrüəl\ n : thin porridge

gru•el•ing, gru•el•ling \-əliŋ\ adj : requiring extreme effort

grue•some \ˈgrüsəm\ adj : horribly repulsive

gruff \ˈgrəf\ adj : rough in speech or manner —**gruff•ly** adv

grum•ble \ˈgrəmbəl\ vb **-bled; -bling** : mutter in discontent —**grum•bler** \-blər\ n

grumpy \-pē\ adj **grump•i•er; -est** : cross —**grump•i•ly** adv —**grump•i•ness** n

grun•ion \ˈgrənyən\ n : fish of the California coast

grunt \ˈgrənt\ n : deep guttural sound —**grunt** vb

gua•no \ˈgwänō\ n : excrement of seabirds used as fertilizer

guar•an•tee \ˌgarənˈtē\ n **1** : assurance of the fulfillment of a condition **2** : something given or held as a security ~ vb **-teed; -tee•ing 1** : promise to be responsible for **2** : state with certainty —**guar•an•tor** \ˌgarənˈtȯr\ n

guar•an•ty \ˈgarəntē\ n, pl **-ties 1** : promise to answer for another's failure to pay a debt **2** : guarantee **3** : pledge ~ vb **-tied; -ty•ing** : guarantee

guard \ˈgärd\ n **1** : defensive position **2** : act of protecting **3** : an individual or group that guards against danger **4** : protective or safety device ~ vb **1** : protect or watch over **2** : take pre-

cautions —**guard•house** n —**guard•room** n

guard•ian \ˈgärdēən\ n : one who has responsibility for the care of the person or property of another —**guard•ian•ship** n

gua•va \ˈgwävə\ n : shrubby tropical tree or its mildly acid fruit

gu•ber•na•to•ri•al \ˌgübənəˈtōrēəl, ˌgyü-\ adj : relating to a governor

guer•ril•la, gue•ril•la \gəˈrilə\ n : soldier engaged in small-scale harassing tactics

guess \ˈges\ vb **1** : form an opinion from little evidence **2** : state correctly solely by chance **3** : think or believe —**guess** n

guest \ˈgest\ n **1** : person to whom hospitality (as of a house) is extended **2** : patron of a commercial establishment (as a hotel) **3** : person not a regular cast member who appears on a program

guf•faw \gəˈfȯ, ˈgəf,ȯ\ n : loud burst of laughter —**guf•faw** \gəˈfȯ\ vb

guide \ˈgīd\ n **1** : one that leads or gives direction to another **2** : device on a machine to direct motion ~ vb **guid•ed; guid•ing 1** : show the way to **2** : direct —**guid•able** adj —**guid•ance** \ˈgīdᵊns\ n —**guide•book** n

guide•line \-,līn\ n : summary of procedures regarding policy or conduct

guild \ˈgild\ n : association

guile \ˈgīl\ n : craftiness —**guile•ful** adj —**guile•less** adj —**guile•less•ness** n

guil•lo•tine \ˈgilə,tēn; ˌgēyəˈtēn, ˈgēyə,-\ n : machine for beheading persons —**guillotine** vb

guilt \ˈgilt\ n **1** : fact of having committed an offense **2** : feeling of responsibility for offenses —**guilt•i•ly** adv —**guilt•i•ness** n —**guilty** \ˈgiltē\ adj

guin•ea \ˈginē\ n **1** : old gold coin of United Kingdom **2** : 21 shillings

guinea pig n : small So. American rodent

guise \ˈgīz\ n : external appearance

gui•tar \gəˈtär, gi-\ n : 6-stringed musical instrument played by plucking

gulch \ˈgəlch\ n : ravine

gulf \ˈgəlf\ n **1** : extension of an ocean or a sea into the land **2** : wide gap

1gull \ˈgəl\ n : seabird with webbed feet

2gull vb : make a dupe of ~ n : dupe —**gull•ible** adj

gul•let \ˈgələt\ n : throat

gul•ly \ˈgəlē\ n, pl **-lies** : trench worn by running water

gulp \'gəlp\ vb : swallow hurriedly or greedily —**gulp** n

¹gum \'gəm\ n : tissue along the jaw at the base of the teeth

²gum n **1** : sticky plant substance **2** : gum usu. of sweetened chicle prepared for chewing —**gum·my** adj

gum·bo \'gəmbō\ n : thick soup

gum·drop n : gumlike candy

gump·tion \'gəmpshən\ n : initiative

gun \'gən\ n **1** : cannon **2** : portable firearm **3** : discharge of a gun **4** : something like a gun ~ vb **-nn-** : hunt with a gun —**gun·fight** n — **gun·fight·er** n —**gun·fire** n —**gun·man** \-mən\ n —**gun·pow·der** n — **gun·shot** n —**gun·smith** n

gun·boat n : small armed ship

gun·ner \'gənər\ n : person who uses a gun

gun·nery sergeant \'gənərē-\ n : noncommissioned officer in the marine corps ranking next below a first sergeant

gun·ny·sack \'gənē,sak\ n : burlap sack

gun·sling·er \'gən,slinər\ n : skilled gunman in the old West

gun·wale \'gənᵊl\ n : upper edge of a boat's side

gup·py \'gəpē\ n, pl **-pies** : tiny tropical fish

gur·gle \'gərgəl\ vb **-gled; -gling** : make a sound like that of a flowing and gently splashing liquid —**gurgle** n

gu·ru \'gü,rü\ n, pl **-rus 1** : personal religious teacher in Hinduism **2** : expert

gush \'gəsh\ vb : pour forth violently or enthusiastically —**gush·er** \'gəshər\ n

gushy \-ē\ adj **gush·i·er; -est** : effusively sentimental

gust \'gəst\ n **1** : sudden brief rush of wind **2** : sudden outburst —**gust** vb —**gusty** adj

gus·ta·to·ry \'gəstə,tōrē\ adj : relating to the sense of taste

gus·to \'gəstō\ n : zest

gut \'gət\ n **1** pl : intestines **2** : digestive canal **3** pl : courage ~ vb **-tt-** : eviscerate

gut·ter \'gətər\ n : channel for carrying off rainwater

gut·tur·al \'gətərəl\ adj : sounded in the throat —**guttural** n

¹guy \'gī\ n : rope, chain, or rod attached to something to steady it —**guy** vb

²guy n : person

guz·zle \'gəzəl\ vb **-zled; -zling** : drink greedily

gym \'jim\ n : gymnasium

gym·na·si·um \jim'nāzēəm, -zhəm\ n, pl **-si·ums** or **-sia** \-zēə, -zhə\ : place for indoor sports

gym·nas·tics \jim'nastiks\ n : physical exercises performed in a gymnasium —**gym·nast** \'jim,nast\ n —**gym·nas·tic** adj

gy·ne·col·o·gy \,gīnə'käləjē, ,jin-\ n : branch of medicine dealing with the diseases of women —**gy·ne·co·log·ic** \-ikə'läjik\, **gy·ne·co·log·i·cal** \-ikəl\ adj —**gy·ne·col·o·gist** \-ə'käləjist\ n

gyp \'jip\ n **1** : cheat **2** : trickery —**gyp** vb

gyp·sum \'jipsəm\ n : calcium-containing mineral

gy·rate \'jī,rāt\ vb **-rat·ed; -rat·ing** : revolve around a center —**gy·ra·tion** \jī'rāshən\ n

gy·ro·scope \'jīrō,skōp\ n : wheel mounted to spin rapidly about an axis that is free to turn in various directions

H

h \'āch\ n, pl **h's** or **hs** \'āchəz\ : 8th letter of the alphabet

hab·er·dash·er \'habər,dashər\ n : men's clothier —**hab·er·dash·ery** \-ərē\ n

hab·it \'habət\ n **1** : monk's or nun's clothing **2** : usual behavior **3** : addiction —**hab·it-form·ing** adj

hab·it·able \-əbəl\ adj : capable of being lived in

hab·i·tat \'habə,tat\ n : place where a plant or animal naturally occurs

hab·i·ta·tion \,habə'tāshən\ n **1** : occupancy **2** : dwelling place

ha·bit·u·al \hə'bichəwəl\ adj **1** : commonly practiced or observed **2** : doing, practicing, or acting by habit —**ha·bit·u·al·ly** adv —**ha·bit·u·al·ness** n

ha·bit·u·ate \ha'bichə,wāt\ vb **-at·ed;** **-at·ing** : accustom

ha·ci·en·da \,häsē'endə\ n : ranch house

¹hack \'hak\ vb **1** : cut with repeated irregular blows **2** : cough in a short dry manner **3** : manage successfully —**hack** n —**hack·er** n

²hack n **1** : horse or vehicle for hire **2** : saddle horse **3** : writer for hire — **hack** adj —**hack·man** \-mən\ n

hack·le \'hakəl\ n **1** : long feather on the neck or back of a bird **2** pl : hairs that can be erected **3** pl : temper

hack·ney \-nē\ n, pl **-neys 1** : horse for riding or driving **2** : carriage for hire

hack·neyed \-nēd\ adj : trite

hack·saw n : saw for metal

had past of HAVE

had·dock \'hadək\ n, pl **haddock** : Atlantic food fish

Ha·des \'hādēz\ n **1** : mythological abode of the dead **2** : often not cap : hell

haft \'haft\ n : handle of a weapon or tool

hag \'hag\ n **1** : witch **2** : ugly old woman

hag·gard \'hagərd\ adj : worn or emaciated —**hag·gard·ly** adv

hag·gle \'hagəl\ vb **-gled; -gling** : argue in bargaining —**hag·gler** n

¹hail \'hāl\ n **1** : precipitation in small lumps of ice **2** : something like a rain of hail ~ vb : rain hail —**hail·stone** n —**hail·storm** n

²hail vb **1** : greet or salute **2** : summon ~ n : expression of greeting or praise —often used as an interjection

hair \'har\ n : threadlike growth from the skin —**hair·brush** n —**hair·cut** n —**hair·dress·er** n —**haired** adj —**hair·i·ness** n —**hair·less** adj —**hair·pin** n —**hair·style** n —**hair·styl·ing** n —**hair·styl·ist** n —**hairy** adj

hair·breadth \-,bredth\, **hairs·breadth** \'harz-\ n : tiny distance or margin

hair·do \-,dü\ n, pl **-dos** : style of wearing hair

hair·line n **1** : thin line **2** : outline of the hair on the head

hair·piece n : toupee

hair·rais·ing adj : causing terror or astonishment

hake \'hāk\ n : marine food fish

hal·cy·on \'halsēən\ adj : prosperous or most pleasant

¹hale \'hāl\ adj : healthy or robust

²hale vb **haled; hal·ing 1** : haul **2** : compel to go

half \'haf, 'háf\ n, pl **halves** \'havz, 'hávz\ : either of 2 equal parts ~ adj **1** : being a half or nearly a half **2** : partial —**half** adv

half brother n : brother related through one parent only

half·heart·ed \-'härtəd\ adj : without enthusiasm —**half·heart·ed·ly** adv —**half·heart·ed·ness** n

half–life n : time for half of something to undergo a process

half sister n : sister related through one parent only

half·way adj : midway between 2 points —**half·way** adv

half–wit \-,wit\ n : foolish person —**half–wit·ted** \-,witəd\ adj

hal·i·but \'haləbət\ n, pl **halibut** : large edible marine flatfish

hal·i·to·sis \,halə'tōsəs\ n : bad breath

hall \'hól\ n **1** : large public or college or university building **2** : lobby **3** : auditorium

hal·le·lu·jah \,halə'lüyə\ interj —used to express praise, joy, or thanks

hall·mark \'hól,märk\ n : distinguishing characteristic

hal·low \'halō\ vb : consecrate —**hal·lowed** \-ōd, -əwəd\ adj

Hal·low·een \,halə'wēn, ,häl-\ n : evening of October 31 observed esp. by children in merrymaking and masquerading

hal·lu·ci·na·tion \hə,lüs°n'āshən\ n : perception of objects that are not real —**hal·lu·ci·nate** \hə'lüs°n,āt\ vb —**hal·lu·ci·na·to·ry** \-'lüs°nə,tōrē\ adj

hal·lu·ci·no·gen \hə'lüs°nəjən\ n : substance that induces hallucinations —**hal·lu·ci·no·gen·ic** \-,lüs°nə'jenik\ adj

hall·way n : entrance hall

ha·lo \'hālō\ n, pl **-los** or **-loes** : circle of light appearing to surround a shining body

¹halt \'hólt\ adj : lame

²halt vb : stop or cause to stop —**halt** n

hal·ter \'hóltər\ n **1** : rope or strap for leading or tying an animal **2** : brief blouse held up by straps ~ vb : catch (an animal) with a halter

halt·ing \'hóltiŋ\ adj : uncertain —**halt·ing·ly** adv

halve \'hav, 'hav\ vb **halved; halv·ing 1** : divide into halves **2** : reduce to half

halves pl of HALF

ham \'ham\ n **1** : thigh—usu. pl. **2** : cut esp. of pork from the thigh **3** : showy actor **4** : amateur radio operator ~ vb **-mm-** : overlay a part —**ham** adj

ham·burg·er \'ham,bərgər\, **ham·burg** \-,bərg\ n : ground beef or a sandwich made with this

ham·let \'hamlət\ n : small village

ham·mer \'hamər\ n **1** : hand tool for pounding **2** : gun part whose striking explodes the charge ~ vb : beat, drive, or shape with a hammer —**hammer out** vb : produce with effort

ham·mer·head n **1** : striking part of a hammer **2** : shark with a hammerlike head

ham·mock \'hamək\ n : swinging bed hung by cords at each end

¹ham·per \'hampər\ vb : impede

²hamper n : large covered basket

ham·ster \'hamstər\ n : stocky short-tailed rodent

ham·string \'ham,striŋ\ vb **-strung** \-,strəŋ\; **-string·ing** \-,striŋiŋ\ **1** : cripple by cutting the leg tendons **2** : make ineffective or powerless

hand \'hand\ n **1** : end of a front limb adapted for grasping **2** : side **3** : promise of marriage **4** : handwriting **5** : assistance or participation **6** : applause **7** : cards held by a player **8** : worker ~ vb : lead, assist, give, or pass with the hand —**hand·clasp** n —**hand·craft** vb —**hand·ful** n —**hand·gun** n —**hand·less** adj —**hand·made** adj —**hand·rail** n —**hand·saw** n —**hand·wo·ven** adj —**hand·writ·ing** n —**hand·writ·ten** adj

hand·bag n : woman's purse

hand·ball n : game played by striking a ball with the hand

hand·bill n : printed advertisement or notice distributed by hand

hand·book n : concise reference book

hand·cuffs n pl : locking bracelets that bind the wrists together —**handcuff** vb

hand·i·cap \'handē,kap\ n **1** : advantage given or imposed to equalize a competition **2** : disadvantage —**handicap** vb —**hand·i·capped** adj —**hand·i·cap·per** n

hand·i·craft \'handē,kraft\ n **1** : manual skill **2** : article made by hand —

hand·i·craft·er n —**hand·i·crafts·man** \-,kraftsmən\ n

hand·i·work \-,wərk\ n : work done personally or by the hands

hand·ker·chief \'haŋkərchəf, -,chēf\ n, pl **-chiefs** \-chəfs, -,chēfs\ : small piece of cloth carried for personal use

han·dle \'hand³l\ n : part to be grasped ~ vb **-dled; -dling 1** : touch, hold, or manage with the hands **2** : deal with **3** : deal or trade in —**han·dle·bar** n —**han·dled** \-d³ld\ adj —**han·dler** \'handlər\ n

hand·maid·en n : female attendant

hand·out n : something given out

hand·pick vb : select personally

hand·shake n : clasping of hands (as in greeting)

hand·some \'hansəm\ adj **-som·er; -est 1** : sizable **2** : generous **3** : nice-looking —**hand·some·ly** adv —**hand·some·ness** n

hand·spring n : somersault on the hands

hand·stand n : a balancing upside down on the hands

handy \'handē\ adj **hand·i·er; -est 1** : conveniently near **2** : easily used **3** : dexterous —**hand·i·ly** adv —**hand·i·ness** n

handy·man \-,man\ n : one who does odd jobs

hang \'haŋ\ vb **hung** \'həŋ\ **hang·ing 1** : fasten or remain fastened to an elevated point without support from below **2** : suspend by the neck until dead—past tense often **hanged 3** : droop ~ n **1** : way a thing hangs **2** : an understanding of something —**hang·er** n —**hang·ing** n

han·gar \'haŋər\ n : airplane shelter

hang·dog \'haŋ,dóg\ adj : ashamed or guilty

hang·man \-mən\ n : public executioner

hang·nail n : loose skin near a fingernail

hang·out n : place where one likes to spend time

hang·over n : sick feeling following heavy drinking

hank \'haŋk\ n : coil or loop

han·ker \'haŋkər\ vb : desire strongly —**han·ker·ing** n

han·ky-pan·ky \,haŋkē'paŋkē\ n : questionable or underhanded activity

han·som \'hansəm\ n : 2-wheeled covered carriage

Ha·nuk·kah \'känəkə, 'hän-\ n : 8-day Jewish holiday commemorating the rededication of the Temple of Jerusalem after its defilement by Antiochus of Syria

hap·haz·ard \hap'hazǝrd\ adj : having no plan or order —**hap·haz·ard·ly** adv

hap·less \'haplǝs\ adj : unfortunate — **hap·less·ly** adv —**hap·less·ness** n

hap·pen \'hapǝn\ vb 1 : take place 2 : be fortunate to encounter something unexpectedly —often used with infinitive

hap·pen·ing \-ǝniŋ\ n : occurrence

hap·py \'hapē\ adj -**pi·er; -est** 1 : fortunate 2 : content, pleased, or joyous —**hap·pi·ly** \'hapǝlē\ adv —**hap·pi·ness** n

ha·rangue \hǝ'raŋ\ n : ranting or scolding speech —**harangue** vb —**ha·rangu·er** \-'raŋǝr\ n

ha·rass \hǝ'ras, 'harǝs\ vb 1 : disturb and impede by repeated raids 2 : annoy continually —**ha·rass·ment** n

har·bin·ger \'härbǝnjǝr\ n : one that announces or foreshadows what is coming

har·bor \-bǝr\ n : protected body of water suitable for anchorage ~ vb 1 : give refuge to 2 : hold as a thought or feeling

hard \'härd\ adj 1 : not easily penetrated 2 : firm or definite 3 : close or searching 4 : severe or unfeeling 5 : strenuous or difficult 6 : physically strong or intense —**hard** adv —**hard·ness** n

hard·en \'härdᵊn\ vb : make or become hard or harder —**hard·en·er** n

hard·head·ed \,härd'hedǝd\ adj 1 : stubborn 2 : realistic —**hard·head·ed·ly** adv —**hard·head·ed·ness** n

hard·heart·ed \-'härtǝd\ adj : lacking sympathy —**hard·heart·ed·ly** adv —**hard·heart·ed·ness** n

hard·ly \'härdlē\ adv 1 : only just 2 : certainly not

hard·nosed \-,nōzd\ adj : tough or uncompromising

hard·ship \-,ship\ n : suffering or privation

hard·tack \-,tak\ n : hard biscuit

hard·ware n 1 : cutlery or tools made of metal 2 : physical components of a vehicle or apparatus

hard·wood n : wood of a broad-leaved usu. deciduous tree —**hardwood** adj

har·dy \'härdē\ adj -**di·er; -est** : able to

withstand adverse conditions —**har·di·ly** adv —**har·di·ness** n

hare \'har\ n, pl **hare** or **hares** : long-eared mammal related to the rabbit

hare·brained \-,brānd\ adj : foolish

hare·lip n : deformity in which the upper lip is vertically split —**hare·lipped** \-,lipt\ adj

ha·rem \'harǝm\ n : house or part of a house allotted to women in a Muslim household or the women and servants occupying it

hark \'härk\ vb : listen

har·le·quin \'härlikǝn, -kwǝn\ n : clown

har·lot \'härlǝt\ n : prostitute

harm \'härm\ n 1 : physical or mental damage 2 : mischief ~ vb : cause harm —**harm·ful** \-fǝl\ adj —**harm·ful·ly** adv —**harm·ful·ness** n —**harm·less** adj —**harm·less·ly** adv —**harm·less·ness** n

har·mon·ic \här'mänik\ adj 1 : of or relating to musical harmony 2 : pleasing to hear —**har·mon·i·cal·ly** \-iklē\ adv

har·mon·i·ca \här'mänikǝ\ n : small wind instrument with metallic reeds

har·mo·ny \'härmǝnē\ n, pl -**nies** 1 : musical combination of sounds 2 : pleasing arrangement of parts 3 : lack of conflict 4 : internal calm —**har·mo·ni·ous** \här'mōnēǝs\ adj —**har·mo·ni·ous·ly** adv —**har·mo·ni·ous·ness** n —**har·mo·ni·za·tion** \,härmǝnǝ'zāshǝn\ n —**har·mo·nize** \'härmǝ,nīz\ vb

har·ness \'härnǝs\ n : gear of a draft animal ~ vb 1 : put a harness on 2 : put to use

harp \'härp\ n : musical instrument with many strings plucked by the fingers ~ vb 1 : play on a harp 2 : dwell on a subject tiresomely —**harp·er** n —**harp·ist** n

har·poon \här'pün\ n : barbed spear used in hunting whales —**harpoon** vb —**har·poon·er** n

harp·si·chord \'härpsi,kȯrd\ n : keyboard instrument with strings that are plucked

har·py \'härpē\ n, pl -**pies** : shrewish woman

har·row \'harō\ n : implement used to break up soil ~ vb 1 : cultivate with a harrow 2 : distress

har·ry \'harē\ vb -**ried; -ry·ing** : torment by or as if by constant attack

harsh \'härsh\ adj 1 : disagreeably

rough 2 : severe —**harsh•ly** adv — **harsh•ness** n

har•um-scar•um \,harəm'skarəm\ adv : recklessly

har•vest \'härvəst\ n 1 : act or time of gathering in a crop 2 : mature crop —**harvest** vb —**har•vest•er** n

has pres 3d sing of HAVE

hash \'hash\ vb : chop into small pieces ~ n : chopped meat mixed with potatoes and browned

hasp \'hasp\ n : hinged strap fastener esp. for a door

has•sle \'hasəl\ n 1 : quarrel 2 : struggle 3 : cause of annoyance —**hassle** vb

has•sock \'hasək\ n : cushion used as a seat or leg rest

haste \'hāst\ n 1 : rapidity of motion 2 : rash action 3 : excessive eagerness —**hast•i•ly** \'hāstəlē\ adv —**hast•i•ness** \-stēnəs\ n —**hasty** \-stē\ adj

has•ten \'hāsᵊn\ vb : hurry

hat \'hat\ n : covering for the head

¹hatch \'hach\ n : small door or opening —**hatch•way** n

²hatch vb : emerge from an egg —**hatch•ery** \-ərē\ n

hatch•et \'hachət\ n : short-handled ax

hate \'hāt\ n 1 : intense hostility and aversion ~ vb **hat•ed; hat•ing** 1 : express or feel hate 2 : dislike —**hate•ful** \-fəl\ adj —**hate•ful•ly** adv —**hate•ful•ness** n —**hat•er** n

ha•tred \'hātrəd\ n : hate

hat•ter \'hatər\ n : one that makes or sells hats

haugh•ty \'hótē\ adj **-ti•er; -est** : disdainfully proud —**haugh•ti•ly** adv —**haugh•ti•ness** n

haul \'hól\ vb 1 : draw or pull 2 : transport or carry ~ n 1 : amount collected 2 : load or the distance it is transported —**haul•er** n

haunch \'hónch\ n : hip or hindquarter —usu. pl.

haunt \'hónt\ vb 1 : visit often 2 : visit or inhabit as a ghost ~ n : place frequented —**haunt•er** n —**haunt•ing•ly** adv

have \'hav, in sense 2 before "to" usu 'haf\ vb **had** \'had\; **hav•ing** \'haviŋ\; **has** \'haz, in sense 2 before "to" usu 'has\ 1 : hold in possession, service, or affection 2 : be compelled or forced to 3 —used as an auxiliary with the past participle to form the present perfect, past perfect, or future perfect 4 : obtain or receive 5 : un-

dergo 6 : cause to 7 : bear —**have to do with** : have in the way of connection or relation with or effect on

ha•ven \'hāvən\ n : place of safety

hav•oc \'havək\ n 1 : wide destruction 2 : great confusion

¹hawk \'hók\ n : bird of prey with a strong hooked bill and sharp talons

²hawk vb : offer for sale by calling out in the street —**hawk•er** n

haw•ser \'hózər\ n : large rope

haw•thorn \'hó,thórn\ n : spiny shrub or tree with pink or white fragrant flowers

hay \'hā\ n : herbs (as grass) cut and dried for use as fodder —**hay** vb —**hay•loft** n —**hay•mow** \-,maú\ n —**hay•stack** n

hay•cock \'hā,käk\ n : small pile of hay

hay•rick \-,rik\ n : large outdoor stack of hay

hay•seed \'hā,sēd\ n : bumpkin

hay•wire adj : being out of order

¹haze \'hāz\ n : fine dust, smoke, or light vapor in the air that reduces visibility

²haze vb **hazed; haz•ing** : harass by abusive and humiliating tricks

ha•zel \'hāzəl\ n 1 : shrub or small tree bearing edible nuts (**ha•zel•nuts**) 2 : light brown color

hazy \'hāzē\ adj **haz•i•er; -est** 1 : obscured by haze 2 : vague or indefinite —**haz•i•ly** adv —**haz•i•ness** n

he \'hē\ pron 1 : that male one 2 : a or the person

head \'hed\ n 1 : front or upper part of the body 2 : mind 3 : upper or higher end 4 : director or leader 5 : place of leadership or honor ~ adj : principal or chief ~ vb 1 : provide with or form a head 2 : put, stand, or be at the head 3 : point or proceed in a certain direction —**head•ache** n —**head•band** n —**head•dress** n —**head•ed** adj —**head•first** adv or adj —**head•gear** n —**head•less** adj —**head•rest** n —**head•ship** n —**head•wait•er** n

head•ing \-iŋ\ n 1 : direction in which a plane or ship heads 2 : something (as a title) standing at the top or beginning

head•land \'hedlənd, -,land\ n : promontory

head·light n : light on the front of a vehicle

head·line n : introductory line of a newspaper story printed in large type

head·long \-'lȯŋ\ adv 1 : head foremost 2 : in a rash or reckless manner — **head·long** \-,lȯŋ\ adj

head·mas·ter n : man who is head of a private school

head·mis·tress n : woman who is head of a private school

head-on adj : having the front facing in the direction of initial contact — **head-on** adv

head·phone n : an earphone held on by a band over the head—usu. pl.

head·quar·ters n sing or pl : command or administrative center

head·stone n : stone at the head of a grave

head·strong adj : stubborn or willful

head·wa·ters n pl : source of a stream

head·way n : forward motion

heady \'hedē\ adj **head·i·er; -est** 1 : intoxicating 2 : shrewd

heal \'hēl\ vb : make or become sound or whole —**heal·er** n

health \'helth\ n : sound physical or mental condition

health·ful \-fəl\ adj : beneficial to health —**health·ful·ly** adv —**health·ful·ness** n

healthy \'helthē\ adj **health·i·er; -est** : enjoying or typical of good health —**health·i·ly** adv —**health·i·ness** n

heap \'hēp\ n : pile ~ vb : throw or lay in a heap

hear \'hir\ vb **heard** \'hǝrd\; **hear·ing** \'hiriŋ\ 1 : perceive by the ear 2 : heed 3 : learn

hear·ing n 1 : process or power of perceiving sound 2 : earshot 3 : session in which witnesses are heard

hear·ken \'härkǝn\ vb : give attention

hear·say n : rumor

hearse \'hǝrs\ n : vehicle for carrying the dead to the grave

heart \'härt\ n 1 : hollow muscular organ that keeps up the circulation of the blood 2 : playing card of a suit marked with a red heart 3 : whole personality or the emotional or moral part of it 4 : courage 5 : essential part —**heart·beat** n —**heart·ed** adj

heart·ache n : anguish of mind

heart·break n : crushing grief —**heart·break·er** n —**heart·break·ing** adj —**heart·bro·ken** adj

heart·burn n : burning distress in the heart area after eating

heart·en \'härtᵊn\ vb : encourage

hearth \'härth\ n 1 : area in front of a fireplace 2 : home —**hearth·stone** n

heart·less \'härtləs\ adj : cruel

heart·rend·ing \-,rendiŋ\ adj : causing intense grief or anguish

heart·sick adj : very despondent —**heart·sick·ness** n

heart·strings n pl : deepest emotions

heart·throb n : sweetheart

heart·warm·ing adj : inspiring sympathetic feeling

heart·wood n : central portion of wood

hearty \'härtē\ adj **heart·i·er; -est** 1 : vigorously healthy 2 : nourishing —**heart·i·ly** adv —**heart·i·ness** n

heat \'hēt\ vb : make or become warm or hot ~ n 1 : condition of being hot 2 : form of energy that causes a body to rise in temperature 3 : intensity of feeling —**heat·ed·ly** adv —**heat·er** n

heath \'hēth\ n 1 : often evergreen shrubby plant of wet acid soils 2 : tract of wasteland —**heathy** adj

hea·then \'hēthǝn\ n, pl **-thens** or **-then** : uncivilized or godless person —**heathen** adj

heath·er \'hethǝr\ n : evergreen heath with lavender flowers —**heath·ery** adj

heat·stroke n : disorder that follows prolonged exposure to excessive heat

heave \'hēv\ vb **heaved** or **hove** \'hōv\; **heav·ing** 1 : rise or lift upward 2 : throw 3 : rise and fall ~ n 1 : an effort to lift or raise 2 : throw

heav·en \'hevǝn\ n 1 pl : sky 2 : abode of the Deity and of the blessed dead 3 : place of supreme happiness —**heav·en·ly** adj —**heav·en·ward** adv or adj

heavy \'hevē\ adj **heav·i·er; -est** 1 : having great weight 2 : hard to bear 3 : greater than the average —**heav·i·ly** adv —**heav·i·ness** n —**heavy·weight** n

heavy-duty adj : able to withstand unusual strain

heavy·set adj : stocky and compact in build

heck·le \'hekǝl\ vb **-led; -ling** : harass with gibes —**heck·ler** \'heklǝr\ n

hec·tic \'hektik\ adj : filled with excitement, activity, or confusion —**hec·ti·cal·ly** \-tiklē\ adv

hedge \'hej\ n 1 : fence or boundary of

shrubs or small trees **2** : means of protection ~ *vb* **hedged; hedg·ing 1** : protect oneself against loss **2** : evade the risk of commitment —**hedg·er** *n*

hedge·hog *n* : spiny mammal (as a porcupine)

he·do·nism \'hēd³n,izəm\ *n* : way of life devoted to pleasure —**he·do·nist** \-³nist\ *n* —**he·do·nis·tic** \,hēd-³n'istik\ *adj*

heed \'hēd\ *vb* : pay attention ~ *n* : attention —**heed·ful** \-fəl\ *adj* —**heed·ful·ly** *adv* —**heed·ful·ness** *n* —**heed·less** *adj* —**heed·less·ly** *adv* —**heed·less·ness** *n*

¹heel \'hēl\ *n* **1** : back of the foot **2** : crusty end of a loaf of bread **3** : solid piece forming the back of the sole of a shoe —**heel·less** \'hēlləs\ *adj*

²heel *vb* : tilt to one side

heft \'heft\ *n* : weight ~ *vb* : judge the weight of by lifting

hefty \'heftē\ *adj* **heft·i·er; -est** : big and bulky

he·ge·mo·ny \hi'jemənē\ *n* : preponderant influence over others

heif·er \'hefər\ *n* : young cow

height \'hīt, 'hītth\ *n* **1** : highest part or point **2** : distance from bottom to top **3** : altitude

height·en \'hīt³n\ *vb* : increase in amount or degree

hei·nous \'hānəs\ *adj* : shockingly evil —**hei·nous·ly** *adv* —**hei·nous·ness** *n*

heir \'ar\ *n* : one who inherits or is entitled to inherit property

heir·ess \'arəs\ *n* : female heir esp. to great wealth

heir·loom \'ar,lüm\ *n* : something handed on from one generation to another

held *past of* HOLD

he·li·cal \'helikəl, 'hē-\ *adj* : spiral

he·li·cop·ter \'helə,käptər, 'hē-\ *n* : aircraft supported in the air by rotors

he·lio·trope \'hēlyə,trōp\ *n* : garden herb with small fragrant white or purple flowers

he·li·um \'hēlēəm\ *n* : very light nonflammable gaseous chemical element

he·lix \'hēliks\ *n, pl* -**li·ces** \'helə,sēz, 'hē-\ : something spiral

hell \'hel\ *n* **1** : nether world in which the dead continue to exist **2** : realm of the devil **3** : place or state of torment or destruction —**hell·ish** *adj*

hell·gram·mite \'helgrə,mīt\ *n* : aquatic insect larva

hel·lion \'helyən\ *n* : troublesome person

hel·lo \hə'lō, he-\ *n, pl* -**los** : expression of greeting

helm \'helm\ *n* : lever or wheel for steering a ship —**helms·man** \'helmzmən\ *n*

hel·met \'helmət\ *n* : protective covering for the head

help \'help\ *vb* **1** : supply what is needed **2** : be of use **3** : refrain from or prevent ~ *n* **1** : something that helps or a source of help **2** : one who helps another —**help·er** *n* —**help·ful** \-fəl\ *adj* —**help·ful·ly** *adv* —**help·ful·ness** *n* —**help·less** *adj* —**help·less·ly** *adv* —**help·less·ness** *n*

help·ing \'helpiŋ\ *n* : portion of food

help·mate *n* **1** : helper **2** : wife

help·meet \-,mēt\ *n* : helpmate

hel·ter-skel·ter \,heltər'skeltər\ *adv* : in total disorder

hem \'hem\ *n* **1** : border of an article of cloth doubled back and stitched down ~ *vb* -**mm- 1** : sew a hem **2** : surround restrictively —**hem·line** *n*

he·ma·tol·o·gy \,hēmə'täləjē\ *n* : study of the blood and blood-forming organs —**hema·to·log·ic** \-mət³l'äjik\ *adj* —**he·ma·tol·o·gist** \-'täləjist\ *n*

hemi·sphere \'hemə,sfir\ *n* : one of the halves of the earth divided by the equator into northern and southern parts (**northern hemisphere, southern hemisphere**) or by a meridian into eastern and western parts (**eastern hemisphere, western hemisphere**) —**hemi·spher·ic** \,hemə-'sfirik, -'sfer-\, **hemi·spher·i·cal** \-'sfirikəl, -'sfer-\ *adj*

hem·lock \'hem,läk\ *n* **1** : poisonous herb related to the carrot **2** : evergreen tree related to the pines

he·mo·glo·bin \'hēmə,glōbən\ *n* : iron-containing compound found in red blood cells

he·mo·phil·ia \,hēmə'filēə\ *n* : hereditary tendency to severe prolonged bleeding —**he·mo·phil·i·ac** \-ē,ak\ *adj or n*

hem·or·rhage \'hemərij\ *n* : large discharge of blood —**hemorrhage** *vb* —**hem·or·rhag·ic** \,hemə'rajik\ *adj*

hem·or·rhoids \'hemə,roidz\ *n pl* : swollen mass of dilated veins at or just within the anus

hemp \'hemp\ *n* : tall Asian herb grown

for its tough fiber **—hemp·en** \'hem'pən\ adj

hen \'hen\ n : female domestic fowl

hence \'hens\ adv 1 : away 2 : therefore 3 : from this source or origin

hence·forth adv : from this point on

hence·for·ward adv : henceforth

hench·man \'henchmən\ n : trusted follower

hen·na \'henə\ n : reddish brown dye from a tropical shrub used esp. on hair

hen·peck \'hen,pek\ vb : subject (one's husband) to persistent nagging

he·pat·ic \hi'patik\ adj : relating to or resembling the liver

hep·a·ti·tis \,hepə'tītəs\ n, pl **-tit·i·des** \-'titə,dēz\ : disease in which the liver becomes inflamed

her \'hər\ adj : of or relating to her or herself ~ \ər, ('hər\ pron, objective case of SHE

her·ald \'herəld\ n 1 : official crier or messenger 2 : harbinger ~ vb : give notice

her·ald·ry \'herəldrē\ n, pl **-ries** : practice of devising and granting stylized emblems (as for a family) **—he·ral·dic** \he'raldik, hə-\ adj

herb \'ərb, 'hərb\ n 1 : seed plant that lacks woody tissue 2 : plant or plant part valued for medicinal or savory qualities **—her·ba·ceous** \,ər'bāshəs, ,hər-\ adj **—herb·age** \'ərbij, 'hər-\ n **—herb·al** \-bəl\ n or adj **—herb·al·ist** \-bəlist\ n

her·bi·cide \'ərbə,sīd, 'hər-\ n : agent that destroys plants **—her·bi·cid·al** \,ərbə'sīdᵊl, ,hər-\ adj

her·biv·o·rous \,ər'bivərəs, ,hər-\ adj : feeding on plants **—her·bi·vore** \'ərbə,vōr, 'hər-\ n

her·cu·le·an \,hərkyə'lēən, ,hər'kyü-lēən\ adj : of extraordinary power, size, or difficulty

herd \'hərd\ n : group of animals of one kind ~ vb : assemble or move in a herd **—herd·er** n **—herds·man** \'hərdzmən\ n

here \'hir\ adv 1 : in, at, or to this place 2 : now 3 : at or in this point or particular 4 : in the present life or state ~ n : this place **—here·abouts** \'hirə,baùts\, **here·about** \-,baùt\ adv

here·af·ter adv : in some future time or state ~ n : existence beyond earthly life

here·by adv : by means of this

he·red·i·tary \hə'redə,terē\ adj 1 : genetically passed or passable from parent to offspring 2 : passing by inheritance

he·red·i·ty \-ətē\ n : the passing of characteristics from parent to offspring

here·in adv : in this

here·of adv : of this

here·on adv : on this

her·e·sy \'herəsē\ n, pl **-sies** : opinion or doctrine contrary to church dogma **—her·e·tic** \-,tik\ n **—he·ret·i·cal** \hə'retikəl\ adj

here·to adv : to this document

here·to·fore \'hirtü,fōr\ adv : up to this time

here·un·der adv : under this

here·un·to adv : to this

here·upon adv : on this

here·with adv 1 : with this 2 : hereby

her·i·tage \'herətij\ n 1 : inheritance 2 : birthright

her·maph·ro·dite \hər'mafrə,dīt\ n : animal or plant having both male and female reproductive organs **—her·maphrodite** adj **—her·maph·ro·dit·ic** \-,mafrə'ditik\ adj

her·met·ic \hər'metik\ adj : sealed airtight **—her·met·i·cal·ly** \-iklē\ adv

her·mit \'hərmət\ n : one who lives in solitude

her·nia \'hərnēə\ n, pl **-ni·as** or **-ni·ae** \-nē,ē, -nē,ī\ : protrusion of a bodily part through the weakened wall of its enclosure **—her·ni·ate** \-nē,āt\ vb

he·ro \'hērō, 'hirō\ n, pl **-roes** : one that is much admired or shows great courage **—he·ro·ic** \hi'rōik\ adj **—he·ro·i·cal·ly** \-iklē\ adv **—he·ro·ics** \-iks\ n pl **—he·ro·ism** \'herə,wizəm\ n

her·o·in \'herəwən\ n : strongly addictive narcotic

her·o·ine \'herəwən\ n : woman of heroic achievements or qualities

her·on \'herən\ n : long-legged long-billed wading bird

her·pes \'hərpēz\ n : virus disease characterized by the formation of blisters

her·pe·tol·o·gy \,hərpə'täləjē\ n : study of reptiles and amphibians **—her·pe·tol·o·gist** \-pə'täləjist\ n

her·ring \'heriŋ\ n, pl **-ring** or **-rings** : narrow-bodied Atlantic food fish

hers \'hərz\ pron : one or the ones belonging to her

her·self \hər'self\ pron : she, her —used reflexively or for emphasis

hertz \'herts, 'hərts\ n, pl **hertz** : unit of

frequency equal to one cycle per second

hes·i·tant \'hezətənt\ *adj* : tending to hesitate —**hes·i·tance** \-təns\ *n* —**hes·i·tan·cy** \-tənsē\ *n* —**hes·i·tant·ly** *adv*

hes·i·tate \'hezə,tāt\ *vb* -**tat·ed; -tat·ing 1** : hold back esp. in doubt **2** : pause —**hes·i·ta·tion** \,hezə'tāshən\ *n*

het·er·o·ge·neous \,hetərə'jēnēəs, -nyəs\ *adj* : consisting of dissimilar ingredients or constituents —**het·er·o·ge·ne·i·ty** \-jə'nēətē\ *n* —**het·er·o·ge·neous·ly** *adv*

het·er·o·sex·u·al \,hetərō'sekshəwəl\ *adj* : oriented toward the opposite sex — **heterosexual** *n* —**het·er·o·sex·u·al·i·ty** \-,seksha'walətē\ *n*

hew \'hyü\ *vb* **hewed; hewed** *or* **hewn** \'hyün\; **hew·ing 1** : cut or shape with or as if with an ax **2** : conform strictly —**hew·er** *n*

hex \'heks\ *vb* : put an evil spell on — **hex** *n*

hexa·gon \'heksə,gän\ *n* : 6-sided polygon —**hex·ag·o·nal** \hek'sagənᵊl\ *adj*

hey·day \'hā,dā\ *n* : time of flourishing

hi·a·tus \hī'ātəs\ *n* : lapse in continuity

hi·ba·chi \hi'bächē\ *n* : brazier

hi·ber·nate \'hībər,nāt\ *vb* -**nat·ed; -nat·ing** : pass the winter in a torpid or resting state —**hi·ber·na·tion** \,hībər'nāshən\ *n* —**hi·ber·na·tor** \'hībər,nātər\ *n*

hic·cup \'hikəp\ *vb* : -**cuped; -cup·ing** : to inhale spasmodically and make a peculiar sound ~ *n pl* : attack of hiccuping

hick \'hik\ *n* : awkward provincial person —**hick** *adj*

hick·o·ry \'hikərē\ *n, pl* -**ries** : No. American hardwood tree —**hickory** *adj*

¹hide \'hīd\ *vb* **hid** \'hid\; **hid·den** \'hidᵊn\ *or* **hid; hid·ing** : put or remain out of sight —**hid·er** *n*

²hide *n* : animal skin

hide·bound \'hīd,baùnd\ *adj* : inflexible or conservative

hid·eous \'hidēəs\ *adj* : very ugly — **hid·eous·ly** *adv* —**hid·eous·ness** *n*

hie \'hī\ *vb* **hied; hy·ing** *or* **hie·ing** : hurry

hi·er·ar·chy \'hīə,rärkē\ *n, pl* -**chies** : persons or things arranged in a graded series —**hi·er·ar·chi·cal** \,hīə'rärkikəl\ *adj*

hi·er·o·glyph·ic \,hīərə'glifik\ *n* : char-

acter in the picture writing of the ancient Egyptians

high \'hī\ *adj* **1** : having large extension upward **2** : elevated in pitch **3** : exalted in character **4** : of greater degree or amount than average **5** : expensive **6** : excited or stupefied by alcohol or a drug ~ *adv* : at or to a high place or degree ~ *n* **1** : elevated point or level **2** : automobile gear giving the highest speed —**highly** *adv*

high·boy *n* : high chest of drawers on legs

high·brow \-,braù\ *n* : person of superior learning or culture —**highbrow** *adj*

high-flown *adj* : pretentious

high-hand·ed *adj* : willful and arrogant —**high-hand·ed·ly** *adv* —**high-hand·ed·ness** *n*

high·land \'hīland\ *n* : hilly country — **high·land·er** \-ləndər\ *n*

high·light *n* : event or detail of major importance ~ *vb* **1** : emphasize **2** : be a highlight of

high·ness \-nəs\ *n* **1** : quality or degree of being high **2** —used as a title (as for kings)

high-rise *adj* : having several stories

high school *n* : school usu. including grades 9 to 12 or 10 to 12

high-spir·it·ed *adj* : lively

high-strung \'hī'strəŋ\ *adj* : very nervous or sensitive

high·way *n* : public road

high·way·man \-mən\ *n* : one who robs travelers on a road

hi·jack \'hī,jak\ *vb* : steal esp. by commandeering a vehicle —**hijack** *n* — **hi·jack·er** *n*

hike \'hīk\ *vb* **hiked; hik·ing 1** : raise quickly **2** : take a long walk ~ *n* **1** : long walk **2** : increase —**hik·er** *n*

hi·lar·i·ous \hi'larēəs, hī'-\ *adj* : extremely funny —**hi·lar·i·ous·ly** *adv* —**hi·lar·i·ty** \-ətē\ *n*

hill \'hil\ *n* : place where the land rises —**hill·side** *n* —**hill·top** *n* —**hilly** *adj*

hill·bil·ly \'hil,bilē\ *n, pl* -**lies** : person from a backwoods area

hill·ock \'hilək\ *n* : small hill

hilt \'hilt\ *n* : handle of a sword

him \'him\ *pron, objective case of* HE

him·self \him'self\ *pron* : he, him — used reflexively or for emphasis

¹hind \'hīnd\ *n* : female deer

²hind *adj* : back

hin·der \'hindər\ *vb* : obstruct or hold back

hind·most *adj* : farthest to the rear

hind·quarter *n* : back half of a complete side of a carcass

hin·drance \'hindrəns\ *n* : something that hinders

hind·sight *n* : understanding of an event after it has happened

Hin·du·ism \'hindü,izəm\ *n* : body of religious beliefs and practices native to India —**Hin·du** *n or adj*

hinge \'hinj\ *n* : jointed piece on which a swinging part (as a door) turns ~ *vb* **hinged; hing·ing** 1 : attach by or furnish with hinges 2 : depend

hint \'hint\ *n* 1 : indirect suggestion 2 : clue 3 : very small amount —**hint** *vb*

hin·ter·land \'hintər,land\ *n* : remote region

hip \'hip\ *n* : part of the body on either side just below the waist —**hip·bone** *n*

hip·po·pot·a·mus \,hipə'pätəməs\ *n, pl* **-mus·es** *or* **-mi** \-,mī\ : large thick-skinned African river animal

hire \'hīr\ *n* 1 : payment for labor 2 : employment 3 : one who is hired ~ *vb* **hired; hir·ing** : employ for pay

hire·ling \-liŋ\ *n* : one who serves another only for gain

hir·sute \'hər,süt, 'hir-\ *adj* : hairy

his \'hiz\ *adj* : of or belonging to him ~ *pron* : ones belonging to him

hiss \'his\ *vb* 1 : make a sibilant sound 2 : show dislike by hissing —**hiss** *n*

his·to·ri·an \his'tōrēən\ *n* : writer of history

his·to·ry \'histərē\ *n, pl* **-ries** 1 : chronological record of significant events 2 : study of past events 3 : an established record —**his·tor·ic** \his-'tórik\, **his·tor·i·cal** \-ikəl\ *adj* —**his·tor·i·cal·ly** \-klē\ *adv*

his·tri·on·ics \,histrē'äniks\ *n pl* : exaggerated display of emotion

hit \'hit\ *vb* **hit; hit·ting** 1 : reach with a blow 2 : come or cause to come in contact 3 : affect detrimentally ~ *n* 1 : blow 2 : great success —**hit·ter** *n*

hitch \'hich\ *vb* 1 : move by jerks 2 : catch by a hook 3 : hitchhike ~ *n* 1 : jerk 2 : sudden halt

hitch·hike \'hich,hīk\ *vb* : travel by securing free rides from passing vehicles —**hitch·hik·er** *n*

hith·er \'hithər\ *adv* : to this place

hith·er·to \-,tü\ *adv* : up to this time

hive \'hīv\ *n* 1 : container housing honeybees 2 : colony of bees —**hive** *vb*

hives \'hīvz\ *n sing or pl* : allergic disorder with itchy skin patches

HMO \,āch,em'ō\ *n* : comprehensive health-care organization financed by clients

hoard \'hōrd\ *n* : hidden accumulation —**hoard** *vb* —**hoard·er** *n*

hoar·frost \'hōr,fróst\ *n* : frost

hoarse \'hōrs\ *adj* **hoars·er; -est** 1 : harsh in sound 2 : speaking in a harsh strained voice —**hoarse·ly** *adv* —**hoarse·ness** *n*

hoary \'hōrē\ *adj* **hoar·i·er; -est** : gray or white with age —**hoar·i·ness** *n*

hoax \'hōks\ *n* : act intended to trick or dupe —**hoax** *vb* —**hoax·er** *n*

hob·ble \'häbəl\ *vb* **-bled; -bling** : limp along ~ *n* : hobbling movement

hob·by \'häbē\ *n, pl* **-bies** : interest engaged in for relaxation —**hob·by·ist** \-ēist\ *n*

hob·gob·lin \'häb,gäblən\ *n* 1 : mischievous goblin 2 : bogey

hob·nail \-,nāl\ *n* : short nail for studding shoe soles —**hob·nailed** \-,nāld\ *adj*

hob·nob \-,näb\ *vb* **-bb-** : associate socially

ho·bo \'hōbō\ *n, pl* **-boes** : tramp

¹hock \'häk\ *n* : joint or region in the hind limb of a quadruped corresponding to the human ankle

²hock *n or vb* : pawn

hock·ey \'häkē\ *n* : game played on ice or a field by 2 teams

hod \'häd\ *n* : carrier for bricks or mortar

hodge·podge \'häj,päj\ *n* : heterogeneous mixture

hoe \'hō\ *n* : long-handled tool for cultivating or weeding —**hoe** *vb*

hog \'hóg, 'häg\ *n* 1 : domestic adult swine 2 : glutton ~ *vb* : take selfishly —**hog·gish** *adj*

hogs·head \'hógz,hed, 'hägz-\ *n* : large cask or barrel

hog·wash *n* : nonsense

hoist \'hóist\ *vb* : lift ~ *n* 1 : lift 2 : apparatus for hoisting

hok·ey \'hōkē\ *adj* **hok·i·er; -est** 1 : tiresomely simple or sentimental 2 : phony

¹hold \'hōld\ *vb* **held** \'held\; **hold·ing** 1 : possess 2 : restrain 3 : have a grasp on 4 : remain or keep in a particular situation or position **5** : contain **6** : regard **7** : cause to occur **8** : occupy esp. by appointment or election ~ *n* **1** : act or manner of holding **2** : restraining or controlling influence —**hold·er** *n* —**hold forth** : speak at length —**hold to** : adhere to —**hold with** : agree with

²hold *n* : cargo area of a ship

hold·ing \'hōldiŋ\ *n* : property owned — usu. pl.

hold·up *n* **1** : robbery at the point of a gun **2** : delay

hole \'hōl\ *n* **1** : opening into or through something **2** : hollow place (as a pit) **3** : den —**hole** *vb*

hol·i·day \'hälə,dā\ *n* **1** : day of freedom from work **2** : vacation —**holiday** *vb*

ho·li·ness \'hōlēnəs\ *n* : quality or state of being holy—used as a title for a high religious official

ho·lis·tic \hō'listik\ *adj* : relating to a whole (as the body)

hol·ler \'hälər\ *vb* : cry out —**holler** *n*

hol·low \'hälō\ *adj* **-low·er** **-əwər\; -est 1** : sunken **2** : having a cavity within **3** : sounding like a noise made in an empty place **4** : empty of value or meaning ~ *vb* : make or become hollow —*n* **1** : surface depression **2** : cavity —**hol·low·ness** *n*

hol·ly \'hälē\ *n, pl* **-lies** : evergreen tree or shrub with glossy leaves

hol·ly·hock \-,häk, -,hók\ *n* **1** : tall perennial herb with showy flowers

ho·lo·caust \'hälə,kóst, 'hō-, 'hó-\ *n* : thorough destruction esp. by fire

hol·stein \'hōl,stēn, -,stīn\ *n* : large black-and-white dairy cow

hol·ster \'hōlstər\ *n* : case for a pistol

ho·ly \'hōlē\ *adj* **-li·er; -est** : sacred **2** : spiritually pure

hom·age \'ämij, 'hä-\ *n* : reverent regard

home \'hōm\ *n* **1** : residence **2** : congenial environment **3** : place of origin or refuge ~ *vb* **homed; hom·ing** : go or return home —**home·bred** *adj* —**home·com·ing** *n* —**home·grown** *adj* —**home·land** \-,land\ *n* —**home·less** *adj* —**home·made** \-'mād\ *adj*

home·ly \-lē\ *adj* **-li·er; -est** : plain or unattractive —**home·li·ness** *n*

home·mak·er *n* : one who manages a household —**home·mak·ing** *n*

home·sick *adj* : longing for home — **home·sick·ness** *n*

home·spun \-,spən\ *adj* : simple

home·stead \-,sted\ *n* : home and land

occupied and worked by a family — **home·stead·er** \-ər\ *n*

home·stretch *n* **1** : last part of a racetrack **2** : final stage

home·ward \-wərd\, **home·wards** \-wərdz\ *adv* : toward home —**home·ward** *adj*

home·work *n* : school lessons to be done outside the classroom

hom·ey \'hōmē\ *adj* **hom·i·er; -est** : characteristic of home

ho·mi·cide \'hämə,sīd, 'hō-\ *n* : the killing of one human being by another — **hom·i·cid·al** \,hämə'sīd^əl, ,hō-\ *adj*

hom·i·ly \'häməlē\ *n, pl* **-lies** : sermon

hom·i·ny \'hämənē\ *n* : type of processed hulled corn

ho·mo·ge·neous \,hōmə'jēnēəs, -nyəs\ *adj* : of the same or a similar kind — **ho·mo·ge·ne·i·ty** \-jə'nēətē\ *n* —**ho·mo·ge·neous·ly** *adv*

ho·mog·e·nize \hō'mäjə,nīz, hə-\ *vb* **-nized; -niz·ing** : make the particles in (as milk) of uniform size and even distribution —**ho·mog·e·ni·za·tion** \-,mäjənə'zāshən\ *n* —**ho·mog·e·niz·er** *n*

ho·mo·graph \'hämə,graf, 'hō-\ *n* : one of 2 or more words (as the noun *conduct* and the verb *conduct*) spelled alike but different in origin or meaning or pronunciation

hom·onym \'hämə,nim, 'hō-\ *n* **1** : homophone **2** : homograph **3** : one of 2 or more words (as *pool* of water and *pool* the game) spelled and pronounced alike but different in meaning

ho·mo·phone \'hämə,fōn, 'hō-\ *n* : one of 2 or more words (as *to, too,* and *two*) pronounced alike but different in origin or meaning or spelling

Ho·mo sa·pi·ens \,hōmō'sapēənz, -'sā-\ *n* : humankind

ho·mo·sex·u·al \,hōmə'sekshəwəl\ *adj* : oriented toward one's own sex — **homosexual** *n* —**ho·mo·sex·u·al·i·ty** \-,sekshə'walətē\ *n*

hone \'hōn\ *vb* : sharpen with or as if with an abrasive stone

hon·est \'änəst\ *adj* **1** : free from deception **2** : trustworthy **3** : frank —**hon·est·ly** *adv* —**hon·esty** \-əstē\ *n*

hon·ey \'hənē\ *n, pl* **-eys** : sweet sticky substance made by bees (**hon·ey·bees**) from the nectar of flowers

hon·ey·comb *n* : mass of 6-sided wax

cells built by honeybees or something like it ~ *vb* : make or become full of holes like a honeycomb

hon·ey·moon \'hän-ē-\ *n* : holiday taken by a newly married couple —**honeymoon** *vb*

hon·ey·suck·le \-,səkəl\ *n* : shrub or vine with flowers rich in nectar

honk \'häŋk, 'hoŋk\ *n* : cry of a goose or a similar sound —**honk** *vb* — **honk·er** *n*

hon·or \'änər\ *n* **1** : good name **2** : outward respect or symbol of this **3** : privilege **4** : person of superior rank or position —used esp. as a title **5** : something or someone worthy of respect **6** : integrity ~ *vb* **1** : regard with honor **2** : confer honor on **3** : fulfill the terms of —**hon·or·able** \'änərəbəl\ *adj* —**hon·or·ably** \-blē\ *adv* —**hon·or·ar·i·ly** \,änə'rerəlē\ *adv* —**hon·or·ary** \'änə,rerē\ *adj* —**hon·or·ee** \,änə'rē\ *n*

hood \'hud\ *n* **1** : part of a garment that covers the head **2** : covering over an automobile engine compartment —**hood·ed** *adj*

-hood \,hud\ *n suffix* **1** : state, condition, or quality **2** : individuals sharing a state or character

hood·lum \'hudləm, 'hud-\ *n* : thug

hood·wink \'hud,wiŋk\ *vb* : deceive

hoof \'huf, 'huf\ *n, pl* **hooves** \'huvz, 'huvz\ *or* **hoofs** : horny covering of the toes of some mammals (as horses or cattle) —**hoofed** \'huft, 'huft\ *adj*

hook \'huk\ *n* : curved or bent device for catching, holding, or pulling ~ *vb* : seize or make fast with a hook —**hook·er** *n*

hook·worm *n* : parasitic intestinal worm

hoo·li·gan \'huligən\ *n* : thug

hoop \'hup\ *n* : circular strip, figure, or object

hoot \'hut\ *vb* **1** : shout in contempt **2** : make the cry of an owl —**hoot** *n* —**hoot·er** *n*

¹hop \'häp\ *vb* -**pp**- : move by quick springy leaps —**hop** *n*

²hop *n* : vine whose ripe dried flowers are used to flavor malt liquors

hope \'hop\ *vb* **hoped; hop·ing** : desire with expectation of fulfillment ~ *n* **1** : act of hoping **2** : something hoped for —**hope·ful** \-fəl\ *adj* —**hope·fully** *adv* —**hope·ful·ness** *n* —**hope·less** *adj* —**hope·less·ly** *adv* —**hope·less·ness** *n*

hop·per \'häpər\ *n* : container that releases its contents through the bottom

horde \'hord\ *n* : throng or swarm

ho·ri·zon \hə'rīzᵊn\ *n* : apparent junction of earth and sky

hor·i·zon·tal \,hórə'zäntᵊl\ *adj* : parallel to the horizon —**hor·i·zon·tal·ly** *adv*

hor·mone \'hór,mōn\ *n* : cell product in body fluids that has a specific effect on other cells —**hor·mon·al** \hór-'mōnᵊl\ *adj*

horn \'hórn\ *n* **1** : hard bony projection on the head of a hoofed animal **2** : brass wind instrument —**horned** *adj* —**horn·less** *adj*

hor·net \'hórnət\ *n* : large social wasp

horny \'hórnē\ *adj* **horn·i·er; -est 1** : made of horn **2** : hard or callous **3** : sexually aroused

horo·scope \'hórə,skōp\ *n* : astrological forecast

hor·ren·dous \hó'rendəs\ *adj* : horrible

hor·ri·ble \'hórəbəl\ *adj* **1** : having or causing horror **2** : highly disagreeable —**hor·ri·ble·ness** *n* —**hor·ri·bly** \-blē\ *adv*

hor·rid \'hórəd\ *adj* : horrible —**hor·rid·ly** *adv*

hor·ri·fy \'hórə,fī\ *vb* -**fied; -fy·ing** : cause to feel horror

hor·ror \'hórər\ *n* **1** : intense fear, dread, or dismay **2** : intense repugnance **3** : something horrible

hors d'oeuvre \ór'dərv\ *n, pl* **hors d'oeuvres** \-'dərvz\ : appetizer

horse \'hórs\ *n* : large solid-hoofed domesticated mammal —**horse·back** *n or adv* —**horse·hair** *n* —**horse·hide** *n* —**horse·less** *adj* —**horse·man** \-mən\ *n* —**horse·man·ship** *n* —**horse·wom·an** *n* —**hors·ey, horsy** *adj*

horse·fly *n* : large fly with bloodsucking female

horse·play *n* : rough boisterous play

horse·pow·er *n* : unit of mechanical power

horse·rad·ish *n* : herb with a pungent root used as a condiment

horse·shoe *n* : U-shaped protective metal plate fitted to the rim of a horse's hoof

hor·ti·cul·ture \'hórtə,kəlchər\ *n* : science of growing fruits, vegetables, and flowers —**hor·ti·cul·tur·al** \,hórtə'kəlchərəl\ *adj* —**hor·ti·cul·tur·ist** \-rist\ *n*

ho·san·na \hō'zanə, -'zän-\ *interj* —

used as a cry of acclamation and adoration —**hosanna** n

hose \'hōz\ n 1 pl **hose** : stocking or sock 2 pl **hos•es** : flexible tube for conveying fluids ~ vb **hosed; hos•ing** : spray, water, or wash with a hose

ho•siery \'hōzhərē, 'hōzə-\ n : stockings or socks

hos•pice \'häspəs\ n 1 : lodging (as for travelers) maintained by a religious order 2 : facility or program for caring for dying persons

hos•pi•ta•ble \hä'spitəbəl, 'häs,pit-\ adj : given to generous and cordial reception of guests —**hos•pi•ta•bly** \-blē\ adv

hos•pi•tal \'häs,pit³l\ n : institution where the sick or injured receive medical care —**hos•pi•tal•i•za•tion** \,häs‚pit³lə'zāshən\ n —**hos•pi•tal•ize** \'häs,pit³l,īz\ vb

hos•pi•tal•i•ty \,häspə'talətē\ n, pl **-ties** : hospitable treatment, reception, or disposition

¹host \'hōst\ n 1 : army 2 : multitude

²host n : one who receives or entertains guests —**host** vb

³host n : eucharistic bread

hos•tage \'hästij\ n : person held to guarantee that promises be kept or demands met

hos•tel \'häst³l\ n : lodging for youth —**hos•tel•er** n

hos•tel•ry \-rē\ n, pl **-ries** : hotel

host•ess \'hōstəs\ n : woman who is host

hos•tile \'häst³l, -,tīl\ adj : openly or actively unfriendly or opposed to someone or something —**hostile** n —**hos•tile•ly** adv —**hos•til•i•ty** \häs'tilətē\ n

hot \'hät\ adj -**tt**- 1 : having a high temperature 2 : giving a sensation of heat or burning 3 : ardent 4 : pungent —**hot** adv —**hot•ly** adv —**hot•ness** n

hot•bed n : environment that favors rapid growth

hot dog n : frankfurter

ho•tel \hō'tel\ n : building where lodging and personal services are provided

hot•head•ed adj : impetuous —**hot•head** n —**hot•head•ed•ly** adv —**hot•head•ed•ness** n

hot•house n : greenhouse

hound \'haůnd\ n : long-eared hunting dog ~ vb : pursue relentlessly

hour \'aůər\ n 1 : 24th part of a day 2 : time of day —**hour•ly** adv or adj

hour•glass n : glass vessel for measuring time

house \'haůs\ n, pl **hous•es** \'haůzəz\ 1 : building to live in 2 : household 3 : legislative body 4 : business firm ~ \'haůz\ vb **housed; hous•ing** : provide with or take shelter —**house•boat** \'haůs,bōt\ n —**house•clean** \'haůs,klēn\ vb —**house•clean•ing** n —**house•ful** \-,fůl\ n —**house•maid** n —**house•wares** n pl —**house•work** n

house•bro•ken \-,brōkən\ adj : trained in excretory habits acceptable in indoor living

house•fly n : two-winged fly common about human habitations

house•hold \-,hōld\ n : those who dwell as a family under the same roof ~ adj 1 : domestic 2 : common or familiar —**house•hold•er** n

house•keep•ing \-,kēpiŋ\ n : care and management of a house or institution —**house•keep•er** n

house•warm•ing n : party to celebrate moving into a house

house•wife \'haůs,wīf\ n : married woman in charge of a household —**house•wife•ly** adj —**house•wif•ery** \-,wīfərē\ n

hous•ing \'haůziŋ\ n 1 : dwellings for people 2 : protective covering

hove past of HEAVE

hov•el \'həvəl, 'häv-\ n : small wretched house

hov•er \'həvər, 'häv-\ vb 1 : remain suspended in the air 2 : move about in the vicinity

how \'haů\ adv 1 : in what way or condition 2 : for what reason 3 : to what extent ~ conj : the way or manner in which

how•ev•er \haů'evər\ conj : in whatever manner ~ adv 1 : to whatever degree or in whatever manner 2 : in spite of that

how•it•zer \'haůətsər\ n : short cannon

howl \'haůl\ vb : emit a loud long doleful sound like a dog —**howl** n —**howl•er** n

hoy•den \'hóid³n\ n : girl or woman of saucy or carefree behavior

hub \'həb\ n : central part of a circular object (as of a wheel) —**hub•cap** n

hub•bub \'həb,əb\ n : uproar

hu•bris \'hyübrəs\ n : excessive pride

huck•le•ber•ry \'həkəl,berē\ n 1 : shrub

related to the blueberry or its berry **2** : blueberry

huck·ster \'həkstər\ *n* : peddler

hud·dle \'həd°l\ *vb* **-dled; -dling 1** : crowd together **2** : confer **—huddle** *n*

hue \'hyü\ *n* : color or gradation of color **—hued** \'hyüd\ *adj*

huff \'həf\ *n* : fit of pique **—huffy** *adj*

hug \'həg\ *vb* **-gg- 1** : press tightly in the arms **2** : stay close to **—hug** *n*

huge \'hyüj\ *adj* **hug·er; hug·est** : very large or extensive **—huge·ly** *adv* **— huge·ness** *n*

hu·la \'hülə\ *n* : Polynesian dance

hulk \'həlk\ *n* **1** : bulky or unwieldy person or thing **2** : old ship unfit for service **—hulk·ing** *adj*

hull \'həl\ *n* **1** : outer covering of a fruit or seed **2** : frame or body of a ship or boat ~ *vb* : remove the hulls of **— huller** *n*

hul·la·ba·loo \'hələbə,lü\ *n, pl* **-loos** : uproar

hum \'həm\ *vb* **-mm- 1** : make a prolonged sound like that of the speech sound \m\ **2** : be busily active **3** : run smoothly **4** : sing with closed lips **— hum** *n* **—hum·mer** *n*

hu·man \'hyümən, 'yü-\ *adj* **1** : of or relating to the species people belong to **2** : by, for, or like people **—human** *n* **—hu·man·kind** *n* **—hu·man·ly** *adv* **—hu·man·ness** *n*

hu·mane \hyü'mān, ,yü-\ *adj* : showing compassion or consideration for others **—hu·mane·ly** *adv* **—hu·mane·ness** *n*

hu·man·ism \'hyümə,nizəm, 'yü-\ *n* : doctrine or way of life centered on human interests or values **—hu·man·ist** \-nist\ *n or adj* **—hu·man·is·tic** \,hyümə'nistik, ,yü-\ *adj*

hu·man·i·tar·i·an \hyü,manə'terēən, yü-\ *n* : person promoting human welfare **—humanitarian** *adj* **—hu·man·i·tar·i·an·ism** *n*

hu·man·i·ty \hyü'manətē, yü-\ *n, pl* **-ties 1** : human or humane quality or state **2** : the human race

hu·man·ize \'hyümə,nīz, 'yü-\ *vb* **-ized; -iz·ing** : make human or humane **— hu·man·i·za·tion** \,hyümənə'zāshən, ,yü-\ *n* **—hu·man·iz·er** *n*

hu·man·oid \'hyümə,nóid, 'yü-\ *adj* : having human form **—humanoid** *n*

hum·ble \'həmbəl\ *adj* **-bler; -blest 1** : not proud or haughty **2** : not pretentious ~ *vb* **-bled; -bling** : make humble **—hum·ble·ness** *n* **—hum·bler** *n* **—hum·bly** \-blē\ *adv*

hum·bug \'həm,bəg\ *n* : nonsense

hum·drum \-,drəm\ *adj* : monotonous

hu·mid \'hyüməd, 'yü-\ *adj* : containing or characterized by moisture **—hu·mid·i·fi·ca·tion** \hyü,midəfə'kāshən\ *n* **—hu·mid·i·fi·er** \-'midə,fiər\ *n* **— hu·mid·i·fy** \-,fī\ *vb* **—hu·mid·ly** *adv*

hu·mid·i·ty \hyü'midətē, yü-\ *n, pl* **-ties** : atmospheric moisture

hu·mi·dor \'hyümə,dór, 'yü-\ *n* : humidified storage case (as for cigars)

hu·mil·i·ate \hyü'milē,āt, yü-\ *vb* **-at·ed; -at·ing** : injure the self-respect of **— hu·mil·i·at·ing·ly** *adv* **—hu·mil·i·ation** \-,milē'āshən\ *n*

hu·mil·i·ty \hyü'milətē, yü-\ *n* : humble quality or state

hum·ming·bird \'həmiŋ,bərd\ *n* : tiny American bird that can hover

hum·mock \'həmək\ *n* : mound or knoll **—hum·mocky** \-məkē\ *adj*

hu·mor \'hyümər, 'yü-\ *n* **1** : mood **2** : quality of being laughably ludicrous or incongruous **3** : appreciation of what is ludicrous or incongruous **4** : something intended to be funny ~ *vb* : comply with the wishes or mood of **—hu·mor·ist** \-ərist\ *n* **—hu·mor·less** *adj* **—hu·mor·less·ly** *adv* **—hu·mor·less·ness** *n* **—hu·mor·ous** \'hyümərəs, 'yü-\ *adj* **—hu·mor·ous·ly** *adv* **—hu·mor·ous·ness** *n*

hump \'həmp\ *n* : rounded protuberance **—humped** *adj*

hump·back \'həmp-\ *n* : hunchback **—hump·backed** *adj*

hu·mus \'hyüməs, 'yü-\ *n* : dark organic part of soil

hunch \'hənch\ *vb* : assume or cause to assume a bent or crooked posture ~ *n* : strong intuitive feeling

hunch·back *n* **1** : back with a hump **2** : person with a crooked back **— hunch·backed** *adj*

hun·dred \'həndrəd\ *n, pl* **-dreds** or **-dred** : 10 times 10 **—hundred** *adj* **—hun·dredth** \-drədth\ *adj or n*

¹hung *past of* HANG

²hung *adj* : unable to reach a verdict

hun·ger \'həŋgər\ *n* **1** : craving or urgent need for food **2** : strong desire **—hunger** *vb* **—hun·gri·ly** \-grəlē\ *adv* **—hun·gry** *adj*

hunk \'həŋk\ *n* : large piece

hun·ker \'həŋkər\ *vb* : settle in for a sustained period—used with *down*

hunt \'hənt\ *vb* **1** : pursue for food or sport **2** : try to find ~ *n* : act or instance of hunting —**hunt·er** *n*

hur·dle \'hərd^əl\ *n* **1** : barrier to leap over in a race **2** : obstacle —**hurdle** *vb* —**hur·dler** *n*

hurl \'hərl\ *vb* : throw with violence —**hurl** *n* —**hurl·er** *n*

hur·rah \hu̇·rä, -'rȯ\ *interj* —used to express joy or approval

hur·ri·cane \'hərə,kān\ *n* : tropical storm with winds of 74 miles per hour or greater

hur·ry \'hərē\ *vb* **-ried; -ry·ing** : go or cause to go with haste ~ *n* : extreme haste —**hur·ried·ly** *adv* —**hur·ried·ness** *n*

hurt \'hərt\ *vb* **hurt; hurt·ing 1** : feel or cause pain **2** : do harm to ~ *n* **1** : bodily injury **2** : harm —**hurt·ful** \-fəl\ *adj* —**hurt·ful·ness** *n*

hur·tle \'hərt^əl\ *vb* **-tled; -tling** : move rapidly or forcefully

hus·band \'həzbənd\ *n* : married man ~ *vb* : manage prudently

hus·band·ry \-bəndrē\ *n* **1** : careful use **2** : agriculture

hush \'həsh\ *vb* : make or become quiet ~ *n* : silence

husk \'həsk\ *n* : outer covering of a seed or fruit ~ *vb* : strip the husk from —**husk·er** *n*

¹hus·ky \'həskē\ *adj* **-ki·er; -est** : hoarse —**hus·ki·ly** *adv* —**hus·ki·ness** *n*

²husky *adj* **-ki·er; -est** : burly —**husk·i·ness** *n*

³husky *n, pl* **-kies** : working dog of the arctic

hus·sy \'həsē, -zē\ *n, pl* **-sies 1** : brazen woman **2** : mischievous girl

hus·tle \'həsəl\ *vb* **-tled; -tling 1** : hurry **2** : work energetically —**hustle** *n* —**hus·tler** \'həslər\ *n*

hut \'hət\ *n* : small often temporary dwelling

hutch \'həch\ *n* **1** : cupboard with open shelves **2** : pen for an animal

hy·a·cinth \'hīə,sinth\ *n* : bulbous herb grown for bell-shaped flowers

hy·brid \'hībrəd\ *n* : offspring of genetically differing parents —**hybrid** *adj* —**hy·brid·iza·tion** \,hībrədə-'zāshən\ *n* —**hy·brid·ize** \'hībrəd-,īz\ *vb* —**hy·brid·iz·er** *n*

hy·drant \'hīdrənt\ *n* : pipe from which water may be drawn to fight fires

hy·drau·lic \hī'dro̊lik\ *adj* : operated by liquid forced through a small hole —**hy·drau·lics** \-liks\ *n*

hy·dro·car·bon \,hīdrə'kärbən\ *n* : organic compound of carbon and hydrogen

hy·dro·elec·tric \,hīdrōi'lektrik\ *adj* : producing electricity by waterpower —**hy·dro·elec·tric·i·ty** \-,lek'trisətē\ *n*

hy·dro·gen \'hīdrəjən\ *n* : very light gaseous colorless odorless flammable chemical element

hydrogen bomb *n* : powerful bomb that derives its energy from the union of atomic nuclei

hy·dro·pho·bia \,hīdrə'fōbēə\ *n* : rabies

hy·dro·plane \'hīdrə,plān\ *n* : speedboat that skims the water

hy·drous \'hīdrəs\ *adj* : containing water

hy·e·na \hī'ēnə\ *n* : nocturnal carnivorous mammal of Asia and Africa

hy·giene \'hī,jēn\ *n* : conditions or practices conducive to health —**hy·gien·ic** \hī'jenik, -'jēn-; ,hījē'enik\ *adj* —**hy·gien·i·cal·ly** \-iklē\ *adv* —**hy·gien·ist** \hī'jēnist, -'jen-; 'hī,jēn-\ *n*

hy·grom·e·ter \hī'grämətər\ *n* : instrument for measuring atmospheric humidity

hying *pres part of* HIE

hymn \'him\ *n* : song of praise esp. to God —**hymn** *vb*

hym·nal \'himnəl\ *n* : book of hymns

hype \'hīp\ *vb* **hyped; hyp·ing** : publicize extravagantly —**hype** *n*

hyper- *prefix* **1** : above or beyond **2** : excessively or excessive

hyperacid	hypernationalistic
hyperacidity	
hyperactive	hyperreactive
hyperacute	hyperrealistic
hyperaggressive	hyperromantic
hypercautious	hypersensitive
hypercorrect	hypersensitiveness
hypercritical	
hyperemotional	hypersensitivity
hyperenergetic	hypersexual
hyperexcitable	hypersusceptible
hyperfastidious	hypertense
hyperintense	hypervigilant
hypermasculine	

hy·per·bo·le \hī'pərbəlē\ *n* : extravagant exaggeration

hy·per·ten·sion \'hīpər,tenchən\ *n*

: high blood pressure —**hy·per·ten·sive** \,hīpər'tensiv\ *adj or n*

hy·phen \'hīfən\ *n* : punctuation mark - used to divide or compound words —**hyphen** *vb*

hy·phen·ate \'hīfə,nāt\ *vb* -**at·ed; -at·ing** : connect or divide with a hyphen —**hy·phen·ation** \,hīfə'nāshən\ *n*

hyp·no·sis \hip'nōsəs\ *n, pl* -**no·ses** \-,sēz\ : induced state like sleep in which the subject is responsive to suggestions of the inducer (**hyp·no·tist** \'hipnətist\)—**hyp·no·tism** \'hipnə,tizəm\ *n* —**hyp·no·tiz·able** \,hipnə'tīzəbəl\ *adj* —**hyp·no·tize** \'hipnə,tīz\ *vb*

hyp·not·ic \hip'nätik\ *adj* : relating to hypnosis —**hypnotic** *n* —**hyp·not·i·cal·ly** \-iklē\ *adv*

hy·po·chon·dria \,hīpə'kändrēə\ *n* : morbid concern for one's health —**hy·po·chon·dri·ac** \-drē,ak\ *adj or n*

hy·poc·ri·sy \hip'äkrəsē\ *n, pl* -**sies** : a feigning to be what one is not —**hyp·o·crite** \'hipə,krit\ *n* —**hyp·o·crit·i·cal** \,hipə'kritikəl\ *adj* —**hyp·o·crit·i·cal·ly** *adv*

hy·po·der·mic \,hīpə'dərmik\ *adj* : administered or used in making an injection beneath the skin ~ *n* : hypodermic syringe

hy·pot·e·nuse \hī'pätə,nüs, -,nüz, -,nyüs, -,nyüz\ *n* : side of a right-angled triangle opposite the right angle

hy·poth·e·sis \hī'päthəsəs\ *n, pl* -**e·ses** \-,sēz\ : assumption made in order to test its consequences —**hy·poth·e·size** \-,sīz\ *vb* —**hy·po·thet·i·cal** \,hīpə-'thetikəl\ *adj* —**hy·po·thet·i·cal·ly** *adv*

hys·ter·ec·to·my \,histə'rektəmē\ *n, pl* -**mies** : surgical removal of the uterus

hys·te·ria \his'terēə, -tir-\ *n* : uncontrollable fear or outburst of emotion —**hys·ter·i·cal** \-'terikəl\ *adj* —**hys·ter·i·cal·ly** *adv*

hys·ter·ics \-'teriks\ *n pl* : uncontrollable laughter or crying

I

i \'ī\ *n, pl* **i's** *or* **is** \'īz\ : 9th letter of the alphabet

I \'ī\ *pron* : the speaker

-ial *adj suffix* : of, relating to, or characterized by

-ian —see -AN

ibis \'ībəs\ *n, pl* **ibis** *or* **ibis·es** : wading bird with a down-curved bill

-ible —see -ABLE

ibu·pro·fen \,ībyü'prōfən\ *n* : drug used to relieve inflammation, pain, and fever

-ic \ik\ *adj suffix* **1** : of, relating to, or being **2** : containing **3** : characteristic of **4** : marked by **5** : caused by

—**-i·cal** \ikəl\ *adj suffix* : -ic —**-i·cal·ly** \iklē, -kəlē\ *adv suffix*

ice \'īs\ *n* **1** : frozen water **2** : flavored frozen dessert ~ *vb* **iced; ic·ing 1** : freeze **2** : chill **3** : cover with icing

ice·berg \'īs,bərg\ *n* : large floating mass of ice

ice·box *n* : refrigerator

ice·break·er *n* : ship equipped to cut through ice

ice cream *n* : sweet frozen food

ice–skate *vb* : skate on ice —**ice skater** *n*

ich·thy·ol·o·gy \,ikthē'äləjē\ *n* : study of fishes —**ich·thy·ol·o·gist** \-jist\ *n*

ici·cle \'ī,sikəl\ *n* : hanging mass of ice

ic·ing \'īsiŋ\ *n* : sweet usu. creamy coating for baked goods

icon \'ī,kän\ *n* **1** : religious image **2** : small picture on a computer screen identified with an available function

icon·o·clast \ī'känə,klast\ *n* : attacker of cherished beliefs or institutions —**icon·o·clasm** \-,klazəm\ *n*

icy \'īsē\ *adj* **ic·i·er; -est 1** : covered with or consisting of ice **2** : very cold —**ic·i·ly** *adv* —**ic·i·ness** *n*

id \'id\ *n* : unconscious instinctual part of the mind

idea \ī'dēə\ *n* **1** : something imagined in the mind **2** : purpose or plan

ide·al \ī'dēəl\ *adj* **1** : imaginary **2** : perfect ~ *n* **1** : standard of excellence **2** : model **3** : aim —**ide·al·ly** *adv*

ide·al·ism \ī'dēə,lizəm\ *n* : adherence to ideals —**ide·al·ist** \-list\ *n* —**ide·**

al·is·tic \ī,dēə'listik\ adj —ide·al·is·ti·cal·ly \-tiklē\ adv

ide·al·ize \ī'dēə,līz\ vb -ized; -iz·ing : think of or represent as ideal — ide·al·i·za·tion \-,dēələ'zāshən\ n

iden·ti·cal \ī'dentikəl\ adj 1 : being the same 2 : exactly or essentially alike

iden·ti·fi·ca·tion \ī,dentəfə'kāshən\ n 1 : act of identifying 2 : evidence of identity

iden·ti·fy \ī'dentə,fī\ vb -fied; -fy·ing 1 : associate 2 : establish the identity of —iden·ti·fi·able \ī,dentə'fīəbəl\ adj —iden·ti·fi·er \ī'dentə,fīər\ n

iden·ti·ty \ī'dentətē\ n, pl -ties 1 : sameness of essential character 2 : individuality 3 : fact of being what is supposed

ide·ol·o·gy \,īdē'äləjē, ,id-\ n, pl -gies : body of beliefs —ide·o·log·i·cal \,īdēə'läjikəl, ,id-\ adj

id·i·om \'idēəm\ n 1 : language peculiar to a person or group 2 : expression with a special meaning —id·i·om·at·ic \,idēə'matik\ adj —id·i·om·at·i·cal·ly \-iklē\ adv

id·io·syn·cra·sy \,idēō'siŋkrəsē\ n, pl -sies : personal peculiarity —id·io·syn·crat·ic \-sin'kratik\ adj —id·io·syn·crat·i·cal·ly \-'kratiklē\ adv

id·i·ot \'idēət\ n : mentally retarded or foolish person —id·i·o·cy \-əsē\ n —id·i·ot·ic \,idē'ätik\ adj —id·i·ot·i·cal·ly \-iklē\ adv

idle \'īd⁼l\ adj idler; idlest 1 : worthless 2 : inactive 3 : lazy ~ vb idled; idling : spend time doing nothing —idle·ness n —idler n —idly \'īdlē\ adv

idol \'īd⁼l\ n 1 : image of a god 2 : object of devotion —idol·i·za·tion \,īd⁼lə'zāshən\ n —idol·ize \'īd⁼līz\ vb

idol·a·ter, idol·a·tor \ī'dälətər\ n : worshiper of idols —idol·a·trous \-trəs\ adj —idol·a·try \-trē\ n

idyll \'īd⁼l\ n : period of peace and contentment —idyl·lic \ī'dilik\ adj

-ier —see -ER

if \'if\ conj 1 : in the event that 2 : whether 3 : even though

-i·fy \ə,fī\ vb suffix : -fy

ig·loo \'iglü\ n, pl -loos : hut made of snow blocks

ig·nite \ig'nīt\ vb -nit·ed; -nit·ing : set afire or catch fire —ig·nit·able \-'nītəbəl\ adj

ig·ni·tion \ig'nishən\ n 1 : a setting on

fire 2 : process or means of igniting fuel

ig·no·ble \ig'nōbəl\ adj : not honorable —ig·no·bly \-blē\ adv

ig·no·min·i·ous \,ignə'minēəs\ adj 1 : dishonorable 2 : humiliating —ig·no·min·i·ous·ly adv —ig·no·mi·ny \'ignə,minē, ig'nämənē\ n

ig·no·ra·mus \,ignə'rāməs\ n : ignorant person

ig·no·rant \'ignərənt\ adj 1 : lacking knowledge 2 : showing a lack of knowledge or intelligence 3 : unaware —ig·no·rance \-rəns\ n —ig·no·rant·ly adv

ig·nore \ig'nōr\ vb -nored; -nor·ing : refuse to notice

igua·na \i'gwänə\ n : large tropical American lizard

ilk \'ilk\ n : kind

ill \'il\ adj worse \'wərs\; worst \'wərst\ 1 : sick 2 : bad 3 : rude or unacceptable 4 : hostile ~ adv worse; worst 1 : with displeasure 2 : harshly 3 : scarcely 4 : badly ~ n 1 : evil 2 : misfortune 3 : sickness

il·le·gal \il'lēgəl\ adj : not lawful —il·le·gal·i·ty \ili'galətē\ n —il·le·gal·ly \il'lēgəlē\ adv

il·leg·i·ble \il'lejəbəl\ adj : not legible —il·leg·i·bil·i·ty \il,lejə'bilətē\ n —il·leg·i·bly \il'lejəblē\ adv

il·le·git·i·mate \,ili'jitəmət\ adj 1 : born of unmarried parents 2 : illegal —il·le·git·i·ma·cy \-əməsē\ n —il·le·git·i·mate·ly adv

il·lic·it \il'lisət\ adj : not lawful —il·lic·it·ly adv

il·lim·it·able \il'limətəbəl\ adj : boundless —il·lim·it·ably \-blē\ adv

il·lit·er·ate \il'litərət\ adj : unable to read or write —il·lit·er·a·cy \-ərəsē\ n —illiterate n

ill-na·tured \'il-'nāchərd\ adj : cross —ill-na·tured·ly adv

ill·ness \'ilnəs\ n : sickness

il·log·i·cal \il'läjikəl\ adj : contrary to sound reasoning —il·log·i·cal·ly adv

ill-starred \'il'stärd\ adj : unlucky

il·lu·mi·nate \il'ümə,nāt\ vb -nat·ed; -nat·ing 1 : light up 2 : make clear —il·lu·mi·nat·ing·ly \-,nātiŋlē\ adv —il·lu·mi·na·tion \-,ümə'nāshən\ n

ill-use \-'yüz\ vb : abuse —ill-use \-'yüs\ n

il·lu·sion \il'üzhən\ n 1 : mistaken idea 2 : misleading visual image il·lu·so·ry \il'üsərē, -'üz-\ adj : based on or producing illusion

il·lus·trate \'iləs,trāt\ vb -trat·ed; -trat·ing 1 : explain by example 2 : provide with pictures or figures —il·lus·tra·tor \-ər\ n

il·lus·tra·tion \,iləs'trāshən\ n 1 : example that explains 2 : pictorial explanation

il·lus·tra·tive \il'əstrətiv\ adj : designed to illustrate —il·lus·tra·tive·ly adv

il·lus·tri·ous \-'trēəs\ adj : notably or brilliantly outstanding —il·lus·tri·ous·ness n

ill will n : unfriendly feeling

im·age \'imij\ n 1 : likeness 2 : visual counterpart of an object formed by a lens or mirror 3 : mental picture ~ vb -aged; -ag·ing : create a representation of

im·ag·ery \'imijrē\ n 1 : images 2 : figurative language

imag·i·nary \im'ajə,nerē\ adj : existing only in the imagination

imag·i·na·tion \im,ajə'nāshən\ n 1 : act or power of forming a mental image 2 : creative ability —imag·i·na·tive \im'ajənətiv, -ə,nātiv\ adj —imag·i·na·tive·ly adv

imag·ine \im'ajən\ vb -ined; -in·ing : form a mental picture of something not present —imag·in·able \-'ajənəbəl\ adj —imag·in·ably \-blē\ adv

im·bal·ance \im'baləns\ n : lack of balance

im·be·cile \'imbəsəl, -,sil\ n : idiot —imbecile, im·be·cil·ic \,imbə'silik\ adj —im·be·cil·i·ty \-'silətē\ n

im·bibe \im'bīb\ vb -bibed; -bib·ing : drink —im·bib·er n

im·bro·glio \im'brōlyō\ n, pl -glios : complicated situation

im·bue \-'byü\ vb -bued; -bu·ing : fill (as with color or a feeling)

im·i·tate \'imə,tāt\ vb -tat·ed; -tat·ing 1 : follow as a model 2 : mimic —im·i·ta·tive \-,tātiv\ adj —im·i·ta·tor \-ər\ n

im·i·ta·tion \,imə'tāshən\ n 1 : act of imitating 2 : copy —imitation adj

im·mac·u·late \im'akyələt\ adj : without stain or blemish —im·mac·u·late·ly adv

im·ma·te·ri·al \,imə'tirēəl\ adj 1 : spiritual 2 : not relevant —im·ma·te·ri·al·i·ty \-,tirē'alətē\ n

im·ma·ture \,imə'tùr, -'tyùr\ adj : not yet mature —im·ma·tu·ri·ty \-ətē\ n

im·mea·sur·able \im'ezhərəbəl\ adj : indefinitely extensive —immeasur·ably \-blē\ adv

im·me·di·a·cy \im'ēdēəsē\ n, pl -cies : quality or state of being urgent

im·me·di·ate \-ēət\ adj 1 : direct 2 : being next in line 3 : made or done at once 4 : not distant —im·me·di·ate·ly adv

im·me·mo·ri·al \,imə'mōrēəl\ adj : old beyond memory

im·mense \im'ens\ adj : vast —im·mense·ly adv —im·men·si·ty \-'ensətē\ n

im·merse \im'ərs\ vb -mersed; -mers·ing 1 : plunge or dip esp. into liquid 2 : engross —im·mer·sion \-'ərzhən\ n

im·mi·grant \'imigrənt\ n : one that immigrates

im·mi·grate \'imə,grāt\ vb -grat·ed; -grat·ing : come into a place and take up residence —im·mi·gra·tion \,imə'grāshən\ n

im·mi·nent \'imənənt\ adj : ready to take place —im·mi·nence \-nəns\ n —im·mi·nent·ly adv

im·mo·bile \im'ōbəl\ adj : incapable of being moved —im·mo·bil·i·ty \,imō'bilətē\ n —im·mo·bi·lize \im'ōbə,līz\ vb

im·mod·er·ate \im'ädərət\ adj : not moderate —im·mod·er·a·cy \-ərəsē\ n —im·mod·er·ate·ly adv

im·mod·est \im'ädəst\ adj : not modest —im·mod·est·ly adv —im·mod·es·ty \-əstē\ n

im·mo·late \'imə,lāt\ vb -lat·ed; -lat·ing : offer in sacrifice —im·mo·la·tion \,imə'lāshən\ n

im·mor·al \im'ōrəl\ adj : not moral —im·mor·al·i·ty \,imō'ralətē, ,imə-\ n —im·mor·al·ly adv

im·mor·tal \im'ört⁽ə⁾l\ adj 1 : not mortal 2 : having lasting fame ~ n : one exempt from death or oblivion —im·mor·tal·i·ty \,im,ör'talətē\ n —im·mor·tal·ize \im'ört⁽ə⁾l,īz\ vb

im·mov·able \im'üvəbəl\ adj 1 : stationary 2 : unyielding —im·mov·abil·i·ty \,im,üvə'bilətē\ n —im·mov·ably adv

im·mune \im'yün\ adj : not liable esp. to disease —im·mu·ni·ty \im'yünətē\ n —im·mu·ni·za·tion \,imyənə-

'zāshən\ *n* —**im·mu·nize** \'imyə-,nīz\ *vb*

im·mu·nol·o·gy \,imyə'näləjē\ *n* : science of immunity to disease —**im·mu·no·log·ic** \-yən[e]'äjik\, **im·mu·no·log·i·cal** \-ikəl\ *adj* —**im·mu·nol·o·gist** \,imyə'näləjist\ *n*

im·mu·ta·ble \im'yütəbəl\ *adj* : unchangeable —**im·mu·ta·bil·i·ty** \im-,yütə'bilətē\ *n* —**im·mu·ta·bly** *adv*

imp \'imp\ *n* **1** : demon **2** : mischievous child

im·pact \im'pakt\ *vb* **1** : press close **2** : have an effect on ~ \'im,pakt\ *n* **1** : forceful contact **2** : influence

im·pact·ed \im'paktəd\ *adj* : wedged between the jawbone and another tooth

im·pair \im'par\ *vb* : diminish in quantity, value, or ability —**im·pair·ment** *n*

im·pa·la \im'palə\ *n, pl* **impalas** *or* **impala** : large African antelope

im·pale \im'pāl\ *vb* -**paled;** -**pal·ing** : pierce with something pointed

im·pal·pa·ble \im'palpəbəl\ *adj* : incapable of being felt —**im·pal·pa·bly** *adv*

im·pan·el \im'pan[e]l\ *vb* : enter in or on a panel

im·part \-'pärt\ *vb* : give from or as if from a store

im·par·tial \im'pärshəl\ *adj* : not partial —**im·par·tial·i·ty** \im,pärshē'alətē\ *n* —**im·par·tial·ly** *adv*

im·pass·able \im'pasəbəl\ *adj* : not passable —**im·pass·ably** \-'pasəblē\ *adv*

im·passe \'im,pas\ *n* : inescapable predicament

im·pas·sioned \im'pashənd\ *adj* : filled with passion

im·pas·sive \im'pasiv\ *adj* : showing no feeling or interest —**im·pas·sive·ly** *adv* —**im·pas·siv·i·ty** \,im,pas'ivətē\ *n*

im·pa·tiens \im'pāshənz, -shəns\ *n* : annual herb with showy flowers

im·pa·tient \im'pāshənt\ *adj* : not patient —**im·pa·tience** \-shəns\ *n* —**im·pa·tient·ly** *adv*

im·peach \im'pēch\ *vb* **1** : charge (an official) with misconduct **2** : cast doubt on **3** : remove from office for misconduct —**im·peach·ment** *n*

im·pec·ca·ble \im'pekəbəl\ *adj* : faultless —**im·pec·ca·bly** *adv*

im·pe·cu·nious \,impi'kyünēəs\ *adj* : broke —**im·pe·cu·nious·ness** *n*

im·pede \im'pēd\ *vb* -**ped·ed;** -**ped·ing** : interfere with

im·ped·i·ment \-'pedəmənt\ *n* **1** : hindrance **2** : speech defect

im·pel \-'pel\ *vb* -**pelled;** -**pel·ling** : urge forward

im·pend \-'pend\ *vb* : be about to occur

im·pen·e·tra·ble \im'penətrəbəl\ *adj* : incapable of being penetrated or understood —**im·pen·e·tra·bil·i·ty** \im-,penətrə'bilətē\ *n* —**im·pen·e·tra·bly** *adv*

im·pen·i·tent \im'penətənt\ *adj* : not penitent —**im·pen·i·tence** \-təns\ *n*

im·per·a·tive \im'perativ\ *adj* **1** : expressing a command **2** : urgent ~ *n* **1** : imperative mood or verb form **2** : unavoidable fact, need, or obligation —**im·per·a·tive·ly** *adv*

im·per·cep·ti·ble \,impər'septəbəl\ *adj* : not perceptible —**im·per·cep·ti·bly** *adv*

im·per·fect \im'pərfikt\ *adj* : not perfect —**im·per·fec·tion** *n* —**im·per·fect·ly** *adv*

im·pe·ri·al \im'pirēəl\ *adj* **1** : relating to an empire or an emperor **2** : royal

im·pe·ri·al·ism \im'pirē,lizəm\ *n* : policy of controlling other nations —**im·pe·ri·al·ist** \-list\ *n* or *adj* —**im·pe·ri·al·is·tic** \-,pirēə'listik\ *adj* —**im·pe·ri·al·is·ti·cal·ly** \-tiklē\ *adv*

im·per·il \im'perəl\ *vb* -**iled** *or* -**illed;** -**il·ing** *or* -**il·ling** : endanger

im·pe·ri·ous \im'pirēəs\ *adj* : arrogant or domineering —**im·pe·ri·ous·ly** *adv*

im·per·ish·able \im'perishəbəl\ *adj* : not perishable

im·per·ma·nent \-'pərmənənt\ *adj* : not permanent —**im·per·ma·nent·ly** *adv*

im·per·me·able \-'pərmēəbəl\ *adj* : not permeable

im·per·mis·si·ble \,impər'misəbəl\ *adj* : not permissible

im·per·son·al \im'pərs[e]nəl\ *adj* : not involving human personality or emotion —**im·per·son·al·i·ty** \im,pərs[e]n'alətē\ *n* —**im·per·son·al·ly** *adv*

im·per·son·ate \im'pərs[e]n,āt\ *vb* -**at·ed;** -**at·ing** : assume the character of —**im·per·son·a·tion** \-,pərs[e]n'āshən\ *n* —**im·per·son·a·tor** \-'pərs[e]n,ātər\ *n*

im·per·ti·nent \im'pərt[e]nənt\ *adj* **1** : irrelevant **2** : insolent —**im·per-**

ti·nence \-ᵊnəns\ n —im·per·ti·nent·ly adv

im·per·turb·able \,impər'tərbəbəl\ adj : calm and steady

im·per·vi·ous \im'pərvēəs\ adj : incapable of being penetrated or affected

im·pet·u·ous \im'pechəwəs\ adj : impulsive —im·pet·u·os·i·ty \im,pechə'wäsətē\ n —im·pet·u·ous·ly adv

im·pe·tus \'impətəs\ n : driving force

im·pi·ety \im'pīətē\ n : quality or state of being impious

im·pinge \im'pinj\ vb -pinged; -ping·ing : encroach —im·pinge·ment \-mənt\ n

im·pi·ous \'impēəs, im'pī-\ adj : not pious

imp·ish \'impish\ adj : mischievous — imp·ish·ly adv —imp·ish·ness n

im·pla·ca·ble \im'plakəbəl, -'plā-\ adj : not capable of being appeased or changed —im·pla·ca·bil·i·ty \im,plakə'bilətē, -,plā-\ n —im·pla·ca·bly \im'plakəblē\ adv

im·plant \im'plant\ vb 1 : set firmly or deeply 2 : fix in the mind or spirit ~ \'im,plant\ n : something implanted in tissue —im·plan·ta·tion \,im,plan'tāshən\ n

im·plau·si·ble \im'plózəbəl\ adj : not plausible —im·plau·si·bil·i·ty \im,plózə'bilətē\ n

im·ple·ment \'impləmənt\ n : tool, utensil ~ \-,ment\ vb : put into practice — im·ple·men·ta·tion \,impləmən'tāshən\ n

im·pli·cate \'implə,kāt\ vb -cat·ed; -cat·ing : involve

im·pli·ca·tion \,implə'kāshən\ n 1 : an implying 2 : something implied

im·plic·it \im'plisət\ adj 1 : understood though only implied 2 : complete and unquestioning —im·plic·it·ly adv

im·plode \im'plōd\ vb -plod·ed; -plod·ing : burst inward —im·plo·sion \-'plōzhən\ n —im·plo·sive \-'plōsiv\ adj

im·plore \im'plōr\ vb -plored; -plor·ing : entreat

im·ply \-'plī\ vb -plied; -ply·ing : express indirectly

im·po·lite \,impə'līt\ adj : not polite

im·pol·i·tic \im'pälə,tik\ adj : not politic

im·pon·der·a·ble \im'pändərəbəl\ adj : incapable of being precisely evaluated —imponderable n

im·port \im'pōrt\ vb 1 : mean 2 : bring in from an external source ~ \'im,pōrt\ n 1 : meaning 2 : importance 3 : something imported —im·por·ta·tion \,im,pōr'tāshən\ n —im·port·er n

im·por·tant \im'pōrtənt\ adj : having great worth, significance, or influence —im·por·tance \-ᵊns\ n —impor·tant·ly adv

im·por·tu·nate \im'pōrchənət\ adj : troublesome persistent or urgent

im·por·tune \,impər'tün, -'tyün; im'pōrchən\ vb -tuned; -tun·ing : urge or beg persistently —im·por·tu·ni·ty \,impər'tünətē, -'tyü-\ n

im·pose \im'pōz\ vb -posed; -pos·ing 1 : establish as compulsory 2 : take unwarranted advantage of —im·po·si·tion \,impə'zishən\ n

im·pos·ing \im'pōziŋ\ adj : impressive —im·pos·ing·ly adv

im·pos·si·ble \im'päsəbəl\ adj 1 : incapable of occurring 2 : enormously difficult —im·pos·si·bil·i·ty \im,päsə'bilətē\ n —im·pos·si·bly \im'päsəblē\ adv

im·post \im,pōst\ n : tax

im·pos·tor, im·pos·ter \im'pästər\ n : one who assumes an identity or title to deceive —im·pos·ture \-'päschər\ n

im·po·tent \'impətənt\ adj 1 : lacking power 2 : sterile —im·po·tence \-pətəns\ n —im·po·ten·cy \-ᵊnsē\ n —im·po·tent·ly adv

im·pound \im'paůnd\ vb : seize and hold in legal custody —im·pound·ment n

im·pov·er·ish \im'pävərish\ vb : make poor —im·pov·er·ish·ment n

im·prac·ti·ca·ble \im'praktikəbəl\ adj : not practicable

im·prac·ti·cal \-'praktikəl\ adj : not practical

im·pre·cise \,impri'sīs\ adj : not precise —im·pre·cise·ly adv —im·pre·cise·ness n —im·pre·ci·sion \-'sizhən\ n

im·preg·na·ble \im'pregnəbəl\ adj : able to resist attack —im·preg·na·bil·i·ty \im,pregnə'bilətē\ n

im·preg·nate \im'preg,nāt\ vb -nat·ed; -nat·ing 1 : make pregnant 2 : cause to be filled, permeated, or saturated —im·preg·na·tion \,im,preg'nāshən\ n

im·pre·sa·rio \ˌimprəˈsärēˌ ō\ *n, pl* **-ri·os** : one who sponsors an entertainment

¹im·press \imˈpres\ *vb* 1 : apply with or produce by pressure 2 : press, stamp, or print in or upon 3 : produce a vivid impression of 4 : affect (as the mind) forcibly

²im·press \imˈpres\ *vb* : force into naval service —**im·press·ment** *n*

im·pres·sion \imˈpreshən\ *n* 1 : mark made by impressing 2 : marked influence or effect 3 : printed copy 4 : vague notion or recollection —**im·pres·sion·able** \-ˈpreshənəbəl\ *adj*

im·pres·sive \imˈpresiv\ *adj* : making a marked impression —**im·pres·sive·ly** *adv* —**im·pres·sive·ness** *n*

im·pri·ma·tur \ˌimprəˈmäˌtùr\ *n* : official approval (as of a publication by a censor)

im·print \imˈprint, ˈimˌ-\ *vb* : stamp or mark by or as if by pressure ~ \ˈimˌ-\ *n* : something imprinted or printed

im·pris·on \imˈprizᵊn\ *vb* : put in prison —**im·pris·on·ment** \-mənt\ *n*

im·prob·a·ble \imˈpräbəbəl\ *adj* : unlikely to be true or to occur —**im·prob·a·bil·i·ty** \im,präbəˈbilətē\ *n* —**im·prob·a·bly** *adv*

im·promp·tu \imˈprämptü, -tyü\ *adj* : not planned beforehand —**impromptu** *adv or n*

im·prop·er \imˈpräpər\ *adj* : not proper —**im·prop·er·ly** *adv*

im·pro·pri·ety \ˌimprəˈprīətē\ *n, pl* **-eties** : state or instance of being improper

im·prove \imˈprüv\ *vb* **-proved; -prov·ing** : grow or make better —**im·prov·able** \-ˈprüvəbəl\ *adj* —**im·prove·ment** *n*

im·prov·i·dent \imˈprävədənt\ *adj* : not providing for the future —**im·prov·i·dence** \-əns\ *n*

im·pro·vise \ˈimprəˌvīz\ *vb* **-vised; -vis·ing** : make, invent, or arrange offhand —**im·pro·vi·sa·tion** \im,prävəˈzāshən, ˌimprəvə-\ *n* —**im·pro·vis·er, im·pro·vi·sor** \ˈimprəˌvīzər\ *n*

im·pru·dent \imˈprüdᵊnt\ *adj* : not prudent —**im·pru·dence** \-ᵊns\ *n*

im·pu·dent \ˈimpyədənt\ *adj* : insolent —**im·pu·dence** \-əns\ *n* —**im·pu·dent·ly** *adv*

im·pugn \imˈpyün\ *vb* : attack as false

im·pulse \ˈimˌpəls\ *n* 1 : moving force 2 : sudden inclination

im·pul·sive \imˈpəlsiv\ *adj* : acting on impulse —**im·pul·sive·ly** *adv* —**im·pul·sive·ness** *n*

im·pu·ni·ty \imˈpyünətē\ *n* : exemption from punishment or harm

im·pure \imˈpyùr\ *adj* : not pure —**im·pu·ri·ty** \-ˈpyùrətē\ *n*

im·pute \imˈpyüt\ *vb* **-put·ed; -put·ing** : credit to or blame on a person or cause —**im·pu·ta·tion** \ˌimpyəˈtāshən\ *n*

in \ˈin\ *prep* 1 —used to indicate location, inclusion, situation, or manner 2 : into 3 : during ~ *adv* : to or toward the inside ~ *adj* : located inside

in- \in\ *prefix* 1 : not 2 : lack of

inability	incoherently
inaccessibility	incombustible
inaccessible	incommensurate
inaccuracy	incommodious
inaccurate	incommunicable
inaction	incompatibility
inactive	incompatible
inactivity	incomplete
inadequacy	incompletely
inadequate	incompleteness
inadequately	incomprehensible
inadmissibility	inconclusive
inadmissible	incongruent
inadvisability	inconsecutive
inadvisable	inconsiderate
inapparent	inconsiderately
inapplicable	inconsiderateness
inapposite	inconsistency
inappositely	inconsistent
inappositeness	inconsistently
inappreciative	inconspicuous
inapproachable	inconspicuously
inappropriate	inconstancy
inappropriately	inconstant
inappropriateness	inconstantly
inapt	inconsumable
inarguable	incontestable
inartistic	incontestably
inartistically	incorporeal
inattention	incorporeally
inattentive	incorrect
inattentively	incorrectly
inattentiveness	incorrectness
inaudible	incorruptible
inaudibly	inculpable
inauspicious	incurable
inauthentic	incurious
incapability	indecency
incapable	indecent
incautious	indecently
incoherence	indecipherable
incoherent	

indecisive
indecisively
indecisiveness
indecorous
indecorously
indecorousness
indefensible
indefinable
indefinably
indescribable
indescribably
indestructibility
indestructible
indigestible
indiscernible
indiscreet
indiscreetly
indiscretion
indisputable
indisputably
indistinct
indistinctly
indistinctness
indivisibility
indivisible
ineducable
ineffective
ineffectively
ineffectiveness
ineffectual
ineffectually
ineffectualness
inefficiency
inefficient
inefficiently
inelastic
inelasticity
inelegance
inelegant
ineligibility
ineligible
ineradicable
inessential
inexact
inexactly
inexpedient
inexpensive
inexperience
inexperienced
inexpert
inexpertly
inexpertness
inexplicable
inexplicably
inexplicit
inexpressible
inexpressibly
inextinguishable

inextricable
infeasibility
infeasible
infelicitous
infelicity
infertile
infertility
inflexibility
inflexible
inflexibly
infrequent
infrequently
inglorious
ingloriously
ingratitude
inhumane
inhumanely
injudicious
injudiciously
injudiciousness
inoffensive
inoperable
inoperative
insalubrious
insensitive
insensitivity
inseparable
insignificant
insincere
insincerely
insincerity
insolubility
insoluble
instability
insubstantial
insufficiency
insufficient
insufficiently
insupportable
intangibility
intangible
intangibly
intolerable
intolerably
intolerance
intolerant
intractable
invariable
invariably
inviable
invisibility
invisible
invisibly
involuntarily
involuntary
invulnerability
invulnerable
invulnerably

in·ad·ver·tent \,inəd'vərtᵊnt\ *adj* : unintentional —**in·ad·ver·tence** \-ᵊns\ *n*
—**in·ad·ver·ten·cy** \-ᵊnsē\ *n* : in-ad·ver·tent·ly *adv*

in·alien·able \in'ālyənəbəl, -'ālēənə-\ *adj* : incapable of being transferred or given up —**in·alien·abil·i·ty** \in-,ālyənə'bilətē, -'ālēənə-\ *n* —**in-alien·ably** *adv*

inane \in'ān\ *adj* : silly or stupid —**inan·i·ty** \in'anətē\ *n*

in·an·i·mate \in'anəmət\ *adj* : not animate or animated —**in·an·i·mate·ly** *adv* —**in·an·i·mate·ness** *n*

in·ap·pre·cia·ble \,inə'prēshəbəl\ *adj* : too small to be perceived —**in·ap-pre·cia·bly** *adv*

in·ar·tic·u·late \,inär'tikyələt\ *adj* : without the power of speech or effective expression —**in·ar·tic·u·late·ly** *adv*

in·as·much as \,inaz'məchaz\ *conj* : because

in·at·ten·tion \,inə'tenchən\ *n* : failure to pay attention

in·au·gu·ral \in'ógyərəl, -gərəl\ *adj* : relating to an inauguration ~ *n* 1 : inaugural speech 2 : inauguration

in·au·gu·rate \in'ógyə,rāt, -gə-\ *vb* -**rat·ed; -rat·ing** 1 : install in office 2 : start —**in·au·gu·ra·tion** \-,ógyə-'rāshən, -gə-\ *n*

in·board \'in,bōrd\ *adv* : inside a vehicle or craft —**inboard** *adj*

in·born \'in,bórn\ *adj* : present from birth

in·bred \'in,bred\ *adj* : deeply ingrained in one's nature

in·breed·ing \'in,brēdiŋ\ *n* : interbreeding of closely related individuals —**in·breed** \-,brēd\ *vb*

in·cal·cu·la·ble \in'kalkyələbəl\ *adj* : too large to be calculated —**in·cal-cu·la·bly** *adv*

in·can·des·cent \,inkan'desᵊnt\ *adj* 1 : glowing with heat 2 : brilliant —**in·can·des·cence** \-ᵊns\ *n*

in·can·ta·tion \,in,kan'tāshən\ *n* : use of spoken or sung charms or spells as a magic ritual

in·ca·pac·i·tate \,inkə'pasə,tāt\ *vb* -**tat-ed; -tat·ing** : disable

in·ca·pac·i·ty \,inkə'pasətē\ *n, pl* -**ties** : quality or state of being incapable

in·car·cer·ate \in'kärsə,rāt\ *vb* -**at·ed; -at·ing** : imprison —**in·car·cer·a·tion** \in,kärsə'rāshən\ *n*

in·car·nate \in'kärnət, -,nāt\ *adj* : having bodily form and substance —**in·car·nate** \-ˌnāt\ *vb* —**in·car·na·tion** \-ˌkär'nāshən\ *n*

in·cen·di·ary \in'sendē,erē\ *adj* **1** : pertaining to or used to ignite fire **2** : tending to excite —**incendiary** *n*

in·cense \'in,sens\ *n* : material burned to produce a fragrant odor or its smoke ~ \in'sens\ *vb* —**censed; -cens·ing** : make very angry

in·cen·tive \in'sentive\ *n* : inducement to do something

in·cep·tion \in'sepshən\ *n* : beginning

in·ces·sant \in'sesªnt\ *adj* : continuing without interruption —**in·ces·sant·ly** *adv*

in·cest \'in,sest\ *n* : sexual intercourse between close relatives —**in·ces·tu·ous** \in'seschəwəs\ *adj*

inch \'inch\ *n* : unit of length equal to 1/12 foot ~ *vb* : move by small degrees

in·cho·ate \in'kōət, 'inkə,wāt\ *adj* : new and not fully formed or ordered

in·ci·dent \'insədənt\ *n* : occurrence —**in·ci·dence** \-əns\ *n* —**incident** *adj*

in·ci·den·tal \,insə'dentªl\ *adj* **1** : subordinate, nonessential, or attendant **2** : met by chance ~ *n* **1** : something incidental **2** *pl* : minor expenses that are not itemized —**in·ci·den·tal·ly** *adv*

in·cin·er·ate \in'sinə,rāt\ *vb* **-at·ed; -at·ing** : burn to ashes —**in·cin·er·a·tor** \-ˌrātər\ *n*

in·cip·i·ent \in'sipēənt\ *adj* : beginning to be or appear

in·cise \in'sīz\ *vb* **-cised; -cis·ing** : carve into

in·ci·sion \in'sizhən\ *n* : surgical cut

in·ci·sive \in'sīsiv\ *adj* : keen and discerning —**in·ci·sive·ly** *adv*

in·ci·sor \in'sīzər\ *n* : tooth for cutting

in·cite \in'sīt\ *vb* **-cit·ed; -cit·ing** : arouse to action —**in·cite·ment** *n*

in·ci·vil·i·ty \,insə'vilətē\ *n* : rudeness

in·clem·ent \in'klemənt\ *adj* : stormy —**in·clem·en·cy** \-ənsē\ *n*

in·cline \in'klīn\ *vb* **-clined; -clin·ing 1** : bow **2** : tend toward an opinion **3** : slope ~ *n* : slope —**in·cli·na·tion** \,inklə'nāshən\ *n* —**in·clin·er** *n*

inclose, inclosure *var of* ENCLOSE, ENCLOSURE

in·clude \in'klüd\ *vb* **-clud·ed; -clud·ing** : take in or comprise —**in·clu·sion** \in'klüzhən\ *n* —**in·clu·sive** \-'klüsiv\ *adj*

in·cog·ni·to \,in,käg'nētō, in'kägnə,tō\

adv or adj : with one's identity concealed

in·come \'in,kəm\ *n* : money gained (as from work or investment)

in·com·ing \'in,kəmiŋ\ *adj* : coming in

in·com·mu·ni·ca·do \,inkə,myünə-'kädō\ *adv* : without means of communication

in·com·pa·ra·ble \in'kämpərəbəl\ *adj* : eminent beyond comparison

in·com·pe·tent \in'kämpətənt\ *adj* : lacking sufficient knowledge or skill —**in·com·pe·tence** \-pətəns\ *n* —**in·com·pe·ten·cy** \-ənsē\ *n* —**incompetent** *n*

in·con·ceiv·able \,inkən'sēvəbəl\ *adj* **1** : impossible to comprehend **2** : unbelievable —**in·con·ceiv·ably** \-blē\ *adv*

in·con·gru·ous \in'käŋgrəwəs\ *adj* : inappropriate or out of place —**incon·gru·i·ty** \,inkən'grüətē, -,kän-\ *n* —**in·con·gru·ous·ly** *adv*

in·con·se·quen·tial \,in,känsə'kwenchəl\ *adj* : unimportant —**in·con·se·quence** \in'känsə,kwens\ *n* —**in·con·se·quen·tial·ly** *adv*

in·con·sid·er·able \,inkən'sidərəbəl\ *adj* : trivial

in·con·sol·able \,inkən'sōləbəl\ *adj* : incapable of being consoled —**in·con·sol·ably** *adv*

in·con·ve·nience \,inkən'vēnyəns\ *n* **1** : discomfort **2** : something that causes trouble or annoyance ~ *vb* : cause inconvenience to —**in·con·ve·nient** \,inkən'vēnyənt\ *adj* —**in·con·ve·nient·ly** *adv*

in·cor·po·rate \in'kórpə,rāt\ *vb* **-rat·ed; -rat·ing 1** : blend **2** : form into a legal body —**in·cor·po·rat·ed** *adj* —**in·cor·po·ra·tion** \-ˌkórpə'rāshən\ *n*

in·cor·ri·gi·ble \in'kórəjəbəl\ *adj* : incapable of being corrected or reformed —**in·cor·ri·gi·bil·i·ty** \-ˌkórəjə'bilətē\ *n*

in·crease \in'krēs, 'in,krēs\ *vb* **-creased; -creas·ing** : make or become greater ~ \'in,-, in'-\ *n* **1** : enlargement in size **2** : something added —**in·creas·ing·ly** \-'krēsiŋlē\ *adv*

in·cred·i·ble \in'kredəbəl\ *adj* : too extraordinary to be believed —**incred·i·bil·i·ty** \in,kredə'bilətē\ *n* —**in·cred·i·bly** \in'kredəblē\ *adv*

in·cred·u·lous \in'krejələs\ *adj* : skeptical —**in·cre·du·li·ty** \,inkri'dülətē, -'dyü-\ *n* —**in·cred·u·lous·ly** *adv*

in·cre·ment \'iŋkrəmənt, 'in-\ n : increase or amount of increase —**incremen·tal** \,iŋkrə'ment³l, ,in-\ adj

in·crim·i·nate \in'krimə,nāt\ vb -**nated; -nating** : show to be guilty of a crime —**in·crim·i·na·tion** \-,krimə'nāshən\ n —**in·crim·i·na·to·ry** \-'krimənə,tōrē\ adj

in·cu·bate \'iŋkyə,bāt, 'in-\ vb -**bated; -bating** : keep (as eggs) under conditions favorable for development —**in·cu·ba·tion** \,iŋkyə'bāshən, ,in-\ n —**in·cu·ba·tor** \'iŋkyə,bātər, 'in-\ n

in·cul·cate \in'kəl,kāt, 'in,kəl-\ vb -**cated; -cating** : instill by repeated teaching —**in·cul·ca·tion** \,in,kəl-'kāshən\ n

in·cum·bent \in'kəmbənt\ n : holder of an office — adj : obligatory —**incum·ben·cy** \-bənsē\ n

in·cur \in'kər\ vb -**rr-** : become liable or subject to

in·cur·sion \in'kərzhən\ n : invasion

in·debt·ed \in'detəd\ adj : owing something —**in·debt·ed·ness** n

in·de·ci·sion \,indi'sizhən\ n : inability to decide

in·deed \in'dēd\ adv : without question

in·de·fat·i·ga·ble \,indi'fatigəbəl\ adj : not tiring —**in·de·fat·i·ga·bly** \-blē\ adv

in·def·i·nite \in'defənət\ adj 1 : not defining or identifying 2 : not precise 3 : having no fixed limit —**indef·i·nite·ly** adv

in·del·i·ble \in'deləbəl\ adj : not capable of being removed or erased —**indel·i·bly** adv

in·del·i·cate \in'delikət\ adj : improper —**in·del·i·ca·cy** \in'deləkəsē\ n

in·dem·ni·fy \in'demnə,fī\ vb -**fied; -fy·ing** : repay for a loss —**in·demni·fi·ca·tion** \-,demnəfə'kāshən\ n

in·dem·ni·ty \in'demnətē\ n, pl -**ties** : security against loss or damage

¹in·dent \in'dent\ vb : leave a space at the beginning of a paragraph

²indent vb : force inward so as to form a depression or dent

in·den·ta·tion \,in,den'tashən\ n 1 : notch, recess, or dent 2 : action of indenting 3 : space at the beginning of a paragraph

in·den·ture \in'denchər\ n : contract binding one person to work for another for a given period —usu. in pl. ~ vb -**tured; -tur·ing** : bind by indentures

Independence Day n : July 4 observed as a legal holiday in commemoration of the adoption of the Declaration of Independence in 1776

in·de·pen·dent \,ində'pendənt\ adj 1 : not governed by another 2 : not requiring or relying on something or somebody else 3 : not easily influenced —**in·de·pen·dence** \-dəns\ n —**independent** n —**in·de·pen·dent·ly** adv

in·de·ter·mi·nate \,indi'tərmənət\ adj : not definitely determined —**inde·ter·mi·na·cy** \-nəsē\ n —**inde·ter·mi·nate·ly** adv

in·dex \'in,deks\ n, pl -**dex·es** or -**di·ces** \-də,sēz\ 1 : alphabetical list of items (as topics in a book) 2 : a number that serves as a measure or indicator of something ~ vb 1 : provide with an index 2 : serve as an index of

index finger n : forefinger

in·di·cate \'ində,kāt\ vb -**cated; -cating** 1 : point out or to 2 : show indirectly 3 : state briefly —**in·di·ca·tion** \,ində'kāshən\ n —**in·di·ca·tor** \'ində-,kātər\ n

in·dic·a·tive \in'dikətiv\ adj : serving to indicate

in·dict \in'dīt\ vb : charge with a crime —**in·dict·able** adj —**in·dict·ment** n

in·dif·fer·ent \in'difrənt\ adj 1 : having no preference 2 : showing neither interest nor dislike 3 : mediocre —**indif·fer·ence** \-'difrəns\ n —**in·dif·fer·ent·ly** adv

in·dig·e·nous \in'dijənəs\ adj : native to a particular region

in·di·gent \'indijənt\ adj : needy —**in·di·gence** \-jəns\ n

in·di·ges·tion \,indi'jeschən, -də-\ n : discomfort from inability to digest food

in·dig·na·tion \,indig'nāshən\ n : anger aroused by something unjust or unworthy —**in·dig·nant** \in'dignənt\ adj —**in·dig·nant·ly** adv

in·dig·ni·ty \in'dignətē\ n, pl -**ties** 1 : offense against self-respect 2 : humiliating treatment

in·di·go \'indi,gō\ n, pl -**gos** or -**goes** 1 : blue dye 2 : deep reddish blue color

in·di·rect \,ində'rekt, -dī-\ adj : not straight or straightforward —**in·di·rec·tion** \-'rekshən\ n —**in·di·rect·ly** adv —**in·di·rect·ness** n

in·dis·crim·i·nate \,indis'krimənət\ adj 1 : not careful or discriminating 2

: haphazard —**in·dis·crim·i·nate·ly** adv

in·dis·pens·a·ble \,indis'pensəbəl\ adj : absolutely essential —**in·dis·pens·abil·i·ty** \-,pensə'bilətē\ n —**indis·pensable** n —**in·dis·pens·ably** \-'pensəblē\ adv

in·dis·posed \-'pōzd\ adj : slightly ill —**in·dis·po·si·tion** \in,dispə'zishən\ n

in·dis·sol·u·ble \,indis'älyəbəl\ adj : not capable of being dissolved or broken

in·di·vid·u·al \,ində'vijəwəl\ n 1 : single member of a category 2 : person —**individual** adj —**in·di·vid·u·al·ly** adv

in·di·vid·u·al·ist \-əwəlist\ n : person who is markedly independent in thought or action

in·di·vid·u·al·i·ty \-,vijə'walətē\ n : special quality that distinguishes an individual

in·di·vid·u·al·ize \-'vijəwə,līz\ vb -ized; -iz·ing 1 : make individual 2 : treat individually

in·doc·tri·nate \in'däktrə,nāt\ vb -nat·ed; -nat·ing : instruct in fundamentals (as of a doctrine) —**in·doc·tri·na·tion** \in,däktrə'nāshən\ n

in·do·lent \'indələnt\ adj : lazy —**in·do·lence** \-ləns\ n

in·dom·i·ta·ble \in'dämətəbəl\ adj : invincible —**in·dom·i·ta·bly** \-blē\ adv

in·door \'in'dōr\ adj : relating to the inside of a building

in·doors \in'dōrz\ adv : in or into a building

in·du·bi·ta·ble \in'dübətəbəl, -'dyü-\ adj : being beyond question —**in·du·bi·ta·bly** \-blē\ adv

in·duce \in'düs, -'dyüs\ vb -duced; -duc·ing 1 : persuade 2 : bring about —**in·duce·ment** n —**in·duc·er** n

in·duct \in'dəkt\ vb 1 : put in office 2 : admit as a member 3 : enroll (as for military service) —**in·duct·ee** \in-,dək'tē\ n

in·duc·tion \in'dəkshən\ n 1 : act or instance of inducting 2 : reasoning from particular instances to a general conclusion

in·duc·tive \in'dəktiv\ adj : reasoning by induction

in·dulge \in'dəlj\ vb -dulged; -dulg·ing : yield to the desire of or for —**in·dulgence** \-'dəljəns\ n —**in·dul·gent** \-jənt\ adj —**in·dul·gent·ly** adv

in·dus·tri·al \in'dəstrēəl\ adj 1 : relating

to industry 2 : heavy-duty —**in·dus·tri·al·ist** \-əlist\ n —**in·dus·tri·al·iza·tion** \-,dəstrēələ'zāshən\ n —**in·dus·tri·al·ize** \-'dəstrēə,līz\ vb —**in·dus·tri·al·ly** adv

in·dus·tri·ous \in'dəstrēəs\ adj : diligent or busy —**in·dus·tri·ous·ly** adv —**in·dus·tri·ous·ness** n

in·dus·try \'indəstrē\ n, pl -tries 1 : diligence 2 : manufacturing enterprises or activity

in·e·bri·at·ed \i'nēbrē,ātəd\ adj : drunk —**ine·bri·a·tion** \-,ēbrē'āshən\ n

in·ef·fa·ble \in'efəbəl\ adj : incapable of being expressed in words —**in·ef·fa·bly** \-blē\ adv

in·ept \in'ept\ adj 1 : inappropriate or foolish 2 : generally incompetent —**in·ep·ti·tude** \in'eptə,tüd, -,tyüd\ n —**in·ept·ly** adv —**in·ept·ness** n

in·equal·i·ty \,ini'kwälətē\ n : quality of being unequal or uneven

in·ert \in'ərt\ adj 1 : powerless to move or act 2 : sluggish —**in·ert·ly** adv —**in·ert·ness** n

in·er·tia \in'ərshə\ n : tendency of matter to remain at rest or in motion —**in·er·tial** \-shəl\ adj

in·es·cap·a·ble \,inə'skāpəbəl\ adj : inevitable —**in·es·cap·ably** \-blē\ adv

in·es·ti·ma·ble \in'estəməbəl\ adj : incapable of being estimated —**in·es·ti·ma·bly** \-blē\ adv

in·ev·i·ta·ble \in'evətəbəl\ adj : incapable of being avoided or escaped —**in·ev·i·ta·bil·i·ty** \in,evətə'bilətē\ n —**in·ev·i·ta·bly** \in'evətəblē\ adv

in·ex·cus·able \inik'skyüzəbəl\ adj : being without excuse or justification —**in·ex·cus·ably** \-blē\ adv

in·ex·haust·ible \,inig'zóstəbəl\ adj : incapable of being used up or tired out —**in·ex·haust·ibly** \-blē\ adv

in·ex·o·ra·ble \in'eksərəbəl\ adj : unyielding or relentless —**in·ex·o·ra·bly** adv

in·fal·li·ble \in'faləbəl\ adj : incapable of error —**in·fal·li·bil·i·ty** \in-,falə'bilətē\ n —**in·fal·li·bly** adv

in·fa·mous \'infəməs\ adj : having the worst kind of reputation —**in·fa·mous·ly** adv

in·fa·my \-mē\ n, pl -mies : evil reputation

in·fan·cy \'infənsē\ n, pl -cies 1 : early childhood 2 : early period of existence

infant 173 infringe

in·fant \'infant\ *n* : baby

in·fan·tile \'infən,tīl, -t^əl, -,tēl\ *adj* 1 : relating to infants 2 : childish

in·fan·try \'infəntrē\ *n, pl* **-tries** : soldiers that fight on foot

in·fat·u·ate \in'facha,wāt\ *vb* **-at·ed; -at·ing** : inspire with foolish love or admiration —**in·fat·u·a·tion** \-,facha-'wāshən\ *n*

in·fect \in'fekt\ *vb* : contaminate with disease-producing matter —**in·fec·tion** \-'fekshən\ *n* —**in·fec·tious** \-shəs\ *adj* —**in·fec·tive** \-'fektiv\ *adj*

in·fer \in'fər\ *vb* **-rr-** : deduce —**in·fer·ence** \'infərəns\ *n* —**in·fer·en·tial** \,infə'renchəl\ *adj*

in·fe·ri·or \in'firēər\ *adj* 1 : being lower in position, degree, rank, or merit 2 : of lesser quality —**inferior** *n* —**in·fe·ri·or·i·ty** \in,firē'orətē\ *n*

in·fer·nal \in'fərn^əl\ *adj* : of or like hell—often used as a general expression of disapproval —**in·fer·nal·ly** *adv*

in·fer·no \in'fərnō\ *n, pl* **-nos** : place or condition suggesting hell

in·fest \in'fest\ *vb* : swarm or grow in or over —**in·fes·ta·tion** \,in,fes'tāshən\ *n*

in·fi·del \'infəd^əl, -fə,del\ *n* : one who does not believe in a particular religion

in·fi·del·i·ty \,infə'delətē, -fī-\ *n, pl* **-ties** : lack of faithfulness

in·field \'in,fēld\ *n* : baseball field inside the base lines —**in·field·er** *n*

in·fil·trate \in'fil,trāt, 'infil-\ *vb* **-trat·ed; -trat·ing** : enter or become established in without being noticed —**in·fil·tra·tion** \,infil'trāshən\ *n*

in·fi·nite \'infənət\ *adj* 1 : having no limit or extending indefinitely 2 : vast —**infinite** *n* —**in·fi·nite·ly** *adv* —**in·fin·i·tude** \in'finə,tüd, -tyüd\ *n*

in·fin·i·tes·i·mal \,in,finə'tesəməl\ *adj* : immeasurably small —**in·fin·i·tes·i·mal·ly** *adv*

in·fin·i·tive \in'finətiv\ *n* : verb form in English usu. used with *to*

in·fin·i·ty \in'finətē\ *n, pl* **-ties** 1 : quality or state of being infinite 2 : indefinitely great number or amount

in·firm \in'fərm\ *adj* : feeble from age —**in·fir·mi·ty** \-'fərmətē\ *n*

in·fir·ma·ry \in'fərmərē\ *n, pl* **-ries** : place for the care of the sick

in·flame \in'flām\ *vb* **-flamed; -flam·ing** 1 : excite to intense action or feeling 2 : affect or become affected with inflammation —**in·flam·ma·to·ry** \-'flamə,tōrē\ *adj*

in·flam·ma·ble \in'flaməbəl\ *adj* : flammable

in·flam·ma·tion \,inflə'māshən\ *n* : response to injury in which an affected area becomes red and painful and congested with blood

in·flate \in'flāt\ *vb* **-flat·ed; -flat·ing** 1 : swell or puff up (as with gas) 2 : expand or increase abnormally —**in·flat·able** *adj*

in·fla·tion \in'flāshən\ *n* 1 : act of inflating 2 : continual rise in prices —**in·fla·tion·ary** \-shə,nerē\ *adj*

in·flec·tion \in'flekshən\ *n* 1 : change in pitch or loudness of the voice 2 : change in form of a word —**in·flect** \-'flekt\ *vb* —**in·flec·tion·al** \-'flekshənəl\ *adj*

in·flict \in'flikt\ *vb* : give by or as if by hitting —**in·flic·tion** \-'flikshən\ *n*

in·flu·ence \'in,flüəns\ *n* 1 : power or capacity of causing an effect in indirect or intangible ways 2 : one that exerts influence ~ *vb* **-enced; -enc·ing** : affect or alter by influence —**in·flu·en·tial** \,inflü'enchəl\ *adj*

in·flu·en·za \,inflü'enzə\ *n* : acute very contagious virus disease

in·flux \'in,fləks\ *n* : a flowing in

in·form \in'form\ *vb* : give information or knowledge to —**in·for·mant** \-ənt\ *n* —**in·form·er** *n*

in·for·mal \in'forməl\ *adj* 1 : without formality or ceremony 2 : for ordinary or familiar use —**in·for·mal·i·ty** \,infor'malətē, -fər-\ *n* —**in·for·mal·ly** *adv*

in·for·ma·tion \,infər'māshən\ *n* : knowledge obtained from investigation, study, or instruction —**in·for·ma·tion·al** \-shənəl\ *adj*

in·for·ma·tive \in'formətiv\ *adj* : giving knowledge

in·frac·tion \in'frakshən\ *n* : violation

in·fra·red \,infrə'red\ *adj* : being, relating to, or using radiation of wavelengths longer than those of red light —**infrared** *n*

in·fra·struc·ture \'infrə,strəkchər\ *n* : foundation of a system or organization

in·fringe \in'frinj\ *vb* **-fringed; -fring-**

ing : violate another's right or privilege —**in·fringe·ment** n

in·fu·ri·ate \in'fyürē,āt\ vb -**at·ed; -at·ing** : make furious —**in·fu·ri·at·ing·ly** \-,ātiŋlē\ adv

in·fuse \in'fyüz\ vb -**fused; -fus·ing 1** : instill a principle or quality in **2** : steep in liquid without boiling — **in·fu·sion** \-'fyüzhən\ n

1·ing \iŋ\ vb suffix or adj suffix —used to form the present participle and sometimes an adjective resembling a present participle

2·ing n suffix **1** : action or process **2** : something connected with or resulting from an action or process

in·ge·nious \in'jēnyəs\ adj : very clever —**in·ge·nious·ly** adv —**in·ge·nious·ness** n

in·ge·nue, in·gé·nue \'anjə,nü, 'än-; 'aⁿzhə-, 'äⁿ-\ n : naive young woman

in·ge·nu·i·ty \,injə'nüətē, -'nyü-\ n, pl -**ities** : skill or cleverness in planning or inventing

in·gen·u·ous \in'jenyəwəs\ adj : innocent and candid —**in·gen·u·ous·ly** adv —**in·gen·u·ous·ness** n

in·gest \in'jest\ vb : eat —**in·ges·tion** \-'jeschən\ n

in·gle·nook \'iŋgəl,nůk\ n : corner by the fireplace

in·got \'iŋgət\ n : block of metal

in·grained \in'grānd\ adj : deep-seated

in·grate \'in,grāt\ n : ungrateful person

in·gra·ti·ate \in'grāshē,āt\ vb -**at·ed; -at·ing** : gain favor for (oneself) — **in·gra·ti·at·ing** adj

in·gre·di·ent \in'grēdēənt\ n : one of the substances that make up a mixture

in·grown \'in,grōn\ adj : grown in and esp. into the flesh

in·hab·it \in'habət\ vb : live or dwell in —**in·hab·it·able** adj —**in·hab·it·ant** \-ətənt\ n

in·hale \in'hāl\ vb -**haled; -hal·ing** : breathe in —**in·hal·ant** \-ənt\ n — **in·ha·la·tion** \,inhə'lāshən, ,inə-\ n —**in·hal·er** n

in·here \in'hir\ vb -**hered; -her·ing** : be inherent

in·her·ent \in'hirənt, -'her-\ adj : being an essential part of something —**in·her·ent·ly** adv

in·her·it \in'herət\ vb : receive from one's ancestors —**in·her·it·able** \-əbəl\ adj —**in·her·i·tance** \-ətəns\ n —**in·her·i·tor** \-ətər\ n

in·hib·it \in'hibət\ vb : hold in check — **in·hi·bi·tion** \,inhə'bishən, ,inə-\ n

in·hu·man \in'hyümən, -'yü-\ adj : cruel or impersonal —**in·hu·man·i·ty** \-hyü'manətē, -yü-\ n —**in·hu·man·ly** adv —**in·hu·man·ness** n

in·im·i·cal \in'imikəl\ adj : hostile or harmful —**in·im·i·cal·ly** adv

in·im·i·ta·ble \in'imətəbəl\ adj : not capable of being imitated

in·iq·ui·ty \in'ikwətē\ n, pl -**ties** : wickedness —**in·iq·ui·tous** \-wətəs\ adj

in·i·tial \in'ishəl\ adj **1** : of or relating to the beginning **2** : first ~ n : 1st letter of a word or name ~ vb -**tialed** or -**tialled; -tial·ing** or -**tial·ling** : put initials on —**in·i·tial·ly** adv

in·i·ti·ate \in'ishē,āt\ vb -**at·ed; -at·ing 1** : start **2** : induct into membership **3** : instruct in the rudiments of something —**ini·ti·ate** \-'ishēət\ n —**ini·ti·a·tion** \-,ishē'āshən\ n —**ini·ti·a·to·ry** \-'ishēə,tōrē\ adj

ini·tia·tive \in'ishətiv\ n **1** : first step **2** : readiness to undertake something on one's own

in·ject \in'jekt\ vb : force or introduce into something —**in·jec·tion** \-'jekshən\ n

in·junc·tion \in'jəŋkshən\ n : court writ requiring one to do or to refrain from doing a specified act

in·jure \'injər\ vb -**jured; -jur·ing** : do damage, hurt, or a wrong to

in·ju·ry \'injərē\ n, pl -**ries 1** : act that injures **2** : hurt, damage, or loss sustained —**in·ju·ri·ous** \in'júrēəs\ adj

in·jus·tice \in'jəstəs\ n : unjust act

ink \'iŋk\ n : usu. liquid and colored material for writing and printing ~ vb : put ink on —**ink·well** \-,wel\ n — **inky** adj

in·kling \'iŋkliŋ\ n : hint or idea

in·land \'in,land, -lənd\ n : interior of a country —**inland** adj or adv

in-law \'in,lò\ n : relative by marriage

in·lay \in'lā, 'in,lā\ vb -**laid** \-'lād\; -**lay·ing** : set into a surface for decoration ~ \'in,lā\ n **1** : inlaid work **2** : shaped filling cemented into a tooth

in·let \'in,let, -lət\ n : small bay

in·mate \'in,māt\ n : person confined to an asylum or prison

in me·mo·ri·am \,inmə'mōrēəm\ prep : in memory of

in·most \'in,mōst\ adj : deepest within

inn \'in\ n : hotel

in·nards \'inərdz\ n pl : internal parts

in·nate \in'āt\ adj 1 : inborn 2 : inherent —**in·nate·ly** adv

in·ner \'inər\ adj : being on the inside

in·ner·most \'inər,mōst\ adj : farthest inward

in·ner·sole \,inər'sōl\ n : insole

in·ning \'iniŋ\ n : baseball team's turn at bat

inn·keep·er \'in,kēpər\ n : owner of an inn

in·no·cent \'inəsənt\ adj 1 : free from guilt 2 : harmless 3 : not sophisticated —**in·no·cence** \-səns\ n —**innocent** n —**in·no·cent·ly** adv

in·noc·u·ous \in'äkyəwəs\ adj 1 : harmless 2 : inoffensive

in·no·va·tion \,inə'vāshən\ n : new idea or method —**in·no·vate** \'inə,vāt\ vb —**in·no·va·tive** \'inə,vātiv\ adj —**in·no·va·tor** \-,vātər\ n

in·nu·en·do \,inyə'wendō\ n, pl -dos or -does : insinuation

in·nu·mer·a·ble \in'ümərəbəl, -'yüm-\ adj : countless

in·oc·u·late \in'äkyə,lāt\ vb -lat·ed; -lat·ing : treat with something esp. to establish immunity —**in·oc·u·la·tion** \-,äkyə'lāshən\ n

in·op·por·tune \in,äpər'tün, -'tyün\ adj : inconvenient —**in·op·por·tune·ly** adv

in·or·di·nate \in'órd°nət\ adj : unusual or excessive —**in·or·di·nate·ly** adv

in·or·gan·ic \,in,ór'ganik\ adj : made of mineral matter

in·pa·tient \'in,pāshənt\ n : patient who stays in a hospital

in·put \'in,put\ n : something put in —**input** vb

in·quest \'in,kwest\ n : inquiry esp. before a jury

in·quire \in'kwīr\ vb -quired; -quir·ing 1 : ask 2 : investigate —**in·quir·er** n —**in·quir·ing·ly** adv —**in·qui·ry** \'in,kwīrē, in'kwīrē; 'inkwərē, 'iŋ-\ n

in·qui·si·tion \,inkwə'zishən, ,iŋ-\ n 1 : official inquiry 2 : severe questioning —**in·quis·i·tor** \in'kwizətər\ n —**in·quis·i·to·ri·al** \-,kwizə'tōrēəl\ adj

in·quis·i·tive \in'kwizətiv\ adj : curious —**in·quis·i·tive·ly** adv —**in·quis·i·tive·ness** n

in·road \'in,rōd\ n : encroachment

in·rush \'in,rəsh\ n : influx

in·sane \in'sān\ adj 1 : not sane 2 : absurd —**in·sane·ly** adv —**in·san·i·ty** \in'sanətē\ n

in·sa·tia·ble \in'sāshəbəl\ adj : incapable of being satisfied —**in·sa·tia·bil·i·ty** \in,sāshə'bilətē\ n —**in·sa·tia·bly** adv

in·scribe \in'skrīb\ vb 1 : write 2 : engrave 3 : dedicate (a book) to someone —**in·scrip·tion** \-'skripshən\ n

in·scru·ta·ble \in'skrütəbəl\ adj : mysterious —**in·scru·ta·bly** adv

in·seam \'in,sēm\ n : inner seam (of a garment)

in·sect \'in,sekt\ n : small usu. winged animal with 6 legs

in·sec·ti·cide \in'sektə,sīd\ n : insect poison —**in·sec·ti·cid·al** \in,sektə'sīd°l\ adj

in·se·cure \,insi'kyùr\ adj 1 : uncertain 2 : unsafe 3 : fearful —**in·se·cure·ly** adv —**in·se·cu·ri·ty** \-'kyùrətē\ n

in·sem·i·nate \in'semə,nāt\ vb -nat·ed; -nat·ing : introduce semen into —**in·sem·i·na·tion** \-,semə'nāshən\ n

in·sen·si·ble \in'sensəbəl\ adj 1 : unconscious 2 : unable to feel 3 : unaware —**in·sen·si·bil·i·ty** \in,sensə'bilətē\ n —**in·sen·si·bly** adv

in·sen·tient \in'senchənt\ adj : lacking feeling —**in·sen·tience** \-chəns\ n

in·sert \in'sərt\ vb : put in —**insert** \'in-,sərt\ n —**in·ser·tion** \in'sərshən\ n

in·set \'in,set\ vb inset or in·set·ted; in·set·ting : set in —**inset** n

in·shore \'in'shōr\ adj 1 : situated near shore 2 : moving toward shore ~ adv : toward shore

in·side \in'sīd, 'in,sīd\ n 1 : inner side 2 pl : innards ~ prep 1 : in or into the inside of 2 : within ~ adv 1 : on the inner side 2 : into the interior —**inside** adj —**in·sid·er** \in'sīdər\ n

inside of prep : inside

in·sid·i·ous \in'sidēəs\ adj 1 : treacherous 2 : seductive —**in·sid·i·ous·ly** adv —**in·sid·i·ous·ness** n

in·sight \'in,sīt\ n : understanding —**in·sight·ful** \'in'sītfəl-\ adj

in·sig·nia \in'signēə\, **in·signe** \-,nē\ n, pl -nia or -ni·as : badge of authority or office

in·sin·u·ate \in'sinyə,wāt\ vb -at·ed; -at·ing 1 : imply 2 : bring in artfully —**in·sin·u·a·tion** \-,sinyə'wāshən\ n

in·sip·id \in'sipəd\ adj 1 : tasteless 2

: not stimulating —**in·si·pid·i·ty** \ˌinsə'pidətē\ n

in·sist \in'sist\ vb : be firmly demanding —**in·sis·tence** \-'sistəns\ n —**in·sis·tent** \-tənt\ adj —**in·sis·tent·ly** adv

insofar as \ˌinsō'färaz\ conj : to the extent that

in·sole \'in,sōl\ n : inside sole of a shoe

in·so·lent \'insələnt\ adj : contemptuously rude —**in·so·lence** \-ləns\ n

in·sol·vent \in'sälvənt\ adj : unable or insufficient to pay debts —**in·sol·ven·cy** \-vənsē\ n

in·som·nia \in'sämnēə\ n : inability to sleep

in·so·much as \ˌinsō'məchaz\ conj : inasmuch as

insomuch that conj : to such a degree that

in·sou·ci·ance \in'süsēəns, aⁿsü'syäⁿs\ n : lighthearted indifference —**insou·ci·ant** \in'süsēənt, aⁿsü'syäⁿ\ adj

in·spect \in'spekt\ vb : view closely and critically —**in·spec·tion** \-'spekshən\ n —**in·spec·tor** \-tər\ n

in·spire \in'spīr\ vb -**spired; -spir·ing** 1 : inhale 2 : influence by example 3 : bring about 4 : stir to action —**in·spi·ra·tion** \ˌinspə'rāshən\ n —**in·spi·ra·tion·al** \-'rāshənəl\ adj —**in·spir·er** n

in·stall, in·stal \in'stól\ vb -**stalled; -stall·ing** 1 : induct into office 2 : set up for use —**in·stal·la·tion** \ˌinstə-'lāshən\ n

in·stall·ment \in'stólmənt\ n : partial payment

in·stance \'instəns\ n 1 : request or instigation 2 : example

in·stant \'instənt\ n : moment ~ adj 1 : immediate 2 : ready to mix —**in·stan·ta·neous** \ˌinstən'tānēəs\ adj —**in·stan·ta·neous·ly** adv —**in·stant·ly** adv

in·stead \in'sted\ adv : as a substitute or alternative

instead of prep : as a substitute for or alternative to

in·step \'in,step\ n : part of the foot in front of the ankle

in·sti·gate \'instə,gāt\ vb -**gat·ed; -gat·ing** : incite —**in·sti·ga·tion** \ˌinstə'gā-shən\ n —**in·sti·ga·tor** \'instə,gātər\ n

in·still \in'stil\ vb -**stilled; -still·ing** : impart gradually

in·stinct \'in,stiŋkt\ n 1 : natural talent

2 : natural inherited or subconsciously motivated behavior —**in·stinc·tive** \in'stiŋktiv\ adj —**in·stinc·tive·ly** adv —**in·stinc·tu·al** \in-'stiŋkchəwəl\ adj

in·sti·tute \'instə,tüt, -,tyüt\ vb -**tut·ed; -tut·ing** : establish, start, or organize ~ n 1 : organization promoting a cause 2 : school

in·sti·tu·tion \ˌinstə'tüshən, -'tyü-\ n 1 : act of instituting 2 : custom 3 : corporation or society of a public character —**in·sti·tu·tion·al** \-shənəl\ adj —**in·sti·tu·tion·al·ize** \-,īz\ vb —**in·sti·tu·tion·al·ly** adv

in·struct \in'strəkt\ vb 1 : teach 2 : give an order to —**in·struc·tion** \-'strəkshən\ n —**in·struc·tion·al** \-shənəl\ adj —**in·struc·tive** \in-'strəktiv\ adj —**in·struc·tor** \in-'strəktər\ n —**in·struc·tor·ship** n

in·stru·ment \'instrəmənt\ n 1 : something that produces music 2 : means 3 : device for doing work and esp. precision work 4 : legal document —**in·stru·men·tal** \ˌinstrə'ment³l\ adj —**in·stru·men·tal·ist** \-ist\ n —**in·stru·men·tal·i·ty** \ˌinstrəmən-'talətē, -,men-\ n —**in·stru·men·ta·tion** \ˌinstrəmən'tāshən, -,men-\ n

in·sub·or·di·nate \ˌinsə'bórd³nət\ adj : not obeying —**in·sub·or·di·na·tion** \-,bórd³n'āshən\ n

in·suf·fer·able \in'səfərəbəl\ adj : unbearable —**in·suf·fer·ably** \-blē\ adv

in·su·lar \'insülər, -syü-\ adj 1 : relating to or residing on an island 2 : narrow-minded —**in·su·lar·i·ty** \ˌinsü'larətē, -syü-\ n

in·su·late \'insə,lāt\ vb -**lat·ed; -lat·ing** : protect from heat loss or electricity —**in·su·la·tion** \ˌinsə'lāshən\ n —**in·su·la·tor** \'insə,lātər\ n

in·su·lin \'insələn\ n : hormone used by diabetics

in·sult \in'səlt\ vb : treat with contempt ~ \'in,səlt\ n : insulting act or remark —**in·sult·ing·ly** \-iŋlē\ adv

in·su·per·able \in'süpərəbəl\ adj : too difficult —**in·su·per·ably** \-blē\ adv

in·sure \in'shúr\ vb -**sured; -sur·ing** 1 : guarantee against loss 2 : make certain —**in·sur·able** \-əbəl\ adj —**in·sur·ance** \-əns\ n —**in·sured** \in-'shúrd\ n —**in·sur·er** n

in·sur·gent \in'sərjənt\ *n* : rebel —**in·surgence** \-jəns\ *n* —**in·sur·gen·cy** \-jənse\ *n* —**in·sur·gent** *adj*

in·sur·mount·able \,insər'maúntəbəl\ *adj* : too great to be overcome —**in·sur·mount·ably** \-blē\ *adv*

in·sur·rec·tion \,insə'rekshən\ *n* : revolution —**in·sur·rec·tion·ist** *n*

in·tact \in'takt\ *adj* : undamaged

in·take \'in,tāk\ *n* **1** : opening through which something enters **2** : act of taking in **3** : amount taken in

in·te·ger \'intijər\ *n* : number that is not a fraction and does not include a fraction

in·te·gral \'intigrəl\ *adj* : essential

in·te·grate \'intə,grāt\ *vb* -**grat·ed**; -**grat·ing** **1** : unite **2** : end segregation of or at —**in·te·gra·tion** \,intə'grāshən\ *n*

in·teg·ri·ty \in'tegrətē\ *n* **1** : soundness **2** : adherence to a code of values **3** : completeness

in·tel·lect \'int^əl,ekt\ *n* : power of knowing or thinking —**in·tel·lec·tu·al** \,int^əl'ekchəwəl\ *adj or n* —**in·tel·lec·tu·al·ism** \-chəwə,lizəm\ *n* —**in·tel·lec·tu·al·ly** *adv*

in·tel·li·gence \in'teləjəns\ *n* **1** : ability to learn and understand **2** : mental acuteness **3** : information

in·tel·li·gent \in'teləjənt\ *adj* : having or showing intelligence —**in·tel·li·gent·ly** *adv*

in·tel·li·gi·ble \in'teləjəbəl\ *adj* : understandable —**in·tel·li·gi·bil·i·ty** \-,telojə'bilətē\ *n* —**in·tel·li·gi·bly** *adv*

in·tem·per·ance \in'tempərəns\ *n* : lack of moderation —**in·tem·per·ate** \-pərət\ *adj* —**in·tem·per·ate·ness** \-pərət'nes\ *n*

in·tend \in'tend\ *vb* : have as a purpose

in·tend·ed \-'tendəd\ *n* : engaged person —**intended** *adj*

in·tense \in'tens\ *adj* **1** : extreme **2** : deeply felt —**in·tense·ly** *adv* —**in·ten·si·fi·ca·tion** \-,tensəfə'kāshən\ *n* —**in·ten·si·fy** \-'tensə,fī\ *vb* —**in·ten·si·ty** \in'tensətē\ *n* —**in·ten·sive** \in-'tensiv\ *adj* —**in·ten·sive·ly** *adv*

¹in·tent \in'tent\ *n* : purpose —**in·ten·tion** \-'tenchən\ *n* —**in·ten·tion·al** \-'tenchənəl\ *adj* —**in·ten·tion·al·ly** *adv*

²intent *adj* : concentrated —**in·tent·ly** *adv* —**in·tent·ness** *n*

in·ter \in'tər\ *vb* -**rr**- : bury

inter- *prefix* : between or among

interagency
interatomic
interbank
interborough
intercampus
interchurch
intercity
interclass
intercoastal
intercollegiate
intercolonial
intercommunal
intercommunity
intercompany
intercontinental
intercounty
intercultural
interdenominational
interdepartmental
interdivisional
interelectronic
interethnic
interfaculty
interfamily
interfiber
interfraternity
intergalactic
intergang
intergovernmental
intergroup
interhemispheric

interindustry
interinstitutional
interisland
interlibrary
intermolecular
intermountain
interoceanic
interoffice
interparticle
interparty
interpersonal
interplanetary
interpopulation
interprovincial
interracial
interregional
interreligious
interscholastic
intersectional
interstate
interstellar
intersystem
interterm
interterminal
intertribal
intertroop
intertropical
interuniversity
interurban
intervalley
intervillage
interwar
interzonal
interzone

in·ter·ac·tion \,intər'akshən\ *n* : mutual influence —**in·ter·act** \-'akt\ *vb* —**in·ter·ac·tive** *adj*

in·ter·breed \,intər'brēd\ *vb* -**bred** \-'bred\; -**breed·ing** : breed together

in·ter·ca·late \in'tərkə,lāt\ *vb* -**lat·ed**; -**lat·ing** : insert —**in·ter·ca·la·tion** \-,tərkə'lāshən\ *n*

in·ter·cede \,intər'sēd\ *vb* -**ced·ed**; -**ced·ing** : act to reconcile —**in·ter·ces·sion** \-'seshən\ *n* —**in·ter·ces·sor** \-'sesər\ *n*

in·ter·cept \,intər'sept\ *vb* : interrupt the progress of —**intercept** \'intər,sept\ *n* —**in·ter·cep·tion** \,intər'sepshən\ *n* —**in·ter·cep·tor** \-'septər\ *n*

in·ter·change \,intər'chānj\ *vb* **1** : exchange **2** : change places ~ \'intər,chānj\ *n* **1** : exchange **2** : junction of highways —**in·ter·change·able** \,intər'chānjəbəl\ *adj*

in·ter·course \'intər,kōrs\ *n* **1** : relations

between persons or nations **2** : copulation

in·ter·de·pen·dent \ˌintərdi'pendənt\ *adj* : mutually dependent —**in·ter·de·pen·dence** \-dəns\ *n*

in·ter·dict \ˌintər'dikt\ *vb* **1** : prohibit **2** : destroy or cut (an enemy supply line) —**in·ter·dic·tion** \-'dikshən\ *n*

in·ter·est \'intrəst, -tə,rest\ *n* **1** : right **2** : benefit **3** : charge for borrowed money **4** : readiness to pay special attention **5** : quality that causes interest ~ *vb* **1** : concern **2** : get the attention of —**in·ter·est·ing** *adj* —**in·ter·est·ing·ly** *adv*

in·ter·face \'intər,fās\ *n* : common boundary —**in·ter·fa·cial** \ˌintər'fā-shəl\ *adj*

in·ter·fere \ˌintər'fir\ *vb* -**fered**; -**fer·ing 1** : collide or be in opposition **2** : try to run the affairs of others —**in·ter·fer·ence** \-'firəns\ *n*

in·ter·im \'intərəm\ *n* : time between —**interim** *adj*

in·te·ri·or \in'tirēər\ *adj* : being on the inside ~ *n* **1** : inside **2** : inland area

in·ter·ject \ˌintər'jekt\ *vb* : stick in between

in·ter·jec·tion \-'jekshən\ *n* : an exclamatory word —**in·ter·jec·tion·al·ly** \-shənəlē\ *adv*

in·ter·lace \ˌintər'lās\ *vb* : cross or cause to cross one over another

in·ter·lin·e·ar \ˌintər'linēər\ *adj* : between written or printed lines

in·ter·lock \ˌintər'läk\ *vb* **1** : interlace **2** : connect for mutual effect —**inter·lock** \'intər,läk\ *n*

in·ter·lop·er \ˌintər'lōpər\ *n* : intruder or meddler

in·ter·lude \'intər,lüd\ *n* : intervening period

in·ter·mar·ry \ˌintər'marē\ *vb* **1** : marry each other **2** : marry within a group —**in·ter·mar·riage** \-'marij\ *n*

in·ter·me·di·ary \ˌintər'mēdē,erē\ *n, pl* -**aries** : agent between individuals or groups —**intermediary** *adj*

in·ter·me·di·ate \ˌintər'mēdēət\ *adj* : between extremes —**intermediate** *n*

in·ter·ment \in'tərmənt\ *n* : burial

in·ter·mi·na·ble \in'tərmənəbəl\ *adj* : endless —**in·ter·mi·na·bly** *adv*

in·ter·min·gle \ˌintər'miŋgəl\ *vb* : mingle

in·ter·mis·sion \ˌintər'mishən\ *n* : break in a performance

in·ter·mit·tent \-'mit³nt\ *adj* : coming at intervals —**in·ter·mit·tent·ly** *adv*

in·ter·mix \ˌintər'miks\ *vb* : mix together —**in·ter·mix·ture** \-'mikschər\ *n*

¹in·tern \'in,tərn, in'tərn\ *vb* : confine esp. during a war —**in·tern·ee** \ˌin,tər'nē\ *n* —**in·tern·ment** *n*

²in·tern \'in,tərn\ *n* : advanced student (as in medicine) gaining supervised experience ~ *vb* : act as an intern —**in·tern·ship** *n*

in·ter·nal \in'tərn³l\ *adj* **1** : inward **2** : inside of the body **3** : relating to or existing in the mind —**in·ter·nal·ly** *adv*

in·ter·na·tion·al \ˌintər'nashənəl\ *adj* : affecting 2 or more nations ~ *n* : something having international scope —**in·ter·na·tion·al·ism** \-,i-zəm\ *n* —**in·ter·na·tion·al·ize** \-,īz\ *vb* —**in·ter·na·tion·al·ly** *adv*

in·ter·nist \'in,tərnist\ *n* : specialist in nonsurgical medicine

in·ter·play \'intər,plā\ *n* : interaction

in·ter·po·late \in'tərpə,lāt\ *vb* -**lat·ed**; -**lat·ing** : insert —**in·ter·po·la·tion** \-,tərpə'lāshən\ *n*

in·ter·pose \ˌintər'pōz\ *vb* -**posed**; -**pos·ing 1** : place between **2** : intrude —**in·ter·po·si·tion** \-pə'zishən\ *n*

in·ter·pret \in'tərprət\ *vb* : explain the meaning of —**in·ter·pre·ta·tion** \in-,tərprə'tāshən\ *n* —**in·ter·pre·ta·tive** \-'tərprə,tātiv\ *adj* —**in·ter·pret·er** *n* —**in·ter·pre·tive** \-'tərprətiv\ *adj*

in·ter·re·late \ˌintər'lāt\ *vb* : have a mutual relationship —**in·ter·re·lat·ed·ness** \-'lātədnəs\ *n* —**in·ter·re·la·tion** \-'lāshən\ *n* —**in·ter·re·la·tion·ship** *n*

in·ter·ro·gate \in'terə,gāt\ *vb* -**gat·ed**; -**gat·ing** : question —**in·ter·ro·ga·tion** \-,terə'gāshən\ *n* —**in·ter·rog·a·tive** \,intə'rägətiv\ *adj or n* —**in·ter·rog·a·tor** \-'terə,gātər\ *n* —**in·ter·rog·a·to·ry** \,intə'rägə,tōrē\ *adj*

in·ter·rupt \,intə'rəpt\ *vb* : intrude so as to hinder or end continuity —**in·ter·rupt·er** *n* —**in·ter·rup·tion** \-'rəp-shən\ *n* —**in·ter·rup·tive** \-'rəptiv\ *adj*

in·ter·sect \,intər'sekt\ *vb* **1** : cut across or divide **2** : cross —**in·ter·sec·tion** \-'sekshən\ *n*

in·ter·sperse \,intər'spərs\ *vb* -**spersed**;

-spers•ing : insert at intervals —**in-ter•sper•sion** \-'spərzhən\ n

in•ter•stice \in'tərstəs\ n, pl **-stic•es** \-stə,sēz, -stəsəz\ : space between —**in•ter•sti•tial** \,intər'stishəl\ adj

in•ter•twine \,intər'twīn\ vb : twist together —**in•ter•twine•ment** n

in•ter•val \'intərvəl\ n 1 : time between 2 : space between

in•ter•vene \,intər'vēn\ vb **-vened; -ven•ing** 1 : happen between events 2 : intercede —**in•ter•ven•tion** \-'venchən\ n

in•ter•view \'intər,vyü\ n : a meeting to get information —**interview** vb —**in•ter•view•er** n

in•ter•weave \,intər'wēv\ vb **-wove** \-'wōv\, **-wo•ven** \-'wōvən\, **-weav•ing** : weave together —**in•ter•wo•ven** \-'wōvən\ adj

in•tes•tate \in'tes,tāt, -tət\ adj : not leaving a will

in•tes•tine \in'testən\ n : tubular part of the digestive system after the stomach including a long narrow upper part (**small intestine**) followed by a broader shorter lower part (**large intestine**) —**in•tes•ti•nal** \-tən³l\ adj

in•ti•mate \'intə,māt\ vb **-mat•ed; -mat•ing** : hint ~ \'intəmət\ adj 1 : very friendly 2 : suggesting privacy 3 : very personal ~ n : close friend —**in•ti•ma•cy** \'intəməsē\ n —**in•ti•mate•ly** adv —**in•ti•ma•tion** \,intə'māshən\ n

in•tim•i•date \in'timə,dāt\ vb **-dat•ed; -dat•ing** : make fearful —**in•tim•i•da•tion** \-,timə'dāshən\ n

in•to \'intü\ prep 1 : to the inside of 2 : to the condition of 3 : against

in•to•na•tion \,intō'nāshən\ n : way of singing or speaking

in•tone \in'tōn\ vb **-toned; -ton•ing** : chant

in•tox•i•cate \in'täksə,kāt\ vb **-cat•ed; -cat•ing** : make drunk —**in•tox•i•cant** \-sikənt\ n or adj —**in•tox•i•ca•tion** \-,täksə'kāshən\ n

in•tra•mu•ral \,intrə'myürəl\ adj : within a school

in•tran•si•gent \in'transəjənt\ adj : uncompromising —**in•tran•si•gence** \-jəns\ n —**intransigent** n

in•tra•ve•nous \,intrə'vēnəs\ adj : by way of the veins —**in•tra•ve•nous•ly** adv

in•trep•id \in'trepəd\ adj : fearless —**in•tre•pid•i•ty** \,intrə'pidətē\ n

in•tri•cate \'intrikət\ adj : very complex and delicate —**in•tri•ca•cy** \-trikəsē\ n —**in•tri•cate•ly** adv

in•trigue \in'trēg\ vb **-trigued; -trigu•ing** 1 : scheme 2 : arouse curiosity of ~ n : secret scheme —**in•trigu•ing•ly** \-iŋlē\ adv

in•trin•sic \in'trinzik, -sik\ adj : essential —**in•trin•si•cal•ly** \-ziklē, -si-\ adv

in•tro•duce \,intrə'düs, -'dyüs\ vb **-duced; -duc•ing** 1 : bring in esp. for the 1st time 2 : cause to be acquainted 3 : bring to notice 4 : put in —**in•tro•duc•tion** \'dəkshən\ n —**in•tro•duc•to•ry** \'dəktərē\ adj

in•tro•spec•tion \,intrə'spekshən\ n : examination of one's own thoughts or feelings —**in•tro•spec•tive** \-'spektiv\ adj —**in•tro•spec•tive•ly** adv

in•tro•vert \'intrə,vərt\ n : shy or reserved person —**in•tro•ver•sion** \,intrə'vərzhən\ n —**introvert** adj —**in•tro•vert•ed** \'intrə,vərtəd\ adj

in•trude \in'trüd\ vb **-trud•ed; -trud•ing** 1 : thrust in 2 : encroach —**in•trud•er** n —**in•tru•sion** \-'trüzhən\ n —**in•tru•sive** \-'trüsiv\ adj —**in•tru•sive•ness** n

in•tu•ition \,intü'ishən, -tyü-\ n : quick and ready insight —**in•tu•it** \in'tüət, -'tyü-\ vb —**in•tu•i•tive** \-ətiv\ adj —**in•tu•i•tive•ly** adv

in•un•date \'inən,dāt\ vb **-dat•ed; -dat•ing** : flood —**in•un•da•tion** \,inən•'dāshən\ n

in•ure \in'ür, -'yür\ vb **-ured; -ur•ing** : accustom to accept something undesirable

in•vade \in'vād\ vb **-vad•ed; -vad•ing** : enter for conquest —**in•vad•er** n —**in•va•sion** \-'vāzhən\ n

¹in•val•id \in'valəd\ adj : not true or legal —**in•va•lid•i•ty** \,invə'lidətē\ n —**in•val•id•ly** adv

²in•va•lid \'invələd\ adj : sickly ~ n : one chronically ill —**in•val•i•date** \in'valə,dāt\ vb : make invalid —**in•val•i•da•tion** \in,valə'dāshən\ n

in•valu•able \in'valyəwəbəl\ adj : extremely valuable

in•va•sive \in'vāsiv\ adj : involving entry into the body

in•vec•tive \in'vektiv\ n : abusive language —**invective** adj

in·veigh \in'vā\ vb : protest or complain forcefully

in·vei·gle \in'vāgəl, -'vē-\ vb -**gled**; -**gling** : win over or get by flattery

in·vent \in'vent\ vb 1 : think up 2 : create for the 1st time —**in·ven·tion** \-'venchən\ n —**in·ven·tive** \-'ventiv\ adj —**in·ven·tive·ness** n —**in·ven·tor** \-'ventər\ n

in·ven·to·ry \'invən,tōrē\ n, pl -**ries** 1 : list of goods 2 : stock —**inventory** vb

in·verse \in'vərs, 'in,vərs\ adj or n : opposite —**in·verse·ly** adv

in·vert \in'vərt\ vb 1 : turn upside down or inside out 2 : reverse —**in·ver·sion** \-'verzhən\ n

in·ver·te·brate \in'vərtəbrət, -,brāt\ adj : lacking a backbone ~ n : invertebrate animal

in·vest \in'vest\ vb 1 : give power or authority to 2 : endow with a quality 3 : commit money to someone else's use in hope of profit —**in·vest·ment** \-mənt\ n —**in·ves·tor** \-'vestər\ n

in·ves·ti·gate \in'vestə,gāt\ vb -**gat·ed**; -**gat·ing** : study closely and systematically —**in·ves·ti·ga·tion** \-,vestə-'gāshən\ n —**in·ves·ti·ga·tive** \-'vestə,gātiv\ adj —**in·ves·ti·ga·tor** \-'vestə-,gātər\ n

in·ves·ti·ture \in'vestə,chùr, -chər\ n : act of establishing in office

in·vet·er·ate \in'vetərət\ adj : acting out of habit

in·vid·i·ous \in'vidēəs\ adj : harmful or obnoxious —**in·vid·i·ous·ly** adv

in·vig·o·rate \in'vigə,rāt\ vb -**rat·ed**; -**rat·ing** : give life and energy to —**in·vig·o·ra·tion** \-,vigə'rāshən\ n

in·vin·ci·ble \in'vinsəbəl\ adj : incapable of being conquered —**in·vin·ci·bil·i·ty** \in,vinsə'bilətē\ n —**in·vin·ci·bly** \in'vinsəblē\ adv

in·vi·o·la·ble \in'vīələbəl\ adj : safe from violation or desecration —**in·vi·o·la·bil·i·ty** \in,vīələ'bilətē\ n

in·vi·o·late \in'vīəlat\ adj : not violated or profaned

in·vite \in'vīt\ vb -**vit·ed**; -**vit·ing** 1 : entice 2 : increase the likelihood of 3 : request the presence or participation of 4 : encourage —**in·vi·ta·tion** \,invə'tāshən\ n —**in·vit·ing** \in'vītiŋ\ adj

in·vo·ca·tion \,invə'kāshən\ n 1 : prayer 2 : incantation

in·voice \'in,vòis\ n : itemized bill for goods shipped ~ vb -**voiced**; -**voic·ing** : bill

in·voke \in'vōk\ vb -**voked**; -**vok·ing** 1 : call on for help 2 : cite as authority 3 : conjure 4 : carry out

in·volve \in'välv\ vb -**volved**; -**volv·ing** 1 : draw in as a participant 2 : relate closely 3 : require as a necessary part 4 : occupy fully —**in·volve·ment** n —**in·volved** \-'välvd\ adj : intricate

¹in·ward \'inwərd\ adj : inside

²inward, in·wards \-wərdz\ adv : toward the inside, center, or inner being

in·ward·ly adv 1 : mentally or spiritually 2 : internally 3 : to oneself

io·dide \'ī,dīd\ n : compound of iodine

io·dine \'ī,dīn, -ədⁿn\ n 1 : nonmetallic chemical element 2 : solution of iodine used as an antiseptic

io·dize \'ī,dīz\ vb -**dized**; -**diz·ing** : treat with iodine or an iodide

ion \'īən, 'ī,än\ n : electrically charged particle —**ion·ic** \ī'änik\ adj —**ion·iz·able** \'īə,nīzəbəl\ adj —**ion·iza·tion** \,īənə'zāshən\ n —**ion·ize** \'īə,nīz\ vb —**ion·iz·er** \'īə,nīzər\ n

-ion n suffix 1 : act or process 2 : state or condition

ion·o·sphere \ī'änə,sfir\ n : layer of the upper atmosphere containing ionized gases —**ion·o·spher·ic** \ī,änə'sfirik, -'sfer-\ adj

io·ta \ī'ōtə\ n : small quantity

IOU \,ī,ō'yü\ n : acknowledgment of a debt

iras·ci·ble \ir'asəbəl, ī'ras-\ adj : marked by hot temper —**iras·ci·bil·i·ty** \-,asə'bilətē, -,ras-\ n

irate \ī'rāt\ adj : roused to intense anger —**irate·ly** adv

ire \'īr\ n : anger

ir·i·des·cence \,irə'desⁿns\ n : rainbow-like play of colors —**ir·i·des·cent** \-ⁿnt\ adj

iris \'īrəs\ n, pl **iris·es** or **iri·des** \'īrə,dēz, 'ir-\ 1 : colored part around the pupil of the eye 2 : plant with long leaves and large showy flowers

irk \'ərk\ vb : annoy —**irk·some** \-səm\ adj —**irk·some·ly** adv

iron \'īərn\ n 1 : heavy metallic chemical element 2 : something made of iron 3 : heated device for pressing clothes 4 : hardness, determination ~

vb : press or smooth out with an iron —**iron·ware** *n* —**iron·work** *n* —**iron·work·er** *n* —**iron·works** *n pl*

iron·clad \-'klad\ *adj* **1** : sheathed in iron armor **2** : strict or exacting

iron·ing \'iərniŋ\ *n* : clothes to be ironed

iron·wood \-ˌwud\ *n* : tree or shrub with very hard wood or this wood

iro·ny \'īrənē\ *n, pl* **-nies 1** : use of words to express the opposite of the literal meaning **2** : incongruity between the actual and expected result of events —**iron·ic** \ī'ränik\, **iron·i·cal** \-ikəl\ *adj* —**iron·i·cal·ly** \-iklē\ *adv*

ir·ra·di·ate \ir'ādē,āt\ *vb* **-at·ed; -at·ing** : treat with radiation —**ir·ra·di·a·tion** \-ˌādē'āshən\ *n*

ir·ra·tio·nal \ir'ashənəl\ *adj* **1** : incapable of reasoning **2** : not based on reason —**ir·ra·tio·nal·i·ty** \-ˌashə'nalətē\ *n* —**ir·ra·tio·nal·ly** *adv*

ir·rec·on·cil·able \ir,ekən'sīləbəl\ *adj* : impossible to reconcile —**ir·rec·on·cil·abil·i·ty** \-ˌsīlə'bilətē\ *n*

ir·re·cov·er·able \ˌiri'kəvərəbəl\ *adj* : not capable of being recovered —**ir·re·cov·er·ably** \-blē\ *adv*

ir·re·deem·able \ˌiri'dēməbəl\ *adj* : not redeemable

ir·re·duc·ible \ˌiri'düsəbəl, -'dyü-\ *adj* : not reducible —**ir·re·duc·ibly** \-blē\ *adv*

ir·re·fut·able \ˌiri'fyütəbəl, ir'refyət-\ *adj* : impossible to refute

ir·reg·u·lar \ir'egyələr\ *adj* : not regular or normal —**irregular** *n* —**ir·reg·u·lar·i·ty** \ir,egyə'larətē\ *n* —**ir·reg·u·lar·ly** *adv*

ir·rel·e·vant \ir'eləvənt\ *adj* : not relevant —**ir·rel·e·vance** \-vəns\ *n*

ir·re·li·gious \ˌiri'lijəs\ *adj* : not following religious practices

ir·rep·a·ra·ble \ir'epərəbəl\ *adj* : impossible to make good, undo, or remedy

ir·re·place·able \ˌiri'plāsəbəl\ *adj* : not replaceable

ir·re·press·ible \-'presəbəl\ *adj* : impossible to repress or control

ir·re·proach·able \-'prōchəbəl\ *adj* : blameless

ir·re·sist·ible \-'zistəbəl\ *adj* : impossible to successfully resist —**ir·re·sist·ibly** \-blē\ *adv*

ir·res·o·lute \ir'ezəlüt\ *adj* : uncertain —**ir·res·o·lute·ly** *adv* —**ir·res·o·lu·tion** \-,ezə'lüshən\ *n*

ir·re·spec·tive of \ˌiri'spektiv-\ *prep* : without regard to

ir·re·spon·si·ble \ˌiri'spänsəbəl\ *adj* : not responsible —**ir·re·spon·si·bil·i·ty** \-,spänsə'bilətē\ *n* —**ir·re·spon·si·bly** *adv*

ir·re·triev·able \ˌiri'trēvəbəl\ *adj* : not retrievable

ir·rev·er·ence \ir'evərəns\ *n* **1** : lack of reverence **2** : irreverent act or utterance —**ir·rev·er·ent** \-rənt\ *adj*

ir·re·vers·ible \ˌiri'vərsəbəl\ *adj* : incapable of being reversed

ir·re·vo·ca·ble \ir'evəkəbəl\ *adj* : incapable of being revoked —**ir·re·vo·ca·bly** \-blē\ *adv*

ir·ri·gate \'irə,gāt\ *vb* **-gat·ed; -gat·ing** : supply with water by artificial means —**ir·ri·ga·tion** \ˌirə'gāshən\ *n*

ir·ri·tate \'irə,tāt\ *vb* **-tat·ed; -tat·ing 1** : excite to anger **2** : make sore or inflamed —**ir·ri·ta·bil·i·ty** \ˌirətə-'bilətē\ *n* —**ir·ri·ta·ble** \'irətəbəl\ *adj* —**ir·ri·ta·bly** \'irətəblē\ *adv* —**ir·ri·tant** \'irətənt\ *adj or n* —**ir·ri·tat·ing·ly** *adv* —**ir·ri·ta·tion** \ˌirə-'tāshən\ *n*

is *pres 3d sing of* BE

-ish \ish\ *adj suffix* **1** : characteristic of **2** : somewhat

Is·lam \is'läm, iz-, -'lam\ *n* : religious faith of Muslims —**Is·lam·ic** \-ik\ *adj*

is·land \'īlənd\ *n* : body of land surrounded by water —**is·land·er** \'īləndər\ *n*

isle \'īl\ *n* : small island

is·let \'īlət\ *n* : small island

-ism \ˌizəm\ *n suffix* **1** : act or practice **2** : characteristic manner **3** : condition **4** : doctrine

iso·late \'īsə,lāt\ *vb* **-lat·ed; -lat·ing** : place or keep by itself —**iso·la·tion** \ˌīsə'lāshən\ *n*

iso·met·rics \ˌīsə'metriks\ *n sing or pl* : exercise against unmoving resistance —**isometric** *adj*

isos·ce·les \ī'säsə,lēz\ *adj* : having 2 equal sides

iso·tope \'īsə,tōp\ *n* : species of atom of a chemical element —**iso·to·pic** \ˌīsə'täpik, -tō-\ *adj*

is·sue \'ishü\ *vb* **-sued; -su·ing 1** : go, come, or flow out **2** : descend from a specified ancestor **3** : emanate or result **4** : put forth or distribute officially ~ *n* **1** : action of issuing **2**

: offspring **3** : result **4** : point of controversy **5** : act of giving out or printing **6** : quantity given out or printed —**is•su•ance** \i-shəwəns\ n —**is•su•er** n

-ist \ist\ n suffix **1** : one that does **2** : one that plays **3** : one that specializes in **4** : follower of a doctrine

isth•mus \isməs\ n : narrow strip of land connecting 2 larger portions

it \it\ pron **1** : that one —used of a lifeless thing or an abstract entity **2** —used as an anticipatory subject or object ~ n : player who tries to catch others (as in a game of tag)

ital•ic \ə-talik, i-, ī-\ n : style of type with slanting letters —**italic** adj —**ital•i•ci•za•tion** \ə,taləsə'zāshən, i-, ī-\ n —**ital•i•cize** \ə'talə,sīz, i-, ī-\ vb

itch \ich\ n **1** : uneasy irritating skin sensation **2** : skin disorder **3** : persistent desire —**itch** vb —**itchy** adj

item \ītəm\ n **1** : particular in a list, account, or series **2** : piece of news —**item•iza•tion** \,ītəmə'zāshən\ n —**item•ize** \ītə,mīz\ vb

itin•er•ant \ī'tinərənt, ə-\ adj : traveling from place to place

itin•er•ary \ī'tinə,rerē, ə-\ n, pl **-ar•ies** : route or outline of a journey

its \its\ adj : relating to it

it•self \it'self\ pron : it—used reflexively or for emphasis

-ity \ətē\ n suffix : quality, state, or degree

-ive \iv\ adj suffix : that performs or tends toward an action

ivo•ry \īvərē\ n, pl **-ries 1** : hard creamy-white material of elephants' tusks **2** : pale yellow color

ivy \īvē\ n, pl **ivies** : trailing woody vine with evergreen leaves

-ize \,īz\ vb suffix **1** : cause to be, become, or resemble **2** : subject to an action **3** : treat or combine with **4** : engage in an activity

J

j \jā\ n, pl **j's** or **js** \jāz\ : 10th letter of the alphabet

jab \jab\ vb **-bb-** : thrust quickly or abruptly ~ n : short straight punch

jab•ber \jabər\ vb : talk rapidly or unintelligibly —**jabber** n

jack \jak\ n **1** : mechanical device to raise a heavy body **2** : small flag **3** : small 6-pointed metal object used in a game (**jacks**) **4** : electrical socket ~ vb **1** : raise with a jack **2** : increase

jack•al \jakəl, -,ȯl\ n : wild dog

jack•ass n **1** : male ass **2** : stupid person

jack•et \jakət\ n : garment for the upper body

jack•ham•mer \jak,hamər\ n : pneumatic tool for drilling

jack•knife \jak,nīf\ n : pocketknife ~ vb : fold like a jackknife

jack-o'-lan•tern \jakə,lantərn\ n : lantern made of a carved pumpkin

jack•pot \jak,pät\ n : sum of money won

jack•rab•bit \-,rabət\ n : large hare of western No. America

jade \jād\ n : usu. green gemstone

jad•ed \jādəd\ adj : dulled or bored by having too much

jag•ged \jagəd\ adj : sharply notched

jag•uar \jag,wär, jagyə-\ n : black-spotted tropical American cat

jai alai \hī,lī\ n : game with a ball propelled by a basket on the hand

jail \jāl\ n : prison —**jail** vb —**jail•break** n —**jail•er, jail•or** n

ja•la•pe•ño \,hälə'pān,yō, -,pēnō\ n : Mexican hot pepper

ja•lopy \jə'läpē\ n, pl **-lopies** : dilapidated vehicle

jal•ou•sie \jaləsē\ n : door or window with louvers

jam \jam\ vb **-mm- 1** : press into a tight position **2** : cause to become wedged and unworkable ~ n **1** : crowded mass that blocks or impedes **2** : difficult situation **3** : thick sweet food made of cooked fruit

jamb \jam\ n : upright framing piece of a door

jam•bo•ree \jambə'rē\ n : large festive gathering

jan·gle \'jaŋgəl\ *vb* **-gled; -gling :** make a harsh ringing sound —**jangle** *n*

jan·i·tor \'janətər\ *n* **:** person who has the care of a building —**jan·i·to·ri·al** \,janə'tōrēəl\ *adj*

Jan·u·ary \'janyə,werē\ *n* **:** 1st month of the year having 31 days

¹jar \'jär\ *vb* **-rr- 1 :** have a harsh or disagreeable effect **2 :** vibrate or shake ~ *n* **1 :** jolt **2 :** painful effect

²jar *n* **:** wide-mouthed container

jar·gon \'järgən, -,gän\ *n* **:** special vocabulary of a group

jas·mine \'jazmən\ *n* **:** climbing shrub with fragrant flowers

jas·per \'jaspər\ *n* **:** red, yellow, or brown opaque quartz

jaun·dice \'jóndəs\ *n* **:** yellowish discoloration of skin, tissues, and body fluids

jaun·diced \-dəst\ *adj* **:** exhibiting envy or hostility

jaunt \'jónt\ *n* **:** short pleasure trip

jaun·ty \'jóntē\ *adj* **-ti·er; -est :** lively in manner or appearance —**jaun·ti·ly** \'jónt°lē\ *adv* —**jaun·ti·ness** *n*

jave·lin \'javələn\ *n* **:** light spear

jaw \'jó\ *n* **1 :** either of the bony or cartilaginous structures that support the mouth **2 :** one of 2 movable parts for holding or crushing ~ *vb* **:** talk indignantly or at length —**jaw·bone** \-,bōn\ *n* —**jawed** \'jód\ *adj*

jay \'jā\ *n* **:** noisy brightly colored bird

jay·bird *n* **:** jay

jay·walk *vb* **:** cross a street carelessly —**jay·walk·er** *n*

jazz \'jaz\ *vb* **:** enliven ~ *n* **1 :** kind of American music involving improvisation **2 :** empty talk —**jazzy** *adj*

jeal·ous \'jeləs\ *adj* **:** suspicious of a rival or of one believed to enjoy an advantage —**jeal·ous·ly** *adv* —**jeal·ou·sy** \-əsē\ *n*

jeans \'jēnz\ *n pl* **:** pants made of durable twilled cotton cloth

jeep \'jēp\ *n* **:** 4-wheel army vehicle

jeer \'jir\ *vb* **1 :** speak or cry out in derision **2 :** ridicule ~ *n* **:** taunt

Je·ho·vah \ji'hōvə\ *n* **:** God

je·june \ji'jün\ *adj* **:** dull or childish

jell \'jel\ *vb* **1 :** come to the consistency of jelly **2 :** take shape

jel·ly \'jelē\ *n, pl* **-lies :** a substance (as food) with a soft somewhat elastic consistency —**jelly** *vb*

jel·ly·fish *n* **:** sea animal with a saucer-shaped jellylike body

jen·ny \'jenē\ *n, pl* **-nies :** female bird or donkey

jeop·ar·dy \'jepərdē\ *n* **:** exposure to death, loss, or injury —**jeop·ar·dize** \-ər,dīz\ *vb*

jerk \'jərk\ *vb* **1 :** give a sharp quick push, pull, or twist **2 :** move in short abrupt motions ~ *n* **1 :** short quick pull or twist **2 :** stupid or foolish person —**jerk·i·ly** *adv* —**jerky** *adj*

jer·kin \'jərkən\ *n* **:** close-fitting sleeveless jacket

jer·ry-built \'jerē,bilt\ *adj* **:** built cheaply and flimsily

jer·sey \'jərzē\ *n, pl* **-seys 1 :** plain knit fabric **2 :** knitted shirt

jest \'jest\ *n* **:** witty remark —**jest** *vb*

jest·er \'jestər\ *n* **:** one employed to entertain a court

¹jet \'jet\ *n* **:** velvet-black coal used for jewelry

²jet *vb* **-tt- 1 :** spout or emit in a stream **2 :** travel by jet ~ *n* **1 :** forceful rush of fluid through a narrow opening **2 :** jet-propelled airplane

jet-propelled *adj* **:** driven by an engine (**jet engine**) that produces propulsion (**jet propulsion**) by the rearward discharge of a jet of fluid

jet·sam \'jetsəm\ *n* **:** jettisoned goods

jet·ti·son \'jetəsən\ *vb* **1 :** throw (goods) overboard **2 :** discard —**jettison** *n*

jet·ty \'jetē\ *n, pl* **-ties :** pier or wharf

Jew \'jü\ *n* **:** one whose religion is Judaism —**Jew·ish** *adj*

jew·el \'jüəl\ *n* **1 :** ornament of precious metal **2 :** gem ~ *vb* **-eled** *or* **-elled; -el·ing** *or* **-el·ling :** adorn with jewels —**jew·el·er, jew·el·ler** \-ər\ *n* —**jew·el·ry** \-rē\ *n*

jib \'jib\ *n* **:** triangular sail

jibe \'jīb\ *vb* **jibed; jib·ing :** be in agreement

jif·fy \'jifē\ *n, pl* **-fies :** short time

jig \'jig\ *n* **:** lively dance ~ *vb* **-gg- :** dance a jig

jig·ger \'jigər\ *n* **:** measure used in mixing drinks

jig·gle \'jigəl\ *vb* **-gled; -gling :** move with quick little jerks —**jiggle** *n*

jig·saw *n* **:** machine saw with a narrow blade that moves up and down

jilt \'jilt\ *vb* **:** drop (a lover) unfeelingly

jim·my \'jimē\ *n, pl* **-mies :** small crowbar ~ *vb* **-mied; -my·ing :** pry open

jim·son·weed \'jimsən,wēd\ *n* **:** coarse poisonous weed

jin·gle \'jiŋgəl\ *vb* **-gled; -gling :** make

a light tinkling sound ~ *n* **1** : light tinkling sound **2** : short verse or song

jin·go·ism \'jiŋgō,izəm\ *n* : extreme chauvinism or nationalism —**jin·go·ist** \-ist\ *n* —**jin·go·is·tic** \,jiŋgō'istik\ *adj*

jinx \'jiŋks\ *n* : one that brings bad luck —**jinx** *vb*

jit·ney \'jitnē\ *n, pl* **-neys** : small bus

jit·ters \'jitərz\ *n pl* : extreme nervousness —**jit·tery** \-ərē\ *adj*

job \'jäb\ *n* **1** : something that has to be done **2** : regular employment —**job·hold·er** *n* —**job·less** *adj*

job·ber \'jäbər\ *n* : middleman

jock·ey \'jäkē\ *n, pl* **-eys** : one who rides a horse in a race ~ *vb* **-eyed; -ey·ing** : manipulate or maneuver adroitly

jo·cose \jō'kōs\ *adj* : jocular

joc·u·lar \'jäkyələr\ *adj* : marked by jesting —**joc·u·lar·i·ty** \,jäkyə'larətē\ *n* —**joc·u·lar·ly** *adv*

jo·cund \'jäkənd\ *adj* : full of mirth or gaiety

jodh·purs \'jädpərz\ *n pl* : riding breeches

¹jog \'jäg\ *vb* **-gg- 1** : give a slight shake or push to **2** : run or ride at a slow pace ~ *n* **1** : slight shake **2** : slow pace —**jog·ger** *n*

²jog *n* : brief abrupt change in direction or line

join \'join\ *vb* **1** : come or bring together **2** : become a member of —**join·er** *n*

joint \'joint\ *n* **1** : point of contact between bones **2** : place where 2 parts connect **3** : often disreputable place ~ *adj* : common to 2 or more —**joint·ed** *adj* —**joint·ly** *adv*

joist \'joist\ *n* : beam supporting a floor or ceiling

joke \'jōk\ *n* : something said or done to provoke laughter ~ *vb* **joked; jok·ing** : make jokes —**jok·er** *n* —**jok·ing·ly** \'jōkiŋlē\ *adv*

jol·li·ty \'jälətē\ *n, pl* **-ties** : gaiety or merriment

jol·ly \'jälē\ *adj* **-li·er; -est** : full of high spirits

jolt \'jōlt\ *vb* **1** : move with a sudden jerky motion **2** : give a jolt to ~ *n* **1** : abrupt jerky blow or movement **2** : sudden shock —**jolt·er** *n*

jon·quil \'jänkwəl\ *n* : narcissus with white or yellow flowers

josh \'jäsh\ *vb* : tease or joke

jos·tle \'jäsəl\ *vb* **-tled; -tling** : push or shove

jot \'jät\ *n* : least bit ~ *vb* **-tt-** : write briefly and hurriedly

jounce \'jauns\ *vb* **jounced; jounc·ing** : jolt —**jounce** *n*

jour·nal \'jərn²l\ *n* **1** : brief account of daily events **2** : periodical (as a newspaper)

jour·nal·ism \'jərn²l,izəm\ *n* : business of reporting or printing news —**jour·nal·ist** \-ist\ *n* —**jour·nal·is·tic** \,jərn²l'istik\ *adj*

jour·ney \'jərnē\ *n, pl* **-neys** : a going from one place to another ~ *vb* **-neyed; -ney·ing** : make a journey

jour·ney·man \-mən\ *n* : worker who has learned a trade and works for another person

joust \'jaust\ *n* : combat on horseback between 2 knights with lances —**joust** *n*

jo·vial \'jōvēəl\ *adj* : marked by good humor —**jo·vi·al·i·ty** \,jōvē'alətē\ *n* —**jo·vi·al·ly** \'jōvēəlē\ *adv*

joy \'joi\ *n* **1** : feeling of happiness **2** : source of happiness —**joy** *vb* —**joy·ful** *adj* —**joy·ful·ly** *adv* —**joy·less** *adj* —**joy·ous** \'joiəs\ *adj* —**joy·ous·ly** *adv* —**joy·ous·ness** *n*

joy·ride *n* : reckless ride for pleasure —**joy·rid·er** *n* —**joy·rid·ing** *n*

ju·bi·lant \'jübələnt\ *adj* : expressing great joy —**ju·bi·lant·ly** *adv* —**ju·bi·la·tion** \,jübə'lāshən\ *n*

ju·bi·lee \'jübə,lē\ *n* **1** : 50th anniversary **2** : season or occasion of celebration

Ju·da·ism \'jüdə,izəm\ *n* : religion developed among the ancient Hebrews —**Ju·da·ic** \jü'dāik\ *adj*

judge \'jəj\ *vb* **judged; judg·ing 1** : form an opinion **2** : decide as a judge ~ *n* **1** : public official authorized to decide questions brought before a court **2** : one who gives an authoritative opinion —**judge·ship** *n*

judg·ment, judge·ment \'jəjmənt\ *n* **1** : decision or opinion given after judging **2** : capacity for judging —**judg·men·tal** \,jəj'ment²l\ *adj* —**judg·men·tal·ly** *adv*

ju·di·ca·ture \'jüdikə,chúr\ *n* : administration of justice

ju·di·cial \jü'dishəl\ *adj* : relating to judicature or the judiciary —**ju·di·cial·ly** *adv*

ju·di·cia·ry \jü'dishē,erē, -'dishərē\ *n*

: system of courts of law or the judges of them —**judiciary** *adj*

ju·di·cious \ju'dishəs\ *adj* : having or characterized by sound judgment —**ju·di·cious·ly** *adv*

ju·do \'jüdō\ *n* : form of wrestling —**judo·ist** *n*

jug \'jəg\ *n* : large deep container with a narrow mouth and a handle

jug·ger·naut \'jəgər,nȯt\ *n* : massive inexorable force or object

jug·gle \'jəgəl\ *vb* **-gled; -gling 1** : keep several objects in motion in the air at the same time **2** : manipulate for an often tricky purpose —**jug·gler** \'jə-glər\ *n*

jug·u·lar \'jəgyələr\ *adj* : in or on the throat or neck

juice \'jüs\ *n* **1** : extractable fluid contents of cells or tissues **2** : electricity —**juic·er** *n* —**juic·i·ly** \'jüsəlē\ *adv* —**juic·i·ness** \-sēnəs\ *n* —**juicy** \'jüsē\ *adj*

ju·jube \'jü,jüb, 'jüjù,bē\ *n* : gummy candy

juke·box \'jük,bäks\ *n* : coin-operated machine for playing music recordings

ju·lep \'jüləp\ *n* : mint-flavored bourbon drink

Ju·ly \jù'lī\ *n* : 7th month of the year having 31 days

jum·ble \'jəmbəl\ *vb* **-bled; -bling** : mix in a confused mass —**jumble** *n*

jum·bo \'jəmbō\ *n, pl* **-bos** : very large version —**jumbo** *adj*

jump \'jəmp\ *vb* **1** : rise into or through the air esp. by muscular effort **2** : pass over **3** : give a start **4** : rise or increase sharply ~ *n* **1** : a jumping **2** : sharp sudden increase **3** : initial advantage

1jump·er \'jəmpər\ *n* : one that jumps

2jumper *n* : sleeveless one-piece dress

jumpy \'jəmpē\ *adj* **jump·i·er; -est** : nervous or jittery

junc·tion \'jəŋkshən\ *n* **1** : a joining **2** : place or point of meeting

junc·ture \'jəŋkchər\ *n* **1** : joint or connection **2** : critical time or state of affairs

June \'jün\ *n* : 6th month of the year having 30 days

jun·gle \'jəŋgəl\ *n* : thick tangled mass of tropical vegetation

ju·nior \'jünyər\ *n* **1** : person who is younger or of lower rank than another **2** : student in the next-to-last year ~ *adj* : younger or lower in rank

ju·ni·per \'jünəpər\ *n* : evergreen shrub or tree

1junk \'jəŋk\ *n* **1** : discarded articles **2** : shoddy product ~ *vb* : discard or scrap —**junky** *adj*

2junk *n* : flat-bottomed ship of Chinese waters

jun·ket \'jəŋkət\ *n* : trip made by an official at public expense

jun·ta \'hùntə, 'jəntə, 'həntə\ *n* : group of persons controlling a government

ju·ris·dic·tion \,jùrəs'dikshən\ *n* **1** : right or authority to interpret and apply the law **2** : limits within which authority may be exercised —**ju·ris·dic·tion·al** \-shənəl\ *adj*

ju·ris·pru·dence \-'prüdəns\ *n* **1** : system of laws **2** : science or philosophy of law

ju·rist \'jùrist\ *n* : judge

ju·ror \'jùrər\ *n* : member of a jury

ju·ry \'jùrē\ *n, pl* **-ries** : body of persons sworn to give a verdict on a matter

just \'jəst\ *adj* **1** : reasonable **2** : correct or proper **3** : morally or legally right **4** : deserved ~ *adv* **1** : exactly **2** : very recently **3** : barely **4** : only **5** : quite **6** : possibly —**just·ly** *adv* —**just·ness** *n*

jus·tice \'jəstəs\ *n* **1** : administration of what is just **2** : judge **3** : administration of law **4** : fairness

jus·ti·fy \'jəstə,fī\ *vb* **-fied; -fy·ing** : prove to be just, right, or reasonable —**jus·ti·fi·a·ble** *adj* —**jus·ti·fi·ca·tion** \,jəstəfə'kāshən\ *n*

jut \'jət\ *vb* **-tt-** : stick out

jute \'jüt\ *n* : strong glossy fiber from a tropical plant

ju·ve·nile \'jüvə,nīl, -vənᵊl\ *adj* : relating to children or young people ~ *n* : young person

jux·ta·pose \'jəkstə,pōz\ *vb* **-posed; -pos·ing** : place side by side —**jux·ta·po·si·tion** \,jəkstəpə'zishən\ *n*

K

k \'kā\ *n, pl* **k's** *or* **ks** \'kāz\ : 11th letter of the alphabet

kai·ser \'kīzər\ *n* : German ruler

kale \'kāl\ *n* : curly cabbage

ka·lei·do·scope \kə'līdə,skōp\ *n* : device containing loose bits of many colored materials reflecting in many patterns — **ka·lei·do·scop·ic** \-,līdə'skäpik\ *adj* — **ka·lei·do·scop·i·cal·ly** \-iklē\ *adv*

kan·ga·roo \,kaŋgə'rü\ *n, pl* **-roos** : large leaping Australian mammal

ka·o·lin \'kāələn\ *n* : fine white clay

kar·at \'karət\ *n* : unit of gold content

ka·ra·te \kə'rätē\ *n* : art of self-defense by crippling kicks and punches

ka·ty·did \'kātē,did\ *n* : large American grasshopper

kay·ak \'kī,ak\ *n* : Eskimo canoe

ka·zoo \kə'zü\ *n, pl* **-zoos** : toy musical instrument

keel \'kēl\ *n* : central lengthwise strip on the bottom of a ship —**keeled** \'kēld\ *adj*

keen \'kēn\ *adj* **1** : sharp **2** : severe **3** : enthusiastic **4** : mentally alert — **keen·ly** *adv* —**keen·ness** *n*

keep \'kēp\ *vb* **kept** \'kept\; **keep·ing 1** : perform **2** : guard **3** : maintain **4** : retain in one's possession **5** : detain **6** : continue in good condition **7** : refrain ~ *n* **1** : fortress **2** : means by which one is kept —**keep·er** *n*

keep·ing \'kēpiŋ\ *n* : conformity

keep·sake \'kēp,sāk\ *n* : souvenir

keg \'keg\ *n* : small cask or barrel

kelp \'kelp\ *n* : coarse brown seaweed

ken \'ken\ *n* : range of sight or understanding

ken·nel \'kenᵊl\ *n* : dog shelter —**kennel** *vb*

ker·chief \'kərchəf, -,chēf\ *n* : square of cloth worn as a head covering

ker·nel \'kərnᵊl\ *n* **1** : inner softer part of a seed or nut **2** : whole seed of a cereal **3** : central part

ker·o·sene, ker·o·sine \'kerə,sēn, ,kerə'-\ *n* : thin flammable oil from petroleum

ketch·up \'kechəp, 'ka-\ *n* : spicy tomato sauce

ket·tle \'ketᵊl\ *n* : vessel for boiling liquids

ket·tle·drum \-,drum\ *n* : brass or copper kettle-shaped drum

¹key \'kē\ *n* **1** : usu. metal piece to open a lock **2** : explanation **3** : lever pressed by a finger in playing an instrument or operating a machine **4** : leading individual or principle **5** : system of musical tones or pitch ~ *vb* : attune ~ *adj* : basic —**key·hole** *n* —**key up** *vb* : make nervous

²key *n* : low island or reef

key·board *n* : arrangement of keys

key·note \-,nōt\ *n* **1** : 1st note of a scale **2** : central fact, idea, or mood ~ *vb* **1** : set the keynote of **2** : deliver the major speech

key·stone *n* : wedge-shaped piece at the crown of an arch

kha·ki \'kakē, 'käk-\ *n* : light yellowish brown color

khan \'kän, 'kan\ *n* : Mongol leader

kib·butz \kib'úts, -'üts\ *n, pl* **-but·zim** \-,út'sēm, -,üt-\ : Israeli communal farm or settlement

ki·bitz·er \'kibətsər, kə'bit-\ *n* : one who offers unwanted advice —**kib·itz** \'kibəts\ *vb*

kick \'kik\ *vb* **1** : strike out or hit with the foot **2** : object strongly **3** : recoil ~ *n* **1** : thrust with the foot **2** : recoil of a gun **3** : stimulating effect — **kick·er** *n*

kid \'kid\ *n* **1** : young goat **2** : child ~ *vb* **-dd- 1** : deceive as a joke **2** : tease —**kid·der** *n* —**kid·ding·ly** *adv*

kid·nap \'kid,nap\ *vb* **-napped** *or* **-naped** \-,napt\; **-nap·ping** *or* **-nap·ing** : carry a person away by illegal force —**kid·nap·per, kid·nap·er** *n*

kid·ney \'kidnē\ *n, pl* **-neys** : either of a pair of organs that excrete urine

kill \'kil\ *vb* **1** : deprive of life **2** : finish **3** : use up (time) ~ *n* : act of killing —**kill·er** *n*

kiln \'kil, 'kiln\ *n* : heated enclosure for burning, firing, or drying —**kiln** *vb*

ki·lo \'kēlō\ *n, pl* **-los** : kilogram

ki·lo·cy·cle \'kilə,sīkəl\ n : kilohertz

ki·lo·gram \'kēlə,gram, 'kilə-\ n : basic metric mass unit nearly equal to the mass of 1000 cubic centimeters of water at its maximum density

ki·lo·hertz \'kilə,hərts, 'kēlə-, -,herts\ n : 1000 hertz

ki·lo·me·ter \kil'ämətər, 'kilə,mēt-\ n : 1000 meters

ki·lo·volt \'kilə,vōlt\ n : 1000 volts

ki·lo·watt \'kilə,wät\ n : 1000 watts

kilt \'kilt\ n : knee-length pleated skirt

kil·ter \'kiltər\ n : proper condition

ki·mo·no \kə'mōnō\ n, pl -nos : loose robe

kin \'kin\ n 1 : one's relatives 2 : kinsman

kind \'kīnd\ n 1 : essential quality 2 : group with common traits 3 : variety ~ adj 1 : of a sympathetic nature 2 : arising from sympathy — **kind·heart·ed** adj — **kind·ness** n

kin·der·gar·ten \'kindər,gärtᵊn\ n : class for young children — **kin·der·gart·ner** \-,gärtnər\ n

kin·dle \'kindᵊl\ vb -dled; -dling 1 : set on fire or start burning 2 : stir up

kin·dling \'kindliŋ, 'kinlən\ n : material for starting a fire

kind·ly \'kīndlē\ adj -li·er; -est : of a sympathetic nature ~ adv 1 : sympathetically 2 : courteously — **kind·li·ness** n

kin·dred \'kindrəd\ n 1 : related individuals 2 : kin ~ adj : of a like nature

kin·folk \'kin,fōk\, **kinfolks** n pl : kin

king \'kiŋ\ n : male sovereign — **king·dom** \-dəm\ n — **king·less** adj — **king·ly** adj — **king·ship** n

king·fish·er \-,fishər\ n : bright-colored crested bird

kink \'kiŋk\ n 1 : short tight twist or curl 2 : cramp — **kinky** adj

kin·ship n : relationship

kins·man \'kinzmən\ n : male relative

kins·wom·an \-,wúmən\ n : female relative

kip·per \'kipər\ n : dried or smoked fish — **kipper** vb

kiss \'kis\ vb : touch with the lips as a mark of affection — **kiss** n

kit \'kit\ n : set of articles (as tools or parts)

kitch·en \'kichən\ n : room with cooking facilities

kite \'kīt\ n 1 : small hawk 2 : covered framework flown at the end of a string

kith \'kith\ n : familiar friends

kit·ten \'kitᵊn\ n : young cat — **kit·ten·ish** adj

¹**kit·ty** \'kitē\ n, pl -ties : kitten

²**kitty** n, pl -ties : fund or pool (as in a card game)

kit·ty-cor·ner, **kit·ty-cor·nered** var of CATERCORNER

ki·wi \'kē,wē\ n : small flightless New Zealand bird

klep·to·ma·nia \,kleptə'mānēə\ n : neurotic impulse to steal — **klep·to·ma·ni·ac** \-nē,ak\ n

knack \'nak\ n 1 : clever way of doing something 2 : natural aptitude

knap·sack \'nap,sak\ n : bag for carrying supplies on one's back

knave \'nāv\ n : rogue — **knav·ery** \'nāvərē\ n — **knav·ish** \'nāvish\ adj

knead \'nēd\ vb 1 : work and press with the hands 2 : massage — **knead·er** n

knee \'nē\ n : joint in the middle part of the leg — **kneed** \'nēd\ adj

knee·cap \'nē,kap\ n : bone forming the front of the knee

kneel \'nēl\ vb **knelt** \'nelt\ or **kneeled**; **kneel·ing** : rest on one's knees

knell \'nel\ n : stroke of a bell

knew past of KNOW

knick·ers \'nikərz\ n pl : pants gathered at the knee

knick·knack \'nik,nak\ n : small decorative object

knife \'nīf\ n, pl **knives** \'nīvz\ : sharp blade with a handle ~ vb **knifed**; **knif·ing** : stab or cut with a knife

knight \'nīt\ n 1 : mounted warrior of feudal times 2 : man honored by a sovereign ~ vb : make a knight of — **knight·hood** n — **knight·ly** adv

knit \'nit\ vb **knit** or **knit·ted**; **knit·ting** 1 : link firmly or closely 2 : form a fabric by interlacing yarn or thread ~ n : knitted garment — **knit·ter** n

knob \'näb\ n : rounded protuberance or handle — **knobbed** \'näbd\ adj — **knob·by** \'näbē\ adj

knock \'näk\ vb 1 : strike with a sharp blow 2 : collide 3 : find fault with ~ n : sharp blow — **knock out** vb : make unconscious

knock·er n : device hinged to a door to knock with

knoll \'nōl\ n : small round hill

knot \'nät\ n 1 : interlacing (as of string) that forms a lump 2 : base of a woody branch in the stem 3 : group 4 : one nautical mile per hour ~ *vb* **-tt-** : tie in or with a knot —**knot•ty** *adj*

know \'nō\ *vb* **knew** \'nü, 'nyü\; **known** \'nōn\; **know•ing 1** : perceive directly or understand **2** : be familiar with —**know•able** *adj* —**know•er** *n*

know•ing \'nōiŋ\ *adj* : shrewdly and keenly alert —**know•ing•ly** *adv*

knowl•edge \'nälij\ *n* **1** : understanding gained by experience **2** : range of information —**knowl•edge•able** *adj*

knuck•le \'nəkəl\ *n* : rounded knob at a finger joint

ko•ala \kō'älə\ *n* : gray furry Australian animal

kohl•ra•bi \kōl'rabē, -'räb-\ *n, pl* **-bies** : cabbage that forms no head

Ko•ran \kə'ran, -'rän\ *n* : book of Islam containing revelations made to Muhammad by Allah

ko•sher \'kōshər\ *adj* : ritually fit for use according to Jewish law

kow•tow \kaù'taù, 'kaù,taù\ *vb* : show excessive deference

kryp•ton \'krip,tän\ *n* : gaseous chemical element used in lamps

ku•dos \'kyü,däs, 'kü-, -,dōz\ *n* : fame and renown

kum•quat \'kəm,kwät\ *n* : small citrus fruit

L

l \'el\ *n, pl* **l's** *or* **ls** \'elz\ : 12th letter of the alphabet

lab \'lab\ *n* : laboratory

la•bel \'lābəl\ *n* **1** : identification slip **2** : identifying word or phrase ~ *vb* **-beled** *or* **-belled**; **-bel•ing** *or* **-bel•ling** : put a label on

la•bi•al \'lābēəl\ *adj* : of or relating to the lips

la•bor \'lābər\ *n* **1** : physical or mental effort **2** : physical efforts of childbirth **3** : task **4** : people who work manually ~ *vb* : work esp. with great effort —**la•bor•er** *n*

lab•o•ra•to•ry \'labrə,tōrē\ *n, pl* **-ries** : place for experimental testing

Labor Day *n* : 1st Monday in September observed as a legal holiday in recognition of working people

la•bo•ri•ous \lə'bōrēəs\ *adj* : requiring great effort —**la•bo•ri•ous•ly** *adv*

lab•y•rinth \'labə,rinth\ *n* : maze —**lab•y•rin•thine** \,labə'rinthən\ *adj*

lace \'lās\ *n* **1** : cord or string for tying **2** : fine net usu. figured fabric ~ *vb* **laced**; **lac•ing 1** : tie **2** : adorn with lace —**lacy** \'lāsē\ *adj*

lac•er•ate \'lasə,rāt\ *vb* **-at•ed**; **-at•ing** : tear roughly —**lac•er•a•tion** \,lasə'rāshən\ *n*

lach•ry•mose \'lakrə,mōs\ *adj* : tearful

lack \'lak\ *vb* : be missing or deficient in ~ *n* : deficiency

lack•a•dai•si•cal \,lakə'dāzikəl\ *adj*

: lacking spirit —**lack•a•dai•si•cal•ly** \-klē\ *adv*

lack•ey \'lakē\ *n, pl* **-eys 1** : footman or servant **2** : toady

lack•lus•ter \'lak,ləstər\ *adj* : dull

la•con•ic \lə'känik\ *adj* : sparing of words —**la•con•i•cal•ly** \-iklē\ *adv*

lac•quer \'lakər\ *n* : glossy surface coating —**lacquer** *vb*

la•crosse \lə'krös\ *n* : ball game played with long-handled rackets

lac•tate \'lak,tāt\ *vb* **-tat•ed**; **-tat•ing** : secrete milk —**lac•ta•tion** \lak-'tāshən\ *n*

lac•tic \'laktik\ *adj* : relating to milk

la•cu•na \lə'künə, -'kyü-\ *n, pl* **-nae** \-,nē\ *or* **-nas** : blank space or missing part

lad \'lad\ *n* : boy

lad•der \'ladər\ *n* : device with steps or rungs for climbing

lad•en \'lādᵊn\ *adj* : loaded

la•dle \'lādᵊl\ *n* : spoon with a deep bowl —**ladle** *vb*

la•dy \'lādē\ *n, pl* **-dies 1** : woman of rank or authority **2** : woman

la•dy•bird \'lādē,bərd\ *n* : ladybug

la•dy•bug \-,bəg\ *n* : brightly colored beetle

lag \'lag\ *vb* **-gg-** : fail to keep up ~ *n* **1** : a falling behind **2** : interval

la•ger \'lägər\ *n* : beer

lag•gard \'lagərd\ *adj* : slow ~ *n* : one that lags —**lag•gard•ly** *adv or adj* —**lag•gard•ness** *n*

la·gniappe \'lan,yap\ n : bonus

la·goon \lə'gün\ n : shallow sound, channel, or pond near or connecting with a larger body of water

laid past of LAY

lain past part of LIE

lair \'lar\ n : den

lais·sez-faire \,les,ā'far\ n : doctrine opposing government interference in business

la·ity \'läətē\ n : people of a religious faith who are not clergy members

lake \'lāk\ n : inland body of water

la·ma \'lämə\ n : Buddhist monk

lamb \'lam\ n : young sheep or its flesh used as food

lam·baste, lam·bast \lam'bāst, -'bast\ vb 1 : beat 2 : censure

lam·bent \'lambənt\ adj : light or bright —**lam·ben·cy** \-bənsē\ n —**lam·bent·ly** adv

lame \'lām\ adj **lam·er; lam·est** 1 : having a limb disabled 2 : weak ~ vb **lamed; lam·ing** : make lame —**lame·ly** adv —**lame·ness** n

la·mé \lä'mā, la-\ n : cloth with tinsel threads

lame·brain \'lām,brān\ n : fool

la·ment \lə'ment\ vb 1 : mourn 2 : express sorrow for ~ n 1 : mourning 2 : complaint —**lam·en·ta·ble** \'laməntəbəl, lə'mentə-\ adj —**lam·en·ta·bly** \-blē\ adv —**lam·en·ta·tion** \,lamən'tāshən\ n

lam·i·nat·ed \'lamə,nātəd\ adj : made of thin layers of material —**lam·i·nate** \-,nāt\ vb —**lam·i·nate** \-nət\ n or adj —**lam·i·na·tion** \,lamə'nāshən\ n

lamp \'lamp\ n : device for producing light or heat

lam·poon \lam'pün\ n : satire —**lampoon** vb

lam·prey \'lamprē\ n, pl **-preys** : sucking eellike fish

lance \'lans\ n : spear ~ vb **lanced; lanc·ing** : pierce or open with a lancet

lance corporal n : enlisted man in the marine corps ranking above a private first class and below a corporal

lan·cet \'lansət\ n : pointed surgical instrument

land \'land\ n 1 : solid part of the surface of the earth 2 : country ~ vb 1 : go ashore 2 : catch or gain 3 : touch the ground or a surface —**land·less** adj —**land·own·er** n

land·fill n : dump

land·ing \'landiŋ\ n 1 : action of one that

lands 2 : place for loading passengers and cargo 3 : level part of a staircase

land·la·dy \'land,lādē\ n : woman landlord

land·locked adj : enclosed by land

land·lord n : owner of property

land·lub·ber \-,ləbər\ n : one with little sea experience

land·mark \-,märk\ n 1 : object that marks a boundary or serves as a guide 2 : event that marks a turning point

land·scape \-,skāp\ n : view of natural scenery ~ vb **-scaped; -scap·ing** : beautify a piece of land (as by decorative planting)

land·slide n 1 : slipping down of a mass of earth 2 : overwhelming victory

land·ward \'landwərd\ adj : toward the land —**landward** adv

lane \'lān\ n : narrow way

lan·guage \'laŋgwij\ n : words and the methods of combining them for communication

lan·guid \'laŋgwəd\ adj 1 : weak 2 : sluggish —**lan·guid·ly** adv —**languid·ness** n

lan·guish \'laŋgwish\ vb : become languid or discouraged

lan·guor \'laŋgər\ n : listless indolence —**lan·guor·ous** adj —**lan·guor·ous·ly** adv

lank \'laŋk\ adj 1 : thin 2 : limp

lanky adj **lank·i·er; -est** : tall and thin

lan·o·lin \'lan³lən\ n : fatty wax from sheep's wool used in ointments

lan·tern \'lantərn\ n : enclosed portable light

¹**lap** \'lap\ n 1 : front part of the lower trunk and thighs of a seated person 2 : overlapping part 3 : one complete circuit completing a course (as around a track or pool) ~ vb **-pp-** : fold over

²**lap** vb **-pp-** 1 : scoop up with the tongue 2 : splash gently

lap·dog n : small dog

la·pel \lə'pel\ n : fold of the front of a coat

lap·i·dary \'lapə,derē\ n : one who cuts and polishes gems ~ adj : relating to gems

lapse \'laps\ n 1 : slight error 2 : termination of a right or privilege 3 : interval ~ vb **lapsed; laps·ing** 1 : slip 2 : subside 3 : cease

lap·top \'lap,täp\ adj : of a size that may be used on one's lap

lar·board \'iärbərd\ n : port side

lar·ce·ny \'lärs⁰nē\ n, pl **-nies** : theft — **lar·ce·nous** \'lärs⁰nəs\ adj

larch \'lärch\ n : tree like a pine that loses its needles

lard \'lärd\ n : pork fat

lar·der \'lärdər\ n : pantry

large \'lärj\ adj **larg·er; larg·est** : greater than average —**large·ly** adv —**large·ness** n

lar·gesse, lar·gess \lär'zhes, -'jes; 'lär,-\ n : liberal giving

lar·i·at \'lareət\ n : lasso

1lark \'lärk\ n : small songbird

2lark vb : romp

lar·va \'lärvə\ n, pl **-vae** \-,vē\ : wormlike form of an insect —**lar·val** \-vəl\ adj

lar·yn·gi·tis \,larən'jītəs\ n : inflammation of the larynx

lar·ynx \'lariŋks\ n, pl **-ryn·ges** \lə'rin,jēz\ or **-ynx·es** : upper part of the trachea —**la·ryn·ge·al** \,larən-'jēəl, lə'rinjēəl\ adj

la·sa·gna \lə'zänyə\ n : flat noodles baked usu. with tomato sauce, meat, and cheese

las·civ·i·ous \lə'sivēəs\ adj : lewd — **las·civ·i·ous·ness** n

la·ser \'lāzər\ n : device that produces an intense light beam

1lash \'lash\ vb : whip ~ n **1** : stroke esp. of a whip **2** : eyelash

2lash vb : bind with a rope or cord

lass \'las\ n : girl

lass·ie \'lasē\ n : girl

las·si·tude \'lasə,tüd, -,tyüd\ n **1** : fatigue **2** : listlessness

las·so \'lasō, la'sü\ n, pl **-sos** or **-soes** : rope with a noose for catching livestock —**lasso** vb

1last \'last\ vb : continue in existence or operation

2last adj **1** : final **2** : previous **3** : least likely ~ adv **1** : at the end **2** : most recently **3** : in conclusion ~ n : something that is last —**last·ly** adv —**at last** : finally

3last n : form on which a shoe is shaped

latch \'lach\ vb : catch or get hold ~ n : catch that holds a door closed

late \'lāt\ adj **lat·er; lat·est** : coming or staying after the proper time **2** : advanced toward the end **3** : recently deceased **4** : recent —**late** adv —**late·com·er** \-,kəmər\ n —**late·ly** adv —**late·ness** n

la·tent \'lāt⁰nt\ adj : present but not visible or expressed —**la·ten·cy** \-⁰nsē\ n

lat·er·al \'latərəl\ adj : on or toward the side —**lat·er·al·ly** adv

la·tex \'lā,teks\ n, pl **-ti·ces** \'lātə,sēz, 'lat-\ or **-tex·es** : emulsion of synthetic rubber or plastic

lath \'lath, 'lath\ n, pl **laths** or **lath** : building material (as a thin strip of wood) used as a base for plaster — **lath** vb —**lath·ing** \-iŋ\ n

lathe \'lāth\ n : machine that rotates material for shaping

lath·er \'lathər\ n : foam ~ vb : form or spread lather

lat·i·tude \'latə,tüd, -,tyüd\ n **1** : distance north or south from the earth's equator **2** : freedom of action

la·trine \lə'trēn\ n : toilet

lat·ter \'latər\ adj **1** : more recent **2** : being the second of **2** —**lat·ter·ly** adv

lat·tice \'latəs\ n : framework of crossed strips

laud vb or n : praise —**laud·able** adj —**laud·ably** adv

laugh \'laf, 'läf\ vb : show mirth, joy, or scorn with a smile and explosive sound —**laugh** n —**laugh·able** adj —**laugh·ing·ly** \-iŋlē\ adv

laugh·ing·stock \'lafiŋ,stäk, 'läf-\ n : object of ridicule

laugh·ter \'laftər, 'läf-\ n : action or sound of laughing

1launch \'lonch\ vb **1** : hurl or send off **2** : set afloat **3** : start —**launch** n —**launch·er** n

2launch n : small open boat

laun·der \'londər\ vb : wash or iron fabrics —**laun·der·er** n —**laun·dress** \-drəs\ n —**laun·dry** \-drē\ n

lau·re·ate \'lorēət\ n : recipient of honors —**laureate** adj

lau·rel \'lorəl\ n **1** : small evergreen tree **2** : honor

la·va \'lävə, 'lav-\ n : volcanic molten rock

lav·a·to·ry \'lavə,torē\ n, pl **-ries** : bathroom

lav·en·der \'lavəndər\ n **1** : aromatic plant used for perfume **2** : pale purple color

lav·ish \'lavish\ adj : expended profusely ~ vb : expend or give freely —**lav·ish·ly** adv —**lav·ish·ness** n

law \'lo\ n **1** : established rule of conduct **2** : body of such rules **3** : principle of construction or procedure **4** : rule stating uniform behavior under uniform conditions **5** : lawyer's profession —

law·break·er *n* —law·giv·er *n* —
law·less *adj* —law·less·ly *adv* —law·
less·ness *n* —law·mak·er *n* —law·
man \-mən\ *n* —law·suit *n*

law·ful \'lófəl\ *adj* : permitted by law —
law·ful·ly *adv*

lawn \'lón\ *n* : grass-covered yard

law·yer \'lóyər\ *n* : legal practitioner

lax \'laks\ *adj* : not strict or tense —
lax·i·ty \'laksətē\ *n* —lax·ly *adv*

lax·a·tive \'laksətiv\ *n* : drug relieving
constipation

¹lay \'lā\ *vb* laid \'lād\; lay·ing 1 : put
or set down 2 : produce eggs 3 : bet
4 : impose as a duty or burden 5 : put
forward ~ *n* : way something lies or
is laid

²lay *past of* LIE

³lay *n* : song

⁴lay *adj* : of the laity —lay·man \-mən\
n —lay·wom·an \-,wúmən\ *n*

lay·er \'lāər\ *n* 1 : one that lays 2 : one
thickness over or under another

lay·off \'lā,óf\ *n* : temporary dismissal
of a worker

lay·out \'lā,aút\ *n* : arrangement

la·zy \'lāzē\ *adj* -zi·er; -est : disliking
activity or exertion —la·zi·ly \'lāzəlē\
adv —la·zi·ness *n*

lea \'lē, 'lā\ *n* : meadow

leach \'lēch\ *vb* : remove (a soluble part)
with a solvent

¹lead \'lēd\ *vb* led \'led\; lead·ing 1
: guide on a way 2 : direct the activity
of 3 : go at the head of 4 : tend to a
definite result ~ *n* : position in front
—lead·er *n* —lead·er·less *adj* —
lead·er·ship *n*

²lead \'led\ *n* 1 : heavy bluish white
chemical element 2 : marking substance in a pencil —lead·en \'led³n\
adj

leaf \'lēf\ *n, pl* leaves \'lēvz\ 1 : green
outgrowth of a plant stem 2 : leaflike
thing ~ *vb* 1 : produce leaves 2 : turn
book pages —leaf·age \'lēfij\ *n* —
leafed \'lēft\ *adj* —leaf·less *adj* —
leafy *adj* —leaved \'lēfd\ *adj*

leaf·let \'lēflət\ *n* : pamphlet

¹league \'lēg\ *n* : unit of distance equal
to about 3 miles

²league *n* : association for a common
purpose —league *vb* —leagu·er *n*

leak \'lēk\ *vb* 1 : enter or escape through
a leak 2 : become or make known ~
n : opening that accidentally admits
or lets out a substance —leak·age
\'lēkij\ *n* —leaky *adj*

¹lean \'lēn\ *vb* 1 : bend from a vertical
position 2 : rely on for support 3
: incline in opinion

²lean *adj* 1 : lacking in flesh 2 : lacking
richness —lean·ness \'lēnnəs\ *n*

leap \'lēp\ *vb* leapt *or* leaped \'lēpt,
'lept\; leap·ing : jump —leap *n*

leap year *n* : 366-day year

learn \'lərn\ *vb* 1 : gain understanding
or skill by study or experience 2
: memorize 3 : find out —learn·er *n*

learned \'lərnəd\ *adj* : having great learning —learn·ed·ness *n*

learn·ing \-iŋ\ *n* : knowledge

lease \'lēs\ *n* : contract transferring real
estate for a term and rent ~ for rent —
vb leased; leas·ing : grant by or hold
under a lease

leash \'lēsh\ *n* : line to hold an animal
—leash *vb*

least \'lēst\ *adj* 1 : lowest in importance
or position 2 : smallest 3 : scantiest
~ *n* : one that is least ~ *adv* : in the
smallest or lowest degree

leath·er \'lethər\ *n* : dressed animal skin
—leath·ern \-ərn\ *adj* —leathery *adj*

¹leave \'lēv\ *vb* left \'left\; leav·ing 1
: bequeath 2 : allow or cause to remain 3 : have as a remainder 4 : go
away ~ *n* 1 : permission 2
: authorized absence 3 : departure

²leave *vb* leaved; leav·ing : leaf

leav·en \'levən\ *n* : substance for producing fermentation ~ *vb* : raise
dough with a leaven

leaves *pl of* LEAF

lech·ery \'lechərē\ *n* : inordinate indulgence in sex —lech·er \'lechər\ *n* —
lech·er·ous \-chərəs\ *adj* —lech·er·
ous·ly *adv* —lech·er·ous·ness *n*

lec·ture \'lekchər\ *n* 1 : instructive talk
2 : reprimand —lecture *vb* —lec·tur·
er *n* —lec·ture·ship *n*

led *past of* LEAD

ledge \'lej\ *n* : shelflike projection

led·ger \'lejər\ *n* : account book

lee \'lē\ *n* : side sheltered from the wind
—lee *adj*

leech \'lēch\ *n* : segmented freshwater
worm that feeds on blood

leek \'lēk\ *n* : onionlike herb

leer \'lir\ *n* : suggestive or malicious
look —leer *vb*

leery \'lirē\ *adj* : suspicious or wary

lees \'lēz\ *n pl* : dregs

lee·ward \'lēwərd, 'lúərd\ *adj* : situated
away from the wind ~ *n* : the lee side

lee·way \'lē,wā\ n : allowable margin

¹left \'left\ adj : on the same side of the body as the heart ~ n : left hand — **left** adv

²left past of LEAVE

leg \'leg\ n 1 : limb of an animal that supports the body 2 : something like a leg 3 : clothing to cover the leg ~ vb **-gg-** : walk or run — **legged** \'legəd\ adj — **leg·less** adj

leg·a·cy \'legəsē\ n, pl **-cies** : inheritance

le·gal \'lēgəl\ adj 1 : relating to law or lawyers 2 : lawful — **le·gal·is·tic** \,lēgə'listik\ adj — **le·gal·i·ty** \li-'galətē\ n — **le·gal·ize** \'lēgə,līz\ vb — **le·gal·ly** \-gəlē\ adv

leg·ate \'legət\ n : official representative

le·ga·tion \li'gāshən\ n 1 : diplomatic mission 2 : official residence and office of a diplomat

leg·end \'lejənd\ n 1 : story handed down from the past 2 : inscription 3 : explanation of map symbols — **leg·end·ary** \-ən,derē\ adj

leg·er·de·main \,lejərdə'mān\ n : sleight of hand

leg·ging, leg·gin \'legən, -iŋ\ n : leg covering

leg·i·ble \'lejəbəl\ adj : capable of being read — **leg·i·bil·i·ty** \,lejə'bilətē\ n — **leg·i·bly** \'lejəblē\ adv

le·gion \'lējən\ n 1 : large army unit 2 : multitude 3 : association of former servicemen — **le·gion·ary** \-,erē\ n — **le·gion·naire** \,lējən'ar\ n

leg·is·late \'lejə,slāt\ vb **-lated; -lating** : enact or bring about with laws — **leg·is·la·tion** \,lejə'slāshən\ n — **leg·is·la·tive** \'lejə,slātiv\ adj — **leg·is·la·tor** \-ər\ n

leg·is·la·ture \'lejə,slāchər\ n : organization with authority to make laws

le·git·i·mate \li'jitəmət\ adj 1 : lawfully begotten 2 : genuine 3 : conforming with law or accepted standards — **le·git·i·ma·cy** \-məsē\ n — **le·git·i·mate·ly** adv — **le·git·i·mize** \-,mīz\ vb

le·gume \'leg,yüm, li'gyüm\ n : plant bearing pods — **le·gu·mi·nous** \li-'gyümənəs\ adj

lei \'lā\ n : necklace of flowers

lei·sure \'lēzhər, 'lezh-, 'lāzh-\ n 1 : free time 2 : ease 3 : convenience — **lei·sure·ly** adj or adv

lem·ming \'lemiŋ\ n : short-tailed rodent

lem·on \'lemən\ n : yellow citrus fruit — **lem·ony** adj

lem·on·ade \,lemə'nād\ n : sweetened lemon beverage

lend \'lend\ vb **lent** \'lent\; **lend·ing 1** : give for temporary use 2 : furnish — **lend·er** n

length \'leŋth\ n 1 : longest dimension 2 : duration in time 3 : piece to be joined to others — **length·en** \'leŋthən\ vb — **length·wise** adv or adj — **lengthy** adj

le·nient \'lēnēənt, -nyənt\ adj : of mild and tolerant disposition or effect — **le·ni·en·cy** \'lēnēənsē -nyənsē\ n — **le·ni·ent·ly** adv

len·i·ty \'lenətē\ n : leniency

lens \'lenz\ n 1 : curved piece for forming an image in an optical instrument 2 : transparent body in the eye that focuses light rays

Lent \'lent\ n : 40-day period of penitence and fasting from Ash Wednesday to Easter — **Lent·en** \-ᵊn\ adj

len·til \'lentᵊl\ n : legume with flat edible seeds

le·o·nine \'lēə,nīn\ adj : like a lion

leop·ard \'lepərd\ n : large tawny black-spotted cat

le·o·tard \'lēə,tärd\ n : close-fitting garment

lep·er \'lepər\ n : person with leprosy

lep·re·chaun \'leprə,kän\ n : mischievous Irish elf

lep·ro·sy \'leprəsē\ n : chronic bacterial disease — **lep·rous** \-rəs\ adj

les·bi·an \'lezbēən\ n : female homosexual — **lesbian** adj — **les·bi·an·ism** \-,izəm\ n

le·sion \'lēzhən\ n : abnormal area in the body due to injury or disease

less \'les\ adj : fewer 2 : of lower rank, degree, or importance 3 : smaller ~ adv 1 : to a lesser degree ~ n, pl **less** : smaller portion ~ prep : minus — **less·en** \-ᵊn\ vb

-less \ləs\ adj suffix 1 : not having 2 : unable to act or be acted on

les·see \le'sē\ n : tenant under a lease

less·er \'lesər\ adj : of less size, quality, or significance

les·son \'lesᵊn\ n 1 : reading or exercise to be studied by a pupil 2 : something learned

les·sor \'les,ór, le'sór\ n : one who transfers property by a lease

lest \,lest\ conj : for fear that

¹let \'let\ n : hindrance or obstacle

²let \vb let; **let·ting 1** : cause to **2** : rent **3** : permit

-let \lət\ n suffix : small one

le·thal \'lēthəl\ adj : deadly **—le·thal·ly** adv

leth·ar·gy \'lethərjē\ n **1** : drowsiness **2** : state of being lazy or indifferent **—le·thar·gic** \li'thärjik\ adj

let·ter \'letər\ n **1** : unit of an alphabet **2** : written or printed communication **3** pl : literature or learning **4** : literal meaning ~ vb : mark with letters **—let·ter·er** n

let·tuce \'letəs\ n : garden plant with crisp leaves

leu·ke·mia \lü'kēmēə\ n : cancerous blood disease **—leu·ke·mic** \-mik\ adj or n

lev·ee \'levē\ n : embankment to prevent flooding

lev·el \'levəl\ n **1** : device for establishing a flat surface **2** : horizontal surface **3** : position in a scale ~ vb -eled or -elled; -el·ing or -el·ling **1** : make flat or level **2** : aim **3** : raze — adj **1** : having an even surface **2** : of the same height or rank **—lev·el·er** n **—lev·el·ly** adv **—lev·el·ness** n

le·ver \'levər, 'lē-\ n : bar for prying or dislodging something **—le·ver·age** \'levərij, 'lēv-\ n

le·vi·a·than \li'vīəthən\ n **1** : large sea animal **2** : enormous thing

lev·i·ty \'levətē\ n : unseemly frivolity

levy \'levē\ n, pl **lev·ies** : imposition or collection of a tax ~ vb lev·ied; levy·ing **1** : impose or collect legally **2** : enlist for military service **3** : wage

lewd \'lüd\ adj **1** : sexually unchaste **2** : vulgar **—lewd·ly** adv **—lewd·ness** n

lex·i·cog·ra·phy \,leksə'kägrəfē\ n : dictionary making **—lex·i·cog·rapher** \-fər\ n **—lex·i·co·graph·i·cal** \-kō'grafikəl\ or **lex·i·co·graph·ic** \-ik\ adj

lex·i·con \'leksə,kän\ n, pl **-i·ca** \-sikə\ or **-icons** : dictionary

li·a·ble \'līəbəl\ adj **1** : legally obligated **2** : probable **3** : susceptible **—li·a·bil·i·ty** \,līə'bilətē\ n

li·ai·son \'lēə,zän, lē'ā-\ n **1** : close bond **2** : communication between groups

li·ar \'līər\ n : one who lies

li·bel \'lībəl\ n : action, crime, or an instance of injuring a person's reputation esp. by something written ~ vb -beled or -belled; -bel·ing or -bel-

ling : make or publish a libel **—li·bel·er** n **—li·bel·ist** n **—li·bel·ous, li·bel·lous** \-bələs\ adj

lib·er·al \'librəl, 'libə-\ adj : not stingy, narrow, or conservative **—liberal** n **—lib·er·al·ism** \-,izəm\ n **—lib·er·al·i·ty** \,libə'ralətē\ n **—lib·er·al·ize** \'librə,līz, 'libə-\ vb **—lib·er·al·ly** \-rəlē\ adv

lib·er·ate \'libə,rāt\ vb -at·ed; -at·ing : set free **—lib·er·a·tion** \,libə'rāshən\ n **—lib·er·a·tor** \'libə,rātər\ n

lib·er·tine \'libər,tēn\ n : one who leads a dissolute life

lib·er·ty \'libərtē\ n, pl **-ties 1** : quality or state of being free **2** : action going beyond normal limits

li·bi·do \lə'bēdō, -'bīd-\ n, pl **-dos** : sexual drive **—li·bid·i·nal** \lə'bidənəl\ adj **—li·bid·i·nous** \-əs\ adj

li·brary \'lī,brerē\ n, pl **-brar·ies 1** : place where books are kept for use **2** : collection of books **—li·brar·i·an** \lī'brerēən\ n

li·bret·to \lə'bretō\ n, pl **-tos** or **-ti** \-ē\ : text of an opera **—li·bret·tist** \-ist\ n

lice pl of LOUSE

li·cense, li·cence \'līsⁿns\ n **1** : legal permission to engage in some activity **2** : document or tag providing proof of a license **3** : irresponsible use of freedom **—license** vb **—li·cens·ee** \,līsⁿn'sē\ n

li·cen·tious \lī'senchəs\ adj : disregarding sexual restraints **—li·cen·tious·ly** adv **—li·cen·tious·ness** n

li·chen \'līkən\ n : complex lower plant made up of an alga and a fungus

lic·it \'lisət\ adj : lawful

lick \'lik\ vb **1** : draw the tongue over **2** : beat ~ n **1** : stroke of the tongue **2** : small amount

lic·o·rice \'likərish, -rəs\ n : dried root of a European legume or candy flavored by it

lid \'lid\ n **1** : movable cover **2** : eyelid

¹lie \'lī\ vb lay \'lā\; lain \'lān\; ly·ing \'līiŋ\ **1** : be in, rest in, or assume a horizontal position **2** : occupy a certain relative position ~ n : position in which something lies

²lie vb lied; ly·ing \'līiŋ\ : tell a lie ~ n : untrue statement

liege \'lēj\ n : feudal superior or vassal

lien \'lēn, 'lēən\ n : legal claim on the property of another

lieu·ten·ant \lü'tenənt\ n 1 : representative 2 : first lieutenant or second lieutenant 3 : commissioned officer in the navy ranking next below a lieutenant commander —**lieu·ten·an·cy** \-ənsē\ n

lieutenant colonel n : commissioned officer (as in the army) ranking next below a colonel

lieutenant commander n : commissioned officer in the navy ranking next below a commander

lieutenant general n : commissioned officer (as in the army) ranking next below a general

lieutenant junior grade n, pl **lieutenants junior grade** : commissioned officer in the navy ranking next below a lieutenant

life \'līf\ n, pl **lives** \'līvz\ 1 : quality that distinguishes a vital and functional being from a dead body or inanimate matter 2 : physical and mental experiences of an individual 3 : biography 4 : period of existence 5 : way of living 6 : liveliness —**life·less** adj — **life·like** adj

life·blood n : basic source of strength and vitality

life·boat n : boat for saving lives at sea

life·guard n : one employed to safeguard bathers

life·long adj : continuing through life

life·sav·ing n : art or practice of saving lives —**life·sav·er** \-,sāvər\ n

life·style \'līf,stīl\ n : a way of life

life·time n : duration of an individual's existence

lift \'lift\ vb 1 : move upward or cause to move upward 2 : put an end to — **lift** n —**lift·er** n

lift·off \'lift,óf\ n : vertical takeoff of a rocket

lig·a·ment \'ligəmənt\ n : band of tough tissue that holds bones together

lig·a·ture \'ligə,chúr, -chər\ n : something that binds or ties

¹light \'līt\ n 1 : radiation that makes vision possible 2 : daylight 3 : source of light 4 : public knowledge 5 : aspect 6 : celebrity 7 : flame for lighting ~ adj 1 : bright 2 : weak in color ~ vb **lit** \'lit\ or **light·ed; light·ing** 1 : make or become light 2 : cause to burn —**light·er** n —**light·ness** n — **light·proof** adj

²light adj : not heavy, serious, or abundant —**light** adv —**light·ly** adv — **light·ness** n —**light·weight** adj

³light vb **light·ed** or **lit** \'lit\; **light·ing** : settle or dismount

¹light·en \'līt^ən\ vb 1 : make light or bright 2 : give out flashes of lightning

²lighten vb 1 : relieve of a burden 2 : become lighter

light·heart·ed \-'härtəd\ adj : free from worry —**light·heart·ed·ly** adv — **light·heart·ed·ness** n

light·house n : structure with a powerful light for guiding sailors

light·ning \'lītniŋ\ n : flashing discharge of atmospheric electricity

light-year \'līt,yir\ n : distance traveled by light in one year equal to about 5.88 trillion miles

lig·nite \'lig,nīt\ n : brownish black soft coal

¹like \'līk\ vb **liked; lik·ing** 1 : enjoy 2 : desire ~ n : preference —**lik·able, like·able** \'līkəbəl\ adj

²like adj : similar ~ prep 1 : similar or similarly to 2 : typical of 3 : such as ~ n : counterpart ~ conj : as or as if —**like·ness** n —**like·wise** adv

-like \,līk\ adj comb form : resembling or characteristic of

like·li·hood \'līklē,hüd\ n : probability

like·ly \'līklē\ adj **-li·er; -est** 1 : probable 2 : believable ~ adv : in all probability

lik·en \'līkən\ vb : compare

lik·ing \'līkiŋ\ n : favorable regard

li·lac \'līlək, -,lak, -,läk\ n : shrub with clusters of fragrant pink, purple, or white flowers

lilt \'lilt\ n : rhythmical swing or flow

lily \'lilē\ n, pl **lil·ies** : tall bulbous herb with funnel-shaped flowers

lima bean \'līmə-\ n : flat edible seed of a plant or the plant itself

limb \'lim\ n 1 : projecting appendage used in moving or grasping 2 : tree branch —**limb·less** adj

lim·ber \'limbər\ adj : supple or agile ~ vb : make or become limber

lim·bo \'limbō\ n, pl **-bos** : place or state of confinement or oblivion

¹lime \'līm\ n : caustic white oxide of calcium

²lime n : small green lemonlike citrus fruit —**lime·ade** \-,ād\ n

lime·light n : center of public attention

lim·er·ick \'limərik\ n : light poem of 5 lines

lime·stone \n\ : rock that yields lime when burned

lim·it \'limət\ n 1 : boundary 2 : something that restrains or confines ~ vb : set limits on **—lim·i·ta·tion** \,limə'tāshən\ n **—lim·it·less** adj

lim·ou·sine \'limə,zēn, ,limə'-\ n : large luxurious sedan

limp \'limp\ vb : walk lamely ~ n : limping movement or gait ~ adj : lacking firmness and body **—limp·ly** adv **—limp·ness** n

lim·pid \'limpəd\ adj : clear or transparent

lin·den \'lindən\ n : tree with large heart-shaped leaves

¹line \'līn\ vb **lined; lin·ing** : cover the inner surface of **—lin·ing** n

²line n 1 : cord, rope, or wire 2 : row or something like a row 3 : note 4 : course of action or thought 5 : state of agreement 6 : occupation 7 : limit 8 : transportation system 9 : long narrow mark ~ vb **lined; lin·ing** 1 : mark with a line 2 : place in a line 3 : form a line

lin·eage \'linēij\ n : descent from a common ancestor

lin·eal \'linēəl\ adj 1 : linear 2 : in a direct line of ancestry

lin·ea·ments \'linēəmənts\ n pl : features or contours esp. of a face

lin·ear \'linēər\ adj 1 : straight 2 : long and narrow

lin·en \'linən\ n 1 : cloth or thread made of flax 2 : household articles made of linen cloth

lin·er \'līnər\ n 1 : one that lines 2 : ship or airplane belonging to a line

line·up \'līn,əp\ n 1 : line of persons for inspection or identification 2 : list of players in a game

-ling \liŋ\ n suffix 1 : one linked with 2 : young, small, or minor one

lin·ger \'liŋgər\ vb : be slow to leave or act **—lin·ger·er** n

lin·ge·rie \,länjə'rā, ,laⁿzhə-, -'rē\ n : women's underwear

lin·go \'liŋgō\ n, pl **-goes** : usu. strange language

lin·guist \'liŋgwist\ n 1 : person skilled in speech or languages 2 : student of language **—lin·guis·tic** \liŋ'gwistik\ adj **—lin·guis·tics** n pl

lin·i·ment \'linəmənt\ n : liquid medication rubbed on the skin

link \'liŋk\ n 1 : connecting structure (as a ring of a chain) 2 : bond **—link** vb **—link·age** \-ij\ n **—link·er** n

li·no·leum \lə'nōlēəm\ n : floor covering with hard surface

lin·seed \'lin,sēd\ n : seeds of flax yielding an oil (linseed oil)

lint \'lint\ n : fine fluff or loose short fibers from fabric

lin·tel \'lintᵊl\ n : horizontal piece over a door or window

li·on \'līən\ n : large cat of Africa and Asia **—li·on·ess** \'līənəs\ n

li·on·ize \'līə,nīz\ vb **-ized; -iz·ing** : treat as very important **—li·on·iza·tion** \,līənə'zāshən\ n

lip \'lip\ n 1 : either of the 2 fleshy folds surrounding the mouth 2 : edge of something hollow **—lipped** \'lipt\ adj **—lip·read·ing** n

li·po·suc·tion \'lipə,səkshən, 'lī-\ n : surgical removal of fat deposits (as from the thighs)

lip·stick \'lip,stik\ n : stick of cosmetic to color lips

liq·ue·fy \'likwə,fī\ vb **-fied; -fy·ing** : make or become liquid **—liq·ue·fi·er** \'likwə,fīər\ n

li·queur \li'kər\ n : sweet or aromatic alcoholic liquor

liq·uid \'likwəd\ adj 1 : flowing freely like water 2 : neither solid nor gaseous 3 : of or convertible to cash **—liquid** n **—liq·uid·i·ty** \lik'widətē\ n

liq·ui·date \'likwə,dāt\ vb **-dat·ed; -dat·ing** 1 : pay off 2 : dispose of **—liq·ui·da·tion** \,likwə'dāshən\ n

li·quor \'likər\ n : liquid substance and esp. a distilled alcoholic beverage

lisp \'lisp\ vb : pronounce s and z imperfectly **—lisp** n

lis·some \'lisəm\ adj : supple or agile

¹list \'list\ n 1 : series of names or items ~ vb 1 : make a list of 2 : put on a list

²list vb : tilt or lean over ~ n : slant

lis·ten \'lisᵊn\ vb 1 : pay attention in order to hear 2 : heed **—lis·ten·er** \'lisⁿər\ n

list·less \'listləs\ adj : having no desire to act **—list·less·ly** adv **—list·less·ness** n

lit \'lit\ past of LIGHT

lit·a·ny \'litᵊnē\ n, pl **-nies** 1 : prayer said as a series of responses to a leader 2 : long recitation

li·ter \'lētər\ n : unit of liquid measure equal to about 1.06 quarts

lit·er·al \\'litərəl\\ *adj* : being exactly as stated —**lit·er·al·ly** *adv*

lit·er·ary \\'litə,rerē\\ *adj* : relating to literature

lit·er·ate \\'litərət\\ *adj* : able to read and write —**lit·er·a·cy** \\'litərəsē\\ *n*

lit·er·a·ture \\'litərə,chùr, -chər\\ *n* : writings of enduring interest

lithe \\'līth, 'līth\\ *adj* **1** : supple **2** : graceful —**lithe·some** \\-səm\\ *adj*

lith·o·graph \\'lithə,graf\\ *n* : print from a drawing on metal or stone —**li·thog·ra·pher** \\lith'ägrəfər, 'lithə,grafər\\ *n* —**lith·o·graph·ic** \\,lithə'grafik\\ *adj* —**li·thog·ra·phy** \\lith'ägrəfē\\ *n*

lit·i·gate \\'litə,gāt\\ *vb* -**gat·ed**; -**gat·ing** : carry on a lawsuit —**lit·i·gant** \\'litigənt\\ *n* —**lit·i·ga·tion** \\,litə-'gāshən\\ *n* —**li·ti·gious** \\lə'tijəs, li-\\ *adj* —**li·ti·gious·ness** *n*

lit·mus \\'litməs\\ *n* : coloring matter that turns red in acid solutions and blue in alkaline

lit·ter \\'litər\\ *n* **1** : animal offspring of one birth **2** : stretcher **3** : rubbish **4** : material to absorb animal waste ~ *vb* **1** : give birth to young **2** : strew with litter

lit·tle \\'litəl\\ *adj* **lit·tler** *or* **less** \\'les\\ *or* **less·er** \\'lesər\\; **lit·tlest** *or* **least** \\'lēst\\ **1** : not big **2** : not much **3** : not important — *adv* **less** \\'les\\; **least** \\'lēst\\ **1** : slightly **2** : not often ~ *n* : small amount —**lit·tle·ness** *n*

lit·ur·gy \\'litərjē\\ *n, pl* -**gies** : rite of worship —**li·tur·gi·cal** \\lə'tərjikəl\\ *adj* —**li·tur·gi·cal·ly** \\-klē\\ *adv* —**lit·ur·gist** \\'litərjist\\ *n*

liv·a·ble \\'livəbəl\\ *adj* : suitable for living in or with —**liv·a·bil·i·ty** \\,livə'bilətē\\ *n*

¹live \\'liv\\ *vb* **lived**; **liv·ing** **1** : be alive **2** : conduct one's life **3** : subsist **4** : reside

²live \\'līv\\ *adj* **1** : having life **2** : burning **3** : connected to electric power **4** : not exploded **5** : of continuing interest **6** : involving the actual presence of real people

live·li·hood \\'līvlē,hùd\\ *n* : means of subsistence

live·long \\'liv'lòn\\ *adj* : whole

live·ly \\'līvlē\\ *adj* -**li·er**; -**est** : full of life and vigor —**live·li·ness** *n*

liv·en \\'līvən\\ *vb* : enliven

liv·er \\'livər\\ *n* : organ that secretes bile

liv·ery \\'livərē\\ *n, pl* -**er·ies** **1** : servant's uniform **2** : care of horses for pay —**liv·er·ied** \\-rēd\\ *adj* —**liv·ery·man** \\-mən\\ *n*

lives *pl of* LIFE

live·stock \\'līv,stäk\\ *n* : farm animals

liv·id \\'livəd\\ *adj* **1** : discolored by bruising **2** : pale **3** : enraged

liv·ing \\'livin\\ *adj* : having life ~ *n* : livelihood

liz·ard \\'lizərd\\ *n* : reptile with 4 legs and a long tapering tail

lla·ma \\'lämə\\ *n* : So. American mammal related to the camel

load \\'lōd\\ *n* **1** : cargo **2** : supported weight **3** : burden **4** : a large quantity—usu. pl. ~ *vb* **1** : put a load on **2** : burden **3** : put ammunition in

¹loaf \\'lōf\\ *n, pl* **loaves** \\'lōvz\\ : mass of bread

²loaf *vb* : waste time —**loaf·er** *n*

loam \\'lōm, 'lüm\\ *n* : soil —**loamy** *adj*

loan \\'lōn\\ *n* **1** : money borrowed at interest **2** : something lent temporarily **3** : grant of use ~ *vb* : lend

loath \\'lōth, 'lōth\\ *adj* : very reluctant

loathe \\'lōth\\ *vb* **loathed**; **loath·ing** : hate

loath·ing \\'lōthin\\ *n* : extreme disgust

loath·some \\'lōthsəm, 'lōth-\\ *adj* : repulsive

lob \\'läb\\ *vb* -**bb**- : throw or hit in a high arc —**lob** *n*

lob·by \\'läbē\\ *n, pl* -**bies** **1** : public waiting room at the entrance of a building **2** : persons lobbying ~ *vb* -**bied**; -**by·ing** : try to influence legislators —**lob·by·ist** *n*

lobe \\'lōb\\ *n* : rounded part —**lo·bar** \\'lōbər\\ *adj* —**lobed** \\'lōbd\\ *adj*

lo·bot·o·my \\lō'bätəmē\\ *n, pl* -**mies** : surgical severance of nerve fibers in the brain

lob·ster \\'läbstər\\ *n* : marine crustacean with 2 large pincerlike claws

lo·cal \\'lōkəl\\ *adj* : confined to or serving a limited area —**local** *n* —**lo·cal·ly** *adv*

lo·cale \\lō'kal\\ *n* : setting for an event

lo·cal·i·ty \\lō'kalətē\\ *n, pl* -**ties** : particular place

lo·cal·ize \\'lōkə,līz\\ *vb* -**ized**; -**iz·ing** : confine to a definite place —**lo·cal·i·za·tion** \\,lōkələ'zāshən\\ *n*

lo·cate \\'lō,kāt, lō'kāt\\ *vb* -**cat·ed**; -**cat·ing** **1** : settle **2** : find a site for **3**

: discover the place of —**lo·ca·tion** \lō′kāshən\ *n*

¹lock \′läk\ *n* : tuft or strand of hair

²lock *n* **1** : fastener using a bolt **2** : enclosure in a canal to raise or lower boats ~ *vb* **1** : make fast with a lock **2** : confine **3** : interlock

lock·er \′läkər\ *n* : storage compartment

lock·et \′läkət\ *n* : small case worn on a necklace

lock·jaw *n* : tetanus

lock·out *n* : closing of a plant by an employer during a labor dispute

lock·smith \-,smith\ *n* : one who makes or repairs locks

lo·co·mo·tion \,lōkə′mōshən\ *n* : power of moving —**lo·co·mo·tive** \-′mōtiv\ *adj*

lo·co·mo·tive \-′mōtiv\ *n* : vehicle that moves railroad cars

lo·co·weed \′lōkō,wēd\ *n* : western plant poisonous to livestock

lo·cust \′lōkəst\ *n* **1** : migratory grasshopper **2** : cicada **3** : tree with hard wood or this wood

lo·cu·tion \lō′kyüshən\ *n* : way of saying something

lode \′lōd\ *n* : ore deposit

lode·stone *n* : magnetic rock

lodge \′läj\ *vb* **lodged; lodg·ing 1** : provide quarters for **2** : come to rest **3** : file ~ *n* **1** : special house (as for hunters) **2** : animal's den **3** : branch of a fraternal organization —**lodg·er** \′läjər\ *n* —**lodg·ing** *n* —**lodg·ment, lodge·ment** \-mənt\ *n*

loft \′lȯft\ *n* **1** : attic **2** : upper floor (as of a warehouse)

lofty \′lȯftē\ *adj* **loft·i·er; -est 1** : noble **2** : proud **3** : tall or high —**loft·i·ly** *adv* —**loft·i·ness** *n*

log \′lȯg, ′läg\ *n* **1** : unshaped timber **2** : daily record of a ship's or plane's progress ~ *vb* **-gg- 1** : cut (trees) for lumber **2** : enter in a log —**log·ger** \-ər\ *n*

log·a·rithm \′lȯgə,rithəm, ′läg-\ *n* : exponent to which a base number is raised to produce a given number

loge \′lōzh\ *n* : box in a theater

log·ger·head \′lȯgər,hed, ′läg-\ *n* : large Atlantic sea turtle —**at loggerheads** : in disagreement

log·ic \′läjik\ *n* **1** : science of reasoning **2** : sound reasoning —**log·i·cal** \-ikəl\ *adj* —**log·i·cal·ly** *adv* —**lo·gi·cian** \lō′jishən\ *n*

lo·gis·tics \lō′jistiks\ *n sing or pl* : procurement and movement of people and supplies —**lo·gis·tic** *adj*

logo \′lōgō, ′lȯg-, ′läg-\ *n, pl* **log·os** \-ōz\ : advertising symbol

loin \′lȯin\ *n* **1** : part of the body on each side of the spine between the hip and lower ribs **2** *pl* : pubic regions

loi·ter \′lȯitər\ *vb* : remain around a place idly —**loi·ter·er** *n*

loll \′läl\ *vb* : lounge

lol·li·pop, lol·ly·pop \′läli,päp\ *n* : hard candy on a stick

lone \′lōn\ *adj* **1** : alone or isolated **2** : only —**lone·li·ness** *n* —**lone·ly** *adj* —**lon·er** \′lōnər\ *n*

lone·some \-səm\ *adj* : sad from lack of company —**lone·some·ly** *adv* —**lone·some·ness** *n*

long \′lȯŋ\ *adj* **lon·ger** \′lȯŋgər\; **longest** \′lȯŋgəst\ **1** : extending far or for a considerable time **2** : having a specified length **3** : tedious **4** : well supplied—used with *on* — *adv* : for a long time ~ *n* : long period ~ *vb* : feel a strong desire —**long·ing** \′lȯŋiŋ\ *n* —**long·ing·ly** *adv*

lon·gev·i·ty \län′jevətē\ *n* : long life

long·hand *n* : handwriting

long·horn *n* : cattle with long horns

lon·gi·tude \′länjə,tüd, -,tyüd\ *n* : angular distance east or west from a meridian

lon·gi·tu·di·nal \,länjə′tüdənəl, -′tyüd-\ *adj* : lengthwise —**lon·gi·tu·di·nal·ly** *adv*

long·shore·man \′lȯŋ′shōrmən\ *n* : one who loads and unloads ships

look \′lük\ *vb* **1** : see **2** : seem **3** : direct one's attention **4** : face ~ *n* **1** : action of looking **2** : appearance of the face **3** : aspect —**look after** : take care of —**look for 1** : expect **2** : search for

look·out *n* **1** : one who watches **2** : careful watch

¹loom \′lüm\ *n* : frame or machine for weaving

²loom *vb* : appear large and indistinct or impressive

loon \′lün\ *n* : black-and-white diving bird

loo·ny, loo·ney \′lünē\ *adj* **-ni·er; -est** : crazy

loop \′lüp\ *n* **1** : doubling of a line that leaves an opening **2** : something like a loop —**loop** *vb*

loop·hole \'lüp,hōl\ *n* : means of evading

loose \'lüs\ *adj* **loos·er; -est** 1 : not fixed tight 2 : not restrained 3 : not dense 4 : slack 5 : not exact ~ *vb* **loosed; loos·ing** 1 : release 2 : untie or relax —**loose** *adv* —**loose·ly** *adv* —**loos·en** \'lüs³n\ *vb* —**loose·ness** *n*

loot \'lüt\ *n or vb* : plunder —**loot·er** *n*

lop \'läp\ *vb* **-pp-** : cut off

lope \'lōp\ *n* : bounding gait —**lope** *vb*

lop·sid·ed \'läp'sīdəd\ *adj* 1 : leaning to one side 2 : not symmetrical —**lop·sid·ed·ly** *adv* —**lop·sid·ed·ness** *n*

lo·qua·cious \lō'kwāshəs\ *adj* : very talkative —**lo·quac·i·ty** \-'kwasətē\ *n*

lord \'lȯrd\ *n* 1 : one with authority over others 2 : British nobleman

lord·ly \-lē\ *adj* **-li·er; -est** : haughty

lord·ship \-,ship\ *n* : rank of a lord

Lord's Supper *n* : Communion

lore \'lōr\ *n* : traditional knowledge

lose \'lüz\ *vb* **lost** \'lȯst\; **los·ing** \'lüziŋ\ 1 : have pass from one's possession 2 : be deprived of 3 : waste 4 : be defeated in 5 : fail to keep to or hold 6 : get rid of —**los·er** *n*

loss \'lȯs\ *n* 1 : something lost 2 *pl* : killed, wounded, or captured soldiers 3 : failure to win

lost \'lȯst\ *adj* 1 : not used, won, or claimed 2 : unable to find the way

lot \'lät\ *n* 1 : object used in deciding something by chance 2 : share 3 : fate 4 : plot of land 5 : much

loth \'lōth, 'lōth\ *var of* LOATH

lo·tion \'lōshən\ *n* : liquid to rub on the skin

lot·tery \'lätərē\ *n, pl* **-ter·ies** : drawing of lots with prizes going to winners

lo·tus \'lōtəs\ *n* 1 : legendary fruit that causes forgetfulness 2 : water lily

loud \'laȯd\ *adj* 1 : high in volume of sound 2 : noisy 3 : obtrusive in color or pattern —**loud** *adv* —**loud·ly** *adv* —**loud·ness** *n*

loud·speak·er *n* : device that amplifies sound

lounge \'laȯnj\ *vb* **lounged; loung·ing** : act or move lazily ~ *n* : room with comfortable furniture

lour \'laȯər\ *var of* LOWER

louse \'laȯs\ *n, pl* **lice** \'līs\ : parasitic wingless usu. flat insect

lousy \'laȯzē\ *adj* **lous·i·er; -est** 1 : infested with lice 2 : not good —**lous·i·ly** *adv* —**lous·i·ness** *n*

lout \'laȯt\ *n* : stupid awkward person —**lout·ish** *adj* —**lout·ish·ly** *adv*

lou·ver, lou·vre \'lüvər\ *n* : opening having parallel slanted slats for ventilation or such a slat

love \'ləv\ *n* 1 : strong affection 2 : warm attachment 3 : beloved person ~ *vb* **loved; lov·ing** 1 : feel affection for 2 : enjoy greatly —**lov·able** \-əbəl\ *adj* —**love·less** *adj* —**lov·er** *n* —**lov·ing·ly** *adv*

love·lorn \-,lȯrn\ *adj* : deprived of love or of a lover

love·ly \'ləvlē\ *adj* **-li·er; -est** : beautiful —**love·li·ness** *n* —**lovely** *adv*

¹low \'lō\ *vb or n* : moo

²low *adj* **low·er; low·est** 1 : not high or tall 2 : below normal level 3 : not loud 4 : humble 5 : sad 6 : less than usual 7 : falling short of a standard 8 : unfavorable — ~ *n* 1 : something low 2 : automobile gear giving the slowest speed —**low** *adv* —**low·ness** *n*

low·brow \'lō,braȯ\ *n* : person with little taste or intellectual interest

¹low·er \'laȯər\ *vb* 1 : scowl 2 : become dark and threatening

²low·er \'lōər\ *adj* : relatively low (as in rank)

³low·er \'lōər\ *vb* 1 : drop 2 : let descend 3 : reduce in amount

low·land \'lōlənd, -,land\ *n* : low flat country

low·ly \'lōlē\ *adj* **-li·er; -est** 1 : humble 2 : low in rank —**low·li·ness** *n*

loy·al \'lȯiəl\ *adj* : faithful to a country, cause, or friend —**loy·al·ist** *n* —**loy·al·ly** *adv* —**loy·al·ty** \'lȯiəltē\ *n*

loz·enge \'läzᵊnj\ *n* : small medicated candy

lu·bri·cant \'lübrikənt\ *n* : material (as grease) to reduce friction

lu·bri·cate \-,kāt\ *vb* **-cat·ed; -cat·ing** : apply a lubricant to —**lu·bri·ca·tion** \,lübrə'kāshən\ *n* —**lu·bri·ca·tor** \'lübrə,kātər\ *n*

lu·cid \'lüsəd\ *adj* 1 : mentally sound 2 : easily understood —**lu·cid·i·ty** \lü-'sidətē\ *n* —**lu·cid·ly** *adv* —**lu·cid·ness** *n*

luck \'lək\ *n* 1 : chance 2 : good fortune —**luck·i·ly** *adv* —**luck·i·ness** *n* —**luck·less** *adj* —**lucky** *adj*

lu·cra·tive \'lükrətiv\ *adj* : profitable —**lu·cra·tive·ly** *adv* —**lu·cra·tive·ness** *n*

lu·di·crous \'lüdəkrəs\ *adj* : comically

ridiculous —**lu·di·crous·ly** adv —
lu·di·crous·ness n

lug \'ləg\ vb -**gg**- : drag or carry laboriously

lug·gage \'ləgij\ n : baggage

lu·gu·bri·ous \lu̇'gübrēəs\ adj
: mournful often to an exaggerated
degree —**lu·gu·bri·ous·ly** adv —**lu·**
gu·bri·ous·ness n

luke·warm \'lük'wȯrm\ adj 1
: moderately warm 2 : not enthusiastic

lull \'ləl\ vb : make or become quiet or
relaxed ~ n : temporary calm

lul·la·by \'lələ,bī\ n, pl -**bies** : song to
lull children to sleep

lum·ba·go \,ləm'bāgō\ n : rheumatic
back pain

lum·ber \'ləmbər\ n : timber dressed for
use ~ vb : cut logs —**lum·ber·man**
n —**lum·ber·yard** n

lum·ber·jack \-,jak\ n : logger

lu·mi·nary \'lümə,nerē\ n, pl -**nar·ies**
: very famous person

lu·mi·nes·cence \,lümə'nes⁰ns\ n : low-
temperature emission of light —**lu·**
mi·nes·cent \-⁰nt\ adj

lu·mi·nous \'lümənəs\ adj : emitting
light —**lu·mi·nance** \-nəns\ n —**lu·**
mi·nos·i·ty \,lümə'näsətē\ n —**lu·mi·**
nous·ly adv

lump \'ləmp\ n 1 : mass of irregular
shape 2 : abnormal swelling ~ vb
: heap together —**lump·ish** adj —
lumpy adj

lu·na·cy \'lünəsē\ n, pl -**cies** : state of
insanity

lu·nar \'lünər\ adj : of the moon

lu·na·tic \'lünə,tik\ adj : insane —**lu·**
na·tic n

lunch \'lənch\ n : noon meal ~ vb : eat
lunch

lun·cheon \'lənchən\ n : usu. formal
lunch

lung \'ləŋ\ n : breathing organ in the
chest —**lunged** \'ləŋd\ adj

lunge \'lənj\ n 1 : sudden thrust 2
: sudden move forward —**lunge** vb

lurch \'lərch\ n : sudden swaying —
lurch vb

lure \'lu̇r\ n 1 : something that attracts
2 : artificial fish bait ~ vb **lured**; **lur·**
ing : attract

lu·rid \'lu̇rəd\ adj 1 : gruesome 2
: sensational —**lu·rid·ly** adv

lurk \'lərk\ vb : lie in wait

lus·cious \'ləshəs\ adj 1 : pleasingly
sweet in taste or smell 2 : sensually
appealing —**lus·cious·ly** adv —**lus·**
cious·ness n

lush \'ləsh\ adj : covered with abundant
growth

lust \'ləst\ n 1 : intense sexual desire 2
: intense longing —**lust** vb —**lust·ful**
adj

lus·ter, lus·tre \'ləstər\ n 1 : brightness
from reflected light 2 : magnificence
—**lus·ter·less** adj —**lus·trous** \-trəs\
adj

lusty \'ləstē\ adj **lust·i·er**; -**est** : full of
vitality —**lust·i·ly** adv —**lust·i·ness**
n

lute \'lüt\ n : pear-shaped stringed instrument —**lute·nist, lu·ta·nist**
\'lüt⁰nist\ n

lux·u·ri·ant \,ləg'zhu̇rēənt, ,lək'shu̇r-\
adj 1 : growing plentifully 2 : rich and
varied —**lux·u·ri·ance** \-ēəns\ n —
lux·u·ri·ant·ly adv

lux·u·ri·ate \-ē,āt\ vb -**at·ed**; -**at·ing**
: revel

lux·u·ry \'ləkshərē, 'ləgzh-\ n, pl -**ries**
1 : great comfort 2 : something add-
ing to pleasure or comfort —**lux·u·ri·**
ous \,ləg'zhu̇rēəs, ,lək'shu̇r-\ adj —
lux·u·ri·ous·ly adv

-**ly** \lē\ adv suffix 1 : in a specified way
2 : from a specified point of view

ly·ce·um \lī'sēəm, 'līsē-\ n : hall for public lectures

lye \'lī\ n : caustic alkaline substance

lying pres part of LIE

lymph \'limf\ n : bodily liquid consisting chiefly of blood plasma and white
blood cells —**lym·phat·ic** \lim'fatik\
adj

lynch \'linch\ vb : put to death by mob
action —**lynch·er** n

lynx \'liŋks\ n, pl **lynx** or **lynx·es**
: wildcat

lyre \'līr\ n : ancient Greek stringed instrument

lyr·ic \'lirik\ adj 1 : suitable for singing
2 : expressing direct personal emotion
~ n 1 : lyric poem 2 pl : words of a
song —**lyr·i·cal** \-ikəl\ adj

M

m \'em\ *n, pl* **m's** *or* **ms** \'emz\ : 13th letter of the alphabet

ma'am \'mam\ *n* : madam

ma·ca·bre \mə'käb, -'käbər, -'käbrə\ *adj* : gruesome

mac·ad·am \mə'kadəm\ *n* : pavement of cemented broken stone **—mac·ad·am·ize** \-,īz\ *vb*

mac·a·ro·ni \,makə'rōnē\ *n* : tube-shaped pasta

mac·a·roon \,makə'rün\ *n* : cookie of ground almonds or coconut

ma·caw \mə'kò\ *n* : large long-tailed parrot

¹mace \'mās\ *n* **1** : heavy spiked club **2** : ornamental staff as a symbol of authority

²mace *n* : spice from the fibrous coating of the nutmeg

ma·chete \mə'shetē\ *n* : large heavy knife

mach·i·na·tion \,makə'nāshən, ,mash-shə-\ *n* : plot or scheme **—machi·nate** \'makə,nāt, 'mash-\ *vb*

ma·chine \mə'shēn\ *n* : combination of mechanical or electrical parts ~ *vb* **-chined; -chin·ing** : modify by machine-operated tools **—ma·chin·able** *adj* **—ma·chin·ery** \-ərē\ *n* **—machin·ist** *n*

mack·er·el \'makərəl\ *n, pl* **-el** *or* **-els** : No. Atlantic food fish

mack·i·naw \'makə,nò\ *n* : short heavy plaid coat

mac·ra·mé \,makrə'mā\ *n* : coarse lace or fringe made by knotting

mac·ro \'makrō\ *adj* : very large

mac·ro·cosm \'makrə,käzəm\ *n* : universe

mad \'mad\ *adj* **-dd- 1** : insane or rabid **2** : rash and foolish **3** : angry **4** : carried away by enthusiasm **—mad·den** \'madᵊn\ *vb* **—mad·den·ing·ly** \'madᵊninlē\ *adv* **—mad·ly** *adv* **—mad·ness** *n*

mad·am \'madəm\ *n, pl* **mes·dames** \mā'däm\ —used in polite address to a woman

ma·dame \mə'dam, *before a surname also* 'madəm\ *n, pl* **mes·dames** \mā-

'däm\ —used as a title for a woman not of English-speaking nationality

mad·cap \'mad,kap\ *adj* : wild or zany **—madcap** *n*

made *past of* MAKE

Ma·dei·ra \mə'dirə\ *n* : amber-colored dessert wine

ma·de·moi·selle \,madmwə'zel, -mə-'zel\ *n, pl* **ma·de·moi·selles** \-'zelz\ *or* **mes·de·moi·selles** \,mādmwə'zel\ : an unmarried girl or woman —used as a title for a woman esp. of French nationality

mad·house *n* **1** : insane asylum **2** : place of great uproar or confusion

mad·man \-,man, -mən\ *n* : lunatic

mad·ri·gal \'madrigəl\ *n* : elaborate song for several voice parts

mad·wom·an \'mad,wümən\ *n* : woman who is insane

mael·strom \'mālstrəm\ *n* **1** : whirlpool **2** : tumult

mae·stro \'mīstrō\ *n, pl* **-stros** *or* **-stri** \-,strē\ : eminent composer or conductor

Ma·fia \'mäfēə\ *n* : secret criminal organization

ma·fi·o·so \,mäfē'ōsō\ *n, pl* **-si** \-sē\ : member of the Mafia

mag·a·zine \'magə,zēn\ *n* **1** : storehouse **2** : publication issued at regular intervals **3** : cartridge container in a gun

ma·gen·ta \mə'jentə\ *n* : deep purplish red color

mag·got \'magət\ *n* : wormlike fly larva **—mag·goty** *adj*

mag·ic \'majik\ *n* **1** : art of using supernatural powers **2** : extraordinary power or influence **3** : sleight of hand **—magic, mag·i·cal** \-ikəl\ *adj* **—mag·i·cal·ly** *adv* **—ma·gi·cian** \mə-'jishən\ *n*

mag·is·te·ri·al \,majə'stirēəl\ *adj* **1** : authoritative **2** : relating to a magistrate

mag·is·trate \'majə,strāt\ *n* : judge **—mag·is·tra·cy** \-strəsē\ *n*

mag·ma \'magmə\ *n* : molten rock

mag·nan·i·mous \mag'nanəməs\ *adj* : noble or generous **—mag·na·nim-**

i·ty \ˌmagnəˈnimətē\ n —**mag·nan·i·mous·ly** adv —**mag·nan·i·mous·ness** n

mag·ne·sia \magˈnēzhə, -shə\ n : oxide of magnesium used as a laxative

mag·ne·sium \magˈnēzēəm, -zhəm\ n : silver-white metallic chemical element

mag·net \ˈmagnət\ n 1 : body that attracts iron 2 : something that attracts —**mag·net·ic** \magˈnetik\ adj —**mag·net·i·cal·ly** \-iklē\ adv —**mag·ne·tism** \ˈmagnəˌtizəm\ n

mag·ne·tite \ˈmagnəˌtīt\ n : black iron ore

mag·ne·tize \ˈmagnəˌtīz\ vb -tized; -tiz·ing 1 : attract like a magnet 2 : give magnetic properties to —**mag·ne·tiz·able** adj —**mag·ne·ti·za·tion** \ˌmagnətəˈzāshən\ n —**mag·ne·tiz·er** n

mag·nif·i·cent \magˈnifəsənt\ adj : splendid —**mag·nif·i·cence** \-səns\ n —**mag·nif·i·cent·ly** adv

mag·ni·fy \ˈmagnəˌfī\ vb -fied; -fy·ing 1 : intensify 2 : enlarge —**mag·ni·fi·ca·tion** \ˌmagnəfəˈkāshən\ n —**mag·ni·fi·er** \ˈmagnəˌfīər\ n

mag·ni·tude \ˈmagnəˌtüd, -ˌtyüd\ n 1 : greatness of size or extent 2 : quantity

mag·no·lia \magˈnōlyə\ n : shrub with large fragrant flowers

mag·pie \ˈmagˌpī\ n : long-tailed black-and-white bird

ma·hog·a·ny \məˈhägənē\ n, pl -nies : tropical evergreen tree or its reddish brown wood

maid \ˈmād\ n 1 : unmarried young woman 2 : female servant

maid·en \ˈmādᵊn\ n : unmarried young woman ~ adj : unmarried 2 : first —**maid·en·hood** \-ˌhůd\ n —**maid·en·ly** adj

maid·en·hair \-ˌhar\ n : fern with delicate feathery fronds

¹mail \ˈmāl\ n 1 : something sent or carried in the postal system 2 : postal system ~ vb : send by mail —**mail·box** n —**mail·man** \-ˌman, -mən\ n

²mail n : armor of metal links or plates

maim \ˈmām\ vb : seriously wound or disfigure

main \ˈmān\ n 1 : force 2 : ocean 3 : principal pipe, duct, or circuit of a utility system ~ adj : chief —**main·ly** adv

main·frame \ˈmānˌfrām\ n : large fast computer

main·land \ˈmānˌland, -lənd\ n : part of a country on a continent

main·stay n : chief support

main·stream n : prevailing current or direction of activity or influence —**mainstream** adj

main·tain \mānˈtān\ vb 1 : keep in an existing state (as of repair) 2 : sustain 3 : declare —**main·tain·abil·i·ty** \-ˌtānəˈbilətē\ n —**main·tain·able** \-ˈtānəbəl\ adj —**main·te·nance** \ˈmāntᵊnəns\ n

mai·tre d'hô·tel \ˌmātrədōˈtel, ˌme-\ n : head of a dining room staff

maize \ˈmāz\ n : corn

maj·es·ty \ˈmajəstē\ n, pl -ties 1 : sovereign power or dignity —used as a title 2 : grandeur or splendor —**ma·jes·tic** \məˈjestik\ adj —**ma·jes·ti·cal·ly** \-tiklē\ adv

ma·jor \ˈmājər\ adj 1 : larger or greater 2 : noteworthy or conspicuous ~ n 1 : commissioned officer (as in the army) ranking next below a lieutenant colonel 2 : main field of study ~ vb -jored; -jor·ing : pursue an academic major

ma·jor·do·mo \ˌmājərˈdōmō\ n, pl -mos : head steward

major general n : commissioned officer (as in the army) ranking next below a lieutenant general

ma·jor·i·ty \məˈjorətē\ n, pl -ties 1 : age of full civil rights 2 : quantity more than half

make \ˈmāk\ vb made \ˈmād\; mak·ing 1 : cause to exist, occur, or appear 2 : fashion or manufacture 3 : formulate in the mind 4 : constitute 5 : prepare 6 : cause to be or become 7 : carry out or perform 8 : compel 9 : gain 10 : have an effect —used with for ~ n : brand —**mak·er** n —**make do** vb : get along with what is available —**make good** vb 1 : repay 2 : succeed —**make out** vb 1 : draw up or write 2 : discern or understand 3 : fare —**make up** vb 1 : invent 2 : become reconciled 3 : compensate for

make–be·lieve n : a pretending to believe ~ adj : imagined or pretended

make·shift n : temporary substitute —**makeshift** adj

make·up \-ˌəp\ n 1 : way in which something is constituted 2 : cosmetics

mal·ad·just·ed \,malə'jəstəd\ *adj* : poorly adjusted (as to one's environment) —**mal·ad·just·ment** \-'jəstmənt\ *n*

mal·adroit \,malə'dròit\ *adj* : clumsy or inept

mal·a·dy \'malədē\ *n, pl* **-dies** : disease or disorder

mal·aise \mə'lāz, ma-\ *n* : sense of being unwell

mal·a·mute \'malə,myüt\ *n* : powerful heavy-coated dog

mal·a·prop·ism \'malə,präp,izəm\ *n* : humorous misuse of a word

ma·lar·ia \mə'lerēə\ *n* : disease transmitted by a mosquito —**ma·lar·i·al** \-əl\ *adj*

ma·lar·key \mə'lärkē\ *n* : foolishness

mal·con·tent \,malkən'tent\ *n* : discontented person —**malcontent** *adj*

male \'māl\ *adj* 1 : relating to the sex that performs a fertilizing function 2 : masculine ~ *n* : male individual —**male·ness** *n*

male·dic·tion \,malə'dikshən\ *n* : curse

male·fac·tor \'malə,faktər\ *n* : one who commits an offense esp. against the law

ma·lef·i·cent \mə'lefəsənt\ *adj* : harmful

ma·lev·o·lent \mə'levələnt\ *adj* : malicious or spiteful —**ma·lev·o·lence** \-ləns\ *n*

mal·fea·sance \mal'fēz'ns\ *n* : misconduct by a public official

mal·for·ma·tion \,malfor'māshən\ *n* : distortion or faulty formation —**mal·formed** \mal'formd\ *adj*

mal·func·tion \mal'fəŋkshən\ *vb* : fail to operate properly —**malfunction** *n*

mal·ice \'maləs\ *n* : desire to cause pain or injury to another —**ma·li·cious** \mə'lishəs\ *adj* —**ma·li·cious·ly** *adv*

ma·lign \mə'līn\ *adj* 1 : wicked 2 : malignant ~ *vb* : speak evil of

ma·lig·nant \mə'lignənt\ *adj* 1 : harmful 2 : likely to cause death —**ma·lig·nan·cy** \-nənsē\ *n* —**ma·lig·nant·ly** *adv* —**ma·lig·ni·ty** \-nətē\ *n*

ma·lin·ger \mə'liŋgər\ *vb* : pretend illness to avoid duty —**ma·lin·ger·er** *n*

mall \'mol\ *n* 1 : shaded promenade 2 : concourse providing access to rows of shops

mal·lard \'malərd\ *n, pl* **-lard** *or* **-lards** : common wild duck

mal·le·a·ble \'malēəbəl\ *adj* 1 : easily shaped 2 : adaptable —**mal·le·a·bil·i·ty** \,malēə'bilətē\ *n*

mal·let \'malət\ *n* : hammerlike tool

mal·nour·ished \mal'nərisht\ *adj* : poorly nourished

mal·nu·tri·tion \,malnü'trishən, -nyü-\ *n* : inadequate nutrition

mal·odor·ous \mal'ōdərəs\ *adj* : foulsmelling —**mal·odor·ous·ly** *adv* —**mal·odor·ous·ness** *n*

mal·prac·tice \-'praktəs\ *n* : failure of professional duty

malt \'molt\ *n* : sprouted grain used in brewing

mal·treat \mal'trēt\ *vb* : treat badly —**mal·treat·ment** *n*

ma·ma, mam·ma \'mämə\ *n* : mother

mam·mal \'maməl\ *n* : warm-blooded vertebrate animal that nourishes its young with milk —**mam·ma·li·an** \mə'mālēən, ma-\ *adj or n*

mam·ma·ry \'mamərē\ *adj* : relating to the milk-secreting glands (**mammary glands**) of mammals

mam·mo·gram \'mamə,gram\ *n* : X-ray photograph of the breasts

mam·moth \'maməth\ *n* : large hairy extinct elephant ~ *adj* : enormous

man \'man\ *n, pl* **men** \'men\ 1 : human being 2 : adult male 3 : mankind ~ *vb* **-nn-** : supply with people for working —**man·hood** *n* —**man·hunt** *n* —**man·like** *adj* —**man·li·ness** *n* —**man·ly** *adj or adv* —**man–made** *adj* —**man·nish** *adj* —**man·nish·ly** *adv* —**man·nish·ness** *n* —**man-size, man-sized** *adj*

man·a·cle \'manikəl\ *n* : shackle for the hands or wrists —**manacle** *vb*

man·age \'manij\ *vb* **-aged; -ag·ing** 1 : control 2 : direct or carry on business or affairs 3 : cope —**man·age·abil·i·ty** \,manijə'bilətē\ *n* —**man·age·able** \'manijəbəl\ *adj* —**man·age·able·ness** *n* —**man·age·ably** \-blē\ *adv* —**man·age·ment** \'manijmənt\ *n* —**man·ag·er** \'manijər\ *n* —**man·a·ge·ri·al** \,manə'jirēəl\ *adj*

man·da·rin \'mandərən\ *n* : Chinese imperial official

man·date \'man,dāt\ *n* : authoritative command

man·da·to·ry \'mandə,tōrē\ *adj* : obligatory

man·di·ble \'mandəbəl\ *n* : lower jaw —**man·dib·u·lar** \man'dibyələr\ *adj*

man·do·lin \,mandə'lin, 'mand'lən\ *n* : stringed musical instrument

man·drake \'man,drāk\ n : herb with a large forked root

mane \'mān\ n : animal's neck hair — **maned** \'mānd\ adj

ma·neu·ver \mə'nüvər, -'nyü-\ n 1 : planned movement of troops or ships 2 : military training exercise 3 : clever or skillful move or action — **maneuver** vb — **ma·neu·ver·abil·i·ty** \-,nüvərə'bilətē, -,nyü-\ n

man·ful \'manfəl\ adj : courageous — **man·ful·ly** adv

man·ga·nese \'maŋgə,nēz, -,nēs\ n : gray metallic chemical element

mange \'mānj\ n : skin disease of domestic animals — **mangy** \'mānjē\ adj

man·ger \'mānjər\ n : feeding trough for livestock

man·gle \'maŋgəl\ vb -**gled**; -**gling** 1 : mutilate 2 : bungle — **man·gler** n

man·go \'maŋgō\ n, pl -**goes** : juicy yellowish red tropical fruit

man·grove \'man,grōv, 'maŋ-\ n : tropical tree growing in salt water

man·han·dle vb : handle roughly

man·hole n : entry to a sewer

ma·nia \'mānēə, -nyə\ n 1 : insanity marked by uncontrollable emotion or excitement 2 : excessive enthusiasm — **ma·ni·ac** \-nē,ak\ n — **ma·ni·a·cal** \mə'nīəkəl\ adj — **man·ic** \'manik\ adj or n

man·i·cure \'manə,kyùr\ n : treatment for the fingernails ~ vb -**cured**; -**cur·ing** 1 : do manicure work on 2 : trim precisely — **man·i·cur·ist** \-,kyùrist\ n

¹**man·i·fest** \'manə,fest\ adj : clear to the senses or to the mind ~ vb : make evident — **man·i·fes·ta·tion** \,manəfə'stāshən\ n — **man·i·fest·ly** adv

²**manifest** n : invoice of cargo or list of passengers

man·i·fes·to \,manə'festō\ n, pl -**tos** or -**toes** : public declaration of policy or views

man·i·fold \'manə,fōld\ adj : marked by diversity or variety ~ n : pipe fitting with several outlets for connections

ma·nila paper \mə'nilə-\ n : durable brownish paper

ma·nip·u·late \mə'nipyə,lāt\ vb -**lat·ed**; -**lat·ing** 1 : treat or operate manually or mechanically 2 : influence esp. by cunning — **ma·nip·u·la·tion** \mə-,nipyə'lāshən\ n — **ma·nip·u·la·tive** \-'nipyə,lātiv, -lətiv\ adj — **ma·nip·u·la·tor** \-,lātər\ n

man·kind \'man'kīnd\ n : human race

man·na \'manə\ n : something valuable that comes unexpectedly

manned \'mand\ adj : carrying or performed by a man

man·ne·quin \'manikən\ n : dummy used to display clothes

man·ner \'manər\ n 1 : kind 2 : usual way of acting 3 : artistic method 4 pl : social conduct

man·nered \-ərd\ adj 1 : having manners of a specified kind 2 : artificial

man·ner·ism \'manə,rizəm\ n : individual peculiarity of action

man·ner·ly \-lē\ adj : polite — **man·ner·li·ness** n — **mannerly** adv

man–of–war \,manə'wór, -əv'wór\ n, pl **men–of–war** \,men-\ : warship

man·or \'manər\ n : country estate — **ma·no·ri·al** \mə'nórēəl\ adj

man·pow·er n : supply of people available for service

man·sard \'man,särd\ n : roof with two slopes on all sides and the lower slope the steeper

manse \'mans\ n : parsonage

man·ser·vant n, pl **men·ser·vants** : a male servant

man·sion \'manchən\ n : very big house

man·slaugh·ter n : unintentional killing of a person

man·tel \'mantᵊl\ n : shelf above a fireplace

man·tis \'mantəs\ n, pl -**tis·es** or -**tes** \'man,tēz\ : large green insect-eating insect with stout forelegs

man·tle \'mantᵊl\ n 1 : sleeveless cloak 2 : something that covers, enfolds, or envelops — **mantle** vb

man·tra \'mantrə\ n : mystical chant

man·u·al \'manyəwəl\ adj : involving the hands or physical force ~ n : handbook — **man·u·al·ly** adv

man·u·fac·ture \,manyə'fakchər, ,manə-\ n : process of making wares by hand or by machinery ~ vb -**tured**; -**tur·ing** : make from raw materials — **man·u·fac·tur·er** n

ma·nure \mə'nùr, -'nyùr\ n : animal excrement used as fertilizer

manu·script \'manyə,skript\ n 1 : something written or typed 2 : document submitted for publication

many \'menē\ adj **more** \'mōr\; **most** \'mōst\ : consisting of a large number — **many** n or pron

map \'map\ n : representation of a geographical area ~ vb -**pp**- 1 : make a map of **2** : plan in detail —**map·pa·ble** \-əbəl\ *adj* —**map·per** *n*

ma·ple \'mäpəl\ *n* : tree with hard light= colored wood

mar \'mär\ *vb* -**rr**- : damage

mar·a·schi·no \,marə'skēnō, -'shē-\ *n, pl* -**nos** : preserved cherry

mar·a·thon \'marə,thän\ *n* **1** : long-distance race **2** : test of endurance — **mar·a·thon·er** \-,thänər\ *n*

ma·raud \mə'rόd\ *vb* : roam about in search of plunder —**ma·raud·er** *n*

mar·ble \'märbəl\ *n* **1** : crystallized limestone **2** : small glass ball used in a children's game (**marbles**)

mar·bling \-bəliŋ\ *n* : intermixture of fat and lean in meat

march \'märch\ *vb* : move with regular steps or in a purposeful manner ~ *n* **1** : distance covered in a march **2** : measured stride **3** : forward movement **4** : music for marching — **march·er** *n*

March *n* : 3d month of the year having 31 days

mar·chio·ness \'märshənəs\ *n* : woman holding the rank of a marquess

Mar·di Gras \'märdē,grä\ *n* : Tuesday before the beginning of Lent often observed with parades and merrymaking

mare \'mar\ *n* : female horse

mar·ga·rine \'märjərən\ *n* : butter substitute made usu. from vegetable oils

mar·gin \'märjən\ *n* **1** : edge **2** : spare amount, measure, or degree

mar·gin·al \-jənəl\ *adj* **1** : relating to or situated at a border or margin **2** : close to the lower limit of acceptability — **mar·gin·al·ly** *adv*

mari·gold \'marə,gōld\ *n* : garden plant with showy flower heads

mari·jua·na \,marə'wänə, -'hwä-\ *n* : intoxicating drug obtained from the hemp plant

ma·ri·na \mə'rēnə\ *n* : place for mooring pleasure boats

mari·nate \'marə,nāt\ *vb* -**nat·ed; -nat-ing** : soak in a savory sauce

ma·rine \mə'rēn\ *adj* **1** : relating to the sea **2** : relating to marines ~ *n* : infantry soldier associated with a navy

mar·i·ner \'marənər\ *n* : sailor

mari·o·nette \,marēə'net\ *n* : puppet

mar·i·tal \'marət³l\ *adj* : relating to marriage

mari·time \'marə,tīm\ *adj* : relating to the sea or commerce on the sea

mar·jo·ram \'märjərəm\ *n* : aromatic mint used as a seasoning

mark \'märk\ *n* **1** : something aimed at **2** : something (as a line) designed to record position **3** : visible sign **4** : written symbol **5** : grade **6** : lasting impression **7** : blemish ~ *vb* **1** : designate or set apart by a mark or make a mark on **2** : characterize **3** : remark —**mark·er** *n*

marked \'märkt\ *adj* : noticeable — **mark·ed·ly** \'märkədlē\ *adv*

mar·ket \'märkət\ *n* **1** : buying and selling of goods or the place this happens **2** : demand for commodities **3** : store ~ *vb* : sell —**mar·ket·able** *adj*

mar·ket·place *n* **1** : market **2** : world of trade or economic activity

marks·man \'märksmən\ *n* : good shooter —**marks·man·ship** *n*

mar·lin \'märlən\ *n* : large oceanic fish

mar·ma·lade \'märmə,lād\ *n* : jam with pieces of fruit and rind

mar·mo·set \'märmə,set\ *n* : small bushy-tailed monkey

mar·mot \'märmət\ *n* : burrowing rodent

1ma·roon \mə'rün\ *vb* : isolate without hope of escape

2maroon *n* : dark red color

mar·quee \mär'kē\ *n* : canopy over an entrance

mar·quess \'märkwəs\, **mar·quis** \'märkwəs, mär'kē\ *n, pl* -**quess·es** *or* -**quis·es** *or* -**quis** : British noble ranking next below a duke

mar·quise \mär'kēz\ *n, pl* **mar·quises** \-'kēz, -'kēzəz\ : marchioness

mar·riage \'marij\ *n* **1** : state of being married **2** : wedding ceremony — **mar·riage·able** *adj*

mar·row \'marō\ *n* : soft tissue in the cavity of bone

mar·ry \'marē\ *vb* -**ried; -ry·ing** **1** : join as husband and wife **2** : take or give in marriage —**mar·ried** *adj or n*

marsh \'märsh\ *n* : soft wet land — **marshy** *adj*

mar·shal \'märshəl\ *n* **1** : leader of ceremony **2** : usu. high military or administrative officer ~ *vb* -**shaled** *or* -**shalled; -shal·ing** *or* -**shal·ling** **1** : arrange in order, rank, or position **2** : lead with ceremony

marsh·mal·low \'märsh,melō, -,malō\ *n* : spongy candy

mar·su·pi·al \mär'süpēəl\ *n* : mammal

that nourishes young in an abdominal pouch —**marsupial** adj

mart \\'märt\\ n : market

mar·ten \\'märt³n\\ n, pl **-ten** or **-tens** : weasellike mammal with soft fur

mar·tial \\'märshǝl\\ adj 1 : relating to war or an army 2 : warlike

mar·tin \\'märt³n\\ n : small swallow

mar·ti·net \\,märt³n'et\\ n : strict disciplinarian

mar·tyr \\'märtǝr\\ n : one who dies or makes a great sacrifice for a cause ~ vb : make a martyr of —**mar·tyr·dom** \\-dǝm\\ n

mar·vel \\'märvǝl\\ vb **-veled** or **-velled**; **-vel·ing** or **-vel·ling** : feel surprise or wonder ~ n : something amazing —**mar·vel·ous, mar·vel·lous** \\'märvǝlǝs\\ adj —**mar·vel·ous·ly** adv —**mar·vel·ous·ness** n

Marx·ism \\'märk,sizǝm\\ n : political and social principles of Karl Marx —**Marx·ist** \\-sist\\ n or adj

mas·cara \\mas'karǝ\\ n : eye cosmetic

mas·cot \\'mas,kät, -kǝt\\ n : one believed to bring good luck

mas·cu·line \\'maskyǝlǝn\\ adj : relating to the male sex —**mas·cu·lin·i·ty** \\,maskyǝ'linǝtē\\ n

mash \\'mash\\ n 1 : crushed steeped grain for fermenting 2 : soft pulpy mass ~ vb 1 : reduce to a pulpy mass 2 : smash —**mash·er** n

mask \\'mask\\ n : disguise for the face ~ vb 1 : disguise 2 : cover to protect —**mask·er** n

mas·och·ism \\'masǝ,kizǝm, 'maz-\\ n : pleasure in being abused —**mas·och·ist** \\-kist\\ n —**mas·och·is·tic** \\,ma-sǝ'kistik, ,maz-\\ adj

ma·son \\'mās³n\\ n : workman who builds with stone or brick —**ma·son·ry** \\-rē\\ n

mas·quer·ade \\,maskǝ'rād\\ n 1 : costume party 2 : disguise ~ vb **-ad·ed; -ad·ing** 1 : disguise oneself 2 : take part in a costume party —**mas·quer·ad·er** n

¹mass \\'mas\\ n 1 : large amount of matter or number of things 2 : expanse or magnitude 3 : great body of people — usu. pl. ~ vb : form into a mass —**mass·less** \\-lǝs\\ adj —**massy** adj

Mass n : worship service of the Roman Catholic Church

mas·sa·cre \\'masikǝr\\ n : wholesale slaughter —**massacre** vb

mas·sage \\mǝ'säzh, -'säj\\ n : a rubbing of the body —**massage** vb

mas·seur \\ma'sǝr\\ n : man who massages

mas·seuse \\-'sœz, -'süz\\ n : woman who massages

mas·sive \\'masiv\\ adj 1 : being a large mass 2 : large in scope —**mas·sive·ly** adv —**mas·sive·ness** n

mast \\'mast\\ n : tall pole esp. for supporting sails —**mast·ed** adj

mas·ter \\'mastǝr\\ n 1 : male teacher 2 : holder of an academic degree between a bachelor's and a doctor's 3 : one highly skilled 4 : one in authority ~ vb 1 : subdue 2 : become proficient in —**mas·ter·ful** \\-fǝl\\ adj —**mas·ter·ful·ly** adv —**mas·ter·ly** adj —**mas·tery** \\'mastǝrē\\ n

master chief petty officer n : petty officer of the highest rank in the navy

master gunnery sergeant n : noncommissioned officer in the marine corps ranking above a master sergeant

mas·ter·piece \\'mastǝr,pēs\\ n : great piece of work

master sergeant n 1 : noncommissioned officer in the army ranking next below a sergeant major 2 : noncommissioned officer in the air force ranking next below a senior master sergeant 3 : noncommissioned officer in the marine corps ranking next below a master gunnery sergeant

mas·ter·work n : masterpiece

mas·tic \\'mastik\\ n : pasty glue

mas·ti·cate \\'mastǝ,kāt\\ vb **-cat·ed; -cat·ing** : chew —**mas·ti·ca·tion** \\,mastǝ'kāshǝn\\ n

mas·tiff \\'mastǝf\\ n : large dog

mast·odon \\'mastǝ,dän\\ n : extinct elephantlike animal

mas·toid \\'mas,tóid\\ n : bone behind the ear —**mastoid** adj

mas·tur·ba·tion \\,mastǝr'bāshǝn\\ n : stimulation of sex organs by hand —**mas·tur·bate** \\'mastǝr,bāt\\ vb

¹mat \\'mat\\ n 1 : coarse woven or plaited fabric 2 : mass of tangled strands 3 : thick pad ~ vb **-tt-** : form into a mat

²mat vb **-tt-** 1 : make matte 2 : provide (a picture) with a mat ~ or **matt** or **matte** n : border around a picture

³mat var of MATTE

ma·ta·dor \\'matǝ,dór\\ n : bullfighter

¹match \\'mach\\ n 1 : one equal to another **2** : one able to cope with another **3** : suitable pairing **4** : game **5** : marriage ~ *vb* **1** : set in competition **2** : marry **3** : be or provide the equal of **4** : fit or go together —**match·less** *adj* —**match·mak·er** *n*

²**match** *n* : piece of wood or paper material with a combustible tip

mate \'māt\ *n* **1** : companion **2** : subordinate officer on a ship **3** : one of a pair ~ *vb* **mat·ed; mat·ing 1** : fit together **2** : come together as a pair **3** : copulate

ma·te·ri·al \mə'tirēəl\ *adj* **1** : natural **2** : relating to matter **3** : important **4** : of a physical or worldly nature ~ *n* : stuff something is made of —**ma·te·ri·al·ly** *adv*

ma·te·ri·al·ism \mə'tirēə,lizəm\ *n* **1** : theory that matter is the only reality **2** : preoccupation with material and not spiritual things —**ma·te·ri·al·ist** \-list\ *n or adj* —**ma·te·ri·al·is·tic** \-,tirēə'listik\ *adj*

ma·te·ri·al·ize \mə'tirēə,līz\ *vb* **-ized; -iz·ing** : take or cause to take bodily form —**ma·te·ri·al·i·za·tion** \mə-,tirēələ'zāshən\ *n*

ma·te·ri·el, ma·te·ri·el \mə,tirē'el\ *n* : military supplies

ma·ter·nal \mə'tərnᵊl\ *adj* : motherly —**ma·ter·nal·ly** *adv*

ma·ter·ni·ty \mə'tərnətē\ *n, pl* **-ties 1** : state of being a mother **2** : hospital's childbirth facility ~ *adj* **1** : worn during pregnancy **2** : relating to the period close to childbirth

math \'math\ *n* : mathematics

math·e·mat·ics \,mathə'matiks\ *n pl* : science of numbers and of shapes in space —**math·e·mat·i·cal** \-ikəl\ *adj* —**math·e·mat·i·cal·ly** *adv* —**math·e·ma·ti·cian** \,mathəmə'tishən\ *n*

mat·i·nee, mat·i·née \,matᵊn'ā\ *n* : afternoon performance

mat·ins \'matᵊnz\ *n* : morning prayers

ma·tri·arch \'mātrē,ärk\ *n* : woman who rules a family —**ma·tri·ar·chal** \,mātrē'ärkəl\ *adj* —**ma·tri·ar·chy** \'mātrē,ärkē\ *n*

ma·tri·cide \'matrə,sīd, 'mā-\ *n* : murder of one's mother —**ma·tri·cid·al** \,matrə'sīdᵊl, ,mā-\ *adj*

ma·tric·u·late \mə'trikyə,lāt\ *vb* **-lat·ed; -lat·ing** : enroll in school —**ma·tric·u·la·tion** \-,trikyə'lāshən\ *n*

mat·ri·mo·ny \'matrə,mōnē\ *n* : marriage —**mat·ri·mo·ni·al** \,matrə-'mōnēəl\ *adj* —**mat·ri·mo·ni·al·ly** *adv*

ma·trix \'mātriks\ *n, pl* **-tri·ces** \'mā-trə,sēz, 'ma-\ *or* **-trix·es** \'mātriksəz\ : something (as a mold) that gives form, foundation, or origin to something else enclosed in it

ma·tron \'mātrən\ *n* **1** : dignified mature woman **2** : woman supervisor —**ma·tron·ly** *adj*

matte \'mat\ *adj* : not shiny

mat·ter \'matər\ *n* **1** : subject of interest **2** *pl* : circumstances **3** : trouble **4** : physical substance ~ *vb* : be important

mat·tock \'matək\ *n* : a digging tool

mat·tress \'matrəs\ *n* : pad to sleep on

ma·ture \mə'tur, -'tyur, -'chur\ *adj* **-tur·er; -est 1** : carefully considered **2** : fully grown or developed **3** : due for payment ~ *vb* **-tured; -tur·ing 1** : become mature —**mat·u·ra·tion** \,machə'rāshən\ *n* —**ma·ture·ly** *adv* —**ma·tu·ri·ty** \-ətē\ *n*

maud·lin \'mȯdlən\ *adj* : excessively sentimental

maul \'mȯl\ *n* : heavy hammer ~ *vb* **1** : beat **2** : handle roughly

mau·so·le·um \,mȯsə'lēəm, ,mȯzə-\ *n, pl* **-leums** *or* **-lea** \-'lēə\ : large aboveground tomb

mauve \'mōv, 'mȯv\ *n* : lilac color

ma·ven, ma·vin \'māvən\ *n* : expert

mav·er·ick \'mavrik\ *n* **1** : unbranded range animal **2** : nonconformist

maw \'mȯ\ *n* **1** : stomach **2** : throat, esophagus, or jaws

mawk·ish \'mȯkish\ *adj* : sickly sentimental —**mawk·ish·ly** *adv* —**mawk·ish·ness** *n*

max·im \'maksəm\ *n* : proverb

max·i·mum \'maksəməm\ *n, pl* **-ma** \-səmə\ *or* **-mums 1** : greatest quantity **2** : upper limit **3** : largest number —**maximum** *adj* —**max·i·mize** \-sə-,mīz\ *vb*

may \'mā\ *verbal auxiliary, past* **might** \'mīt\, *pres sing & pl* **may 1** : have permission **2** : be likely to **3** —used to express desire, purpose, or contingency

May \'mā\ *n* : 5th month of the year having 31 days

may·ap·ple *n* : woodland herb having edible fruit

may·be \'mābē\ *adv* : perhaps

may·flow·er *n* : spring-blooming herb

may·fly *n* : fly with an aquatic larva

may·hem \'mā,hem, 'māəm\ n 1 : crippling or mutilation of a person 2 : needless damage

may·on·naise \'māə,nāz\ n : creamy white sandwich spread

may·or \'māər, 'mer\ n : chief city official —**may·or·al** \-əl\ adj — **may·or·al·ty** \-əltē\ n

maze \'māz\ n : confusing network of passages —**mazy** adj

ma·zur·ka \mə'zərkə\ n : Polish dance

me \'mē\ pron, objective case of I

mead \'mēd\ n : alcoholic beverage brewed from honey

mead·ow \'medō\ n : low-lying usu. level grassland —**mead·ow·land** \-,land\ n

mead·ow·lark \ n : songbird with a yellow breast

mea·ger, mea·gre \'mēgər\ adj 1 : thin 2 : lacking richness or strength — **mea·ger·ly** adv —**mea·ger·ness** n

¹meal \'mēl\ n 1 : food to be eaten at one time 2 : act of eating —**meal·time** n

²meal n : ground grain —**mealy** adj

¹mean \'mēn\ adj 1 : humble 2 : worthy of or showing little regard 3 : stingy 4 : malicious —**mean·ly** adv — **mean·ness** n

²mean \'mēn\ vb **meant** \'ment\; **mean·ing** \'mēnin\ 1 : intend 2 : serve to convey, show, or indicate 3 : be important

³mean n 1 : middle point 2 pl : something that helps gain an end 3 pl : material resources 4 : sum of several quantities divided by the number of quantities ~ adj : being a mean

me·an·der \mē'andər\ vb -**dered; -der·ing** 1 : follow a winding course 2 : wander aimlessly —**meander** n

mean·ing \'mēnin\ n 1 : idea conveyed or intended to be conveyed 2 : aim —**mean·ing·ful** \-fəl\ adj —**mean·ing·ful·ly** adv —**mean·ing·less** adj

mean·time \'mēn,tīm\ n : intervening time —**meantime** adv

mean·while \-,hwīl\ n : meantime ~ adv 1 : meantime 2 : at the same time

mea·sles \'mēzəlz\ n pl : disease that is marked by red spots on the skin

mea·sly \'mēzlē\ adj -**sli·er; -est** : contemptibly small in amount

mea·sure \'mezhər, 'māzh-\ n 1 : moderate amount 2 : dimensions or amount 3 : something to show amount 4 : unit or system of measurement 5 : act of measuring 6 : means to an end ~ vb -**sured; -sur·ing** 1 : find out or mark off size or amount of 2 : have a specified measurement —**mea·sur·able** \'mezhərəbəl, 'māzh-\ adj —**mea·sur·ably** \-blē\ adv —**mea·sure·less** adj — **mea·sure·ment** n —**mea·sur·er** n

meat \'mēt\ n 1 : food 2 : animal flesh used as food —**meat·ball** n —**meaty** adj

me·chan·ic \mi'kanik\ n : worker who repairs cars

me·chan·i·cal \mi'kanikəl\ adj 1 : relating to machines or mechanics 2 : involuntary —**me·chan·i·cal·ly** adv

me·chan·ics \-iks\ n sing or pl 1 : branch of physics dealing with energy and forces in relation to bodies 2 : mechanical details

mech·a·nism \'mekə,nizəm\ n 1 : piece of machinery 2 : technique for gaining a result 3 : basic processes producing a phenomenon —**mech·a·nis·tic** \,mekə'nistik\ adj —**mech·a·ni·za·tion** \mekənə'zāshən\ n — **mech·a·nize** \'mekə,nīz\ vb — **mech·a·niz·er** n

med·al \'medᵊl\ n 1 : religious pin or pendant 2 : coinlike commemorative metal piece

med·al·ist, med·al·list \'medᵊlist\ n : person awarded a medal

me·dal·lion \mə'dalyən\ n : large medal

med·dle \'medᵊl\ vb -**dled; -dling** 1 : interfere —**med·dler** \'medᵊlər\ n —**med·dle·some** \'medᵊlsəm\ adj

me·dia \'mēdēə\ n pl : communications organizations

me·di·an \'mēdēən\ n : middle value in a range —**median** adj

me·di·ate \'mēdē,āt\ vb -**at·ed; -at·ing** : help settle a dispute —**me·di·a·tion** \,mēdē'āshən\ n —**me·di·a·tor** \'mē-dē,ātər\ n

med·ic \'medik\ n : medical worker esp. in the military

med·i·ca·ble \'medikəbəl\ adj : curable

med·ic·aid \'medi,kād\ n : government program of medical aid for the poor

med·i·cal \'medikəl\ adj : relating to medicine —**med·i·cal·ly** \-klē\ adv

medi·care \'medi,ker\ n : government program of medical care for the aged

med·i·cate \'medi,kāt\ vb -**cat·ed; -cat·ing** : treat with medicine

med·i·ca·tion \,medə'kāshən\ n 1 : act of medicating 2 : medicine

med·i·cine \'medəsən\ *n* **1** : preparation used to treat disease **2** : science dealing with the cure of disease —**med·ic·i·nal** \mə'dis⁹nəl\ *adj* —**medic·i·nal·ly** *adv*

me·di·eval, me·di·ae·val \,mēdē'ēval, ,med-, ,mid-; ;mē'dē-, ,me-, ,mi-\ *adj* : of or relating to the Middle Ages —**me·di·eval·ist** \-ist\ *n*

me·di·o·cre \,mēdē'ōkər\ *adj* : not very good —**me·di·oc·ri·ty** \-'äkrətē\ *n*

med·i·tate \'medə,tāt\ *vb* -**tat·ed; -tat·ing** : contemplate —**med·i·ta·tion** \,medə'tāshən\ *n* —**med·i·ta·tive** \'medə,tātiv\ *adj* —**med·i·ta·tive·ly** *adv*

me·di·um \'mēdēəm\ *n, pl* -**diums** or -**dia** \-ēə\ **1** : middle position or degree **2** : means of effecting or conveying something **3** : surrounding substance **4** : means of communication **5** : mode of artistic expression —**medium** *adj*

med·ley \'medlē\ *n, pl* -**leys** : series of songs performed as one

meek \'mēk\ *adj* **1** : mild-mannered **2** : lacking spirit —**meek·ly** *adv* —**meek·ness** *n*

meer·schaum \'mirshəm, -,shom\ *n* : claylike tobacco pipe

¹meet \'mēt\ *vb* **met** \'met\; **meet·ing 1** : run into **2** : join **3** : oppose **4** : assemble **5** : satisfy **6** : be introduced to ~ *n* : sports team competition

²meet *adj* : proper

meet·ing \'mētiŋ\ *n* : a getting together —**meet·ing·house** *n*

mega·byte \'megə,bīt\ *n* : unit of computer storage capacity

mega·hertz \-,hərts, -,herts\ *n* : one million hertz

mega·phone \'megə,fōn\ *n* : cone-shaped device to intensify or direct the voice

mel·an·choly \'melən,kälē\ *n* : depression —**mel·an·chol·ic** \,melən'kälik\ *adj* —**melancholy** *adj*

mel·a·no·ma \,melə'nōmə\ *n, pl* -**mas** : usu. malignant skin tumor

me·lee \'mā,lā, mā'lā\ *n* : brawl

me·lio·rate \'mēlyə,rāt, 'mēlēə-\ *vb* -**rat·ed; -rat·ing** : improve —**me·lio·ra·tion** \,mēlyə'rāshən, ,mēlēə-\ *n* —**me·lio·ra·tive** \'mēlyə,rātiv, 'mēlēə-\ *adj*

mel·lif·lu·ous \me'lifləwəs, mə-\ *adj* : sweetly flowing —**mel·lif·lu·ous·ly** *adv* —**mel·lif·lu·ous·ness** *n*

mel·low \'melō\ *adj* **1** : grown gentle or mild **2** : rich and full —**mellow** *vb* —**mel·low·ness** *n*

melo·dra·ma \'melə,drämə, -,dram-\ *n* : overly theatrical play —**melo·dra·mat·ic** \,melədrə'matik\ *adj* —**melo·dra·mat·i·cal·ly** \-tiklē\ *adv*

mel·o·dy \'melədē\ *n, pl* -**dies 1** : agreeable sound **2** : succession of musical notes —**me·lod·ic** \mə'lädik\ *adj* —**me·lod·i·cal·ly** \-iklē\ *adv* —**me·lo·di·ous** \mə'lōdēəs\ *adj* —**me·lo·di·ous·ly** *adv* —**me·lo·di·ous·ness** *n*

mel·on \'melən\ *n* : gourdlike fruit

melt \'melt\ *vb* **1** : change from solid to liquid usu. by heat **2** : dissolve or disappear gradually **3** : move or be moved emotionally

mem·ber \'membər\ *n* **1** : part of a person, animal, or plant **2** : one of a group **3** : part of a whole —**mem·ber·ship** \-,ship\ *n*

mem·brane \'mem,brān\ *n* : thin layer esp. in an organism —**mem·bra·nous** \-brənəs\ *adj*

me·men·to \mi'mentō\ *n, pl* -**tos** or -**toes** : souvenir

memo \'memō\ *n, pl* **mem·os** : memorandum

mem·oirs \'mem,wärz\ *n pl* : autobiography

mem·o·ra·bil·ia \,memərə'bilēə, -'bil-yə\ *n pl* **1** : memorable things **2** : mementos

mem·o·ra·ble \'memərəbəl\ *adj* : worth remembering —**mem·o·ra·bil·i·ty** \,memərə'bilətē\ *n* —**mem·o·ra·ble·ness** *n* —**mem·o·ra·bly** \-blē\ *adv*

mem·o·ran·dum \,memə'randəm\ *n, pl* -**dums** or -**da** \-də\ : informal note

me·mo·ri·al \mə'mōrēəl\ *n* : something (as a monument) meant to keep remembrance alive —**memorial** *adj* —**me·mo·ri·al·ize** *vb*

Memorial Day *n* : last Monday in May or formerly May 30 observed as a legal holiday in commemoration of dead servicemen

mem·o·ry \'memrē, 'memə-\ *n, pl* -**ries 1** : power of remembering **2** : something remembered **3** : commemoration **4** : time within which past events are remembered —**mem·o·ri·za·tion** \,memərə'zāshən\ *n* —**mem·o·rize** \'memə,rīz\ *vb* —**mem·o·riz·er** *n*

men *pl of* MAN

men·ace \'menəs\ *n* : threat of danger ~

vb **-aced; -ac·ing 1** : threaten **2** : endanger **—men·ac·ing·ly** *adv*

me·nag·er·ie \mə'najərē\ *n* : collection of wild animals

mend \'mend\ *vb* **1** : improve **2** : repair **3** : heal **—mend** *n* **—mend·er** *n*

men·da·cious \men'dāshəs\ *adj* : dishonest **—men·da·cious·ly** *adv* **—men·dac·i·ty** \-'dasətē\ *n*

men·di·cant \'mendikənt\ *n* : beggar **—men·di·can·cy** \-kənsē\ *n* **—mendicant** *adj*

men·ha·den \men'hādⁿn, mən-\ *n, pl* **-den** : fish related to the herring

me·nial \'mēnēəl, -nyəl\ *adj* **1** : relating to servants **2** : humble **~** *n* : domestic servant **—me·ni·al·ly** *adv*

men·in·gi·tis \menən'jītəs\ *n, pl* **-git·i·des** \-'jitə‚dēz\ : disease of the brain and spinal cord

meno·pause \'menə‚pöz\ *n* : time when menstruation ends **—meno·paus·al** \menə'pözəl\ *adj*

me·no·rah \mə'nōrə\ *n* : candelabrum used in Jewish worship

men·stru·a·tion \menstrə'wāshən, men'strā-\ *n* : monthly discharge of blood from the uterus **—men·stru·al** \'menstrəwəl\ *adj* **—men·stru·ate** \'menstrə‚wāt, -‚strāt\ *vb*

-ment \mənt\ *n suffix* **1** : result or means of an action **2** : action or process **3** : place of an action **4** : state or condition

men·tal \'mentⁿl\ *adj* : relating to the mind or its disorders **—men·tal·i·ty** \men'talətē\ *n* **—men·tal·ly** *adv*

men·thol \'men‚thöl, -‚thōl\ *n* : soothing substance from oil of peppermint **—men·tho·lat·ed** \-thə‚lātəd\ *adj*

men·tion \'menchən\ *vb* : refer to **—mention** *n*

men·tor \'men‚tör, 'mentər\ *n* : instructor

menu \'menyü\ *n* **1** : restaurant's list of food **2** : list of offerings

me·ow \mē'aů\ *n* : characteristic cry of a cat **—meow** *vb*

mer·can·tile \'mərkən‚tēl, -‚tīl\ *adj* : relating to merchants or trade

mer·ce·nary \'mərsⁿn‚erē\ *n, pl* **-nar·ies** : hired soldier **~** *adj* : serving only for money

mer·chan·dise \'mərchən‚dīz, -‚dīs\ *n* : goods bought and sold **~** *vb* **-dised; -dis·ing** : buy and sell **—mer·chan·dis·er** *n*

mer·chant \'mərchənt\ *n* : one who buys and sells

merchant marine *n* : commercial ships

mer·cu·ri·al \mər'kyürēəl\ *adj* : unpredictable **—mer·cu·ri·al·ly** *adv* **—mer·cu·ri·al·ness** *n*

mer·cu·ry \'mərkyərē\ *n* : heavy liquid metallic chemical element

mer·cy \'mərsē\ *n, pl* **-cies 1** : show of pity or leniency **2** : divine blessing **—mer·ci·ful** \-sifəl\ *adj* **—mer·ci·ful·ly** *adv* **—mer·ci·less** \-siləs\ *adj* **—mer·ci·less·ly** *adv* **—mercy** *adj*

mere \'mir\ *adj, superlative* **mer·est** : nothing more than **—mere·ly** *adv*

merge \'mərj\ *vb* **merged; merg·ing 1** : unite **2** : blend **—merg·er** \'mərjər\ *n*

me·rid·i·an \mə'ridēən\ *n* : imaginary circle on the earth's surface passing through the poles **—meridian** *adj*

me·ringue \mə'raŋ\ *n* : baked dessert topping of beaten egg whites

me·ri·no \mə'rēnō\ *n, pl* **-nos 1** : kind of sheep **2** : fine soft woolen yarn

mer·it \'merət\ *n* **1** : praiseworthy quality **2** *pl* : rights and wrongs of a legal case **~** *vb* : deserve **—mer·i·to·ri·ous** \merə'tōrēəs\ *adj* **—mer·i·to·ri·ous·ly** *adv* **—mer·i·to·ri·ous·ness** *n*

mer·maid \'mər‚mād\ *n* : legendary female sea creature

mer·ry \'merē\ *adj* **-ri·er; -est** : full of high spirits **—mer·ri·ly** *adv* **—mer·riment** \'merimənt\ *n* **—merry·mak·er** \'merē‚mākər\ *n* **—merry·mak·ing** \merē‚mākiŋ\ *n*

merry-go-round *n* : revolving amusement ride

me·sa \'māsə\ *n* : steep flat-topped hill

mesdames *pl of* MADAM *or of* MADAME *or of* MRS.

mesdemoiselles *pl of* MADEMOISELLE

mesh \'mesh\ *n* **1** : one of the openings in a net **2** : net fabric **3** : working contact **~** *vb* : fit together properly **—meshed** \'mesht\ *adj*

mes·mer·ize \'mezmə‚rīz\ *vb* **-ized; -iz·ing** : hypnotize

mess \'mes\ *n* **1** : meal eaten by a group **2** : confused, dirty, or offensive state **~** *vb* **1** : make dirty or untidy **2** : putter **3** : interfere **—messy** *adj*

mes·sage \'mesij\ *n* : news, information, or a command sent by one person to another

mes·sen·ger \'mesⁿnjər\ *n* : one who carries a message or does an errand

Mes·si·ah \mə̇ˈsīə\ n 1 : expected deliverer of the Jews 2 : Jesus Christ 3 not cap : great leader

messieurs pl of MONSIEUR

Messrs. pl of MR.

mes·ti·zo \me·ˈstēzō\ n, pl -zos : person of mixed blood

met past of MEET

me·tab·o·lism \mə̇ˈtabə,lizəm\ n : biochemical processes necessary to life —**met·a·bol·ic** \,metə·ˈbälik\ adj —**me·tab·o·lize** \mə̇ˈtabə,līz\ vb

met·al \ˈmetᵊl\ n : shiny substance that can be melted and shaped and conducts heat and electricity —**me·tal·lic** \mə̇ˈtalik\ adj —**met·al·ware** n —**met·al·work** n —**met·al·work·er** n —**met·al·work·ing** n

met·al·lur·gy \ˈmetᵊl,ərjē\ n : science of metals —**met·al·lur·gi·cal** \,metᵊl·ˈərjikəl\ adj —**met·al·lur·gist** \ˈmetᵊl,ərjist\ n

meta·mor·pho·sis \,metə·ˈmórfəsəs\, n, pl -pho·ses \-,sēz\ : sudden and drastic change (as of form) —**metamorphose** \-,fōz, -,fōs\ vb

met·a·phor \ˈmetə,fòr, -fər\ n : use of a word denoting one kind of object or idea in place of another to suggest a likeness between them —**met·a·phor·i·cal** \,metə·ˈfòrikəl\ adj

meta·phys·ics \,metə·ˈfiziks\ n : study of the causes and nature of things —**meta·phys·i·cal** \-ˈfizəkəl\ adj

mete \ˈmēt\ vb **met·ed; met·ing** : allot

me·te·or \ˈmētēər, -ē,ór\ n : small body that produces a streak of light as it burns up in the atmosphere

me·te·or·ic \,mētē·ˈórik\ adj 1 : relating to a meteor 2 : sudden and spectacular —**me·te·or·i·cal·ly** \-ik·lē\ adv

me·te·or·ite \ˈmētēə,rīt\ n : meteor that reaches the earth

me·te·or·ol·o·gy \,mētēə·ˈräləjē\ n : science of weather —**me·te·o·ro·log·ic** \,mētē,órə·ˈläjik, -mētē,órə·ˈläjik\, **me·te·o·ro·log·i·cal** \-ˈläjikəl\ adj —**me·te·o·rol·o·gist** \-ēə·ˈrälətjist\ n

¹me·ter \ˈmētər\ n : rhythm in verse or music

²meter n : unit of length equal to 39.37 inches

³meter n : measuring instrument

meth·a·done \ˈmethə,dōn\ n : synthetic addictive narcotic

meth·ane \ˈmeth,ān\ n : colorless odorless flammable gas

meth·a·nol \ˈmethə,nól, -,nōl\ n : volatile flammable poisonous liquid

meth·od \ˈmethəd\ n 1 : procedure for achieving an end 2 : orderly arrangement or plan —**me·thod·i·cal** \mə̇ˈthädikəl\ adj —**me·thod·i·cal·ly** \-klē\ adv —**me·thod·i·cal·ness** n

me·tic·u·lous \mə̇ˈtikyələs\ adj : extremely careful in attending to detail —**me·tic·u·lous·ly** adv —**me·tic·u·lous·ness** n

met·ric \ˈmetrik\, **met·ri·cal** \-trikəl\ adj : relating to meter or the metric system —**met·ri·cal·ly** adv

metric system n : system of weights and measures using the meter and kilogram

met·ro·nome \ˈmetrə,nōm\ n : instrument that ticks regularly to mark a beat in music

me·trop·o·lis \mə̇ˈträpələs\ n : major city —**met·ro·pol·i·tan** \,metrə·ˈpälətᵊn\ adj

met·tle \ˈmetᵊl\ n : spirit or courage —**met·tle·some** \-səm\ adj

mez·za·nine \ˈmezᵊn,ēn, ,mezᵊn·ˈēn\ n 1 : intermediate level between 2 main floors 2 : lowest balcony

mez·zo-so·pra·no \,metsōsə·ˈpranō, ,medz-\ n : voice between soprano and contralto

mi·as·ma \mī·ˈazmə\ n 1 : noxious vapor 2 : harmful influence —**mi·as·mic** \-mik\ adj

mi·ca \ˈmīkə\ n : mineral separable into thin transparent sheets

mice pl of MOUSE

mi·cro \ˈmīkrō\ adj : very small

mi·crobe \ˈmī,krōb\ n : disease-causing microorganism —**mi·cro·bi·al** \mī·ˈkrōbēəl\ adj

mi·cro·bi·ol·o·gy \,mīkrōbī·ˈäləjē\ n : biology dealing with microscopic life —**mi·cro·bi·o·log·i·cal** \ˈmīkrō,bīə·ˈläjikəl\ adj —**mi·cro·bi·ol·o·gist** \,mīkrōbī·ˈäləjist\ n

mi·cro·com·put·er \ˈmīkrōkəm,pyütər\ n : small computer that uses a microprocessor

mi·cro·cosm \ˈmīkrə,käzəm\ n : one thought of as a miniature universe

mi·cro·film \-,film\ n : small film recording printed matter —**microfilm** vb

mi·crom·e·ter \mī·ˈkrämətər\ n : instrument for measuring minute distances

mi·cro·min·ia·tur·ized \,mīkrō·ˈminēachə‚rīzd, -'minichə-\ *adj* : reduced to a very small size —**mi·cro·min·ia·tur·iza·tion** \-‚minēə‚chürə'zāshən, -‚mini‚chür-, -‚chər-\ *n*

mi·cron \'mī‚krän\ *n* : one millionth of a meter

mi·cro·or·gan·ism \‚mīkrō'órgə‚nizəm\ *n* : very tiny living thing

mi·cro·phone \'mīkrə‚fōn\ *n* : instrument for changing sound waves into variations of an electric current

mi·cro·pro·ces·sor \‚mīkrō'präsesər\ *n* : miniaturized computer processing unit on a single chip

mi·cro·scope \-‚skōp\ *n* : optical device for magnifying tiny objects —**mi·cro·scop·ic** \‚mīkrə'skäpik\ *adj* —**mi·cro·scop·i·cal·ly** *adv* —**mi·cros·co·py** \mī'kräskəpē\ *n*

mi·cro·wave \'mīkrə‚wāv\ *n* 1 : short radio wave 2 : oven that cooks food using microwaves ~ *vb* : heat or cook in a microwave oven —**mi·cro·wav·able, mi·cro·wave·able** \‚mīkrə'wā-vəbəl\ *adj*

mid \'mid\ *adj* : middle —**mid·point** *n* —**mid·stream** *n* —**mid·sum·mer** *n* —**mid·town** *n or adj* —**mid·week** *n* —**mid·win·ter** *n* —**mid·year** *n*

mid·air *n* : a point in the air well above the ground

mid·day *n* : noon

mid·dle \'midᵊl\ *adj* 1 : equally distant from the extremes 2 : being at neither extreme ~ *n* : middle part or point

Middle Ages *n pl* : period from about A.D. 500 to about 1500

mid·dle·man \-‚man\ *n* : dealer or agent between the producer and consumer

mid·dling \'midliŋ, -lən\ *adj* 1 : of middle or medium size, degree, or quality 2 : mediocre

midge \'mij\ *n* : very tiny fly

midg·et \'mijət\ *n* : very small person or thing

mid·land \'midlənd, -‚land\ *n* : interior of a country

mid·most *adj* : being nearest the middle —**midmost** *adv*

mid·night *n* : 12 o'clock at night

mid·riff \'mid‚rif\ *n* : mid-region of the torso

mid·ship·man \'mid‚shipmən, ‚mid-'ship-\ *n* : student naval officer

midst \'midst\ *n* : position close to or surrounded by others —**midst** *prep*

mid·way \'mid‚wā\ *n* : concessions and amusements at a carnival ~ *adv* : in the middle

mid·wife \'mid‚wīf\ *n* : person who aids at childbirth —**mid·wife·ry** \mid-'wīfərē, -'wīf-\ *n*

mien \'mēn\ *n* : appearance

miff \'mif\ *vb* : upset or peeve

¹might \'mīt\ *past of* MAY —used to express permission or possibility or as a polite alternative to *may*

²might *n* : power or resources

mighty \'mītē\ *adj* **might·i·er; -est** 1 : very strong 2 : great —**might·i·ly** *adv* —**might·i·ness** *n* —**mighty** *adv*

mi·graine \'mī‚grān\ *n* : severe headache often with nausea

mi·grant \'mīgrənt\ *n* : one who moves frequently to find work

mi·grate \'mī‚grāt\ *vb* **-grat·ed; -grat·ing** 1 : move from one place to another 2 : pass periodically from one region or climate to another —**mi·gra·tion** \mī'grāshən\ *n* —**mi·gra·to·ry** \'mīgrə‚tōrē\ *adj*

mild \'mīld\ *adj* 1 : gentle in nature or behavior 2 : moderate in action or effect —**mild·ly** *adv* —**mild·ness** *n*

mil·dew \'mil‚dü, -‚dyü\ *n* : whitish fungal growth —**mildew** *vb*

mile \'mīl\ *n* : unit of length equal to 5280 feet

mile·age \'mīlij\ *n* 1 : allowance per mile for traveling expenses 2 : amount or rate of use expressed in miles

mile·stone *n* : significant point in development

mi·lieu \mēl'yü, -'yœ̄\ *n, pl* **-lieus** *or* **-lieux** \-'yüz, -'yœ̄\ : surroundings or setting

mil·i·tant \'milətənt\ *adj* : aggressively active or hostile —**mil·i·tan·cy** \-tənsē\ *n* —**militant** *n* —**mil·i·tant·ly** *adv*

mil·i·tar·ism \'milətə‚rizəm\ *n* : dominance of military ideals or of a policy of aggressive readiness for war —**mil·i·ta·rist** \-rist\ *n* —**mil·i·tar·is·tic** \‚milətə'ristik\ *adj*

mil·i·tary \'milə‚terē\ *adj* 1 : relating to soldiers, arms, or war 2 : relating to or performed by armed forces ~ *n* : armed forces or the people in them —**mil·i·tar·i·ly** \‚milə'terəlē\ *adv*

mil·i·tate \-‚tāt\ *vb* **-tat·ed; -tat·ing** : have an effect

mi·li·tia \mə'lishə\ *n* : civilian soldiers —**mi·li·tia·man** \-mən\ *n*

milk \'milk\ *n* : white nutritive fluid secreted by female mammals for feeding their young ~ *vb* 1 : draw off the milk of 2 : draw something from as if by milking —**milk·er** *n* —**milk·i·ness** \-ēnəs\ *n* —**milky** *adj*

milk·man \-,man, -mən\ *n* : man who sells or delivers milk

milk·weed *n* : herb with milky juice

¹mill \'mil\ *n* 1 : building in which grain is ground into flour 2 : manufacturing plant 3 : machine used esp. for forming or processing ~ *vb* 1 : subject to a process in a mill 2 : move in a circle —**mill·er** *n*

²mill *n* : 1/10 cent

mil·len·ni·um \mə'lenēəm\ *n, pl* **-nia** \-ēə\ *or* **-niums** : a period of 1000 years

mil·let \'milət\ *n* : cereal and forage grass with small seeds

mil·li·gram \'milə,gram\ *n* : 1/1000 gram

mil·li·liter \-,lētər\ *n* : 1/1000 liter

mil·li·me·ter \-,mētər\ *n* : 1/1000 meter

mil·li·ner \'milənər\ *n* : person who makes or sells women's hats —**mil·li·nery** \'milə,nerē\ *n*

mil·lion \'milyən\ *n, pl* **millions** *or* **million** : 1000 thousands —**million** *adj* —**mil·lionth** \-yənth\ *adj or n*

mil·lion·aire \,milyə'nar, 'milyə,nar\ *n* : person worth a million or more (as of dollars)

mil·li·pede \'milə,pēd\ *n* : longbodied arthropod with 2 pairs of legs on most segments

mill·stone *n* : either of 2 round flat stones used for grinding grain

mime \'mīm\ *n* 1 : mimic 2 : pantomime —**mime** *vb*

mim·eo·graph \'mimēə,graf\ *n* : machine for making many stencil copies —**mimeograph** *vb*

mim·ic \'mimik\ *n* : one that mimics ~ *vb* **-icked; -ick·ing** 1 : imitate closely 2 : ridicule by imitation —**mim·ic·ry** \'mimikrē\ *n*

min·a·ret \,minə'ret\ *n* : tower attached to a mosque

mince \'mins\ *vb* **minced; minc·ing** 1 : cut into small pieces 2 : choose (one's words) carefully 3 : walk in a prim affected manner

mind \'mīnd\ *n* 1 : memory 2 : the part of an individual that feels, perceives, and esp. reasons 3 : intention 4 : normal mental condition 5 : opinion 6 : intellectual ability ~ *vb* 1 : attend to 2 : obey 3 : be concerned about 4 : be careful —**mind·ed** *adj* —**mind·less** \'mīndləs\ *adj* —**mind·less·ly** *adv* —**mind·less·ness** *n*

mind·ful \-fəl\ *adj* : aware or attentive —**mind·ful·ly** *adv* —**mind·ful·ness** *n*

¹mine \'mīn\ *pron* : that which belongs to me

²mine \'mīn\ *n* 1 : excavation from which minerals are taken 2 : explosive device placed in the ground or water for destroying enemy vehicles or vessels that later pass ~ *vb* **mined; min·ing** 1 : get ore from 2 : place military mines in —**mine·field** *n* —**min·er** *n*

min·er·al \'minərəl\ *n* 1 : crystalline substance not of organic origin 2 : useful natural substance (as coal) obtained from the ground —**mineral** *adj*

min·er·al·o·gy \,minə'räləjē, -'ral-\ *n* : science dealing with minerals —**min·er·al·og·i·cal** \,minərə'läjikəl\ *adj* —**min·er·al·o·gist** \,minə'räləjist, -'ral-\ *n*

min·gle \'miŋgəl\ *vb* **-gled; -gling** : bring together or mix

mini- *comb form* : miniature or of small dimensions

min·ia·ture \'minēə,chùr, 'mini,chùr, -chər\ *n* : tiny copy or very small version —**miniature** *adj* —**min·ia·tur·ist** \-,chùrist, -chər-\ *n* —**min·ia·tur·ize** \-ēəchə,rīz, -ichə-\ *vb*

mini·bike \'minē,bīk\ *n* : small motorcycle

mini·bus \-,bəs\ *n* : small bus

mini·com·put·er \-kəm,pyütər\ *n* : computer intermediate between a mainframe and a microcomputer in size and speed

mini·course \-,kōrs\ *n* : short course of study

min·i·mal \'minəməl\ *adj* : relating to or being a minimum —**min·i·mal·ly** *adv*

min·i·mize \'minə,mīz\ *vb* **-mized; -miz·ing** 1 : reduce to a minimum 2 : underestimate intentionally

min·i·mum \'minəməm\ *n, pl* **-ma** \-mə\ *or* **-mums** : lowest quantity or amount —**minimum** *adj*

min·ion \'minyən\ *n* 1 : servile dependent 2 : subordinate official

mini·se·ries \'minē,sirēz\ *n* : television story in several parts

mini·skirt \-ˌskərt\ n : very short skirt

min·is·ter \'minəstər\ n 1 : Protestant member of the clergy 2 : high officer of state 3 : diplomatic representative ~ vb : give aid or service —**min·is·te·ri·al** \ˌminə'stirēəl\ adj —**min·is·tra·tion** n

min·is·try \'minəstrē\ n, pl **-tries** 1 : office or duties of a minister 2 : body of ministers 3 : government department headed by a minister

mini·van \'minē,van\ n : small van

mink \'miŋk\ n, pl **mink** or **minks** : weasellike mammal or its soft brown fur

min·now \'minō\ n, pl **-nows** : small freshwater fish

mi·nor \'mīnər\ adj 1 : less in size, importance, or value 2 : not serious ~ n 1 : person not yet of legal age 2 : secondary field of academic specialization

mi·nor·i·ty \mə'nórətē, mī-\ n, pl **-ties** 1 : time or state of being a minor 2 : smaller number (as of votes) 3 : part of a population differing from others (as in race or religion)

min·strel \'minstrəl\ n 1 : medieval singer of verses 2 : performer in a program usu. of black American songs and jokes —**min·strel·sy** \-sē\ n

¹**mint** \'mint\ n 1 : fragrant herb that yields a flavoring oil 2 : mint-flavored piece of candy —**minty** adj

²**mint** n 1 : place where coins are made 2 : vast sum ~ adj : unused —**mint** vb —**mint·er** n

min·u·et \ˌminyə'wet\ n : slow graceful dance

mi·nus \'mīnəs\ prep 1 : diminished by 2 : lacking ~ n : negative quantity or quality

mi·nus·cule \'minəs,kyül, min'əs-, min·is·cule \'minəs-\ adj : very small

¹**min·ute** \'minət\ n 1 : 60th part of an hour or of a degree 2 : short time 3 pl : official record of a meeting

²**mi·nute** \mī'nüt, mə-, -'nyüt\ adj **-nut·er; -est** 1 : very small 2 : marked by close attention to details —**mi·nute·ly** adv —**mi·nute·ness** n

mir·a·cle \'mirikəl\ n 1 : extraordinary event taken as a sign of divine intervention in human affairs 2 : marvel —**mi·rac·u·lous** \mə'rakyələs\ adj —**mi·rac·u·lous·ly** adv

mi·rage \mə'räzh\ n : distant illusion caused by atmospheric conditions (as in the desert)

mire \'mīr\ n : heavy deep mud ~ vb : mired; mir·ing : stick or sink in mire —**miry** adj

mir·ror \'mirər\ n : smooth surface (as of glass) that reflects images ~ vb : reflect in or as if in a mirror

mirth \'mərth\ n : gladness and laughter —**mirth·ful** adj —**mirth·ful·ly** adv —**mirth·ful·ness** n —**mirth·less** adj

mis·an·thrope \'misˀn,thrōp\ n : one who hates mankind —**mis·an·throp·ic** \ˌmisˀn'thräpik\ adj —**mis·an·thro·py** \mis'anthrəpē\ n

mis·ap·pre·hend \ˌmis,aprə'hend\ vb : misunderstand —**mis·ap·pre·hen·sion** n

mis·ap·pro·pri·ate \ˌmisə'prōprē,āt\ vb : take dishonestly for one's own use —**mis·ap·pro·pri·a·tion** n

mis·be·got·ten \ˌmisbi'gätˀn\ adj 1 : illegitimate 2 : ill-conceived

mis·be·have \ˌmisbi'hāv\ vb : behave improperly —**mis·be·hav·er** n —**mis·be·hav·ior** n

mis·cal·cu·late \mis'kalkyə,lāt\ vb : calculate wrongly —**mis·cal·cu·la·tion** n

mis·car·ry \mis'karē, 'mis,karē\ vb 1 : give birth prematurely before the fetus can survive 2 : go wrong or be unsuccessful —**mis·car·riage** \-rij\ n

mis·ce·ge·na·tion \mis,ejə'nāshən, ˌmisijə'nā-\ n : marriage between persons of different races

mis·cel·la·neous \ˌmisə'lānēəs\ adj : consisting of many things of different kinds —**mis·cel·la·neous·ly** adv —**mis·cel·la·neous·ness** n

mis·cel·la·ny \'misə,lānē\ n, pl **-nies** : collection of various things

mis·chance \mis'chans\ n : bad luck

mis·chief \'mischəf\ n : conduct esp. of a child that annoys or causes minor damage

mis·chie·vous \'mischəvəs\ adj 1 : causing annoyance or minor injury 2 : irresponsibly playful —**mis·chie·vous·ly** adv —**mis·chie·vous·ness** n

mis·con·ceive \ˌmiskən'sēv\ vb : interpret incorrectly —**mis·con·cep·tion** n

mis·con·duct \mis'kändəkt\ n 1 : mismanagement 2 : bad behavior

mis·con·strue \ˌmiskən'strü\ vb : misinterpret —**mis·con·struc·tion** n

mis·cre·ant \'miskrēənt\ n : one who behaves criminally or viciously —**miscreant** adj

mis·deed \mis'dēd\ n : wrong deed

mis·de·mean·or \,misdi'mēnər\ n : crime less serious than a felony

mi·ser \'mīzər\ n : person who hoards and is stingy with money —**miser·li·ness** \-lēnəs\ n —**mi·ser·ly** adj

mis·er·a·ble \'mizərəbəl\ adj 1 : wretchedly deficient 2 : causing extreme discomfort 3 : shameful —**mis·er·a·ble·ness** n —**mis·er·a·bly** \-blē\ adv

mis·ery \'mizərē\ n, pl **-er·ies** : suffering and want caused by distress or poverty

mis·fire \mis'fīr\ vb 1 : fail to fire 2 : miss an intended effect —**misfire** \'mis,fīr\ n

mis·fit \'mis,fit, mis'fit\ n : person poorly adjusted to his environment

mis·for·tune \mis'fórchən\ n 1 : bad luck 2 : unfortunate condition or event

mis·giv·ing \mis'givin\ n : doubt or concern

mis·guid·ed \mis'gīdəd\ adj : mistaken, uninformed, or deceived

mis·hap \'mis,hap\ n : accident

mis·in·form \,mis°n'fórm\ vb : give wrong information to —**mis·in·for·ma·tion** \,mis,infər'māshən\ n

mis·in·ter·pret \,mis°n'tərprət\ vb : understand or explain wrongly —**mis·in·ter·pre·ta·tion** \-,tərprə-'tā-shən\ n

mis·judge \mis'jəj\ vb : judge incorrectly or unjustly —**mis·judg·ment** n

mis·lay \mis'lā\ vb **-laid; -lay·ing** : misplace

mis·lead \mis'lēd\ vb **-led; -lead·ing** : lead in a wrong direction or into error —**mis·lead·ing·ly** adv

mis·man·age \mis'manij\ vb : manage badly —**mis·man·age·ment** n

mis·no·mer \mis'nōmər\ n : wrong name

mi·sog·y·nist \mə'säjənist\ n : one who hates or distrusts women —**mi·sog·y·nis·tic** \mə,säjə'nistik\ adj —**mi·sog·y·ny** \-nē\ n

mis·place \mis'plās\ vb : put in a wrong or unremembered place

mis·print \'mis,print, mis'-\ n : error in printed matter

mis·pro·nounce \,misprə'naúns\ vb : pronounce incorrectly —**mis·pro·nun·ci·a·tion** n

mis·quote \mis'kwōt\ vb : quote incorrectly —**mis·quo·ta·tion** \,miskwō-'tāshən\ n

mis·read \mis'rēd\ vb **-read; -read·ing** : read or interpret incorrectly

mis·rep·re·sent \,mis,repri'zent\ vb : represent falsely or unfairly —**mis·rep·re·sen·ta·tion** n

mis·rule \mis'rül\ vb : govern badly ~ n 1 : bad or corrupt government 2 : disorder

¹miss \'mis\ vb 1 : fail to hit, reach, or contact 2 : notice the absence of 3 : fail to obtain 4 : avoid 5 : omit —**miss** n

²miss n : young unmarried woman or girl —often used as a title

mis·sal \'misəl\ n : book containing what is said at mass during the year

mis·shap·en \mis'shāpən\ adj : distorted

mis·sile \'misəl\ n : object (as a stone or rocket) thrown or shot

miss·ing \'misin\ adj : absent or lost

mis·sion \'mishən\ n 1 : ministry sent by a church to spread its teaching 2 : group of diplomats sent to a foreign country 3 : task

mis·sion·ary \'mishə,nerē\ adj : relating to religious missions ~ n, pl **-ar·ies** : person sent to spread religious faith

mis·sive \'misiv\ n : letter

mis·spell \mis'spel\ vb : spell incorrectly —**mis·spell·ing** n

mis·state \mis'stāt\ vb : state incorrectly —**mis·state·ment** n

mis·step \'mis,step\ n 1 : wrong step 2 : mistake

mist \'mist\ n : particles of water falling as fine rain

mis·take \mə'stāk\ n 1 : misunderstanding or wrong belief 2 : wrong action or statement —**mistake** vb

mis·tak·en \-'stākən\ adj : having a wrong opinion or incorrect information —**mis·tak·en·ly** adv

mis·ter \'mistər\ n : sir —used without a name in addressing a man

mis·tle·toe \'misəl,tō\ n : parasitic green shrub with waxy white berries

mis·treat \mis'trēt\ vb : treat badly —**mis·treat·ment** n

mis·tress \'mistrəs\ n 1 : woman in control 2 : a woman not his wife with whom a married man has recurrent sexual relations

mis·tri·al \'mis'trīəl\ n : trial that has no legal effect

mis·trust \-'trəst\ n : lack of confidence ~ vb : have no confidence in —**mis·trust·ful** \-fəl\ adj —**mis·trust·ful·ly** adv —**mis·trust·ful·ness** n

misty \'mistē\ adj **mist·i·er; -est** 1 : obscured by mist 2 : tearful —**mist·i·ly** adv —**mist·i·ness** n

mis·un·der·stand \,mis,əndər'stand\ vb 1 : fail to understand 2 : interpret incorrectly

mis·un·der·stand·ing \-'standiŋ\ n 1 : wrong interpretation 2 : disagreement

mis·use \mis'yüz\ vb 1 : use incorrectly 2 : mistreat —**mis·use** \-'yüs\ n

mite \'mīt\ n 1 : tiny spiderlike animal 2 : small amount

mi·ter, mi·tre \'mītər\ n 1 : bishop's headdress 2 : angular joint in wood ~ vb -**tered** or -**tred; -ter·ing** or -**tring** : bevel the ends of for a miter joint

mit·i·gate \'mitə,gāt\ vb -**gat·ed; -gat·ing** : make less severe —**mit·i·ga·tion** \,mitə'gāshən\ n —**mit·i·ga·tive** \'mitə,gātiv\ adj

mi·to·sis \mī'tōsəs\ n, pl -**to·ses** \-,sēz\ : process of forming 2 cell nuclei from one —**mi·tot·ic** \-'tätik\ adj

mitt \'mit\ n : mittenlike baseball glove

mit·ten \'mitᵊn\ n : hand covering without finger sections

mix \'miks\ vb : combine or join into one mass or group ~ n : commercially prepared food mixture —**mix·able** adj —**mix·er** n —**mix up** vb : confuse

mix·ture \'mikschər\ n : act or product of mixing

mix–up n : instance of confusion

mne·mon·ic \ni'mänik\ adj : relating to or assisting memory

moan \'mōn\ n : low prolonged sound of pain or grief —**moan** vb

moat \'mōt\ n : deep wide trench around a castle

mob \'mäb\ n 1 : large disorderly crowd 2 : criminal gang ~ vb -**bb**- : crowd around and attack or annoy

mo·bile \'mōbəl, -,bēl, -,bīl\ adj : capable of moving or being moved ~ \'mō,bēl\ n : suspended art construction with freely moving parts —**mo·bil·i·ty** \mō'bilətē\ n

mo·bi·lize \'mōbə,līz\ vb -**lized; -liz·ing** : assemble and make ready for war

duty —**mo·bi·li·za·tion** \,mōbələ-'zāshən\ n

moc·ca·sin \'mäkəsən\ n 1 : heelless shoe 2 : venomous U.S. snake

mo·cha \'mōkə\ n 1 : mixture of coffee and chocolate 2 : dark brown color

mock \'mäk, 'mȯk\ vb 1 : ridicule 2 : mimic in derision ~ adj 1 : simulated 2 : phony —**mock·er** n —**mock·ery** \-ərē\ n —**mock·ing·ly** adv

mock·ing·bird \'mäkiŋ,bərd, 'mȯk-\ n : songbird that mimics other birds

mode \'mōd\ n 1 : particular form or variety 2 : style —**mod·al** \-ᵊl\ adj —**mod·ish** \'mōdish\ adj

mod·el \'mädᵊl\ n 1 : structural design 2 : miniature representation 3 : something worthy of copying 4 : one who poses for an artist or displays clothes 5 : type or design ~ vb -**eled** or -**elled; -el·ing** or -**el·ling** 1 : shape 2 : work as a model ~ adj 1 : serving as a pattern 2 : being a miniature representation of

mo·dem \'mōdəm, -,dem\ n : device by which a computer communicates with another computer over telephone lines

mod·er·ate \'mädərət\ adj : avoiding extremes ~ \'mädə,rāt\ vb -**at·ed; -at·ing** 1 : lessen the intensity of 2 : act as a moderator —**moderate** n —**mod·er·ate·ly** adv —**mod·er·ate·ness** n —**mod·er·a·tion** \,mädə-'rāshən\ n

mod·er·a·tor \'mädə,rātər\ n : one who presides

mod·ern \'mädərn\ adj : relating to or characteristic of the present —**modern** n —**mo·der·ni·ty** \mə'dərnətē\ n —**mod·ern·iza·tion** \,mädərnə'zā-shən\ n —**mod·ern·ize** \'mädər,nīz\ vb —**mod·ern·iz·er** \'mädər,nīzər\ n —**mod·ern·ly** adv —**modern·ness** n

mod·est \'mädəst\ adj 1 : having a moderate estimate of oneself 2 : reserved or decent in thoughts or actions 3 : limited in size, amount, or aim —**mod·est·ly** adv —**mod·es·ty** \-əstē\ n

mod·i·cum \'mädikəm\ n : small amount

mod·i·fy \'mädə,fī\ vb -**fied; -fy·ing** 1 : limit the meaning of 2 : change —**mod·i·fi·ca·tion** \,mädəfə'kāshən\ n —**mod·i·fi·er** \'mädə,fīər\ n

mod·u·lar \'mäjələr\ adj : built with

standardized units —**mod·u·lar·ized** \-lə₁rīzd\ adj

mod·u·late \'mäjə₁lāt\ vb **-lat·ed; -lat·ing** 1 : keep in proper measure or proportion 2 : vary a radio wave —**mod·u·la·tion** \₁mäjə'lāshən\ n —**mod·u·la·tor** \'mäjə₁lātər\ n —**mod·u·la·to·ry** \-lə₁tōrē\ adj

mod·ule \'mäjül\ n : standardized unit

mo·gul \'mōgəl\ n : important person

mo·hair \'mō₁har\ n : fabric made from the hair of the Angora goat

moist \'mȯist\ adj : slightly or moderately wet —**moist·en** \'mȯis⁹n\ vb —**moist·en·er** \'mȯis⁹nər\ n —**moist·ly** adv —**moist·ness** n

mois·ture \'mȯischər\ n : small amount of liquid that causes dampness —**mois·tur·ize** \-chə₁rīz\ vb —**mois·tur·iz·er** n

mo·lar \'mōlər\ n : grinding tooth — **molar** adj

mo·las·ses \mə'lasəz\ n : thick brown syrup from raw sugar

¹mold \'mōld\ n : crumbly organic soil

²mold n : frame or cavity for forming ~ vb : shape in or as if in a mold — **mold·er** n

³mold n : surface growth of fungus ~ vb : become moldy —**mold·i·ness** \'mōldēnəs\ n —**moldy** adj

mold·er \'mōldər\ vb : crumble

mold·ing \'mōldiŋ\ n : decorative surface, plane, or strip

¹mole \'mōl\ n : spot on the skin

²mole n : small burrowing mammal — **mole·hill** n

mol·e·cule \'mäli₁kyül\ n : small particle of matter —**mo·lec·u·lar** \mə-'lekyələr\ adj

mole·skin \-₁skin\ n : heavy cotton fabric

mo·lest \mə'lest\ vb 1 : annoy or disturb 2 : force physical and usu. sexual contact on —**mo·les·ta·tion** \₁mōl₁es'tāshən, ₁mäl-\ n —**mo·lest·er** n

mol·li·fy \'mälə₁fī\ vb **-fied; -fy·ing** : soothe in temper —**mol·li·fi·ca·tion** \₁mäləfə'kāshən\ n

mol·lusk, mol·lusc \'mäləsk\ n : shelled aquatic invertebrate —**mol·lus·can** \mə'ləskən\ adj

mol·ly·cod·dle \'mälē₁kädᵊl\ vb **-dled; -dling** : pamper

molt \'mōlt\ vb : shed hair, feathers, outer skin, or horns periodically — **molt** n —**molt·er** n

mol·ten \'mōlt⁹n\ adj : fused or liquefied by heat

mom \'mäm, 'mȯm\ n : mother

mo·ment \'mōmənt\ n 1 : tiny portion of time 2 : time of excellence 3 : importance

mo·men·tar·i·ly \₁mōmən'terəlē\ adv 1 : for a moment 2 : at any moment

mo·men·tary \'mōmən₁terē\ adj : continuing some a moment —**mo·men·tar·i·ness** n

mo·men·tous \mō'mentəs\ adj : very important —**mo·men·tous·ly** adv —**mo·men·tous·ness** n

mo·men·tum \-əm\ n, pl **-ta** \-ə\ or **-tums** : force of a moving body

mon·arch \'mänərk, -₁ärk\ n : ruler of a kingdom or empire —**mo·nar·chi·cal** \mə'närkikəl\ adj

mon·ar·chist \'mänərkist\ n : believer in monarchical government —**mon·ar·chism** \-₁kizəm\ n

mon·ar·chy \'mänərkē\ n, pl **-chies** : realm of a monarch

mon·as·tery \'mänə₁sterē\ n, pl **-ter·ies** : house for monks

mo·nas·tic \mə'nastik\ adj : relating to monasteries, monks, or nuns —**mo·nastic** n —**mo·nas·ti·cal·ly** \-tiklē\ adv —**mo·nas·ti·cism** \-tə₁sizəm\ n

Mon·day \'məndā, -dē\ n : 2d day of the week

mon·e·tary \'mänə₁terē, 'mən-\ adj : relating to money

mon·ey \'mənē\ n, pl **-eys** or **-ies** \'mənēz\ 1 : something (as coins or paper currency) used in buying 2 : wealth —**mon·eyed** \-ēd\ adj —**mon·ey·lend·er** n

mon·ger \'məŋgər, 'mäŋ-\ n : dealer

mon·gol·ism \'mäŋgə₁lizəm\ n : congenital mental retardation —**Mongol·oid** \-gə₁lȯid\ adj or n

mon·goose \'män₁güs, 'mäŋ-\ n, pl **-goos·es** : small agile mammal esp. of India

mon·grel \'mäŋgrəl, 'məŋ-\ n : offspring of mixed breed

mon·i·tor \'mänətər\ n 1 : student assistant 2 : television screen ~ vb : watch or observe esp. for quality

monk \'məŋk\ n : member of a religious order living in a monastery —**monk·ish** adj

mon·key \'məŋkē\ n, pl **-keys** : small long-tailed arboreal primate ~ vb 1 : fool 2 : tamper

mon·key·shines \-₁shīnz\ n pl : pranks

monks•hood \'məŋks,hùd\ n : poisonous herb with showy flowers

mon•o•cle \'mänikəl\ n : eyeglass for one eye

mo•nog•a•my \mə'nägəmē\ n 1 : marriage with one person at a time 2 : practice of having a single mate for a period of time —mo•nog•a•mist \mə'nägəmist\ n —mo•nog•a•mous \-məs\ adj

mono•gram \'mänə,gram\ n : sign of identity made of initials —monogram vb

mono•graph \-,graf\ n : learned treatise

mono•lin•gual \,mänə'liŋgwəl\ adj : using only one language

mono•lith \'mänᵊl,ith\ n 1 : single great stone 2 : single uniform massive whole —mono•lith•ic \,mänᵊl'ithik\ adj

mono•logue \'mänᵊl,òg\ n : long speech —mono•logu•ist \-,ògist\, mo•nol•o•gist \mə'näləjist, 'mänᵊl,ògist\ n

mono•nu•cle•o•sis \,mänō,nüklē'ōsəs, -,nyü-\ n : acute infectious disease

mo•nop•o•ly \mə'näpəlē\ n, pl -lies 1 : exclusive ownership or control of a commodity 2 : one controlling a monopoly —mo•nop•o•list \-list\ n —mo•nop•o•lis•tic \mə,näpə'listik\ adj —mo•nop•o•li•za•tion \-lə'zāshən\ n —mo•nop•o•lize \mə'näpə,līz\ vb

mono•rail \'mänə,rāl\ n : single rail for a vehicle or a vehicle or system using it

mono•syl•lab•ic \,mänəsə'labik\ adj : consisting of or using words of only one syllable —mono•syl•la•ble \'mänə,siləbəl\ n

mono•the•ism \'mänōthē,izəm\ n : doctrine or belief that there is only one deity —mono•the•ist \-,thēist\ n —mono•the•is•tic \,mänōthē'istik\ adj

mono•tone \'mänə,tōn\ n : succession of words in one unvarying tone

mo•not•o•nous \mə'nätᵊnəs\ adj 1 : sounded in one unvarying tone 2 : tediously uniform —mo•not•o•nous•ly adv —mo•not•o•nous•ness n —mo•not•o•ny \-ᵊnē\ n

mon•ox•ide \mə'näk,sīd\ n : oxide containing one atom of oxygen in a molecule

mon•sieur \məs'yər, məsh-\ n, pl mes•sieurs \-yərz, mā'syərz\ : man of high rank or station —used as a title for a man esp. of French nationality

mon•si•gnor \män'sēnyər\ n, pl monsi-gnors or mon•si•gno•ri \,män,sēn'yōrē\ : Roman Catholic prelate —used as a title

mon•soon \män'sün\ n : periodic rainy season

mon•ster \'mänstər\ n 1 : abnormal or terrifying animal 2 : ugly, wicked, or cruel person —mon•stros•i•ty \män'sträsətē\ n —mon•strous \'mänstrəs\ adj —mon•strous•ly adv

mon•tage \män'täzh\ n : artistic composition of several different elements

month \'mənth\ n : 12th part of a year —month•ly adv or adj or n

mon•u•ment \'mänyəmənt\ n : structure erected in remembrance

mon•u•men•tal \,mänyə'mentᵊl\ adj 1 : serving as a monument 2 : outstanding 3 : very great —mon•u•men•tal•ly adv

moo \'mü\ vb : make the noise of a cow —moo n

mood \'müd\ n : state of mind or emotion

moody \'müdē\ adj mood•i•er; -est 1 : sad 2 : subject to changing moods and esp. to bad moods —mood•i•ly \'müd²lē\ adv —mood•i•ness \-ēnəs\ n

moon \'mün\ n : natural satellite (as of earth) —moon•beam n —moon•light n —moon•lit adj

moon•light \-,līt\ vb -ed; -ing : hold a 2d job —moon•light•er n

moon•shine n 1 : moonlight 2 : meaningless talk 3 : illegally distilled liquor

¹moor \'mùr\ n : open usu. swampy wasteland —moor•land \-,lənd, -,land\ n

²moor vb : fasten with line or anchor

moor•ing \-iŋ\ n : place where boat can be moored

moose \'müs\ n, pl moose : large heavy-antlered deer

moot \'müt\ adj : open to question

mop \'mäp\ n : floor-cleaning implement ~ vb -pp- : use a mop on

mope \'mōp\ vb moped; mop•ing : be sad or listless

mo•ped \'mō,ped\ n : low-powered motorbike

mo•raine \mə'rān\ n : glacial deposit of earth and stones

mor•al \'mòrəl\ adj 1 : relating to principles of right and wrong 2 : conforming to a standard of right behavior 3 : relating to or acting on the mind, character, or will ~ *n* **1** : point of a story **2** *pl* : moral practices or teachings —**mor·al·ist** \'mȯrəlist\ *n* —**mor·al·is·tic** \,mȯrə'listik\ *adj* —**mor·al·i·ty** \mə'ralətē\ *n* —**mor·al·ize** \'mȯrə,līz\ *vb* —**mor·al·ly** *adv*

mo·rale \mə'ral\ *n* : emotional attitude

mo·rass \mə'ras\ *n* : swamp

mor·a·to·ri·um \,mȯrə'tōrēəm\ *n, pl* **-ri·ums** *or* **-ria** \-ēə\ : suspension of activity

mo·ray \'mȯr,ā, mə'rā\ *n* : savage eel

mor·bid \'mȯrbəd\ *adj* **1** : relating to disease **2** : gruesome —**mor·bid·i·ty** \mȯr'bidətē\ *n* —**mor·bid·ly** *adv* —**mor·bid·ness** *n*

mor·dant \'mȯrdᵊnt\ *adj* : sarcastic —**mor·dant·ly** *adv*

more \'mȯr\ *adj* **1** : greater **2** : additional ~ *adv* **1** : in addition **2** : to a greater degree ~ *n* **1** : greater quantity **2** : additional amount ~ *pron* : additional ones

mo·rel \mə'rel\ *n* : pitted edible mushroom

more·over \mōr'ōvər\ *adv* : in addition

mo·res \'mȯr,āz, -ēz\ *n, pl* : customs

morgue \'mȯrg\ *n* : temporary holding place for dead bodies

mor·i·bund \'mȯrə,bənd\ *adj* : dying

morn \'mȯrn\ *n* : morning

morn·ing \'mȯrniŋ\ *n* : time from sunrise to noon

mo·ron \'mȯr,än\ *n* **1** : mentally retarded person **2** : very stupid person —**mo·ron·ic** \mə'ränik\ *adj* —**mo·ron·i·cal·ly** *adv*

mo·rose \mə'rōs\ *adj* : sullen —**mo·rose·ly** *adv* —**mo·rose·ness** *n*

mor·phine \'mȯr,fēn\ *n* : addictive painkilling drug

mor·row \'märō\ *n* : next day

Morse code \'mȯrs-\ *n* : code of dots and dashes or long and short sounds used for transmitting messages

mor·sel \'mȯrsəl\ *n* : small piece or quantity

mor·tal \'mȯrtᵊl\ *adj* **1** : causing or subject to death **2** : extreme —**mortal** *n* —**mor·tal·i·ty** \mȯr'talətē\ *n* —**mor·tal·ly** \'mȯrtᵊlē\ *adv*

mor·tar \'mȯrtər\ *n* **1** : strong bowl **2** : short-barreled cannon **3** : masonry material used to cement bricks or stones in place —**mortar** *vb*

mort·gage \'mȯrgij\ *n* : transfer of property rights as security for a loan —**mortgage** *vb* —**mort·gag·ee** \,mȯr-

gi'jē\ *n* —**mort·ga·gor** \,mȯrgi'jȯr\ *n*

mor·ti·fy \'mȯrtə,fī\ *vb* **-fied; -fy·ing** **1** : subdue by abstinence or self-inflicted pain **2** : humiliate —**mor·ti·fi·ca·tion** \,mȯrtəfə'kāshən\ *n*

mor·tu·ary \'mȯrchə,werē\ *n, pl* **-ar·ies** : place where dead bodies are kept until burial

mo·sa·ic \mō'zāik\ *n* : inlaid stone decoration —**mosaic** *adj*

Mos·lem \'mäzləm\ *var of* MUSLIM

mosque \'mäsk\ *n* : building where Muslims worship

mos·qui·to \mə'skētō\ *n, pl* **-toes** : biting bloodsucking insect

moss \'mȯs\ *n* : green seedless plant —**mossy** *adj*

most \'mōst\ *adj* **1** : majority of **2** : greatest ~ *adv* : to the greatest or a very great degree ~ *n* : greatest amount ~ *pron* : greatest number or part

-most \,mōst\ *adj suffix* : most : most toward

most·ly \'mōstlē\ *adv* : mainly

mote \'mōt\ *n* : small particle

mo·tel \mō'tel\ *n* : hotel with rooms accessible from the parking lot

moth \'mȯth\ *n* : small pale insect related to the butterflies

moth·er \'məthər\ *n* **1** : female parent **2** : source ~ *vb* **1** : give birth to **2** : cherish or protect —**moth·er·hood** \-,húd\ *n* —**moth·er·land** \-,land\ *n* —**moth·er·less** *adj* —**moth·er·ly** *adj*

mother–in–law *n, pl* **mothers–in–law** : spouse's mother

mo·tif \mō'tēf\ *n* : dominant theme

mo·tion \'mōshən\ *n* **1** : act or instance of moving **2** : proposal for action ~ *vb* : direct by a movement —**motion·less** *adj* —**mo·tion·less·ly** *adv* —**mo·tion·less·ness** *n*

motion picture *n* : movie

mo·ti·vate \'mōtə,vāt\ *vb* **-vat·ed; -vat·ing** : provide with a motive —**mo·ti·va·tion** \,mōtə'vāshən\ *n* —**mo·ti·va·tor** \'mōtə,vātər\ *n*

mo·tive \'mōtiv\ *n* : cause of a person's action ~ *adj* **1** : moving to action **2** : relating to motion —**mo·tive·less** *adj*

mot·ley \'mätlē\ *adj* : of diverse colors or elements

mo·tor \'mōtər\ *n* : unit that supplies power or motion ~ *vb* : travel by automobile —**mo·tor·ist** \-ist\ n —**mo·tor·ize** \'mōtə,rīz\ vb

mo·tor·bike n : lightweight motorcycle

mo·tor·boat n : engine-driven boat

mo·tor·car n : automobile

mo·tor·cy·cle n : 2-wheeled automotive vehicle —**mo·tor·cy·clist** n

mo·tor·truck n : automotive truck

mot·tle \'mät³l\ vb -**tled**; -**tling** : mark with spots of different color

mot·to \'mätō\ n, pl -**toes** : brief guiding rule

mould \'mōld\ var of MOLD

mound \'maůnd\ n : pile (as of earth)

¹**mount** \'maůnt\ n : mountain

²**mount** vb 1 : increase in amount 2 : get up on 3 : put in position ~ n 1 : frame or support 2 : horse to ride —**mount·able** adj —**mount·er** n

moun·tain \'maůnt³n\ n : elevated land higher than a hill —**moun·tain·ous** \'maůnt³nəs\ adj —**moun·tain·top** n

moun·tain·eer \,maůnt³n'ir\ n : mountain resident or climber

moun·te·bank \'maůnti,bank\ n : impostor

mourn \'mōrn\ vb : feel or express grief —**mourn·er** n —**mourn·ful** \-fəl\ adj —**mourn·ful·ly** adv —**mourn·ful·ness** n —**mourn·ing** n

mouse \'maůs\ n, pl **mice** \'mīs\ 1 : small rodent 2 : device for controlling cursor movement on a computer display —**mouse·trap** n or vb —**mousy**, **mous·ey** \'maůsē, -zē\ adj

mousse \'müs\ n 1 : light chilled dessert 2 : foamy hair-styling preparation

mous·tache \'məs,tash, məs'tash\ var of MUSTACHE

mouth \'maůth\ n : opening through which an animal takes in food ~ \'maůth\ vb 1 : speak 2 : repeat without comprehension or sincerity 3 : form soundlessly with the lips —**mouthed** \'maůthd, 'maůtht\ adj —**mouth·ful** \-,fůl\ n

mouth·piece n 1 : part (as of a musical instrument) held in or to the mouth 2 : spokesman

mou·ton \'mü,tän\ n : processed sheepskin

move \'müv\ vb **moved**; **mov·ing** 1 : go or cause to go to another point 2 : change residence 3 : change or cause to change position 4 : take or cause to take action 5 : make a formal request 6 : stir the emotions ~ n 1 : act or instance of moving 2 : step taken

to achieve a goal —**mov·able**, **move·able** \-əbəl\ adj —**move·ment** n —**mov·er** n

mov·ie \'müvē\ n : projected picture in which persons and objects seem to move

¹**mow** \'maů\ n : part of a barn where hay or straw is stored

²**mow** \'mō\ vb **mowed**; **mowed** or **mown** \'mōn\; **mow·ing** : cut with a machine —**mow·er** n

Mr. \'mistər\ n, pl **Messrs.** \'mesərz\ — conventional title for a man

Mrs. \'misəz, -əs, esp South 'mizəz, -əs\ n, pl **Mes·dames** \mā'däm, -'dam\ — conventional title for a married woman

Ms. \'miz\ — conventional title for a woman

much \'məch\ adj **more** \'mōr\; **most** \'mōst\ : great in quantity, extent, or degree ~ adv **more**; **most** : to a great degree or extent ~ n : great quantity, extent, or degree

mu·ci·lage \'myüsəlij\ n : weak glue

muck \'mək\ n : manure, dirt, or mud —**mucky** adj

mu·cus \'myükəs\ n : slippery protective secretion of membranes (**mucous membranes**) lining body cavities —**mu·cous** \-kəs\ adj

mud \'məd\ n : soft wet earth —**mud·di·ly** \'məd³lē\ adv —**mud·di·ness** \-ēnəs\ n —**mud·dy** adj or vb

mud·dle \'məd³l\ vb -**dled**; -**dling** 1 : make, be, or act confused 2 : make a mess of —**muddle** n —**mud·dle·head·ed** \,məd³l'hedəd\ adj

mu·ez·zin \mü'ez³n, myü-\ n : Muslim who calls the hour of daily prayer

¹**muff** \'məf\ n : tubular hand covering

²**muff** vb : bungle —**muff** n

muf·fin \'məfən\ n : soft cake baked in a cup-shaped container

muf·fle \'məfəl\ vb -**fled**; -**fling** 1 : wrap up 2 : dull the sound of —**muf·fler** \'məflər\ n

muf·ti \'məftē\ n : civilian clothes

¹**mug** \'məg\ n : drinking cup ~ vb -**gg**- : make faces

²**mug** vb -**gg**- : assault with intent to rob —**mugger** n

mug·gy \'məgē\ adj -**gi·er**; -**est** : hot and humid —**mug·gi·ness** n

Mu·ham·mad·an \mō'hamədən, -'häm-\; mü-\ n : Muslim —**Mu·ham·mad·an·ism** \-,izəm\ n

mu·lat·to \mü'lätō, -'lat-\ n, pl -**toes** or

-tos : person of mixed black and white ancestry

mul·ber·ry \'məl,berē\ *n* : tree with small edible fruit

mulch \'məlch\ *n* : protective ground covering —**mulch** *vb*

mulct \'məlkt\ *n or vb* : fine

¹mule \'myül\ *n* **1** : offspring of a male ass and a female horse **2** : stubborn person —**mul·ish** \'myülish\ *adj* —**mul·ish·ly** *adv* —**mul·ish·ness** *n*

²mule *n* : backless shoe

mull \'məl\ *vb* : ponder

mul·let \'mələt\ *n, pl* **-let** *or* **-lets** : marine food fish

multi- *comb form* **1** : many or multiple **2** : many times over

multiarmed	multimember
multibarreled	multimillion
multibillion	multimillionaire
multibranched	multipart
multibuilding	multipartite
multicenter	multiparty
multichambered	multiplant
multichannel	multipolar
multicolored	multiproblem
multicounty	multiproduct
multicultural	multipurpose
multidimen-	multiracial
sional	multiroom
multidirectional	multisense
multidisciplin-	multiservice
ary	multisided
multidiscipline	multispeed
multidivisional	multistage
multifaceted	multistep
multifamily	multistory
multifilament	multisyllabic
multifunction	multitalented
multifunctional	multitrack
multigrade	multiunion
multiheaded	multiunit
multihospital	multiuse
multihued	multivitamin
multilane	multiwarhead
multilevel	multiyear
multimedia	

mul·ti·far·i·ous \,məltə'farēəs\ *adj* : diverse

mul·ti·lat·er·al \,məlti'latərəl, -,tī-\ *adj* : having many sides or participants

mul·ti·lin·gual \-'liŋgwəl\ *adj* : knowing or using several languages —**mul·ti·lin·gual·ism** \-gwə,lizəm\ *n*

mul·ti·na·tion·al \-'nashənəl\ *adj* **1** : re-

lating to several nations or nationalities **2** : having divisions in several countries —**multinational** *n*

mul·ti·ple \'məltəpəl\ *adj* **1** : several or many **2** : various ~ *n* : product of one number by another

multiple sclerosis \-sklə'rōsəs\ *n* : brain or spinal disease affecting muscle control

mul·ti·pli·ca·tion \,məltəplə'kāshən\ *n* **1** : increase **2** : short method of repeated addition

mul·ti·plic·i·ty \,məltə'plisətē\ *n, pl* **-ties** : great number or variety

mul·ti·ply \'məltə,plī\ *vb* **-plied; -ply·ing 1** : increase in number **2** : perform multiplication —**mul·ti·pli·er** \-,plī-ər\ *n*

mul·ti·tude \'məltə,tüd, -,tyüd\ *n* : great number —**mul·ti·tu·di·nous** \,məltə-'tüd°nəs, -'tyü-\ *adj*

¹mum \'məm\ *adj* : silent

²mum *n* : chrysanthemum

mum·ble \'məmbəl\ *vb* **-bled; -bling** : speak indistinctly —**mumble** *n* —**mum·bler** *n*

mum·mer \'məmər\ *n* **1** : actor esp. in a pantomime **2** : disguised merrymaker —**mum·mery** *n*

mum·my \'məmē\ *n, pl* **-mies** : embalmed body —**mum·mi·fi·ca·tion** \,məmifə'kāshən\ *n* —**mum·mi·fy** \'məmi,fī\ *vb*

mumps \'məmps\ *n sing or pl* : virus disease with swelling esp. of the salivary glands

munch \'mənch\ *vb* : chew

mun·dane \,mən'dān, 'mən,-\ *adj* **1** : relating to the world **2** : lacking concern for the ideal or spiritual — **mun·dane·ly** *adv*

mu·nic·i·pal \myü'nisəpəl\ *adj* : of or relating to a town or city —**mu·nic·i·pal·i·ty** \myü,nisə'palətē\ *n*

mu·nif·i·cent \myü'nifəsənt\ *adj* : generous —**mu·nif·i·cence** \-səns\ *n*

mu·ni·tion \myü'nishən\ *n* : armaments

mu·ral \'myürəl\ *adj* : relating to a wall ~ *n* : wall painting —**mu·ral·ist** *n*

mur·der \'mərdər\ *n* : unlawful killing of a person ~ *vb* : commit a murder —**murderer** *n* —**mur·der·ess** \-əs\ *n* —**mur·der·ous** \-əs\ *adj* —**mur·der·ous·ly** *adv*

murk \'mərk\ *n* : darkness —**murk·i·ly** \'mərkəlē\ *adv* —**murk·i·ness** \-kē-nəs\ *n* —**murky** *adj*

mur·mur \'mərmər\ *n* **1** : muttered

complaint **2** : low indistinct sound — **murmur** vb — **mur·mur·er** n — **mur·mur·ous** adj

mus·ca·tel \ˌməskəˈtel\ n : sweet wine

mus·cle \ˈməsəl\ n **1** : body tissue capable of contracting to produce motion **2** : strength ~ vb **-cled; -cling** : force one's way — **mus·cled** adj — **mus·cu·lar** \ˈməskyələr\ adj — **mus·cu·lar·i·ty** \ˌməskyəˈlarətē\ n

muscular dystrophy n : disease marked by progressive wasting of muscles

mus·cu·la·ture \ˈməskyələˌchu̇r\ n : bodily muscles

¹**muse** \ˈmyüz\ vb **mused; mus·ing** : ponder — **mus·ing·ly** adv

²**muse** n : source of inspiration

mu·se·um \myu̇ˈzēəm\ n : institution displaying objects of interest

mush \ˈməsh\ n **1** : corn meal boiled in water or something of similar consistency **2** : sentimental nonsense — **mushy** adj

mush·room \ˈməshˌru̇m, -ˌru̇m\ n : cap-like organ of a fungus ~ vb : grow rapidly

mu·sic \ˈmyüzik\ n : vocal or instrumental sounds — **mu·si·cal** \-zikəl\ adj or n — **mu·si·cal·ly** adv

mu·si·cian \myu̇ˈzishən\ n : composer or performer of music — **mu·si·cian·ly** adj — **mu·si·cian·ship** n

musk \ˈməsk\ n : strong-smelling substance from an Asiatic deer used in perfume — **musk·i·ness** \ˈməskēnəs\ n — **musky** adj

mus·kel·lunge \ˈməskəˌlənj\ n, pl **-lunge** : large No. American pike

mus·ket \ˈməskət\ n : former shoulder firearm — **mus·ke·teer** \ˌməskəˈtir\ n

musk·mel·on \ˈməskˌmelən\ n : small edible melon

musk-ox \ˈməskˌäks\ n : shaggy-coated wild ox of the arctic

musk·rat \-ˌrat\ n, pl **-rat** or **-rats** : No. American aquatic rodent

Mus·lim \ˈməzləm, ˈmu̇s-, ˈmu̇z-\ n : adherent of Islam — **Muslim** adj

mus·lin \ˈməzlən\ n : cotton fabric

muss \ˈməs\ n : untidy state ~ vb : disarrange — **muss·i·ly** \ˈməsəlē\ adv — **muss·i·ness** \-ēnəs\ n — **mussy** adj

mus·sel \ˈməsəl\ n : edible mollusk

must \ˈməst\ vb —used as an auxiliary esp. to express a command, obligation, or necessity ~ \ˈməst\ n : something necessary

mus·tache \ˈməsˌtash, məsˈ-\ n : hair of the human upper lip

mus·tang \ˈməsˌtaŋ\ n : wild horse of Western America

mus·tard \ˈməstərd\ n : pungent yellow seasoning

mus·ter \ˈməstər\ vb **1** : assemble **2** : rouse ~ n : assembled group

musty \ˈməstē\ adj **mus·ti·er; -est** : stale — **mus·ti·ly** adv — **mus·ti·ness** n

mu·ta·ble \ˈmyütəbəl\ adj : changeable — **mu·ta·bil·i·ty** \ˌmyütəˈbilətē\ n

mu·tant \ˈmyütᵊnt\ adj : relating to or produced by mutation — **mutant** n

mu·tate \ˈmyüˌtāt\ vb **-tat·ed; -tat·ing** : undergo mutation — **mu·ta·tive** \ˈmyüˌtātiv, ˈmyütət-\ adj

mu·ta·tion \myu̇ˈtāshən\ n : change in a hereditary character — **mu·ta·tion·al** adj

mute \ˈmyüt\ adj **mut·er; mut·est 1** : unable to speak **2** : silent ~ n **1** : one who is mute **2** : muffling device ~ vb **mut·ed; mut·ing** : muffle — **mute·ly** adv — **mute·ness** n

mu·ti·late \ˈmyütᵊlˌāt\ vb **-lat·ed; -lat·ing** : damage seriously (as by cutting off or altering an essential part) — **mu·ti·la·tion** \ˌmyütᵊlˈāshən\ n — **mu·ti·la·tor** \ˈmyütᵊlˌātər\ n

mu·ti·ny \ˈmyütᵊnē\ n, pl **-nies** : rebellion — **mu·ti·neer** \ˌmyütᵊnˈir\ n — **mu·ti·nous** \ˈmyütᵊnəs\ adj — **mu·ti·nous·ly** adv — **mutiny** vb

mutt \ˈmət\ n : mongrel

mut·ter \ˈmətər\ vb **1** : speak indistinctly or softly **2** : grumble — **mutter** n

mut·ton \ˈmətᵊn\ n : flesh of a mature sheep — **mut·tony** adj

mu·tu·al \ˈmyüchəwəl\ adj **1** : given or felt by one another in equal amount **2** : common — **mu·tu·al·ly** adv

muz·zle \ˈməzəl\ n **1** : nose and jaws of an animal **2** : muzzle covering to immobilize an animal's jaws **3** : discharge end of a gun ~ vb **-zled; -zling** : restrain with or as if with a muzzle

my \ˈmī\ adj **1** : relating to me or myself **2** —used interjectionally esp. to express surprise

my·nah, my·na \ˈmīnə\ n : dark crested Asian bird

my·o·pia \mīˈōpēə\ n : nearsightedness — **my·o·pic** \-ˈōpik, -ˈäpik\ adj — **my·o·pi·cal·ly** adv

myr·i·ad \ˈmirēəd\ n : indefinitely large number — **myriad** adj

myrrh \'mər\ *n* : aromatic plant gum

myr·tle \'mərt³l\ *n* : shiny evergreen

my·self \mī'self\ *pron* : I, me —used reflexively or for emphasis

mys·tery \'mistərē\ *n, pl* **-ter·ies 1** : religious truth **2** : something not understood **3** : puzzling or secret quality or state —**mys·te·ri·ous** \mis'tirēəs\ *adj* —**mys·te·ri·ous·ly** *adv* —**mys·te·ri·ous·ness** *n*

mys·tic \'mistik\ *adj* : mystical or mysterious ~ *n* : one who has mystical experiences —**mys·ti·cism** \-tə-,sizəm\ *n*

mys·ti·cal \'mistikəl\ *adj* **1** : spiritual **2** : relating to direct communion with God —**mys·ti·cal·ly** *adj*

mys·ti·fy \'mistə,fī\ *vb* **-fied; -fy·ing** : perplex —**mys·ti·fi·ca·tion** \,mistəfə'kāshən\ *n*

mys·tique \mis'tēk\ *n* : aura of mystery surrounding something

myth \'mith\ *n* **1** : legendary narrative explaining a belief or phenomenon **2** : imaginary person or thing —**myth·i·cal** \-ikəl\ *adj*

my·thol·o·gy \mith'äləjē\ *n, pl* **-gies** : body of myths —**myth·o·log·i·cal** \,mithə'läjikəl\ *adj* —**my·thol·o·gist** \mith'äləjist\ *n*

N

n \'en\ *n, pl* **n's** *or* **ns** \'enz\ : 14th letter of the alphabet

nab \'nab\ *vb* **-bb-** : seize or arrest

na·dir \'nā,dir, 'nādər\ *n* : lowest point

¹nag \'nag\ *n* : old or decrepit horse

²nag *vb* **-gg- 1** : complain **2** : scold or urge continually **3** : be persistently annoying ~ *n* : one who nags habitually

na·iad \'nāəd, 'nī-, -,ad\ *n, pl* **-iads** *or* **-ia·des** \-ə,dēz\ : mythological water nymph

nail \'nāl\ *n* **1** : horny sheath at the end of each finger and toe **2** : pointed metal fastener ~ *vb* : fasten with a nail —**nail·er** *n*

na·ive, na·ïve \nä'ēv\ *adj* **-iv·er; -est 1** : innocent and unsophisticated **2** : easily deceived —**na·ive·ly** *adv* —**na·ive·ness** *n*

na·ïve·té \,nä,ēvə'tā, nä'ēvə,-\ *n* : quality or state of being naive

na·ked \'nākəd, 'nekəd\ *adj* **1** : having no clothes on **2** : uncovered **3** : plain or obvious **4** : unaided —**na·ked·ly** *adv* —**na·ked·ness** *n*

nam·by–pam·by \,nambē'pambē\ *adj* : weak or indecisive

name \'nām\ *n* **1** : word by which a person or thing is known **2** : disparaging word for someone **3** : distinguished reputation ~ *vb* **named; nam·ing 1** : give a name to **2** : mention or identify by name **3** : nominate or appoint ~ *adj* **1** : relating to a name **2** : prominent —**name·able** *adj* —**name·less** *adj* —**name·less·ly** *adv*

name·ly \'nāmlē\ *adv* : that is to say

name·sake \-,sāk\ *n* : one named after another

¹nap \'nap\ *vb* **-pp- 1** : sleep briefly **2** : be off guard ~ *n* : short sleep

²nap *n* : soft downy surface —**nap·less** *adj* —**napped** \'napt\ *adj*

na·palm \'nā,pälm, -,päm\ *n* : gasoline in the form of a jelly

nape \'nāp, 'nap\ *n* : back of the neck

naph·tha \'nafthə\ *n* : flammable solvent

nap·kin \'napkən\ *n* : small cloth for use at the table

nar·cis·sism \'närsə,sizəm\ *n* : self-love —**nar·cis·sist** \-sist\ *n or adj* —**nar·cis·sis·tic** \,närsə'sistik\ *adj*

nar·cis·sus \när'sisəs\ *n, pl* **-cis·sus** *or* **-cis·sus·es** *or* **-cis·si** \-'sis,ī, -,ē\ : plant with flowers usu. borne separately

nar·cot·ic \när'kätik\ *n* : painkilling addictive drug —**narcotic** *adj*

nar·rate \'nar,āt\ *vb* **nar·rat·ed; nar·rat·ing** : tell (a story) —**nar·ra·tion** \na'rāshən\ *n* —**nar·ra·tive** \'narətiv\ *n or adj* —**nar·ra·tor** \'nar,ātər\ *n*

nar·row \'narō\ *adj* **1** : of less than standard width **2** : limited **3** : not liberal **4** : barely successful ~ *vb* : make narrow—**nar·row·ly** *adv* —**nar·row·ness** *n*

nar·row–mind·ed \,narō'mīndəd\ *adj* : shallow, provincial, or bigoted

nar·rows \'narōz\ *n pl* : narrow passage

nar·whal \'när,hwäl, 'närwəl\ *n* : sea mammal with a tusk

nasal \'nāzəl\ *adj* : relating to or uttered through the nose —**na·sal·ly** *adv*

nas·tur·tium \nə'stərshəm, na-\ *n* : herb with showy flowers

nas·ty \'nastē\ *adj* **nas·ti·er; -est** 1 : filthy 2 : indecent 3 : malicious or spiteful 4 : difficult or disagreeable 5 : unfair —**nas·ti·ly** \'nastəlē\ *adv* —**nas·ti·ness** \-tēnəs\ *n*

na·tal \'nāt³l\ *adj* : relating to birth

na·tion \'nāshən\ *n* 1 : people of similar characteristics 2 : community with its own territory and government —**na·tion·al** \'nashənəl\ *adj or n* —**na·tion·al·ly** *adv* —**na·tion·hood** *n* —**na·tion·wide** *adj*

na·tion·al·ism \'nashənəl,izəm\ *n* : devotion to national interests, unity, and independence —**na·tion·al·ist** \-ist\ *n or adj* —**na·tion·al·is·tic** \,nashənəl'istik\

na·tion·al·i·ty \,nashə'nalətē\ *n, pl* **-ties** 1 : national character 2 : membership in a nation 3 : political independence 4 : ethnic group

na·tion·al·ize \'nashənəl,īz\ *vb* **-ized; -iz·ing** 1 : make national 2 : place under government control —**na·tion·al·i·za·tion** \,nashənələ'zāshən\ *n*

na·tive \'nātiv\ *adj* 1 : belonging to a person at or by way of birth 2 : born or produced in a particular place ~ *n* : one who belongs to a country by birth

Na·tiv·i·ty \nə'tivətē, nā-\ *n, pl* **-ties** 1 : birth of Christ 2 *not cap* : birth

nat·ty \'natē\ *adj* **-ti·er; -est** : smartly dressed —**nat·ti·ly** \'nat³lē\ *adv* —**nat·ti·ness** \-ēnəs\ *n*

nat·u·ral \'nachərəl\ *adj* 1 : relating to or determined by nature 2 : not artificial 3 : simple and sincere 4 : lifelike ~ *n* : one having an innate talent —**nat·u·ral·ness** *n*

nat·u·ral·ism \'nachərə,lizəm\ *n* : realism in art and literature —**nat·u·ral·is·tic** \,nachərə'listik\ *adj*

nat·u·ral·ist \-list\ *n* 1 : one who practices naturalism 2 : student of animals or plants

nat·u·ral·ize \-,līz\ *vb* **-ized; -iz·ing** 1 : become or cause to become established 2 : confer citizenship on —**nat·u·ral·i·za·tion** \,nachərələ'zāshən\ *n*

nat·u·ral·ly \'nachərəlē\ *adv* 1 : in a natural way 2 : as might be expected

na·ture \'nāchər\ *n* 1 : basic quality of something 2 : kind 3 : disposition 4 : physical universe 5 : natural environment

naught \'nȯt, 'nät\ *n* 1 : nothing 2 : zero

naugh·ty \'nȯtē, 'nät-\ *adj* **-ti·er; -est** 1 : disobedient or misbehaving 2 : improper —**naught·i·ly** \'nȯt³lē, 'nät-\ *adv* —**naught·i·ness** \-ēnəs\ *n*

nau·sea \'nȯzēə, -shə\ *n* 1 : sickness of the stomach with a desire to vomit 2 : extreme disgust —**nau·seous** \-shəs, -zēəs\ *adj*

nau·se·ate \'nȯzē,āt, -zhē-, -sē-, -shē-\ *vb* **-ated; -at·ing** : affect or become affected with nausea —**nau·se·at·ing·ly** \-,ātiŋlē\ *adv*

nau·ti·cal \'nȯtikəl\ *adj* : relating to ships and sailing —**nau·ti·cal·ly** *adv*

nau·ti·lus \'nȯt³ləs\ *n, pl* **-lus·es** *or* **-li** \-³l,ī, -,ē\ : sea mollusk with a spiral shell

na·val \'nāvəl\ *adj* : relating to a navy

nave \'nāv\ *n* : central part of a church

na·vel \'nāvəl\ *n* : depression in the abdomen

nav·i·ga·ble \'navigəbəl\ *adj* : capable of being navigated —**nav·i·ga·bil·i·ty** \,navigə'bilətē\ *n*

nav·i·gate \'navə,gāt\ *vb* **-gat·ed; -gat·ing** 1 : sail on or through 2 : direct the course of —**nav·i·ga·tion** \,navə'gāshən\ *n* —**nav·i·ga·tor** \'navə,gātər\ *n*

na·vy \'nāvē\ *n, pl* **-vies** 1 : fleet 2 : nation's organization for sea warfare

nay \'nā\ *adv* : no—used in oral voting ~ *n* : negative vote

Na·zi \'nätsē, 'nat-\ *n* : member of a German fascist party from 1933 to 1945 —**Nazi** *adj* —**Na·zism** \'nät,sizəm, 'nat-\, **Na·zi·ism** \-sē,izəm\ *n*

near \'nir\ *adv* : at or close to ~ *prep* : close to ~ *adj* 1 : not far away 2 : very much like ~ *vb* : approach —**near·ly** *adv* —**near·ness** *n*

near·by \nir'bī, 'nir,bī\ *adv or adj* : near

near·sight·ed \'nir'sītəd\ *adj* : seeing well at short distances only —**near·sight·ed·ly** *adv* —**near·sight·ed·ness** *n*

neat \'nēt\ *adj* 1 : not diluted 2 : tastefully simple 3 : orderly and clean —**neat** *adv* —**neat·ly** *adv* —**neat·ness** *n*

neb·u·la \'nebyələ\ *n, pl* **-lae** \-,lē, -,lī\

: large cloud of interstellar gas —
neb·u·lar \-lər\ adj

neb·u·lous \-ləs\ adj : indistinct

nec·es·sary \'nesə,serē\ n, pl **-saries**
1 : indispensable item — adj 1
: inevitable 2 : compulsory 3
: positively needed —**nec·es·sar·i·ly**
\,nesə'serəlē\ adv

ne·ces·si·tate \ni'sesə,tāt\ vb **-tat·ed;**
-tat·ing : make necessary

ne·ces·si·ty \ni'sesətē\ n, pl **-ties** 1 : very
great need 2 : something that is nec-
essary 3 : poverty 4 : circumstances
that cannot be changed

neck \'nek\ n 1 : body part connecting
the head and trunk 2 : part of a garment at the neck 3 : narrow part ~ vb
: kiss and caress —**necked** \'nekt\ adj

neck·er·chief \'nekərchəf, -,chēf\ n, pl
-chiefs \-chəfs, -,chēfs\ : cloth worn
tied about the neck

neck·lace \'nekləs\ n : ornament worn
around the neck

neck·tie n : ornamental cloth tied under
a collar

nec·ro·man·cy \'nekrə,mansē\ n : art of
conjuring up the spirits of the dead —
nec·ro·man·cer \-sər\ n

ne·cro·sis \nə'krōsəs, ne-\ n, pl **-cro·ses**
\-,sēz\ : death of body tissue

nec·tar \'nektər\ n : sweet plant secretion

nec·tar·ine \,nektə'rēn\ n : smooth-
skinned peach

née, nee \'nā\ adj—used to identify a
married woman by maiden name

need \'nēd\ n 1 : obligation 2 : lack of
something or what is lacking 3
: poverty ~ vb 1 : be in want 2 : have
cause for 3 : be under obligation —
need·ful \-fəl\ adj —**need·less** adj —
need·less·ly adv —**needy** adj

nee·dle \'nēd°l\ n 1 : pointed sewing implement or something like it 2
: movable bar in a compass 3 : hollow
instrument for injecting or withdrawing material ~ vb **-dled; -dling**
: incite to action by repeated gibes —
nee·dle·work \-,wərk\ n

nee·dle·point \'nēd°l,point\ n 1 : lace
fabric 2 : embroidery done on canvas —
needlepoint adj

ne·far·i·ous \ni'farēəs\ adj : very
wicked —**ne·far·i·ous·ly** adv

ne·gate \ni'gāt\ vb **-gat·ed; -gat·ing** 1
: deny 2 : nullify —**ne·ga·tion**
\-'gāshən\ n

neg·a·tive \'negətiv\ adj 1 : marked by

denial or refusal 2 : showing a lack of
something suspected or desirable 3
: less than zero 4 : having more electrons than protons 5 : having light and
shadow images reversed ~ n 1
: negative word or vote 2 : a negative
number 3 : negative photographic
image —**neg·a·tive·ly** adv —**neg-**
a·tive·ness n —**neg·a·tiv·i·ty** \,negə-
'tivətē\ n

ne·glect \ni'glekt\ vb 1 : disregard 2
: leave unattended to ~ n 1 : act of
neglecting 2 : condition of being ne-
glected —**ne·glect·ful** adj

neg·li·gee \,neglə'zhā\ n : woman's
loose robe

neg·li·gent \'neglijənt\ adj : marked by
neglect —**neg·li·gence** \-jəns\ n —
neg·li·gent·ly adv

neg·li·gi·ble \'neglijəbəl\ adj : insignificant

ne·go·ti·ate \ni'gōshē,āt\ vb **-at·ed; -at-**
ing 1 : confer with another to settle a
matter 2 : obtain cash for 3 : get
through successfully —**ne·go·tia·ble**
\-shəbəl, -shēə-\ adj—**ne·go·ti·a·tion**
\-,gōshē'āshən, -shē'ā-\ n —**ne·go-**
ti·a·tor \-'gōshē,ātər\ n

Ne·gro \'nēgrō\ n, pl **-groes** : member
of the black race —**Negro** adj —**Ne-**
groid \'nē,gròid\ n or adj, often not
cap

neigh \'nā\ n : cry of a horse —**neigh** vb

neigh·bor \'nābər\ n 1 : one living
nearby 2 : fellowman ~ vb : be near
or next to —**neigh·bor·hood** \-,húd\
n —**neigh·bor·li·ness** n —**neigh-**
bor·ly adv

nei·ther \'nēthər, 'nī-\ pron or adj : not
the one or the other ~ conj 1 : not
either 2 : nor

nem·e·sis \'neməsəs\ n, pl **-e·ses** \-ə,sēz\
1 : old and usu. frustrating rival 2
: retaliation

ne·ol·o·gism \nē'älə,jizəm\ n : new
word

ne·on \'nē,än\ n : gaseous colorless
chemical element that emits a reddish
glow in electric lamps —**neon** adj

neo·phyte \'nēə,fīt\ n : beginner

neph·ew \'nefyü, chiefly Brit 'nev-\ n : a
son of one's brother, sister, brother=
in-law, or sister-in-law

nep·o·tism \'nepə,tizəm\ n : favoritism
shown in hiring a relative

nerd \'nərd\ n : one who is not stylish
or socially at ease —**nerdy** adj

nerve \'nərv\ n 1 : strand of body tissue

that connects the brain with other parts of the body **2** : self-control **3** : daring **4** *pl* : nervousness **—nerved** \\'nərvd\ *adj* **—nerve·less** *adj*

ner·vous \\'nərvəs\ *adj* **1** : relating to or made up of nerves **2** : easily excited **3** : timid or fearful **—ner·vous·ly** *adv* **—ner·vous·ness** *n*

nervy \\'nərvē\ *adj* **nerv·i·er; -est** : insolent or presumptuous

-ness \nəs\ *n suffix* : condition or quality

nest \\'nest\ *n* **1** : shelter prepared by a bird for its eggs **2** : place where insects or fish) are laid and hatched **3** : snug retreat **4** : set of objects fitting one inside or under another ~ *vb* : build or occupy a nest

nes·tle \\'nesəl\ *vb* **-tled; -tling** : settle snugly (as in a nest)

¹net \\'net\ *n* : fabric with spaces between strands or something made of this ~ *vb* **-tt-** : cover with or catch in a net

²net *adj* : remaining after deductions ~ *vb* **-tt-** : have as profit

neth·er \\'nethər\ *adj* : situated below

net·tle \\'netᵊl\ *n* : coarse herb with stinging hairs ~ *vb* **-tled; -tling** : provoke or vex **—net·tle·some** *adj*

net·work *n* : system of crossing or connected elements

neu·ral \\'nurəl, 'nyur-\ *adj* : relating to a nerve

neu·ral·gia \nu̇'raljə, nyu̇-\ *n* : pain along a nerve **—neu·ral·gic** \-jik\ *adj*

neu·ri·tis \nu̇'rītəs, nyu̇-\ *n, pl* **-rit·i·des** \-'ritə,dēz\ *or* **-ri·tis·es** : inflammation of a nerve

neu·rol·o·gy \nu̇'räləjē, nyu̇-\ *n* : study of the nervous system **—neu·ro·log·i·cal** \,nurə'läjikəl, ,nyu̇r-\, **neu·ro·log·ic** \-ik\ *adj* **—neu·rol·o·gist** \nu̇'räləjist, nyu̇-\ *n*

neu·ro·sis \nu̇'rōsəs, nyu̇-\ *n, pl* **-ro·ses** \-,sēz\ : nervous disorder

neu·rot·ic \nu̇'rätik, nyu̇-\ *adj* : relating to neurosis ~ *n* : unstable person **—neu·rot·i·cal·ly** *adv*

neu·ter \\'nütər, 'nyü-\ *adj* : neither masculine nor feminine ~ *vb* : castrate or spay

neu·tral \-trəl\ *adj* **1** : not favoring either side **2** : being neither one thing nor the other **3** : not decided in color **4** : not electrically charged ~ *n* **1** : one that is neutral **2** : position of gears that are not engaged **—neu-**

tral·i·za·tion \,nütrələ'zāshən, ,nyü-\ *n* **—neu·tral·ize** \'nütrə,līz, 'nyü-\ *vb*

neu·tral·i·ty \nü'tralətē, nyü-\ *n* : state of being neutral

neu·tron \\'nü,trän, 'nyü-\ *n* : uncharged atomic particle

nev·er \\'nevər\ *adv* **1** : not ever **2** : not in any degree, way, or condition

nev·er·more *adv* : never again

nev·er·the·less *adv* : in spite of that

new \\'nü, 'nyü\ *adj* **1** : not old or familiar **2** : different from the former **3** : recently discovered or learned **4** : not accustomed **5** : refreshed or regenerated **6** : being such for the first time ~ *adv* : newly **—new·ish** *adj* **—new·ness** *n*

new·born *adj* **1** : recently born **2** : born anew ~ *n, pl* **-born** *or* **-borns** : newborn individual

new·ly \-lē\ *adv* : recently

news \\'nüz, 'nyüz\ *n* : report of recent events **—news·let·ter** *n* **—news·mag·a·zine** *n* **—news·man** \-,mən, -,man\ *n* **—news·pa·per** *n* **—news·pa·per·man** \-,man\ *n* **—news·stand** *n* **—news·wom·an** \-,wu̇mən\ *n* **—news·wor·thy** *adj*

news·cast \-,kast\ *n* : broadcast of news **—news·cast·er** \-,kastər\ *n*

news·print *n* : paper made from wood pulp

newsy \\'nüzē, 'nyü-\ *adj* **news·i·er; -est** : filled with news

newt \\'nüt, 'nyüt\ *n* : small salamander

New Year *n* : New Year's Day

New Year's Day *n* : January 1 observed as a legal holiday

next \\'nekst\ *adj* : immediately preceding or following ~ *adv* **1** : in the time or place nearest **2** : at the first time yet to come ~ *prep* : nearest to

nex·us \\'neksəs\ *n, pl* **-us·es** \-səsəz\ *or* **-us** \-səs, -,süs\ : connection

nib \\'nib\ *n* : pen point

nib·ble \\'nibəl\ *vb* **-bled; -bling** : bite gently or bit by bit ~ *n* : small bite

nice \\'nīs\ *adj* **nic·er; nic·est** **1** : fastidious **2** : very precise or delicate **3** : pleasing **4** : respectable **—nice·ly** *adv* **—nice·ness** *n*

nice·ty \\'nīsətē\ *n, pl* **-ties** **1** : dainty or elegant thing **2** : fine detail **3** : exactness

niche \\'nich\ *n* **1** : recess in a wall **2** : fitting place, work, or use

nick \\'nik\ *n* **1** : small broken area or

chip **2** : critical moment ~ *vb* : make a nick in

nick•el \'nikəl\ *n* **1** : hard silver-white metallic chemical element used in alloys **2** : U.S. 5-cent piece

nick•name \'nik,nām\ *n* : informal substitute name —**nickname** *vb*

nic•o•tine \'nikə,tēn\ *n* : poisonous and addictive substance in tobacco

niece \'nēs\ *n* : a daughter of one's brother, sister, brother-in-law, or sister-in-law

nig•gard•ly \'nigərdlē\ *adj* : stingy — **nig•gard** *n* —**nig•gard•li•ness** *n*

nig•gling \'nigəliŋ\ *adj* : petty and annoying

nigh \'nī\ *adv or adj or prep* : near

night \'nīt\ *n* **1** : period between dusk and dawn **2** : the coming of night — **night** —**night•ly** *adj or adv* — **night•time** *n*

night•clothes *n pl* : garments worn in bed

night•club \-,kləb\ *n* : place for drinking and entertainment open at night

night crawler *n* : earthworm

night•fall *n* : the coming of night

night•gown *n* : gown worn for sleeping

night•in•gale \'nīt²n,gāl, -iŋ-\ *n* : Old World thrush that sings at night

night•mare \'nīt,mar\ *n* : frightening dream —**nightmare** *adj* —**night•mar•ish** \-,marish\ *adj*

night•shade \'nīt,shād\ *n* : group of plants that include poisonous plants and food plants (as the potato and eggplant)

nil \'nil\ *n* : nothing

nim•ble \'nimbəl\ *adj* **-bler; -blest 1** : agile **2** : clever —**nim•ble•ness** *n* —**nim•bly** \-blē\ *adv*

nine \'nīn\ *n* **1** : one more than 8 **2** : 9th in a set or series —**nine** *adj or pron* —**ninth** \'nīnth\ *adj or n*

nine•pins *n* : bowling game using 9 pins

nine•teen \nīn'tēn\ *n* : one more than 18 —**nineteen** *adj or pron* —**nine•teenth** \-'tēnth\ *adj or n*

nine•ty \'nīntē\ *n, pl* **-ties** : 9 times 10 —**nine•ti•eth** \-ēəth\ *adj or n* — **ninety** *adj or pron*

nin•ny \'ninē\ *n, pl* **nin•nies** : fool

¹nip \'nip\ *vb* **-pp- 1** : catch hold of and squeeze tightly **2** : pinch or bite off **3** : destroy the growth or fulfillment of ~ *n* **1** : biting cold **2** : tang **3** : pinch or bite

²nip *n* : small quantity of liquor ~ *vb* **-pp-** : take liquor in nips

nip•per \'nipər\ *n* **1** : one that nips **2** *pl* : pincers **3** : small boy

nip•ple \'nipəl\ *n* : tip of the breast or something resembling it

nip•py \'nipē\ *adj* **-pier; -est 1** : pungent **2** : chilly

nir•va•na \nir'vänə\ *n* : state of blissful oblivion

nit \'nit\ *n* : egg of a parasitic insect

ni•ter \'nītər\ *n* : potassium nitrate used in gunpowder or fertilizer or in curing meat

ni•trate \'nī,trāt, -trət\ *n* : chemical salt used esp. in curing meat

ni•tric acid \'nītrik-\ *n* : liquid acid used in making dyes, explosives, and fertilizers

ni•trite \-,trīt\ *n* : chemical salt used in curing meat

ni•tro•gen \'nītrəjən\ *n* : tasteless odorless gaseous chemical element

ni•tro•glyc•er•in, ni•tro•glyc•er•ine \,nītrō'glisərən\ *n* : heavy oily liquid used as an explosive and as a blood-vessel relaxer

nit•wit \'nit,wit\ *n* : stupid person

no \'nō\ *adv* **1**—used to express the negative **2** : in no respect or degree **3** : not so **4**—used as an interjection of surprise or doubt ~ *adj* **1** : not any **2** : not a ~ *n, pl* **noes** *or* **nos** \'nōz\ **1** : refusal **2** : negative vote

no•bil•i•ty \nō'bilətē\ *n* **1** : quality or state of being noble **2** : class of people of noble rank

no•ble \'nōbəl\ *adj* **-bler; -blest 1** : illustrious **2** : aristocratic **3** : stately **4** : of outstanding character ~ *n* : nobleman —**no•ble•ness** *n* —**no•bly** *adv*

no•ble•man \-mən\ *n* : member of the nobility

no•ble•wom•an \-,wùmən\ *n* : a woman of noble rank

no•body \'nōbədē, -,bädē\ *pron* : no person ~ *n, pl* **-bod•ies** : person of no influence or importance

noc•tur•nal \näk'tərn²l\ *adj* : relating to, occurring at, or active at night

noc•turne \'näk,tərn\ *n* : dreamy musical composition

nod \'näd\ *vb* **-dd- 1** : bend the head downward or forward (as in bowing or going to sleep or as a sign of assent) **2** : move up and down **3** : show by a nod of the head —**nod** *n*

node \'nōd\ *n* : stem part from which a leaf arises —**nod•al** \-^əl\ *adj*

nod•ule \'näjül\ *n* : small lump or swelling —**nod•u•lar** \'näjələr\ *adj*

no•el \nō'el\ *n* **1** : Christmas carol **2** *cap* : Christmas season

noes *pl of* NO

nog•gin \'nägən\ *n* **1** : small mug **2** : person's head

no•how \'nō,haü\ *adv* : in no manner

noise \'nöiz\ *n* : loud or unpleasant sound ~ *vb* **noised; nois•ing** : spread by rumor —**noise•less** *adj* —**noise•less•ly** *adv* —**noise•mak•er** *n* —**nois•i•ly** \'nöizəlē\ *adv* —**nois•i•ness** \-zēnəs\ *n* —**noisy** \'nöizē\ *adj*

noi•some \'nöisəm\ *adj* : harmful or offensive

no•mad \'nō,mad\ *n* : one who has no permanent home —**nomad** *adj* —**no•mad•ic** \nō'madik\ *adj*

no•men•cla•ture \'nōmən,klāchər\ *n* : system of names

nom•i•nal \'nämən^əl\ *adj* **1** : being something in name only **2** : small or negligible —**nom•i•nal•ly** *adv*

nom•i•nate \'nämə,nāt\ *vb* **-nat•ed; -nat•ing** : propose or choose as a candidate —**nom•i•na•tion** \,nämə'nāshən\ *n*

nom•i•na•tive \'nämənətiv\ *adj* : relating to or being a grammatical case marking typically the subject of a verb —**nominative** *n*

nom•i•nee \,nämə'nē\ *n* : person nominated

non- \'nän, ,nän\ *prefix* **1** : not, reverse of, or absence of **2** : not important

nonabrasive	noncandidate	noncontrover-	nonliving
nonabsorbent	non-Catholic	sial	nonmagnetic
nonacademic	non-Christian	noncorrosive	nonmalignant
nonaccredited	nonchurchgoer	noncriminal	nonmedical
nonacid	noncitizen	noncritical	nonmember
nonaddictive	nonclassical	noncumulative	nonmetal
nonadhesive	nonclassified	noncurrent	nonmetallic
nonadjacent	noncombat	nondeductible	nonmilitary
nonadjustable	noncombatant	nondeferrable	nonmusical
nonaffiliated	noncombustible	nondegradable	nonnative
nonaggression	noncommercial	nondelivery	nonnegotiable
nonalcoholic	noncommunist	nondemocratic	nonobjective
nonaligned	noncompliance	nondenomina-	nonobservance
nonappearance	nonconflicting	tional	nonorthodox
nonautomatic	nonconforming	nondestructive	nonparallel
nonbeliever	nonconsecutive	nondiscrimina-	nonparticipant
nonbinding	nonconstructive	tion	nonparticipat-
nonbreakable	noncontagious	nondiscrimina-	ing
noncancerous	noncontrollable	tory	nonpaying
		noneducational	nonpayment
		nonelastic	nonperform-
		nonelected	ance
		nonelective	nonperishable
		nonelectric	nonphysical
		nonelectronic	nonpoisonous
		nonemotional	nonpolitical
		nonenforcement	nonpolluting
		nonessential	nonporous
		nonexclusive	nonpregnant
		nonexistence	nonproductive
		nonexistent	nonprofessional
		nonexplosive	nonprofit
		nonfat	nonracial
		nonfatal	nonradioactive
		nonfattening	nonrated
		nonfictional	nonrealistic
		nonflammable	nonrecurring
		nonflowering	nonrefillable
		nonfunctional	nonrefundable
		nongovernmen-	nonreligious
		tal	nonrenewable
		nongraded	nonrepresenta-
		nonhazardous	tive
		nonhereditary	nonresident
		nonindustrial	nonresponsive
		nonindustriali-	nonrestricted
		zed	nonreversible
		noninfectious	nonsalable
		noninflationary	nonscientific
		nonintegrated	nonscientist
		nonintellectual	nonsegregated
		noninterference	non-self-
		nonintoxicating	governing
		noninvasive	nonsexist
		non-Jewish	nonsexual
		nonlegal	nonsignificant
		nonlethal	nonskier
		nonliterary	nonsmoker

nonsmoking nontechnical

nonspeaking nontoxic

nonspecialist nontraditional

nonspecific nontransferable

nonstandard nontropical

nonstick nontypical

nonstop nonunion

nonstrategic nonuser

nonstudent nonvenomous

nonsugar nonverbal

nonsurgical nonvoter

nonswimmer nonwhite

nontaxable nonworker

nonteaching

non·age \'nänij, 'nōnij\ n : period of youth and esp. legal minority

nonce \'näns\ n : present occasion ~ adj : occurring, used, or made only once

non·cha·lant \,nänshə'länt\ adj : showing indifference **—non·cha·lance** \-'läns\ n **—non·cha·lant·ly** adv

non·com·mis·sioned officer \,nänkə-'mishənd-\ n : subordinate officer in the armed forces appointed from enlisted personnel

non·com·mit·tal \,nänkə'mit³l\ adj : indicating neither consent nor dissent

non·con·duc·tor n : substance that is a very poor conductor

non·con·form·ist n : one who does not conform to an established belief or mode of behavior **—non·con·for·mi·ty** n

non·de·script \,nändi'skript\ adj : lacking distinctive qualities

none \'nən\ pron : not any ~ adv : not at all

non·en·ti·ty n : one of no consequence

none·the·less \,nənthə'les\ adv : nevertheless

non·pa·reil \,nänpə'rel\ adj : having no equal ~ n 1 : one who has no equal 2 : chocolate candy disk

non·par·ti·san adj : not influenced by political party bias

non·per·son n : person without social or legal status

non·plus \,nän'pləs\ vb **-ss-** : perplex

non·pre·scrip·tion adj : available without a doctor's prescription

non·pro·lif·er·a·tion adj : aimed at ending increased use of nuclear arms

non·sched·uled adj : licensed to carry by air without a regular schedule

non·sense \'nän,sens, -səns\ n : foolish or meaningless words or actions —

non·sen·si·cal \nän'sensikəl\ adj — **non·sen·si·cal·ly** adv

non·sup·port n : failure in a legal obligation to provide for someone's needs

non·vi·o·lence n : avoidance of violence esp. in political demonstrations — **non·vi·o·lent** adj

noo·dle \'nüd³l\ n : ribbon-shaped food paste

nook \'nuk\ n 1 : inside corner 2 : private place

noon \'nün\ n : middle of the day — **noon** adj

noon·day \-,dā\ n : noon

no one pron : no person

noon·time n : noon

noose \'nüs\ n : rope loop that slips down tight

nor \nȯr\ conj : and not—used esp. after *neither* to introduce and negate the 2d member of a series

norm \'nȯrm\ n 1 : standard usu. derived from an average 2 : typical widespread practice or custom

nor·mal \'nȯrməl\ adj : average, regular, or standard **—nor·mal·cy** \-sē\ n **—nor·mal·i·ty** \nȯr'malətē\ n **—nor·mal·iza·tion** \,nȯrmələ'zāshən\ n — **nor·mal·ize** \'nȯrmə,līz\ vb **—nor·mal·ly** adv

north \'nȯrth\ adv : to or toward the north ~ adj : situated toward, at, or coming from the north ~ n 1 : direction to the left of one facing east 2 cap : regions to the north — **north·er·ly** \'nȯrtharlē\ adv or adj — **north·ern** \-ərn\ adj **—North·ern·er** n **—north·ern·most** \-,mōst\ adj — **north·ward** \-wərd\ adv or adj — **north·wards** \-wərdz\ adv

north·east \nȯrth'ēst\ n 1 : direction between north and east 2 cap : regions to the northeast **—northeast** adj or adv **—north·east·er·ly** \-ərlē\ adv or adj **—north·east·ern** \-ərn\ adj

northern lights n pl : aurora borealis

north pole n : northernmost point of the earth

north·west \-'west\ n 1 : direction between north and west 2 cap : regions to the northwest **—northwest** adj or adv **—north·west·er·ly** \-ərlē\ adv or adj **—north·west·ern** \-ərn\ adj

nose \'nōz\ n 1 : part of the face containing the nostrils 2 : sense of smell 3 : front part ~ vb **nosed; nos·ing** 1 : detect by smell 2 : push aside with the nose 3 : pry 4 : inch ahead —

nose·bleed n —**nosed** \'nōzd\ adj —
nose out vb : narrowly defeat

nose·gay \-‚gā\ n : small bunch of flowers

nos·tal·gia \nä'staljə, nə-\ n : wistful
yearning for something past —**nos·
tal·gic** \-jik\ adj

nos·tril \'nästrəl\ n : opening of the nose

nos·trum \-trəm\ n : questionable remedy

nosy, nos·ey \'nōzē\ adj **nos·i·er; -est**
: tending to pry

not \'nät\ adv—used to make a statement negative

no·ta·ble \'nōtəbəl\ adj 1 : noteworthy
2 : distinguished ~ n : notable person
—**no·ta·bil·i·ty** \‚nōtə'bilətē\ n —
no·ta·bly \'nōtəblē\ adv

no·ta·rize \'nōtə‚rīz\ vb **-rized; -riz·ing**
: attest as a notary public

no·ta·ry public \'nōtərē-\ n, pl **-ries
public** or **-ry publics** : public official
who attests writings to make them legally authentic

no·ta·tion \nō'tāshən\ n 1 : note 2 : act,
process, or method of marking things
down

notch \'näch\ n : V-shaped hollow —
notch vb

note \'nōt\ vb **not·ed; not·ing** 1 : notice
2 : write down ~ n 1 : musical tone
2 : written comment or record 3
: short informal letter 4 : notice or
heed —**note·book** n

not·ed \'nōtəd\ adj : famous

note·wor·thy \-‚wərthē\ adj : worthy of
special mention

noth·ing \'nəthiŋ\ pron 1 : no thing 2
: no part 3 : one of no value or importance ~ adv : not at all ~ n 1
: something that does not exist 2
: zero 3 : one of little or no importance —**noth·ing·ness** n

no·tice \'nōtəs\ n 1 : warning or announcement 2 : attention ~ vb **-ticed;
-tic·ing** : take notice of —**no·tice-
able** adj —**no·tice·ably** adv

no·ti·fy \'nōtə‚fī\ vb **-fied; -fy·ing** : give
notice of or to —**no·ti·fi·ca·tion**
\‚nōtəfə'kāshən\ n

no·tion \'nōshən\ n 1 : idea or opinion
2 : whim

no·to·ri·ous \nō'tōrēəs\ adj : widely and
unfavorably known —**no·to·ri·ety**
\‚nōtə'rīətē\ n —**no·to·ri·ous·ly** adv

not·with·stand·ing \‚nätwith'standiŋ,
-with-\ prep : in spite of ~ adv
: nevertheless ~ conj : although

nou·gat \'nügət\ n : nuts or fruit pieces
in a sugar paste

nought \'not, 'nät\ var of NAUGHT

noun \'naun\ n : word that is the name
of a person, place, or thing

nour·ish \'nərish\ vb : promote the
growth of —**nour·ish·ing** adj —
nour·ish·ment n

no·va \'nōvə\ n, pl **-vas** or **-vae** \-‚vē,
-‚vī\ : star that suddenly brightens and
then fades gradually

nov·el \'nävəl\ adj : new or strange ~ n
: long invented prose story —**nov-
el·ist** \-əlist\ n

nov·el·ty \'nävəltē\ n, pl **-ties** 1
: something new or unusual 2
: newness 3 : small manufactured article—usu. pl.

No·vem·ber \nō'vembər\ n : 11th month
of the year having 30 days

nov·ice \'nävəs\ n 1 : one preparing to
take vows in a religious order 2 : one
who is inexperienced or untrained

no·vi·tiate \nō'vishət, nə-\ n : period or
state of being a novice

now \'nau\ adv 1 : at the present time or
moment 2 : forthwith 3 : under these
circumstances ~ conj : in view of the
fact ~ n : present time

now·a·days \'nauə‚dāz\ adv : now

no·where \-‚hwer\ adv : not anywhere
—**nowhere** n

nox·ious \'näkshəs\ adj : harmful

noz·zle \'näzəl\ n : device to direct or
control a flow of fluid

nu·ance \'nü‚äns, 'nyü-\ n : subtle distinction or variation

nub \'nəb\ n 1 : knob or lump 2 : gist

nu·bile \'nü‚bīl, 'nyü-, -bəl\ adj 1 : of
marriageable condition or age 2
: sexually attractive

nu·cle·ar \'nüklēər, 'nyü-\ adj 1
: relating to the atomic nucleus or
atomic energy 2 : relating to a weapon
whose power is from a nuclear reaction

nu·cle·us \'nüklēəs, 'nyü-\ n, pl **-clei**
\-klē‚ī\ : central mass or part (as of a
cell or an atom)

nude \'nüd, 'nyüd\ adj **nud·er; nud·est**
: naked ~ n : nude human figure —
nu·di·ty \'nüdətē, 'nyü-\ n

nudge \'nəj\ vb **nudged; nudg·ing**
: touch or push gently —**nudge** n

nud·ism \'nüd‚izəm, 'nyü-\ n : practice
of going nude —**nud·ist** \'nüdist‚
'nyü-\ n

nug·get \'nəgət\ n : lump of gold

nui·sance \'nüs³ns, 'nyü-\ *n* : something annoying

null \'nəl\ *adj* : having no legal or binding force —**nul·li·ty** \'nələtē\ *n*

nul·li·fy \'nələ͵fī\ *vb* **-fied; -fy·ing** : make null or valueless —**nul·li·fi·ca·tion** \͵nələfə'kāshən\ *n*

numb \'nəm\ *adj* : lacking feeling — **numb** *vb* —**numb·ly** *adv* —**numb·ness** *n*

num·ber \'nəmbər\ *n* **1** : total of individuals taken together **2** : indefinite total **3** : unit of a mathematical system **4** : numeral **5** : one in a sequence ~ *vb* **1** : count **2** : assign a number to **3** : comprise in number —**num·ber·less** *adj*

nu·mer·al \'nümərəl, 'nyü-\ *n* : conventional symbol representing a number

nu·mer·a·tor \'nümə͵rātər, 'nyü-\ *n* : part of a fraction above the line

nu·mer·i·cal \nù'merikəl, nyü-\, **nu·mer·ic** \-'merik\ *adj* **1** : relating to numbers **2** : expressed in or involving numbers —**nu·mer·i·cal·ly** *adv*

nu·mer·ol·o·gy \͵nümə'räləjē, ͵nyü-\ *n* : occult study of numbers —**nu·mer·ol·o·gist** \-jist\ *n*

nu·mer·ous \'nümərəs, 'nyü-\ *adj* : consisting of a great number

nu·mis·mat·ics \͵nüməz'matiks, ͵nyü-\ *n* : study or collection of monetary objects —**nu·mis·mat·ic** \-ik\ *adj* — **nu·mis·ma·tist** \nü'mizmətist, nyü-\ *n*

num·skull \'nəm͵skəl\ *n* : stupid person

nun \'nən\ *n* : woman belonging to a religious order —**nun·nery** \-ərē\ *n*

nup·tial \'nəpshəl\ *adj* : relating to marriage or a wedding ~ *n* : marriage or wedding—usu. pl.

nurse \'nərs\ *n* **1** : one hired to care for children **2** : person trained to care for sick people ~ *vb* **nursed; nurs·ing 1** : suckle **2** : care for

nurs·ery \'nərsərē\ *n, pl* **-eries 1** : place where children are cared for **2** : place where young plants are grown

nursing home *n* : private establishment providing care for persons who are unable to care for themselves

nur·ture \'nərchər\ *n* **1** : training or upbringing **2** : food or nourishment ~ *vb* **-tured; -tur·ing 1** : care for or feed **2** : educate

nut \'nət\ *n* **1** : dry hard-shelled fruit or seed with a firm inner kernel **2** : metal block with a screw hole through it **3** : foolish, eccentric, or crazy person **4** : enthusiast —**nut·crack·er** *n* —**nut·shell** *n* —**nut·ty** *adj*

nut·hatch \'nət͵hach\ *n* : small bird

nut·meg \'nət͵meg, -͵māg\ *n* : nutlike aromatic seed of a tropical tree

nu·tri·ent \'nütrēənt, 'nyü-\ *n* : something giving nourishment — **nutrient** *adj*

nu·tri·ment \-trəmənt\ *n* : nutrient

nu·tri·tion \nù'trishən, nyü-\ *n* : act or process of nourishing esp. with food —**nu·tri·tion·al** \-'trishənəl\ *adj* — **nu·tri·tious** \-'trishəs\ *adj* —**nu·tri·tive** \'nütrətiv, 'nyü-\ *adj*

nuts \'nəts\ *adj* **1** : enthusiastic **2** : crazy

nuz·zle \'nəzəl\ *vb* **-zled; -zling 1** : touch with or as if with the nose **2** : snuggle

ny·lon \'nī͵län\ *n* **1** : tough synthetic material used esp. in textiles **2** *pl* : stockings made of nylon

nymph \'nimf\ *n* **1** : lesser goddess in ancient mythology **2** : girl **3** : immature insect

O

o \'ō\ *n, pl* **o's** *or* **os** \'ōz\ **1** : 15th letter of the alphabet **2** : zero

O *var of* OH

oaf \'ōf\ *n* : stupid or awkward person —**oaf·ish** \'ōfish\ *adj*

oak \'ōk\ *n, pl* **oaks** *or* **oak** : tree bearing

a thin-shelled nut or its wood —**oak·en** \'ōkən\ *adj*

oar \'ōr\ *n* : pole with a blade at the end used to propel a boat

oar·lock \-͵läk\ *n* : u-shaped device for holding an oar

oa·sis \ō'āsəs\ *n, pl* **oa·ses** \-,sēz\ : fertile area in a desert

oat \'ōt\ *n* : cereal grass or its edible seed —**oat·cake** *n* —**oat·en** \-ᵊn\ *adj* —**oat·meal** *n*

oath \'ōth\ *n, pl* **oaths** \'ōthz, 'ōths\ 1 : solemn appeal to God as a pledge of sincerity 2 : profane utterance

ob·du·rate \'äbdüret, -dyü-\ *adj* : stubbornly resistant —**ob·du·ra·cy** \-rəsē\ *n*

obe·di·ent \ō'bēdēənt\ *adj* : willing to obey —**obe·di·ence** \-əns\ *n* —**obe·di·ent·ly** *adv*

obei·sance \ō'bēsəns, -'bās-\ *n* : bow of respect or submission

obe·lisk \'äbə,lisk\ *n* : 4-sided tapering pillar

obese \ō'bēs\ *adj* : extremely fat —**obe·si·ty** \-'bēsətē\ *n*

obey \ō'bā\ *vb* **obeyed; obey·ing** 1 : follow the commands or guidance of 2 : behave in accordance with

ob·fus·cate \'äbfə,skāt\ *vb* **-cat·ed; -cat·ing** : confuse —**ob·fus·ca·tion** \,äbfəs'kāshən\ *n*

obit·u·ary \ō'bichə,werē\ *n, pl* **-ar·ies** : death notice

¹**ob·ject** \'äbjikt\ *n* 1 : something that may be seen or felt 2 : purpose 3 : noun or equivalent toward which the action of a verb is directed or which follows a preposition

²**ob·ject** \əb'jekt\ *vb* : offer opposition or disapproval —**ob·jec·tion** \-'jek-shən\ *n* —**ob·jec·tion·able** \-shə-nəbəl\ *adj* —**ob·jec·tion·ably** \-blē\ *adv* —**ob·jec·tor** \-'jektər\ *n*

ob·jec·tive \əb'jektiv\ *adj* 1 : relating to an object or end 2 : existing outside an individual's thoughts or feelings 3 : treating facts without distortion 4 : relating to or being a grammatical case marking objects ~ *n* : aim or end of action —**ob·jec·tive·ly** *adv* —**ob·jec·tive·ness** *n* —**ob·jec·tiv·i·ty** \,äb-jek'tivətē\ *n*

ob·li·gate \'äblə,gāt\ *vb* **-gat·ed; -gat·ing** : bind legally or morally —**ob·li·ga·tion** \,äblə'gāshən\ *n* —**oblig·a·to·ry** \ə'bligə,tōrē, 'äbligə-\ *adj*

oblige \ə'blīj\ *vb* **obliged; oblig·ing** 1 : compel 2 : do a favor for —**oblig·ing** *adj* —**oblig·ing·ly** *adv*

oblique \ō'blēk, -'blīk\ *adj* 1 : lying at a slanting angle 2 : indirect —**oblique-**

ly *adv* —**oblique·ness** *n* —**obliq·ui·ty** \-'blikwətē\ *n*

oblit·er·ate \ə'blitə,rāt\ *vb* **-at·ed; -at·ing** : completely remove or destroy —**oblit·er·a·tion** \-,blitə'rāshən\ *n*

obliv·i·on \ə'blivēən\ *n* 1 : state of having lost conscious awareness 2 : state of being forgotten

obliv·i·ous \-ēəs\ *adj* : not aware or mindful—with *to* or *of* —**obliv·i·ous·ly** *adv* —**obliv·i·ous·ness** *n*

ob·long \'äb,lȯŋ\ *adj* : longer in one direction than in the other with opposite sides parallel —**oblong** *n*

ob·lo·quy \'äbləkwē\ *n, pl* **-quies** 1 : strongly condemning utterance 2 : bad repute

ob·nox·ious \äb'näkshəs, əb-\ *adj* : repugnant —**ob·nox·ious·ly** *adv* —**ob·nox·ious·ness** *n*

oboe \'ōbō\ *n* : slender woodwind instrument with a reed mouthpiece —**obo·ist** \'o,bōist\ *n*

ob·scene \äb'sēn, əb-\ *adj* : repugnantly indecent —**ob·scene·ly** *adv* —**ob·scen·i·ty** \-'senətē\ *n*

ob·scure \äb'skyúr, əb-\ *adj* 1 : dim or hazy 2 : not well known 3 : vague ~ *vb* : make indistinct or unclear —**ob·scure·ly** *adv* —**ob·scu·ri·ty** \-'skyú-rətē\ *n*

ob·se·quies \'äbsəkwēz\ *n pl* : funeral or burial rite

ob·se·qui·ous \əb'sēkwēəs\ *adj* : excessively attentive or flattering —**ob·se·qui·ous·ly** *adv* —**ob·se·qui·ous·ness** *n*

ob·ser·va·to·ry \əb'zərvə,tōrē\ *n, pl* **-ries** : place for observing astronomical phenomena

ob·serve \əb'zərv\ *vb* **-served; -serv·ing** 1 : conform to 2 : celebrate 3 : see, watch, or notice 4 : remark —**ob·serv·able** *adj* —**ob·ser·vance** \-'zərvəns\ *n* —**ob·ser·vant** \-vənt\ *adj* —**ob·ser·va·tion** \,äbsər'vāshən, -zər-\ *n*

ob·sess \äb'ses\ *vb* : preoccupy intensely or abnormally —**ob·ses·sion** \äb-'seshən, əb-\ *n* —**ob·ses·sive** \-'sesiv\ *adj* —**ob·ses·sive·ly** *adv*

ob·so·les·cent \,äbsə'lesᵊnt\ *adj* : going out of use —**ob·so·les·cence** \-ᵊns\ *n*

ob·so·lete \,äbsə'lēt, 'äbsə-\ *adj* : no longer in use

ob·sta·cle \'äbstikəl\ *n* : something that stands in the way or opposes

ob·stet·rics \əb'stetriks\ *n sing or pl* : branch of medicine that deals with childbirth —**obstet·ric** \-rik\ *adj*, **ob·stet·ri·cal** \-rikəl\ *adj* —**ob·ste·tri·cian** \,äbstə'trishən\ *n*

ob·sti·nate \'äbstənət\ *adj* : stubborn — **ob·sti·na·cy** \-nəsē\ *n* —**ob·sti·nate·ly** *adv*

ob·strep·er·ous \əb'strepərəs\ *adj* : uncontrollably noisy or defiant — **ob·strep·er·ous·ness** *n*

ob·struct \əb'strəkt\ *vb* : block or impede —**ob·struc·tion** \-'strəkshən\ *n* —**ob·struc·tive** \-'strəktiv\ *adj* —**ob·struc·tor** \-tər\ *n*

ob·tain \əb'tān\ *vb* 1 : gain by effort 2 : be generally recognized —**ob·tain·able** *adj*

ob·trude \əb'trüd\ *vb* -**trud·ed**; -**trud·ing** 1 : thrust out 2 : intrude —**ob·tru·sion** \-'trüzhən\ *n* —**ob·tru·sive** \-'trüsiv\ *adj* —**ob·tru·sive·ly** *adv* —**ob·tru·sive·ness** *n*

ob·tuse \äb'tüs, əb-, -'tyüs\ *adj* 1 : slow-witted 2 : exceeding 90 but less than 180 degrees —**ob·tuse·ly** *adv* —**ob·tuse·ness** *n*

ob·verse \'äb,vərs, äb'-\ *n* : principal side (as of a coin)

ob·vi·ate \'äbvē,āt\ *vb* -**at·ed**; -**at·ing** : make unnecessary —**ob·vi·a·tion** \,äbvē'āshən\ *n*

ob·vi·ous \'äbvēəs\ *adj* : plain or unmistakable —**ob·vi·ous·ly** *adv* —**obvi·ous·ness** *n*

oc·ca·sion \ə'kāzhən\ *n* 1 : favorable opportunity 2 : cause 3 : time of an event 4 : special event ~ *vb* : cause —**oc·ca·sion·al** \-'kāzhənəl\ *adj* —**oc·ca·sion·al·ly** *adv*

oc·ci·den·tal \,äksə'dent³l\ *adj* : western —**Occidental** *n*

oc·cult \ə'kəlt, 'äk,əlt\ *adj* 1 : secret or mysterious 2 : relating to supernatural agencies —**oc·cult·ism** \-'kəl,tizəm\ *n* —**oc·cult·ist** \-tist\ *n*

oc·cu·pan·cy \'äkyəpənsē\ *n, pl* -**cies** : an occupying

oc·cu·pant \-pənt\ *n* : one who occupies

oc·cu·pa·tion \,äkyə'pāshən\ *n* 1 : vocation 2 : action or state of occupying —**oc·cu·pa·tion·al** \-shənəl\ *adj* —**oc·cu·pa·tion·al·ly** *adv*

oc·cu·py \'äkyə,pī\ *vb* -**pied**; -**py·ing** 1 : engage the attention of 2 : fill up 3 : take or hold possession of 4 : reside in —**oc·cu·pi·er** \-,pīər\ *n*

oc·cur \ə'kər\ *vb* -**rr-** 1 : be found or

met with 2 : take place 3 : come to mind

oc·cur·rence \ə'kərəns\ *n* : something that takes place

ocean \'ōshən\ *n* 1 : whole body of salt water 2 : very large body of water — **ocean·front** *n* —**ocean·go·ing** *adj* — **oce·an·ic** \,ōshē'anik\ *adj*

ocean·og·ra·phy \,ōshə'nägrəfē\ *n* : science dealing with the ocean — **ocean·og·ra·pher** \-fər\ *n* —**ocean·o·graph·ic** \-nə'grafik\ *adj*

oce·lot \'äsə,lät, 'ōsə-\ *n* : medium-sized American wildcat

ocher, ochre \'ōkər\ *n* : red or yellow pigment

o'·clock \ə'kläk\ *adv* : according to the clock

oc·ta·gon \'äktə,gän\ *n* : 8-sided polygon —**oc·tag·o·nal** \äk'tagən³l\ *adj*

oc·tave \'äktiv\ *n* : musical interval of 8 steps or the notes within this interval

Oc·to·ber \äk'tōbər\ *n* : 10th month of the year having 31 days

oc·to·pus \'äktəpəs\ *n, pl* -**pus·es** *or* -**pi** \-,pī\ : sea mollusk with 8 arms

oc·u·lar \'äkyələr\ *adj* : relating to the eye

oc·u·list \'äkyəlist\ *n* 1 : ophthalmologist 2 : optometrist

odd \'äd\ *adj* 1 : being only one of a pair or set 2 : not divisible by two without a remainder 3 : additional to what is usual or to the number mentioned 4 : queer —**odd·ly** *adv* —**odd·ness** *n*

odd·i·ty \'ädətē\ *n, pl* -**ties** : something odd

odds \'ädz\ *n pl* 1 : difference by which one thing is favored 2 : disagreement 3 : ratio between winnings and the amount of the bet

ode \'ōd\ *n* : solemn lyric poem

odi·ous \'ōdēəs\ *adj* : hated —**odi·ous·ly** *adv* —**odi·ous·ness** *n*

odi·um \'ōdēəm\ *n* 1 : merited loathing 2 : disgrace

odor \'ōdər\ *n* : quality that affects the sense of smell —**odor·less** *adj* — **odor·ous** *adj*

od·ys·sey \'ädəsē\ *n, pl* -**seys** : long wandering

o'er \'ōr\ *adv or prep* : OVER

of \'əv, 'äv\ *prep* 1 : from 2 : distinguished by 3 : because of 4 : made or written by 5 : made with, being, or containing 6 : belonging to or connected with 7 : about 8 : that is 9 : concerning 10 : before

off \ˈȯf\ adv 1 : from a place 2 : unattached or removed 3 : to a state of being no longer in use 4 : away from work 5 : at a distance in time or space ~ prep 1 : away from 2 : at the expense of 3 : not engaged in or abstaining from 4 : below the usual level of ~ adj 1 : not operating, up to standard, or correct 2 : remote 3 : provided for

of·fal \ˈȯfəl\ n 1 : waste 2 : viscera and trimmings of a butchered animal

of·fend \ə'fend\ vb 1 : sin or act in violation 2 : hurt, annoy, or insult —of·fend·er n

of·fense, of·fence \ə'fens, 'äf,ens\ n : attack, misdeed, or insult

of·fen·sive \ə'fensiv, 'äf,en-\ adj : causing offense ~ n : attack —of·fen·sive·ly adv —of·fen·sive·ness n

of·fer \ˈȯfər\ vb 1 : present for acceptance 2 : propose 3 : put up (an effort) ~ n 1 : proposal 2 : bid —of·fer·ing n

of·fer·to·ry \ˈȯfər,tōrē\ n, pl -ries : presentation of offerings or its musical accompaniment

off·hand adv or adj : without previous thought or preparation

of·fice \ˈȯfəs\ n 1 : position of authority (as in government) 2 : rite 3 : place where a business is transacted —of·fice·hold·er n

of·fi·cer \ˈȯfəsər\ n 1 : one charged with law enforcement 2 : one who holds an office of trust or authority 3 : one who holds a commission in the armed forces

of·fi·cial \ə'fishəl\ n : one in office ~ adj : authorized or authoritative —of·fi·cial·dom \-dəm\ n —of·fi·cial·ly adv

of·fi·ci·ant \ə'fishēənt\ n : clergy member who officiates at a religious rite

of·fi·ci·ate \ə'fishē,āt\ vb -at·ed; -at·ing : perform a ceremony or function

of·fi·cious \ə'fishəs\ adj : volunteering one's services unnecessarily —of·fi·cious·ly adv —of·fi·cious·ness n

off·ing \ˈȯfiŋ\ n : future

off·set \ˈȯf,set\ vb -set; -set·ting : provide an opposite or equaling effect to

off·shoot \ˈȯf,shüt\ n : outgrowth

off·shore adv : at a distance from the shore ~ adj : moving away from or situated off the shore

off·spring \ˈȯf,spriŋ\ n, pl offspring : one coming into being through animal or plant reproduction

of·ten \ˈȯfən, 'ȯft-\ adv : many times —of·ten·times, oft·times adv

ogle \ˈōgəl\ vb ogled; ogling : stare at lustily —ogle n —ogler \-ələr\ n

ogre \ˈōgər\ n 1 : monster 2 : dreaded person

oh \ˈō\ interj 1—used to express an emotion 2—used in direct address

ohm \ˈōm\ n : unit of electrical resistance —ohm·ic \ˈōmik\ adj —ohm·me·ter \ˈōm,mētər\ n

oil \ˈȯil\ n 1 : greasy liquid substance 2 : petroleum ~ vb : put oil in or on —oil·er n —oil·i·ness \ˈȯilēnəs\ n —oily \ˈȯilē\ adj

oil·cloth n : cloth treated with oil or paint and used for coverings

oil·skin n : oiled waterproof cloth

oink \ˈȯiŋk\ n : natural noise of a hog —oink vb

oint·ment \ˈȯintmənt\ n : oily medicinal preparation

OK or okay \ō'kā\ adv or adj : all right ~ vb OK'd or okayed; OK'·ing or okay·ing : approve ~ n : approval

okra \ˈōkrə, South also -krē\ n : leafy vegetable with edible green pods

old \ˈōld\ adj 1 : of long standing 2 : of a specified age 3 : relating to a past era 4 : having existed a long time —old·ish \ˈōldish\ adj

old·en \ˈōldən\ adj : of or relating to a bygone era

old-fash·ioned \-'fashənd\ adj 1 : out-of-date 2 : conservative

old maid n : spinster

old-tim·er \ˈōld'tīmər\ n 1 : veteran 2 : one who is old

ole·an·der \ˈōlē,andər\ n : poisonous evergreen shrub

oleo·mar·ga·rine \,ōlēō'märjərən\ n : margarine

ol·fac·to·ry \äl'faktərē, ōl-\ adj : relating to the sense of smell

oli·gar·chy \ˈälə,gärkē, 'ōlə-\ n, pl -chies 1 : government by a few people 2 : those holding power in an oligarchy —oli·garch \-,gärk\ n —oli·gar·chic \,älə'gärkik, ,ōlə-\, oli·gar·chi·cal \-kikəl\ adj

ol·ive \ˈäliv, -əv\ n 1 : evergreen tree bearing small edible fruit or the fruit 2 : dull yellowish green color

om·buds·man \ˈäm,bu̇dzmən, äm-'bu̇dz-\ n, pl -men \-mən\ : complaint investigator

om·e·let, om·e·lette \'ämələt\ *n* : beaten eggs lightly fried and folded

omen \'ōmən\ *n* : sign or warning of the future

om·i·nous \'ämənəs\ *adj* : presaging evil —**om·i·nous·ly** *adv* —**om·i·nous·ness** *n*

omit \ō'mit\ *vb* **-tt-** 1 : leave out 2 : fail to perform —**omis·si·ble** \ō'misəbəl\ *adj* —**omis·sion** \-'mishən\ *n*

om·nip·o·tent \äm'nipətənt\ *adj* : almighty —**om·nip·o·tence** \-əns\ *n* —**om·nip·o·tent·ly** *adv*

om·ni·pres·ent \ˌämni'prezᵊnt\ *adj* : ever-present —**om·ni·pres·ence** \-ᵊns\ *n*

om·ni·scient \äm'nishənt\ *adj* : all-knowing —**om·ni·science** \-əns\ *n* —**om·ni·scient·ly** *adv*

om·niv·o·rous \äm'nivərəs\ *adj* 1 : eating both meat and vegetables 2 : avid —**om·niv·o·rous·ly** *adv*

on \'ȯn, 'än\ *prep* 1 : in or to a position over and in contact with 2 : at or to 3 : about 4 : from 5 : with regard to 6 : in a state or process 7 : during the time of ~ *adv* 1 : in or into contact with 2 : forward 3 : into operation

once \'wəns\ *adv* 1 : one time only 2 : at any one time 3 : formerly ~ *n* : one time ~ *conj* : as soon as ~ *adj* : former —**at once** 1 : simultaneously 2 : immediately

once-over *n* : swift examination

on·com·ing *adj* : approaching

one \'wən\ *adj* 1 : being a single thing 2 : being one in particular 3 : being the same in kind ~ *pron* 1 : certain indefinitely indicated person or thing 2 : a person in general ~ *n* 1 : 1st in a series 2 : single person or thing —**one·ness** *n*

oner·ous \'änərəs, 'ōnə-\ *adj* : imposing a burden

one·self \ˌwən'self\ *pron* : one's own self—usu. used reflexively or for emphasis

one-sid·ed \-'sīdəd\ *adj* 1 : occurring on one side only 2 : partial

one·time *adj* : former

one-way *adj* : made for or use in only one direction

on·go·ing *adj* : continuing

on·ion \'ənyən\ *n* : plant grown for its pungent edible bulb or this bulb

on·ly \'ōnlē\ *adj* : alone in its class ~ *adv* 1 : merely or exactly 2 : solely 3

: at the very least 4 : as a result ~ *conj* : but

on·set *n* : start

on·shore *adj* 1 : moving toward shore 2 : lying on or near the shore —**on·shore** *adv*

on·slaught \'än,slȯt, 'ȯn-\ *n* : attack

on·to \'ȯntü, 'än-\ *prep* : to a position or point on

onus \'ōnəs\ *n* : burden (as of obligation or blame)

on·ward \'ȯnwərd, 'än-\ *adv or adj* : forward

on·yx \'äniks\ *n* : quartz used as a gem

ooze \'üz\ *n* : soft mud ~ *vb* **oozed; ooz·ing** : flow or leak out slowly —**oozy** \'üzē\ *adj*

opac·i·ty \ō'pasətē\ *n* : quality or state of being opaque or an opaque spot

opal \'ōpəl\ *n* : gem with delicate colors

opaque \ō'pāk\ *adj* 1 : blocking light 2 : not easily understood 3 : dull-witted —**opaque·ly** *adv*

open \'ōpən\ *adj* 1 : not shut or shut up 2 : not secret or hidden 3 : frank or generous 4 : extended 5 : free from controls 6 : not decided ~ *vb* 1 : make or become open 2 : make or become functional 3 : start ~ *n* : outdoors —**open·er** \-ər\ *n* —**open·ly** *adv* —**open·ness** *n*

open-hand·ed \-'handəd\ *adj* : generous —**open·hand·ed·ly** *adv*

open·ing \'ōpəniŋ\ *n* 1 : act or instance of making open 2 : something that is open 3 : opportunity

op·era \'äpərə, 'äprə\ *n* : drama set to music —**op·er·at·ic** \ˌäpə'ratik\ *adj*

op·er·a·ble \'äpərəbəl\ *adj* 1 : usable or in working condition 2 : suitable for surgical treatment

op·er·ate \'äpə,rāt\ *vb* **-at·ed; -at·ing** 1 : perform work 2 : perform an operation 3 : manage —**op·er·a·tor** \-,rātər\ *n*

op·er·a·tion \ˌäpə'rāshən\ *n* 1 : act or process of operating 2 : surgical work on a living body 3 : military action or mission —**op·er·a·tion·al** \-shənəl\ *adj*

op·er·a·tive \'äpərətiv, -,rāt-\ *adj* : working or having an effect

op·er·et·ta \ˌäpə'retə\ *n* : light opera

oph·thal·mol·o·gy \ˌäf,thal'mäləjē\ *n* : branch of medicine dealing with the eye —**oph·thal·mol·o·gist** \-jist\ *n*

opi·ate \'ōpēət, -pē,āt\ *n* : preparation or derivative of opium

opine \ō'pīn\ *vb* **opined; opin·ing** : express an opinion

opin·ion \ə'pinyən\ *n* 1 : belief 2 : judgment 3 : formal statement by an expert

opin·ion·at·ed \-yə‚nātəd\ *adj* : stubborn in one's opinions

opi·um \'ōpēəm\ *n* : addictive narcotic drug that is the dried juice of a poppy

opos·sum \ə'päsəm\ *n* : common tree-dwelling nocturnal mammal

op·po·nent \ə'pōnənt\ *n* : one that opposes

op·por·tune \‚äpər'tün, -'tyün\ *adj* : suitable or timely —**op·por·tune·ly** *adv*

op·por·tun·ism \-'tü‚nizəm, -'tyü-\ *n* : a taking advantage of opportunities —**op·por·tun·ist** \-nist\ *n* —**op·por·tu·nis·tic** \-tü'nistik, -tyü-\ *adj*

op·por·tu·ni·ty \-'tünətē, -'tyü-\ *n, pl* **-ties** : favorable time

op·pose \ə'pōz\ *vb* **-posed; -pos·ing** : place opposite or against something 2 : resist —**op·po·si·tion** \‚äpə-'zishən\ *n*

op·po·site \'äpəzət\ *n* : one that is opposed ~ *adj* 1 : set facing something that is at the other side or end 2 : opposed or contrary ~ *adv* : on opposite sides ~ *prep* : across from —**op·po·site·ly** *adv*

op·press \ə'pres\ *vb* 1 : persecute 2 : weigh down —**op·pres·sion** \ə-'preshən\ *n* —**op·pres·sive** \-'presiv\ *adj* —**op·pres·sive·ly** *adv* —**op·pres·sor** \-'presər\ *n*

op·pro·bri·ous \ə'prōbrēəs\ *adj* : expressing or deserving opprobrium —**op·pro·bri·ous·ly** *adv*

op·pro·bri·um \-brēəm\ *n* 1 : something that brings disgrace 2 : infamy

opt \'äpt\ *vb* : choose

op·tic \'äptik\ *adj* : relating to vision or the eye

op·ti·cal \'äptikəl\ *adj* : relating to optics, vision, or the eye

op·ti·cian \äp'tishən\ *n* : maker of or dealer in eyeglasses

op·tics \'äptiks\ *n pl* : science of light and vision

op·ti·mal \'äptəməl\ *adj* : most favorable —**op·ti·mal·ly** *adv*

op·ti·mism \'äptə‚mizəm\ *n* : tendency to hope for the best —**op·ti·mist** \-mist\ *n* —**op·ti·mis·tic** \‚äptə'mistik\ *adj* —**op·ti·mis·ti·cal·ly** *adv*

op·ti·mum \'äptəməm\ *n, pl* **-ma** \-mə\ : amount or degree of something most favorable to an end —**optimum** *adj*

op·tion \'äpshən\ *n* 1 : ability to choose 2 : right to buy or sell a stock 3 : alternative —**op·tion·al** \-shənəl\ *adj*

op·tom·e·try \äp'tämətrē\ *n* : profession of examining the eyes —**op·tom·e·trist** \-trist\ *n*

op·u·lent \'äpyələnt\ *adj* : lavish —**op·u·lence** \-ləns\ *n* —**op·u·lent·ly** *adv*

opus \'ōpəs\ *n, pl* **opera** \'ōpərə, 'äpə-\ : work esp. of music

or \'ȯr\ *conj*—used to indicate an alternative

-or \ər\ *n suffix* : one that performs an action

ora·cle \'ȯrəkəl\ *n* 1 : one held to give divinely inspired answers or revelations 2 : wise person or an utterance of such a person —**orac·u·lar** \ȯ-'rakyələr\ *adj*

oral \'ōrəl\ *adj* 1 : spoken 2 : relating to the mouth —**oral·ly** *adv*

or·ange \'ȯrinj\ *n* : reddish yellow citrus fruit 2 : color between red and yellow —**or·ange·ade** \‚ȯrinj'äd\ *n*

orang·u·tan \ə'raŋə‚taŋ, -‚tan\ *n* : large reddish brown ape

ora·tion \ə'rāshən\ *n* : elaborate formal speech

ora·tor \'ȯrətər\ *n* : one noted as a public speaker

ora·to·rio \‚ȯrə'tōrē‚ō\ *n, pl* **-ri·os** : major choral work

ora·to·ry \'ȯrə‚tōrē\ *n* : art of public speaking —**ora·tor·i·cal** \‚ȯrə'tōrikəl\ *adj*

orb \'ȯrb\ *n* : spherical body

or·bit \'ȯrbət\ *n* : path made by one body revolving around another ~ *vb* : revolve around —**or·bit·al** \-əl\ *adj* —**or·bit·er** *n*

or·chard \'ȯrchərd\ *n* : place where fruit or nut trees are grown —**or·chard·ist** \-ist\ *n*

or·ches·tra \'ȯrkəstrə\ *n* 1 : group of musicians 2 : front seats of a theater's main floor —**or·ches·tral** \ȯr'kestrəl\ *adj* —**or·ches·tral·ly** *adv*

or·ches·trate \'ȯrkə‚strāt\ *vb* **-trat·ed; -trat·ing** 1 : compose or arrange for an orchestra 2 : arrange or combine for best effect —**or·ches·tra·tion** \‚ȯrkə'strāshən\ *n*

or·chid \'ȯrkəd\ *n* : plant with showy 3-petal flowers or its flower

or·dain \or̄'dān\ vb 1 : admit to the clergy 2 : decree

or·deal \or̄'dēl, 'or̄,dēl\ n : severely trying experience

order \'or̄dər\ n 1 : rank, class, or special group 2 : arrangement 3 : rule of law 4 : authoritative regulation or instruction 5 : working condition 6 : special request for a purchase or what is purchased ~ vb 1 : arrange 2 : give an order to 3 : place an order for

or·der·ly \-lē\ adj 1 : being in order or tidy 2 : well behaved ~ n, pl -lies 1 : officer's attendant 2 : hospital attendant —**or·der·li·ness** n

or·di·nal \'or̄dᵊnəl\ n : number indicating order in a series

or·di·nance \-ᵊnəns\ n : municipal law

or·di·nary \'or̄dᵊn,erē\ adj : of common occurrence, quality, or ability —**or·di·nar·i·ly** \,or̄dᵊn'erəlē\ adv

or·di·na·tion \,or̄dᵊn'āshən\ n : act of ordaining

ord·nance \'or̄dnəns\ n : military supplies

ore \'or̄\ n : mineral containing a valuable constituent

oreg·a·no \ə'regə,nō\ n : mint used as a seasoning and source of oil

or·gan \'or̄gən\ n 1 : air-powered or electronic keyboard instrument 2 : animal or plant structure with special function 3 : periodical

or·gan·ic \or̄'ganik\ adj 1 : relating to a bodily organ 2 : relating to living things 3 : relating to or containing carbon or its compounds 4 : relating to foods produced without the use of laboratory-made products —**or·gan·i·cal·ly** adv

or·gan·ism \'or̄gə,nizəm\ n : a living thing

or·gan·ist \'or̄gənist\ n : organ player

or·ga·nize \'or̄gə,nīz\ vb -nized; -niz·ing : form parts into a functioning whole —**or·ga·ni·za·tion** \,or̄gənə'zāshən\ n —**or·ga·ni·za·tion·al** \-shənəl\ adj —**or·ga·niz·er** n

or·gasm \'or̄,gazəm\ n : climax of sexual excitement —**or·gas·mic** \or̄'gazmik\ adj

or·gy \'or̄jē\ n, pl -gies : unrestrained indulgence (as in sexual activity)

ori·ent \'or̄ē,ent\ vb 1 : set in a definite position 2 : acquaint with a situation —**ori·en·ta·tion** \,or̄ēən'tāshən\ n

ori·en·tal \,or̄ē'entᵊl\ adj : Eastern —**Oriental** n

or·i·fice \'or̄əfəs\ n : opening

or·i·gin \'or̄əjən\ n 1 : ancestry 2 : rise, beginning, or derivation from a source —**orig·i·nate** \ə'rijə,nāt\ vb —**orig·i·na·tor** \-ər\ n

orig·i·nal \ə'rijənəl\ n : something from which a copy is made ~ adj 1 : first 2 : not copied from something else 3 : inventive —**orig·i·nal·i·ty** n —**orig·i·nal·ly** adv

ori·ole \'or̄ē,ōl, -ēəl\ n : American songbird

or·na·ment \'or̄nəmənt\ n : something that adorns ~ vb : provide with ornament —**or·na·men·tal** \,or̄nə'mentᵊl\ adj —**or·na·men·ta·tion** \-mən'tāshən\ n

or·nate \or̄'nāt\ adj : elaborately decorated —**or·nate·ly** adv —**or·nate·ness** n

or·nery \'or̄nərē, 'än-\ adj : irritable

or·ni·thol·o·gy \,or̄nə'thäləjē\ n, pl -gies : study of birds —**or·ni·tho·log·i·cal** \-thə'läjikəl\ adj —**or·ni·thol·o·gist** \-'thäləjist\ n

or·phan \'or̄fən\ n : child whose parents are dead —**orphan** vb —**or·phan·age** \-ənij\ n

or·tho·don·tics \,or̄thə'däntiks\ n : dentistry dealing with straightening teeth —**or·tho·don·tist** \-'däntist\ n

or·tho·dox \'or̄thə,däks\ adj 1 : conforming to established doctrine 2 cap : of or relating to a Christian church originating in the Eastern Roman Empire —**or·tho·doxy** \-,däksē\ n

or·thog·ra·phy \or̄'thägrəfē\ n : spelling —**or·tho·graph·ic** \,or̄thə'grafik\ adj

or·tho·pe·dics \,or̄thə'pēdiks\ n sing or pl : correction or prevention of skeletal deformities —**or·tho·pe·dic** \-ik\ adj —**or·tho·pe·dist** \-'pēdist\ n

-o·ry \,ōrē, ,ôrē, ərē\ adj suffix 1 : of, relating to, or characterized by 2 : serving for, producing, or maintaining

os·cil·late \'äsə,lāt\ vb -lat·ed; -lat·ing : swing back and forth —**os·cil·la·tion** \,äsə'lāshən\ n

os·mo·sis \äz'mōsəs, äs-\ n : diffusion esp. of water through a membrane —**os·mot·ic** \-'mätik\ adj

os·prey \'äsprē, -,prä\ n, pl -preys : large fish-eating hawk

os·si·fy \'äsə,fï\ *vb* **-fied; -fy·ing** : make or become hardened or set in one's ways

os·ten·si·ble \ä'stensəbəl\ *adj* : seeming —**os·ten·si·bly** \-blē\ *adv*

os·ten·ta·tion \,ästən'tāshən\ *n* : pretentious display —**os·ten·ta·tious** \-shəs\ *adj* —**os·ten·ta·tious·ly** *adv*

os·te·op·a·thy \,ästē'äpəthē\ *n* : system of healing that emphasizes manipulation (as of joints) —**os·te·o·path** \'ästēə,path\ *n* —**os·te·o·path·ic** \,ästēə'pathik\ *adj*

os·te·o·po·ro·sis \,ästēōpə'rōsəs\ *n, pl* **-ro·ses** \-,sēz\ : condition characterized by fragile and porous bones

os·tra·cize \'ästrə,sīz\ *vb* **-cized; -ciz·ing** : exclude by common consent —**os·tra·cism** \-,sizəm\ *n*

os·trich \'ästrich, 'ós-\ *n* : very large flightless bird

oth·er \'əthər\ *adj* **1** : being the one left **2** : alternate **3** : additional ~ *pron* **1** : remaining one **2** : different one

oth·er·wise *adv* **1** : in a different way **2** : in different circumstances **3** : in other respects —**otherwise** *adj*

ot·ter \'ätər\ *n* : fish-eating mammal with webbed feet

ot·to·man \'ätəmən\ *n* : upholstered footstool

ought \'ót\ *verbal auxiliary*—used to express obligation, advisability, or expectation

ounce \'aúns\ *n* **1** : unit of weight equal to about 28.3 grams **2** : unit of capacity equal to about 29.6 milliliters

our \'är, 'aúr\ *adj* : of or relating to us

ours \'aúrz, 'ärz\ *pron* : that which belongs to us

our·selves \är'selvz, aúr-\ *pron* : we, us—used reflexively or for emphasis

-ous \əs\ *adj suffix* : having or having the qualities of

oust \'aúst\ *vb* : expel or eject

oust·er \'aústər\ *n* : expulsion

out \'aút\ *adv* **1** : away from the inside or center **2** : beyond control **3** : to extinction, exhaustion, or completion **4** : in or into the open ~ *vb* : become known ~ *adj* **1** : situated outside **2** : absent ~ *prep* **1** : out through **2** : outward on or along —**out·bound** *adj* —**out·build·ing** *n*

out·age \'aútij\ *n* : period of no electricity

out·board \'aút,bōrd\ *adv* : outside a boat or ship —**outboard** *adj*

out·break \'aút,brāk\ *n* : sudden occurrence

out·burst \-,bərst\ *n* : violent expression of feeling

out·cast \-,kast\ *n* : person cast out by society

out·come \-,kəm\ *n* : result

out·crop \'aút,kräp\ *n* : part of a rock stratum that appears above the ground —**outcrop** *vb*

out·cry \-,krï\ *n* : loud cry

out·dat·ed \aút'dātəd\ *adj* : out-of-date

out·dis·tance *vb* : go far ahead of

out·do \aút'dü\ *vb* **-did** \-'did\; **-done** \-'dən\; **-do·ing** \-'düiŋ\; **-does** \-'dəz\ : do better than

out·doors \aút'dōrz\ *adv* : in or into the open air ~ *n* : open air —**out·door** *adj*

out·er \'aútər\ *adj* **1** : external **2** : farther out —**out·er·most** *adj*

out·field \'aút,fēld\ *n* : baseball field beyond the infield —**out·field·er** \-,fēldər\ *n*

out·fit \'aút,fit\ *n* **1** : equipment for a special purpose **2** : group ~ *vb* **-tt-** : equip —**out·fit·ter** *n*

out·go \'aút,gō\ *n, pl* **outgoes** : expenditure

out·go·ing \'aút,gōiŋ\ *adj* **1** : retiring from a position **2** : friendly

out·grow \aút'grō\ *vb* **-grew** \-'grü\; **-grown** \-'grōn\; **-grow·ing** **1** : grow faster than **2** : grow too large for

out·growth \'aút,grōth\ *n* **1** : product of growing out **2** : consequence

out·ing \'aútiŋ\ *n* : excursion

out·land·ish \aút'landish\ *adj* : very strange —**out·land·ish·ly** *adv*

outlast *vb* : last longer than

out·law \'aút,ló\ *n* : lawless person ~ *vb* : make illegal

out·lay \'aút,lā\ *n* : expenditure

out·let \'aút,let, -lət\ *n* **1** : exit **2** : means of release **3** : market for goods **4** : electrical device that gives access to wiring

out·line \'aút,līn\ *n* **1** : line marking the outer limits **2** : summary ~ *vb* **1** : draw the outline of **2** : indicate the chief parts of

out·live \aút'liv\ *vb* : live longer than

out·look \'aút,lúk\ *n* **1** : viewpoint **2** : prospect for the future

out·ly·ing \'aút,līiŋ\ *adj* : far from a central point

out·ma·neu·ver \,aútmə'nüvər, -'nyü-\

vb : defeat by more skillful maneuvering

out·mod·ed \aút'mōdəd\ *adj* : out-of-date

out·num·ber \-'nəmbər\ *vb* : exceed in number

out of *prep* **1** : out from within **2** : beyond the limits of **3** : among **4** — used to indicate absence or loss **5** : because of **6** : from or with

out-of-date *adj* : no longer in fashion or in use

out·pa·tient *n* : person treated at a hospital who does not stay overnight

out·post *n* : remote military post

out·put *n* : amount produced ~ *vb* -**put·ted** *or* -**put; -put·ting** : produce

out·rage \'aút,rāj\ *n* **1** : violent or shameful act **2** : injury or insult **3** : extreme anger ~ *vb* -**raged; -rag·ing 1** : subject to violent injury **2** : make very angry

out·ra·geous \aút'rājəs\ *adj* : extremely offensive or shameful —**out·ra·geous·ly** *adv* —**out·ra·geous·ness** *n*

out·right *adv* **1** : completely **2** : instantly ~ *adj* **1** : complete **2** : given without reservation

out·set *n* : beginning

out·side \aút'sīd, 'aút,-\ *n* **1** : place beyond a boundary **2** : exterior **3** : utmost limit ~ *adj* **1** : outer **2** : coming from without **3** : remote ~ *adv* : on or to the outside ~ *prep* **1** : on or to the outside of **2** : beyond the limits of

outside of *prep* **1** : outside **2** : besides

out·sid·er \-'sīdər\ *n* : one who does not belong to a group

out·skirts *n pl* : outlying parts (as of a city)

out·smart \aút'smärt\ *vb* : outwit

out·spo·ken *adj* : direct and open in speech —**out·spo·ken·ness** *n*

out·stand·ing *adj* **1** : unpaid **2** : very good —**out·stand·ing·ly** *adv*

out·strip \aút'strip\ *vb* **1** : go faster than **2** : surpass

1out·ward \'aútwərd\ *adj* **1** : being toward the outside **2** : showing outwardly

2outward, out·wards \-wərdz\ *adv* : toward the outside —**out·ward·ly** *adv*

out·wit \aút'wit\ *vb* : get the better of by superior cleverness

ova *pl of* OVUM

oval \'ōvəl\ *adj* : egg-shaped —**oval** *n*

ova·ry \'ōvərē\ *n, pl* -**ries 1** : egg-producing organ **2** : seed-producing part of a flower —**ovar·i·an** \ō'varēən\ *adj*

ova·tion \ō'vāshən\ *n* : enthusiastic applause

ov·en \'əvən\ *n* : chamber (as in a stove) for baking

over \'ōvər\ *adv* **1** : across **2** : upside down **3** : in excess or addition **4** : above **5** : at an end **6** : again ~ *prep* **1** : above in position or authority **2** : more than **3** : along, through, or across **4** : because of ~ *adj* **1** : upper **2** : remaining **3** : ended

over- *prefix* **1** : so as to exceed or surpass **2** : excessive or excessively

overabundance	overcontrol
overabundant	overcook
overachiever	overcorrect
overactive	overcritical
overaggressive	overcrowd
overambitious	overdecorate
overanalyze	overdependence
overanxiety	overdependent
overanxious	overdevelop
overarousal	overdose
overassertive	overdramatic
overbake	overdramatize
overbid	overdress
overbill	overdrink
overbold	overdue
overborrow	overeager
overbright	overeat
overbroad	overeducated
overbuild	overelaborate
overburden	overemotional
overbusy	overemphasis
overbuy	overemphasize
overcapacity	overenergetic
overcapitalize	overenthusiastic
overcareful	overestimate
overcautious	overexaggerate
overcharge	overexaggera-tion
overcivilized	
overclean	overexcite
overcommit	overexcited
overcompensate	overexercise
overcomplicate	overexert
overconcern	overexertion
overconfidence	overexpand
overconfident	overexpansion
overconscien-tious	overexplain
	overexploit
overconsume	overexpose
overconsump-tion	overextend
	overextension

overexuberant
overfamiliar
overfatigued
overfeed
overfertilize
overfill
overfond
overgeneraliza-
    tion
overgeneralize
overgenerous
overglamorize
overgraze
overharvest
overhasty
overheat
overidealize
overimaginative
overimpress
overindebted-
    ness
overindulge
overindulgence
overindulgent
overinflate
overinsistent
overintense
overintensity
overinvestment
overladen
overlarge
overlend
overload
overlong
overloud
overmedicate
overmodest
overmuch
overobvious
overoptimistic
overorganize
overparticular
overpay
overpayment
overplay
overpopulated
overpraise
overprescribe
overpressure
overprice

overprivileged
overproduce
overproduction
overpromise
overprotect
overprotective
overqualified
overrate
overreact
overreaction
overrefined
overregulate
overregulation
overreliance
overrepresented
overrespond
overripe
oversaturate
oversell
oversensitive
overserious
oversexed
oversimple
oversimplify
oversolicitous
overspecialize
overspend
overstaff
overstimula-
    tion
overstock
overstrain
overstress
overstretch
oversubtle
oversupply
oversuspicious
oversweeten
overtax
overtighten
overtip
overtired
overtrain
overtreat
overuse
overutilize
overvalue
overweight
overwork
overzealous

over·awe vb : subdue by awe
over·bear·ing \-'barin\ adj : arrogant
over·blown \-'blōn\ adj : pretentious
over·board adv : over the side into the water
over·cast adj : clouded over ~ n : cloud covering
over·coat n : outer coat
over·come vb -came \-'kām\; -come; -com·ing 1 : defeat 2 : make helpless or exhausted
over·do vb -did; -done; -do·ing; -does : do too much
over·draft n : overdrawn sum
over·draw vb -drew; -drawn; -draw·ing : write checks for more than one's bank balance
over·flow \,ōvər'flō\ vb 1 : flood 2 : flow over —**over·flow** \'ōvər,flō\ n
over·grow vb -grew; -grown; -grow·ing : grow over
over·hand adj : made with the hand brought down from above —**over·hand** adv —**over·hand·ed** \-,handəd\ adv or adj
over·hang vb -hung; -hang·ing : jut out over ~ n : something that overhangs
over·haul vb 1 : repair 2 : overtake
over·head \,ōvər'hed\ adv : aloft ~ \'ōvər,-\ adj : situated above ~ \'ōvər,-\ n : general business expenses
over·hear vb -heard; -hear·ing : hear without the speaker's knowledge
over·joyed adj : filled with joy
over·kill \'ōvər,kil\ n : large excess
over·land \-,land, -lənd\ adv or adj : by, on, or across land
over·lap vb : lap over —**over·lap** \'ōvər,lap\ n
over·lay \,ōvər'lā\ vb -laid; -lay·ing : lay over or across —**over·lay** \'ōvər,lā\ n
over·look \,ōvər'lùk\ vb 1 : look down on 2 : fail to see 3 : ignore 4 : pardon 5 : supervise ~ \'ōvər,-\ n : observation point
over·ly \'ōvərlē\ adv : excessively
over·night adv 1 : through the night 2 : suddenly —**overnight** adj
over·pass n : bridge over a road
over·power vb : conquer
over·reach \,ōvər'rēch\ vb : try or seek too much
over·ride vb -rode; -rid·den; -rid·ing : neutralize action of
over·rule vb : rule against or set aside
over·run vb -ran; -run·ning 1 : swarm

¹**over·age** \,ōvər'āj\ adj : too old
²**over·age** \'ōvərij\ n : surplus
over·all \,ōvər'ól\ adj : including everything
over·alls \'ōvər,ólz\ n pl : pants with an extra piece covering the chest

or flow over **2** : go beyond ~ *n* : an exceeding of estimated costs

over·seas *adv or adj* : beyond or across the sea

over·see \'ō-var'sē\ *vb* **-saw; -seen; -see·ing** : supervise —**over·seer** \'ōvar-,siar\ *n*

over·shad·ow *vb* : exceed in importance

over·shoe *n* : protective outer shoe

over·shoot *vb* **-shot; -shoot·ing** : shoot or pass beyond

over·sight *n* : inadvertent omission or error

over·sleep *vb* **-slept; -sleep·ing** : sleep longer than intended

over·spread *vb* **-spread; -spread·ing** : spread over or above

over·state *vb* : exaggerate —**over·state·ment** *n*

over·stay *vb* : stay too long

over·step *vb* : exceed

overt \ō'vart, 'ō,vart\ *adj* : not secret —**overt·ly** *adv*

over·take *vb* **-took; -tak·en; -tak·ing** : catch up with

over·throw \,ōvar'thrō\ *vb* **-threw; -thrown; -throw·ing 1** : upset **2** : defeat —**over·throw** \'ōvar,-\ *n*

over·time *n* : extra working time —**overtime** *adv*

over·tone *n* **1** : higher tone in a complex musical tone **2** : suggestion

over·ture \'ōvar,chúr, -char\ *n* **1** : opening offer **2** : musical introduction

over·turn *vb* **1** : turn over **2** : nullify

over·view *n* : brief survey

over·ween·ing \,ōvar'wēnin\ *adj* **1** : arrogant **2** : excessive

over·whelm \,ōvar'hwelm\ *vb* : overcome completely —**over·whelm·ing·ly** \-'hwelmin͡lē\ *adv*

over·wrought \,ōvar'rót\ *adj* : extremely excited

ovoid \'ō,vóid\, **ovoi·dal** \ō'vóidᵊl\ *adj* : egg-shaped

ovu·late \'ävya,lāt, 'ōv-\ *vb* **-lat·ed; -lat·ing** : produce eggs from an ovary —**ovu·la·tion** \,ävya'lāshan, ,ōv-\ *n*

ovum \'ōvam\ *n, pl* **ova** \-va\ : female germ cell

owe \'ō\ *vb* **owed; ow·ing 1** : have an obligation to pay **2** : be indebted to or for

owing to *prep* : because of

owl \aul\ *n* : nocturnal bird of prey —**owl·ish** *adj* —**owl·ish·ly** *adv*

own \'ōn\ *adj* : belonging to oneself ~ *vb* **1** : have as property **2** : acknowledge ~ *pron* : one or ones belonging to oneself —**own·er** *n* —**own·er·ship** *n*

ox \'äks\ *n, pl* **ox·en** \'äksan\ : bovine mammal and esp. a castrated bull

ox·ide \'äk,sīd\ *n* : compound of oxygen

ox·i·dize \'äksa,dīz\ *vb* **-dized; -diz·ing** : combine with oxygen —**ox·i·da·tion** \,äksa'dāshan\ *n* —**ox·i·diz·er** *n*

ox·y·gen \'äksijan\ *n* : gaseous chemical element essential for life

oys·ter \'óistar\ *n* : bivalve mollusk —**oys·ter·ing** \-riṇ\ *n*

ozone \'ō,zōn\ *n* : very reactive bluish form of oxygen

P

p \'pē\ *n, pl* **p's** *or* **ps** \'pēz\ : 16th letter of the alphabet

pace \'pās\ *n* **1** : walking step **2** : rate of progress ~ *vb* **paced; pac·ing 1** : go at a pace **2** : cover with slow steps **3** : set the pace of

pace·mak·er *n* : electrical device to regulate heartbeat

pachy·derm \'paki,darm\ *n* : elephant

pa·cif·ic \pa'sifik\ *adj* : calm or peaceful

pac·i·fism \'pasa,fizam\ *n* : opposition to war or violence —**pac·i·fist** \-fist\

n or adj —**pac·i·fis·tic** \,pasa'fistik\ *adj*

pac·i·fy \'pasa,fī\ *vb* **-fied; -fy·ing** : make calm —**pac·i·fi·ca·tion** \,pasa-fa'kāshan\ *n* —**pac·i·fi·er** \'pasa,-fīar\ *n*

pack \'pak\ *n* **1** : compact bundle **2** : group of animals ~ *vb* **1** : put into a container **2** : fill tightly or completely **3** : send without ceremony —**pack·er** *n*

pack·age \'pakij\ *n* : items bundled together ~ *vb* **-aged; -ag·ing** : enclose in a package

pack·et \'pakət\ *n* : small package

pact \'pakt\ *n* : agreement

pad \'pad\ *n* 1 : cushioning part or thing 2 : floating leaf of a water plant 3 : tablet of paper ~ *vb* 1 : furnish with a pad 2 : expand with needless matter —**pad·ding** *n*

pad·dle \'pad°l\ *n* : implement with a flat blade ~ *vb* **-dled; -dling** : move, beat, or stir with a paddle

pad·dock \'padək\ *n* : enclosed area for racehorses

pad·dy \'padē\ *n, pl* **-dies** : wet land where rice is grown

pad·lock *n* : lock with a U-shaped catch —**padlock** *vb*

pae·an \'pēən\ *n* : song of praise

pa·gan \'pāgən\ *n or adj* : heathen —**pa·gan·ism** \-,izəm\ *n*

¹**page** \'pāj\ *n* : messenger ~ *vb* **paged; pag·ing** : summon by repeated calls —**pag·er** *n*

²**page** *n* : single leaf (as of a book) or one side of the leaf

pag·eant \'pajənt\ *n* : elaborate spectacle or procession —**pag·eant·ry** \-əntrē\ *n*

pa·go·da \pə'gōdə\ *n* : tower with roofs curving upward

paid *past of* PAY

pail \'pāl\ *n* : cylindrical container with a handle —**pail·ful** \-,ful\ *n*

pain \'pān\ *n* 1 : punishment or penalty 2 : suffering of body or mind 3 *pl* : great care ~ *vb* : cause or experience pain —**pain·ful** \-fəl\ *adj* —**pain·ful·ly** *adv* —**pain·kill·er** *n* —**pain·kill·ing** *adj* —**pain·less** *adj* —**pain·less·ly** *adv*

pains·tak·ing \'pān,stākiŋ\ *adj* : taking pains —**painstaking** *n* —**pains·tak·ing·ly** *adv*

paint \'pānt\ *vb* 1 : apply color or paint to 2 : portray esp. in color ~ *n* : mixture of pigment and liquid —**paint·brush** *n* —**paint·er** *n* —**paint·ing** *n*

pair \'par\ *n* : a set of two ~ *vb* : put or go together as a pair

pa·ja·mas \pə'jäməz, -'jam-\ *n pl* : loose suit for sleeping

pal \'pal\ *n* : close friend

pal·ace \'paləs\ *n* 1 : residence of a chief of state 2 : mansion —**pa·la·tial** \pə'lāshəl\ *adj*

pal·at·able \'palətəbəl\ *adj* : agreeable to the taste

pal·ate \'palət\ *n* 1 : roof of the mouth 2 : taste —**pal·a·tal** \-ət°l\ *adj*

pa·la·ver \pə'lavər, -'läv-\ *n* : talk —**palaver** *vb*

¹**pale** \'pāl\ *adj* **pal·er; pal·est** 1 : lacking in color or brightness 2 : light in color or shade ~ *vb* **paled; pal·ing** : make or become pale —**pale·ness** *n*

²**pale** *n* 1 : fence stake 2 : enclosed place

pa·le·on·tol·o·gy \,pālē,än'täləjē\ *n* : branch of biology dealing with ancient forms of life known from fossils —**pa·le·on·tol·o·gist** \-,än'täləjist, -ən-\ *n*

pal·ette \'palət\ *n* : board on which paints are laid and mixed

pal·i·sade \,palə'sād\ *n* 1 : high fence 2 : line of cliffs

¹**pall** \'pol\ *n* 1 : cloth draped over a coffin 2 : something that produces gloom

²**pall** *vb* : lose in interest or attraction

pall·bear·er *n* : one who attends the coffin at a funeral

¹**pal·let** \'palət\ *n* : makeshift bed

²**pallet** *n* : portable storage platform

pal·li·ate \'palē,āt\ *vb* **-at·ed; -at·ing** 1 : ease without curing 2 : cover or conceal by excusing —**pal·li·a·tion** \,palē'āshən\ *n* —**pal·li·a·tive** \'palē,ātiv\ *adj or n*

pal·lid \'paləd\ *adj* : pale

pal·lor \'palər\ *n* : paleness

¹**palm** \'päm, 'pälm\ *n* 1 : tall tropical tree crowned with large leaves 2 : symbol of victory

²**palm** *n* : underside of the hand ~ *vb* 1 : conceal in the hand 2 : impose by fraud

palm·ist·ry \'päməstrē, 'pälmə-\ *n* : reading a person's character or future in his palms —**palm·ist** \'pämist, 'pälm-\ *n*

palmy \'pämē, 'pälmē\ *adj* **palm·i·er; -est** : flourishing

pal·o·mi·no \,palə'mēnō\ *n, pl* **-nos** : light-colored horse

pal·pa·ble \'palpəbəl\ *adj* 1 : capable of being touched 2 : obvious —**pal·pa·bly** \-blē\ *adv*

pal·pi·tate \'palpə,tāt\ *vb* **-tat·ed; -tat·ing** : beat rapidly —**pal·pi·ta·tion** \,palpə'tāshən\ *n*

pal·sy \'polzē\ *n, pl* **-sies** 1 : paralysis 2

: condition marked by tremor —**pal·sied** \-zēd\ *adj*

pal·try \'pòltrē\ *adj* **-tri·er; -est** : trivial

pam·per \'pampər\ *vb* : spoil or indulge

pam·phlet \'pamflət\ *n* : unbound publication —**pam·phlet·eer** \,pamflə-'tir\ *n*

pan \'pan\ *n* : broad, shallow, and open container ~ *vb* **1** : wash gravel in a pan to search for gold **2** : criticize severely

pan·a·cea \,panə'sēə\ *n* : remedy for all ills or difficulties

pan·cake *n* : fried flat cake

pan·cre·as \'pankrēəs, 'pan-\ *n* : gland that produces insulin —**pan·cre·at·ic** \,pankrē'atik, ,pan-\ *adj*

pan·da \'pandə\ *n* : black-and-white bearlike animal

pan·de·mo·ni·um \,pandə'mōnēəm\ *n* : wild uproar

pan·der \'pandər\ *n* **1** : pimp **2** : one who caters to others' desires or weaknesses ~ *vb* : act as a pander

pane \'pān\ *n* : sheet of glass

pan·e·gyr·ic \,panə'jirik\ *n* : eulogistic oration —**pan·e·gyr·ist** \-'jirist\ *n*

pan·el \'panᵊl\ *n* **1** : list of persons (as jurors) **2** : discussion group **3** : flat piece of construction material **4** : board with instruments or controls ~ *vb* **-eled** *or* **-elled; -el·ing** *or* **-el·ling** : decorate with panels —**pan·el·ing** *n* —**pan·el·ist** \-ist\ *n*

pang \'pan\ *n* : sudden sharp pain

pan·han·dle \'pan,handᵊl\ *vb* **-dled; -dling** : ask for money on the street —**pan·han·dler** \-ər\ *n*

pan·ic \'panik\ *n* : sudden overpowering fright ~ *vb* **-icked; -ick·ing** : affect or be affected with panic —**pan·icky** \-ikē\ *adj*

pan·o·ply \'panəplē\ *n, pl* **-plies 1** : full suit of armor **2** : impressive array

pan·o·ra·ma \,panə'ramə, -'räm-\ *n* : view in every direction —**pan·o·ram·ic** \-'ramik\ *adj*

pan·sy \'panzē\ *n, pl* **-sies** : low-growing garden herb with showy flowers

pant \'pant\ *vb* **1** : breathe with great effort **2** : yearn ~ *n* : panting sound

pan·ta·loons \,pantᵊl'ünz\ *n pl* : pants

pan·the·on \'panthē,än, -ən\ *n* **1** : the gods of a people **2** : group of famous people

pan·ther \'panthər\ *n* : large wild cat

pant·ies \'pantēz\ *n pl* : woman's or child's short underpants

pan·to·mime \'pantə,mīm\ *n* **1** : play without words **2** : expression by bodily or facial movements ~ *vb* : represent by pantomime

pan·try \'pantrē\ *n, pl* **-tries** : storage room for food and dishes

pants \'pants\ *n pl* **1** : 2-legged outer garment **2** : panties

pap \'pap\ *n* : soft food

pa·pa·cy \'pāpəsē\ *n, pl* **-cies 1** : office of pope **2** : reign of a pope

pa·pal \'pāpəl\ *adj* : relating to the pope

pa·pa·ya \pə'pīə\ *n* : tropical tree with large yellow edible fruit

pa·per \'pāpər\ *n* **1** : pliable substance used to write or print on, to wrap things in, or to cover walls **2** : printed or written document **3** : newspaper —**paper** *adj or vb* —**pa·per·hang·er** *n* —**pa·per·weight** *n* —**pa·pery** \'pāpərē\ *adj*

pa·per·board *n* : cardboard

pa·pier-mâché \,pāpərmə'shā, ,pap-,yämə-, -ma-\ *n* : molding material of waste paper

pa·poose \pa'püs, pə-\ *n* : young child of American Indian parents

pa·pri·ka \pə'prēkə, pa-\ *n* : mild red spice from sweet peppers

pa·py·rus \pə'pīrəs\ *n, pl* **-rus·es** *or* **-ri** \-,rē, -,rī\ **1** : tall grasslike plant **2** : paper from papyrus

par \'pär\ *n* **1** : stated value **2** : common level **3** : accepted standard or normal condition —**par** *adj*

par·a·ble \'parəbəl\ *n* : simple story illustrating a moral truth

para·chute \'parə,shüt\ *n* : large umbrella-shaped device for making a descent through air —**parachute** *vb* —**para·chut·ist** \-,shütist\ *n*

pa·rade \pə'rād\ *n* **1** : pompous display **2** : ceremonial formation and march ~ *vb* **-rad·ed; -rad·ing 1** : march in a parade **2** : show off

par·a·digm \'parə,dīm, -,dim\ *n* : model

par·a·dise \'parə,dīs, -,dīz\ *n* : place of bliss

par·a·dox \'parə,däks\ *n* : statement that seems contrary to common sense yet is perhaps true —**par·a·dox·i·cal** \,parə'däksikəl\ *adj* —**par·a·dox·i·cal·ly** *adv*

par·af·fin \'parəfən\ *n* : white waxy substance used esp. for making candles and sealing foods

par·a·gon \'parə,gän, -gən\ *n* : model of perfection

par·a·graph \'parə,graf\ *n* : unified division of a piece of writing ~ *vb* : divide into paragraphs

par·a·keet \'parə,kēt\ *n* : small slender parrot

par·al·lel \'parə,lel\ *adj* **1** : lying or moving in the same direction but always the same distance apart **2** : similar ~ *n* **1** : parallel line, curve, or surface **2** : line of latitude **3** : similarity ~ *vb* **1** : compare **2** : correspond to —**par·al·lel·ism** \-,izəm\ *n*

par·al·lel·o·gram \,parə'lelə,gram\ *n* : 4-sided polygon with opposite sides equal and parallel

pa·ral·y·sis \pə'raləsəs\ *n, pl* **-y·ses** \-,sēz\ : loss of function and esp. of voluntary motion —**par·a·lyt·ic** \,parə'litik\ *adj or n*

par·a·lyze \'parə,līz\ *vb* **-lyzed; -lyz·ing** : affect with paralysis —**par·a·lyz·ing·ly** *adv*

para·med·ic \,parə'medik\ *n* : person trained to provide initial emergency medical treatment

pa·ram·e·ter \pə'ramətər\ *n* : characteristic element —**para·met·ric** \,parə'metrik\ *adj*

par·a·mount \'parə,maunt\ *adj* : superior to all others

par·amour \'parə,mur\ *n* : illicit lover

para·noia \,parə'nóiə\ *n* : mental disorder marked by irrational suspicion —**para·noid** \'parə,nóid\ *adj or n*

par·a·pet \'parəpət, -,pet\ *n* : protecting rampart in a fort

para·pher·na·lia \,parəfə'nālyə, -fər-\ *n sing or pl* : equipment

para·phrase \'parə,frāz\ *n* : restatement of a text giving the meaning in different words —**paraphrase** *vb*

para·ple·gia \,parə'plējə, -jēə\ *n* : paralysis of the lower trunk and legs —**para·ple·gic** \-jik\ *adj or n*

par·a·site \'parə,sīt\ *n* : organism living on another —**para·sit·ic** \,parə'sitik\ *adj* —**para·sit·ism** \'parəsə,tizəm, -,sīt,iz-\ *n*

para·sol \'parə,sól\ *n* : umbrella used to keep off the sun

para·troops \-,trüps\ *n pl* : troops trained to parachute from an airplane —**para·troop·er** \-,trüpər\ *n*

par·boil \'pär,bóil\ *vb* : boil briefly

par·cel \'pärsəl\ *n* **1** : lot **2** : package ~ *vb* **-celed** or **-celled; -cel·ing** or **-cel·ling** : divide into portions

parch \'pärch\ *vb* : toast or shrivel with dry heat

parch·ment \'pärchmənt\ *n* : animal skin prepared to write on

par·don \'pärdən\ *n* : excusing of an offense ~ *vb* : free from penalty —**par·don·able** \'pärdnəbəl\ *adj* —**par·don·er** \-ənər\ *n*

pare \'par\ *vb* **pared; par·ing** **1** : trim off an outside part **2** : reduce as if by paring —**par·er** *n*

par·e·gor·ic \,parə'górik\ *n* : tincture of opium and camphor

par·ent \'parənt\ *n* : one that begets or brings up offspring —**par·ent·age** \-ij\ *n* —**pa·ren·tal** \pə'rentəl\ *adj* —**par·ent·hood** *n*

pa·ren·the·sis \pə'renthəsəs\ *n, pl* **-the·ses** \-,sēz\ **1** : word or phrase inserted in a passage **2** : one of a pair of punctuation marks ( ) —**par·en·thet·ic** \,parən'thetik\, **par·en·thet·i·cal** \-ikəl\ *adj* —**par·en·thet·i·cal·ly** *adv*

par·fait \pär'fā\ *n* : layered cold dessert

pa·ri·ah \pə'rīə\ *n* : outcast

par·ish \'parish\ *n* : local church community

pa·rish·io·ner \pə'rishənər\ *n* : member of a parish

par·i·ty \'parətē\ *n, pl* **-ties** : equality

park \'pärk\ *n* : land set aside for recreation or for its beauty ~ *vb* : leave a vehicle standing

par·ka \'pärkə\ *n* : usu. hooded heavy jacket

park·way \'pärk,wā\ *n* : broad landscaped thoroughfare

par·lance \'pärləns\ *n* : manner of speaking

par·lay \'pär,lā\ *n* : the risking of a stake plus its winnings —**parlay** *vb*

par·ley \'pärlē\ *n, pl* **-leys** : conference about a dispute —**parley** *vb*

par·lia·ment \'pärləmənt\ *n* : legislative assembly —**par·lia·men·tar·i·an** *n* —**par·lia·men·ta·ry** \,pärlə'mentərē\ *adj*

par·lor \'pärlər\ *n* **1** : reception room **2** : place of business

pa·ro·chi·al \pə'rōkēəl\ *adj* **1** : relating to a church parish **2** : provincial —**pa·ro·chi·al·ism** \-ə,lizəm\ *n*

par·o·dy \'parədē\ *n, pl* **-dies** : humorous or satirical imitation —**parody** *vb*

pa·role \pə'rōl\ *n* : conditional release of a prisoner —**parole** *vb* —**pa·rol·ee** \-,rō'lē, -'rō,lē\ *n*

par·ox·ysm \'parək,sizəm, pə'räk-\ n : convulsion

par·quet \'pär,kā, pär'kā\ n : flooring of patterned wood inlay

par·ra·keet var of PARAKEET

par·rot \'parət\ n : bright-colored tropical bird

par·ry \'parē\ vb **-ried; -ry·ing 1** : ward off a blow **2** : evade adroitly —**parry** n

parse \'pärs\ vb **parsed; pars·ing** : analyze grammatically

par·si·mo·ny \'pärsə,mōnē\ n : extreme frugality —**par·si·mo·ni·ous** \,pärsə-'mōnēəs\ adj —**par·si·mo·ni·ous·ly** adv

pars·ley \'pärslē\ n : garden plant used as a seasoning or garnish

pars·nip \'pärsnəp\ n : carrotlike vegetable with a white edible root

par·son \'pärs⁰n\ n : minister

par·son·age \'pärs⁰nij\ n : parson's house

part \'pärt\ n **1** : one of the units into which a larger whole is divided **2** : function or role ~ vb **1** : take leave **2** : separate **3** : go away **4** : give up

par·take \pär'tāk, pər-\ vb **-took; -tak·en; -tak·ing** : have or take a share — **par·tak·er** n

par·tial \'pärshəl\ adj **1** : favoring one over another **2** : affecting a part only —**par·tial·i·ty** \,pärshē'alətē\ n — **par·tial·ly** \'pärshəlē\ adv

par·tic·i·pate \pər'tisə,pāt, pär-\ vb **-pat·ed; -pat·ing** : take part in something —**par·tic·i·pant** \-pənt\ adj or n —**par·tic·i·pa·tion** \-,tisə'pāshən\ n —**par·tic·i·pa·to·ry** \-'tisəpə,tōrē\ adj

par·ti·ci·ple \'pärtə,sipəl\ n : verb form with functions of both verb and adjective —**par·ti·cip·i·al** \,pärtə'si-pēəl\ adj

par·ti·cle \'pärtikəl\ n : small bit

par·tic·u·lar \pär'tikyələr\ adj **1** : relating to a specific person or thing **2** : individual **3** : hard to please ~ n : detail —**par·tic·u·lar·ly** adv

par·ti·san \'pärtəzən, -sən\ n **1** : adherent **2** : guerrilla —**partisan** adj — **par·ti·san·ship** n

par·tite \'pär,tīt\ adj : divided into parts

par·ti·tion \pər'tishən, pär-\ n **1** : distribution **2** : something that divides —**partition** vb

part·ly \'pärtlē\ adv : in some degree

part·ner \'pärtnər\ n **1** : associate **2**

: companion **3** : business associate — **part·ner·ship** n

part of speech : class of words distinguished esp. according to function

par·tridge \'pärtrij\ n, pl **-tridge** or **-tridg·es** : stout-bodied game bird

par·ty \'pärtē\ n, pl **-ties 1** : political organization **2** : participant **3** : company of persons esp. with a purpose **4** : social gathering

par·ve·nu \'pärvə,nü, -,nyü\ n : social upstart

pass \'pas\ vb **1** : move past, over, or through **2** : go away or die **3** : allow to elapse **4** : go unchallenged **5** : transfer or undergo transfer **6** : render a judgment **7** : occur **8** : enact **9** : undergo testing successfully **10** : be regarded **11** : decline ~ n **1** : low place in a mountain range **2** : act of passing **3** : accomplishment **4** : permission to leave, enter, or move about —**pass·able** adj —**pass·ably** adv —**pass·er** n —**pass·er·by** n

pas·sage \'pasij\ n **1** : process of passing **2** : means of passing **3** : voyage **4** : right to pass **5** : literary selection — **pas·sage·way** n

pass·book n : bankbook

pas·sé \pa'sā\ adj : out-of-date

pas·sen·ger \'pas⁰njər\ n : traveler in a conveyance

pass·ing \'pasiŋ\ n : death

pas·sion \'pashən\ n **1** : strong feeling esp. of anger, love, or desire **2** : object of affection or enthusiasm —**pas·sion·ate** \'pashənət\ adj —**pas·sion·ate·ly** adv —**pas·sion·less** adj

pas·sive \'pasiv\ adj **1** : not active but acted upon **2** : submissive —**passive** n —**pas·sive·ly** adv —**pas·siv·i·ty** \pa'sivətē\ n

Pass·over \'pas,ōvər\ n : Jewish holiday celebrated in March or April in commemoration of the Hebrews' liberation from slavery in Egypt

pass·port \'pas,pōrt\ n : government document needed for travel abroad

pass·word n **1** : word or phrase spoken to pass a guard **2** : sequence of characters needed to get into a computer system

past \'past\ adj **1** : ago **2** : just gone by **3** : having existed before the present **4** : expressing past time ~ prep or adv **1** : beyond ~ n **1** : time gone by **2** : verb tense expressing time gone by **3** : past life

pas·ta \'pästə\ n : fresh or dried shaped dough

paste \'pāst\ n **1** : smooth ground food **2** : moist adhesive ~ vb **past·ed; past·ing** : attach with paste —**pasty** adj

paste·board n : cardboard

pas·tel \pas'tel\ n : light color —**pastel** adj

pas·teur·ize \'paschə,rīz, 'pastə-\ vb **-ized; -iz·ing** : heat (as milk) so as to kill germs —**pas·teur·i·za·tion** \,paschərə'zāshən, ,pastə-\ n

pas·time \'pas,tīm\ n : amusement

pas·tor \'pastər\ n : priest or minister serving a church or parish —**pas·tor·ate** \-tərət\ n

pas·to·ral \'pastərəl\ adj **1** : relating to rural life **2** : of or relating to spiritual guidance or a pastor ~ n : literary work dealing with rural life

pas·try \'pāstrē\ n, pl **-ries** : sweet baked goods

pas·ture \'paschər\ n : land used for grazing ~ vb **-tured; -tur·ing** : graze

pat \'pat\ n **1** : light tap **2** : small mass ~ vb **-tt-** : tap gently ~ adj or adv **1** : apt or glib **2** : unyielding

patch \'pach\ n **1** : piece used for mending **2** : small area distinct from surrounding area ~ vb **1** : mend with a patch **2** : make of fragments **3** : repair hastily —**patchy** \-ē\ adj

patch·work n : something made of pieces of different materials, shapes, or colors

pate \'pāt\ n : crown of the head

pa·tel·la \pə'telə\ n, pl **-lae** \-'tel,ē, -,ī\ or **-las** : kneecap

pa·tent adj **1** \'pat⁹nt, 'pāt-\ : obvious **2** \'pat-\ : protected by a patent ~ \'pat-\ n : document conferring or securing a right ~ \'pat-\ vb : secure by patent —**pat·ent·ly** adv

pa·ter·nal \pə'tərn⁹l\ adj **1** : fatherly **2** : related through or inherited from a father —**pa·ter·nal·ly** adv

pa·ter·ni·ty \pə'tərnətē\ n : fatherhood

path \'path, 'päth\ n **1** : trodden way **2** : route or course —**path·find·er** n —**path·way** n —**path·less** adj

pa·thet·ic \pə'thetik\ adj : pitiful —**pa·thet·i·cal·ly** adv

pa·thol·o·gy \pə'thäləjē\ n, pl **-gies 1** : study of disease **2** : physical abnormality —**path·o·log·i·cal** \,pathə-'läjikəl\ adj —**pa·thol·o·gist** \pə-'thäləjist\ n

pa·thos \'pā,thäs\ n : element evoking pity

pa·tience \'pāshəns\ n : habit or fact of being patient

pa·tient \'pāshənt\ adj : bearing pain or trials without complaint ~ n : one under medical care —**pa·tient·ly** adv

pa·ti·na \pə'tēnə, 'patənə\ n, pl **-nas** \-nəz\ or **-nae** \-,nē, -,nī\ : green film formed on copper and bronze

pa·tio \'patē,ō, 'pät-\ n, pl **-ti·os** **1** : courtyard **2** : paved recreation area near a house

pa·tri·arch \'pātrē,ärk\ n **1** : man revered as father or founder **2** : venerable old man —**pa·tri·ar·chal** \,pātrē'ärkəl\ adj —**pa·tri·ar·chy** \-,ärkē\ n

pa·tri·cian \pə'trishən\ n : person of high birth —**patrician** adj

pat·ri·mo·ny \'patrə,mōnē\ n : something inherited —**pat·ri·mo·ni·al** \,patrə'mōnēəl\ adj

pa·tri·ot \'pātrēət, -,ät\ n : one who loves his or her country —**pa·tri·ot·ic** \,pātrē'ätik\ adj —**pa·tri·ot·i·cal·ly** adv —**pa·tri·o·tism** \'pātrēə,tizəm\ n

pa·trol \pə'trōl\ n **1** : a going around for observation or security **2** : group on patrol ~ vb **-ll-** : carry out a patrol

pa·trol·man \-mən\ n : police officer

pa·tron \'pātrən\ n **1** : special protector **2** : wealthy supporter **3** : customer

pa·tron·age \'patrənij, 'pā-\ n **1** : support or influence of a patron **2** : trade of customers **3** : control of government appointments

pa·tron·ess \'pātrənəs\ n : woman who is a patron

pa·tron·ize \'pātrə,nīz, 'pa-\ vb **-ized; -iz·ing 1** : be a customer of **2** : treat with condescension

¹pat·ter \'patər\ vb : talk glibly or mechanically ~ n : rapid talk

²patter vb : pat or tap rapidly ~ n : quick succession of pats or taps

pat·tern \'patərn\ n **1** : model for imitation or making things **2** : artistic design **3** : noticeable formation or set of characteristics ~ vb : form according to a pattern

pat·ty \'patē\ n, pl **-ties** : small flat cake

pau·ci·ty \'pòsətē\ n : shortage

paunch \'pònch\ n : large belly —**paunchy** adj

pau·per \'pòpər\ n : poor person —**pau·per·ism** \-pə,rizəm\ n —**pau·per·ize** \-pə,rīz\ vb

pause \'póz\ *n* : temporary stop ~ *vb* **paused; paus·ing** : stop briefly

pave \'pāv\ *vb* **paved; pav·ing** : cover to smooth or firm the surface —**pave·ment** \-mənt\ *n* —**pav·ing** *n*

pa·vil·ion \pə'vilyən\ *n* **1** : large tent **2** : light structure used for entertainment or shelter

paw \'pò\ *n* : foot of a 4-legged clawed animal ~ *vb* **1** : handle clumsily or rudely **2** : touch or strike with a paw

pawn \'pòn\ *n* **1** : goods deposited as security for a loan **2** : state of being pledged ~ *vb* : deposit as a pledge —**pawn·bro·ker** *n* —**pawn·shop** *n*

pay \'pā\ *vb* **paid** \'pād\; **pay·ing 1** : make due return for goods or services **2** : discharge indebtedness for **3** : requite **4** : give freely or as fitting **5** : be profitable ~ *n* **1** : status of being paid **2** : something paid —**pay·able** *adj* —**pay·check** *n* —**pay·ee** \pā'ē\ *n* —**pay·er** *n* —**pay·ment** *n*

PC \,pē'sē\ *n, pl* **PCs** *or* **PC's** : microcomputer

pea \'pē\ *n* : round edible seed of a leguminous vine

peace \'pēs\ *n* **1** : state of calm and quiet **2** : absence of war or strife —**peace·able** \-əbəl\ *adj* —**peace·ably** \-blē\ *adv* —**peace·ful** \-fəl\ *adj* —**peace·fully** *adv* —**peace·keep·er** *n* —**peace·keep·ing** *n* —**peace·mak·er** *n* —**peace·time** *n*

peach \'pēch\ *n* : sweet juicy fruit of a flowering tree or this tree

pea·cock \'pē,käk\ *n* : brilliantly colored male pheasant

peak \'pēk\ *n* **1** : pointed or projecting part **2** : top of a hill **3** : highest level ~ *vb* : reach a maximum —**peak** *adj*

peak·ed \'pēkəd\ *adj* : sickly

peal \'pēl\ *n* : loud sound (as of ringing bells) ~ *vb* : give out peals

pea·nut \'pē,nət\ *n* : annual herb that bears underground pods or the pod or the edible seed inside

pear \'par\ *n* : fleshy fruit of a tree related to the apple

pearl \'pərl\ *n* : gem formed within an oyster —**pearly** \'pərlē\ *adj*

peas·ant \'pez²nt\ *n* : tiller of the soil —**peas·ant·ry** \-²ntrē\ *n*

peat \'pēt\ *n* : decayed organic deposit often dried for fuel —**peaty** *adj*

peb·ble \'pebəl\ *n* : small stone —**peb·bly** *adj*

pe·can \pi'kän, -'kan\ *n* : hickory tree bearing a smooth-shelled nut or the nut

pec·ca·dil·lo \,pekə'dilō\ *n, pl* **-loes** *or* **-los** : slight offense

¹peck \'pek\ *n* : unit of dry measure equal to 8 quarts

²peck *vb* : strike or pick up with the bill ~ *n* : quick sharp stroke

pec·tin \'pektən\ *n* : water-soluble plant substance that causes fruit jellies to set —**pec·tic** \-tik\ *adj*

pec·to·ral \'pektərəl\ *adj* : relating to the breast or chest

pe·cu·liar \pi'kyülyər\ *adj* **1** : characteristic of only one **2** : strange —**pe·cu·liar·i·ty** \-,kyül'yarətē, -ē'ar-\ *n* —**pe·cu·liar·ly** *adv*

pe·cu·ni·ary \pi'kyünē,erē\ *adj* : relating to money

ped·a·go·gy \'pedə,gōjē, -,gäj-\ *n* : art or profession of teaching —**ped·a·gog·ic** \,pedə'gäjik, -'gōj-\, **ped·a·gog·i·cal** \-ikəl\ *adj* —**ped·a·gogue** \'pedə,gäg\ *n*

ped·al \'ped³l\ *n* : lever worked by the foot ~ *adj* : relating to the foot ~ *vb* : use a pedal

ped·ant \'ped³nt\ *n* : learned bore —**pe·dan·tic** \pi'dantik\ *adj* —**ped·ant·ry** \'ped³ntrē\ *n*

ped·dle \'ped³l\ *vb* **-dled; -dling** : offer for sale —**ped·dler** \'pedlər\ *n*

ped·es·tal \'pedəst³l\ *n* : support or foot of something upright

pe·des·tri·an \pə'destrēən\ *adj* **1** : ordinary **2** : walking ~ *n* : person who walks

pe·di·at·rics \,pēdē'atriks\ *n* : branch of medicine dealing with children —**pe·di·at·ric** \-trik\ *adj* —**pe·di·a·tri·cian** \,pēdēə'trishən\ *n*

ped·i·gree \'pedə,grē\ *n* : line of ancestors or a record of it

ped·i·ment \'pedəmənt\ *n* : triangular gablelike decoration on a building

peek \'pēk\ *vb* **1** : look furtively **2** : glance —**peek** *n*

peel \'pēl\ *vb* **1** : strip the skin or rind from **2** : lose the outer layer ~ *n* : skin or rind —**peel·ing** *n*

¹peep \'pēp\ *vb or n* : cheep

²peep *vb* **1** : look slyly **2** : begin to emerge ~ *n* : brief look —**peep·er** *n* —**peep·hole** *n*

¹peer \'pir\ *n* **1** : one's equal **2** : nobleman —**peer·age** \-ij\ *n*

²peer *vb* : look intently or curiously

peer·less \-ləs\ *adj* : having no equal

peeve \'pēv\ *vb* **peeved; peev·ing** : make resentful ~ *n* : complaint — **peev·ish** \-ish\ *adj* —**peev·ish·ly** *adv* —**peev·ish·ness** *n*

peg \'peg\ *n* : small pinlike piece ~ *vb* **-gg-** 1 : put a peg into 2 : fix or mark with or as if with pegs

pei·gnoir \pān'wär, pen-\ *n* : negligee

pe·jo·ra·tive \pi'jórətiv\ *adj* : having a negative or degrading effect ~ *n* : a degrading word or phrase —**pe·jo·ra·tive·ly** *adv*

pel·i·can \'pelikən\ *n* : large-billed seabird

pel·la·gra \pə'lagrə, -'läg-\ *n* : protein-deficiency disease

pel·let \'pelət\ *n* : little ball —**pel·let·al** \-∘l\ *adj* —**pel·let·ize** \-,īz\ *vb*

pell-mell \'pel'mel\ *adv* : in confusion or haste

pel·lu·cid \pə'lüsəd\ *adj* : very clear

1pelt \'pelt\ *n* : skin of a fur-bearing animal

2pelt *vb* : strike with blows or missiles

pel·vis \'pelvəs\ *n, pl* **-vis·es** \-vəsəz\ *or* **-ves** \-,vēz\ : cavity formed by the hip bones —**pel·vic** \-vik\ *adj*

1pen \'pen\ *n* : enclosure for animals ~ *vb* **-nn-** : shut in a pen

2pen *n* : tool for writing with ink ~ *vb* **-nn-** : write

pe·nal \'pēn∘l\ *adj* : relating to punishment

pe·nal·ize \'pēn∘l,īz, 'pen-\ *vb* **-ized; -iz·ing** : put a penalty on

pen·al·ty \'pen∘ltē\ *n, pl* **-ties** 1 : punishment for crime 2 : disadvantage, loss, or hardship due to an action

pen·ance \'penəns\ *n* : act performed to show repentance

pence \'pens\ *pl of* PENNY

pen·chant \'penchənt\ *n* : strong inclination

pen·cil \'pensəl\ *n* : writing or drawing tool with a solid marking substance (as graphite) as its core ~ *vb* **-ciled** *or* **-cilled; -cil·ing** *or* **-cil·ling** : draw or write with a pencil

pen·dant \'pendənt\ *n* : hanging ornament

pen·dent, pen·dant \'pendənt\ *adj* : hanging

pend·ing \'pendiŋ\ *prep* : while awaiting ~ *adj* : not yet decided

pen·du·lous \'penjələs, -dyùləs\ *adj* : hanging loosely

pen·du·lum \-ləm\ *n* : a hanging weight that is free to swing

pen·e·trate \'penə,trāt\ *vb* **-trat·ed; -trat·ing** 1 : enter into 2 : permeate 3 : see into —**pen·e·tra·ble** \-trəbəl\ *adj* —**pen·e·tra·tion** \,penə'trāshən\ *n* —**pen·e·tra·tive** \'penə,trātiv\ *adj*

pen·guin \'peŋgwən, 'peŋ-\ *n* : short-legged flightless seabird

pen·i·cil·lin \,penə'silən\ *n* : antibiotic usu. produced by a mold

pen·in·su·la \pə'ninsələ, -'ninchə-\ *n* : land extending out into the water — **pen·in·su·lar** \-lər\ *adj*

pe·nis \'pēnəs\ *n, pl* **-nes** \-,nēz\ *or* **-nis·es** : male organ of copulation

pen·i·tent \'penətənt\ *adj* : feeling sorrow for sins or offenses ~ *n* : penitent person —**pen·i·tence** \-təns\ *n*—**pen·i·ten·tial** \,penə'tenchəl\ *adj*

pen·i·ten·tia·ry \,penə'tenchərē\ *n, pl* **-ries** : state or federal prison

pen·man·ship \'penmən,ship\ *n* : art or practice of writing

pen·nant \'penənt\ *n* : nautical or championship flag

pen·ny \'penē\ *n, pl* **-nies** \-ēz\ *or* **pence** \'pens\ 1 : monetary unit equal to 1/100 pound 2 *pl* **-nies** : cent —**pen·ni·less** \'peniləs\ *adj*

pen·sion \'penchən\ *n* : retirement income ~ *vb* : pay a pension to —**pen·sion·er** *n*

pen·sive \'pensiv\ *adj* : thoughtful —**pen·sive·ly** *adv*

pent \'pent\ *adj* : confined

pent·a·gon \'pentə,gän\ *n* : 5-sided polygon —**pen·tag·o·nal** \pen'tagən∘l\ *adj*

pen·tam·e·ter \pen'tamətər\ *n* : line of verse containing 5 metrical feet

pent·house \'pent,haús\ *n* : rooftop apartment

pen·u·ry \'penyərē\ *n* 1 : poverty 2 : thrifty or stingy manner —**pe·nu·ri·ous** \pə'nùreəs, -'nyùr-\ *adj*

pe·on \'pēän, -ən\ *n, pl* **-ons** *or* **-o·nes** \pā'ōnēz\ : landless laborer in Spanish America —**pe·on·age** \-ənij\ *n*

pe·o·ny \'pēənē\ *n, pl* **-nies** : garden plant having large flowers

peo·ple \'pēpəl\ *n, pl* **people** 1 *pl* : human beings in general 2 *pl* : human beings in a certain group (as a family) or community 3 *pl* **peoples** : tribe, nation, or race ~ *vb* **-pled; -pling** : constitute the population of

pep \'pep\ *n* : brisk energy ~ *vb*

pepped; pep·ping : put pep into — **pep·py** *adj*

pep·per \'pepər\ *n* **1** : pungent seasoning from the berry (**peppercorn**) of a shrub **2** : vegetable grown for its hot or sweet fruit ~ *vb* : season with pepper — **pep·pery** \-ərē\ *adj*

pep·per·mint \-,mint, -mənt\ *n* : pungent aromatic mint

pep·per·o·ni \,pepə'rōnē\ *n* : spicy beef and pork sausage

pep·tic \'peptik\ *adj* : relating to digestion or the effect of digestive juices

per \'pər\ *prep* **1** : by means of **2** : for each **3** : according to

per·am·bu·late \pə'rambyə,lāt\ *vb* **-lat·ed; -lat·ing** : walk — **per·am·bu·la·tion** \-,rambyə'lāshən\ *n*

per·cale \,pər'kāl, 'pər-,; ,pər'kal\ *n* : fine woven cotton cloth

per·ceive \pər'sēv\ *vb* **-ceived; -ceiv·ing** **1** : realize **2** : become aware of through the senses — **per·ceiv·able** *adj*

per·cent \pər'sent\ *adv* : in each hundred ~ *n*, *pl* **-cent** or **-cents** **1** : one part in a hundred **2** : percentage

per·cent·age \pər'sentij\ *n* : part expressed in hundredths

per·cen·tile \pər'sen,tīl\ *n* : a standing on a scale of 0–100

per·cep·ti·ble \pər'septəbəl\ *adj* : capable of being perceived — **per·cep·ti·bly** \-blē\ *adv*

per·cep·tion \pər'sepshən\ *n* **1** : act or result of perceiving **2** : ability to understand

per·cep·tive \pər'septiv\ *adj* : showing keen perception — **per·cep·tive·ly** *adv*

¹perch \'pərch\ *n* : roost for birds ~ *vb* : roost

²perch *n*, *pl* **perch** or **perch·es** : freshwater spiny-finned food fish

per·co·late \'pərkə,lāt\ *vb* **-lat·ed; -lat·ing** : trickle or filter down through a substance — **per·co·la·tor** \-,lātər\ *n*

per·cus·sion \pər'kəshən\ *n* **1** : sharp blow **2** : musical instrument sounded by striking

pe·remp·to·ry \pə'remptərē\ *adj* **1** : imperative **2** : domineering — **pe·remp·to·ri·ly** \-tərəlē\ *adv*

pe·ren·ni·al \pə'renēəl\ *adj* **1** : present at all seasons **2** : continuing from year to year **3** : recurring regularly ~ *n* : perennial plant — **pe·ren·ni·al·ly** *adv*

per·fect \'pərfikt\ *adj* **1** : being without fault or defect **2** : exact **3** : complete ~ \pər'fekt\ *vb* : make perfect — **per·fect·ibil·i·ty** \pər,fektə'bilətē\ *n* — **per·fect·ible** \pər'fektəbəl\ *adj* — **per·fect·ly** *adv* — **per·fect·ness** *n*

per·fec·tion \pər'fekshən\ *n* **1** : quality or state of being perfect **2** : highest degree of excellence — **per·fec·tion·ist** \-shənist\ *n*

per·fid·i·ous \pər'fidēəs\ *adj* : treacherous — **per·fid·i·ous·ly** *adv*

per·fo·rate \'pərfə,rāt\ *vb* **-rat·ed; -rat·ing** : make a hole in — **per·fo·ra·tion** \,pərfə'rāshən\ *n*

per·force \pər'fōrs\ *adv* : of necessity

per·form \pər'fōrm\ *vb* **1** : carry out **2** : do in a set manner **3** : give a performance — **per·form·er** *n*

per·for·mance \pər'fōr,məns\ *n* **1** : act or process of performing **2** : public presentation

per·fume \'pər,fyüm, pər'-\ *n* **1** : pleasant odor **2** : something that gives a scent ~ \pər'-, 'pər,-\ *vb* **-fumed; -fum·ing** : add scent to

per·func·to·ry \pər'fəŋktərē\ *adj* : done merely as a duty — **per·func·to·ri·ly** \-tərəlē\ *adv*

per·haps \pər'haps\ *adv* : possibly but not certainly

per·il \'perəl\ *n* : danger — **per·il·ous** *adj* — **per·il·ous·ly** *adv*

pe·rim·e·ter \pə'rimətər\ *n* : outer boundary of a body or figure

pe·ri·od \'pirēəd\ *n* **1** : punctuation mark . used esp. to mark the end of a declarative sentence or an abbreviation **2** : division of time **3** : stage in a process or development

pe·ri·od·ic \,pirē'ädik\ *adj* : occurring at regular intervals — **pe·ri·od·i·cal·ly** *adv*

pe·ri·od·i·cal \,pirē'ädikəl\ *n* : newspaper or magazine

pe·riph·ery \pə'rifərē\ *n*, *pl* **-er·ies** : outer boundary — **pe·riph·er·al** \-ərəl\ *adj*

peri·scope \'perə,skōp\ *n* : optical instrument for viewing from a submarine

per·ish \'perish\ *vb* : die or spoil — **per·ish·able** \-əbəl\ *adj or n*

per·ju·ry \'pərjərē\ *n* : lying under oath — **per·jure** \'pərjər\ *vb* — **per·jur·er** *n*

¹perk \'pərk\ *vb* **1** : thrust (as the head)

up jauntily 2 : freshen 3 : gain vigor or spirit —**perky** adj

²**perk** vb : percolate

³**perk** n : privilege or benefit in addition to regular pay

per·ma·nent \'pərmənənt\ adj : lasting ~ n : hair wave —**per·ma·nence** \-nəns\ n —**per·ma·nent·ly** adv

per·me·able \'pərmēəbəl\ adj : permitting fluids to seep through —**per·me·a·bil·i·ty** \,pərmēə'bilətē\ n

per·me·ate \'pərmē,āt\ vb -**at·ed; -at·ing** 1 : seep through 2 : pervade —**per·me·ation** \,pərmē'āshən\ n

per·mis·si·ble \pər'misəbəl\ adj : that may be permitted

per·mis·sion \pər'mishən\ n : formal consent

per·mis·sive \pər'misiv\ adj : granting freedom esp. to excess —**per·mis·sive·ly** adv —**per·mis·sive·ness** n

per·mit \pər'mit\ vb -**tt-** 1 : approve 2 : make possible ~ \'pər,-, pər'-\ n : license

per·ni·cious \pər'nishəs\ adj : very harmful —**per·ni·cious·ly** adv

per·ox·ide \pə'räk,sīd\ n : compound (as hydrogen peroxide) in which oxygen is joined to oxygen

per·pen·dic·u·lar \,pərpən'dikyələr\ adj 1 : vertical 2 : meeting at a right angle —**perpendicular** n —**per·pen·dic·u·lar·i·ty** \-,dikyə'larətē\ n —**per·pen·dic·u·lar·ly** adv

per·pe·trate \'pərpə,trāt\ vb -**trat·ed; -trat·ing** : be guilty of doing —**per·pe·tra·tion** \,pərpə'trāshən\ n —**per·pe·tra·tor** \'pərpə,trātər\ n

per·pet·u·al \pər'pechəwəl\ adj 1 : continuing forever 2 : occurring continually —**per·pet·u·al·ly** adv —**per·pe·tu·i·ty** \,pərpə'tüətē, -'tyü-\ n

per·pet·u·ate \pər'pechə,wāt\ vb -**at·ed; -at·ing** : make perpetual —**per·pet·u·a·tion** \-,pechə'wāshən\ n

per·plex \pər'pleks\ vb : confuse —**per·plex·i·ty** \-ətē\ n

per·se·cute \'pərsi,kyüt\ vb -**cut·ed; -cut·ing** : harass, afflict —**per·se·cu·tion** \,pərsi'kyüshən\ n —**per·se·cu·tor** \'pərsi,kyütər\ n

per·se·vere \,pərsə'vir\ vb -**vered; -ver·ing** : persist —**per·se·ver·ance** \-'virəns\ n

per·sist \pər'sist, -'zist\ vb 1 : go on resolutely in spite of difficulties 2 : continue to exist —**per·sis·tence** \-'sistəns, -'zis-\ n —**per·sis·ten·cy**

\-tənsē\ n —**per·sis·tent** \-tənt\ adj —**per·sis·tent·ly** adv

per·son \'pərs³n\ n 1 : human being 2 : human being's body or individuality 3 : reference to the speaker, one spoken to, or one spoken of

per·son·able \'pərs³nəbəl\ adj : having a pleasing personality

per·son·age \'pərs³nij\ n : person of rank or distinction

per·son·al \'pərs³nəl\ adj 1 : relating to a particular person 2 : done in person 3 : affecting one's body 4 : offensive to a certain individual —**per·son·al·ly** adv

per·son·al·i·ty \,pərs³n'alətē\ n, pl -**ties** 1 : manner and disposition of an individual 2 : distinctive or well-known person

per·son·al·ize \'pərs³nə,līz\ vb -**ized; -iz·ing** : mark as belonging to a particular person

per·son·i·fy \pər'sänə,fī\ vb -**fied; -fy·ing** 1 : represent as a human being 2 : be the embodiment of —**per·son·i·fi·ca·tion** \-,sänəfə'kāshən\ n

per·son·nel \,pərs³n'el\ n : body of persons employed

per·spec·tive \pər'spektiv\ n 1 : apparent depth and distance in painting 2 : view of things in their true relationship or importance

per·spi·ca·cious \,pərspə'kāshəs\ adj : showing keen understanding or discernment —**per·spi·cac·i·ty** \-'kasətē\ n

per·spire \pər'spīr\ vb -**spired; -spir·ing** : sweat —**per·spi·ra·tion** \,pərspə'rāshən\ n

per·suade \pər'swād\ vb -**suad·ed; -suad·ing** : win over to a belief or course of action by argument or entreaty —**per·sua·sion** \pər'swāzhən\ n —**per·sua·sive** \-'swāsiv, -ziv\ adj —**per·sua·sive·ly** adv —**per·sua·sive·ness** n

pert \'pərt\ adj : flippant or irreverent

per·tain \pər'tān\ vb 1 : belong 2 : relate

per·ti·nent \'pərt³nənt\ adj : relevant —**per·ti·nence** \-əns\ n

per·turb \pər'tərb\ vb : make uneasy —**per·tur·ba·tion** \,pərtər'bāshən\ n

pe·ruse \pə'rüz\ vb -**rused; -rus·ing** : read attentively —**pe·rus·al** \-'rüzəl\ n

per·vade \pər'vād\ vb -**vad·ed; -vad·ing** : spread through every part of —**per·va·sive** \-'vāsiv, -ziv\ adj

per·verse \pər'vərs\ adj 1 : corrupt 2 : unreasonably contrary —**per·verse·ly** adv —**per·verse·ness** n — **per·version** \pər'vərzhən\ n — **per·ver·si·ty** \-'vərsətē\ n

per·vert \pər'vərt\ vb : corrupt or distort ~ \'pər,-\ n : one that is perverted

pe·so \'pāsō\ n, pl **-sos** : monetary unit (as of Mexico)

pes·si·mism \'pesə,mizəm\ n : inclination to expect the worst —**pes·si·mist** \-mist\ n —**pes·si·mis·tic** \,pesə'mistik\ adj

pest \'pest\ n 1 : nuisance 2 : plant or animal detrimental to humans or their crops —**pes·ti·cide** \'pestə,sīd\ n

pes·ter \'pestər\ vb **-tered; -ter·ing** : harass with petty matters

pes·ti·lence \'pestələns\ n : plague —**pes·ti·lent** \-lənt\ adj

pes·tle \'pesəl, 'pest³l\ n : implement for grinding substances in a mortar

pet \'pet\ n 1 : domesticated animal kept for pleasure 2 : favorite ~ vb **-tt-** : stroke gently or lovingly

pet·al \'pet³l\ n : modified leaf of a flower head

pe·tite \pə'tēt\ adj : having a small trim figure

pe·ti·tion \pə'tishən\ n : formal written request ~ vb : make a request —**pe·ti·tion·er** n

pet·ri·fy \'petrə,fī\ vb **-fied; -fy·ing** 1 : change into stony material 2 : make rigid or inactive (as from fear) —**pet·ri·fac·tion** \,petrə'fakshən\ n

pe·tro·leum \pə'trōlēəm\ n : raw oil obtained from the ground

pet·ti·coat \'petē,kōt\ n : skirt worn under a dress

pet·ty \'petē\ adj **-ti·er; -est** 1 : minor 2 : of no importance 3 : narrow-minded or mean —**pet·ti·ly** \'pet³lē\ adv —**pet·ti·ness** n

petty officer n : subordinate officer in the navy or coast guard

pet·u·lant \'pechələnt\ adj : irritable —**pet·u·lance** \-ləns\ n —**pet·u·lant·ly** adv

pe·tu·nia \pi'tünyə, -'tyü-\ n : tropical herb with bright flowers

pew \'pyü\ n : bench with a back used in a church

pew·ter \'pyütər\ n : alloy of tin used for household utensils

pH \,pē'āch\ n : number expressing relative acidity and alkalinity

pha·lanx \'fā,laŋks\ n, pl **-lanx·es** or **-lan·ges** \fə'lan,jēz\ 1 : body (as of troops) in compact formation 2 pl **phalanges** : digital bone of the hand or foot

phal·lus \'faləs\ n, pl **-li** \'fal,ī\ or **-lus·es** : penis —**phal·lic** \'falik\ adj

phantasy var of FANTASY

phan·tom \'fantəm\ n : something that only appears to be real —**phantom** adj

pha·raoh \'ferō, 'fārō\ n : ruler of ancient Egypt

phar·ma·ceu·ti·cal \,färmə'sütikəl\ adj : relating to pharmacy or the making and selling of medicinal drugs —**pharmaceutical** n

phar·ma·col·o·gy \,färmə'käləjē\ n : science of drugs esp. as related to medicinal uses —**phar·ma·co·log·i·cal** \-ikəl\ adj —**phar·ma·col·o·gist** \-'käləjist\ n

phar·ma·cy \'färməsē\ n, pl **-cies** 1 : art or practice of preparing and dispensing medical drugs 2 : drugstore —**phar·ma·cist** \-sist\ n

phar·ynx \'fariŋks\ n, pl **pha·ryn·ges** \fə'rin,jēz\ : space behind the mouth into which the nostrils, esophagus, and windpipe open —**pha·ryn·ge·al** \fə'rinjəl, ,faron'jēəl\ adj

phase \'fāz\ n 1 : particular appearance or stage in a recurring series of changes 2 : stage in a process —**phase in** vb : introduce in stages —**phase out** vb : discontinue gradually

pheas·ant \'fez³nt\ n, pl **-ant** or **-ants** : long-tailed brilliantly colored game bird

phe·nom·e·non \fi'nämə,nän, -nən\ n, pl **-na** \-nə\ or **-nons** 1 : observable fact or event 2 pl **-nons** : prodigy —**phe·nom·e·nal** \-'nämən³l\ adj

phi·lan·der·er \fə'landərər\ n : one who makes love without serious intent

phi·lan·thro·py \fə'lanthrəpē\ n, pl **-pies** : charitable act or gift or an organization that distributes such gifts —**phil·an·throp·ic** \,filan'thräpik\ adj —**phi·lan·thro·pist** \fə'lanthrəpist\ n

phi·lat·e·ly \fə'lat³lē\ n : collection and study of postage stamps —**phi·lat·e·list** \-³list\ n

phi·lis·tine \'filə,stēn, fə'listən\ n : one who is smugly indifferent to intellectual or artistic values —**philistine** adj

phi·lo·den·dron \,filə'dendrən\ n, pl

-drons *or* **-dra** \-drə\ : plant grown for its showy leaves

phi•los•o•pher \fə'läsəfər\ *n* **1** : reflective thinker **2** : student of philosophy

phi•los•o•phy \fə'läsəfē\ *n, pl* **-phies 1** : critical study of fundamental beliefs **2** : sciences and liberal arts exclusive of medicine, law, and theology **3** : system of ideas **4** : sum of personal convictions —**phil•o•soph•ic** \,filə-'säfik\, **phil•o•soph•i•cal** \-ikəl\ *adj* —**phil•o•soph•i•cal•ly** \-klē\ *adv* —**phi•los•o•phize** \fə'läsə,fīz\ *vb*

phle•bi•tis \fli'bītəs\ *n* : inflammation of a vein

phlegm \'flem\ *n* : thick mucus in the nose and throat

phlox \'fläks\ *n, pl* **phlox** *or* **phlox•es** : herb grown for its flower clusters

pho•bia \'fōbēə\ *n* : irrational persistent fear

phoe•nix \'fēniks\ *n* : legendary bird held to burn itself to death and rise fresh and young from its ashes

phone \'fōn\ *n* : telephone ~ *vb* **phoned; phon•ing** : call on a telephone

pho•neme \'fō,nēm\ *n* : basic distinguishable unit of speech —**pho•ne•mic** \fō'nēmik\ *adj*

pho•net•ics \fə'netiks\ *n* : study of speech sounds —**pho•net•ic** \-ik\ *adj* —**pho•ne•ti•cian** \,fōnə'tishən\ *n*

pho•nics \'fäniks\ *n* : method of teaching reading by stressing sound values of syllables and words

pho•no•graph \'fōnə,graf\ *n* : instrument that reproduces sounds from a grooved disc

pho•ny, pho•ney \'fōnē\ *adj* **-ni•er; -est** : not sincere or genuine —**phony** *n*

phos•phate \'fäs,fāt\ *n* : chemical salt used in fertilizers —**phos•phat•ic** \fäs'fatik\ *adj*

phos•phor \'fäsfər\ *n* : phosphorescent substance

phos•pho•res•cence \,fäsfə'res³ns\ *n* : luminescence from absorbed radiation —**phos•pho•res•cent** \-³nt\ *adj* —**phos•pho•res•cent•ly** *adv*

phos•pho•rus \'fäsfərəs\ *n* : poisonous waxy chemical element —**phos•phor•ic** \fäs'förik, -'fär-\ *adj* —**phos•pho•rous** \'fäsfərəs, fäs'fōrəs\ *adj*

pho•to \'fōtō\ *n, pl* **-tos** : photograph —**photo** *vb or adj*

pho•to•copy \'fōtə,käpē\ *n* : photographic copy (as of a printed page) —**photocopy** *vb*

pho•to•elec•tric \,fōtōi'lektrik\ *adj* : relating to an electrical effect due to the interaction of light with matter

pho•to•gen•ic \,fōtə'jenik\ *adj* : suitable for being photographed

pho•to•graph \'fōtə,graf\ *n* : picture taken by photography —**photograph** *vb* —**pho•tog•ra•pher** \fə'tägrəfər\ *n*

pho•tog•ra•phy \fə'tägrəfē\ *n* : process of using light to produce images on a sensitized surface —**pho•to•graph•ic** \,fōtə'grafik\ *adj* —**pho•to•graph•i•cal•ly** *adv*

pho•to•syn•the•sis \,fōtō'sinthəsəs\ *n* : formation of carbohydrates by chlorophyll-containing plants exposed to sunlight —**pho•to•syn•the•size** \-,sīz\ *vb* —**pho•to•syn•thet•ic** \-sin'thetik\ *adj*

phrase \'frāz\ *n* **1** : brief expression **2** : group of related words that express a thought ~ *vb* **phrased; phras•ing** : express in a particular manner

phrase•ol•o•gy \,frāzē'äləjē\ *n, pl* **-gies** : manner of phrasing

phy•lum \'fīləm\ *n, pl* **-la** \-lə\ : major division of the plant or animal kingdom

phys•i•cal \'fizikəl\ *adj* **1** : relating to nature **2** : material as opposed to mental or spiritual **3** : relating to the body ~ *n* : medical examination —**phys•i•cal•ly** \-klē\ *adv*

phy•si•cian \fə'zishən\ *n* : doctor of medicine

physician's assistant *n* : person certified to provide basic medical care under a physician's supervision

phys•i•cist \'fizəsist\ *n* : specialist in physics

phys•ics \'fiziks\ *n* : science that deals with matter and motion

phys•iog•no•my \,fizē'ägnəmē\ *n, pl* **-mies** : facial appearance esp. as a reflection of inner character

phys•i•ol•o•gy \,fizē'äləjē\ *n* : functional processes in an organism —**phys•i•o•log•i•cal** \-ēə'läjikəl\, **phys•i•o•log•ic** \-ik\ *adj* —**phys•i•ol•o•gist** \-ē'äləjist\ *n*

phy•sique \fə'zēk\ *n* : build of a person's body

pi \'pī\ *n, pl* **pis** \'pīz\ : symbol π denoting the ratio of the circumference of a circle to its diameter or the ratio itself

pi·a·nist \pē'anist, 'pēanist\ *n* : one who plays the piano

pi·a·no \pē'anō\ *n, pl* **-anos** : musical instrument with strings sounded by hammers operated from a keyboard

pi·az·za \pē'azə, -'äz-, -tsə\ *n, pl* **-zas** *or* **-ze** \-tsā\ : public square in a town

pic·a·yune \,pikē'yün\ *adj* : trivial or petty

pic·co·lo \'pikə,lō\ *n, pl* **-los** : small shrill flute

1pick \'pik\ *vb* **1** : break up with a pointed instrument **2** : remove bit by bit **3** : gather by plucking **4** : select **5** : rob **6** : provoke **7** : unlock with a wire **8** : eat sparingly ~ *n* **1** : act of choosing **2** : choicest one —**pick·er** *n* —**pick up** *vb* **1** : improve **2** : put in order

2pick *n* : pointed digging tool

pick·ax *n* : pick

pick·er·el \'pikərəl\ *n, pl* **-el** *or* **-els** : small pike

pick·et \'pikət\ *n* **1** : pointed stake (as for a fence) **2** : worker demonstrating on strike ~ *vb* : demonstrate as a picket

pick·le \'pikəl\ *n* **1** : brine or vinegar solution for preserving foods or a food preserved in a pickle **2** : bad state —**pickle** *vb*

pick·pock·et *n* : one who steals from pockets

pick·up \'pik,əp\ *n* **1** : revival or acceleration **2** : light truck with an open body

pic·nic \'pik,nik\ *n* : outing with food usu. eaten in the open ~ *vb* **-nicked; -nick·ing** : go on a picnic

pic·to·ri·al \pik'tōrēəl\ *adj* : relating to pictures

pic·ture \'pikchər\ *n* **1** : representation by painting, drawing, or photography **2** : vivid description **3** : copy **4** : movie ~ *vb* **-tured; -tur·ing** : form a mental image of

pic·tur·esque \,pikchə'resk\ *adj* : attractive or charming enough for a picture —**pic·tur·esque·ness** *n*

pie \'pī\ *n* : pastry crust and a filling

pie·bald \'pī,bȯld\ *adj* : blotched with white and black

piece \'pēs\ *n* **1** : part of a whole **2** : one of a group or set **3** : single item **4** : product of creative work ~ *vb* **pieced; piec·ing** : join into a whole

piece·meal \'pēs,mēl\ *adv or adj* : gradually

pied \'pīd\ *adj* : colored in blotches

pier \'pir\ *n* **1** : support for a bridge span **2** : deck or wharf built out over water **3** : pillar

pierce \'pirs\ *vb* **pierced; pierc·ing** **1** : enter or thrust into or through **2** : penetrate **3** : see through

pi·e·ty \'pīətē\ *n, pl* **-eties** : devotion to religion

pig \'pig\ *n* **1** : young swine **2** : dirty or greedy individual **3** : iron casting — **pig·gish** \-ish\ *adj* —**pig·let** \-lət\ *n* — **pig·pen** *n* —**pig·sty** *n*

pi·geon \'pijən\ *n* : stout-bodied short= legged bird

pi·geon·hole *n* : small open compartment for letters or documents ~ *vb* **1** : place in a pigeonhole **2** : classify

pig·gy·back \'pigē,bak\ *adv or adj* : up on the back and shoulders

pig·head·ed \-'hedəd\ *adj* : stubborn

pig·ment \'pigmənt\ *n* : coloring matter —**pig·men·ta·tion** *n*

pigmy *var of* PYGMY

pig·tail *n* : tight braid of hair

1pike \'pīk\ *n, pl* **pike** *or* **pikes** : large freshwater fish

2pike *n* : former weapon consisting of a long wooden staff with a steel point

3pike *n* : turnpike

pi·laf, pi·laff \pi'läf, 'pē,läf\, **pi·lau** \pi-'lȯ, -'lȯ; 'pēlȯ, -lȯ\ *n* : dish of seasoned rice

1pile \'pīl\ *n* : supporting pillar driven into the ground

2pile *n* : quantity of things thrown on one another ~ *vb* **piled; pil·ing** : heap up, accumulate

3pile *n* : surface of fine hairs or threads —**piled** *adj*

piles \'pīlz\ *n pl* : hemorrhoids

pil·fer \'pilfər\ *vb* : steal in small quantities

pil·grim \'pilgrəm\ *n* **1** : one who travels to a shrine or holy place in devotion **2** *cap* : one of the English settlers in America in 1620

pil·grim·age \-grəmij\ *n* : pilgrim's journey

pill \'pil\ *n* : small rounded mass of medicine —**pill·box** *n*

pil·lage \'pilij\ *vb* **-laged; -lag·ing** : loot and plunder —**pillage** *n*

pil·lar \'pilər\ *n* : upright usu. supporting column —**pil·lared** *adj*

pil·lo·ry \'pilərē\ *n, pl* **-ries** : wooden frame for public punishment with holes for the head and hands ~ *vb*

-ried; -ry·ing 1 : set in a pillory **2** : expose to public scorn

pil·low \'pilō\ *n* : soft cushion for the head **—pil·low·case** *n*

pi·lot \'pīlət\ *n* **1** : helmsman **2** : person licensed to take ships into and out of a port **3** : guide **4** : one that flies an aircraft or spacecraft ~ *vb* : act as pilot of **—pi·lot·less** *adj*

pi·men·to \pə'mentō\ *n, pl* **-tos** *or* **-to 1** : allspice **2** : pimiento

pi·mien·to \pə'mentō, -'myen-\ *n, pl* **-tos** : mild red sweet pepper

pimp \'pimp\ *n* : man who solicits clients for a prostitute **—pimp** *vb*

pim·ple \'pimpəl\ *n* : small inflamed swelling on the skin **—pim·ply** \-pəlē\ *adj*

pin \'pin\ *n* **1** : fastener made of a small pointed piece of wire **2** : ornament or emblem fastened to clothing with a pin **3** : wooden object used as a target in bowling ~ *vb* **-nn- 1** : fasten with a pin **2** : hold fast or immobile **—pin·hole** *n*

pin·a·fore \'pinə,fōr\ *n* : sleeveless dress or apron fastened at the back

pin·cer \'pinsər\ *n* **1** *pl* : gripping tool with 2 jaws **2** : pincerlike claw

pinch \'pinch\ *vb* **1** : squeeze between the finger and thumb or between the jaws of a tool **2** : compress painfully **3** : restrict **4** : steal ~ *n* **1** : emergency **2** : painful effect **3** : act of pinching **4** : very small quantity

pin·cush·ion *n* : cushion for storing pins

pine \'pīn\ *n* : evergreen cone-bearing tree or its wood

²pine *vb* **pined; pin·ing 1** : lose health through distress **2** : yearn for intensely

pine·ap·ple *n* : tropical plant bearing an edible juicy fruit

pin·feath·er *n* : new feather just coming through the skin

¹pin·ion \'pinyən\ *vb* : restrain by binding the arms

²pinion *n* : small gear

¹pink \'piŋk\ *n* **1** : plant with narrow leaves and showy flowers **2** : highest degree

²pink *n* : light red color **—pink** *adj* **—pink·ish** *adj*

pink·eye *n* : contagious eye inflammation

pin·na·cle \'pinikəl\ *n* : highest point

pi·noch·le \'pē,nəkəl\ *n* : card game played with a 48-card deck

pin·point *vb* : locate, hit, or aim with great precision

pint \'pīnt\ *n* : 1/2 quart

pin·to \'pin,tō\ *n, pl* **pintos** : spotted horse or pony

pin·worm *n* : small parasitic intestinal worm

pi·o·neer \,pīə'nir\ *n* **1** : one that originates or helps open up a new line of thought or activity **2** : early settler ~ *vb* : act as a pioneer

pi·ous \'pīəs\ *adj* **1** : conscientious in religious practices **2** : affectedly religious **—pi·ous·ly** *adv*

pipe \'pīp\ *n* **1** : tube that produces music when air is forced through **2** : bagpipe **3** : long tube for conducting a fluid **4** : smoking tool ~ *vb* **piped; pip·ing 1** : play on a pipe **2** : speak in a high voice **3** : convey by pipes **—pip·er** *n*

pipe·line *n* **1** : line of pipe **2** : channel for information

pip·ing \'pīpiŋ\ *n* **1** : music of pipes **2** : narrow fold of material used to decorate edges or seams

pi·quant \'pēkənt\ *adj* **1** : tangy **2** : provocative or charming **—pi·quan·cy** \-kənsē\ *n*

pique \'pēk\ *n* : resentment ~ *vb* **piqued; piqu·ing 1** : offend **2** : arouse by provocation

pi·qué, pi·que \pi'kā\ *n* : durable ribbed clothing fabric

pi·ra·cy \'pīrəsē\ *n, pl* **-cies 1** : robbery on the seas **2** : unauthorized use of another's production or invention

pi·ra·nha \pə'ranyə, -'ränə\ *n* : small So. American fish with sharp teeth

pi·rate \'pīrət\ *n* : one who commits piracy **—pirate** *vb* **—pi·rat·i·cal** \pə'ratikəl, pī-\ *adj*

pir·ou·ette \,pirə'wet\ *n* : ballet turn on the toe or ball of one foot **—pirouette** *vb*

pis *pl of* PI

pis·ta·chio \pə'stashē,ō, -'stäsh-\ *n, pl* **-chios** : small tree bearing a greenish edible seed or its seed

pis·til \'pist⁰l\ *n* : female reproductive organ in a flower **—pis·til·late** \'pistə,lāt\ *adj*

pis·tol \'pist⁰l\ *n* : firearm held with one hand

pis·ton \'pistən\ *n* : sliding piece that receives and transmits motion usu. inside a cylinder

¹pit \'pit\ *n* **1** : hole or shaft in the

ground **2** : sunken or enclosed place for a special purpose **3** : hell **4** : hollow or indentation ~ *vb* **-tt- 1** : form pits in **2** : become marred with pits

²pit *n* : stony seed of some fruits ~ *vb* **-tt-** : remove the pit from

pit bull *n* : powerful compact dog bred for fighting

¹pitch \'pich\ *n* : resin from conifers — **pitchy** *adj*

²pitch *vb* **1** : erect and fix firmly in place **2** : throw **3** : set at a particular tone level **4** : fall headlong ~ *n* **1** : action or manner of pitching **2** : degree of slope **3** : relative highness of a tone **4** : sales talk —**pitched** *adj*

¹pitch•er \'pichər\ *n* : container for liquids

²pitcher *n* : one that pitches (as in baseball)

pitch•fork *n* : long-handled fork for pitching hay

pit•e•ous \'pitēəs\ *adj* : arousing pity — **pit•e•ous•ly** *adv*

pit•fall \'pit,fȯl\ *n* : hidden danger

pith \'pith\ *n* **1** : spongy plant tissue **2** : essential or meaningful part —**pithy** *adj*

piti•able \'pitēəbəl\ *adj* : pitiful

piti•ful \'pitifəl\ *adj* **1** : arousing or deserving pity **2** : contemptible —**piti•ful•ly** *adv*

pit•tance \'pitⁿs\ *n* : small portion or amount

pi•tu•itary \pə'tüə,terē, -'tyü-\ *adj* : relating to or being a small gland attached to the brain

pity \'pitē\ *n, pl* **pi•ties 1** : sympathetic sorrow **2** : something to be regretted ~ *vb* **pit•ied; pity•ing** : feel pity for —**piti•less** *adj* —**piti•less•ly** *adv*

piv•ot \'pivət\ *n* : fixed pin on which something turns ~ *vb* : turn on or as if on a pivot —**piv•ot•al** *adj*

pix•ie, pixy \'piksē\ *n, pl* **pix•ies** : mischievous sprite

piz•za \'pētsə\ *n* : thin pie of bread dough spread with a spiced mixture (as of tomatoes, cheese, and meat)

piz•zazz, pi•zazz \pə'zaz\ *n* : glamour

piz•ze•ria \,pētsə'rēə\ *n* : pizza restaurant

plac•ard \'plakərd, -,ärd\ *n* : poster ~ *vb* : display placards in or on

pla•cate \'plā,kāt, 'plak,āt\ *vb* **-cat•ed; -cat•ing** : appease —**pla•ca•ble** \'plakəbəl, 'plākə-\ *adj*

place \'plās\ *n* **1** : space or room **2** : indefinite area **3** : a particular building, locality, area, or part **4** : relative position in a scale or sequence **5** : seat **6** : job ~ *vb* **placed; plac•ing 1** : put in a place **2** : identify —**place•ment** *n*

pla•ce•bo \plə'sēbō\ *n, pl* **-bos** : something inactive prescribed as a remedy for its psychological effect

pla•cen•ta \plə'sentə\ *n, pl* **-tas** *or* **-tae** \-,ē\ : structure in a uterus by which a fetus is nourished —**pla•cen•tal** \-'sent^əl\ *adj*

plac•id \'plasəd\ *adj* : undisturbed or peaceful —**pla•cid•i•ty** \pla'sidətē\ *n* —**plac•id•ly** *adv*

pla•gia•rize \'plājə,rīz\ *vb* **-rized; -riz•ing** : use (words or ideas) of another as if your own —**pla•gia•rism** \-,rizəm\ *n* —**pla•gia•rist** \-rist\ *n*

plague \'plāg\ *n* **1** : disastrous evil **2** : destructive contagious bacterial disease ~ *vb* **plagued; plagu•ing 1** : afflict with disease or disaster **2** : harass

plaid \'plad\ *n* : woolen fabric with a pattern of crossing stripes or the pattern itself —**plaid** *adj*

plain \'plān\ *n* : expanse of relatively level treeless country ~ *adj* **1** : lacking ornament **2** : not concealed or disguised **3** : easily understood **4** : frank **5** : not fancy or pretty —**plain•ly** *adv* —**plain•ness** \'plānnəs\ *n*

plain•tiff \'plāntəf\ *n* : complaining party in a lawsuit

plain•tive \'plāntiv\ *adj* : expressive of suffering or woe —**plain•tive•ly** *adv*

plait \'plāt, 'plat\ *n* **1** : pleat **2** : braid of hair or straw —**plait** *vb*

plan \'plan\ *n* **1** : drawing or diagram **2** : method for accomplishing something ~ *vb* **-nn- 1** : form a plan of **2** : intend —**plan•less** *adj* —**plan•ner** *n*

¹plane \'plān\ *vb* **planed; plan•ing** : smooth or level off with a plane ~ *n* : smoothing or shaping tool —**plan•er** *n*

²plane *n* **1** : level surface **2** : level of existence, consciousness, or development **3** : airplane ~ *adj* **1** : flat **2** : dealing with flat surfaces or figures

plan•et \'planət\ *n* : celestial body that revolves around the sun —**plan•e•tary** \-ə,terē\ *adj*

plan•e•tar•i•um \,planə'terēəm\ *n, pl* **-iums** *or* **-ia** \-ēə\ : building or room housing a device to project images of celestial bodies

plank \'plank\ n 1 : heavy thick board 2 : article in the platform of a political party —**plank·ing** n

plank·ton \'plaŋktən\ n : tiny aquatic animal and plant life —**plank·ton·ic** \plaŋk'tänik\ adj

plant \'plant\ vb 1 : set in the ground to grow 2 : place firmly or forcibly ~ n 1 : living thing without sense organs that cannot move about 2 : land, buildings, and machinery used esp. in manufacture

¹**plan·tain** \'plant³n\ n : short-stemmed herb with tiny greenish flowers

²**plantain** n : banana plant with starchy greenish fruit

plan·ta·tion \plan'tāshən\ n : agricultural estate usu. worked by resident laborers

plant·er \'plantər\ n 1 : plantation owner 2 : plant container

plaque \'plak\ n 1 : commemorative tablet 2 : film layer on a tooth

plas·ma \'plazmə\ n : watery part of blood —**plas·mat·ic** \plaz'matik\ adj

plas·ter \'plastər\ n 1 : medicated dressing 2 : hardening paste for coating walls and ceilings~ vb : cover with plaster —**plas·ter·er** n

plas·tic \'plastik\ adj 1 : capable of being molded ~ n : material that can be formed into rigid objects, films, or filaments —**plas·tic·i·ty** \plas'tisətē\ n

plate \'plāt\ n 1 : flat thin piece 2 : plated metalware 3 : shallow usu. circular dish 4 : denture or the part of it that fits to the mouth 5 : something printed from an engraving ~ vb **plat·ed**; **plat·ing** : overlay with metal —**plat·ing** n

pla·teau \pla'tō\ n, pl **-teaus** or **-teaux** \-tōz\ : large level area of high land

plat·form \'plat,fȯrm\ n 1 : raised flooring or stage 2 : declaration of principles for a political party

plat·i·num \'plat³nəm\ n : heavy grayish-white metallic chemical element

plat·i·tude \'platə,tüd, -,tyüd\ n : trite remark —**plat·i·tu·di·nous** \platə'tüd³nəs, -'tyüd-\ adj

pla·toon \plə'tün\ n : small military unit

platoon sergeant n : noncommissioned officer in the army ranking below a first sergeant

plat·ter \'platər\ n : large serving plate

platy·pus \'platipəs\ n : small aquatic egg-laying mammal

plau·dit \'plȯdət\ n : act of applause

plau·si·ble \'plȯzəbəl\ adj : reasonable or believeable —**plau·si·bil·i·ty** \,plȯzə'bilətē\ n —**plau·si·bly** \-blē\ adv

play \'plā\ n 1 : action in a game 2 : recreational activity 3 : light or fitful movement 4 : free movement 5 : stage representation of a drama ~ vb 1 : engage in recreation 2 : move or toy with aimlessly 3 : perform music 4 : act in a drama —**play·act·ing** n —**play·er** n —**play·ful** \-fəl\ adj —**play·ful·ly** adv —**play·ful·ness** n —**play·pen** n —**play·suit** n —**play·thing** n

play·ground n : place for children to play

play·house n 1 : theater 2 : small house for children to play in

playing card n : one of a set of 24 to 78 cards marked to show its rank and suit and used to play a game of cards

play·mate n : companion in play

play-off n : contest or series of contests to determine a champion

play·wright \-,rīt\ n : writer of plays

pla·za \'plazə, 'pläz-\ n 1 : public square 2 : shopping mall

plea \'plē\ n 1 : defendant's answer to charges 2 : urgent request

plead \'plēd\ vb **plead·ed** \'plēdəd\ or **pled** \'pled\; **plead·ing** 1 : argue for or against in court 2 : answer to a charge or indictment 3 : appeal earnestly —**plead·er** n

pleas·ant \'plez³nt\ adj 1 : giving pleasure 2 : marked by pleasing behavior or appearance —**pleas·ant·ly** adv —**pleas·ant·ness** n

pleas·ant·ries \-³ntrēz\ n pl : pleasant and casual conversation

please \'plēz\ vb **pleased**; **pleas·ing** 1 : give pleasure or satisfaction to 2 : desire or intend

pleas·ing \'plēziŋ\ adj : giving pleasure —**pleas·ing·ly** adv

plea·sur·able \'plezhərəbəl\ adj : pleasant —**plea·sur·ably** \-blē\ adv

plea·sure \'plezhər\ n 1 : desire or inclination 2 : enjoyment 3 : source of delight

pleat \'plēt\ vb : arrange in pleats ~ n : fold in cloth

ple·be·ian \pli'bēən\ n : one of the common people ~ adj : ordinary

pledge \'plej\ n 1 : something given as security 2 : promise or vow ~ vb **pledged; pledg·ing 1** : offer as or bind by a pledge 2 : promise

ple·na·ry \'plēnərē, 'plen-\ adj : full

pleni·po·ten·tia·ry \,plenəpə'tenchə-rē, -'tenchē,erē\ n : diplomatic agent having full authority —**plenipotentiary** adj

plen·i·tude \'plenə,tüd, -,tyüd\ n 1 : completeness 2 : abundance

plen·te·ous \'plentēəs\ adj : existing in plenty

plen·ty \'plentē\ n : more than adequate number or amount —**plen·ti·ful** \'plentifəl\ adj —**plen·ti·ful·ly** adv

pleth·o·ra \'plethərə\ n : excess

pleu·ri·sy \'plúrəsē\ n : inflammation of the chest membrane

pli·able \'plīəbəl\ adj : flexible

pli·ant \'plīənt\ adj : flexible —**pli·an·cy** \-ənsē\ n

pli·ers \'plīərz\ n pl : pinching or gripping tool

¹plight \'plīt\ vb : pledge

²plight n : bad state

plod \'pläd\ vb **-dd- 1** : walk heavily or slowly 2 : work laboriously and monotonously —**plod·der** n —**plod·ding·ly** \-iŋlē\ adv

plot \'plät\ n 1 : small area of ground 2 : ground plan 3 : main story development (as of a book or movie) 4 : secret plan for doing something ~ vb **-tt- 1** : make a plot or plan of 2 : plan or contrive —**plot·ter** n

plo·ver \'pləvər, 'plōvər\ n, pl **-ver** or **-vers** : shorebird related to the sandpiper

plow, plough \'plaú\ n 1 : tool used to turn soil 2 : device for pushing material aside ~ vb 1 : break up with a plow 2 : cleave or move through like a plow —**plow·man** \-mən, -,man\ n

plow·share \-,sher\ n : plow part that cuts the earth

ploy \'plói\ n : clever maneuver

pluck \'plək\ vb 1 : pull off or out 2 : tug or twitch ~ n 1 : act or instance of plucking 2 : spirit or courage

plucky \'pləkē\ adj **pluck·i·er; -est** : courageous or spirited

plug \'pləg\ n 1 : something for sealing an opening 2 : electrical connector at the end of a cord 3 : piece of favorable publicity ~ vb **-gg- 1** : stop or make tight or secure by inserting a plug 2 : publicize

plum \'pləm\ n 1 : smooth-skinned juicy fruit 2 : fine reward

plum·age \'plümij\ n : feathers of a bird **plum·aged** \-mijd\ adj

plumb \'pləm\ n : weight on the end of a line (**plumb line**) to show vertical direction ~ adv 1 : vertically 2 : completely ~ vb : sound or test with a plumb ~ adj : vertical

plumb·er \'pləmər\ n : one who repairs usu. water pipes and fixtures

plumb·ing \'pləmiŋ\ n : system of water pipes in a building

plume \'plüm\ n : large, conspicuous, or showy feather ~ vb **plumed; plum·ing 1** : provide or deck with feathers 2 : indulge in pride —**plumed** \'plümd\ adj

plum·met \'pləmət\ vb : drop straight down

¹plump \'pləmp\ vb : drop suddenly or heavily ~ adv 1 : straight down 2 : in a direct manner

²plump adj : having a full rounded form —**plump·ness** n

plun·der \'pləndər\ vb : rob or take goods by force (as in war) ~ n : something taken in plundering —**plun·der·er** n

plunge \'plənj\ vb **plunged; plung·ing 1** : thrust or drive with force 2 : leap or dive into water 3 : begin an action suddenly 4 : dip or move suddenly forward or down ~ n : act or instance of plunging —**plung·er** n

plu·ral \'plúrəl\ adj : relating to a word form denoting more than one —**plu·ral** n

plu·ral·i·ty \plú'ralətē\ n, pl **-ties** : greatest number of votes cast when not a majority

plu·ral·ize \'plúrə,līz\ vb **-ized; -iz·ing** : make plural —**plu·ral·i·za·tion** \,plúrələ'zāshən\ n

plus \'pləs\ prep : with the addition of ~ n 1 : sign + (**plus sign**) in mathematics to indicate addition 2 : added or positive quantity 3 : advantage ~ adj : being more or in addition ~ conj : and

plush \'pləsh\ n : fabric with a long pile ~ adj : luxurious —**plush·ly** adv —**plushy** adj —**plush·ness** n

plu·toc·ra·cy \plü'täkrəsē\ n, pl **-cies 1** : government by the wealthy 2 : a controlling class of the wealthy —**plu·to·crat** \'plütə,krat\ n —**plu·to·crat·ic** \,plütə'kratik\ adj

plu·to·ni·um \plü'tōnēəm\ n : radioactive chemical element

¹ply \'plī\ n, pl **plies** : fold, thickness, or strand of which something is made

²ply vb **plied; ply·ing 1** : use or work at 2 : keep supplying something to 3 : travel regularly usu. by sea

ply·wood n : sheets of wood glued and pressed together

pneu·mat·ic \nu̇'matik, nyü-\ adj **1** : moved by air pressure 2 : filled with compressed air —**pneu·mat·i·cal·ly** adv

pneu·mo·nia \nu̇'mōnyə, nyü-\ n : inflammatory lung disease

¹poach \'pōch\ vb : cook in simmering liquid

²poach vb : hunt or fish illegally — **poach·er** n

pock \'päk\ n : small swelling on the skin or its scar —**pock·mark** n —**pock·marked** adj

pock·et \'päkət\ n **1** : small open bag sewn into a garment 2 : container or receptacle 3 : isolated area or group ~ vb : put in a pocket —**pock·et·ful** \-,fu̇l\ n

pock·et·book n **1** : purse 2 : financial resources

pock·et·knife n : knife with a folding blade carried in the pocket

pod \'päd\ n **1** : dry fruit that splits open when ripe 2 : compartment on a ship or craft

po·di·a·try \pə'dīətrē, pō-\ n : branch of medicine dealing with the foot —**po·di·a·trist** \pə'dīətrist, pō-\ n

po·di·um \'pōdēəm\ n, pl **-di·ums** or **-dia** \-ēə\ : dais

po·em \'pōəm\ n : composition in verse

po·et \'pōət\ n : writer of poetry

po·et·ry \'pōətrē\ n **1** : metrical writing 2 : poems —**po·et·ic** \pō'etik\, **po·et·i·cal** \-ikəl\ adj

po·grom \'pōgrəm, pə'gräm, 'pägrəm\ n : organized massacre

poi·gnant \'pȯinyənt\ adj **1** : emotionally painful 2 : deeply moving —**poi·gnan·cy** \-nyənsē\ n

poin·set·tia \pȯin'setēə, -'setə\ n : showy tropical American plant

point \'pȯint\ n **1** : individual often essential detail 2 : purpose 3 : particular place, time, or stage 4 : sharp end 5 : projecting piece of land 6 : dot or period 7 : division of the compass 8 : unit of counting ~ vb **1** : sharpen 2 : indicate direction by extending a finger 3 : direct attention to 4 : aim —**point·ed·ly** \-ədlē\ adv —**point·less** adj

point-blank adj **1** : so close to a target that a missile fired goes straight to it 2 : direct —**point-blank** adv

point·er \'pȯintər\ n **1** : one that points out 2 : large short-haired hunting dog 3 : hint or tip

poise \'pȯiz\ vb **poised; pois·ing** : balance ~ n : self-possessed calmness

poi·son \'pȯiz°n\ n : chemical that can injure or kill ~ vb **1** : injure or kill with poison 2 : apply poison to 3 : affect destructively —**poi·son·er** n —**poi·son·ous** \'pȯiz°nəs\ adj

poke \'pōk\ vb **poked; pok·ing 1** : prod 2 : dawdle ~ n : quick thrust

¹pok·er \'pōkər\ n : rod for stirring a fire

²pok·er n : card game for gambling

po·lar \'pōlər\ adj : relating to a geographical or magnetic pole

po·lar·ize \'pōlə,rīz\ vb **-ized; -iz·ing 1** : cause to have magnetic poles 2 : break up into opposing groups — **po·lar·i·za·tion** \,pōlərə'zāshən\ n

¹pole \'pōl\ n : long slender piece of wood or metal

²pole n **1** : either end of the earth's axis 2 : battery terminal 3 : either end of a magnet

pole·cat \'pōl,kat\ n, pl **polecats** or **polecat 1** : European carnivorous mammal 2 : skunk

po·lem·ics \pə'lemiks\ n sing or pl : practice of disputation —**po·lem·i·cal** \-ikəl\ adj —**po·lem·i·cist** \-əsist\ n

po·lice \pə'lēs\ n, pl **police 1** : department of government that keeps public order and enforces the laws 2 : members of the police ~ vb **-liced; -lic·ing** : regulate and keep in order —**po·lice·man** \-mən\ n —**po·lice·wom·an** n

police officer n : member of the police

pol·i·cy \'päləsē\ n, pl **-cies** : course of action selected to guide decisions

²policy n, pl **-cies** : insurance contract —**pol·i·cy·hold·er** n

po·lio \'pōlē,ō\ n : poliomyelitis —**polio** adj

po·lio·my·eli·tis \-,mīə'lītəs\ n : acute virus disease of the spinal cord

pol·ish \'pälish\ vb **1** : make smooth and glossy 2 : develop or refine ~ n **1** : shiny surface 2 : refinement

po·lite \pə'līt\ *adj* **-lit·er; -est** : marked by courteous social conduct **—po·lite·ly** *adv* **—po·lite·ness** *n*

pol·i·tic \'pälə,tik\ *adj* : shrewdly tactful

politically correct *adj* : seeking to avoid offending members of a different group

pol·i·tics \'pälə,tiks\ *n sing or pl* : practice of government and managing of public affairs **—po·lit·i·cal** \pə'litikəl\ *adj* **—po·lit·i·cal·ly** *adv* **—pol·i·ti·cian** \,pälə'tishən\ *n*

pol·ka \'pōlkə\ *n* : lively couple dance **—polka** *vb*

pol·ka dot \'pōkə,dät\ *n* : one of a series of regular dots in a pattern

poll \'pōl\ *n* **1** : head **2** : place where votes are cast —usu. pl. **3** : a sampling of opinion ~ *vb* **1** : cut off **2** : receive or record votes **3** : question in a poll **—poll·ster** \-stər\ *n*

pol·len \'pälən\ *n* : spores of a seed plant

pol·li·na·tion \,pälə'nāshən\ *n* : the carrying of pollen to fertilize the seed **—pol·li·nate** \'pälə,nāt\ *vb* **—pol·li·na·tor** \-ər\ *n*

pol·lute \pə'lüt\ *vb* **-lut·ed; -lut·ing** : contaminating with waste products **—pol·lut·ant** \-'lüt⁼ᵊnt\ *n* **—pol·lut·er** *n* **—pol·lu·tion** \-'lüshən\ *n*

pol·ly·wog, pol·li·wog \'pälē,wäg\ *n* : tadpole

po·lo \'pōlō\ *n* : game played by 2 teams on horseback using long-handled mallets to drive a wooden ball

pol·ter·geist \'pōltər,gīst\ *n* : mischievous ghost

pol·troon \päl'trün\ *n* : coward

poly·es·ter \'pälē,estər\ *n* : synthetic fiber

po·lyg·a·my \pə'ligəmē\ *n* : marriage to several spouses at the same time **—po·lyg·a·mist** \-mist\ *n* **—po·lyg·a·mous** \-məs\ *adj*

poly·gon \'päli,gän\ *n* : closed plane figure with straight sides

poly·mer \'päləmər\ *n* : chemical compound of molecules joined in long strings **—po·lym·er·i·za·tion** \pə,limərə'zäshən\ *n* **—po·lym·er·ize** \pə'limə,rīz\ *vb*

poly·tech·nic \,päli'teknik\ *adj* : relating to many technical arts or applied sciences

poly·the·ism \'pälithē,izəm\ *n* : worship of many gods **—poly·the·ist** \-,thēist\ *adj or n*

poly·un·sat·u·rat·ed \,päle,ən'sachə-

,rātəd\ *adj* : having many double or triple bonds in a molecule

pome·gran·ate \'päm,granət, 'pämə-\ *n* : tropical reddish fruit with many seeds

pom·mel \'pəməl, 'päm-\ *n* **1** : knob on the hilt of a sword **2** : knob at the front of a saddle ~ \'pəməl\ *vb* **-meled** *or* **-melled; -mel·ing** *or* **-mel·ling** : pummel

pomp \'pämp\ *n* **1** : brilliant display **2** : ostentation

pom·pous \'pämpəs\ *adj* : pretentiously dignified **—pom·pos·i·ty** \päm-'päsətē\ *n* **—pomp·ous·ly** *adv*

pon·cho \'pänchō\ *n, pl* **-chos** : blanketlike cloak

pond \'pänd\ *n* : small body of water

pon·der \'pändər\ *vb* : consider

pon·der·ous \'pändərəs\ *adj* **1** : very heavy **2** : clumsy **3** : oppressively dull

pon·tiff \'päntəf\ *n* : pope **—pon·tif·i·cal** \pän'tifikəl\ *adj*

pon·tif·i·cate \pän'tifə,kāt\ *vb* **-cat·ed; -cat·ing** : talk pompously

pon·toon \pän'tün\ *n* : flat-bottomed boat or float

po·ny \'pōnē\ *n, pl* **-nies** : small horse

po·ny·tail \-,tāl\ *n* : hair arrangement like the tail of a pony

poo·dle \'püd⁼ᵊl\ *n* : dog with a curly coat

¹pool \'pül\ *n* **1** : small body of water **2** : puddle

²pool *n* **1** : amount contributed by participants in a joint venture **2** : game of pocket billiards ~ *vb* : combine in a common fund

poor \'pu̇r, 'pȯr\ *adj* **1** : lacking material possessions **2** : less than adequate **3** : arousing pity **4** : unfavorable **—poor·ly** *adv*

¹pop \'päp\ *vb* **-pp- 1** : move suddenly **2** : burst with or make a sharp sound **3** : protrude ~ *n* **1** : sharp explosive sound **2** : flavored soft drink

²pop *adj* : popular

pop·corn \'päp,kȯrn\ *n* : corn whose kernels burst open into a light mass when heated

pope \'pōp\ *n, often cap* : head of the Roman Catholic Church

pop·lar \'päplər\ *n* : slender quick-growing tree

pop·lin \'päplən\ *n* : strong plain-woven fabric with crosswise ribs

pop·over \'päp,ōvər\ *n* : hollow muffin made from egg-rich batter

pop·py \'päpē\ n, pl **-pies** : herb with showy flowers

pop·u·lace \'päpyələs\ n 1 : common people 2 : population

pop·u·lar \'päpyələr\ adj 1 : relating to the general public 2 : widely accepted 3 : commonly liked —**pop·u·lar·i·ty** \,päpyə'larətē\ n —**pop·u·lar·ize** \'päpyələ,rīz\ vb —**pop·u·lar·ly** \-lərlē\ adv

pop·u·late \'päpyə,lāt\ vb **-lat·ed; -lat·ing** : inhabit or occupy

pop·u·la·tion \,päpyə'lāshən\ n : people or number of people in an area

pop·u·list \'päpyəlist\ n : advocate of the rights of the common people —**pop·u·lism** \-,lizəm\ n

pop·u·lous \'päpyələs\ adj : densely populated —**pop·u·lous·ness** n

por·ce·lain \'pórsələn\ n : fine-grained ceramic ware

porch \'pórch\ n : covered entrance

por·cu·pine \'pórkyə,pīn\ n : mammal with sharp quills

¹**pore** \'pór\ vb **pored; por·ing** : read attentively

²**pore** n : tiny hole (as in the skin) —**pored** adj

pork \'pórk\ n : pig meat

pork barrel n : government projects benefiting political patrons

por·nog·ra·phy \pór'nägrəfē\ n : depiction of erotic behavior intended to cause sexual excitement —**porno·graph·ic** \,pórnə'grafik\ adj

po·rous \'pórəs\ adj : permeable to fluids —**po·ros·i·ty** \pə'räsətē\ n

por·poise \'pórpəs\ n 1 : small whale with a blunt snout 2 : dolphin

por·ridge \'pórij\ n : soft boiled cereal

por·rin·ger \'pórənjər\ n : low one-handled metal bowl or cup

¹**port** \'pórt\ n 1 : harbor 2 : city with a harbor

²**port** n 1 : inlet or outlet (as in an engine) for a fluid 2 : porthole

³**port** n : left side of a ship or airplane looking forward —**port** adj

⁴**port** n : sweet wine

por·ta·ble \'pórtəbəl\ adj : capable of being carried —**portable** n

por·tage \'pórtij, pór'täzh\ n : carrying of boats overland between navigable bodies of water or the route where this is done —**portage** vb

por·tal \'pórt⁹l\ n : entrance

por·tend \pór'tend\ vb : give a warning of beforehand

por·tent \'pór,tent\ n : something that foreshadows a coming event —**por·ten·tous** \pór'tentəs\ adj

por·ter \'pórtər\ n : baggage carrier

por·ter·house \-,haús\ n : choice cut of steak

port·fo·lio \pórt'fōlē,ō\ n, pl **-lios** 1 : portable case for papers 2 : office or function of a diplomat 3 : investor's securities

port·hole \'pórt,hōl\ n : window in the side of a ship or aircraft

por·ti·co \'pórti,kō\ n, pl **-coes** or **-cos** : colonnade forming a porch

por·tion \'pórshən\ n : part or share of a whole ~ vb : divide into or allot portions

port·ly \'pórtlē\ adj **-li·er; -est** : somewhat stout

por·trait \'pórtrət, -,trāt\ n : picture of a person —**por·trait·ist** \-ist\ n —**por·trai·ture** \'pórtrə,chúr\ n

por·tray \pór'trā\ vb 1 : make a picture of 2 : describe in words 3 : play the role of —**por·tray·al** n

por·tu·la·ca \,pórchə'lakə\ n : tropical herb with showy flowers

pose \'pōz\ vb **posed; pos·ing** 1 : assume a posture or attitude 2 : propose 3 : pretend to be what one is not ~ n 1 : sustained posture 2 : pretense —**pos·er** n

posh \'päsh\ adj : elegant

po·si·tion \pə'zishən\ n 1 : stand taken on a question 2 : place or location 3 : status 4 : job —**position** vb

pos·i·tive \'päzətiv\ adj 1 : definite 2 : confident 3 : relating to or being an adjective or adverb form that denotes no increase 4 : greater than zero 5 : having a deficiency of electrons 6 : affirmative —**pos·i·tive·ly** adv —**pos·i·tive·ness** n

pos·se \'päsē\ n : emergency assistants of a sheriff

pos·sess \pə'zes\ vb 1 : have as property or as a quality 2 : control —**pos·ses·sion** \-'zeshən\ n —**pos·ses·sor** \-'zesər\ n

pos·ses·sive \pə'zesiv\ adj 1 : relating to a grammatical case denoting ownership 2 : jealous —**possessive** n —**pos·ses·sive·ness** n

pos·si·ble \'päsəbəl\ adj 1 : that can be done 2 : potential —**pos·si·bil·i·ty** \,päsə'bilətē\ n —**pos·si·bly** adv

pos·sum \'päsəm\ n : opossum

¹post \'pōst\ n : upright stake serving to support or mark ~ vb : put up or announce by a notice

²post vb **1** : mail **2** : inform

³post n **1** : sentry's station **2** : assigned task **3** : army camp ~ vb : station

post- prefix : after or subsequent to

postadolescent	postinoculation
postattack	postmarital
postbaccalau-	postmenopausal
reate	postnatal
postbiblical	postnuptial
postcollege	postproduction
postcolonial	postpuberty
postelection	postrecession
postexercise	postretirement
postflight	postrevolu-
postgame	tionary
postgraduate	postseason
postgraduation	postsecondary
postharvest	postsurgical
posthospital	posttreatment
postimperial	posttrial
postinaugural	postvaccination
postindustrial	postwar

post•age \'pōstij\ n : fee for mail

post•al \'pōstᵊl\ adj : relating to the mail

post•card n : card for mailing a message

post•date \'pōst'dāt\ vb : assign a date to that is later than the actual date of execution

post•er \'pōstər\ n : large usu. printed notice

pos•te•ri•or \pō'stirēər, pä-\ adj **1** : later **2** : situated behind ~ n : buttocks

pos•ter•i•ty \pä'sterətē\ n : all future generations

post•haste \'pōst'hāst\ adv : speedily

post•hu•mous \'päschəməs\ adj : occurring after one's death —**post•hu•mous•ly** adv

post•man \'pōstmən, -,man\ n : mail carrier

post•mark n : official mark on mail —**postmark** vb

post•mas•ter n : chief of a post office

post me•ri•di•em \'pōstmə'ridēəm, -ē-,em\ adj : being after noon

post•mor•tem \'pōst'mórtəm\ adj : occurring or done after death ~ n **1** : medical examination of a corpse **2** : analysis after an event

post office n : agency or building for mail service

post•op•er•a•tive \,pōst'äpərətiv, -'äpə-,rāt-\ adj : following surgery

post•paid adv : with postage paid by the sender

post•par•tum \-'pärtəm\ adj : following childbirth —**postpartum** adv

post•pone \-'pōn\ vb -**poned; -pon•ing** : put off to a later time —**post•pone•ment** n

post•script \'pōst,skript\ n : added note

pos•tu•lant \'päschələnt\ n : candidate for a religious order

pos•tu•late \'päschə,lāt\ vb -**lat•ed; -lat•ing** : assume as true ~ n : assumption

pos•ture \'päschər\ n : bearing of the body ~ vb -**tured; -tur•ing** : strike a pose

po•sy \'pōzē\ n, pl -**sies** : flower or bunch of flowers

pot \'pät\ n : rounded container ~ vb -**tt-** : place in a pot —**pot•ful** n

po•ta•ble \'pōtəbəl\ adj : drinkable

pot•ash \'pät,ash\ n : white chemical salt of potassium used esp. in agriculture

po•tas•si•um \pə'tasēəm\ n : silver-white metallic chemical element

po•ta•to \pə'tātō\ n, pl -**toes** : edible plant tuber

pot•bel•ly n : paunch —**pot•bel•lied** adj

po•tent \'pōtᵊnt\ adj : powerful or effective —**po•ten•cy** \-ᵊnsē\ n

po•ten•tate \'pōtᵊn,tāt\ n : powerful ruler

po•ten•tial \pə'tenchəl\ adj : capable of becoming actual ~ n **1** : something that can become actual **2** : degree of electrification with reference to a standard —**po•ten•ti•al•i•ty** \pə,tenchē'alətē\ n —**po•ten•tial•ly** adv

poth•er \'päthər\ n : fuss

pot•hole \'pät,hōl\ n : large hole in a road surface

po•tion \'pōshən\ n : liquid medicine or poison

pot•luck n : whatever food is available

pot•pour•ri \,pōpù'rē\ n **1** : mix of flowers, herbs, and spices used for scent **2** : miscellaneous collection

pot•shot n **1** : casual or easy shot **2** : random critical remark

pot•ter \'pätər\ n : pottery maker

pot•tery \'pätərē\ n, pl -**teries** : objects (as dishes) made from clay

pouch \'paùch\ n **1** : small bag **2** : bodily sac

poul•tice \'pōltəs\ n : warm medicated dressing —**poultice** vb

poul•try \'pōltrē\ n : domesticated fowl

pounce \'paùns\ vb **pounced; pounc•ing** : spring or swoop upon and seize

¹pound \'paund\ n **1** : unit of weight equal to 16 ounces **2** : monetary unit (as of the United Kingdom) —**poundage** \-ij\ n

²pound n : shelter for stray animals

³pound vb **1** : crush by beating **2** : strike heavily **3** : drill **4** : move along heavily

pour \'pōr\ vb **1** : flow or supply esp. copiously **2** : rain hard

pout \'paut\ vb : look sullen —**pout** n

pov·er·ty \'pävərtē\ n **1** : lack of money or possessions **2** : poor quality

pow·der \'paudər\ n : dry material of fine particles ~ vb : sprinkle or cover with powder —**pow·dery** adj

pow·er \'paudər\ n **1** : position of authority **2** : ability to act **3** : one that has power **4** : physical might **5** : force or energy used to do work ~ vb : supply with power —**pow·er·ful** \-fəl\ adj —**pow·er·ful·ly** adv —**pow·er·less** adj

pow·er·house n : dynamic or energetic person

pow·wow \'pau̇‚wau̇\ n : conference

pox \'päks\ n, pl **pox** or **pox·es** : disease marked by skin rash

prac·ti·ca·ble \'praktikəbəl\ adj : feasible —**prac·ti·ca·bil·i·ty** \‚praktikə'bilətē\ n

prac·ti·cal \'praktikəl\ adj **1** : relating to practice **2** : virtual **3** : capable of being put to use **4** : inclined to action as opposed to speculation —**prac·ti·cal·i·ty** \‚prakti'kalətē\ n —**prac·ti·cal·ly** \'praktiklē\ adv

prac·tice, prac·tise \'praktəs\ vb **-ticed** or **-tised; -tic·ing** or **-tis·ing 1** : perform repeatedly to become proficient **2** : do or perform customarily **3** : be professionally engaged in ~ n **1** : actual performance **2** : habit **3** : exercise for proficiency **4** : exercise of a profession

prac·ti·tio·ner \prak'tishənər\ n : one who practices a profession

prag·ma·tism \'pragmə‚tizəm\ n : practical approach to problems —**prag·mat·ic** \prag'matik\ adj —**prag·mat·i·cal·ly** adv

prai·rie \'prerē\ n : broad grassy rolling tract of land

praise \'prāz\ vb **praised; prais·ing 1** : express approval of **2** : glorify —**praise** n —**praise·wor·thy** adj

prance \'prans\ vb **pranced; pranc·ing**

1 : spring from the hind legs **2** : swagger —**prance** n —**pranc·er** n

prank \'praŋk\ n : playful or mischievous act —**prank·ster** \-stər\ n

prate \'prāt\ vb **prat·ed; prat·ing** : talk long and foolishly

prat·fall \'prat‚fȯl\ n : fall on the buttocks

prat·tle \'pratᵊl\ vb **-tled; -tling** : babble —**prattle** n

prawn \'prȯn\ n : shrimplike crustacean

pray \'prā\ vb **1** : entreat **2** : ask earnestly for something **3** : address God or a god

prayer \'prer\ n **1** : earnest request **2** : an addressing of God or a god **3** : words used in praying —**prayer·ful** adj —**prayer·ful·ly** adv

praying mantis n : mantis

pre- prefix : before, prior to, or in advance

preadmission	predrill
preadolescence	preelection
preadolescent	preelectric
preadult	preemployment
preanesthetic	preestablish
prearrange	preexist
prearrangement	preexistence
preassembled	preexistent
preassign	prefight
prebattle	preform
prebiblical	pregame
prebreakfast	preheat
precalculus	preinaugural
precancel	preindustrial
precancellation	preinterview
preclear	prejudge
preclearance	prekindergarten
precollege	prelaunch
precolonial	prelife
precombustion	premarital
precompute	premenopausal
preconceive	premenstrual
preconception	premix
preconcert	premodern
precondition	premodify
preconstructed	premoisten
preconvention	premold
precook	prenatal
precool	prenotification
precut	prenotify
predawn	prenuptial
predefine	preopening
predeparture	preoperational
predesignate	preoperative
predetermine	preordain
predischarge	prepackage

prepay
preplan
preprocess
preproduction
preprofessional
preprogram
prepubertal
prepublication
prepunch
prepurchase
prerecorded
preregister
preregistration
prerehearsal
prerelease
preretirement
prerevolution-
ary
prerinse
presale
preschool

preseason
preselect
preset
preshrink
preshrunk
presoak
presort
prestamp
presterilize
prestrike
presurgery
presweeten
pretape
pretelevision
pretournament
pretreat
pretreatment
pretrial
prewar
prewash
prewrap

preach \'prēch\ *vb* **1** : deliver a sermon **2** : advocate earnestly —**preach·er** *n* —**preach·ment** *n*

pre·am·ble \'prē,ambəl\ *n* : introduction

pre·can·cer·ous \,prē'kansərəs\ *adj* : likely to become cancerous

pre·car·i·ous \pri'kareəs\ *adj* : dangerously insecure —**pre·car·i·ous·ly** *adv* —**pre·car·i·ous·ness** *n*

pre·cau·tion \pri'kôshən\ *n* : care taken beforehand —**pre·cau·tion·ary** \-shə,nerē\ *adj*

pre·cede \pri'sēd\ *vb* -**ced·ed; -ced·ing** : be, go, or come ahead of —**pre·ce·dence** \presədəns, pri'sēd°ns\ *n*

prec·e·dent \'presədənt\ *n* : something said or done earlier that serves as an example

pre·cept \'prē,sept\ *n* : rule of action or conduct

pre·cinct \'prē,siŋkt\ *n* **1** : district of a city **2** *pl* : vicinity

pre·cious \'preshəs\ *adj* **1** : of great value **2** : greatly cherished **3** : affected

prec·i·pice \'presəpəs\ *n* : steep cliff

pre·cip·i·tate \pri'sipə,tāt\ *vb* -**tat·ed; -tat·ing** **1** : cause to happen quickly or abruptly **2** : cause to separate out of a liquid **3** : fall as rain, snow, or hail ~ *n* : solid matter precipitated from a liquid ~ \-'sipətət, -ə,tāt\ *adj* : unduly hasty —**pre·cip·i·tate·ly** *adv* —**pre·cip·i·tate·ness** *n* —**pre·cip·i·tous** \pri'sipətəs\ *adj* —**pre·cip·i·tous·ly** *adv*

pre·cip·i·ta·tion \pri,sipə'tāshən\ *n* **1** : rash haste **2** : rain, snow, or hail

pré·cis \prā'sē\ *n, pl* **pré·cis** \-'sēz\ : concise summary of essentials

pre·cise \pri'sīs\ *adj* **1** : definite **2** : highly accurate —**pre·cise·ly** *adv* —**pre·cise·ness** *n*

pre·ci·sion \pri'sizhən\ *n* : quality or state of being precise

pre·clude \pri'klüd\ *vb* -**clud·ed; -clud·ing** : make impossible

pre·co·cious \pri'kōshəs\ *adj* : exceptionally advanced —**pre·co·cious·ly** *adv* —**pre·coc·i·ty** \-'käsətē\ *n*

pre·cur·sor \pri'kərsər\ *n* : harbinger

pred·a·to·ry \'predə,tōrē\ *adj* : preying upon others —**pred·a·tor** \'predətər\ *n*

pre·de·ces·sor \'predə,sesər, 'prēd-\ *n* : a previous holder of a position

pre·des·tine \prē'destən\ *vb* : settle beforehand —**pre·des·ti·na·tion** \-,destə'nāshən\ *n*

pre·dic·a·ment \pri'dikəmənt\ *n* : difficult situation

pred·i·cate \'predikət\ *n* : part of a sentence that states something about the subject ~ \'predə,kāt\ *vb* -**cat·ed; -cat·ing** **1** : affirm **2** : establish —**pred·i·ca·tion** \,predə'kāshən\ *n*

pre·dict \pri'dikt\ *vb* : declare in advance —**pre·dict·abil·i·ty** \-,diktə'bilətē\ *n* —**pre·dict·able** \-'diktəbəl\ *adj* —**pre·dict·ably** \-blē\ *adv* —**pre·dic·tion** \-'dikshən\ *n*

pre·di·lec·tion \,pred°l'ekshən, ,prēd-\ *n* : established preference

pre·dis·pose \,prēdis'pōz\ *vb* : cause to be favorable or susceptible to something beforehand —**pre·dis·po·si·tion** \,prē,dispə'zishən\ *n*

pre·dom·i·nate \pri'dämə,nāt\ *vb* : be superior —**pre·dom·i·nance** \-nəns\ *n* —**pre·dom·i·nant** \-nənt\ *adj* —**pre·dom·i·nant·ly** *adv*

pre·em·i·nent \prē'emənənt\ *adj* : having highest rank —**pre·em·i·nence** \-nəns\ *n* —**pre·em·i·nent·ly** *adv*

pre·empt \prē'empt\ *vb* **1** : seize for oneself **2** : take the place of —**pre·emp·tion** \-'empshən\ *n* —**pre·emp·tive** \-'emptiv\ *adj*

preen \'prēn\ *vb* : dress or smooth up (as feathers)

pre·fab·ri·cat·ed \'prē'fabrə,kātəd\ *adj* : manufactured for rapid assembly elsewhere —**pre·fab·ri·ca·tion** \,prē-,fabri'kāshən\ n

pref·ace \'prefəs\ n : introductory comments ~ vb -aced; -ac·ing : introduce with a preface —**pref·a·to·ry** \'prefe-,tōrē\ adj

pre·fect \'prē,fekt\ n : chief officer or judge —**pre·fec·ture** \-,fekchər\ n

pre·fer \pri'fər\ vb -rr- 1 : like better 2 : bring (as a charge) against a person —**pref·er·a·ble** \'prefərəbəl\ adj —**pref·er·a·bly** adv —**pref·er·ence** \-ərəns\ n —**pref·er·en·tial** \,prefə-'renchəl\ adj

pre·fer·ment \pri'fərmənt\ n : promotion

pre·fig·ure \prē'figyər\ vb : foreshadow

¹pre·fix \'prē,fiks, prē'fiks\ vb : place before

²pre·fix \'prē,fiks\ n : affix at the beginning of a word

preg·nant \'pregnənt\ adj 1 : containing unborn young 2 : meaningful —**preg·nan·cy** \-nənsē\ n

pre·hen·sile \prē'hensəl, -,sīl\ adj : adapted for grasping

pre·his·tor·ic \,prēhis'torik\, **pre·his·tor·i·cal** \-ikəl\ adj : relating to the period before written history

prej·u·dice \'prejədəs\ n 1 : damage esp. to one's rights 2 : unreasonable attitude for or against something ~ vb -diced; -dic·ing 1 : damage 2 : cause to have prejudice —**prej·u·di·cial** \,prejə'dishəl\ adj

prel·ate \'prelət\ n : clergy member of high rank —**prel·a·cy** \-əsē\ n

pre·lim·i·nary \pri'limə,nerē\ n, pl -nar·ies : something that precedes or introduces —**preliminary** adj

pre·lude \'prel,üd, -,yüd; 'prā,lüd\ n : introductory performance, event, or musical piece

pre·ma·ture \,prēmə'tùər, -'tyùr, -'chùr\ adj : coming before the usual or proper time —**pre·ma·ture·ly** adv

pre·med·i·tate \pri'medə,tāt\ vb : plan beforehand —**pre·med·i·ta·tion** \-,medə'tāshən\ n

pre·mier \pri'mir, -'myir; 'prēmēər\ adj 1 : first in rank or importance ~ n : prime minister —**pre·mier·ship** n

pre·miere \pri'myer, -'mir\ n : 1st performance ~ vb -miered; -mier·ing : give a 1st performance of

prem·ise \'preməs\ n 1 : statement made or implied as a basis of argument 2 pl

: piece of land with the structures on it

pre·mi·um \'prēmēəm\ n 1 : bonus 2 : sum over the stated value 3 : sum paid for insurance 4 : high value

pre·mo·ni·tion \,prēmə'nishən, ,premə-\ n : feeling that something is about to happen —**pre·mon·i·to·ry** \pri'mänə,tōrē\ adj

pre·oc·cu·pied \prē'äkyə,pīd\ adj : lost in thought

pre·oc·cu·py \-,pī\ vb : occupy the attention of —**pre·oc·cu·pa·tion** \prē-,äkyə'pāshən\ n

pre·pare \pri'par\ vb -pared; -par·ing 1 : make or get ready often beforehand 2 : put together or compound —**prep·a·ra·tion** \,prepə'rāshən\ n —**pre·pa·ra·to·ry** \pri'parə,tōrē\ adj —**pre·pared·ness** \-'parədnəs\ n

pre·pon·der·ant \pri'pändərənt\ adj : having great weight, power, importance, or numbers —**pre·pon·der·ance** \-rəns\ n —**pre·pon·der·ant·ly** adv

prep·o·si·tion \,prepə'zishən\ n : word that combines with a noun or pronoun to form a phrase —**prep·o·si·tion·al** \-'zishənəl\ adj

pre·pos·sess·ing \,prēpə'zesiŋ\ adj : tending to create a favorable impression

pre·pos·ter·ous \pri'pästərəs\ adj : absurd

pre·req·ui·site \prē'rekwəzət\ n : something required beforehand —**prerequisite** adj

pre·rog·a·tive \pri'rägətiv\ n : special right or power

pre·sage \'presij, pri'sāj\ vb -saged; -sag·ing 1 : give a warning of 2 : predict —**pre·sage** \'presij\ n

pres·by·ter \'prezbətər\ n : priest or minister

pre·science \'prēshəns, 'presh-\ n : foreknowledge of events —**pre·scient** \-ənt\ adj

pre·scribe \pri'skrīb\ vb -scribed; -scrib·ing 1 : lay down as a guide 2 : direct the use of as a remedy

pre·scrip·tion \pri'skripshən\ n : written direction for the preparation and use of a medicine or the medicine prescribed

pres·ence \'prez°ns\ n 1 : fact or condition of being present 2 : appearance or bearing

¹pres·ent \'prez^ᵊnt\ *n* : gift

²pre·sent \pri'zent\ *vb* **1** : introduce **2** : bring before the public **3** : make a gift to or of **4** : bring before a court for inquiry —**pre·sent·able** *adj* —**pre·sen·ta·tion** \,prē,zen'tāshən, ,prez-ᵊn-\ *n* —**pre·sent·ment** \pri'zent-mənt\ *n*

³pres·ent \'prez^ᵊnt\ *adj* : now existing, in progress, or attending ~ *n* : present time

pre·sen·ti·ment \pri'zentəmənt\ *n* : premonition

pres·ent·ly \'prez^ᵊntlē\ *adv* **1** : soon **2** : now

present participle *n* : participle that typically expresses present action

pre·serve \pri'zərv\ *vb* -**served**; -**serv·ing 1** : keep safe from danger or spoilage **2** : maintain ~ *n* **1** : preserved fruit —often in pl. **2** : area for protection of natural resources —**pres·er·va·tion** \,prezər'vāshən\ *n* —**pre·ser·va·tive** \pri'zərvətiv\ *adj or n* —**pre·serv·er** \-'zərvər\ *n*

pre·side \pri'zīd\ *vb* -**sid·ed**; -**sid·ing 1** : act as chairman **2** : exercise control

pres·i·dent \'prezədənt\ *n* **1** : one chosen to preside **2** : chief official (as of a company or nation) —**pres·i·den·cy** \-ənsē\ *n* —**pres·i·den·tial** \,prezə'denchəl\ *adj*

press \'pres\ *n* **1** : crowded condition **2** : machine or device for exerting pressure and esp. for printing **3** : pressure **4** : printing or publishing establishment **5** : news media and esp. newspapers ~ *vb* **1** : lie against and exert pressure on **2** : smooth with an iron or squeeze with something heavy **3** : urge **4** : crowd **5** : force one's way —**press·er** *n*

press·ing *adj* : urgent

pres·sure \'preshər\ *n* **1** : burden of distress or urgent business **2** : direct application of force —**pressure** *vb* —**pres·sur·i·za·tion** \,preshərə'zāshən\ *n* —**pres·sur·ize** \-,īz\ *vb*

pres·ti·dig·i·ta·tion \,prestə,dijə'tāshən\ *n* : sleight of hand

pres·tige \pres'tēzh, -'tēj\ *n* : estimation in the eyes of people —**pres·ti·gious** \-'tijəs\ *adj*

pres·to \'prestō\ *adv or adj* : quickly

pre·sume \pri'züm\ *vb* -**sumed**; -**sum·ing 1** : assume authority without right to do so **2** : take for granted —**pre·**

sum·able \-'zümәbәl\ *adj* —**pre·sum·ably** \-blē\ *adv*

pre·sump·tion \pri'zəmpshən\ *n* **1** : presumptuous attitude or conduct **2** : belief supported by probability —**pre·sump·tive** \-tiv\ *adj*

pre·sump·tu·ous \pri'zəmpchəwəs\ *adj* : too bold or forward —**pre·sump·tu·ous·ly** *adv*

pre·sup·pose \,prēsə'pōz\ *vb* : take for granted —**pre·sup·po·si·tion** \,prē,səpə'zishən\ *n*

pre·tend \pri'tend\ *vb* **1** : act as if something is real or true when it is not **2** : act in a way that is false **3** : lay claim —**pre·tend·er** *n*

pre·tense, pre·tence \'prē,tens, pri'tens\ *n* **1** : insincere effort **2** : deception —**pre·ten·sion** \pri'tenchən\ *n*

pre·ten·tious \pri'tenchəs\ *adj* : overly showy or self-important —**pre·ten·tious·ly** *adv* —**pre·ten·tious·ness** *n*

pre·ter·nat·u·ral \,prētər'nachərəl\ *adj* **1** : exceeding what is natural **2** : inexplicable by ordinary means —**pre·ter·nat·u·ral·ly** *adv*

pre·text \'prē,tekst\ *n* : falsely stated purpose

pret·ty \'pritē, 'pùrt-\ *adj* -**ti·er**; -**est** : pleasing by delicacy or attractiveness ~ *adv* : in some degree —**pre·tied**; -**ty·ing** : make pretty —**pret·ti·ly** \'pritᵊlē\ *adv* —**pret·ti·ness** *n*

pret·zel \'pretsəl\ *n* : twisted thin bread that is glazed and salted

pre·vail \pri'vāl\ *vb* **1** : triumph **2** : urge successfully **3** : be frequent, widespread, or dominant

prev·a·lent \'prevələnt\ *adj* : widespread —**prev·a·lence** \-ləns\ *n*

pre·var·i·cate \pri'varə,kāt\ *vb* -**cat·ed**; -**cat·ing** : deviate from the truth —**pre·var·i·ca·tion** \-,varə'kāshən\ *n* —**pre·var·i·ca·tor** \-'varə,kātər\ *n*

pre·vent \pri'vent\ *vb* : keep from happening or acting —**pre·vent·able** *adj* —**pre·ven·tion** \-'venchən\ *n* —**pre·ven·tive** \-'ventiv\ *adj or n* —**pre·ven·ta·tive** \-'ventətiv\ *adj or n*

pre·view \'prē,vyü\ *vb* : view or show beforehand —**preview** *n*

pre·vi·ous \'prēvēəs\ *adj* : having gone, happened, or existed before —**pre·vi·ous·ly** *adv*

prey \'prā\ *n, pl* **preys 1** : animal taken for food by another **2** : victim ~ *vb* **1** : seize and devour animals as prey **2** : have a harmful effect on

price \'prīs\ *n* : cost ~ *vb* **priced; pricing** : set a price on

price·less \-ləs\ *adj* : too precious to have a price

pric·ey \'prīsē\ *adj* **pric·i·er; -est** : expensive

prick \'prik\ *n* **1** : tear or small wound made by a point **2** : something sharp or pointed ~ *vb* : pierce slightly with a sharp point —**prick·er** *n*

prick·le \'prikəl\ *n* **1** : small sharp spine or thorn **2** : slight stinging pain ~ *vb* **-led; -ling** : tingle —**prick·ly** \'priklē\ *adj*

pride \'prīd\ *n* : quality or state of being proud ~ *vb* **prid·ed; prid·ing** : indulge in pride —**pride·ful** *adj*

priest \'prēst\ *n* : person having authority to perform the sacred rites of a religion —**priest·hood** *n* —**priest·li·ness** \-lēnəs\ *n* —**priest·ly** *adj*

priest·ess \'prēstəs\ *n* : woman who is a priest

prig \'prig\ *n* : one who irritates by rigid or pointed observance of proprieties —**prig·gish** \-ish\ *adj* —**prig·gish·ly** *adv*

prim \'prim\ *adj* **-mm-** : stiffly formal and proper —**prim·ly** *adv* —**prim·ness** *n*

pri·mal \'prīməl\ *adj* **1** : original or primitive **2** : most important

pri·ma·ry \'prī,merē, 'prīmərē\ *adj* : first in order of time, rank, or importance ~ *n, pl* **-ries** : preliminary election —**pri·mar·i·ly** \prī'merəlē\ *adv*

primary school *n* : elementary school

pri·mate *n* **1** \'prī,māt, -mət\ : highest-ranking bishop **2** \-,māt\ : mammal of the group that includes humans and monkeys

prime \'prīm\ *n* : earliest or best part of period ~ *adj* : standing first (as in significance or quality) ~ *vb* **primed; prim·ing 1** : fill or load **2** : lay a preparatory coating on

prime minister *n* : chief executive of a parliamentary government

¹prim·er \'primər\ *n* : small introductory book

²prim·er \'prīmər\ *n* **1** : device for igniting an explosive **2** : material for priming a surface

pri·me·val \prī'mēvəl\ *adj* : relating to the earliest ages

prim·i·tive \'primətiv\ *adj* **1** : relating to or characteristic of an early stage of development **2** : of or relating to a tribal people or culture ~ *n* : one that is primitive —**prim·i·tive·ly** *adv* —**prim·i·tive·ness** *n*

pri·mor·di·al \prī'mordēəl\ *adj* : primeval

primp \'primp\ *vb* : dress or groom in a finicky manner

prim·rose \'prim,rōz\ *n* : low herb with clusters of showy flowers

prince \'prins\ *n* **1** : ruler **2** : son of a king or queen —**prince·ly** *adj*

prin·cess \'prinsəs, -,ses\ *n* **1** : daughter of a king or queen **2** : wife of a prince

prin·ci·pal \'prinsəpəl\ *adj* : most important ~ *n* **1** : leading person **2** : head of a school **3** : sum lent at interest —**prin·ci·pal·ly** *adv*

prin·ci·pal·i·ty \,prinsə'palətē\ *n, pl* **-ties** : territory of a prince

prin·ci·ple \'prinsəpəl\ *n* **1** : general or fundamental law **2** : rule or code of conduct or devotion to such a code

print \'print\ *n* **1** : mark or impression made by pressure **2** : printed state or form **3** : printed matter **4** : copy made by printing **5** : cloth with a figure stamped on it ~ *vb* **1** : produce impressions of (as from type) **2** : write in letters like those of printer's type —**print·able** *adj* —**print·er** *n*

print·ing \'printiŋ\ *n* : art or business of a printer

print·out \'print,aut\ *n* : printed output produced by a computer —**print out** *vb*

¹pri·or \'prīər\ *n* : head of a religious house —**pri·o·ry** \'prīərē\ *n*

²prior *adj* : coming before in time, order, or importance —**pri·or·i·ty** \prī'órətē\ *n*

pri·or·ess \'prīərəs\ *n* : nun who is head of a religious house

prism \'prizəm\ *n* : transparent 3-sided object that separates light into colors —**pris·mat·ic** \priz'matik\ *adj*

pris·on \'priz²n\ *n* : place where criminals are confined

pris·on·er \'priz²nər\ *n* : person on trial or in prison

pris·sy \'prisē\ *adj* **-si·er; -est** : overly prim —**pris·si·ness** *n*

pris·tine \'pris,tēn, pris'-\ *adj* : pure

pri·va·cy \'prīvəsē\ *n, pl* **-cies** : quality or state of being apart from others

pri·vate \'prīvət\ *adj* **1** : belonging to a particular individual or group **2** : carried on independently **3**

: withdrawn from company or observation ~ *n* : enlisted person of the lowest rank in the marine corps or of one of the two lowest ranks in the army —**pri·vate·ly** *adv*

pri·va·teer \ˌprīvə'tir\ *n* : private ship armed to attack enemy ships and commerce

private first class *n* : enlisted person ranking next below a corporal in the army and next below a lance corporal in the marine corps

pri·va·tion \prī'vāshən\ *n* : lack of what is needed for existence

priv·i·lege \'privəlij\ *n* : right granted as an advantage or favor —**priv·i·leged** *adj*

privy \'privē\ *adj* 1 : private or secret 2 : having access to private or secret information ~ *n*, *pl* **priv·ies** : outdoor toilet —**priv·i·ly** \'privəlē\ *adv*

¹**prize** \'prīz\ *n* 1 : something offered or striven for in competition or in contests of chance 2 : something very desirable —**prize** *adj* —**prize·win·ner** *n* —**prize·win·ning** *adj*

²**prize** *vb* **prized; priz·ing** : value highly

³**prize** *vb* **prized; priz·ing** : pry

prize·fight *n* : professional boxing match —**prize·fight·er** *n* —**prize·fight·ing** *n*

¹**pro** \'prō\ *n* : favorable argument or person —*adv* : in favor

²**pro** *n* or *adj* : professional

prob·a·ble \'präbəbəl\ *adj* : seeming true or real or to have a good chance of happening —**prob·a·bil·i·ty** \ˌpräbə'bilətē\ *n* —**prob·a·bly** \'präbəblē\ *adv*

pro·bate \'prō,bāt\ *n* : judicial determination of the validity of a will ~ *vb* -**bat·ed; -bat·ing** : establish by probate

pro·ba·tion \prō'bāshən\ *n* 1 : period of testing and trial 2 : freedom for a convict during good behavior under supervision —**pro·ba·tion·ary** \-shə,nerē\ *adj* —**pro·ba·tion·er** *n*

probe \'prōb\ *n* 1 : slender instrument for examining a cavity 2 : investigation ~ *vb* **probed; prob·ing** 1 : examine with a probe 2 : investigate

pro·bi·ty \'prōbətē\ *n* : honest behavior

prob·lem \'präbləm\ *n* 1 : question to be solved 2 : source of perplexity or vexation —**problem** *adj* —**prob·lem·at·ic** \ˌpräblə'matik\ *adj* —**prob·lem·at·i·cal** \-ikəl\ *adj*

pro·bos·cis \prə'bäsəs\ *n, pl* **-cis·es** also **-ci·des** \-ə,dēz\ : long flexible snout

pro·ce·dure \prə'sējər\ *n* 1 : way of doing something 2 : series of steps in regular order —**pro·ce·dur·al** \-'sējərəl\ *adj*

pro·ceed \prō'sēd\ *vb* 1 : come forth 2 : go on in an orderly way 3 : begin and carry on an action 4 : advance

pro·ceed·ing *n* 1 : procedure 2 *pl* : something said or done or its official record

pro·ceeds \'prō,sēdz\ *n pl* : total money taken in

pro·cess \'präs,es, 'prōs-\ *n, pl* **-cess·es** \-ˌesəz, -əsəz, -ə,sēz\ 1 : something going on 2 : natural phenomenon marked by gradual changes 3 : series of actions or operations directed toward a result 4 : summons 5 : projecting part ~ *vb* : subject to a process —**pro·ces·sor** \-ər\ *n*

pro·ces·sion \prə'seshən\ *n* : group moving along in an orderly way

pro·ces·sion·al \-'seshənəl\ *n* : music for a procession

pro·claim \prō'klām\ *vb* : announce publicly or with conviction —**proc·la·ma·tion** \ˌpräklə'māshən\ *n*

pro·cliv·i·ty \prō'klivətē\ *n, pl* **-ties** : inclination

pro·cras·ti·nate \prə'krastə,nāt\ *vb* -**nat·ed; -nat·ing** : put something off until later —**pro·cras·ti·na·tion** \-,krastə'nāshən\ *n* —**pro·cras·ti·na·tor** \-'krastə,nātər\ *n*

pro·cre·ate \'prōkrē,āt\ *vb* -**at·ed; -at·ing** : produce offspring —**pro·cre·ation** \,prōkrē'āshən\ *n* —**pro·cre·ative** \'prōkrē,ātiv\ *adj* —**pro·cre·ator** \-,ātər\ *n*

proc·tor \'präktər\ *n* : supervisor of students (as at an examination) —**proc·tor** *vb*

pro·cure \prə'kyùr\ *vb* -**cured; -cur·ing** : get possession of —**pro·cur·able** \-'kyùrəbəl\ *adj* —**pro·cure·ment** *n* —**pro·cur·er** *n*

prod \'präd\ *vb* **-dd-** : push with or as if with a pointed instrument —**prod** *n*

prod·i·gal \'prädigəl\ *adj* : recklessly extravagant or wasteful —**prodigal** *n* —**prod·i·gal·i·ty** \,prädə'galətē\ *n*

pro·di·gious \prə'dijəs\ *adj* : ex-

pro·di·gious·ly \prə'dijəs|ē\ *adj* **1** : traordinary in size or degree — **pro·di·gious·ly** *adv*

prod·i·gy \'prädəjē\ *n, pl* **-gies** : extraordinary person or thing

pro·duce \prə'düs, -'dyüs\ *vb* **-duced; -duc·ing 1** : present to view **2** : give birth to **3** : bring into existence ~ \'präd,üs, 'prōd-, -,yüs\ *n* **1** : product **2** : agricultural products —**pro·duc·er** \prə'düsər, -'dyü-\ *n*

prod·uct \'präd,əkt\ *n* **1** : number resulting from multiplication **2** : something produced

pro·duc·tion \prə'dəkshən\ *n* : act, process, or result of producing —**pro·duc·tive** \-'dəktiv\ *adj* —**pro·duc·tive·ness** *n* —**pro·duc·tiv·i·ty** \,prō-,dək'tivətē, ,prä-\ *n*

pro·fane \prō'fān\ *vb* **-faned; -fan·ing** : treat with irreverence — *adj* **1** : not concerned with religion **2** : serving to debase what is holy —**pro·fane·ly** *adv* —**pro·fane·ness** *n* —**pro·fan·i·ty** \prō'fanətē\ *n*

pro·fess \prə'fes\ *vb* **1** : declare openly **2** : confess one's faith in —**pro·fessed·ly** \-ədlē\ *adv*

pro·fes·sion \prə'feshən\ *n* **1** : open declaration of belief **2** : occupation requiring specialized knowledge and academic training

pro·fes·sion·al \prə'feshənəl\ *adj* **1** : of, relating to, or engaged in a profession **2** : playing sport for pay —**professional** *n* —**pro·fes·sion·al·ism** *n* —**pro·fes·sion·al·ize** *vb* —**pro·fes·sion·al·ly** *adv*

pro·fes·sor \prə'fesər\ *n* : university or college teacher —**pro·fes·so·ri·al** \,prōfə'sōrēəl, ,präfə-\ *adj* —**pro·fes·sor·ship** *n*

prof·fer \'präfər\ *vb* **-fered; -fer·ing** : offer —**proffer** *n*

pro·fi·cient \prə'fishənt\ *adj* : very good at something —**pro·fi·cien·cy** \-ənsē\ *n* —**proficient** *n* —**pro·fi·cient·ly** *adv*

pro·file \'prō,fīl\ *n* : picture in outline —**profile** *vb*

prof·it \'präfət\ *n* **1** : valuable return **2** : excess of the selling price of goods over cost ~ *vb* : gain a profit —**prof·it·able** \'präfətəbəl\ *adj* —**prof·it·ably** *adv* —**prof·it·less** *adj*

prof·i·teer \,präfə'tir\ *n* : one who makes an unreasonable profit —**prof·iteer** *vb*

prof·li·gate \'präfligət, -lə,gāt\ *adj* **1** : shamelessly immoral **2** : wildly extravagant —**prof·li·ga·cy** \-gəsē\ *n* —**profligate** *n* —**prof·li·gate·ly** *adv*

pro·found \prə'faůnd\ *adj* **1** : marked by intellectual depth or insight **2** : deeply felt —**pro·found·ly** *adv* —**pro·fun·di·ty** \-'fəndətē\ *n*

pro·fuse \prə'fyüs\ *adj* : pouring forth liberally —**pro·fuse·ly** *adv* —**pro·fu·sion** \-'fyüzhən\ *n*

pro·gen·i·tor \prō'jenətər\ *n* : direct ancestor

prog·e·ny \'präjənē\ *n, pl* **-nies** : offspring

pro·ges·ter·one \prō'jestə,rōn\ *n* : female hormone

prog·no·sis \präg'nōsəs\ *n, pl* **-no·ses** \-,sēz\ : prospect of recovery from disease

prog·nos·ti·cate \präg'nästə,kāt\ *vb* **-cat·ed; -cat·ing** : predict from signs or symptoms —**prog·nos·ti·ca·tion** \-,nästə'kāshən\ *n* —**prog·nos·ti·ca·tor** \-'nästə,kātər\ *n*

pro·gram \'prō,gram, -grəm\ *n* **1** : outline of the order to be pursued or the subjects included (as in a performance) **2** : plan of procedure **3** : coded instructions for a computer ~ *vb* **-grammed** *or* **-gramed; -gram·ming** *or* **-gram·ing 1** : enter in a program **2** : provide a computer with a program —**pro·gram·ma·bil·i·ty** \,prō,gramə'bilətē\ *n* —**pro·gram·ma·ble** \'prō,graməbəl\ *adj* —**pro·gram·mer** \'prō,gramər\ *n*

prog·ress \'prägrəs, -,res\ *n* : movement forward or to a better condition ~ \prə'gres\ *vb* **1** : move forward **2** : improve —**pro·gres·sive** \-'gresiv\ *adj* —**pro·gres·sive·ly** *adv*

pro·gres·sion \prə'greshən\ *n* **1** : act of progressing **2** : continuous connected series

pro·hib·it \prō'hibət\ *vb* : prevent by authority

pro·hi·bi·tion \,prōə'bishən\ *n* **1** : act of prohibiting **2** : legal restriction on sale or manufacture of alcoholic beverages —**pro·hi·bi·tion·ist** \-'bishənist\ *n* —**pro·hib·i·tive** \prō'hibətiv\ *adj* —**pro·hib·i·tive·ly** *adv* —**pro·hib·i·to·ry** \-'hibə,tōrē\ *adj*

proj·ect \'präj,ekt, -ikt\ *n* : planned undertaking ~ \prə'jekt\ *vb* **1** : design or plan **2** : protrude **3** : throw forward —**pro·jec·tion** \-'jekshən\ *n*

pro·jec·tile \prə'jekt^əl\ *n* : missile hurled by external force

pro·jec·tor \-'jektər\ *n* : device for projecting pictures on a screen

pro·le·tar·i·an \,prōlə'terēən\ *n* : member of the proletariat —**proletarian** *adj*

pro·le·tar·i·at \-ēət\ *n* : laboring class

pro·lif·er·ate \prə'lifə,rāt\ *vb* **-at·ed; -at·ing** : grow or increase in number rapidly —**pro·lif·er·a·tion** \-,lifə'rāshən\ *n*

pro·lif·ic \prə'lifik\ *adj* : producing abundantly —**pro·lif·i·cal·ly** *adv*

pro·logue \'prō,lòg, -,läg\ *n* : preface

pro·long \prə'lòn\ *vb* : lengthen in time or extent —**pro·lon·ga·tion** \,prō-,lòn'gāshən\ *n*

prom \'präm\ *n* : formal school dance

prom·e·nade \,prämə'nād, -'näd\ *n* : leisurely walk **2** : place for strolling —**promenade** *vb*

prom·i·nence \'prämənəns\ *n* **1** : quality, state, or fact of being readily noticeable or distinguished **2** : something that stands out —**prom·i·nent** \-nənt\ *adj* —**prom·i·nent·ly** *adv*

pro·mis·cu·ous \prə'miskyəwəs\ *adj* : having a number of sexual partners —**prom·is·cu·i·ty** \,prämis'kyüətē, ,prō,mis-\ *n* —**pro·mis·cu·ous·ly** *adv* —**pro·mis·cu·ous·ness** *n*

prom·ise \'präməs\ *n* **1** : statement that one will do or not do something **2** : basis for expectation —**promise** *vb* —**prom·is·so·ry** \-ə,sōrē\ *adj*

prom·is·ing \'präməsin\ *adj* : likely to succeed —**prom·is·ing·ly** *adv*

prom·on·to·ry \'prämən,tōrē\ *n, pl* **-ries** : point of land jutting into the sea

pro·mote \prə'mōt\ *vb* **-mot·ed; -mot·ing 1** : advance in rank **2** : contribute to the growth, development, or prosperity of —**pro·mot·er** *n* —**pro·mo·tion** \-'mōshən\ *n* —**pro·mo·tion·al** \-'mōshənəl\ *adj*

¹prompt \'prämpt\ *vb* **1** : incite **2** : give a cue to (an actor or singer) —**prompt·er** *n*

²prompt *adj* : ready and quick —**prompt·ly** *adv* —**prompt·ness** *n*

prone \'prōn\ *adj* **1** : having a tendency **2** : lying face downward —**prone·ness** \'prōnnəs\ *n*

prong \'pròn\ *n* : sharp point of a fork —**pronged** \'pròn\ *adj*

pro·noun \'prō,naùn\ *n* : word used as a substitute for a noun

pro·nounce \prə'naùns\ *vb* **-nounced; -nounc·ing 1** : utter officially or as an opinion **2** : say or speak esp. correctly —**pro·nounce·able** *adj* —**pro·nounce·ment** *n* —**pro·nun·ci·a·tion** \-,nənsē'āshən\ *n*

pro·nounced \-'naùnst\ *adj* : decided

¹proof \'prüf\ *n* **1** : evidence of a truth or fact **2** : trial impression or print

²proof *adj* : designed for successful in resisting or repelling

proof·read *vb* : read and mark corrections in —**proof·read·er** *n*

prop \'präp\ *vb* **-pp- 1** : support **2** : sustain —**prop** *n*

pro·pa·gan·da \,präpə'gandə, ,prōpə-\ *n* : the spreading of ideas or information to further or damage a cause —**pro·pa·gan·dist** \-dist\ *n* —**pro·pa·gan·dize** \-,dīz\ *vb*

prop·a·gate \'präpə,gāt\ *vb* **-gat·ed; -gat·ing 1** : reproduce biologically **2** : cause to spread —**prop·a·ga·tion** \,präpə'gāshən\ *n*

pro·pane \'prō,pān\ *n* : heavy flammable gaseous fuel

pro·pel \prə'pel\ *vb* **-ll-** : drive forward —**pro·pel·lant, pro·pel·lent** *n or adj*

pro·pel·ler \prə'pelər\ *n* : hub with revolving blades that propels a craft

pro·pen·si·ty \prə'pensətē\ *n, pl* **-ties** : particular interest or inclination

prop·er \'präpər\ *adj* **1** : suitable or right **2** : limited to a specified thing **3** : correct **4** : strictly adhering to standards of social manners, dignity, or good taste —**prop·er·ly** *adv*

prop·er·ty \'präpərtē\ *n, pl* **-ties 1** : quality peculiar to an individual **2** : something owned **3** : piece of real estate **4** : ownership

proph·e·cy \'präfəsē\ *n, pl* **-cies** : prediction

proph·e·sy \-,sī\ *vb* **-sied; -sy·ing** : predict —**proph·e·si·er** \-,sīər\ *n*

proph·et \'präfət\ *n* : one who utters revelations or predicts events —**proph·et·ess** \-əs\ *n* —**pro·phet·ic** \prə'fetik\, **pro·phet·i·cal** \-ikəl\ *adj* —**pro·phet·i·cal·ly** *adv*

pro·pin·qui·ty \prə'pinkwətē\ *n* : nearness

pro·pi·ti·ate \prō'pishē,āt\ *vb* **-at·ed; -at·ing** : gain or regain the favor of —**pro·pi·ti·a·tion** \-,pishē'āshən\ *n* —**pro·pi·ti·a·to·ry** \-'pishēə,tōrē\ *adj*

pro·pi·tious \prə'pishəs\ *adj* : favorable

pro·po·nent \prə'pōnənt\ *n* : one who argues in favor of something

pro·por·tion \prə'pōrshən\ *n* **1** : relation of one part to another or to the whole with respect to magnitude, quantity, or degree **2** : symmetry **3** : share ~ *vb* : adjust in size in relation to others **—pro·por·tion·al** \-shənəl\ *adj* **—pro·por·tion·al·ly** *adv* **—pro·por·tion·ate** \-shənət\ *adj* **—pro·por·tion·ate·ly** *adv*

pro·pose \prə'pōz\ *vb* **-posed; -pos·ing** **1** : plan or intend **2** : make an offer of marriage **3** : present for consideration **—pro·pos·al** \-'pōzəl\ *n*

prop·o·si·tion \ˌpräpə'zishən\ *n* : something proposed ~ *vb* : suggest sexual intercourse to

pro·pound \prə'paùnd\ *vb* : set forth for consideration

pro·pri·etor \prə'prīətər\ *n* : owner **—pro·pri·etary** \prə'prīəˌterē\ *adj* **—pro·pri·etor·ship** *n* **—pro·pri·etress** \-'prīətrəs\ *n*

pro·pri·ety \prə'prīətē\ *n, pl* **-eties** : standard of acceptability in social conduct

pro·pul·sion \prə'pəlshən\ *n* **1** : action of propelling **2** : driving power **—pro·pul·sive** \-siv\ *adj*

pro·sa·ic \prō'zāik\ *adj* : dull

pro·scribe \prō'skrīb\ *vb* **-scribed; -scrib·ing** : prohibit **—pro·scrip·tion** \-'skripshən\ *n*

prose \'prōz\ *n* : ordinary language

pros·e·cute \'präsiˌkyüt\ *vb* **-cut·ed; -cut·ing** **1** : follow to the end **2** : seek legal punishment of **—pros·e·cu·tion** \ˌpräsi'kyüshən\ *n* **—pros·e·cu·tor** \'präsiˌkyütər\ *n*

pros·e·lyte \'präsəˌlīt\ *n* : new convert **—pros·e·ly·tize** \'präsələˌtīz\ *vb*

pros·pect \'präsˌpekt\ *n* **1** : extensive view **2** : something awaited **3** : potential buyer ~ *vb* : look for mineral deposits **—pro·spec·tive** \prə'spektiv, 'präsˌpek-\ *adj* **—pro·spec·tive·ly** *adv* **—pros·pec·tor** \-ˌpektər, -'pek-\ *n*

pro·spec·tus \prə'spektəs\ *n* : introductory description of an enterprise

pros·per \'präspər\ *vb* : thrive or succeed **—pros·per·ous** \-pərəs\ *adj*

pros·per·i·ty \präs'perətē\ *n* : economic well-being

pros·tate \'präsˌtāt\ *n* : glandular body

about the base of the male urethra **—prostate** *adj*

pros·the·sis \präs'thēsəs, 'prästhə-\ *n, pl* **-the·ses** \-ˌsēz\ : artificial replacement for a body part **—pros·thet·ic** \präs'thetik\ *adj*

pros·ti·tute \'prästəˌtüt, -ˌtyüt\ *vb* **-tut·ed; -tut·ing** **1** : offer sexual activity for money **2** : put to corrupt or unworthy purposes ~ *n* : one who engages in sexual activities for money **—pros·ti·tu·tion** \ˌprästə'tüshən, -'tyü-\ *n*

pros·trate \'präsˌtrāt\ *adj* : stretched out with face on the ground ~ *vb* **-trat·ed; -trat·ing** **1** : fall or throw (oneself) into a prostrate position **2** : reduce to helplessness **—pros·tra·tion** \präs'trāshən\ *n*

pro·tag·o·nist \prō'tagənist\ *n* : main character in a drama or story

pro·tect \prə'tekt\ *vb* : shield from injury **—pro·tec·tor** \-tər\ *n*

pro·tec·tion \prə'tekshən\ *n* **1** : act of protecting **2** : one that protects **—pro·tec·tive** \-'tektiv\ *adj*

pro·tec·tor·ate \-tərət\ *n* : state dependent upon the authority of another state

pro·té·gé \'prōtəˌzhā\ *n* : one under the care and protection of an influential person

pro·tein \'prō,tēn\ *n* : complex combination of amino acids present in living matter

pro·test \'prō,test\ *n* **1** : organized public demonstration of disapproval **2** : strong objection ~ \prə'test\ *vb* **1** : assert positively **2** : object strongly **—prot·es·ta·tion** \ˌprätəs'tāshən\ *n* **—pro·test·er, pro·tes·tor** \'prō,testər\ *n*

Prot·es·tant \'prätəstənt\ *n* : Christian not of a Catholic or Orthodox church **—Prot·es·tant·ism** \'prätəstəntˌizəm\ *n*

pro·to·col \'prōtəˌkól\ *n* : diplomatic etiquette

pro·ton \'prō,tän\ *n* : positively charged atomic particle

pro·to·plasm \'prōtəˌplazəm\ *n* : complex colloidal living substance of plant and animal cells **—pro·to·plas·mic** \ˌprōtə'plazmik\ *adj*

pro·to·type \'prōtəˌtīp\ *n* : original model

pro·to·zo·an \ˌprōtə'zōən\ *n* : single-celled lower invertebrate animal

pro·tract \prō'trakt\ vb : prolong

pro·trac·tor \-'traktər\ n : instrument for drawing and measuring angles

pro·trude \prō'trüd\ vb -trud·ed; -trud·ing : stick out or cause to stick out —**pro·tru·sion** \-'trüzhən\ n

pro·tu·ber·ance \prō'tübərəns, -'tyü-\ n : something that protrudes —**pro·tu·ber·ant** adj

proud \'praůd\ adj 1 : having or showing excessive self-esteem 2 : highly pleased 3 : having proper self-respect 4 : glorious —**proud·ly** adv

prove \'prüv\ vb **proved; proven** or **prov·en** \'prüvən\; **prov·ing** 1 : test by experiment or by a standard 2 : establish the truth of by argument or evidence 3 : turn out esp. after trial or test —**prov·able** \'prüvəbəl\ adj

prov·en·der \'prävəndər\ n : dry food for domestic animals

prov·erb \'präv,ərb\ n : short meaningful popular saying —**pro·ver·bi·al** \prə'vərbēəl\ adj

pro·vide \prə'vīd\ vb -vid·ed; -vid·ing 1 : take measures beforehand 2 : make a stipulation 3 : supply what is needed —**pro·vid·er** n

pro·vid·ed conj : if

prov·i·dence \'prävədəns\ n 1 often cap : divine guidance 2 cap : God 3 : quality of being provident

prov·i·dent \-ədənt\ adj 1 : making provision for the future 2 : thrifty —**prov·i·dent·ly** adv

prov·i·den·tial \,prävə'denchəl\ adj 1 : relating to Providence 2 : opportune

pro·vid·ing conj : provided

prov·ince \'prävəns\ n 1 : administrative district 2 pl : all of a country outside the metropolis 3 : sphere

pro·vin·cial \prə'vinchəl\ adj 1 : relating to a province 2 : limited in outlook —**pro·vin·cial·ism** \-,izəm\ n

pro·vi·sion \prə'vizhən\ n 1 : act of providing 2 : stock of food —usu. in pl. 3 : stipulation ~ vb : supply with provisions

pro·vi·sion·al \-'vizhənəl\ adj : provided for a temporary need —**pro·vi·sion·al·ly** adv

pro·vi·so \prə'vīzō\ n, pl -sos or -soes : stipulation

pro·voke \prə'vōk\ vb -voked; -vok·ing 1 : incite to anger 2 : stir up on purpose —**prov·o·ca·tion** \,prävə-

'kāshən\ n —**pro·voc·a·tive** \prə-'väkətiv\ adj

prow \'praů\ n : bow of a ship

prow·ess \'praůəs\ n 1 : valor 2 : extraordinary ability

prowl \'praůl\ vb : roam about stealthily —**prowl** n —**prowl·er** n

prox·i·mate \'präksəmət\ adj : very near

prox·im·i·ty \präk'simətē\ n : nearness

proxy \'präksē\ n, pl **prox·ies** : authority to act for another —**proxy** adj

prude \'prüd\ n : one who shows extreme modesty —**prud·ery** \'prüdərē\ n —**prud·ish** \'prüdish\ adj

pru·dent \'prüdᵊnt\ adj 1 : shrewd 2 : cautious 3 : thrifty —**pru·dence** \-ᵊns\ n —**pru·den·tial** \prü'denchəl\ adj —**pru·dent·ly** adv

¹prune \'prün\ n : dried plum

²prune vb **pruned; prun·ing** : cut off unwanted parts

pru·ri·ent \'prürēənt\ adj : lewd —**pru·ri·ence** \-ēəns\ n

¹pry \'prī\ vb **pried; pry·ing** : look closely or inquisitively

²pry vb **pried; pry·ing** : raise, move, or pull apart with a lever

psalm \'säm, 'sälm\ n : sacred song or poem —**psalm·ist** n

pseu·do·nym \'südᵊn,im\ n : fictitious name —**pseu·don·y·mous** \sü'dänəməs\ adj

pso·ri·a·sis \sə'rīəsəs\ n : chronic skin disease

psy·che \'sīkē\ n : soul or mind

psy·chi·a·try \sə'kīətrē, sī-\ n : branch of medicine dealing with mental, emotional, and behavioral disorders —**psy·chi·at·ric** \,sīkē'atrik\ adj —**psy·chi·a·trist** \sə'kīətrist, sī-\ n

psy·chic \'sīkik\ adj 1 : relating to the psyche 2 : sensitive to supernatural forces ~ n : person sensitive to supernatural forces —**psy·chi·cal·ly** adv

psy·cho·anal·y·sis \,sīkōə'naləsəs\ n : study of the normally hidden content of the mind esp. to resolve conflicts —**psy·cho·an·a·lyst** \-'anᵊlist\ n —**psy·cho·an·a·lyt·ic** \-,anᵊl'itik\ adj —**psy·cho·an·a·lyze** \-'anᵊl,īz\ vb

psy·chol·o·gy \sī'käləjē\ n, pl -gies 1 : science of mind and behavior 2 : mental and behavioral aspect (as of an individual) —**psy·cho·log·i·cal** \,sīkə'läjikəl\ adj —**psy·cho·log·i·cal·ly** adv —**psy·chol·o·gist** \sī-'käləjist\ n

psy·cho·path \'sīkə,path\ *n* : mentally ill or unstable person —**psy·cho·path·ic** \,sīkə'pathik\ *adj*

psy·cho·sis \sī'kōsəs\ *n, pl* **-cho·ses** \-,sēz\ : mental derangement (as paranoia) —**psy·chot·ic** \-'kätik\ *adj or n*

psy·cho·so·mat·ic \,sīkəsə'matik\ *adj* : relating to bodily symptoms caused by mental or emotional disturbance

psy·cho·ther·a·py \,sīkō'therəpē\ *n* : treatment of mental disorder by psychological means —**psy·cho·ther·a·pist** \-pist\ *n*

pto·maine \'tō,mān\ *n* : bacterial decay product

pu·ber·ty \'pyübərtē\ *n* : time of sexual maturity

pu·bic \'pyübik\ *adj* : relating to the lower abdominal region

pub·lic \'pəblik\ *adj* 1 : relating to the people as a whole 2 : civic 3 : not private 4 : open to all 5 : well-known ~ *n* : people as a whole —**pub·lic·ly** *adv*

pub·li·ca·tion \,pəblə'kāshən\ *n* 1 : process of publishing 2 : published work

pub·lic·i·ty \pə'blisətē\ *n* 1 : news information given out to gain public attention 2 : public attention

pub·li·cize \'pəblə,sīz\ *vb* **-cized; -cizing** : bring to public attention —**pub·li·cist** \-sist\ *n*

pub·lish \'pəblish\ *vb* 1 : announce publicly 2 : reproduce for sale esp. by printing —**pub·lish·er** *n*

puck·er \'pəkər\ *vb* : pull together into folds or wrinkles ~ *n* : wrinkle

pud·ding \'pudiŋ\ *n* : creamy dessert

pud·dle \'pədᵊl\ *n* : very small pool of water

pudgy \'pəjē\ *adj* **pudg·i·er; -est** : short and plump

pu·er·ile \'pyurəl\ *adj* : childish

puff \'pəf\ *vb* 1 : blow in short gusts 2 : pant 3 : enlarge ~ *n* 1 : short discharge (as of air) 2 : slight swelling 3 : something light and fluffy —**puffy** *adj*

pug \'pəg\ *n* : small stocky dog

pu·gi·lism \'pyüjə,lizəm\ *n* : boxing —**pu·gi·list** \-list\ *n* —**pu·gi·lis·tic** \,pyüjə'listik\ *adj*

pug·na·cious \,pəg'nāshəs\ *adj* : prone to fighting —**pug·nac·i·ty** \-'nasətē\ *n*

puke \'pyük\ *vb* **puked; puk·ing** : vomit —**puke** *n*

pul·chri·tude \'pəlkrə,tüd, -,tyüd\ *n* : beauty —**pul·chri·tu·di·nous** \,pəlkrə'tüd⁰nəs, -'tyüd-\ *adj*

pull \'pul\ *vb* 1 : exert force so as to draw (something) toward or out 2 : move 3 : stretch or tear ~ *n* 1 : act of pulling 2 : influence 3 : device for pulling something —**pull·er** *n*

pul·let \'pulət\ *n* : young hen

pul·ley \'pulē\ *n, pl* **-leys** : wheel with a grooved rim

Pull·man \'pulmən\ *n* : railroad car with berths

pull·over \'pul,ōvər\ *adj* : put on by being pulled over the head —**pullover** *n*

pul·mo·nary \'pulmə,nerē, 'pəl-\ *adj* : relating to the lungs

pulp \'pəlp\ *n* 1 : soft part of a fruit or vegetable 2 : soft moist mass (as of mashed wood) —**pulpy** *adj*

pul·pit \'pul,pit\ *n* : raised desk used in preaching

pul·sate \'pəl,sāt\ *vb* **-sat·ed; -sat·ing** : expand and contract rhythmically —**pul·sa·tion** \,pəl'sāshən\ *n*

pulse \'pəls\ *n* : arterial throbbing caused by heart contractions —**pulse** *vb*

pul·ver·ize \'pəlvə,rīz\ *vb* **-ized; -iz·ing** : beat or grind into a powder

pu·ma \'pümə, 'pyü-\ *n* : cougar

pum·ice \'pəməs\ *n* : light porous volcanic glass used in polishing

pum·mel \'pəməl\ *vb* **-meled; -mel·ing** : beat

¹pump \'pəmp\ *n* : device for moving or compressing fluids ~ *vb* 1 : raise (as water) with a pump 2 : fill by means of a pump with *up* 3 : move like a pump —**pump·er** *n*

²pump *n* : woman's low shoe

pum·per·nick·el \'pəmpər,nikəl\ *n* : dark rye bread

pump·kin \'pəŋkən, 'pəmpkən\ *n* : large usu. orange fruit of a vine related to the gourd

pun \'pən\ *n* : humorous use of a word in a way that suggests two or more interpretations —**pun** *vb*

¹punch \'pənch\ *vb* 1 : strike with the fist 2 : perforate with a punch ~ *n* : quick blow with the fist —**punch·er** *n*

²punch *n* : tool for piercing or stamping

³punch n : mixed beverage often including fruit juice

punc·til·i·ous \pəŋk'tiléəs\ adj : marked by precise accordance with conventions

punc·tu·al \'pəŋkchəwəl\ adj : prompt —**punc·tu·al·i·ty** \,pəŋkchə'walətē\ n —**punc·tu·al·ly** adv

punc·tu·ate \'pəŋkchə,wāt\ vb -**at·ed;** -**at·ing** : mark with punctuation

punc·tu·a·tion \,pəŋkchə'wāshən\ n : standardized marks in written matter to clarify the meaning and separate parts

punc·ture \'pəŋkchər\ n : act or result of puncturing ~ vb -**tured;** -**tur·ing** : make a hole in

pun·dit \'pəndət\ n 1 : learned person 2 : expert or critic

pun·gent \'pənjənt\ adj : having a sharp or stinging odor or taste —**pun·gen·cy** \-jənsē\ n —**pun·gent·ly** adv

pun·ish \'pənish\ vb : impose a penalty on or for —**pun·ish·able** adj —**pun·ish·ment** n

pu·ni·tive \'pyünətiv\ adj : inflicting punishment

pun·kin var of PUMPKIN

¹punt \'pənt\ n : long narrow flat-bottomed boat ~ vb : propel (a boat) by pushing with a pole

²punt vb : kick a ball dropped from the hands ~ n : act of punting a ball

pu·ny \'pyünē\ adj -**ni·er;** -**est** : slight in power or size

pup \'pəp\ n : young dog

pu·pa \'pyüpə\ n, pl -**pae** \-,pē, -,pī\ or -**pas** : insect (as a moth) when it is in a cocoon —**pu·pal** \-pəl\ adj

¹pu·pil \'pyüpəl\ n : young person in school

²pupil n : dark central opening of the iris of the eye

pup·pet \'pəpət\ n : small doll moved by hand or by strings —**pup·pe·teer** \,pəpə'tir\ n

pup·py \'pəpē\ n, pl -**pies** : young dog

pur·chase \'pərchəs\ vb -**chased;** -**chas·ing** : obtain in exchange for money ~ n 1 : act of purchasing 2 : something purchased 3 : secure grasp —**pur·chas·er** n

pure \'pyür\ adj **pur·er; pur·est** : free of foreign matter, contamination, or corruption —**pure·ly** adv

pu·ree \pyu'rā, -'rē\ n : thick liquid mass of food —**puree** vb

pur·ga·to·ry \'pərgə,tōrē\ n, pl -**ries** : intermediate state after death for purification by expiating sins —**pur·ga·tor·i·al** \,pərgə'tōrēəl\ adj

purge \'pərj\ vb **purged; purg·ing** 1 : purify esp. from sin 2 : have or cause emptying of the bowels 3 : to get rid of ~ n 1 : act or result of purging 2 : something that purges —**pur·ga·tive** \'pərgətiv\ adj or n

pu·ri·fy \'pyürə,fī\ vb -**fied;** -**fy·ing** : make or become pure —**pu·ri·fi·ca·tion** \,pyürəfə'kāshən\ n —**pu·ri·fi·er** \-,fīər\ n

Pu·rim \'pürim\ n : Jewish holiday celebrated in February or March in commemoration of the deliverance of the Jews from the massacre plotted by Haman

pu·ri·tan \'pyürətªn\ n : one who practices or preaches a very strict moral code —**pu·ri·tan·i·cal** \,pyürə'tanikəl\ adj —**pu·ri·tan·i·cal·ly** adv

pu·ri·ty \'pyürətē\ n : quality or state of being pure

purl \'pərl\ n : stitch in knitting ~ vb : knit in purl stitch

pur·loin \pər'lȯin, 'pər,lȯin\ vb : steal

pur·ple \'pərpəl\ n : bluish red color —**pur·plish** \'pərpəlish\ adj

pur·port \pər'pōrt\ vb : convey outwardly as the meaning ~ \'pər,pōrt\ n : meaning —**pur·port·ed·ly** \-ədlē\ adv

pur·pose \'pərpəs\ n 1 : something (as a result) aimed at 2 : resolution ~ vb -**posed;** -**pos·ing** : intend —**pur·pose·ful** \-fəl\ adj —**pur·pose·ful·ly** adv —**pur·pose·less** adj —**pur·pose·ly** adv

purr \'pər\ n : low murmur typical of a contented cat —**purr** vb

¹purse \'pərs\ n 1 : bag or pouch for money and small objects 2 : financial resource 3 : prize money

²purse vb **pursed; purs·ing** : pucker

pur·su·ance \pər'süəns\ n : act of carrying out or into effect

pur·su·ant to \-'süənt-\ prep : according to

pur·sue \pər'sü\ vb -**sued;** -**su·ing** 1 : follow in order to overtake 2 : seek to accomplish 3 : proceed along 4 : engage in —**pur·su·er** n

pur·suit \pər'süt\ n 1 : act of pursuing 2 : occupation

pur•vey \pər'vā\ vb -**veyed; -vey•ing** : supply (as provisions) usu. as a business —**pur•vey•or** \-ər\ n

pus \'pəs\ n : thick yellowish fluid (as in a boil)

push \'push\ vb 1 : press against to move forward 2 : urge on or provoke ~ n 1 : vigorous effort 2 : act of pushing —**push•cart** n —**push•er** \'pushər\ n

pushy \'pushē\ adj **push•i•er; -est** : objectionably aggressive

pu•sil•lan•i•mous \,pyüsə'lanəməs\ adj : cowardly

pussy \'püsē\ n, pl **puss•ies** : cat

pus•tule \'pəschül\ n : pus-filled pimple

put \'put\ vb **put; put•ting** 1 : bring to a specified position or condition 2 : subject to pain, suffering, or death 3 : impose or cause to exist 4 : express 5 : cause to be used or employed —**put off** vb : postpone or delay —**put out** vb : bother or inconvenience —**put up** vb 1 : prepare for storage 2 : lodge 3 : contribute or pay —**put up with** : endure

pu•tre•fy \'pyütrə,fī\ vb -**fied; -fy•ing** : make or become putrid —**pu•tre•fac•tion** \,pyütrə'fakshən\ n

pu•trid \'pyütrəd\ adj : rotten —**pu•trid•i•ty** \pyü'tridətē\ n

put•ty \'pətē\ n, pl -**ties** : doughlike cement —**putty** vb

puz•zle \'pəzəl\ vb -**zled; -zling** 1 : confuse 2 : attempt to solve —with out or over ~ n : something that confuses or tests ingenuity —**puz•zle•ment** n —**puz•zler** \-ələr\ n

pyg•my \'pigmē\ n, pl -**mies** : dwarf —**pygmy** adj

py•lon \'pī,län, -lən\ n : tower or tall post

pyr•a•mid \'pirə,mid\ n : structure with a square base and 4 triangular sides meeting at a point

pyre \'pīr\ n : material heaped for a funeral fire

py•ro•ma•nia \,pīrō'mānēə\ n : irresistible impulse to start fires —**py•ro•ma•ni•ac** \-nē,ak\ n

py•ro•tech•nics \,pīrō'tekniks\ n pl : spectacular display (as of fireworks) —**py•ro•tech•nic** \-nik\ adj

Pyr•rhic \'pirik\ adj : achieved at excessive cost

py•thon \'pī,thän, -thən\ n : very large constricting snake

Q

q \'kyü\ n, pl **q's** or **qs** \'kyüz\ : 17th letter of the alphabet

¹quack \'kwak\ vb : make a cry like that of a duck —**quack** n

²quack n : one who pretends to have medical or healing skill —**quack** adj —**quack•ery** \-ərē\ n —**quack•ish** adj

quad•ran•gle \'kwäd,raŋgəl\ n : rectangular courtyard

quad•rant \'kwädrənt\ n : 1/4 of a circle

quad•ri•lat•er•al \,kwädrə'latərəl\ n : 4-sided polygon

qua•drille \kwä'dril, kə-\ n : square dance for 4 couples

quad•ru•ped \'kwädrə,ped\ n : animal having 4 feet

qua•dru•ple \kwä'drüpəl, -'drəp-; 'kwädrüpəl\ vb -**pled; -pling** : multiply by 4 ~ adj : being 4 times as great or as many

qua•dru•plet \kwä'drəplət, -'drüp-; 'kwädrəp-\ n : one of 4 offspring born at one birth

quaff \'kwäf, 'kwaf\ vb : drink deeply or repeatedly —**quaff** n

quag•mire \'kwag,mīr, 'kwäg-\ n : soft land or bog

qua•hog \'kō,hóg, 'kwó-, 'kwō-, -,häg\ n : thick-shelled clam

¹quail \'kwāl\ n, pl **quail** or **quails** : short-winged plump game bird

²quail vb : cower in fear

quaint \'kwänt\ adj : pleasingly old-fashioned or odd —**quaint•ly** adv —**quaint•ness** n

quake \'kwāk\ vb **quaked; quak•ing** : shake or tremble ~ n : earthquake

qual•i•fi•ca•tion \,kwäləfə'kāshən\ n 1 : limitation or stipulation 2 : special skill or experience for a job

qual•i•fy \'kwälə,fī\ vb -**fied; -fy•ing** 1

: modify or limit **2** : fit by skill or training for some purpose **3** : become eligible **—qual·i·fied** *adj* **—qual·i·fi·er** \-ˌfīər\ *n*

qual·i·ty \'kwälətē\ *n, pl* **-ties 1** : peculiar and essential character, nature, or feature **2** : excellence or distinction

qualm \'kwäm, 'kwälm, 'kwóm\ *n* : sudden feeling of doubt or uneasiness

quan·da·ry \'kwändrē\ *n, pl* **-ries** : state of perplexity or doubt

quan·ti·ty \'kwäntətē\ *n, pl* **-ties 1** : something that can be measured or numbered **2** : considerable amount

quan·tum theory \'kwäntəm-\ *n* : theory in physics that radiant energy (as light) is composed of separate packets of energy

quar·an·tine \'kwórənˌtēn\ *n* **1** : restraint on the movements of persons or goods to prevent the spread of pests or disease **2** : place or period of quarantine **—quarantine** *vb*

quar·rel \'kwórəl\ *n* : basis of conflict **—quarrel** *vb* **—quar·rel·some** \-səm\ *adj*

¹quar·ry \'kwórē\ *n, pl* **quarries** : prey

²quarry *n, pl* **-ries** : excavation for obtaining stone **—quarry** *vb*

quart \'kwórt\ *n* : unit of liquid measure equal to .95 liter or of dry measure equal to 1.10 liters

quar·ter \'kwórtər\ *n* **1** : 1/4 part **2** : 1/4 of a dollar **3** : city district **4** *pl* : place to live esp. for a time **5** : mercy ~ *vb* : divide into 4 equal parts

quar·ter·ly \'kwórtərlē\ *adv or adj* : at 3-month intervals ~ *n, pl* **-lies** : periodical published 4 times a year

quar·ter·mas·ter *n* **1** : ship's helmsman **2** : army supply officer

quar·tet \kwór'tet\ *n* **1** : music for 4 performers **2** : group of 4

quar·to \'kwórtō\ *n, pl* **-tos** : book printed on pages cut 4 from a sheet

quartz \'kwórts\ *n* : transparent crystalline mineral

quash \'kwäsh, 'kwósh\ *vb* **1** : set aside by judicial action **2** : suppress summarily and completely

qua·si \'kwäˌzī, -ˌsī; 'kwäzē, 'kwäs-; 'kwäzē\ *adj* : similar or nearly identical

qua·train \'kwäˌträn\ *n* : unit of 4 lines of verse

qua·ver \'kwāvər\ *vb* : tremble or trill **—quaver** *n*

quay \'kē, 'kā, 'kwā\ *n* : wharf

quea·sy \'kwēzē\ *adj* **-si·er; -est** : nauseated **—quea·si·ly** \-zəlē\ *adv* **—quea·si·ness** \-zēnəs\ *n*

queen \'kwēn\ *n* **1** : wife or widow of a king **2** : female monarch **3** : woman of rank, power, or attractiveness **4** : fertile female of a social insect **—queen·ly** *adj*

queer \'kwir\ *adj* : differing from the usual or normal **—queer·ly** *adv* **—queer·ness** *n*

quell \'kwel\ *vb* : put down by force

quench \'kwench\ *vb* **1** : put out **2** : satisfy (a thirst) **—quench·able** *adj* **—quench·er** *n*

quer·u·lous \'kwerələs, -yələs\ *adj* : fretful or whining **—quer·u·lous·ly** *adv* **—quer·u·lous·ness** *n*

que·ry \'kwirē, 'kwer-\ *n, pl* **-ries** : question **—query** *vb*

quest \'kwest\ *n or vb* : search

ques·tion \'kweschən\ *n* **1** : something asked **2** : subject for debate **3** : dispute ~ *vb* **1** : ask questions **2** : doubt or dispute **3** : subject to analysis **—ques·tion·er** *n*

ques·tion·able \'kweschənəbəl\ *adj* **1** : not certain **2** : of doubtful truth or morality **—ques·tion·ably** \-blē\ *adv*

question mark *n* : a punctuation mark ? used esp. at the end of a sentence to indicate a direct question

ques·tion·naire \ˌkweschə'nar\ *n* : set of questions

queue \'kyü\ *n* **1** : braid of hair **2** : a waiting line ~ *vb* **queued; queu·ing** *or* **queue·ing** : line up

quib·ble \'kwibəl\ *n* : minor objection **—quibble** *vb* **—quib·bler** *n*

quick \'kwik\ *adj* **1** : rapid **2** : alert or perceptive ~ *n* : sensitive area of living flesh **—quick** *adv* **—quick·ly** *adv* **—quick·ness** *n*

quick·en \'kwikən\ *vb* **1** : come to life **2** : increase in speed

quick·sand *n* : deep mass of loose sand and water

quick·sil·ver *n* : mercury

qui·es·cent \kwī'esᵊnt\ *adj* : being at rest **—qui·es·cence** \-əns\ *n*

qui·et \'kwīət\ *adj* **1** : marked by little motion or activity **2** : gentle **3** : free from noise **4** : not showy **5** : secluded ~ *vb* : pacify **—quiet** *adv or n* **—qui·et·ly** *adv* **—qui·et·ness** *n*

qui·etude \'kwīə,tüd, -,tyüd\ *n* : quietness or repose

quill \'kwil\ *n* **1** : a large stiff feather **2** : porcupine's spine

quilt \'kwilt\ *n* : padded bedspread ~ *vb* : stitch or sew in layers with padding in between

quince \'kwins\ *n* : hard yellow apple-like fruit

qui·nine \'kwī,nīn\ *n* : bitter drug used against malaria

quin·tes·sence \kwin'tesᵊns\ *n* **1** : purest essence of something **2** : most typical example —**quin·tes·sen·tial** \,kwintə'senchəl\ *adj* —**quin·tes·sen·tial·ly** *adv*

quin·tet \kwin'tet\ *n* **1** : music for 5 performers **2** : group of 5

quin·tu·ple \kwin'tüpəl, -'tyüp-, -'təp-; 'kwintəp-\ *adj* **1** : having 5 units or members **2** : being 5 times as great or as many —**quintuple** *n or vb*

quin·tu·plet \-plət\ *n* : one of 5 offspring at one birth

quip \'kwip\ *vb* -**pp**- : make a clever remark —**quip** *n*

quire \'kwīr\ *n* : 24 or 25 sheets of paper of the same size and quality

quirk \'kwərk\ *n* : peculiarity of action or behavior —**quirky** *adj*

quit \'kwit\ *vb* quit; quit·ting **1** : stop **2** : leave —**quit·ter** *n*

quite \'kwīt\ *adv* **1** : completely **2** : to a considerable extent

quits \'kwits\ *adj* : even or equal with another (as by repaying a debt)

¹quiver \'kwivər\ *n* : case for arrows

²quiver *vb* : shake or tremble —**quiver** *n*

quix·ot·ic \kwik'sätik\ *adj* : idealistic to an impractical degree —**quix·ot·i·cal·ly** \-tik(ə)lē\ *adv*

quiz \'kwiz\ *n, pl* quiz·zes : short test ~ *vb* -**zz**- : question closely

quiz·zi·cal \'kwizikəl\ *adj* **1** : teasing **2** : curious

quoit \'kóit, 'kwóit, 'kwät\ *n* : ring thrown at a peg in a game (**quoits**)

quon·dam \'kwändəm, -,dam\ *adj* : former

quo·rum \'kwórəm\ *n* : required number of members present

quo·ta \'kwōtə\ *n* : proportional part or share

quotation mark *n* : one of a pair of punctuation marks ' ' or ' ' used esp. to indicate the beginning and the end of a quotation

quote \'kwōt\ *vb* quot·ed; quot·ing **1** : repeat (another's words) exactly **2** : state (a price) —**quot·able** *adj* —**quo·ta·tion** \kwō'tāshən\ *n* —**quote** *n*

quo·tient \'kwōshənt\ *n* : number obtained from division

R

r \'är\ *n, pl* r's *or* rs \'ärz\ : 18th letter of the alphabet

rab·bet \'rabət\ *n* : groove in a board

rab·bi \'rab,ī\ *n* : Jewish religious leader —**rab·bin·ic** \rə'binik\, **rab·bin·i·cal** \-ikəl\ *adj*

rab·bin·ate \'rabənət, -,nāt\ *n* : office of a rabbi

rab·bit \'rabət\ *n, pl* -bit *or* -bits : long-eared burrowing mammal

rab·ble \'rabəl\ *n* : mob

ra·bid \'rabəd\ *adj* **1** : violent **2** : fanatical **3** : affected with rabies —**ra·bid·ly** *adv*

ra·bies \'rābēz\ *n, pl* rabies : acute deadly virus disease

rac·coon \ra'kün\ *n, pl* -coon *or* -coons : tree-dwelling mammal with a black mask and a bushy ringed tail

¹race \'rās\ *n* **1** : strong current of water **2** : contest of speed **3** : election campaign ~ *vb* raced; rac·ing **1** : run in a race **2** : rush —**race·course** *n* —**rac·er** *n* —**race·track** *n*

²race *n* **1** : family, tribe, people, or nation of the same stock **2** : division of mankind based on hereditary traits —**ra·cial** \'rāshəl\ *adj* —**ra·cial·ly** *adv*

race·horse *n* : horse used for racing

rac·ism \'rās,izəm\ *n* : discrimination based on the belief that some races are by nature superior —**rac·ist** \-ist\ *n*

rack \'rak\ *n* **1** : framework for display or storage **2** : instrument that stretches the body for torture ~ *vb* : torture with or as if with a rack

¹rack·et \'rakət\ *n* : bat with a tight netting across an open frame

²rack·et n 1 : confused noise 2 : fraudulent scheme —rack·e·teer \,rakə'tir\ n —rack·e·teer·ing n

ra·con·teur \,rak,än'tər\ n : storyteller

racy \'rāsē\ adj rac·i·er; -est : risqué —rac·i·ly adv —rac·i·ness n

ra·dar \'rā,där\ n : radio device for determining distance and direction of distant objects

ra·di·al \'rādēəl\ adj : having parts arranged like rays coming from a common center —ra·di·al·ly adv

ra·di·ant \'rādēənt\ adj 1 : glowing 2 : beaming with happiness 3 : transmitted by radiation —ra·di·ance \-əns\ n —ra·di·ant·ly adv

ra·di·ate \'rādē,āt\ vb -at·ed; -at·ing 1 : issue rays or in rays 2 : spread from a center —ra·di·a·tion \,rādē'āshən\ n

ra·di·a·tor \'rādē,ātər\ n : cooling or heating device

rad·i·cal \'radikəl\ adj 1 : fundamental 2 : extreme ~ n : person favoring extreme changes —rad·i·cal·ism \-,izəm\ n —rad·i·cal·ly adv

radii pl of RADIUS

ra·dio \'rādē,ō\ n, pl -di·os 1 : wireless transmission or reception of sound by means of electric waves 2 : radio receiving set ~ vb : send a message to by radio —radio adj

ra·dio·ac·tiv·i·ty \,rādēō,ak'tivətē\ n : property of an element that emits energy through nuclear disintegration —ra·dio·ac·tive \-'aktiv\ adj

ra·di·ol·o·gy \,rādē'äləjē\ n : medical use of radiation —ra·di·ol·o·gist \-jist\ n

rad·ish \'radish\ n : pungent fleshy root usu. eaten raw

ra·di·um \'rādēəm\ n : metallic radioactive chemical element

ra·di·us \'rādēəs\ n, pl -dii \-ē,ī\ 1 : line from the center of a circle or sphere to the circumference or surface 2 : area defined by a radius

ra·don \'rā,dän\ n : gaseous radioactive chemical element

raff·ish \'rafish\ adj : flashily vulgar —raff·ish·ly adv —raff·ish·ness n

raf·fle \'rafəl\ n : lottery among people who have bought tickets ~ vb -fled; -fling : offer in a raffle

¹raft \'raft\ n : flat floating platform ~ vb : travel or transport by raft

²raft n : large amount or number

raf·ter \'raftər\ n : beam supporting a roof

¹rag \'rag\ n : waste piece of cloth

²rag n : composition in ragtime

rag·a·muf·fin \'ragə,məfən\ n : ragged dirty person

rage \'rāj\ n 1 : violent anger 2 : vogue ~ vb raged; rag·ing 1 : be extremely angry or violent 2 : be out of control

ragged \'ragəd\ adj : torn —rag·ged·ly adv —rag·ged·ness n

ra·gout \ra'gü\ n : meat stew

rag·time n : syncopated music

rag·weed n : coarse weedy herb with allergenic pollen

raid \'rād\ n : sudden usu. surprise attack —raid vb —raid·er n

¹rail \'rāl\ n 1 : bar serving as a guard or barrier 2 : bar forming a track for wheeled vehicles 3 : railroad

²rail vb : scold someone vehemently —rail·er n

rail·ing \'rāliŋ\ n : rail or a barrier of rails

rail·lery \'rālərē\ n, pl -ler·ies : good-natured ridicule

rail·road \'rāl,rōd\ n : road for a train laid with iron rails and wooden ties ~ vb : force something hastily —rail·road·er n —rail·road·ing n

rail·way \-,wā\ n : railroad

rai·ment \'rāmənt\ n : clothing

rain \'rān\ n 1 : water falling in drops from the clouds 2 : shower of objects ~ vb : fall as or like rain —rain·coat n —rain·drop n —rain·fall n —rain·mak·er n —rain·mak·ing n —rain·storm n —rain·water n —rainy adj

rain·bow \-,bō\ n : arc of colors formed by the sun shining through moisture

raise \'rāz\ vb raised; rais·ing 1 : lift 2 : arouse 3 : erect 4 : collect 5 : breed, grow, or bring up 6 : increase 7 : make light ~ n : increase esp. in pay —rais·er n

rai·sin \'rāzᵊn\ n : dried grape

ra·ja, ra·jah \'räjə\ n : Indian prince

¹rake \'rāk\ n : garden tool for smoothing or sweeping ~ vb raked; rak·ing 1 : gather, loosen, or smooth with or as if with a rake 2 : sweep with gunfire

²rake n : dissolute man

rak·ish \'rākish\ adj : smart or jaunty —rak·ish·ly adv —rak·ish·ness n

ral·ly \'ralē\ vb -lied; -ly·ing 1 : bring or come together 2 : revive or recover

3 : make a comeback ~ *n, pl* **-lies 1**
: act of rallying **2** : mass meeting

ram \\ram\ *n* **1** : male sheep **2** : beam
used in battering down walls or doors
~ *vb* **-mm- 1** : force or drive in or
through **2** : strike against violently

RAM \\ram\ *n* : main internal storage
area in a computer

ram·ble \\rambəl\ *vb* **-bled; -bling**
: wander **—ramble** ~ *n* **—ram·bler**
\-blər\ *n*

ram·bunc·tious \ram'bəŋkshəs\ *adj*
: unruly

ram·i·fi·ca·tion \,raməfə'kāshən\ *n*
: consequence

ram·i·fy \'ramə,fī\ *vb* **-fied; -fy·ing**
: branch out

ramp \\ramp\ *n* : sloping passage or
connecting roadway

ram·page \'ram,pāj, ram'pāj\ *vb*
-paged; -pag·ing : rush about wildly
~ \'ram,-\ *n* : violent or riotous action
or behavior

ram·pant \\rampənt\ *adj* : widespread
—ram·pant·ly *adv*

ram·part \\ram,pärt\ *n* : embankment of
a fortification

ram·rod *n* : rod used to load or clean a
gun ~ *adj* : strict or inflexible

ram·shack·le \\ram,shakəl\ *adj* : shaky

ran *past of* RUN

ranch \\ranch\ *n* **1** : establishment for
the raising of cattle, sheep, or horses
2 : specialized farm ~ *vb* : operate a
ranch **—ranch·er** *n*

ran·cid \\ransəd\ *adj* : smelling or tast-
ing as if spoiled **—ran·cid·i·ty** \ran-
'sidətē\ *n*

ran·cor \\raŋkər\ *n* : bitter deep-seated
ill will **—ran·cor·ous** *adj*

ran·dom \\randəm\ *adj* : occurring by
chance **—ran·dom·ly** *adv* **—ran·
dom·ness** *n* **—at random** : without
definite aim or method

ran·dom·ize \\randə,mīz\ *vb* **-ized; -iz·
ing** : select, assign, or arrange in a
random way

rang *past of* RING

range \\rānj\ *n* **1** : series of things in a
row **2** : open land for grazing **3**
: cooking stove **4** : variation within
limits **5** : place for target practice **6**
: extent ~ *vb* **ranged; rang·ing 1**
: arrange **2** : roam at large, freely, or
over **3** : vary within limits

rang·er \\rānjər\ *n* : officer who manages and protects public lands

rangy \\rānjē\ *adj* **rang·i·er, -est** : being
slender with long limbs **—rang·i·ness**
n

¹rank \\raŋk\ *adj* **1** : vigorous in growth
2 : unpleasantly strong-smelling **—**
rank·ly *adv* **—rank·ness** *n*

²rank *n* **1** : line of soldiers **2** : orderly
arrangement **3** : grade of official
standing **4** : position within a group
~ *vb* **1** : arrange in formation or according to class **2** : take or have a relative position

rank and file *n* : general membership

ran·kle \\raŋkəl\ *vb* **-kled; -kling**
: cause anger, irritation, or bitterness

ran·sack \\ran,sak\ *vb* : search through
and rob

ran·som \\ransəm\ *n* : something de-
manded for the freedom of a captive
~ *vb* : gain the freedom of by paying
a price **—ran·som·er** *n*

rant \\rant\ *vb* : talk or scold violently
—rant·er *n* **—rant·ing·ly** *adv*

¹rap \\rap\ *n* : sharp blow or rebuke ~
vb **-pp-** : strike or criticize sharply

²rap *vb* **-pp-** : talk freely

ra·pa·cious \rə'pāshəs\ *adj* **1** : excessively greedy **2** : ravenous **—ra·pa·
cious·ly** *adv* **—ra·pa·cious·ness** *n* **—**
ra·pac·i·ty \-'pasətē\ *n*

¹rape \\rāp\ *n* : herb grown as a forage
crop and for its seeds (**rape·seed**)

²rape *vb* **raped; rap·ing** : force to have
sexual intercourse **—rape** *n* **—rap·er**
n **—rap·ist** \\rāpist\ *n*

rap·id \\rapəd\ *adj* : very fast **—ra·pid·
i·ty** \rə'pidətē\ *n* **—rap·id·ly** *adv*

rap·ids \-ədz\ *n pl* : place in a stream
where the current is swift

ra·pi·er \\rāpēər\ *n* : narrow 2-edged
sword

rap·ine \\rapən, -,īn\ *n* : plunder

rap·port \ra'pōr\ *n* : harmonious relationship

rapt \\rapt\ *adj* : engrossed **—rapt·ly**
adv **—rapt·ness** *n*

rap·ture \\rapchər\ *n* : spiritual or emotional ecstasy **—rap·tur·ous** \-chə-
rəs\ *adj* **—rap·tur·ous·ly** *adv*

¹rare \\rar\ *adj* **rar·er; rar·est** : having
a portion relatively uncooked

²rare *adj* **rar·er; rar·est 1** : not dense
2 : unusually fine **3** : seldom met with
—rare·ly *adv* **—rare·ness** *n* **—rar·
i·ty** \\rarətē\ *n*

rar·e·fy \\rarə,fī\ *vb* **-fied; -fy·ing**

: make or become rare, thin, or less dense —**rar·e·fac·tion** \,rarə'fak-shən\ *n*

rar·ing \'rarən, -iŋ\ *adj* : full of enthusiasm

ras·cal \'raskəl\ *n* : mean, dishonest, or mischievous person —**ras·cal·i·ty** \ras'kalətē\ *n* —**ras·cal·ly** \'raskəlē\ *adj*

¹rash \'rash\ *adj* : too hasty in decision or action —**rash·ly** *adv* —**rash·ness** *n*

²rash *n* : a breaking out of the skin with red spots

rasp \'rasp\ *vb* 1 : rub with or as if with a rough file 2 : to speak in a grating tone ~ *n* : coarse file

rasp·ber·ry \'raz,berē\ *n* : edible red or black berry

rat \'rat\ *n* : destructive rodent larger than the mouse ~ *vb* : betray or inform on

ratch·et \'rachət\ *n* : notched device for allowing motion in one direction

rate \'rāt\ *n* 1 : quantity, amount, or degree measured in relation to some other quantity 2 : rank ~ *vb* **rat·ed; rat·ing** 1 : estimate or determine the rank or quality of 2 : deserve

rath·er \'rathər, 'rəth-, 'räth-\ *adv* 1 : preferably 2 : on the other hand 3 : more properly 4 : somewhat

rat·i·fy \'ratə,fī\ *vb* **-fied; -fy·ing** : approve and accept formally —**rat·i·fi·ca·tion** \,ratəfə'kāshən\ *n*

rat·ing \'rātiŋ\ *n* : classification according to grade

ra·tio \'rāshēō\ *n, pl* **-tios** : relation in number, quantity, or degree between things

ra·tion \'rashən, 'rāshən\ *n* : share or allotment (as of food) ~ *vb* : use or allot sparingly

ra·tio·nal \'rashənəl\ *adj* 1 : having reason or sanity 2 : relating to reason —**ra·tio·nal·ly** *adv*

ra·tio·nale \,rashə'nal\ *n* 1 : explanation of principles of belief or practice 2 : underlying reason

ra·tio·nal·ize \'rashənə,līz\ *vb* **-ized; -iz·ing** : justify (as one's behavior or weaknesses) esp. to oneself —**ra·tio·nal·i·za·tion** \,rashənələ'zāshən\ *n*

rat·tan \ra'tan, rə-\ *n* : palm with long stems used esp. for canes and wickerwork

rat·tle \'rat³l\ *vb* **-tled; -tling** 1 : make a series of clattering sounds 2 : say

briskly 3 : confuse or upset ~ *n* 1 : series of clattering sounds 2 : something (as a toy) that rattles

rat·tler \'ratlər\ *n* : rattlesnake

rat·tle·snake *n* : American venomous snake with a rattle at the end of the tail

rat·ty \'ratē\ *adj* **rat·ti·er; -est** : shabby

rau·cous \'rȯkəs\ *adj* : harsh or boisterous —**rau·cous·ly** *adv* —**rau·cous·ness** *n*

rav·age \'ravij\ *n* : destructive effect ~ *vb* **-aged; -ag·ing** : lay waste —**rav·ag·er** *n*

rave \'rāv\ *vb* **raved; rav·ing** 1 : talk wildly in or as if in delirium 2 : talk with extreme enthusiasm ~ *n* 1 : act of raving 2 : enthusiastic praise

rav·el \'ravəl\ *vb* **-eled** or **-elled; -el·ing** or **-el·ling** 1 : unravel 2 : tangle ~ *n* 1 : something tangled 2 : loose thread

ra·ven \'rāvən\ *n* : large black bird ~ *adj* : black and shiny

rav·en·ous \'ravənəs\ *adj* : very hungry —**rav·en·ous·ly** *adv* —**rav·en·ous·ness** *n*

ra·vine \rə'vēn\ *n* : narrow steep-sided valley

rav·ish \'ravish\ *vb* 1 : seize and take away by violence 2 : overcome with joy or delight 3 : rape —**rav·ish·er** *n* —**rav·ish·ment** *n*

raw \'rȯ\ *adj* **raw·er** \'rȯər\; **raw·est** \'rȯəst\ 1 : not cooked 2 : not processed 3 : not trained 4 : having the surface rubbed off 5 : cold and damp 6 : vulgar —**raw·ness** *n*

raw·hide \'rȯ,hīd\ *n* : untanned skin of cattle

ray \'rā\ *n* 1 : thin beam of radiant energy (as light) 2 : tiny bit

ray·on \'rā,än\ *n* : fabric made from cellulose fiber

raze \'rāz\ *vb* **razed; raz·ing** : destroy or tear down

ra·zor \'rāzər\ *n* : sharp cutting instrument used to shave off hair

re- \rē, 'rē, 'rē\ *prefix* 1 : again or anew 2 : back or backward

reaccelerate	readdress
reaccept	readjust
reacclimatize	readjustment
reaccredit	readmit
reacquaint	readopt
reacquire	reaffirm
reactivate	realign
reactivation	realignment

reallocate
reanalysis
reanalyze
reappear
reappearance
reapply
reappoint
reapportion
reappraisal
reappraise
reapprove
reargue
rearrange
rearrest
reassemble
reassert
reassess
reassessment
reassign
reassignment
reattach
reattain
reawaken
rebalance
rebaptize
rebid
rebind
reborn
rebroadcast
rebuild
rebury
recalculate
recapture
recast
recertification
recertify
rechannel
recharge
rechargeable
recheck
rechristen
recirculate
recirculation
reclassification
reclassify
recolonize
recombine
recompute
reconceive
reconnect
reconquer
reconquest
reconsider
reconsideration
reconsolidate
reconstruct
recontaminate
reconvene

reconvict
recopy
re-create
recross
redecorate
rededicate
rededication
redefine
redeposit
redesign
redevelop
rediscover
rediscovery
redissolve
redistribute
redraft
redraw
reemerge
reemergence
reemphasize
reenergize
reengage
reenlist
reenlistment
reenroll
reenter
reequip
reestablish
reestablishment
reestimate
reevaluate
reevaluation
reexamination
reexamine
refinance
refire
refloat
refocus
refold
reformulate
refreeze
refuel
regain
regrow
regrowth
rehear
reheat
rehire
rehospitaliza-
  tion
rehospitalize
reidentify
reignite
reimplant
reimpose
reincorporate
reindict
reinfection

reinflate
reinject
reinjection
reinoculate
reinsert
reinsertion
reinspect
reinstall
reinstitute
reintegrate
reintegration
reinter
reintroduce
reinvent
reinvestigate
reinvestigation
reinvigorate
rejudge
rekindle
reknit
relabel
relandscape
relaunch
relearn
relight
reline
reload
remarriage
remarry
rematch
remelt
remobilize
remoisten
remold
remotivate
rename
renegotiate
reoccupy
reoccur
reoccurrence
reoperate
reorchestrate
reorganization
reorganize
reorient
repack
repave
rephotograph
replan
replaster
replay
replot
repolish
repopulate
repressurize
reprice
reprint
reprocess

reprogram
reread
rereading
rerecord
reregister
reroof
reroute
resalable
resale
reschedule
reseal
resegregate
resell
resentence
reset
resettle
resew
reshoot
reshow
resocialization
resod
resolidify
restage
restart
restate
restatement
restimulate
restock
restructure
restudy
restyle
resubmit
resupply
resurface
resurvey
resynthesis
resynthesize
retarget
reteach
retell
retest
rethink
retighten
retrain
retranslate
retransmit
retry
retune
retype
reupholster
reusable
reuse
reutilize
revaccinate
revaccination
revisit
rewash
reweave

rewind   rewrap
rewire

reach \'rēch\ *vb* 1 : stretch out 2 : touch or try to touch or grasp 3 : extend to or arrive at 4 : communicate with ~ *n* 1 : act of reaching 2 : distance one can reach 3 : ability to reach —**reach·able** *adj* —**reach·er** *n*

re·act \rē'akt\ *vb* 1 : act in response to some influence or stimulus 2 : undergo chemical change —**re·ac·tive** \-'aktiv\ *adj*

re·ac·tion \rē'akshən\ *n* 1 : action or emotion caused by and directly related to or counter to another action 2 : chemical change

re·ac·tion·ary \-shə‚nerē\ *adj* : relating to or favoring return to an earlier political order or policy —**reactionary** *n*

re·ac·tor \rē'aktər\ *n* 1 : one that reacts 2 : device for the controlled release of nuclear energy

read \'rēd\ *vb* **read** \'red\; **read·ing** \'rēdiŋ\ 1 : understand written language 2 : utter aloud printed words 3 : interpret 4 : study 5 : indicate — *adj* \'red\: informed by reading —**read·a·bil·i·ty** \‚rēdə'bilətē\ *n* —**read·able** *adj* —**read·ably** *adv* —**read·er** *n* —**read·er·ship** *n*

read·ing \'rēdiŋ\ *n* 1 : something read or for reading 2 : particular version, interpretation, or performance 3 : data indicated by an instrument

ready \'redē\ *adj* **readi·er; -est** 1 : prepared or available for use or action 2 : willing to do something ~ *vb* **read·ied; ready·ing** : make ready ~ *n* : state of being ready —**read·i·ly** *adv* —**read·i·ness** *n*

re·al \'rēl\ *adj* 1 : relating to fixed or immovable things (as land) 2 : genuine 3 : not imaginary ~ *adv* : very —**re·al·ness** *n* —**for real** 1 : in earnest 2 : genuine

real estate *n* : property in houses and land

re·al·ism \'rēə‚lizəm\ *n* 1 : disposition to deal with facts practically 2 : faithful portrayal of reality —**real·ist** \-list\ *adj or n* —**re·al·is·tic** \‚rēə'listik\ *adj* —**re·al·is·ti·cal·ly** \-ti-klē\ *adv*

re·al·i·ty \rē'alətē\ *n, pl* **-ties** 1 : quality or state of being real 2 : something real

re·al·ize \'rēə‚līz\ *vb* **-ized; -iz·ing** 1 : make actual 2 : obtain 3 : be aware of —**re·al·iz·able** *adj* —**re·al·i·za·tion** \‚rēələ'zāshən\ *n*

re·al·ly \'rēlē, 'ril-\ *adv* : in truth

realm \'relm\ *n* 1 : kingdom 2 : sphere

¹**ream** \'rēm\ *n* : quantity of paper that is 480, 500, or 516 sheets

²**ream** *vb* : enlarge, shape, or clean with a specially shaped tool (**reamer**)

reap \'rēp\ *vb* : cut or clear (as a crop) with a scythe or machine —**reap·er** *n*

¹**rear** \'rir\ *vb* 1 : raise upright 2 : breed or bring up 3 : rise on the hind legs

²**rear** *n* 1 : back 2 : position at the back of something ~ *adj* : being at the back —**rear·ward** \-wərd\ *adj or adv*

rear admiral *n* : commissioned officer in the navy or coast guard ranking next below a vice admiral

rea·son \'rēz²n\ *n* 1 : explanation or justification 2 : motive for action or belief 3 : power or process of thinking ~ *vb* 1 : use the faculty of reason 2 : try to persuade another —**rea·son·er** *n* —**rea·son·ing** \'rēz²niŋ\ *n*

rea·son·able \'rēz²nəbəl\ *adj* 1 : being within the bounds of reason 2 : inexpensive —**rea·son·able·ness** *n* —**rea·son·ably** \-blē\ *adv*

re·as·sure \‚rēə'shu̇r\ *vb* : restore one's confidence —**re·as·sur·ance** \-'shu̇rəns\ *n* —**re·as·sur·ing·ly** *adv*

re·bate \'rē‚bāt\ *n* : return of part of a payment —**rebate** *vb*

reb·el \'rebəl\ *n* : one that resists authority ~ \ri'bel\ *vb* **-belled; -bel·ling** 1 : resist authority 2 : feel or exhibit anger —**rebel** \'rebəl\ *adj*

re·bel·lion \ri'belyən\ *n* : resistance to authority and esp. to one's government

re·bel·lious \-yəs\ *adj* 1 : engaged in rebellion 2 : inclined to resist authority —**re·bel·lious·ly** *adv* —**re·bel·lious·ness** *n*

re·birth \'rē'bərth\ *n* 1 : new or second birth 2 : revival

re·bound \'rē'baund, ri-\ *vb* 1 : spring back on striking something 2 : recover from a reverse ~ \'rē‚-\ *n* 1 : action of rebounding 2 : reaction to a reverse

re·buff \ri'bəf\ *vb* : refuse or repulse rudely —**rebuff** *n*

re·buke \-'byük\ *vb* **-buked; -buk·ing** : reprimand sharply —**rebuke** *n*

re·bus \'rēbəs\ *n* : riddle representing syllables or words with pictures

re·but \ri'bət\ *vb* **-but·ted; -but·ting** : refute —**re·but·ter** *n*

re·but·tal \-ᵊl\ *n* : opposing argument

re·cal·ci·trant \ri'kalsətrənt\ *adj* **1** : stubbornly resisting authority **2** : resistant to handling or treatment —**re·cal·ci·trance** \-trəns\ *n*

re·call \ri'kól\ *vb* **1** : call back **2** : remember **3** : revoke ~ \ri'-, 'rē-\ *n* **1** : a summons to return **2** : remembrance **3** : act of revoking

re·cant \ri'kant\ *vb* : take back (something said) publicly

re·ca·pit·u·late \,rēkə'pichə,lāt\ *vb* **-lated; -lating** : summarize —**re·ca·pit·u·la·tion** \-,pichə'lāshən\ *n*

re·cede \ri'sēd\ *vb* **-ced·ed; -ced·ing 1** : move back or away **2** : slant backward

re·ceipt \-'sēt\ *n* **1** : act of receiving **2** : something (as payment) received — usu. in pl. **3** : writing acknowledging something received

re·ceive \ri'sēv\ *vb* **-ceived; -ceiv·ing 1** : take in or accept **2** : greet or entertain (visitors) **3** : pick up radio waves and convert into sounds or pictures — **re·ceiv·able** *adj*

re·ceiv·er \ri'sēvər\ *n* **1** : one that receives **2** : one having charge of property or money involved in a lawsuit **3** : apparatus for receiving radio waves —**re·ceiv·er·ship** *n*

re·cent \'rēsᵊnt\ *adj* **1** : having lately come into existence **2** : of the present time or time just past —**re·cent·ly** *adv* —**re·cent·ness** *n*

re·cep·ta·cle \ri'septikəl\ *n* : container

re·cep·tion \ri'sepshən\ *n* **1** : act of receiving **2** : social gathering at which guests are formally welcomed

re·cep·tion·ist \-shənist\ *n* : person employed to greet callers

re·cep·tive \ri'septiv\ *adj* : open and responsive to ideas, impressions, or suggestions —**re·cep·tive·ly** *adv* —**re·cep·tive·ness** *n* —**re·cep·tiv·i·ty** \,rē,sep'tivətē\ *n*

re·cess \'rē,ses, ri'ses\ *n* **1** : indentation in a line or surface **2** : suspension of a session for rest ~ *vb* **1** : make a recess in or put into a recess **2** : interrupt a session for a recess

re·ces·sion \ri'seshən\ *n* **1** : departing procession **2** : period of reduced economic activity

rec·i·pe \'resə,pē\ *n* : instructions for making something

re·cip·i·ent \ri'sipēənt\ *n* : one that receives

re·cip·ro·cal \ri'siprəkəl\ *adj* **1** : affecting each in the same way **2** : so related that one is equivalent to the other — **re·cip·ro·cal·ly** *adv* —**re·ci·proc·i·ty** \,resə'präsətē\ *n*

re·cip·ro·cate \-,kāt\ *vb* **-cat·ed; -cat·ing** : make a return for something done or given —**re·cip·ro·ca·tion** \-,siprə'kāshən\ *n*

re·cit·al \ri'sītᵊl\ *n* **1** : public reading or recitation **2** : music or dance concert or exhibition by pupils —**re·cit·al·ist** \-ᵊlist\ *n*

rec·i·ta·tion \,resə'tāshən\ *n* : a reciting or recital

re·cite \ri'sīt\ *vb* **-cit·ed; -cit·ing 1** : repeat verbatim **2** : recount —**re·cit·er** *n*

reck·less \'rekləs\ *adj* : lacking caution —**reck·less·ly** *adv* —**reck·less·ness** *n*

reck·on \'rekən\ *vb* **1** : count or calculate **2** : consider

reck·on·ing *n* **1** : act or instance of reckoning **2** : settling of accounts

re·claim \ri'klām\ *vb* **1** : change to a desirable condition **2** : obtain from a waste product or by-product **3** : demand or obtain the return of —**re·claim·able** *adj* —**rec·la·ma·tion** \,reklə'māshən\ *n*

re·cline \ri'klīn\ *vb* **-clined; -clin·ing** : lean backward or lie down

re·cluse \'rek,lüs, ri'klüs\ *n* : one who leads a secluded or solitary life

rec·og·ni·tion \,rekig'nishən\ *n* : act of recognizing or state of being recognized

re·cog·ni·zance \ri'känəzəns, -'käg-\ *n* : promise recorded before a court

rec·og·nize \'rekig,nīz\ *vb* **-nized; -niz·ing 1** : identify as previously known **2** : take notice of **3** : acknowledge esp. with appreciation —**rec·og·niz·able** \'rekig,nīzəbəl\ *adj* —**rec·og·niz·ably** \-blē\ *adv*

re·coil \ri'kóil\ *vb* : draw or spring back ~ \'rē,-, ri'-\ *n* : action of recoiling

re·col·lect \,rekə'lekt\ *vb* : remember

rec·ol·lec·tion \,rekə'lekshən\ *n* **1** : act or power of recollecting **2** : something recollected

rec·om·mend \,rekə'mend\ *vb* **1**

: present as deserving of acceptance or trial **2** : advise —**rec·om·mend·able** \-'mendəbəl\ *adj*

rec·om·men·da·tion \,rekəmən'dāshən\ *n* **1** : act of recommending **2** : something recommended or that recommends

rec·om·pense \'rekəm,pens\ *n* : compensation —**recompense** *vb*

rec·on·cile \'rekən,sīl\ *vb* -**ciled; -cil·ing 1** : cause to be friendly again **2** : adjust or settle **3** : bring to acceptance —**rec·on·cil·able** *adj* —**rec·on·cile·ment** *n* —**rec·on·cil·er** *n* —**rec·on·cil·i·a·tion** \,rekən,silē'āshən\ *n*

rec·on·dite \'rekən,dīt, ri'kän-\ *adj* **1** : hard to understand **2** : little known

re·con·di·tion \,rēkən,dishən\ *vb* : restore to good condition

re·con·nais·sance \ri'känəzəns, -səns\ *n* : exploratory survey of enemy territory

re·con·noi·ter, re·con·noi·tre \,rēkə'nóitər, ,rekə-\ *vb* -**tered** *or* -**tred; -ter·ing** *or* -**tring** : make a reconnaissance of

re·cord \ri'kórd\ *vb* **1** : set down in writing **2** : register permanently **3** : indicate **4** : preserve (as sound or images) for later reproduction ~ \'rekərd\ *n* **1** : something recorded **2** : best performance

re·cord·er \ri'kórdər\ *n* **1** : person or device that records **2** : wind instrument with finger holes

¹**re·count** \ri'kaúnt\ *vb* : relate in detail

²**re·count** \'rē'-\ *vb* : count again —**re·count** \'rē,-, ,rē'-\ *n*

re·coup \ri'küp\ *vb* : make up for (an expense or loss)

re·course \'rē,kórs, ri'-\ *n* : source of aid or a turning to such a source

re·cov·er \ri'kəvər\ *vb* **1** : regain position, poise, or health **2** : recoup —**re·cov·er·able** *adj* —**re·cov·ery** \-'kə-vərē\ *n*

rec·re·a·tion \,rekrē'āshən\ *n* : a refreshing of strength or spirits as a change from work or study —**rec·re·a·tion·al** \-shənəl\ *adj*

re·crim·i·na·tion \ri,krimə'nāshən\ *n* : retaliatory accusation —**re·crim·i·nate** *vb*

re·cruit \ri'krüt\ *n* : newly enlisted member ~ *vb* : enlist the membership or services of —**re·cruit·er** *n* —**re·cruit·ment** *n*

rect·an·gle \'rek,taŋgəl\ *n* : 4-sided fig-

ure with 4 right angles —**rect·an·gu·lar** \rek'taŋgələr\ *adj*

rec·ti·fy \'rektə,fī\ *vb* -**fied; -fy·ing** : make or set right —**rec·ti·fi·ca·tion** \,rektəfə'kāshən\ *n*

rec·ti·tude \'rektə,tüd, -,tyüd\ *n* : moral integrity

rec·tor \'rektər\ *n* : pastor

rec·to·ry \'rektərē\ *n, pl* -**ries** : rector's residence

rec·tum \'rektəm\ *n, pl* -**tums** *or* -**ta** \-tə\ : last part of the intestine joining the colon and anus —**rec·tal** \-t⁹l\ *adj*

re·cum·bent \ri'kəmbənt\ *adj* : lying down

re·cu·per·ate \ri'küpə,rāt, -'kyü-\ *vb* -**at·ed; -at·ing** : recover (as from illness) —**re·cu·per·a·tion** \-,küpə-'rāshən, -,kyü-\ *n* —**re·cu·per·a·tive** \-'küpərātiv, -'kyü-\ *adj*

re·cur \ri'kər\ *vb* -**rr- 1** : return in thought or talk **2** : occur again —**re·cur·rence** \-'kərəns\ *n* —**re·cur·rent** \-ənt\ *adj*

re·cy·cle \rē'sīkəl\ *vb* : process (as glass or cans) in order to regain a material for human use —**re·cy·cla·ble** \-kələbəl\ *adj*

red \'red\ *n* **1** : color of blood or of the ruby **2** *cap* : communist —**red** *adj* —**red·dish** *adj* —**red·ness** *n*

red·den \'red⁹n\ *vb* : make or become red or reddish

re·deem \ri'dēm\ *vb* **1** : regain, free, or rescue by paying a price **2** : atone for **3** : free from sin **4** : convert into something of value —**re·deem·able** *adj* —**re·deem·er** *n*

re·demp·tion \-'dempshən\ *n* : act of redeeming —**re·demp·tive** \-tiv\ *adj* —**re·demp·to·ry** \-tərē\ *adj*

red·head \-,hed\ *n* : one having red hair —**red·head·ed** \-'hedəd\ *adj*

red·o·lent \'red⁹lənt\ *adj* **1** : having a fragrance **2** : suggestive —**red·o·lence** \-əns\ *n* —**red·o·lent·ly** *adv*

re·dou·ble \rē'dəbəl\ *vb* **1** : make twice as great in size or amount **2** : intensify

re·doubt \ri'daút\ *n* : small fortification

re·doubt·able \-əbəl\ *adj* : arousing dread

re·dound \ri'daúnd\ *vb* : have an effect

re·dress \ri'dres\ *vb* : set right ~ *n* **1** : relief or remedy **2** : compensation

red tape *n* : complex obstructive official routine

re·duce \ri'düs, -'dyüs\ *vb* -**duced; -duc·ing 1** : lessen **2** : put in a lower rank

3 : lose weight —**re·duc·er** *n* —**re·duc·i·ble** \-'düsəbəl, -'dyü-\ *adj*

re·duc·tion \ri'dəkshən\ *n* **1** : act of reducing **2** : amount lost in reducing **3** : something made by reducing

re·dun·dant \ri'dəndənt\ *adj* : using more words than necessary —**re·dun·dan·cy** \-dənsē\ *n* —**re·dun·dant·ly** *adv*

red·wood *n* : tall coniferous timber tree

reed \'rēd\ *n* **1** : tall slender grass of wet areas **2** : elastic strip that vibrates to produce tones in certain wind instruments —**reedy** *adj*

reef \'rēf\ *n* : ridge of rocks or sand at or near the surface of the water

reek \'rēk\ *n* : strong or disagreeable fume or odor ~ *vb* : give off a reek

¹**reel** \'rēl\ *n* : revolvable device on which something flexible is wound or a quantity of something wound on it ~ *vb* **1** : wind on a reel **2** : pull in by reeling —**reel·able** *adj* —**reel·er** *n*

²**reel** *vb* **1** : whirl or waver as from a blow **2** : walk or move unsteadily ~ *n* : reeling motion

³**reel** *n* : lively dance

re·fer \ri'fər\ *vb* **-rr- 1** : direct or send to some person or place **2** : submit for consideration or action **3** : have connection **4** : mention or allude to something —**re·fer·able** \'refərəbəl, ri-'fərə-\ *adj* —**re·fer·ral** \ri'fərəl\ *n*

ref·er·ee \,refə'rē\ *n* **1** : one to whom an issue is referred for settlement **2** : sports official ~ *vb* **-eed; -ee·ing** : act as referee

ref·er·ence \'refərəns\ *n* **1** : act of referring **2** : a bearing on a matter **3** : consultation for information **4** : person who can speak for one's character or ability or a recommendation given by such a person

ref·er·en·dum \,refə'rendəm\ *n, pl* **-da** \-də\ *or* **-dums** : a submitting of legislative measures for voters' approval or rejection

re·fill \,rē'fil\ *vb* : fill again —**re·fill** \'rē-,-\ *n* —**re·fill·able** *adj*

re·fine \ri'fīn\ *vb* **-fined; -fin·ing 1** : free from impurities or waste matter **2** : improve or perfect **3** : free or become free of what is coarse or uncouth —**re·fine·ment** \-mənt\ *n* —**re·fin·er** *n*

re·fin·ery \ri'fīnərē\ *n, pl* **-er·ies** : place for refining (as oil or sugar)

re·flect \ri'flekt\ *vb* **1** : bend or cast back

(as light or heat) **2** : bring as a result **3** : cast reproach or blame **4** : ponder —**re·flec·tion** \-'flekshən\ *n* —**re·flec·tive** \-tiv\ *adj* —**re·flec·tor** \ri-'flektər\ *n*

re·flex \'rē,fleks\ *n* : automatic response to a stimulus ~ *adj* **1** : bent back **2** : relating to a reflex —**re·flex·ly** *adv*

re·flex·ive \ri'fleksiv\ *adj* : of or relating to an action directed back upon the doer or the grammatical subject —**re·flexive** *n* —**re·flex·ive·ly** *adv* —**re·flex·ive·ness** *n*

re·form \ri'fórm\ *vb* : make or become better esp. by correcting bad habits —**reform** *n* —**re·form·able** *adj* —**re·for·ma·tive** \-'fórmətiv\ *adj* —**re·form·er** *n*

re·for·ma·to·ry \ri'fórmə,tōrē\ *n, pl* **-ries** : penal institution for reforming young offenders

re·fract \ri'frakt\ *vb* : subject to refraction

re·frac·tion \-'frakshən\ *n* : the bending of a ray (as of light) when it passes from one medium into another —**re·frac·tive** \-tiv\ *adj*

re·frac·to·ry \ri'fraktərē\ *adj* : obstinate or unmanageable

re·frain \ri'frān\ *vb* : hold oneself back ~ *n* : verse recurring regularly in a song —**re·frain·ment** *n*

re·fresh \ri'fresh\ *vb* **1** : make or become fresh or fresher **2** : supply or take refreshment —**re·fresh·er** *n* —**re·fresh·ing·ly** *adv*

re·fresh·ment \-mənt\ *n* **1** : act of refreshing **2** *pl* : light meal

re·frig·er·ate \ri'frijə,rāt\ *vb* **-at·ed; -at·ing** : chill or freeze (food) for preservation —**re·frig·er·ant** \-ərənt\ *adj or n* —**re·frig·er·a·tion** \-,frijə'rāshən\ *n* —**re·frig·er·a·tor** \-'frijə,rātər\ *n*

ref·uge \'ref,yüj\ *n* **1** : protection from danger **2** : place that provides protection

ref·u·gee \,refyü'jē\ *n* : person who flees for safety

re·fund \ri'fənd, 'rē,fənd\ *vb* : give or put back (money) ~ \'rē-,-\ *n* **1** : act of refunding **2** : sum refunded —**re·fund·able** *adj*

re·fur·bish \ri'fərbish\ *vb* : renovate

¹**re·fuse** \ri'fyüz\ *vb* **-fused; -fus·ing** : decline to accept, do, or give — **re·fus·al** \-'fyüzəl\ *n*

²ref·use \'ref,yüs, -,yüz\ n : worthless matter

re·fute \ri'fyüt\ vb **-fut·ed; -fut·ing** : prove to be false —**ref·u·ta·tion** \,refyü'tāshən\ n —**re·fut·er** \ri'fyütər\ n

re·gal \'rēgəl\ adj 1 : befitting a king 2 : stately —**re·gal·ly** adv

re·gale \ri'gāl\ vb **-galed; -gal·ing** 1 : entertain richly or agreeably 2 : delight

re·ga·lia \ri'gālyə\ n pl 1 : symbols of royalty 2 : insignia of an office or order 3 : finery

re·gard \ri'gärd\ n 1 : consideration 2 : feeling of approval and liking 3 pl : friendly greetings 4 : relation ~ vb 1 : pay attention to 2 : show respect for 3 : have an opinion of 4 : look at 5 : relate to —**re·gard·ful** adj —**re·gard·less** adj

re·gard·ing prep : concerning

regardless of \ri'gärdləs-\ prep : in spite of

re·gen·er·ate \ri'jenərət\ adj 1 : formed or created again 2 : spiritually reborn ~ \-'jenə,rāt\ vb 1 : reform completely 2 : replace (a lost body part) by new tissue growth 3 : give new life to —**re·gen·er·a·tion** \-,jenə'rāshən\ n —**re·gen·er·a·tive** \-'jenə,rātiv\ adj —**re·gen·er·a·tor** \-,rātər\ n

re·gent \'rējənt\ n 1 : person who rules during the childhood, absence, or incapacity of the sovereign 2 : member of a governing board —**re·gen·cy** \-jənsē\ n

re·gime \rā'zhēm, ri-\ n : government in power

reg·i·men \'rejəmən\ n : systematic course of treatment or training

reg·i·ment \'rejəmənt\ n : military unit ~ \-,ment\ vb 1 : organize rigidly for control 2 : make orderly —**reg·i·men·tal** \,rejə'ment³l\ adj —**reg·i·men·ta·tion** \-mən'tāshən\ n

re·gion \'rējən\ n : indefinitely defined area —**re·gion·al** \'rejənəl\ adj —**re·gion·al·ly** adv

reg·is·ter \'rejəstər\ n 1 : record of items or details or a book for keeping such a record 2 : device to regulate ventilation 3 : counting or recording device 4 : range of a voice or instrument ~ vb 1 : enter in a register 2 : record automatically 3 : get special care for mail by paying more postage

reg·is·trar \-,strär\ n : official keeper of records

reg·is·tra·tion \,rejə'strāshən\ n 1 : act of registering 2 : entry in a register

reg·is·try \'rejəstrē\ n, pl **-tries** 1 : enrollment 2 : place of registration 3 : official record book

re·gress \ri'gres\ vb : go or cause to go back or to a lower level —**re·gres·sion** \-'greshən\ n —**re·gres·sive** adj

re·gret \ri'gret\ vb **-tt-** 1 : mourn the loss or death of 2 : be very sorry for ~ n 1 : sorrow or the expression of sorrow 2 pl : message declining an invitation —**re·gret·ful** \-fəl\ adj —**re·gret·ful·ly** adv —**re·gret·ta·ble** \-əbəl\ adj —**re·gret·ta·bly** \-blē\ adv —**re·gret·ter** n

reg·u·lar \'regyələr\ adj 1 : conforming to what is usual, normal, or average 2 : steady, uniform, or unvarying —**regular** n —**reg·u·lar·i·ty** \,regyə'larətē\ n —**reg·u·lar·ize** \'regyələ-,rīz\ vb —**reg·u·lar·ly** adv

reg·u·late \'regyə,lāt\ vb **-lat·ed; -lat·ing** 1 : govern according to rule 2 : adjust to a standard —**reg·u·la·tive** \-,lātiv\ adj —**reg·u·la·tor** \-,lātər\ n —**reg·u·la·to·ry** \-lə,tōrē\ adj

reg·u·la·tion \,regyə'lāshən\ n 1 : act of regulating 2 : rule dealing with details of procedure

re·gur·gi·tate \rē'gərjə,tāt\ vb **-tat·ed; -tat·ing** : vomit —**re·gur·gi·ta·tion** \-,gərjə'tāshən\ n

re·ha·bil·i·tate \,rēhə'bilə,tāt\ vb **-tat·ed; -tat·ing** 1 : reinstate 2 : make good or usable again —**re·ha·bil·i·ta·tion** \-,bilə'tāshən\ n

re·hears·al \ri'hərsəl\ n : practice session or performance

re·hearse \-'hərs\ vb **-hearsed; -hears·ing** 1 : repeat or recount 2 : engage in a rehearsal of —**re·hears·er** n

reign \'rān\ n : sovereign's authority or rule ~ vb : rule as a sovereign

re·im·burse \,rēəm'bərs\ vb **-bursed; -burs·ing** : repay —**re·im·burs·able** adj —**re·im·burse·ment** n

rein \'rān\ n 1 : strap fastened to a bit to control an animal 2 : restraining influence ~ vb : direct by reins

re·in·car·na·tion \,rē,in,kär'nāshən\ n : rebirth of the soul —**re·in·car·nate** \,rēin'kär,nāt\ vb

rein·deer \'rān,dir\ n : caribou

re·in·force \,rēən'fōrs\ vb : strengthen

or support —**re·in·force·ment** n — **re·in·forc·er** n

re·in·state \,rēən'stāt\ vb : restore to a former position —**re·in·state·ment** n

re·it·er·ate \rē'itə,rāt\ vb : say again — **re·it·er·a·tion** \-,itə'rāshən\ n

re·ject \ri'jekt\ vb 1 : refuse to grant or consider 2 : refuse to admit, believe, or receive 3 : throw out as useless or unsatisfactory ~ \'rē,-\ n : rejected person or thing —**re·jec·tion** \-'jekshən\ n

re·joice \ri'jois\ vb -joiced; -joic·ing : feel joy —**re·joic·er** n

re·join vb 1 \'rē'join\ : join again 2 \ri'-\ : say in answer

re·join·der \ri'joindər\ n : answer

re·ju·ve·nate \ri'jüvə,nāt\ vb -nat·ed; -nat·ing : make young again —**re·ju·ve·na·tion** \-,jüvə'nāshən\ n

re·lapse \ri'laps, 'rē,laps\ n : recurrence of illness after a period of improvement ~ \ri'-\ vb : suffer a relapse

re·late \ri'lāt\ vb -lat·ed; -lat·ing 1 : give a report of 2 : show a connection between 3 : have a relationship —**re·lat·able** adj —**re·lat·er, re·la·tor** n

re·la·tion \-'lāshən\ n 1 : account 2 : connection 3 : relationship 4 : reference 5 pl : dealings

re·la·tion·ship \-,ship\ n : the state of being related or interrelated

rel·a·tive \'relətiv\ n : person connected with another by blood or marriage ~ adj : considered in comparison with something else —**rel·a·tive·ly** adv —**rel·a·tive·ness** n

re·lax \ri'laks\ vb 1 : make or become less tense or rigid 2 : make less severe 3 : seek rest or recreation —**re·lax·er** n

re·lax·a·tion \,rē,lak'sāshən\ n 1 : lessening of tension 2 : recreation

re·lay \'rē,lā\ n : fresh supply (as of horses or people) arranged to relieve others ~ \'rē,-, ri'-\ vb -layed; -lay·ing : pass along in stages

re·lease \ri'lēs\ vb -leased; -leas·ing 1 : free from confinement or oppression 2 : relinquish 3 : permit publication, performance, exhibition, or sale ~ n 1 : relief from trouble 2 : discharge from an obligation 3 : act of releasing or what is released

rel·e·gate \'relə,gāt\ vb -gat·ed; -gat·ing 1 : remove to some less prominent position 2 : assign to a particular class

or sphere —**rel·e·ga·tion** \,relə-'gāshən\ n

re·lent \ri'lent\ vb : become less severe

re·lent·less \-ləs\ adj : mercilessly severe or persistent —**re·lent·less·ly** adv —**re·lent·less·ness** n

rel·e·vance \'reləvəns\ n : relation to the matter at hand —**rel·e·vant** \-vənt\ adj —**rel·e·vant·ly** adv

re·li·able \ri'līəbəl\ adj : fit to be trusted —**re·li·abil·i·ty** \-,līə'bilətē\ n —**re·li·able·ness** n —**re·li·ably** \-'līəblē\ adv

re·li·ance \ri'līəns\ n : act or result of relying

re·li·ant \ri'līənt\ adj : dependent

rel·ic \'relik\ n 1 : object venerated because of its association with a saint or martyr 2 : remaining trace

re·lief \ri'lēf\ n 1 : lightening of something oppressive 2 : welfare

re·lieve \ri'lēv\ vb -lieved; -liev·ing 1 : free from a burden or distress 2 : release from a post or duty 3 : break the monotony of —**re·liev·er** n

re·li·gion \ri'lijən\ n 1 : service and worship of God 2 : set or system of religious beliefs —**re·li·gion·ist** n

re·li·gious \ri'lijəs\ adj 1 : relating or devoted to an ultimate reality or deity 2 : relating to religious beliefs or observances 3 : faithful, fervent, or zealous —**re·li·gious·ly** adv

re·lin·quish \-'liŋkwish, -'lin-\ vb 1 : renounce 2 : let go of —**re·lin·quish·ment** n

rel·ish \'relish\ n 1 : keen enjoyment 2 : highly seasoned sauce (as of pickles) ~ vb : enjoy —**rel·ish·able** adj

re·live \rē'liv\ vb : live over again (as in the imagination)

re·lo·cate \,rē'lō,kāt, ,rēlō'kāt\ vb : move to a new location —**re·lo·ca·tion** \,rēlō'kāshən\ n

re·luc·tant \ri'ləktənt\ adj : feeling or showing doubt or unwillingness —**re·luc·tance** \ri'ləktəns\ n —**re·luc·tant·ly** adv

re·ly \ri'lī\ vb -lied; -ly·ing : place faith or confidence—often with on

re·main \ri'mān\ vb 1 : be left after others have been removed 2 : be something yet to be done 3 : stay behind 4 : continue unchanged

re·main·der \-'māndər\ n : that which is left over

re·mains \-'mānz\ n pl 1 : remaining part or trace 2 : dead body

re·mark \ri'märk\ *vb* : express as an observation ~ *n* : passing comment

re·mark·able \-'märkəbəl\ *adj* : extraordinary —**re·mark·able·ness** *n* —**re·mark·ably** \-blē\ *adv*

re·me·di·al \ri'mēdēəl\ *adj* : intended to remedy or improve

rem·e·dy \'remədē\ *n, pl* **-dies** 1 : medicine that cures 2 : something that corrects an evil or compensates for a loss ~ *vb* **-died; -dy·ing** : provide or serve as a remedy for

re·mem·ber \ri'membər\ *vb* 1 : think of again 2 : keep from forgetting 3 : convey greetings from

re·mem·brance \-brəns\ *n* 1 : act of remembering 2 : something that serves to bring to mind

re·mind \ri'mīnd\ *vb* : cause to remember —**re·mind·er** *n*

rem·i·nisce \remə'nis\ *vb* **-nisced; -nisc·ing** : indulge in reminiscence

rem·i·nis·cence \-'nis³ns\ *n* 1 : recalling of a past experience 2 : account of a memorable experience

rem·i·nis·cent \-³nt\ *adj* 1 : relating to reminiscence 2 : serving to remind —**rem·i·nis·cent·ly** *adv*

re·miss \ri'mis\ *adj* : negligent or careless in performance of duty —**re·miss·ly** *adv* —**re·miss·ness** *n*

re·mis·sion \ri'mishən\ *n* 1 : act of forgiving 2 : a period of relief from or easing of symptoms of a disease

re·mit \ri'mit\ *vb* **-tt-** 1 : pardon 2 : send money in payment

re·mit·tance \ri'mit³ns\ *n* : sum of money remitted

rem·nant \'remnənt\ *n* : small part or trace remaining

re·mod·el \rē'mäd³l\ *vb* : alter the structure of

re·mon·strance \ri'mänstrəns\ *n* : act or instance of remonstrating

re·mon·strate \ri'män,strāt\ *vb* **-strat·ed; -strat·ing** : speak in protest, reproof, or opposition —**re·mon·stra·tion** \ri,män'strāshən, remən-\

re·morse \ri'mórs\ *n* : distress arising from a sense of guilt —**re·morse·ful** *adj* —**re·morse·less** *adj*

re·mote \ri'mōt\ *adj* **-mot·er; -est** 1 : far off in place or time 2 : hard to reach or find 3 : acting, acted on, or controlled indirectly or from afar 4 : slight 5 : distant in manner —**re·mote·ly** *adv* —**re·mote·ness** *n*

re·move \ri'müv\ *vb* **-moved; -mov·ing**

1 : move by lifting or taking off or away 2 : get rid of —**re·mov·able** *adj* —**re·mov·al** \-vəl\ *n* —**re·mov·er** *n*

re·mu·ner·ate \ri'myünə,rāt\ *vb* **-at·ed; -at·ing** : pay —**re·mu·ner·a·tion** *n* —**re·mu·ner·a·tor** \-,rātər\ *n*

re·mu·ner·a·tive \ri'myünərativ, -,rāt-\ *adj* : gainful

re·nais·sance \renə'säns, -'zäns\ *n* : rebirth or revival

re·nal \'rēn³l\ *adj* : relating to the kidneys

rend \'rend\ *vb* **rent** \'rent\; **rend·ing** : tear apart forcibly

ren·der \'rendər\ *vb* 1 : extract by heating 2 : hand over or give up 3 : do (a service) for another 4 : cause to be or become

ren·dez·vous \'rändi,vü, -dā-\ *n, pl* **rendez·vous** \-,vüz\ 1 : place appointed for a meeting 2 : meeting at an appointed place ~ *vb* **-voused; -vous·ing** : meet at a rendezvous

ren·di·tion \ren'dishən\ *n* : version

ren·e·gade \'reni,gād\ *n* : deserter of one faith or cause for another

re·nege \ri'nig, -'neg, -'nēg, -'nāg\ *vb* **-neged; -neg·ing** : go back on a promise —**re·neg·er** *n*

re·new \ri'nü, -'nyü\ *vb* 1 : make or become new, fresh, or strong again 2 : begin again 3 : grant or obtain an extension of —**re·new·able** *adj* —**re·new·al** *n* —**re·new·er** *n*

re·nounce \ri'naúns\ *vb* **-nounced; -nounc·ing** : give up, refuse, or resign —**re·nounce·ment** *n*

ren·o·vate \'renə,vāt\ *vb* **-vat·ed; -vat·ing** : make like new again —**ren·o·va·tion** \renə'vāshən\ *n* —**ren·o·va·tor** \'renə,vātər\ *n*

re·nown \ri'naún\ *n* : state of being widely known and honored —**re·nowned** \-'naúnd\ *adj*

¹**rent** \'rent\ *n* : money paid or due periodically for the use of another's property ~ *vb* : hold or give possession and use of for rent —**rent·al** *n* or *adj* —**rent·er** *n*

²**rent** *n* : a tear in cloth

re·nun·ci·a·tion \ri,nənsē'āshən\ *n* : act of renouncing

¹**re·pair** \ri'par\ *vb* : go

²**repair** *vb* : restore to good condition ~ *n* 1 : act or instance of repairing 2 : condition —**re·pair·er** *n* —**re·pair·man** \-,man\ *n*

rep·a·ra·tion \,repə'rāshən\ n : money paid for redress—usu. pl.

rep·ar·tee \,repər'tē\ n : clever replies

re·past \ri'past, 'rē,past\ n : meal

re·pa·tri·ate \rē'pātrē,āt\ vb -at·ed; -at·ing : send back to one's own country —re·pa·tri·ate \-trēət, -trē,āt\ n —re·pa·tri·a·tion \-,pātrē'āshən\ n

re·pay \rē'pā\ vb -paid; -pay·ing : pay back —re·pay·able adj —re·pay·ment n

re·peal \ri'pēl\ vb : annul by legislative action —repeal n —re·peal·er n

re·peat \ri'pēt\ vb : say or do again ~ n 1 : act of repeating 2 : something repeated —re·peat·able adj —re·peat·ed·ly adv —re·peat·er n

re·pel \ri'pel\ vb -pelled; -pel·ling 1 : drive away 2 : disgust —re·pel·lent \-'pelənt\ adj or n

re·pent \ri'pent\ vb 1 : turn from sin 2 : regret —re·pen·tance \-ri'pent°ns\ n —re·pen·tant \-°nt\ adj

re·per·cus·sion \,rēpər'kəshən, ,rep-\ n : effect of something done or said

rep·er·toire \'repər,twär\ n : pieces a company or performer can present

rep·er·to·ry \'repər,tōrē\ n, pl -ries 1 : repertoire 2 : theater with a resident company doing several plays

rep·e·ti·tion \,repə'tishən\ n : act or instance of repeating

rep·e·ti·tious \-'tishəs\ adj : tediously repeating —rep·e·ti·tious·ly adv —rep·e·ti·tious·ness n

re·pet·i·tive \ri'petətiv\ adj : repetitious —re·pet·i·tive·ly adv —re·pet·i·tive·ness n

re·pine \ri'pīn\ vb re·pined; re·pin·ing : feel or express discontent

re·place \ri'plās\ vb 1 : restore to a former position 2 : take the place of 3 : put something new in the place of —re·place·able adj —re·place·ment n —re·plac·er n

re·plen·ish \ri'plenish\ vb : stock or supply anew —re·plen·ish·ment n

re·plete \ri'plēt\ adj : full —re·plete·ness n —re·ple·tion \-'plēshən\ n

rep·li·ca \'replikə\ n : exact copy

rep·li·cate \'replə,kāt\ vb -cat·ed; -cat·ing : duplicate or repeat —rep·li·cate \-likət\ n —rep·li·ca·tion \-lə'kāshən\ n

re·ply \ri'plī\ vb -plied; -ply·ing : say or do in answer ~ n, pl -plies : answer

re·port \ri'pōrt\ n 1 : rumor 2 : statement of information (as events or causes) 3 : explosive noise ~ vb 1 : give an account of 2 : present an account of (an event) as news 3 : present oneself 4 : make known to authorities —re·port·age \ri'pōrtij, ,repər'täzh, ,rep,ȯr'-\ n —re·port·ed·ly adv —re·port·er n —re·por·to·ri·al \,repər'tōrēəl\ adj

re·pose \ri'pōz\ vb -posed; -pos·ing : lay or lie at rest ~ n 1 : state of resting 2 : calm or peace —re·pose·ful adj

re·pos·i·to·ry \ri'päzə,tōrē\ n, pl -ries : place where something is stored

re·pos·sess \,rēpə'zes\ vb : regain possession and legal ownership of —re·pos·ses·sion \-'zeshən\ n

rep·re·hend \,repri'hend\ vb : censure —rep·re·hen·sion \-'henchən\ n

rep·re·hen·si·ble \-'hensəbəl\ adj : deserving condemnation —rep·re·hen·si·bly adv

rep·re·sent \,repri'zent\ vb 1 : serve as a sign or symbol of 2 : act or speak for 3 : describe as having a specified quality or character —rep·re·sen·ta·tion \,repri,zen'tāshən\ n

rep·re·sen·ta·tive \,repri'zentətiv\ adj 1 : standing or acting for another 2 : carried on by elected representatives ~ n 1 : typical example 2 : one that represents another 3 : member of usu. the lower house of a legislature —rep·re·sen·ta·tive·ly adv —rep·re·sen·ta·tive·ness n

re·press \ri'pres\ vb : restrain or suppress —re·pres·sion \-'preshən\ n —re·pres·sive \-'presiv\ adj

re·prieve \ri'prēv\ n 1 : a delay in punishment 2 : temporary respite —re·prieve vb

rep·ri·mand \'reprə,mand\ n : formal or severe criticism —reprimand vb

re·pris·al \ri'prīzəl\ n : act in retaliation

re·prise \ri'prēz\ n : musical repetition

re·proach \ri'prōch\ n 1 : disgrace 2 : rebuke ~ vb : express disapproval to —re·proach·ful adj —re·proach·ful·ly adv —re·proach·ful·ness n

rep·ro·bate \'reprə,bāt\ n : scoundrel —reprobate adj

rep·ro·ba·tion \,reprə'bāshən\ n : strong disapproval

re·pro·duce \,rēprə'düs, -'dyüs\ vb 1 : produce again or anew 2 : produce offspring —re·pro·duc·ible \-'düsəbəl, -'dyü-\ adj —re·pro·duc-

tion \-'dəkshən\ *n* —**re•pro•duc•tive** \-'dəktiv\ *adj*

re•proof \ri'prüf\ *n* : blame or censure for a fault

re•prove \ri'prüv\ *vb* **-proved; -prov•ing** : express disapproval to or of

rep•tile \'rept³l, -,tīl\ *n* : air-breathing scaly vertebrate —**rep•til•ian** \rep-'tileⁱən\ *adj or n*

re•pub•lic \ri'pəblik\ *n* : country with representative government

re•pub•li•can \-likən\ *adj* 1 : relating to or resembling a republic 2 : supporting a republic —**republican** *n* —**re•pub•li•can•ism** *n*

re•pu•di•ate \ri'pyüdē,āt\ *vb* **-at•ed; -at•ing** : refuse to have anything to do with —**re•pu•di•a•tion** \-,pyüdē-'āshən\ *n*

re•pug•nant \ri'pəgnənt\ *adj* : contrary to one's tastes or principles —**re•pug•nance** \-nəns\ *n* —**re•pug•nant•ly** *adv*

re•pulse \ri'pəls\ *vb* **-pulsed; -puls•ing** 1 : drive or beat back 2 : rebuff 3 : be repugnant to —**repulse** *n* —**re•pul•sion** \-'pəlshən\ *n*

re•pul•sive \-siv\ *adj* : arousing aversion or disgust —**re•pul•sive•ly** *adv* —**re•pul•sive•ness** *n*

rep•u•ta•ble \'repyətəbəl\ *adj* : having a good reputation —**rep•u•ta•bly** \-blē\ *adv*

rep•u•ta•tion \,repyə'tāshən\ *n* : one's character or public esteem

re•pute \ri'pyüt\ *vb* **-put•ed; -put•ing** : think of as being ~ *n* : reputation —**re•put•ed** *adj* —**re•put•ed•ly** *adv*

re•quest \ri'kwest\ *n* : act or instance of asking for something or a thing asked for —*vb* 1 : make a request of 2 : ask for —**re•quest•er** *n*

re•qui•em \'rekwēəm, 'rāk-\ *n* : Mass for a dead person or a musical setting for this

re•quire \ri'kwīr\ *vb* **-quired; -quir•ing** 1 : insist on 2 : call for as essential —**re•quire•ment** *n*

req•ui•site \'rekwəzət\ *adj* : necessary —**requisite** *n*

req•ui•si•tion \,rekwə'zishən\ *n* : formal application or demand —**requisition** *vb*

re•quite \ri'kwīt\ *vb* **-quit•ed; -quit•ing** : make return for or to —**re•quit•al** \-'kwīt³l\ *n*

re•scind \ri'sind\ *vb* : repeal or cancel —**re•scis•sion** \-'sizhən\ *n*

res•cue \'reskyü\ *vb* **-cued; -cu•ing** : set

free from danger or confinement —**rescue** *n* —**res•cu•er** *n*

re•search \ri'sərch, 'rē,sərch\ *n* : careful or diligent search esp. for new knowledge —**research** *vb* —**re•search•er** *n*

re•sem•ble \ri'zembəl\ *vb* **-sem•bled; -sem•bling** : be like or similar to —**re•sem•blance** \-'zembləns\ *n*

re•sent \ri'zent\ *vb* : feel or show annoyance at —**re•sent•ful** *adj* —**re•sent•ful•ly** *adv* —**re•sent•ment** *n*

res•er•va•tion \,rezər'vāshən\ *n* 1 : act of reserving or something reserved 2 : limiting condition

re•serve \ri'zərv\ *vb* **-served; -serv•ing** 1 : store for future use 2 : set aside for special use ~ *n* 1 : something reserved 2 : restraint in words or bearing 3 : military forces withheld from action or not part of the regular services —**re•served** *adj*

res•er•voir \'rezər,vwär, -,vwȯr, -,vȯr, -,vȯi\ *n* : place where something (as water) is kept in store

re•side \ri'zīd\ *vb* **-sid•ed; -sid•ing** 1 : make one's home 2 : be present

res•i•dence \'rezədəns\ *n* 1 : act or fact of residing in a place 2 : place where one lives —**res•i•dent** \-ənt\ *adj or n* —**res•i•den•tial** \,rezə'denchəl\ *adj*

res•i•due \'rezə,dü, -,dyü\ *n* : part remaining —**re•sid•u•al** \ri'zijəwəl\ *adj*

re•sign \ri'zīn\ *vb* 1 : give up deliberately 2 : give (oneself) over without resistance —**res•ig•na•tion** \,rezig-'nāshən\ *n* —**re•sign•ed•ly** \-'zīnədlē\ *adv*

re•sil•ience \ri'zilyəns\ *n* : ability to recover or adjust easily

re•sil•ien•cy \-yənsē\ *n* : resilience

re•sil•ient \-yənt\ *adj* : elastic

res•in \'rez³n\ *n* : substance from the gum or sap of trees —**res•in•ous** *adj*

re•sist \ri'zist\ *vb* 1 : withstand the force or effect of 2 : fight against —**re•sist•ible** \-'zistəbəl\ *adj* —**re•sist•less** *adj*

re•sis•tance \ri'zistəns\ *n* 1 : act of resisting 2 : ability of an organism to resist disease 3 : opposition to electric current

re•sis•tant \-tənt\ *adj* : giving resistance

res•o•lute \'rezə,lüt\ *adj* : having a fixed purpose —**res•o•lute•ly** *adv* —**res•o•lute•ness** *n*

res•o•lu•tion \,rezə'lüshən\ *n* 1 : process of resolving 2 : firmness of purpose 3 : statement of the opinion, will, or intent of a body

re·solve \ri'zälv\ vb **-solved; -solv·ing 1** : find an answer to **2** : make a formal resolution ~ n **1** : something resolved **2** : steadfast purpose —**re·solv·able** adj

res·o·nant \'rezᵊnənt\ adj **1** : continuing to sound **2** : relating to intensification or prolongation of sound (as by a vibrating body) —**res·o·nance** \-əns\ n —**res·o·nant·ly** adv

re·sort \ri'zórt\ n **1** : source of help **2** : place to go for vacation ~ vb **1** : go often or habitually **2** : have recourse

re·sound \ri'zaúnd\ vb : become filled with sound

re·sound·ing \-iŋ\ adj : impressive —**re·sound·ing·ly** adv

re·source \'rē,sórs, ri'sórs\ n **1** : new or reserve source **2** pl : available funds **3** : ability to handle situations —**re·source·ful** adj —**re·source·ful·ness** n

re·spect \ri'spekt\ n **1** : relation to something **2** : high or special regard **3** : detail ~ vb : consider deserving of high regard —**re·spect·er** n —**re·spect·ful** adj —**re·spect·ful·ly** adv —**re·spect·ful·ness** n

re·spect·able \ri'spektəbəl\ adj **1** : worthy of respect **2** : fair in size, quantity, or quality —**re·spect·abil·i·ty** \-,spektə'bilətē\ n —**re·spect·ably** \-'spektəblē\ adv

re·spec·tive \-tiv\ adj : individual and specific

re·spec·tive·ly \-lē\ adv **1** : as relating to each **2** : each in the order given

res·pi·ra·tion \,respə'rāshən\ n : act or process of breathing —**re·spi·ra·to·ry** \'respərə,tōrē, ri'spīrə-\ adj —**re·spire** \ri'spīr\ vb

res·pi·ra·tor \'respə,rātər\ n : device for artificial respiration

re·spite \'respət\ n : temporary delay or rest

re·splen·dent \ri'splendənt\ adj : shining brilliantly —**re·splen·dence** \-dəns\ n —**re·splen·dent·ly** adv

re·spond \ri'spänd\ vb **1** : answer **2** : react —**re·spon·dent** \-'spändənt\ n or adj —**re·spond·er** n

re·sponse \ri'späns\ n **1** : act of responding **2** : answer

re·spon·si·ble \ri'spänsəbəl\ adj **1** : answerable for acts or decisions **2** : able to fulfill obligations **3** : having important duties —**re·spon·si·bil·i·ty** \ri,spänsə'bilətē\ n —**re·spon·si·ble·ness** n —**re·spon·si·bly** \-blē\ adv

re·spon·sive \-siv\ adj : quick to respond —**re·spon·sive·ly** adv —**re·spon·sive·ness** n

¹rest \'rest\ n **1** : sleep **2** : freedom from work or activity **3** : state of inactivity **4** : something used as a support ~ vb **1** : get rest **2** : cease action or motion **3** : give rest to **4** : sit or lie fixed or supported **5** : depend —**rest·ful** adj —**rest·ful·ly** adv

²rest n : remainder

res·tau·rant \'restərənt, -tə,ränt\ n : public eating place

res·ti·tu·tion \,restə'tüshən, -'tyü-\ n : act or fact of restoring something or repaying someone

res·tive \'restiv\ adj : uneasy or fidgety —**res·tive·ly** adv —**res·tive·ness** n

rest·less \'restləs\ adj **1** : lacking or giving no rest **2** : always moving **3** : uneasy —**rest·less·ly** adv —**rest·less·ness** n

re·store \ri'stōr\ vb **-stored; -stor·ing 1** : give back **2** : put back into use or into a former state —**re·stor·able** adj —**res·to·ra·tion** \,restə'rāshən\ n —**re·stor·ative** \ri'stōrətiv\ n or adj —**re·stor·er** n

re·strain \ri'strān\ vb : limit or keep under control —**re·strain·able** adj —**re·strained** \-'strānd\ adj —**re·strain·ed·ly** \-'strānədlē\ adv —**re·strain·er** n

restraining order n : legal order directing one person to stay away from another

re·straint \-'strānt\ n **1** : act of restraining **2** : restraining force **3** : control over feelings

re·strict \ri'strikt\ vb **1** : confine within bounds **2** : limit use of —**re·stric·tion** \-'strikshən\ n —**re·stric·tive** \-tiv\ adj —**re·stric·tive·ly** adv

re·sult \ri'zəlt\ vb : come about because of something else ~ n **1** : thing that results **2** : something obtained by calculation or investigation —**re·sul·tant** \-'zəltᵊnt\ adj or n

re·sume \ri'züm\ vb **-sumed; -sum·ing** : return to or take up again after interruption —**re·sump·tion** \-'zəmpshən\ n

ré·su·mé, re·su·me, re·su·mé \'rezə,mā, ,rezə'-\ n : summary of one's career and qualifications

re·sur·gence \ri'sərjəns\ n : a rising again —**re·sur·gent** \-jənt\ adj

res·ur·rect \,rezə'rekt\ vb **1** : raise from

the dead **2** : bring to attention or use again —**res·ur·rec·tion** \-'rekshən\ n

re·sus·ci·tate \ri'səsə,tāt\ vb **-tat·ed; -tat·ing** : bring back from apparent death —**re·sus·ci·ta·tion** \ri,səsə-'tāshən, ,rē-\ n —**re·sus·ci·ta·tor** \-,tātər\ n

re·tail \'rē,tāl\ vb : sell in small quantities directly to the consumer ~ n : business of selling to consumers — **retail** adj or adv —**re·tail·er** n

re·tain \ri'tān\ vb **1** : keep or hold onto **2** : engage the services of

re·tain·er n **1** : household servant **2** : retaining fee

re·tal·i·ate \ri'talē,āt\ vb **-at·ed; -at·ing** : return (as an injury) in kind — **re·tal·i·a·tion** \-,talē'āshən\ n —**re·tal·ia·to·ry** \-'talyə,tōrē\ adj

re·tard \ri'tärd\ vb : hold back —**re·tar·da·tion** \,rē,tär'dāshən, ri-\ n

re·tard·ed \ri'tärdəd\ adj : slow or limited in intellectual development

retch \'rech\ vb : try to vomit

re·ten·tion \ri'tenchən\ n **1** : state of being retained **2** : ability to retain —**re·ten·tive** \-'tentiv\ adj

ret·i·cent \'retəsənt\ adj : tending not to talk —**ret·i·cence** \-səns\ n —**ret·i·cent·ly** adv

ret·i·na \'ret²nə\ n, pl **-nas** or **-nae** \-²n-,ē\ : sensory membrane lining the eye —**ret·i·nal** \'ret²nəl\ adj

ret·i·nue \'ret²n,ü, -,yü\ n : attendants or followers of a distinguished person

re·tire \ri'tīr\ vb **-tired; -tir·ing 1** : withdraw for privacy **2** : end a career **3** : go to bed —**re·tir·ee** \ri,tī'rē\ n —**re·tire·ment** n

re·tir·ing \ri'tīriŋ\ adj : shy

re·tort \ri'tórt\ vb : say in reply ~ n : quick, witty, or cutting answer

re·trace \,rē'trās\ vb : go over again or in reverse

re·tract \ri'trakt\ vb **1** : draw back or in **2** : withdraw a charge or promise — **re·tract·able** adj —**re·trac·tion** \-'trakshən\ n

re·treat \ri'trēt\ n **1** : act of withdrawing **2** : place of privacy or safety or meditation and study ~ vb : make a retreat

re·trench \ri'trench\ vb : cut down (as expenses) —**re·trench·ment** n

ret·ri·bu·tion \,retrə'byushən\ n : retaliation —**re·trib·u·tive** \ri'tribyətiv\ adj —**re·trib·u·to·ry** \-yə,tōrē\ adj

re·trieve \ri'trēv\ vb **-trieved; -triev·ing 1** : search for and bring in game **2**

: recover —**re·triev·able** adj —**re·triev·al** \-'trēvəl\ n

re·triev·er \-'trēvər\ n : dog for retrieving game

ret·ro·ac·tive \,retrō'aktiv\ adj : made effective as of a prior date —**ret·ro·ac·tive·ly** adv

ret·ro·grade \'retrə,grād\ adj **1** : moving backward **2** : becoming worse

ret·ro·gress \,retrə'gres\ vb : move backward —**ret·ro·gres·sion** \-'greshən\ n

ret·ro·spect \'retrə,spekt\ n : review of past events —**ret·ro·spec·tion** \,retrə'spekshən\ n —**ret·ro·spec·tive** \-'spektiv\ adj —**ret·ro·spec·tive·ly** adv

re·turn \ri'tərn\ vb **1** : go or come back **2** : pass, give, or send back to an earlier possessor **3** : answer **4** : bring in as a profit **5** : give or do in return — n **1** : act of returning or something returned **2** pl : report of balloting results **3** : statement of taxable income **4** : profit —**return** adj —**re·turn·able** adj or n —**re·turn·er** n

re·union \rē'yünyən\ n **1** : act of reuniting **2** : a meeting of persons after a separation

re·vamp \,rē'vamp\ vb : renovate or revise

re·veal \ri'vēl\ vb **1** : make known **2** : show plainly

rev·eil·le \'revəlē\ n : military signal sounded about sunrise

rev·el \'revəl\ vb **-eled** or **-elled; -el·ing** or **-el·ling 1** : take part in a revel **2** : take great pleasure ~ n : wild party or celebration —**rev·el·er, rev·el·ler** \-ər\ n —**rev·el·ry** \-rē\ n

rev·e·la·tion \,revə'lāshən\ n **1** : act of revealing **2** : something enlightening or astonishing

re·venge \ri'venj\ vb **-venged; -veng·ing** : avenge ~ n **1** : desire for retaliation **2** : act of retaliation —**re·venge·ful** adj —**re·veng·er** n

rev·e·nue \'revə,nü, -,nyü\ n : money collected by a government

re·ver·ber·ate \ri'vərbə,rāt\ vb **-at·ed; -at·ing** : resound in a series of echoes —**re·ver·ber·a·tion** \-,vərbə'rāshən\ n

re·vere \ri'vir\ vb **-vered; -ver·ing** : show honor and devotion to —**rev·er·ence** \'revərəns\ n —**rev·er·ent** \-rənt\ adj —**rev·er·ent·ly** adv

rev·er·end \'revərənd\ adj : worthy of reverence ~ n : clergy member

rev·er·ie \'revərē\ n, pl **-er·ies** : daydream

re·verse \ri'vərs\ adj 1 : opposite to a previous or normal condition 2 : acting in an opposite way ~ vb **-versed; -vers·ing 1** : turn upside down or completely around 2 : change to the contrary or in the opposite direction ~ n 1 : something contrary 2 : change for the worse 3 : back of something —**re·ver·sal** \-səl\ n —**re·verse·ly** adv —**re·vers·ible** \-'vərsəbəl\ adj

re·vert \ri'vərt\ vb : return to an original type or condition —**re·ver·sion** \-'vərzhən\ n

re·view \ri'vyü\ n 1 : formal inspection 2 : general survey 3 : critical evaluation 4 : second or repeated study or examination ~ vb 1 : examine or study again 2 : reexamine judicially 3 : look back over 4 : examine critically 5 : inspect —**re·view·er** n

re·vile \ri'vīl\ vb **-viled; -vil·ing** : abuse verbally —**re·vile·ment** n —**re·vil·er** n

re·vise \-'vīz\ vb **-vised; -vis·ing 1** : look over something written to correct or improve 2 : make a new version of —**re·vis·able** adj —**revise** n —**re·vis·er, re·vi·sor** \-'vīzər\ n —**re·vi·sion** \-'vizhən\ n

re·viv·al \-'vīvəl\ n 1 : act of reviving or state of being revived 2 : evangelistic meeting

re·vive \-'vīv\ vb **-vived; -viv·ing** : bring back to life or consciousness or into use —**re·viv·er** n

rev·o·ca·tion \revə'kāshən\ n : act or instance of revoking

re·voke \ri'vōk\ vb **-voked; -vok·ing** : annul by recalling —**re·vok·er** n

re·volt \ri'vōlt\ vb 1 : throw off allegiance 2 : cause or experience disgust or shock ~ n : rebellion or revolution —**re·volt·er** n

re·volt·ing \-iŋ\ adj : extremely offensive —**re·volt·ing·ly** adv

rev·o·lu·tion \revə'lüshən\ n 1 : rotation 2 : progress in an orbit 3 : sudden, radical, or complete change (as overthrow of a government) —**rev·o·lu·tion·ary** \-shə,nerē\ adj or n

rev·o·lu·tion·ize \-shə,nīz\ vb **-ized; -iz·ing** : change radically —**rev·o·lu·tion·iz·er** n

re·volve \ri'välv\ vb **-volved; -volv·ing 1** : ponder 2 : move in an orbit 3 : rotate —**re·volv·able** adj

re·volv·er \ri'välvər\ n : pistol with a revolving cylinder

re·vue \ri'vyü\ n : theatrical production of brief numbers

re·vul·sion \ri'vəlshən\ n : complete dislike or repugnance

re·ward \ri'word\ vb : give a reward to or for ~ n : something offered for service or achievement

re·write \,rē'rīt\ vb **-wrote; -writ·ten; -writ·ing** : revise —**rewrite** n

rhap·so·dy \'rapsədē\ n, pl **-dies 1** : expression of extravagant praise 2 : flowing free-form musical composition —**rhap·sod·ic** \rap'sädik\ adj —**rhap·sod·i·cal·ly** \-iklē\ adv —**rhap·so·dize** \'rapsə,dīz\ vb

rhet·o·ric \'retərik\ n : art of speaking or writing effectively —**rhe·tor·i·cal** \ri'tórikəl\ adj —**rhet·o·ri·cian** \,retə'rishən\ n

rheu·ma·tism \'rümə,tizəm, 'rüm-\ n : disorder marked by inflammation or pain in muscles or joints —**rheu·mat·ic** \rü'matik\ adj

rhine·stone \'rīn,stōn\ n : a colorless imitation gem

rhi·no \'rīnō\ n, pl **-no** or **-nos** : rhinoceros

rhi·noc·er·os \rī'näsərəs\ n, pl **-noc·er·os·es** or **-noc·er·os** or **-noc·eri** \-'näsə,rī\ : large thick-skinned mammal with 1 or 2 horns on the snout

rho·do·den·dron \,rōdə'dendrən\ n : flowering evergreen shrub

rhom·bus \'rämbəs\ n, pl **-bus·es** or **-bi** \-,bī\ : parallelogram with equal sides

rhu·barb \'rü,bärb\ n : garden plant with edible stalks

rhyme \'rīm\ n 1 : correspondence in terminal sounds 2 : verse that rhymes ~ vb **rhymed; rhym·ing** : make or have rhymes

rhythm \'rithəm\ n : regular succession of sounds or motions —**rhyth·mic** \'rithmik\, **rhyth·mi·cal** \-mikəl\ adj —**rhyth·mi·cal·ly** adv

rhythm and blues n : popular music based on blues and black folk music

rib \'rib\ n 1 : curved bone joined to the spine 2 : riblike thing ~ vb **-bb- 1** : furnish or mark with ribs 2 : tease —**rib·ber** n

rib·ald \'ribəld\ adj : coarse or vulgar —**rib·ald·ry** \-əldrē\ n

rib·bon \'ribən\ *n* **1** : narrow strip of fabric used esp. for decoration **2** : strip of inked cloth (as in a typewriter)

ri·bo·fla·vin \,rībə'flāvən, 'rībə-\ *n* : growth-promoting vitamin

rice \'rīs\ *n, pl* **rice** : starchy edible seeds of an annual cereal grass

rich \'rich\ *adj* **1** : having a lot of money or possessions **2** : valuable **3** : containing much sugar, fat, or seasoning **4** : abundant **5** : deep and pleasing in color or tone **6** : fertile —**rich·ly** *adv* —**rich·ness** *n*

rich·es \'richəz\ *n pl* : wealth

rick·ets \'rikəts\ *n* : childhood bone disease

rick·ety \'rikətē\ *adj* : shaky

rick·sha, rick·shaw \'rik,shȯ\ *n* : small covered 2-wheeled carriage pulled by one person

ric·o·chet \'rikə,shā, *Brit also* -,shet\ *vb* **-cheted** \-,shād\ *or* **-chet·ted** \-,shetəd\; **-chet·ing** \-,shāiŋ\ *or* **-chet·ting** \-,shetiŋ\ : bounce off at an angle —**ricochet** *n*

rid \'rid\ *vb* **rid; rid·ding** : make free of something unwanted —**rid·dance** \'rid³ns\ *n*

rid·den \'rid³n\ *adj* : overburdened with—used in combination

¹rid·dle \'rid³l\ *n* : puzzling question ~ *vb* **-dled; -dling** : speak in riddles

²riddle *vb* **-dled; -dling** : fill full of holes

ride \'rīd\ *vb* **rode** \'rōd\; **rid·den** \'rid³n\; **rid·ing** \'rīdiŋ\ **1** : be carried along **2** : sit on and cause to move **3** : travel over a surface **4** : tease or nag ~ *n* **1** : trip on an animal or in a vehicle **2** : mechanical device ridden for amusement

rid·er *n* **1** : one that rides **2** : attached clause or document —**rid·er·less** *adj*

ridge \'rij\ *n* **1** : range of hills **2** : raised line or strip **3** : line of intersection of 2 sloping surfaces —**ridgy** *adj*

rid·i·cule \'ridə,kyül\ *vb* **-culed; -cul·ing** : laugh at or make fun of —**ridi·cule** *n*

ri·dic·u·lous \rə'dikyələs\ *adj* : arousing ridicule —**ri·dic·u·lous·ly** *adv* —**ri·dic·u·lous·ness** *n*

rife \'rīf\ *adj* : abounding —**rife** *adv*

riff·raff \'rif,raf\ *n* : mob

¹ri·fle \'rīfəl\ *vb* **-fled; -fling** : ransack esp. with intent to steal —**ri·fler** \-flər\ *n*

²rifle *n* : long shoulder weapon with

spiral grooves in the bore —**ri·fle·man** \-mən\ *n* —**ri·fling** *n*

rift \'rift\ *n* : separation —**rift** *vb*

¹rig \'rig\ *vb* **-gg-** **1** : fit out with rigging **2** : set up esp. as a makeshift ~ *n* **1** : distinctive shape, number, and arrangement of sails and masts of a sailing ship **2** : equipment **3** : carriage with its horse

²rig *vb* **-gg-** : manipulate esp. by deceptive or dishonest means

rig·ging \'rigiŋ, -ən\ *n* : lines that hold and move the masts, sails, and spars of a sailing ship

right \'rīt\ *adj* **1** : meeting a standard of conduct **2** : correct **3** : genuine **4** : normal **5** : opposite of left ~ *n* **1** : something that is correct, just, proper, or honorable **2** : something to which one has a just claim **3** : something that is on the right side ~ *adv* **1** : according to what is right **2** : immediately **3** : completely **4** : on or to the right ~ *vb* **1** : restore to a proper state **2** : bring or become upright again —**right·er** *n* —**right·ness** *n* —**right·ward** \-wərd\ *adj*

right angle *n* : angle whose sides are perpendicular to each other —**right-an·gled** \'rīt'aŋgəld\ *or* **right-an·gle** \-gəl\ *adj*

right·eous \'rīchəs\ *adj* : acting or being in accordance with what is just or moral —**right·eous·ly** *adv* —**right·eous·ness** *n*

right·ful \'rītfəl\ *adj* : lawful —**right·ful·ly** \-ē\ *adv* —**right·ful·ness** *n*

right·ly \'rītlē\ *adv* **1** : justly **2** : properly **3** : correctly

rig·id \'rijəd\ *adj* : lacking flexibility —**ri·gid·i·ty** \rə'jidətē\ *n* —**rig·id·ly** *adv*

rig·ma·role \'rigmə,rōl, 'rigə-\ *n* **1** : meaningless talk **2** : complicated often unnecessary procedure

rig·or \'rigər\ *n* : severity —**rig·or·ous** *adj* —**rig·or·ous·ly** *adv*

rig·or mor·tis \,rigər'mȯrtəs\ *n* : temporary stiffness of muscles occurring after death

rile \'rīl\ *vb* **riled; ril·ing** : anger

rill \'ril\ *n* : small brook

rim \'rim\ *n* : edge esp. of something curved ~ *vb* **-mm-** : border

¹rime \'rīm\ *n* : frost —**rimy** \'rīmē\ *adj*

²rime *var of* RHYME

rind \'rīnd\ *n* : usu. hard or tough outer layer

¹ring \'riŋ\ *n* **1** : circular band used as

an ornament or for holding or fastening **2** : something circular **3** : place for contest or display **4** : group with a selfish or dishonest aim ~ *vb* : surround —**ringed** \'riŋd\ *adj* —**ring·like** *adj*

²**ring** *vb* **rang** \'raŋ\; **rung** \'rəŋ\; **ring·ing 1** : sound resonantly when struck **2** : cause to make a metallic sound by striking **3** : resound **4** : call esp. by a bell ~ *n* **1** : resonant sound or tone **2** : act or instance of ringing

ring·er \'riŋər\ *n* **1** : one that sounds by ringing **2** : illegal substitute **3** : one that closely resembles another

ring·lead·er \'riŋˌlēdər\ *n* : leader esp. of troublemakers

ring·let *n* : long curl

ring·worm *n* : contagious skin disease caused by fungi

rink \'riŋk\ *n* : enclosed place for skating

rinse \'rins\ *vb* **rinsed; rins·ing 1** : cleanse usu. with water only **2** : treat (hair) with a rinse ~ *n* : liquid used for rinsing —**rins·er** *n*

ri·ot \'rīət\ *n* **1** : violent public disorder **2** : random or disorderly profusion —**riot** *vb* —**ri·ot·er** *n* —**ri·ot·ous** *adj*

rip \'rip\ *vb* **-pp-** : cut or tear open ~ *n* : rent made by ripping —**rip·per** *n*

ripe \'rīp\ *adj* **rip·er; rip·est** : fully grown, developed, or prepared —**ripe·ly** *adv* —**rip·en** \'rīpən\ *vb* —**ripe·ness** *n*

rip-off *n* : theft —**rip off** *vb*

rip·ple \'ripəl\ *vb* **-pled; -pling 1** : become lightly ruffled on the surface **2** : sound like rippling water —**ripple** *n*

rise \'rīz\ *vb* **rose** \'rōz\; **ris·en** \'riz³n\; **ris·ing** \'rīziŋ\ **1** : get up from sitting, kneeling, or lying **2** : take arms **3** : appear above the horizon **4** : ascend **5** : gain a higher position or rank **6** : increase ~ *n* **1** : act of rising **2** : origin **3** : elevation **4** : increase **5** : upward slope **6** : area of high ground —**ris·er** \'rīzər\ *n*

risk \'risk\ *n* : exposure to loss or injury —**risk** *vb* —**risk·i·ness** *n* —**risky** *adj*

ris·qué \ris'kā\ *adj* : nearly indecent

rite \'rīt\ *n* **1** : set form for conducting a ceremony **2** : liturgy of a church **3** : ceremonial action

rit·u·al \'richəwəl\ *n* : rite —**ritual** *adj* —**rit·u·al·ism** \-ˌizəm\ *n* —**rit·u·al·is·tic** \ˌrichəwəl'istik\ *adj* —**rit·u·al·is·ti·cal·ly** \-tiklē\ *adv* —**rit·u·al·ly** \'richəwəlē\ *adv*

ri·val \'rīvəl\ *n* **1** : competitor **2** : peer ~ *vb* **-valed** *or* **-valled; -val·ing** *or* **-val·ling 1** : be in competition with **2** : equal —**rival** *adj* —**ri·val·ry** \-rē\ *n*

riv·er \'rivər\ *n* : large natural stream of water —**riv·er·bank** *n* —**riv·er·bed** *n* —**riv·er·boat** *n* —**riv·er·side** *n*

riv·et \'rivət\ *n* : headed metal bolt ~ *vb* : fasten with a rivet —**riv·et·er** *n*

riv·u·let \'rivyələt\ *n* : small stream

roach \'rōch\ *n* : cockroach

road \'rōd\ *n* : open way for vehicles, persons, and animals —**road·bed** *n* —**road·side** *n or adj* —**road·way** *n*

road·block *n* : obstruction on a road

road·run·ner *n* : large fast-running bird

roam \'rōm\ *vb* : wander

roan \'rōn\ *adj* : of a dark color sprinkled with white ~ *n* : animal with a roan coat

roar \'rōr\ *vb* : utter a full loud prolonged sound —**roar** *n* —**roar·er** *n*

roast \'rōst\ *vb* **1** : cook by dry heat **2** : criticize severely ~ *n* : piece of meat suitable for roasting —**roast** *adj* —**roast·er** *n*

rob \'räb\ *vb* **-bb- 1** : steal from **2** : commit robbery —**rob·ber** *n*

rob·bery \'räbərē\ *n, pl* **-ber·ies** : theft of something from a person by use of violence or threat

robe \'rōb\ *n* **1** : long flowing outer garment **2** : covering for the lower body ~ *vb* **robed; rob·ing** : clothe with or as if with a robe

rob·in \'räbən\ *n* : No. American thrush with a reddish breast

ro·bot \'rō,bät, -bət\ *n* **1** : machine that looks and acts like a human being **2** : efficient but insensitive person —**ro·bot·ic** \rō'bätik\ *adj*

ro·bust \rō'bəst, 'rō,bəst\ *adj* : strong and vigorously healthy —**ro·bust·ly** *adv* —**ro·bust·ness** *n*

¹**rock** \'räk\ *vb* : sway or cause to sway back and forth ~ *n* **1** : rocking movement **2** : popular music marked by repetition and a strong beat

²**rock** *n* : mass of hard mineral material —**rock** *adj* —**rocky** *adj*

rock·er *n* **1** : curved piece on which a chair rocks **2** : chair that rocks

rock·et \'räkət\ *n* **1** : self-propelled firework or missile **2** : jet engine that carries its own oxygen ~ *vb* : rise abruptly and rapidly —rock·et·ry \-ətrē\ n

rod \'räd\ n 1 : straight slender stick 2 : unit of length equal to 5 yards

rode past of RIDE

ro·dent \'rōd²nt\ n : usu. small gnawing mammal

ro·deo \'rōdē,ō, rō'dāō\ n, pl -de·os : contest of cowboy skills

roe \'rō\ n : fish eggs

rogue \'rōg\ n : dishonest or mischievous person —rogu·ery \'rōgərē\ n —rogu·ish \'rōgish\ adj —rogu·ish·ly adv —rogu·ish·ness n

roil \'roil\ vb 1 : make cloudy or muddy by stirring up 2 : make angry

role \'rōl\ n 1 : part to play 2 : function

roll \'rōl\ n 1 : official record or list of names 2 : something rolled up or rounded 3 : bread baked in a small rounded mass 4 : sound of rapid drum strokes 5 : heavy reverberating sound 6 : rolling movement ~ vb 1 : move by turning over 2 : move on wheels 3 : flow in a continuous stream 4 : swing from side to side 5 : shape or be shaped in rounded form 6 : press with a roller

roll·er n 1 : revolving cylinder 2 : rod on which something is rolled up 3 : long heavy ocean wave

roller skate n : a skate with wheels instead of a runner —roller-skate vb

rol·lick·ing \'rälikin\ adj : full of good spirits

Ro·man Catholic \'rōmən-\ n : member of a Christian church led by a pope —Roman Catholic adj —Roman Catholicism n

ro·mance \rō'mans, 'rō,mans\ n 1 : medieval tale of knightly adventure 2 : love story 3 : love affair ~ vb -manced; -manc·ing 1 : have romantic fancies 2 : have a love affair with —ro·manc·er n

ro·man·tic \rō'mantik\ adj 1 : visionary or imaginative 2 : appealing to one's emotions —ro·man·ti·cal·ly \-iklē\ adv

romp \'rämp\ vb : play actively and noisily —romp n

roof \'rüf, 'rüf\ n, pl roofs \'rüfs, 'rüfs; 'rüvz, 'rüvz\ : upper covering part of a building ~ vb : cover with a roof —roofed \'rüft, 'rüft\ adj —roof·ing n —roof·less adj —roof·top n

¹rook \'rük\ n : crowlike bird

²rook vb : cheat

rook·ie \'rükē\ n : novice

room \'rüm, 'rüm\ n 1 : sufficient space 2 : partitioned part of a building ~ vb : occupy lodgings —room·er n — room·ful n —roomy adj

room·mate n : one sharing the same lodgings

roost \'rüst\ n : support on which birds perch ~ vb : settle on a roost

roost·er \'rüstər, 'rüs-\ n : adult male domestic chicken

¹root \'rüt, 'rut\ n 1 : leafless underground part of a seed plant 2 : rootlike thing or part 3 : source 4 : essential core ~ vb : form, fix, or become fixed by roots —root·less adj —root·let \-lət\ n —root·like adj

²root \'rüt\ vb : turn up with the snout

³root \'rüt, 'rut\ vb : applaud or encourage noisily —root·er n

rope \'rōp\ n : large strong cord of strands of fiber ~ vb : roped; rop·ing 1 : tie with a rope 2 : lasso

ro·sa·ry \'rōzərē\ n, pl -ries 1 : string of beads used in praying 2 : Roman Catholic devotion

¹rose past of RISE

²rose \'rōz\ n 1 : prickly shrub with bright flowers 2 : purplish red —rose adj —rose·bud n —rose·bush n

rose·mary \'rōz,merē\ n, pl -mar·ies : fragrant shrubby mint

ro·sette \rō'zet\ n : rose-shaped ornament

Rosh Ha·sha·nah \,räshhä'shänə, ,rōsh-\ n : Jewish New Year observed as a religious holiday in September or October

ros·in \'räz²n\ n : brittle resin

ros·ter \'rästər\ n : list of names

ros·trum \'rästrəm\ n, pl -trums or -tra \-trä\ : speaker's platform

rosy \'rōzē\ adj ros·i·er; -est 1 : of the color rose 2 : hopeful —ros·i·ly adv —ros·i·ness n

rot \'rät\ vb -tt- : undergo decomposition ~ n 1 : decay 2 : disease in which tissue breaks down

ro·ta·ry \'rōtərē\ adj 1 : turning on an axis 2 : having a rotating part

ro·tate \'rō,tāt\ vb -tat·ed; -tat·ing 1 : turn about an axis or a center 2 : alternate in a series —ro·ta·tion \rō-'tāshən\ n —ro·ta·tor \'rō,tātər\ n

rote \'rōt\ n : repetition from memory

ro·tor \'rōtər\ n 1 : part that rotates 2 : system of rotating horizontal blades for supporting a helicopter

rot·ten \'rätən\ adj 1 : having rotted 2 : corrupt 3 : extremely unpleasant or inferior —**rot·ten·ness** n

ro·tund \rō'tənd\ adj : rounded —**ro·tun·di·ty** \-'təndətē\ n

ro·tun·da \rō'təndə\ n : building or room with a dome

roué \rü'ā\ n : man given to debauched living

rouge \'rüzh, 'rüj\ n : cosmetic for the cheeks —**rouge** vb

rough \'rəf\ adj 1 : not smooth 2 : not calm 3 : harsh, violent, or rugged 4 : crudely or hastily done ~ n : rough state or something in that state ~ vb 1 : roughen 2 : manhandle 3 : make roughly —**rough·ly** adv —**rough·ness** n

rough·age \'rəfij\ n : coarse bulky food

rough·en \'rəfən\ vb : make or become rough

rough·neck \'rəf,nek\ n : rowdy

rou·lette \rü'let\ n : gambling game using a whirling numbered wheel

¹round \'raúnd\ adj 1 : having every part the same distance from the center 2 : cylindrical 3 : complete 4 : approximate 5 : blunt 6 : moving in or forming a circle ~ n 1 : round or curved thing 2 : series of recurring actions or events 3 : period of time or a unit of action 4 : fired shot 5 : cut of beef ~ vb 1 : make or become round 2 : go around 3 : finish 4 : express as an approximation —**round·ish** adj —**round·ly** adv —**round·ness** n

²round prep or adv : around

round·about adj : indirect

round·up \'raúnd,əp\ n 1 : gathering together of range cattle 2 : summary —**round up** vb

rouse \'raúz\ vb **roused; rous·ing** 1 : wake from sleep 2 : stir up

rout \'raút\ n 1 : state of wild confusion 2 : disastrous defeat ~ vb : defeat decisively

route \'rüt, 'raút\ n : line of travel ~ vb **rout·ed; rout·ing** : send by a selected route

rou·tine \rü'tēn\ n 1 : regular course of procedure 2 : an often repeated speech, formula, or part —**routine** adj —**rou·tine·ly** adv

rove \'rōv\ vb **roved; rov·ing** : wander or roam —**rov·er** n

¹row \'rō\ vb 1 : propel a boat with oars 2 : carry in a rowboat ~ n : act of

rowing —**row·boat** n —**row·er** \'rōər\ n

²row n : number of objects in a line

³row \'raú\ n : noisy quarrel —**row** vb

row·dy \'raúdē\ adj **-di·er; -est** : coarse or boisterous in behavior —**row·di·ness** n —**rowdy** n

roy·al \'roíəl\ adj : relating to or befitting a king ~ n : person of royal blood —**roy·al·ly** adv

roy·al·ty \'roíəltē\ n, pl **-ties** 1 : state of being royal 2 : royal persons 3 : payment for use of property

rub \'rəb\ vb **-bb-** 1 : use pressure and friction on a body 2 : scour, polish, erase, or smear by pressure and friction 3 : chafe with friction ~ n : difficulty

rub·ber \'rəbər\ n 1 : one that rubs 2 : waterproof elastic substance or something made of it —**rubber** adj —**rub·ber·ize** \-,īz\ vb —**rub·bery** adj

rub·bish \'rəbish\ n : waste or trash

rub·ble \'rəbəl\ n : broken fragments esp. of a destroyed building

ru·ble \'rübəl\ n : monetary unit of Russia

ru·by \'rübē\ n, pl **-bies** : precious red stone or its color —**ruby** adj

rud·der \'rədər\ n : steering device at the rear of a ship or aircraft

rud·dy \'rədē\ adj **-di·er; -est** : reddish —**rud·di·ness** n

rude \'rüd\ adj **rud·er; rud·est** 1 : roughly made 2 : impolite —**rude·ly** adv —**rude·ness** n

ru·di·ment \'rüdəmənt\ n 1 : something not fully developed 2 : elementary principle —**ru·di·men·ta·ry** \,rüdə-'mentərē\ adj

rue \'rü\ vb **rued; ru·ing** : feel regret for ~ n : regret —**rue·ful** \-fəl\ adj —**rue·ful·ly** adv —**rue·ful·ness** n

ruf·fi·an \'rəfēən\ n : brutal person

ruf·fle \'rəfəl\ vb **-fled; -fling** 1 : draw into or provide with pleats 2 : roughen the surface of 3 : irritate ~ n : strip of fabric pleated on one edge —**ruf·fly** \'rəfəlē, -flē\ adj

rug \'rəg\ n : piece of heavy fabric used as a floor covering

rug·ged \'rəgəd\ adj 1 : having a rough uneven surface 2 : severe 3 : strong —**rug·ged·ly** adv —**rug·ged·ness** n

ru·in \'rüən\ n 1 : complete collapse or destruction 2 : remains of something destroyed —usu. in pl. **3** : cause of destruction ~ *vb* **1** : destroy **2** : damage beyond repair **3** : bankrupt

ru·in·ous \'rüənəs\ *adj* : causing ruin —**ru·in·ous·ly** *adv*

rule \'rül\ *n* **1** : guide or principle for governing action **2** : usual way of doing something **3** : government **4** : straight strip (as of wood or metal) marked off in units for measuring ~ *vb* **ruled; rul·ing 1** : govern **2** : give as a decision —**rul·er** *n*

rum \'rəm\ *n* : liquor made from molasses or sugarcane

rum·ble \'rəmbəl\ *vb* **-bled; -bling** : make a low heavy rolling sound —**rumble** *n*

ru·mi·nant \'rümənənt\ *n* : hoofed mammal (as a cow or deer) that chews the cud —**ruminant** *adj*

ru·mi·nate \'rümə,nāt\ *vb* **-nat·ed; -nat·ing** : contemplate —**ru·mi·na·tion** \,rümə'nāshən\ *n*

rum·mage \'rəmij\ *vb* **-maged; -mag·ing** : search thoroughly

rum·my \'rəmē\ *n* : card game

ru·mor \'rümər\ *n* **1** : common talk **2** : widespread statement not authenticated —**rumor** *vb*

rump \'rəmp\ *n* : rear part of an animal

rum·ple \'rəmpəl\ *vb* **-pled; -pling** : tousle or wrinkle —**rumple** *n*

rum·pus \'rəmpəs\ *n* : disturbance

run \'rən\ *vb* **ran** \'ran\; **run; run·ning 1** : go rapidly or hurriedly **2** : enter a race or election **3** : operate **4** : continue in force **5** : flow rapidly **6** : take a certain direction **7** : manage **8** : incur ~ *n* **1** : act of running **2** : brook **3** : continuous series **4** : usual kind **5** : freedom of movement **6** : lengthwise ravel

run·around *n* : evasive or delaying action esp. in response to a request

run·away \'rənə,wā\ *n* : fugitive ~ *adj* **1** : fugitive **2** : out of control

run·down *adj* : being in poor condition

¹rung *past part of* RING

²rung \'rən\ *n* : horizontal piece of a chair or ladder

run·ner \'rənər\ *n* **1** : one that runs **2** : thin piece or part on which something slides **3** : slender creeping branch of a plant

run·ner–up *n, pl* **run·ners–up** : competitor who finishes second

run·ning \'rəniŋ\ *adj* **1** : flowing **2** : continuous

runt \'rənt\ *n* : small person or animal —**runty** *adj*

run·way \'rən,wā\ *n* : strip on which aircraft land and take off

ru·pee \rü'pē, 'rü,-\ *n* : monetary unit (as of India)

rup·ture \'rəpchər\ *n* **1** : breaking or tearing apart **2** : hernia ~ *vb* **-tured; -tur·ing** : cause or undergo rupture

ru·ral \'rurəl\ *adj* : relating to the country or agriculture

ruse \'rüs, 'rüz\ *n* : trick

¹rush \'rəsh\ *n* : grasslike marsh plant

²rush *vb* **1** : move forward or act with too great haste **2** : perform in a short time ~ *n* : violent forward motion ~ *adj* : requiring speed —**rush·er** *n*

rus·set \'rəsət\ *n* **1** : reddish brown color **2** : a baking potato —**russet** *adj*

rust \'rəst\ *n* **1** : reddish coating on exposed iron **2** : reddish brown color —**rust** *vb* —**rusty** *adj*

rus·tic \'rəstik\ *adj* : relating to or suitable for the country or country dwellers ~ *n* : rustic person —**rus·ti·cal·ly** *adv*

rus·tle \'rəsəl\ *vb* **-tled; -tling 1** : make or cause a rustle **2** : forage food **3** : steal cattle from the range ~ *n* : series of small sounds —**rus·tler** \-ələr\ *n*

rut \'rət\ *n* **1** : track worn by wheels or feet **2** : set routine —**rut·ted** *adj*

ruth·less \'rüthləs\ *adj* : having no pity —**ruth·less·ly** *adv* —**ruth·less·ness** *n*

-ry \rē\ *n suffix* : -ery

rye \'rī\ *n* **1** : cereal grass grown for grain **2** : whiskey from rye

S

s \'es\ *n, pl* **s's** *or* **ss** \'esəz\ : 19th letter of the alphabet

¹-s \s *after sounds* f, k, <u>k</u>, p, t, th; əz *after sounds* ch, j, s, sh, z, zh; z *after*

other sounds —used to form the plural of most nouns

2-s *vb suffix* —used to form the 3d person singular present of most verbs

Sab·bath \'sabəth\ *n* **1** : Saturday observed as a day of worship by Jews and some Christians **2** : Sunday observed as a day of worship by Christians

sa·ber, sa·bre \'sābər\ *n* : curved cavalry sword

sa·ble \'sābəl\ *n* **1** : black **2** : dark brown mammal or its fur

sab·o·tage \'sabə,täzh\ *n* : deliberate destruction or hampering ~ *vb* **-taged; -tag·ing** : wreck through sabotage

sab·o·teur \,sabə'tər\ *n* : person who sabotages

sac \'sak\ *n* : anatomical pouch

sac·cha·rin \'sakərən\ *n* : low-calorie artificial sweetener

sac·cha·rine \-ərən\ *adj* : nauseatingly sweet

sa·chet \sa'shā\ *n* : small bag with perfumed powder (**sachet powder**)

1sack \'sak\ *n* : bag ~ *vb* : fire

2sack *vb* : plunder a captured place

sack·cloth *n* : rough garment worn as a sign of penitence

sac·ra·ment \'sakrəmənt\ *n* : formal religious act or rite —**sac·ra·men·tal** \,sakrə'ment°l\ *adj*

sa·cred \'sākrəd\ *adj* **1** : set apart for or worthy of worship **2** : worthy of reverence **3** : relating to religion —**sa·cred·ly** *adv* —**sa·cred·ness** *n*

sac·ri·fice \'sakrə,fīs\ *n* **1** : the offering of something precious to a deity or the thing offered **2** : loss or deprivation ~ *vb* **-ficed; -fic·ing** : offer or give up as a sacrifice —**sac·ri·fi·cial** \,sakrə'fishəl\ *adj*

sac·ri·lege \'sakrəlij\ *n* : violation of something sacred —**sac·ri·le·gious** \,sakrə'lijəs, -'lējəs\ *adj*

sac·ro·sanct \'sakrō,saŋkt\ *adj* : sacred

sad \'sad\ *adj* **-dd- 1** : affected with grief or sorrow **2** : causing sorrow —**sad·den** \'sad°n\ *vb* —**sad·ly** *adv* —**sad·ness** *n*

sad·dle \'sad°l\ *n* : seat for riding on horseback ~ *vb* **-dled; -dling** : put a saddle on

sa·dism \'sā,dizəm, 'sad,iz-\ *n* : delight in cruelty —**sa·dist** \'sādist, 'sad-\ *n* —**sa·dis·tic** \sə'distik\ *adj* —**sa·dis·ti·cal·ly** *adv*

sa·fa·ri \sə'färē, -'far-\ *n* : hunting expedition in Africa

safe \'sāf\ *adj* **saf·er; saf·est 1** : free from harm **2** : providing safety ~ *n* : container to keep valuables safe —**safe·keep·ing** *n* —**safe·ly** *adv*

safe·guard *n* : measure or device for preventing accidents —**safeguard** *vb*

safe·ty \'sāftē\ *n, pl* **-ties 1** : freedom from danger **2** : protective device

saf·flow·er \'saf,laúər\ *n* : herb with seeds rich in edible oil

saf·fron \'safrən\ *n* : orange powder from a crocus flower used in cooking

sag \'sag\ *vb* **-gg-** : droop, sink, or settle —**sag** *n*

sa·ga \'sägə\ *n* : story of heroic deeds

sa·ga·cious \sə'gāshəs\ *adj* : shrewd —**sa·gac·i·ty** \-'gasətē\ *n*

1sage \'sāj\ *adj* : wise or prudent ~ *n* : wise man —**sage·ly** *adv*

2sage *n* : mint used in flavoring

sage·brush *n* : low shrub of the western U.S.

said *past of* SAY

sail \'sāl\ *n* **1** : fabric used to catch the wind and move a boat or ship **2** : trip on a sailboat ~ *vb* **1** : travel on a ship or sailboat **2** : move with ease or grace —**sail·boat** *n* —**sail·or** \'sālər\ *n*

sail·fish *n* : large fish with a very large dorsal fin

saint \'sānt, *before a name* ,sānt *or* sənt\ *n* : holy or godly person —**saint·ed** \-əd\ *adj* —**saint·hood** \,hud\ *n* —**saint·li·ness** *n* —**saint·ly** *adj*

1sake \'sāk\ *n* **1** : purpose or reason **2** : one's good or benefit

2sa·ke, sa·ki \'säkē\ *n* : Japanese rice wine

sa·la·cious \sə'lāshəs\ *adj* : sexually suggestive —**sa·la·cious·ly** *adv*

sal·ad \'saləd\ *n* : dish usu. of raw lettuce, vegetables, or fruit

sal·a·man·der \'salə,mandər\ *n* : lizard-like amphibian

sa·la·mi \sə'lämē\ *n* : highly seasoned dried sausage

sal·a·ry \'salərē\ *n, pl* **-ries** : regular payment for services

sale \'sāl\ *n* **1** : transfer of ownership of property for money **2** : selling at bargain prices **3** : *sales pl* : activities involved in selling —**sal·able, sale·able** \'sāləbəl\ *adj* —**sales·man** \-mən\ *n* —**sales·per·son** *n* —**sales·wom·an** *n*

sa·lient \'sālyənt\ *adj* : standing out conspicuously

sa·line \'sā,lēn, -,līn\ *adj* : containing salt —**sa·lin·i·ty** \sā'linətē, sə-\ *n*

sa·li·va \sə'līvə\ *n* : liquid secreted into the mouth —**sal·i·vary** \'salə,verē\ *adj* —**sal·i·vate** \-,vāt\ *vb* —**sal·i·va·tion** \,salə'vāshən\ *n*

sal·low \'salō\ *adj* : of a yellowish sickly color

sal·ly \'salē\ *n, pl* -**lies** 1 : quick attack on besiegers 2 : witty remark —**sally** *vb*

salm·on \'samən\ *n, pl* **salmon** 1 : food fish with pink or red flesh 2 : deep yellowish pink color

sa·lon \sə'län, 'sal,än, sa'lōⁿ\ *n* : elegant room or shop

sa·loon \sə'lün\ *n* 1 : public cabin on a passenger ship 2 : barroom

sal·sa \'sòlsə, 'säl-\ *n* : spicy sauce of tomatoes, onions, and hot peppers

salt \'sòlt\ *n* 1 : white crystalline substance that consists of sodium and chlorine 2 : compound formed usu. from acid and metal —**salt** *vb or adj* —**salt·i·ness** *n* —**salty** *adj*

salt·wa·ter *adj* : relating to or living in salt water

sa·lu·bri·ous \sə'lübrēəs\ *adj* : good for health

sal·u·tary \'salyə,terē\ *adj* : health-giving or beneficial

sal·u·ta·tion \,salyə'tāshən\ *n* : greeting

sa·lute \sə'lüt\ *vb* -**lut·ed; -lut·ing** : honor by ceremony or formal movement —**salute** *n*

sal·vage \'salvij\ *n* : something saved from destruction ~ *vb* -**vaged; -vag·ing** : rescue or save

sal·va·tion \sal'vāshən\ *n* : saving of a person from sin or danger

salve \'sav, 'sàv\ *n* : medicinal ointment ~ *vb* **salved; salv·ing** : soothe

sal·ver \'salvər\ *n* : small tray

sal·vo \'salvō\ *n, pl* -**vos** *or* -**voes** : simultaneous discharge of guns

same \'sām\ *adj* : being the one referred to ~ *pron* : the same one or ones ~ *adv* : in the same manner —**same·ness** *n*

sam·ple \'sampəl\ *n* : piece or part that shows the quality of a whole ~ *vb* -**pled; -pling** : judge by a sample

sam·pler \'samplər\ *n* : piece of needlework testing skill in embroidering

san·a·to·ri·um \,sanə'tōrēəm\ *n, pl* -**riums** *or* -**ria** \-ēə\ : hospital for the chronically ill

sanc·ti·fy \'saŋktə,fī\ *vb* -**fied; -fy·ing** : make holy —**sanc·ti·fi·ca·tion** \,saŋktəfə'kāshən\ *n*

sanc·ti·mo·nious \,saŋktə'mōnēəs\ *adj* : hypocritically pious —**sanc·ti·mo·nious·ly** *adv*

sanc·tion \'saŋkshən\ *n* 1 : authoritative approval 2 : coercive measure —usu. pl ~ *vb* : approve

sanc·ti·ty \'saŋktətē\ *n, pl* -**ties** : quality or state of being holy or sacred

sanc·tu·ary \'saŋkchə,werē\ *n, pl* -**ar·ies** 1 : consecrated place 2 : place of refuge

sand \'sand\ *n* : loose granular particles of rock ~ *vb* : smooth with an abrasive —**sand·bank** *n* —**sand·er** *n* —**sand·storm** *n* —**sandy** *adj*

san·dal \'sand²l\ *n* : shoe consisting of a sole strapped to the foot

sand·pa·per *n* : abrasive paper —**sand·paper** *vb*

sand·pip·er \-,pīpər\ *n* : long-billed shorebird

sand·stone *n* : rock made of naturally cemented sand

sand·wich \'sand,wich\ *n* : 2 or more slices of bread with a filling between them ~ *vb* : squeeze or crowd in

sane \'sān\ *adj* **san·er; san·est** 1 : mentally healthy 2 : sensible —**sane·ly** *adv*

sang *past of* SING

san·gui·nary \'saŋgwə,nerē\ *adj* : bloody

san·guine \'saŋgwən\ *adj* 1 : reddish 2 : cheerful

san·i·tar·i·um \,sanə'terēəm\ *n, pl* -**i·ums** *or* -**ia** \-ēə\ : sanatorium

san·i·tary \'sanə,terē\ *adj* 1 : relating to health 2 : free from filth or infective matter

san·i·ta·tion \,sanə'tāshən\ *n* : protection of health by maintenance of sanitary conditions

san·i·ty \'sanətē\ *n* : soundness of mind

sank *past of* SINK

¹**sap** \'sap\ *n* 1 : fluid that circulates through a plant 2 : gullible person

²**sap** *vb* -**pp-** 1 : undermine 2 : weaken or exhaust gradually

sa·pi·ent \'sāpēənt, 'sapē-\ *adj* : wise —**sa·pi·ence** \-əns\ *n*

sap·ling \'sapliŋ\ *n* : young tree

sap·phire \'saf,īr\ *n* : hard transparent blue gem

sap·py \\'sapē\ *adj* **-pi·er; -est 1** : full of sap **2** : overly sentimental

sap·suck·er \\'sap,səkər\ *n* : small No. American woodpecker

sar·casm \\'sär,kazəm\ *n* **1** : cutting remark **2** : ironical criticism or reproach —**sar·cas·tic** \sär'kastik\ *adj* —**sar·cas·ti·cal·ly** *adv*

sar·coph·a·gus \sär'käfəgəs\ *n, pl* **-gi** \-,gī, -,jī\ : large stone coffin

sar·dine \sär'dēn\ *n* : small fish preserved for use as food

sar·don·ic \sär'dänik\ *adj* : disdainfully humorous —**sar·don·i·cal·ly** *adv*

sa·rong \sə'ròŋ, -'räŋ\ *n* : loose garment worn esp. by Pacific islanders

sar·sa·pa·ril·la \,saspə'rilə, ,särs-\ *n* : dried roots of a tropical American plant used esp. for flavoring or a carbonated drink flavored with this

sar·to·ri·al \sär'tōrēəl\ *adj* : relating to a tailor or men's clothes

¹sash \\'sash\ *n* : broad band worn around the waist or over the shoulder

²sash *n, pl* **sash 1** : frame for a pane of glass in a door or window **2** : movable part of a window

sas·sa·fras \\'sasə,fras\ *n* : No. American tree or its dried root bark

sassy \\'sasē\ *adj* **sass·i·er; -est** : saucy

sat *past of* SIT

Sa·tan \\'sāt⁰n\ *n* : devil —**sa·tan·ic** \sə'tanik, sā-\ *adj* —**sa·tan·i·cal·ly** *adv*

satch·el \\'sachəl\ *n* : small bag

sate \\'sāt\ *vb* **sat·ed; sat·ing** : satisfy fully

sat·el·lite \\'sat⁰l,īt\ *n* **1** : toady **2** : body or object that revolves around a larger celestial body

sa·ti·ate \\'sāshē,āt\ *vb* **-ated; -ating** : sate —**sa·ti·e·ty** \sə'tīətē\ *n*

sat·in \\'sat⁰n\ *n* : glossy fabric —**sat·iny** *adj*

sat·ire \\'sa,tīr\ *n* : literary ridicule done with humor —**sa·tir·ic** \sə'tirik\, **sa·tir·i·cal** \-ikəl\ *adj* —**sa·tir·i·cal·ly** *adv* —**sat·i·rist** \\'satərist\ *n* —**sat·i·rize** \-ə,rīz\ *vb*

sat·is·fac·tion \,satəs'fakshən\ *n* : state of being satisfied —**sat·is·fac·to·ri·ly** \-'faktərəlē\ *adv* —**sat·is·fac·to·ry** \-'faktərē\ *adj*

sat·is·fy \\'satəs,fī\ *vb* **-fied; -fy·ing 1** : make happy **2** : pay what is due to or on —**sat·is·fy·ing·ly** *adv*

sat·u·rate \\'sachə,rāt\ *vb* **-rated; -rating** : soak or charge thoroughly —**sat·u·ra·tion** \,sachə'rāshən\ *n*

Sat·ur·day \\'satərdā, -dē\ *n* : 7th day of the week

sat·ur·nine \\'satər,nīn\ *adj* : sullen

sa·tyr \\'sātər, 'sat-\ *n* : pleasure-loving forest god of ancient Greece

sauce \\'sòs\ *n* : fluid dressing or topping for food —**sauce·pan** *n*

sau·cer \\'sòsər\ *n* : small shallow dish under a cup

saucy \\'sasē, 'sòsē\ *adj* **sauc·i·er; -est** : insolent —**sauc·i·ly** *adv* —**sauc·i·ness** *n*

sauer·kraut \\'saùər,kraùt\ *n* : finely cut and fermented cabbage

sau·na \\'saùnə\ *n* : steam or dry heat bath or a room or cabinet used for such a bath

saun·ter \\'sòntər, 'sänt-\ *vb* : stroll

sau·sage \\'sòsij\ *n* : minced and highly seasoned meat

sau·té \sò'tā, sō-\ *vb* **-téed** *or* **-téd; -té·ing** : fry in a little fat —**sauté** *n*

sav·age \\'savij\ *adj* **1** : wild **2** : cruel ~ *n* : person belonging to a primitive society —**sav·age·ly** *adv* —**sav·age·ness** *n* —**sav·age·ry** *n*

¹save \\'sāv\ *vb* **saved; sav·ing 1** : rescue from danger **2** : guard from destruction **3** : redeem from sin **4** : put aside as a reserve —**sav·er** *n*

²save *prep* : except

sav·ior, sav·iour \\'sāvyər\ *n* **1** : one who saves **2** *cap* : Jesus Christ

sa·vor \\'sāvər\ *n* : special flavor ~ *vb* : taste with pleasure —**sa·vory** *adj*

¹saw *past of* SEE

²saw \\'sò\ *n* : cutting tool with teeth ~ *vb* **sawed; sawed** *or* **sawn; saw·ing** : cut with a saw —**saw·dust** \-,dəst\ *n* —**saw·mill** *n* —**saw·yer** \-yər\ *n*

saw·horse *n* : support for wood being sawed

sax·o·phone \\'saksə,fōn\ *n* : wind instrument with a reed mouthpiece and usu. a bent metal body

say \\'sā\ *vb* **said** \\'sed\; **say·ing** \\'sāiŋ\; **says** \\'sez\ **1** : express in words **2** : state positively ~ *n, pl* **says** \\'sāz\ **1** : expression of opinion **2** : power of decision

say·ing \\'sāiŋ\ *n* : commonly repeated statement

scab \\'skab\ *n* **1** : protective crust over a sore or wound **2** : worker taking a striker's job ~ *vb* **-bb- 1** : become covered with a scab **2** : work as a scab —**scab·by** *adj*

scab·bard \'skabərd\ *n* : sheath for the blade of a weapon

scaf·fold \'skafəld, -,ōld\ *n* **1** : raised platform for workmen **2** : platform on which a criminal is executed

scald \'skȯld\ *vb* **1** : burn with hot liquid or steam **2** : heat to the boiling point

¹scale \'skāl\ *n* : weighing device ~ *vb* **scaled; scal·ing** : weigh

²scale *n* **1** : thin plate esp. on the body of a fish or reptile **2** : thin coating or layer ~ *vb* **scaled; scal·ing** : strip of scales —**scaled** \'skāld\ *adj* —**scale·less** *adj* —**scaly** *adj*

³scale *n* **1** : graduated series **2** : size of a sample (as a model) in proportion to the size of the actual thing **3** : standard of estimation or judgment **4** : series of musical tones ~ *vb* **scaled; scal·ing 1** : climb by a ladder **2** : arrange in a graded series

scal·lion \'skalyən\ *n* : bulbless onion

scal·lop \'skäləp, 'skal-\ *n* **1** : marine mollusk **2** : rounded projection on a border

scalp \'skalp\ *n* : skin and flesh of the head ~ *vb* **1** : remove the scalp from **2** : resell at a greatly increased price —**scalp·er** *n*

scal·pel \'skalpəl\ *n* : surgical knife

scamp \'skamp\ *n* : rascal

scam·per \'skampər\ *vb* : run nimbly —**scamper** *n*

scan \'skan\ *vb* **-nn- 1** : read (verses) so as to show meter **2** : examine closely or hastily **3** : examine with a sensing device —**scan** *n* —**scan·ner** *n*

scan·dal \'skandᵊl\ *n* **1** : disgraceful situation **2** : malicious gossip —**scan·dal·ize** *vb* —**scan·dal·ous** *adj*

scant \'skant\ *adj* : barely sufficient ~ *vb* : stint —**scant·i·ly** *adv* —**scanty** *adj*

scape·goat \'skāp,gōt\ *n* : one that bears the blame for others

scap·u·la \'skapyələ\ *n, pl* **-lae** \-,lē\ *or* **-las** : shoulder blade

scar \'skär\ *n* : mark where a wound has healed —**scar** *vb*

scar·ab \'skarəb\ *n* : large dark beetle or an ornament representing one

scarce \'skers\ *adj* **scarc·er; scarc·est** : lacking in quantity or number —**scarc·i·ty** \'skersətē\ *n*

scarce·ly \'skerslē\ *adv* **1** : barely **2** : almost not

scare \'sker\ *vb* **scared; scar·ing** : frighten ~ *n* : fright —**scary** *adj*

scare·crow \'sker,krō\ *n* : figure for scaring birds from crops

scarf \'skärf\ *n, pl* **scarves** \'skärvz\ *or* **scarfs** : cloth worn about the shoulders or the neck

scar·let \'skärlət\ *n* : bright red color —**scarlet** *adj*

scarlet fever *n* : acute contagious disease marked by fever, sore throat, and red rash

scath·ing \'skāṯẖiŋ\ *adj* : bitterly severe

scat·ter \'skatər\ *vb* **1** : spread about irregularly **2** : disperse

scav·en·ger \'skavənjər\ *n* **1** : person that collects refuse or waste **2** : animal that feeds on decayed matter —**scav·enge** \'skavənj\ *vb*

sce·nar·io \sə'narē,ō, -'när-\ *n, pl* **-i·os 1** : plot of a play or movie **2** : possible sequence of events

scene \'sēn\ *n* **1** : single situation in a play or movie **2** : stage setting **3** : view **4** : display of emotion —**sce·nic** \'sēnik\ *adj*

scen·ery \'sēnərē\ *n, pl* **-er·ies 1** : painted setting for a stage **2** : picturesque view

scent \'sent\ *vb* **1** : smell **2** : fill with odor ~ *n* **1** : odor **2** : sense of smell **3** : perfume —**scent·ed** \'sentəd\ *adj*

scep·ter \'septər\ *n* : staff signifying authority

scep·tic \'skeptik\ *var of* SKEPTIC

sched·ule \'skejül, *esp Brit* 'shedyül\ *n* : list showing sequence of events ~ *vb* **-uled; -ul·ing** : make a schedule of

scheme \'skēm\ *n* **1** : crafty plot **2** : systematic design ~ *vb* **schemed; schem·ing** : form a plot —**sche·mat·ic** \ski'matik\ *adj* —**schem·er** *n*

schism \'sizəm, 'skiz-\ *n* : split —**schis·mat·ic** \siz'matik, skiz-\ *n or adj*

schizo·phre·nia \,skitsə'frēnēə\ *n* : severe mental illness —**schiz·oid** \'skit,sȯid\ *adj or n* —**schizo·phren·ic** \,skitsə'frenik\ *adj or n*

schol·ar \'skälər\ *n* : student or learned person —**schol·ar·ly** *adj*

schol·ar·ship \-,ship\ *n* **1** : qualities or learning of a scholar **2** : money given to a student to pay for education

scho·las·tic \skə'lastik\ *adj* : relating to schools, scholars, or scholarship

¹school \'skül\ *n* **1** : institution for learning **2** : pupils in a school **3** : group with shared beliefs ~ *vb* : teach —**school·boy** *n* —**school·girl** *n* —

school•house n —**school•mate** n —
school•room n —**school•teach•er** n
²**school** n : large number of fish swimming together

schoo•ner \'skünər\ n : sailing ship

sci•ence \'sīəns\ n : branch of systematic study esp. of the physical world —**sci•en•tif•ic** \sīən'tifik\ adj —**sci•en•tif•i•cal•ly** adv —**sci•en•tist** \'sīəntist\ n

scin•til•late \'sint⁰l,āt\ vb -**lat•ed**; -**lat•ing** : flash —**scin•til•la•tion** \,sint⁰l-'āshən\ n

scin•til•lat•ing adj : brilliantly lively or witty

sci•on \'sīən\ n : descendant

scis•sors \'sizərz\ n pl : small shears

scoff \'skäf\ vb : mock —**scoff•er** n

scold \'skōld\ n : person who scolds ~ vb : criticize severely

scoop \'sküp\ n : shovellike utensil ~ vb 1 : take out with a scoop 2 : dig out

scoot \'süt\ vb : move swiftly

scoot•er \'skütər\ n : child's foot-propelled vehicle

¹**scope** \'skōp\ n 1 : extent 2 : room for development

²**scope** n : viewing device (as a microscope)

scorch \'skórch\ vb : burn the surface of

score \'skōr\ n, pl **scores** 1 or pl **score** : twenty 2 : cut 3 : record of points made (as in a game) 4 : debt 5 : music of a composition ~ vb **scored; scor•ing** 1 : record 2 : mark with lines 3 : gain an advantage 4 : assign a grade to 5 : compose a score for —**score•less** adj —**scor•er** n

scorn \'skórn\ n : emotion involving both anger and disgust ~ vb : hold in contempt —**scorn•er** n —**scorn•ful** \-fəl\ adj —**scorn•ful•ly** adv

scor•pi•on \'skórpēən\ n : poisonous long-tailed animal

scoun•drel \'skaúndrəl\ n : villain

¹**scour** \'skaúər\ vb : examine thoroughly

²**scour** vb : rub in order to clean

scourge \'skərj\ n 1 : whip 2 : punishment ~ vb **scourged; scourg•ing** 1 : lash 2 : punish severely

scout \'skaút\ vb : inspect or observe to get information ~ n : person sent out to get information

scow \'skaú\ n : large flat-bottomed boat with square ends

scowl \'skaúl\ vb : make a frowning expression of displeasure —**scowl** n

scrag•gly \'skraglē\ adj : irregular or unkempt

scram \'skram\ vb -**mm-** : go away at once

scram•ble \'skrambəl\ vb -**bled; -bling** 1 : clamber clumsily around 2 : struggle for possession of something 3 : mix together 4 : cook (eggs) by stirring during frying —**scramble** n

¹**scrap** \'skrap\ n 1 : fragment 2 : discarded material ~ vb -**pp-** : get rid of as useless

²**scrap** vb -**pp-** : fight —**scrap** n —**scrap•per** n

scrap•book n : blank book in which mementos are kept

scrape \'skrāp\ vb **scraped; scrap•ing** 1 : remove by drawing a knife over 2 : clean or smooth by rubbing 3 : draw across a surface with a grating sound 4 : damage by contact with a rough surface 5 : gather or proceed with difficulty ~ n 1 : act of scraping 2 : predicament —**scrap•er** n

scratch \'skrach\ vb 1 : scrape or dig with or as if with claws or nails 2 : cause to move gratingly 3 : delete by or as if by drawing a line through ~ n : mark or sound made in scratching —**scratchy** adj

scrawl \'skról\ vb : write hastily and carelessly —**scrawl** n

scraw•ny \'skrónē\ adj -**ni•er; -est** : very thin

scream \'skrēm\ vb : cry out loudly and shrilly ~ n : loud shrill cry

screech \'skrēch\ vb or n : shriek

screen \'skrēn\ n : device or partition used to protect or decorate 2 : surface on which pictures appear (as in movies) ~ vb : shield or separate with or as if with a screen

screw \'skrü\ n 1 : grooved fastening device 2 : propeller ~ vb 1 : fasten by means of a screw 2 : move spirally

screw•driv•er \'skrü,drīvər\ n : tool for turning screws

scrib•ble \'skribəl\ vb -**bled; -bling** : write hastily or carelessly —**scrib•ble** n —**scrib•bler** \-ələr\ n

scribe \'skrīb\ n : one who writes or copies writing

scrimp \'skrimp\ vb : economize greatly

scrip \'skrip\ n 1 : paper money for less than a dollar 2 : certificate entitling one to something (as stock)

script \'skript\ n : text (as of a play)

scrip·ture \'skripchər\ *n* : sacred writings of a religion —**scrip·tur·al** \'skripchərəl\ *adj*

scroll \'skrōl\ *n* **1** : roll of paper for writing a document **2** : spiral or coiled design

scro·tum \'skrōtəm\ *n, pl* **-ta** \-ə\ *or* **-tums** : pouch containing the testes

scrounge \'skraunj\ *vb* **scrounged; scroung·ing** : collect by or as if by foraging

¹scrub \'skrəb\ *n* : stunted tree or shrub or a growth of these —**scrub** *adj* —**scrub·by** *adj*

²scrub *vb* **-bb-** : clean or wash by rubbing —**scrub** *n*

scruff \'skrəf\ *n* : loose skin of the back of the neck

scrump·tious \'skrəmpshəs\ *adj* : delicious

scru·ple \'skrüpəl\ *n* : reluctance due to ethical considerations —**scruple** *vb* —**scru·pu·lous** \-pyələs\ *adj* —**scru·pu·lous·ly** *adv*

scru·ti·ny \'skrüt²nē\ *n, pl* **-nies** : careful inspection —**scru·ti·nize** \-²n,īz\ *vb*

scud \'skəd\ *vb* **-dd-** : move speedily

scuff \'skəf\ *vb* : scratch, scrape, or wear away —**scuff** *n*

scuf·fle \'skəfəl\ *vb* **-fled; -fling** **1** : struggle at close quarters **2** : shuffle one's feet —**scuffle** *n*

scull \'skəl\ *n* **1** : oar **2** : racing shell propelled with sculls ~ *vb* : propel a boat by an oar over the stern

scul·lery \'skələrē\ *n, pl* **-ler·ies** : room for cleaning dishes and cookware

sculpt \'skəlpt\ *vb* : sculpture

sculp·ture \'skəlpchər\ *n* : work of art carved or molded ~ *vb* **-tured; -tur·ing** : form as sculpture —**sculp·tor** \-tər\ *n* —**sculp·tur·al** \-chərəl\ *adj*

scum \'skəm\ *n* : slimy film on a liquid

scur·ri·lous \'skərələs\ *adj* : vulgar or abusive

scur·ry \'skərē\ *vb* **-ried; -ry·ing** : scamper

scur·vy \'skərvē\ *n* : vitamin-deficiency disease

¹scut·tle \'skət²l\ *n* : pail for coal

²scuttle *vb* **-tled; -tling** : sink (a ship) by cutting holes in its bottom

³scuttle *vb* **-tled; -tling** : scamper

scythe \'sīth\ *n* : tool for mowing by hand —**scythe** *vb*

sea \'sē\ *n* **1** : large body of salt water **2** : ocean **3** : rough water —**sea** *adj* —**sea·coast** *n* —**sea·food** *n* —**sea·port** *n* —**sea·shore** *n* —**sea·wa·ter** *n*

sea·bird *n* : bird frequenting the open ocean

sea·board *n* : country's seacoast

sea·far·er \-,farər\ *n* : seaman —**sea·far·ing** \-,farin\ *adj or n*

sea horse *n* : small fish with a horselike head

¹seal \'sēl\ *n* : large sea mammal of cold regions —**seal·skin** *n*

²seal *n* **1** : device for stamping a design **2** : something that closes ~ *vb* **1** : affix a seal to **2** : close up securely **3** : determine finally —**seal·ant** \-ənt\ *n* —**seal·er** *n*

sea lion *n* : large Pacific seal with external ears

seam \'sēm\ *n* **1** : line of junction of 2 edges **2** : layer of a mineral ~ *vb* : join by sewing —**seam·less** *adj*

sea·man \'sēmən\ *n* **1** : one who helps to handle a ship **2** : naval enlisted man ranking next below a petty officer third class —**sea·man·ship** *n*

seaman apprentice *n* : naval enlisted man ranking next below a seaman

seaman recruit *n* : naval enlisted man of the lowest rank

seam·stress \'sēmstrəs\ *n* : woman who sews

seamy \'sēmē\ *adj* **seam·i·er; -est** : unpleasant or sordid

sé·ance \'sā,äns\ *n* : meeting for communicating with spirits

sea·plane *n* : airplane that can take off from and land on the water

sear \'sir\ *vb* : scorch —**sear** *n*

search \'sərch\ *vb* **1** : look through **2** : seek —**search** *n* —**search·er** *n* —**search·light** *n*

sea·sick *adj* : nauseated by the motion of a ship —**sea·sick·ness** *n*

¹sea·son \'sēz²n\ *n* **1** : division of the year **2** : customary time for something —**sea·son·al** \'sēz²nəl\ *adj* —**sea·son·al·ly** *adv*

²season *vb* **1** : add spice to (food) **2** : make strong or fit for use —**sea·son·ing** \-²nin\ *n*

sea·son·able \'sēznəbəl\ *adj* : occurring at a suitable time —**sea·son·ably** \-blē\ *adv*

seat \'sēt\ *n* **1** : place to sit **2** : chair, bench, or stool for sitting on **3** : place that serves as a capital or center ~ *vb*

1 : place in or on a seat 2 : provide seats for

sea·weed n : marine alga

sea·wor·thy adj : strong enough to hold up to a sea voyage

se·cede \si'sēd\ vb **-ced·ed; -ced·ing** : withdraw from a body (as a nation)

se·clude \si'klüd\ vb **-clud·ed; -clud·ing** : shut off alone —**se·clu·sion** \si-'klüzhən\ n

1sec·ond \'sekənd\ adj : next after the 1st ~ n 1 : one that is second 2 : one who assists (as in a duel) —**second, sec·ond·ly** adv

2second n 1 : 60th part of a minute 2 : moment

sec·ond·ary \'sekən,derē\ adj 1 : second in rank or importance 2 : coming after the primary or elementary

sec·ond·hand adj 1 : not original 2 : used before

second lieutenant n : lowest ranking commissioned officer of the army, air force, or marines

se·cret \'sēkrət\ adj 1 : hidden 2 : kept from general knowledge —**se·cre·cy** \-krəsē\ n —**secret** n —**se·cre·tive** \'sēkrətiv, si'krēt-\ adj —**se·cret·ly** adv

sec·re·tar·i·at \,sekrə'terēət\ n : administrative department

sec·re·tary \'sekrə,terē\ n, pl **-tar·ies** 1 : one hired to handle correspondence and other tasks for a superior 2 : official in charge of correspondence or records 3 : head of a government department —**sec·re·tar·i·al** \,sekrə-'terēəl\ adj

1se·crete \si'krēt\ vb **-cret·ed; -cret·ing** : produce as a secretion

2se·crete \si'krēt, 'sēkrət\ vb **-cret·ed; -cret·ing** : hide

se·cre·tion \si'krēshən\ n 1 : process of secreting 2 : product of glandular activity

sect \'sekt\ n : religious group

sec·tar·i·an \sek'terēən\ adj 1 : relating to a sect 2 : limited in character or scope ~ n : member of a sect

sec·tion \'sekshən\ n : distinct part —**sec·tion·al** \-shənəl\ adj

sec·tor \'sektər\ n 1 : part of a circle between 2 radii 2 : distinctive part

sec·u·lar \'sekyələr\ adj 1 : not sacred 2 : not monastic

se·cure \si'kyür\ adj **-cur·er; -est** : free from danger or loss ~ vb 1 : fasten safely 2 : get —**se·cure·ly** adv

se·cu·ri·ty \si'kyùrətē\ n, pl **-ties** 1 : safety 2 : something given to guarantee payment 3 pl : bond or stock certificates

se·dan \si'dan\ n 1 : chair carried by 2 men 2 : enclosed automobile

1se·date \si'dāt\ adj : quiet and dignified —**se·date·ly** adv

2sedate vb **-dat·ed; -dat·ing** : dose with sedatives —**se·da·tion** \si'dāshən\ n

sed·a·tive \'sedətiv\ adj : serving to relieve tension ~ n : sedative drug

sed·en·tary \'sed³n,terē\ adj : characterized by much sitting

sedge \'sej\ n : grasslike marsh plant

sed·i·ment \'sedəmənt\ n : material that settles to the bottom of a liquid or is deposited by water or a glacier —**sed·i·men·ta·ry** \,sedə'mentərē\ adj —**sed·i·men·ta·tion** \-mən'tā-shən, -,men-\ n

se·di·tion \si'dishən\ n : revolution against a government —**se·di·tious** \-əs\ adj

se·duce \si'düs, -'dyüs\ vb **-duced; -duc·ing** 1 : lead astray 2 : entice to sexual intercourse —**se·duc·er** n —**se·duc·tion** \-'dəkshən\ n —**se·duc·tive** \-tiv\ adj

sed·u·lous \'sejələs\ adj : diligent

1see \'sē\ vb **saw** \'sò\; **seen** \'sēn\; **see·ing** 1 : perceive by the eye 2 : have experience of 3 : understand 4 : make sure 5 : meet with or escort

2see n : jurisdiction of a bishop

seed \'sēd\ n, pl **seed** or **seeds** 1 : part by which a plant is propagated 2 : source ~ vb 1 : sow 2 : remove seeds from —**seed·less** adj

seed·ling \-liŋ\ n : young plant grown from seed

seedy \-ē\ adj **seed·i·er; -est** 1 : full of seeds 2 : shabby

seek \'sēk\ vb **sought** \'sòt\; **seek·ing** 1 : search for 2 : try to reach or obtain —**seek·er** n

seem \'sēm\ vb : give the impression of being —**seem·ing·ly** adv

seem·ly \-lē\ adj **seem·li·er; -est** : proper or fit

seep \'sēp\ vb : leak through fine pores or cracks —**seep·age** \'sēpij\ n

seer \'sēər\ n : one who foresees or predicts events

seer·suck·er \'sir,səkər\ n : light puckered fabric

see·saw \'sē,sò\ n : board balanced in the middle —**seesaw** vb

seethe \'sēth\ *vb* **seethed; seeth·ing** : become violently agitated

seg·ment \'segmənt\ *n* : division of a thing —**seg·ment·ed** \-,mentəd\ *adj*

seg·re·gate \'segri,gāt\ *vb* **-gat·ed; -gat·ing 1** : cut off from others **2** : separate by races —**seg·re·ga·tion** \,segri-'gāshən\ *n*

seine \'sān\ *n* : large weighted fishing net ~ *vb* : fish with a seine

seis·mic \'sīzmik, 'sīs-\ *adj* : relating to an earthquake

seis·mo·graph \-mə,graf\ *n* : apparatus for detecting earthquakes

seize \'sēz\ *vb* **seized; seiz·ing** : take by force —**sei·zure** \'sēzhər\ *n*

sel·dom \'seldəm\ *adv* : not often

se·lect \sə'lekt\ *adj* **1** : favored **2** : discriminating ~ *vb* : take by preference —**se·lec·tive** \-'lektiv\ *adj*

se·lec·tion \sə'lekshən\ *n* : act of selecting or thing selected

se·lect·man \si'lekt,man, -mən\ *n* : New England town official

self \'self\ *n, pl* **selves** \'selvz\ : essential person distinct from others

self- *comb form* **1** : oneself or itself **2** : of oneself or itself **3** : by oneself or automatic **4** : to, for, or toward oneself

self-addressed
self-adminis-
tered
self-analysis
self-appointed
self-assertive
self-assurance
self-assured
self-awareness
self-cleaning
self-closing
self-complacent
self-conceit
self-confessed
self-confidence
self-confident
self-contained
self-contempt
self-contradic-
tion
self-contradic-
tory
self-control
self-created
self-criticism
self-defeating

self-defense
self-denial
self-denying
self-destruction
self-destructive
self-determina-
tion
self-determined
self-discipline
self-doubt
self-educated
self-employed
self-employment
self-esteem
self-evident
self-explanatory
self-expression
self-fulfilling
self-fulfillment
self-governing
self-government
self-help
self-image
self-importance
self-important
self-imposed

self-improve-
ment
self-indulgence
self-indulgent
self-inflicted
self-interest
self-love
self-operating
self-pity
self-portrait
self-possessed
self-possession
self-preserva-
tion
self-proclaimed
self-propelled
self-propelling
self-protection

self-reliance
self-reliant
self-respect
self-respecting
self-restraint
self-sacrifice
self-satisfaction
self-satisfied
self-service
self-serving
self-starting
self-styled
self-sufficiency
self-sufficient
self-supporting
self-taught
self-winding

self-cen·tered *adj* : concerned only with one's own self

self-con·scious *adj* : uncomfortably aware of oneself as an object of observation —**self-con·scious·ly** *adv* —**self-con·scious·ness** *n*

self·ish \'selfish\ *adj* : excessively or exclusively concerned with one's own well-being —**self·ish·ly** *adv* —**self·ish·ness** *n*

self·less \'selfləs\ *adj* : unselfish —**self·less·ness** *n*

self-made *adj* : having succeeded by one's own efforts

self-right·teous *adj* : strongly convinced of one's own righteousness

self·same \'self,sām\ *adj* : precisely the same

sell \'sel\ *vb* **sold** \'sōld\; **sell·ing 1** : transfer (property) esp. for money **2** : deal in as a business **3** : be sold —**sell·er** *n*

selves *pl of* SELF

se·man·tic \si'mantik\ *adj* : relating to meaning in language —**se·man·tics** \-iks\ *n sing or pl*

sem·a·phore \'semə,fōr\ *n* **1** : visual signaling apparatus **2** : signaling by flags

sem·blance \'sembləns\ *n* : appearance

se·men \'sēmən\ *n* : male reproductive fluid

se·mes·ter \sə'mestər\ *n* : half a school year

semi- \,semi, 'sem-, -,ī\ *prefix* **1** : half **2** : partial

semi·co·lon \'semi,kōlən\ *n* : punctuation mark ;

semi·con·duc·tor *n* : substance between

a conductor and a nonconductor in ability to conduct electricity —semi·con·duct·ing adj

semi·fi·nal \'adj : being next to the final —semifinal n

semi·for·mal adj : being or suitable for an occasion of moderate formality

sem·i·nal \'semən°l\ adj 1 : relating to seed or semen 2 : causing or influencing later development

sem·i·nar \'semə,när\ n : conference or conferencelike study

sem·i·nary \'semə,nerē\ n, pl -nar·ies : school and esp. a theological school —sem·i·nar·i·an \,semə'nerēən\ n

sen·ate \'senət\ n : upper branch of a legislature —sen·a·tor \-ər\ n —sen·a·to·ri·al \,senə'tōrēəl\ adj

send \'send\ vb sent \'sent\; send·ing 1 : cause to go 2 : propel —send·er n

se·nile \'sēn,īl, 'sen-\ adj : mentally deficient through old age —se·nil·i·ty \si'nilətē\ n

se·nior \'sēnyər\ adj : older or higher ranking —senior n —se·nior·i·ty \,sēn'yörətē\ n

senior chief petty officer n : petty officer in the navy or coast guard ranking next below a master chief petty officer

senior master sergeant n : noncommissioned officer in the air force ranking next below a chief master sergeant

sen·sa·tion \sen'sāshən\ n 1 : bodily feeling 2 : condition of excitement or the cause of it —sen·sa·tion·al \-shənəl\ adj

sense \'sens\ n 1 : meaning 2 : faculty of perceiving something physical 3 : sound mental capacity ~ vb sensed; sens·ing 1 : perceive by the senses 2 : detect automatically —sense·less adj —sense·less·ly adv

sen·si·bil·i·ty \,sensə'bilətē\ n, pl -ties : delicacy of feeling

sen·si·ble \'sensəbəl\ adj 1 : capable of sensing or being sensed 2 : aware or conscious 3 : reasonable —sen·si·bly \-blē\ adv

sen·si·tive \'sensətiv\ adj 1 : subject to excitation by or responsive to stimuli 2 : having power of feeling 3 : easily affected —sen·si·tive·ness n —sen·si·tiv·i·ty \,sensə'tivətē\ n

sen·si·tize \'sensə,tīz\ vb -tized; -tiz·ing : make or become sensitive

sen·sor \'sen,sòr, -sər\ n : device that responds to a physical stimulus

sen·so·ry \'sensərē\ adj : relating to sensation or the senses

sen·su·al \'senchəwəl, -shəwəl\ adj 1 : pleasing the senses 2 : devoted to the pleasures of the senses —sen·su·al·ist n —sen·su·al·i·ty \,senchə'walətē\ n —sen·su·al·ly adv

sen·su·ous \'senchəwəs\ adj : having strong appeal to the senses

sent past of SEND

sen·tence \'sent°ns, -°nz\ n 1 : judgment of a court 2 : grammatically self-contained speech unit ~ vb -tenced; -tenc·ing : impose a sentence on

sen·ten·tious \sen'tenchəs\ adj : using pompous language

sen·tient \'senchēənt\ adj : capable of feeling

sen·ti·ment \'sentəmənt\ n 1 : belief 2 : feeling

sen·ti·men·tal \,sentə'ment°l\ adj : influenced by tender feelings —sen·ti·men·tal·ism n —sen·ti·men·tal·ist n —sen·ti·men·tal·i·ty \-,men'talətē, -,mən-\ n —sen·ti·men·tal·ize \-'men·t°l,īz\ vb —sen·ti·men·tal·ly adv

sen·ti·nel \'sent°nəl\ n : sentry

sen·try \'sentrē\ n, pl -tries : one who stands guard

se·pal \'sēpəl, 'sep-\ n : modified leaf in a flower calyx

sep·a·rate \'sepə,rāt\ vb -rat·ed; -rat·ing 1 : set or keep apart 2 : become divided or detached ~ \'seprət, 'sepə-\ adj 1 : not connected or shared 2 : distinct from each other —sep·a·ra·ble \'sepərəbəl\ adj —sep·a·rate·ly adv —sep·a·ra·tion \,sepə'rāshən\ n —sep·a·ra·tor \'sepə,rātər\ n

se·pia \'sēpēə\ n : brownish gray

Sep·tem·ber \sep'tembər\ n : 9th month of the year having 30 days

se·pul·chre, se·pul·cher \'sepəlkər\ n : burial vault —se·pul·chral \sə-'pəlkrəl\ adj

se·quel \'sēkwəl\ n 1 : consequence or result 2 : continuation of a story

se·quence \'sēkwəns\ n : continuous or connected series —se·quen·tial \si-'kwenchəl\ adj —se·quen·tial·ly adv

se·ques·ter \si'kwestər\ vb : segregate

se·quin \'sēkwən\ n : spangle

se·quoia \si'kwóiə\ n : huge California coniferous tree

se·ra pl of SERUM

ser·aph \'serəf\ n, pl **-a·phim** \-ə,fim\ or **-aphs** : angel —**se·raph·ic** \sə'rafik\ adj

sere \'sir\ adj : dried up or withered

ser·e·nade \,serə'nād\ n : music sung or played esp. to a woman being courted —**serenade** vb

ser·en·dip·i·ty \,serən'dipətē\ n : good luck in finding things not sought for —**ser·en·dip·i·tous** \-əs\ adj

se·rene \sə'rēn\ adj : tranquil —**se·rene·ly** adv —**se·ren·i·ty** \sə'renətē\ n

serf \'sərf\ n : peasant obligated to work the land —**serf·dom** \-dəm\ n

serge \'sərj\ n : twilled woolen cloth

ser·geant \'särjənt\ n : noncommissioned officer (as in the army) ranking next below a staff sergeant

sergeant first class n : noncommissioned officer in the army ranking next below a master sergeant

sergeant major n, pl **sergeants major** or **sergeant majors 1** : noncommissioned officer serving as an enlisted adviser in a headquarters **2** : noncommissioned officer in the marine corps ranking above a first sergeant

se·ri·al \'sirēəl\ adj : being or relating to a series or sequence ~ n : story appearing in parts —**se·ri·al·ly** adv

se·ries \'sirēz\ n, pl **series** : number of things in order

se·ri·ous \'sirēəs\ adj **1** : subdued in appearance or manner **2** : sincere **3** : of great importance —**se·ri·ous·ly** adv —**se·ri·ous·ness** n

ser·mon \'sərmən\ n : lecture on religion or behavior

ser·pent \'sərpənt\ n : snake —**ser·pen·tine** \-pən,tēn, -,tīn\ adj

ser·rat·ed \ser,ātəd\ adj : saw-toothed

se·rum \'sirəm\ n, pl **-rums** or **-ra** \-ə\ : watery part of blood

ser·vant \'sərvənt\ n : person employed for domestic work

serve \'sərv\ vb **served; serv·ing 1** : work through or perform a term of service **2** : be of use **3** : prove adequate **4** : hand out (food or drink) **5** : be of service to —**serv·er** n

ser·vice \'sərvəs\ n **1** : act or means of serving **2** : meeting for worship **3** : branch of public employment or the persons in it **4** : set of dishes or silverware **5** : benefit ~ vb **-viced; -vic·ing** : repair —**service·able** adj —

ser·vice·man \-,man, -mən\ n —**ser·vice·wom·an** n

ser·vile \'sərvəl, -,vīl\ adj : behaving like a slave —**ser·vil·i·ty** \sər'vilətē\ n

serv·ing \'sərviŋ\ n : helping

ser·vi·tude \'sərvə,tüd, -,tyüd\ n : slavery

ses·a·me \'sesəmē\ n : annual herb or its seeds that are used in flavoring

ses·sion \'seshən\ n : meeting

set \'set\ vb **set; set·ting 1** : cause to sit **2** : place **3** : settle, arrange, or adjust **4** : cause to be or do **5** : become fixed or solid **6** : sink below the horizon ~ adj : settled ~ n **1** : group classed together **2** : setting for the scene of a play or film **3** : electronic apparatus **4** : collection of mathematical elements —**set forth** : begin a trip —**set off** vb : set forth —**set out** vb : begin a trip or undertaking —**set up** vb **1** : assemble or erect **2** : cause

set·back n : reverse

set·tee \se'tē\ n : bench or sofa

set·ter \'setər\ n : large long-coated hunting dog

set·ting \'setiŋ\ n : the time, place, and circumstances in which something occurs

set·tle \'setᵊl\ vb **-tled; -tling 1** : come to rest **2** : sink gradually **3** : establish in residence **4** : adjust or arrange **5** : calm **6** : dispose of (as by paying) **7** : decide or agree on —**set·tle·ment** \-mənt\ n —**set·tler** \'setᵊlər\ n

sev·en \'sevən\ n : one more than 6 —**seven** adj or pron —**sev·enth** \-ənth\ adj or adv or n

sev·en·teen \,sevən'tēn\ n : one more than 16 —**seventeen** adj or pron —**sev·en·teenth** \-'tēnth\ adj or n

sev·en·ty \'sevəntē\ n, pl **-ties** : 7 times 10 —**sev·en·ti·eth** \-tēəth\ adj or n —**seventy** adj or pron

sev·er \'sevər\ vb **-ered; -er·ing** : cut off or apart —**sev·er·ance** \'sevrəns, -vərəns\ n

sev·er·al \'sevrəl, 'sevə-\ adj **1** : distinct **2** : consisting of an indefinite but not large number —**sev·er·al·ly** adv

se·vere \sə'vir\ adj **-ver·er; -est 1** : strict **2** : restrained or unadorned **3** : painful or distressing **4** : hard to endure —**se·vere·ly** adv —**se·ver·i·ty** \-'verətē\ n

sew \'sō\ vb **sewed; sewn** \'sōn\ or **sewed; sew·ing** : join or fasten by stitches —**sew·ing** n

sew·age \'süij\ *n* : liquid household waste

¹sew·er \'sōər\ *n* : one that sews

²sew·er \'süər\ *n* : pipe or channel to carry off waste matter

sex \'seks\ *n* **1** : either of 2 divisions into which organisms are grouped according to their reproductive roles or the qualities which differentiate them **2** : copulation —**sexed** \'sekst\ *adj* —**sex·less** *adj* —**sex·u·al** \'sekshəwəl\ *adj* —**sex·u·al·i·ty** \,seksha'walətē\ *n* —**sex·u·al·ly** *adv* —**sexy** *adj*

sex·ism \'sek,sizəm\ *n* : discrimination based on sex and esp. against women —**sex·ist** \sexist\ *adj or n*

sex·tant \'sekstənt\ *n* : instrument for navigation

sex·tet \sek'stet\ *n* **1** : music for 6 performers **2** : group of 6

sex·ton \'sekstən\ *n* : church caretaker

shab·by \'shabē\ *adj* **-bi·er; -est 1** : worn and faded **2** : dressed in worn clothes **3** : not generous or fair —**shab·bi·ly** *adv* —**shab·bi·ness** *n*

shack \'shak\ *n* : hut

shack·le \'shakəl\ *n* : metal device to bind legs or arms ~ *vb* **-led; -ling** : bind or fasten with shackles

shad \'shad\ *n* : Atlantic food fish

shade \'shād\ *n* **1** : space sheltered from the light esp. of the sun **2** : gradation of color **3** : small difference **4** : something that shades ~ *vb* **shad·ed; shad·ing 1** : shelter from light and heat **2** : add shades of color to **3** : show slight differences esp. in color or meaning

shad·ow \'shadō\ *n* **1** : shade cast upon a surface by something blocking light **2** : trace **3** : gloomy influence ~ *vb* **1** : cast a shadow **2** : follow closely —**shad·owy** *adj*

shady \'shādē\ *adj* **shad·i·er; -est 1** : giving shade **2** : of dubious honesty

shaft \'shaft\ *n* **1** : long slender cylindrical part **2** : deep vertical opening (as of a mine)

shag \'shag\ *n* : shaggy tangled mat

shag·gy \'shagē\ *adj* **-gi·er; -est 1** : covered with long hair or wool **2** : not neat and combed

shake \'shāk\ *vb* **shook** \'shúk\; **shak·en** \'shākən\; **shak·ing 1** : move or cause to move quickly back and forth **2** : distress **3** : clasp (hands) as friendly gesture —**shake** *n* —**shak·er** \-ər\ *n*

shake–up *n* : reorganization

shaky \'shākē\ *adj* **shak·i·er; -est** : not sound, stable, or reliable —**shak·i·ly** *adv* —**shak·i·ness** *n*

shale \'shāl\ *n* : stratified rock

shall \'shal\ *vb, past* **should** \'shúd\; *pres sing & pl* **shall** —used as an auxiliary to express a command, futurity, or determination

shal·low \'shalō\ *adj* **1** : not deep **2** : not intellectually profound

shal·lows \-ōz\ *n pl* : area of shallow water

sham \'sham\ *adj or n or vb* : fake

sham·ble \'shambəl\ *vb* **-bled; -bling** : shuffle along —**sham·ble** *n*

sham·bles \'shambəlz\ *n* : state of disorder

shame \'shām\ *n* **1** : distress over guilt or disgrace **2** : cause of shame or regret ~ *vb* **shamed; sham·ing 1** : make ashamed **2** : disgrace —**shame·ful** \-fəl\ *adj* —**shame·ful·ly** \-ē\ *adv* —**shame·less** *adj* —**shame·less·ly** *adv*

shame·faced \'shām'fāst\ *adj* : ashamed

sham·poo \sham'pü\ *vb* : wash one's hair ~ *n, pl* **-poos** : act of or preparation used in shampooing

sham·rock \'sham,räk\ *n* : plant of legend with 3-lobed leaves

shank \'shaŋk\ *n* : part of the leg between the knee and ankle

shan·ty \'shantē\ *n, pl* **-ties** : hut

shape \'shāp\ *vb* **shaped; shap·ing** : form esp. in a particular structure or appearance ~ *n* **1** : distinctive appearance or arrangement of parts **2** : condition —**shape·less** \-ləs\ *adj* —**shape·li·ness** *n* —**shape·ly** *adj*

shard \'shärd\ *n* : broken piece

share \'sher\ *n* **1** : portion belonging to one **2** : interest in a company's stock ~ *vb* **shared; shar·ing** : divide or use with others —**share·hold·er** *n* —**shar·er** *n*

share·crop·per \-,kräpər\ *n* : farmer who works another's land in return for a share of the crop —**share·crop** *vb*

shark \'shärk\ *n* : voracious sea fish

sharp \'shärp\ *adj* **1** : having a good point or cutting edge **2** : alert, clever, or sarcastic **3** : vigorous or fierce **4** : having prominent angles or a sudden change in direction **5** : distinct **6** : higher than the true pitch ~ *adv* : exactly ~ *n* : sharp note —**sharp·ly** *adv* —**sharp·ness** *n*

sharp·en \'shärpən\ *vb* : make sharp — **sharp·en·er** \-ənər\ *n*

sharp·shoot·er *n* : expert marksman — **sharp·shoot·ing** *n*

shat·ter \'shatər\ *vb* : smash or burst into fragments —**shat·ter·proof** \-,prüf\ *adj*

shave \'shāv\ *vb* **shaved; shaved** or **shav·en** \'shāvən\; **shav·ing 1** : cut off with a razor **2** : make bare by cutting the hair from **3** : slice very thin ~ *n* : act or instance of shaving — **shav·er** *n*

shawl \'shȯl\ *n* : loose covering for the head or shoulders

she \'shē\ *pron* : that female one

sheaf \'shēf\ *n, pl* **sheaves** \'shēvz\ : bundle esp. of grain stalks

shear \'shir\ *vb* **sheared; sheared** or **shorn** \'shȯrn\; **shear·ing 1** : trim wool from **2** : cut off with scissorlike action

shears \'shirz\ *n pl* : cutting tool with 2 blades fastened so that the edges slide by each other

sheath \'shēth\ *n, pl* **sheaths** \'shēthz, 'shēths\ : covering (as for a blade)

sheathe \'shēth\ *vb* **sheathed; sheath·ing** : put into a sheath

shed \'shed\ *vb* **shed; shed·ding 1** : give off (as tears or hair) **2** : cause to flow or diffuse ~ *n* : small storage building

sheen \'shēn\ *n* : subdued luster

sheep \'shēp\ *n, pl* **sheep** : domesticated mammal covered with wool —**sheep·skin** *n*

sheep·ish \'shēpish\ *adj* : embarrassed by awareness of a fault

sheer \'shir\ *adj* **1** : pure **2** : very steep **3** : very thin or transparent —**sheer** *adv*

sheet \'shēt\ *n* : broad flat piece (as of cloth or paper)

sheikh, sheik \'shēk, 'shāk\ *n* : Arab chief —**sheikh·dom, sheik·dom** \-dəm\ *n*

shelf \'shelf\ *n, pl* **shelves** \'shelvz\ **1** : flat narrow structure used for storage or display **2** : sandbank or rock ledge

shell \'shel\ *n* **1** : hard or tough outer covering **2** : case holding explosive powder and projectile for a weapon **3** : light racing boat with oars ~ *vb* **1** : remove the shell of **2** : bombard — **shelled** \'sheld\ *adj* —**shell·er** *n*

shel·lac \shə'lak\ *n* : varnish ~ *vb* **-lacked; -lack·ing 1** : coat with shellac **2** : defeat —**shel·lack·ing** *n*

shell·fish *n* : water animal with a shell

shel·ter \'sheltər\ *n* : something that gives protection ~ *vb* : give refuge to

shelve \'shelv\ *vb* **shelved; shelv·ing 1** : place or store on shelves **2** : dismiss or put aside

she·nan·i·gans \shə'nanigənz\ *n pl* : mischievous or deceitful conduct

shep·herd \'shepərd\ *n* : one that tends sheep ~ *vb* : act as a shepherd or guardian

shep·herd·ess \'shepərdəs\ *n* : woman who tends sheep

sher·bet \'shərbət, sher·bert \-bərt\ *n* : fruit-flavored frozen dessert

sher·iff \'sherəf\ *n* : county law officer

sher·ry \'sherē\ *n, pl* **-ries** : type of wine

shield \'shēld\ *n* **1** : broad piece of armor carried on the arm **2** : something that protects —**shield** *vb*

shier *comparative of* SHY

shiest *superlative of* SHY

shift \'shift\ *vb* **1** : change place, position, or direction **2** : get by ~ *n* **1** : loose-fitting dress **2** : an act or instance of shifting **3** : scheduled work period

shift·less \-ləs\ *adj* : lazy

shifty \'shiftē\ *adj* **shift·i·er; -est** : tricky or untrustworthy

shil·le·lagh \shə'lālē\ *n* : club or stick

shil·ling \'shiliŋ\ *n* : former British coin

shil·ly–shal·ly \'shilē,shalē\ *vb* **-shal·lied; -shal·ly·ing 1** : hesitate **2** : dawdle

shim·mer \'shimər\ *vb or n* : glimmer

shin \'shin\ *n* : front part of the leg below the knee ~ *vb* **-nn-** : climb by sliding the body close along

shine \'shīn\ *vb* **shone** \-shōn\ *or* **shined; shin·ing 1** : give off or cause to give off light **2** : be outstanding **3** : polish ~ *n* : brilliance

shin·gle \'shiŋgəl\ *n* **1** : small thin piece used in covering roofs or exterior walls —**shingle** *vb*

shin·gles \'shiŋgəlz\ *n pl* : acute inflammation of spinal nerves

shin·ny \'shinē\ *vb* **-nied; -ny·ing** : shin

shiny \'shīnē\ *adj* **shin·i·er; -est** : bright or polished

ship \'ship\ *n* **1** : large oceangoing vessel **2** : aircraft or spacecraft ~ *vb* **-pp- 1** : put on a ship **2** : transport by carrier —**ship·board** *n* —**ship·build·er** *n* —**ship·per** *n* —**ship·wreck** *n or vb* — **ship·yard** *n*

-ship \,ship\ *n suffix* **1** : state, condition,

or quality **2** : rank or profession **3** : skill **4** : something showing a state or quality

ship·ment \\'shē-mənt\\ n : an act of shipping or the goods shipped

ship·ping \\'shipiṇ\\ n **1** : ships **2** : transportation of goods

ship·shape adj : tidy

shire \\'shīr, *in place-name compounds* ,shir, shər\\ n : British county

shirk \\'shərk\\ vb : evade —**shirk·er** n

shirr \\'shər\\ vb **1** : gather (cloth) by drawing up parallel lines of stitches **2** : bake (eggs) in a dish

shirt \\'shərt\\ n : garment for covering the torso —**shirt·less** adj

shiv·er \\'shivər\\ vb : tremble —**shiver** n —**shiv·ery** adj

shoal \\'shōl\\ n : shallow place (as in a river)

¹shock \\'shäk\\ n : pile of sheaves set up in a field

²shock n **1** : forceful impact **2** : violent mental or emotional disturbance **3** : effect of a charge of electricity **4** : depression of the vital bodily processes ~ vb **1** : strike with surprise, horror, or disgust **2** : subject to an electrical shock —**shock·proof** adj

³shock n : bushy mass of hair

shod·dy \\'shäde\\ adj -**di·er; -est** : poorly made or done —**shod·di·ly** \\'shäd²lē\\ adv —**shod·di·ness** n

shoe \\'shü\\ n **1** : covering for the human foot **2** : horseshoe ~ vb **shod** \\'shäd\\ **shoe·ing** : put horseshoes on —**shoe·lace** n —**shoe·ma·ker** n

shone past of SHINE

shook past of SHAKE

shoot \\'shüt\\ vb **shot** \\'shät\\; **shoot·ing 1** : propel (as an arrow or bullet) **2** : wound or kill with a missile **3** : discharge (a weapon) **4** : drive (as a ball) at a goal **5** : photograph **6** : move swiftly ~ n : new plant growth —**shoot·er** n

shop \\'shäp\\ n : place where things are made or sold ~ vb -**pp**- : visit stores —**shop·keep·er** n —**shop·per** n

shop·lift vb : steal goods from a store —**shop·lift·er** \\-,liftər\\ n

¹shore \\'shōr\\ n : land along the edge of water —**shore·line** n

²shore vb **shored; shor·ing** : prop up ~ n : something that props

shore·bird n : bird of the seashore

shorn past part of SHEAR

short \\'shȯrt\\ adj **1** : not long or tall or

extending far **2** : brief in time **3** : curt **4** : not having or being enough ~ adv : curtly ~ n **1** pl : short drawers or trousers **2** : short circuit —**short·en** \\-³n\\ vb —**short·ly** adv —**short·ness** n

short·age \\'shȯrtij\\ n : deficiency

short·cake n : dessert of biscuit with sweetened fruit

short·change vb : cheat esp. by giving too little change

short circuit n : abnormal electric connection —**short-circuit** vb

short·com·ing n : fault or failing

short·cut \\-,kət\\ n **1** : more direct route than that usu. taken **2** : quicker way of doing something

short·hand n : method of speed writing

short-lived \\'shȯrt'līvd, -,livd\\ adj : of short life or duration

short·sight·ed adj : lacking foresight

shot \\'shät\\ n **1** : act of shooting **2** : attempt (as at making a goal) **3** : small pellets forming a charge **4** : range or reach **5** : photograph **6** : injection of medicine **7** : small serving of liquor —**shot·gun** n

should \\'shud\\ past of SHALL —used as an auxiliary to express condition, obligation, or probability

shoul·der \\'shōldər\\ n **1** : part of the body where the arm joins the trunk **2** : part that projects or lies to the side ~ vb : push with or bear on the shoulder

shoulder blade n : flat triangular bone at the back of the shoulder

shout \\'shau̇t\\ vb : give voice loudly —**shout** n

shove \\'shəv\\ vb **shoved; shov·ing** : push along or away —**shove** n

shov·el \\'shəvəl\\ n : broad tool for digging or lifting ~ vb -**eled** or -**elled; -el·ing** or -**el·ling** : take up or dig with a shovel

show \\'shō\\ vb **showed** \\'shōd\\; **shown** \\'shōn\\ or **showed; show·ing 1** : present to view **2** : reveal or demonstrate **3** : teach **4** : prove **5** : conduct or escort **6** : appear or be noticeable ~ n **1** : demonstrative display **2** : spectacle **3** : theatrical, radio, or television program —**show·case** n

show off vb **1** : display proudly **2** : act so as to attract attention — **show up** vb : arrive

show·down n : decisive confrontation

show·er \\'shau̇ər\\ n **1** : brief fall of rain

2 : bath in which water sprinkles down on the person or a facility for such a bath **3** : party at which someone gets gifts ~ *vb* **1** : rain or fall in a shower **2** : bathe in a shower —**show•ery** *adj*

showy \'shō\ *adj* **show•i•er; -est** : very noticeable or overly elaborate —**show•i•ly** *adv* —**show•i•ness** *n*

shrap•nel \'shrapn³l\ *n. pl* **shrapnel** : metal fragments of a bomb

shred \'shred\ *n* : narrow strip cut or torn off ~ *vb* **-dd-** : cut or tear into shreds

shrew \'shrü\ *n* **1** : scolding woman **2** : mouselike mammal —**shrew•ish** \-ish\ *adj*

shrewd \'shrüd\ *adj* : clever —**shrewd•ly** *adv* —**shrewd•ness** *n*

shriek \'shrēk\ *n* : shrill cry —**shriek** *vb*

shrill \'shril\ *adj* : piercing and high-pitched —**shril•ly** *adv*

shrimp \'shrimp\ *n* : small sea crustacean

shrine \'shrīn\ *n* **1** : tomb of a saint **2** : hallowed place

shrink \'shriŋk\ *vb* **shrank** \'shraŋk\ *or* **shrunk** \'shrəŋk\; **shrunk•en** \'shrəŋkən\; **shrink•ing** : draw back or away **2** : become smaller —**shrink•able** *adj*

shrink•age \'shriŋkij\ *n* : amount lost by shrinking

shriv•el \'shrivəl\ *vb* **-eled** *or* **-elled; -el•ing** *or* **-el•ling** : shrink or wither into wrinkles

shroud \'shraůd\ *n* **1** : cloth put over a corpse **2** : cover or screen ~ *vb* : veil or screen from view

shrub \'shrəb\ *n* : low woody plant —**shrub•by** *adj*

shrub•bery \'shrəbərē\ *n. pl* **-ber•ies** : growth of shrubs

shrug \'shrəg\ *vb* **-gg-** : hunch the shoulders up in doubt, indifference, or uncertainty —**shrug** *n*

shuck \'shək\ *vb* : strip of a shell or husk —**shuck** *n*

shud•der \'shədər\ *vb* : tremble —**shudder** *n*

shuf•fle \'shəfəl\ *vb* **-fled; -fling 1** : mix together **2** : walk with a sliding movement —**shuffle** *n*

shuf•fle•board \'shəfəl‚bōrd\ *n* : game of sliding disks into a scoring area

shun \'shən\ *vb* **-nn-** : keep away from

shunt \'shənt\ *vb* : turn off to one side

shut \'shət\ *vb* **shut; shut•ting 1** : bar passage into or through (as by moving a lid or door) **2** : suspend activity —**shut out** *vb* : exclude —**shut up** *vb* : stop or cause to stop talking

shut–in *n* : invalid

shut•ter \'shətər\ *n* **1** : movable cover for a window **2** : camera part that exposes film

shut•tle \'shət³l\ *n* **1** : part of a weaving machine that carries thread back and forth **2** : vehicle traveling back and forth over a short route ~ *vb* **-tled; -tling** : move back and forth frequently

shut•tle•cock \'shət³l‚käk\ *n* : light conical object used in badminton

shy \'shī\ *adj* **shi•er** *or* **shy•er** \'shīər\; **shi•est** *or* **shy•est** \'shīəst\ **1** : sensitive and hesitant in dealing with others **2** : wary **3** : lacking ~ *vb* **shied; shy•ing** : draw back (as in fright) —**shy•ly** *adv* —**shy•ness** *n*

sib•i•lant \'sibələnt\ *adj* : having the sound of the *s* or the *sh* in *sash* —**sibilant** *n*

sib•ling \'sibliŋ\ *n* : brother or sister

sick \'sik\ *adj* **1** : not in good health **2** : nauseated **3** : relating to or meant for the sick —**sick•bed** *n* —**sick•en** \-ən\ *vb* —**sick•ly** *adj* —**sick•ness** *n*

sick•le \'sikəl\ *n* : curved short-handled blade

side \'sīd\ *n* **1** : part to left or right of an object or the torso **2** : edge or surface away from the center or at an angle to top and bottom or ends **3** : contrasting or opposing position or group —**sid•ed** *adj*

side•board *n* : piece of dining-room furniture for table service

side•burns \-‚bərnz\ *n pl* : whiskers in front of the ears

side•long \'sīd‚loŋ\ *adv or adj* : to or along the side

side•show *n* : minor show at a circus

side•step *vb* **1** : step aside **2** : avoid

side•swipe \-‚swīp\ *vb* : strike with a glancing blow —**sideswipe** *n*

side•track *vb* : lead aside or astray

side•walk *n* : paved walk at the side of a road

side•ways \-‚wāz\ *adv or adj* **1** : to or from the side **2** : with one side to the front

sid•ing \'sīdiŋ\ *n* **1** : short railroad track **2** : material for covering the outside of a building

si•dle \'sīd³l\ *vb* **-dled; -dling** : move sideways or unobtrusively

siege \'sēj\ *n* : persistent attack (as on a fortified place)

si•es•ta \sē'estə\ *n* : midday nap

sieve \'siv\ *n* : utensil with holes to separate particles

sift \'sift\ *vb* 1 : pass through a sieve 2 : examine carefully —**sift•er** *n*

sigh \'sī\ *n* : audible release of the breath (as to express weariness) —**sigh** *vb*

sight \'sīt\ *n* 1 : something seen or worth seeing 2 : process, power, or range of seeing 3 : device used in aiming 4 : view or glimpse ~ *vb* : get sight of —**sight•ed** *adj* —**sight•less** *adj* —**sight-see•ing** *adj* —**sight•seer** \-,sēər\ *n*

sign \'sīn\ *n* 1 : symbol 2 : gesture expressing a command or thought 3 : public notice to advertise or warn 4 : trace ~ *vb* 1 : mark with or make a sign 2 : write one's name on —**sign•er** *n*

sig•nal \'signəl\ *n* 1 : sign of command or warning 2 : electronic transmission ~ *vb* -**naled** *or* -**nalled**; -**nal•ing** *or* -**nal•ling** : communicate or notify by signals ~ *adj* : distinguished

sig•na•to•ry \'signə,tōrē\ *n, pl* -**ries** : person or government that signs jointly with others

sig•na•ture \'signə,chùr\ *n* : one's name written by oneself

sig•net \'signət\ *n* : small seal

sig•nif•i•cance \sig'nifikəns\ *n* 1 : meaning 2 : importance —**sig•nif•i•cant** \-kənt\ *adj* —**sig•nif•i•cant•ly** *adv*

sig•ni•fy \'signə,fī\ *vb* -**fied**; -**fy•ing** 1 : show by a sign 2 : mean —**sig•ni•fi•ca•tion** \,signəfə'kāshən\ *n*

si•lence \'sīləns\ *n* : state of being without sound ~ *vb* -**lenced**; -**lenc•ing** : keep from making noise or sound —**si•lenc•er** *n*

si•lent \'sīlənt\ *adj* : having or producing no sound —**si•lent•ly** *adv*

sil•hou•ette \,silə'wet\ *n* : outline filled in usu. with black —-**ett•ed**; -**ett•ing** : represent by a silhouette

sil•i•ca \'silikə\ *n* : mineral found as quartz and opal

sil•i•con \'silikən, -,kän\ *n* : nonmetallic chemical element

silk \'silk\ *n* 1 : fine strong lustrous protein fiber from moth larvae (**silk-worms** \-,wərmz\) 2 : thread or cloth made from silk —**silk•en** \'silkən\ *adj* —**silky** *adj*

sill \'sil\ *n* : bottom part of a window frame or a doorway

sil•ly \'silē\ *adj* **sil•li•er**; -**est** : foolish or stupid —**sil•li•ness** *n*

si•lo \'sīlō\ *n, pl* -**los** : tall building for storing animal feed

silt \'silt\ *n* : fine earth carried by rivers ~ *vb* : obstruct or cover with silt

sil•ver \'silvər\ *n* 1 : white ductile metallic chemical element 2 : silverware ~ *adj* : having the color of silver —**sil•very** *adj*

sil•ver•ware \-,war\ *n* : eating and serving utensils esp. of silver

sim•i•lar \'simələr\ *adj* : resembling each other in some ways —**sim•i•lar•i•ty** \,simə'larətē\ *n* —**sim•i•lar•ly** \'simələrlē\ *adv*

sim•i•le \'simə,lē\ *n* : comparison of unlike things using *like* or *as*

sim•mer \'simər\ *vb* : stew gently

sim•per \'simpər\ *vb* : give a silly smile —**simper** *n*

sim•ple \'simpəl\ *adj* -**pler**; -**plest** 1 : free from dishonesty, vanity, or pretense 2 : of humble origin or modest position 3 : not complex 4 : lacking education, experience, or intelligence —**sim•ple•ness** *n* —**sim•ply** \-plē\ *adv*

sim•ple•ton \'simpəltən\ *n* : fool

sim•plic•i•ty \sim'plisətē\ *n* : state or fact of being simple

sim•pli•fy \'simplə,fī\ *vb* -**fied**; -**fy•ing** : make easier —**sim•pli•fi•ca•tion** \,simpləfə'kāshən\ *n*

sim•u•late \'simyə,lāt\ *vb* -**lat•ed**; -**lat•ing** : create the effect or appearance of —**sim•u•la•tion** \,simyə'lāshən\ *n* —**sim•u•la•tor** \'simyə,lātər\ *n*

si•mul•ta•ne•ous \,sīməl'tānēəs\ *adj* : occurring or operating at the same time —**si•mul•ta•ne•ous•ly** *adv* —**si•mul•ta•ne•ous•ness** *n*

sin \'sin\ *n* : offense against God ~ *vb* -**nn**- : commit a sin —**sin•ful** \-fəl\ *adj* —**sin•less** *adj* —**sin•ner** *n*

since \'sins\ *adv* 1 : from a past time until now 2 : backward in time ~ *prep* 1 : in the period after 2 : continuously from ~ *conj* 1 : from the time when 2 : because

sin•cere \sin'sir\ *adj* -**cer•er**; -**cer•est** : genuine or honest —**sin•cere•ly** *adv* —**sin•cer•i•ty** \-'serətē\ *n*

si•ne•cure \'sīni,kyùr, 'sini-\ *n* : well-paid job that requires little work

sin·ew \'sinyü\ n 1 : tendon 2 : physical strength —**sin·ewy** adj

sing \'siŋ\ vb **sang** \'saŋ\ or **sung** \'səŋ\; **sung**; **sing·ing** : produce musical tones with the voice —**sing·er** n

singe \'sinj\ vb **singed**; **singe·ing** : scorch lightly

sin·gle \'siŋgəl\ adj 1 : one only 2 : unmarried ~ n : separate one —**sin·gle·ness** n —**sin·gly** \-glē\ adv —**single out** vb : select or set aside

sin·gu·lar \'siŋgyələr\ adj 1 : relating to a word form denoting one 2 : outstanding or superior 3 : queer —**singular** n —**sin·gu·lar·i·ty** \,siŋgyə-'larətē\ n —**sin·gu·lar·ly** \'siŋgyə-lərlē\ adv

sin·is·ter \'sinəstər\ adj : threatening evil

sink \'siŋk\ vb **sank** \'saŋk\ or **sunk** \'səŋk\; **sunk**; **sink·ing** 1 : submerge or descend 2 : grow worse 3 : make by digging or boring 4 : invest ~ n : basin with a drain

sink·er \'siŋkər\ n : weight to sink a fishing line

sin·u·ous \'sinyəwəs\ adj : winding in and out —**sin·u·os·i·ty** \,sinyə-'wäsətē\ n —**sin·u·ous·ly** adv

si·nus \'sīnəs\ n : skull cavity usu. connecting with the nostrils

sip \'sip\ vb **-pp-** : drink in small quantities —**sip** n

si·phon \'sīfən\ n : tube that draws liquid by suction —**siphon** vb

sir \'sər\ n 1 —used before the first name of a knight or baronet 2 —used as a respectful form of address

sire \'sīr\ n : father ~ vb **sired**; **sir·ing** : beget

si·ren \'sīrən\ n 1 : seductive woman 2 : wailing warning whistle

sir·loin \'sər,lȯin\ n : cut of beef

sirup var of SYRUP

si·sal \'sīsəl, -zəl\ n : strong rope fiber

sis·sy \'sisē\ n, pl **-sies** : timid or effeminate boy

sis·ter \'sistər\ n : female sharing one or both parents with another person —**sis·ter·hood** n,hüd\ n —**sis·ter·ly** adj

sis·ter-in-law n, pl **sis·ters-in-law** : sister of one's spouse or wife of one's brother

sit \'sit\ vb **sat** \'sat\; **sit·ting** 1 : rest on the buttocks or haunches 2 : roost 3 : hold a session 4 : pose for a portrait 5 : have a location 6 : rest or fix in place —**sit·ter** n

site \'sīt\ n : place

sit·u·at·ed \'sichə,wātəd\ adj : located

sit·u·a·tion \,sichə'wāshən\ n 1 : location 2 : condition 3 : job

six \'siks\ n : one more than 5 —**six** adj or pron —**sixth** \'siksth\ adj or adv or n

six·teen \siks'tēn\ n : one more than 15 —**sixteen** adj or pron —**six·teenth** \-'tēnth\ adj or n

six·ty \'sikstē\ n, pl **-ties** : 6 times 10 —**six·ti·eth** \-tēəth\ adj or n —**sixty** adj or pron

siz·able, size·able \'sīzəbəl\ adj : quite large —**siz·ably** \-blē\ adv

size \'sīz\ n : measurement of the amount of space something takes up —**siz**- : grade according to size

siz·zle \'sizəl\ vb **-zled**; **-zling** : fry with a hissing sound —**sizzle** n

skate \'skāt\ n 1 : metal runner on a shoe for gliding over ice 2 : roller skate —**skate** vb —**skat·er** n

skein \'skān\ n : loosely twisted quantity of yarn or thread

skel·e·ton \'skelətᵊn\ n : bony framework —**skel·e·tal** \-ətᵊl\ adj

skep·tic \'skeptik\ n : one who is critical or doubting —**skep·ti·cal** \-tikəl\ adj —**skep·ti·cism** \-tə,sizəm\ n

sketch \'skech\ n 1 : rough drawing 2 : short story or essay —**sketch** vb —**sketchy** adj

skew·er \'skyüər\ n : long pin for holding roasting meat —**skewer** vb

ski \'skē\ n, pl **skis** : long strip for gliding over snow or water —**ski** vb —**ski·er** n

skid \'skid\ n 1 : plank for supporting something or on which it slides 2 : act of skidding ~ vb **-dd-** : slide sideways

skiff \'skif\ n : small boat

skill \'skil\ n : developed or learned ability —**skilled** \'skild\ adj —**skill·ful** \-fəl\ adj —**skill·ful·ly** \-fal\ adv

skil·let \'skilət\ n : pan for frying

skim \'skim\ vb **-mm-** 1 : take off from the top of a liquid 2 : read or move over swiftly ~ adj : having the cream removed —**skim·mer** n

skimp \'skimp\ vb : give too little of something —**skimpy** adj

skin \'skin\ n 1 : outer layer of an animal body 2 : rind ~ vb **-nn-** : take the skin from —**skin·less** adj —**skinned** adj —**skin·tight** adj

skin diving *n* : sport of swimming under water with a face mask and flippers

skin-flint \'skin,flint\ *n* : stingy person

skin-ny \'skinē\ *adj* -ni-er; -est : very thin

skip \'skip\ *vb* -pp- **1** : move with leaps **2** : read past or ignore —**skip** *n*

skip-per \'skipər\ *n* : ship's master — **skipper** *vb*

skir-mish \'skərmish\ *n* : minor combat —**skirmish** *vb*

skirt \'skərt\ *n* : garment or part of a garment that hangs below the waist ~ *vb* : pass around the edge of

skit \'skit\ *n* : brief usu. humorous play

skit-tish \'skitish\ *adj* : easily frightened

skulk \'skəlk\ *vb* : move furtively

skull \'skəl\ *n* : bony case that protects the brain

skunk \'skəŋk\ *n* : mammal that can forcibly eject an ill-smelling fluid

sky \'skī\ *n, pl* **skies** **1** : upper air **2** : heaven —**sky-line** *n* —**sky-ward** \-wərd\ *adv or adj*

sky-lark \'skī,lärk\ *n* : European lark noted for its song

sky-light *n* : window in a roof or ceiling

sky-rock-et *n* : shooting firework ~ *vb* : rise suddenly

sky-scrap-er \-,skrāpər\ *n* : very tall building

slab \'slab\ *n* : thick slice

slack \'slak\ *adj* **1** : careless **2** : not taut **3** : not busy ~ *n* **1** : part hanging loose **2** *pl* : casual trousers —**slack-en** *vb* —**slack-ly** *adv* —**slack-ness** *n*

slag \'slag\ *n* : waste from melting of ores

slain *past part of* SLAY

slake \'slāk\ *vb* **slaked; slak-ing** : quench

slam \'slam\ *n* : heavy jarring impact ~ *vb* -mm- : shut, strike, or throw violently and loudly

slan-der \'slandər\ *n* : malicious gossip ~ *vb* : hurt (someone) with slander —**slan-der-er** *n* —**slan-der-ous** *adj*

slang \'slaŋ\ *n* : informal nonstandard vocabulary —**slangy** *adj*

slant \'slant\ *vb* **1** : slope ~ *n* : present with a special viewpoint ~ *n* : sloping direction, line, or plane

slap \'slap\ *vb* -pp- : strike sharply with the open hand —**slap** *n*

slash \'slash\ *vb* **1** : cut with sweeping strokes **2** : reduce sharply ~ *n* : gash

slat \'slat\ *n* : thin narrow flat strip

slate \'slāt\ *n* **1** : dense fine-grained layered rock **2** : roofing tile or writing tablet of slate **3** : list of candidates ~ *vb* **slat-ed; slat-ing** : designate

slat-tern \'slatərn\ *n* : untidy woman — **slat-tern-ly** *adj*

slaugh-ter \'slotər\ *n* **1** : butchering of livestock for market **2** : great and cruel destruction of lives ~ *vb* : commit slaughter upon —**slaugh-ter-house** *n*

slave \'slāv\ *n* : one owned and forced into service by another ~ *vb* **slaved; slav-ing** : work as or like a slave —**slave** *adj* —**slav-ery** \'slāvərē\ *n*

sla-ver \'slavər, 'slāv-\ *vb or n* : slobber

slav-ish \'slāvish\ *adj* : of or like a slave —**slav-ish-ly** *adv*

slay \'slā\ *vb* **slew** \'slü\; **slain** \'slān\; **slay-ing** : kill —**slay-er** *n*

slea-zy \'slēzē, 'slā-\ *adj* -zi-er; -est : shabby or shoddy

sled \'sled\ *n* : vehicle on runners —**sled** *vb*

¹sledge \'slej\ *n* : sledgehammer

²sledge *n* : heavy sled

sledge-ham-mer *n* : heavy long-handled hammer —**sledgehammer** *adj or vb*

sleek \'slēk\ *adj* : smooth or glossy — **sleek** *vb*

sleep \'slēp\ *n* : natural suspension of consciousness ~ *vb* **slept** \'slept\; **sleep-ing** : rest in a state of sleep —**sleep-er** *n* —**sleep-less** *adj* —**sleep-walk-er** *n*

sleepy \'slēpē\ *adj* **sleep-i-er; -est** **1** : ready for sleep **2** : quietly inactive —**sleep-i-ly** \'slēpəlē\ *adv* —**sleep-i-ness** \-pēnəs\ *n*

sleet \'slēt\ *n* : frozen rain —**sleet** *vb* — **sleety** *adj*

sleeve \'slēv\ *n* : part of a garment for the arm —**sleeve-less** *adj*

sleigh \'slā\ *n* : horse-drawn sled with seats ~ *vb* : drive or ride in a sleigh

sleight of hand : skillful manual manipulation or a trick requiring it

slen-der \'slendər\ *adj* **1** : thin esp. in physique **2** : scanty

sleuth \'slüth\ *n* : detective

slew \'slü\ *past of* SLAY

slice \'slīs\ *n* : thin flat piece ~ *vb* **sliced; slic-ing** : cut a slice from

slick \'slik\ *adj* **1** : very smooth **2** : clever —**slick** *vb*

slick-er \'slikər\ *n* : raincoat

slide \'slīd\ *vb* **slid** \'slid\; **slid-ing** \'slīdiŋ\ : move smoothly along a surface ~ *n* **1** : act of sliding **2** : surface

on which something slides **3**
: transparent picture for projection

slier comparative of SLY

sliest superlative of SLY

slight \'slīt\ adj **1** : slender **2** : frail **3**
: small in degree ~ vb **1** : ignore or
treat as unimportant —**slight** n —
slight·ly adv

slim \'slim\ adj **-mm- 1** : slender **2**
: scanty ~ vb **-mm- :** make or become
slender

slime \'slīm\ n : dirty slippery film (as
on water) —**slimy** adj

sling \'slin̄\ vb **slung** \'slən̄\; **sling·ing**
: hurl with or as if with a sling ~ n **1**
: strap for swinging and hurling
stones **2** : looped strap or bandage to
lift or support

sling·shot n : forked stick with elastic
bands for shooting pebbles

slink \'slin̄k\ vb **slunk** \'slən̄k\; **slink·ing** : move stealthily or sinuously —
slinky adj

¹slip \'slip\ vb **-pp- 1** : escape quietly or
secretly **2** : slide along smoothly **3**
: make a mistake **4** : to pass without
being noticed or done **5** : fall off from
a standard ~ n **1** : ship's berth **2**
: sudden mishap **3** : mistake **4**
: woman's undergarment

²slip n **1** : plant shoot **2** : small strip (as
of paper)

slip·per \'slipər\ n : shoe that slips on
easily

slip·pery \'slipərē\ adj **-peri·er; -est 1**
: slick enough to slide on **2** : tricky
—**slip·peri·ness** n

slip·shod \'slip,shäd\ adj : careless

slit \'slit\ vb **slit; slit·ting** : make a slit
in ~ n **1** : long narrow cut

slith·er \'slithər\ vb : glide along like a
snake —**slith·ery** adj

sliv·er \'slivər\ n : splinter

slob \'släb\ n : untidy person

slob·ber \'släbər\ vb : dribble saliva —
slobber n

slo·gan \'slōgən\ n : word or phrase expressing the aim of a cause

sloop \'slüp\ n : one-masted sailboat

slop \'släp\ n : food waste for animal
feed ~ vb **-pp- :** spill

slope \'slōp\ vb **sloped; slop·ing**
: deviate from the vertical or horizontal ~ n : upward or downward slant

slop·py \'släpē\ adj **-pi·er; -est 1**
: muddy **2** : untidy

slot \'slät\ n : narrow opening

sloth \'slöth, 'slóth\ n, pl **sloths** \with ths

or thz\ **1** : laziness **2** : slow-moving
mammal —**sloth·ful** adj

slouch \'slaúch\ n **1** : drooping posture
2 : lazy or incompetent person ~ vb
: walk or stand with a slouch

¹slough \'slü, 'slaú\ n : swamp

²slough \'sləf\, **sluff** vb : cast off (old
skin)

slov·en·ly \'sləvənlē\ adj : untidy

slow \'slō\ adj **1** : sluggish or stupid **2**
: moving, working, or happening at
less than the usual speed ~ vb **1**
: make slow **2** : go slower —**slow** adv
—**slow·ly** adv —**slow·ness** n

sludge \'sləj\ n : slushy mass (as of
treated sewage)

slug \'sləg\ n **1** : mollusk related to the
snails **2** : bullet **3** : metal disk ~ vb
-gg- : strike forcibly —**slug·ger** n

slug·gish \'sləgish\ adj : slow in movement or flow —**slug·gish·ly** adv —
slug·gish·ness n

sluice \'slüs\ n : channel for water ~ vb
sluiced; sluic·ing : wash in running
water

slum \'sləm\ n : thickly populated area
marked by poverty

slum·ber \'sləmbər\ vb or n : sleep

slump \'sləmp\ vb **1** : sink suddenly **2**
: slouch —**slump** n

slung past of SLING

slunk past of SLINK

¹slur \'slər\ vb **-rr- :** run (words or
notes) together —**slur** n

²slur n : malicious or insulting remark

slurp \'slərp\ vb : eat or drink noisily —
slurp n

slush \'sləsh\ n : partly melted snow —
slushy adj

slut \'slət\ n **1** : untidy woman **2** : lewd
woman —**slut·tish** adj

sly \'slī\ adj **sli·er** \'slīər\; **sli·est** \'slīəst\
: given to or showing secrecy and de-
ception —**sly·ly** adv —**sly·ness** n

¹smack \'smak\ n : characteristic flavor
~ vb : have a taste or hint

²smack vb **1** : move (the lips) so as to
make a sharp noise **2** : kiss or slap
with a loud noise ~ n **1** : sharp noise
made by the lips **2** : noisy slap

³smack adv : squarely and sharply

⁴smack n : fishing boat

small \'smól\ adj **1** : little in size or
amount **2** : few in number **3** : trivial
—**small·ish** adj —**small·ness** n

small·pox \'smól,päks\ n : contagious
virus disease

smart \'smärt\ vb **1** : cause or feel stinging pain **2** : endure distress ~ *adj* **1** : intelligent or resourceful **2** : stylish —**smart** *n* —**smart•ly** *adv* —**smart•ness** *n*

smash \'smash\ *vb* : break or be broken into pieces ~ *n* **1** : smashing blow **2** : act or sound of smashing

smat•ter•ing \'smatəriŋ\ *n* **1** : superficial knowledge **2** : small scattered number or amount

smear \'smir\ *n* : greasy stain ~ *vb* **1** : spread (something sticky) **2** : smudge **3** : slander

smell \'smel\ *vb* **smelled** \'smeld\ *or* **smelt** \'smelt\; **smell•ing 1** : perceive the odor of **2** : have or give off an odor ~ *n* **1** : sense by which one perceives odor **2** : odor —**smelly** *adj*

¹**smelt** \'smelt\ *n, pl* **smelts** *or* **smelt** : small food fish

²**smelt** *vb* : melt or fuse (ore) in order to separate the metal —**smelt•er** *n*

smile \'smīl\ *n* : facial expression with the mouth turned up usu. to show pleasure —**smile** *vb*

smirk \'smərk\ *vb* : wear a conceited smile —**smirk** *n*

smite \'smīt\ *vb* **smote** \'smōt\; **smit•ten** \'smit°n\ *or* **smote; smit•ing** \'smītiŋ\ **1** : strike heavily or kill **2** : affect strongly

smith \'smith\ *n* : worker in metals and esp. a blacksmith

smithy \'smithē\ *n, pl* **smith•ies** : a smith's workshop

smock \'smäk\ *n* : loose dress or protective coat

smog \'smäg, 'smog\ *n* : fog and smoke —**smog•gy** *adj*

smoke \'smōk\ *n* : sooty gas from burning ~ *vb* **smoked; smok•ing 1** : give off smoke **2** : inhale the fumes of burning tobacco **3** : cure (as meat) with smoke —**smoke•less** *adj* —**smok•er** *n* —**smoky** *adj*

smoke•stack *n* : chimney through which smoke is discharged

smol•der, smoul•der \'smōldər\ *vb* **1** : burn and smoke without flame **2** : be suppressed but active —**smolder** *n*

smooth \'smüth\ *adj* **1** : having a surface without irregularities **2** : not jarring or jolting ~ *vb* : make smooth —**smooth•ly** *adv* —**smooth•ness** *n*

smor•gas•bord \'smórgəs,bȯrd\ *n* : buffet consisting of many foods

smoth•er \'sməthər\ *vb* **1** : kill by depriving of air **2** : cover thickly

smudge \'sməj\ *vb* **smudged; smudging** : soil or blur by rubbing ~ *n* **1** : thick smoke **2** : dirty spot

smug \'sməg\ *adj* **-gg-** : content in one's own virtue or accomplishment —**smug•ly** *adv* —**smug•ness** *n*

smug•gle \'sməgəl\ *vb* **-gled; -gling** : import or export secretly or illegally —**smug•gler** \'sməglər\ *n*

smut \'smət\ *n* **1** : something that soils **2** : indecent language or matter **3** : disease of plants caused by fungi —**smut•ty** *adj*

snack \'snak\ *n* : light meal

snag \'snag\ *n* : unexpected difficulty ~ *vb* **-gg-** : become caught on something that sticks out

snail \'snāl\ *n* : small mollusk with a spiral shell

snake \'snāk\ *n* : long-bodied limbless reptile —**snake•bite** *n*

snap \'snap\ *vb* **-pp- 1** : bite at something **2** : utter angry words **3** : break suddenly with a sharp sound ~ *n* **1** : act or sound of snapping **2** : fastening that closes with a click **3** : something easy to do —**snap•per** *n* —**snap•pish** *adj* —**snap•py** *adj*

snap•drag•on *n* : garden plant with spikes of showy flowers

snap•shot \'snap,shät\ *n* : casual photograph

snare \'snar\ *n* : trap for catching game ~ *vb* : capture or hold with or as if with a snare

¹**snarl** \'snärl\ *n* : tangle ~ *vb* : cause to become knotted

²**snarl** *vb or n* : growl

snatch \'snach\ *vb* **1** : try to grab something suddenly **2** : seize or take away suddenly ~ *n* **1** : act of snatching **2** : something brief or fragmentary

sneak \'snēk\ *vb* : move or take in a furtive manner ~ *n* : one who acts in a furtive manner —**sneak•i•ly** \'snē-kəlē\ *adv* —**sneak•ing•ly** *adv* —**sneaky** *adj*

sneak•er \'snēkər\ *n* : sports shoe

sneer \'snir\ *vb* : smile scornfully —**sneer** *n*

sneeze \'snēz\ *vb* **sneezed; sneez•ing** : force the breath out with sudden and involuntary violence —**sneeze** *n*

snick•er \'snikər\ *n* : partly suppressed laugh —**snicker** *vb*

snide \'snīd\ *adj* : subtly ridiculing

sniff \'snif\ *vb* **1** : draw air audibly up

the nose 2 : detect by smelling —**sniff** n

snip \snip\ n : fragment snipped off ~ vb -**pp**- : cut off by bits

¹**snipe** \snīp\ n, pl **snipes** or **snipe** : game bird of marshy areas

²**snipe** vb **sniped; snip·ing** : shoot at an enemy from a concealed position —**snip·er** n

snips \snips\ n pl : scissorslike tool

sniv·el \snivəl\ vb -**eled** or -**elled**; -**el·ing** or -**el·ling** 1 : have a running nose 2 : whine

snob \snäb\ n : one who acts superior to others —**snob·bery** \-ərē\ n —**snob·bish** adj —**snob·bish·ly** adv —**snob·bish·ness** n

snoop \snüp\ vb : pry in a furtive way ~ n : prying person

snooze \snüz\ vb **snoozed; snooz·ing** : take a nap —**snooze** n

snore \snōr\ vb **snored; snor·ing** : breathe with a hoarse noise while sleeping —**snore** n

snort \snȯrt\ vb : force air noisily through the nose —**snort** n

snout \snaút\ n : long projecting muzzle (as of a swine)

snow \snō\ n : crystals formed from water vapor ~ vb : fall as snow —**snow·ball** n —**snow·bank** n —**snow·drift** n —**snow·fall** n —**snow·plow** n —**snow·storm** n —**snowy** adj

snow·shoe n : frame of wood strung with thongs for walking on snow

snub \snəb\ vb -**bb**- : ignore or avoid through disdain —**snub** n

¹**snuff** \snəf\ vb : put out (a candle) —**snuff·er** n

²**snuff** vb : draw forcibly into the nose ~ n : pulverized tobacco

snug \snəg\ adj -**gg**- 1 : warm, secure, and comfortable 2 : fitting closely —**snug·ly** adv —**snug·ness** n

snug·gle \snəgəl\ vb -**gled; -gling** : curl up comfortably

so \sō\ adv 1 : in the manner or to the extent indicated 2 : in the same way 3 : therefore 4 : finally 5 : thus ~ conj : for that reason

soak \sōk\ vb 1 : lie in a liquid 2 : absorb ~ n : act of soaking

soap \sōp\ n : cleaning substance —**soap** vb —**soapy** adj

soar \sōr\ vb : fly upward on or as if on wings

sob \säb\ vb -**bb**- : weep with convulsive heavings of the chest —**sob** n

so·ber \sōbər\ adj 1 : not drunk 2 : serious or solemn —**so·ber·ly** adv

so·bri·ety \sə'brīətē, sō-\ n : quality or state of being sober

soc·cer \säkər\ n : game played by kicking a ball

so·cia·ble \sōshəbəl\ adj : friendly —**so·cia·bil·i·ty** \,sōshə'bilətē\ n —**so·cia·bly** \sōshəblē\ adv

so·cial \sōshəl\ adj 1 : relating to pleasant companionship 2 : naturally living or growing in groups 3 : relating to human society ~ n : social gathering —**so·cial·ly** adv

so·cial·ism \sōshə,lizəm\ n : social system based on government control of the production and distribution of goods —**so·cial·ist** \sōshəlist\ n or adj —**so·cial·is·tic** \,sōshə'listik\ adj

so·cial·ize \sōshə,līz\ vb -**ized; -iz·ing** 1 : regulate by socialism 2 : adapt to social needs 3 : participate in a social gathering —**so·cial·i·za·tion** \,sōshələ'zāshən\ n

social work n : services concerned with aiding the poor and socially maladjusted —**social worker** n

so·ci·ety \sə'sīətē\ n, pl -**et·ies** 1 : companionship 2 : community life 3 : rich or fashionable class 4 : voluntary group

so·ci·ol·o·gy \,sōsē'äləjē\ n : study of social relationships —**so·ci·o·log·i·cal** \-ə'läjikəl\ adj —**so·ci·ol·o·gist** \-'äləjist\ n

¹**sock** \säk\ n, pl **socks** or **sox** : short stocking

²**sock** vb or n : punch

sock·et \säkət\ n : hollow part that holds something

sod \säd\ n : turf ~ vb -**dd**- : cover with sod

so·da \sōdə\ n 1 : carbonated water or a soft drink 2 : ice cream drink made with soda

sod·den \säd°n\ adj 1 : lacking spirit 2 : soaked or soggy

so·di·um \sōdēəm\ n : soft waxy silver white metallic chemical element

so·fa \sōfə\ n : wide padded chair

soft \sȯft\ adj 1 : not hard, rough, or harsh 2 : nonalcoholic —**soft·en** \sȯfən\ vb —**soft·en·er** \-ənər\ n —**soft·ly** adv —**soft·ness** n

soft·ball n : game like baseball

soft·ware \sȯft,war\ n : computer programs

sog·gy \'säge\ *adj* **-gi·er; -est** : heavy with moisture —**sog·gi·ness** \-ēnəs\ *n*

¹soil \'soil\ *vb* : make or become dirty ~ *n* : embedded dirt

²soil *n* : loose surface material of the earth

so·journ \'sō,jərn, sō'jərn\ *n* : temporary stay ~ *vb* : reside temporarily

so·lace \'säləs\ *n or vb* : comfort

so·lar \'sōlər\ *adj* : relating to the sun or the energy in sunlight

sold *past of* SELL

sol·der \'sädər, 'sod-\ *n* : metallic alloy melted to join metallic surfaces ~ *vb* : cement with solder

sol·dier \'sōljər\ *n* : person in military service ~ *vb* : serve as a soldier — **sol·dier·ly** *adj or adv*

¹sole \'sōl\ *n* : bottom of the foot or a shoe —**soled** *adj*

²sole *n* : flatfish caught for food

³sole *adj* : single or only —**sole·ly** *adv*

sol·emn \'säləm\ *adj* **1** : dignified and ceremonial **2** : highly serious —**so·lem·ni·ty** \sə'lemnətē\ *n* —**sol·emn·ly** *adv*

so·lic·it \sə'lisət\ *vb* : ask for —**so·lic·i·ta·tion** \-,lisə'tāshən\ *n*

so·lic·i·tor \sə'lisətər\ *n* **1** : one that solicits **2** : lawyer

so·lic·i·tous \sə'lisətəs\ *adj* : showing or expressing concern —**so·lic·i·tous·ly** *adv* —**so·lic·i·tude** \sə'lisə,tüd, -,tyüd\ *n*

sol·id \'säləd\ *adj* **1** : not hollow **2** : having 3 dimensions **3** : hard **4** : of good quality **5** : of one character ~ *n* **1** : 3-dimensional figure **2** : substance in solid form —**solid** *adv* —**so·lid·i·ty** \sə'lidətē\ *n* —**sol·id·ly** *adv* —**sol·id·ness** *n*

sol·i·dar·i·ty \sälə'darətē\ *n* : unity of purpose

so·lid·i·fy \sə'lidə,fī\ *vb* **-fied; -fy·ing** : make or become solid —**so·lid·i·fi·ca·tion** \-,lidəfə'kāshən\ *n*

so·lil·o·quy \sə'liləkwē\ *n, pl* **-quies** : dramatic monologue —**so·lil·o·quize** \-,kwīz\ *vb*

sol·i·taire \'sälə,tar\ *n* **1** : solitary gem **2** : card game for one person

sol·i·tary \-,terē\ *adj* **1** : alone **2** : secluded **3** : single

sol·i·tude \-,tüd, -,tyüd\ *n* : state of being alone

so·lo \'sōlō\ *n, pl* **-los** : performance by only one person ~ *adv* : alone —**solo** *adj or vb* —**so·lo·ist** *n*

sol·stice \'sälstəs\ *n* : time of the year when the sun is farthest north or south of the equator

sol·u·ble \'sälyəbəl\ *adj* **1** : capable of being dissolved **2** : capable of being solved —**sol·u·bil·i·ty** \,sälyə'bilətē\ *n*

so·lu·tion \sə'lüshən\ *n* **1** : answer to a problem **2** : homogeneous liquid mixture

solve \'sälv\ *vb* **solved; solv·ing** : find a solution for —**solv·able** *adj*

sol·vent \'sälvənt\ *adj* **1** : able to pay all debts **2** : dissolving or able to dissolve ~ *n* : substance that dissolves or disperses another substance —**sol·ven·cy** \-vənsē\ *n*

som·ber, som·bre \'sämbər\ *adj* **1** : dark **2** : grave —**som·ber·ly** *adv*

som·bre·ro \säm'brerō\ *n, pl* **-ros** : broad-brimmed hat

some \'səm\ *adj* **1** : one unspecified **2** : unspecified or indefinite number of **3** : at least a few or a little ~ *pron* : a certain number or amount

-some \səm\ *adj suffix* : characterized by a thing, quality, state, or action

some·body \'səmbədē, -,bäd-\ *pron* : some person

some·day \'səm,dā\ *adv* : at some future time

some·how \-,haü\ *adv* : by some means

some·one \-,wən\ *pron* : some person

som·er·sault \'səmər,solt\ *n* : body flip —**somersault** *vb*

some·thing \'səmthin\ *pron* : some undetermined or unspecified thing

some·time \'səm,tīm\ *adv* : at a future, unknown, or unnamed time

some·times \-,tīmz\ *adv* : occasionally

some·what \-,hwət, -,hwät\ *adv* : in some degree

some·where \-,hwer\ *adv* : in, at, or to an unknown or unnamed place

som·no·lent \'sämnələnt\ *adj* : sleepy —**som·no·lence** \-ləns\ *n*

son \'sən\ *n* : male offspring

so·nar \'sō,när\ *n* : device that detects and locates underwater objects using sound waves

so·na·ta \sə'nätə\ *n* : instrumental composition

song \'soṅ\ *n* : music and words to be sung

song·bird *n* : bird with musical tones

son·ic \'sänik\ *adj* : relating to sound waves or the speed of sound

son-in-law \ n, pl **sons-in-law** : husband of one's daughter

son·net \'sänət\ n : poem of 14 lines

so·no·rous \sə'nōrəs, 'sänərəs\ adj 1 : loud, deep, or rich in sound 2 : impressive —**so·nor·i·ty** \sə'nórətē\ n

soon \'sün\ adv 1 : before long 2 : promptly 3 : early

soot \'sut, 'sət, 'süt\ n : fine black substance formed by combustion —**sooty** adj

soothe \'süth\ vb **soothed**; **sooth·ing** : calm or comfort —**sooth·er** n

sooth·say·er \'süth,sāər\ n : prophet —**sooth·say·ing** \-iŋ\ n

sop \'säp\ n : conciliatory bribe, gift, or concession ~ vb -**pp**- 1 : dip in a liquid 2 : soak 3 : mop up

so·phis·ti·cat·ed \sə'fistə,kātəd\ adj 1 : complex 2 : wise, cultured, or shrewd in human affairs —**so·phis·ti·ca·tion** \-,fistə'kāshən\ n

soph·ist·ry \'säfəstrē\ n : subtly fallacious reasoning or argument —**soph·ist** \'säfist\ n

soph·o·more \'säf°m,ōr, 'säf,mōr\ n : 2d-year student

so·po·rif·ic \,säpə'rifik, ,sōp-\ adj : causing sleep or drowsiness

so·pra·no \sə'pranō\ n, pl -**nos** : highest singing voice

sor·cery \'sórsərē\ n : witchcraft —**sor·cer·er** \-rər\ n —**sor·cer·ess** \-rəs\ n

sor·did \'sórdəd\ adj : filthy or vile —**sor·did·ly** adv —**sor·did·ness** n

sore \'sōr\ adj **sor·er**; **sor·est** 1 : causing pain or distress 2 : severe or intense 3 : angry ~ n : sore usu. infected spot on the body —**sore·ly** adv —**sore·ness** n

sor·ghum \'sórgəm\ n : forage grass

so·ror·i·ty \sə'rórətē\ n, pl -**ties** : women's student social group

¹sor·rel \'sórəl\ n : brownish orange to light brown color or an animal of this color

²sorrel n : herb with sour juice

sor·row \'särō\ n : deep distress, sadness, or regret or a cause of this —**sor·row·ful** \-fəl\ adj —**sor·row·ful·ly** adv

sor·ry \'särē\ adj -**ri·er**; -**est** 1 : feeling sorrow, regret, or penitence 2 : dismal

sort \'sórt\ n 1 : kind 2 : nature ~ vb : classify —**out of sorts** : grouchy

sor·tie \'sórtē, sór'tē\ n : military attack esp. against besiegers

SOS \,es,ō'es\ n : call for help

so-so \'sō'sō\ adj or adv : barely acceptable

sot \'sät\ n : drunkard —**sot·tish** adj

souf·flé \sü'flā\ n : baked dish made light with beaten egg whites

sought past of SEEK

soul \'sōl\ n 1 : immaterial essence of an individual life 2 : essential part 3 : person

soul·ful \'sōlfəl\ adj : full of or expressing deep feeling —**soul·ful·ly** adv

¹sound \'saund\ adj 1 : free from fault, error, or illness 2 : firm or hard 3 : showing good judgment —**sound·ly** adv —**sound·ness** n

²sound n 1 : sensation of hearing 2 : energy of vibration sensed in hearing 3 : something heard ~ vb 1 : make or cause to make a sound 2 : seem —**sound·less** adj —**sound·less·ly** adv —**sound·proof** adj or vb

³sound n : wide strait ~ vb 1 : measure the depth of (water) 2 : investigate

soup \'süp\ n : broth usu. containing pieces of solid food —**soupy** adj

sour \'sauər\ adj 1 : having an acid or tart taste 2 : disagreeable ~ vb : become or make sour —**sour·ish** adj —**sour·ly** adv —**sour·ness** n

source \'sōrs\ n 1 : point of origin 2 : one that provides something needed

souse \'saus\ vb **soused**; **sous·ing** 1 : pickle 2 : immerse 3 : intoxicate ~ n 1 : something pickled 2 : drunkard

south \'sauth\ adv : to or toward the south ~ adj : situated toward, at, or coming from the south ~ n 1 : direction to the right of sunrise 2 cap : regions to the south —**south·er·ly** \'sətharlē\ adv or adj —**south·ern** \'səthərn\ adj —**South·ern·er** n —**south·ern·most** \-,mōst\ adj —**south·ward** \'sauthwərd\ adv or adj —**south·wards** \-wərdz\ adv

southeast \sauth'ēst, naut saú'ēst\ n 1 : direction between south and east 2 cap : regions to the southeast —**southeast** adj or adv —**south·east·er·ly** adv or adj —**south·east·ern** \-ərn\ adj

south pole n : the southernmost point of the earth

southwest \sauth'west, naut saú'west\ n 1 : direction between south and west 2 cap : regions to the southwest —**southwest** adj or adv —**south·west-**

er·ly *adv or adj* —**south·west·ern** \-ərn\ *adj*

sou·ve·nir \'süvə,nir\ *n* : something that is a reminder of a place or event

sov·er·eign \'sävərən\ *n* **1** : supreme ruler **2** : gold coin of the United Kingdom ~ *adj* **1** : supreme **2** : independent —**sov·er·eign·ty** \-tē\ *n*

¹sow \'saü\ *n* : female swine

²sow \'sō\ *vb* **sowed; sown** \'sōn\ *or* **sowed, sow·ing 1** : plant or strew with seed **2** : scatter abroad —**sow·er** \'sōər\ *n*

sox *pl of* SOCK

soy·bean \'söi,bēn\ *n* : legume with edible seeds

spa \'spä\ *n* : resort at a mineral spring

space \'spās\ *n* **1** : period of time **2** : area in, around, or between **3** : region beyond earth's atmosphere **4** : accommodations ~ *vb* **spaced; spac·ing** : place at intervals —**space·craft** *n* —**space·flight** *n* —**space·man** *n* —**space·ship** *n*

spa·cious \'spāshəs\ *adj* : large or roomy —**spa·cious·ly** *adv* —**spa·cious·ness** *n*

¹spade \'spād\ *n or vb* : shovel —**spade·ful** *n*

²spade *n* : playing card marked with a black figure like an inverted heart

spa·ghet·ti \spə'getē\ *n* : pasta strings

span \'span\ *n* **1** : amount of time **2** : distance between supports ~ *vb* **-nn-** : extend across

span·gle \'spaŋgəl\ *n* : small disk of shining metal or plastic —**spangle** *vb*

span·iel \'spanyəl\ *n* : small or medium-sized dog with drooping ears and long wavy hair

spank \'spaŋk\ *vb* : hit on the buttocks with an open hand

¹spar \'spär\ *n* : pole or boom

²spar *vb* **-rr-** : practice boxing

spare \'spar\ *adj* **1** : held in reserve **2** : thin or scanty ~ *vb* **spared; spar·ing 1** : reserve or avoid using **2** : avoid punishing or killing —**spare** *n*

spar·ing \'sparin\ *adj* : thrifty —**spar·ing·ly** *adv*

spark \'spärk\ *n* **1** : tiny hot and glowing particle **2** : smallest beginning or germ **3** : visible electrical discharge ~ *vb* **1** : emit or produce sparks **2** : stir to activity

spar·kle \'spärkəl\ *vb* **-kled; -kling 1**

: flash **2** : effervesce ~ *n* : gleam —**spark·ler** \-klər\ *n*

spar·row \'sparō\ *n* : small singing bird

sparse \'spärs\ *adj* **spars·er; spars·est** : thinly scattered —**sparse·ly** *adv*

spasm \'spazəm\ *n* **1** : involuntary muscular contraction **2** : sudden, violent, and temporary effort or feeling —**spas·mod·ic** \spaz'mädik\ *adj* —**spas·mod·i·cal·ly** *adv*

spas·tic \'spastik\ *adj* : relating to, marked by, or affected with muscular spasm —**spastic** *n*

¹spat \'spat\ *past of* SPIT

²spat *n* : petty dispute

spa·tial \'spāshəl\ *adj* : relating to space —**spa·tial·ly** *adv*

spat·ter \'spatər\ *vb* : splash with drops of liquid —**spatter** *n*

spat·u·la \'spachələ\ *n* : flexible knife-like utensil

spawn \'spön\ *vb* **1** : produce eggs or offspring **2** : bring forth ~ *n* : egg cluster —**spawn·er** *n*

spay \'spā\ *vb* : remove the ovaries of (a female)

speak \'spēk\ *vb* **spoke** \'spōk\; **spo·ken** \'spōkən\; **speak·ing 1** : utter words **2** : express orally **3** : address an audience **4** : use (a language) in talking —**speak·er** *n*

spear \'spir\ *n* : long pointed weapon ~ *vb* : strike or pierce with a spear

spear·head *n* : leading force, element, or influence —**spearhead** *vb*

spear·mint *n* : aromatic garden mint

special \'speshəl\ *adj* **1** : unusual or unique **2** : particularly favored **3** : set aside for a particular use —**special** *n* —**spe·cial·ly** *adv*

spe·cial·ist \'speshəlist\ *n* **1** : person who specializes in a particular branch of learning or activity **2** : any of four enlisted ranks in the army corresponding to the grades of corporal through sergeant first class

spe·cial·ize \'speshə,līz\ *vb* **-ized; -iz·ing** : concentrate one's efforts —**spe·cial·iza·tion** \,speshələ'zāshən\ *n*

spe·cial·ty \'speshəltē\ *n, pl* **-ties** : area or field in which one specializes

spe·cie \'spēshē, -sē\ *n* : money in coin

spe·cies \'spēshēz, -sēz\ *n, pl* **species** : biological grouping of closely related organisms

spe·cif·ic \spi'sifik\ *adj* : definite or exact —**spe·cif·i·cal·ly** *adv*

spec•i•fi•ca•tion \,spesəfə'kāshən\ n 1 : act or process of specifying 2 : detailed description of work to be done —usu. pl.

spec•i•fy \'spesə,fī\ vb **-fied; -fy•ing** : mention precisely or by name

spec•i•men \-əmən\ n : typical example

spe•cious \'spēshəs\ adj : apparently but not really genuine or correct

speck \'spek\ n : tiny particle or blemish —**speck** vb

speck•led \'spekəld\ adj : marked with spots

spec•ta•cle \'spektikəl\ n 1 : impressive public display 2 pl : eyeglasses

spec•tac•u•lar \spek'takyələr\ adj : sensational or showy

spec•ta•tor \'spek,tātər\ n : person who looks on

spec•ter, spec•tre \'spektər\ n 1 : ghost 2 : haunting vision

spec•tral \'spektrəl\ adj : relating to or resembling a specter or spectrum

spec•trum \'spektrəm\ n, pl **-tra** \-trə\ or **-trums** : series of colors formed when white light is dispersed into its components

spec•u•late \'spekyə,lāt\ vb **-lat•ed; -lat•ing** 1 : think about things yet unknown 2 : risk money in a business deal in hope of high profit —**spec•u•la•tion** \,spekyə'lāshən\ n —**spec•u•la•tive** \'spekyə,lātiv\ adj —**spec•u•la•tor** \-,lātər\ n

speech \'spēch\ n 1 : power, act, or manner of speaking 2 : talk given to an audience —**speech•less** adj

speed \'spēd\ n 1 : quality of being fast 2 : rate of motion or performance ~ vb **sped** \'sped\ or **speed•ed; speed•ing** : go at a great or excessive rate of speed —**speed•boat** n —**speed•er** n —**speed•i•ly** \'spēdᵊlē\ adv —**speed•up** \-,əp\ n —**speedy** adj

speed•om•e•ter \spi'dämətər\ n : instrument for indicating speed

¹**spell** \'spel\ n : influence of or like magic

²**spell** vb 1 : name, write, or print the letters of 2 : mean —**spell•er** n

³**spell** vb : substitute for or relieve (someone) ~ n 1 : turn at work 2 : period of time

spell•bound adj : held by a spell

spend \'spend\ vb **spent** \'spent\; **spend•ing** 1 : pay out 2 : cause or allow to pass —**spend•er** n

spend•thrift \'spend,thrift\ n : wasteful person

sperm \'spərm\ n, pl **sperm** or **sperms** : semen or a germ cell in it

spew \'spyü\ vb : gush out in a stream

sphere \'sfir\ n 1 : figure with every point on its surface at an equal distance from the center 2 : round body 3 : range of action or influence —**spher•i•cal** \'sfirikəl, 'sfer-\ adj

spher•oid \'sfir-\ n : spherelike figure

spice \'spīs\ n 1 : aromatic plant product for seasoning food 2 : interesting quality —**spice** vb —**spicy** adj

spi•der \'spīdər\ n : small insectlike animal with 8 legs —**spi•dery** adj

spig•ot \'spigət, 'spikət\ n : faucet

spike \'spīk\ n : very large nail ~ vb **spiked; spik•ing** : fasten or pierce with a spike —**spiked** \'spīkt\ adj

spill \'spil\ vb 1 : fall, flow, or run out unintentionally 2 : divulge ~ n 1 : act of spilling 2 : something spilled —**spill•able** adj

spill•way n : passage for surplus water

spin \'spin\ vb **spun** \'spən\; **spin•ning** 1 : draw out fiber and twist into thread 2 : form thread from a sticky body fluid 3 : revolve or cause to revolve extremely fast ~ n : rapid rotating motion —**spin•ner** n

spin•ach \'spinich\ n : garden herb with edible leaves

spi•nal \'spinᵊl\ adj : relating to the backbone —**spi•nal•ly** adv

spinal cord n : thick strand of nervous tissue that extends from the brain along the back within the backbone

spin•dle \'spindᵊl\ n 1 : stick used for spinning thread 2 : shaft around which something turns

spin•dly \'spindlē\ adj : tall and slender

spine \'spin\ n 1 : backbone 2 : stiff sharp projection on a plant or animal —**spine•less** adj —**spiny** adj

spin•et \'spinət\ n : small piano

spin•ster \'spinstər\ n : woman who has never married

spi•ral \'spirəl\ adj : circling or winding around a single point or line —**spiral** n or vb —**spi•ral•ly** adv

spire \'spir\ n : steeple —**spiry** adj

spir•it \'spirət\ n 1 : life-giving force 2 cap : presence of God 3 : ghost 4 : mood 5 : vivacity or enthusiasm 6 pl : alcoholic liquor ~ vb : carry off secretly —**spir•it•ed** adj —**spir•it•less** adj

spir·i·tu·al \'spirichəwəl\ *adj* **1** : relating to the spirit or sacred matters **2** : deeply religious ~ *n* : religious folk song —**spir·i·tu·al·i·ty** \,spirichə'walətē\ *n* —**spir·i·tu·al·ly** *adv*

spir·i·tu·al·ism \'spirichəwə,lizəm\ *n* : belief that spirits communicate with the living —**spir·i·tu·al·ist** \-list\ *n or adj*

¹spit \'spit\ *n* **1** : rod for holding and turning meat over a fire **2** : point of land that runs into the water

²spit *vb* **spit** *or* **spat** \'spat\; **spit·ting** : eject saliva from the mouth ~ *n* **1** : saliva **2** : perfect likeness

spite \'spīt\ *n* : petty ill will ~ *vb* **spit·ed; spit·ing** : annoy or offend —**spite·ful** \-fəl\ *adj* —**spite·ful·ly** *adv* —**in spite of** : in defiance or contempt of

spit·tle \'spit⁰l\ *n* : saliva

spit·toon \spi'tün\ *n* : receptacle for spit

splash \'splash\ *vb* : scatter a liquid on —**splash** *n*

splat·ter \'splatər\ *vb* : spatter —**splatter** *n*

splay \'splā\ *vb* : spread out or apart —**splay** *n or adj*

spleen \'splēn\ *n* **1** : organ for maintenance of the blood **2** : spite or anger

splen·did \'splendəd\ *adj* **1** : impressive in beauty or brilliance **2** : outstanding —**splen·did·ly** *adv*

splen·dor \'splendər\ *n* **1** : brilliance **2** : magnificence

splice \'splīs\ *vb* **spliced; splic·ing** : join (2 things) end to end —**splice** *n*

splint \'splint\ *n* **1** : thin strip of wood **2** : something that keeps an injured body part in place

splin·ter \'splintər\ *n* : thin needlelike piece ~ *vb* : break into splinters

split \'split\ *vb* **split; split·ting** : divide lengthwise or along a grain —**split** *n*

splotch \'splách\ *n* : blotch

splurge \'splərj\ *vb* **splurged; splurg·ing** : indulge oneself —**splurge** *n*

splut·ter \'splətər\ *n* : sputter —**splutter** *vb*

spoil \'spoil\ *vb* **spoiled** \'spoild, 'spoilt\ *or* **spoilt** \'spoilt\; **spoil·ing** **1** : pillage **2** : ruin **3** : rot —**spoil·age** \'spoilij\ *n* —**spoil·er** *n*

¹spoke \'spōk\ *past of* SPEAK

²spoke *n* : rod from the hub to the rim of a wheel

spo·ken *past part of* SPEAK

spokes·man \'spōksmən\ *n* : person who speaks for others

spokes·wom·an \-,wümən\ *n* : woman who speaks for others

sponge \'spənj\ *n* **1** : porous water-absorbing mass that forms the skeleton of some marine animals **2** : spongelike material used for wiping ~ *vb* **sponged; spong·ing 1** : wipe with a sponge **2** : live at another's expense —**spongy** \'spənjē\ *adj*

spon·sor \'spänsər\ *n* : one who assumes responsibility for another or who provides financial support —**sponsor** *vb* —**spon·sor·ship** *n*

spon·ta·ne·ous \spän'tānēəs\ *adj* : done, produced, or occurring naturally or without planning —**spon·ta·ne·i·ty** \,späntən'ēətē\ *n* —**spon·ta·ne·ous·ly** \spän'tānēəslē\ *adv*

spoof \'spüf\ *vb* : make good-natured fun of —**spoof** *n*

spook \'spük\ *n* **1** : ghost ~ *vb* : frighten —**spooky** *adj*

spool \'spül\ *n* : cylinder on which something is wound

spoon \'spün\ *n* : utensil consisting of a small shallow bowl with a handle —**spoon** *vb* —**spoon·ful** \-,fül\ *n*

spoor \'spur, 'spōr\ *n* : track or trail esp. of a wild animal

spo·rad·ic \spə'radik\ *adj* : occasional —**spo·rad·i·cal·ly** *adv*

spore \'spōr\ *n* : primitive usu. one-celled reproductive body

sport \'spōrt\ *vb* **1** : show off ~ *n* **1** : physical activity engaged in for pleasure **2** : jest **3** : person who shows good sportsmanship —**sport·ive** \-iv\ *adj* —**sporty** *adj*

sports·cast \'spōrts,kast\ *n* : broadcast of a sports event —**sports·cast·er** \-,kastər\ *n*

sports·man \-mən\ *n* : one who enjoys hunting and fishing

sports·man·ship \-mən,ship\ *n* : ability to be gracious in winning or losing

spot \'spät\ *n* **1** : blemish **2** : distinctive small part **3** : location ~ *vb* **-tt- 1** : mark with spots **2** : see or recognize ~ *adj* : made at random or in limited numbers —**spot·less** *adj* —**spot·less·ly** *adv*

spot·light *n* **1** : intense beam of light **2** : center of public interest —**spotlight** *vb*

spot·ty \'spätē\ *adj* **-ti·er; -est** : uneven in quality

spouse \'spaús\ *n* : one's husband or wife

spout \'spaút\ *vb* **1** : shoot forth in a stream **2** : say pompously ~ *n* **1** : opening through which liquid spouts **2** : jet of liquid

sprain \'sprān\ *n* : twisting injury to a joint ~ *vb* : injure with a sprain

sprat \'sprat\ *n* : small or young herring

sprawl \'sprȯl\ *vb* : lie or sit with limbs spread out —**sprawl** *n*

¹spray \'sprā\ *n* : branch or arrangement of flowers

²spray *n* **1** : mist **2** : device that discharges liquid as a mist —**spray** *vb* —**spray·er** *n*

spread \'spred\ *vb* **spread**; **spread·ing** **1** : open up or unfold **2** : scatter or smear over a surface **3** : cause to be known or to exist over a wide area ~ *n* **1** : extent to which something is spread **2** : cloth cover **3** : something intended to be spread —**spread·er** *n*

spread·sheet \'spred,shēt\ *n* : accounting program for a computer

spree \'sprē\ *n* : burst of indulging in something

sprig \'sprig\ *n* : small shoot or twig

spright·ly \'sprītlē\ *adj* **-li·er**; **-est** : lively —**spright·li·ness** *n*

spring \'spriŋ\ *vb* **sprang** \'spraŋ\ or **sprung** \'sprəŋ\; **sprung**; **spring·ing** **1** : move or grow quickly or by elastic force **2** : come from by descent **3** : make known suddenly ~ *n* **1** : source **2** : flow of water from underground **3** : season between winter and summer **4** : elastic body or device (as a coil of wire) **5** : leap **6** : elastic power —**springy** *adj*

sprin·kle \'spriŋkəl\ *vb* **-kled**; **-kling** : scatter in small drops or particles ~ *n* : light rainfall —**sprin·kler** *n*

sprint \'sprint\ *n* : short run at top speed —**sprint** *vb* —**sprint·er** *n*

sprite \'sprīt\ *n* : elf or elfish person

sprock·et \'spräkət\ *n* : toothed wheel whose teeth engage the links of a chain

sprout \'spraút\ *vb* : send out new growth ~ *n* : plant shoot

¹spruce \'sprüs\ *n* : conical evergreen tree

²spruce *adj* **spruc·er**; **spruc·est** : neat and stylish in appearance ~ *vb* **spruced**; **spruc·ing** : make or become neat

spry \'sprī\ *adj* **spri·er** or **spry·er** \'sprīər\; **spri·est** or **spry·est** \'sprīəst\ : agile and active

spume \'spyüm\ *n* : froth

spun *past of* SPIN

spunk \'spəŋk\ *n* : courage —**spunky** *adj*

spur \'spər\ *n* **1** : pointed device used to urge on a horse **2** : something that urges to action **3** : projecting part ~ *vb* **-rr-** : urge on —**spurred** *adj*

spu·ri·ous \'spyúrēəs\ *adj* : not genuine

spurn \'spərn\ *vb* : reject

¹spurt \'spərt\ *n* : burst of effort, speed, or activity ~ *vb* : make a spurt

²spurt *n* : gush out~ *n* : sudden gush

sput·ter \'spətər\ *vb* **1** : talk hastily and indistinctly in excitement **2** : make popping sounds —**sputter** *n*

spy \'spī\ *vb* **spied**; **spy·ing** : watch or try to gather information secretly —**spy** *n*

squab \'skwäb\ *n, pl* **squabs** or **squab** : young pigeon

squab·ble \'skwäbəl\ *n or vb* : dispute

squad \'skwäd\ *n* : small group

squad·ron \'skwädrən\ *n* : small military unit

squal·id \'skwäləd\ *adj* : filthy or wretched

squall \'skwȯl\ *n* : sudden violent brief storm —**squally** *adj*

squa·lor \'skwälər\ *n* : quality or state of being squalid

squan·der \'skwändər\ *vb* : waste

square \'skwar\ *n* **1** : instrument for measuring right angles **2** : flat figure that has 4 equal sides and 4 right angles **3** : open area in a city **4** : product of number multiplied by itself ~ *adj* **squar·er**; **squar·est** **1** : being a square in form **2** : having sides meet at right angles **3** : multiplied by itself **4** : being a square unit of area **5** : honest ~ *vb* **squared**; **squar·ing** **1** : form into a square **2** : multiply (a number) by itself **3** : conform **4** : settle —**square·ly** *adv*

¹squash \'skwäsh, 'skwȯsh\ *vb* **1** : press flat **2** : suppress

²squash *n, pl* **squash·es** or **squash** : garden vegetable

squat \'skwät\ *vb* **-tt-** **1** : stoop or sit on one's heels **2** : settle on land one does not own ~ *n* : act or posture of squatting ~ *adj* **squat·ter**; **squat·test** : short and thick —**squat·ter** *n*

squaw \'skwȯ\ *n* : American Indian woman

squawk \\'skwȯk\ *n* : harsh loud cry — **squawk** *vb*

squeak \\'skwēk\ *vb* : make a thin high-pitched sound —**squeak** *n* — **squeaky** *adj*

squeal \\'skwēl\ *vb* 1 : make a shrill sound or cry 2 : protest —**squeal** *n*

squea·mish \\'skwēmish\ *adj* : easily nauseated or disgusted

squeeze \\'skwēz\ *vb* **squeezed; squeezing** 1 : apply pressure to 2 : extract by pressure —**squeeze** *n* —**squeez·er** *n*

squelch \\'skwelch\ *vb* : suppress (as with a retort) —**squelch** *n*

squid \\'skwid\ *n*, *pl* **squid** *or* **squids** : 10-armed long-bodied sea mollusk

squint \\'skwint\ *vb* : look with the eyes partly closed —**squint** *n* *or adj*

squire \\'skwīr\ *n* 1 : knight's aide 2 : country landholder 3 : lady's devoted escort ~ *vb* **squired; squir·ing** : escort

squirm \\'skwərm\ *vb* : wriggle

squir·rel \\'skwərəl\ *n* : rodent with a long bushy tail

squirt \\'skwərt\ *vb* : eject liquid in a spurt —**squirt** *n*

stab \\'stab\ *n* 1 : wound made by a pointed weapon 2 : quick thrust 3 : attempt ~ *vb* **-bb-** : pierce or wound with or as if with a pointed weapon

¹sta·ble \\'stābəl\ *n* : building for domestic animals ~ *vb* **-bled; -bling** : keep in a stable

²stable *adj* **sta·bler; sta·blest** 1 : firmly established 2 : mentally and emotionally healthy 3 : steady —**sta·bil·i·ty** \stə'bilətē\ *n* —**sta·bil·iza·tion** \ˌstābələ'zāshən\ *n* —**sta·bi·lize** \\'stābəˌlīz\ *vb* —**sta·bi·liz·er** *n*

stac·ca·to \stə'kätō\ *adj* : disconnected

stack \\'stak\ *n* : large pile ~ *vb* : pile up

sta·di·um \\'stādēəm\ *n* : outdoor sports arena

staff \\'staf\ *n*, *pl* **staffs** \\'stafs, stavz\ *or* **staves** \\'stavz, 'stāvz\ 1 : rod or supporting cane 2 : people assisting a leader 3 : 5 horizontal lines on which music is written ~ *vb* : supply with workers —**staff·er** *n*

staff sergeant *n* : noncommissioned officer ranking next above a sergeant in the army, air force, or marine corps

stag \\'stag\ *n*, *pl* **stags** *or* **stag** : male deer ~ *adj* : only for men ~ *adv* : without a date

stage \\'stāj\ *n* 1 : raised platform for a speaker or performers 2 : theater 3 : step in a process ~ *vb* **staged; stag·ing** : produce (a play)

stage·coach *n* : passenger coach

stag·ger \\'stagər\ *vb* 1 : reel or cause to reel from side to side 2 : overlap or alternate —**stagger** *n* —**stag·ger·ing·ly** *adv*

stag·nant \\'stagnənt\ *adj* : not moving or active —**stag·nate** \-ˌnāt\ *vb* —**stag·na·tion** \stag'nāshən\ *n*

¹staid \\'stād\ *adj* : sedate

²staid *past of* STAY

stain \\'stān\ *vb* 1 : discolor 2 : dye (as wood) 3 : disgrace ~ *n* 1 : discolored area 2 : mark of guilt 3 : coloring preparation —**stain·less** *adj*

stair \\'star\ *n* 1 : step in a series for going from one level to another 2 *pl* : flight of steps —**stair·way** *n*

stair·case *n* : series of steps with their framework

stake \\'stāk\ *n* 1 : usu. small post driven into the ground 2 : bet 3 : prize in a contest ~ *vb* **staked; stak·ing** 1 : mark or secure with a stake 2 : bet

sta·lac·tite \stə'lakˌtīt\ *n* : icicle-shaped deposit hanging in a cavern

sta·lag·mite \stə'lagˌmīt\ *n* : icicle-shaped deposit on a cavern floor

stale \\'stāl\ *adj* **stal·er; stal·est** 1 : having lost good taste and value from age 2 : no longer new, strong, or effective —**stale·ness** *n*

stale·mate \\'stālˌmāt\ *n* : deadlock — **stalemate** *vb*

¹stalk \\'stȯk\ *vb* 1 : walk stiffly or proudly 2 : pursue stealthily

²stalk *n* : plant stem —**stalked** \\'stȯkt\ *adj*

¹stall \\'stȯl\ *n* 1 : compartment in a stable 2 : booth where articles are sold

²stall *vb* : bring or come to a standstill unintentionally

³stall *vb* : delay, evade, or keep a situation going to gain advantage or time

stal·lion \\'stalyən\ *n* : male horse

stal·wart \\'stȯlwərt\ *adj* : strong or brave

sta·men \\'stāmən\ *n* : flower organ that produces pollen

stam·i·na \\'staminə\ *n* : endurance

stam·mer \\'stamər\ *vb* : hesitate in speaking —**stammer** *n*

stamp \\'stamp\ *vb* 1 : pound with the sole of the foot or a heavy implement 2 : impress or imprint 3 : cut out with a die 4 : attach a postage stamp to ~

n **1** : device for stamping **2** : act of stamping **3** : government seal showing a tax or fee has been paid

stam·pede \stam'pēd\ *n* : headlong rush of frightened animals ~ *vb* **-ped·ed; -ped·ing** : flee in panic

¹stance \'stans\ *n* : way of standing

¹stanch \'stȯnch, 'stänch\ *vb* : stop the flow of (as blood)

²stanch *var of* STAUNCH

stan·chion \'stanchən\ *n* : upright support

stand \'stand\ *vb* **stood** \'stůd\; **stand·ing 1** : be at rest in or assume an upright position **2** : remain unchanged **3** : be steadfast **4** : maintain a relative position or rank **5** : set upright **6** : undergo or endure ~ *n* **1** : act or place of standing, staying, or resisting **2** : sales booth **3** : structure for holding something upright **4** : group of plants growing together **5** *pl* : tiered seats **6** : opinion or viewpoint

stan·dard \'standərd\ *n* **1** : symbolic figure or flag **2** : model, rule, or guide **3** : upright support —**standard** *adj* — **stan·dard·i·za·tion** \,standərdə'zā-shən\ *n* —**stan·dard·ize** \'standərd,īz\ *vb*

standard time *n* : time established over a region or country

stand·ing \'standiŋ\ *n* **1** : relative position or rank **2** : duration

stand·still *n* : state of rest

stank *past of* STINK

stan·za \'stanzə\ *n* : division of a poem

¹sta·ple \'stāpəl\ *n* : U-shaped wire fastener —**staple** *vb* —**sta·pler** \-plər\ *n*

²staple *n* : chief commodity or item —**staple** *adj*

star \'stär\ *n* **1** : celestial body visible as a point of light **2** : 5- or 6-pointed figure representing a star **3** : leading performer ~ *vb* **-rr- 1** : mark with a star **2** : play the leading role —**star·dom** \'stärdəm\ *n* —**star·less** *adj* —**star·light** *n* —**star·ry** *adj*

star·board \'stärbərd\ *n* : right side of a ship or airplane looking forward —**starboard** *adj*

starch \'stärch\ *n* : nourishing carbohydrate from plants also used in adhesives and laundering ~ *vb* : stiffen with starch —**starchy** *adj*

stare \'star\ *vb* **stared; star·ing** : look intently with wide-open eyes —**stare** *n* —**star·er** *n*

stark \'stärk\ *adj* **1** : absolute **2** : severe

or bleak ~ *adv* : completely —**stark·ly** *adv*

star·ling \'stärliŋ\ *n* : bird related to the crows

start \'stärt\ *vb* **1** : twitch or jerk (as from surprise) **2** : perform or show performance of the first part of an action or process ~ *n* **1** : sudden involuntary motion **2** : beginning —**start·er** *n*

star·tle \'stärt⁴l\ *vb* **-tled; -tling** : frighten or surprise suddenly

starve \'stärv\ *vb* **starved; starv·ing 1** : suffer or die from hunger **2** : kill with hunger —**star·va·tion** \stär-'vāshən\ *n*

stash \'stash\ *vb* : store in a secret place for future use —**stash** *n*

state \'stāt\ *n* **1** : condition of being **2** : condition of mind **3** : nation or a political unit within it ~ *vb* **stat·ed; stat·ing 1** : express in words **2** : establish —**state·hood** \-,hůd\ *n*

state·ly \'stātlē\ *adj* **-li·er; -est** : having impressive dignity —**state·li·ness** *n*

state·ment \'stātmənt\ *n* **1** : something stated **2** : financial summary

state·room *n* : private room on a ship

states·man \'stātsmən\ *n* : one skilled in government or diplomacy —**states·man·like** *adj* —**states·man·ship** *n*

stat·ic \'statik\ *adj* **1** : relating to bodies at rest or forces in equilibrium **2** : not moving **3** : relating to stationary charges of electricity ~ *n* : noise on radio or television from electrical disturbances

sta·tion \'stāshən\ *n* **1** : place of duty **2** : regular stop on a bus or train route **3** : social standing **4** : place where radio or television programs originate ~ *vb* : assign to a station

sta·tion·ary \'stāshə,nerē\ *adj* **1** : not moving or not movable **2** : not changing

sta·tio·nery \'stāshə,nerē\ *n* : letter paper with envelopes

sta·tis·tic \stə'tistik\ *n* : single item of statistics

sta·tis·tics \-tiks\ *n pl* : numerical facts collected for study —**sta·tis·ti·cal** \-tikəl\ *adj* —**sta·tis·ti·cal·ly** *adv* — **stat·is·ti·cian** \,statə'stishən\ *n*

stat·u·ary \'stachə,werē\ *n. pl* **-ar·ies** : collection of statues

stat·ue \'stachü\ *n* : solid 3-dimensional likeness —**stat·u·ette** \,stachə'wet\ *n*

stat·u·esque \,stachə'wesk\ *adj* : tall and shapely

stat·ure \'stachər\ n 1 : height 2 : status gained by achievement

sta·tus \'stātəs, 'stat-\ n : relative situation or condition

sta·tus quo \-'kwō\ n : existing state of affairs

stat·ute \'stachüt\ n : law —**stat·u·to·ry** \'stacha,tōrē\ adj

staunch \'stonch\ adj : steadfast —**staunch·ly** adv

stave \'stāv\ n : narrow strip of wood ~ vb **staved** or **stove** \'stōv\; **stav·ing** 1 : break a hole in 2 : drive away

staves pl of STAFF

¹stay \'stā\ n : support ~ vb **stayed**; **stay·ing** : prop up

²stay vb **stayed** \'stād\ or **staid** \'stād\; **stay·ing** 1 : pause 2 : remain 3 : reside 4 : stop or postpone 5 : satisfy for a time ~ n : a staying

stead \'sted\ n : one's place, job, or function —**in good stead** : to advantage

stead·fast \-,fast\ adj : faithful or determined —**stead·fast·ly** adv

steady \'stedē\ adj **stead·i·er; -est** 1 : firm in position or sure in movement 2 : calm or reliable 3 : constant 4 : regular ~ vb **stead·ied; steady·ing** : make or become steady —**stead·i·ly** \'stedªlē\ adv —**stead·i·ness** n — **steady** adv

steak \'stāk\ n : thick slice of meat

steal \'stēl\ vb **stole** \'stōl\; **sto·len** \'stōlən\; **steal·ing** 1 : take and carry away wrongfully and with intent to keep 2 : move secretly or slowly

stealth \'stelth\ n : secret or unobtrusive procedure —**stealth·i·ly** \-thəlē\ adv —**stealthy** adj

steam \'stēm\ n : vapor of boiling water ~ vb : give off steam —**steam·boat** n —**steam·ship** n —**steamy** adj

steed \'stēd\ n : horse

steel \'stēl\ n : tough carbon-containing iron ~ vb : fill with courage —**steel** adj —**steely** adj

¹steep \'stēp\ adj : having a very sharp slope or great elevation —**steep·ly** adv —**steep·ness** n

²steep vb : soak in a liquid

stee·ple \'stēpəl\ n : usu. tapering church tower

stee·ple·chase n : race over hurdles

¹steer \'stir\ n : castrated ox

²steer vb 1 : direct the course of (as a ship or car) 2 : guide

steer·age \'stirij\ n : section in a ship for people paying the lowest fares

stein \'stīn\ n : mug

stel·lar \'stelər\ adj : relating to stars or resembling a star

¹stem \'stem\ n : main upright part of a plant ~ vb **-mm-** 1 : derive 2 : make progress against —**stem·less** adj —**stemmed** adj

²stem vb **-mm-** : stop the flow of

stench \'stench\ n : stink

sten·cil \'stensəl\ n : printing sheet cut with letters to let ink pass through —**stencil** vb

ste·nog·ra·phy \stə'nägrəfē\ n : art or process of writing in shorthand —**ste·nog·ra·pher** \-fər\ n —**steno·graph·ic** \,stenə'grafik\ adj

sten·to·ri·an \sten'tōrēən\ adj : extremely loud and powerful

step \'step\ n 1 : single action of a leg in walking or running 2 : rest for the foot in going up or down 3 : degree, rank, or stage 4 : way of walking ~ vb **-pp-** 1 : move by steps 2 : press with the foot

step- \'step-\ comb form : related by a remarriage and not by blood

step·lad·der n : light portable set of steps in a hinged frame

steppe \'step\ n : dry grassy treeless land esp. of Asia

-ster \stər\ n suffix 1 : one that does, makes, or uses 2 : one that is associated with or takes part in 3 : one that is

ste·reo \'sterē,ō, 'stir-\ n, pl **-reos** : stereophonic sound system —**stereo** adj

ste·reo·phon·ic \,sterēə'fänik, ,stir-\ adj : relating to a 3-dimensional effect of reproduced sound

ste·reo·type \'sterēə,tīp, 'stir-\ n : gross often mistaken generalization —**stereotype** vb —**ste·reo·typ·i·cal** \,sterē·ə'tipikəl\ adj —**ste·reo·typ·i·cal·ly** adv

ste·reo·typed \'sterēə,tīpt, 'stir-\ adj : lacking originality or individuality

ster·ile \'sterəl\ adj 1 : unable to bear fruit, crops, or offspring 2 : free from disease germs —**ste·ril·i·ty** \stə'rilətē\ n —**ster·il·i·za·tion** \,sterələ'zāshən\ n —**ster·il·ize** \-ə,līz\ vb —**ster·il·iz·er** n

ster·ling \'stərliŋ\ adj 1 : being or made of an alloy of 925 parts of silver with 75 parts of copper 2 : excellent

¹stern \'stərn\ adj : severe —**stern·ly** adv —**stern·ness** n

²stern n : back end of a boat

ster•num \'stərnəm\ n, pl -nums or -na \-nə\ : long flat chest bone joining the 2 sets of ribs

stetho•scope \'stethə,skōp\ n : instrument used for listening to sounds in the chest

steve•dore \'stēvə,dōr\ n : worker who loads and unloads ships

stew \'stü, 'styü\ n 1 : dish of boiled meat and vegetables 2 : state of worry or agitation —stew vb

stew•ard \'stüərd, 'styü-\ n 1 : manager of an estate or an organization 2 : person on a ship or airliner who looks after passenger comfort — stew•ard•ship n

stew•ard•ess \-əs\ n : woman who is a steward (as on an airplane)

¹stick \'stik\ n 1 : cut or broken branch 2 : long thin piece of wood or something resembling it

²stick vb stuck \'stək\; stick•ing 1 : stab 2 : thrust or project 3 : hold fast to something 4 : attach 5 : become jammed or fixed

stick•er \'stikər\ n : adhesive label

stick•ler \'stiklər\ n : one who insists on exactness or completeness

sticky \'stikē\ adj stick•i•er; -est 1 : adhesive or gluey 2 : muggy 3 : difficult

stiff \'stif\ adj 1 : not bending easily 2 : tense 3 : formal 4 : strong 5 : severe —stiff•en \'stifən\ vb —stiff•en•er \-ənər\ n —stiff•ly adv —stiff•ness n

sti•fle \'stīfəl\ vb -fled; -fling 1 : smother or suffocate 2 : suppress

stig•ma \'stigmə\ n, pl -ma•ta \stig-'mätə, 'stigmətə\ or -mas 1 : mark of disgrace —stig•ma•tize \'stigmə,tīz\ vb

stile \'stīl\ n : steps for crossing a fence

sti•let•to \stə'letō\ n, pl -tos or -toes : slender dagger

¹still \'stil\ adj 1 : motionless 2 : silent ~ vb : make or become still ~ adv 1 : without motion 2 : up to and during this time 3 : in spite of that ~ n : silence —still•ness n

²still n : apparatus used in distillation

still•born adj : born dead —still•birth n

stilt \'stilt\ n : one of a pair of poles for walking

stilt•ed \'stiltəd\ adj : not easy and natural

stim•u•lant \'stimyələnt\ n : substance

that temporarily increases the activity of an organism —stimulant adj

stim•u•late \-,lāt\ vb -lat•ed; -lat•ing : make active —stim•u•la•tion \,stim-yə'lāshən\ n

stim•u•lus \'stimyələs\ n, pl -li \-,lī\ : something that stimulates

sting \'stiŋ\ vb stung \'stəŋ\; sting•ing 1 : prick painfully 2 : cause to suffer acutely ~ n : act of stinging or a resulting wound —sting•er n

stin•gy \'stinjē\ adj stin•gi•er; -est : not generous —stin•gi•ness n

stink \'stiŋk\ vb stank \'staŋk\ or stunk \'stəŋk\; stunk; stink•ing : have a strong offensive odor —stink n —stink•er n

stint \'stint\ vb : be sparing or stingy ~ n 1 : restraint 2 : quantity or period of work

sti•pend \'stī,pend, -pənd\ n : money paid periodically

stip•ple \'stipəl\ vb -pled; -pling : engrave, paint, or draw with dots instead of lines —stipple n

stip•u•late \'stipyə,lāt\ vb -lat•ed; -lat•ing : demand as a condition —stip•u•la•tion \,stipyə'lāshən\ n

stir \'stər\ vb -rr- 1 : move slightly 2 : prod or push into activity 3 : mix by continued circular movement ~ n : act or result of stirring

stir•rup \'stərəp\ n : saddle loop for the foot

stitch \'stich\ n 1 : loop formed by a needle in sewing 2 : sudden sharp pain ~ vb 1 : fasten or decorate with stitches 2 : sew

stock \'stäk\ n 1 : block or part of wood 2 : original from which others derive 3 : farm animals 4 : supply of goods 5 : money invested in a large business 6 pl : instrument of punishment like a pillory with holes for the feet or feet and hands ~ vb : provide with stock

stock•ade \stä'kād\ n : defensive or confining enclosure

stock•ing \'stäkiŋ\ n : close-fitting covering for the foot and leg

stock•pile n : reserve supply —stock•pile vb

stocky \'stäkē\ adj stock•i•er; -est : short and relatively thick

stock•yard n : yard for livestock to be slaughtered or shipped

stodgy \'stäjē\ adj stodg•i•er; -est 1 : dull 2 : old-fashioned

sto•ic \'stōik\, sto•i•cal \-ikəl\ adj

: showing indifference to pain —**stoic** n —**sto·i·cal·ly** adv —**sto·i·cism** \'stōə,sizəm\ n

stoke \'stōk\ vb **stoked; stok·ing** : stir up a fire or supply fuel to a furnace —**stok·er** n

¹**stole** \'stōl\ past of STEAL

²**stole** n : long wide scarf

stolen past part of STEAL

stol·id \'stäləd\ adj : having or showing little or no emotion —**stol·id·ly** \'stäləd(ə)lē\ adv

stom·ach \'stəmək, -ik\ n 1 : saclike digestive organ 2 : abdomen 3 : appetite or desire ~ vb : put up with —**stom·ach·ache** n

stomp \'stämp, 'stòmp\ vb : stamp

stone \'stōn\ n 1 : hardened earth or mineral matter 2 : small piece of rock 3 : seed that is hard or has a hard covering ~ vb **stoned; ston·ing** : pelt or kill with stones —**stony** adj

stood past of STAND

stool \'stül\ n 1 : seat usu. without back or arms 2 : footstool 3 : discharge of feces

¹**stoop** \'stüp\ vb 1 : bend over 2 : lower oneself ~ n 1 : act of bending over 2 : bent position of shoulders

²**stoop** n : small porch at a house door

stop \'stäp\ vb -**pp**- 1 : block an opening 2 : end or cause to end 3 : pause for rest or a visit in a journey ~ n 1 : plug 2 : act or place of stopping 3 : delay in a journey —**stop·light** n —**stop·page** \-ij\ n —**stop·per** n

stop·gap n : temporary measure or thing

stor·age \'stōrij\ n : safekeeping of goods (as in a warehouse)

store \'stōr\ vb **stored; stor·ing** : put aside for future use ~ n 1 : something stored 2 : retail business establishment —**store·house** n —**store·keep·er** n —**store·room** n

stork \'stòrk\ n : large wading bird

storm \'stòrm\ n 1 : heavy fall of rain or snow 2 : violent outbreak ~ vb 1 : rain or snow heavily 2 : rage 3 : make an attack against —**stormy** adj

¹**sto·ry** \'stōrē\ n, pl -**ries** 1 : narrative 2 : report —**sto·ry·tell·er** n

²**story** n, pl -**ries** : floor of a building

stout \'staùt\ adj 1 : firm or strong 2 : thick or bulky —**stout·ly** adv —**stout·ness** n

¹**stove** \'stōv\ n : apparatus for providing heat (as for cooking or heating)

²**stove** past of STAVE

stow \'stō\ vb 1 : pack in a compact mass 2 : put or hide away

strad·dle \'stradᵊl\ vb -**dled; -dling** : stand over or sit on with legs on opposite sides —**straddle** n

strafe \'strāf\ vb **strafed; straf·ing** : fire upon with machine guns from a low-flying airplane

strag·gle \'stragəl\ vb -**gled; -gling** : wander or become separated from others —**strag·gler** \-ələr\ n

straight \'strāt\ adj 1 : having no bends, turns, or twists 2 : just, proper, or honest 3 : neat and orderly ~ adv : in a straight manner —**straight·en** \'strātᵊn\ vb

straight·for·ward \strāt'fòrwərd\ adj : frank or honest

straight·way adv : immediately

¹**strain** \'strān\ n 1 : lineage 2 : trace

²**strain** vb 1 : exert to the utmost 2 : filter or remove by filtering 3 : injure by improper use ~ n 1 : excessive tension or exertion 2 : bodily injury from excessive effort —**strain·er** n

strait \'strāt\ n 1 : narrow channel connecting 2 bodies of water 2 pl : distress

strait·en \'strātᵊn\ vb 1 : hem in 2 : make distressing or difficult

¹**strand** \'strand\ vb 1 : drive or cast upon the shore 2 : leave helpless

²**strand** n 1 : twisted fiber of a rope 2 : length of something ropelike

strange \'strānj\ adj **strang·er; strang·est** 1 : unusual or queer 2 : new —**strange·ly** adv —**strange·ness** n

strang·er \'strānjər\ n : person with whom one is not acquainted

stran·gle \'straŋgəl\ vb -**gled; -gling** : choke to death —**stran·gler** \-glər\ n

stran·gu·la·tion \,straŋgyə'lāshən\ n : act or process of strangling

strap \'strap\ n : narrow strip of flexible material used esp. for fastening ~ vb 1 : secure with a strap 2 : beat with a strap —**strap·less** n

strap·ping \'strapiŋ\ adj : robust

strat·a·gem \'stratəjəm, -,jem\ n : deceptive scheme or maneuver

strat·e·gy \'stratəjē\ n, pl -**gies** : carefully worked out plan of action —**strat·e·gic** \strə'tējik\ adj —**strat·e·gist** \'stratəjist\ n

strat·i·fy \'stratə,fī\ vb -**fied; -fy·ing**

: form or arrange in layers —**strat·i·fi·ca·tion** \,stratəfə'kāshən\ n

strato·sphere \'stratə,sfir\ n : earth's atmosphere from about 7 to 31 miles above the surface

stra·tum \'strātəm, 'strat-\ n, pl **-ta** \'strātə, 'strat-\ : layer

straw \'strȯ\ n 1 : grass stems after grain is removed 2 : tube for drinking ~ adj : made of straw

straw·ber·ry \'strȯ,berē\ n : juicy red pulpy fruit

stray \'strā\ vb : wander or deviate ~ n : person or animal that strays ~ adj : separated from or not related to anything close by

streak \'strēk\ n 1 : mark of a different color 2 : narrow band of light 3 : trace 4 : run (as of luck) or series ~ vb 1 : form streaks in or on 2 : move fast

stream \'strēm\ n 1 : flow of water on land 2 : steady flow (as of water or air) ~ vb 1 : flow in a stream 2 : pour out streams

stream·er \'strēmər\ n : long ribbon or ribbonlike flag

stream·lined \-,līnd, -'līnd\ adj 1 : made with contours to reduce air or water resistance 2 : simplified 3 : modernized —**streamline** vb

street \'strēt\ n : thoroughfare esp. in a city or town

street·car n : passenger vehicle running on rails in the streets

strength \'streŋth\ n 1 : quality of being strong 2 : toughness 3 : intensity

strength·en \'streŋthən\ vb : make, grow, or become stronger —**strength·en·er** \'streŋthənər\ n

stren·u·ous \'strenyəwəs\ adj 1 : vigorous 2 : requiring or showing energy —**stren·u·ous·ly** adv

stress \'stres\ n 1 : pressure or strain that tends to distort a body 2 : relative prominence given to one thing among others 3 : state of physical or mental tension or something inducing it ~ vb : put stress on —**stress·ful** \'stresfəl\ adj

stretch \'strech\ vb 1 : spread or reach out 2 : draw out in length or breadth 3 : make taut 4 : exaggerate 5 : become extended without breaking ~ n 1 : act of extending beyond normal limits

stretch·er \'strechər\ n : device for carrying a sick or injured person

strew \'strü\ vb **strewed; strewed** or

strewn \'strün\; **strew·ing 1** : scatter 2 : cover by scattering something over

strick·en \'strikən\ adj : afflicted with disease

strict \'strikt\ adj 1 : allowing no escape or evasion 2 : precise —**strict·ly** adv —**strict·ness** n

stric·ture \'strikchər\ n : hostile criticism

stride \'strīd\ vb **strode** \'strōd\; **strid·den** \'strid°n\; **strid·ing** : walk or run with long steps ~ n 1 : long step 2 : manner of striding

stri·dent \'strīd°nt\ adj : loud and harsh

strife \'strīf\ n : conflict

strike \'strīk\ vb **struck** \'strək\; **struck**; **strik·ing** \'strīkiŋ\ 1 : hit sharply 2 : delete 3 : produce by impressing 4 : cause to sound 5 : afflict 6 : occur to or impress 7 : cause (a match) to ignite by rubbing 8 : refrain from working 9 : find 10 : take on (as a pose) ~ n 1 : act or instance of striking 2 : work stoppage 3 : military attack —**strik·er** n —**strike out** vb : start out vigorously —**strike up** vb : start

strik·ing \'strīkiŋ\ adj : very noticeable —**strik·ing·ly** adv

string \'striŋ\ n 1 : line usu. of twisted threads 2 : series 3 pl : stringed instruments ~ vb **strung** \'strəŋ\; **string·ing** 1 : thread on or with a string 2 : hang or fasten by a string

stringed \'striŋd\ adj : having strings

strin·gent \'strinjənt\ adj : severe

stringy \'striŋē\ adj **string·i·er; -est** : tough or fibrous

¹strip \'strip\ vb **-pp-** 1 : take the covering or clothing from 2 : undress —**strip·per** n

²strip n : long narrow flat piece

stripe \'strīp\ n : distinctive line or long narrow section ~ vb **striped** \'strīpt\; **strip·ing** : make stripes on —**striped** \'strīpt, 'strīpəd\ adj

strive \'strīv\ vb **strove** \'strōv\; **striv·en** \'strivən\ or **strived; striv·ing** \'strī-viŋ\ 1 : struggle 2 : try hard

strode past of STRIDE

stroke \'strōk\ vb **stroked; strok·ing** : rub gently ~ n 1 : act of swinging or striking 2 : sudden action

stroll \'strōl\ vb : walk leisurely —**stroll** n —**stroll·er** n

strong \'strȯŋ\ adj 1 : capable of exerting great force or of withstanding stress or violence **2** : healthy **3** : zealous —**strong·ly** adv

strong·hold n : fortified place

struck past of STRIKE

struc·ture \'strək·chər\ n **1** : building **2** : arrangement of elements ~ vb **-tured; -tur·ing** : make into a structure —**struc·tur·al** \-chərəl\ adj

strug·gle \'strəgəl\ vb **-gled; -gling 1** : make strenuous efforts to overcome an adversary **2** : proceed with great effort ~ n **1** : strenuous effort **2** : intense competition for superiority

strum \'strəm\ vb **-mm-** : play (a musical instrument) by brushing the strings with the fingers

strum·pet \'strəmpət\ n : prostitute

strung past of STRING

strut \'strət\ vb **-tt-** : walk in a proud or showy manner ~ n **1** : proud walk **2** : supporting bar or rod

strych·nine \'strik,nīn, -nən, -,nēn\ n : bitter poisonous substance

stub \'stəb\ n : short end or section ~ vb **-bb-** : strike against something

stub·ble \'stəbəl\ n : short growth left after cutting —**stub·bly** adj

stub·born \'stəbərn\ adj **1** : determined not to yield **2** : hard to control —**stub·born·ly** adv —**stub·born·ness** n

stub·by \'stəbē\ adj : short, blunt, and thick

stuc·co \'stəkō\ n, pl **-cos** or **-coes** : plaster for coating outside walls —**stuc·coed** \'stəkōd\ adj

stuck past of STICK

stuck-up \'stək'əp\ adj : conceited

1stud \'stəd\ n : male horse kept for breeding

2stud n **1** : upright beam for holding wall material **2** : projecting nail, pin, or rod ~ vb **-dd-** : supply or dot with studs

stu·dent \'stüd°nt, 'styü-\ n : one who studies

stud·ied \'stədēd\ adj : premeditated

stu·dio \'stüdē,ō, 'styü-\ n, pl **-dios 1** : artist's workroom **2** : place where movies are made or television or radio shows are broadcast

stu·di·ous \'stüdēəs, 'styü-\ adj : devoted to study —**stu·di·ous·ly** adv

study \'stədē\ n, pl **stud·ies 1** : act or process of learning something **2** : branch of learning **3** : careful examination **4** : room for reading or studying ~ vb **stud·ied; study·ing**

: apply the attention and mind to a subject

stuff \'stəf\ n **1** : personal property **2** : raw or fundamental material **3** : unspecified material or things ~ vb : fill by packing things in —**stuff·ing** n

stuffy \'stəfē\ adj **stuff·i·er; -est 1** : lacking fresh air **2** : unimaginative or pompous

stul·ti·fy \'stəltə,fī\ vb **-fied; -fy·ing 1** : cause to appear foolish **2** : impair or make ineffective **3** : have a dulling effect on

stum·ble \'stəmbəl\ vb **-bled; -bling 1** : lose one's balance or fall in walking or running **2** : speak or act clumsily **3** : happen by chance —**stumble** n

stump \'stəmp\ n : part left when something is cut off ~ vb : confuse —**stumpy** adj

stun \'stən\ vb **-nn- 1** : make senseless or dizzy by or as if by a blow **2** : bewilder

stung past of STING

stunk past of STINK

stun·ning \'stənin\ adj **1** : astonishing or incredible **2** : strikingly beautiful —**stun·ning·ly** adv

1stunt \'stənt\ vb : hinder the normal growth or progress of

2stunt n : spectacular feat

stu·pe·fy \'stüpə,fī, 'styü-\ vb **-fied; -fy·ing 1** : make insensible by or as if by drugs **2** : amaze

stu·pen·dous \stü'pendəs, styü-\ adj : very big or impressive —**stu·pen·dous·ly** adv

stu·pid \'stüpəd, 'styü-\ adj : not sensible or intelligent —**stu·pid·i·ty** \stü-'pidətē, styü-\ n —**stu·pid·ly** adv

stu·por \'stüpər, 'styü-\ n : state of being conscious but not aware or sensible

stur·dy \'stərdē\ adj **-di·er; -est** : strong —**stur·di·ly** \'stərd°lē\ adv —**stur·di·ness** n

stur·geon \'stərjən\ n : fish whose roe is caviar

stut·ter \'stətər\ vb or n : stammer

1sty \'stī\ n, pl **sties** : pig pen

2sty, stye \'stī\ n, pl **sties** or **styes** : inflamed swelling on the edge of an eyelid

style \'stīl\ n **1** : distinctive way of speaking, writing, or acting **2** : elegant or fashionable way of living ~ vb **styled; styl·ing 1** : name **2** : give a particular design or style to —**styl-**

ish \'stīlish\ adj —**styl·ish·ly** adv —
styl·ish·ness n —**styl·ist** \-ist\ n —
styl·ize \'stīˌlīz\ vb

sty·lus \'stīləs\ n, pl **-li** \-ˌlī\ \'stīˌlī\ 1
: pointed writing tool 2 : phonograph
needle

sty·mie \'stīmē\ vb **-mied; -mie·ing**
: block or frustrate

suave \'swäv\ adj : well-mannered and
gracious —**suave·ly** adv

1sub \'səb\ n or vb : substitute

2sub n : submarine

sub- \ˌsəb, 'səb\ prefix 1 : under or beneath 2 : subordinate or secondary 3
: subordinate portion of 4 : with repetition of a process so as to form,
stress, or deal with subordinate parts
or relations 5 : somewhat 6 : nearly

subacute	subindustry
subagency	sublease
subagent	sublethal
subarctic	sublevel
subarea	subliterate
subatmospheric	subnetwork
subaverage	suboceanic
subbase	suborder
subbasement	subpar
subbranch	subpart
subcabinet	subplot
subcategory	subpolar
subclass	subprincipal
subclassification	subprocess
subclassify	subprogram
subcommission	subproject
subcommittee	subregion
subcommunity	subsea
subcomponent	subsection
subcontract	subsense
subcontractor	subspecialty
subculture	subspecies
subdean	substage
subdepartment	subsurface
subdistrict	subsystem
subentry	subtemperate
subfamily	subtheme
subfreezing	subtopic
subgroup	subtotal
subhead	subtreasury
subheading	subtype
subhuman	subunit
subindex	subvariety

sub·con·scious \ˌsəb'känchəs\ adj
: existing without conscious awareness ~ n : part of the mind concerned
with subconscious activities —**sub·
con·scious·ly** adv

sub·di·vide \ˌsəbdə'vīd, 'səbdəˌvīd\ vb
1 : divide into several parts 2 : divide
(land) into building lots —**sub·di·vi·
sion** \-'vizhən, -ˌvizh-\ n

sub·due \səb'dü, -'dyü\ vb **-dued; -du·
ing** 1 : bring under control 2 : reduce
the intensity of

sub·ject \'səbjikt\ n 1 : person under the
authority of another 2 : something being discussed or studied 3 : word or
word group about which something is
said in a sentence ~ adj 1 : being under one's authority 2 : prone 3
: dependent on some condition or act
~ \səb'jekt\ vb 1 : bring under control
2 : cause to undergo —**sub·jec·tion**
\-'jekshən\ n

sub·jec·tive \ˌsəb'jektiv\ adj : deriving
from an individual viewpoint or bias
—**sub·jec·tive·ly** adv —**sub·jec·tiv·i·
ty** \-ˌjek'tivətē\ n

sub·ju·gate \'səbjiˌgāt\ vb **-gat·ed; -gat·
ing** : bring under one's control —**sub·
ju·ga·tion** \ˌsəbji'gāshən\ n

sub·junc·tive \səb'jəŋktiv\ adj : relating
to a verb form which expresses possibility or contingency —**subjunctive**
n

sub·let \'səbˌlet\ vb **-let; -let·ting** : rent
(a property) from a lessee

sub·lime \sə'blīm\ adj : splendid —**sub·
lime·ly** adv

sub·ma·rine \'səbməˌrēn, ˌsəbmə'-\ adj
: existing, acting, or growing under
the sea ~ n : underwater boat

sub·merge \səb'mərj\ vb **-merged;
-merg·ing** : put or plunge under the
surface of water —**sub·mer·gence**
\-'mərjəns\ n —**sub·mers·ible** \səb-
'mərsəbəl\ adj or n —**sub·mer·sion**
\-'mərzhən\ n

sub·mit \səb'mit\ vb **-tt-** 1 : yield 2
: give or offer —**sub·mis·sion** \-'mi-
shən\ n —**sub·mis·sive** \-'misiv\ adj

sub·nor·mal \ˌsəb'nórməl\ adj : falling
below what is normal

sub·or·di·nate \sə'bórdənət\ adj : lower
in rank ~ n : one that is subordinate
~ \sə'bórdəˌnāt\ vb **-nat·ed; -nat·ing**
: place in a lower rank or class —**sub·
or·di·na·tion** \-ˌbórdən'āshən\ n

sub·poe·na \sə'pēnə\ n : summons to
appear in court ~ vb **-naed; -na·ing**
: summon with a subpoena

sub·scribe \səb'skrīb\ vb **-scribed;
-scrib·ing** 1 : give consent or ap-

proval **2** : agree to support or to receive and pay for **—sub·scrib·er** n

sub·scrip·tion \səb'skripshən\ n : order for regular receipt of a publication

sub·se·quent \'səbsikwənt, -sə₁kwent\ adj : following after **—sub·se·quent·ly** \-ˌkwentlē, -kwənt-\ adv

sub·ser·vi·ence \səb'sərvēəns\ n : obsequious submission **—sub·ser·vi·en·cy** \-ənsē\ n **—sub·ser·vi·ent** \-ənt\ adj

sub·side \səb'sīd\ vb **-sid·ed; -sid·ing** : die down in intensity

sub·sid·iary \səb'sidē₁erē\ adj **1** : furnishing support **2** : of secondary importance ~ n : company controlled by another company

sub·si·dize \'səbsə₁dīz\ vb **-dized; -diz·ing** : aid with a subsidy

sub·si·dy \'səbsədē\ n, pl **-dies** : gift of supporting funds

sub·sist \səb'sist\ vb : acquire the necessities of life **—sub·sis·tence** \-'sistəns\ n

sub·stance \'səbstəns\ n **1** : essence or essential part **2** : physical material **3** : wealth

sub·stan·dard \ˌsəb'standərd\ adj : falling short of a standard or norm

sub·stan·tial \səb'stanchəl\ adj **1** : plentiful **2** : considerable **—sub·stan·tial·ly** adv

sub·stan·ti·ate \səb'stanchē₁āt\ vb **-at·ed; -at·ing** : verify **—sub·stan·ti·a·tion** \-₁stanchē'āshən\ n

sub·sti·tute \'səbstə₁tüt, -₁tyüt\ n : replacement ~ vb **-tut·ed; -tut·ing** : put or serve in place of another **—substitute** adj **—sub·sti·tu·tion** \ˌsəbstə'tüshən, -'tyü-\ n

sub·ter·fuge \'səbtər₁fyüj\ n : deceptive trick

sub·ter·ra·nean \ˌsəbtə'rānēən\ adj : lying or being underground

sub·ti·tle \'səb₁tīt²l\ n : movie caption

sub·tle \'sət²l\ adj **-tler** \-ər\; **-tlest** \-ist\ **1** : hardly noticeable **2** : clever **—sub·tle·ty** \-tē\ n **—sub·tly** \-ₗlē\ adv

sub·tract \səb'trakt\ vb : take away (as one number from another) **—sub·trac·tion** \-'trakshən\ n

sub·urb \'səb₁ərb\ n : residential area adjacent to a city **—sub·ur·ban** \sə'bərbən\ adj or n **—sub·ur·ban·ite** \-bə₁nīt\ n

sub·vert \səb'vərt\ vb : overthrow or ruin **—sub·ver·sion** \-'vərzhən\ n **—sub·ver·sive** \-'vərsiv\ adj

sub·way \'səb₁wā\ n : underground electric railway

suc·ceed \sək'sēd\ vb **1** : follow (someone) in a job, role, or title **2** : attain a desired object or end

suc·cess \-'ses\ n **1** : favorable outcome **2** : gaining of wealth and fame **3** : one that succeeds **—suc·cess·ful** \-fəl\ adj **—suc·cess·ful·ly** adv

suc·ces·sion \sək'seshən\ n **1** : order, act, or right of succeeding **2** : series

suc·ces·sive \-'sesiv\ adj : following in order **—suc·ces·sive·ly** adv

suc·ces·sor \-'sesər\ n : one that succeeds another

suc·cinct \sək'siŋkt, sə'siŋkt\ adj : brief **—suc·cinct·ly** adv **—suc·cinct·ness** n

suc·cor \'səkər\ n or vb : help

suc·co·tash \'səkə₁tash\ n : beans and corn cooked together

suc·cu·lent \'səkyələnt\ adj : juicy **—suc·cu·lence** \-ləns\ n **—succulent** n

suc·cumb \sə'kəm\ vb **1** : yield **2** : die

such \'səch\ adj **1** : of this or that kind **2** : having a specified quality **—such** pron or adv

suck \'sək\ vb **1** : draw in liquid with the mouth **2** : draw liquid from by or as if by mouth **—suck** n

suck·er \'səkər\ n **1** : one that sucks or clings **2** : easily deceived person

suck·le \'səkəl\ vb **-led; -ling** : give or draw milk from the breast or udder

suck·ling \'səkliŋ\ n : young unweaned mammal

su·crose \'sü₁krōs, -₁krōz\ n : cane or beet sugar

suc·tion \'səkshən\ n **1** : act of sucking **2** : act or process of drawing in by partially exhausting the air

sud·den \'səd²n\ adj **1** : happening unexpectedly **2** : steep **3** : hasty **—sud·den·ly** adv **—sud·den·ness** n

suds \'sədz\ n pl : soapy water esp. when frothy **—sudsy** \'sədzē\ adj

sue \'sü\ vb **sued; su·ing 1** : petition **2** : bring legal action against

suede, suède \'swād\ n : leather with a napped surface

su·et \'süət\ n : hard beef fat

suf·fer \'səfər\ vb **1** : experience pain, loss, or hardship **2** : permit **—suf·fer·er** n

suf·fer·ing \-əriŋ\ n : pain or hardship

suf·fice \sə'fīs\ vb **-ficed; -fic·ing** : be sufficient

suf·fi·cient \sə'fishənt\ adj : adequate

—suf·fi·cien·cy \-ənsē\ n —suf·fi-
cient·ly adv

suf·fix \'səf,iks\ n : letters added at the
end of a word —suffix \'səfiks,
sə'fiks\ vb —suf·fix·a·tion \,səf-
,ik'sāshən\ n

suf·fo·cate \'səfə,kāt\ vb -cat·ed; -cat·
ing : suffer or die or cause to die from
lack of air —suf·fo·cat·ing·ly adv —
suf·fo·ca·tion \,səfə'kāshən\ n

suf·frage \'səfrij\ n : right to vote

suf·fuse \sə'fyüz\ vb -fused; -fus·ing
: spread over or through

sug·ar \'shùgər\ n : sweet substance ~
vb : mix, cover, or sprinkle with sugar
—sug·ar·cane n —sug·ary adj

sug·gest \sə'jest, səg-\ vb 1 : put into
someone's mind 2 : remind one by
association of ideas —sug·gest·ible
\-'jestəbəl\ adj —sug·ges·tion \-'jes-
chən\ n

sug·ges·tive \-'jestiv\ adj : suggesting
something improper —sug·ges·tive-
ly adv —sug·ges·tive·ness n

sui·cide \'süə,sīd\ n 1 : act of killing
oneself purposely 2 : one who commits suicide —sui·cid·al \,süə'sīdᵊl\
adj

suit \'süt\ n 1 : action in court to recover
a right or claim 2 : number of things
used or worn together 3 : one of the
4 sets of playing cards ~ vb 1 : be
appropriate or becoming to 2 : meet
the needs of —suit·abil·i·ty \,sütə-
'bilətē\ n —suit·able \'sütəbəl\ adj—
suit·ably adv

suit·case n : case for a traveler's clothing

suite \'swēt, for 2 also 'süt\ n 1 : group
of rooms 2 : set of matched furniture

suit·or \'sütər\ n : one who seeks to
marry a woman

sul·fur \'səlfər\ n : nonmetallic yellow
chemical element —sul·fu·ric \,səl-
'fyùrik\ adj —sul·fu·rous \-'fyùrəs,
'səlfərəs, 'səlfyə-\ adj

sulk \'səlk\ vb : be moodily silent or irritable —sulk n

sulky \'səlkē\ adj : inclined to sulk ~ n
: light 2-wheeled horse-drawn cart —
sulk·i·ly \'səlkəlē\ adv —sulk·i·ness
\-kēnəs\ n

sul·len \'sələn\ adj 1 : gloomily silent 2
: dismal —sul·len·ly adv —sul·len-
ness n

sul·ly \'səlē\ vb -lied; -ly·ing : cast
doubt or disgrace on

sul·tan \'səltᵊn\ n : sovereign of a Muslim state —sul·tan·ate \-,āt\ n

sul·try \'səltrē\ adj -tri·er; -est 1 : very
hot and moist 2 : sexually arousing

sum \'səm\ n 1 : amount 2 : gist 3
: result of addition ~ vb -mm- : find
the sum of

su·mac \'shü,mak, 'sü-\ n : shrub with
spikes of berries

sum·ma·ry \'səmərē\ adj 1 : concise 2
: done without delay or formality ~
n, pl -ries : concise statement —sum-
mar·i·ly \sə'merəlē, 'səmərəlē\ adv
—sum·ma·rize \'səmə,rīz\ vb

sum·ma·tion \sə'māshən\ n : a sum-
ming up esp. in court

sum·mer \'səmər\ n : season in which
the sun shines most directly —sum·
mery adj

sum·mit \'səmət\ n 1 : highest point 2
: high-level conference

sum·mon \'səmən\ vb 1 : send for or call
together 2 : order to appear in court
—sum·mon·er n

sum·mons \'səmənz\ n, pl sum·mons·es
: an order to answer charges in court

sump·tu·ous \'səmpchəwəs\ adj : lavish

sun \'sən\ n 1 : shining celestial body
around which the planets revolve 2
: light of the sun ~ vb -nn- : expose
to the sun —sun·beam n —sun·
block n —sun·burn n or vb —sun-
glass·es n pl —sun·light n —sun·ny
adj —sun·rise n —sun·set n —sun-
shine n —sun·tan n

sun·dae \'səndē\ n : ice cream with topping

Sun·day \'səndā, -dē\ n : 1st day of the
week

sun·di·al \-,dīəl\ n : device for showing
time by the sun's shadow

sun·dries \'səndrēz\ n, pl : various small
articles

sun·dry \-drē\ adj : several

sun·fish n : perchlike freshwater fish

sun·flow·er n : tall plant grown for its
oil-rich seeds

sung past of SING

sunk past of SINK

sunk·en \'səŋkən\ adj 1 : submerged 2
: fallen in

sun·spot n : dark spot on the sun

sun·stroke n : heatstroke from the sun

sup \'səp\ vb -pp- : eat the evening meal

super \'süpər\ adj : very fine

super- \,süpər, 'sü-\ prefix 1 : higher in
quantity, quality, or degree than 2 : in

addition **3** : exceeding a norm **4** : in excessive degree or intensity **5** : surpassing others of its kind **6** : situated above, on, or at the top of **7** : more inclusive than **8** : superior in status or position

superabundance	superpatriotism
superabundant	superplane
superambitious	superpolite
superathlete	superport
superbomb	superpowerful
superclean	superrich
supercolossal	supersalesman
superconvenient	superscout
supercop	supersecrecy
superdense	supersecret
supereffective	supersensitive
superefficiency	supersize
superefficient	supersized
superfast	superslick
supergood	supersmooth
supergovern-	supersoft
ment	superspecial
supergroup	superspecialist
superhero	superspy
superheroine	superstar
superhuman	superstate
superintellec-	superstrength
tual	superstrong
superintellig-	supersystem
ence	supertanker
superintelligent	superthick
superman	superthin
supermodern	supertight
superpatriot	superweapon
superpatriotic	superwoman

su·perb \su'pərb\ *adj* : outstanding — **su·perb·ly** *adv*

su·per·cil·ious \,süpər'silēəs\ *adj* : haughtily contemptuous

su·per·fi·cial \,süpər'fishəl\ *adj* : relating to what is only apparent — **su·per·fi·ci·al·i·ty** \-,fishē'alətē\ *n* — **su·per·fi·cial·ly** *adv*

su·per·flu·ous \su'pərfləwəs\ *adj* : more than necessary — **su·per·flu·i·ty** \,süpər'flüətē\ *n*

su·per·im·pose \,süpərim'pōz\ *vb* : lay over or above something

su·per·in·tend \,süpərin'tend\ *vb* : have charge and oversight of — **su·per·in·ten·dence** \-'tendəns\ *n* — **su·per·in·ten·den·cy** \-dənsē\ *n* — **su·per·in·ten·dent** \-dənt\ *n*

su·pe·ri·or \su'pirēər\ *adj* **1** : higher, better, or more important **2** : haughty

—**superior** *n* —**su·pe·ri·or·i·ty** \-,pirē'órətē\ *n*

su·per·la·tive \su'pərlətiv\ *adj* **1** : relating to or being an adjective or adverb form that denotes an extreme level **2** : surpassing others —**superlative** *n* —**su·per·la·tive·ly** *adv*

su·per·mar·ket \'süpər,märkət\ *n* : self-service grocery store

su·per·nat·u·ral \,süpər'nachərəl\ *adj* : beyond the observable physical world —**su·per·nat·u·ral·ly** *adv*

su·per·pow·er \'süpər,paủər\ *n* : politically and militarily dominant nation

su·per·sede \,süpər'sēd\ *vb* -**sed·ed**; -**sed·ing** : take the place of

su·per·son·ic \-'sänik\ *adj* : faster than the speed of sound

su·per·sti·tion \,süpər'stishən\ *n* : beliefs based on ignorance, fear of the unknown, or trust in magic —**su·per·sti·tious** \-əs\ *adj*

su·per·struc·ture \'süpər,strəkchər\ *n* : something built on a base or as a vertical extension

su·per·vise \'süpər,vīz\ *vb* -**vised**; -**vis·ing** : have charge of —**su·per·vi·sion** \,süpər'vizhən\ *n* —**su·per·vi·sor** \'süpər,vīzər\ *n* —**su·per·vi·so·ry** \,süpər'vīzərē\ *adj*

su·pine \su'pīn\ *adj* **1** : lying on the back **2** : indifferent or abject

sup·per \'səpər\ *n* : evening meal

sup·plant \sə'plant\ *vb* : take the place of

sup·ple \'səpəl\ *adj* -**pler**; -**plest** : able to bend easily

sup·ple·ment \'səpləmənt\ *n* : something that adds to or makes up for a lack —**supplement** *vb* —**sup·ple·men·tal** \,səplə'mentᵊl\ *adj* —**sup·ple·men·ta·ry** \-'mentərē\ *adj*

sup·pli·ant \'səplēənt\ *n* : one who supplicates

sup·pli·cate \'səplə,kāt\ *vb* -**cat·ed**; -**cat·ing** **1** : pray to God **2** : ask earnestly and humbly —**sup·pli·cant** \-likənt\ *n* —**sup·pli·ca·tion** \,səplə'kāshən\ *n*

sup·ply \sə'plī\ *vb* -**plied**; -**ply·ing** : furnish ~ *n, pl* -**plies 1** : amount needed or available **2** *pl* : provisions —**sup·pli·er** \-'plīər\ *n*

sup·port \sə'pōrt\ *vb* **1** : take sides with **2** : provide with food, clothing, and shelter **3** : hold up or serve as a foundation for —**support** *n* —**sup·port·able** *adj* —**sup·port·er** *n*

sup·pose \sə'pōz\ vb **-posed; -pos·ing 1** : assume to be true **2** : expect **3** : think probable **—sup·po·si·tion** \,səpə-'zishən\ n

sup·pos·i·to·ry \sə'päzə,tōrē\ n, pl **-ries** : medicated material for insertion (as into the rectum)

sup·press \sə'pres\ vb **1** : put an end to by authority **2** : keep from being known **3** : hold back **—sup·pres·sant** \sə'pres³nt\ n **—sup·pres·sion** \-'preshən\ n

su·prem·a·cy \sù'preməsē\ n, pl **-cies** : supreme power or authority

su·preme \sù'prēm\ adj **1** : highest in rank or authority **2** : greatest possible **—su·preme·ly** adv

Supreme Being n : God

sur·charge \'sər,chärj\ n **1** : excessive load or burden **2** : extra fee or cost

sure \'shùr\ adj **sur·er; sur·est 1** : confident **2** : reliable **3** : not to be disputed **4** : bound to happen ~ adv : surely **—sure·ness** n

sure·ly \'shùrlē\ adv **1** : in a sure manner **2** : without doubt **3** : indeed

sure·ty \'shùrətē\ n, pl **-ties 1** : guarantee **2** : one who gives a guarantee for another person

surf \'sərf\ n : waves that break on the shore ~ vb : ride the surf **—surf·board** n **—surf·er** n **—surf·ing** n

sur·face \'sərfəs\ n **1** : the outside of an object **2** : outward aspect ~ vb **-faced; -fac·ing** : rise to the surface

sur·feit \'sərfət\ n **1** : excess **2** : excessive indulgence (as in food or drink) **3** : disgust caused by excess ~ vb : feed, supply, or indulge to the point of surfeit

surge \'sərj\ vb **surged; surg·ing** : rise and fall in or as if in waves ~ n : sudden increase

sur·geon \'sərjən\ n : physician who specializes in surgery

sur·gery \'sərjərē\ n, pl **-ger·ies** : medical treatment involving cutting open the body

sur·gi·cal \'sərjikəl\ adj : relating to surgeons or surgery **—sur·gi·cal·ly** adv

sur·ly \'sərlē\ adj **-li·er; -est** : having a rude nature **—sur·li·ness** n

sur·mise \sər'mīz\ vb **-mised; -mis·ing** : guess **—surmise** n

sur·mount \-'maùnt\ vb **1** : prevail over **2** : get to or be the top of

sur·name \'sər,nām\ n : family name

sur·pass \sər'pas\ vb : go beyond or exceed **—sur·pass·ing·ly** adv

sur·plice \'sərpləs\ n : loose white outer ecclesiastical vestment

sur·plus \'sər,pləs\ n : quantity left over

sur·prise \sə'prīz, sər-\ vb **-prised; -pris·ing 1** : come upon or affect unexpectedly **2** : amaze **—surprise** n **—sur·pris·ing** adj **—sur·pris·ing·ly** adv

sur·ren·der \sə'rendər\ vb : give up oneself or a possession to another ~ n : act of surrendering

sur·rep·ti·tious \,sərəp'tishəs\ adj : done, made, or acquired by stealth **—sur·rep·ti·tious·ly** adv

sur·rey \'sərē\ n, pl **-reys** : horse-drawn carriage

sur·ro·gate \'sərəgāt, -gət\ n : substitute

sur·round \sə'raùnd\ vb : enclose on all sides

sur·round·ings \sə'raùndiŋz\ n pl : objects, conditions, or area around something

sur·veil·lance \sər'vāləns, -'vālyəns, -'vāəns\ n : careful watch

sur·vey \sər'vā\ vb **-veyed; -vey·ing 1** : look over and examine closely **2** : make a survey of (as a tract of land) ~ \'sər,-\ n, pl **-veys 1** : inspection **2** : process of measuring (as land) **—sur·vey·or** \-ər\ n

sur·vive \sər'vīv\ vb **-vived; -viv·ing 1** : remain alive or in existence **2** : outlive or outlast **—sur·viv·al** n **—sur·vi·vor** \-'vīvər\ n

sus·cep·ti·ble \sə'septəbəl\ adj : likely to allow or be affected by something **—sus·cep·ti·bil·i·ty** \-,septə'bilətē\ n

sus·pect \'səs,pekt, sə'spekt\ adj **1** : regarded with suspicion **2** : questionable ~ \'səs,pekt\ n : one who is suspected (as of a crime) ~ \sə'spekt\ vb **1** : have doubts of **2** : believe guilty without proof **3** : guess

sus·pend \sə'spend\ vb **1** : temporarily stop or keep from a function or job **2** : withhold (judgment) temporarily **3** : hang

sus·pend·er \sə'spendər\ n : one of 2 supporting straps holding up trousers and passing over the shoulders

sus·pense \sə'spens\ n : excitement and uncertainty as to outcome **—sus·pense·ful** adj

sus·pen·sion \sə'spenchən\ n : act of

suspending or the state or period of being suspended

sus·pi·cion \sə'spishən\ *n* 1 : act of suspecting something 2 : trace

sus·pi·cious \-əs\ *adj* 1 : arousing suspicion 2 : inclined to suspect —**sus·pi·cious·ly** *adv*

sus·tain \sə'stān\ *vb* 1 : provide with nourishment 2 : keep going 3 : hold up 4 : suffer 5 : support or prove

sus·te·nance \'səstənəns\ *n* 1 : nourishment 2 : something that sustains or supports

svelte \'sfelt\ *adj* : slender and graceful

swab \'swäb\ *n* 1 : mop 2 : wad of absorbent material for applying medicine ~ *vb* -**bb**- : use a swab on

swad·dle \'swäd³l\ *vb* -**dled**; -**dling** \'swädᵊliŋ\ : bind (an infant) in bands of cloth

swag·ger \'swagər\ *vb* -**gered**; -**ger·ing** 1 : walk with a conceited swing 2 : boast —**swagger** *n*

¹**swal·low** \'swälō\ *n* : small migratory bird

²**swallow** *vb* 1 : take into the stomach through the throat 2 : envelop or take in 3 : accept too easily —**swallow** *n*

swam *past of* SWIM

swamp \'swämp\ *n* : wet spongy land ~ *vb* : deluge (as with water) —**swampy** *adj*

swan \'swän\ *n* : white long-necked swimming bird

swap \'swäp\ *vb* -**pp**- : trade —**swap** *n*

swarm \'swȯrm\ *n* 1 : mass of honeybees leaving a hive to start a new colony 2 : large crowd ~ *vb* : gather in a swarm

swar·thy \'swȯrthē, -thē\ *adj* -**thi·er**; -**est** : dark in complexion

swash·buck·ler \'swäsh,bəklər\ *n* : swaggering or daring soldier or adventurer —**swash·buck·ling** \-,bəkliŋ\ *adj*

swat \'swät\ *vb* -**tt**- : hit sharply —**swat** *n* —**swat·ter** *n*

swatch \'swäch\ *n* : sample piece (as of fabric)

swath \'swäth, 'swȯth\, **swathe** \'swäth, 'swȯth, 'swäth\ *n* : row or path cut (as through grass)

swathe \'swäth, 'swȯth, 'swäth\ *vb* **swathed**; **swath·ing** : wrap with or as if with a bandage

sway \'swā\ *vb* 1 : swing gently from side to side 2 : influence ~ *n* 1

: gentle swinging from side to side 2 : controlling power or influence

swear \'swar\ *vb* **swore** \'swōr\; **sworn** \'swōrn\; **swear·ing** 1 : make or cause to make a solemn statement under oath 2 : use profane language —**swear·er** *n* —**swear·ing** *n*

sweat \'swet\ *vb* **sweat** *or* **sweat·ed**; **sweat·ing** 1 : excrete salty moisture from skin glands 2 : form drops of moisture on the surface 3 : work or cause to work hard —**sweat** *n* —**sweaty** *adj*

sweat·er \'swetər\ *n* : knitted jacket or pullover

sweat·shirt \'swet,shərt\ *n* : loose collarless heavy cotton jersey pullover

sweep \'swēp\ *vb* **swept** \'swept\; **sweep·ing** 1 : remove or clean by a brush or a single forceful wipe (as of the hand) 2 : move over with speed and force (as of the hand) 3 : move or extend in a wide curve ~ *n* 1 : a clearing off or away 2 : single forceful wipe or swinging movement 3 : scope —**sweep·er** *n* —**sweep·ing** *adj*

sweep·stakes \'swēp,stāks\ *n, pl* **sweep·stakes** : contest in which the entire prize may go to the winner

sweet \'swēt\ *adj* 1 : being or causing the pleasing taste typical of sugar 2 : not stale or spoiled 3 : not salted 4 : pleasant 5 : much loved ~ *n* : something sweet —**sweet·en** \'swēt³n\ *vb* —**sweet·ly** *adv* —**sweet·ness** *n* —**sweet·en·er** \-ᵊnər\ *n*

sweet·heart *n* : person one loves

sweet potato *n* : sweet yellow edible root of a tropical vine

swell \'swel\ *vb* **swelled** *or* **swol·len** \'swōlən\; **swell·ing** 1 : enlarge 2 : bulge 3 : fill or be filled with emotion ~ *n* 1 : long rolling ocean wave 2 : condition of bulging —**swell·ing** *n*

swel·ter \'sweltər\ *vb* : be uncomfortable from excessive heat

swept *past of* SWEEP

swerve \'swərv\ *vb* **swerved**; **swerv·ing** : move abruptly aside from a course —**swerve** *n*

¹**swift** \'swift\ *adj* 1 : moving with great speed 2 : occurring suddenly —**swift·ly** *adv* —**swift·ness** *n*

²**swift** *n* : small insect-eating bird

swig \'swig\ *vb* -**gg**- : drink in gulps —**swig** *n*

swill \'swil\ vb : swallow greedily ~ n 1 : animal food of refuse and liquid 2 : garbage

swim \'swim\ vb **swam** \'swam\; **swum** \'swəm\; **swim·ming** 1 : propel oneself in water 2 : float in or be surrounded with a liquid 3 : be dizzy ~ n : act or period of swimming —**swim·mer** n

swin·dle \'swind°l\ vb -**dled**; -**dling** \-iŋ\ : cheat (someone) of money or property —**swindle** n —**swin·dler** \-ər\ n

swine \'swīn\ n, pl **swine** : short-legged hoofed mammal with a snout —**swin·ish** \'swīnish\ adj

swing \'swiŋ\ vb **swung** \'swəŋ\; **swing·ing** 1 : move or cause to move rapidly in an arc 2 : sway or cause to sway back and forth 3 : hang so as to sway or sag 4 : turn on a hinge or pivot 5 : manage or handle successfully ~ n 1 : act or instance of swinging 2 : swinging movement (as in trying to hit something) 3 : suspended seat for swinging —**swing** adj —**swing·er** n

swipe \'swīp\ n : strong sweeping blow ~ vb **swiped**; **swip·ing** 1 : strike or wipe with a sweeping motion 2 : steal esp. with a quick movement

swirl \'swərl\ vb : move or cause to move in a circle —**swirl** n

swish \'swish\ n : hissing, sweeping, or brushing sound —**swish** vb

switch \'swich\ n 1 : slender flexible whip or twig 2 : blow with a switch 3 : shift, change, or reversal 4 : device that opens or closes an electrical circuit ~ vb 1 : punish or urge on with a switch 2 : change or reverse roles, positions, or subjects 3 : operate a switch of

switch·board n : panel of switches to make and break telephone connections

swiv·el \'swivəl\ vb -**eled** or -**elled**; -**el·ing** or -**el·ling** : swing or turn on a pivot —**swivel** n

swollen past part of SWELL

swoon \'swün\ n : faint —**swoon** vb

swoop \'swüp\ vb : make a swift diving attack —**swoop** n

sword \'sōrd\ n : thrusting or cutting weapon with a long blade

sword·fish n : large ocean fish with a long swordlike projection

swore past of SWEAR

sworn past part of SWEAR

swum past part of SWIM

swung past of SWING

syc·a·more \'sikə,mōr\ n : shade tree

sy·co·phant \'sikəfənt\ n : servile flatterer —**syc·o·phan·tic** \,sikə'fantik\ adj

syl·la·ble \'siləbəl\ n : unit of a spoken word —**syl·lab·ic** \sə'labik\ adj

syl·la·bus \'siləbəs\ n, pl -**bi** \-,bī\ or -**bus·es** : summary of main points (as of a course of study)

syl·van \'silvən\ adj 1 : living or located in a wooded area 2 : abounding in woods

sym·bol \'simbəl\ n : something that represents or suggests another thing —**sym·bol·ic** \sim'bälik\ adj —**sym·bol·i·cal·ly** adv

sym·bol·ism \'simbə,lizəm\ n : representation of meanings with symbols

sym·bol·ize \'simbə,līz\ vb -**ized**; -**izing** : serve as a symbol of —**sym·bol·i·za·tion** \,simbələ'zāshən\ n

sym·me·try \'simətrē\ n, pl -**tries** : regularity and balance in the arrangement of parts —**sym·met·ri·cal** \sə'metrikəl\ adj —**sym·met·ri·cal·ly** adv

sym·pa·thize \'simpə,thīz\ vb -**thized**; -**thiz·ing** : feel or show sympathy —**sym·pa·thiz·er** n

sym·pa·thy \'simpəthē\ n, pl -**thies** 1 : ability to understand or share the feelings of another 2 : expression of sorrow for another's misfortune —**sym·pa·thet·ic** \,simpə'thetik\ adj —**sym·pa·thet·i·cal·ly** adv

sym·pho·ny \'simfənē\ n, pl -**nies** : composition for an orchestra or the orchestra itself —**sym·phon·ic** \sim'fänik\ adj

sym·po·sium \sim'pōzēəm\ n, pl -**sia** \-zēə\ or -**siums** : conference at which a topic is discussed

symp·tom \'simptəm\ n : unusual feeling or reaction that is a sign of disease —**symp·tom·at·ic** \,simptə'matik\ adj

syn·a·gogue, syn·a·gog \'sinə,gäg, -,gōg\ n : Jewish house of worship

syn·chro·nize \'siŋkrə,nīz, 'sin-\ vb -**nized**; -**niz·ing** 1 : occur or cause to occur at the same instant 2 : cause to agree in time —syn·chro·ni·za·tion \,siŋkrənə'zāshən, ,sin-\ n

syn·co·pa·tion \,siŋkə'pāshən, ,sin-\ n : shifting of the regular musical accent to the weak beat —syn·co·pate \'siŋkə,pāt, 'sin-\ vb

syn·di·cate \'sindikət\ n : business association ~ \-də,kāt\ vb -cat·ed; -cat·ing 1 : form a syndicate 2 : publish through a syndicate —syn·di·ca·tion \,sində'kā-shən\ n

syn·drome \'sin,drōm\ n : particular group of symptoms

syn·onym \'sinə,nim\ n : word with the same meaning as another —syn·on·y·mous \sə'nänəməs\ adj —syn·on·y·my \-mē\ n

syn·op·sis \sə'näpsəs\ n, pl -op·ses \-,sēz\ : condensed statement or outline

syn·tax \'sin,taks\ n : way in which words are put together —syn·tac·tic

\sin'taktik\ or syn·tac·ti·cal \-tikəl\ adj

syn·the·sis \'sinthəsəs\ n, pl -the·ses \-,sēz\ : combination of parts or elements into a whole —syn·the·size \-,sīz\ vb

syn·thet·ic \sin'thetik\ adj : artificially made —synthetic n —syn·thet·i·cal·ly adv

syph·i·lis \'sifələs\ n : venereal disease

sy·ringe \sə'rinj, 'sirinj\ n : plunger device for injecting or withdrawing liquids

syr·up \'sərəp, 'sirəp\ n : thick sticky sweet liquid —syr·upy adj

sys·tem \'sistəm\ n 1 : arrangement of units that function together 2 : regular order —sys·tem·at·ic \,sistə'matik\ adj —sys·tem·at·i·cal·ly adv —sys·tem·a·tize \'sistəmə,tīz\ vb

sys·tem·ic \sis'temik\ adj : relating to the whole body

T

t \'tē\ n, pl t's or ts \'tēz\ : 20th letter of the alphabet

tab \'tab\ n 1 : short projecting flap 2 pl : careful watch

tab·by \'tabē\ n, pl -bies : domestic cat

tab·er·na·cle \'tabər,nakəl\ n : house of worship

ta·ble \'tābəl\ n 1 : piece of furniture having a smooth slab fixed on legs 2 : supply of food 3 : arrangement of data in columns 4 : short list —ta·ble·cloth n —ta·ble·top n —ta·ble·ware n —tab·u·lar \'tabyələr\ adj

ta·ble·spoon n 1 : large serving spoon 2 : measuring spoon holding ½ fluid ounce —ta·ble·spoon·ful \-,fu̇l\ n

tab·let \'tablət\ n 1 : flat slab suited for an inscription 2 : collection of sheets of paper glued together at one edge 3 : disk-shaped pill

tab·loid \'tab,lȯid\ n : newspaper of small page size

ta·boo \tə'bü, ta-\ adj : banned esp. as

immoral or dangerous —taboo n or vb

tab·u·late \'tabyə,lāt\ vb -lat·ed; -lat·ing : put in the form of a table —tab·u·la·tion \,tabyə'lāshən\ n —tab·u·la·tor \'tabyə,lātər\ n

tac·it \'tasət\ adj : implied but not expressed —tac·it·ly adv —tac·it·ness n

tac·i·turn \'tasə,tərn\ adj : not inclined to talk

tack \'tak\ n 1 : small sharp nail 2 : course of action ~ vb 1 : fasten with tacks 2 : add on

tack·le \'takəl, naut often 'tāk-\ n 1 : equipment 2 : arrangement of ropes and pulleys 3 : act of tackling ~ vb -led; -ling 1 : seize or throw down 2 : start dealing with

¹tacky \'takē\ adj tack·i·er; -est : sticky to the touch

²tacky adj tack·i·er; -est : cheap or gaudy

tact \'takt\ n : sense of the proper thing to say or do —tact·ful \-fəl\ adj —tact·ful·ly adv —tact·less adj —tact·less·ly adv

tac·tic \'taktik\ *n* : action as part of a plan

tac·tics \'taktiks\ *n sing or pl* 1 : science of maneuvering forces in combat 2 : skill of using available means to reach an end —**tac·ti·cal** \-tikəl\ *adj* —**tac·ti·cian** \tak'tishən\ *n*

tac·tile \'takt³l, -,tīl\ *adj* : relating to or perceptible through the sense of touch

tad·pole \'tad,pōl\ *n* : larval frog or toad with tail and gills

taf·fe·ta \'tafətə\ *n* : crisp lustrous fabric (as of silk)

taf·fy \'tafē\ *n, pl* -**fies** : candy stretched until porous

¹tag \'tag\ *n* 1 : piece of hanging or attached material ~ *vb* -**gg**- 1 : provide or mark with a tag 2 : follow closely

²tag *n* : children's game of trying to catch one another ~ *vb* : touch a person in tag

tail \'tāl\ *n* 1 : rear end or a growth extending from the rear end of an animal 2 : back or last part 3 : the reverse of a coin ~ *vb* : follow —**tailed** \'tāld\ *adj* —**tail·less** *adj*

tail·gate \-,gāt\ *n* : hinged gate on the back of a vehicle that can be lowered for loading ~ *vb* -**gat·ed**; -**gat·ing** : drive too close behind another vehicle

tail·light *n* : red warning light at the back of a vehicle

tai·lor \'tālər\ *n* : one who makes or alters garments ~ *vb* 1 : fashion or alter (clothes) 2 : make or adapt for a special purpose

tail·spin *n* : spiral dive by an airplane

taint \'tānt\ *vb* : affect or become affected with something bad and esp. decay ~ *n* : trace of decay or corruption

take \'tāk\ *vb* **took** \'tůk\; **tak·en** \'tākən\; **tak·ing** 1 : get into one's possession 2 : become affected by 3 : receive into one's body (as by eating) 4 : pick out or remove 5 : use for transportation 6 : need or make use of 7 : lead, carry, or cause to go to another place 8 : undertake and do, make, or perform ~ *n* : amount taken —**take·over** *n* —**tak·er** *n* —**take advantage of** : profit by —**take exception** : object —**take off** *vb* 1 : remove 2 : go away 3 : mimic 4 : begin flight —**take over** *vb* : assume control or possession of or responsibility for —**take place** : happen

take·off *n* : act or instance of taking off

talc \'talk\ *n* : soft mineral used in making toilet powder (**tal·cum powder** \'talkəm-\)

tale \'tāl\ *n* 1 : story or anecdote 2 : falsehood

tal·ent \'talənt\ *n* : natural mental or creative ability —**tal·ent·ed** *adj*

tal·is·man \'taləsmən, -əz-\ *n, pl* -**mans** : object thought to act as a charm

talk \'tȯk\ *vb* 1 : express one's thoughts in speech 2 : discuss 3 : influence to a position or course of action by talking ~ *n* 1 : act of talking 2 : formal discussion 3 : rumor 4 : informal lecture —**talk·ative** \-ətiv\ *adj* —**talk·er** *n*

tall \'tȯl\ *adj* : extending to a great or specified height —**tall·ness** *n*

tal·low \'talō\ *n* : hard white animal fat used esp. in candles

tal·ly \'talē\ *n, pl* -**lies** : recorded amount ~ *vb* -**lied**; -**ly·ing** 1 : add or count up 2 : match

tal·on \'talən\ *n* : bird's claw

tam \'tam\ *n* : tam-o'-shanter

tam·bou·rine \,tambə'rēn\ *n* : small drum with loose disks at the sides

tame \'tām\ *adj* **tam·er**; **tam·est** 1 : changed from being wild to being controllable by man 2 : docile 3 : dull ~ *vb* **tamed**; **tam·ing** : make or become tame —**tam·able, tame·able** *adj* —**tame·ly** *adv* —**tam·er** *n*

tam-o'-shan·ter \'tamə,shantər\ *n* : Scottish woolen cap with a wide flat circular crown

tamp \'tamp\ *vb* : drive down or in by a series of light blows

tam·per \'tampər\ *vb* : interfere so as to change for the worse

tan \'tan\ *vb* -**nn**- 1 : change (hide) into leather esp. by soaking in a liquid containing tannin 2 : make or become brown (as by exposure to the sun) ~ *n* 1 : brown skin color induced by the sun 2 : light yellowish brown —**tan·ner** *n* —**tan·nery** \'tanərē\ *n*

tan·dem \'tandəm\ *adv* : one behind another

tang \'tan\ *n* : sharp distinctive flavor —**tangy** *adj*

tan·gent \'tanjənt\ *adj* : touching a curve or surface at only one point ~ *n* 1 : tangent line, curve, or surface 2 : abrupt change of course —**tan·gen·tial** \tan'jenchəl\ *adj*

tan·ger·ine \'tanjə,rēn, ,tanjə'-\ *n* : deep orange citrus fruit

tan·gi·ble \'tanjəbəl\ *adj* **1** : able to be touched **2** : substantially real **—tangi·bly** *adv*

tan·gle \'tangəl\ *vb* **-gled; -gling** : unite in intricate confusion ~ *n* : tangled twisted mass

tan·go \'tanggō\ *n, pl* **-gos** : dance of Latin-American origin **—tango** *vb*

tank \'tank\ *n* **1** : large artificial receptacle for liquids **2** : armored military vehicle **—tank·ful** *n*

tan·kard \'tankərd\ *n* : tall one-handled drinking vessel

tank·er \'tankər\ *n* : vehicle or vessel with tanks for transporting a liquid

tan·nin \'tanən\ *n* : substance of plant origin used in tanning and dyeing

tan·ta·lize \'tant³l,īz\ *vb* **-lized; -liz·ing** : tease or torment by keeping something desirable just out of reach **—tan·ta·liz·er** *n* **—tan·ta·liz·ing·ly** *adv*

tan·ta·mount \'tantə,maúnt\ *adj* : equivalent in value or meaning

tan·trum \'tantrəm\ *n* : fit of bad temper

¹tap \'tap\ *n* **1** : faucet **2** : act of tapping ~ *vb* **-pp- 1** : pierce so as to draw off fluid **2** : connect into **—tap·per** *n*

²tap *vb* **-pp- :** rap lightly ~ *n* : light stroke or its sound

tape \'tāp\ *n* **1** : narrow flexible strip (as of cloth, plastic, or metal) **2** : tape measure ~ *vb* **taped; tap·ing 1** : fasten with tape **2** : record on tape

tape measure *n* : strip of tape marked in units for use in measuring

ta·per \'tāpər\ *n* **1** : slender wax candle **2** : gradual lessening of width in a long object ~ *vb* **1** : make or become smaller toward one end **2** : diminish gradually

tap·es·try \'tapəstrē\ *n, pl* **-tries** : heavy handwoven ruglike wall hanging

tape·worm *n* : long flat intestinal worm

tap·i·o·ca \,tapē'ōkə\ *n* : a granular starch used esp. in puddings

tar \'tär\ *n* : thick dark sticky liquid distilled (as from coal) ~ *vb* **-rr- :** treat or smear with tar

ta·ran·tu·la \tə'ranchələ, -'rant³lə\ *n* : large hairy usu. harmless spider

tar·dy \'tärdē\ *adj* **-di·er; -est** : late **—tar·di·ly** \'tärd³lē\ *adv* **—tar·di·ness** *n*

tar·get \'tärgət\ *n* **1** : mark to shoot at **2** : goal to be achieved ~ *vb* **1** : make a target of **2** : establish as a goal

tar·iff \'tarəf\ *n* **1** : duty or rate of duty imposed on imported goods **2** : schedule of tariffs, rates, or charges

tar·nish \'tärnish\ *vb* : make or become dull or discolored **—tarnish** *n*

tar·pau·lin \tär'pólən, 'tärpə-\ *n* : waterproof protective covering

¹tar·ry \'tarē\ *vb* **-ried; -ry·ing** : be slow in leaving

²tar·ry \'tärē\ *adj* : resembling or covered with tar

¹tart \'tärt\ *adj* **1** : pleasantly sharp to the taste **2** : caustic **—tart·ly** *adv* **—tart·ness** *n*

²tart *n* : small pie

tar·tan \'tärt³n\ *n* : woolen fabric with a plaid design

tar·tar \'tärtər\ *n* : hard crust on the teeth

task \'task\ *n* : assigned work

task·mas·ter *n* : one that burdens another with labor

tas·sel \'tasəl, 'täs-\ *n* : hanging ornament made of a bunch of cords fastened at one end

taste \'tāst\ *vb* **tast·ed; tast·ing 1** : test or determine the flavor of **2** : eat or drink in small quantities **3** : have a specific flavor ~ *n* **1** : small amount tasted **2** : bit **3** : special sense that identifies sweet, sour, bitter, or salty qualities **4** : individual preference **5** : critical appreciation of quality **—taste·ful** \-fəl\ *adj* **—taste·ful·ly** *adv* **—taste·less** *adj* **—taste·less·ly** *adv* **—tast·er** *n*

tasty \'tāstē\ *adj* **tast·i·er; -est** : pleasing to the sense of taste **—tast·i·ness** *n*

tat·ter \'tatər\ *n* **1** : part torn and left hanging **2** *pl* : tattered clothing ~ *vb* : make or become ragged

tat·tle \'tat³l\ *vb* **-tled; -tling** : inform on someone **—tat·tler** *n*

tat·tle·tale *n* : one that tattles

tat·too \ta'tü\ *vb* : mark the skin with indelible designs or figures **—tattoo** *n*

taught *past of* TEACH

taunt \'tónt\ *n* : sarcastic challenge or insult **—taunt** *vb* **—taunt·er** *n*

taut \'tót\ *adj* : tightly drawn **—taut·ly** *adv* **—taut·ness** *n*

tav·ern \'tavərn\ *n* : establishment where liquors are sold to be drunk on the premises

taw·dry \'tódrē\ *adj* **-dri·er; -est** : cheap and gaudy **—taw·dri·ly** \'tódrəlē\ *adv*

taw·ny \'tȯnē\ adj **-ni·er; -est** : brownish orange

tax \'taks\ vb 1 : impose a tax on 2 : charge 3 : put under stress ~ n 1 : charge by authority for public purposes 2 : strain —**tax·able** adj —**tax·a·tion** \tak'sāshən\ n —**tax·pay·er** n —**tax·pay·ing** adj

taxi \'taksē\ n, pl **tax·is** \-sēz\ : automobile transporting passengers for a fare ~ vb **tax·ied; taxi·ing** or **taxy·ing; tax·is** or **tax·ies** 1 : transport or go by taxi 2 : move along the ground before takeoff or after landing

taxi·cab \'taksē,kab\ n : taxi

taxi·der·my \'taksə,dərmē\ n : skill or job of stuffing and mounting animal skins —**taxi·der·mist** \-mist\ n

tea \'tē\ n : cured leaves of an oriental shrub or a drink made from these —**tea·cup** n —**tea·pot** n

teach \'tēch\ vb **taught** \'tȯt\; **teaching** 1 : tell or show the fundamentals or skills of something 2 : cause to know the consequences 3 : impart knowledge of —**teach·able** adj —**teach·er** n —**teach·ing** n

teak \'tēk\ n : East Indian timber tree or its wood

tea·ket·tle \'tē,ket⁀l\ n : covered kettle with a handle and spout for boiling water

teal \'tēl\ n, pl **teal** or **teals** : small short-necked wild duck

team \'tēm\ n 1 : draft animals harnessed together 2 : number of people organized for a game or work ~ vb : form or work together as a team — **team** adj —**team·mate** n —**team·work** n

team·ster \'tēmstər\ n 1 : one that drives a team of animals 2 : one that drives a truck

¹tear \'tir\ n : drop of salty liquid that moistens the eye —**tear·ful** \-fəl\ adj —**tear·ful·ly** adv

²tear \'tar\ vb **tore** \'tōr\; **torn** \'tōrn\; **tear·ing** 1 : separate or pull apart by force 2 : move or act with violence or haste ~ n : act or result of tearing

tease \'tēz\ vb **teased; teas·ing** : annoy by goading, coaxing, or tantalizing ~ n 1 : act of teasing or state of being teased 2 : one that teases

tea·spoon \'tē,spün\ n 1 : small spoon for stirring or sipping 2 : measuring spoon holding ⅙ fluid ounce —**tea·spoon·ful** \-,fül\ n

teat \'tēt\ n : protuberance through which milk is drawn from an udder or breast

tech·ni·cal \'teknikəl\ adj 1 : having or relating to special mechanical or scientific knowledge 2 : by strict interpretation of rules —**tech·ni·cal·ly** adv

tech·ni·cal·i·ty \,teknə'kalətē\ n, pl **-ties** : detail meaningful only to a specialist

technical sergeant n : noncommissioned officer in the air force ranking next below a master sergeant

tech·ni·cian \tek'nishən\ n : person with the technique of a specialized skill

tech·nique \tek'nēk\ n : manner of accomplishing something

tech·nol·o·gy \tek'näləjē\ n, pl **-gies** : applied science —**tech·no·log·i·cal** \,teknə'läjikəl\ adj

te·dious \'tēdēəs\ adj : wearisome from length or dullness —**te·dious·ly** adv —**te·dious·ness** n

te·di·um \'tēdēəm\ n : tedious state or quality

tee \'tē\ n : mound or peg on which a golf ball is placed before beginning play —**tee** vb

teem \'tēm\ vb : become filled to overflowing

teen·age \'tēn,āj\, **teen·aged** \-,ājd\ adj : relating to people in their teens — **teen·ag·er** \-,ājər\ n

teens \'tēnz\ n pl : years 13 to 19 in a person's life

tee·pee var of TEPEE

tee·ter \'tētər\ vb 1 : move unsteadily 2 : seesaw —**teeter** n

teeth pl of TOOTH

teethe \'tēth\ vb **teethed; teeth·ing** : grow teeth

tele·cast \'teli,kast\ vb **-cast; -cast·ing** : broadcast by television —**telecast** n —**tele·cast·er** n

tele·com·mu·ni·ca·tion \'teləkəmyünə'kāshən\ n : communication at a distance (as by radio or telephone)

tele·gram \'telə,gram\ n : message sent by telegraph

tele·graph \-,graf\ n : system for communication by electrical transmission of coded signals ~ vb : send by telegraph —**te·leg·ra·pher** \tə'legrəfər\ n —**tele·graph·ic** \,telə'grafik\ adj

te·lep·a·thy \tə'lepəthē\ n : apparent communication without known sensory means **—tele·path·ic** \,tel-ə'pathik\ *adj* **—tele·path·i·cal·ly** *adv*

tele·phone \'telə,fōn\ *n* : instrument or system for electrical transmission of spoken words ~ *vb* **-phoned; -phon·ing** : communicate with by telephone **—tele·phon·er** *n*

tele·scope \-,skōp\ *n* : tube-shaped optical instrument for viewing distant objects ~ *vb* **-scoped; -scop·ing** : slide or cause to slide inside another similar section **—tele·scop·ic** \,telə'skäpik\ *adj*

tele·vise \'telə,vīz\ *vb* **-vised; -vis·ing** : broadcast by television

tele·vi·sion \-,vizhən\ *n* : transmission and reproduction of images by radio waves

tell \'tel\ *vb* **told** \'tōld\; **tell·ing** 1 : count 2 : relate in detail 3 : reveal 4 : give information or an order to 5 : find out by observing

tell·er \'telər\ *n* 1 : one that relates or counts 2 : bank employee handling money

te·mer·i·ty \tə'merətē\ *n, pl* **-ties** : boldness

temp \'temp\ *n* 1 : temperature 2 : temporary worker

tem·per \'tempər\ *vb* 1 : dilute or soften 2 : toughen ~ *n* 1 : characteristic attitude or feeling 2 : toughness 3 : disposition or control over one's emotions

tem·per·a·ment \'tempərəmənt\ *n* : characteristic frame of mind **—tem·per·a·men·tal** \,tempra'ment⁺l\ *adj*

tem·per·ance \'temprəns\ *n* : moderation in or abstinence from indulgence and esp. the use of intoxicating drink

tem·per·ate \'tempərət\ *adj* : moderate

tem·per·a·ture \'tempər,chùr, -prə-,chùr, -chər\ *n* 1 : degree of hotness or coldness 2 : fever

tem·pest \'tempəst\ *n* : violent storm **—tem·pes·tu·ous** \tem'peschəwəs\ *adj*

¹tem·ple \'tempəl\ *n* : place of worship

²temple *n* : flattened space on each side of the forehead

tem·po \'tempō\ *n, pl* **-pi** \-,pē\ *or* **-pos** : rate of speed

tem·po·ral \'tempərəl\ *adj* : relating to time or to secular concerns

tem·po·rary \'tempə,rerē\ *adj* : lasting for a short time only **—tem·po·rar·i·ly** \,tempə'rerəlē\ *adv*

tempt \'tempt\ *vb* 1 : coax or persuade

to do wrong 2 : attract or provoke **—tempt·er** *n* **—tempt·ing·ly** *adv* **—tempt·ress** \'temptrəs\ *n*

temp·ta·tion \temp'tāshən\ *n* 1 : act of tempting 2 : something that tempts

ten \'ten\ *n* 1 : one more than 9 2 : 10th in a set or series 3 : thing having 10 units **—ten** *adj or pron* **—tenth** \'tenth\ *adj or adv or n*

ten·a·ble \'tenəbəl\ *adj* : capable of being held or defended **—ten·a·bil·i·ty** \,tenə'bilətē\ *n*

te·na·cious \tə'nāshəs\ *adj* 1 : holding fast 2 : retentive **—te·na·cious·ly** *adv* **—te·nac·i·ty** \tə'nasətē\ *n*

ten·ant \'tenənt\ *n* : one who occupies a rented dwelling **—ten·an·cy** \-ənsē\ *n*

¹tend \'tend\ *vb* : take care of or supervise something

²tend *vb* 1 : move in a particular direction 2 : show a tendency

ten·den·cy \'tendənsē\ *n, pl* **-cies** : likelihood to move, think, or act in a particular way

¹ten·der \'tendər\ *adj* 1 : soft or delicate 2 : expressing or responsive to love or sympathy 3 : sensitive (as to touch) **—ten·der·ly** *adv* **—ten·der·ness** *n*

²tender \'tendər\ *n* 1 : one that tends 2 : boat providing transport to a larger ship 3 : vehicle attached to a steam locomotive for carrying fuel and water

³tender *n* 1 : offer of a bid for a contract 2 : something that may be offered in payment **—tender** *vb*

ten·der·ize \'tendə,rīz\ *vb* **-ized; -iz·ing** : make (meat) tender **—ten·der·iz·er** \'tendə,rīzər\ *n*

ten·der·loin \'tendər,lóin\ *n* : tender beef or pork strip from near the backbone

ten·don \'tendən\ *n* : cord of tissue attaching muscle to bone **—ten·di·nous** \-dənəs\ *adj*

ten·dril \'tendrəl\ *n* : slender coiling growth of some climbing plants

ten·e·ment \'tenəmənt\ *n* 1 : house divided into apartments 2 : shabby dwelling

te·net \'tenət\ *n* : principle of belief

ten·nis \'tenəs\ *n* : racket-and-ball game played across a net

ten·or \'tenər\ *n* 1 : general drift or meaning 2 : highest natural adult male voice

ten·pin \'ten,pin\ *n* : bottle-shaped pin bowled in a game (**tenpins**)

¹**tense** \'tens\ n : distinct verb form that indicates time

²**tense** adj **tens·er; tens·est 1** : stretched tight **2** : marked by nervous tension —**tense** vb —**tense·ly** adv —**tense·ness** n —**ten·si·ty** \'tensətē\ n

ten·sile \'tensəl, -,sīl\ adj : relating to tension

ten·sion \'tenchən\ n **1** : tense condition **2** : state of mental unrest or of potential hostility or opposition

tent \'tent\ n : collapsible shelter

ten·ta·cle \'tentikəl\ n : long flexible projection of an insect or mollusk —**ten·ta·cled** \-kəld\ adj —**ten·tac·u·lar** \ten'takyələr\ adj

ten·ta·tive \'tentətiv\ adj : subject to change or discussion —**ten·ta·tive·ly** adv

ten·u·ous \'tenyəwəs\ adj **1** : not dense or thick **2** : flimsy or weak —**ten·u·ous·ly** adv —**ten·u·ous·ness** n

ten·ure \'tenyər\ n : act, right, manner, or period of holding something —**ten·ured** \-yərd\ adj

te·pee \'tē,pē\ n : conical tent

tep·id \'tepəd\ adj : moderately warm

term \'tərm\ n **1** : period of time **2** : mathematical expression **3** : special word or phrase **4** pl : conditions **5** pl : relations ~ vb : name

ter·mi·nal \'tərmən³l\ n **1** : end **2** : device for making an electrical connection **3** : station at end of a transportation line —**terminal** adj

ter·mi·nate \'tərmə,nāt\ vb **-nat·ed; -nat·ing** : bring or come to an end —**ter·mi·na·ble** \-nəbəl\ adj —**ter·mi·na·tion** \,tərmə'nāshən\ n

ter·mi·nol·o·gy \,tərmə'näləjē\ n : terms used in a particular subject

ter·mi·nus \'tərmənəs\ n, pl **-ni** \-,nī\ or **-nus·es 1** : end **2** : end of a transportation line

ter·mite \'tər,mīt\ n : wood-eating insect

tern \'tərn\ n : small sea bird

ter·race \'terəs\ n **1** : balcony or patio **2** : bank with a flat top ~ vb **-raced; -rac·ing** : landscape in a series of banks

ter·ra-cot·ta \,terə'kätə\ n : reddish brown earthenware

ter·rain \tə'rān\ n : features of the land

ter·ra·pin \'terəpən\ n : No. American turtle

ter·rar·i·um \tə'rareēəm\ n, pl **-ia** \-ēə\ or **-i·ums** : container for keeping plants or animals

ter·res·tri·al \tə'restrēəl\ adj **1** : relating to the earth or its inhabitants **2** : living or growing on land

ter·ri·ble \'terəbəl\ adj **1** : exciting terror **2** : distressing **3** : intense **4** : of very poor quality —**ter·ri·bly** \-blē\ adv

ter·ri·er \'terēər\ n : small dog

ter·rif·ic \tə'rifik\ adj **1** : exciting terror **2** : extraordinary

ter·ri·fy \'terə,fī\ vb **-fied; -fy·ing** : fill with terror —**ter·ri·fy·ing·ly** adv

ter·ri·to·ry \'terə,tōrē\ n, pl **-ries** : particular geographical region —**ter·ri·to·ri·al** \,terə'tōrēəl\ adj

ter·ror \'terər\ n : intense fear and panic or a cause of it

ter·ror·ism \-,izəm\ n : systematic covert warfare to produce terror for political coercion —**ter·ror·ist** \-ist\ adj or n

ter·ror·ize \-,īz\ vb **-ized; -iz·ing 1** : fill with terror **2** : coerce by threat or violence

ter·ry \'terē\ n, pl **-ries** : absorbent fabric with a loose pile

terse \'tərs\ adj **ters·er; ters·est** : concise —**terse·ly** adv —**terse·ness** n

ter·tia·ry \'tərshē,erē\ adj : of 3d rank, importance, or value

test \'test\ n : examination or evaluation ~ vb : examine by a test —**test·er** n

tes·ta·ment \'testəmənt\ n **1** cap : division of the Bible **2** : will —**tes·ta·men·ta·ry** \,testə'mentərē\ adj

tes·ti·cle \'testikəl\ n : testis

tes·ti·fy \'testə,fī\ vb **-fied; -fy·ing 1** : give testimony **2** : serve as evidence

tes·ti·mo·ni·al \,testə'mōnēəl\ n **1** : favorable recommendation **2** : tribute —**testimonial** adj

tes·ti·mo·ny \'testə,mōnē\ n, pl **-nies** : statement given as evidence in court

tes·tis \'testəs\ n, pl **-tes** \-,tēz\ : male reproductive gland

tes·ty \'testē\ adj **-ti·er; -est** : easily annoyed

tet·a·nus \'tet³nəs\ n : bacterial disease producing violent spasms

tête-à-tête \,tātə'tāt\ adv : privately ~ n : private conversation ~ adj : private

teth·er \'tethər\ n : leash ~ vb : restrain with a leash

text \'tekst\ n **1** : author's words **2** : main body of printed or written matter on a page **3** : textbook **4** : scriptural passage used as the theme of a sermon **5** : topic —**tex·tu·al** \'teksch∂w∂l\ adj

text·book \-ˌbûk\ n : book on a school subject

tex·tile \'tekˌstīl, 'tekst∂l\ n : fabric

tex·ture \'teksch∂r\ n **1** : feel and appearance of something **2** : structure

than \'than\ conj or prep —used in comparisons

thank \'thaŋk\ vb : express gratitude to

thank·ful \-f∂l\ adj : giving thanks —**thank·ful·ly** adv —**thank·ful·ness** n

thank·less adj : not appreciated

thanks \'thaŋks\ n pl : expression of gratitude

Thanks·giv·ing \thaŋks'giviŋ\ n : 4th Thursday in November observed as a legal holiday for giving thanks for divine goodness

that \'that\ pron, pl **those** \'thōz\ **1** : something indicated or understood **2** : the one farther away ~ adj, pl **those** : being the one mentioned or understood or farther away ~ conj or pron —used to introduce a clause ~ adv : to such an extent

thatch \'thach\ vb : cover with thatch — n : covering of matted straw

thaw \'thȯ\ vb : melt or cause to melt — thaw n

the \th∂, before vowel sounds usu thē\ definite article : that particular one ~ adv —used before a comparative or superlative

the·ater, **the·atre** \'thē∂t∂r\ n **1** : building or room for viewing a play or movie **2** : dramatic arts

the·at·ri·cal \thē'atrik∂l\ adj **1** : relating to the theater **2** : involving exaggerated emotion

thee \'thē\ pron, archaic objective case of THOU

theft \'theft\ n : act of stealing

their \'ther\ adj : relating to them

theirs \'therz\ pron : their one or ones

the·ism \'thē,iz∂m\ n : belief in the existence of a god or gods —**the·ist** \-ist\ n or adj —**the·is·tic** \thē'istik\ adj

them \'them\ pron, objective case of THEY

theme \'thēm\ n **1** : subject matter **2** : essay **3** : melody developed in a piece of music —**the·mat·ic** \thi'matik\ adj

them·selves \th∂m'selvz, them-\ pron pl

: they, them —used reflexively or for emphasis

then \'then\ adv **1** : at that time **2** : soon after that **3** : in addition **4** : in that case **5** : consequently ~ n : that time ~ adj : existing at that time

thence \'thens, 'thens\ adv : from that place or fact

the·oc·ra·cy \thē'äkr∂sē\ n, pl **-cies** : government by officials regarded as divinely inspired —**the·o·crat·ic** \,thē∂'kratik\ adj

the·ol·o·gy \thē'äl∂jē\ n, pl **-gies** : study of religion —**the·o·lo·gian** \,thē∂-'lōj∂n\ n —**the·o·log·i·cal** \-'läjik∂l\ adj

the·o·rem \'thē∂r∂m, 'thir∂m\ n : provable statement of truth

the·o·ret·i·cal \,thē∂'retik∂l\ adj : relating to or being theory —**the·o·ret·i·cal·ly** adv

the·o·rize \'thē∂,rīz\ vb **-rized; -riz·ing** : put forth theories —**the·o·rist** n

the·o·ry \'thē∂rē, 'thirē\ n, pl **-ries 1** : general principles of a subject **2** : plausible or scientifically acceptable explanation **3** : judgment, guess, or opinion

ther·a·peu·tic \,ther∂'pyütik\ adj : offering or relating to remedy — **ther·a·peu·ti·cal·ly** adv

ther·a·py \'ther∂pē\ n, pl **-pies** : treatment for mental or physical disorder —**ther·a·pist** \-pist\ n

there \'ther\ adv **1** : in, at, or to that place **2** : in that respect ~ pron — used to introduce a sentence or clause ~ n : that place or point

there·abouts, **there·about** \,ther∂-'baûts, 'ther∂-,-, -'baût\ adv : near that place, time, number, or quantity

there·af·ter \thar'aft∂r\ adv : after that

there·by \thar'bī, 'thar,bī\ adv **1** : by that **2** : connected with or with reference to that

there·fore \'thar,fōr\ adv : for that reason

there·in \thar'in\ adv **1** : in or into that place, time, or thing **2** : in that respect

there·of \-'∂v, -'äv\ adv **1** : of that or it **2** : from that

there·upon \'thar∂,pȯn, -,pän; ,thar∂-'pȯn, -'pän\ adv **1** : on that matter **2** : therefore **3** : immediately after that

there·with \thar'with, -'with\ adv : with that

ther·mal \'th∂rm∂l\ adj : relating to,

caused by, or conserving heat —**ther·mal·ly** adv

ther·mo·dy·nam·ics \,thərmōdī'na-miks\ n : physics of heat

ther·mom·e·ter \thər'mämətər\ n : instrument for measuring temperature —**ther·mo·met·ric** \,thərmə'metrik\ adj —**ther·mo·met·ri·cal·ly** adv

ther·mos \'thərməs\ n : double-walled bottle used to keep liquids hot or cold

ther·mo·stat \'thərmə,stat\ n : automatic temperature control —**ther·mo·stat·ic** \,thərmə'statik\ adj —**ther·mo·stat·i·cal·ly** adv

the·sau·rus \thi'sórəs\ n. pl **-sau·ri** \-'sór,ī\ or **-sau·rus·es** \-'sórəsəz\ : book of words and esp. synonyms

these pl of THIS

the·sis \'thēsəs\ n, pl **the·ses** \'thē,sēz\ 1 : proposition to be argued for 2 : essay embodying results of original research

thes·pi·an \'thespēən\ adj : dramatic ~ n : actor

they \'thā\ pron 1 : those ones 2 : people in general

thi·a·mine \'thīəmən, -,mēn\ n : essential vitamin

thick \'thik\ adj 1 : having relatively great mass from front to back or top to bottom 2 : viscous ~ n : most crowded or thickest part —**thick·ly** adv —**thick·ness** n

thick·en \'thikən\ vb : make or become thick —**thick·en·er** \-ənər\ n

thick·et \'thikət\ n : dense growth of bushes or small trees

thick–skinned \-'skind\ adj : insensitive to criticism

thief \'thēf\ n, pl **thieves** \'thēvz\ : one that steals

thieve \'thēv\ vb **thieved; thiev·ing** : steal —**thiev·ery** n

thigh \'thī\ n : upper part of the leg

thigh·bone \'thī,bōn\ n : femur

thim·ble \'thimbəl\ n : protective cap for the finger in sewing —**thim·ble·ful** n

thin \'thin\ adj **-nn-** 1 : having relatively little mass from front to back or top to bottom 2 : not closely set or placed 3 : relatively free flowing 4 : lacking substance, fullness, or strength ~ vb **-nn-** : make or become thin —**thin·ly** adv —**thin·ness** n

thing \'thiŋ\ n 1 : matter of concern 2

: event or act 3 : object 4 pl : possessions

think \'thiŋk\ vb **thought** \'thót\; **think·ing** 1 : form or have in the mind 2 : have as an opinion 3 : ponder 4 : devise by thinking 5 : imagine —**think·er** n

thin–skinned adj : extremely sensitive to criticism

third \'thərd\ adj : being number 3 in a countable series ~ n 1 : one that is third 2 : one of 3 equal parts —**third, third·ly** adv

third dimension n : thickness or depth —**third–dimensional** adj

third world n : less developed nations of the world

thirst \'thərst\ n 1 : dryness in mouth and throat 2 : intense desire ~ vb : feel thirst —**thirsty** adj

thir·teen \,thər'tēn\ n : one more than 12 —**thirteen** adj or pron —**thir·teenth** \-'tēnth\ adj or n

thir·ty \'thərtē\ n, pl **thirties** : 3 times 10 —**thir·ti·eth** \-ēəth\ adj or n —**thirty** adj or pron

this \'this\ pron, pl **these** \'thēz\ : something close or under immediate discussion ~ adj, pl **these** : being the one near, present, just mentioned, or more immediately under observation ~ adv : to such an extent or degree

this·tle \'thisəl\ n : tall prickly herb

thith·er \'thithər\ adv : to that place

thong \'thóŋ\ n : strip of leather or hide

tho·rax \'thór,aks\ n, pl **-rax·es** or **-ra·ces** \'thórə,sēz\ 1 : part of the body between neck and abdomen 2 : middle of 3 divisions of an insect body —**tho·rac·ic** \thə'rasik\ adj

thorn \'thórn\ n : sharp spike on a plant or a plant bearing these —**thorny** adj

thor·ough \'thərō\ adj : omitting or overlooking nothing —**thor·ough·ly** adv —**thor·ough·ness** n

thor·ough·bred \'thərə,bred\ n 1 cap : light speedy racing horse 2 : one of excellent quality —**thoroughbred** adj

thor·ough·fare \'thərə,far\ n : public road

those pl of THAT

thou \'thaú\ pron, archaic : you

though \'thō\ adv : however ~ conj 1 : despite the fact that 2 : granting that

thought \'thót\ past of THINK ~ n 1 : process of thinking 2 : serious consideration 3 : idea

thought·ful \-fəl\ adj 1 : absorbed in or

showing thought **2** : considerate of others **—thought·ful·ly** *adv* **—thought·ful·ness** *n*

thought·less \-ləs\ *adj* **1** : careless or reckless **2** : lacking concern for others **—thought·less·ly** *adv*

thou·sand \'thau̇z°nd\ *n, pl* **-sands** or **-sand** : 10 times 100 **—thousand** *adj* **—thou·sandth** \-°nth\ *adj or n*

thrash \'thrash\ *vb* **1** : thresh **2** : beat **3** : move about violently **—thrash·er** *n*

thread \'thred\ *n* **1** : fine line of fibers **2** : train of thought **3** : ridge around a screw ~ *vb* **1** : pass thread through **2** : put on a thread **3** : make one's way through or between

thread·bare *adj* **1** : worn so that the thread shows **2** : trite

threat \'thret\ *n* **1** : expression of intention to harm **2** : thing that threatens

threat·en \'thret°n\ *vb* **1** : utter threats **2** : show signs of being near or impending **—threat·en·ing·ly** *adv*

three \'thrē\ *n* **1** : one more than 2 **2** : 3d in a set or series **—three** *adj or pron*

three·fold \'thrē,fōld\ *adj* : triple **—three·fold** \-'fōld\ *adv*

three·score *adj* : being 3 times 20

thresh \'thresh, 'thrash\ *vb* : beat to separate grain **—thresh·er** *n*

thresh·old \'thresh,ōld\ *n* **1** : sill of a door **2** : beginning stage

threw *past of* THROW

thrice \'thrīs\ *adv* : 3 times

thrift \'thrift\ *n* : careful management or saving of money **—thrift·i·ly** \'thriftəlē\ *adv* **—thrift·less** *adj* **—thrifty** *adj*

thrill \'thril\ *vb* **1** : have or cause to have a sudden sharp feeling of excitement **2** : tremble **—thrill** *n* **—thrill·er** *n* **—thrill·ing·ly** *adv*

thrive \'thrīv\ *vb* **throve** \'thrōv\ or **thrived**; **thriv·en** \'thrivən\ **1** : grow vigorously **2** : prosper

throat \'thrōt\ *n* **1** : front part of the neck **2** : passage to the stomach **—throat·ed** *adj* **—throaty** *adj*

throb \'thräb\ *vb* **-bb-** : pulsate **—throb** *n*

throe \'thrō\ *n* **1** : pang or spasm **2** *pl* : hard or painful struggle

throne \'thrōn\ *n* : chair representing power or sovereignty

throng \'thrȯŋ\ *n or vb* : crowd

throt·tle \'thrät°l\ *vb* **-tled; -tling** : choke ~ *n* : valve regulating volume of fuel and air delivered to engine cylinders

through \'thrü\ *prep* **1** : into at one side and out at the other side of **2** : by way of **3** : among, between, or all around **4** : because of **5** : throughout the time of ~ \'thrü\ *adv* **1** : from one end or side to the other **2** : from beginning to end **3** : to the core **4** : into the open ~ *adj* **1** : going directly from origin to destination **2** : finished

through·out \thrü'au̇t\ *adv* **1** : everywhere **2** : from beginning to end ~ *prep* **1** : in or to every part of **2** : during the whole of

throve *past of* THRIVE

throw \'thrō\ *vb* **threw** \'thrü\; **thrown** \'thrōn\; **throw·ing** **1** : propel through the air **2** : cause to fall or fall off **3** : put suddenly in a certain position or condition **4** : move quickly as if throwing **5** : put on or off hastily **—throw** *n* **—throw·er** \'thrōər\ *n* **—throw up** *vb* : vomit

thrush \'thrəsh\ *n* : songbird

thrust \'thrəst\ *vb* **thrust; thrust·ing** **1** : shove forward **2** : stab or pierce **—thrust** *n*

thud \'thəd\ *n* : dull sound of something falling **—thud** *vb*

thug \'thəg\ *n* : ruffian or gangster

thumb \'thəm\ *n* **1** : short thick division of the hand opposing the fingers **2** : glove part for the thumb ~ *vb* : leaf through with the thumb **—thumb·nail** *n*

thump \'thəmp\ *vb* : strike with something thick or heavy causing a dull sound **—thump** *n*

thun·der \'thəndər\ *n* : sound following lightning **—thunder** *vb* **—thun·der·clap** *n* **—thun·der·ous** \'thəndərəs\ *adj* **—thun·der·ous·ly** *adv*

thun·der·bolt \-,bōlt\ *n* : discharge of lightning with thunder

thun·der·show·er \'thəndər,shau̇ər\ *n* : shower with thunder and lightning

thun·der·storm *n* : storm with thunder and lightning

Thurs·day \'thərzdā, -dē\ *n* : 5th day of the week

thus \'thəs\ *adv* **1** : in this or that way **2** : to this degree or extent **3** : because of this or that

thwart \'thwȯrt\ *vb* : block or defeat

thy \'thī\ *adj, archaic* : your

thyme \'tīm, 'thīm\ *n* : cooking herb

thy·roid \'thī,rȯid\ *adj* : relating to a

large endocrine gland (**thyroid gland**)

thy·self \thī'self\ *pron, archaic* : yourself

ti·ara \tē'arə, -'är-\ *n* : decorative formal headband

tib·ia \'tibēə\ *n, pl* **-i·ae** \-ē,ē\ : bone between the knee and ankle

tic \'tik\ *n* : twitching of facial muscles

¹tick \'tik\ *n* : small 8-legged blood-sucking animal

²tick *n* **1** : light rhythmic tap or beat **2** : check mark ~ *vb* **1** : make ticks **2** : mark with a tick **3** : operate

tick·er \'tikər\ *n* **1** : something (as a watch) that ticks **2** : telegraph instrument that prints on paper tape

tick·et \'tikət\ *n* **1** : tag showing price, payment of a fee or fare, or a traffic offense **2** : list of candidates ~ *vb* : put a ticket on

tick·ing \'tikiŋ\ *n* : fabric covering of a mattress

tick·le \'tikəl\ *vb* **-led; -ling 1** : please or amuse **2** : touch lightly causing uneasiness, laughter, or spasmodic movements —**tickle** *n*

tick·lish \'tiklish\ *adj* **1** : sensitive to tickling **2** : requiring delicate handling —**tick·lish·ly** *adv* —**tick·lish·ness** *n*

tid·al wave \'tīdᵊl-\ *n* : high sea wave following an earthquake

tid·bit \'tid,bit\ *n* : choice morsel

tide \'tīd\ *n* : alternate rising and falling of the sea ~ *vb* **tid·ed; tid·ing** : be enough to allow (one) to get by for a time —**tid·al** \'tīdᵊl\ *adj* —**tide·wa·ter** *n*

tid·ings \'tīdiŋz\ *n pl* : news or message

ti·dy \'tīdē\ *adj* **-di·er; -est 1** : well ordered and cared for **2** : large or substantial —**ti·di·ness** *n* —**tidy** *vb*

tie \'tī\ *n* **1** : line or ribbon for fastening, uniting, or closing **2** : cross support to which railroad rails are fastened **3** : uniting force **4** : equality in score or tally or a deadlocked contest **5** : necktie ~ *vb* **tied; ty·ing** *or* **tie·ing 1** : fasten or close by wrapping and knotting a tie **2** : form a knot in **3** : gain the same score or tally as an opponent

tier \'tir\ *n* : one of a steplike series of rows

tiff \'tif\ *n* : petty quarrel —**tiff** *vb*

ti·ger \'tīgər\ *n* : very large black-striped cat —**ti·ger·ish** \-gərish\ *adj* —**ti·gress** \-grəs\ *n*

tight \'tīt\ *adj* **1** : fitting close together esp. so as not to allow air or water in **2** : held very firmly **3** : taut **4** : fitting too snugly **5** : difficult **6** : stingy **7** : evenly contested **8** : low in supply —**tight** *adv* —**tight·en** \-ᵊn\ *vb* —**tight·ly** *adv* —**tight·ness** *n*

tights \'tīts\ *n pl* : skintight garments

tight·wad \'tīt,wäd\ *n* : stingy person

tile \'tīl\ *n* : thin piece of stone or fired clay used on roofs, floors, or walls ~ *vb* : cover with tiles

¹till \'til\ *prep or conj* : until

²till *vb* : cultivate (soil) —**till·able** *adj*

³till *n* : money drawer

¹till·er \'tilər\ *n* : one that cultivates soil

²til·ler \'tilər\ *n* : lever for turning a boat's rudder

tilt \'tilt\ *vb* : cause to incline ~ *n* : slant

tim·ber \'timbər\ *n* **1** : cut wood for building **2** : large squared piece of wood **3** : wooded land or trees for timber ~ *vb* : cover, frame, or support with timbers —**tim·bered** *adj* —**tim·ber·land** \-,land\ *n*

tim·bre \'tambər, 'tim-\ *n* : sound quality

time \'tīm\ *n* **1** : period during which something exists or continues or can be accomplished **2** : point at which something happens **3** : customary hour **4** : age **5** : tempo **6** : moment, hour, day, or year as indicated by a clock or calendar **7** : one's experience during a particular period ~ *vb* **timed; tim·ing 1** : arrange or set the time of **2** : determine or record the time, duration, or rate of —**time·keep·er** *n* —**time·less** *adj* —**time·less·ness** *n* —**time·li·ness** *n* —**time·ly** *adv* —**tim·er** *n*

time·piece *n* : device to show time

times \'tīmz\ *prep* : multiplied by

time·ta·ble \'tīm,tābəl\ *n* : table of departure and arrival times

tim·id \'timəd\ *adj* : lacking in courage or self-confidence —**ti·mid·i·ty** \tə'midətē\ *n* —**tim·id·ly** *adv*

tim·o·rous \'timərəs\ *adj* : fearful —**tim·o·rous·ly** *adv* —**tim·o·rous·ness** *n*

tim·pa·ni \'timpənē\ *n pl* : set of kettledrums —**tim·pa·nist** \-nist\ *n*

tin \'tin\ *n* **1** : soft white metallic chemical element **2** : metal food can

tinc·ture \'tiŋkchər\ n : alcoholic solution of a medicine

tin·der \'tindər\ n : substance used to kindle a fire

tine \'tīn\ n : one of the points of a fork

tin·foil \'tin,foil\ n : thin metal sheeting

tinge \'tinj\ vb **tinged**; **tinge·ing** or **ting·ing** \'tinjiŋ\ **1** : color slightly **2** : affect with a slight odor ~ n : slight coloring or flavor

tin·gle \'tiŋgəl\ vb **-gled**; **-gling** : feel a ringing, stinging, or thrilling sensation —**tingle** n

tin·ker \'tiŋkər\ vb : experiment in repairing something —**tin·ker·er** n

tin·kle \'tiŋkəl\ vb **-kled**; **-kling** : make or cause to make a high ringing sound —**tinkle** n

tin·sel \'tinsəl\ n : decorative thread or strip of glittering metal or paper

tint \'tint\ n **1** : slight or pale coloration **2** : color shade ~ vb : give a tint to

ti·ny \'tīnē\ adj **-ni·er**; **-est** : very small

¹tip \'tip\ vb **-pp- 1** : overturn **2** : lean ~ n : act or state of tipping

²tip n : pointed end of something ~ vb **-pp- 1** : furnish with a tip **2** : cover the tip of

³tip n : small sum given for a service performed ~ vb : give a tip to

⁴tip n : piece of confidential information ~ vb **-pp-** : give confidential information to

tip–off \'tip,óf\ n : indication

tip·ple \'tipəl\ vb **-pled**; **-pling** : drink intoxicating liquor esp. habitually or excessively —**tip·pler** n

tip·sy \'tipsē\ adj **-si·er**; **-est** : unsteady or foolish from alcohol

tip·toe \'tip,tō\ n : the toes of the feet ~ adv or adj : supported on tiptoe ~ vb **-toed**; **-toe·ing** : walk quietly or on tiptoe

tip–top n : highest point ~ adj : excellent

ti·rade \'tī'rād, 'tī,-\ n : prolonged speech of abuse

¹tire \'tīr\ vb **tired**; **tir·ing 1** : make or become weary **2** : wear out the patience of —**tire·less** adj —**tire·less·ly** adv —**tire·less·ness** n —**tire·some** \-səm\ adj —**tire·some·ly** adv —**tire·some·ness** n

²tire n : rubber cushion encircling a car wheel

tired \'tīrd\ adj : weary

tis·sue \'tishü\ n **1** : soft absorbent paper **2** : layer of cells forming a basic structural element of an animal or plant body

ti·tan·ic \tī'tanik, tə-\ adj : gigantic

ti·ta·ni·um \tī'tānēəm, tə-\ n : gray light strong metallic chemical element

tithe \'tīth\ n : tenth part paid or given esp. for the support of a church —**tithe** vb —**tith·er** n

tit·il·late \'tit²l,āt\ vb **-lat·ed**; **-lat·ing** : excite pleasurably —**tit·il·la·tion** \,tit²l'āshən\ n

ti·tle \'tīt²l\ n **1** : legal ownership **2** : distinguishing name **3** : designation of honor, rank, or office **4** : championship —**ti·tled** adj

tit·ter \'titər\ n : nervous or affected laugh —**titter** vb

tit·u·lar \'tichələr\ adj **1** : existing in title only **2** : relating to or bearing a title

tiz·zy \'tizē\ n, pl **tizzies** : state of agitation or worry

TNT \,tē,en'tē\ n : high explosive

to \'tü\ prep **1** : in the direction of **2** : at, on, or near **3** : resulting in **4** : before or until **5** —used to show a relationship or object of a verb **6** —used with an infinitive ~ adv **1** : forward **2** : to a state of consciousness

toad \'tōd\ n : tailless leaping amphibian

toad·stool \-,stül\ n : mushroom esp. when inedible or poisonous

toady \'tōdē\ n, pl **toad·ies** : one who flatters to gain favors —**toady** vb

toast \'tōst\ vb **1** : make (as a slice of bread) crisp and brown **2** : drink in honor of someone or something **3** : warm ~ n **1** : toasted sliced bread **2** : act of drinking in honor of someone —**toast·er** n

to·bac·co \tə'bakō\ n, pl **-cos** : broadleaved herb or its leaves prepared for smoking or chewing

to·bog·gan \tə'bägən\ n : long flat-bottomed light sled ~ vb : coast on a toboggan

to·day \tə'dā\ adv **1** : on or for this day **2** : at the present time ~ n : present day or time

tod·dle \'täd²l\ vb **-dled**; **-dling** : walk with tottering steps like a young child —**toddle** n —**tod·dler** \²lər\ n

to–do \tə'dü\ n, pl **to–dos** \-'düz\ : disturbance or fuss

toe \'tō\ n : one of the 5 end divisions of the foot —**toe·nail** n

tof·fee, tof·fy \'tôfē, 'tä-\ n, pl **toffees** or

toffies : candy made of boiled sugar and butter

to·ga \'tōgə\ *n* : loose outer garment of ancient Rome

to·geth·er \tə'gethər\ *adv* **1** : in or into one place or group **2** : in or into contact or association **3** : at one time **4** : as a group —**to·geth·er·ness** *n*

togs \'tägz, 'tógz\ *n pl* : clothing

toil \'toil\ *vb* : work hard and long — **toil** *n* —**toil·er** *n* —**toil·some** *adj*

toi·let \'toilət\ *n* **1** : dressing and grooming oneself **2** : bathroom **3** : water basin to urinate and defecate in

to·ken \'tōkən\ *n* **1** : outward sign or expression of something **2** : small part representing the whole **3** : piece resembling a coin

told *past of* TELL

tol·er·a·ble \'tälərəbəl\ *adj* **1** : capable of being endured **2** : moderately good —**tol·er·a·bly** \-blē\ *adv*

tol·er·ance \'tälərəns\ *n* **1** : lack of opposition for beliefs or practices differing from one's own **2** : capacity for enduring **3** : allowable deviation — **tol·er·ant** *adj* —**tol·er·ant·ly** *adv*

tol·er·ate \'tälə,rāt\ *vb* **-at·ed; -at·ing 1** : allow to be or to be done without opposition **2** : endure or resist the action of —**tol·er·a·tion** \,tälə'rāshən\ *n*

¹toll \'tōl\ *n* **1** : fee paid for a privilege or service **2** : cost of achievement in loss or suffering —**toll·booth** *n* —**toll·gate** *n*

²toll *vb* **1** : cause the sounding of (a bell) **2** : sound with slow measured strokes ~ *n* : sound of a tolling bell

tom·a·hawk \'tämə,hók\ *n* : light ax used as a weapon by American Indians

to·ma·to \tə'mātō, -'mät-\ *n, pl* **-toes** : tropical American herb or its fruit

tomb \'tüm\ *n* : house, vault, or grave for burial

tom·boy \'täm,bói\ *n* : girl who behaves in a manner usu. considered boyish

tomb·stone \'tüm\ *n* : stone marking a grave

tom·cat \'täm,kat\ *n* : male cat

tome \'tōm\ *n* : large or weighty book

to·mor·row \tə'märō\ *adv* : on or for the day after today —**tomorrow** *n*

tom-tom \'täm,täm\ *n* : small-headed drum beaten with the hands

ton \'tən\ *n* : unit of weight equal to 2000 pounds

tone \'tōn\ *n* **1** : vocal or musical sound **2** : sound of definite pitch **3** : manner of speaking that expresses an emotion or attitude **4** : color quality **5** : healthy condition **6** : general character or quality ~ *vb* : soften or muffle —often used with *down* —**ton·al** \-ᵊl\ *adj* —**to·nal·i·ty** \tō'nalətē\ *n*

tongs \'täŋz, 'tóŋz\ *n pl* : grasping device of 2 joined or hinged pieces

tongue \'təŋ\ *n* **1** : fleshy movable organ of the mouth **2** : language **3** : something long and flat and fastened at one end —**tongued** \'təŋd\ *adj* — **tongue·less** *adj*

ton·ic \'tänik\ *n* : something (as a drug) that invigorates or restores health — **tonic** *adj*

to·night \tə'nīt\ *adv* : on this night ~ *n* : present or coming night

ton·sil \'tänsəl\ *n* : either of a pair of oval masses in the throat —**ton·sil·lec·to·my** \,tänsə'lektəmē\ *n* —**ton·sil·li·tis** \-'lītəs\ *n*

too \'tü\ *adv* **1** : in addition **2** : excessively

took *past of* TAKE

tool \'tül\ *n* : device worked by hand ~ *vb* : shape or finish with a tool

toot \'tüt\ *vb* : sound or cause to sound esp. in short blasts —**toot** *n*

tooth \'tüth\ *n, pl* **teeth** \'tēth\ **1** : one of the hard structures in the jaws for chewing **2** : one of the projections on the edge of a gear wheel —**tooth·ache** *n* —**tooth·brush** *n* —**toothed** \'tütht\ *adj* —**tooth·less** *adj* —**tooth·paste** *n* —**tooth·pick** *n*

tooth·some \'tüthsəm\ *adj* **1** : delicious **2** : attractive

¹top \'täp\ *n* **1** : highest part or level of something **2** : lid or covering ~ *vb* **-pp- 1** : cover with a top **2** : surpass **3** : go over the top of ~ *adj* : being at the top —**topped** *adj*

²top *n* : spinning toy

to·paz \'tō,paz\ *n* : hard gem

top·coat *n* : lightweight overcoat

top·ic \'täpik\ *n* : subject for discussion or study

top·i·cal \-ikəl\ *adj* **1** : relating to or arranged by topics **2** : relating to current or local events —**top·i·cal·ly** *adv*

top·most \'täp,mōst\ *adj* : highest of all

top-notch \-'näch\ *adj* : of the highest quality

to·pog·ra·phy \tə'pägrəfē\ *n* **1** : art of mapping the physical features of a place **2** : outline of the form of a place

—**to·pog·ra·pher** \-fər\ *n* —**top·o·graph·ic** \,täpə'grafik\, **top·o·graph·i·cal** \-ikəl\ *adj*

top·ple \'täpəl\ *vb* **-pled; -pling** : fall or cause to fall

top·sy-tur·vy \,täpsē'tərvē\ *adv or adj* **1** : upside down **2** : in utter confusion

torch \'torch\ *n* : flaming light —**torch·bear·er** *n* —**torch·light** *n*

tore *past of* TEAR

tor·ment \'tor,ment\ *n* : extreme pain or anguish or a source of this ~ *vb* **1** : cause severe anguish to **2** : harass —**tor·men·tor** \-ər\ *n*

torn *past part of* TEAR

tor·na·do \tor'nādō\ *n, pl* **-does** *or* **-dos** : violent destructive whirling wind

tor·pe·do \tor'pēdō\ *n, pl* **-does** : self-propelled explosive submarine missile ~ *vb* : hit with a torpedo

tor·pid \'torpəd\ *adj* **1** : having lost motion or the power of exertion **2** : lacking vigor —**tor·pid·i·ty** \tor'pidətē\ *n*

tor·por \'torpər\ *n* : extreme sluggishness or lethargy

torque \'tork\ *n* : turning force

tor·rent \'torənt\ *n* **1** : rushing stream **2** : tumultuous outburst —**tor·ren·tial** \to'renchəl, tə-\ *adj*

tor·rid \'torəd\ *adj* **1** : parched with heat **2** : impassioned

tor·sion \'torshən\ *n* : a twisting or being twisted —**tor·sion·al** \'torshənəl\ *adj* —**tor·sion·al·ly** *adv*

tor·so \'torsō\ *n, pl* **-sos** *or* **-si** \-,sē\ : trunk of the human body

tor·til·la \tor'tēyə\ *n* : round flat cornmeal or wheat flour bread

tor·toise \'tortəs\ *n* : land turtle

tor·tu·ous \'torchəwəs\ *adj* **1** : winding **2** : tricky

tor·ture \'torchər\ *n* **1** : use of pain to punish or force **2** : agony ~ *vb* **-tured; -tur·ing** : inflict torture on —**tor·tur·er** *n*

toss \'tos, 'täs\ *vb* **1** : move to and fro or up and down violently **2** : throw with a quick light motion **3** : move restlessly —**toss** *n*

toss-up *n* **1** : a deciding by flipping a coin **2** : even chance

tot \'tät\ *n* : small child

to·tal \'tōt°l\ *n* : entire amount ~ *vb* **-taled** *or* **-talled; -tal·ing** *or* **-tal·ling** **1** : add up **2** : amount to —**total** *adj* —**to·tal·ly** *adv*

to·tal·i·tar·i·an \tō,talə'terēən\ *adj* : relating to a political system in which the government has complete control over the people —**totalitarian** *n* —**to·tal·i·tar·i·an·ism** \-ēə,nizəm\ *n*

to·tal·i·ty \tō'talətē\ *n, pl* **-ties** : whole amount or entirety

tote \'tōt\ *vb* **tot·ed; tot·ing** : carry

to·tem \'tōtəm\ *n* : often carved figure used as a family or tribe emblem

tot·ter \'tätər\ *vb* **1** : sway as if about to fall **2** : stagger

touch \'təch\ *vb* **1** : make contact with so as to feel **2** : be or cause to be in contact **3** : take into the hands or mouth **4** : treat or mention a subject **5** : relate or concern **6** : move to sympathetic feeling ~ *n* **1** : light stroke **2** : act or fact of touching or being touched **3** : sense of feeling **4** : trace **5** : state of being in contact —**touch up** *vb* : improve with minor changes

touch·down \'təch,daun\ *n* : scoring of 6 points in football

touch·stone *n* : test or criterion of genuineness or quality

touchy \'təchē\ *adj* **touch·i·er; -est 1** : easily offended **2** : requiring tact

tough \'təf\ *adj* **1** : strong but elastic **2** : not easily chewed **3** : severe or disciplined **4** : stubborn ~ *n* : rowdy —**tough·ly** *adv* —**tough·ness** *n*

tough·en \'təfən\ *vb* : make or become tough

tou·pee \tü'pā\ *n* : small wig for a bald spot

tour \'tur\ *n* **1** : period of time spent at work or on an assignment **2** : journey with a return to the starting point ~ *vb* : travel over to see the sights —**tour·ist** \'turist\ *n*

tour·na·ment \'turnəmənt, 'tər-\ *n* **1** : medieval jousting competition **2** : championship series of games

tour·ney \-nē\ *n, pl* **-neys** : tournament

tour·ni·quet \'turnikət, 'tər-\ *n* : tight bandage for stopping blood flow

tou·sle \'tauzəl\ *vb* **-sled; -sling** : disheval (as someone's hair)

tout \'taut, 'tüt\ *vb* : praise or publicize loudly

tow \'tō\ *vb* : pull along behind —**tow** *n*

to·ward, to·wards \'tōrd, tə'word, 'tōrdz, tə'wordz\ *prep* **1** : in the direction of **2** : with respect to **3** : in part payment on

tow·el \'tauəl\ *n* : absorbent cloth or paper for wiping or drying

tow·er \'tau̇ər\ n : tall structure ~ vb : rise to a great height —**tow·ered** \'tau̇ərd\ adj —**tow·er·ing** adj

tow·head \'tō,hed\ n : person having whitish blond hair —**tow·head·ed** \-,hedəd\ adj

town \'tau̇n\ n 1 : small residential area 2 : city —**towns·peo·ple** \'tau̇nz-,pēpəl\ n pl

town·ship \'tau̇n,ship\ n 1 : unit of local government 2 : 36 square miles of U.S. public land

tox·ic \'täksik\ adj : poisonous —**tox·ic·i·ty** \täk'sisətē\ n

tox·in \'täksən\ n : poison produced by an organism

toy \'tȯi\ n : something for a child to play with ~ vb : amuse oneself or play with something ~ adj 1 : designed as a toy 2 : very small

¹**trace** \'trās\ vb **traced; trac·ing** 1 : mark over the lines of (a drawing) 2 : follow the trail or the development of ~ n 1 : track 2 : tiny amount or residue —**trace·able** adj —**trac·er** n

²**trace** n : line of a harness

tra·chea \'trākēə\ n, pl **-che·ae** \-kē,ē\ : windpipe —**tra·che·al** \-kēəl\ adj

track \'trak\ n 1 : trail left by wheels or footprints 2 : racing course 3 : train rails 4 : awareness of a progression 5 : looped belts propelling a vehicle ~ vb 1 : follow the trail of 2 : make tracks on —**track·er** n

track-and-field adj : relating to athletic contests of running, jumping, and throwing events

¹**tract** \'trakt\ n 1 : stretch of land 2 : system of body organs

²**tract** n : pamphlet of propaganda

trac·ta·ble \'traktəbəl\ adj : easily controlled

trac·tion \'trakshən\ n : gripping power to permit movement —**trac·tion·al** \-shənəl\ adj —**trac·tive** \'traktiv\ adj

trac·tor \'traktər\ n 1 : farm vehicle used esp. for pulling 2 : truck for hauling a trailer

trade \'trād\ n 1 : one's regular business 2 : occupation requiring skill 3 : the buying and selling of goods 4 : act of trading ~ vb **trad·ed; trad·ing** 1 : give in exchange for something 2 : buy and sell goods 3 : be a regular customer —**trades·peo·ple** \'trādz-,pēpəl\ n pl

trade-in \'trād,in\ n : an item traded to a merchant at the time of a purchase

trade·mark \'trād,märk\ n : word or mark identifying a manufacturer —**trademark** vb

trades·man \'trādzmən\ n : shopkeeper

tra·di·tion \trə'dishən\ n : belief or custom passed from generation to generation —**tra·di·tion·al** \-'dishənəl\ adj —**tra·di·tion·al·ly** adv

tra·duce \trə'düs, -'dyüs\ vb **-duced; -duc·ing** : lower the reputation of —**tra·duc·er** n

traf·fic \'trafik\ n 1 : business dealings 2 : movement along a route ~ vb : do business —**traf·fick·er** n —**traffic light** n

trag·e·dy \'trajədē\ n, pl **-dies** 1 : serious drama describing a conflict and having a sad ending 2 : disastrous event

trag·ic \'trajik\ adj : being a tragedy —**trag·i·cal·ly** adv

trail \'trāl\ vb 1 : hang down and drag along the ground 2 : draw along behind 3 : follow the track of 4 : dwindle ~ n 1 : something that trails 2 : path or evidence left by something

trail·er \'trālər\ n 1 : vehicle intended to be hauled 2 : dwelling designed to be towed to a site

train \'trān\ n 1 : trailing part of a gown 2 : retinue or procession 3 : connected series 4 : group of linked railroad cars ~ vb 1 : cause to grow as desired 2 : make or become prepared or skilled 3 : point —**train·ee** n —**train·er** n —**train·load** n

traipse \'trāps\ vb **traipsed; traips·ing** : walk

trait \'trāt\ n : distinguishing quality

trai·tor \'trātər\ n : one who betrays a trust or commits treason —**trai·tor·ous** adj

tra·jec·to·ry \trə'jektərē\ n, pl **-ries** : path of something moving through air or space

tram·mel \'traməl\ vb **-meled** or **-melled; -mel·ing** or **-mel·ling** : impede —**trammel** n

tramp \'tramp\ vb 1 : walk or hike 2 : tread on ~ n : beggar or vagrant

tram·ple \'trampəl\ vb **-pled; -pling** : walk or step on so as to bruise or crush —**trample** n —**tram·pler** \-plər\ n

tram·po·line \,trampə'lēn, 'trampə,-\ n : resilient sheet or web supported by springs and used for bouncing —**tram·po·lin·ist** \-ist\ n

trance \\trans\ *n* **1** : sleeplike condition **2** : state of mystical absorption

tran·quil \\traŋkwəl, 'tran-\ *adj* : quiet and undisturbed —**tran·quil·ize** \-kwə,līz\ *vb* —**tran·quil·iz·er** *n* —**tran·quil·li·ty** *or* **tran·quil·i·ty** \tran-'kwilətē, traŋ-\ *n* —**tran·quil·ly** *adv*

trans·act \trans'akt, tranz-\ *vb* : conduct (business)

trans·ac·tion \-'akshən\ *n* **1** : business deal **2** *pl* : records of proceedings

trans·cend \trans'end\ *vb* : rise above or surpass —**tran·scen·dent** \-'endənt\ *adj* —**tran·scen·den·tal** \,trans-,en'dentᵊl, -ən-\ *adj*

tran·scribe \trans'krīb\ *vb* -**scribed**; -**scrib·ing** : make a copy, arrangement, or recording of —**tran·scrip·tion** \trans'kripshən\ *n*

tran·script \\trans,kript\ *n* : official copy

tran·sept \\trans,ept\ *n* : part of a church that crosses the nave at right angles

trans·fer \trans'fər, 'trans,fər\ *vb* -**rr-** **1** : move from one person, place, or situation to another **2** : convey ownership of **3** : print or copy by contact **4** : change to another vehicle or transportation line ~ \'trans,fər\ *n* **1** : act or process of transferring **2** : one that transfers or is transferred **3** : ticket permitting one to transfer —**trans·fer·able** \trans'fərəbəl\ *adj* —**trans·fer·al** \-əl\ *n* —**trans·fer·ence** \-əns\ *n*

trans·fig·ure \trans'figyər\ *vb* -**ured**; -**ur·ing** **1** : change the form or appearance of **2** : glorify —**trans·fig·u·ra·tion** \,trans,figyə'rāshən\ *n*

trans·fix \trans'fiks\ *vb* **1** : pierce through **2** : hold motionless

trans·form \-'fórm\ *vb* **1** : change in structure, appearance, or character **2** : change (an electric current) in potential or type —**trans·for·ma·tion** \,transfər'māshən\ *n* —**trans·form·er** \trans'fórmər\ *n*

trans·fuse \trans'fyüz\ *vb* -**fused**; -**fus·ing** **1** : diffuse into or through **2** : transfer (as blood) into a vein —**trans·fu·sion** \-'fyüzhən\ *n*

trans·gress \trans'gres, tranz-\ *vb* : sin —**trans·gres·sion** \-'greshən\ *n* —**trans·gres·sor** \-'gresər\ *n*

tran·sient \'tranchənt\ *adj* : not lasting or staying long —**transient** *n* —**tran·sient·ly** *adv*

tran·sis·tor \tranz'istər, trans-\ *n* : small

electronic device used in electronic equipment —**tran·sis·tor·ize** \-tə,rīz\ *vb*

tran·sit \\transət, 'tranz-\ *n* **1** : movement across, or through **2** : local and esp. public transportation **3** : surveyor's instrument

tran·si·tion \trans'ishən, tranz-\ *n* : passage from one state, stage, or subject to another —**tran·si·tion·al** \-'ishənəl\ *adj*

tran·si·to·ry \'transə,tōrē, 'tranz-\ *adj* : of brief duration

trans·late \trans'lāt, tranz-\ *vb* -**lat·ed**; -**lat·ing** : change into another language —**trans·lat·able** *adj* —**trans·la·tion** \-'lāshən\ *n* —**trans·la·tor** \-'lātər\ *n*

trans·lu·cent \trans'lüsᵊnt, tranz-\ *adj* : not transparent but clear enough to allow light to pass through —**trans·lu·cence** \-ᵊns\ *n* —**trans·lu·cen·cy** \-ᵊnsē\ *n* —**trans·lu·cent·ly** *adv*

trans·mis·sion \-'mishən\ *n* **1** : act or process of transmitting **2** : system of gears between a car engine and drive wheels

trans·mit \-'mit\ *vb* -**tt-** **1** : transfer from one person or place to another **2** : pass on by inheritance **3** : broadcast —**trans·mis·si·ble** \-'misəbəl\ *adj* —**trans·mit·ta·ble** \-'mitəbəl\ *adj* —**trans·mit·tal** \-'mitᵊl\ *n* —**trans·mit·ter** *n*

tran·som \\transəm\ *n* : often hinged window above or beside a door

trans·par·ent \trans'parənt\ *adj* **1** : clear enough to see through **2** : obvious —**trans·par·en·cy** \-ənsē\ *n* —**trans·par·ent·ly** *adv*

tran·spire \trans'pīr\ *vb* -**spired**; -**spir·ing** : take place —**tran·spi·ra·tion** \,transpə'rāshən\ *n*

trans·plant \trans'plant\ *vb* **1** : dig up and move to another place **2** : transfer from one body part or person to another —**transplant** \'trans,-\ *n* —**trans·plan·ta·tion** \,trans,plan'tāshən\ *n*

trans·port \trans'pōrt\ *vb* **1** : carry or deliver to another place **2** : carry away by emotion ~ \'trans,-\ *n* **1** : act of transporting **2** : rapture **3** : ship or plane for carrying troops or supplies —**trans·por·ta·tion** \,transpər'tāshən\ *n* —**trans·port·er** *n*

trans·pose \trans'pōz\ *vb* -**posed**; -**pos·ing** : change the position, sequence, or key —**trans·po·si·tion** \,transpə-'zishən\ n

trans·ship \tran'ship, trans-\ vb : transfer from one mode of transportation to another —**trans·ship·ment** n

trans·verse \trans'vərs, tranz-\ adj : lying across —**trans·verse** \'trans-,vərs, 'tranz-\ n —**trans·verse·ly** adv

trap \'trap\ n 1 : device for catching animals 2 : something by which one is caught unawares 3 : device to allow one thing to pass through while keeping other things out ~ vb -**pp**- : catch in a trap —**trap·per** n

trap·door n : door in a floor or roof

tra·peze \tra'pēz\ n : suspended bar used by acrobats

trap·e·zoid \'trapə,zȯid\ n : plane 4-sided figure with 2 parallel sides —**trap·e·zoi·dal** \,trapə'zȯid²l\ adj

trap·pings \'trapiŋz\ n pl 1 : ornamental covering 2 : outward decoration or dress

trash \'trash\ n : something that is no good —**trashy** adj

trau·ma \'traúmə, 'trȯ-\ n : bodily or mental injury —**trau·mat·ic** \trȯ-'matik, trau-\ adj

tra·vail \trə'vāl, 'trav,āl\ n : painful work or exertion ~ vb : labor hard

trav·el \'travəl\ vb -**eled** or -**elled**; -**el·ing** or -**el·ling** 1 : take a trip or tour 2 : move or be carried from point to point ~ n : journey —often pl. —**trav·el·er, trav·el·ler** n

tra·verse \trə'vərs, tra'vərs, 'travərs\ vb -**versed**; -**vers·ing** 1 : go or extend across —**tra·verse** \'travərs\ n

trav·es·ty \'travəstē\ n, pl -**ties** : imitation that makes crude fun of something —**travesty** vb

trawl \'trȯl\ vb : fish or catch with a trawl ~ n : large cone-shaped net —**trawl·er** n

tray \'trā\ n : shallow flat-bottomed receptacle for holding or carrying something

treach·er·ous \'trechərəs\ adj : disloyal or dangerous —**treach·er·ous·ly** adv

treach·ery \'trechərē\ n, pl -**er·ies** : betrayal of a trust

tread \'tred\ vb **trod** \'träd\; **trod·den** \'träd³n\ or **trod; tread·ing** 1 : step on or over 2 : walk 3 : press or crush with the feet ~ n 1 : way of walking 2 : sound made in walking 3 : part on which a thing runs

trea·dle \'tred³l\ n : foot pedal operating a machine —**treadle** vb

tread·mill n 1 : mill worked by walking persons or animals 2 : wearisome routine

trea·son \'trēz³n\ n : attempt to overthrow the government —**trea·son·able** \'trēz³nəbəl\ adj —**trea·son·ous** \-³nəs\ adj

trea·sure \'trezhər, 'trāzh-\ n 1 : wealth stored up 2 : something of great value ~ vb -**sured; -sur·ing** : keep as precious

trea·sur·er \'trezhərər, 'trāzh-\ n : officer who handles funds

trea·sury \'trezhərē, 'trāzh-\ n, pl -**sur·ies** : place or office for keeping and distributing funds

treat \'trēt\ vb 1 : have as a topic 2 : pay for the food or entertainment of 3 : act toward or regard in a certain way 4 : give medical care to ~ n 1 : food or entertainment paid for by another 2 : something special and enjoyable —**treat·ment** \-mənt\ n

trea·tise \'trētəs\ n : systematic written exposition or argument

trea·ty \'trētē\ n, pl -**ties** : agreement between governments

tre·ble \'trebəl\ n 1 : highest part in music 2 : upper half of the musical range ~ adj : triple in number or amount ~ vb -**bled; -bling** : make triple —**tre·bly** adv

tree \'trē\ n : tall woody plant ~ vb **treed; tree·ing** : force up a tree —**tree·less** adj

trek \'trek\ n : difficult trip ~ vb -**kk**- : make a trek

trel·lis \'treləs\ n : structure of crossed strips

trem·ble \'trembəl\ vb -**bled; -bling** 1 : shake from fear or cold 2 : move or sound as if shaken

tre·men·dous \tri'mendəs\ adj : amazingly large, powerful, or excellent —**tre·men·dous·ly** adv

trem·or \'tremər\ n : a trembling

trem·u·lous \'tremyələs\ adj : trembling or quaking

trench \'trench\ n : long narrow cut in land

tren·chant \'trenchənt\ adj : sharply perceptive

trend \'trend\ n : prevailing tendency, direction, or style ~ vb : move in a particular direction —**trendy** \'trendē\ adj

trep·i·da·tion \ˌtrepəˈdāshən\ *n* : nervous apprehension

tres·pass \ˈtrespəs, -ˌpas\ *n* **1** : sin **2** : unauthorized entry onto someone's property ~ *vb* **1** : sin **2** : enter illegally —**tres·pass·er** *n*

tress \ˈtres\ *n* : long lock of hair

tres·tle \ˈtresəl\ *n* **1** : support with a horizontal piece and spreading legs **2** : framework bridge

tri·ad \ˈtrīˌad, -əd\ *n* : union of 3

tri·age \trēˈäzh, ˈtrēˌäzh\ *n* : system of dealing with cases (as patients) according to priority guidelines intended to maximize success

tri·al \ˈtrīəl\ *n* **1** : hearing and judgment of a matter in court **2** : source of great annoyance **3** : test use or experimental effort —**trial** *adj*

tri·an·gle \ˈtrīˌaŋgəl\ *n* : plane figure with 3 sides and 3 angles —**tri·an·gu·lar** \trīˈaŋgyələr\ *adj*

tribe \ˈtrīb\ *n* : social group of numerous families —**trib·al** \ˈtrībəl\ *adj* —**tribes·man** \ˈtrībzmən\ *n*

trib·u·la·tion \ˌtribyəˈlāshən\ *n* : suffering from oppression

tri·bu·nal \trīˈbyünəl, tri-\ *n* **1** : court **2** : something that decides

trib·u·tary \ˈtribyəˌterē\ *n, pl* **-tar·ies** : stream that flows into a river or lake

trib·ute \ˈtribˌyüt\ *n* **1** : payment to acknowledge submission **2** : tax **3** : gift or act showing respect

trick \ˈtrik\ *n* **1** : scheme to deceive **2** : prank **3** : deceptive or ingenious feat **4** : mannerism **5** : knack **6** : tour of duty ~ *vb* : deceive by cunning —**trick·ery** \-ərē\ *n* —**trick·ster** \-stər\ *n*

trick·le \ˈtrikəl\ *vb* **-led; -ling** : run in drops or a thin stream —**trickle** *n*

tricky \ˈtrikē\ *adj* **trick·i·er; -est** **1** : inclined to trickery **2** : requiring skill or caution

tri·cy·cle \ˈtrīˌsikəl\ *n* : 3-wheeled bicycle

tri·dent \ˈtrīdᵊnt\ *n* : 3-pronged spear

tri·en·ni·al \trīˈenēəl\ *adj* : lasting, occurring, or done every 3 years —**triennial** *n*

tri·fle \ˈtrīfəl\ *n* : something of little value or importance ~ *vb* **-fled; -fling** **1** : speak or act in a playful or flirting way **2** : toy —**tri·fler** *n*

tri·fling \ˈtrīfliŋ\ *adj* : trivial

trig·ger \ˈtrigər\ *n* : finger-piece of a firearm lock that fires the gun ~ *vb*

: set into motion —**trigger** *adj* —**trig·gered** \-ərd\ *adj*

trig·o·nom·e·try \ˌtrigəˈnämətrē\ *n* : mathematics dealing with triangular measurement —**trig·o·no·met·ric** \-nəˈmetrik\ *adj*

trill \ˈtril\ *n* **1** : rapid alternation between 2 adjacent tones **2** : rapid vibration in speaking ~ *vb* : utter in or with a trill

tril·lion \ˈtrilyən\ *n* : 1000 billions —**trillion** *adj* —**tril·lionth** \-yənth\ *adj or n*

tril·o·gy \ˈtriləjē\ *n, pl* **-gies** : 3-part literary or musical composition

trim \ˈtrim\ *vb* **-mm- 1** : decorate **2** : make neat or reduce by cutting ~ *adj* **-mm-** : neat and compact ~ *n* **1** : state or condition **2** : ornaments —**trim·ly** *adv* —**trim·mer** *n*

trim·ming \ˈtrimiŋ\ *n* : something that ornaments or completes

Trin·i·ty \ˈtrinətē\ *n* : divine unity of Father, Son, and Holy Spirit

trin·ket \ˈtriŋkət\ *n* : small ornament

trio \ˈtrēō\ *n, pl* **tri·os 1** : music for 3 performers **2** : group of 3

trip \ˈtrip\ *vb* **-pp- 1** : step lightly **2** : stumble or cause to stumble **3** : make or cause to make a mistake **4** : release (as a spring or switch) ~ *n* **1** : journey **2** : stumble **3** : drug-induced experience

tri·par·tite \trīˈpärˌtīt\ *adj* : having 3 parts or parties

tripe \ˈtrīp\ *n* **1** : animal's stomach used as food **2** : trash

tri·ple \ˈtripəl\ *vb* **-pled; -pling** : make 3 times as great ~ *n* : group of 3 ~ *adj* **1** : having 3 units **2** : being 3 times as great or as many

trip·let \ˈtriplət\ *n* **1** : group of 3 **2** : one of 3 offspring born together

trip·li·cate \ˈtriplikət\ *adj* : made in 3 identical copies ~ *n* : one of 3 copies

tri·pod \ˈtrīˌpäd\ *n* : a stand with 3 legs —**tripod, tri·po·dal** \ˈtripədᵊl, ˈtrīˌpäd-\ *adj*

tri·sect \ˈtrīˌsekt, trīˈ-\ *vb* : divide into 3 usu. equal parts —**tri·sec·tion** \ˈtrīˌsekshən\ *n*

trite \ˈtrīt\ *adj* **trit·er; trit·est** : commonplace

tri·umph \ˈtrīəmf\ *n, pl* **-umphs** : victory or great success ~ *vb* : obtain or celebrate victory —**tri·um·phal** \ˈtrīˈəmfəl\ *adj* —**tri·um·phant** \-fənt\ *adj* —**tri·um·phant·ly** *adv*

tri·um·vi·rate \trī'əmvərət\ *n* : ruling body of 3 persons

triv·et \'trivət\ *n* **1** : 3-legged stand **2** : stand to hold a hot dish

triv·ia \'trivēə\ *n sing or pl* : unimportant details

triv·i·al \'trivēəl\ *adj* : of little importance —**triv·i·al·i·ty** \,trivē'alətē\ *n*

trod *past of* TREAD

trod·den *past part of* TREAD

troll \'trōl\ *n* : dwarf or giant of folklore inhabiting caves or hills

trol·ley \'trälē\ *n, pl* **-leys** : streetcar run by overhead electric wires

trol·lop \'träləp\ *n* : untidy or immoral woman

trom·bone \träm'bōn, 'träm,-\ *n* : musical instrument with a long sliding tube —**trom·bon·ist** \-'bōnist, -,bō-\ *n*

troop \'trüp\ *n* **1** : cavalry unit **2** *pl* : soldiers **3** : collection of people or things ~ *vb* : move or gather in crowds

troop·er \'trüpər\ *n* **1** : cavalry soldier **2** : police officer on horseback or state police officer

tro·phy \'trōfē\ *n, pl* **-phies** : prize gained by a victory

trop·ic \'träpik\ *n* **1** : either of the 2 parallels of latitude one 23½ degrees north of the equator (**tropic of Cancer** \-'kansər\) and one 23½ degrees south of the equator (**tropic of Capri·corn** \-'kaprə,kórn\) **2** *pl* : region lying between the tropics —**tropic, trop·i·cal** \-ikəl\ *adj*

trot \'trät\ *n* : moderately fast gait esp. of a horse with diagonally paired legs moving together ~ *vb* **-tt-** : go at a trot —**trot·ter** *n*

troth \'träth, 'trȯth, 'trōth\ *n* **1** : pledged faithfulness **2** : betrothal

trou·ba·dour \'trübə,dōr\ *n* : medieval lyric poet

trou·ble \'trəbəl\ *vb* **-bled; -bling 1** : disturb **2** : afflict **3** : make an effort ~ *n* **1** : cause of mental or physical distress **2** : effort —**trou·ble·mak·er** *n* —**trou·ble·some** *adj* —**trou·ble·some·ly** *adv*

trough \'trȯf\ *n, pl* **troughs** \'trȯfs, 'trȯvz\ **1** : narrow container for animal feed or water **2** : long channel or depression (as between waves)

trounce \'traúns\ *vb* **trounced; trouncing** : thrash, punish, or defeat severely

troupe \'trüp\ *n* : group of stage performers —**troup·er** *n*

trou·sers \'traúzərz\ *n pl* : long pants —**trouser** *adj*

trous·seau \trüsō, trü'sō\ *n, pl* **-seaux** \-sōz, -'sōz\ *or* **-seaus** : bride's collection of clothing and personal items

trout \'traút\ *n, pl* **trout** : freshwater food and game fish

trow·el \'traúəl\ *n* **1** : tool for spreading or smoothing **2** : garden scoop —**trowel** *vb*

troy \'trȯi\ *n* : system of weights based on a pound of 12 ounces

tru·ant \'trüənt\ *n* : student absent from school without permission —**tru·an·cy** \-ənsē\ *n* —**truant** *adj*

truce \'trüs\ *n* : agreement to halt fighting

truck \'trək\ *n* **1** : wheeled frame for moving heavy objects **2** : automotive vehicle for transporting heavy loads ~ *vb* : transport on a truck —**truck·er** *n* —**truck·load** *n*

truck·le \'trəkəl\ *vb* **-led; -ling** : yield slavishly to another

tru·cu·lent \'trakyələnt\ *adj* : aggressively self-assertive —**tru·cu·lence** \-ləns\ *n* —**tru·cu·len·cy** \-lənsē\ *n* —**tru·cu·lent·ly** *adv*

trudge \'trəj\ *vb* **trudged; trudg·ing** : walk or march steadily and with difficulty

true \'trü\ *adj* **tru·er; tru·est 1** : loyal **2** : in agreement with fact or reality **3** : genuine ~ *adv* **1** : truthfully **2** : accurately ~ *vb* **trued; tru·ing** : make balanced or even —**tru·ly** *adv*

true-blue *adj* : loyal

truf·fle \'trəfəl\ *n* **1** : edible fruit of an underground fungus **2** : ball-shaped chocolate candy

tru·ism \'trü,izəm\ *n* : obvious truth

trump \'trəmp\ *n* : card of a designated suit any of whose cards will win over other cards ~ *vb* : take with a trump

trumped-up \'trəmpt'əp\ *adj* : made-up

trum·pet \'trəmpət\ *n* : tubular brass wind instrument with a flaring end ~*vb* **1** : blow a trumpet **2** : proclaim loudly —**trum·pet·er** *n*

trun·cate \'trəŋ,kāt, 'trən-\ *vb* **-cat·ed; -cat·ing** : cut short —**trun·ca·tion** \,trəŋ'kāshən\ *n*

trun·dle \'trənd°l\ *vb* **-dled; -dling** : roll along

trunk \'trəŋk\ *n* **1** : main part (as of a

body or tree) **2** : long muscular nose of an elephant **3** : storage chest **4** : storage space in a car **5** : shorts

truss \'trəs\ *vb* : bind tightly ~ *n* **1** : set of structural parts forming a framework **2** : appliance worn to hold a hernia in place

trust \'trəst\ *n* **1** : reliance on another **2** : assured hope **3** : credit **4** : property held or managed in behalf of another **5** : combination of firms that reduces competition **6** : something entrusted to another's care **7** : custody ~ *vb* **1** : depend **2** : hope **3** : entrust **4** : have faith in —**trust·ful** \-fəl\ *adj* —**trust·ful·ly** *adv* —**trust·ful·ness** *n* —**trust·worthi·ness** *n* —**trust·wor·thy** *adj*

trust·ee \ˌtrəs'tē\ *n* : person holding property in trust —**trust·ee·ship** *n*

trusty \'trəstē\ *adj* **trust·i·er; -est** : dependable

truth \'trüth\ *n, pl* **truths** \'trüthz, 'trüths\ **1** : real state of things **2** : true or accepted statement **3** : agreement with fact or reality —**truth·ful** \-fəl\ *adj* —**truth·ful·ly** *adv* —**truth·ful·ness** *n*

try \'trī\ *vb* **tried; try·ing 1** : conduct the trial of **2** : put to a test **3** : strain **4** : make an effort at ~ *n, pl* **tries** : act of trying

try·out *n* : competitive test of performance esp. for athletes or actors —**try out** *vb*

tryst \'trist, 'trīst\ *n* : secret rendezvous of lovers

tsar \'zär, 'tsär, 'sär\ *var of* CZAR

T–shirt \'tē,shərt\ *n* : collarless pullover shirt with short sleeves

tub \'təb\ *n* **1** : wide bucketlike vessel **2** : bathtub

tu·ba \'tübə, 'tyü-\ *n* : large low-pitched brass wind instrument

tube \'tüb, 'tyüb\ *n* **1** : hollow cylinder **2** : round container from which a substance can be squeezed **3** : airtight circular tube of rubber inside a tire **4** : electronic device consisting of a sealed usu. glass container with electrodes inside —**tubed** \'tübd, 'tyübd\ *adj* —**tube·less** *adj*

tu·ber \'tübər, 'tyü-\ *n* : fleshy underground growth (as of a potato) —**tu·ber·ous** \-rəs\ *adj*

tu·ber·cu·lo·sis \tu̇ˌbərkyə'lōsəs, tyü-\ *n, pl* **-lo·ses** \-ˌsēz\ : bacterial disease esp. of the lungs —**tu·ber·cu·lar**

\-'bərkyələr\ *adj* —**tu·ber·cu·lous** \-ləs\ *adj*

tub·ing \'tübiŋ, 'tyü-\ *n* : series or arrangement of tubes

tu·bu·lar \'tübyələr, 'tyü-\ *adj* : of or like a tube

tuck \'tək\ *vb* **1** : pull up into a fold **2** : put into a snug often concealing place **3** : make snug in bed —with *in* **1** : fold in a cloth

tuck·er \'təkər\ *vb* : fatigue

Tues·day \'tüzdā, 'tyüz-, -dē\ *n* : 3d day of the week

tuft \'təft\ *n* : clump (as of hair or feathers) —**tuft·ed** \'təftəd\ *adj*

tug \'təg\ *vb* **-gg- 1** : pull hard **2** : move by pulling ~ *n* **1** : act of tugging **2** : tugboat

tug·boat *n* : boat for towing or pushing ships through a harbor

tug-of-war \ˌtəgə'wȯr\ *n, pl* **tugs-of-war** : pulling contest between 2 teams

tu·ition \tu̇'ishən, 'tyü-\ *n* : cost of instruction

tu·lip \'tüləp, 'tyü-\ *n* : herb with cup-shaped flowers

tum·ble \'təmbəl\ *vb* **-bled; -bling 1** : perform gymnastic feats of rolling and turning **2** : fall or cause to fall suddenly **3** : toss ~ *n* : act of tumbling

tum·bler \'təmblər\ *n* **1** : acrobat **2** : drinking glass **3** : obstruction in a lock that can be moved (as by a key)

tu·mid \'tüməd, 'tyü-\ *adj* : turgid

tum·my \'təmē\ *n, pl* **-mies** : belly

tu·mor \'tümər 'tyü-\ *n* : abnormal and useless growth of tissue —**tu·mor·ous** *adj*

tu·mult \'tü,məlt 'tyü-\ *n* **1** : uproar **2** : violent agitation of mind or feelings —**tu·mul·tu·ous** \tu̇'məlchəwəs, tyü-\ *adj*

tun \'tən\ *n* : large cask

tu·na \'tünə, 'tyü-\ *n, pl* **-na** *or* **-nas** : large sea food fish

tun·dra \'təndrə\ *n* : treeless arctic plain

tune \'tün, 'tyün\ *n* **1** : melody **2** : correct musical pitch **3** : harmonious relationship ~ *vb* **tuned; tun·ing 1** : bring or come into harmony **2** : adjust in musical pitch **3** : adjust a receiver so as to receive a broadcast **4** : put in first-class working order —**tun·able** *adj* —**tune·ful** \-fəl\ *adj* —**tun·er** *n*

tung·sten \'təŋstən\ *n* : metallic element used for electrical purposes and in hardening alloys (as steel)

tu·nic \'tünik, 'tyü-\ n 1 : ancient knee-length garment 2 : hip-length blouse or jacket

tun·nel \'tən³l\ n : underground passageway ~ vb -neled or -nelled; -nel·ing or -nel·ling : make a tunnel through or under something

tur·ban \'tərbən\ n : wound headdress worn esp. by Muslims

tur·bid \'tərbəd\ adj 1 : dark with stirred-up sediment 2 : confused — **tur·bid·i·ty** \,tər'bidətē\ n

tur·bine \'tərbən, -,bīn\ n : engine turned by the force of gas or water on fan blades

tur·bo·jet \'tərbō,jet\ n : airplane powered by a jet engine having a turbine-driven air compressor or the engine itself

tur·bo·prop \'tərbō,präp\ n : airplane powered by a propeller turned by a jet engine-driven turbine

tur·bu·lent \'tərbyələnt\ adj 1 : causing violence or disturbance 2 : marked by agitation or tumult —**tur·bu·lence** \-ləns\ n —**tur·bu·lent·ly** adv

tu·reen \tə'rēn, tyu-\ n : deep bowl for serving soup

turf \'tərf\ n : upper layer of soil bound by grass and roots

tur·gid \'tərjəd\ adj 1 : swollen 2 : too highly embellished in style —**tur·gid·i·ty** \,tər'jidətē\ n

tur·key \'tərkē\ n, pl **-keys** : large American bird raised for food

tur·moil \'tər,moil\ n : extremely agitated condition

turn \'tərn\ vb 1 : move or cause to move around an axis 2 : twist (a mechanical part) to operate 3 : wrench 4 : cause to face or move in a different direction 5 : reverse the sides or surfaces of 6 : upset 7 : go around 8 : become or cause to become 9 : seek aid from a source ~ n 1 : act or instance of turning 2 : change 3 : place at which something turns 4 : place, time, or opportunity to do something in order —**turn·er** n —**turn down** vb : decline to accept —**turn in** vb 1 : deliver or report to authorities 2 : go to bed —**turn off** vb : stop the functioning of —**turn out** vb 1 : expel 2 : produce 3 : come together 4 : prove to be in the end —**turn over** vb : transfer —**turn up** vb 1 : discover or appear 2 : happen unexpectedly

turn·coat n : traitor

turn·ip \'tərnəp\ n : edible root of an herb

turn·out \'tərn,aút\ n 1 : gathering of people for a special purpose 2 : size of a gathering

turn·over n 1 : upset or reversal 2 : filled pastry 3 : volume of business 4 : movement (as of goods or people) into, through, and out of a place

turn·pike \'tərn,pīk\ n : expressway on which tolls are charged

turn·stile \-,stīl\ n : post with arms pivoted on the top that allows people to pass one by one

turn·ta·ble n : platform that turns a phonograph record

tur·pen·tine \'tərpən,tīn\ n : oil distilled from pine-tree resin and used as a solvent

tur·pi·tude \'tərpə,tüd, -,tyüd\ n : inherent baseness

tur·quoise \'tər,kóiz, -,kwóiz\ n : blue or greenish gray gemstone

tur·ret \'tərət\ n 1 : little tower on a building 2 : revolving tool holder or gun housing

tur·tle \'tərt³l\ n : reptile with the trunk enclosed in a bony shell

tur·tle·dove n : wild pigeon

tur·tle·neck n : high close-fitting collar that can be turned over or a sweater or shirt with this collar

tusk \'təsk\ n : long protruding tooth (as of an elephant) —**tusked** \'təskt\ adj

tus·sle \'təsəl\ n or vb : struggle

tu·te·lage \'tüt³lij, 'tyüt-\ n 1 : act of protecting 2 : instruction esp. of an individual

tu·tor \'tütər, 'tyü-\ n : private teacher ~ vb : teach usu. individually

tux·e·do \,tək'sēdō\ n, pl **-dos** or **-does** : semiformal evening clothes for a man

TV \,tē'vē, 'tē,vē\ n : television

twain \'twān\ n : two

twang \'twaŋ\ n 1 : harsh sound like that of a plucked bowstring 2 : nasal speech or resonance ~ vb : sound or speak with a twang

tweak \'twēk\ vb : pinch and pull playfully —**tweak** n

tweed \'twēd\ n 1 : rough woolen fabric 2 pl : tweed clothing —**tweedy** adj

tweet \'twēt\ n : chirping note —**tweet** vb

twee·zers \'twēzərz\ *n pl* : small pincer-like tool

twelve \'twelv\ *n* **1** : one more than 11 **2** : 12th in a set or series **3** : something having 12 units —**twelfth** \'twelfth\ *adj or n* —**twelve** *adj or pron*

twen·ty \'twentē\ *n, pl* -**ties** : 2 times 10 —**twen·ti·eth** \-ēəth\ *adj or n* —**twenty** *adj or pron*

twen·ty–twen·ty, 20–20 *adj* : being vision of normal sharpness

twice \'twīs\ *adv* **1** : on 2 occasions **2** : 2 times

twig \'twig\ *n* : small branch —**twig·gy** *adj*

twi·light \'twī,līt\ *n* : light from the sky at dusk or dawn —**twilight** *adj*

twill \'twil\ *n* : fabric with a weave that gives an appearance of diagonal lines in the fabric

twilled \'twild\ *adj* : made with a twill weave

twin \'twin\ *n* : either of 2 offspring born together ~ *adj* **1** : born with one another or as a pair at one birth **2** : made up of 2 similar parts

twine \'twīn\ *n* : strong twisted thread ~ *vb* **twined; twin·ing 1** : twist together **2** : coil about a support —**twin·er** *n* —**twiny** *adj*

twinge \'twinj\ *vb* **twinged; twing·ing** *or* **twinge·ing** : affect with or feel a sudden sharp pain ~ *n* : sudden sharp stab (as of pain)

twin·kle \'twiŋkəl\ *vb* -**kled; -kling** : shine with a flickering light ~ *n* **1** : wink **2** : intermittent shining —**twin·kler** \-klər\ *n*

twirl \'twərl\ *vb* : whirl round ~ *n* **1** : act of twirling **2** : coil —**twirl·er** *n*

twist \'twist\ *vb* **1** : unite by winding (threads) together **2** : wrench **3** : move in or have a spiral shape **4** : follow a winding course ~ *n* **1** : act or result of twisting **2** : unexpected development

twist·er \'twistər\ *n* : tornado

¹twit \'twit\ *n* : fool

²twit *vb* -**tt**- : taunt

twitch \'twich\ *vb* : move or pull with a sudden motion ~ *n* : act of twitching

twit·ter \'twitər\ *vb* : make chirping noises ~ *n* : small intermittent noise

two \'tü\ *n, pl* **twos 1** : one more than one **2** : the 2d in a set or series **3** : something having 2 units —**two** *adj or pron*

two·fold \'tü,fōld\ *adj* : double —**two·fold** \-'fōld\ *adv*

two·some \'tüsəm\ *n* : couple

-ty *n suffix* : quality, condition, or degree

ty·coon \tī'kün\ *n* : powerful and successful businessman

tying *pres part of* TIE

tyke \'tīk\ *n* : small child

tym·pa·num \'timpənəm\ *n, pl* -**na** \-nə\ : eardrum or the cavity which it closes externally —**tym·pan·ic** \tim'panik\ *adj*

type \'tīp\ *n* **1** : class, kind, or group set apart by common characteristics **2** : special design of printed letters ~ *vb* **typed; typ·ing 1** : write with a typewriter **2** : identify or classify as a particular type

type·writ·er *n* : keyboard machine that produces printed material by striking a ribbon with raised letters —**type·write** *vb*

ty·phoid \'tī,fȯid, tī'-\ *adj* : relating to or being a communicable bacterial disease (**typhoid fever**)

ty·phoon \tī'fün\ *n* : hurricane of the western Pacific ocean

ty·phus \'tīfəs\ *n* : severe disease with fever, delirium, and rash

typ·i·cal \'tipikəl\ *adj* : having the essential characteristics of a group —**typ·i·cal·i·ty** \,tipə'kalətē\ *n* —**typ·i·cal·ly** *adv* —**typ·i·cal·ness** *n*

typ·i·fy \'tipə,fī\ *vb* -**fied; -fy·ing** : be typical of

typ·ist \'tīpist\ *n* : one who operates a typewriter

ty·pog·ra·phy \tī'pägrəfē\ *n* **1** : art of printing with type **2** : style, arrangement, or appearance of printed matter —**ty·po·graph·ic** \,tīpə'grafik\, **ty·po·graph·i·cal** \-ikəl\ *adj* —**ty·po·graph·i·cal·ly** *adv*

ty·ran·ni·cal \tə'ranikəl, tī-\ *adj* : relating to a tyrant —**ty·ran·ni·cal·ly** *adv*

tyr·an·nize \'tirə,nīz\ *vb* -**nized; -niz·ing** : rule or deal with in the manner of a tyrant —**tyr·an·niz·er** *n*

tyr·an·ny \'tirənē\ *n, pl* -**nies** : unjust use of absolute governmental power

ty·rant \'tīrənt\ *n* : harsh ruler having absolute power

ty·ro \'tīrō\ *n, pl* -**ros** : beginner

tzar \'zär, 'tsär, 'sär\ *var of* CZAR

U

u \'yü\ *n, pl* **u's** *or* **us** \'yüz\ : 21st letter of the alphabet

ubiquitous \yü'bikwətəs\ *adj* : omnipresent —**ubiquitously** *adv* —**ubiquity** \-wətē\ *n*

udder \'ədər\ *n* : animal sac containing milk glands and nipples

ugly \'əglē\ *adj* **uglier; -est 1** : offensive to look at **2** : mean or quarrelsome —**ugliness** *n*

ukulele \,yükə'lālē\ *n* : small 4-string guitar

ulcer \'əlsər\ *n* : eroded sore —**ulcerous** *adj*

ulcerate \'əlsə,rāt\ *vb* **-ated; -ating** : become affected with an ulcer —**ulceration** \,əlsə'rāshən\ *n* —**ulcerative** \'əlsə,rātiv\ *adj*

ulna \'əlnə\ *n* : bone of the forearm opposite the thumb

ulterior \,əl'tirēər\ *adj* : not revealed

ultimate \'əltəmət\ *adj* : final, maximum, or extreme —**ultimate** *n* —**ultimately** *adv*

ultimatum \,əltə'mātəm, -'mät-\ *n, pl* **-tums** *or* **-ta** \-ə\ : final proposition or demand carrying or implying a threat

ultraviolet \,əltrə'vīələt\ *adj* : having a wavelength shorter than visible light

umbilicus \,əmbə'līkəs, ,əm'bili-\ *n, pl* **-lici** \-bə'lī,kī, -,sī; -'bilə,kī, -,kē\ *or* **-licuses** : small depression on the abdominal wall marking the site of the cord (**umbilical cord**) that joins the unborn fetus to its mother —**umbilical** \,əm'bilikəl\ *adj*

umbrage \'əmbrij\ *n* : resentment

umbrella \,əm'brelə\ *n* : collapsible fabric device to protect from sun or rain

umpire \'əm,pīr\ *n* **1** : arbitrator **2** : sport official —**umpire** *vb*

umpteen \'əmp'tēn\ *adj* : very numerous —**umpteenth** \-'tēnth\ *adj*

un- \,ən, 'ən\ *prefix* **1** : not **2** : opposite of

unable	unaccompanied
unabridged	unaccounted
unacceptable	unacquainted

unaddressed	unconventional
unadorned	unconvention-
unadulterated	ally
unafraid	unconverted
unaided	uncooked
unalike	uncooperative
unambiguous	uncoordinated
unambitious	uncovered
unannounced	uncultivated
unanswered	undamaged
unanticipated	undated
unappetizing	undecided
unappreciated	undeclared
unapproved	undefeated
unarguable	undemocratic
unarguably	undependable
unassisted	undeserving
unattended	undesirable
unattractive	undetected
unauthorized	undetermined
unavailable	undeveloped
unavoidable	undeviating
unbearable	undignified
unbiased	undisturbed
unbranded	undivided
unbreakable	undomesticated
uncensored	undrinkable
unchallenged	unearned
unchangeable	uneducated
unchanged	unemotional
unchanging	unending
uncharacteristic	undurable
uncharged	unenforceable
unchaste	unenlightened
uncivilized	unethical
unclaimed	unexcitable
unclear	unexciting
uncleared	unexplainable
unclothed	unexplored
uncluttered	unfair
uncombed	unfairly
uncomfortable	unfairness
uncomfortably	unfavorable
uncomplimen-	unfavorably
tary	unfeigned
unconfirmed	unfilled
unconsummated	unfinished
uncontested	unflattering
uncontrolled	unforeseeable
uncontroversial	unforeseen

unforgivable
unforgiving
unfulfilled
unfurnished
ungenerous
ungentlemanly
ungraceful
ungrammatical
unharmed
unhealthful
unheated
unhurt
unidentified
unimaginable
unimaginative
unimportant
unimpressed
uninformed
uninhabited
uninjured
uninsured
unintelligent
unintelligible
unintelligibly
unintended
unintentional
unintentionally
uninterested
uninteresting
uninterrupted
uninvited
unjust
unjustifiable
unjustified
unjustly
unknowing
unknowingly
unknown
unleavened
unlicensed
unlikable
unlimited
unlovable
unmanageable
unmarked
unmarried
unmerciful
unmercifully
unmerited
unmolested
unmotivated
unmoving
unnamed
unnecessarily
unnecessary
unneeded
unnoticeable
unnoticed

unobjectionable
unobservable
unobservant
unobtainable
unobtrusive
unobtrusively
unofficial
unopened
unopposed
unorganized
unoriginal
unorthodox
unorthodoxy
unpaid
unpardonable
unpatriotic
unpaved
unpleasant
unpleasantly
unpleasantness
unpopular
unpopularity
unposed
unpredictability
unpredictable
unpredictably
unprejudiced
unprepared
unpretentious
unproductive
unprofitable
unprotected
unproved
unproven
unprovoked
unpunished
unqualified
unquenchable
unquestioning
unreachable
unreadable
unready
unrealistic
unreasonable
unreasonably
unrefined
unrelated
unreliable
unremembered
unrepentant
unrepresented
unrequited
unresolved
unresponsive
unrestrained
unrestricted
unrewarding
unripe

unsafe
unsalted
unsanitary
unsatisfactory
unsatisfied
unscented
unscheduled
unseasoned
unseen
unselfish
unselfishly
unselfishness
unshaped
unshaven
unskillful
unskillfully
unsolicited
unsolved
unsophisticated
unsound
unsoundly
unsoundness
unspecified
unspoiled
unsteadily
unsteadiness
unsteady
unstructured
unsubstantiated
unsuccessful
unsuitable
unsuitably
unsuited
unsupervised
unsupported
unsure

unsurprising
unsuspecting
unsweetened
unsympathetic
untamed
untanned
untidy
untouched
untrained
untreated
untrue
untrustworthy
untruthful
unusable
unusual
unvarying
unverified
unwanted
unwarranted
unwary
unwavering
unweaned
unwed
unwelcome
unwholesome
unwilling
unwillingly
unwillingness
unwise
unwisely
unworkable
unworthily
unworthiness
unworthy
unyielding

un·ac·cus·tomed *adj* **1** : not customary **2** : not accustomed

un·af·fect·ed *adj* **1** : not influenced or changed by something **2** : natural and sincere — **un·af·fect·ed·ly** *adv*

unan·i·mous \yù'nanəməs\ *adj* **1** : showing no disagreement **2** : formed with the agreement of all — **una·nim·i·ty** \ˌyünə'nimətē\ *n* — **unan·i·mous·ly** *adv*

un·armed *adj* : not armed or armored

un·as·sum·ing *adj* : not bold or arrogant

un·at·tached *adj* **1** : not attached **2** : not married or engaged

un·aware *adv* : unawares ~ *adj* : not aware

un·awares \ˌonə'warz\ *adv* **1** : without warning **2** : unintentionally

un·bal·anced *adj* **1** : not balanced **2** : mentally unstable

un·beat·en *adj* : not beaten

un·be·com·ing adj : not proper or suitable —**un·be·com·ing·ly** adv

un·be·liev·able adj 1 : improbable 2 : superlative —**un·be·liev·ably** adv

un·bend vb -**bent**; -**bend·ing** : make or become more relaxed and friendly

un·bend·ing adj : formal and inflexible

un·bind vb -**bound**; -**bind·ing** 1 : remove bindings from 2 : release

un·bolt vb : open or unfasten by withdrawing a bolt

un·born adj : not yet born

un·bo·som vb : disclose thoughts or feelings

un·bowed \ˌənˈbau̇d\ adj : not defeated or subdued

un·bri·dled \ˌənˈbrīdəld\ adj : unrestrained

un·bro·ken adj 1 : not damaged 2 : not interrupted

un·buck·le vb : unfasten the buckle of

un·bur·den vb : relieve (oneself) of anxieties

un·but·ton vb : unfasten the buttons of

un·called-for adj : too harsh or rude for the occasion

un·can·ny \ənˈkanē\ adj 1 : weird 2 : suggesting superhuman powers —**un·can·ni·ly** \-ˈkanəlē\ adv

un·ceas·ing adj : never ceasing —**un·ceas·ing·ly** adv

un·cer·e·mo·ni·ous adj : acting without ordinary courtesy —**un·cer·e·mo·ni·ous·ly** adv

un·cer·tain adj 1 : not determined, sure, or definitely known 2 : subject to chance or change —**un·cer·tain·ly** adv —**un·cer·tain·ty** n

un·chris·tian adj : not consistent with Christian teachings

un·cle \ˈəŋkəl\ n 1 : brother of one's father or mother 2 : husband of one's aunt

un·clean adj : not clean or pure —**un·clean·ness** n

un·clog vb : remove an obstruction from

un·coil vb : release or become released from a coiled state

un·com·mit·ted adj : not pledged to a particular allegiance or course of action

un·com·mon adj 1 : rare 2 : superior —**un·com·mon·ly** adv

un·com·pro·mis·ing adj : not making or accepting a compromise

un·con·cerned adj 1 : disinterested 2 : not anxious or upset —**un·con·cerned·ly** adv

un·con·di·tion·al adj : not limited in any way —**un·con·di·tion·al·ly** adv

un·con·scio·na·ble adj : shockingly unjust or unscrupulous —**un·con·scio·na·bly** adv

un·con·scious adj 1 : not awake or aware of one's surroundings 2 : not consciously done ~ n : part of one's mental life that one is not aware of —**un·con·scious·ly** adv —**un·con·scious·ness** n

un·con·sti·tu·tion·al adj : not according to or consistent with a constitution

un·con·trol·la·ble adj : incapable of being controlled —**un·con·trol·la·bly** adv

un·count·ed adj : countless

un·couth \ˌənˈküth\ adj : rude and vulgar

un·cov·er vb 1 : reveal 2 : expose by removing a covering

unc·tion \ˈəŋkshən\ n 1 : rite of anointing 2 : exaggerated or insincere earnestness

unc·tu·ous \ˈəŋkchəwəs\ adj 1 : oily 2 : insincerely smooth in speech or manner —**unc·tu·ous·ly** adv

un·cut adj 1 : not cut down, into, off, or apart 2 : not shaped by cutting 3 : not abridged

un·daunt·ed adj : not discouraged —**un·daunt·ed·ly** adv

un·de·ni·able adj : plainly true —**un·de·ni·ably** adv

un·der \ˈəndər\ adv : below or beneath something ~ prep 1 : lower than and sheltered by 2 : below the surface of 3 : covered or concealed by 4 : subject to the authority of 5 : less than ~ adj 1 : lying below or beneath 2 : subordinate 3 : less than usual, proper, or desired

un·der·age \ˌəndərˈāj\ adj : of less than legal age

un·der·brush \ˈəndərˌbrəsh\ n : shrubs and small trees growing beneath large trees

un·der·clothes \ˈəndərˌklōz, -ˌklōthz\ n pl : underwear

un·der·cloth·ing \-ˌklōthiŋ\ n : underwear

un·der·cov·er \ˌəndərˈkəvər\ adj : employed or engaged in secret investigation

un·der·cur·rent \ˈəndərˌkərənt\ n : hidden tendency or opinion

un·der·cut \ˌəndərˈkət\ vb -**cut**; -**cut**-

ting : offer to sell or to work at a lower rate than

un·der·de·vel·oped \,əndərdi'veləpt\ *adj* : not normally or adequately developed esp. economically

un·der·dog \'əndər,dóg\ *n* : contestant given least chance of winning

un·der·done \,əndər'dən\ *adj* : not thoroughly done or cooked

un·der·es·ti·mate \,əndər'estə,māt\ *vb* : estimate too low

un·der·ex·pose \,əndərik'spōz\ *vb* : give less than normal exposure to —**un·der·ex·po·sure** *n*

un·der·feed \,əndər'fēd\ *vb* **-fed; -feed·ing** : feed inadequately

un·der·foot \,əndər'fút\ *adv* **1** : under the feet **2** : in the way of another

un·der·gar·ment \'əndər,gärmənt\ *n* : garment to be worn under another

un·der·go \,əndər'gō\ *vb* **-went; -gone; -go·ing 1** : endure **2** : go through (as an experience)

un·der·grad·u·ate \,əndər'grajəwət\ *n* : university or college student

un·der·ground \,əndər'graúnd\ *adv* **1** : beneath the surface of the earth **2** : in secret ~ \'əndər,-\ *adj* **1** : being or growing under the surface of the ground **2** : secret ~ \'əndər,-\ *n* : secret political movement or group

un·der·growth \'əndər,grōth\ *n* : low growth on the floor of a forest

un·der·hand \'əndər,hand\ *adv or adj* **1** : with secrecy and deception **2** : with the hand kept below the waist

un·der·hand·ed \,əndər'handəd\ *adj or adv* : underhand —**un·der·hand·ed·ly** *adv* —**un·der·hand·ed·ness** *n*

un·der·line \'əndər,līn\ *vb* **1** : draw a line under **2** : stress —**underline** *n*

un·der·ling \'əndərliŋ\ *n* : inferior

un·der·ly·ing \,əndər,lïiŋ\ *adj* : basic

un·der·mine \,əndər'mīn\ *vb* **1** : excavate beneath **2** : weaken or wear away secretly or gradually

un·der·neath \,əndər'nēth\ *prep* : directly under ~ *adv* **1** : below a surface or object **2** : on the lower side

un·der·nour·ished \,əndər'nərisht\ *adj* : insufficiently nourished —**un·der·nour·ish·ment** *n*

un·der·pants \'əndər,pants\ *n pl* : short undergarment for the lower trunk

un·der·pass \-,pas\ *n* : passageway crossing underneath another

un·der·pin·ning \'əndər,piniŋ\ *n* : support

un·der·priv·i·leged *adj* : poor

un·der·rate \,əndər'rāt\ *vb* : rate or value too low

un·der·score \'əndər,skōr\ *vb* **1** : underline **2** : emphasize —**underscore** *n*

un·der·sea \,əndər'sē\ *adj* : being, carried on, or used beneath the surface of the sea ~ \,əndər'sē\, **un·der·seas** \-'sēz\ *adv* : beneath the surface of the sea

under secretary *n* : deputy secretary

un·der·sell \,əndər'sel\ *vb* **-sold; -sel·ing** : sell articles cheaper than

un·der·shirt \,əndər,shərt\ *n* : shirt worn as underwear

un·der·shorts \'əndər,shórts\ *n pl* : short underpants

un·der·side \'əndər,sīd, ,əndər'sīd\ *n* : side or surface lying underneath

un·der·sized \,əndər'sīzd\ *adj* : unusually small

un·der·stand \,əndər'stand\ *vb* **-stood** \-'stúd\; **-stand·ing 1** : be aware of the meaning of **2** : deduce **3** : have a sympathetic attitude —**un·der·stand·able** \-'standəbəl\ *adj* —**un·der·stand·ably** \-blē\ *adv*

un·der·stand·ing \,əndər'standiŋ\ *n* **1** : intelligence **2** : ability to comprehend and judge **3** : mutual agreement ~ *adj* : sympathetic

un·der·state \,əndər'stāt\ *vb* **1** : represent as less than is the case **2** : state with restraint —**un·der·state·ment** *n*

un·der·stood \,əndər'stúd\ *adj* **1** : agreed upon **2** : implicit

un·der·study \'əndər,stədē, ,əndər'-\ *vb* : study another actor's part in order to substitute —**understudy** \'əndər,-\ *n*

un·der·take \,əndər'tāk\ *vb* **-took; -tak·en; -tak·ing 1** : attempt (a task) or assume (a responsibility) **2** : guarantee

un·der·tak·er \'əndər,tākər\ *n* : one in the funeral business

un·der·tak·ing \'əndər,tākiŋ, ,əndər'-\ *n* **1** : something (as work) that is undertaken **2** : promise

under-the-counter *adj* : illicit

un·der·tone \'əndər,tōn\ *n* : low or subdued tone or utterance

un·der·tow \-,tō\ *n* : current beneath the waves that flows seaward

un·der·val·ue \,əndər'valyü\ *vb* : value too low

un·der·wa·ter \-'wótər, -'wät-\ *adj*

: being or used below the surface of the water —**underwater** adv

under way adv : in motion or in progress

un·der·wear \'əndər,war\ n : clothing worn next to the skin and under ordinary clothes

under·world \'əndər,wərld\ n 1 : place of departed souls 2 : world of organized crime

un·der·write \'əndər,rīt, ,əndər,-\ vb -wrote; -writ·ten; -writ·ing 1 : provide insurance for 2 : guarantee financial support of —**un·der·writ·er** n

un·dies \'əndēz\ n pl : underwear

un·do vb -did; -done; -do·ing 1 : unfasten 2 : reverse 3 : ruin —**un·do·ing** n

un·doubt·ed adj : certain —**un·doubt·ed·ly** adv

un·dress vb : remove one's clothes ~ n : state of being naked

un·due adj : excessive —**un·du·ly** adv

un·du·late \'ənjə,lāt\ vb -lat·ed; -lat·ing : rise and fall regularly —**un·du·la·tion** \,ənjə'lāshən\ n

un·dy·ing adj : immortal or perpetual

un·earth vb : dig up or discover

un·earth·ly adj : supernatural

un·easy adj 1 : awkward or embarrassed 2 : disturbed or worried —**un·eas·i·ly** adv —**un·eas·i·ness** n

un·em·ployed adj : not having a job —**un·em·ploy·ment** n

un·equal adj : not equal or uniform —**un·equal·ly** adv

un·equaled, un·equalled adj : having no equal

un·equiv·o·cal adj : leaving no doubt —**un·equiv·o·cal·ly** adv

un·err·ing adj : infallible —**un·err·ing·ly** adv

un·even adj 1 : not smooth 2 : not regular or consistent —**un·even·ly** adv —**un·even·ness** n

un·event·ful adj : lacking interesting or noteworthy incidents —**un·event·ful·ly** adv

un·ex·pect·ed \anik'spektəd\ adj : not expected —**un·ex·pect·ed·ly** adv

un·fail·ing adj : steadfast —**un·fail·ing·ly** adv

un·faith·ful adj : not loyal —**un·faith·ful·ly** adv —**un·faith·ful·ness** n

un·fa·mil·iar adj 1 : not well known 2 : not acquainted —**un·fa·mil·iar·i·ty** n

un·fas·ten vb : release a catch or lock

un·feel·ing adj : lacking feeling or compassion —**un·feel·ing·ly** adv

un·fit adj : not suitable —**un·fit·ness** n

un·flap·pa·ble \,ən'flapəbəl\ adj : not easily upset or panicked —**un·flap·pa·bly** adv

un·fold vb 1 : open the folds of 2 : reveal 3 : develop

un·for·get·ta·ble adj : memorable —**un·for·get·ta·bly** adv

un·for·tu·nate adj 1 : not lucky or successful 2 : deplorable —**unfortunate** n —**un·for·tu·nate·ly** adv

un·found·ed adj : lacking a sound basis

un·freeze vb -froze; -fro·zen; -freez·ing : thaw

un·friend·ly adj : not friendly or kind —**un·friend·li·ness** n

un·furl vb : unfold or unroll

un·gain·ly adj : clumsy —**un·gain·li·ness** n

un·god·ly adj : wicked —**un·god·li·ness** n

un·grate·ful adj : not thankful for favors —**un·grate·ful·ly** adv —**un·grate·ful·ness** n

un·guent \'əŋgwənt, 'ən-\ n : ointment

un·hand vb : let go

un·hap·py adj 1 : unfortunate 2 : sad —**un·hap·pi·ly** adv —**un·hap·pi·ness** n

un·healthy adj 1 : not wholesome 2 : not well

un·heard-of \,ən'hərdəv, -,äv\ adj : unprecedented

un·hinge \,ən'hinj\ vb 1 : take from the hinges 2 : make unstable esp. mentally

un·hitch vb : unfasten

un·ho·ly adj : sinister or shocking —**un·ho·li·ness** n

un·hook vb : release from a hook

uni·cel·lu·lar \,yüni'selyələr\ adj : having or consisting of a single cell

uni·corn \'yünə,kórn\ n : legendary animal with one horn in the middle of the forehead

uni·cy·cle \'yüni,sīkəl\ n : pedal-powered vehicle with only a single wheel

uni·di·rec·tion·al \,yünidə'rekshənəl, -dī-\ adj : working in only a single direction

uni·form \'yünə,fórm\ adj : not changing or showing any variation ~ n : distinctive dress worn by members of a particular group —**uni·form·i·ty** \,yünə'fórmətē\ n —**u·ni·form·ly** adv

uni·fy \'yünə,fĭ\ vb **-fied; -fy·ing** : make into a coherent whole **—uni·fi·ca·tion** \,yünəfə'kāshən\ n

uni·lat·er·al \,yünə'latərəl\ adj : having, affecting, or done by one side only **—uni·lat·er·al·ly** adv

un·im·peach·able adj : blameless

un·in·hib·it·ed adj : free of restraint **—un·in·hib·it·ed·ly** adv

union \'yünyən\ n **1** : act or instance of joining 2 or more things into one or the state of being so joined **2** : confederation of nations or states **3** : organization of workers (**labor union, trade union**)

union·ize \'yünyə,nīz\ vb **-ized; -iz·ing** : form into a labor union **—union·i·za·tion** \,yünyənə'zāshən\ n

unique \yủ'nēk\ adj **1** : being the only one of its kind **2** : very unusual **—unique·ly** adv **—unique·ness** n

uni·son \'yünəsən, -nəzən\ n **1** : sameness in pitch **2** : exact agreement

unit \'yünət\ n **1** : smallest whole number **2** : definite amount or quantity used as a standard of measurement **3** : single part of a whole **—unit** adj

unite \yủ'nīt\ vb **unit·ed; unit·ing** : put or join together

uni·ty \'yünətē\ n, pl **-ties 1** : quality or state of being united or a unit **2** : harmony

uni·ver·sal \,yünə'vərsəl\ adj **1** : relating to or affecting everyone or everything **2** : present or occurring everywhere **—uni·ver·sal·ly** adv

uni·verse \'yünə,vərs\ n : the complete system of all things that exist

uni·ver·si·ty \,yünə'vərsətē\ n, pl **-ties** : institution of higher learning

un·kempt \,ən'kempt\ adj : not neat or combed

un·kind adj : not kind or sympathetic **—un·kind·li·ness** n **—un·kind·ly** adv **—un·kind·ness** n

un·law·ful adj : illegal **—un·law·ful·ly** adv

un·leash vb : free from control or restraint

un·less \ən'les\ conj : except on condition that

un·like \ən'līk, 'ən,līk\ adj **1** : not similar **2** : not equal ~ prep : different from **—un·like·ly** \ən'līklē\ adv **—un·like·ness** \-nəs\ n **—un·like·li·hood** \-lēhủd\ n

un·load vb **1** : take (cargo) from a ve-

hicle, vessel, or plane **2** : take a load from **3** : discard

un·lock vb **1** : unfasten through release of a lock **2** : release or reveal

un·lucky adj **1** : experiencing bad luck **2** : likely to bring misfortune **—un·luck·i·ly** adv

un·mis·tak·able adj : not capable of being mistaken or misunderstood **—un·mis·tak·ably** adv

un·moved adj **1** : not emotionally affected **2** : remaining in the same place or position

un·nat·u·ral adj **1** : not natural or spontaneous **2** : abnormal **—un·nat·u·ral·ly** adv **—un·nat·u·ral·ness** n

un·nerve vb : deprive of courage, strength, or steadiness

un·oc·cu·pied adj **1** : not busy **2** : not occupied

un·pack vb **1** : remove (things packed) from a container **2** : remove the contents of (a package)

un·par·al·leled adj : having no equal

un·plug vb **1** : unclog **2** : disconnect from an electric circuit by removing a plug

un·prec·e·dent·ed adj : unlike or superior to anything known before

un·prin·ci·pled adj : unscrupulous

un·ques·tion·able adj : acknowledged as beyond doubt **—un·ques·tion·ably** adv

un·rav·el vb **1** : separate the threads of **2** : solve

un·re·al adj : not real or genuine **—un·re·al·i·ty** n

un·rea·son·ing adj : not using or being guided by reason

un·re·lent·ing adj : not yielding or easing **—un·re·lent·ing·ly** adv

un·rest n : turmoil

un·ri·valed, un·ri·valled adj : having no rival

un·roll vb **1** : unwind a roll of **2** : become unrolled

un·ruf·fled adj : not agitated or upset

un·ruly \,ən'rülē\ adj : not readily controlled or disciplined **—un·rul·i·ness** n

un·scathed \,ən'skāthd\ adj : unharmed

un·sci·en·tif·ic adj : not in accord with the principles and methods of science

un·screw vb : loosen or remove by withdrawing screws or by turning

un·scru·pu·lous adj : being or acting in total disregard of conscience, ethical principles, or rights of others **—un-**

scru•pu•lous•ly *adv* **—un•scru•pu•lous•ness** *n*

un•seal *vb* : break or remove the seal of

un•sea•son•able *adj* : not appropriate or usual for the season **—un•sea•son•ably** *adv*

un•seem•ly \ˌən'sēmlē\ *adj* : not polite or in good taste **—un•seem•li•ness** *n*

un•set•tle *vb* : disturb **—un•set•tled** *adj*

un•sight•ly \ˌən'sītlē\ *adj* : not attractive

un•skilled *adj* : not having or requiring a particular quality

un•snap *vb* : loosen by undoing a snap

un•speak•able \ˌən'spēkəbəl\ *adj* : extremely bad **—un•speak•ably** \-blē\ *adv*

un•sta•ble *adj* **1** : not mentally or physically balanced **2** : tending to change

un•stop *vb* **1** : unclog **2** : remove a stopper from

un•stop•pa•ble \ˌən'stäpəbəl\ *adj* : not capable of being stopped

un•strung \ˌən'strəŋ\ *adj* : nervously tired or anxious

un•sung \ˌən'səŋ\ *adj* : not celebrated in song or verse

un•tan•gle *vb* **1** : free from a state of being tangled **2** : find a solution to

un•think•able \ˌən'thiŋkəbəl\ *adj* : not to be thought of or considered possible

un•think•ing *adj* : careless **—un•think•ing•ly** *adv*

un•tie *vb* **-tied; -ty•ing** *or* **-tie•ing** : open by releasing ties

un•til \ˌən'til\ *prep* : up to the time of ~ *conj* : to the time that

un•time•ly *adj* **1** : premature **2** : coming at an unfortunate time

un•to \ˌən'tü, 'ən,-\ *prep* : to

un•told *adj* **1** : not told **2** : too numerous to count

un•to•ward \ˌən'tōrd\ *adj* **1** : difficult to manage **2** : inconvenient

un•truth *n* **1** : lack of truthfulness **2** : lie

un•used *adj* **1** \ˌən'yüst, -'yüzd\ : not accustomed to **2** \-'yüzd\ : not used

un•well *adj* : sick

un•wieldy \ˌən'wēldē\ *adj* : too big or awkward to manage easily

un•wind *vb* **-wound; -wind•ing 1** : undo something that is wound **2** : become unwound **3** : relax

un•wit•ting *adj* **1** : not knowing **2** : not intended **—un•wit•ting•ly** *adv*

un•wont•ed *adj* **1** : unusual **2** : not accustomed by experience

un•wrap *vb* : remove the wrappings from

un•writ•ten *adj* : made or passed on only in speech or through tradition

un•zip *vb* : zip open

up \'əp\ *adv* **1** : in or to a higher position or level **2** : from beneath a surface or level **3** : in or into an upright position **4** : out of bed **5** : to or with greater intensity **6** : into existence, evidence, or knowledge **7** : away **8** — used to indicate a degree of success, completion, or finality **9** : in or into parts ~ *adj* **1** : in the state of having risen **2** : raised to or at a higher level **3** : moving, inclining, or directed upward **4** : in a state of greater intensity **5** : at an end ~ *vb* **upped** *or in l* **up; upped; up•ping; ups** *or in l* **up 1** : act abruptly **2** : move or cause to move upward ~ *prep* **1** : to, toward, or at a higher point of **2** : along or toward the beginning of

up•braid \ˌəp'brād\ *vb* : criticize or scold

up•bring•ing \'əp,briŋiŋ\ *n* : process of bringing up and training

up•com•ing \əp'kəmiŋ\ *adj* : approaching

up•date \ˌəp'dāt\ *vb* : bring up to date **—update** \'əp,dāt\ *n*

up•end \ˌəp'end\ *vb* **1** : stand or rise on end **2** : overturn

up•grade \'əp,grād\ *n* **1** : upward slope **2** : increase ~ \'əp,-, ,əp'-\ *vb* : raise to a higher position

up•heav•al \ˌəp'hēvəl\ *n* **1** : a heaving up (as of part of the earth's crust) **2** : violent change

up•hill \'əp'hil\ *adv* : upward on a hill or incline ~ \'əp,-\ *adj* **1** : going up **2** : difficult

up•hold \ˌəp'hōld\ *vb* **-held; -hold•ing 1** : support or defend **—up•hold•er** *n*

up•hol•ster \ˌəp'hōlstər\ *vb* : cover (furniture) with padding and fabric (**up•hol•stery** \-stərē\) **—up•hol•ster•er** *n*

up•keep \'əp,kēp\ *n* : act or cost of keeping up or maintaining

up•land \'əplənd, -,land\ *n* : high land **—upland** *adj*

up•lift \ˌəp'lift\ *vb* **1** : lift up **2** : improve the condition or spirits of **—up•lift** \'əp,-\ *n*

up•on \ə'pȯn, -'pän\ *prep* : on

up•per \'əpər\ *adj* : higher in position, rank, or order ~ *n* : top part of a shoe

upper·hand *n* : advantage

up·per·most \'əpər,mōst\ *adv* : in or into the highest or most prominent position —**uppermost** *adj*

up·pi·ty \'əpətē\ *adj* : acting with a manner of undue importance

up·right \'əp,rīt\ *adj* 1 : vertical 2 : erect in posture 3 : morally correct ~ *n* : something that stands upright —**up·right** *adv* —**up·right·ly** *adv* —**up·right·ness** *n*

up·ris·ing \'əp,rīziŋ\ *n* : revolt

up·roar \'əp,rōr\ *n* : state of commotion or violent disturbance

up·roar·i·ous \,əp'rōrēəs\ *adj* 1 : marked by uproar 2 : extremely funny —**up·roar·i·ous·ly** *adv*

up·root \,əp'rüt, -'rüt\ *vb* : remove by or as if by pulling up by the roots

up·set \,əp'set\ *vb* **-set; -set·ting** 1 : force or be forced out of the usual position 2 : disturb emotionally or physically ~ \'əp,-\ *n* 1 : act of throwing into disorder 2 : minor physical disorder ~ *adj* : emotionally disturbed or agitated

up·shot \'əp,shät\ *n* : final result

up·side down \,əp,sīd'daún\ *adv* 1 : turned so that the upper and lower parts are reversed 2 : in or into confusion or disorder —**upside-down** *adj*

up·stairs \'əp,starz, ,əp'-\ *adv* : up the stairs or to the next floor ~ *adj* : situated on the floor above ~ *n sing or pl* : part of a building above the ground floor

up·stand·ing \,əp'standiŋ, 'əp,-\ *adj* : honest

up·start \'əp,stärt\ *n* : one who claims more personal importance than is warranted —**upstart** *adj*

up·swing \'əp,swiŋ\ *n* : marked increase (as in activity)

up·tight \,əp'tīt\ *adj* 1 : tense 2 : angry 3 : rigidly conventional

up–to–date *adj* : current —**up-to-date·ness** *n*

up·town \'əp,taún\ *n* : upper part of a town or city —**uptown** *adj or adv*

up·turn \'əp,tərn\ *n* : improvement or increase

up·ward \'əpwərd\, **up·wards** \-wərdz\ *adv* 1 : in a direction from lower to higher 2 : toward a higher or greater state or number ~ *adj* : directed toward or situated in a higher place —**up·ward·ly** *adv*

up·wind \,əp'wind\ *adv or adj* : in the direction from which the wind is blowing

ura·ni·um \yú'rānēəm\ *n* : metallic radioactive chemical element

ur·ban \'ərbən\ *adj* : characteristic of a city

ur·bane \,ər'bān\ *adj* : polished in manner —**ur·ban·i·ty** \,ər'banətē\ *n*

ur·ban·ite \'ərbə,nīt\ *n* : city dweller

ur·chin \'ərchən\ *n* : mischievous youngster

-ure *n suffix* : act or process

ure·thra \yú'rēthrə\ *n, pl* **-thras** *or* **-thrae** \-,thrē\ : canal that carries off urine from the bladder —**ure·thral** \-thrəl\ *adj*

urge \'ərj\ *vb* **urged; urging** 1 : earnestly plead for or insist on (an action) 2 : try to persuade 3 : impel to a course of activity ~ *n* : force or impulse that moves one to action

ur·gent \'ərjənt\ *adj* 1 : calling for immediate attention 2 : urging insistently —**ur·gen·cy** \-jənsē\ *n* —**ur·gent·ly** *adv*

uri·nal \'yúrən°l\ *n* : receptacle to urinate in

uri·nate \'yúrə,nāt\ *vb* **-nated; -nat·ing** : discharge urine —**uri·na·tion** \,yúrə'nāshən\ *n*

urine \'yúrən\ *n* : liquid waste material from the kidneys —**uri·nary** \-ə,nerē\ *adj*

urn \'ərn\ *n* 1 : vaselike or cuplike vessel on a pedestal 2 : large coffee pot

us \'əs\ *pron, objective case of* WE

us·able \'yüzəbəl\ *adj* : suitable or fit for use —**us·abil·i·ty** \,yüzə'bilətē\ *n*

us·age \'yüsij, -zij\ *n* 1 : customary practice 2 : way of doing or of using something

use \'yüs\ *n* 1 : act or practice of putting something into action 2 : state of being used 3 : way of using 4 : privilege, ability, or power to use something 5 : utility or function 6 : occasion or need to use ~ \'yüz\ *vb* **used** \'yüzd; ''used to'' *usu* 'yüstə\; **using** \'yüziŋ\ 1 : put into action or service 2 : consume 3 : behave toward 4 : to make use of 5 —used in the past tense with *to* to indicate a former practice —**use·ful** \'yüsfəl\ *adj* —**use·ful·ly** *adv* —**use·ful·ness** *n* —**use·less** \'yüsləs\ *adj* —**use·less·ly** *adv* —**use·less·ness** *n* —**us·er** *n*

used \'yüzd\ *adj* : not new

ush·er \'əshər\ *n* : one who escorts people to their seats ~ *vb* : conduct to a place

ush·er·ette \,əshə'ret\ *n* : woman or girl who is an usher

usu·al \'yüzhəwəl\ *adj* : being what is expected according to custom or habit —**usu·al·ly** \'yüzhəwəlē\ *adv*

usurp \yü'sərp, -'zərp\ *vb* : seize and hold by force or without right —**usur·pa·tion** \,yüsər'pāshən, -zər-\ *n* —**usurp·er** *n*

usu·ry \'yüzhərē\ *n, pl* -**ries 1** : lending of money at excessive interest or the rate or amount of such interest —**usu·rer** \-zhərər\ *n* —**usu·ri·ous** \yu-'zhürēəs\ *adj*

uten·sil \yù'tensəl\ *n* **1** : eating or cooking tool **2** : useful tool

uter·us \'yütərəs\ *n, pl* **uteri** \-,rī\ : organ for containing and nourishing an unborn offspring —**uter·ine** \-,rīn, -rən\ *adj*

util·i·tar·i·an \yü,tilə'terēən\ *adj* : being or meant to be useful rather than beautiful

util·i·ty \yü'tilətē\ *n, pl* -**ties 1** : usefulness **2** : regulated business providing a public service (as electricity)

uti·lize \'yüt⁰l,īz\ *vb* -**lized; -liz·ing** : make use of —**uti·li·za·tion** \,yüt⁰lə'zāshən\ *n*

ut·most \'ət,mōst\ *adj* **1** : most distant **2** : of the greatest or highest degree or amount —**utmost** *n*

uto·pia \yù'tōpēə\ *n* : place of ideal perfection —**uto·pi·an** \-pēən\ *adj or n*

ut·ter \'ətər\ *adj* : absolute ~ *vb* : express with the voice —**ut·ter·er** \-ərər\ *n* —**ut·ter·ly** *adv*

ut·ter·ance \'ətərəns\ *n* : what one says

V

v \'vē\ *n, pl* **v's** *or* **vs** \'vēz\ : 22d letter of the alphabet

va·can·cy \'vākənsē\ *n, pl* -**cies 1** : state of being vacant **2** : unused or unoccupied place or office

va·cant \-kənt\ *adj* **1** : not occupied, filled, or in use **2** : devoid of thought or expression —**va·cant·ly** *adv*

va·cate \-,kāt\ *vb* -**cat·ed; -cat·ing 1** : annul **2** : leave unfilled or unoccupied

va·ca·tion \vā'kāshən, və-\ *n* : period of rest from routine —**vacation** *vb* —**va·ca·tion·er** *n*

vac·ci·nate \'vaksə,nāt\ *vb* -**nat·ed; -nat·ing** : administer a vaccine usu. by injection

vac·ci·na·tion \,vaksə'nāshən\ *n* : act of or the scar left by vaccinating

vac·cine \vak'sēn, 'vak,-\ *n* : substance to induce immunity to a disease

vac·il·late \'vasə,lāt\ *vb* -**lat·ed; -lat·ing** : waver between courses or opinions —**vac·il·la·tion** \,vasə'lāshən\ *n*

vac·u·ous \'vakyəwəs\ *adj* **1** : empty **2** : dull or inane —**va·cu·i·ty** \va'kyüətē, və-\ *n* —**vac·u·ous·ly** *adv* —**vac·u·ous·ness** *n*

vac·u·um \'vak,yüm, -yəm\ *n, pl* **vac·u·ums** *or* **vac·ua** \-yəwə\ : empty space with no air ~ *vb* : clean with a vacuum cleaner

vacuum cleaner *n* : appliance that cleans by suction

vag·a·bond \'vagə,bänd\ *n* : wanderer with no home —**vagabond** *adj*

va·ga·ry \'vāgərē, və'gerē\ *n, pl* -**ries** : whim

va·gi·na \və'jīnə\ *n, pl* -**nae** \-,nē\ *or* -**nas** : canal that leads out from the uterus —**vag·i·nal** \'vajən⁰l\ *adj*

va·grant \'vāgrənt\ *n* : person with no home and no job —**va·gran·cy** \-grənsē\ *n* —**vagrant** *adj*

vague \'vāg\ *adj* **vagu·er; vagu·est** : not clear, definite, or distinct —**vague·ly** *adv* —**vague·ness** *n*

vain \'vān\ *adj* **1** : of no value **2** : unsuccessful **3** : conceited —**vain·ly** *adv*

va·lance \'valəns, 'vāl-\ *n* : border drapery

vale \'vāl\ *n* : valley

vale·dic·to·ri·an \,valə,dik'tōrēən\ *n* : student giving the farewell address at commencement

vale·dic·to·ry \-'diktərē\ adj : bidding farewell —**valedictory** n

va·lence \'vāləns\ n : degree of combining power of a chemical element

val·en·tine \'valən,tīn\ n : sweetheart or a card sent to a sweetheart or friend on St. Valentine's Day

va·let \'valət, 'val,ā, va'lā\ n : male personal servant

val·iant \'valyənt\ adj : brave or heroic —**val·iant·ly** adv

val·id \'valəd\ adj 1 : proper and legally binding 2 : founded on truth or fact —**va·lid·i·ty** \və'lidətē, va-\ n —**val·id·ly** adv

val·i·date \'valə,dāt\ vb -dat·ed; -dat·ing : establish as valid —**val·i·da·tion** \,valə'dāshən\ n

va·lise \və'lēs\ n : suitcase

val·ley \'valē\ n, pl -leys : long depression between ranges of hills

val·or \'valər\ n : bravery or heroism —**val·or·ous** \'valərəs\ adj

valu·able \'valyəwəbəl\ adj 1 : worth a lot of money 2 : being of great importance or use —**valuable** n

val·u·a·tion \,valyə'wāshən\ n 1 : act or process of valuing 2 : market value of a thing

val·ue \'valyü\ n 1 : fair return or equivalent for something exchanged 2 : how much something is worth 3 : distinctive quality (as of a color or sound) 4 : guiding principle or ideal—usu. pl. ~ vb val·ued; valu·ing 1 : estimate the worth of 2 : appreciate the importance of —**val·ue·less** adj —**val·u·er** n

valve \'valv\ n : structure or device to control flow of a liquid or gas —**valved** \'valvd\ adj —**valve·less** adj

vam·pire \'vam,pīr\ n 1 : legendary night-wandering dead body that sucks human blood 2 : bat that feeds on the blood of animals

¹**van** \'van\ n : vanguard

²**van** n : enclosed truck

va·na·di·um \və'nādēəm\ n : soft ductile metallic chemical element

van·dal \'vandᵊl\ n : person who willfully defaces or destroys property —**van·dal·ism** \-,izəm\ n —**van·dal·ize** \-,īz\ vb

vane \'vān\ n : bladelike device designed to be moved by force of the air or water

van·guard \'van,gärd\ n 1 : troops moving at the front of an army 2 : forefront of an action or movement

va·nil·la \və'nilə\ n : a flavoring made from the pods of a tropical orchid or this orchid

van·ish \'vanish\ vb : disappear suddenly

van·i·ty \'vanətē\ n, pl -ties 1 : futility or something that is futile 2 : undue pride in oneself 3 : makeup case or table

van·quish \'vankwish, 'van-\ vb 1 : overcome in battle or in a contest 2 : gain mastery over

van·tage \'vantij\ n : position of advantage or perspective

va·pid \'vapəd, 'vāpəd\ adj : lacking spirit, liveliness, or zest —**va·pid·i·ty** \va'pidətē\ n —**vap·id·ly** \'vapədlē\ adv —**vap·id·ness** n

va·por \'vāpər\ n 1 : fine separated particles floating in and clouding the air 2 : gaseous form of an ordinarily liquid substance —**va·por·ous** \-pərəs\ adj

va·por·ize \'vāpə,rīz\ vb -ized; -iz·ing : convert into vapor —**va·por·iza·tion** \,vāpərə'zāshən\ n —**va·por·iz·er** n

vari·able \'verēəbəl\ adj : apt to vary —**var·i·abil·i·ty** \,verēə'bilətē\ n —**vari·able** n —**vari·ably** adv

vari·ance \'verēəns\ n 1 : instance or degree of variation 2 : disagreement or dispute 3 : legal permission to build contrary to a zoning law

vari·ant \-ənt\ n : something that differs from others of its kind —**variant** adj

vari·a·tion \,verē'āshən\ n : instance or extent of varying

vari·cose \'varə,kōs\ adj : abnormally swollen and dilated

var·ied \'verēd\ adj : showing variety —**var·ied·ly** adv

vari·e·gat·ed \'verēə,gātəd\ adj : having patches, stripes, or marks of different colors —**vari·e·gate** \-,gāt\ vb —**vari·e·ga·tion** \,verēə'gāshən\ n

va·ri·ety \və'rīətē\ n, pl -eties 1 : state of being different 2 : collection of different things 3 : something that differs from others of its kind

var·i·ous \'verēəs\ adj : being many and unlike —**var·i·ous·ly** adv

var·nish \'värnish\ *n* : liquid that dries to a hard glossy protective coating ~ *vb* : cover with varnish

var·si·ty \'värsətē\ *n, pl* **-ties** : principal team representing a school

vary \'verē\ *vb* **var·ied; vary·ing 1** : alter **2** : make or be of different kinds

vas·cu·lar \'vaskyələr\ *adj* : relating to a channel for the conveyance of a body fluid (as blood or sap)

vase \'vās, 'vāz\ *n* : tall usu. ornamental container to hold flowers

vas·sal \'vasəl\ *n* **1** : one acknowledging another as feudal lord **2** : one in a dependent position —**vas·sal·age** \-əlij\ *n*

vast \'vast\ *adj* : very great in size, extent, or amount —**vast·ly** *adv* —**vast·ness** *n*

vat \'vat\ *n* : large tub- or barrel-shaped container

vaude·ville \'vȯdvəl, 'väd-, 'vȯd-, -,vil, -əvəl, -ə,vil\ *n* : stage entertainment of unrelated acts

¹vault \'vȯlt\ *n* **1** : masonry arch **2** : usu. underground storage or burial room ~ *vb* : form or cover with a vault —**vault·ed** *adj* —**vaulty** *adj*

²vault *vb* : spring over esp. with the help of the hands or a pole — *n* : act of vaulting —**vault·er** *n*

vaunt \'vȯnt\ *vb* : boast —**vaunt** *n*

veal \'vēl\ *n* : flesh of a young calf

veer \'vir\ *vb* : change course esp. gradually —**veer** *n*

vege·ta·ble \'vejtəbəl, 'vejə-\ *adj* **1** : relating to or obtained from plants **2** : like that of a plant ~ *n* **1** : plant **2** : plant grown for food

vege·tar·i·an \,vejə'terēən\ *n* : person who eats no meat —**vegetarian** *adj* —**vege·tar·i·an·ism** \-ēə,nizəm\ *n*

vege·tate \'vejə,tāt\ *vb* **-tat·ed; -tat·ing** : lead a dull inert life

vege·ta·tion \,vejə'tāshən\ *n* : plant life —**vege·ta·tion·al** \-shənəl\ *adj* —**vege·ta·tive** \'vejə,tātiv\ *adj*

ve·he·ment \'vēəmənt\ *adj* : showing strong esp. violent feeling —**ve·he·mence** \-məns\ *n* —**ve·he·ment·ly** *adv*

ve·hi·cle \'vē,hikəl, 'vēəkəl\ *n* **1** : medium through which something is expressed, applied, or administered **2** : structure for transporting something esp. on wheels —**ve·hic·u·lar** \vē-'hikyələr\ *adj*

veil \'vāl\ *n* **1** : sheer material to hide something or to cover the face and head **2** : something that hides ~ *vb* : cover with a veil

vein \'vān\ *n* **1** : rock fissure filled with deposited mineral matter **2** : vessel that carries blood toward the heart **3** : sap-carrying tube in a leaf **4** : distinctive element or style of expression —**veined** \'vānd\ *adj*

ve·loc·i·ty \və'läsətē\ *n, pl* **-ties** : speed

ve·lour, ve·lours \və'lùr\ *n, pl* **velours** \-'lùrz\ : fabric with a velvetlike pile

vel·vet \'velvət\ *n* : fabric with a short soft pile —**velvet** *adj* —**vel·vety** *adj*

ve·nal \'vēnᵊl\ *adj* : capable of being corrupted esp. by money —**ve·nal·i·ty** \vi'nalətē\ *n* —**ve·nal·ly** *adv*

vend \'vend\ *vb* : sell —**vend·ible** *adj* —**ven·dor** \'vendər\ *n*

ven·det·ta \ven'detə\ *n* : feud marked by acts of revenge

ve·neer \və'nir\ *n* **1** : thin layer of fine wood glued over a cheaper wood **2** : superficial display ~ *vb* : overlay with a veneer

ven·er·a·ble \'venərəbəl\ *adj* : deserving of respect

ven·er·ate \'venə,rāt\ *vb* **-at·ed; -at·ing** : respect esp. with reverence —**ven·er·a·tion** \,venə'rāshən\ *n*

venereal disease \və'nirēəl-\ *n* : contagious disease spread through copulation

ven·geance \'venjəns\ *n* : punishment in retaliation for an injury or offense

venge·ful \'venjfəl\ *adj* : filled with a desire for revenge —**venge·ful·ly** *adv*

ve·nial \'vēnēəl\ *adj* : capable of being forgiven

ven·i·son \'venəsən, -əzən\ *n* : deer meat

ven·om \'venəm\ *n* **1** : poison secreted by certain animals **2** : ill will —**ven·om·ous** \-əməs\ *adj*

vent \'vent\ *vb* **1** : provide with or let out at a vent **2** : give expression to ~ *n* : opening for passage or for relieving pressure

ven·ti·late \'ventᵊl,āt\ *vb* **-lat·ed; -lat·ing** : allow fresh air to circulate through —**ven·ti·la·tion** \,ventᵊl-'āshən\ *n* —**ven·ti·la·tor** \'ventᵊl-,ātər\ *n*

ven·tri·cle \'ventrikəl\ *n* : heart chamber that pumps blood into the arteries

ven·tril·o·quist \ven'trilə,kwist\ *n* : one who can make the voice appear to come from another source —**ven·tril·o·quism** \-,kwizəm\ *n* —**ven·tril·o·quy** \-kwē\ *n*

ven·ture \'venchər\ *vb* -**tured;** -**tur·ing** 1 : risk or take a chance on 2 : put forward (an opinion) ~ *n* : speculative business enterprise

ven·ture·some \-səm\ *adj* : brave or daring —**ven·ture·some·ly** *adv* —**ven·ture·some·ness** *n*

ven·ue \'venyü\ *n* : scene of an action or event

ve·rac·i·ty \və'rasətē\ *n, pl* -**ties** : truthfulness or accuracy —**ve·ra·cious** \və'rāshəs\ *adj*

ve·ran·da, ve·ran·dah \və'randə\ *n* : large open porch

verb \'vərb\ *n* : word that expresses action or existence

ver·bal \'vərbəl\ *adj* 1 : having to do with or expressed in words 2 : oral 3 : relating to or formed from a verb —**ver·bal·i·za·tion** \,vərbələ'zāshən\ *n* —**ver·bal·ize** \'vərbə,līz\ *vb* —**ver·bal·ly** \-ē\ *adv*

verbal auxiliary *n* : auxiliary verb

ver·ba·tim \vər'bātəm\ *adv* or *adj* : using the same words

ver·biage \'vərbēij\ *n* : excess of words

ver·bose \vər'bōs\ *adj* : using more words than are needed —**ver·bos·i·ty** \-'bäsətē\ *n*

ver·dant \'vərdᵊnt\ *adj* : green with growing plants —**ver·dant·ly** *adv*

ver·dict \'vərdikt\ *n* : decision of a jury

ver·dure \'vərjər\ *n* : green growing vegetation or its color

verge \'vərj\ *vb* **verged; verg·ing** : be almost on the point of happening or doing something ~ *n* 1 : edge 2 : threshold

ver·i·fy \'verə,fī\ *vb* -**fied;** -**fy·ing** : establish the truth, accuracy, or reality of —**ver·i·fi·able** *adj* —**ver·i·fi·ca·tion** \,verəfə'kāshən\ *n*

ver·i·ly \'verəlē\ *adv* : truly or confidently

ver·i·si·mil·i·tude \,verəsə'milə,tüd\ *n* : appearance of being true

ver·i·ta·ble \'verətəbəl\ *adj* : actual or true —**ver·i·ta·bly** *adv*

ver·i·ty \'verətē\ *n, pl* -**ties** : truth

ver·mi·cel·li \,vərmə'chelē, -'sel-\ *n* : thin spaghetti

ver·min \'vərmən\ *n, pl* **vermin** : small animal pest

ver·mouth \vər'müth\ *n* : dry or sweet wine flavored with herbs

ver·nac·u·lar \vər'nakyələr\ *adj* : relating to a native language or dialect and esp. its normal spoken form ~ *n* : vernacular language

ver·nal \'vərnᵊl\ *adj* : relating to spring

ver·sa·tile \'vərsət∘l\ *adj* : having many abilities or uses —**ver·sa·til·i·ty** \,vərsə'tilətē\ *n*

¹**verse** \'vərs\ *n* 1 : line or stanza of poetry 2 : poetry 3 : short division of a chapter in the Bible

²**verse** *vb* **versed; versing** : make familiar by experience, study, or practice

ver·sion \'vərzhən\ *n* 1 : translation of the Bible 2 : account or description from a particular point of view

ver·sus \'vərsəs\ *prep* : opposed to or against

ver·te·bra \'vərtəbrə\ *n, pl* -**brae** \-,brā, -,brē\ *or* -**bras** : segment of the backbone —**ver·te·bral** \vər'tēbrəl, 'vərtə-\ *adj*

ver·te·brate \'vərtəbrət, -,brāt\ *n* : animal with a backbone —**vertebrate** *adj*

ver·tex \'vər,teks\ *n, pl* **ver·ti·ces** \'vərtə,sēz\ 1 : point of intersection of lines or surfaces 2 : highest point

ver·ti·cal \'vərtikəl\ *adj* : rising straight up from a level surface —**vertical** *n*—**ver·ti·cal·i·ty** \,vərtə'kalətē\ *n*—**ver·ti·cal·ly** *adv*

ver·ti·go \'vərti,gō\ *n, pl* -**goes** *or* -**gos** : dizziness

verve \'vərv\ *n* : liveliness or vividness

very \'verē\ *adj* **veri·er; -est** 1 : exact 2 : exactly suitable 3 : mere or bare 4 : precisely the same ~ *adv* 1 : to a high degree 2 : in actual fact

ves·i·cle \'vesikəl\ *n* : membranous cavity —**ve·sic·u·lar** \və'sikyələr\ *adj*

ves·pers \'vespərz\ *n pl* : late afternoon or evening worship service

ves·sel \'vesəl\ *n* 1 : a container (as a barrel, bottle, bowl, or cup) for a liquid 2 : craft for navigation esp. on water 3 : tube in which a body fluid is circulated

¹**vest** \'vest\ *vb* 1 : give a particular authority, right, or property to 2 : clothe with or as if with a garment

²**vest** *n* : sleeveless garment usu. worn under a suit coat

vestibular 370 viewer

ves·ti·bule \'vestə,byül\ *n* : enclosed entrance —**ves·tib·u·lar** \ve'stibyələr\ *adj*

ves·tige \'vestij\ *n* : visible trace or remains —**ves·ti·gial** \ve'stijēəl\ *adj* — **ves·ti·gial·ly** *adv*

vest·ment \'vestmənt\ *n* : clergy member's garment

ves·try \'vestrē\ *n, pl* **-tries** : church storage room for garments and articles

vet·er·an \'vetərən\ *n* **1** : former member of the armed forces **2** : person with long experience —**veteran** *adj*

Veterans Day *n* : 4th Monday in October or formerly November 11 observed as a legal holiday in commemoration of the end of war in 1918 and 1945

vet·er·i·nar·i·an \,vetərən'erēən\ *n* : doctor of animals —**vet·er·i·nary** \'vetərən,erē\ *adj*

ve·to \'vētō\ *n, pl* **-toes 1** : power to forbid and esp. the power of a chief executive to prevent a bill from becoming law **2** : exercise of the veto ~ *vb* **1** : forbid **2** : reject a legislative bill

vex \'veks\ *vb* **vexed; vex·ing** : trouble, distress, or annoy —**vex·a·tion** \vek-'sāshən\ *n* —**vex·a·tious** \-shəs\ *adj*

via \'vīə, 'vēə\ *prep* : by way of

vi·a·ble \'vīəbəl\ *adj* **1** : capable of surviving or growing **2** : practical or workable —**vi·a·bil·i·ty** \,vīə'bilətē\ *n* —**vi·a·bly** \'vīəblē\ *adv*

via·duct \'vīə,dəkt\ *n* : elevated roadway or railway bridge

vi·al \'vīəl\ *n* : small bottle

vi·brant \'vībrənt\ *adj* **1** : vibrating **2** : pulsing with vigor or activity **3** : sounding from vibration —**vi·bran·cy** \-brənsē\ *n*

vi·brate \'vī,brāt\ *vb* **-brat·ed; -brat·ing 1** : move or cause to move quickly back and forth or side to side **2** : respond sympathetically —**vi·bra·tion** \vī'brāshən\ *n* —**vi·bra·tor** \'vī-,brātər\ *n* —**vi·bra·to·ry** \'vībrə,tōrē\ *adj*

vic·ar \'vikər\ *n* : parish clergy member —**vic·ar·i·ate** \-ēət\ *n*

vi·car·i·ous \vī'karēəs\ *adj* : sharing in someone else's experience through imagination or sympathetic feelings —**vi·car·i·ous·ly** *adv* —**vi·car·i·ous·ness** *n*

vice \'vīs\ *n* **1** : immoral habit **2** : depravity

vice- \,vīs\ *prefix* : one that takes the place of

vice-chancellor vice president
vice-consul vice presidential
vice presidency vice-regent

vice admiral *n* : commissioned officer in the navy or coast guard ranking above a rear admiral

vice·roy \'vīs,rói\ *n* : provincial governor who represents the sovereign

vice versa \,vīsi'vərsə, ,vīs'vər-\ *adv* : with the order reversed

vi·cin·i·ty \və'sinətē\ *n, pl* **-ties** : surrounding area

vi·cious \'vishəs\ *adj* **1** : wicked **2** : savage **3** : malicious —**vi·cious·ly** *adv* —**vi·cious·ness** *n*

vi·cis·si·tude \və'sisə,tüd, vī-, -,tyüd\ *n* : irregular, unexpected, or surprising change —usu. used in pl.

vic·tim \'viktəm\ *n* : person killed, hurt, or abused

vic·tim·ize \'viktə,mīz\ *vb* **-ized; -iz·ing** : make a victim of —**vic·tim·i·za·tion** \,viktəmə'zāshən\ *n* —**vic·tim·iz·er** \'viktə,mīzər\ *n*

vic·tor \'viktər\ *n* : winner

Vic·to·ri·an \vik'tōrēən\ *adj* : relating to the reign of Queen Victoria of England or the art, taste, or standards of her time ~ *n* : one of the Victorian period

vic·to·ri·ous \vik'tōrēəs\ *adj* : having won a victory —**vic·to·ri·ous·ly** *adv*

vic·to·ry \'viktərē\ *n, pl* **-ries** : success in defeating an enemy or opponent or in overcoming difficulties

vict·uals \'vitᵊlz\ *n pl* : food

vid·eo \'vidē,ō\ *adj* : relating to the television image

vid·eo·cas·sette \,vidē,ōkə'set\ *n* : cassette containing videotape

vid·eo·tape \'vidēō,tāp\ *vb* : make a recording of (a television production) on special tape —**videotape** *n*

vie \'vī\ *vb* **vied; vy·ing** : contend —**vi·er** \'vīər\ *n*

view \'vyü\ *n* **1** : process of seeing or examining **2** : opinion **3** : area of landscape that can be seen **4** : range of vision **5** : purpose or object ~ *vb* **1** : look at **2** : think about or consider —**view·er** *n*

view·point *n* : position from which something is considered

vig·il \'vijǝl\ *n* **1** : day of devotion before a religious feast **2** : act or time of keeping awake **3** : long period of keeping watch (as over a sick or dying person)

vig·i·lant \'vijǝlǝnt\ *adj* : alert esp. to avoid danger —**vig·i·lance** \-lǝns\ *n* —**vig·i·lant·ly** *adv*

vig·i·lan·te \,vijǝ'lantē\ *n* : one of a group independent of the law working to suppress crime

vi·gnette \vin'yet\ *n* : short descriptive literary piece

vig·or \'vigǝr\ *n* **1** : energy or strength **2** : intensity or force —**vig·or·ous** \'vigǝrǝs\ *adj* —**vig·or·ous·ly** *adv* —**vig·or·ous·ness** *n*

vile \'vīl\ *adj* **vil·er; vil·est** : thoroughly bad or contemptible —**vile·ly** *adv* —**vile·ness** *n*

vil·i·fy \'vilǝ,fī\ *vb* **-fied; -fy·ing** : speak evil of —**vil·i·fi·ca·tion** \,vilǝfǝ-'kāshǝn\ *n* —**vil·i·fi·er** \'vilǝ,fīǝr\ *n*

vil·la \'vilǝ\ *n* : country estate

vil·lage \'vilij\ *n* : small country town —**vil·lag·er** *n*

vil·lain \'vilǝn\ *n* : bad person —**vil·lain·ess** \-ǝnǝs\ *n* —**vil·lainy** *n*

vil·lain·ous \-ǝnǝs\ *adj* : evil or corrupt —**vil·lain·ous·ly** *adv* —**vil·lain·ous·ness** *n*

vim \'vim\ *n* : energy

vin·di·cate \'vindǝ,kāt\ *vb* **-cat·ed; -cat·ing 1** : avenge **2** : exonerate **3** : justify —**vin·di·ca·tion** \,vindǝ'kāshǝn\ *n* —**vin·di·ca·tor** \'vindǝ,kātǝr\ *n*

vin·dic·tive \vin'diktiv\ *adj* : seeking or meant for revenge —**vin·dic·tive·ly** *adv* —**vin·dic·tive·ness** *n*

vine \'vīn\ *n* : climbing or trailing plant

vin·e·gar \'vinigǝr\ *n* : acidic liquid obtained by fermentation —**vin·e·gary** \-gǝrē\ *adj*

vine·yard \'vinyǝrd\ *n* : plantation of grapevines

vin·tage \'vintij\ *n* **1** : season's yield of grapes or wine **2** : period of origin ~ *adj* : of enduring interest

vi·nyl \'vīnⁿl\ *n* : strong plastic

vi·o·la \vē'ōlǝ\ *n* : instrument of the violin family tuned lower than the violin —**vi·o·list** \-list\ *n*

vi·o·late \'vīǝ,lāt\ *vb* **-lat·ed; -lat·ing 1** : act with disrespect or disregard of **2** : rape **3** : desecrate —**vi·o·la·tion** \,vīǝ'lāshǝn\ *n* —**vi·o·la·tor** \'vīǝ-,lātǝr\ *n*

vi·o·lence \'vīǝlǝns\ *n* : intense physical force that causes or is intended to cause injury or destruction —**vi·o·lent** \-lǝnt\ *adj* —**vi·o·lent·ly** *adv*

vi·o·let \'vīǝlǝt\ *n* **1** : small flowering plant **2** : reddish blue

vi·o·lin \,vīǝ'lin\ *n* : bowed stringed instrument —**vi·o·lin·ist** \-nist\ *n*

VIP \,vē,ī'pē\ *n, pl* **VIPs** \-'pēz\ : very important person

vi·per \'vīpǝr\ *n* **1** : venomous snake **2** : treacherous or malignant person

vi·ra·go \vǝ'rägō, -'rä-; 'virǝ,gō\ *n, pl* **-goes** *or* **-gos** : shrew

vi·ral \'vīrǝl\ *adj* : relating to or caused by a virus

vir·gin \'vǝrjǝn\ *n* **1** : unmarried woman **2** : a person who has never had sexual intercourse ~ *adj* **1** : chaste **2** : natural and unspoiled —**vir·gin·al** \-ᵊl\ *adj* —**vir·gin·al·ly** *adv* —**vir·gin·i·ty** \vǝr'jinǝtē\ *n*

vir·gule \'vǝrgyül\ *n* : mark / used esp. to denote "or" or "per"

vir·ile \'virǝl\ *adj* : masculine —**vi·ril·i·ty** \vǝ'rilǝtē\ *n*

vir·tu·al \'vǝrchǝwǝl\ *adj* : being in effect but not in fact or name —**vir·tu·al·ly** *adv*

vir·tue \'vǝrchü\ *n* **1** : moral excellence **2** : effective or commendable quality **3** : chastity

vir·tu·os·i·ty \,vǝrchǝ'wäsǝtē\ *n, pl* **-ties** : great skill (as in music)

vir·tu·o·so \,vǝrchǝ'wōsō, -zō\ *n, pl* **-sos** *or* **-si** \-,sē, -,zē\ : highly skilled performer esp. of music —**virtuoso** *adj*

vir·tu·ous \'vǝrchǝwǝs\ *adj* **1** : morally good **2** : chaste —**vir·tu·ous·ly** *adv*

vir·u·lent \'virǝlǝnt, -yǝlǝnt\ *adj* **1** : extremely severe or infectious **2** : full of malice —**vir·u·lence** \-lǝns\ *n* —**vir·u·lent·ly** *adv*

vi·rus \'vīrǝs\ *n* **1** : tiny disease-causing agent **2** : a computer program that performs a malicious action (as destroying data)

vi·sa \'vēzǝ, -sǝ\ *n* : authorization to enter a foreign country

vis·age \'vizij\ *n* : face

vis·cera \'visǝrǝ\ *n pl* : internal bodily organs esp. of the trunk

vis·cer·al \'visǝrǝl\ *adj* **1** : bodily **2** : instinctive **3** : deeply or crudely emotional —**vis·cer·al·ly** *adv*

vis·cid \'visəd\ *adj* : viscous —**vis·cid·i·ty** \vis'idətē\ *n*

vis·count \'vī,kaunt\ *n* : British nobleman ranking below an earl and above a baron

vis·count·ess \-əs\ *n* **1** : wife of a viscount **2** : woman with rank of a viscount

vis·cous \'viskəs\ *adj* : having a thick or sticky consistency —**vis·cos·i·ty** \vis'käsətē\ *n*

vise \'vīs\ *n* : device for clamping something being worked on

vis·i·bil·i·ty \,vizə'bilətē\ *n, pl* **-ties** : degree or range to which something can be seen

vis·i·ble \'vizəbəl\ *adj* **1** : capable of being seen **2** : manifest or apparent —**vis·i·bly** *adv*

vi·sion \'vizhən\ *n* **1** : vivid picture seen in a dream or trance or in the imagination **2** : foresight **3** : power of seeing ~ *vb* : imagine

vi·sion·ary \'vizhə,nerē\ *adj* **1** : given to dreaming or imagining **2** : illusory **3** : not practical ~ *n* : one with great dreams or projects

vis·it \'vizət\ *vb* **1** : go or come to see **2** : stay with for a time as a guest **3** : cause or be a reward, affliction, or punishment ~ *n* : short stay as a guest —**vis·it·able** *adj* —**vis·i·tor** \-ər\ *n*

vis·i·ta·tion \,vizə'tāshən\ *n* **1** : official visit **2** : divine punishment or favor **3** : severe trial

vi·sor \'vīzər\ *n* **1** : front piece of a helmet **2** : part (as on a cap or car windshield) that shades the eyes

vis·ta \'vistə\ *n* : distant view

vi·su·al \'vizhəwəl\ *adj* **1** : relating to sight **2** : visible —**vi·su·al·ly** *adv*

vi·su·al·ize \'vizhəwə,līz\ *vb* **-ized; -iz·ing** : form a mental image of —**vi·su·al·i·za·tion** \,vizhəwələ'zāshən\ *n* —**vi·su·al·iz·er** \'vizhəwə,līzər\ *n*

vi·tal \'vīt³l\ *adj* **1** : relating to, necessary for, or characteristic of life **2** : full of life and vigor **3** : fatal **4** : very important —**vi·tal·ly** *adv*

vi·tal·i·ty \vī'talətē\ *n, pl* **-ties 1** : life force **2** : energy

vital signs *n pl* : body's pulse rate, respiration, temperature, and usu. blood pressure

vi·ta·min \'vītəmən\ *n* : natural organic substance essential to health

vi·ti·ate \'vishē,āt\ *vb* **-at·ed; -at·ing 1** : spoil or impair **2** : invalidate —**vi·ti·a·tion** \,vishē'āshən\ *n* —**vi·ti·a·tor** \'vishē,ātər\ *n*

vit·re·ous \'vitrēəs\ *adj* : relating to or resembling glass

vit·ri·ol \'vitrēəl\ *n* : something caustic, corrosive, or biting —**vit·ri·ol·ic** \,vitrē'älik\ *adj*

vi·tu·per·ate \vī'tüpə,rāt, və, -'tyü-\ *vb* **-at·ed; -at·ing** : abuse in words —**vi·tu·per·a·tion** \-,tüpə'rāshən, -,tyü-\ *n* —**vi·tu·per·a·tive** \-'tüpərətiv, -'tyü-, -pə,rāt-\ *adj* —**vi·tu·per·a·tive·ly** *adv*

vi·va·cious \və'vāshəs, vī-\ *adj* : lively —**vi·va·cious·ly** *adv* —**vi·va·cious·ness** *n* —**vi·vac·i·ty** \-'vasətē\ *n*

viv·id \'vivəd\ *adj* **1** : lively **2** : brilliant **3** : intense or sharp —**viv·id·ly** *adv* —**viv·id·ness** *n*

viv·i·fy \'vivə,fī\ *vb* **-fied; -fy·ing** : give life or vividness to

viv·i·sec·tion \,vivə'sekshən, 'vivə,-\ *n* : experimental operation on a living animal

vix·en \'viksən\ *n* **1** : scolding woman **2** : female fox

vo·cab·u·lary \vō'kabyə,lerē\ *n, pl* **-lar·ies 1** : list or collection of words **2** : stock of words used by a person or about a subject

vo·cal \'vōkəl\ *adj* **1** : relating to or produced by or for the voice **2** : speaking out freely and usu. emphatically

vocal cords *n pl* : membranous folds in the larynx that are important in making vocal sounds

vo·cal·ist \'vōkəlist\ *n* : singer

vo·cal·ize \-,līz\ *vb* **-ized; -iz·ing** : give vocal expression to

vo·ca·tion \vō'kāshən\ *n* : regular employment —**vo·ca·tion·al** \-shənəl\ *adj*

vo·cif·er·ous \vō'sifərəs\ *adj* : noisy and insistent —**vo·cif·er·ous·ly** *adv*

vod·ka \'vädkə\ *n* : colorless distilled grain liquor

vogue \'vōg\ *n* : brief but intense popularity —**vogu·ish** \'vōgish\ *adj*

voice \'vois\ *n* **1** : sound produced through the mouth by humans and many animals **2** : power of speaking **3** : right of choice or opinion ~ *vb* : express in words —**voiced** \'voist\ *adj*

void \'void\ *adj* **1** : containing nothing

2 : lacking —with *of* 3 : not legally binding ~ *n* 1 : empty space 2 : feeling of hollowness — *vb* 1 : discharge (as body waste) 2 : make (as a contract) void —**void·able** *adj* —**void·er** *n*

vol·a·tile \\'välət°l\ *adj* 1 : readily vaporizing at a relatively low temperature 2 : likely to change suddenly —**vol·a·til·i·ty** \\,välə'tilətē\ *n* —**vol·a·til·ize** \\'välət°l,īz\ *vb*

vol·ca·no \\väl'kānō\ *n, pl* -**noes** *or* -**nos** : opening in the earth's crust from which molten rock and steam come out —**vol·ca·nic** \-'kanik\ *adj*

vo·li·tion \\vō'lishən\ *n* : free will —**vo·li·tion·al** \-'lishənəl\ *adj*

vol·ley \\'välē\ *n, pl* -**leys** 1 : flight of missiles (as arrows) 2 : simultaneous shooting of many weapons

vol·ley·ball *n* : game of batting a large ball over a net

volt \\'vōlt\ *n* : unit for measuring the force that moves an electric current

volt·age \\'vōltij\ *n* : quantity of volts

vol·u·ble \\'välyəbəl\ *adj* : fluent and smooth in speech —**vol·u·bil·i·ty** \\,välyə'bilətē\ *n* —**vol·u·bly** \\'välyəblē\ *adv*

vol·ume \\'välyəm\ *n* 1 : book 2 : space occupied as measured by cubic units 3 : amount 4 : loudness of a sound

vo·lu·mi·nous \\və'lümənəs\ *adj* : large or bulky

vol·un·tary \\'välən,terē\ *adj* 1 : done, made, or given freely and without expecting compensation 2 : relating to or controlled by the will —**vol·un·tar·i·ly** *adv*

vol·un·teer \\,välən'tir\ *n* : person who offers to help or work without expecting payment or reward ~ *vb* 1 : offer or give voluntarily 2 : offer oneself as a volunteer

vo·lup·tuous \\və'ləpchəwəs\ *adj* 1 : luxurious 2 : having a full and sexually attractive figure —**vo·lup·tuous·ly** *adv* —**vo·lup·tuous·ness** *n*

vom·it \\'vämət\ *vb* : throw up the contents of the stomach —**vomit** *n*

voo·doo \\'vüdü\ *n, pl* **voodoos** 1 : religion derived from African polytheism and involving sorcery 2 : one who practices voodoo 3 : charm or fetish used in voodoo —**voodoo** *adj* —**voo·doo·ism** \-,izəm\ *n*

vo·ra·cious \\vȯ'rāshəs, və-\ *adj* : greedy or exceedingly hungry — **vo·ra·cious·ly** *adv* —**vo·ra·cious·ness** *n* —**vo·rac·i·ty** \-'rasətē\ *n*

vor·tex \\'vȯr,teks\ *n, pl* **vor·ti·ces** \\'vȯrtə,sēz\ : whirling liquid

vo·ta·ry \\'vōtərē\ *n, pl* -**ries** 1 : devoted participant, adherent, admirer, or worshiper

vote \\'vōt\ *n* 1 : individual expression of preference in choosing or reaching a decision 2 : right to indicate one's preference or the preference expressed ~ *vb* **vot·ed; vot·ing** 1 : cast a vote 2 : choose or defeat by vote —**vote·less** *adj* —**vot·er** *n*

vo·tive \\'vōtiv\ *adj* : consisting of or expressing a vow, wish, or desire

vouch \\'vaüch\ *vb* : give a guarantee or personal assurance

vouch·er \\'vaüchər\ *n* : written record or receipt that serves as proof of a transaction

vouch·safe \\vaüch'sāf\ *vb* -**safed; -saf·ing** : grant as a special favor

vow \\'vaü\ *n* : solemn promise to do something or to live or act a certain way —**vow** *vb*

vow·el \\'vaüəl\ *n* 1 : speech sound produced without obstruction or friction in the mouth 2 : letter representing such a sound

voy·age \\'vȯiij\ *n* : long journey esp. by water or through space ~ *vb* -**aged; -ag·ing** : make a voyage —**voy·ag·er** *n*

vul·ca·nize \\'vəlkə,nīz\ *vb* -**nized; -niz·ing** : treat (as rubber) to make more elastic or stronger

vul·gar \\'vəlgər\ *adj* 1 : relating to the common people 2 : lacking refinement 3 : offensive in manner or language —**vul·gar·ism** \-,rizəm\ *n* —**vul·gar·ize** \-,rīz\ *vb* —**vul·gar·ly** *adv*

vul·gar·i·ty \\,vəl'garətē\ *n, pl* -**ties** 1 : state of being vulgar 2 : vulgar language or act

vul·ner·a·ble \\'vəlnərəbəl\ *adj* : susceptible to attack or damage — **vul·ner·a·bil·i·ty** \\,vəlnərə'bilətē\ *n* —**vul·ner·a·bly** *adv*

vul·ture \\'vəlchər\ *n* : large flesh-eating bird

vul·va \\'vəlvə\ *n, pl* -**vae** \-,vē, -,vī\ : external genital parts of the female

vying *pres part of* VIE

W

w \\'dəbəl,yü\\ *n, pl* **w's** *or* **ws** \\-,yüz\\ : 23d letter of the alphabet

wad \\'wäd\\ *n* **1** : little mass **2** : soft mass of fibrous material **3** : pliable plug to retain a powder charge **4** : considerable amount ~ *vb* **1** : form into a wad **2** : stuff with a wad

wad·dle \\'wäd°l\\ *vb* **-dled; -dling** : walk with short steps swaying from side to side **—waddle** *n*

wade \\'wäd\\ *vb* **wad·ed; wad·ing 1** : step in or through (as water) **2** : move with difficulty **—wade** *n* **—wad·er** *n*

wa·fer \\'wäfər\\ *n* **1** : thin crisp cake or cracker **2** : waferlike thing

waf·fle \\'wäfəl\\ *n* : crisped cake of batter cooked in a hinged utensil (**waffle iron**) ~ *vb* : vacillate

waft \\'wäft, 'waft\\ *vb* : cause to move lightly by wind or waves **—waft** *n*

¹wag \\'wag\\ *vb* **-gg-** : sway or swing from side to side and to and fro **—wag** *n*

²wag *n* : wit **—wag·gish** *adj*

wage \\'wāj\\ *vb* **waged; wag·ing** : engage in ~ *n* **1** : payment for labor or services **2** : compensation

wa·ger \\'wājər\\ *n or vb* : bet

wag·gle \\'wagəl\\ *vb* **-gled; -gling** : wag **—waggle** *n*

wag·on \\'wagən\\ *n* **1** : 4-wheeled vehicle drawn by animals **2** : child's 4-wheeled cart

waif \\'wāf\\ *n* : homeless child

wail \\'wāl\\ *vb* **1** : mourn **2** : make a sound like a mournful cry **—wail** *n*

wain·scot \\'wānskət, -,skōt, -,skät\\ *n* : usu. paneled wooden lining of an interior wall **—wainscot** *vb*

waist \\'wāst\\ *n* **1** : narrowed part of the body between chest and hips **2** : waistlike part **—waist·line** *n*

wait \\'wāt\\ *vb* **1** : remain in readiness or expectation **2** : delay **3** : attend as a waiter ~ *n* **1** : concealment **2** : act or period of waiting

wait·er \\'wātər\\ *n* : person who serves others at tables

wait·per·son \\'wāt,pərsən\\ *n* : a waiter or waitress

wait·ress \\'wātrəs\\ *n* : woman who serves others at tables

waive \\'wāv\\ *vb* **waived; waiv·ing** : give up claim to

waiv·er \\'wāvər\\ *n* : act of waiving right, claim, or privilege

¹wake \\'wāk\\ *vb* **woke** \\'wōk\\; **wo·ken** \\'wōkən\\; **wak·ing 1** : keep watch **2** : bring or come back to consciousness after sleep ~ *n* **1** : state of being awake **2** : watch held over a dead body

²wake *n* : track left by a ship

wake·ful \\'wākfəl\\ *adj* : not sleeping or able to sleep **—wake·ful·ness** *n*

wak·en \\'wākən\\ *vb* : wake

wale \\'wāl\\ *n* : ridge on cloth

walk \\'wȯk\\ *vb* **1** : move or cause to move on foot **2** : pass over, through, or along by walking ~ *n* **1** : a going on foot **2** : place or path for walking **3** : distance to be walked **4** : way of living **5** : way of walking **6** : slow 4-beat gait of a horse **—walk·er** *n*

wall \\'wȯl\\ *n* **1** : structure for defense or for enclosing something **2** : upright enclosing part of a building or room **3** : something like a wall ~ *vb* : provide, separate, surround, or close with a wall **—walled** \\'wȯld\\ *adj*

wal·la·by \\'wäləbē\\ *n, pl* **-bies** : small or medium-sized kangaroo

wal·let \\'wälət\\ *n* : pocketbook with compartments

wall·flow·er *n* **1** : mustardlike plant with showy fragrant flowers **2** : one who remains on the sidelines of social activity

wal·lop \\'wäləp\\ *n* **1** : powerful blow **2** : ability to hit hard ~ *vb* **1** : beat soundly **2** : hit hard

wal·low \\'wälō\\ *vb* **1** : roll about in deep mud **2** : indulge oneself excessively ~ *n* : place for wallowing

wall·pa·per *n* : decorative paper for walls **—wallpaper** *vb*

wal·nut \\'wȯl,nət\\ *n* **1** : nut with a furrowed shell and adherent husk **2** : tree on which this nut grows or its brown wood

wal·rus \'wȯlrəs, -wäl-\ *n, pl* **-rus** *or* **-rus·es** : large seallike mammal of northern seas having ivory tusks

waltz \'wȯlts\ *n* : gliding dance to music having 3 beats to the measure or the music —**waltz** *vb*

wam·pum \'wämpəm\ *n* : strung shell beads used by No. American Indians as money

wan \'wän\ *adj* **-nn-** : sickly or pale — **wan·ly** *adv* —**wan·ness** *n*

wand \'wänd\ *n* : slender staff

wan·der \'wändər\ *vb* **1** : move about aimlessly **2** : stray **3** : become delirious —**wan·der·er** *n*

wan·der·lust \'wändər,ləst\ *n* : strong urge to wander

wane \'wän\ *vb* **waned; wan·ing 1** : grow smaller or less **2** : lose power, prosperity, or influence —**wane** *n*

wan·gle \'waŋgəl\ *vb* **-gled; -gling** : obtain by sly or devious means

want \'wȯnt\ *vb* **1** : lack **2** : need **3** : desire earnestly ~ *n* **1** : deficiency **2** : dire need **3** : something wanted

want·ing \-iŋ\ *adj* **1** : not present or in evidence **2** : falling below standards **3** : lacking in ability ~ *prep* **1** : less or minus **2** : without

wan·ton \'wȯntᵊn\ *adj* **1** : lewd **2** : having no regard for justice or for others' feelings, rights, or safety ~ *n* : lewd or immoral person ~ *vb* : be wanton —**wan·ton·ly** *adv* —**wan·ton·ness** *n*

wa·pi·ti \'wäpətē\ *n, pl* **-ti** *or* **-tis** : elk

war \'wȯr\ *n* **1** : armed fighting between nations **2** : state of hostility or conflict **3** : struggle between opposing forces or for a particular end ~ *vb* **-rr-** : engage in warfare —**war·less** \-ləs\ *adj* —**war·time** *n*

war·ble \'wȯrbəl\ *n* **1** : melodious succession of low pleasing sounds **2** : musical trill ~ *vb* **-bled; -bling** : sing or utter in a trilling way

war·bler \'wȯrblər\ *n* **1** : small thrushlike singing bird **2** : small bright-colored insect-eating bird

ward \'wȯrd\ *n* **1** : a guarding or being under guard or guardianship **2** : division of a prison or hospital **3** : electoral or administrative division of a city **4** : person under protection of a

guardian or a law court ~ *vb* : turn aside —**ward·ship** *n*

1·ward \wərd\ *adj suffix* **1** : that moves, tends, faces, or is directed toward **2** : that occurs or is situated in the direction of

2·ward, -wards *adv suffix* **1** : in a (specified) direction **2** : toward a (specified) point, position, or area

war·den \'wȯrdᵊn\ *n* **1** : guardian **2** : official charged with supervisory duties or enforcement of laws **3** : official in charge of a prison

ward·er \'wȯrdər\ *n* : watchman or warden

ward·robe \'wȯrd,rōb\ *n* **1** : clothes closet **2** : collection of wearing apparel

ware \'war\ *n* **1** : articles for sale —often pl. **2** : items of fired clay

ware·house \-,haús\ *n* : place for storage of merchandise —**warehouse** *vb* —**ware·house·man** \-mən\ *n* —**ware·hous·er** \-,haúzər, -sər\ *n*

war·fare \-,far\ *n* **1** : military operations between enemies **2** : struggle

war·head \-,hed\ *n* : part of a missile holding the explosive material

war·like *adj* : fond of, relating to, or used in war

warm \'wȯrm\ *adj* **1** : having or giving out moderate or adequate heat **2** : serving to retain heat **3** : showing strong feeling **4** : giving a pleasant impression of warmth, cheerfulness, or friendliness ~ *vb* **1** : make or become warm **2** : give warmth or energy to **3** : experience feelings of affection **4** : become increasingly ardent, interested, or competent —**warm·er** *n* —**warm·ly** *adv* —**warm up** *vb* : make ready by preliminary activity

war·mon·ger \'wȯr,məŋgər, -,mäŋ-\ *n* : one who attempts to stir up war

warmth \'wȯrmth\ *n* **1** : quality or state of being warm **2** : enthusiasm

warn \'wȯrn\ *vb* **1** : put on guard **2** : notify in advance —**warn·ing** \-iŋ\ *n or adj*

warp \'wȯrp\ *n* **1** : lengthwise threads in a woven fabric **2** : twist ~ *vb* **1** : twist out of shape **2** : lead astray **3** : distort

war·rant \'wȯrənt, 'wär-\ *n* **1** : authorization **2** : legal writ authorizing action ~ *vb* **1** : declare or maintain positively **2** : guarantee **3** : approve **4** : justify

warrant officer n **1** : officer in the armed forces ranking next below a commissioned officer **2** : commissioned officer in the navy or coast guard ranking below an ensign

war·ran·ty \'wòrəntē, 'wär-\ n, pl **-ties** : guarantee of the integrity of a product

war·ren \'wòrən, 'wär-\ n : area where rabbits are bred and kept

war·rior \'wòryər, 'wòrēər; 'wärē-, 'wäryər\ n : man engaged or experienced in warfare

war·ship \'wòr,ship\ n : naval vessel

wart \'wòrt\ n **1** : small projection on the skin caused by a virus **2** : wartlike protuberance —**warty** adj

wary \'warē\ adj **war·i·er; -est** : careful in guarding against danger or deception

was past 1st & 3d sing of BE

wash \'wòsh, 'wäsh\ vb **1** : cleanse with or as if with a liquid (as water) **2** : wet thoroughly with liquid **3** : flow along the border of **4** : flow in a stream **5** : move or remove by or as if by the action of water **6** : cover or daub lightly with a liquid **7** : undergo laundering ~ n **1** : act of washing or being washed **2** : articles to be washed **3** : surging action of water or disturbed air —**wash·able** \-əbəl\ adj

wash·board n : grooved board to scrub clothes on

wash·bowl n : large bowl for water for washing hands and face

wash·cloth n : cloth used for washing one's face and body

washed-up \'wòsht'əp, 'wäsht-\ adj : no longer capable or usable

wash·er \'wòshər, 'wäsh-\ n **1** : machine for washing **2** : ring used around a bolt or screw to ensure tightness or relieve friction

wash·ing \'wòshiŋ, 'wäsh-\ n : articles to be washed

Washington's Birthday n : the 3d Monday in February or formerly February 22 observed as a legal holiday

wash·out n **1** : washing out or away of earth **2** : failure

wash·room n : bathroom

wasp \'wäsp, 'wòsp\ n : slender-bodied winged insect related to the bees and having a formidable sting

wasp·ish \'wäspish, 'wòs-\ adj : irritable

was·sail \'wäsəl, wä'sāl\ n **1** : toast to someone's health **2** : liquor drunk on festive occasions **3** : riotous drinking —**wassail** vb

waste \'wāst\ n **1** : sparsely settled or barren region **2** : act or an instance of wasting **3** : refuse (as garbage or rubbish) **4** : material (as feces) produced but not used by a living body ~ vb **wast·ed; wast·ing 1** : ruin **2** : spend or use carelessly **3** : lose substance or energy ~ adj **1** : wild and uninhabited **2** : being of no further use —**wast·er** n —**waste·ful** \-fəl\ adj —**waste·ful·ly** adv —**waste·ful·ness** n

waste·bas·ket \-,baskət\ n : receptacle for refuse

waste·land \-,land, -lənd\ n : barren uncultivated land

was·trel \'wāstrəl, 'wästrəl\ n : one who wastes

watch \'wäch, 'wòch\ vb **1** : be or stay awake intentionally **2** : be on the lookout for danger **3** : observe **4** : keep oneself informed about ~ n **1** : act of keeping awake to guard **2** : close observation **3** : one that watches **4** : period of duty on a ship or those on duty during this period **5** : timepiece carried on the person —**watch·er** n

watch·dog n **1** : dog kept to guard property **2** : one that protects

watch·ful \-fəl\ adj : steadily attentive —**watch·ful·ly** adv —**watch·ful·ness** n

watch·man \-mən\ n : person assigned to watch

watch·word n **1** : secret word used as a signal **2** : slogan

wa·ter \'wòtər, 'wät-\ n **1** : liquid that descends as rain and forms rivers, lakes, and seas **2** : liquid containing or resembling water ~ vb **1** : supply with or get water **2** : dilute with or as if with water **3** : form or secrete watery matter

water buffalo n : common oxlike often domesticated Asian buffalo

wa·ter·col·or n **1** : paint whose liquid part is water **2** : picture made with watercolors

wa·ter·course n : stream of water

wa·ter·cress \-,kres\ n : perennial salad plant with white flowers

wa·ter·fall n : steep descent of the water of a stream

wa·ter·fowl n **1** : bird that frequents the water **2 waterfowl** pl : swimming game birds

wa·ter·front *n* : land fronting a body of water

water lily *n* : aquatic plant with floating leaves and showy flowers

wa·ter·logged \-ˌlȯgd, -ˌlägd\ *adj* : filled or soaked with water

wa·ter·mark *n* **1** : mark showing how high water has risen **2** : a marking in paper visible under light ~ *vb* : mark (paper) with a watermark

wa·ter·mel·on *n* : large fruit with sweet juicy sus. red pulp

water moccasin *n* : venomous snake of the southeastern U.S.

wa·ter·pow·er *n* : power of moving water used to run machinery

wa·ter·proof *adj* : not letting water through ~ *vb* : make waterproof —**wa·ter·proof·ing** *n*

wa·ter·shed \-ˌshed\ *n* : dividing ridge between two drainage areas or one of these areas

water ski *n* : ski used on water when the wearer is towed —**wa·ter·ski** *vb* —**wa·ter·ski·er** *n*

wa·ter·spout *n* **1** : pipe from which water is spouted **2** : tornado over a body of water

wa·ter·tight *adj* **1** : so tight as not to let water in **2** : allowing no possibility for doubt or uncertainty

wa·ter·way *n* : navigable body of water

wa·ter·works *n pl* : system by which water is supplied (as to a city)

wa·tery \ˈwȯtərē, ˈwät-\ *adj* **1** : containing, full of, or giving out water **2** : being like water **3** : soft and soggy

watt \ˈwät\ *n* : unit of electric power —**watt·age** \ˈwätij\ *n*

wat·tle \ˈwätᵊl\ *n* **1** : framework of flexible branches used in building **2** : fleshy process hanging usu. about the head or neck (as of a bird) —**wat·tled** \-ᵊld\ *adj*

wave \ˈwāv\ *vb* **waved; wav·ing 1** : flutter **2** : signal with the hands **3** : wave to and fro with the hand **4** : curve up and down like a wave ~ *n* **1** : moving swell on the surface of water **2** : wave-like shape **3** : waving motion **4** : surge **5** : disturbance that transfers energy from point to point —**wave·let** \-lət\ *n* —**wave·like** *adj* —**wavy** *adj*

wave·length \ˈwāvˌleṇth\ *n* **1** : distance from crest to crest in the line of advance of a wave **2** : line of thought that reveals a common understanding

wa·ver \ˈwāvər\ *vb* **1** : fluctuate in opinion, allegiance, or direction **2** : flicker **3** : falter —**waver** *n* —**wa·ver·er** *n* —**wa·ver·ing·ly** *adv*

¹**wax** \ˈwaks\ *n* **1** : yellowish plastic substance secreted by bees **2** : substance like beeswax ~ *vb* : treat or rub with wax esp. for polishing

²**wax** *vb* **1** : grow larger **2** : become

wax·en \ˈwaksən\ *adj* : made of or resembling wax

waxy \ˈwaksē\ *adj* **wax·i·er; -est** : made of, full of, or resembling wax

way \ˈwā\ *n* **1** : thoroughfare for travel or passage **2** : route **3** : course of action **4** : method **5** : detail **6** : usual or characteristic state of affairs **7** : condition **8** : distance **9** : progress along a course —**by the way** : in a digression —**by way of 1** : for the purpose of **2** : by the route through —**out of the way** : remote

way·bill *n* : paper that accompanies a shipment and gives details of goods, route, and charges

way·far·er \ˈwāˌfarər\ *n* : traveler esp. on foot —**way·far·ing** \-ˌfariŋ\ *adj*

way·lay \ˈwāˌlā\ *vb* **-laid** \-ˌlād\; **-lay·ing** : lie in wait for

way·side *n* : side of a road

way·ward \ˈwāwərd\ *adj* **1** : following one's own capricious inclinations **2** : unpredictable

we \ˈwē\ *pron* —used of a group that includes the speaker or writer

weak \ˈwēk\ *adj* **1** : lacking strength or vigor **2** : deficient in vigor of mind or character **3** : of less than usual strength **4** : not having or exerting authority —**weak·en** \ˈwēkən\ *vb* —**weak·ly** *adv*

weak·ling \-liŋ\ *n* : person who is physically, mentally, or morally weak

weak·ly \ˈwēklē\ *adj* : feeble

weak·ness \-nəs\ *n* **1** : quality or state of being weak **2** : fault **3** : object of special liking

wealth \ˈwelth\ *n* **1** : abundant possessions or resources **2** : profusion

wealthy \ˈwelthē\ *adj* **wealth·i·er; -est** : having wealth

wean \ˈwēn\ *vb* **1** : accustom (a young mammal) to take food by means other than nursing **2** : free from dependence

weap·on \ˈwepən\ *n* **1** : something (as a gun) that may be used to fight with **2** : means by which one contends against another —**weap·on·less** *adj*

wear \'war\ *vb* **wore** \'wōr\; **worn** \'wōrn\; **wear·ing 1** : use as an article of clothing or adornment **2** : carry on the person **3** : show an appearance of **4** : decay by use or by scraping **5** : lessen the strength of **6** : endure use ~ *n* **1** : act of wearing **2** : clothing **3** : lasting quality **4** : result of use — **wear·able** \'warəbəl\ *adj* —**wear·er** *n* —**wear out** *vb* **1** : make or become useless by wear **2** : tire

wea·ri·some \'wirēsəm\ *adj* : causing weariness —**wea·ri·some·ly** *adv* —**wea·ri·some·ness** *n*

wea·ry \'wirē\ *adj* **-ri·er; -est 1** : worn out in strength, freshness, or patience **2** : expressing or characteristic of weariness ~ *vb* **-ried; -ry·ing** : make or become weary —**wea·ri·ly** *adv* —**wea·ri·ness** *n*

wea·sel \'wēzəl\ *n* : small slender flesh-eating mammal

weath·er \'wethər\ *n* : state of the atmosphere ~ *vb* **1** : expose to or endure the action of weather **2** : endure

weath·er-beat·en *adj* : worn or damaged by exposure to the weather

weath·er·man \-,man\ *n* : one who forecasts and reports the weather

weath·er·proof *adj* : able to withstand exposure to weather —**weatherproof** *vb*

weather vane *n* : movable device that shows the way the wind blows

weave \'wēv\ *vb* **wove** \'wōv\ *or* **weaved; wo·ven** \'wōvən\ *or* **weaved; weav·ing 1** : form by interlacing strands of material **2** : to make as if by weaving together parts **3** : follow a winding course ~ *n* : pattern or method of weaving —**weav·er** *n*

web \'web\ *n* **1** : cobweb **2** : animal or plant membrane **3** : network ~ *vb* **-bb- 1** : cover or provide with a web — **webbed** \'webd\ *adj*

web·bing \'webiŋ\ *n* : strong closely woven tape

wed \'wed\ *vb* **-dd- 1** : marry **2** : unite

wed·ding \'wediŋ\ *n* : marriage ceremony and celebration

wedge \'wej\ *n* : V-shaped object used for splitting, raising, forcing open, or tightening ~ *vb* **wedged; wedg·ing 1** : tighten or split with a wedge **2** : force into a narrow space

wed·lock \'wed,läk\ *n* : marriage

Wednes·day \'wenzdā, -dē\ *n* : 4th day of the week

wee \'wē\ *adj* : very small

weed \'wēd\ *n* : unwanted plant ~ *vb* **1** : remove weeds **2** : get rid of —**weed·er** *n* —**weedy** *adj*

weeds *n pl* : mourning clothes

week \'wēk\ *n* **1** : 7 successive days **2** : calendar period of 7 days beginning with Sunday and ending with Saturday **3** : the working or school days of the calendar week

week·day \'wēk,dā\ *n* : any day except Sunday and often Saturday

week·end \-,end\ *n* : Saturday and Sunday ~ *vb* : spend the weekend

week·ly \'wēklē\ *adj* : occurring, appearing, or done every week ~ *n, pl* **-lies** : weekly publication —**weekly** *adv*

weep \'wēp\ *vb* **wept** \'wept\; **weep·ing** : shed tears —**weep·er** *n* —**weepy** *adj*

wee·vil \'wēvəl\ *n* : small injurious beetle with a long head usu. curved into a snout —**wee·vily, wee·vil·ly** \'wēvəlē\

weft \'weft\ *n* : crosswise threads or yarn in weaving

weigh \'wā\ *vb* **1** : determine the heaviness of **2** : have a specified weight **3** : consider carefully **4** : raise (an anchor) off the sea floor **5** : press down or burden

weight \'wāt\ *n* **1** : amount that something weighs **2** : relative heaviness **3** : heavy object **4** : burden or pressure **5** : importance ~ *vb* **1** : load with a weight **2** : oppress —**weight·less** \-ləs\ *adj* —**weight·less·ness** *n* —**weighty** \'wātē\ *adj*

weird \'wird\ *adj* **1** : unearthly or mysterious **2** : strange —**weird·ly** *adv* —**weird·ness** *n*

wel·come \'welkəm\ *vb* **-comed; -com·ing** : accept or greet cordially ~ *adj* : received or permitted gladly ~ *n* : cordial greeting or reception

weld \'weld\ *vb* : unite by heating, hammering, or pressing ~ *n* : union by welding —**weld·er** *n*

wel·fare \'wel,far\ *n* **1** : prosperity **2** : government aid for those in need

¹**well** \'wel\ *n* **1** : spring **2** : hole sunk in the earth to obtain a natural deposit (as of oil) **3** : source of supply **4** : open space extending vertically through floors ~ *vb* : flow forth

²**well** *adv* **bet·ter** \'betər\; **best** \'best\ **1** : in a good or proper manner **2** : satisfactorily **3** : fully **4** : intimately

5 : considerably ~ *adj* 1 : satisfactory 2 : prosperous 3 : desirable 4 : healthy

well–adjusted \,welə'jəstəd\ *adj* : well-balanced

well–ad·vised \,weləd'vīzd\ *adj* : prudent

well–balanced \'wel'ba`lənst\ *adj* 1 : evenly balanced 2 : emotionally or psychologically sound

well–being \'wel'bēiŋ\ *n* : state of being happy, healthy, or prosperous

well–bred \-'bred\ *adj* : having good manners

well–done *adj* 1 : properly performed 2 : cooked thoroughly

well–heeled \-'hēld\ *adj* : financially well-off

well–meaning *adj* : having good intentions

well–nigh *adv* : nearly

well–off *adj* : being in good condition esp. financially

well–read \-'red\ *adj* : well informed through reading

well–round·ed \-'raúndəd\ *adj* : broadly developed

well·spring *n* : source

well–to–do \,weltə'dü\ *adj* : prosperous

welsh \'welsh, 'welch\ *vb* 1 : avoid payment 2 : break one's word

Welsh rabbit *n* : melted often seasoned cheese poured over toast or crackers

Welsh rare·bit \-'rarbət\ *n* : Welsh rabbit

welt \'welt\ *n* 1 : narrow strip of leather between a shoe upper and sole 2 : ridge raised on the skin usu. by a blow ~ *vb* : hit hard

wel·ter \'weltər\ *vb* 1 : toss about 2 : wallow ~ *n* : confused jumble

wen \'wen\ *n* : abnormal growth or cyst

wench \'wench\ *n* : young woman

wend \'wend\ *vb* : direct one's course

went *past of* GO

wept *past of* WEEP

were *past 2d sing, past pl. or past subjunctive of* BE

were·wolf \'wer,wúlf, 'wir-, 'wər-\ *n, pl* **-wolves** \-,wúlvz\ : person held to be able to change into a wolf

west \'west\ *adv* : to or toward the west ~ *adj* : situated toward or at or coming from the west ~ *n* 1 : direction of sunset 2 *cap* : regions to the west — **wester·ly** \'westərlē\ *adv or adj* — **west·ward** \-wərd\ *adv or adj* — **west·wards** \-wərdz\ *adv*

west·ern \'western\ *adj* 1 *cap* : of a region designated West 2 : lying toward or coming from the west —**West·ern·er** *n*

wet \'wet\ *adj* **-tt-** 1 : consisting of or covered or soaked with liquid 2 : not dry ~ *n* : moisture ~ *vb* **-tt-** : make or become moist —**wet·ly** *adv* —**wet·ness** *n*

whack \'hwak\ *vb* : strike sharply ~ *n* 1 : sharp blow 2 : proper working order 3 : chance 4 : try

¹**whale** \'hwāl\ *n, pl* **whales** *or* **whale** : large marine mammal ~ *vb* **whaled; whal·ing** : hunt for whales —**whale·boat** *n* —**whal·er** *n*

²**whale** *vb* **whaled; whal·ing** : strike or hit vigorously

whale·bone *n* : horny substance attached to the upper jaw of some large whales (**whalebone whales**)

wharf \'hworf\ *n, pl* **wharves** \'hworvz\ : structure alongside which boats lie to load or unload

what \'hwät\ *pron* 1 —used to inquire the identity or nature of something 2 : that which 3 : whatever ~ *adv* : in what respect ~ *adj* 1 —used to inquire about the identity or nature of something 2 : how remarkable or surprising 3 : whatever

what·ever \hwät'evər\ *pron* 1 : anything or everything that 2 : no matter what ~ *adj* : of any kind at all

what·not \'hwät,nät\ *pron* : any of various other things that might be mentioned

what·so·ever \,hwätsō'evər\ *pron or adj* : whatever

wheal \'hwēl\ *n* : a welt on the skin

wheat \'hwēt\ *n* : cereal grain that yields flour —**wheat·en** *adj*

whee·dle \'hwēdᵊl\ *vb* **-dled; -dling** : coax or tempt by flattery

wheel \'hwēl\ *n* 1 : disk or circular frame capable of turning on a central axis 2 : device of which the main part is a wheel ~ *vb* 1 : convey or move on wheels or a wheeled vehicle 2 : rotate 3 : turn so as to change direction — **wheeled** *adj* —**wheeler** *n* —**wheel·less** *adj*

wheel·bar·row \-,barō\ *n* : one-wheeled vehicle for carrying small loads

wheel·base *n* : distance in inches between the front and rear axles of an automotive vehicle

wheel·chair *n* : chair mounted on

wheels esp. for the use of disabled persons

wheeze \\'hwēz\\ vb **wheezed; wheez·ing** : breathe with difficulty and with a whistling sound —**wheeze** n —**wheezy** adj

whelk \\'hwelk\\ n : large sea snail

whelp \\'hwelp\\ n : one of the young of various carnivorous mammals (as a dog) ~ vb : bring forth whelps

when \\'hwen\\ adv —used to inquire about or designate a particular time ~ conj 1 : at or during the time that 2 : every time that 3 : if 4 : although ~ pron : what time

whence \\'hwens\\ adv or conj : from what place, source, or cause

when·ever \\'hwen'evər\\ conj or adv : at whatever time

where \\'hwer\\ adv 1 : at, in, or to what place 2 : at, in, or to what situation, position, direction, circumstances, or respect ~ conj 1 : at, in, or to what place, position, or circumstance 2 : at, in, or to which place ~ n : place

where·abouts \\-ə,baùts\\ adv : about where ~ n sing or pl : place where a person or thing is

where·as \\hwer'az\\ conj 1 : while on the contrary 2 : since

where·by conj : by, through, or in accordance with which

where·fore \\'hwer,fōr\\ adv 1 : why 2 : therefore ~ n : reason

where·in \\hwer'in\\ adv : in what respect

where·of \\-'əv, -äv\\ conj : of what, which, or whom

where·up·on \\'hwerə,pón, -,pän\\ conj 1 : on which 2 : and then

wher·ev·er \\hwer'evər\\ adv : where ~ conj : at, in, or to whatever place or circumstance

where·with·al \\'hwerwith,ól, -with-\\ n : resources and esp. money

whet \\'hwet\\ vb **-tt-** 1 : sharpen by rubbing (as with a stone) 2 : stimulate —**whet·stone** n

whey \\'hwā\\ n : watery part of sour milk

which \\'hwich\\ adj 1 : being what one or ones out of a group 2 : whichever ~ pron 1 : which one or ones 2 : whichever

which·ev·er \\hwich'evər\\ pron or adj : no matter what one

whiff \\'hwif\\ n 1 : slight gust 2

: inhalation of odor, gas, or smoke 3 : slight trace ~ vb : inhale an odor

while \\'hwil\\ n 1 : period of time 2 : time and effort used ~ conj : during the time that 2 : as long as 3 : although ~ vb : whiled; whil·ing : cause to pass esp. pleasantly

whim \\'hwim\\ n : sudden wish, desire, or change of mind

whim·per \\'hwimpər\\ vb : cry softly —**whimper** n

whim·si·cal \\'hwimzikəl\\ adj 1 : full of whims 2 : erratic —**whim·si·cal·i·ty** \\,hwimzə'kalətē\\ n —**whim·si·cal·ly** adv

whim·sy, whim·sey \\'hwimzē\\ n, pl **-sies** or **-seys** 1 : whim 2 : fanciful creation

whine \\'hwin\\ vb **whined; whin·ing** 1 : utter a usu. high-pitched plaintive cry 2 : complain —**whine** n —**whin·er** n —**whiny** adj

whin·ny \\'hwinē\\ vb **-nied; -ny·ing** : neigh —**whinny** n

whip \\'hwip\\ vb **-pp-** 1 : move quickly 2 : strike with something slender and flexible 3 : defeat 4 : incite 5 : beat into a froth ~ n 1 : flexible device used for whipping 2 : party leader responsible for discipline 3 : thrashing motion —**whip·per** n

whip·cord n 1 : thin tough cord 2 : cloth made of hard-twisted yarns

whip·lash n : injury from a sudden sharp movement of the neck and head

whip·per·snap·per \\'hwipər,snapər\\ n : small, insignificant, or presumptuous person

whip·pet \\'hwipət\\ n : small swift dog often used for racing

whip·poor·will \\'hwipər,wil\\ n : American nocturnal bird

whir \\'hwər\\ vb **-rr-** : move, fly, or revolve with a whir ~ n : continuous fluttering or vibratory sound

whirl \\'hwərl\\ vb 1 : move or drive in a circle 2 : spin 3 : move or turn quickly 4 : reel ~ n 1 : rapid circular movement 2 : state of commotion or confusion 3 : try

whirl·pool n : whirling mass of water having a depression in the center

whirl·wind n : whirling wind storm

whisk \\'hwisk\\ n 1 : quick light sweeping or brushing motion 2 : usu. wire kitchen implement for beating ~ vb 1 : move or convey briskly 2 : beat 3 : brush lightly

whisk broom *n* : small broom

whis·ker \'hwiskər\ *n* **1** *pl* : beard **2** : long bristle or hair near an animal's mouth —**whis·kered** \-kərd\ *adj*

whis·key, whis·ky \'hwiskē\ *n, pl* **-keys** *or* **-kies** : liquor distilled from a fermented mash of grain

whis·per \'hwispər\ *vb* **1** : speak softly **2** : tell by whispering ~ *n* **1** : soft low sound **2** : rumor

whist \'hwist\ *n* : card game

whis·tle \'hwisəl\ *n* **1** : device by which a shrill sound is produced **2** : shrill clear sound made by a whistle or through the lips ~ *vb* **-tled; -tling 1** : make or utter a whistle **2** : signal or call by a whistle **3** : produce by whistling —**whis·tler** *n*

whis·tle–blow·er \'hwisəl,blōər\ *n* : informer

whis·tle–stop *n* : brief political appearance

whit \'hwit\ *n* : bit

white \'hwit\ *adj* **1** : free from color **2** : of the color of new snow or milk **3** : having light skin ~ *n* **1** : color of maximum lightness **2** : white part or thing **3** : person who is light-skinned —**white·ness** *n* —**whit·ish** *adj*

white blood cell *n* : blood cell that does not contain hemoglobin

white·cap \'hwit,kap\ *n* : wave crest breaking into white foam

white–col·lar *adj* : relating to salaried employees with duties not requiring protective or work clothing

white elephant *n* : something costly but of little use or value

white·fish \'hwit,fish\ *n* : freshwater food fish

whit·en \'hwitᵊn\ *vb* : make or become white —**whit·en·er** \'hwitᵊnər\ *n*

white slave *n* : woman or girl held unwillingly for purposes of prostitution —**white slavery** *n*

white·tail \'hwit,tāl\ *n* : No. American deer

white·wash *vb* **1** : whiten with a composition (as of lime and water) **2** : gloss over or cover up faults or wrongdoing —**whitewash** *n*

whith·er \'hwithər\ *adv* **1** : to what place **2** : to what situation, position, degree, or end

¹whit·ing \'hwitiŋ\ *n* : usu. light or silvery food fish

²whiting *n* : pulverized chalk or limestone

whit·tle \'hwitᵊl\ *vb* **-tled; -tling 1** : pare **2** : shape by paring **3** : reduce gradually

whiz, whizz \'hwiz\ *vb* **-zz-** : make a sound like a speeding object —**whiz, whizz** *n*

who \'hü\ *pron* **1** : what or which person or persons **2** : person or persons that **3** : —used to introduce a relative clause

who·dun·it \hü'dənət\ *n* : detective or mystery story

who·ev·er \hü'evər\ *pron* : no matter who

whole \'hōl\ *adj* **1** : being in healthy or sound condition **2** : having all its parts or elements **3** : constituting the total sum of ~ *n* **1** : complete amount or sum **2** : something whole or entire —**on the whole 1** : considering all circumstances **2** : in general —**whole·ness** *n*

whole·heart·ed \'hōl'härtəd\ *adj* : sincere

whole number *n* : integer

whole·sale \'hōl,sāl\ *n* : sale of goods in quantity usu. for resale by a retail merchant ~ *adj* **1** : of or relating to wholesaling **2** : performed on a large scale ~ *vb* **-saled; -sal·ing** : sell at wholesale —**wholesale** *adv* —**whole·sal·er** *n*

whole·some \-səm\ *adj* **1** : promoting mental, spiritual, or bodily health **2** : healthy —**whole·some·ness** *n*

whole wheat *adj* : made of ground entire wheat kernels

whol·ly \'hōlē\ *adv* **1** : totally **2** : solely

whom \'hüm\ *pron, objective case of* WHO

whom·ev·er \hüm'evər\ *pron, objective case of* WHOEVER

whoop \'hwüp, 'hwůp, 'hüp, 'hůp\ *vb* : shout loudly ~ *n* : shout

whooping cough *n* : infectious disease marked by convulsive coughing fits

whop·per \'hwäpər\ *n* : something unusually large or extreme of its kind **2** : monstrous lie

whop·ping \'hwäpiŋ\ *adj* : extremely large

whore \'hōr\ *n* : prostitute

whorl \'hwórl, 'hwərl\ *n* : spiral —**whorled** *adj*

whose \'hüz\ *adj* : of or relating to whom or which ~ *pron* : whose one or ones

who·so·ev·er \,hüsō'evər\ *pron* : whoever

why \'hwī\ *adv* : for what reason, cause, or purpose ~ *conj* 1 : reason for which 2 : for which ~ *n, pl* **whys** : reason — *interj* —used esp. to express surprise

wick \'wik\ *n* : cord that draws up oil, tallow, or wax to be burned

wick·ed \'wikəd\ *adj* 1 : morally bad 2 : harmful or troublesome 3 : very unpleasant 4 : very impressive —**wick·ed·ly** *adv* —**wick·ed·ness** *n*

wick·er \'wikər\ *n* 1 : small pliant branch 2 : wickerwork —**wicker** *adj*

wick·er·work *n* : work made of wickers

wick·et \'wikət\ *n* 1 : small gate, door, or window 2 : frame in cricket or arch in croquet

wide \'wīd\ *adj* **wid·er; wid·est** 1 : covering a vast area 2 : measured at right angles to the length 3 : having a great measure across 4 : opened fully 5 : far from the thing in question ~ *adv* **wid·er; wid·est** 1 : over a great distance 2 : so as to leave considerable space between 3 : fully —**wide·ly** *adv* —**wid·en** \'wīd⁰n\ *vb*

wide–awake *adj* : alert

wide–eyed *adj* 1 : having the eyes wide open 2 : amazed 3 : naive

wide·spread *adj* : widely extended

wid·ow \'widō\ *n* : woman who has lost her husband by death and has not married again ~ *vb* : cause to become a widow —**wid·ow·hood** *n*

wid·ow·er \'widəwər\ *n* : man who has lost his wife by death and has not married again

width \'width\ *n* 1 : distance from side to side 2 : largeness of extent 3 : measured and cut piece of material

wield \'wēld\ *vb* 1 : use or handle esp. effectively 2 : exert —**wield·er** *n*

wie·ner \'wēnər\ *n* : frankfurter

wife \'wīf\ *n, pl* **wives** \'wīvz\ : married woman —**wife·hood** *n* —**wife·less** *adj* —**wife·ly** *adj*

wig \'wig\ *n* : manufactured covering of hair for the head

wig·gle \'wigəl\ *vb* **-gled; -gling** 1 : move with quick jerky or shaking movements 2 : wriggle —**wiggle** *n* —**wig·gler** *n*

wig·gly \-əlē\ *adj* 1 : tending to wiggle 2 : wavy

wig·wag \'wig,wag\ *vb* : signal by a flag or light waved according to a code

wig·wam \'wig,wäm\ *n* : American Indian hut consisting of a framework of poles overlaid with bark, rush mats, or hides

wild \'wīld\ *adj* 1 : living or being in a state of nature and not domesticated or cultivated 2 : unrestrained 3 : turbulent 4 : crazy 5 : uncivilized 6 : erratic ~ *n* 1 : wilderness 2 : undomesticated state ~ *adv* : without control —**wild·ly** *adv* —**wild·ness** *n*

wild·cat \-,kat\ *n* : any of various undomesticated cats (as a lynx) ~ *adj* 1 : not sound or safe 2 : unauthorized

wil·der·ness \'wildərnəs\ *n* : uncultivated and uninhabited region

wild·fire \'wīld,fīr\ *n* : sweeping and destructive fire

wild·fowl *n* : game waterfowl

wild·life \'wīld,līf\ *n* : undomesticated animals

wile \'wīl\ *n* : trick to snare or deceive ~ *vb* **wiled; wil·ing** : lure

will \'wil\ *vb, past* **would** \'wùd\; *pres sing & pl* **will** 1 : wish 2 —used as an auxiliary verb to express (1) desire or willingness (2) customary action (3) simple future time (4) capability (5) determination (6) probability (7) inevitability or (8) a command 3 : dispose of by a will ~ *n* 1 : often determined wish 2 : act, process, or experience of willing 3 : power of controlling one's actions or emotions 4 : legal document disposing of property after death

will·ful, wil·ful \'wilfəl\ *adj* 1 : governed by will without regard to reason 2 : intentional —**will·ful·ly** *adv*

will·ing \'wiliŋ\ *adj* 1 : inclined or favorably disposed in mind 2 : prompt to act 3 : done, borne, or accepted voluntarily or without reluctance —**will·ing·ly** *adv* —**will·ing·ness** *n*

will-o'-the-wisp \,wiləthə'wisp\ *n* 1 : light that appears at night over marshy grounds 2 : misleading or elusive goal or hope

wil·low \'wilō\ *n* : quick-growing shrub or tree with flexible shoots

wil·lowy \'wiləwē\ *adj* : gracefully tall and slender

will·pow·er \'wil,paüər\ *n* : energetic determination

wil·ly–nil·ly \,wilē'nilē\ *adv or adj* : without regard for one's choice

wilt \'wilt\ *vb* **1** : lose or cause to lose freshness and become limp esp. from lack of water **2** : grow weak

wily \'wīlē\ *adj* **wil•i•er; -est** : full of craftiness —**wil•i•ness** *n*

win \'win\ *vb* **won** \'wən\; **win•ning 1** : get possession of esp. by effort **2** : gain victory in battle or a contest **3** : make friendly or favorable ~ *vb* : victory

wince \'wins\ *vb* **winced; winc•ing** : shrink back involuntarily —**wince** *n*

winch \'winch\ *n* : machine for hoisting or pulling with a drum around which rope is wound —**winch** *vb*

¹**wind** \'wind\ *n* **1** : movement of the air **2** : breath **3** : gas in the stomach or intestines **4** : air carrying a scent **5** : intimation ~ *vb* **1** : get a scent of **2** : cause to be out of breath

²**wind** \'wīnd\ *vb* **wound** \'waùnd\; **wind•ing 1** : have or follow a curving course **2** : move or lie to encircle **3** : encircle or cover with something pliable **4** : tighten the spring of ~ *n* : turn or coil —**wind•er** *n*

wind•break \-,brāk\ *n* : trees and shrubs to break the force of the wind

wind•break•er \-,brākər\ *n* : light wind-resistant jacket

wind•fall \'wind,fȯl\ *n* **1** : thing blown down by wind **2** : unexpected benefit

wind instrument *n* : musical instrument (as a flute or horn) sounded by wind and esp. by the breath

wind•lass \'windləs\ *n* : winch esp. for hoisting anchor

wind•mill \'wind,mil\ *n* : machine worked by the wind turning vanes

win•dow \'windō\ *n* **1** : opening in the wall of a building to let in light and air **2** : pane in a window **3** : span of time for something **4** : area of a computer display —**win•dow•less** *adj*

win•dow-shop *vb* : look at the displays in store windows —**win•dow-shop•per** *n*

wind•pipe \'wind,pīp\ *n* : passage for the breath from the larynx to the lungs

wind•shield \'-,shēld\ *n* : transparent screen in front of the occupants of a vehicle

wind•up \'wīnd,əp\ *n* : end —**wind up** *vb*

wind•ward \'windwərd\ *adj* : being in or facing the direction from which the wind is blowing ~ *n* : direction from which the wind is blowing

windy \'windē\ *adj* **wind•i•er; -est 1** : having wind **2** : indulging in useless talk

wine \'wīn\ *n* **1** : fermented grape juice **2** : usu. fermented juice of a plant product (as fruit) used as a beverage ~ *vb* : treat to or drink wine

wing \'wiŋ\ *n* **1** : movable paired appendage for flying **2** : winglike thing **3** *pl* : area at the side of the stage out of sight **4** : faction ~ *vb* **1** : fly **2** : propel through the air —**winged** *adj* —**wing•less** *adj* —**on the wing** : in flight —**under one's wing** : in one's charge or care

wink \'wiŋk\ *vb* **1** : close and open the eyes quickly **2** : avoid seeing or noticing something **3** : twinkle **4** : close and open one eye quickly as a signal or hint ~ *n* **1** : brief sleep **2** : act of winking **3** : instant —**wink•er** *n*

win•ner \'winər\ *n* : one that wins

win•ning \-iŋ\ *n* **1** : victory **2** : money won at gambling ~ *adj* **1** : victorious **2** : charming

win•now \'winō\ *vb* **1** : remove (as chaff) by a current of air **2** : sort or separate something

win•some \'winsəm\ *adj* **1** : causing joy **2** : cheerful or gay —**win•some•ly** *adv* —**win•some•ness** *n*

win•ter \'wintər\ *n* : season between autumn and spring ~ *adj* : sown in autumn for harvest the next spring or summer —**win•ter•time** *n*

win•ter•green \'wintər,grēn\ *n* : low heathlike evergreen plant with red berries

win•try \'wintrē\ *adj* **win•tri•er; -est 1** : characteristic of winter **2** : cold in feeling

wipe \'wīp\ *vb* **wiped; wip•ing 1** : clean or dry by rubbing **2** : remove by rubbing **3** : erase completely **4** : destroy **5** : pass over a surface ~ *n* : act or instance of wiping —**wip•er** *n*

wire \'wīr\ *n* **1** : thread of metal **2** : work made of wire **3** : telegram or cablegram ~ *vb* **1** : provide with wire **2** : bind or mount with wire **3** : telegraph —**wire•less** *adj*

wire•less \-ləs\ *n, chiefly Brit* : radio

wire•tap *vb* : connect into a telephone or telegraph wire to get information —**wiretap** *n* —**wire•tap•per** *n*

wir•ing \'wīriŋ\ *n* : system of wires

wiry \'wīrē\ *adj* **wir•i•er** \'wīrēər\; **-est**

1 : resembling wire 2 : slender yet strong and sinewy **—wir·i·ness** n

wis·dom \'wizdəm\ n 1 : accumulated learning 2 : good sense

wisdom tooth n : last tooth on each half of each human jaw

1wise \'wīz\ n : manner

2wise adj **wis·er; wis·est** 1 : having or showing wisdom, good sense, or good judgment 2 : aware of what is going on **—wise·ly** adv

wise·crack n : clever, smart, or flippant remark ~ vb : make a wisecrack

wish \'wish\ vb 1 : have a desire 2 : express a wish concerning 3 : request ~ n 1 : a wishing or desire 2 : expressed will or desire

wish·bone n : forked bone in front of the breastbone in most birds

wish·ful \-fəl\ adj 1 : expressive of a wish 2 : according with wishes rather than fact

wishy-washy \'wishē,wȯshē, -,wäsh-\ adj : weak or insipid

wisp \'wisp\ n 1 : small bunch of hay or straw 2 : thin strand, strip, fragment, or streak 3 : something frail, slight, or fleeting **—wispy** adj

wis·te·ria \wis'tirēə\ n : pealike woody vine with long clusters of flowers

wist·ful \'wistfəl\ adj : full of longing **—wist·ful·ly** adv **—wist·ful·ness** n

wit \'wit\ n 1 : reasoning power 2 : mental soundness —usu. pl. 3 : quickness and cleverness in handling words and ideas 4 : talent for clever remarks or one noted for witty remarks **—wit·less** adj **—wit·less·ly** adv **—wit·less·ness** n **—wit·ted** adj

witch \'wich\ n 1 : person believed to have magic power 2 : ugly old woman ~ vb : bewitch

witch·craft \'wich,kraft\ n : power or practices of a witch

witch·ery \'wichərē\ n, pl **-er·ies** 1 : witchcraft 2 : charm

witch ha·zel \'wich,hāzəl\ n 1 : shrub having small yellow flowers in fall 2 : alcoholic lotion made from witch hazel bark

witch·hunt n 1 : searching out and persecution of supposed witches 2 : harassment esp. of political opponents

with \'with, 'with\ prep 1 : against, to, or toward 2 : in support of 3 : because of 4 : in the company of 5 : having 6

: despite 7 : containing 8 : by means of

with·draw \with'drȯ, with-\ vb **-drew** \-'drü\; **-drawn** \-'drȯn\; **-draw·ing** \-'drȯiŋ\ 1 : take back or away 2 : call back or retract 3 : go away 4 : terminate one's participation in or use of **—with·draw·al** \-'drȯəl\ n

with·drawn \with'drȯn\ adj : socially detached and unresponsive

with·er \'withər\ vb 1 : shrivel 2 : lose or cause to lose energy, force, or freshness

with·ers \'withərz\ n pl : ridge between the shoulder bones of a horse

with·hold \with'hōld, with-\ vb **-held** \-'held\; **-hold·ing** 1 : hold back 2 : refrain from giving

with·in \with'in, with-\ adv 1 : in or into the interior 2 : inside oneself ~ prep 1 : in or to the inner part of 2 : in the limits or compass of

with·out \with'aut, with-\ prep 1 : outside 2 : lacking 3 : unaccompanied or unmarked by **—without** adv

with·stand \with'stand, with-\ vb **-stood** \-'stüd\; **-stand·ing** : oppose successfully

wit·ness \'witnəs\ n 1 : testimony 2 : one who testifies 3 : one present at a transaction to testify that it has taken place 4 : one who has personal knowledge or experience 5 : something serving as proof ~ vb 1 : bear witness 2 : act as legal witness of 3 : furnish proof of 4 : be a witness of 5 : be the scene of

wit·ti·cism \'witə,sizəm\ n : witty saying or phrase

wit·ting \'witiŋ\ adj : intentional **—wit·ting·ly** adv

wit·ty \'witē\ adj **-ti·er; -est** : marked by or full of wit **—wit·ti·ly** \'witᵊlē\ adv **—wit·ti·ness** n

wives pl of WIFE

wiz·ard \'wizərd\ n 1 : magician 2 : very clever person **—wiz·ard·ry** \-ərdrē\ n

wiz·ened \'wizᵊnd\ adj : dried up

wob·ble \'wäbəl\ vb **-bled; -bling** 1 : move or cause to move with an irregular rocking motion 2 : tremble 3 : waver **—wobble** n **—wob·bly** \'wäbəlē\ adj

woe \'wō\ n 1 : deep suffering 2 : misfortune

woe·be·gone \'wōbi,gȯn\ adj : exhibiting woe, sorrow, or misery

woe·ful \'wōfəl\ *adj* **1** : full of woe **2** : bringing woe —**woe·ful·ly** *adv*

woke *past of* WAKE

woken *past part of* WAKE

wolf \'wulf\ *n, pl* **wolves** \'wulvz\ : large doglike predatory mammal ~ *vb* : eat greedily —**wolf·ish** *adj*

wol·fram \'wulfrəm\ *n* : tungsten

wol·ver·ine \,wulvə'rēn\ *n, pl* **-ines** : flesh–eating mammal related to the weasels

wom·an \'wumən\ *n, pl* **wom·en** \'wimən\ **1** : adult female person **2** : womankind **3** : feminine nature — **wom·an·hood** \-,hud\ *n* —**wom·an·ish** *adj*

wom·an·kind \-,kīnd\ *n* : females of the human race

wom·an·ly \-lē\ *adj* : having qualities characteristic of a woman —**wom·an·li·ness** \-lēnəs\ *n*

womb \'wüm\ *n* : uterus

won *past of* WIN

won·der \'wəndər\ *n* **1** : cause of astonishment or surprise **2** : feeling (as of astonishment) aroused by something extraordinary ~ *vb* **1** : feel surprise **2** : feel curiosity or doubt

won·der·ful \'wəndərfəl\ *adj* **1** : exciting wonder **2** : unusually good —**won·der·ful·ly** *adv* —**won·der·ful·ness** *n*

won·der·land \-,land, -lənd\ *n* **1** : fairylike imaginary realm **2** : place that excites admiration or wonder

won·der·ment \-mənt\ *n* : wonder

won·drous \'wəndrəs\ *adj* : wonderful —**won·drous·ly** *adv* —**won·drous·ness** *n*

wont \'wont, 'wōnt\ *adj* : accustomed ~ *n* : habit —**wont·ed** *adj*

woo \'wü\ *vb* : try to gain the love or favor of —**woo·er** *n*

wood \'wud\ *n* **1** : dense growth of trees usu. smaller than a forest —often pl. **2** : hard fibrous substance of trees and shrubs beneath the bark **3** : wood prepared for some use (as burning) ~ *adj* **1** : wooden **2** : suitable for working with wood **3** *or* **woods** \'wudz\ : living or growing in woods — **wood·chop·per** *n* —**wood·pile** *n* —**wood·shed** *n*

wood·bine \'wud,bīn\ *n* : climbing vine

wood·chuck \-,chək\ *n* : thick-bodied grizzled animal of No. America

wood·craft *n* **1** : skill and practice in matters relating to the woods **2** : skill in making articles from wood

wood·cut \-,kət\ *n* **1** : relief printing surface engraved on wood **2** : print from a woodcut

wood·ed \'wudəd\ *adj* : covered with woods

wood·en \'wud°n\ *adj* **1** : made of wood **2** : lacking resilience **3** : lacking ease, liveliness or interest —**wood·en·ly** *adv* —**wood·en·ness** *n*

wood·land \-lond, -,land\ *n* : land covered with trees

wood·peck·er \'wud,pekər\ *n* : brightly marked bird with a hard bill for drilling into trees

woods·man \'wudzmən\ *n* : person who works in the woods

wood·wind \'wud,wind\ *n* : one of a group of wind instruments (as a flute or oboe)

wood·work *n* : work (as interior house fittings) made of wood

woody \'wudē\ *adj* **wood·i·er; -est 1** : abounding with woods **2** : of, containing, or like wood fibers — **wood·i·ness** *n*

woof \'wuf\ *n* : weft

wool \'wul\ *n* **1** : soft hair of some mammals and esp. the sheep **2** : something (as a textile) made of wool —**wooled** \'wuld\ *adj*

wool·en, wool·len \'wulən\ *adj* **1** : made of wool **2** : relating to the manufacture of woolen products — *n* **1** : woolen fabric **2** : woolen garments —usu. pl.

wool·gath·er·ing *n* : idle daydreaming

wool·ly \'wulē\ *adj* **-li·er; -est 1** : of, relating to, or bearing wool **2** : consisting of or resembling wool **3** : confused or turbulent

woo·zy \'wüzē\ *adj* **-zi·er; -est 1** : confused or somewhat dizzy, nauseated, or weak —**woo·zi·ness** *n*

word \'wərd\ *n* **1** : brief remark **2** : speech sound or series of speech sounds that communicates a meaning **3** : written representation of a word **4** : order **5** : news **6** : promise **7** *pl* : dispute ~ *vb* : express in words —**word·less** *adj*

word·ing \'wərdiŋ\ *n* : verbal expression

word processing *n* : production of structured and printed documents through a computer program (**word processor**) —**word process** *vb*

word·y \\'wərdē\ adj **word·i·er; -est** : using many words —**word·i·ness** n

wore past of WEAR

work \\'wərk\ n 1 : labor 2 : employment 3 : task 4 : something (as an artistic production) produced by mental effort or physical labor 5 pl : place where industrial labor is done 6 pl : moving parts of a mechanism 7 : workmanship ~ adj 1 : suitable for wear while working 2 : used for work ~ vb **worked** \\'wərkt\ or **wrought** \\'ròt\, **work·ing** 1 : bring to pass 2 : create by expending labor upon 3 : bring or get into a form or condition 4 : set or keep in operation 5 : solve 6 : cause to labor 7 : arrange 8 : excite 9 : labor 10 : perform work regularly for wages 11 : function according to plan or design 12 : produce a desired effect —**work·bench** n —**work·man** \-mən\ n —**work·room** n —**in the works** : in preparation

work·able \\'wərkəbəl\ adj 1 : capable of being worked 2 : feasible —**work·able·ness** n

work·a·day \\'wərkə,dā\ adj 1 : relating to or suited for working days 2 : ordinary

work·a·hol·ic \,wərkə'hòlik, -'häl-\ n : compulsive worker

work·day \\'wərk,dā\ n 1 : day on which work is done 2 : period of time during which one is working

work·er \\'wərkər\ n : person who works esp. for wages

work·horse n 1 : horse used for hard work 2 : person who does most of the work of a group task

work·house n : place of confinement for persons who have committed minor offenses

work·ing \\'wərkiŋ\ adj 1 : adequate to allow work to be done 2 : adopted or assumed to help further work or activity ~ n : operation —usu. used in pl.

work·ing·man \\'wərkiŋ,man\ n : worker

work·man·like \-,līk\ adj : worthy of a good workman

work·man·ship \-,ship\ n 1 : art or skill of a workman 2 : quality of a piece of work

work·out \\'wərk,aut\ n : exercise to improve one's fitness

work out vb 1 : bring about by effort 2 : solve 3 : develop 4 : to be successful 5 : perform exercises

work·shop n 1 : small establishment for manufacturing or handicrafts 2 : seminar emphasizing exchange of ideas and practical methods

world \\'wərld\ n 1 : universe 2 : earth with its inhabitants and all things upon it 3 : people in general 4 : great number or quantity 5 : class of persons or their sphere of interest

world·ly \\'wərldlē\ adj 1 : devoted to this world and its pursuits rather than to religion 2 : sophisticated —**world·li·ness** n

world·ly-wise adj : possessing understanding of human affairs

world·wide adj : extended throughout the entire world —**worldwide** adv

worm \\'wərm\ n 1 : earthworm or a similar animal 2 pl : disorder caused by parasitic worms ~ vb 1 : move or cause to move in a slow and indirect way 2 : to free from worms —**wormy** adj

worm·wood \\'wərm,wud\ n 1 : aromatic woody herb (as sagebrush) 2 : something bitter or grievous

worn past part of WEAR

worn-out \\'wòrn'aut\ adj : exhausted or used up by or as if by wear

wor·ri·some \\'wərēsəm\ adj 1 : causing worry 2 : inclined to worry

wor·ry \\'wərē\ vb **-ried; -ry·ing** 1 : shake and mangle with the teeth 2 : disturb 3 : feel or express anxiety ~ n, pl **-ries** 1 : anxiety 2 : cause of anxiety —**wor·ri·er** n

worse \\'wərs\ adj, comparative of BAD or of ILL 1 : bad or evil in a greater degree 2 : more unwell ~ n 1 : one that is worse 2 : greater degree of badness ~ adv, comparative of BAD or of ILL : in a worse manner

wors·en \\'wərsⁿn\ vb : make or become worse

wor·ship \\'wərshəp\ n 1 : reverence toward a divine being or supernatural power 2 : expression of reverence 3 : extravagant respect or devotion ~ vb **-shiped** or **-shipped; -ship·ing** or **-ship·ping** 1 : honor or reverence 2 : perform or take part in worship —**wor·ship·er, wor·ship·per** n

worst \\'wərst\ adj, superlative of BAD or of ILL 1 : most bad, evil, ill, or corrupt 2 : most unfavorable, unpleasant, or painful ~ n : one that is worst ~ adv, *superlative of* ILL *or of* BAD *or* BADLY : to the extreme degree of badness ~ *vb* : defeat

wor·sted \'wústəd, 'wərstəd\ *n* : smooth compact wool yarn or fabric made from such yarn

worth \'wərth\ *prep* **1** : equal in value to **2** : deserving of ~ *n* **1** : monetary value **2** : value of something measured by its qualities **3** : moral or personal merit

worth·less \-ləs\ *adj* **1** : lacking worth **2** : useless —**worth·less·ness** *n*

worth·while \-'hwil\ *adj* : being worth the time or effort spent

wor·thy \'wərthē\ *adj* **-thi·er; -est 1** : having worth or value **2** : having sufficient worth ~ *n, pl* **-thies** : worthy person —**wor·thi·ly** *adv* —**wor·thi·ness** *n*

would \'wúd\ *past of* WILL —used to express (1) preference (2) intent (3) habitual action (4) contingency (5) probability or (6) a request

would–be \'wúd'bē\ *adj* : desiring or pretending to be

¹wound \'wünd\ *n* **1** : injury in which the skin is broken **2** : mental hurt ~ *vb* : inflict a wound to or in

²wound \'waúnd\ *past of* WIND

wove *past of* WEAVE

woven *past part of* WEAVE

wrack \'rak\ *n* : ruin

wraith \'rāth\ *n, pl* **wraiths** \'rāths, 'rāthz\ **1** : ghost **2** : insubstantial appearance

wran·gle \'raŋgəl\ *vb or n* : quarrel —**wran·gler** *n*

wrap \'rap\ *vb* **-pp- 1** : cover esp. by winding or folding **2** : envelop and secure for transportation or storage **3** : enclose, surround, or conceal wholly **4** : coil, fold, draw, or twine about something ~ *n* **1** : wrapper or wrapping **2** : outer garment (as a shawl)

wrap·per \'rapər\ *n* **1** : that in which something is wrapped **2** : one that wraps

wrap·ping *n* : something used to wrap an object

wrath \'rath\ *n* : violent anger —**wrath·ful** \-fəl\ *adj*

wreak \'rēk\ *vb* **1** : inflict **2** : bring about

wreath \'rēth\ *n, pl* **wreaths** \'rēthz, 'rēths\ : something (as boughs) intertwined into a circular shape

wreathe \'rēth\ *vb* **wreathed; wreath·ing 1** : shape into or take on the shape

of a wreath **2** : decorate or cover with a wreath

wreck \'rek\ *n* **1** : broken remains (as of a ship or vehicle) after heavy damage **2** : something disabled or in a state of ruin **3** : an individual who has become weak or infirm **4** : action of breaking up or destroying something ~ *vb* : ruin or damage by breaking up

wreck·age \'rekij\ *n* **1** : act of wrecking **2** : remains of a wreck

wreck·er \-ər\ *n* **1** : automotive vehicle for removing disabled cars **2** : one that wrecks or tears down and removes buildings

wren \'ren\ *n* : small mostly brown singing bird

wrench \'rench\ *vb* **1** : pull with violent twisting or force **2** : injure or disable by a violent twisting or straining ~ *n* **1** : forcible twisting **2** : tool for exerting a twisting force

wrest \'rest\ *vb* **1** : pull or move by a forcible twisting movement **2** : gain with difficulty ~ *n* : forcible twist

wres·tle \'resəl, 'ras-\ *vb* **-tled; -tling 1** : scuffle with and attempt to throw and pin an opponent **2** : compete against in wrestling **3** : struggle (as with a problem) ~ *n* : action or an instance of wrestling —**wres·tler** \'reslər, 'ras-\

wres·tling \'resliŋ\ *n* : sport in which 2 opponents try to throw and pin each other

wretch \'rech\ *n* **1** : miserable unhappy person **2** : vile person

wretch·ed \'rechəd\ *adj* **1** : deeply afflicted, dejected, or distressed **2** : grievous **3** : inferior —**wretch·ed·ly** *adv* —**wretch·ed·ness** *n*

wrig·gle \'rigəl\ *vb* **-gled; -gling 1** : twist and turn restlessly **2** : move along by twisting and turning —**wrig·gle** *n* —**wrig·gler** \'rigələr\ *n*

wring \'riŋ\ *vb* **wrung** \'rəŋ\; **wring·ing 1** : squeeze or twist out moisture **2** : get by or as if by twisting or pressing **3** : twist together in anguish **4** : pain —**wring·er** *n*

wrin·kle \'riŋkəl\ *n* : crease or small fold on a surface (as in the skin or in cloth) ~ *vb* **-kled; -kling** : develop or cause to develop wrinkles —**wrin·kly** \-kəlē\ *adj*

wrist \'rist\ *n* : joint or region between the hand and the arm

writ \'rit\ *n* **1** : something written **2** : legal order in writing

write \'rīt\ *vb* **wrote** \'rōt\; **writ•ten** \'rit°n\; **writ•ing** \'rītiŋ\ **1** : form letters or words on a surface **2** : form the letters or the words of (as on paper) **3** : make up and set down for others to read **4** : write a letter to —**write off** *vb* : cancel

writ•er \'rītər\ *n* : one that writes esp. as a business or occupation

writhe \'rīth\ *vb* **writhed; writh•ing** : twist and turn this way and that

writ•ing \'rītiŋ\ *n* **1** : act of one that writes **2** : handwriting **3** : something written or printed

wrong \'rôŋ\ *n* **1** : unfair or unjust act **2** : something that is contrary to justice **3** : state of being or doing wrong ~ *adj* **wrong•er** \'rôŋər\; **wrong•est** \'rôŋəst\ **1** : sinful **2** : not right according to a standard **3** : unsuitable **4** : incorrect ~ *adv* **1** : in a wrong di-

rection or manner **2** : incorrectly ~ *vb* **wronged; wrong•ing 1** : do wrong to **2** : treat unjustly —**wrong•ly** *adv*

wrong-do•er \-'düər\ *n* : one who does wrong —**wrong•do•ing** \-'düiŋ\ *n*

wrong•ful \-fəl\ *adj* **1** : wrong **2** : illegal —**wrong•ful•ly** *adv* —**wrong•ful•ness** *n*

wrong•head•ed \-'ròŋ'hedəd\ *adj* : stubborn in clinging to wrong opinion or principles —**wrong•head•ed•ly** *adv* —**wrong•head•ed•ness** *n*

wrote *past of* WRITE

wrought \'ròt\ *adj* **1** : formed **2** : hammered into shape **3** : deeply stirred

wrung *past of* WRING

wry \'rī\ *adj* **wri•er** \'rīər\; **wri•est** \'rīəst\ **1** : turned abnormally to one side **2** : twisted **3** : cleverly and often ironically humorous —**wry•ly** *adv* —**wry•ness** *n*

X

x \'eks\ *n, pl* **x's** *or* **xs** \'eksəz\ **1** : 24th letter of the alphabet **2** : unknown quantity ~ *vb* **x-ed; x-ing** *or* **x'ing** : cancel with a series of *x's*—usu. with *out*

xe•non \'zē,nän,'zen,än\ *n* : heavy gaseous chemical element

xe•no•pho•bia \,zenə'fōbēə, ,zēn-\ *n* : fear and hatred of foreign people and things —**xe•no•phobe** \'zenə,fōb, 'zēn-\ *n*

Xmas \'krisməs\ *n* : Christmas

x–ra•di•a•tion *n* **1** : exposure to X rays **2** : radiation consisting of X rays

x–ray \'eks,rā\ *vb* : examine, treat, or photograph with X rays

X ray *n* **1** : radiation of short wavelength that is able to penetrate solids **2** : photograph taken with X rays —**X-ray** *adj*

xy•lo•phone \'zīlə,fōn\ *n* : musical instrument with wooden bars that are struck —**xy•lo•phon•ist** \-,fōnist\ *n*

Y

y \'wī\ *n, pl* **y's** *or* **ys** \'wīz\ : 25th letter of the alphabet

1.-y \ē\ *adj suffix* **1** : composed or full of **2** : like **3** : performing or apt to perform an action

2.-y \ē\ *n suffix, pl* **-ies 1** : state, condition, or quality **2** : activity, place of

business, or goods dealt with **3** : whole group

yacht \'yät\ *n* **1** : luxurious pleasure boat ~ *vb* : race or cruise in a yacht

ya•hoo \'yähü, 'yä-\ *n, pl* **-hoos** : uncouth or stupid person

yak \'yak\ *n* : big hairy Asian ox

yam \\'yam\\ n **1** : edible root of a tropical vine **2** : deep orange sweet potato

yam·mer \\'yamər\\ vb **1** : whimper **2** : chatter —**yammer** n

yank \\'yaŋk\\ n : strong sudden pull —**yank** vb

Yank \\'yaŋk\\ n : Yankee

Yan·kee \\'yaŋkē\\ n : native or inhabitant of New England, the northern U.S., or the U.S.

yap \\'yap\\ vb **-pp-** **1** : yelp **2** : chatter —**yap** n

¹yard \\'yärd\\ n **1** : 3 feet **2** : long spar for supporting and spreading a sail —**yard·age** \\-ij\\ n

²yard n **1** : enclosed roofless area **2** : grounds of a building **3** : work area

yard·arm \\'yärd,ärm\\ n : end of the yard of a square-rigged ship

yard·stick n **1** : measuring stick 3 feet long **2** : standard for judging

yar·mul·ke \\'yäməkə, 'yär-, -məl-\\ n : a small brimless cap worn by Jewish males in a synagogue

yarn \\'yärn\\ n **1** : spun fiber for weaving or knitting **2** : tale

yaw \\'yò\\ vb : deviate erratically from a course —**yaw** n

yawl \\'yòl\\ n : sailboat with 2 masts

yawn \\'yòn\\ vb : open the mouth wide ~ n : deep breath through a wide-open mouth —**yawn·er** n

ye \\'yē\\ pron : you

yea \\'yā\\ adv **1** : yes **2** : truly ~ n : affirmative vote

year \\'yir\\ n **1** : period of about 365 days **2** pl : age

year·book n : annual report of the year's events

year·ling \\'yirliŋ, 'yərlən\\ n : one that is or is rated as a year old

year·ly \\'yirlē\\ adj : annual —**yearly** adv

yearn \\'yərn\\ vb **1** : feel desire esp. for what one cannot have **2** : feel tenderness or compassion

yearn·ing \\-iŋ\\ n : tender or urgent desire

yeast \\'yēst\\ n : froth or sediment in sugary liquids containing a tiny fungus and used in making alcoholic liquors and as a leaven in baking —**yeasty** adj

yell \\'yel\\ vb : utter a loud cry —**yell** n

yel·low \\'yelō\\ adj **1** : of the color yellow **2** : sensational **3** : cowardly ~ vb : make or turn yellow ~ n **1** : color of lemons **2** : yolk of an egg —**yel·low·ish** \\'yeləwish\\ adj

yellow fever n : virus disease marked by prostration, jaundice, fever, and often hemorrhage

yellow jacket n : wasp with yellow stripes

yelp \\'yelp\\ vb : utter a sharp quick shrill cry —**yelp** n

yen \\'yen\\ n : strong desire

yeo·man \\'yōmən\\ n **1** : attendant or officer in a royal or noble household **2** : small farmer **3** : naval petty officer with clerical duties —**yeo·man·ry** \\-rē\\ n

-yer —see **-ER**

yes \\'yes\\ adv —used to express consent or agreement ~ n : affirmative answer

ye·shi·va, ye·shi·vah \\yə'shēvə\\ n, pl **yeshivas** or **ye·shi·voth** \\-,shē'vōt, -'vōth\\ : Jewish school

yes-man \\'yes,man\\ n : person who agrees with every opinion or suggestion of a boss

yes·ter·day \\'yestərdē\\ adv **1** : on the day preceding today **2** : only a short time ago ~ n **1** : day last past **2** : time not long past

yet \\'yet\\ adv **1** : in addition **2** : up to now **3** : so soon as now **4** : nevertheless ~ conj : but

yew \\'yü\\ n : evergreen tree or shrubs with dark stiff poisonous needles

yield \\'yēld\\ vb **1** : surrender **2** : grant **3** : bear as a crop **4** : produce **5** : cease opposition or resistance ~ n : quantity produced or returned

yo·del \\'yōdəl\\ vb **-deled** or **-delled; -del·ing** or **-del·ling** : sing by abruptly alternating between chest voice and falsetto —**yodel** n —**yo·del·er** \\'yōdələr\\ n

yo·ga \\'yōgə\\ n : system of exercises for attaining bodily or mental control and well-being

yo·gi \\'yōgē\\ : person who practices yoga

yo·gurt \\'yōgərt\\ n : fermented slightly acid soft food made from milk

yoke \\'yōk\\ n **1** : neck frame for coupling draft animals or for carrying loads **2** : clamp **3** : slavery **4** : tie or link **5** : piece of a garment esp. at the shoulder ~ vb **yoked; yok·ing** **1** : couple with a yoke **2** : join

yo·kel \\'yōkəl\\ n : naive and gullible country person

yolk \'yōk\ *n* : yellow part of an egg —
	yolked \'yōkt\ *adj*
Yom Kip·pur \,yōmki'pur, ,yäm-,
	-'kipər\ *n* : Jewish holiday observed
	in September or October with fasting
	and prayer as a day of atonement
yon \'yän\ *adj or adv* : YONDER
yon·der \'yändər\ *adv* : at or to that
	place ~ *adj* : distant
yore \'yōr\ *n* : time long past
you \'yü\ *pron* **1** : person or persons ad-
	dressed **2** : person in general
young \'yəŋ\ *adj* **young·er** \'yəŋgər\;
	young·est \'yəŋgəst\ **1** : being in the
	first or an early stage of life, growth,
	or development **2** : recently come into
	being **3** : youthful ~ *n, pl* **young**
	: persons or animals that are young —
	young·ish \-ish\ *adj*
young·ster \-stər\ *n* **1** : young person **2**
	: child
your \'yər, 'yür, 'yōr\ *adj* : relating to
	you or yourself
yours \'yürz, 'yōrz\ *pron* : the ones be-
	longing to you

your·self \yər'self\ *pron, pl* **your·selves**
	\-'selvz\ : you —used reflexively or
	for emphasis
youth \'yüth\ *n, pl* **youths** \'yüthz,
	'yüths\ **1** : period between childhood
	and maturity **2** : young man **3** : young
	persons **4** : state or quality of being
	young, fresh, or vigorous
youth·ful \'yüthfəl\ *adj* **1** : relating to or
	appropriate to youth **2** : young **3**
	: vigorous and fresh —**youth·ful·ly**
	adv —**youth·ful·ness** *n*
yowl \'yaúl\ *vb* : utter a loud long
	mournful cry —**yowl** *n*
yo-yo \'yō,yō\ *n, pl* **-yos** : toy that falls
	from or rises to the hand as it unwinds
	and rewinds on a string
yuc·ca \'yəkə\ *n* : any of several plants
	related to the lilies that grow in dry
	regions
yule \'yül\ *n* : Christmas —**yule·tide**
	\-,tīd\ *n*
yum·my \'yəmē\ *adj* **-mi·er; -est**
	: highly attractive or pleasing

Z

z \'zē\ *n, pl* **z's** *or* **zs** : 26th letter of the
	alphabet
za·ny \'zānē\ *n, pl* **-nies** **1** : clown **2**
	: silly person ~ *adj* **-ni·er; -est** : crazy
	or foolish —**za·ni·ly** *adv* — **za·ni-
	ness** *n*
zeal \'zēl\ *n* : enthusiasm
zeal·ot \'zelət\ *n* : fanatical partisan
zeal·ous \'zeləs\ *adj* : filled with zeal —
	zeal·ous·ly *adv* —**zeal·ous·ness** *n*
ze·bra \'zēbrə\ *n* : horselike African
	mammal marked with light and dark
	stripes
zeit·geist \'tsīt,gīst, 'zīt-\ *n* : general
	spirit of an era
ze·nith \'zēnəth\ *n* : highest point
zeph·yr \'zefər\ *n* : gentle breeze
zep·pe·lin \'zepələn\ *n* : rigid airship
	like a blimp
ze·ro \'zērō\ *n, pl* **-ros** **1** : number rep-
	resented by the symbol 0 or the sym-
	bol itself **2** : starting point **3** : lowest
	point ~ *adj* : having no size or quan-
	tity
zest \'zest\ *n* **1** : quality of enhancing

enjoyment **2** : keen enjoyment —
	zest·ful \-fəl\ *adj* —**zest·ful·ly** *adv* —
	zest·ful·ness *n*
zig·zag \'zig,zag\ *n* : one of a series of
	short sharp turns or angles ~ *adj*
	: having zigzags ~ *adv* : in or by a
	zigzag path ~ *vb* **-gg-** : proceed along
	a zigzag path
zil·lion \'zilyən\ *n* : large indeterminate
	number
zinc \'ziŋk\ *n* : bluish white crystaline
	metallic chemical element
zing \'ziŋ\ *n* **1** : shrill humming noise **2**
	: energy —**zing** *vb*
zin·nia \'zinēə, 'zēnyə\ *n* : American
	herb widely grown for its showy
	flowers
¹zip \'zip\ *vb* **-pp-** : move or act with
	speed ~ *n* : energy
²zip *vb* **-pp-** : close or open with a zip-
	per
zip code *n* : number that identifies a
	U.S. postal delivery area
zip·per \'zipər\ *n* : fastener consisting of
	2 rows of interlocking teeth

zip•py \'zipē\ *adj* **-pi•er; -est** : brisk

zir•con \'zər,kän\ *n* : zirconium-containing mineral sometimes used in jewelry

zir•co•ni•um \,zər'kōnēəm\ *n* : corrosion-resistant gray metallic element

zith•er \'zithər, 'zith-\ *n* : stringed musical instrument played by plucking

zi•ti \'zētē\ *n, pl* **ziti** : short tubular pasta

zo•di•ac \'zōdē,ak\ *n* : imaginary belt in the heavens encompassing the paths of the planets and divided into 12 signs used in astrology —**zo•di•a•cal** \zō'dīəkəl\ *adj*

zom•bie \'zämbē\ *n* : person thought to have died and been brought back to life without free will

zon•al \'zōnᵊl\ *adj* : of, relating to, or having the form of a zone —**zon•al•ly** *adv*

zone \'zōn\ *n* **1** : division of the earth's surface based on latitude and climate

2 : distinctive area ~ *vb* **zoned; zoning 1** : mark off into zones **2** : reserve for special purposes —**zo•na•tion** \zō-'nāshən\ *n*

zoo \'zü\ *n, pl* **zoos** : collection of living animals usu. for public display —**zoo•keep•er** *n*

zo•ol•o•gy \zō'äləjē\ *n* : science of animals —**zo•o•log•i•cal** \,zōə'läjikəl\ *adj* —**zo•ol•o•gist** \zō'äləjist\ *n*

zoom \'züm\ *vb* **1** : move with a loud hum or buzz **2** : move or increase with great speed —**zoom** *n*

zuc•chi•ni \zù'kēnē\ *n, pl* **-ni** *or* **-nis** : summer squash with smooth cylindrical dark green fruits

zwie•back \'swēbak, 'swī-, 'zwē-, 'zwī-\ *n* : biscuit of baked, sliced, and toasted bread

zy•gote \'zī,gōt\ *n* : cell formed by the union of 2 sexual cells —**zy•got•ic** \zī'gätik\ *adj*

Abbreviations

Most of these abbreviations have been given in one form. Variation in use of periods, in type, and in capitalization is frequent and widespread (as *mph, MPH, m.p.h., Mph*).

abbr abbreviation
AC alternating current
acad academic, academy
AD in the year of our Lord
adj adjective
adv adverb, advertisement
advt advertisement
AF air force, audio frequency
agric agricultural, agriculture
AK Alaska
aka also known as
AL, Ala Alabama
alg algebra
Alta Alberta
a.m., AM before noon
Am, Amer America, American
amp ampere
amt amount
anc ancient
anon anonymous
ans answer
ant antonym
APO army post office
approx approximate, approximately
Apr April
apt apartment, aptitude
AR Arkansas
arith arithmetic
Ariz Arizona
Ark Arkansas
art article, artificial
assn association
assoc associate, associated, association
asst assistant
ATM automated teller machine
att attached, attention, attorney
attn attention
atty attorney
Aug August
auth authentic, author, authorized
aux, auxil auxiliary
av avoirdupois

AV audiovisual
ave avenue
avg average
AZ Arizona
BA bachelor of arts
bal balance
bar barometer, barrel
bbl barrel, barrels
BC before Christ, British Columbia
BCE before the Christian Era, before the Common Era
bet between
biog biographer, biographical, biography
biol biologic, biological, biologist, biology
bldg building
blvd boulevard
BO backorder, best offer, body odor, box office, branch office
Brit Britain, British
bro brother, brothers
bros brothers
BS bachelor of science
Btu British thermal unit
bu bureau, bushel
c carat, cent, centimeter, century, chapter, circa, cup
C Celsius, centigrade
ca circa
CA, Cal, Calif California
cal calendar, caliber, calorie
Can, Canad Canada, Canadian
cap capacity, capital, capitalize, capitalized
Capt captain
CB citizens band
CDT central daylight time
cen central
cert certificate, certification, certified, certify
cf compare
chap chapter

chem chemistry
cir circle, circuit, circular, circumference
civ civil, civilian
cm centimeter
co company, county
CO Colorado
c/o care of
COD cash on delivery, collect on delivery
col colonial, colony, color, colored, column, counsel
Col colonel, Colorado
Colo Colorado
comp comparative, compensation, compiled, compiler, composition, compound, comprehensive, comptroller
cong congress, congressional
conj conjunction
Conn Connecticut
cont continued
contr contract, contraction
corp corporal, corporation
corr corrected, correction
cp compare, coupon
CPR cardiopulmonary resuscitation
cr credit, creditor
CSA Confederate States of America
CST Central standard time
ct carat, cent, count, court
CT central time, certified teacher, Connecticut
cu cubic
cur currency, current
CZ Canal Zone
d penny
DA district attorney
dag dekagram
dal dekaliter
dam dekameter
dbl double
DC direct current, District of Columbia
DDS doctor of dental science, doctor of dental surgery
DE Delaware
dec deceased, decrease
Dec December
deg degree
Del Delaware
Dem Democrat, Democratic
dept department

det detached, detachment, detail, determine
dg decigram
dia, diam diameter
diag diagonal, diagram
dict dictionary
dif, diff difference
dim dimension, diminished
dir director
disc discount
dist distance, district
div divided, dividend, division, divorced
dl deciliter
dm decimeter
DMD doctor of dental medicine
DOB date of birth
doz dozen
DP data processing
dr dram, drive, drum
Dr doctor
DST daylight saving time
DUI driving under the influence
DWI driving while intoxicated
dz dozen
e east, eastern, excellent
ea each
ecol ecological, ecology
econ economics, economist, economy
EDT Eastern daylight time
e.g. for example
EKG electrocardiogram, electrocardiograph
elec electric, electrical, electricity
elem elementary
eng engine, engineer, engineering
Eng England, English
esp especially
EST Eastern standard time
ET eastern time
et al and others
etc et cetera
ex example, express, extra
exec executive
f false, female, feminine
F, Fah, Fahr Fahrenheit
Feb February
fed federal, federation
fem female, feminine
FL, Fla Florida
fl oz fluid ounce
FPO fleet post office
fr father, friar, from
Fri Friday

ft feet, foot, fort
fut future
FYI for your information
g gram
Ga, GA Georgia
gal gallery, gallon
gen general
geog geographic, geographical, geography
geol geologic, geological, geology
geom geometric, geometrical, geometry
gm gram
GMT Greenwich mean time
GOP Grand Old Party (Republican)
gov government, governor
govt government
GP general practice, general practitioner
gr grade, grain, gram
gram grammar, grammatical
gt great
GU Guam
hd head
hf half
hgt height
hgwy highway
HI Hawaii
hist historian, historical, history
hon honor, honorable, honorary
hr here, hour
HS high school
ht height
HT Hawaiian time
hwy highway
i intransitive, island, isle
Ia, IA Iowa
ICU intensive care unit
ID Idaho, identification
i.e. that is
IL, Ill Illinois
imp imperative, imperfect
in inch
IN Indiana
inc incomplete, incorporated
ind independent
Ind Indian, Indiana
inf infinitive
int interest
interj interjection
intl, intnl international
ital italic, italicized
Jan January
JD juvenile delinquent

jour journal, journeyman
JP justice of the peace
jr, jun junior
JV junior varsity
Kans Kansas
kg kilogram
km kilometer
KS Kansas
kW kilowatt
Ky, KY Kentucky
l late, left, liter, long
L large
La Louisiana
LA Los Angeles, Louisiana
lat latitude
lb pound
lg large, long
lib liberal, librarian, library
long longitude
m male, masculine, meter, mile
M medium
MA Massachusetts
Man Manitoba
Mar March
masc masculine
Mass Massachusetts
math mathematical, mathematician
max maximum
Md Maryland
MD doctor of medicine, Maryland
MDT mountain daylight time
Me, ME Maine
med medium
mg milligram
mgr manager
MI, Mich Michigan
mid middle
min minimum, minor, minute
Minn Minnesota
misc miscellaneous
Miss Mississippi
ml milliliter
mm millimeter
MN Minnesota
mo month
Mo, MO Missouri
Mon Monday
Mont Montana
mpg miles per gallon
mph miles per hour
MRI magnetic resonance imaging
MS Mississippi
MST Mountain standard time
mt mount, mountain

MT Montana, Mountain time
n neuter, noun
N north, northern
NA North America, not applicable
nat national, native, natural
natl national
naut nautical
NB New Brunswick
NC North Carolina
ND, N Dak North Dakota
NE, Neb, Nebr Nebraska
neg negative
neut neuter
Nev Nevada
Nfld Newfoundland
NH New Hampshire
NJ New Jersey
NM, N Mex New Mexico
no north, number
Nov November
NR not rated
NS Nova Scotia
NV Nevada
NWT Northwest Territories
NY New York
NYC New York City
O Ohio
obj object, objective
occas occasionally
Oct October
off office, officer, official
OH Ohio
OJ orange juice
OK, Okla Oklahoma
Ont Ontario
opp opposite
OR, Ore, Oreg Oregon
orig original, originally
oz ounce, ounces
p page
Pa Pennsylvania
PA Pennsylvania, public address
PAC political action committee
par paragraph, parallel
part participle, particular
pass passenger, passive
pat patent
PC percent, politically correct,
  postcard
pd paid
PD police department
PDT Pacific daylight time
PE physical education
PEI Prince Edward Island

Penn, Penna Pennsylvania
pg page
PIN personal identification
  number
pk park, peak, peck
pkg package
pl place, plural
p.m., PM afternoon
PMS premenstrual syndrome
PO post office
Port Portugal, Portuguese
pos position, positive
poss possessive
pp pages
PQ Province of Quebec
pr pair, price, printed
PR public relations, Puerto Rico
prep preposition
pres present, president
prob probable, probably, problem
prof professor
pron pronoun
prov province
PS postscript, public school
PST Pacific standard time
psych psychology
pt part, payment, pint, point
PT Pacific time, physical therapy
pvt private
qr quarter
qt quantity, quart
Que Quebec
quot quotation
r right, river
rd road, rod, round
RDA recommended daily
  allowance, recommended dietary
  allowance
recd received
reg region, register, registered,
  regular
rel relating, relative, religion
rep report, reporter, representative,
  republic
Rep Republican
res residence
rev reverse, review, revised,
  revision, revolution
Rev reverend
RFD rural free delivery
RI Rhode Island
rm room
rpm revolutions per minute
RR railroad, rural route

RSVP   please reply
rt   right
rte   route
s   small, south, southern
SA   South America
SASE   self-addressed stamped
  envelope
Sask   Saskatchewan
Sat   Saturday
SC   South Carolina
sci   science, scientific
SD, S Dak   South Dakota
secy   secretary
sen   senate, senator, senior
Sept, Sep   September
sing   singular
sm   small
so   south, southern
soph   sophomore
sp   spelling
spec   special, specifically
specif   specific, specifically
SPF   sun protection factor
sq   square
sr   senior
Sr   sister
SSN   Social Security number
SSR   Soviet Socialist Republic
st   street
St   saint
std   standard
subj   subject
Sun   Sunday
supt   superintendent
SWAT   Special Weapons and
  Tactics
syn   synonym
t   teaspoon, temperature, ton,
  transitive, troy, true
T   tablespoon
tbs, tbsp   tablespoon
TD   touchdown
tech   technical, technician,
  technology

Tenn   Tennessee
terr   territory
Tex   Texas
Th, Thu, Thur, Thurs   Thursday
TN   Tennessee
trans   translated, translation,
  translator
tsp   teaspoon
Tu, Tue, Tues   Tuesday
TX   Texas
UK   United Kingdom
UN   United Nations
univ   universal, university
US   United States
USA   United States of America
USSR   Union of Soviet Socialist
  Republics
usu   usual, usually
UT   Utah
UV   ultraviolet
v   verb, versus
Va, VA   Virginia
var   variant, variety
vb   verb
VG   very good
VI   Virgin Islands
vol   volume, volunteer
VP   vice-president
vs   versus
Vt, VT   Vermont
W   west, western
WA, Wash   Washington
Wed   Wednesday
WI, Wis, Wisc   Wisconsin
wk   week, work
wt   weight
WV, W Va   West Virginia
WY, Wyo   Wyoming
XL   extra large, extra long
yd   yard
yr   year, younger, your
YT   Yukon Territory

Handbook of Style

Punctuation

The English writing system uses punctuation marks to separate groups of words for meaning and emphasis; to convey an idea of the variations of pitch, volume, pauses, and intonations of speech; and to help avoid ambiguity. English punctuation marks, together with general rules and bracketed examples of their use, follow.

APOSTROPHE   '

1. **indicates the possessive case of nouns and indefinite pronouns** ⟨the boy's mother⟩ ⟨the boys' mothers⟩ ⟨It is anyone's guess.⟩
2. **marks omissions in contracted words** ⟨didn't⟩ ⟨o'clock⟩
3. **often forms plurals of letters, figures, and words referred to as words** ⟨You should dot your *i*'s and cross your *t*'s.⟩ ⟨several 8's⟩ ⟨She has trouble pronouncing her *the*'s.⟩

BRACKETS   [   ]

1. **set off extraneous data such as editorial additions esp. within quoted material** ⟨wrote that the author was "trying to dazzle his readers with phrases like *jeu de mots* [play on words]"⟩
2. **function as parentheses within parentheses** ⟨Bowman Act (22 Stat., ch. 4, § [or sec.] 4, p. 50)⟩

COLON   :

1. **introduces word, clause, or phrase that explains, illustrates, amplifies, or restates what has gone before** ⟨The sentence was poorly constructed: it lacked both unity and coherence.⟩
2. **introduces a series** ⟨Three countries were represented: England, France, and Belgium.⟩
3. **introduces lengthy quoted material set off from the rest of a text by indentation but not by quotation marks** ⟨I quote from the text of Chapter One:⟩
4. **separates data in time-telling and data in bibliographic**

and biblical references ⟨8:30 a.m.⟩ ⟨New York: Smith Publishing Co.⟩ ⟨John 4:10⟩
5. **separates titles and subtitles (as of books)** ⟨*The Tragic Dynasty: A History of the Romanovs*⟩
6. **follows the salutation in formal correspondence** ⟨Dear Sir:⟩ ⟨Gentlemen:⟩

COMMA ,

1. **separates main clauses joined by a coordinating conjunction (as *and, but, or, nor,* or *for*)** and very short clauses not so joined ⟨She knew very little about him, and he volunteered nothing.⟩ ⟨I came, I saw, I conquered.⟩
2. **sets off an adverbial clause (or a long phrase) that precedes the main clause** ⟨When she found that her friends had deserted her, she sat down and cried.⟩
3. **sets off from the rest of the sentence transitional words and expressions (as *on the contrary, on the other hand*),** conjunctive adverbs (as *consequently, furthermore, however*), and expressions that introduce an illustration or example (as *namely, for example*) ⟨Your second question, on the other hand, remains open.⟩ ⟨The mystery, however, remains unsolved.⟩ ⟨She expects to travel through two countries, namely, France and England.⟩
4. **separates words, phrases, or clauses in series and coordinate adjectives modifying a noun** ⟨Men, women, and children crowded into the square.⟩ ⟨The harsh, cold wind was strong.⟩
5. **sets off from the rest of the sentence parenthetic elements (as nonrestrictive modifiers)** ⟨Our guide, who wore a blue beret, was an experienced traveler.⟩ ⟨We visited Gettysburg, the site of a famous battle.⟩
6. **introduces a direct quotation, terminates a direct quotation that is neither a question nor an exclamation, and encloses split quotations** ⟨John said, "I am leaving."⟩ ⟨"I am leaving," John said.⟩ ⟨"I am leaving," John said with determination, "even if you want me to stay."⟩
7. **sets off words in direct address, absolute phrases, and mild interjections** ⟨You may go, Mary, if you wish.⟩ ⟨I fear the encounter, his temper being what it is.⟩ ⟨Ah, that's my idea of an excellent dinner.⟩
8. **separates a question from the rest of the sentence which it ends** ⟨It's a fine day, isn't it?⟩
9. **indicates the omission of a word or words, and esp. a**

word or words used earlier in the sentence ⟨Common stocks are preferred by some investors; bonds, by others.⟩

10. **is used to avoid ambiguity** ⟨To Mary, Jane was someone special.⟩
11. **is used to group numbers into units of three in separating thousands, millions, etc.; however, it is generally not used in numbers of four figures, in page numbers, in dates, or in street numbers** ⟨Smithville, pop. 100,000⟩ *but* ⟨3600 rpm⟩ ⟨the year 1973⟩ ⟨page 1411⟩ ⟨4507 Smith Street⟩
12. **punctuates an inverted name** ⟨Smith, John W., Jr.⟩
13. **separates a proper name from a following academic, honorary, governmental, or military title** ⟨John Smith, M.D.⟩
14. **sets off geographical names (as state or country from city), items in dates, and addresses from the rest of a text** ⟨Shreveport, Louisiana, is the site of a large air base.⟩ ⟨On Sunday, June 23, 1940, he was wounded.⟩ ⟨Number 10 Downing Street, London, is a famous address.⟩
15. **follows the salutation in informal correspondence and follows the closing line of a formal or informal letter** ⟨Dear Mary,⟩ ⟨Affectionately,⟩ ⟨Very truly yours,⟩

DASH   —

1. **usu. marks an abrupt change or break in the continuity of a sentence** ⟨When in 1960 the stockpile was sold off—indeed, dumped as surplus—natural-rubber sales were hard hit.—Barry Commoner⟩
2. **introduces a summary statement after a series** ⟨Oil, steel, and wheat—these are the sinews of industrialization.⟩
3. **often precedes the attribution of a quotation** ⟨My foot is on my native heath . . . . —Sir Walter Scott⟩

ELLIPSIS   . . .   .

1. **indicates the omission of one or more words within a quoted passage** ⟨The head is not more native to the heart . . . than is the throne of Denmark to thy father.—Shakespeare⟩
2. **indicates halting speech or an unfinished sentence in dialogue** ⟨"I'd like to . . . that is . . . if you don't mind. . . ." He faltered and then stopped speaking.⟩
3. **indicates the omission of one or more sentences within**

a quoted passage or the omission of words at the end of a sentence by using four spaced dots the last of which represents the period ⟨That recovering the manuscripts would be worth almost any effort is without question. . . . The monetary value of a body of Shakespeare's manuscripts would be almost incalculable—Charlton Ogburn⟩

4. **usu. indicates omission of one or more lines of poetry when ellipsis is extended the length of the line**

⟨Thus driven

By the bright shadow of that lovely dream

. . . .

He fled.

—P. B. Shelley⟩

EXCLAMATION POINT   !

1. **terminates an emphatic phrase or sentence** ⟨Get out of here!⟩

2. **terminates an emphatic interjection** ⟨Encore!⟩

HYPHEN   -

1. **marks separation or division of a word at the end of a line** ⟨mill-[end of line]stone⟩

2. **is used between some prefix and word combinations, as prefix + proper name;** ⟨pre-Renaissance⟩ **prefix ending with a vowel + word beginning often with the same vowel** ⟨co-opted⟩ ⟨re-ink⟩; **stressed prefix + word, esp. when this combination is similar to a different one** ⟨re-cover a sofa⟩ *but* ⟨recover from an illness⟩

3. **is used in some compounds, esp. those containing prepositions** ⟨president-elect⟩ ⟨sister-in-law⟩

4. **is often used between elements of a unit modifier in attributive position in order to avoid ambiguity** ⟨He is a small-business man.⟩ ⟨She has gray-green eyes.⟩

5. **suspends the first part of a hyphened compound when used with another hyphened compound** ⟨a six- or eight-cylinder engine⟩

6. **is used in writing out compound numbers between 21 and 99** ⟨thirty-four⟩ ⟨one hundred twenty-eight⟩

7. **is used between the numerator and the denominator in writing out fractions esp. when they are used as modifiers** ⟨a two-thirds majority of the vote⟩

8. **serves instead of the phrase "(up) to and including"**

between **numbers and dates** ⟨pages 40-98⟩ ⟨the decade 1960-69⟩

HYPHEN, DOUBLE   =

is used in the end-of-line division of a hyphened compound to indicate that the compound is hyphened and not closed ⟨self=[end of line]seeker⟩ *but* ⟨self-[end of line]same⟩

PARENTHESES   ( )

1. **set off supplementary, parenthetic, or explanatory material when the interruption is more marked than that usu. indicated by commas** ⟨Three old destroyers (all now out of commission) will be scrapped.⟩ ⟨He is hoping (as we all are) that this time he will succeed.⟩
2. **enclose numerals which confirm a written number in a text** ⟨Delivery will be made in thirty (30) days.⟩
3. **enclose numbers or letters in a series** ⟨We must set forth (1) our long-term goals, (2) our immediate objectives, and (3) the means at our disposal.⟩

PERIOD   .

1. **terminates sentences or sentence fragments that are neither interrogatory nor exclamatory** ⟨Obey the law.⟩ ⟨He obeyed the law.⟩
2. **follows some abbreviations and contractions** ⟨Dr.⟩ ⟨Jr.⟩ ⟨etc.⟩ ⟨cont.⟩

QUESTION MARK   ?

1. **terminates a direct question** ⟨Who threw the bomb?⟩ ⟨''Who threw the bomb?'' he asked.⟩ ⟨To ask the question Who threw the bomb? is unnecessary.⟩
2. **indicates the writer's ignorance or uncertainty** ⟨Omar Khayyém, Persian poet (?-?1123)⟩

QUOTATION MARKS, DOUBLE   " "

1. **enclose direct quotations in conventional usage** ⟨He said, ''I am leaving.''⟩
2. **enclose words or phrases borrowed from others, words used in a special way, and often slang when it is introduced into formal writing** ⟨He called himself ''em-

peror,'' but he was really just a dictator.) ⟨He was arrested for smuggling ''smack.''⟩

3. **enclose titles of short poems, short stories, articles, lectures, chapters of books, songs, short musical compositions, and radio and TV programs** ⟨Robert Frost's ''Dust of Snow''⟩ ⟨Pushkin's ''Queen of Spades''⟩ ⟨The third chapter of *Treasure Island* is entitled ''The Black Spot.''⟩ ⟨''America the Beautiful''⟩ ⟨Ravel's ''Bolero''⟩ ⟨NBC's ''Today Show''⟩

4. **are used with other punctuation marks in the following ways: the period and the comma fall *within* the quotation marks** ⟨''I am leaving,'' he said.⟩ ⟨His camera was described as ''waterproof,'' but ''moisture-resistant'' would have been a better description.⟩ **the semicolon falls *outside* the quotation marks** ⟨He spoke of his ''little cottage in the country''; he might have called it a mansion.⟩ **the dash, the question mark, and the exclamation point fall *within* the quotation marks when they refer to the quoted matter only; they fall *outside* when they refer to the whole sentence** ⟨He asked, ''When did you leave?''⟩ ⟨What is the meaning of ''the open door''?⟩ ⟨The sergeant shouted, ''Halt!''⟩ ⟨Save us from his ''mercy''!⟩

QUOTATION MARKS, SINGLE   ' '

enclose a quotation within a quotation in conventional usage ⟨The witness said, ''I distinctly heard him say, 'Don't be late,' and then I heard the door close.''⟩

SEMICOLON   ;

1. **links main clauses not joined by coordinating conjunctions** ⟨Some people have the ability to write well; others do not.⟩

2. **links main clauses joined by conjunctive adverbs (as *consequently, furthermore, however*** ⟨Speeding is illegal; furthermore, it is very dangerous.⟩

3. **links clauses which themselves contain commas even when such clauses are joined by coordinating conjunctions** ⟨Mr. King, whom you met yesterday, will be our representative on the committee; but you should follow the proceedings carefully yourself, because they are vitally important to us.⟩

VIRGULE   /

1. **separates alternatives** ⟨. . . designs intended for high-heat and/or high-speed applications—F. S. Badger, Jr.⟩
2. **separates successive divisions (as months or years) of an extended period of time** ⟨the fiscal year 1972/73⟩
3. **serves as a dividing line between run-in lines of poetry** ⟨Say, sages, what's the charm on earth/Can turn death's dart aside?—Robert Burns⟩
4. **often represents *per* in abbreviations** ⟨9 ft/sec⟩ ⟨20 km/hr⟩

Italicization

The following are usually italicized in print and underlined in manuscript:

1. **titles of books, magazines, newspapers, plays, movies, works of art, and longer musical compositions** ⟨Eliot's *The Waste Land*⟩ ⟨*Saturday Review*⟩ ⟨*Christian Science Monitor*⟩ ⟨Shakespeare's *Othello*⟩ ⟨the movie *Gone With the Wind*⟩ ⟨Gainsborough's *Blue Boy*⟩ ⟨Mozart's *Don Giovanni*⟩
2. **names of ships and aircraft, and often spacecraft** ⟨M.V. *West Star*⟩ ⟨Lindbergh's *Spirit of St. Louis*⟩ ⟨*Apollo 13*⟩
3. **words, letters, and figures when referred to as words, letters, and figures** ⟨The word *receive* is often misspelled.⟩ ⟨The *g* in *align* is silent.⟩ ⟨The first *2* and the last *0* in the address are barely legible.⟩
4. **foreign words and phrases that have not been naturalized in English** ⟨*che sarà, sarà*⟩ ⟨*ich dien*⟩
5. **New Latin scientific names of genera, species, subspecies, and varieties (but not groups of higher rank) in botanical and zoological names** ⟨a thick-shelled American clam (*Mercenaria mercenaria*)⟩

Capitalization

Capitals are used for two broad purposes in English: they mark a beginning (as of a sentence) and they signal a proper noun or adjective.

1. **The first word of a sentence or sentence fragment is capitalized.** ⟨The play lasted nearly three hours.⟩ ⟨How are you feeling?⟩ ⟨Bravo!⟩
2. **The first word of a direct quotation is capitalized.** ⟨And

God said, Let there be light.—Gen 1:3⟩ ⟨He replied, "We can stay only a few minutes."⟩

3. **The first word of a direct question within a sentence is capitalized.** ⟨That question is this: Is man an ape or an angel?—Benjamin Disraeli⟩

4. **The first word of a line of poetry is conventionally capitalized.**
⟨The best lack all conviction, while the worst
Are full of passionate intensity.—W. B. Yeats⟩

5. **Words in titles are capitalized with the exception of internal conjunctions, prepositions, and articles.** ⟨*The Way of the World*⟩ ⟨*Of Mice and Men*⟩

6. **The first word of the salutation of a letter and the first word of the closing line are capitalized.** ⟨Dear Mary⟩ ⟨My dear Mrs. Smith⟩ ⟨Sincerely yours⟩

7. **The names of persons and places, of organizations and their members, of congresses and councils, and of historical periods and events are capitalized.** ⟨Noah Webster⟩ ⟨Rome⟩ ⟨Texas⟩ ⟨England⟩ ⟨Rotary International⟩ ⟨Baptists⟩ ⟨the Atomic Energy Commission⟩ ⟨the Yalta Conference⟩ ⟨the Middle Ages⟩ ⟨World War II⟩

8. **The names of ships, aircraft, and spacecraft are capitalized.** ⟨Lindbergh's *Spirit of St. Louis*⟩

9. **Words designating peoples and languages are capitalized.** ⟨Canadians⟩ ⟨Iroquois⟩ ⟨Latin⟩

10. **Derivatives of proper names are capitalized when used in their primary sense.** ⟨Roman customs⟩ ⟨Shakespearean comedies⟩ ⟨the Edwardian era⟩

11. **Words of family relationship preceding the name of a person are capitalized.** ⟨Uncle George⟩

12. **Titles preceding the name of a person and epithets used instead of a name are capitalized.** ⟨President Roosevelt⟩ ⟨Professor Harris⟩ ⟨Pope Paul⟩ ⟨Old Hickory⟩ ⟨the Iron Chancellor⟩

13. **The pronoun *I* is capitalized.** ⟨only I know the real story⟩

14. **Words designating the Deity (and pronouns referring thereto) are often capitalized.** ⟨God⟩ ⟨Jehovah⟩ ⟨Allah⟩ ⟨the Supreme Being in His great wisdom⟩

15. **Personifications are capitalized.** ⟨She dwells with Beauty—John Keats⟩

16. **The days of the week, the months of the year, and holidays and holy days are capitalized.** ⟨Tuesday⟩ ⟨June⟩ ⟨Thanksgiving⟩ ⟨Yom Kippur⟩

17. **Names of specific courts of law are capitalized.** ⟨the United States Court of Appeals for the Second Circuit⟩
18. **Names of treaties are capitalized.** ⟨Treaty of Versailles⟩ ⟨Kellogg-Briand Pact⟩
19. **Registered trademarks and other registered marks are capitalized.** ⟨Orlon⟩ ⟨Air Express⟩
20. **Geological eras, periods, epochs, strata, and names of prehistoric divisions are capitalized.** ⟨Silurian period⟩ ⟨Age of Reptiles⟩ ⟨Neolithic age⟩
21. **Planets, constellations, asteroids, stars, and groups of stars are capitalized; however, sun, earth, and moon are not capitalized unless they are listed with other capitalized astronomical names.** ⟨Venus⟩ ⟨Big Dipper⟩ ⟨Sirius⟩
22. **Genera in scientific names in zoology and botany are capitalized; names of species are not.** ⟨a cabbage butterfly ⟨*Pieris rapae*⟩⟩

Plurals

The plurals of English words are regularly formed by the addition of the suffix *-s* or *-es* to the singular, as
⟨dog → dogs⟩ ⟨race → races⟩ ⟨guy → guys⟩ ⟨monarch → monarchs⟩ ⟨grass → grasses⟩ ⟨dish → dishes⟩ ⟨buzz → buzzes⟩ ⟨branch → branches⟩

The plurals of words that follow other patterns, as
⟨army → armies⟩ ⟨duo → duos⟩ ⟨ox → oxen⟩ ⟨foot → feet⟩ ⟨p. → pp.⟩ ⟨sheep → sheep⟩ ⟨phenomenon → phenomena *or* phenomenons⟩ ⟨libretto → librettos *or* libretti⟩ ⟨curriculum → curricula⟩ ⟨alga → algae⟩ ⟨corpus → corpora⟩ ⟨sergeant major → sergeants major *or* sergeant majors⟩ **are given at the appropriate entries in the main body of the dictionary.**